DATE DUE

Germany and the Great Powers
1866-1914

GERMANY
AND THE GREAT POWERS
1866-1914

A Study
in Public Opinion and Foreign Policy

BY

E. MALCOLM CARROLL

OCTAGON BOOKS

A DIVISION OF FARRAR, STRAUS AND GIROUX

New York   1975

Copyright, 1938, by Prentice-Hall, Inc.

Reprinted 1975
by special arrangement with Prentice-Hall, Inc.

OCTAGON BOOKS
A Division of Farrar, Straus & Giroux, Inc.
19 Union Square West
New York, N.Y. 10003

Library of Congress Cataloging in Publication Data

Carroll, Eber Malcolm, 1893-1959.
    Germany and the great powers, 1866-1914.

    Reprint of the ed. published by Prentice-Hall, New York, in
Prentice-Hall history series.

    Includes bibliographical references.
    1. Public opinion—Germany. 2. Germany—Foreign relations
—1871-1918.   3. Europe—Politics—1871-1918.   4. Press—
Germany. I. Title.

DD117.C3   1975   327.43   74-28179
ISBN 0-374-91299-8

Manufactured by Braun-Brumfield, Inc.
Ann Arbor, Michigan

Printed in the United States of America

To the memory of
WILLIAM KENNETH BOYD

Preface

Every book has its roots in the past. This one goes back to 1925, when my interest in the rôle of European public opinion in the history of international relations was first aroused in connection with the origins of the Franco-Prussian War of 1870. After the completion of my book *French Public Opinion on Foreign Affairs, 1870–1914* (published in 1931), I began the investigations which now eventuate in this study.

There is today, it is safe to say, a rather general appreciation among students of history of the importance of public opinion in the development of foreign relations, but, unless I am much mistaken, there is a good deal of skepticism as to its significance in Germany, even during the comparative freedom of the Second Reich. My own vague ideas were at first based upon the revelations of Bismarck's control of the press in Moritz Busch's *Memoirs,* by what I had heard and read of the foreign office's press bureau under William II, and by what the Germans themselves were wont to say of their own political docility and incapacity. My researches show, beyond any doubt, that the official control of the press and of public opinion, although greater than in France and England, was far less complete and that there was more real independence of opinion than is generally believed. Instead of lightening my labors, these conclusions greatly increased them, for it was impossible to assume that what the official and so-called inspired press said was automatically accepted by the press and public opinion in general. First of all, it was necessary to find out with respect to every important question what the government wished the reaction of the public to be, and then, which was far more difficult, what that reaction really was. Without going into the whole question of the causative forces behind German public opinion, I wish to point out the part played time after time by the press of other countries. I have made considerable use of the London press from the early eighties, because of the great influence of its reactions in Germany, but I make no claim to have exhausted this aspect of the problem. For the attitude of the press in other countries, I have relied upon such special studies as are in print, including my own book on French public opinion, and upon other indirect evidence.

Any attempt to estimate the influence of the press and public opinion upon official policy encounters great difficulties in every country. Rarely is it possible to say of a statesman or a diplomat that a given cause determined his decision; the situation is almost invariably far less simple than that. In the usual complex of causes, public opinion is one of those intangibles whose influence may be important even if it cannot be proved by documentary evidence. This is just as true of Germany as of other countries, for it is impossible to escape the conclusion that the men who guided her destinies, although they often spoke of the press and public opinion with contempt, were affected by the broad currents of popular opinion and emotion. My own feeling, however, is that the value of a study of public opinion does not mainly depend upon its immediate influence upon the rulers' decisions. How the public reacted and why are, to my mind, interesting and significant questions for their own sake.

In this book, much more than in my earlier study of French public opinion, I have attempted to trace the development of the official foreign policy. For one thing, the documentary evidence and the secondary literature are far more complete for Germany than they were for France. Since I was undertaking to trace the various trends of opinion on the management of Germany's foreign affairs, it seemed pertinent to, indicate, at least in broad outline, what German foreign policy actually was. For this purpose I have examined the usual sources for the diplomatic history of this period, including the monumental collections of diplomatic correspondence published by all of the great powers of Europe except Italy, and I have frequently relied upon the writings of specialists; but I do not pretend to have made much use of the huge mass of material scattered through the learned and other periodicals of Germany and other countries. Where my researches have led me to conclusions that differ from those of other writers, I have not hesitated to state them. Perhaps the most notable examples of divergence from accepted views are my interpretations of Bismarck and Caprivi, to whom are devoted the greater part of the concluding section of Chapter VII.

The informed reader will decide for himself how successfully I have dealt with the many difficulties of this study. Not the least of these was the maintenance of a detached point of view between the countries concerned and between the parties within Germany. The present situation in Germany and in Europe weighs heavily upon anyone who concerns himself with German history. While a small part of my material was gathered in Munich during the summer of 1935, most of it was assembled before the establishment of the National Socialist régime in 1933, especially in 1931–1932. The book, however, was written during the last five years. There are those who believe that impartiality is impossible in the writing of history; but believing, as I do, that there can be no sound historical writing without impartiality, I have striven to attain and to maintain it to the best of my ability, whatever my personal sympathies may be. In any event, my task has been not to review the hoary war-guilt question but to tell, as accurately as possible, what actually happened and why, in so far as that can be done within the limits of this study.

Among my obligations, the deepest are to the executives of Duke University, who granted me a sabbatical leave during the year 1931–1932. To the University's Research Council I owe grateful thanks for generous grants for the purchase of books and for clerical assistance. To the officials and staffs of the Preussische Staatsbibliothek in Berlin, the Bayerische Staatsbibliothek in Munich, the Städtische Bibliothek in Frankfort, the British Museum, the Bibliothèque Nationale in Paris, the Congressional Library, the Widener Library of Harvard University, and the library of Duke University, I am grateful for many services. Almost every page of this book shows my indebtedness to the scores of scholars who have contributed so much to the richness of our knowledge of the period leading to the World War. The editorial department of Prentice-Hall, Inc., has been of real assistance in preparing the manuscript for the printers and in seeing it through the press. Professor Paul F. Baum, of the Department of English of Duke University, kindly gave many hours to the reading of several of the early chapters in manuscript, and my colleague Dr. William B. Hamilton, of the Department of History, generously shared the task of reading the page proof. For any technical errors and other shortcomings in the book, of course only I am responsible.

E. M. C.

Contents

Illustrations

xiii

Abbreviations

A.B. = *Alldeutsche Blätter.*

A.P.P. = *Die auswärtige Politik Preussens.*

B.D. = *British Documents on the Origins of the World War, 1898–1914.*

B.D.K. = P. Dirr, *Bayerische Dokumente zum Kriegsausbruch und zum Versailler Schuldsspruch.*

B: G.W. = *Bismarck: die gesammelten Werke.*

D.D.F. = *Documents diplomatiques français (1871– 1914).*

D.G. = *Deutsche Gesandtschaftsberichte.*

G.P. = *Die Grosse Politik der europäischen Kabinette.*

I.Z. = *Die internationale Beziehungen im Zeitalter des Imperialismus; Dokumente aus den Archiven der zaristischen und der provisorischen Regierung.*

K.D. = K. Kautsky, ed., *Die deutschen Dokumente zum Kreigsausbruch.*

L.N. = R. Marchand, ed., *Un livre noir; diplomatie d'avant-guerre d'après les documents des archives russes.*

N.A.Z. = *Norddeutsche Allgemeine Zeitung.*

O.D. = *Les origines diplomatiques de la guerre de 1870–1871.*

Ö.-U.A. = *Oesterreich-Ungarns Aussenpolitik von der bosnischen Krise bis zum Kriegsausbruch.*

P.J. = *Preussische Jahrbücher.*

R.N. = H. Oncken, *Die Rheinpolitik Napoleons III, von 1863 bis 1870.*

CHAPTER I

The Dynamics of German Foreign Policy

Fürst Bismarck erkannte zuerst in Deutschland an regier-
ender Stelle, welch' eine Macht das Bewusstsein verleiht, sich
eins mit dem Willen eines ganzes Volkes zu wissen.

Deutsche Rundschau, III, 315
(April 15, 1875).

. . . der Mann kann den Strom der Zeit nicht schaffen
und nicht lenken, er kann nur darauf hinfahren und steuern,
mit mehr oder weniger Erfahrung und Geschick.

Bismarck, April 1, 1895.

Um dieses vorwiegenden Interesses der auswärtigen Politik
für Deutschland und sein öffentliches Wohl muss eben der
Reichstag um so mehr die Gewissheit verlangen, dass die
auswärtige Politik eine Gute ist.   Denn was hülfe ihm alle
seine Sorge für das öffentliche Wohl, vermöge der inneren
Gesetzgebung, wenn ein einziger Fehltritt der auswärtigen
Politik die Arbeit langer Jahre zu Nichte machen könnte?

Vossische Zeitung, February 3, 1878.

If a country ever owed its foreign policy exclusively to the genius
of one man, that country was Germany and the man was Bismarck.   Before him there had been an Austrian and a Prussian
policy and a point of view that represented the interests of the
middle and small states.   For centuries the nation had been sacrificed to local interests and ambitions.   Given a practically complete independence in foreign affairs by the Treaty of Westphalia
(1648), each prince in the Holy Roman Empire was interested
in his own survival and perhaps in adding a few square miles of
territory to his dominions, when the ambitions of Sweden, Denmark, and France, and the duel between the Bourbons and the
Hapsburgs made Germany the cockpit of Europe.   Thanks to

the skill of the Hohenzollerns in profiting by the wars of other countries, Brandenburg-Prussia waxed in strength until she became Austria's chief rival in the Empire. If she fought at last at Austria's side for the overthrow of Napoleon I's hegemony, her purpose, as stated in the Treaty of Kalisch (1813) with Alexander I of Russia, was the recovery of her own powers rather than national unification. From 1815 to 1848, Frederick William III and IV preferred to accept Austria's control of the German Confederation, in part doubtless because of Metternich's tactful treatment of them, rather than to risk the loss of Prussia's identity in a national movement. Even the *Zollverein's* contribution to German unity was indirect and not wholly intentional.[1] To the Frankfort Parliament's offer of the German crown, tainted as it was by its liberal origins, Frederick William IV turned a cold shoulder, helped Austria to crush the liberals in 1849, and only then made the bid for national unity (without Austria) that ended, largely because of Russia's hostility, in the humiliating surrender to Austria at Olmütz (1851). Bismarck, soon to be Prussia's envoy to the Diet of the restored Confederation, drew the obvious conclusion: only if the other powers remained neutral could Prussia hope to expel Austria, force a settlement with France, and unite Germany. He therefore threw his influence in favor of neutrality during the Crimean War (1854–1856) in order to win Russia's good-will and during the Austro-Sardinian War (1859) to conciliate Napoleon III and to prevent Austria from strengthening her position.[2] His aim then and after he became the Prussian Chancellor in 1862 was of course to unite Germany under Prussia's domination. The moderation of the terms he imposed upon Austria in the Treaty of Prague (1866) was the first clear recognition of an essential agreement between Prussian and German interests. It prevented Austria's inevitable bitterness from hardening into a lasting hatred and led to the renewal of the historic association in the Austro-German Alliance of 1879.

Although constitutionally responsible to the Emperor, Bismarck in fact controlled German foreign policy until his fall in 1890,

[1] H. R. von Srbik, *Deutsche Einheit; Idee und Wirklichkeit vom Heiligen Reich bis Königgrätz*, 2 vols. (Munich, 1935), I, 276.

[2] E. Marcks, *Der Aufstieg des Reiches; deutsche Geschichte von 1807–1871/78*, 2 vols. (Berlin, 1936), I, 425, 426, 445, 446.

thanks to his own great prestige and to the sovereign's favor. The few who dared to oppose him were usually crushed. Flight alone saved Count Harry von Arnim from imprisonment when he used his influence as the German ambassador to France in favor of a monarchical restoration instead of working for the consolidation of the Republic as Bismarck desired. The English and liberal sympathies of the court circle, including the Empress, the Crown Prince Frederick William, and the Crown Princess Victoria—the daughter of Queen Victoria—caused Bismarck endless irritation, for these personages were almost beyond his reach, but he had his way in the end. Not only was the Crown Prince denied any real influence, but his wife was not permitted, out of consideration for Russia, to marry her daughter to Prince Alexander of Battenberg or to interfere in other ways, even during Frederick's brief reign in 1888. Neither the ambassadors nor the foreign office officials were anything more than agents for the collection of information and for the carrying out of the Chancellor's instructions. In 1884 Count Münster, the ambassador in London, failed to divert German policy from the acquisition of colonies to that of Heligoland, and, two years later, his estimate of the French *revanche,* after his transfer to Paris, was rejected in favor of the alarmist reports of the military attaché. After 1890 control ceased to be centered so entirely in one man. If the ambassadors gained little in real authority, the officials of the foreign office became much more powerful. Even Marschall von Bieberstein, who apparently displayed a good deal of independence in securing Turkey's friendship during his long and successful career in Constantinople, was merely an exceptionally efficient agent, for the reserve which Bismarck had regarded as fundamental to German policy in the Near East had long since been abandoned. Prince Metternich's well-founded warnings as to the consequences of the naval program upon Anglo-German relations made little or no impression on those who determined German policy, and later it was hoped that the English would value Prince Lichnowsky's friendliness more highly than Berlin did his wisdom. On the other hand, Friedrich von Holstein, a simple *vortragener Rat* in the foreign office, perhaps had more to say about German foreign policy until his resignation in 1906 than Bismarck's successors, although his influence has often been exaggerated. While no one quite took his place, the official heads of the foreign office, von Schoen, Kiderlen-Wächter, and von Jagow, were probably just as influential, and, at specific times, even more so than Bülow or Bethmann-Hollweg. The rôle of William II is less clear. It was neither so vital nor so negligible as many have supposed. Although he usually yielded to his advisers—his temperamental comments upon the diplomatic dispatches were, it is said, usually ignored [3]—he was at least partly responsible for the *Weltpolitik,* for the naval program, for the *Drang nach Osten,* and for Austria's confidence in Germany's support. To a certain extent, the Kruger Telegram was also his work, and his speech-making as well as his injudicious remarks to foreign diplomats often created difficulties for the conduct of foreign affairs.

Like those of other countries, Germany's statesmen and diplomats believed that they were serving the interests of the state and nation. "For me," said Bismarck, "there has been only one compass, one Polar star: the well-being of the state. . . . A doctrinaire I have never been; all party considerations are of secondary importance to me." [4] Yet even his understanding of Germany's interests and his choice of the means of attaining them were in part the results of general forces. Under Bismarck as well as under the lesser men who succeeded him, historical and geographical influences, the outlook of their class, economic and military considerations, and public opinion helped in varying degrees to shape their decisions. A word must suffice for all of these factors except that of public opinion, which is a principal theme of this study. While the new German Empire had not inherited from the past as definite an understanding of its interests as had England, France and Russia, Prussian history nevertheless seemed to teach the value of Russia's friendship and the need of regarding England with suspicion. A long experience established the view that friendly relations should be maintained with Austria

---

[3] See Friedrich Thimme and Max Lenz on this point in L. Franke, *Die Randbemerkungen Wilhelms II. in den Akten der auswärtigen Politik als historische und psychologische Quelle* (Ohlau i. Sehl., 1933), pp. 2, 3. *Cf.* E. Thoma, *Der Einfluss der Randbemerkungen Bismarcks und Kaiser Wilhelms II. auf die deutsche auswärtige Politik* (Tübingen, 1930).

[4] *Provinzial-Correspondenz,* March 2, 1881.

and that France was the great national enemy. If other things than history probably account for the presence of these points of view in Bismarck's policies, those policies, though sometimes distorted and misunderstood, quickly acquired the weight and prestige of traditions after his fall. No factor was more important than Germany's central location in Europe. Not only did it directly affect the decisions of statesmen, but it also made itself felt through most of the other general forces here under consideration. This was notably true, for example, of the part played by the general staff, for geography as well as politics was responsible for the danger of a war upon two fronts. If Bismarck retained full control, lecturing the military when they urged Austria to prepare for war in 1887, the army became more influential under William II. The Schlieffen plan of a holding action against Russia while France was being crushed tended to limit the diplomats' freedom of action and to take the control of events out of their hands in a crisis. At least to some extent, the Moltke-Hötzendorf exchange of letters in 1909 undermined the defensive character of the alliance with Austria, and the general staff's eagerness for the swift seizure of the Liège forts may have helped to precipitate war in 1914. To what extent Germany's foreign policy was influenced by the aristocratic and agrarian background of her statesmen and diplomats is probably impossible to say. While the greater value which they placed upon a friendship with autocratic Russia than upon one with England may have been in part the result of the prejudices of their class against parliamentary institutions, and while many Germans felt that a diplomatic service so composed could not adequately represent an increasingly industrial country, this factor is so difficult to isolate and to evaluate that it is not very useful for the purposes of this study. Far more significant was the exceptionally rapid development of German industry and the increasing concentration of its control, yet economic determinism, important as it was in spite of the lack of supporting evidence in the diplomatic documents, was far from being the whole story. In part Bismarck's colonial policy was intended to help him recover a favorable majority in the Reichstag. Behind the later *Weltpolitik* there were political as well as economic motives; the hope of breaking the Entente Cordiale was just as important as the desire for markets and raw materials in Germany's Moroccan policy. So closely were these general forces associated that it is usually impossible to distinguish between them with any exactness.[5]

None has been more neglected by the historians than public opinion.[6] At first sight, this neglect seems justified. Especially of the press, German as well as foreign observers often spoke with contempt. Bismarck's description of the journalist as "a man who has failed in his profession" became one of his most frequently quoted sayings. In all of his writings and in all of the records of his conversations, there is scarcely a trace of a more favorable judgment—until his dismissal in 1890 caused him to value the good-will of the press.[7] Any divergence from what he regarded as the proper reaction on the part of public opinion excited his wrath. In 1875, probably as a result of the criticism of the official press campaign against France, he condemned the "exaggerated attention" accorded to foreign affairs and expressed the hope that more interest would soon be shown in domestic questions.[8] Opposition to his Russian policy betrayed, in his opinion, the lack of the most elementary political capacity, if it was not outright treason. While the press enjoyed a somewhat better reputation under William II, the gain was far from commensurate with its increased social and economic significance. "An estate without a status," wrote an unfriendly English critic, "despised as a profession . . . the German press offers no attraction to the educated young German. . . . The inevitable result is that its ranks are recruited from the flotsam and jetsam of other professions, almost never from the schools. Indeed, the open

---

[5] While no references are given for the historical illustrations in this and the following paragraphs, they are all discussed at appropriate places in this study.

[6] Among the more recent monographs dealing with German public opinion and foreign affairs are the following: M. Sell, *Das deutsch-englische Abkommen von 1890 über Helgoland und die afrikanischen Kolonien im Lichte der deutschen Presse* (Berlin, 1926); J. F. Scott, *Five Weeks; The Surge of Public Opinion on the Eve of the Great War* (N. Y., 1927); J. Sass, *Die deutschen Weissbücher zur auswärtigen Politik 1870–1914* (Berlin, 1928); A. Jux, *Der Kriegsschrecken des Frühjahrs 1914 in der europäischen Presse* (Berlin, 1929); O. J. Hale, *Germany and the Diplomatic Revolution; A Study in Diplomacy and the Press 1904–1906* (Philadelphia, 1931); H. Schulze, *Die Presse im Urteil Bismarcks* (Leipzig, 1931); E. Leupolt, *Die Aussenpolitik in den bedeutendsten Zeitschriften Deutschlands 1890–1909* (Leipzig, 1933). Cf. J. F. Scott's review article, "The Press and Foreign Policy," *Journal of Modern History*, III, 627–638.

[7] Schulze, *Die Presse im Urteil Bismarcks*, pp. 153, 154.

[8] D. Albers, *Reichstag und Aussenpolitik von 1871–1879* (Berlin, 1927), pp. 14, 15.

contempt of Germans for their own press is astounding. . ." [9]
In no other civilized country, except perhaps Austria, was the
press, asserted another English observer, on "so low a level both
socially and commercially. . ." [10]   Unlike the press in France,[11]
it scarcely ever served as a stepping stone to a political career.
Even Eugen Richter was already a leader of the Progressive party
when he founded the *Freisinnige Zeitung* in 1885.[12]   "It very
seldom happens," wrote Ludwig Bamberger, "that a journalist attains a high political office. . ." [13]   Maximilian Harden regarded
the failure to include a single German correspondent among the
speakers at a reception in New York organized by Herman Ridder, the editor of the *New Yorker Staats Zeitung,* on the occasion
of the American visit of Prince Henry of Prussia as an accurate
index to the official attitude toward the press.   "True, it boasts of
its power, but it doesn't believe in it. . ." [14]   William II told his
English hosts in 1899 that he was German public opinion.

The press nevertheless became increasingly important.   By
1914 there were approximately four thousand newspapers in existence, although the great majority, having a purely local character, of course exerted no appreciable influence upon public
opinion in regard to national problems.   With the fairly liberal
press law of 1874, which removed the stamp tax, largely eliminated the censorship, and limited the actionable offenses chiefly
to *lèse majesté* (*Majestätsbeleidigung*), disappeared the principal
legal obstacle to the expansion of the press as a whole, despite the
rigorous measures against the Social Democratic newspapers from
1878 to 1900.[15]   To a degree greater than in the French press and

[9] One who knows it, "The German Press," *National Review*, December 1904, pp.
634, 635.
[10] G. W. Williams, "The German Press Bureau," *Contemporary Review*, XCVII, 319
(March 1910).
[11] E. M. Carroll, *French Public Opinion and Foreign Affairs, 1871–1914* (N. Y.,
1931), p. 13.
[12] L. Ullstein, *Eugen Richter als Publizist und Herausgeber* (Leipzig, 1930), p. 107.
[13] L. Bamberger, "The German Daily Press," *Nineteenth Century*, vol. 27, p. 29
(Jan. 1890).
[14] M. Harden, "Die Journalisten," *Zukunft*, March 8, 1902. This article was written as an open letter to Ridder.
[15] G. Weill, *Le journal; origines, évolution et rôle de la presse périodique* (Paris,
1934), p. 270. After 1874, the National Liberal *National Zeitung*, which had been
confiscated seven times since 1867, was thereafter proceeded against only once. E. G.
Friehe, *Geschichte der 'National-Zeitung' 1848–1878* (Leipzig, 1933), p. 152. The
great majority of the numerous Social Democratic newspapers were suppressed during
the period from 1878 to 1890.

comparable to that of the English and American newspapers, advertising was developed as the principal source of income, making possible a lower sales price, greater diversity of content, and in some instances a vast increase in bulk. Partly because Berlin never attained a position of supremacy like that of Paris and London, no single journal ever sold as widely as the *Petit Parisien* or the *Daily Mail* or, in general, attained a reputation like the London *Times* or the *Temps* of Paris, but a few Berlin newspapers finally acquired circulations of several hundred thousand and three houses, those of Mosse, Scherl, and Ullstein, owned and published a number of journals toward the end of this period.[16] Most of the larger provincial cities had one or more newspapers of considerable regional and, in some cases, of national and even international significance. In age, dignity, and in influence measured in part by the frequency with which their views were quoted, the *Magdeburgische Zeitung,* the *Hamburger Nachrichten,* the *Allgemeine Zeitung* (first of Augsburg and later of Munich), the *Münchener Neueste Nachrichten,* the *Frankfurter Zeitung,* and the *Kölnische Zeitung* compared favorably with the most important of the Berlin journals.[17] Of the Pan-German press the *Rheinisch-Westfälische Zeitung* of Essen was probably more important, as the organ of the Ruhr industrialists, than the *Berliner Post,* the *Tägliche Rundschau,* or the *Berliner Neueste Nachrichten.* Because they were necessarily addressed to smaller groups, the political reviews shared this prosperity to a smaller extent. The *Grenzboten* and the *Preussische Jahrbücher* remained the most important throughout this period, but a number of newcomers appeared from time to time, among them being Harden's inimitable *Zukunft,* the *Deutsche Revue,* the *Deutsche Rundschau,*

---

[16] The Ullsteins published two morning journals, the *Berliner Zeitung* and the *Berliner Morgenpost,* one at noon, the *Berliner Zeitung am Mittag,* and one in the evening, the *Berliner Abendpost.* Among others Scherl owned the widely circulated *Lokal-Anzeiger,* and Mosse the *Berliner Tageblatt.* In foreign affairs the most influential newspapers were not those of the largest circulation.

[17] Of the nine newspapers in existence more than two centuries, only the *Vossische Zeitung* was published in Berlin. More than a hundred had been established well over a century and at least a thousand for at least fifty years. The great majority were the individual property of families, the Fabers having been in possession of the *Magdeburgische Zeitung* for nine generations. Many other journals had only a little less impressive record. M. Rietschel, *Der Familienbesitz in der deutschen politischen Tagespresse* (Leipzig, 1933), pp. 6, 60–68.

the *Nord und Sud,* the *Gegenwart,* and the *Nation.* Second only to the profit motive as a cause for the expansion of the press was the need of parties and of pressure groups for press organs. With the repeal of the Socialist laws in 1890 the last of the legal barriers to the development of the partisan press disappeared. Besides such daily newspapers as the *Germania* and the *Kölnische Volkszeitung* for the Catholic Center, the *Vorwärts* for the Social Democrats, the *Berliner Post* for the Free Conservatives, the *Kreuz-Zeitung* and *Deutsche Tageszeitung* for the agrarian Conservatives, the *Freisinnige Zeitung* and the *Volks-Zeitung* for the Progressives, most of these parties maintained news circulars for their members which, though primarily intended to report on meetings, party programs, and so forth, sometimes commented upon foreign affairs. With this tremendous expansion inevitably went some improvement in public esteem for the men who were responsible for it. Among the most respected of the editors of the liberal press were Georg Bernhard of the *Vossische Zeitung* and Theodor Wolff of the *Berliner Tageblatt;* A. Stein, for many years the Berlin correspondent of the *Frankfurter Zeitung,* enjoyed Bülow's confidence. The *Post* (Aug. 2, 1902) once noted, though with much amusement, the claim that the best training for the country's future rulers and statesmen was to be found in the editorial rooms.

"Even the church in its heyday," asserted the National Liberal *National Zeitung* (Jan. 25, 1885), "never impressed itself upon the whole people as the newspapers have." Although the liberals and the Social Democrats talked more of the press as the mirror of public opinion while most Conservatives stressed its work in creating opinion, a double function was usually assumed. For example, the Social Democratic *Berliner Volksblatt* (March 15, 1885) described the press as the most effective school for the masses. "Professional scholars and diplomats may be amused by its shortcomings, but what other institution furnishes the kind of instruction upon current questions which alone produces results?" Perhaps the newspapers of no other country contained such substantial fare in serious articles on all sorts of subjects, but their point of view, as elsewhere, was influenced by the underlying prejudices and aspirations of the general public and especially of the party or group to which they were addressed.[18]   "If individual journalists edit the newspapers," wrote the *National Zeitung* (Jan. 25, 1885), "public opinion undoubtedly directs the press as a whole."   As in other countries, the repetition of catchwords such as *ruhmsüchtig* to describe the French temperament, *Krämerpolitik* in regard to English foreign policy, and *Gleichberechtigung* in connection with Germany's claims, especially as against England, created as well as reflected popular sentiment.   In regard to foreign affairs, the press doubtless gave the lead to public opinion in most cases.   Nowhere was the general public more curious about and more interested in conditions abroad, a demand which the press encouraged and satisfied by innumerable and lengthy articles relating to the most remote corners of the globe. But Germans were not noticeably more concerned than other peoples about the technical problems of international relations except in a crisis or when some well-recognized national interest was at stake.   During the Bismarckian period, the liberals frequently lamented the general indifference to foreign affairs which they correctly attributed to the feeling that these problems were in safe hands,[19] but this indifference, as this study shows, was by no means complete.   Even under the great Chancellor and still more under William II, the existence of parties and pressure groups, such as the Social Democrats, the Catholic Center, the Pan-Germans, the Navy League, and the Colonial Society, with special interests to serve or a general point of view to expound, assured on increasingly frequent occasions a lively discussion of foreign affairs.   Hans Delbrück, the editor of the *Preussische Jahrbücher,* complained as late as 1903 that no one was interested in these problems,[20] but he was probably thinking of the small cultivated group for which this review was intended.   "Only above and below is there any activity (*herrscht Bewegung*)," wrote another observer about the same time, "for the center is like a lush green swamp in which he sinks who tries to penetrate

---

[18] Bülow, like most German statesmen, believed that party prejudices were far more influential in determining the reactions of German public opinion in foreign affairs than that of other countries.   B. von Bülow, *Denkwürdigkeiten,* 4 vols. (Berlin, 1931), I, 428.

[19] They often pointed to England as an example to be emulated. *Volks-Zeitung,* Feb. 9, 1884; *Vossische Zeitung,* Sept. 8, 1885.

[20] Leupolt, *Aussenpolitik in den bedeutendsten Zeitschriften,* p. 28.

it." [21]   Nevertheless, all sections of the German press, like that of other countries, showed the effect of increasing international tension.   By 1912, such journals as the *Kölnische Zeitung* (Sept. 25, 1912, March 19, 1913) and the Catholic *Germania* (March 16, 1913) were beginning to appeal for subscribers on the basis of their foreign news service and their editorial comments on the international situation.

To all who believed in the free expression of public opinion the government's influence upon the press was a standing grievance.   The situation differed from that of other countries in degree rather than in principle, for all of the great powers— Russia most and England least of all— [22] used the press in one way or another to enlist the support of public opinion for what they were trying to do in foreign affairs.   While a united nation was practically a necessity for the efficient prosecution of a war, the diplomats everywhere regarded it as a valuable ally in current negotiations.   Even Bismarck cited public sentiment as a reason for insisting upon colonies in 1884.   Moreover, it furnished a convenient reason for refusing concessions which statesmen for other reasons had no intention of granting.   For the launching of trial balloons by which the reactions of other powers might be tested without unduly exposing the government's own hand, the press also served a technical diplomatic function.   Hohenlohe told William II that the *Kölnische Zeitung* was indispensable because its articles were read and studied abroad when the latter, in a moment of pique, directed that the foreign office should sever its relations with this journal. [23]   To the German government the exercise of official influence upon the press seemed especially necessary in order to assure a continuous exposition of its views to the general public, for, contrary to the situation in countries whose governments were controlled by the majority parties, no part of the press could always be counted upon to serve this function.   While Bismarck did not originate this practice, he devel-

---

[21] "Die Wahrheit über das Deutsche Reich," von einem Diplomat, *Deutsche Revue,* Jan. 1904, p. 98.

[22] S. B. Fay, "The Influence of the Pre-War Press in Europe," *Proceedings of the Massachusetts Historical Society,* LXIV, 141.   This article has been translated into German.   *Berliner Monatshefte für internationale Aufklärung,* X, 443.

[23] Hohenlohe, *Denkwürdigkeiten der Reichskanzlerzeit* (Stuttgart, 1931), pp. 291, 292 (Jan. 7, 1897).

oped it to an unprecedented extent, at least so far as Germany was concerned. Newspaper technique, especially the means by which reader interest was aroused, attracted his attention from the beginning of his career.[24]   Eugen Richter once said in the Reichstag that he was just as active a journalist as any deputy.[25] That an openly acknowledged official press, such as the *Staatsanzeiger* and the *Provinzial-Correspondenz*,[26] had only a limited value was clear to him, for he was fond of saying that he would be satisfied if a number of journals placed a certain amount of space at his disposal. What they filled the rest of their columns with was a matter of indifference.   Repeatedly, he and his colleagues, and even the *Norddeutsche Allgemeine Zeitung*,[27] denied the existence of any official influence, but the well-known revelations of Heinrich Wuttke, a bitter critic, and of Moritz Busch, one of his most active agents, make it impossible to take these protests seriously.[28]   From the confiscation in 1866 of the private estates of the Hanoverian royal house was derived a source of revenue—the notorious "reptile fund"—[29] for which no accounting had to be made either to the German or the Prussian parliaments.   This money enabled the press bureau, which was set up in the foreign office about the time of the Franco-Prussian War, to secure the insertion of articles that sometimes were entirely written by government officials with or without the aid of Bismarck's own suggestions in journals that retained some appearance of independence.[30]   Thus public opinion not only could be

[24] See his letter to Hermann Wagener, editor of the *Kreuz-Zeitung,* of July 5, 1848. Schulze, *Presse im Urteil Bismarcks,* pp. 10, 11n.

[25] Ullstein, *Eugen Richter,* p. 102 (May 6, 1881).

[26] Openly controlled by the ministry of the interior, this weekly ceased publication in the early eighties.

[27] This journal was first subsidized in 1862 to counteract the attacks upon Bismarck's "blood and iron" speech.   Within a year, its subscribers declined from 5200 to 1800, and most of the remainder were government officials.   E. Zechlin, "Der Weg zur Einheit und die 'Norddeutsche Allgemeine Zeitung'," *Deutsche Allgemeine Zeitung,* Oct. 1, 1936.   I am indebted to Professor Chester W. Clark for this article, which is in part based upon unpublished material.

[28] H. Wuttke, *Die deutschen Zeitschriften und die Entstehung der öffentlichen Meinung* (2d ed., Leipzig, 1875); M. Busch, *Tagebuchblätter,* 3 vols. (Leipzig, 1899).

[29] Apparently so named originally because it was intended to enable Bismarck to drive the "reptiles"—that is, his opponents—into their holes, but later the word was applied to the journals which accepted money from this source.

[30] In other respects, however, the German press, at least after 1870, was by common repute relatively free from corruption.   Whatever the reason may have been, the fact remains that no foreign government distributed largess to it as Russia did in France in 1912, 1913.

influenced but, if necessary, manufactured. Thus, the Progressive *Volks-Zeitung* (April 25, 1877) complained that the *National Zeitung* of Berlin quoted an editorial in the *Weser Zeitung* (Bremen) as expressing public opinion, that the *Norddeutsche* repeated this procedure with reference to the *National Zeitung,* and that all three articles had originated in the press bureau.[31] Since Busch's diaries are most specific for the official sources of articles appearing in the *Grenzboten,* it is obviously not always possible to distinguish even in Bismarck's time between inspired and uninspired statements in the daily newspapers. Clearly, however, the editorials of the *Norddeutsche Allgemeine Zeitung* and those of other journals which it quoted with approval, those of the *Provinzial-Correspondenz,* and the Berlin dispatches which appeared in the *Kölnische Zeitung* and were repeated elsewhere had an official origin. In general, only Conservative, National Liberal, and perhaps occasionally Centrist newspapers were used for this purpose, for the independence of at least the Progressive, the Social Democratic, and usually the Centrist journals was beyond question. Even Bismarck, after burning his fingers in the crisis of 1875, announced the end of this official influence, and in 1891 Caprivi made different arrangements for the disposal of the "reptile fund." [32] In neither instance, however, did any real change occur. Caprivi and his successors found it impossible to do without a dependable press; Bülow indeed seems at first to have given extraordinarily close attention to the problem.[33] From 1894, Otto Hammann remained at the head of the press bureau, with thirty or forty newspapers more or less at his disposal.[34] "For its domestic and foreign policies," wrote a leading Catholic review as late as 1908, "Berlin directs the largest orchestra the world has ever seen." [35] It would be a mistake to assume that money was the sole means by which this influence was exerted, for the government had other and perhaps even more

---

31 According to Wuttke, articles were placed in foreign journals and then re-translated, as evidence of public opinion in those countries. Wuttke, *Deutsche Zeitschriften,* p. 291. No wonder that this pamphlet was regarded as Wuttke's testament as a publicist. "Die Grossmacht-Presse," *Historisch-Politische Blätter,* vol. 150, p. 596 (Oct. 1912).

32 *Staatsanzeiger,* April 2, 1891. Cf. *Reichsbote,* April 3, 1891.

33 M. Harden, *"Norddeutsche Allgemeine Zeitung,"* Zukunft, Aug. 30, 1902.

34 Fay, "Pre-War Press," *Proc. of Mass. Hist. Soc.,* LXIV, 128.

35 "Das Pressorchester," *Historisch-Politische Blätter,* vol. 141, p. 916 (May 1908).

valuable favors at its command, such as news and paid announce-
ments of official business; [36] nor should the degree to which German public opinion was regimented be exaggerated. There was
some point to the *Norddeutsche Allgemeine Zeitung's* (April 11,
1888) claim that even an approximately complete control of the
German press was a physical impossibility.

Especially since Germany's defeat in the World War, many
have placed a large share of the responsibility for the increasing
hostility of world opinion upon the official press policy.[37] However well-founded may be the charges of the failure to enlighten
the outside world as to the true character of her aims and methods
and, in particular, of permitting, because of the long delay in laying cables to the New World, the English Reuter Agency and the
French *Agence Havas* to enjoy almost a monopoly of European
news, it was guilty of another and scarcely less costly failure.
Rarely was it possible for the general public to gain a clear impression of the official policy from the inspired press—in contrast
to the lucid, if not always wholly accurate, outline in the speeches
of Bismarck and his successors. Instead of clarity, confusion was
more frequently the result. Under Bismarck the paucity of information was especially criticized, and what appeared in the
press was often self-contradictory, for some articles were intended
for foreign readers and others for home consumption. Uncertainty greatly increased after his fall and with the adoption of the
Weltpolitik. "It is only necessary," wrote an observer in 1900,
"to leaf through last year's file of an important journal to see how
contradictory are the directions from official sources." [38] The
Conservative *Kreuz-Zeitung* (Nov. 23, 1898) complained that
public opinion was increasingly presented with accomplished facts
(*vollendeten Tatsachen*), with little if any preparation of opinion.
Hoping to profit by Germany's supposed "free hand" and from
the quarrels of other powers by the acquisition of colonies, the

---

[36] *Cf.* Richter's speech, April 6, 1891, printed as a pamphlet under the title, *"Die
geheimen Ausgaben, und der Welfenfonds* (Berlin, 1891). Ullstein, *Eugen Richter,*
pp. 130, 131.

[37] P. Eltzbacher, *Die Presse als Werkzeug der auswärtigen Politik* (Jena, 1918),
passim.

[38] M. von Brandt, "Die deutsche Presse und die auswärtige Politik," *Deutsche Revue,*
May 1900, p. 201. The existence of press bureaus in other departments as well as the
foreign office—especially in the marine—added to the confusion.

government doubtless found it inexpedient to explain its policy fully, but the self-contradictions of the official press sometimes created difficulties even with Germany's allies. In 1902, Bülow warned the Italian ambassador that only those articles of the *Kölnische Zeitung* reflected the government's views which originated from the Wolff Agency or which were clipped by the *Norddeutsche Allgemeine Zeitung*.[39] Under William II the official press policy was to no small degree the cause of the increasing lack of confidence in the government's foreign policy.

The *Hamburgischer Korrespondent* doubtless expressed the official point of view when it warned public opinion, "which usually derives its strength from irrational instincts," not to interfere with the conduct of negotiations and when it stressed the value of the support of "a strong and independent public opinion."[40] If the great majority usually followed Bismarck's leadership after 1866 without question, there were few Germans, or few parties and groups, who were prepared after his fall to support the official policy regardless of circumstances. By 1911, the Conservatives and the Pan-Germans tried their best to influence the conduct of foreign affairs while the negotiations during the Agadir crisis were still in progress. Besides the opposition parties, there were others who desired a closer agreement with public opinion—so long as that opinion agreed substantially with their own. Such was the trend of the Pan-German propaganda. Occasionally a more moderate voice was raised for a definite effort to influence the official foreign policy. Had the German nation, asked Alfred Schäffle in the *Zukunft* (Sept. 21, 1895), done all it could to prevent "dangerous and costly adventures in foreign affairs?" Even more than in democratic countries means were lacking for the establishment of a popular control. From the repeated efforts of the Progressive and Social Democratic deputies since 1866 to force the government to copy England's *Blue Books,* in the hope that some indirect influence would result, appeared a total of forty-eight *White Books,* but their contents were usually thin and only remotely connected with the great problems of international

---

[39] Bülow, Jan. 12, 1902. *Die Grosse Politik der europäischen Politik,* 40 vols. (Berlin, 1922–1927) XVIII, 746. This work will hereafter be cited as *G. P.*
[40] *Post,* Jan. 13, 1899.

relations.[41] The right of interpellation on foreign affairs was rarely asserted, and even less frequently granted, so that these problems were debated in the Reichstag only at fairly long intervals in connection with the annual appropriation for the foreign office, with army and navy bills, and with colonial questions.[42] The Bundesrat's committee on foreign affairs, which Bavaria had insisted upon in order to assure that the federated states would be regularly informed as to what was going on, met only once under Bismarck, not at all under Caprivi, once under Hohenlohe, and twice under Bülow. It was not until the severe crisis over William II's *Daily Telegraph* interview in the autumn of 1908 that meetings were held with any sort of regularity.[43] In comparison with Bismarck, his successors dealt more tactfully with the Reichstag—and with the press—but there was no real change of policy. In November 1900 Bülow expatiated with his usual suavity upon his understanding and approval of the need for a full explanation of the government's foreign policy, yet he had that summer consented to the dispatch of an expeditionary force to China without calling the Reichstag into a special session for an appropriation—an oversight which the spokesmen of almost every party denounced as an outright violation of the constitution.[44]

The prospect for a democratic control of foreign affairs was even slighter in Germany than in France and England. Even the occasional proposal for a Reichstag committee on foreign affairs was not acted upon.[45] As a platform from which party leaders could speak to the nation and from which the government could explain as much or as little as it pleased, the Reichstag served an important purpose, but it had no direct influence upon foreign policy. Whether public opinion in general and the press in particular counted for something in its formulation is a more debatable question. Impressed by the extent of official influence upon the press, by the supposed docility of German opinion, and

[41] Sass, *Deutsche Weissbücher*, pp. 110–113.
[42] Albers, *Reichstag und Aussenpolitik*, pp. 9, 10. Not until 1878, and then only on Bismarck's suggestion, did the rightist parties sponsor an interpellation relating to foreign affairs. *National Zeitung*, Feb. 10, 1878.
[43] Sass, *op. cit.*, pp. 66, 67n.
[44] *Stenographische Berichte der Verhandlungen des deutschen Reichstages*, X Leg. Per., II Sess., I, 11, 17, 18, 21, 49, 104 (Nov. 19, 20, 23, 1900).
[45] Sass, *op. cit.*, p. 106.

Kladderadatsch, November 22, 1908.

Figure 1.—The proposed standing committee of the
Reichstag on foreign affairs.

by the political incapacity which Germans themselves have been the first to acknowledge, most students have dismissed it without much careful consideration. Even Professor Sydney B. Fay, one of the historians who most fully recognize the importance of these factors in the history of international relations, finds only one incident in which the press exerted a decisive influence—he attributed Bülow's failure to respond to Chamberlain's friendly speech in the autumn of 1899 to the anti-English campaign during the Boer War—and concludes that the press was less influential in Germany than in England, France, or even Russia.[46]   None of Germany's rulers and diplomats, nor indeed those of other countries, perhaps ever admitted that they were influenced by the press. "I never read newspapers," said William II, "what those muttonheads write means nothing to me."[47]   Yet the *Post* (Nov. 7, 1908) asserted that the leading articles of eight or nine journals were placed before him each morning and the archives are said to contain volumes of these clippings, with occasional comments from the imperial pen.[48]   Even the printed diplomatic documents reveal William's sensitiveness to press criticism during the Agadir crisis.   No one knew better than Bismarck how extensive the official influence was, yet visitors often found him immersed in "a sea of newspapers."[49]   To be sure, the reader of a newspaper, especially if he occupies a position of great power, is not necessarily influenced by it.   Yet the press was responsible in large measure for that climate of opinion, one of the imponderables which are just as important in history as Bismarck said they were in politics, which influenced rulers and commoners alike.[50]

Bismarck once said that it was the business of statesmen to understand and to give effect to the aspirations of the nation. To him, however, these aspirations were not at all identical with public opinion as expressed in the newspapers.[51]   In practice, this reservation perhaps meant that the statesman's own reactions

[46] Fay, "Pre-War Press," *Proc. of Mass. Hist. Soc.*, LXIV, p. 141.

[47] J. Ziekursch, *Politische Geschichte des neuen deutschen Kaiserreiches*, 4 vols. (Berlin, 1925–1930), IV, 10.

[48] It also spoke of the Empress as an industrious reader of the press, naming itself, the *National Zeitung, Reichsbote, Kreuz-Zeitung*, and *Lokal-Anzeiger* as her favorites.

[49] Schulze, *Die Presse im Urteil Bismarcks*, p. 8 (Jan. 12, 1873).

[50] "Sogar der russische Selbstherrscher wäre heute nicht im Stande eine Politik zu treiben, welche den Gesinnungen und Tendenzen seines Volkes widerspräche, . . ." *Preussische Jahrbücher*, vol. 31, p. 580 (May 15, 1873). This periodical will hereafter be cited as *P. J.*

[51] F. Tönnies, *Kritik der öffentliche Meinung* (Berlin, 1922), p. 164.

were the best guide to the people's true desires. It would seem to follow that where official action was in accord with public opinion this agreement was either more or less accidental or the result of official propaganda or of the tendency of men, whether officials or private citizens, to react to the more elementary situations, like a serious menace, in essentially the same way. That Bismarck finally came around to a view of the Near Eastern crisis in 1878 and its meaning for Germany not unlike that of the opposition parties and press perhaps illustrates the first of these hypotheses. The third and last does not rule out public opinion as a contributing influence. During the *Einkreisung* scare in 1908 the general public, the press, and the government probably influenced each other. The strong protest against France's annexation of Luxemburg in 1867 was almost certainly a reason why Bismarck openly declared against it, so vital was then his prestige as the champion of national unity, and public opinion was clearly one cause of his colonial policy. The fact that a large part of the German people in 1905 did not regard Morocco as worth a war probably influenced the course of events by weakening Bülow's bluff. Despite William II's boasted indifference to the press, he was himself a pretty accurate barometer for its changing moods of pessimism and of overconfidence and for its fits of passion. However, the Pan-German and ultra-nationalist journals perhaps exerted their greatest influence beyond the frontiers. Thanks to the general belief abroad that the German newspapers were completely under official control as far as foreign affairs were concerned, they were assiduously read for light in regard to Germany's intentions. In the British foreign office, Eyre Crowe paid far more attention to the *Alldeutsche Blätter,* the Pan-German organ, than to the *Berliner Tageblatt* or the *Frankfurter Zeitung,* the two most important liberal journals. A German observer feared that the activities of the extremists would result in disaster. "The names and articles of the writers who are preparing international unpleasantnesses (*Unangenehmlichkeiten*) for us will quickly be forgotten, grass will soon grow over their printer's ink, but who knows but that many a mother's son will atone for their misdoings." [52]

---

[52] Brandt, "Die deutsche Presse und auswärtige Politik," *Deutsche Revue,* May 1900, pp. 200, 201.

CHAPTER II

Bismarck's Diplomacy
and German National Sentiment, 1866-1871

Die staatliche Consolidirung von acht und dreissig Millionen Deutscher ist in sicherer Aussicht. Wehe dem, der an diesen Staat des deutsche Volk rührt!
A. Wagner, "Die Entwicklung der europäischen Staatsterritorien und das Nationalitätsprincip," *Preussische Jahrbücher,* vol. 19 (1867) p. 548.

Ich musste . . . für einen Beweis grosser Kurzsichtigkeit halten, . . . dass man nicht verstanden hat, wie das ganze Auftreten Frankreichs nur dazu beigetragen hat, den notwendigen Prozess zu beschleunigen . . .
Bismarck, March 15, 1867.

. . . ein zu nationaler Macht und Selbstständigkeit erwachtes Deutschland die sicherste Garantie des Weltfriedens sei!
Berliner Post, May 15, 1867.

I

The reactions of Germans to international politics as the second half of the nineteenth century began were chiefly influenced, like those of other peoples, by historical memories, geographical conditions, and by the feeling of a common nationality. There was nothing essentially unique in the grievances which they had inherited from the past. The Germans were by no means the only people who blamed others for their misfortunes and forgot their own considerable responsibility. Their contributions to the long record of disunion and weakness while other countries were acquiring strong central governments were numerous: the Italian ambitions of their medieval Emperors, their religious conflicts, the selfishness of local rulers, the international outlook of the Catholics, and the cosmopolitan ideas of the eighteenth century, to name only those which made their influence felt prior to the nineteenth century. Far more vivid memories were left, however, of the use which Germany's neighbors had made of her divisions. In more recent times, there has been no lack of an appreciation of the consequences of her central location in Europe between France, Austria, and Russia, with England facing her across the North Sea. Her historians are prone to emphasize the weakness of this position as a constant invitation to foreign intervention, whereas her neighbors have often been alarmed by its potential strength. The results for the German people, however, were the same. At one time or another the armies of almost every great power devastated her fields and towns. Jealousy and fear of Prussia, alone of the German states strong enough since Frederick William the Great Elector (1640–1688) to play the part of a European power, made of the secondary states the tools of Austria's domination of the Holy Roman Empire and of the German Confederation for more than three centuries. France advanced to the Rhine, annexing Alsace-Lorraine, and exploited Germany's religious divisions and the selfish interests of her princes to keep her in a state of anarchy. In the absence of a strong central authority during the development of the foreign policies of the great powers, the postulate of a weak Germany became a basic assumption of European politics. It was made a part of the status quo by the Peace of Westphalia (1648) and the Treaty of Vienna (1815). The first Napoleon's unintentional but valuable contributions to German unity were insignificant in comparison with the memories of his ruthless exploitation. The impression of Europe as an inimical force and of Germany as its innocent victim became an inseparable part of German thought and emotion in regard to foreign affairs. Nor is it strange, after Richelieu, Louis XIV, and Napoleon I, that France was regarded as the hereditary foe, except perhaps in the Rhineland and in South Germany and among a small circle of liberal intellectuals.

The thesis that the peace of Europe and the security of the other countries must be assured at Germany's expense elicited nothing but derision, for it had the appearance of a device for the establishment of France's hegemony. After 1815, it was, however, Austria that controlled the German Confederation. Even in Prussia tradition and the aversion of conservative opinion to revolutionary changes assured support for Austria's domination. Bismarck accepted it until his experiences as the Prussian envoy to the Diet (1851–1858) convinced him that Austria would never accept Prussia as an equal partner. In 1840 the response to the crisis over the Rhine frontier, which Thiers worked up as a diversion from France's diplomatic defeat in the Near East, showed that a French menace was still certain to evoke an explosion of national sentiment. Nevertheless, the ideal of German unity was kept alive during the period of police repression after 1815. There was no Mazzini to define the place in Europe of a liberal German state, but the liberals doubtless desired a friendly collaboration with England and even with France, from whom they had borrowed their chief political ideas. Pacifism was not a tenet of their creed, in spite of their hatred of Prussian militarism. The liberal majority in the Frankfort Parliament (1848–1849) aided Prussia in her war with Denmark for the possession of Schleswig-Holstein and it began the construction of a German fleet.[1] Lack of political experience rather than an aversion in principle to the use of force explains the failure in 1848 to arm the nation against Austria's inevitable counter-attack after she had refused the crown of a Great Germany. Prussia, however, administered the *coup de grâce* to the brief period of liberal control when Frederick William IV rejected the offer of the crown of a Small Germany, in which no part of Austria would be included. From the point of view of the Hohenzollerns and of the ruling class, a divided Germany and even Austrian domination was preferable to absorption by a united nation.

Italy's victory with French aid in the Austro-Sardinian War (1859–1860) gave birth in Germany to a sense of impending change. The liberals, with a national organization in Rudolph Bennigsen's *National-Verein,* turned toward Prussia as the only

---

[1] V. Valentin, *Geschichte der deutschen Revolution, 1848–1849,* 2 vols. (Berlin, 1931), II, 25, 26, 337–344.

source of effective leadership.[2] Her part in the national rising against Napoleon, the prestige that accrued to her from the economic benefits of the *Zollverein,* and her position as the strongest German state outweighed their dislike of her militarist and authoritarian régime. Frederick William IV's abortive attempt to enlist the small states against Austria in 1850, although it ended in the humiliation of Olmütz (1851), was a gratifying display of courage in the service of the national cause. It seemed possible that the Regent, Prince William, whose willingness to aid Austria in 1859 had cooled when the latter refused to concede anything more than a partnership in the command of the federal army,[3] might work with the liberals. By permitting the first free elections for the Landtag since the grant of the reactionary constitution of 1851, he made it possible for them to win a working majority and, in 1859, he accepted a moderate ministry. It was a fateful moment for Germany. Instead of granting the increase of the army on which he had set his heart, the liberals defied him, fearing that a stronger military force would be turned against themselves and hoping that this issue might be used to secure the control of the Prussian state by establishing the principle of ministerial responsibility. This decision sealed their fate. Henceforth there could be no question of an alliance between the Prussian Crown and German liberalism. The attack began in September 1862 with Bismarck's appointment as Minister-President, with the mission of increasing the army with—or if necessary without—the Landtag's consent. He warned the Budget Committee that Germany's problems could only be solved by "blood and iron," not by "debates and parliamentary majorities,"[4] and when the Landtag voted the necessary appropriations for only one year, he dissolved it and proceeded to build up the army by executive decrees. Thereupon liberal opinion at once began to turn toward

---

[2] E. Zechlin, *Bismarck und die Grundlegung der deutschen Grossmacht* (Stuttgart, 1930), p. 235.

[3] H. Friedjung, *Der Kampf um die Vorherrschaft in Deutschland, 1859–1886,* 2 vols. (Stuttgart, 1916), I, 13, 14.

[4] In an effort to counteract the bad impression abroad, he explained to Loftus, the British ambassador, that his meaning had been misrepresented by an unofficial stenographer. He had, he said, merely urged the need of an adequate army for the support of Prussia's policy. Loftus, Oct. 18, 1862. *Die auswärtige Politik Preussens 1858–1871,* III, 45. This work will henceforth be cited as *A. P. P.*

Austria. The *Reform-Verein,* in whose organization Austria had been active,[5] made considerable progress, especially as it seemed that the February Patent (1861) had laid the foundation of a parliamentary régime in Vienna. On the essential question of her control in Germany, Austria had no intention of yielding, but it was to her advantage to conciliate German opinion.

Bismarck's unconstitutional methods contributed to the unpopularity of his foreign policy. Not only were the Catholics and other Great Germans passionately opposed to the exclusion of Austria from a united Germany, not only did the Prussian Conservatives regard German unity as a menace to their special privileges and to Prussia's independence,[6] but the liberals lost their former sympathy for his hostility toward Austria and his readiness to coöperate with France if it served his purpose.[7] Bismarck was therefore forced to play almost a lone hand, for only his assiduous attendance upon the King perhaps forestalled opposition from that quarter.[8] Yet, even in these circumstances, the public opinion which he sometimes contemptuously described as bereft of political sense may not summarily be dismissed as without influence upon his decisions. From the first, his purpose remained the expansion of Prussia's power,[9] but he also hoped to secure in the support of the German nation a source of strength which he by no means underestimated. Public opinion was a significant, if unacknowledged, force pressing for positive and reasonably speedy achievements; defeat would mean the end of his own career and the repudiation of his policy. A change in public sentiment, he was confident, would promptly follow definite progress toward union. "I know my Prussians well," he

[5] H. Ruider, *Bismarck und die öffentliche Meinung in Bayern, 1864–1866* (Munich, 1924), p. 7.

[6] They accepted, though with many misgivings, his leadership as their strongest defense against the liberals. G. Ritter, *Die preussischen Konservativen und Bismarcks deutsche Politik, 1858 bis 1871* (Heidelberg, 1913), pp. 73–75 *passim.* On the army question, they supported Bismarck in order, according to a recent sociological and economic interpretation of German history from 1866 to 1914, to prevent the development of the *Landwehr* as a sort of bourgeois national guard. W. Hallgarten, *Vorkriegs Imperialismus; die soziologischen Grundlagen der Aussenpolitik europäischer Grossmächte bis 1914* (Paris, 1935), p. 91.

[7] Zechlin, *Bismarck,* p. 237.

[8] See his statement to Courcel, the French ambassador, in May 1885. Courcel, May 28, 1885. *Documents diplomatiques français,* (1), VI, 42. This collection will henceforth be cited as *D. D. F.*

[9] This thesis is developed by G. Franz, *Bismarcks Nationalgefühl* (Leipzig, 1926).

once said, "they have something of the Frenchman in them. Just give them a little fame and influence abroad, and you can do anything with them." [10]

Too large a part in his success may be attributed to Bismarck's genius. Extraordinarily adroit in making use of favorable conditions and events—one essential test of statesmanship—for their existence he was not often entirely or even chiefly responsible. Chance favored him continually. Russia's grievances against Austria dating from the Crimean War (1854–1856) and her desire to rid herself of the Treaty of Paris made it easier for him to win her favor, and the Polish insurrection of 1863, which threatened Prussia's control of her own Polish provinces, gave him an opportunity to do Russia a favor. That France was ruled at this critical juncture by Napoleon III and not by a Thiers was the most fortunate of all these favorable circumstances, since Napoleon, dreaming of a mission for the reorganization of Europe along national lines, had partly broken with France's historic policy of keeping Germany weak and divided. At first Napoleon thought of Prussia as a German Sardinia and of Bismarck as a German Cavour, more than once offering him an alliance with a considerable extension of territory for Prussia in North Germany. Napoleon III, like his uncle, must be included among the founders of united Germany. Scarcely a year after Bismarck's appointment as Chancellor, a convenient crisis was precipitated by Christian IX's integration of Schleswig-Holstein with his Danish territory, in violation of the London Convention (1852). Aided by Austria's jealousy and suspicions of Prussia, he was able to entice her into the alliance of January 1864, into the war against Denmark (1864), and into the dangerous complications of a joint administration of the duchies. The threat of foreign intervention, which Bismarck had feared most of all, was averted by Christian's obstinate demand for both duchies.[11] A lesser man might have bungled these opportunities, but without the assistance of Austria's blunders, such as her consent in the Gastein Convention (1865) to undertake the separate administration of Holstein,

---

[10] C. W. Clark, *Franz Joseph and Bismarck; The Diplomacy of Austria before the War of 1866* (Cambridge, 1934), p. 480.

[11] L. D. Steefel, *The Schleswig-Holstein Question* (Cambridge, 1932), p. 242.

his progress must have been slower. Each advance toward the undivided possession of both duchies and a final settlement with Austria was carefully calculated in the light of her probable reaction. His offers of compensation in return for Austria's peaceful withdrawal from Holstein, because they never went beyond a money payment or vague references to territorial concessions, were undoubtedly made with little expectation, or even desire, of their acceptance.[12]   He probably foresaw that Austria would be unwilling to pay the price of alliances with Italy and France by the voluntary cession of Venetia and by a promise of her support of France's desire for the left bank of the Rhine.

As Bismarck's intention to provoke a war with Austria became clear in the spring of 1866, public opinion in Prussia as well as in all Germany declared its disapproval in no uncertain terms.[13] Attacks against him in the press reached unprecedented heights and a flood of petitions to the King protested against his policy. Nor did his proposal for the reform of the Confederation (June 10) satisfy the liberals, for they, somewhat unfairly, discounted it as an insincere gesture. From the Great German point of view, war with Austria meant a lamentable break with German traditions, a fratricidal conflict, and therefore treason to the German cause. The majority of Germans undoubtedly not only expected but also hoped for Prussia's defeat when the armies took the field in June. All Germany, with varying degrees of zeal, stood with Austria. Apart from the mistakes of Austria's diplomacy, which compelled a diversion of a part of her army against Prussia's Italian ally, there was nothing accidental in Prussia's victory at Königgrätz (July 3). It was the merited achievement of Moltke, the Prussian organization, the needle-gun, and the Prussian schoolmaster.

As Bismarck had expected, the swift and decisive success of the armies promptly changed Prussian and, to a certain extent, German public opinion. Demands for extensive territorial annexations and for complete unity poured into the general head-

---

[12] Clark, *Franz Joseph and Bismarck,* pp. 479, 480.
[13] See the brief summaries of contemporary pamphlets in H. Rosenberg, *Die Nationalpolitische Publizistik Deutschlands vom Eintritt der neuen Ära in Preussen bis zum Ausbruch des deutschen Krieges,* 2 vols. (Munich, 1935), II, Nos. 1261–1324.

quarters. German and Prussian liberalism was among the casualties of the war. Soon the *National-Verein* divided, with the majority, as the National Liberal party, going over to Bismarck, while the minority remained in opposition as the Progressive party. The Landtag paid its tribute to success by legalizing the unconstitutional régime of the past four years. Even Ludwig Bamberger, a Progressive leader, deprecated his party's fear of Prussia's domination of a united Germany, arguing that the conquered would eventually subdue the conqueror.[14] The nationally minded minority in the secondary states tacitly abandoned the struggle for *Freiheit* in favor of *Einheit* under Prussia's leadership. This movement of opinion was powerfully stimulated by the danger of French intervention. After Königgrätz Napoleon III could no longer hope to act as an arbiter between two combatants who had bled themselves white. Prussia clearly did not intend to content herself with the relatively modest gains in North Germany which he had graciously allotted to her in his letter of June 11 to the *corps législatif*. Although his illness and the weakness of the French army prevented a military demonstration on the Rhine, the exposure of Prussia's right flank caused Bismarck to accept Napoleon's offer of diplomatic mediation and to give him a voice in the peace negotiations. More symptomatic of German national sentiment, however, were the threats of war in the National Liberal press.[15]

In the Treaty of Prague, Bismarck attained his two immediate purposes, the exclusion of Austria and the unity of Germany north of the Main River under Prussia's leadership. He promptly annexed Schleswig-Holstein, Nassau, Hesse-Cassel, and Frankfort, and began negotiations for the North German Confederation. That Austria escaped with a moderate indemnity was the result more of Bismarck's desire to keep the door open for a future alliance than of French influence, but Napoleon did se-

---

[14] L. Bamberger, *M. de Bismarck* (Paris, 1868), p. 224. *Cf.* his letter to *Le Temps* (Jan. 27, 1867) of January 12, 1867, in reply to Edgar Quinet's articles on Franco-German relations. The economic advantages of union, no matter how achieved, naturally attracted many bankers, merchants, and industrialists. Hallgarten, *Vorkriegs Imperialismus*, p. 95.

[15] *Kölnische Zeitung, Magdeburgische Zeitung, National Zeitung* (Berlin), July 6; H. von Treitschke, *Zehn Jahre deutscher Kämpfe, 1865–1874* (Berlin, 1874), p. 93 (July 10).

cure the promise of a plebiscite in North Schleswig, the recognition of the independence of the South German states, and a provision for an eventual federal organization south of the Main.[16] To balance these concessions to France, Bismarck insisted upon and secured the formal mention of prospective national ties between the two German confederations. Prussian opinion was acutely disappointed by these terms. It declared with one accord that the Main line was merely a temporary barrier to complete unity,[17] a coaling station before the Prussian locomotive proceeded further. That Prussia was more bitterly hated than ever in South Germany and that the crossing of the Main would mean war with France, as the *Kölnische Zeitung* (July 27) admitted, was no deterrent even for moderate opinion.[18] Treitschke spoke more plainly than most in declaring that the Treaty of Prague should be set aside, even at the price of war, if the South Germans would coöperate.[19] That the general trend of Prussian public opinion was agreeable to Bismarck was suggested by the attitude of the inspired and official press. The *Kölnische Zeitung* (Aug. 5) at first affirmed Prussia's intention to respect the treaty and then (Aug. 21) it wrote of the "temporary separation" between the North and the South. On August 1, the *Provinzial-Correspondenz,* published by the Prussian ministry of the interior, spoke of their union as the inevitable result of common interests. The chasm between Bismarck and German national sentiment, caused by the constitutional conflict, had been closed.

II

Austria's defeat awakened Europe for the first time to Bismarck's capacities and to Prussia's power. Nowhere was the reaction entirely favorable. The rise of a strong military power upon the ruins of the weak Confederation, which had served as

---

[16] The French diplomats hoped for a future alliance between Austria and a South German Confederation. Wendland, Paris, July 14. H. Oncken, *Die Rheinpolitik Napoleons III, von 1863 bis 1870 und der Ursprung des Krieges von 1870–71,* 3 vols. (Stuttgart, 1926), I, 348, 350. This work will henceforth be cited as *R. N.* de Lhuys, Paris, July 23. *Les Origines diplomatiques de la guerre de 1870–1871,* A. Aulard, ed., 29 vols. (1910–1932), XI, 165, 166. This work will henceforth be cited as *O. D.*

[17] *National Zeitung, Post* (Berlin), Aug. 3, 1866.

[18] *Volks-Zeitung* (Berlin), Aug. 12; *Vossische Zeitung* (Berlin), Sept. 20.

[19] *Zehn Jahre,* p. 137 (Aug. 10).

a basis of the balance of power since 1815, affected more or less
adversely the security and interests of every European country.
Even Russia and England, less immediately concerned than the
other great powers, were disturbed by the fate of the secondary
German states because of dynastic interests, although their sympathies and jealousy were neutralized by the use which might be
made of the new power for the advancement of Russia's aims in
the Black Sea and by England's traditional desire for a balance
to France.[20]   The danger of active resistance to the completion of
German unity by other countries, if not of a direct attack upon
the achievements of 1866, was more immediate.   Impotent for
the moment, Austria nevertheless publicly identified herself with
a policy of revenge (November 1866) by the appointment of
Beust, Bismarck's Saxon enemy, as Minister-President, and the
cession of Venetia to Italy freed her rear.   Italy could and did
hope for a solution of the Roman question either as the price of
an alliance with France or as a result of a Franco-Prussian war.
Far more menacing was France's dissatisfaction.   For the moment, the government of Napoleon III had decided against war,
but war remained as a possible diversion from its increasing political difficulties at home, as a satisfaction for the chauvinists, and
as a means of rehabilitating France's diminished prestige abroad.
Much would depend upon the outcome of her efforts between
July 1866 and May 1867 to secure territorial compensations as a
balance to Prussia's gains.

   In dealing with Napoleon's efforts to secure such compensations, Bismarck's hands were less free than in the period leading
to the Austro-Prussian War.   War was clearly inadvisable before
Prussia had consolidated her gains, before she had satisfactorily
clarified her relations with the South German states, and before
she had secured some assurance that the other powers would remain neutral.   Success had given German public opinion an importance that Bismarck had earlier contemptuously denied, for
Prussia's new prestige with German national sentiment would be
a powerful support in the further development of German unity.
Her reputation as the champion of the national cause served re-

---

[20] A. Loftus, *Diplomatic Reminiscences*, (2), 2 vols. (London, 1894), I, 99.

peatedly as a reason or excuse for the refusal of Napoleon's demands, but the violent objection of public opinion to any concessions was also, as in the Luxemburg crisis, a restraint upon Bismarck's freedom of action. National susceptibilities played no inconsiderable part in the failure of the search for compensations which would strengthen Napoleon at home.

Even Drouhyn de Lhuys, Napoleon's foreign minister, saw the danger of arousing German national sentiment. Benedetti was instructed (Aug. 5) to present the first demands—the frontier of 1814 (Saarbruck and Landau), Luxemburg, the Bavarian Palatinate, Mainz, and a part of Hesse—in such a way as to prevent their use in exciting "Germany's nationalist passions against us"; [21] but rumors of these or similar demands at once aroused a storm of protest. Complete unity, it was said, would be the sole result.[22] Bismarck's refusal was certain,[23] for the territory in question would establish France upon both banks of the middle Rhine, from which she could dictate the course of events in Germany. He suspected, moreover, that Napoleon's real aim was to discredit Prussia with German national sentiment.[24] His use of this unwise and ill-considered initiative was masterly. By attributing his refusal to the King's opposition and to the irresistible passions of public opinion rather than to his own objections,[25] he left the door open to further negotiations concerning territory as to whose fate German sentiment might be less sensitive. At the same time, he inflamed public opinion by communicating the French demands to a correspondent of the *Siècle,* a Republican journal of Paris, although he added an assurance of his own desire of peace,[26] while, in view of possible war, he thought of inciting a Hungarian revolution and of alliances with Italy and Russia.[27] But the storm of indignation following the *Siècle's* revelations (Aug. 11) [28] persuaded Napoleon to yield

[21] de Lhuys, Aug. 3. *O. D.,* XI, 359, 360.
[22] *National Zeitung,* Aug. 9; *Allgemeine Zeitung* (Augsburg), Aug. 10.
[23] Bismarck's marginal comment. Goltz, Paris, July 11. *R. N.,* I, 341.
[24] Bismarck, July 8. *R. N.,* II, 33.
[25] Benedetti, Aug. 6, July 26. *O. D.,* XI, 219–225, 392–402.
[26] J. Vilbort, *L'Oeuvre de M. de M. Bismarck, 1863–1866* (Paris, 1869), pp. 521, 522.
[27] Bismarck, Aug. 9. *Bismarck: Die gesammelten Werke,* F. Thimme, ed., VI, 114, 115. This work will henceforth be cited as *B: G. W.*
[28] *Kölnische Zeitung,* Aug. 12.

rather than have all Germany against him for "a very small profit."[29]   On August 12 Bismarck acknowledged that no complications were to be expected;[30] three days later, the official *Provinzial-Correspondenz* expressed the extraordinary opinion that the German people should be grateful for Napoleon's moderation.[31] Such encouragement as anti-Prussian opinion derived from the prospect of French interference was overshadowed by the popular protest against France's demands for German soil. Nationalists wrote of a "fresh, joyful war,"[32] and a National Liberal newspaper in Bavaria declared that a demand for Alsace-Lorraine should be the only reply.[33]   The fear of France's armed intervention together with his own judicious concessions in the terms of peace enabled Bismarck to conclude secret offensive and defensive alliances with Wurtemberg (Aug. 13), Baden (Aug. 17), and Bavaria (Aug. 22), providing for reciprocal guarantees of frontiers and military coöperation under the supreme command of the King of Prussia.   He had thus averted a possible defeat, had stimulated national sentiment, and had erected at least a temporary bridge across the Main River.

Moreover, Napoleon continued to play into Bismarck's hands. Encouraged by the latter's earlier suggestion of Belgium as a suitable satisfaction,[34] although Bismarck's purpose had obviously been to divert France's attention from the Rhine and to open the way for Anglo-French complications, Benedetti proposed within ten days of his first rebuff an alliance stipulating Prussia's support of France's annexation of Belgium and King William's aid in the purchase of Luxemburg from the King of Holland.   Seeing no need of a second forthright refusal, for the fate of neither Belgium nor Luxemburg seemed essential to his German policy, Bismarck demanded and secured—doubtless without seriously expecting positive results but rather to assure a profit to Prussia whatever the outcome might be—France's specific recognition of

[29] Napoleon III, Aug. 12.   *O. D.,* XII, 70, 71.

[30] Bismarck, Aug. 12.   *B: G. W.,* VI, 122.

[31] Bismarck had instructed the press to blame the French political parties for the crisis and to praise the Emperor's unselfishness. Bismarck, Nikolsburg, July 31. *Ibid.,* VI, 96. Cf. *Haude und Spenersche Zeitung* (Berlin), Aug. 12; *Magdeburgische Zeitung,* Aug. 17; *Post,* Aug. 19.

[32] *National Zeitung,* Aug. 14; *Frankfurter Journal,* in *Allgemeine Zeitung,* Aug. 15.

[33] *Fränkische Zeitung,* Aug. 15.

[34] Behaine, Berlin, July 25.   *O. D.,* XI, 203–205.

a federal union between North and South Germany as an essential condition to further negotiations.[35] This maneuver, which has recently been interpreted as proof of his readiness to make serious sacrifices in the interest of a peaceful settlement with France,[36] was the logical reply to a proposal that might lead to a notable expansion of French territory. Undaunted by this condition, Napoleon was ready to sign by the end of August,[37] but Bismarck was in no hurry.[38] Whatever the latter's original attitude may have been, France's refusal to agree that the unification of Germany should precede and serve as the signal for her action in Belgium naturally antagonized Bismarck;[39] and King William, fearing for Prussia's prestige in Germany in the event of a transaction of this kind, refused his approval.[40] The negotiations, never officially broken off, left in Bismarck's hands the famous draft of the alliance which he later used to insure England's neutrality during the Franco-Prussian War.

At the close of 1866 and the beginning of 1867 mutual suspicion continued to block every move for Franco-Prussian diplomatic coöperation. In France's suggestion of common action in defense of the Papacy's temporal power against the young Italian state, Bismarck saw a plan to divide Prussia and Italy.[41] His own proposal of the Near Eastern question in connection with the Cretan rebellion was no more acceptable to Paris, where a prior understanding in regard to Western European questions was preferred.[42] On none of these questions was there a sharp break, nor was it Bismarck's intention that there should be one.[43] Since his revelation of the first French demands, he had made no important appeal to national sentiment. With the temporary suspension of pressure from France, German opinion enjoyed a brief breathing spell, especially after the dismissal of de Lhuys in September 1866. This minister had been most intimately associated

---

[35] Benedetti, Aug. 23.   O. D., XII, 173–175.
[36] B: G. W., VI, 150 n.
[37] Napoleon, Aug. 26.   O. D., XII, 192, 193.
[38] Goltz, Paris, Sept. 11.   R. N., II, 101–109.
[39] Benedetti, Aug. 23.   O. D., XII, 173–175.
[40] William I's comments, Goltz, Paris, Sept. 11.   R. N., II, 101–109.
[41] B: G. W., VI, 212 (Dec. 25, 1866), 216 (Jan. 6, 1867), 217 (Jan. 7); A. P. P., VIII, 169–171 (Nov. 27, 1866), 183–187 (Dec. 6).
[42] Benedetti, Jan. 26, 1867.   O. D., XIV, 186; Moustier, Paris, Feb. 20.   Ibid., XIV, 332; R. N., II, 218, 219; Goltz, Paris, March 1.   Ibid., II, 227.
[43] Bismarck. Jan. 26, 27, 1867.   B: G. W., VI, 244–246.

with the demands of August 5, and his fall meant, according to the Prussian ambassador, "the adoption of a definitely friendly policy toward Prussia." [44]   With official encouragement, the press interpreted it as the repudiation of the policy of compensations.[45] That France intended to keep the peace, at least for the immediate future, and even that she had reconciled herself to the new situation in Germany were the conclusions commonly drawn from the circular (September 16, 1866) of *ad interim* foreign minister La Valette, in which the threefold division of the German Confederation had been represented, with forced optimism, as advantageous to France.[46]   There was, however, no illusion as to France's stand in regard to the crossing of the Main.

But new clouds were gathering upon the Western frontier. A rapidly growing dissatisfaction with Bismarck's evasiveness as to the proposed alliance increased the French government's impatience for tangible gains. With Bismarck's tacit encouragement, negotiations gradually focussed upon Luxemburg, which had been a member of the German Confederation since the Treaty of 1815, but whose juristic ties with Germany had been severed by the events of 1866. Bismarck's interest in the fate of this small state was slight. In September 1866 he told the British ambassador "that Prussia has no personal interest or wish with respect to Luxemburg" and that "it is a question which does not materially or politically affect Prussia, and we are prepared for any arrangement which may be agreeable to the King Grand Duke." [47] Prussia's right to garrison the fortress of Luxemburg, acquired by a separate treaty in 1817 on behalf of the Confederation, was, he conceded, at least open to question,[48] and he defended his low estimate of its strategic value even against Moltke's expert opin-

---

[44] Goltz, Aug. 30, 1866. *A. P. P.*, VIII, 53.

[45] *Norddeutsche Allgemeine Zeitung*, Sept. 4. This journal, which Bismarck began to subsidize in the autumn of 1862 (E. Zechlin in the *Deutsche Allgemeine Zeitung*, Oct. 1, 1936), will henceforth be cited as *N. A. Z.* It will be referred to in the text as the *Norddeutsche*. *Kölnische Zeitung*, Sept. 5; *Vossische Zeitung*, Sept. 5; Treitschke, *Zehn Jahre*, p. 162 (Sept. 10). *Cf.* T. von Bernhardi, *Tagebücher aus den Jahren 1866 und 1867*, 7 vols. (Leipzig, 1897), VII, 276.

[46] *Neue Preussische Zeitung*, Sept. 19. This ultra-conservative journal will henceforth be cited as *Kreuz-Zeitung*, according to the usual practice which doubtless was suggested by the Iron Cross which appears in the masthead. *N. A. Z.*, Sept. 19; *Magdeburgische Zeitung*, Sept. 20; *Kölnische Zeitung*, Sept. 25.

[47] Loftus, Berlin, Sept. 1. *A. P. P.*, VIII, 55.

[48] Bismarck, March 10. *R. N.*, II, 237.

ion.[49] Although he believed that Luxemburg would merely whet France's appetite for the Rhineland[50] and that its acquisition would be resented by German public opinion, he continued the negotiations in an apparently accommodating spirit, partly in order to gain time for the completion of the North German Confederation. The carefulness of his advice as to France's procedure in arranging its purchase suggests, if it does not prove, that he was not in principle opposed to the transaction. Time and again he explained that he would be able to win his sovereign's consent and to resist the wrath of public opinion only on the condition that Prussia should not be implicated in the preliminary discussions, that a demonstration by conservative groups in Luxemburg should be incited to ask for the withdrawal of the Prussian garrison, and that the purchase should be presented to King William as a *fait accompli*.[51] It was clearly his intention to reserve his freedom of action in order to prevent France from compromising Prussia with German national sentiment.[52]

Franco-Prussian relations, in the meantime, grew steadily worse. A resolution of the Liberals in the Bavarian Landtag (Jan. 18) approving union with the North against a foreign enemy, Hohenlohe's pronouncement (Jan. 19) for eventual union, and the warm response of the official Prussian press, raised for France the specter of a united Germany[53] and led to a full-dress debate of France's relations with Germany in the *corps législatif* (March 14–18). Thiers' glorification of the traditional policy of intervention, although the official Prussian press discounted its significance,[54] electrified German opinion as a reminder of historic grievances against France.[55] Tension was greatly increased by the publication, delayed out of consideration for the French government

[49] *B: G. W.*, VI, 92 (July 31, 1866), 235 (Jan. 14, 1867); *R. N.*, II, 34, 35 (Aug. 8, 1866), 201 (Feb. 15, 1867).

[50] Bismarck's comment, Feb. 8, 1867. *R. N.*, 200; *ibid.*, II, 202 (Feb. 15).

[51] *R. N.*, II, 87, 88 (Aug. 20, 1866), 143 (Dec. 19), 148 (Dec. 20), 182, 183 (Jan. 13, 1867); *B: G. W.*, VI, 212, 213 (Jan. 13, 1867); Benedetti, Jan. 17, 1867. *O. D.*, XIV, 133; Moustier, Paris, March 4. *Ibid.*, XV, 38–41.

[52] Bismarck, Dec. 20, 1866. *R. N.*, II, 148.

[53] *Provinzial-Correspondenz*, Jan. 23, 1867; *N. A. Z.*, Jan. 24. For Benedetti's protest against these articles see *O. D.*, XIV, 176–180 (Jan. 25); *B: G. W.*, VI, 243, 244 (Jan. 25).

[54] *N. A. Z.*, *Kölnische Zeitung*, March 19.

[55] *Vossische Zeitung, Frankfurter Zeitung*, March 17; *Kreuz-Zeitung*, March 19; *National Zeitung*, March 20.

until the last day of the debate,[56] of the offensive and defensive
alliances with the South German states in order to strengthen
Hohenlohe's political position in Bavaria and to help him to introduce the Prussian military system.[57]   Not even Königgrätz
had aroused greater consternation in France than these disclo-
sures,[58] but the alliances awakened boundless enthusiasm in
North Germany as a timely and effective reply to Thiers and as
a promise of complete unity in the near future.[59]   In South Germany, the national press announced that the independence of the
four southern states had virtually ceased to exist.[60]   Bitter talk of
treason, of great popular indignation, and of a violation of the
Bavarian constitution filled, however, the Catholic press.[61]   In
Prussia, Progressive opinion continued to hope, though with
diminishing confidence, for a liberal constitution in North Germany, but it yielded to none in the vigor of its denunciation of
French interference and of its protest against any concessions.[62]

Such was the immediate background of the Luxemburg crisis
and of the definitive failure to reconcile France to the new order
in Germany.   Alarmed by multiplying storm signals, King William of Holland refused to sell Luxemburg to France without
first consulting Prussia and insisted as a condition for further
conversations that Napoleon should come to an understanding
with her King—exactly the circumstances which Bismarck had
urgently advised the French to avoid.[63]   French diplomacy
doubtless had a hand in the street demonstrations and perhaps in
the appearance of seditious appeals to the Prussian garrison in
Luxemburg.[64]   Bismarck therefore broke no specific promise

---

[56] Bismarck, March 8. *B: G. W.*, VI, 296.
[57] *Memoirs of Prince Chlodwig of Hohenlohe-Schillingsfuerst*, 2 vols. (N. Y., 1906),
II, 191; *B: G. W.*, VI, 300, 301 (March 10); Méloizes, Munich, March 19. *O. D.*,
XV, 111; Loftus, Berlin, March 27. *A. P. P.*, VIII, 518.
[58] *Temps*, March 21; *Liberté*, March 22; *National Zeitung*, March 23, Paris, March
21; Perglas to Louis II, Paris, March 25. *R. N.*, II, 259.
[59] *Vossische Zeitung, Frankfurter Zeitung*, March 22.
[60] *Schwäbische Merkur* (Stuttgart), in O. Elben, *Geschichte des 'Schwäbischen Merkurs,'
1785–1885* (Stuttgart, 1885), p. 104.
[61] *Volksbote* (Munich), *Bayerische Kurier* (Munich), March 21.
[62] *Volks-Zeitung*, March 21; *Frankfurter Zeitung*, March 24.
[63] Moustier, Paris, March 17. *O. D.*, XV, 94, 95; Baudin, Hague, March 23. *Ibid.*,
XV, 139; Perponcher to Bismarck, Hague, March 25, 26. *A. P. P.*, VIII, 509, 512,
513; Benedetti, Berlin, March 22, 24, *O. D.*, XV, 136–138, 146.
[64] Bismarck, March 30. *A. P. P.*, VIII, 534; E. Brandenburg, *Die Reichsgründung*,
2d ed., 2 vols. (Leipzig, 1924), II, 257.

when, to the King of Holland's communication of the French proposal, he replied that the signatory powers of the treaty of 1839, the federated German governments, and the North German Reichstag, must be consulted.[65]   Already signs, of a violent explosion of German national sentiment had appeared, not as might be supposed as a result of calculated indiscretions in Berlin, but caused by rumors in the Paris press that the purchase had been or was about to be completed with Prussia's aid.[66]   Instead of fanning the flames, newspapers close to the Prussian government minimized Luxemburg's importance to Germany and, by questioning the legality of Prussia's claims, occasioned charges of Bismarck's guilty complicity in Napoleon's designs.[67]

Public opinion, as Bismarck had foreseen, promptly saw in Luxemburg a symbol of German unity and in the refusal of Prussia's consent to its sale a test of her leadership. "Prussia," declared Max Duncker, a Progressive politician, "must not begin her rôle as Germany's leader and defender by giving German territory away." [68]   A young state like the North German Confederation could not afford, wrote another politician, a retreat as its first act in foreign affairs.[69]   Significant of the reaction of German national sentiment was the *Magdeburgische Zeitung's* (March 30) warning to Bismarck that "the shameful gift of Luxemburg to France would nullify all of his earlier successes." For the Conservative *Post* (March 29) the transaction would mean a humiliating acknowledgement of Germany's inferiority to France. The Treaties of Lunéville and Tilsit, wrote the *Frankfurter Zeitung* (March 29), were tragic necessities, but now, after a great deal of brave talk of defending every inch of German soil, "to yield would mean a cowardly acknowledgment of inferiority." In general, liberal opinion was concerned with Luxemburg's German nationality as a reason for resistance,[70] the

---

[65] *R. N.*, II, 260.

[66] *Post*, March 14; *National Zeitung*, March 16; *Kreuz-Zeitung*, March 20; *Allgemeine Zeitung*, March 25, Paris, March 22. *Cf.* Brandenburg, *Reichsgründung*, II, 257.

[67] *Kölnische Zeitung*, March 29.

[68] Bernhardi, *Tagebuchblätter*, VII, 352 (March 29). For a similar point of view, see *Allgemeine Zeitung*, April 3.

[69] K. Saumer, *Zur Erinnerung an Franz von Roggenbach* (Wiesbaden, 1909), pp. 116, 117. Napoleon was told that this was a reason why Prussia could not support his plans. Goltz, April 2. *R. N.*, II, 276–278.

[70] *Frankfurter Zeitung*, March 29; *Vossische Zeitung*, March 28.

Progressive *Volks-Zeitung* (March 31) reminding its readers that the Frankfort Parliament had claimed Luxemburg with Limburg and Holstein for united Germany.   More important from the viewpoint of Bismarck's German policy was the indignant protest of the Catholic press in Bavaria.   "Who dares now," exclaimed the *Augsburger Postzeitung* (March 26), "to speak of Prussia's German mission!"   The *Bayerische Kurier* (Munich, March 30) recalled King William's promise never to agree to the cession of a German village.   In spite of this sudden enthusiasm for German national interests, Hohenlohe, the Bavarian Minister-President, expected to be set aside in the event of war on account of his loyalty to the alliance with Prussia and of his support of national unity.[71]

Articulate opinion, at least north of the Main, loudly proclaimed that war was preferable to France's annexation of Luxemburg.   "All classes and all shades of opinion," wrote Loftus, the British ambassador, at the height of the crisis, "are unanimous in their determination to oppose even by force of arms the cession of the Grand Duchy to France."[72]   The *Vossische Zeitung* (March 28) doubted that Napoleon really desired war, but said that if he did, "it might better come now than later and be fought to a definitive solution!"   All parties in the North German Reichstag were reported as prepared to accept an immediate war if it were true that Napoleon was bent upon a conflict.[73]   Forgiveness of Prussia's sins and the possession of Metz and Strassburg were mentioned by a Catholic Bavarian newspaper as the rewards of a challenge to France.[74]   Doubtless hoping to prevent a last-minute sale, Bismarck told the governments of Holland and England that he would prefer immediate war to concessions "which the excited public opinion would not accept."[75]   Public opinion had become a valuable ally for Bismarck, not necessarily for war, but for his diplomatic purposes.   The excitement among Prussia's friends, he assured the Prussian envoy at Stuttgart, was unob-

---

[71] Werthern, Munich, April 2.   *A. P. P.,* VIII, 567.

[72] *Ibid.,* VIII, 614 (April 6).

[73] H. Oncken, *Rudolf von Bennigsen,* 2 vols. (Stuttgart, 1910), II, 35 (April 1).

[74] *Korrespondent von und für Deutschland* (Nuremberg), April 4.

[75] Bylandt to Zuylen, Berlin, April 4.   *A, P, P.,* VIII, 588.   *Cf.* Bismarck to Bernstorff, April 11.   *Ibid.,* VIII, 637.

jectionable,[76] and he drew France's attention to the pressure of public opinion, excited, he claimed, by Prussia's enemies within Germany, as a reason why he should not be presented with an accomplished fact, for he would then be "compelled to subordinate every other consideration to the defense of our situation in Germany."[77]   By agreeing to France's desires he would, he told Benedetti, lose control of the decision for peace or war.[78] With swift and sure strokes, he prepared France's defeat, while trying at the same time to avoid an open offense to her susceptibilities.[79] He asked England and Russia to advise the King of Holland against the sale as the easiest way to avoid war;[80] and on the same day he made sure that King William would accept Napoleon's invitation to visit the Paris exhibition as a conciliatory gesture.[81]

On April 1, Bennigsen's interpellation, presented with Bismarck's knowledge and approval,[82] brought the crisis to the attention of the Reichstag of the recently constituted North German Confederation. According to this National Liberal leader, Luxemburg was German territory, whose defense was necessary in order to preclude further efforts to weaken Germany. Any weakness would lead to war. Bismarck's reply was distinctly more moderate. Mild in that it omitted any reference to Luxemburg's German nationality and in its acknowledgment that the Luxemburgers had expressed no desire for union with Germany, it nevertheless stated Bismarck's position clearly enough by declaring that the signatory powers of the treaty of 1839, the federated German states, and the North German Reichstag must be consulted, and that "the federated governments are confident that no foreign power would violate undoubted rights of the German states and of a German population."[83]   It was, however, no part of his program to claim Luxemburg for united Germany.

[76] B: G. W., VI, 320 (March 30).

[77] Ibid., VI, 320 (March 30).

[78] Benedetti, June 15. O. D., XVII, 229–248.

[79] That he sincerely desired peace was the opinion of Loftus and Wimpffen, the British and Austrian ambassadors. A. P. P., VIII, 615, 617 (April 6).

[80] R. N., II, 269 (March 30).

[81] William to Napoleon, March 30. Ibid., II, 268, 269.

[82] Oncken, Bennigsen, II, 35.

[83] Stenographische Berichte über die Verhandlungen des Reichstages des Norddeutschen Bundes . . . , I, 487–489.

The nationalist press at once accepted Bismarck's speech as an adequate guarantee that there would be no surrender to France.[84] As always it emphasized Prussia's prestige, for whose conservation the *National Zeitung* (April 6) would have the government arouse public opinion. "The occasion," it wrote, "may be insignificant, but our honor is involved. . . . Prestige rules the world in small as in great things." For the *Magdeburgische Zeitung* (April 26) the essential objective should be to convince Germans of their equality with the French.[85]   Opposition and South German opinion continued to charge Bismarck with yielding to France.[86] "Luxemburg," the Progressive *Volks-Zeitung* (April 4) affirmed, "has been sold." In Munich, the Catholic *Volksbote* (April 9) argued that the South German states would be justified in remaining neutral in a Franco-Prussian war because Bismarck had at first encouraged France's pretensions, and its first (April 3) reaction to Bismarck's speech was that it left the public as much in the dark as it had been before. Nevertheless, it was clear that public opinion in South Germany had turned sharply against France.[87]   Even Prussia's opponents in Bavaria were being swept, according to French diplomats, by the wave of passionate resentment into common action with her for the defense of national territory.[88]

After 1871 Bismarck denied on many occasions that prestige had ever been an objective of German foreign policy, but it was certainly one of his primary interests at the height of the Luxemburg crisis. He believed that France intended to compel him to choose between war and a surrender which would irreparably damage Prussia's standing in Germany.[89]   For England's benefit, he wrote that "Prussia must choose war rather than risk the loss of the nation's respect and divorce herself from German national sentiment." He therefore rejected England's proposal for the

---

[84] *Magdeburgische Zeitung,* April 3. *Cf.* the liberal *Frankfurter Zeitung,* April 3.

[85] Bismarck expressed the same point of view in a letter to Goltz in Paris, April 29. *B: G. W.,* VI, 371.

[86] The *Kreuz-Zeitung* (April 7) attributed this attitude to political motives.

[87] *Korrespondent von und für Deutschland,* April 10; *Fränkische Zeitung* (Ansbach, Bavaria), April 13.

[88] d'Astorg, Darmstadt, April 10. *O. D.,* XV, 362; Méloizes, Munich, April 7. *Ibid.,* XV, 323.

[89] Bismarck to Goltz, April 6. *R. N.,* II, 293, 294.

neutralizat'on of Luxemburg and for the withdrawal of the Prussian garrison as an acceptable compromise.[90]   To Hohenlohe, he had already represented the possibly impending war as required by national sentiment rather than by Prussian interests,[91] a view which he communicated to all of the South German capitals (April 12) the day after h:s refusal of England's suggestion.[92] With France's final renunciation of Luxemburg, Bismarck was noticeably less impressed by the need of yielding to the pressure of national sentiment, for her insistence upon the withdrawal of the Prussian garrison seemed reasonable to the other powers.   It was this unfavorable development of the international situation that made him receptive to a compromise settlement.   On Austria's initiative, Gorchakov, the Russian Chancellor, not only clearly indicated Russia's approval of a reasonable arrangement, but he also mildly lectured Bismarck for his constant reference to the necessity of propitiating public opinion and rejected, as an unacceptable sacrifice of Russia's influence with the Balkan peoples, the suggestion of an Austro-Russo-German understanding based upon a guarantee of Austria's Turkish frontier.[93]   Even Bismarck's hints of a possible bargain with France at Belgium's expense failed to win England for an alliance in the defense of Belgium.[94]   Reserving at first his own ultimate decision in view of the uncertain reactions of German national sentiment,[95] he at length accepted England's suggestion of a conference,[96] although he refused to commit himself publicly before its meeting to accept the neutrality of Luxemburg under the pressure of France's military preparations.[97]   In the end, the terms agreed upon at the London Conference provided, as England had already advised, the evacuation of the Prussian garrison and the neutralization of Luxemburg under a parallel guarantee of the powers.   It was also arranged, as a guarantee that neither the French nor the

---

[90] Bismarck, April 11. *B: G. W.,* VI, 349.
[91] *Ibid.,* VI, 333 (April 3).
[92] *Ibid.,* VI, 350–352 (April 12).
[93] Reuss, St. Petersburg, April 13, 17. *A. P. P.,* VIII, 648, 690–692.
[94] Loftus, Berlin, April 13; Bernstorff, London, April 15, 16. *Ibid.,* VIII, 651, 652, 673, 676, 677.
[95] *R. N.,* II, 331 (April 15); Bismarck to Reuss, April 18. *A. P. P.,* VIII, 697.
[96] *B: G. W.,* VI, 364 (April 26).
[97] *Ibid.,* VI, 370 (April 27).

Germans would change this settlement, that Luxemburg should never be alienated by the King of Holland.

Unfortunately, this solution solved none of the fundamental issues between France and Prussia. In France, the failure to acquire Luxemburg or other territory was attributed to Bismarck's deceit; and in Germany, public opinion, embittered by the definitive loss of German territory, was more firmly convinced than ever of France's systematic hostility. "As usual," King William wrote to the Queen, "the affair ends with an insult from France." [98] Whatever satisfaction may have been felt at the maintenance of peace, almost every section of the press agreed that Prussia, not France, had been defeated. Official assurances that sufficient guarantees had been secured for Prussian and German interests and for an enduring peace were unavailing.[99] To the official press should be left, according to the National Liberal *Magdeburgische Zeitung* (May 15), this hollow optimism. In return for the sacrifice of Luxemburg's last ties with Germany, Prussia, wrote the liberal *Frankfurter Zeitung* (May 18), had secured a worthless guarantee of her neutrality. Treitschke's organ doubted that even peace had been obtained.[100] In Kiel, according to the French diplomatic agent, patriots were crying "Treason!" and charging Bismarck with weakness.[101] South German opinion was especially bitter. "I have heard," wrote a National Liberal politician in Munich, "the most unedifying things. . . ." [102] Both the *Bayerische Kurier* (April 24) and the *Augsburger Postzeitung* (May 13) asserted that Germany as well as Prussia had lost in Luxemburg a defensive position of great importance. The *Volksbote* (May 14), another Catholic journal, reminded its readers, like many others, of King William's promise never to agree to the sacrifice of a single German village. Events had proved, according to the *Allgemeine Zeitung* (May 15), the truth of France's official thesis that the dissolution of the German Confederation had weakened Germany. It even foresaw (May 24) Luxemburg's eventual annexation by France. The dissatis-

---

98 *A. P. P.*, VIII, 829 (May 10).
99 *Provinzial-Correspondenz*, May 16. Cf. *Kreuz-Zeitung*, May 17.
100 *P. J.*, vol. 19, pp. 613, 614 (May 12).
101 de Valves, May 15. *O. D.*, XVII, 27.
102 Oncken, *Bennigsen*, II, 72 (May 19).

faction in France convinced many in North and South Germany alike that the result would be merely a truce. To King William, convinced that Paris was bent upon war, delay settled nothing (*aufgeschoben ist nicht aufgehoben*).[103] France and Austria were expected to be more sensitive than ever to any semblance of a move to cross the Main.[104] To one observer, the crisis had been France's first shot in a campaign against the alliances with the South German states,[105] and others expected Napoleon to revive projects once abandoned.[106] Nor had Bismarck, as the nationalist *Fränkische Zeitung* (Ansbach, Bavaria, May 17) surmised, perhaps spoken his last word. The feeling that war was inevitable began more frequently to find public expression.[107] No possible solution of the crisis, wrote the *National Zeitung* (May 1), could establish a permanent peace, since the real causes of the crisis still existed; the great need was haste in uniting Germany.

III

Even Prussia's opponents had felt for a moment as Germans. That the unity which the crisis had revealed as existing upon really national issues should influence relations with North Germany was sometimes conceded by Bavarian liberals and Catholics alike.[108] Offensive and defensive alliances had emerged intact. Hohenlohe had pledged Bavaria's loyalty,[109] but it was more significant that Varnbüler of Wurtemberg, who was supposed to be peculiarly sensitive to the public opinion of his little country, recognized the Luxemburg affair as a legitimate *casus foederis,* although after more than a little prodding by Bismarck.[110] Hesse-Darmstadt had no alliance with Prussia, but Dalwigk, her anti-Prussian Minister-President, told Bismarck that

---

103 William I to Schweinitz, April 13. *Briefwechsel des Botschafters General von Schweinitz* (Berlin, 1928), p. 35.

104 "Luxemburg und die Mainlinie," *Grenzboten,* 1867, II, 234–236.

105 S. von Aurach, *Der luxemburger Handel und die französischen Rheingelüste* (Munich, 1867), p. 67.

106 Perglas to Louis II, Paris, May 8. *R. N.,* II, 383. Cf. *Magdeburgische Zeitung,* April 26.

107 *Betrachtungen über die auswärtige Politik Bayerns* (Munich, 1868).   .

108 *Süddeutschland, zunächst Bayern und der Norddeutsche Bund* (Munich, 1868), pp. 8, 9; *Augsburger Postzeitung,* May 10.

109 Hohenlohe, *Memoirs,* I, 216, 217 (April 23).

110 Pfuel, Karlsruhe, April 14. *A. P. P.,* VIII, 663; Varnbüler, Stuttgart, April 20. *Ibid.,* VIII, 717.

"Hesse would support Prussia to the last drop of her blood in defense of German territory and interests."[111] Napoleon's demands for German territory in 1866 had made these alliances possible; after the Luxemburg crisis, the South German states promised to reorganize their military forces according to the Prussian model.[112]

To Bismarck the moment for complete unity had not yet arrived, but he did not hesitate to use every occasion for advancing toward this ultimate goal. He invited Dalwigk to petition for Hesse's admission to the North German Confederation, perhaps to force him to show his true colors, and followed his refusal with an assurance to the North German parliament of his receptiveness to such requests.[113] When Tauffkirchen, commissioned by Hohenlohe to win Bismarck's approval for an Austro-Prussian alliance as a basis for national unity, which would then be presented to Vienna, arrived in Berlin, he responded cordially, agreeing to guarantee Austria's territorial integrity against Russia, Turkey, and Italy, for he had nothing to lose and much to gain in a move that might detach Austria from France.[114] Beust's insistence upon a free hand for Austria, and to a lesser extent, France's pressure on Munich, brought failure to this scheme, from which Bismarck could not, after all, have expected much.[115] A noteworthy step toward union was taken, though the states of the South were won for it only by the threat of dropping this useful economic union altogether, by the renewal of the *Zollverein* in 1867, with a provision that the South German delegates would meet with the North German parliament to form its governing body (*Zollparlement*). This was the high-water mark of the movement for a united Germany until 1870, but the failure of the negotiations for a South German Confederation, which France

[111] *Die Tagebücher des Freiherrn von Dalwigk. . .* , W. Schüssler, ed., (Stuttgart, 1920), p. 321 (April 14); Wentzel, Darmstadt, April 14. *A. P. P.*, VIII, 662.

[112] A. Rapp, *Die Württemberger und die Nationalfrage, 1863–1871* (Stuttgart, 1910), pp. 224, 225; E. Vogt, *Die hessische Politik in der Zeit der Reichsgründung, 1866–1871* (Munich, 1914), p. 140.

[113] *Verhandlungen*, I, 639 (April 9).

[114] K. A. von Müller, "Die Tauffkirchen Mission nach Berlin und Wien," in *Riezler-Denkschrift* (Gotha, 1913), p. 358; Hohenlohe, *Memoirs*, I, 214–216; W. Schüssler, *Bismarcks Kampf um Süddeutschland 1867* (Berlin, 1929), pp. 176 *passim*.

[115] H. Plehn, *Bismarcks auswärtige Politik nach der Reichsgründung* (Munich, 1920), p. 15; Hohenlohe, *Memoirs*, I, 221; R. N., II, 386 (May 9, 1867) and note.

and Austria had provided for in the Treaty of Prague as a defense of the Main line, thanks chiefly to the smaller states' jealousy of Bavaria, was at least a negative advantage.

As the echoes of the Luxemburg crisis subsided, tension momentarily relaxed, but the problem of German unity remained more definitely than ever the main issue between Prussia and France. Bismarck reminded France early in 1870 that "peace will be strengthened in proportion to the recognition of the principle of the right of each nation to settle its own affairs." [116]   The chance of a peaceful compromise, never really promising, was lost with the failure to assure a substantial expansion of French territory. In the absence of acute crises, despite the general feeling that war was inevitable, there was no immediate occasion for the public discussion of a war as the most effective means for the completion of national unity.   A few saw in the American Civil War a precedent for the use of force to overcome the increasing resistance of South Germany,[117] but the general tendency was for a peaceful and evolutionary development.[118]   Time and the force of circumstances were relied upon to convert the South Germans to the advantages of union.[119]   The Treaty of Prague was not considered even a legal obstacle, for ingenious commentators refused to accept the French thesis that a South German Confederation must be the first step and argued that the recognition of the independence of the South German states and of an eventual national bond between them and North Germany opened the way for the peaceful passage of the Main line whenever one of these states should ask for admission to the North German Confederation.[120]   That France could not easily object to this procedure was an advantage frequently noted.   Bismarck himself

---

[116] Bismarck to Werther, Jan. 11.   B: G. W., VI b, pp. 202, 203.

[117] Zur Orientierung im neuen Deutschland (Heidelberg, 1868), p. 59.

[118] H. von Sybel, Das neue Deutschland und Frankreich, Sendschreiben an Herrn Forçade (Bonn, 1866); Orientierung im neuen Deutschland, p. 56; K. C. Planck, Süddeutschland und der deutsche Nationalstaat (Stuttgart, 1868), p. 15; Das Parlament ist der Friede, von einem Süddeutschen (Munich, 1869).

[119] P. Volksmuth, Herr von Ketteler, Bischof von Mainz, und der sogenannte Beruf Preussens (Berlin, 1867); Cf. Ketteler, Deutschland nach dem Krieg von 1866 (Mainz, 1866).

[120] "Die Stuttgart-Conferenz," Grenzboten, 1867, I, 276; L. K. Aegidi, Die Mainlinie. Ein Beitrag zur Interpretation des Prager Friedens (Bonn, 1869), p. 11; P. Römer, Die Verfassung des Norddeutschen Bundes und die süddeutsche, insbesondere der württemberger Freiheit (Tübingen, 1867), pp. 69, 70.

approved it after the failure of the Tauffkirchen mission, although he of course reserved the decision as to the timeliness of any request for union.

For France and Bismarck alike, the attitude of the South German governments and public opinion became of paramount concern. Most of the French diplomats at last saw what had been obvious from the first to a few, that threats, demands for territorial compensation, and interference in German affairs only played into Bismarck's hands.[121] The principal objective of French foreign policy undoubtedly remained the defense of the Main line as the southern limit of German unity rather than an attack upon the achievements of 1866. The choice, from the point of view of the French government, was not between the peaceful acceptance of German unity and war, the dilemma which was repeatedly placed before the French authorities,[122] but rather as to the means by which the further progress of German unity might be prevented. No definite decision could be made between peace or war with relation to unpredictable events. By insisting upon Austria's approval as a necessary condition before even a South German Confederation might propose a national union with the North, France nevertheless virtually vetoed the evolutionary program, for Austria would never give her consent;[123] but her policy in the South German capitals became distinctly more tactful in order to neutralize the influence of Bismarck's moderate attitude. Nothing more was heard of compensations. Overt intervention was avoided, with highly satisfactory results in a strong resurgence of particularist sentiment. Even in Baden, where the proximity of France inspired much sympathy for Prussia's military power, national sentiment failed to maintain the gains of 1866–1867, for there, as in the other states of the South, a delegation was elected to the *Zollparlement* pledged to oppose the inclusion of political questions within its functions.

---

[121] Karlsruhe, July 11, 1866. *O. D.*, XI, 5, 6; Munich, Aug. 5. *Ibid.*, XI, 285, 286; Berlin, Jan. 2, 1867. *Ibid.*, XIV, 11–14; Stuttgart, Jan. 3, 1868. *Ibid.*, XX, 128, 129, etc.

[122] Moustier, Paris, June (5–7), 1867. *Ibid.*, XVII, 181; Benedetti, Berlin, Jan. 5, 1868. *Ibid.*, XX, 139; Goltz, Paris, June 28, 1867. *R. N.*, II, 429. *Ibid.*, II, 468, 469; J. Fröbel, *Ein Lebenslauf*, 2 vols. (Stuttgart, 1891), II, 531.

[123] Benedetti, Berlin, March 2, 1867. *O. D.*, XIV, 400.

In spite of the obvious difficulties of independence as a permanent status for the South German states against the acknowledged or implicit pretensions of Prussia, Austria, and France (and South German opinion was painfully aware of them), the particularist reaction was even more pronounced elsewhere than in Baden. Dalwigk asked France and Austria more than once to intervene after the Luxemburg crisis and even offered to provide an occasion by petitioning for Hesse's admission to the North German Confederation.[124]   In Stuttgart, Varnbüler warned France against the Tauffkirchen mission, and his generally anti-Prussian attitude again reflected the main trend of opinion in Wurtemberg.[125] National sentiment was strong among the middle classes of the Bavarian cities and towns, but the peasants, the nobility, and the Catholics everywhere were generally more attached than ever to Bavarian independence.[126]   The task of converting these groups seemed hopeless to one advocate of national unity. "They have," he said, "no comprehension of German history."[127]   There is no more reliable evidence of this reaction than the pamphlets that poured from the press, especially in Bavaria.   One asserted that Hohenlohe's support of the alliance with Prussia could not be reconciled with his promise to defend the independence of Bavaria.[128]   Another insisted that the vociferous national sentiment was characteristic of a small group of agitators who spoke in legislative assemblies, wrote in the press, and taught in the universities; and said that Prussia, not France, was the real enemy.[129] Still another insisted that the ability of the South German states to survive had been demonstrated during the Luxemburg crisis.[130] But the most widely read and commented upon, was a pamphlet by Streubel, a former lieutenant in the Saxon army, under the

---

[124] Bruck to Beust, Darmstadt, Dec. 17, 1868. *R. N.*, III, 82; Rochefoucauld, Darmstadt, June 10, 1869. *O. D.*, XXV, 25. *Cf.* Vogt, *Hessische Politik*, p. 175.

[125] Metternich, Paris, April 25, 1867. *R. N.*, II, 355.

[126] Planck, *Süddeutschland und der deutsche Nationalstaat*, p. 10. *Cf.* Radowitz, *Aufzeichnungen und Erinnerungen*, 2 vols. (Berlin, 1925), I, 159. J. Ziekursch, *Politische Geschichte*, I, 241.

[127] Römer, *Verfassung des Norddeutschen Bundes*, pp. iii, iv.

[128] *Betrachtungen über die auswärtige Politik Bayerns*, pp. 8–12. The French *chargé d'affaires* in Munich attributed this anonymous pamphlet to Austrian influence. Le Sourd, Feb. 2, 1869. *O. D.*, XXIII, 214–217.

[129] An English translation of this pamphlet appeared. *Who is the Real Enemy of Germany?* (London, 1868).

[130] *Süddeutschland, zunächst Bayern und der Norddeutsche Bund*, p. 89.

pseudonym of Arkolay.[131]   He called for the denunciation of the alliances with Prussia, for a close friendship with Austria, and for a neutral position between Prussia and France, because Prussia, without Austria's aid, was too weak to defend more than North Germany.   Austria, he maintained, could divide the Prussian army by concentrating troops on the Bohemian frontier, while France attacked across the Middle Rhine and launched another army against the coast of North Germany.   Bismarck dismissed Streubel's strategy as "wretched nonsense" (*elendstes Gewäsch*) and instructed Prussia's agents to ignore the pamphlet.[132]   It enjoyed, nevertheless, a phenomenal success, appearing simultaneously in the four South German capitals, with a sale in each of four to six thousand copies.   The demand was so great a month after its publication, according to a French diplomat, that it could scarcely be satisfied.[133]   In Bavaria, the pamphlet occasioned a lively discussion among the army officers and a copy was sent to King Ludwig with the inscription, "Read, O King, and decide for the welfare of your people!" [134]   It elicited a number of scandalized replies; [135] but even the common-sense argument that neutrality would make of South Germany the battleground of the great powers [136] failed to check the trend of opinion of which Streubel's pamphlet was an extreme example.

Since active intervention would obviously strengthen these antinational tendencies, Bismarck, like the French diplomats, adopted a policy of reserve, pledging himself publicly in a circular of September 7, 1867 and in a speech to the North German parliament, September 24, 1867 against any semblance of pressure.

---

131 *Der Anschluss Süddeutschlands an die Staaten der preussischen Hegemonie, sein sicherer Untergang bei einem französisch-preussischen Krieg, Mahnungen an alle Patrioten, mit wissenschaftlichen Gründen dargethan,* von einem deutschen Offizier, Arkolay (Zurich, 1869).   There is a French translation.   *L'Allemagne du Sud sous l'hégémonie prussienne, sa perte certaine en cas de guerre entre la France et la Prusse,* par un officier allemand (Arcolay) (Paris, 1869).

132 Bismarck, Feb. 20, 1869.   *B: G. W.,* VI b, 32, 33.

133 Saint-Vallier, Stuttgart, March 23, 25, 1869.   *O. D.,* XXIV, 91, 92, 214.

134 Werthern, Munich, March 11.   *B: G. W.,* VI b, p. 32.

135 G. Morin, *Ueber Arkolays falsche "Mahnungen" an alle falschen Patrioten.   Eine gründliche Widerlegung dieser Vaterlandsverrätherischen Schrift,* von einem Süddeutschen (Munich, 1869); *Erwiderung auf die undeutsche Mahnung eines süddeutschen Offiziers* (Arkolay), von einem süddeutschen Offizier (Munich, 1869); *Entegnung auf die Arkolaysche Broschüre,* von einem deutschen Patrioten (Leipzig, 1869).

136 A. von Suckow, *Wo Süddeutschland Schutz für sein Dasein findet* (Stuttgart, 1869).   Suckow was soon to become the Wurtemberger Minister of War.

Nor was this considerate attitude exclusively reserved for his public pronouncements. Prussia's diplomatic agents were directed to refrain from encouraging the South German states to organize a central military commission; and Bismarck reprimanded the envoy in Stuttgart when he used the newspaper press for this purpose.[137] The national cause, he wrote, would best be served "at present by avoiding every sign of zeal, haste, or concern as to the obstructive intrigues of our opponents." [138] In the autumn of 1869, he rejected Baden's petition for union with North Germany, although it conformed to the evolutionary program, on the ground that it would endanger peace with France and weaken national opinion in Bavaria. He did what he could to strengthen Hohenlohe's political position,[139] but, after the latter's defeat in the election for the Bavarian Landtag in November 1869, he accepted the appointment of the pro-Austrian Bray.[140] In time, this tactful treatment might have achieved results, although the immediate prospects were far from encouraging.

It seemed possible to German observers that France's hostility to a united Germany might be rendered harmless by developments in France. In November 1869, Bismarck spoke to the King of a revolution, of the evolution of German opinion, and of a European war, in which Germany would remain neutral, as among the possible peaceful solutions of the German question.[141] From the growth of the opposition parties in France, as shown by the elections of 1869, he expected a strengthening of Napoleon's resistance to the war party, and he instructed the South German newspapers which were accessible to Prussian influence to note his satisfaction with the Ollivier ministry of January 2, 1870, "since it means peace with us." [142] Domestic affairs, he wrote to the Prussian military attaché in Paris, would divert France from foreign complications.[143] Official encouragement was given the

---

[137] Bismarck, Feb. 28, March 3, 1869. *B: G. W.*, VI b, pp. 3, 4, 7.

[138] Bismarck, March 25, 1869. *Ibid.*, VI b, pp. 35, 36.

[139] *B: G. W.*, VI b, pp. 165–168.

[140] Bismarck, Feb. 13, 25, 1870. *B: G. W.*, VI b, pp. 243, 259.

[141] *Ibid.*, VI b, pp. 165–168 (Nov. 20).

[142] M. Busch, *Tagebuchblätter*, 3 vols. (Leipzig, 1899), I, 6, 7. (Feb. 27, 1870). *Cf.* Bismarck, Feb. 28. *R. N.*, II, 324–328; *Kölnische Zeitung*, March 10, 1870.

[143] *Denkwürdigkeiten des General Feldmarschalls Alfred von Waldersee*, 3 vols., H. O. Meissner, ed. (Stuttgart, 1922), I, 49.

view that Prussia's moderate policy in South Germany had accustomed France and Europe in general to the idea of German unity.[144] Since Napoleon's personal good-will continued to be lauded, the strengthening of his control by the plebiscite of May 7, 1870 aroused comparatively little apprehension, although the liberal *Frankfurter Zeitung* (April 23) foresaw a graver danger to peace than to the liberties of Frenchmen. These illusions were partially corrected when Gramont was summoned in May 1870 from his post as ambassador to Austria to become the foreign minister, for his anti-Prussian activities in Vienna were well-known. Henceforth it was expected that France's courtship of Austria would be pressed more zealously than ever.[145] "What nefarious plans Napoleon must be contemplating," was Bismarck's comment to Benedetti, "to appoint so stupid a man!"[146]

The French government, of course, had not abandoned its opposition to German unity. There is no satisfactory proof that it ever pledged itself to accept a united Germany, even if union were accomplished peacefully with the consent of the South Germans,[147] for Ollivier, who expressed himself in this sense to Dr. Levysohn, the Paris correspondent of the *Kölnische Zeitung*,[148] had by no means final authority in foreign affairs. On the contrary, Daru, Gramont's predecessor as foreign minister, had already solemnly warned the Prussian ambassador, while assuring him of France's acceptance of the status quo and of her reserve in German affairs: "Make no mistake," he said, "if the status quo is changed or if imprudent moves betray the intention of changing those terms which are the foundations of peace and mutual confidence, national susceptibilities will be aroused. The imperial government would then be forced to submit the question to the Chambers and to appeal to public opinion. . . ."[149] Moreover,

---

[144] "Die deutsche Suden und der Lasker'sche Antrag," *Grenzboten*, 1870, I, 412, 416; Treitschke, "Badens Eintritt in den Bund," *P. J.*, vol. 25, p. 335 (1870); *Provinzial-Correspondenz*, in *Weimarsche Zeitung*, Jan. 1, 1870.

[145] *Kölnische Zeitung*, May 17; *National Zeitung*, May 18; *Weimarsche Zeitung*, May 18. *Cf.* d'Astorg, Darmstadt, May 21. *O. D.*, XXVII, 330; Rothan, Hamburg, May 22. *Ibid.*, XXVII, 307-309.

[146] Hohenlohe, *Memoirs*, II, 66 (Nov. 4, 1871).

[147] For the contrary view, see R. H. Lord, *The Origins of the War of 1870* (Cambridge, 1924), p. 3.

[148] E. Ollivier, *L'empire libéral*, 15 vols. (Paris, 1911), XIII, 78, 79.

[149] Daru, Paris, Feb. 20, 23, 1870. *O. D.*, XXVI, 334, 335, 342-344.

French diplomacy had been working since the Luxemburg crisis for alliances with Austria and Italy, not to destroy what had been accomplished in 1866, since Austria dared not risk offending the susceptibilities of German national sentiment and since she desired France's support in Balkan questions at least as much as in Germany,[150] but to defend the Main line. At Napoleon's meeting with Francis Joseph in Salzburg, August 1867, and by a subsequent exchange of letters, a general and vague agreement was arranged for the defense of the status quo and against a direct intervention, which would strengthen German national sentiment. Napoleon was still less successful with Italy because of his refusal to pay her price, the withdrawal of the French garrison in Rome.

In spite of the secrecy of these Franco-Austro-Italian negotiations, abundant evidence as well as the logic of the situation called Bismarck's attention to France's efforts to arouse and organize Europe against the completion of German unity.[151] The Salzburg interview, the visit of Archduke Albrecht to Paris in the spring of 1870, and Gramont's appointment all indicated a Franco-Austrian understanding; but Bismarck was justifiably skeptical of an arrangement between France and Italy. In September 1869, partly as a result of France's suggestions, Beust toured South Germany, encouraging resistance to Prussia and hope for Austrian and French aid.[152] A few weeks later Bismarck heard of the efforts of the French ambassador to Russia to secure the Tsar's intervention for the execution of Article V of the Treaty of Prague providing for a plebiscite in North Schleswig. His first impulse, as he informed the Prussian minister of war, was to take the public into his confidence, but the French government, rather than risk a crisis on this dangerous issue, promptly disavowed its ambassador.[153] In February 1870, the French persuaded Clarendon, the British foreign secretary, to present Bismarck with a proposal for a mutual and simultaneous disarmament, chiefly in

---

[150] Beust's memorandum, Vienna, July 20, 1868. *R. N.,* III, 14, 15; Metternich, Paris, Aug. 19. *Ibid.,* III, 19, 20; Beust to Metternich, Nov. 6, Dec. 22, 1868. *Ibid.,* III, 60, 83, 84.

[151] *N. A. Z.,* March 24, 1869, March 4, 1870.

[152] Cadore, Munich, Sept. 15. *O. D.,* XXV, 223, 224; Saint-Vallier, Stuttgart, Sept. 16. *Ibid.,* XXV, 225 f.; d'Astorg, Darmstadt, Sept. 23. *Ibid.,* XXV, 230–232.

[153] Fleury, St. Petersburg, Nov. 13, 1869. *Ibid.,* XXV, 377–383; Bismarck, Nov. 20. *B: G. W.,* VI b, p. 163; d'Auvergne, Paris, Nov. 28. *O. D.,* XXVI, 21–24.

the hope of turning England, and perhaps even liberal opinion in Germany, against Prussia.   After a first evasive reply, calculated to conciliate England, Bismarck definitely rejected it.[154]   He was still less impressed by France's offer to reduce her annual contingent of recruits by ten thousand, arguing that the legal number had in fact never been called to the colors.   The meaning of these events was plain.   It was emphasized by an unofficial but obviously inspired announcement in Gramont's organ, the *Constitutionnel* (May 18), that France must now make her voice heard in all important questions, that none might be settled or even discussed without consulting France.   To this flourish of the trumpets, the official *Norddeutsche Allgemeine Zeitung* (May 21) replied by quietly inquiring as to the nature of these questions.

Bismarck had not remained inactive while French diplomacy wove its web of intrigue.   The most he could hope for from the other powers was neutrality, for none was disposed to accept an alliance against France or to support his plans for the completion of German unity.   Nevertheless, his efforts were more fruitful in positive results than Napoleon's grandiose schemes.   Russia's benevolent neutrality was still assured by the prospect of relief from the servitude of the Treaty of Paris, and timely references to France's alleged designs upon Belgium kept England's suspicions alive.   Troubles in the Balkans diverted Austria's attention to a certain extent and turned that country toward France in questions which led to friction with Russia.[155]   None of these maneuvers endangered peace, but this could not be said of the Hohenzollern candidature for the Spanish throne.   In September 1868 a revolution dethroned Queen Isabella, whose government had been friendly, even subservient, to France, and brought the anti-French parties into power.   Nevertheless, it was only after the provisional government's own candidates had been eliminated that Prince Leopold, whose father, Prince Anthony, was the head of the Sigmaringen branch of the Prussian house, was seriously considered.   Bismarck may not have been the first to suggest this name, but he gave it his support soon after the revolution and

---

[154] H. Michael, *Bismarck, England und Europa (vorwiegend von 1866–1870)*, (Munich, 1930), ch. 10.
[155] *Ibid.*, ch. 8.

worked in Spain and Germany for its success. His motives and
aims are still far from clear. According to the German point of
view, the Hohenzollern candidature was an incident in the
French and Prussian diplomatic campaigns and was Bismarck's
reply to France's negotiations with Austria and Italy, while the
traditional view in France explains it as a carefully planned
maneuver for the purpose of provoking a war. Neither explanation is entirely adequate. Once launched, the project might serve
various purposes. In the war with France, which he doubtless
regarded as inevitable, a Hohenzollern King of Spain would force
France to use a part of her army for the defense of the Spanish
frontier—a sufficient advantage in itself to explain his interest.
Bismarck, however, must have anticipated France's resentment,
and, in fact, newspaper rumors of the candidacy in March 1869
elicited a specific warning from Paris.[156] He intended to present
Leopold's establishment in Madrid as an accomplished fact; as to
France's reaction, that was her affair. His interests would be
served in one sense if she accepted it peacefully, in another if she
made it an occasion for war. There is no doubt, however, that
he had thought of the various means by which France might be
provoked to declare war. Only a few weeks before Benedetti's
warning, Bismarck had assured Russia that this could easily be
done by concentrating troops on the frontier or by using Spain
for this purpose.[157]

The particularist reaction of South German opinion after the
Luxemburg crisis was perhaps the most serious danger of war, because France, although she had not agreed to a peaceful unification of Germany, could not easily have forced a crisis on any
incident arising from a gradual and pacific merging of South
with North Germany, certainly not without precipitating the
result which she wished to avoid. Her retreat in the Schleswig
plebiscite question and, to a certain extent, her policy in South
Germany showed a desire, which was encouraged by Austria, to
avoid an issue over questions relating to German unification. In
the Spanish question, which closely affected the interests and

[156] Benedetti, Berlin, March 27, 1869. Benedetti, *Ma mission en Prusse* (Paris,
1871), pp. 302–304.
[157] Bismarck to Reuss, March 9, 1869. *B: G. W.*, VI b, p. 11.

security of France, Bismarck did not exercise the same restraint. On June 19, 1870, he secured the renewal of the Spanish offer to Prince Leopold and, a few days later (June 21–23), King William's reluctant approval of its acceptance by the Sigmaringen Hohenzollerns. Thus was prepared a surprise for France which she was certain to regard as a challenge. France had her own diplomatic secrets, but even if she had succeeded in establishing a triple alliance with Austria and Italy, its purpose would probably have been the defense of the status quo. If her opposition to German unity was morally reprehensible, her stand upon the status quo was at least legally defensible, while Bismarck's Spanish policy threatened to disturb the existing balance of power to France's positive detriment, to diminish still further her already seriously compromised prestige abroad and that of her government at home, and to weaken her military position. For the decisions which precipitated the crisis Bismarck was chiefly responsible.

IV

Planned in secret and unrelated to those questions which stirred Germans, the Hohenzollern candidature was conceived and developed without any connection with public opinion. Casual references to it in the press had excited little curiosity and even less feeling that Germany's national interests were involved, and Bismarck showed no concern as to the probable reactions of German opinion. Since he intended that France should be forced to choose between peace and war, his purpose would manifestly be served best by an indifferent public, until France should have committed herself definitely to one course or the other. The premature announcement of Leopold's acceptance after the unexpected adjournment of the Cortes (June 23) caused, in fact, little excitement in Germany. Beginning with July 4, the German press copied the Havas Agency's Madrid dispatch from the Paris newspapers either without comment or with speculation as to the identity of the Sigmaringen prince.[158] Nevertheless, national

---

[158] *Elberfelder Zeitung,* July 4; *Vossische Zeitung,* July 5; *Weimarsche Zeitung,* July 5; *Fränkische Zeitung,* July 6. Thile, Bismarck's representative at the foreign office, also mentioned this uncertainty in his first interview with Le Sourd, the French *chargé d'affaires. O. D.,* XXVIII, 31, July 4.

sentiment needed no coaching to repudiate France's immediate inference that the Prussian government was responsible, and to affirm its indifference. On July 4, a Paris correspondent of the *Kölnische Zeitung* (July 5) wrote substantially in this sense, whereas the first instructions from Varzin, where Bismarck was then residing, were not received in Berlin until 8:15 p.m. on the following day (July 5).[159] The effect of Bismarck's influence upon the press thenceforth was chiefly to strengthen the natural disposition of opinion to oppose France and to suggest arguments such as Spain's exclusive responsibility for the candidature. Official policy was therefore at first in substantial accord with public opinion. Acting in the spirit of Bismarck's general directions but without his immediate instructions, the Prussian foreign office replied to France's precipitate questions, July 4, that the candidature did not exist for the Prussian government, that it was the exclusive concern of Spain and the Hohenzollern Sigmaringens.

Thenceforth every word of the inspired French press and of French statesmen was scanned for light as to France's intentions. Because of its well-known connections with Gramont, particular significance was attributed to the *Constitutionnel*. Through its article of July 4, which attributed not only the candidature but the Spanish revolution of 1868 as well to Bismarck's intrigues, it suggested that the Empire of Charles V was about to be restored and predicted disturbing European repercussions;[160] and through another of July 5, affirming France's determination to oppose the candidature, German opinion was prepared for a strong stand by the French and even for the possibility of war.[161] This was also the impression which Werther, the Prussian ambassador, took (July 5) to the King at Ems, from an interview with Ollivier and Gramont of the preceding day. They had asked him to warn King William that the candidature, if persisted in, would compromise peace, that public opinion in France would compel the

---

159 Lord, *Origins*, p. 128. Until the publication of this document, July 7 was accepted as the date of Bismarck's earliest instructions to the press from the evidence in Busch's *Tagebuchblätter*. It was therefore easy for Schulz to show that the press had anticipated these directions. E. Schulz, *Bismarcks Einfluss auf die deutsche Presse (Juli 1870)* (Halle, 1910) (Halle, 1910), pp. 17, 18. R. Fester incorporated Schulz's conclusions in his work, *Die Genesis der Emser Depesche* (Berlin, 1915), p. 53.

160 O. D., XXVIII, 22, n.2. It is here identified as the product of Gramont's pen.

161 These articles were clipped by practically every German newspaper of any significance. *Cf.* d'Astorg, Darmstadt, July 6. *Ibid.*, XXVIII, 70, 71.

Emperor to act if he did not secure its withdrawal.[162]   When Werther asked if what had been said was meant as a threat of war, Ollivier replied, according to a press report of unknown origin, which is accepted as authentic in a recent account of the crisis by a French diplomat, *"Oui, il y a menace de guerre."*[163] At any rate, Werther was sufficiently impressed, for his first words at Ems were, "The devil is abroad in Paris; it looks very much like war," and, of course, Bismarck and the foreign office were at once informed as to these reasons for alarm.[164]   Meanwhile, both the inspired and the unofficial press discounted the moderate and peaceful tendencies of French opinion as exceptional and without significance.[165]

This estimate of France's attitude was strongly supported by Gramont's fateful declaration of July 6 in the *corps législatif,* for it committed France to an inflexible resistance.   Henceforth war was the probable alternative if Prussia refused to order Leopold's withdrawal, since the French authorities would certainly regard any other course as an insupportable humiliation.   He hoped that the "friendship of the Spanish and the wisdom of the German people" would dispose of this threat to the interests and honor of France.   "But should it be otherwise," he concluded, "strong in your support and in that of the nation, we should know how to do our duty without hesitation and without weakness."   According to a German scholar, the response in Germany was an unanimous protest by all classes that Spain's selection of a king was no concern of France.[166]   On the issue of the candidature, however, the anti-national opinion in South Germany sympathized with France, agreeing that she was threatened with an intolerable situation upon her frontiers.[167]   *"Es kann der Beste*

---

[162] Werther, Paris, July 5.   Lord, *Origins,* p. 126.

[163] C. Saurel, *Juillet 1870, le drame de la dépêche d'Ems* (Paris, 1930) pp. 136, 137.   Werther's own report does not contain this damning admission, nor does it appear in Gramont's account in a dispatch to the French ambassador in London. Werther, Paris, July 5.   Lord, *Origins,* pp. 125–127.   *Cf.* Gramont, July 5.   O. D., XXVIII, 39, 40.

[164] Waldersee, *Denkwürdigkeiten,* I, 71; Abeken, Ems, July 7.   Lord, *Origins,* p. 138.

[165] *Kölnische Zeitung,* July 7, Paris, July 6; *N. A. Z.,* July 9, Paris, July 6; *Vossische Zeitung,* July 10, Paris, July 7.

[166] H. Hesselbarth, *Die Entstehung des deutsch-französischen Krieges* (Gotha, 1910), p. 17.

[167] *Augsburger Postzeitung,* July 6.

nicht in Frieden leben," the *Bayerische Vaterland* (July 5) wrote, quoting Schiller in France's defense, *"wenn es dem bösen Nachbar nicht gefällt."* Of the claim that Bismarck had been responsible for the Spanish revolution it declared (July 7): "That sounds exactly like Prussia." Prussia's opponents refused to believe that she had had no part in the candidature [168] and they sharply rejected the thesis that the alliances of 1866 would apply to a war occasioned by it.[169] With these exceptions, Gramont's statement stiffened German opinion in the belief that France intended to use the candidature as an excuse for war. Bismarck wrote, *"Wir auch,"* to his threats and sent his comments to Busch as a guide for the press.[170] The press should deny that the German people were involved,[171] and, with the exception of the *Norddeutsche Allgemeine Zeitung,* it should deal very roughly with Gramont.[172] Patriotic sentiment, however, needed no encouragement. The *Kölnische Zeitung* (July 7) had already asked, "Are they mad?" and the *Magdeburgische Zeitung* (July 7) asserted a threat of war had been made. The unfortunate effect of Gramont's declaration was best illustrated by the democratic *Frankfurter Zeitung's* change of attitude. At first it had explained (July 6) the candidature as Bismarck's maneuver to secure the election of the government's candidates in the approaching Landtag elections, but two days later it acknowledged "to our great astonishment" that France was determined upon war. "The peace of Europe," it declared (July 8), "depends upon Napoleon III, not upon Spain and Prussia."

After Gramont's definition of France's position, Bismarck's systematic denial of official responsibility by the King and the Prussian government increased the danger of war, but it also strengthened the reserve and detachment of the press.[173] On July 9, he directed that it should write of Leopold's establishment

---

168 *Volksbote,* July 9; *Bayerische Kurier,* July 10; *Beobachter* (Stuttgart) July 12, in Rapp, *Die Württemberger,* p. 364. *Cf.* Saint-Vallier, Stuttgart, July 10. *O. D.,* XXVIII, 210.

169 *Volksbote,* July 8. Bray was reported as expressing the same opinion. Cadore, Munich, July 8. *O. D.,* XXVIII, 137.

170 Busch, *Tagebuchblätter,* I, 34. 35 (July 9).

171 Bucher, Varzin, July 7. Lord, *Origins,* p. 137.

172 Bismarck, July 8. Busch, *Tagebuchblätter,* I, 33, 34.

173 French diplomatic agents frequently noted the moderation of the press. Rothan, Hamburg, July 8. *O. D.,* XXVIII, 112 etc.

in Spain as an advantage for Germany but not as a question which would justify a war.[174] The press, reflecting the general tendencies of opinion, dwelt more frequently and fervently upon the second than upon the first theme. German sentiment did not in fact accept the candidature as a national interest.[175] "In no case," wrote the *National Zeitung* (July 6), "can Prussia assume the responsibility for it or guarantee its success." For the moderate *Vossische Zeitung* (July 8) the interests of the German nation and the Hohenzollern dynasty were distinctly different considerations. "All parties," it said, "have the same interest in preventing a confusion between national and dynastic interests." Bismarck should assume no obligations which must later be satisfied "with blood and iron." Good wishes, according to the strongly nationalist *Magdeburgische Zeitung* (July 8), were all that Prussia could give Leopold: "We will wage no war on Spain's account" (July 9). "It may be France's interest, it is not ours, to identify the German with the Spanish question." The *Neue Stettiner Zeitung* (July 13) was prepared to wager that the Landtag would not even pay the prince's travelling expenses to Madrid. In spite of its official connections, the *Kölnische Zeitung* carried Bismarck's instructions far beyond their limits. After affirming Prussia's indifference, it wrote (July 7): "We can only wish in all sincerity that Spain will elect another King," and, the next day, "The Prussian government can, and doubtless will, dissuade Prince Leopold from an enterprise that is entirely against its interests." On July 11, it reported the unanimous decision of the press against a war on this issue. The *Weimarsche Zeitung* (July 10) likewise admitted that the King could advise, if not command, the prince to withdraw his acceptance.

Of course, Bismarck had no such intention.[176] He had insisted from the first that the King should yield nothing to France's demands. Concern for Prussia's prestige in Germany does not appear in the dispatches from Varzin, as it frequently had during

---

[174] Busch, *Tagebuchblätter*, I, 35, 36.

[175] Chateaurenard, Dresden, July 9. *O. D.*, XXVIII, 170; Rothan, Hamburg, July 9. *Ibid.*, XXVIII, 176; d'Astorg, Darmstadt, July 11. *Ibid.*, XXVIII, 237.

[176] The circular of July 5 in which Fester, a leading German authority upon the crisis, believed that Bismarck had announced the withdrawal of the candidature has not materialized from the Prussian archives. Fester, *Genesis der Emser Depesche*, pp. 35, 36; Lord, *Origins*, p. 39.

the Luxemburg crisis, and the chauvinist *Berliner Börsen-Zeitung* (July 11) was alone in the opinion that "the slightest surrender to France's unjust demands would mean a humiliation of Prussia that would cost her all of her material and moral gains of recent years." Never enthusiastic in regard to the candidature and now alarmed by the danger of war, King William sent Colonel Strantz, July 10, without Bismarck's knowledge, to Sigmaringen with a letter advising the withdrawal of Leopold's name in the interest of peace. On July 12, yielding to this and other appeals from the disinterested powers, Prince Anthony renounced the candidature in behalf of his son, who was inaccessible for the moment, in wires to Marshal Prim in Madrid and the Spanish ambassador in Paris. At the same time, he communicated his decision to the German press in terms that suggested Prince Leopold's own responsibility for the renunciation.[177]

If the equanimity of German opinion, which Prussian diplomats frequently cited as an example for France, was seriously disturbed, it was the result for the most part of well-founded suspicions of France's purposes based upon the aggressive tone of the inspired Paris press. Even French diplomats warned their superiors of its dangerous effect.[178] On July 10, the *Moniteur Universel,* generally accepted as Ollivier's organ,[179] insisted that a satisfactory settlement must include guarantees of the literal execution of the Treaty of Prague, Prussia's evacuation of the fortress of Mainz, and the abrogation of her military alliances with the South German states. No wonder that many attributed to France the purpose of recovering her former predominance and of striking a blow at German unity.[180] It was a natural inference that she would not be content with Leopold's renunciation.[181] For

---

[177] R. Fester, *Briefe, Aktenstücke und Regesten zur Geschichte der Hohenzollernschen Thronkandidatur in Spanien,* 2 vols. (Leipzig, 1913), II, 93, 94.

[178] Saint-Vallier, Stuttgart, July 12. *O. D.,* XXVIII, 265 (quoting Varnbüler); d'Astorg, Darmstadt, July 12. *Ibid.,* XXVIII, 274. See especially, Saint-Vallier, Stuttgart, July 15. *Ibid.,* XXVIII, 422–424.

[179] Solms, Paris, July 10. Lord, *Origins,* p. 183. Cf. *Vossische Zeitung,* July 13. The essential passage appears in *O. D.,* XXVIII, 256 n.

[180] *Neue Stettiner Zeitung,* July 7, 10; *Weimarsche Zeitung,* July 9; *Kreuz-Zeitung, Magdeburgische Zeitung, Elberfelder Zeitung,* July 10; *Augsburger Anzeigerblatt,* July 13.

[181] *Elberfelder Zeitung,* July 11; *National Zeitung, Augsburger Postzeitung, Frankfurter Zeitung,* July 12; *Kreuz-Zeitung,* July 13, Paris, July 10; *Allgemeine Zeitung,* July 13, Paris, July 10; *Volksbote,* July 13. Cf. Cadore, Munich, July 12. *O. D.,* XXVIII, 225, 226.

Bismarck's part, he declared then as later that France wished to force a crisis on a question which would probably not excite German national sentiment.[182]

Nevertheless, these expectations aroused little enthusiasm for the candidature, for public opinion still refused to accept it as a German interest.[183]   Only an undeniably unjust demand that the King should order Leopold to withdraw, said the Conservative *Kreuz-Zeitung* (July 14), writing before the publication of the Ems Dispatch, would give the candidature a national character. "A war on this question," Keudell, the King's adjutant wrote later, "would have been extremely unpopular."[184]   The reaction to Leopold's renunciation was therefore generally favorable, for it removed an unpopular issue.   It won the hearty approval of the liberal press.   "For us," wrote the Progressive *Volks-Zeitung* (July 13), "Leopold's success would not have meant a Prussian victory, nor do we feel his withdrawal as a defeat.   We hold no grudge on account of the chauvinist outburst in Paris, for it had its counterpart here."   It meant, said the *Vossische Zeitung* (July 13), an assurance of peace.[185]   Prussia's critics in South Germany, of course, were well satisfied.[186]   Even the official *Norddeutsche Allgemeine Zeitung* (July 14) spoke of the renunciation as the end of the crisis, without, however, definitely approving it.   In accordance with Bismarck's point of view, it denied that the King was responsible, predicted that France would still cause trouble, and asserted that further concessions after Gramont's brusque methods were impossible.   The Conservative and nationalist press, however, reacted more cordially, although it compared Germany's moderation with France's chauvinism and questioned the permanence of peace.[187]   To the *Kölnische Zeitung* (July 12) it seemed that Leopold had done "what any man of intelligence and heart would have done in his place. . . . Peace

[182] Bismarck, Varzin, July 9. Lord, *Origins,* p. 165; Bismarck, *Gedanken und Erinnerungen,* 2 vols. (Stuttgart, 1898), II, 82. There was probably much truth in this view. Gramont frankly acknowledged it as did also the inspired Paris press. Metternich, Paris, July 8.   *R. N.,* III, 405.   Cf. *Constitutionnel,* July 8; *Liberté,* July 9.
[183] Chateaurenard, Dresden, July 12.   *O. D.,* XXVIII, 277, 278.
[184] R. von Keudell, *Fürst Bismarck und Fürsten Bismarck* (Berlin, 1901), p. 444. Cf. *Magdeburgische Zeitung,* July 12; *Frankfurter Zeitung,* July 15.
[185] Cf. *Allgemeine Zeitung,* July 13.
[186] *Nürnberger Tagblatt,* July 13.
[187] *Haude und Spenersche Zeitung,* July 13.

is considered certain." Peace had been assured for the moment, said the *National Zeitung* (July 14), even if its permanence could not be guaranteed. The National Liberal *Schwäbische Merkur* (Stuttgart, July 15) was willing that France should claim a victory. Of particular interest are the *Magdeburgische Zeitung's* (July 14) comments, for they confirm the unattractiveness of the candidature as an issue with France, even from the point of view of nationalist opinion. "Prince Leopold's decision," it pointed out, "has at least one advantage: we are now once more upon German soil, ready to crush the disturber of peace if he will not remain quiet." There is no doubt that opinion was distinctly relieved, but its approval was given with the condition that no further demands would be addressed to Prussia. Gramont, wrote the Crown Prince Frederick William to his mother-in-law, Queen Victoria, "must now show his cards and prove whether war is necessary for him, or whether he is content to do without bloodshed. Should fresh demands be made upon us, however, he will meet a unanimous expression of German feeling and anger that will cost him dear." [188]

A majority of the Paris newspapers indeed called for the acceptance of the renunciation as an adequate, if not a dramatic, satisfaction. [189] The British and Austrian ambassadors warned Gramont that new demands would inflame national sentiment in Germany; [190] but so great was his disappointment at the failure of his plan to associate Prussia publicly and officially with Leopold's renunciation that he dictated on the spur of the moment a virtual letter of apology, which Werther was to ask the King to sign. This inexcusable action, however, had no direct influence upon events, for Werther, instead of sending it over the telegraph, arrived in Ems with it after Benedetti's crucial interview on the promenade during the morning of July 13 and after Abeken's report of it to Bismarck had been drafted. [191] In

[188] *The Letters of Queen Victoria,* 2d Series, 2 vols. (London, 1926), II, 29, 30 (July 13).

[189] Carroll, *French Public Opinion and Foreign Affairs,* p. 30. For further details, see Carroll, "French Public Opinion on War with Prussia in 1870", *American Historical Review,* XXXI, 690.

[190] Lyons, Paris, July 12. Fester, *Briefe, Aktenstücke,* II, 110; Beust, Vienna, July 13. *R. N.,* III, 433, 434. *Cf.* Saint-Vallier, Stuttgart, July 13. *O. D.,* XXVIII, 300, 301.

[191] Lord, *Origins,* pp. 79, 80, 81.

the meantime, Benedetti had been directed to secure from the King a guarantee that the candidature would never be revived. To this new demand, presented in the course of an unconventional interview for which the King had taken the initiative, the reply was a definite refusal. Nevertheless, no insult had been given or received, and the King apparently was willing that negotiations should continue in·Berlin with Bismarck.

On July 12, Bismarck left Varzin for Berlin and Ems, determined to prevent any concessions which might nullify his policy. It seemed too late when, after his arrival in Berlin, he heard of Leopold's renunciation, and he is said for a moment to have thought of resigning. This disappointment was understandable; for Leopold's withdrawal, if France accepted it as an adequate satisfaction, would transfer from France to Prussia the responsibility for the further development of the crisis. Thus, the essential advantage which Bismarck's policy had hitherto assured Prussia would be lost. Nevertheless he remained in office, not because he had himself decided to assume the aggressive, but probably because he believed that France, with a little goading on his part, would blunder again. As elsewhere in Germany the atmosphere in Berlin was electric; further demands were certain, it was believed.[192] Ministerial statements in the *corps législatif* permitted the worst conclusion as to the intentions of the French government. "No illusion is now possible," exclaimed the Conservative *Post* (July 13), "The French government is determined to freshen its glory even at the expense of the peace of Europe." "They are saying in Paris," asserted the *Kreuz-Zeitung* (July 13), "that the *aigle noir* will only cease to be France's *bête noir* if we promise to obey France in the future." France, wrote the moderate *Vossische Zeitung* (July 13), "is determined upon war *à tout prix.*" Scarcely any of the Berlin newspapers doubted that France would promptly present new demands, and all agreed that they should be rejected. Is it therefore too much to assume that Bismarck was influenced by this state of mind or that he shared it? At any rate, he received fairly

---

[192] *Frankfurter Journal,* July 12. (This National Liberal newspaper is not to be confused with the better-known *Frankfurter Zeitung.*)   Cf. *Allgemeine Zeitung,* July 15, Berlin, July 13.

definite reports of France's intentions during the afternoon of July 13 from Gorchakov, then in Berlin for a few hours, and from the Prussian envoy at Stuttgart,[193] although, as Professor Lord has shown, authentic information as to Gramont's letter of apology did not reach him until the essential decisions had been made.[194]   He immediately informed the press that a meeting of the Reichstag during the following week was to be expected as a result of France's dissatisfaction with the renunciation.[195]

Meanwhile, Bismarck had bent every effort and resorted to every stratagem to save something from the wreckage of his policy. To prevent France from claiming a diplomatic victory, he directed the press to keep the King's name in the background and to announce that France had first heard the news from the Spanish ambassador in Paris.[196]   He bombarded Ems with telegrams, urging William to shun every semblance of approving the renunciation,[197] and asked Busch to scotch any press report that it had been the work of the King.[198]   Not content with efforts to minimize the damage already done, he also attempted to recover the advantage for Prussia as the injured party. For this purpose, he explained his own acceptance of the new situation in quarters where this information would do the most good, that is to the King and the Crown Prince for England's benefit, and to the Italian ambassador and a confidant of the Bavarian Minister-President; and he permitted a suggestion that he intended to return to Varzin to appear in the press. Other maneuvers, which may best be interpreted as calculated to goad France into precipitate action, are more significant. During the evening of July 12, he advised the King to recall Werther from Paris on leave and to explain the measure as a reply to Gramont's declaration of July 6.[199]   To Loftus, the British ambassador, he spoke on the following afternoon, after his interview with Gorchakov, of Prussia's own need for guarantees and for an explanation of Gramont's attitude, rightly expecting his ominous remarks to

[193] Lord, *Origins*, pp. 96, 97.
[194] *Ibid.*, p. 81.
[195] *Kölnische Zeitung, Elberfelder Zeitung*, July 13, evening editions.
[196] Bismarck's comment, Werther, Paris, July 12. Lord, *op. cit.*, pp. 201, 202.
[197] *Ibid.*, pp. 202, 203 (July 12).
[198] Busch, *Tagebuchblätter*, I, 40 (July 13).
[199] Lord, *Origins*, p. 205.

be immediately communicated to France.[200] Now unquestionably bent upon war, whatever his original purposes had been, he was prepared as a last resort to launch a diplomatic offensive of his own. There is no satisfactory evidence, however, that he thought of immediate action, for there was still a good chance that France would save him the trouble, and good reasons existed for avoiding it if possible. If France remained quiet, the imponderables of the German as well as the international situation would have almost certainly been unfavorable to a reopening of the crisis by Prussia, for England and Russia were advising France to accept the renunciation as a satisfactory solution and national sentiment in Germany was astir only at the prospect of further demands by France. In the absence of such demands, even Bismarck might not easily have won German opinion, and especially the South German governments, for a sudden change to the offensive. At any rate, he had made no definite arrangements with the military authorities, for von Roon and von Moltke met him at dinner that evening in a pessimistic mood.

The first result of their conversation was a telegram to the King recommending that France should be asked to explain her intentions, but a certain delay was still envisaged to permit William's return to Berlin for consultation as to the form of the note. Even this plan could not have been regarded as the final word, for Abeken's report of Benedetti's interview with the King that morning had, according to Bismarck's classic account, a most depressing effect. By striking out those parts which indicated the possible continuance of the negotiations, Bismarck not only abbreviated it but also sharpened its tone. What had sounded like an invitation to a parley, said the admiring von Roon, was now a fanfare. Rushed into print, the Ems Dispatch appeared that evening on the streets of Berlin between the hours of nine and ten as the sole contents of a special edition of the *Norddeutsche Allgemeine Zeitung*.[201] A few hours later it was sent in substantially the same form to the Prussian diplomatic agents

---

[200] Le Sourd, July 13; *O. D.*, XXVIII, 321, 322; Loftus, July 13. Loftus, *Diplomatic Reminiscences 1862–1879*, 2d Series, 2 vols. (London, 1894), I, 274 ff.

[201] The form of its publication has no particular importance, for the Berlin newspapers not infrequently used this method of announcing important news after the printing of their latest editions.

in Germany and abroad for communication to the governments to which they were accredited, with a special reference to Benedetti's provocation for use at Munich, London, and St. Petersburg. By this suddenly devised expedient, Bismarck intended, obviously, to prevent further negotiations, to provoke France to a declaration of war, to insure the neutrality of the foreign powers and the sympathy of foreign opinion, and finally to arouse German national sentiment. Whatever may be thought of its morality, and Bismarck's own revelations later as to its origins played into the hands of Germany's enemies, the Ems Dispatch served these purposes to perfection, although it was the excuse, rather than the cause, of France's virtual declaration of war (July 15), as the author has shown elsewhere.[202]

Since the final decision was made in Paris, the effect of the Ems Dispatch upon German opinion has usually been briefly dismissed as relatively unimportant. It assured, nevertheless, the enthusiastic acceptance of the war and, if France had remained quiet, it would have given Bismarck the support of public opinion for his own demand for an explanation. By the Ems Dispatch the issue ceased to be dynastic in character and became a national interest; for the first time during the crisis national sentiment clearly identified itself with the person of the Prussian King. To secure the desired effect, the press, led by the official *Norddeutsche Allgemeine Zeitung* (July 15), added fanciful but graphic details as to Benedetti's discourteous conduct. The worst offender was the chauvinist *Berliner Börsen-Zeitung* (July 15), for it represented the ambassador as following William to the door of his hotel with his importunities.[203] The identity between the Prussian King and the German nation was affirmed on all sides. Voicing national sentiment as well as official instructions, the *Kölnische Zeitung* (July 14) asserted that "the excesses of the French government have succeeded in making the affair of the Prussian King the concern of every German." The executive committee of the National Liberal Party protested to the King against France's insult to "Your Majesty and in you to the

---

[202] Carroll, *French Public Opinion*, pp. 31–35.
[203] Noted by *National Zeitung*, July 15; *Börsenhalle* (Hamburg), *Haude und Spenersche Zeitung*, in *Kölnische Zeitung*, July 16.

German nation." [204]   Bismarck's aggressive purposes appeared in substantially identical dispatches from Berlin to provincial newspapers.   From France rather than from Prussia were due guarantees such as would prevent her from precipitating war during the next generation.[205]   "The Duke of Gramont stated his demands before a public tribunal," said the *Süddeutsche Presse* (July 14), a Munich newspaper which sometimes reflected the views of the Prussian as well as those of the Bavarian government, "France must withdraw them."   The moderate *Vossische Zeitung* (July 16) felt that Prussia might legitimately require guarantees against Napoleon's *Frivolitäten*.   Nevertheless, few ventured to rejoice at the prospect of war or even to argue its advantages as a means of completing German unity.   For this reason the *Weimarsche Zeitung* (July 15) thought of it at least as "almost desirable."   No one doubted the probability of war, but the blame was attributed almost universally to France.   This was the sense of the phrase *"die Würfel sind gefallen,"* which came naturally to the pen of most commentators.   Prussia, it was said, could do nothing to prevent it, since still more drastic demands would have followed the King's surrender to Benedetti.[206]

Until France's virtual declaration of war on July 15, mediation by the neutral powers offered a possible, if remote, hope of peace. Neither Bismarck nor public opinion were, however, receptive. The King was reported as favorably disposed on July 14,[207] and the *Kölnische Zeitung* mentioned foreign mediation as a possible solution on the same day.   Bismarck informed England nevertheless that William would be painfully affected by her proposal of a settlement, although it was in fact based upon the King's specific approval of Leopold's renunciation and upon France's withdrawal of her demand for guarantees.   Public opinion in Germany, he declared, now preferred war to further concessions.[208]   Nothing short of guarantees for Germany's present and

[204] *National Zeitung*, July 16. For similar statements see, *Weimarsche Zeitung*, July 17.
[205] *Magdeburgische Zeitung*, July 14; *Schwäbische Merkur* (Stuttgart), July 16.
[206] *Post*, July 14; *Kölnische Zeitung*, *Kreuz-Zeitung*, July 15; *Allgemeine Zeitung*, July 16, Paris, July 14. Cf. *Constitutionnel*, July 15, Berlin, July 14.
[207] O. Lorenz, *Kaiser Wilhelm und die Begründung des Reichs 1866–1871* (Jena, 1902), p. 263.
[208] Bernstorff, London, July 14. Lord, *Origins*, pp. 244, 245. *Cf.* Bismarck, July 14. *Ibid.*, p. 248.

future security against France would be acceptable, he wrote in reply to a rumor, attributed to Bray, the Bavarian Minister-President, of new proposals.[209] Bismarck's veto meant the end of this never substantial hope of peace, for France's later suggestions to Austria and Italy for their mediation was intended either to impress these potential allies, or, as Gramont acknowledged, to destroy Prussia's alliances with the South German states.[210]

Not until the approach of war did South Germany become an important factor. France's diplomatic agents had correctly informed Paris that the South German governments and public opinion would not accept a war over the Hohenzollern candidature as one for Germany's national interests.[211] They had also faithfully depicted the effect of the French chauvinist press[212] and predicted that new demands after Leopold's renunciation would lead to the fulfillment by the South German states of their obligations in the alliances.[213] But all this good advice went for nothing. To Gramont, bent upon the humiliation of Prussia at any cost, it merely meant that the South Germans had never been reliable friends. Their reactions had no influence upon his final decision.[214] In the meantime, Bismarck had pressed for an assurance of Bavaria's loyalty. In his conversations with Cadore, the French minister, Bray had spoken (July 12) of the general suspicion that France was seeking an excuse for war,[215] but to Werthern, Prussia's representative, he had stressed the problem of an unfavorable public opinion toward the alliance, while affirming his own good-will. In Darmstadt, Dalwigk likewise avoided the issue as long as possible by retiring (July 14) to his country estate.[216] The Ems Dispatch assured to Prussia the ultimate coöperation of South Germany, but the Catholic press of Bavaria continued to resist the general current. Prussia, said the *Augsburger Postzeitung* (July 15), desired war just as much as France,

[209] M. Doeberl, *Bayern und die Bismarcksche Reichsgründung* (Munich, 1926), p. 30.
[210] *R. N.*, III, 447, 448, 460, 461 (July 16, 19).
[211] d'Astorg, Darmstadt, July 11, quoting the *Volksblätter*. *O. D.*, XXVIII, 237, 238; Cadore, Munich, July 12. *Ibid*, XXVIII, 290.
[212] Saint-Vallier, Stuttgart, July 12. *Ibid.*, XXVIII, 264, 265; d'Astorg, Darmstadt, July 12. *Ibid.*, XXVIII, 274.
[213] Saint-Vallier, Stuttgart, July 13, *Ibid.*, XXVIII, 300.
[214] *Cf.* Saint-Vallier, July 15, ministerial note. *Ibid.*, XXVIII, 422-430.
[215] Cadore, July 13. *Ibid.*, XXVIII, 332.
[216] d'Astorg, Darmstadt, July 15. *Ibid.*, XXVIII, 412.

and the *Volksbote* (July 16) agreed with the French view that Prince Leopold might change his mind again. Although the *Bayerische Kurier* (July 16) had characterized Benedetti's demands as a provocation, it declared (July 17) for complete neutrality until Bavarian soil should be menaced. A committee of the Landtag recommended a policy of neutrality by a vote of six to three, and Jörg, the editor of the Catholic *Historisch-Politische Blätter* and the parliamentary leader of the Catholics, denied that the German question was involved.[217] The Landtag, however, reversed this report by approving the government's decision to respect the alliance with Prussia. "The Spanish question no longer exists," averred Bray during the crucial debate, quoting Bismarck's reference to Benedetti's alleged provocation, "the German question is beginning."[218] Having made its choice on the probably correct assumption that neutrality was impossible, the government turned against the Catholic press. On July 17, the *Bayerische Vaterland* was suppressed four times, the *Volksbote* three times, and the *Bayerische Kurier* twice. Only the intervention of the police is said to have saved Dr. Sigl, the editor of the *Bayerische Vaterland,* from violence at the hands of a nationalist mob.[219] "The Main," exulted the *Süddeutsche Presse* (July 20), "has been bridged." For many weeks the Catholic press appeared in mutilated form, but the *Volksbote* (July 21) nevertheless acknowledged that Germany was fighting for unity and France for revenge.

V

No nation ever went to war more convinced that its cause was just than the German people in 1870. Bismarck's secret machinations, of course, were unknown. The official version of the crisis was accepted for the most part without question, and even the publication of Radziwill's more detailed account of the interview between King William and Benedetti apparently occasioned no doubts as to the accuracy of the Ems Dispatch. On July 19 the

---

217 *Erlanger Tagblatt, Augsburger Postzeitung,* July 20.
218 *Bayerische Kurier,* July 19.
219 Nevertheless, the Prussian King and Queen were greeted in Munich with only moderate enthusiasm a few days later. Hohenlohe, *Denkwürdigkeiten,* II, 14.

King again affirmed Prussia's complete indifference to the Spanish question, but the candidature had by this time lost its importance. The future status of Germany and a new balance of power had become the real issues. "The war," according to a resolution adopted by a mass meeting at Stuttgart, "is a national war. It will decide the future of our people. France forced it in order to thrust Germany back into her condition of former weakness and to seize her territory."[220] "Neither the candidature nor the justifiable refusal of Benedetti's demands is the real cause," said the nationalist *Münchener Neueste Nachrichten* (July 14), "it is France's hatred and fear of Germany's potential world power." To all it was immediately evident that national unity was the goal for which they were to fight.[221] The last of Bismarck's wars was the first to begin with the enthusiastic support of public opinion. "We go to war with entirely different feelings from those of 1866," wrote the *Elberfelder Zeitung* (July 16), "it is a campaign against the hereditary foe whose century-old aim has been Germany's destruction." Progressive opinion was swept along with the current. "For the first time," said the *Volks-Zeitung* (July 21), "we send our brothers and sons to war with our love and blessings rather than with our regrets." On July 30 it called upon the nation to rise against Napoleon.

From the belief that the Germans were fighting for their own just interests to the conviction that the war was a crusade for those of Europe was a natural and easy transition. This evolution deserves more than passing attention, since it explains something of the state of mind in Germany at the beginning of the new era. It was in part based upon a moral condemnation of the French manner of life.[222] What could Germany learn, asked Treitschke, from a country where party conflicts had destroyed belief in the spiritual values of life?[223] France's defeat, it was

---

[220] *Schwäbische Volkszeitung*, in *National Zeitung*, July 19. See the manifesto of the Progressives at Mainz. *Bismarcks grosses Spiel; Die geheimen Tagebücher Ludwig Bambergers*, E. Feder, ed. (Frankfurt, 1932), pp. 125, 126.

[221] *National Zeitung*, July 30.

[222] Waldersee, *Denkwürdigkeiten*, I, 60, 61. *Cf.* J. Vetter, *Deutschlands Sieg über Welsches Wesen und Deutschlands Recht auf Elsass-Lothringen* (Karlsruhe, 1870, 6th ed.), p. 4. This pamphlet was approved by the official *Provinzial-Correspondenz*, in *Kölnische Zeitung*, Aug. 19.

[223] "Was fordern wir von Frankreich?" *P. J.*, vol. 26, pp. 369, 370.

Kladderadatsch, January 1, 1871.

Figure 2.—A part of that power which always wills evil
but always works good.

asserted, would put an end to the harmful prestige of French civilization in Germany and would mean the triumph of German virtue over French vice and chauvinism.[224] The war, therefore, seemed a moral crusade, but the feeling that France's power must be diminished was more significant. Her domination had been established at Germany's expense and at the price of perpetual uncertainty for all Europe. Throughout her history France had been the chief disturber of peace (*der Störenfried*). Strauss spoke for many of his countrymen in telling Thiers (in Switzerland) that Germany was fighting the spirit of Louis XIV. To exorcise this evil spirit forever, wrote one observer, Germany was prepared to fight to the end.[225] The executive committee of the National Liberal Party drew up an elaborate indictment of France's sins on the day (July 15) of her virtual declaration of war. A state of perpetual unrest in Europe, it affirmed, was the life principle of Bonapartism. The Poles had been encouraged to revolt and then left to their fate. At one time or another France had picked a quarrel or threatened the independence of every country in Europe, while pretending a hypocritical respect for the sovereignty of other states and the right of the self-determination of peoples. "We are fighting," it concluded, "for the best of causes, the civilization and peace of Europe against the cursed system of Bonapartism." [226] It followed, therefore, that Europe should welcome Germany's success or, if necessary, that it should intervene in her behalf.[227] "The completion of the German state," said the *National Zeitung* (Aug. 25), "alone guarantees the permanence of peace." Prophetic of the future was the wrathful reaction to the theory of the balance of power of which the French made so much. "The effort to set up a real balance," wrote one observer, "has as little chance of enduring success as the communist program for an equal distribution of

---

[224] Vetter, *Deutschlands Sieg,* p. 4. Du Bois-Raymond, the Rector of the University of Berlin, spoke in the crowded *Aula* in this sense. *Über dem deutschen Krieg . . .* (Berlin, 1870), p. 39. *Cf.* C. Rohrbach, *Wofür wir kämpfen! Ein Rundblick von jetzt in die kommenden Lage* (Gotha, 1870).
[225] *Grenzboten,* 1870, III, 85.
[226] *National Zeitung,* July 16.
[227] *Der gegenwärtige Krieg, die neutralen Mächte und ihre Interessen* (Berlin, 1870). *Cf.* W. Pauli, *Napoleons Absichten und Hoffnungen, Europas Pflicht, Andenken an 1870* (Hanau, Aug. 4, 2d ed.), p. 3.

property." There had always been and would always be a predominant power. Ranke had written of the transition from the
Spanish to the French hegemony in Richelieu's time, and "the
future historian will sum up our own period in the removal of
the hegemony of Europe from Paris to Berlin." [228]   The Progressive *Volks-Zeitung* (Aug. 28) protested against the increasing
talk of this kind as provocative of new wars of liberation, but
public opinion was more generally impressed by the image of a
powerful Germany as the guardian of the peace of Europe.

On September 2, a series of brilliant victories culminating at
Sedan in the capture of Napoleon and the surrender of France's
last important army in the field assured to the new Germany and
her rulers the power, sooner or later, to dictate terms of peace.
Two days after the fall of the Empire and the organization of the
Provisional Government, Jules Favre, the new minister of
foreign affairs, appealed (September 6) to European opinion,
and indirectly to Germany, for lenient terms, on the ground that
the new French government and public opinion had opposed
the war. King William, he argued, had said that Germany was
fighting the government and not the people of France. With an
eye to French opinion, he declared in conclusion that France
would fight to the end rather than cede an inch of her soil or a
stone of her fortresses. For Bismarck and the military chieftains,
Favre's distinction between the government and people of France
carried no greater weight than is usual in such circumstances, for
only the intervention of the neutral powers would influence their
opinion as to the terms of peace. That danger had for the
moment been averted by Bismarck's publication in the London
Times of Benedetti's draft treaty (1867) for the annexation of
Belgium and by his approval of Russia's plan to tear up the
Treaty of Paris. As for Favre's plea for mercy, it merely irritated him. After their first interview, September 19, as the
siege of Paris was about to begin, Bismarck said of the Frenchman that he had, like an actor, painted his face to depict grief
over the fate of his country.

Nevertheless, some German observers acknowledged that

---

[228] *Grenzboten*, 1870, III, 496, 497.

French public opinion was not responsible for the war. Even the *Kölnische Zeitung* (July 25) wrote that the great majority of Frenchmen had been herded like cattle into the conflict "in order to strengthen a trembling throne by military victories and conquests." A traveller who had recently returned from France said that the French Chamber was more representative of the government than of the people and that the mobs which had demanded war had been paid by the government. In his judgment the extravagances of the Paris chauvinists were no better index to French opinion than the reactions of the German courtiers were for the views of the German people.[229] Bismarck admitted privately that the majority in France had been peaceful, but this was, in his opinion, unimportant, inasmuch as the chauvinist minority would always determine the government's action in a crisis.[230] On September 12 he directed the press to deny that the war was merely against Napoleon and his dynasty. It should write of the declaration of war as the work "of the immense majority of the French people as represented in the Chambers and the army." [231]

Bismarck need not have taken this precaution, for German opinion had definitely rejected the moderate view of France's action. To the opinions of the traveller quoted above, the editor of the *Magdeburgische Zeitung* (July 22) replied: "It is a lie to distinguish between Bonaparte and the French. Both are equally proud, selfish, and domineering." It affirmed two days later that "the French nation, not Louis Napoleon, is the author of the war." According to Treitschke, the appreciation of German literature and philosophy in France had been based upon the assumption of Germany's weakness. Since 1866, he pointed out, the *Revue Germanique,* the leading organ of French students of things German, had ceased publication, and the *Temps,* edited by Alsatians, had been as hateful as the rest of the French press.[232] Du Bois-Raymond, the Rector of the University of Berlin, speaking as "one of purely Celtic blood and in considerable measure

---

[229] *Magdeburgische Zeitung,* July 22.
[230] Busch, *Tagebuchblätter,* I, 169 (Sept. 3).
[231] Bismarck, Rheims, Sept. 12. B: G. W., VI b, pp. 242, 243. The N. A. Z. (Sept. 9) had already expressed this point of view.
[232] P. J., vol. 26, p. 390 (Aug. 30).

of French training," said that Germany had an account to settle with the French people. "The French people," he declared, "is the more dangerous criminal than Louis Napoleon because it is eternal." [233] "The real guilt," exclaimed a Protestant pastor, "lies with the French people." [234] The liberal Ludwig Bamberger, just returned from Paris, insisted that the entire nation must assume the responsibility for the chauvinist minority, although the thirty-eight millions of Frenchmen taken individually were peace-loving.[235]

No protestation of innocence on behalf of the French people, no change of government, could persuade German opinion or the German rulers that France should be dealt with leniently. "The bandits will remain," wrote Bismarck for Russia's benefit, "even if their captain is changed." [236] "According to our experiences with France," wrote Adolph Wagner, an influential professor of political economy at the University of Berlin, "a Robespierre or Napoleon, a Rochefort or Jules Favre, a Thiers or a Guizot, a Consul or an Emperor, an hereditary King or an elective sovereign, makes not the slightest difference." [237] To Favre's version of Napoleon III's more famous pronouncement, *"La république, c'est la paix,"* Bismarck instructed the press to reply, *"La France, c'est la guerre."* [238] "Not so much Napoleon as all of France," affirmed the *Kreuz-Zeitung* (Sept. 6), "is fully responsible for the war, and France must bear the consequences." Back of the demand for drastic terms was in part, however, the general and well-founded belief that defeat would mean the destruction of what had already been accomplished in the long struggle for unity. Even the Progressive *Volks-Zeitung* (Sept. 2) agreed that France's war aims would justify the separation of Alsace-Lorraine from France, although it did not go so far as to approve the annexation of these provinces. A few liberals advised France to

---

233 *Über den deutschen Krieg; Rede am 3 August, 1870* (Berlin, 1870), p. 15.

234 Bottscher, *Was fordern wir von Frankreich?* (Hanover, 1870), p. 4.

235 Bamberger, *Die geheimen Tagebücher*, pp. 106–116. Cf. *National Zeitung*, July 22.

236 Bismarck, Saarbrücken, Aug. 10. *B: G. W.*, VI b, p. 442. *Cf.* William I to Alexander II, Aug. 31. *Ibid.*, VI b, 459.

237 A. Wagner, *Elsass und Lothringen und ihre Wiedergewinnung* (Leipzig, 1870), p. 2.

238 Busch, *Tagebuchblätter*, I, 204 (Sept. 18).

approach Prussia contritely, acknowledging her willingness to accept the consequences of her sins, with a plea for moderate terms, in order that she might devote herself without impossible handicaps to the tasks of reconstruction.[239]   By no means is it certain that the course of events would have changed materially if France had followed this advice.   It was quite generally said with official encouragement that Germany's military superiority had not yet been sufficiently impressed upon France, for the French could and did persuade themselves that the discredited Empire was alone responsible for their reverses.   "The persistent legend of France's invincibility," said the *Provinzial-Correspondenz* (Oct. 19), "makes it imperative that every Frenchman should see her powerlessness.   Had peace been made after Sedan, the illusions which Paris and France still cherish would soon have regained irresistible force."   The *Norddeutsche Allgemeine Zeitung* (Sept. 11) had already expressed substantially the same view.   "Not until the people of Paris and of all France have drunk the bitter dregs of defeat, not until their military strength has been completely broken and the hope of new armies has been destroyed, . . . not until Paris itself has been captured and the consciousness of defeat has attained its full strength will there be reason to hope that the experiences of this year will serve the cause of peace."   Later, when it was a question of a heavier bombardment of Paris, Bismarck cited a Prussian criminal court official who habitually dealt the last three blows "with especial force—*zum heilsamer Gedächtnis*." [240]   He perhaps thought for a moment of halting the armies after Sedan, not to make peace, but in order to avoid foreign mediation and to permit France, as he said, to stew in her own juice.[241]   In any case, he had no confidence in the stability of the Provisional Government and doubted its ability to sign a treaty in the name of the French nation.[242]   Excited by victory, public opinion needed no word from official circles to demand the thorough chastisement of

---

[239] *Offene Antwort an Herrn Jules Favre auf sein Manifest vom 6 September 1870* (Zurich, Sept. 1870); *Frankfurter Zeitung*, Sept. 7.

[240] Busch, *Tagebuchblätter*, II, 89 (Jan. 26, 1871).

[241] K. Jacob, *Bismarck und die Erwerbung Elsass-Lothringens, 1870–1871* (Strassburg, 1905), pp. 44, 45.

[242] Bismarck, Rheims, Sept. 12.   *B: G. W.,* VI b, p. 488.

France. That Germany should not sheath her sword "until France's arrogance has been entirely destroyed" was the opinion of one war-time sheet.[243] "There can be no talk of peace," wrote the *Kölnische Zeitung* (Aug. 13), "until the enemy sees that his defeat has not been due to accidental circumstances." Even the difficult negotiations with the South German states for the completion of German unity were advanced as an argument against peace before their conclusion. "France's humiliation," said the *National Zeitung* (Aug. 13), "is a guarantee against disunion in Germany." For these reasons, German opinion agreed with Bismarck in rejecting Favre's plea for moderate terms and held that peace must be dictated in Paris.[244]

On August 31, the official *Provinzial-Correspondenz* spoke of the historic wrong Germany had suffered, but until the first German victories few called for the recovery of Alsace-Lorraine. During the crisis only one Berlin newspaper, the chauvinist *Börsen-Zeitung* (July 13), had taken its stand for the acquisition of Alsace.[245] Hostilities had scarcely started, however, when the nationalist and Conservative journals began to agitate, not at first for the reunion of the Alsatians and Lorrainers with the Fatherland as a step toward national unity, but for the establishment of a better strategic frontier. Germany's watch should be, according to the *Kreuz-Zeitung* (July 17), on the Meuse instead of on the Rhine. On July 18, the Berlin correspondent of the *Allgemeine Zeitung* (July 21) wrote that the German problem would not be solved until the French had been driven beyond the Vosges. By the first days of August, practically the entire press had joined in the demand for Alsace and at least a part of Lorraine. The *Provinzial-Correspondenz* wrote approvingly of the popular movement for a rectification of the frontier,[246] and the *Norddeutsche* (Aug. 19) announced the appointment of governor generals for the "reconquered German provinces of Alsace-Lorraine." Two weeks later, the union with Alsace of the five

[243] *Hoch Deutschland! Hurrah Preussen!* (Berlin, Aug. 1870).
[244] *Volks-Zeitung,* Sept. 6; *Kölnische Zeitung,* Sept. 6.   Cf. *Kreuz-Zeitung,* Aug. 21.
[245] G. Körner, *Die norddeutsche Publizistik und die Reichsgründung im Jahre 1870* (Hanover, 1908), p. 249. Because Busch wrote, August 11, of the annexation of Alsace as a new idea, Körner believed that this article had not been officially inspired. For the opposing view, see Jacob, *Bismarck und die Erwerbung Elsass-Lothringens,* p. 8.
[246] *N. A. Z.,* Aug. 5.

northern *arrondissements* of the departments of the Moselle and Meurthe was announced.[247]   Bismarck, at the same time, definitely placed territorial annexation among Germany's war aims in his diplomatic circulars.   The supposed certainty of another attack by France to avenge her defeat and the desire of South Germany for a bulwark against it account to a large extent for

Kladderadatsch, September 4, 1870.

Figure 3.—To be safe from the beast, we must clip his claws.

this momentous decision.   "Even his great popularity," wrote the *Norddeutsche Allgemeine Zeitung* (Sept. 25), "would not suffice to check the indignation of public opinion if Germany's necessary demands were not pressed with sufficient force"; but it would be rash to conclude that Bismarck's decision was primarily determined by the desires of the German people.

The German nationality of the Alsatians and Lorrainers, which was ignored in Bismarck's speeches to the Reichstag on Germany's peace terms,[248] was of major concern to public opinion. That their sympathies at the moment were French, though gen-

---

247 *N. A. Z.,* Aug. 21.
248 Franz, *Bismarcks Nationalgefühl,* p. 86.

erally admitted, received no consideration as a serious argument against annexation. Germany, it was believed, would soon make them forget France. "German schools, teachers, officials, and universities will work wonders," wrote a pamphleteer; "they will be good Germans in a quarter of a century." [249] The satisfaction arising from a common life, wrote another, would soon accomplish their assimilation.[250] According to the *National Zeitung* (Aug. 17), most Alsatians had never acquired more than a veneer of French civilization, while the advantages by which the French state had won their loyalty during the Revolution would be more than offset by the merits of the German administrative system.[251] Professor Wagner admitted that the difficulties of their assimilation would be great, but he insisted that Germany's honor, her security, and the real interests of the people of Alsace-Lorraine required a solution of the problem.[252] Treitschke spurned the doctrine of the self-determination of peoples in connection with any fraction of the German nation. "This territory is ours," he said, "by the right of the sword, and annexation follows from the right of the German nation to prevent the loss of any of its sons. Those of us who know Germany and France know better what is salutary for the Alsatians than those unfortunates do themselves. . . . We will make them good Germans in spite of themselves (*Wir wollen ihnen wider ihren Willen ihr eigenes Selbst zurückgeben*)." [253] The suggestion that Alsace might be made a neutral buffer state between France and Germany was denounced.[254] Too weak to defend its neutrality, Alsace would, according to official opinion, always lean upon France.[255] A Progressive politician rejected the project on the ground that it would prevent punitive action by Germany in the event of France's assuming the aggressive again.[256] Nationalist opinion

---

[249] F. Volger, *Elsass, Lothringen und unsere Friedensbedingungen* (Anklam, 1870), p. 3.

[250] Bottscher, *Was fordern wir von Frankreich?* p. 16.

[251] *Cf.* Vetter, *Deutschlands Sieg*, p. 38.

[252] Wagner, *Elsass und Lothringen*, p. 36.

[253] *P. J.*, vol. 26, p. 371 (Aug. 31). This article received von Sybel's approval. *Kölnische Zeitung*, Sept. 19.

[254] *Grenzboten*, 1870, IV, 8.

[255] *N. A. Z.*, Oct. 9. Cf. *National Zeitung*, Nov. 20; Bismarck, Sept. 6. B: *G. W.*, VI b, pp. 480, 481.

[256] Franz Duncker, in the *Volks-Zeitung*, Sept. 14.

also justified annexation as a demonstration of Prussia's leadership and of her ability to defend South Germany.[257] But historical memories had an equal, perhaps even a greater, influence than the claims of race in the public demand for the two provinces. Gneisenau's phrase of 1815, "What the sword has done, the pen has destroyed," was revised and repeated in innumerable journals: "What the sword has won should not now be given away by the pen." There was no reason for alarm on this score, for Bismarck was in substantial agreement with the trend of opinion, which he had at least encouraged. He acknowledged to a correspondent of the *Pall Mall Gazette* (London) the great difficulties which their annexation would occasion, but he insisted that the possession of Strassburg and Metz was necessary in order to limit France's offensive strength.[258]

The few who championed moderate terms could make no headway. Of those who agitated publicly, Johann Jacobi, the editor of the democratic *Zukunft,* was interned for a time, and the Social Democratic executive committee of Braunschweig, which addressed an open letter "To all German Workers," was imprisoned.[259] Bismarck, who had approved Jacobi's internment at first, later ordered his release, but he directed the press to write of the opponents of annexation "as Republicans in the first place and only then a little German. . . . Their party comes before their Fatherland." [260] They were, he declared, "French in sentiment and opinion." [261] Some were so powerful as to be beyond Bismarck's reach, but the Queen, though supported by a few of the German princes, was unable to influence King William,[262] and the Crown Prince in the end accepted Bismarck's program.[263] A textile firm in Baden protested against the annexa-

[257] *Kreuz-Zeitung,* Sept. 3; *National Zeitung,* Sept. 8.

[258] *National Zeitung,* Sept. 9.

[259] *Kreuz-Zeitung,* Sept. 27. Socialist leaders who were responsible for the printing of Marx's letter against annexations, which was at least partly responsible for the committee's action, were also arrested. K. Kautsky, *Elsass-Lothringen: Eine historische Studie* (Stuttgart, 1917), p. 48; H. Nagel, *Die Stellung der Sozialdemokratie zu Bismarcks auswärtige Politik in der Zeit von 1871-1890 (ausschliesslich der Kolonialpolitik)* (Berlin, 1930), p. 13.

[260] *B: G. W.,* VI b, 522-534. Cf. *N. A. Z.,* Oct. 28.

[261] Busch, *Tagebuchblätter,* I, 200 (Sept. 16).

[262] Waldersee, *Denkwürdigkeiten,* I, 98, 99 (Sept. 24).

[263] *Kaiser Friedrich Wilhelm III; das Kriegstagebuch von 1870/71* (Berlin, 1926), p. 119.

tion of Alsace as a dangerous competitor.[264] The inclusion of Metz in the proposed annexations caused, however, vigorous protest from a few newspapers of whose nationalism there could be no doubt. Among them the *Kölnische Zeitung* was the most important, but it could only name the *Westfälische Zeitung* (Essen) and the *Ostpreussische Zeitung* (Königsberg) in support of its position. "In Metz," it wrote (Sept. 11, 18), "French has been spoken for a thousand years. It is just as French as Nancy . . . or Paris. Heaven spare us the claims of conquest on the basis of the boundaries of the Holy Roman Empire. . . . We should arouse all Europe against us and lead to a coalition for which France would wait in vain if we won the best of all victories: moderation and self-restraint. . . . By raising the German flag in Metz we invite the mistrust, fear, and hate of all other countries, with the certainty that all our sacrifices will not establish an enduring peace." [265] Bismarck may privately have doubted the wisdom of annexing Metz,[266] but he certainly did not welcome a publicity campaign against it. Metz was included in the terms which he confided to Russia in September [267] and to the Crown Prince in October.[268] In any event, so irritated was he by the *Kölnische Zeitung's* stand that he said, "They will yet force me to demand the Meuse frontier." [269]

Of greater significance was the reaction in Germany to the mounting concern abroad at France's defeat. Russia advised moderate terms of peace as late as January 1871 and counselled the annexation of Luxemburg instead of Alsace-Lorraine as less productive of future complications. Bismarck rejected this excellent suggestion, but Russia's good-will was too important to risk by a display of bad temper. He reserved his displeasure for England, whose eleventh hour offer of mediation smacked of partiality for France.[270] Her neutrality, thanks to France's superior power upon the sea, worked to the latter's advantage in

---

[264] H. Goldschmidt, *Bismarck und die Friedenshändler 1871* (Berlin, 1929), pp. 6, 7.

[265] See also, *Kölnische Zeitung,* Sept. 21, 23.

[266] Busch, *Tagebuchblätter,* II, 168, 169.

[267] Bismarck, Meaux, Sept. 16. *B: G. W.,* VI b, p. 499.

[268] *Kriegstagebuch,* p. 183 (Versailles, Oct. 26).

[269] Busch, *Tagebuchblätter,* I, 253 (Sept. 30).

[270] Bismarck, July 18. *B: G. W.,* VI b, pp. 397, 398; Busch, *Tagebuchblätter,* II, 85 Jan. 25).

the importation of munitions. The German press was instructed to write of England's "fraudulent neutrality,"[271] and Bismarck charged Granville, the British foreign minister, with a personal animus dating from the Crimean War.[272] Bismarck was prepared to accept England's open hostility rather than to agree "to terms that would be inacceptable to the German nation."[273] To the end of the war, the danger of foreign intervention alarmed Bismarck and embittered public opinion.[274] Advice of moderation from abroad merely strengthened the popular demand for annexations. In permitting France to declare war against inoffensive Germany, the neutral powers, it was said, had forfeited every claim to be heard in the negotiations.[275] It was only too obvious that Europe refused to accept Germany's own estimate of her services to the general interest and that the usual reaction was one of suspicion and hostility to the new German Empire proclaimed at Versailles, January 28, 1871. Treitschke had foreseen at an early date the reluctance of the other countries to accept the disturbing influence of a united Germany upon the balance of power. "We are surrounded," he said, "by secret enemies."[276] Others despaired of a just appreciation abroad of Germany's worth. "It is easier," wrote the *Grenzboten,* "to accept the smooth superficiality of French civilization in spite of its inner corruption than to appreciate properly the depths of the German spirit. This war has shown that in essentials Germany can never hope to be understood by other peoples than those of German blood."[277]

The full responsibility for the terms of peace was Bismarck's. He had been systematically ignored by the generals in the conduct of the war to the extent that he was sometimes forced to depend upon the press for information, but the King's support gave him complete control of the negotiations for the armistice

[271] Busch, *Tagebuchblätter,* II, 47, 48.
[272] Bismarck, July 26. *B: G. W.,* VI b, pp. 423–425.
[273] Bismarck, Aug. 11. *B: G. W.,* VI b, pp. 442–444.
[274] Washington was sounded, without success, as to the prospects of American pressure against intervention by the neutral powers. Bismarck, Aug. 27. *Ibid.,* VI b, 464.
[275] *Offene Antwort an Herrn Jules Favre* (Leipzig, 1870), pp. 49, 50; Treitschke, "Was fordern wir von Frankreich?" *P. J.* vol. 26, p. 376. According to the *N. A. Z.* (Oct. 5), this was the sense of daily petitions to the King.
[276] "Friedenshoffnungen," *P. J.,* vol. 26, p. 500 (Sept. 25).
[277] 1870, IV, 70.

and the terms of peace. Like most Germans, he was convinced that France would inevitably seek revenge for her loss of prestige even without territorial annexations. He refused the Crown Prince's last-minute plea to leave Metz to the French. In reply to the demonstrations in Paris of the bitter-enders against an armistice, the *Norddeutsche* (Feb. 2) protested against the slightest deviation from the demands required by Germany's security as playing into the hands of her sworn enemies. Nevertheless, Bismarck yielded something, perhaps having in mind, as the official *Provinzial-Correspondenz* (Feb. 8) pointed out, that the two nations must after all live together as neighbors. The concession of Belfort and of a smaller indemnity than had originally been contemplated failed, of course, to soften the bitterness caused by the loss of Alsace with Metz and the adjacent territory, the indemnity of five billion francs, and the occupation of sixteen departments in northern France as security for its payment. Such were the terms of the definitive Treaty of Frankfort, May 10, 1871—with additional provisions for the extension of the most-favored-nation clause to German commerce and a transitional period (until October 1872) during which the people of Alsace and Lorraine might choose between German and French nationalities.

For those who had insisted upon France's complete exhaustion, the abandonment of the claim to Belfort was deplorable. "Who," asked the *National Zeitung* (March 1), "had supposed that to be possible?" To the Reichstag and in the official press, Bismarck described the settlement as a just satisfaction of past wrongs, an adequate guarantee against future dangers, and an assurance to Germany of the reasonable fruits of her victory.[278] With official approval, it was argued that Germany was aiding France's recovery by the moderation of the terms of peace.[279] According to a popular weekly, good results might follow even from France's concentration of her energies upon the *revanche,* since it would restore a "lost dignity to her literature, chastity to her art, and moderation to her words"; and the material benefits of hard

---

[278] *N. A. Z.*, March 3, May 14, 1871.
[279] *National Zeitung*, March 12; *Provinzial-Correspondenz*, in *N. A. Z.*, May 20; *Magdeburgische Zeitung*, May 20.

work and discipline might eventually turn her thoughts from war.[280] Criticism of the peace terms was, however, more outspoken than had seemed probable from the trend of opinion during the war. The Crown Prince expected an unfavorable reaction by the non-German world.[281] Continuing the independence it had shown in the question of Metz, the *Kölnische Zeitung* (Feb. 28) welcomed the concession of Belfort for the surprising reason "that every renunciation of French soil is a gain." The hostile criticism of the small Socialist minority was to be expected,[282] but more significant, because it had supported territorial annexations during the war, was the opinion of the Progressive party that a grave mistake had been made. Undoubtedly a contributing cause was the irreconcilable opposition into which this group had been forced by the failure of the imperial constitution to provide for a responsible ministry. But there was an unmistakable note of sincerity in its concern for the future. It was during the electoral campaign for the first imperial Reichstag that the Progressives most forcibly expressed their views. "It is an unprecedented illusion," wrote the *Volks-Zeitung* (March 1), "to expect a real peace from the terms of peace. France makes peace because she cannot continue the war. The situation points to a renewed and a better prepared war, not to peace." Since the treaty could not now be changed, only a Progressive majority in the Reichstag would divert France from thoughts of war to her domestic problems, as a demonstration of the will for peace on the part of the German people. This alone would neutralize the universal suspicion aroused by the new German Empire.[283]

Even before Königgratz, when Bismarck was the object of almost universal execration, public opinion was not without influence upon his foreign policy. The King's support enabled

---

280 *Illustrierte Zeitung* (Leipzig), March 11.

281 *Kriegstagebuch*, p. 389 (Feb. 25).

282 Bebel warned that France would always seek to recover Alsace-Lorraine and that Germany would be compelled repeatedly to increase her army. Nagel, *Stellung der Sozialdemokratie*, pp. 13, 14.

283 *Volks-Zeitung*, March 3, 8. The Progressive candidates, including Jacobi, carried all six electoral districts in Berlin, but elsewhere the party failed to check the wave of nationalist sentiment that piled up a safe majority for the Conservative and nationalist parties.

him to maneuver Austria into war without regard to its immediate reactions, but he gambled everything for which he stood upon a speedy success. Failure, he knew, would mean his own downfall and the indefinite adjournment of national unity. Austria's defeat and its results changed Bismarck's attitude toward public opinion. No longer could he afford to be indifferent to its immediate reactions, for he now personified the popular aspirations for unity and a powerful fatherland. That he placed a high value upon the support of the masses, despite his social background and his conservative political philosophy, is shown by the provision for universal manhood suffrage in the election of the Reichstag of the North German Confederation (1867). The conservation of his new prestige was one of his principal tasks and one of his greatest achievements during the four years before the war with France.

Not the least of his many difficulties was the eagerness of the extremists for the immediate attainment of unity and the sensitiveness of patriotic sentiment even to the appearance of yielding in foreign affairs, especially to France. He doubtless regarded the Treaty of Prague as a merely temporary arrangement, but, unlike the extremists, he saw the need of caution, if the South Germans were ever to become good citizens of the new Germany, and of diplomatic preparations for the war with France, which he probably regarded as inevitable. Prussia's triumph in fact increased the attachment of public sentiment in the South to the independence of the separate states. Against this growth of particularism, neither Bismarck's calculated moderation nor his influence upon a part of the South German press would have availed without the aid of France's provocations. Only against France were the great majority of Germans able to forget their differences. Her demands for territorial compensations after Königgrätz were directly responsible for the alliances of 1866 and for the reorganization of the South German armies on the Prussian model in 1867. The renewal of the *Zollverein* was the single step toward union that owed little to the French danger.

Public opinion was therefore a fairly constant source of concern during the negotiations with France, with the result that Bismarck lost some of the freedom of action which he had enjoyed before

1866. In Napoleon's bids for Belgium and Luxemburg, he saw an opportunity to gain time for the consolidation of the achievements of 1866 and to improve the diplomatic situation, and perhaps, though he probably was more hopeful of deceiving Napoleon than of attaining positive results, to trade his own support of Napoleon's ambitions for an acceptance of German unity. So far did he go that national sentiment was outraged during the Luxemburg crisis by his alleged consent to France's acquisition of territory that was German by blood and history. Exploited to the limit by the liberals and by South German particularists, this charge caused Bismarck to block Napoleon's designs rather than to compromise his prestige as the champion of the German cause; yet he was blamed for the loss of Luxemburg by the declaration of her neutrality.

In the diplomatic preparations for the Franco-Prussian War, public opinion had little or no part. Even France finally learned that direct interference in German affairs usually played Bismarck's game. To the German people, the preliminaries of the Hohenzollern candidature were practically unknown and, in any event, they probably would have aroused little interest. The press did not need Bismarck's instructions to say that the question concerned Prince Leopold and Spain alone, that the candidature was not a national interest, and to watch France's every move with a suspicious eye. From these views to the position that Germany would not fight to place a Hohenzollern prince upon the Spanish throne and to an approval of Leopold's resignation seemed a logical step to many of the most important journals, although the prospect that France would present new and drastic demands was doubtless one reason for this attitude of cautious reserve. Bismarck may not have been entirely pleased by the vigor with which the press asserted that the German nation had no interest in the Spanish question, but whatever harm resulted was soon remedied by the historic Ems Dispatch. That the dynastic question had been superseded by a national issue was the practically unanimous conclusion. The French ambassador had insulted the German nation in the person of King William. With comparatively unimportant exceptions, the resulting national union was maintained in the rejection of Favre's appeal for moderate terms of peace, in the demands for the prosecution of the war until France was completely crushed and for the annexation of Alsace-Lorraine, in the belief that Germany was fighting for the interests of Europe, and in the approval of the Treaty of Frankfort. Most Germans agreed with Bismarck that France would attack as soon as possible to avenge the defeat of her armies and to recover her lost prestige, and that her action in a crisis would always be determined by the chauvinist minority. Few foresaw that the loss of Alsace-Lorraine would load the dice in favor of the chauvinists during the coming years of peace and would make of France a permanent ally of Germany's other enemies.

CHAPTER III

The New Empire
and a Nervous Europe, 1871-1875

Im Gegentheil sollten wir uns bemühn, die Verstimmungen,
die unser Heranwachsen zu einer wirklichen Grossmacht
hervorgerufen hat, durch den ehrlichen and friedliebenden
Gebrauch unsrer Schwerkraft abzuschwächen, um die Welt
zu überzeugen, dass eine deutsche Hegemonie nützlicher und
unparteiischer, auch unschädlicher für die Freiheit andrer
wirkt als eine französische, russische oder englische.
                    Bismarck, *Gedanken und Erinnerungen*, II, 267.

For the first time in modern history, the great majority of Germans were satisfied with their position in Europe. They felt no strong resentment on account of the fact that millions of fellow Germans still lived beyond the frontiers and that Germany had no colonies. Only France, they thought, might reasonably resent Germany's predominance, but her defeat was generally regarded as a service to Europe.[1] "We have fought for our neighbors," wrote the *National Zeitung* (Feb. 12, 1871), "as well as for ourselves." "By destroying France's hegemony," said a new weekly, "we have restored freedom to ourselves and to all nations; yes, even that great nation . . . if it ever achieves the humility of self-knowledge, will thank us for the saving punishment which . . . almost unwillingly we have imposed upon it."[2] Official assurances of peaceful intentions accompanied the establishment of the Empire. It would be, according to the Emperor's proclamation, January 18, 1871, a bulwark against war.[3] "If it depends upon the German people," affirmed the official *Staats-Anzeiger*,

---

[1] *Europa nach dem letzten Krieg* (Berlin, 1871), p. 19.
[2] *Im neuen Reich; Wochenschrift für das Leben des deutschen Volkes in Staat, Wissenschaft und Kunst* (A. Dove, ed.), I, 1 (Jan. 1871).
[3] *N. A. Z.*, Jan. 19.

"Europe's guns may remain silent and her peoples may turn their attention to domestic problems."[4] The Emperor assured the first Imperial Reichstag that Germany would accord the same respect to all countries, strong or weak, which she expected for herself, and that the spirit of her civilization, her constitution, and the organization of her army were guarantees against the abuse of her power.[5] The efforts of the Catholics, already organized as the Center party, to enlist Germany's aid for the restoration of the Pope's temporal power, elicited only an official declaration, in which the representatives of the other parliamentary groups concurred, against interference in the affairs of other peoples.[6]

Nevertheless, Germany's victories inspired in nationalist circles an overweening pride. "The star of Marengo and of Austerlitz," the *National Zeitung* (March 19, 1871) boasted, "has paled forever before the sun of Sedan." To the National Liberal *Magdeburgische Zeitung* (May 12, 1871), it was self-evident that "the control of war and peace has now passed to Germany." With official encouragement, agitation began during the summer of 1871 for the celebration of September 2, the anniversary of Sedan, as the national holiday. There was, however, serious opposition. A year later, even a National Liberal journal admitted that the French had never celebrated a defeat of the German armies in this offensive manner,[7] but the manifest wishes of the government, coupled with the argument that the celebration would be an expression of national unity rather than a reminder of the humiliation of France, finally carried the day. Only the Catholics and the Social Democrats remained aloof at the dedication of the *Siegessäule*, September 2, 1873, in Berlin.[8] Repeated warn-

---

[4] *N. A. Z.,* Jan. 25.

[5] *Stenographische Berichte über die Verhandlungen des Deutschen Reichstages,* I Leg. Per., I Sess., I, 2 (March 21, 1871). This set will hereafter be cited as *Verhandlungen.*

[6] *Ibid.,* 1871, III (*Anlagen*), no. 11, p. 61. For an analysis of the debate, see Albers, *Reichstag und Aussenpolitik,* pp. 52–57.

[7] *Haude und Spenersche Zeitung,* Aug. 18, 1872. Hereafter cited as *Spenersche Zeitung.*

[8] *Germania,* Aug. 23, 1873. Sedan Day never acquired a place in the affection of the German people comparable to that of Bastille Day in France and not much was heard of it after the few first years. For the Catholic hierarchy the fact that Italian troops had occupied Rome on this date was decisive. M. L., "Die Sedanfeier und Bischof Ketteler," *Die Gegenwart,* VI, 145 (Sept. 5, 1874).

ings against excessive talk of Germany's hegemony came from the Progressive *Volks-Zeitung* (June 27, 1871), and von Sybil, the historian, pointed to France's exaggerated pride as an example to be avoided.[9] To be sure, this understandable expression of national pride was less important to Europe than the direction of German policy. Official affirmations of peaceful intentions made no serious or lasting impression beyond the German frontiers. The French were by no means alone in rejecting the German interpretation of events since 1866 and in doubting the sincerity of her satisfaction with the status quo. That each of Prussia's wars had added to her territory and power seemed more significant than the German argument that they had all been essentially defensive. The possession of the strongest army in Europe, it was feared, might tempt Germany's rulers to new adventures. Queen Victoria, a few years later, echoed Disraeli's opinion that Bismarck was a new Bonaparte and that "he must be bridled."[10] According to Odo Russell, the British ambassador to Berlin, Bismarck's purpose was "the supremacy of the German race in Europe and in the world."[11] "Germany," wrote the *Times* (March 22, 1871) in recognition of Germany's moderation, "bears her triumphs with a meekness which is too consistent to be affected," but the vogue of the alarmist pamphlet *The Battle of Dorking* was more indicative of popular sentiment in England at the the close of the Franco-Prussian war. Sweden was reported as fearful for her security and Denmark was said to have erected coastal defenses.[12] Rumor credited Germany with plans for the absorption of Austria's German provinces or for the annexation of Holland.[13] These reactions of foreign observers were straws in the wind; but several years were to elapse before the supposed German menace resulted in counter diplomatic measures.

That Europe remained suspicious and alarmed astonished and

---

[9] For his lecture at the University of Bonn, see *N. A. Z.*, March 3, 1872.

[10] A. F. Moneypenny, G. E. Buckle, *The Life of Benjamin Disraeli, Earl Beaconsfield*, 6 vols. (New York, 1920), V, 421. Cf. *Letters of Queen Victoria* (2), II, 399.

[11] Lord Newton, *Lord Lyons: a Record of British Diplomacy*, 2 vols. (London, 1913), II, 41 (1873).

[12] Ziekursch, *Politische Geschichte*, II, 7; Plehn, *Bismarcks auswärtige Politik*, pp. 2, 3. Cf. "Der Deutschenhass in Zürich," *Im neuen Reich*, I, 485.

[13] N. Japekse, *Europa und Bismarcks Friedenspolitik* (Berlin, 1927), p. 20.

angered German observers. "How often," exclaimed the *National Zeitung* (Aug. 21, 1873), naïvely unconscious that its own way of expressing Germany's peaceful purposes was one of the reasons for these suspicions, "must Germany repeat that she covets no foreign territory and that she merely requests (*verlangt*) the honor of being the strong guardian of the peace of Europe?" Differences of opinion existed as to the measures Germany should undertake in view of this willful obtuseness. During the Reichstag elections in 1871 and later, the Progressives argued for the establishment of ministerial responsibility and other liberal reforms as the only effective means of disarming foreign suspicion.[14] Schweinitz, for example, then the military attaché in St. Petersburg, believed that Germany's foreign policy should be moderate and conciliatory.[15] While prodigal of peaceful assurances, the government relied more upon the strength of the army. The war was scarcely over when a publicist who sometimes expressed official views warned that the jealousy aroused by the establishment of a great German state would require redoubled attention to its military strength.[16] When the government asked the Reichstag in 1874 for a perpetual grant with which to maintain the army at its constitutional strength of one per cent of the population, Moltke cited (Feb. 16, 1874), while Bismarck listened with approval, the unfriendly attitude of Europe as well as France's hostility.[17] Even Bismarck was powerless to change the fundamental causes of Germany's fears, for they were the natural consequences of the recent changes in the balance of power. His famous *cauchemar des alliances* was an implicit recognition of the advantages which might accrue to France from these suspicions. The maintenance of the status quo, the prevention of hostile alliances, and the isolation of France were therefore prescribed by Germany's situation as the necessary aims of Bismarck's foreign policy.

---

[14] *Volks-Zeitung*, March 8, 1871. The relative importance of this party should not be exaggerated, for it elected only a total of thirty-seven of three hundred and eighty-four deputies. Most of its successes were in Berlin.

[15] Vienna, Sept. 30, 1872. *Briefwechsel des Botschafters General v. Schweinitz* (Berlin, 1928), p. 88.

[16] C. Rössler, *Graf Bismarck und das deutsche Volk* (Berlin, 1871), pp. 56, 57.

[17] *Verhandlungen*, II Leg. Per., I Sess., I, 80; H. E. Brockhaus, *Stunden bei Bismarck 1871–1878* (Leipzig, 1929), pp. 88, 89.

In spite of her defeat, France continued to occupy first place in Bismarck's calculations. He left to Austria and Russia the initiative in clarifying their relations with the new Germany, but the application of the peace terms and the formulation of a general policy for Franco-German relations required immediate decisions in Berlin. When von Arnim, the ambitious ambassador in Paris, used his influence in favor of an Orleanist restoration, Bismarck warned him against the dangers to Germany and Europe of a policy based upon questionable premises, though the Chancellor did not himself approach the problem of Franco-German relations with an open mind.[18] His brusque and offensive treatment of France's representatives during the negotiation of the armistice was not that of a statesman who admitted even the possibility of a reconciliation. To Favre's complaint that the sick and the blind had been fired upon during the siege of Paris, he replied: "I fail to see the grounds for your complaint. . . . You do much worse, you are shooting at our sound and healthy men," and he pretended to wonder that the French had not yet eaten the women and children who, according to Favre, still thronged the boulevards.[19] Fresh from the negotiations at Frankfort, he compared the typical Frenchman to a hunted fox: "If the hunter shoots him, he never admits that he is done for but gnashes his teeth in impotent rage, and when the hunter at last puts him in his pouch, he puts all his strength into one final bite."[20] The annexation of Alsace-Lorraine confirmed the presumption in his own mind and on the part of public opinion against the possibility of a reconciliation. In his opinion, nothing was to be gained by speculation as to France's future aims and policy: "they will fall upon us as soon as they feel strong enough."[21] It was only a question of the time France would require for the reorganization of her army and the acquisition of alliances, because any party in power would be forced by public sentiment and its own previous advocacy of the *revanche* to precipitate war when the moment arrived for action.[22] He insisted, therefore, upon the

[18] Bismarck, Dec. 20, 1872. *G. P.,* I, 157, 158.
[19] Busch, *Tagebuchblätter,* II, 75, 89 (Jan. 24, 26, 1871).
[20] Brockhaus, *Stunden mit Bismarck,* p. 22 (May 13, 1871).
[21] *Bismarck-Erinnerungen des Staataministers Freiherrn von Ballhausen* (Stuttgart, 1921), p. 27 (Jan. 25, 1875).
[22] Bismarck, Feb. 2, 1873. *G. P.,* I, 162–164.

fulfillment of the terms of peace to the last detail,[23] although he did not follow the first Napoleon's example after the Treaty of Tilsit (1807) in weakening France still further by exacting more than was specifically stated in the bond.[24]   Only after a personal appeal to the Emperor did the conciliatory Manteuffel, the commander of the army of occupation, secure the order for the first step in the evacuation of the occupied departments, which Bismarck had held up following a comparatively unimportant variation from the agreement in the first payment on the indemnity.[25] When the Chancellor consented to the full payment before the expiration of the agreed time limit [26] and to the withdrawal of the last German troops, this concession was due quite as much to the eagerness of German opinion for demobilization as to any desire to avoid further friction between the army of occupation and the civilian population or to strengthen Thiers' political position in France.   Expediency alone prevented his active intervention in French politics.   He preferred a form of government strong enough to carry out the terms of peace but sufficiently weak to delay France's reorganization at home and the establishment of alliances abroad.   Next to a Bonapartist restoration, his first choice, he desired Thiers' maintenance in power as a statesman of his own realistic stamp, and, after him, the Republic, as the form of government least capable of making France dangerous again.[27]   Because Bismarck's favor was a handicap rather than an advantage to any party in France, its practical influence was probably slight and was apparently neutralized by von Arnim's support of an Orleanist restoration, which, in Bismarck's opinion,[28] contributed to Thiers' defeat in the National Assembly (May 1873) by a coalition of the Monarchist groups.

---

[23] Next to the payment of the indemnity, according to *Im neuen Reich* (vol. I, 491), the purpose of the occupation was to assure the creation of a legal government, "to repress the Socialist elements, yes, to safeguard all Latin Europe from a new revolution of incalculable consequence."

[24] K. Linnebach, *Deutschland als Sieger im besiegten Frankreich* (Berlin, 1924), pp. 71, 72.

[25] *D. D. F.,* (1), I, 48–50. Cf. *G. P.,* I, 60; H. Hertzfeld, *Deutschland und das geschlagene Frankreich* (Berlin, 1924), pp. 71, 72.

[26] The last payment was made September 5, 1873.

[27] Hohenlohe, *Denkwürdigkeiten,* 2 vols. (Berlin, 1897–1901), II, 118, 119 (May 2, 1874). *Cf.* G. Rosen, *Der Stellungsnahme der Politik Bismarcks zur Frage der Staatsform in Frankreich von 1871 bis 1890* (Detmold, 1924).

[28] Hohenlohe, *op. cit.,* II, 107 (Feb. 18, 1874).

The violent reaction in France to the terms of peace at first occasioned little concern. Although the treaty was regarded as a model of moderation, the first hysterical demands for revenge were heard with a kind of condescending sympathy. To the *National Zeitung* (March 7, 1871), the threatened "war of revenge" was essentially a phrase which "the victors may allow the defeated as a release for their passions." A popular weekly, the *Illustrierte Zeitung* of Leipzig advised against a reply in kind. "How bitter we should be," it wrote (March 11, 1871), "if Germany lay crushed and defeated at Napoleon's feet." Judicial procedure, according to the *Kölnische Zeitung* (March 23, 1871), had once permitted the loser an hour at the close of a suit in which to abuse the court; France, after her defeat, might be allowed a similarly harmless satisfaction. Upon France alone, it was generally said, would depend the development of Franco-German relations. If the Germans were sincere, as they doubtless were, in denying the existence of an irreconcilable hatred of the French, they were, nevertheless, easily excited by evidence that France was bent upon the recovery of her strength, that her national pride was reasserting itself, and that she refused to accept the new status quo. She would, Germany was informed, punctually fulfill her obligations, "which the world acknowledges are exceptionally hard," [29] but Thiers made no secret of France's intention to use Germany's difficulties with other countries, preferably by peaceful means, for the recovery of Alsace-Lorraine.[30] It was a question of fundamentally different interpretations of the Treaty of Frankfort. While Germany regarded it as definitive and perpetual, every French newspaper, as von Arnim informed Thiers, made it clear that it was unbearable and temporary.[31] To German observers it was also obvious that France in general and Thiers in particular hoped for an alliance with Russia,[32] although they could not know that Thiers counted upon

---

[29] Gabriac, Aug. 14, 1871. *D. D. F.*, (1), I, 62, 63. It was, wrote one observer, all that Germany could ask of France. *Im neuen Reich*, 1872, II, 70.

[30] A moderate observer wrote of Thiers: "Niemand versteht so gut, schöngeformte Versicherungen der Friedensliebe nach auswärts zu senden und zugleich vertraulich dem Lande zu verrathen, dass die Kräfte Frankreichs für eine Zeit neuer Thaten gesammelt werden." "Frankreich und der Friede," *Im neuen Reich*, 1872, II, 70.

[31] Arnim, Jan. 15, 1872. *G. P.*, I, 108, 109.

[32] The *Kladderadatsch's* cartoons constantly played upon this theme during the two

an irreconcilable Russo-German antagonism and that he had instructed the French ambassador to be receptive to any advances by the Russian government.[33]

The danger of a Franco-Russian alliance seemed too remote to alarm public opinion,[34] but the nationalist press was quick to castigate the revival of national pride in France.[35] Thiers' review of the army at Versailles after the fall of the Paris Commune was the first cause of irritation. In reply to the *Journal Officiel's* claim that the army had saved European civilization and that it would enable France to recover her rightful place as a great nation, the National Liberal *Magdeburgische Zeitung* (July 5, 1871) wrote: "It is true, the Frenchman has no memory; he is already forgetting the recent frightful events and nothing remains except the old pretentious pride and self-exaltation." "Only a complete self-abnegation," according to the *Preussische Jahrbücher,* "can bring the French to surrender their claim to pre-eminence in Europe." [36] The *National Zeitung* (July 12, 1871) expressed in extreme form the contempt and suspicion which were especially characteristic of the National Liberal press. Only fear, it declared, could restrain the French. "The astonishing thing for men of common sense is their complete denial of facts. Readers of their speeches and press must constantly remind themselves that these people were not the victors. . . . They are not to be measured by ordinary standards: they are a special people, 'the people of ideas,' and to live they must always contemplate an adventure. . . . Their weakness is the sole guarantee against another war." The Progressive *Volks-Zeitung* (June 7, 1871) added its voice to the chorus. "Even amid the ruins of Paris and under the burden of boundless suffering, the French are reverting to their favorite illusion of being the great, the incomparable nation. . . . As only the French nation could build a Paris, it alone, they claim, is capable of destroying it."

years of his power. See especially the numbers for April 7, June 23, Aug. 4, 11, 15, 1872.

[33] Thiers, Sept. 4, 1871. *D. D. F.*, (I), I, 73, 74.

[34] Not until years later did the Socialist leaders use this menace in their attack upon Bismarck's foreign policy. Nagel, *Stellung der Sozialdemokratie,* pp. 24–27.

[35] L. Richter, "Die französische politische Presse im Jahre 1873," *Die Gegenwart; Wochenschrift für Literatur, Kunst und öffentliches Leben* (Paul Lindau, ed.), III, 178 (March 22, 1873).

[36] *P. J.,* vol. 30, pp. 475, 476 (Oct. 10, 1872).

Talk of the French people's instinctive aggressiveness and domineering tendencies soon revived, with the official *Norddeutsche's* encouragement, when (Sept. 17, 1871) it spoke of the "self-glorification, passion for military glory and credulity" of Frenchmen as the perfect tool for the first Napoleon's ambitions. In 1873 an anonymous pamphleteer again attributed the responsibility for the war to the French people and depicted Louis XIV as typical of the aggressive spirit with which Germany had to contend.[37] The same symptoms of vainglory and overconfidence were seen in the satisfaction produced by France's rapid payment of the indemnity and by the successful loans which had made it possible.[38]

Still more important in the development of German opinion and policy toward France was the difficulty which most Germans experienced in reconciling themselves to France's inevitable efforts to recover her strength. It ranked with Alsace-Lorraine and France's refusal to accept the status quo as one of the chief obstacles to better relations. Bismarck doubtless reasoned that her recovery could not permanently be prevented, since he included no provisions in the Treaty of Frankfort for the reduction or limitation of the French army. As long as Thiers remained in power, the reorganization of the French army did not greatly perturb him, for he placed a good deal of confidence in Thiers' sense of political realities,[39] but his comparative indifference at once changed to alarm when France acquired a government under MacMahon, whose monarchist and clerical tendencies in his opinion gave a more dangerous significance to France's rearmament. In Germany, the opposition parties were normally skeptical as to the French menace, doubtless in part because of political reasons. Foreseeing the use of France as an argument for increased armaments, the Progressives questioned the effectiveness of her preparations, and the Catholics, although they excelled in their vituperative criticism of Thiers after his refusal

[37] *Unser Krieg mit Ludwig dem Vierzehnten* (Gutersloh, 1873), p. 7.
[38] *Volks-Zeitung,* July 2, 1871; *N. A. Z.,* July 2, 1871; *Kölnische Zeitung,* July 29, 1872; *National Zeitung,* July 31, 1872.
[39] Thiers also found in Bismarck a kindred spirit. After his fall (May 1873), he told Hohenlohe that Bismarck had been as generous in the peace negotiations as possible. Hohenlohe, *Denkwürdigkeiten,* II, 129 (July 16, 1874).

to work for the restoration of the Papacy's temporal power, had little to say against the military efforts of the clerical government which succeeded him. Not even the nationalists questioned France's right to an army sufficiently large for self-defense. The *raison d'être* of the French army was the crux of the matter. Since German opinion was practically a unit in believing that France was in no danger of an attack, the extent of her rearmament seemed excessive even to many members of the opposition and to mean warlike purposes. That a great army was necessary to assure her "legitimate position" in Europe, as Thiers repeatedly asserted, carried no conviction for those who believed this phrase to be merely a blind to cover France's passion for predominant power and the recovery of Alsace-Lorraine. Nationalist opinion was distinctly less confident than Bismarck of Thiers' moderation, for the agreement of March 1873—providing for the last payments of the French indemnity and for the withdrawal of the German troops—which the official press represented as a service to peace,[40] was from its point of view a leap in the dark; for no one could be sure that France had taken her recent lesson to heart. No other German, said the skeptical *Magdeburgische Zeitung* (March 19, 1873), would have approved an equally moderate settlement.

Only the Catholics in Germany found any satisfaction in Thiers' defeat (May 1873) and in the organization of Marshal MacMahon's monarchist and clerical government. According to Bismarck, the change meant that France, now in a position to count upon the sympathy of the Catholic and conservative powers, had a better chance to find allies,[41] and this prospect promptly increased his concern as to her rearmament. German opinion did not at once share his alarm, thanks to the greater feeling of security which accompanied the development of close diplomatic relations with Austria and Russia. It was in Central and Eastern Europe that Bismarck, facing new problems, had shown to best advantage his diplomatic skill. Until 1871, his foreign policy had centered, for the most part, upon the solution

---

[40] *Provinzial-Correspondenz*, March 19, 1873.

[41] In the anti-clericalism of the Republicans, *Im neuen Reich* (1873, I, 972) saw an ally against the Church in the *Kulturkampf*.

of the German problem. The new Germany found herself for
the first time squarely in the main current of European politics
between Western and Eastern Europe. That she was drawn in
both directions and that she never succeeded in making a definite
choice between them was one of Germany's tragedies. Western
in her civilization, in her increasing commercial and industrial
development, and in the political aspirations and sympathies of
her liberals, she was turned back toward Central and Eastern
Europe by the hatred of her powerful Conservatives for the parliamentary institutions of the Western countries, by France's
hostility, and by England's coolness or at least her refusal to
establish close diplomatic relations with a continental power.
Bismarck's task was therefore to assure Germany's security in the
presence of the increasingly dangerous Austro-Russian rivalry in
the Balkans, and, at the same time, by Germany's relations with
these countries, to strengthen her position with reference to the
Western powers. An inescapable consequence of Germany's
geographical location, this remained one of the permanent problems of German foreign policy under Bismarck and his successors.

Since no immediate crisis required haste, Bismarck was content at first to permit the interests of Austria and Russia to
determine their relations with Germany. He probably foresaw
that each would seek Germany's support, thus giving him an
opportunity to establish friendly relations with both and perhaps to improve their relations with each other. The success of
this plan, which was the essence of his policy in Eastern Europe
with only temporary variations to the end of his career, required
the cool detachment with which he was eminently endowed.
German opinion, however, did not share this impartiality. Not
until the Near-Eastern crisis and the Russo-Turkish War (1877–
1878) did the issue present itself definitely as the choice between
the friendship of Austria and that of Russia, but even in these
early years German opinion declared quite clearly in favor of
the former. To the great satisfaction of public opinion, therefore, the first step in the strengthening of Germany's diplomatic
position was a reconciliation with Austria, which Bismarck's
moderation in 1866 had made possible, which the defeat of France

and the obvious impossibility of restoring the old order in Germany had indicated as Austria's logical policy, and which the desire of the Hungarians for Germany's friendship against Russia finally made a reality. In 1871, Andrássy, who had said that Austria should "offer her hand to Germany and show her fist to Russia," [42] became Beust's successor, and promptly thereafter the two Emperors, William and Francis Joseph, met at Ischl and Gastein. Their tacit agreement to forget old quarrels and the beginning of an association which was to last until the collapse of the Dual Monarchy in 1918, won practically unanimous approval in Germany, thanks to the power of sentiment and traditions, to the religious ties which profoundly influenced German Catholic opinion, and to the ideal of Greater Germany. On this issue, the enthusiasm of the chief opposition parties, the Progressives and the Centrists, was not surpassed by that of Bismarck's most loyal followers. Nevertheless, there were some who advised against going too fast or too far, because the Hohenwart ministry's pro-Slavic tendencies aroused doubts as to Austria's future; [43] and consideration for Russia's reaction moved the official press to question the need of a formal alliance between states whose friendship was assured by common interests and mutual sympathy.[44]

Less simple was the problem of relations with Russia. Her services before and during the war with France pointed logically to an enduring diplomatic association, if not a definite alliance.[45] In spite of the unpleasant shock that followed her advice of moderation in the terms of peace and especially her suggestion in favor of the annexation of Luxemburg in the place of Alsace-Lorraine, William telegraphed the Tsar, February 27, 1871, that "Prussia will never forget that it is thanks to you that the war remained localized." Several considerations restrained Bismarck from initiating negotiations for a diplomatic understanding with

---

[42] Busch, *Tagebuchblätter*, II, 46.

[43] *Magdeburgische Zeitung, Provinzial-Correspondenz*, Aug. 16, 1871; *N. A. Z.*, Sept. 7.

[44] *Provinzial-Correspondenz*, Aug. 16, 1871; *N. A. Z.*, Sept. 7, 9.

[45] Moltke, however, had little confidence in Russia's friendship, which, in his opinion, had been the result of common hostility to France and of family ties. The two nations were divided by religion and material interests. F. von Schmerfeld, *Die deutschen Aufmarschpläne, 1871–1890* (Berlin, 1929), p. 5 (April 25).

Russia after the war.   To the probability that Austria would take offense was added the possibility that Russia, having won her freedom from the Treaty of Paris, would be unwilling to aid in the further strengthening of Germany's position, or that she would require impossible concessions.   It was, therefore, better strategy to wait for Russia to make the first move.   Bismarck never acknowledged that the hostility of German opinion to a formal alliance with Russia was a determining cause of his policy; and yet even he was doubtless not entirely immune to popular feeling, if for no other reason than that it might be a source of weakness. The attitude of public opinion at any rate requires some attention, because it influenced Russia's attitude toward Germany.

As a general rule, those groups which were most friendly to Austria were likewise extremely hostile toward Russia.   Sympathy for England as well as for Austria and their hatred of autocratic institutions turned the liberals against Germany's eastern neighbor.   *Grossdeutsch* traditions and sentiment presented serious obstacles to a Russo-German friendship, just as they worked in favor of a rapprochement with Austria.   Bismarck disclaimed any political interest in the fate of the Germans of Russia's Baltic provinces, who were, during these years, the victims of an active Russification program, but it aroused much sympathy in Germany in spite of the apparently systematic neglect of the situation by the news agencies.   The well-known anti-German tendencies and Francophile sympathies of the Pan-Slavic movement not only nourished hostile opinion in Germany [46] but they seriously affected Russo-German diplomatic relations.   From the opposition and pro-Austrian groups came forthright criticism of a Russian alliance.   The Progressive *Volks-Zeitung* (Jan. 7, 1871) said that the Pan-Slavic agitation was "a provocation of the German nation."   Religious differences as well as partiality for Austria turned Catholic opinion against Russia, and Bismarck's manifestly friendly attitude toward her became one of the items in the Catholic indictment of the Empire.   In that friendship Catholic observers found an argument in favor of their opposition to Bismarck's policy since 1866.   Dependence upon Russia, as-

---

[46] *Französen-Cultus und Deutschenhass,* von XXX (Berlin, 1871), pp. 5, 6.

serted the leading Catholic review of South Germany, was the inevitable result. "Emperor William is only the nominal victor, the real one is Tsar Alexander. The German people lost their independence on the battlefields of France." [47]   An alliance with Russia found its adherents chiefly among Bismarck's loyal followers and among the Conservatives, although, from the Chancellor's point of view, the Emperor's unwavering preference for Russia was more important. They stressed such general considerations as the family relationships between the two reigning houses, gratitude for Russia's past services, and its usefulness as a defense of conservative principles. Supporting arguments were found in the absence of any conflicts between the imperialist interests of the two countries. Germany's lack of an important commercial stake in the Near East, it was said, would enable her to support Russia's desire to open the Straits and even her desire to control their Southern shore. That Russia was at odds with England in Central Asia was not considered a valid reason for objection, for, in the words of an ardent advocate of an alliance, "the world will be entirely indifferent to the decline and fall of England's power in that region." [48]   The strong anti-English tendency of Conservative opinion in Germany worked in Russia's favor, but even nationalist opinion had its reservations as to a formal alliance. For those who thought of the Russians as barbarous, and Treitschke wrote of this as a general characteristic of German opinion,[49] it was difficult to accept Russia as an equal. Nor was an alliance considered a necessity, for it was held that united Germany need not fear even the numerical superiority of the Russian masses.[50] Bismarck, for the reasons stated above, agreed with those who were not eager for a definite alliance. Writing at the close of 1870, the frequently inspired *Grenzboten* asserted that a Russo-German alliance would be "only an *ad hoc* combination which should entail no permanent obligations." [51]

Once more Russia's interests served Bismarck's purposes. In-

[47] *Historisch-politische Blätter*, 1871, XIII, 393.

[48] *Russland und Deutschland*, von XXX, (Berlin, 1871), p. 23. Cf. *Europa nach dem letzten Kriege*, von dem Verfasser von *Russland und Deutschland* (Berlin, 1871).

[49] H. Holborn, *Bismarcks europäische Politik zu Beginn der siebzige Jahre und die Mission Radowitz* (Berlin, 1925), pp. 16, 17.

[52] On Victor Emmanuel's visit, see *Provinzial-Correspondenz*, Sept. 24, 1873.

[51] 1870, III, 339.

creasingly disturbed by the signs of Austro-German intimacy, the Tsar virtually invited himself to Berlin on the occasion of Francis Joseph's visit in September 1872. From a Russian source came the suggestion that led to a Russo-German defensive alliance in May 1873 providing for a mutual promise of military aid to the extent of two hundred thousand men against an attack upon either by a third power. In October of the same year, the unwillingness of either Russia or Austria to permit the other to enjoy a monopoly of Germany's friendship enabled Bismarck, as he had foreseen, to unite them with Germany in the more famous League of the Three Emperors. After a general affirmation of a common interest against revolutionary movements, this agreement provided for consultation in view of common action against an attack by a fourth power upon any one of its three members. These arrangements presented on paper a far more imposing appearance than their real importance merited, because they only partially expressed the interests of the countries concerned. In spite of the apparently solid guarantees of the Alliance of May 1873, Germany's support of Russia in the event of an attack by Austria was as doubtful as that of Germany by Russia against a French aggression. The agreement was, in fact, quietly ignored by both countries. Less specific, the League reflected more accurately the relations between its three members; under the severe strain of the war scare of 1875, it also weakened, and finally, under the test of the Near Eastern crisis, broke up. As a demonstration of France's isolation and as a bridge between Austria and Russia, it nevertheless remained Bismarck's ideal solution for Germany's diplomatic problems.

Of the negotiations between these powers the general public knew nothing, but the interviews between the chiefs of state, especially the visits to Berlin by Alexander of Russia in September 1872 and by Victor Emmanuel of Italy a year later, were sufficient to indicate the drawing together of the Central and Eastern powers. The absence of binding engagements, for the official press did not admit that definite engagements had been arranged,[52] itself contributed to the general feeling of satisfaction.

---

[52] On Victor Emmanuel's visit, see *Provinzial-Correspondenz*, Sept. 24, 1873.

It reassured the opponents of a close union with Russia and apparently justified the conclusion that an association had been achieved between countries whose interests were in a defense of the status quo. Russia's participation seemed an unmistakable warning to France that her support could not be counted upon for a war of revenge [53] and an implicit recognition of the annexation of Alsace-Lorraine.[54] That the Progressives never quite reconciled themselves to an association of any kind with Russia and that the Centrists scented an international conspiracy against the Roman Church [55] did not seriously diminish the popularity of Bismarck's achievement. Somewhat exaggerated estimates of its importance were expressed with the encouragement of the official press. The *Norddeutsche* (Sept. 6) wrote of the Berlin meeting as an event of world significance, and the *Preussische Jahrbücher* thought that it closed a historical period with something of the authority of a European congress.[56] The facts, of course, did not warrant these conclusions. The general agreement for the defense of the territorial status quo did not extend to the rearmament of France or to her revival as a great power. Russia, in particular, had no intention of identifying herself with Germany against France on the latter issue. Alexander told Gontaut-Biron in Berlin that France had no reason to be alarmed, and Gorchakov assured him that Germany could not legitimately object to France's rearmament. "You are right," he said, "in doing what you think is necessary. I have told you before, and I am glad to say it again, Russia needs a strong France." [57] The Berlin meeting was the occasion for still another display of sympathy for France. Irritated by Germany's intimacy with Russia, England sent a naval squadron to Le Havre, and Thiers, after passing it in review, wrote that "the Berlin tableau, instead of being a menace or an injury, has brought us honors and strength." [58] With uncommon perspicacity the Progressive

[53] *Kölnische Zeitung*, Sept. 7, 19, 1872; *Spenersche Zeitung*, Aug. 1, Sept. 6, 1872; *N. A. Z.*, Sept. 13 1872; *P. J.*, vol. 30 p. 226 (Aug. 1872).

[54] *N. A. Z.*, Sept. 18, 1872; *Spenersche Zeitung*, Sept. 25, 1872.

[55] *Germania*, Sept. 7, 1872.

[56] *P. J.*, vol. 30, p. 332 (Sept. 8, 1872).

[57] Gontaut-Biron, Sept. 14, 1872. *D. D. F.*, (1), I, 184.

[58] Thiers, Sept. 26, 1872. *Ibid.*, (1), I, 188, 189. To Lord Odo Russell, Gorchakov frankly acknowledged, at the very time he was entering the League of the Three Em-

Volks-Zeitung (Sept. 1872) wrote that Russia's friendship was more effective as a guarantee for France than for Germany.

So far as the territorial question was concerned, Germany, nevertheless, had little reason for alarm. On this issue she could count upon at least the moral support of Europe and therefore upon the isolation of France. Until 1873 Bismarck had used the general desire for peace to Germany's advantage, but the impairment of Germany's favorable diplomatic position during the next two years resulted largely, if not entirely, from the extension of his conflict with the Catholics in Germany to the arena of international politics. A competent German historian has recently, though not quite convincingly, attributed the inception of the *Kulturkampf* to Bismarck's foreign policy, on the ground that the conflict with the Church was intended to attract Austria and Italy and thus to confirm France's isolation.[59] In spite of the plain threat of an international as well as a purely German offensive against the Church in the *Kreuz-Zeitung's* article (June 22, 1871), which is generally supposed to have contained Bismarck's declaration of war, the older theory that he was led gradually by events to carry his attack across the German frontiers is still a more satisfactory explanation.[60] At any rate, it was not until the dogged resistance of the German Catholics evoked applause and encouragement abroad that he began to subordinate his foreign policy to the needs of the church conflict. A consideration of that struggle from the point of view of German domestic politics does not lie within the province of this study, but it should at least be noted here that the attempt to use Germany's great influence abroad for the purposes of a questionable domestic policy was a serious error. For once Bismarck failed to

perors, Russia's desire "for a strong and prudent France, *une France forte et sage.*" Not only did he regard France's future as "of primary importance to the peace of Europe," but Russia "would object to" any foreign interference in France. Russell to Granville, Sept. 12. W. Taffs, "Unprinted Documents," *Slavonic Review*, VIII, 704, 705.

[59] A. Wahl, *Deutsche Geschichte von der Reichsgründung bis zum Ausbruch des Weltkrieges (1871 bis 1914)*, 4 vols. (Stuttgart, 1926–32), I, 342.

[60] For the relevant text, see Wahl, *Vom Bismarck der 70er Jahre*, pp. 36, 37. In his unpublished doctoral dissertation, "Bismarck und der Ausbruch des Kulturkampfes," Dr. Paul Sattler corrects the common error of dating this article June 19 and attributes it to H. Wagener, who frequently expounded Bismarck's ideas in the Reichstag. He concludes after an elaborate argument that the threat of an international campaign was Wagener's, not Bismarck's.

analyze correctly the interests and probable reactions of those countries of whom he asked or demanded action against the church.   He wrote in his memoirs at the close of his long career that Germany's problem after 1871 was to use her power honorably and moderately in order that Europe might be reconciled to her hegemony,[61] but it can scarcely be said that the course upon which he embarked in 1873 was true to his own teaching.   From the *Kulturkampf* within Germany he may have anticipated, as the official *Norddeutsche* (Feb. 3, 1874) put it, "the beginning of a new period of civilization," yet it was upon the fear of Germany, rather than an appreciation of cultural values, that he counted to secure action against the church by other countries.   The responsibility, of course, was Bismarck's.   Nevertheless, the international as well as the domestic attack upon the church found some support even in a section of Progressive opinion.

The effect of this new phase of his foreign policy upon Germany's diplomatic position was not less unfortunate because it probably developed according to circumstances and not as the result of a carefully considered plan.   Foreign opinion scented a systematic campaign as he brought pressure to bear upon one country after another for legislative action to prevent and to penalize interference in the German conflict.[62]   Alarm and suspicion became more general than ever, especially when Bismarck turned against France.   He had at first declared that relations with France would not be affected by Thiers' fall and the organization of the MacMahon-Broglie government, that they would be "solely determined by France's attitude toward us and especially toward her treaty obligations." [63]   His agreement with Thiers for the final payment of the indemnity and for the evacuation of the army of occupation was faithfully carried out.   Even the official press at first maintained a fairly equable tone, and public opinion, more confident thanks to Austria's and Russia's friendship, showed no signs of panic.   For the German Catholics the recent changes in France were in fact a source of encourage-

---

[61] See excerpt at the head of this chapter.

[62] Schulze-Delitzsch told an audience in Leipzig, Jan. 8, 1874, that all civilized nations were on Germany's side in the struggle with the Church. *Gegenwart*, V, 99 (Feb. 14, 1874).

[63] *Provinzial-Correspondenz*, May 28, 1873.

ment. In Bismarck's opinion, however, they meant increased danger. He believed that the papacy's support together with the monarchist complexion of the new French government would greatly improve France's chances to acquire allies and that Germany's avowed or secret enemies everywhere would be encouraged.[64] According to his loyal followers in the press, the apparent triumph of French clericalism meant that the *revanche* had been strengthened. "For Rome," wrote the *National Zeitung* (June 1, 1873), "it is an imperative need to keep the *revanche* alive."

From Bismarck's point of view, the political situation in France therefore greatly increased the significance of the demonstrations of sympathy for the German Catholics in the pastoral letters of the French bishops after the enactment of the Falk laws in Prussia, May 1873. A legitimate occasion for representations to France appeared in the letter of the Bishop of Nancy, August 3, 1873, directing the clergy of his diocese, which included a part of German Lorraine, to read prayers for the return of the lost provinces to France, but Bismarck unwisely and with ultimately harmful consequences to his country decided to make a major issue of it. He allowed a month to pass before demanding, on the eve of the final evacuation of the occupied territory, satisfactory measures against the repetition of the offensive pastoral letters, under the threat of harsher frontier regulations.[65] Since Broglie, the French foreign minister, could not yield without offending the Catholics—the strongest support for his government—he tried to evade the issue by arguing that the government could not be held responsible for statements by the bishops. In his reply, Bismarck demanded not only a public and official remonstrance, but also the prosecution of the Bishop of Nancy in a French court, and he wrote, at the same time, of circumstances that would justify a preventive war.[66] For the lesser demand, the circular of the French minister of public worship advising moderation to the bishops, which was officially communicated to the

---

[64] Bismarck, June 4, 1873. *G. P.,* I, 189 and n.
[65] Bismarck, Sept. 3, 1873. *Ibid.,* I, 211.
[66] Bismarck, Oct. 30, 1873. *Ibid.,* I, 221. He later defended himself from the charge of meddling in French affairs on the ground that the bishop's letter had been addressed to German as well as to French subjects. *Verhandlungen,* I Leg. Per., II Sess., I, 484, 485 (Dec. 4, 1874).

German government, seemed an adequate satisfaction even to the official German press. Unfortunately, however, it occurred to Bismarck that the incident might be used in the Reichstag elections of January 10, 1874 to secure a majority for a harsher prosecution of the *Kulturkampf* at home and for the enactment of the government's army bill. The latter was, for the moment, the more important issue, since a permanent appropriation for the maintenance of the peace army at one per cent of the population would mean the Reichstag's surrender of all control over the army. It seemed reasonable to expect that a convenient Franco-German crisis would win votes for the government's bill. On the morning of the election, the *National Zeitung* (Jan. 10, 1874) declared that no effective action against the bishops could be expected from the French government and that Germany must herself secure adequate satisfaction. "France must say," it concluded, "whether she desires peace or war."

The results of the election, however, were disappointing; the Center party doubled its popular vote and increased the number of its representatives in the Reichstag from about forty to ninety-five. A small majority was still assured for the military bill if all of the one hundred and fifty-two National Liberals voted with the smaller government parties, but enough to defeat it were certain to join the Centrists, Progressives, Social Democrats, and the national minority groups on the issue of the parliamentary control of the army.[67] That "a third of the elected representatives of the German people are avowed enemies of the Empire," as the *National Zeitung* (Jan. 17, 1874) exclaimed, was a severe shock to nationalist opinion. Such was the situation in Germany when Bismarck told Gontaut-Biron, January 13, that the affair of the bishops was still open.[68] Not only in the interest of peaceful relations but also in that of "our domestic conflicts," as he acknowledged in a marginal comment of January 17,[69] something more must be done, even if he had to initiate a suit in a French court himself. The same menacing tone appeared in the official *Norddeutsche* (Jan. 16). The danger to peace, affirmed that

[67] "Die Reichstagswahlen," *Grenzboten*, 1874, I, 153.
[68] Gontaut-Biron, Jan. 14. *D. D. F.*, (1), I, 296, 297.
[69] Bülow's memorandum, Jan. 17. *G. P.*, I, 233.

official journal, comes from Paris, where "war was in the air a few days ago." Since peace would be impossible if France acted as the satellite of Rome, the affair of the bishops, it continued, required close attention. "The more plainly we state that a breach will inevitably follow the continued appearance of these letters, the more effective will be our efforts for the maintenance of peace." Gontaut-Biron discounted the seriousness of the crisis on the ground that Bismarck was chiefly interested in the passage of the army bill, but his government, less optimistic, again yielded by suppressing Louis Veuillot's *Univers,* the leading organ of the French clericals, for a period of two months.[70] Neither Bismarck nor his devoted followers were at first willing to accept this as an adequate satisfaction, although the *Spenersche Zeitung* (Jan. 21) proclaimed it as a notable triumph.[71] MacMahon would betray his real desire for trouble (*Handel und Krieg*), said the *National Zeitung* (Jan. 22, 1874), unless he at once proceeded against the bishops, for war would follow the continued interference by the French clergy and press in German affairs. Nor was this merely a press maneuver, for Bismarck incorporated similar views in a diplomatic circular on the following day to the European capitals, with the significant exception of St. Petersburg. He was, he wrote, determined to avoid war, but if France supported the papacy's hostile schemes, "we will consider ourselves threatened and we must then think of defending ourselves."[72] At this point, however, Bismarck suddenly became more circumspect. The official press hinted that the suppression of the *Univers* might be an adequate satisfaction. Even the *Provinzial-Correspondenz* (Jan. 28, 1874), which had at first rejected this action as in no way affecting the bishops, ended by admitting that Germany would reserve her decision as to the next step, and the *Norddeutsche* (Jan. 25) declared that time would show if Germany would have to resort to the French courts.

---

[70] Decazes, the French foreign minister, hoped that Bismarck might thereby be dissuaded from his contemplated judicial action. Decazes, Jan. 19. *D. D. F.,* (1), I, 299, 300. The *Schreckschuss,* according to the Paris correspondent (Jan. 29, 1874) of the *Grenzboten* (1874, I, 192) had had its desired effect. Never had the semi-official press been more conciliatory.

[71] Bismarck later wrote that von Arnim had used this journal as a support for his own policy in Paris. Bismarck, *Gedanken und Erinnerungen,* II, 165.

[72] *G. P.,* I, 235,n.

As the day (Feb. 16, 1874) approached for the first and crucial debate on the army bill, unfavorable international developments turned Bismarck for the moment against further pressure upon France. He suspected, as he informed the German ambassador in St. Petersburg (Jan. 21, 1874), that the Francophile circles at the Russian court had influenced the conduct of Russian diplomacy.[73] Even his confidence in the Tsar's personal friendship was not entirely justified, for Alexander had spoken reassuringly of Bismarck's attitude to Le Flô, the French ambassador. "Between ourselves," he said, "it is just one of his tricks." [74] Austria also assured France of her sympathy. "You have done well," said Francis Joseph after hearing the French version of the situation; "Bismarck is on the wrong track and will lose." [75] A few days later in St. Petersburg the Austrian and Russian rulers assured France of their desire for her speedy recovery. "A powerful France," they said, "is more than ever necessary for the balance of power in Europe." [76] What had been said in confidence by Germany's associates in the League of the Three Emperors to her enemy less than six months after its establishment was of course unknown, though perhaps not unsuspected by Bismarck, but England had spoken directly and plainly through her sovereign. Less than a week before the army debate a letter from Queen Victoria to the Emperor William arrived (Feb. 10) in Berlin deprecating any aggression against France.[77] These circumstances required a withdrawal from his advanced position, but he covered his retreat with a parting salvo. Speaking in defense of the military bill in Bismarck's presence and obviously with his approval,[78] Moltke attributed the necessity of guarding with the sword for fifty years what had been won in six months, to France's entirely natural desire for revenge, which through her political parties would nullify the peaceful sentiment of the majority of her people.[79] Not a word did he say, however, of the dangerous character of French clericalism, and on the following day (Feb. 17)

---

[73] Holborn, *Bismarcks europäische Politik*, pp. 20, 21.
[74] Le Flô, Jan. 29. *D. D. F.*, (1), I, 308, 309.
[75] Harcourt, Vienna, Feb. 11. *Ibid.*, (1), I, 311.
[76] Le Flô, Feb. 17. *D. D. F.*, (1), I, 313.
[77] *Letters of Queen Victoria*, (2), II; 313, 314.
[78] Brockhaus, *Stunden mit Bismarck*, p. 88.
[79] *Verhandlungen*, I Leg. Per., I Sess., I, 80–82 (Feb. 16, 1874).

Bismarck instructed von Arnim in Paris to say nothing more about the bishops.[80] Henceforth foreign affairs played no significant part in the agitation throughout Germany for the enactment of a military law satisfactory to the government. In spite of numerous public meetings and hundreds of petitions for the passage of the original bill, which the opposition denounced as officially inspired, even the National Liberals refused to accept it *in toto,* for Bennigsen, their leader, insisted that public opinion expected the government to yield something.[81] The result of Bismarck's reluctance to add a constitutional conflict to the *Kulturkampf* was the passage of the famous Septennate, in which the government's recommendation as to the size of the army was accepted but with a grant for only seven years.[82] Bismarck's change of tactics came too late to prevent a not inconsiderable damage to Germany's diplomatic position. In Decazes France had a foreign minister with the courage and the skill to exploit Bismarck's mistakes. He had kept in close touch with the neutral capitals, where he represented Bismarck's purpose as the extension of the *Kulturkampf* rather than war, thus showing his own moderation.[83] After the crisis had quietly ended, he urged the powers to continue their close observation of events, for no one could say when or under what conditions Bismarck's pretensions might again cause trouble.[84] That Bismarck was aware of Decazes' activities is a reasonable inference, since the political observer of the *Deutsche Rundschau* not long thereafter attributed to the French statesman a systematic campaign for the sympathy of the European powers against Germany's ceaseless provocations.[85]

In Germany these events produced some uneasiness, though not enough to weaken Bismarck's reputation for infallibility. Without evoking a protest of any significance, he dismissed the Center party's request for a meeting of the Bundesrat's committee on foreign affairs during the debate on the budget, December 1874,

---

[80] Bismarck, Feb. 17. *G. P.,* I, 238.
[81] He described the movement as the most impressive manifestation of public opinion since 1848. *Verhandlungen,* I Leg. Per., I Sess., I, 756 (April 12, 1874).
[82] Ballhausen, *Bismarck-Erinnerungen,* p. 51.
[83] Decazes, Jan. 18. *D. D. F.,* (1), I, 298, 299.
[84] *Ibid.,* (1), I, 322, 323 (March 27).
[85] I, 170, 171 (Oct. 1874).

with the astonishing misrepresentation that the year had been the least disturbed of his career.[86] But the facts scarcely warranted this optimism. Not only were relations with France definitely worse, but a rift had appeared in the League of the Three Emperors when Russia refused to follow Bismarck's example in recognizing the anti-clerical government in Spain.[87] He was now also on the point of launching his most ambitious diplomatic offensive since 1870 for the development of the international *Kulturkampf*, for the general improvement of Germany's diplomatic situation, and more specifically for the weakening of France. The first move was to send Radowitz, a personal confidant, on a special mission to St. Petersburg (February 1875) for the ostensible purpose of arranging minor differences in Serbia, but in reality to fathom Russia's relations with France.[88] That he was instructed to offer a free hand in the Near East in return for Germany's freedom of action against France has long been suspected, although no satisfactory proof has been unearthed,[89] but this offer, in any event, was undoubtedly to be reserved until Russia's favorable reaction should be ascertained. This encouragement was never forthcoming. To the argument that France should be shown by a closer Russo-German understanding that Russia's sympathies had limits, the discouraging reply was given that new arrangements were unnecessary, since France was already fully aware of Russia's point of view. In short, the effort to free Germany's rear ended with a distinct rebuff. Gorchakov, Bismarck was informed, had acted "as if it were inconsiderate to expect him to say anything of Russia's policy toward France." [90] Nor was this, in the long run, the most serious result, for Radowitz's activities occasioned rumors in St. Petersburg of Germany's intention to precipitate a preventive war that strengthened De-

---

[86] A rumor that Bismarck had approved the theory of a preventive war in a diplomatic document occasioned this attempt to use the German parliament's one constitutional check upon his conduct of foreign affairs. *Verhandlungen*, II Leg. Per., II Sess., I, 482 (Dec. 4, 1874).

[87] Holborn, *Bismarcks europäische Politik*, p. 53.

[88] Karolyi, Berlin, April 17, 1875. E. von Wertheimer, *Graf Julius Andrássy, sein Leben and seine Zeit,* 3 vols. (Stuttgart, 1913), I, 225.

[89] W. L. Langer, *European Alliances and Alignments* (N. Y., 1931), p. 42.

[90] Radowitz, March 7, 1875. Holborn, *Bismarcks europäische Politik*, p. 144. *Cf.* Radowitz's own version, Radowitz, *Aufzeichnungen und Erinnerungen*, I, ch. XIX.

cazes' hands at a critical point during the approaching war scare.

Bismarck was also active in other directions, with equally discouraging results, in the development of his international *Kulturkampf*. On February 3, 1875, he asked Belgium to restrain her bishops and press from interfering in German affairs. Instead of yielding immediately, the Belgian government played for time and communicated Bismarck's second and harsher note to France and England. England's traditional interest in Belgium's independence and neutrality, and the victory of the Conservative party under Disraeli's leadership in the election of 1874, assured her sympathetic reaction. Since the Belgian affair paralleled the more important crisis with France, it helped to align England against Germany. Italy also refused to do Bismarck's bidding when he asked her to reduce the papacy's privileges under the law of guarantees; for France's withdrawal of the "Orénoque" during the autumn of 1874 [91] and the diminishing danger that French foreign policy would be controlled by church influences cooled Italy's interest in a measure which might involve active coöperation against France. Even Russia was negotiating with the Vatican as to the status of her Roman Catholic subjects. [92] By none of these moves had Bismarck strengthened either his offensive against the church or Germany's diplomatic position.

France, of course, seemed to Bismarck the principal source of opposition. His difficulties resulted to a large extent from the existence of a strong France as a rallying point for Germany's enemies. It was not unreasonable to expect a more yielding disposition on their part to follow a decisive diplomatic victory at her expense or the slowing up of her armaments under Germany's pressure. In spite of the rearmament, from which she derived a measure of self-confidence and a more pronounced will to stand her ground, France was still the weakest of the great powers and French opinion was still under the influence of the shattering experience of 1870. At any rate, the prize was worth a certain risk. Instead of accepting the decision by which the National Assembly wrote into the Organic Laws a provision for a successor to

---

[91] Since 1870, France had kept this warship at Cività Vecchia for the Pope's use if he should decide to leave Italy.

[92] An agreement was concluded March 2, 1875.

Marshal MacMahon at the end of seven years—a measure that appreciably lessened the danger of a monarchical restoration—as a promise of improved relations between France and Germany, he acted as if it had no significance for his foreign policy, although he had earlier counted upon positive advantages from the permanent establishment of the Republic.[93]   The official and nationalist

Kladderadatsch, June 14, 1874.

Figure 4.—If this peace lasts twenty-five years longer,
we will all have to—join the soldiers!

press either paid no attention or denied that the event had any importance for Germany.[94]   "It is," wrote the *Magdeburgische Zeitung* (March 17), "a matter of indifference to us which flag flies in France, for we know that every party burns with zeal for the *revanche*."

The debate on the Organic Laws was soon followed by incidents leading to the famous war scare of 1875.   Reports of large purchases of horses in Germany for the French army were followed by Bismarck's declaration (March 2) of an embargo

---

[93] "Eine Republik," he had told Hohenlohe, "und innere Wirren seien eine Garantie des Friedens."   Hohenlohe, *Denkwürdigkeiten*, II, 118, 119 (May 2, 1874).
[94] *Kölnische Zeitung*, Feb. 26; *N. A. Z.*, March 3; *Post*, March 5.

against their export, in spite of the doubts as to the value of this measure expressed by Bülow, the military attaché in Paris.[95]   It was obviously a preliminary warning;[96] Bismarck admitted to the Russian ambassador that such measures usually smelled of powder, but he insisted that the real reason for the order was the need of safeguarding the interests of the German peasants.[97]   For the moment it was not his purpose to excite opinion against France; the official press was silent, while the more independent journals attributed the measure to technical and economic reasons.[98]   More significant of nationalist opinion was the *Kladderadatsch's* cartoon (March 14) representing a charge of the Uhlans across the French frontier as the only acceptable way to send horses into France.   Indignant denials in no way diminished

Kladderadatsch, March 14, 1875.

Figure 5.—Horses may be exported from Germany to France only if an Uhlan is mounted on each and every one—wherefrom may Heaven long protect us.

Bismarck's determination to force something like a settlement with France on the issues arising from her recovery.   It was the general staff, however, rather than Bismarck, that first took exception to the National Assembly's approval with little or no debate (March 12) of an amendment to the pending army organization bill adding a fourth battalion to every infantry regi-

[95] Bülow, March 1, *G. P.*, I, 246, 247. Hohenlohe, the ambassador, thought that the continued attachment to the *revanche* justified measures against France's rearmament. *Ibid.*, I, 245, 246 (March 2).

[96] Herzfeld, the best of the German authorities for the crisis, argues that the embargo had no other purpose than to prevent Germany's coöperation in France's rearmament. H. Herzfeld, *Die deutsch-französische Kriegsgefahr von 1875* (Berlin, 1922), pp. 19, 20.

[97] Faverney, St. Petersburg, March 18. *D. D. F.*, (1), I, 385.

[98] On the general reaction of the press, see *National Zeitung*, March 5.

ment and an additional regiment to the Foreign Legion. Within a week Moltke informed Bismarck that the French army had at one stroke been increased by one hundred and forty-four battalions or 144,000 men.[99] Only a few nationalist newspapers at first scented a menace, and those that did found it in the almost complete absence of discussion before its enactment—another sign, in their opinion, that the French parties all thought alike on questions relating to the army.[100] Bismarck probably had not yet made up his mind to act, for the official *Norddeutsche,* after giving close attention to the earlier debate, passed over the amendment in silence. Even as late as the end of March, when the *National Zeitung* (March 30) and the *Kölnische Zeitung* (April 1) called attention to the ominous character of France's military preparations and wrote of 1877 as the date of their approximate completion, these journals explained the fourth-battalion amendment as a provision for skeleton formations to expedite the mobilization of more men in the event of war and not as meaning an immediate increase in the peace strength of the army.[101] On April 2 the *Norddeutsche* declared that the "full significance of the measure will first appear at the moment of mobilization." This in fact was also Bülow's opinion in Paris.[102] His superiors, however, did not agree; for the *Militär-Wochenblatt,* which stood in close relations with the general staff, announced about the middle of April that the French army was being increased by 144,000 men.[103]

The falling of the diplomatic barometer probably explains Bismarck's increased concern with France's military preparations.[104] That he wished the French to feel the presence of dan-

---

[99] Krause, March 18. *G. P.,* I, 248, 249. Some observers believed that the sudden addition of large numbers of soldiers to the French army would be a source of weakness instead of strength. "Frankreich und der Friede," *Im neuen Reich,* 1875, I, 2.

[100] The retention of General Cissey as minister of war in a number of ministries aroused much comment. *National Zeitung,* March 12; *Magdeburgische Zeitung,* April 9. The amendment was not mentioned in the Progressive *Volks-Zeitung's* (March 21) weekly comment.

[101] Herzfeld admits that this was the real effect of the measure, but he claims that German observers needed time to reach this conclusion. See his *Deutsch-französische Kriegsgefahr,* p. 24.

[102] Bülow, April 11. *G. P.,* I, 250–253.

[103] *Kreuz-Zeitung,* April 30. Moltke later expressed the same opinion to Nothomb, the Belgian Minister. Gontaut-Biron, May 7. *D. D. F.,* (1), V, 441.

[104] For his remarks regarding a Franco-Russian alliance to Hohenlohe, see the latter's *Denkwürdigkeiten,* II, 152 (March 22).

ger had been shown by his prohibition of the export of horses. He now used the approaching interview between Francis Joseph and Victor Emmanuel in Venice (April 4, 5) as the occasion for a press campaign. The failure to invite the German Emperor to this meeting and the hopes for diplomatic support which this neglect of Germany inspired in a section of the French press led many German observers to suspect the possibility of an Austro-Italian understanding, which Russia might join for the isolation of Germany.[105] The *Kölnische Zeitung's* famous article, April 5, launching the attack upon France, therefore reflected to some extent the nervousness of German opinion. Although in appearance a letter from a Vienna correspondent, it was in reality the work of Ludwig Aegidi, an official of the press bureau of the German foreign office, who told the editors that "every word in it has been weighed as if it were a state document."[106] The article stressed the diplomatic rather than the military danger, but instead of pointing to a Franco-Austro-Russian alliance, which was Bismarck's real preoccupation,[107] as the most serious danger, it discussed in detail the possibility of a Catholic League between France, Austria, Italy, and the papacy, and represented Andrássy's control of Austrian policy as its chief obstacle. And Andrássy, it concluded, might be driven from power by the clerical party and the anti-German military authorities.[108] In spite of its official origins, this article might speedily have been forgotten, as others of a similar nature had been, if the *Post's* much more influential editorial "Is War in Sight?" (April 9) had not promptly followed it. Again, Bismarck's responsibility, at least for the general arguments, is almost certain; its author was Constantine Rössler of the press bureau,[109] and Bismarck's denials were weakened by his acknowledgment of the article's services in clarifying

---

[105] *National Zeitung*, March 25; *Post*, April 4; *Kölnische Zeitung*, April 4. Francis Joseph's trip along the Dalmatian coast greatly diminished, according to the *Frankfurter Zeitung* (April 1), the significance of the Venice interview.

[106] Ziekursch, *Politische Geschichte*, II, 41. Cf. *D. D. F.*, (1), I, 395.

[107] *Cf.* Hohenlohe, *Denkwürdigkeiten*, II, 152 (March 21). *Cf.* Russell, Berlin, Feb. 3, 1875; W. Taffs, "The War Scare of 1875," I, *Slavonic Review*, IX, 336.

[108] The *Frankfurter Zeitung* (April 7) traced the idea of a Catholic league of this composition to the clerical journal *Voca della Verità*, and characterized it as a dream. Nevertheless, Bismarck's *Kulturkampf* was, in its opinion, bringing together moderate groups abroad, which the Pope might win by a few concessions. It concluded that a suspension of the conflict would be the best defense.

[109] Herzfeld, *Deutsch-französische Kriegsgefahr*, p. 31n.

the international situation.[110]   In general, it endorsed the *Köl-nische Zeitung's* views, but its own account of the menace in France's military efforts and in her political situation was chiefly responsible for the fear of war that now began to oppress all Europe.   So great were the burdens of France's armaments, according to Rössler, that no country would undertake them if it were not planning an immediate war.   The Republicans and the Orleanists had perhaps not arranged their differences for this purpose,[111] but there was, nevertheless, a group in the National Assembly which was working for war before its dissolution. War was therefore in sight, but the threatening clouds might still break up.   Bismarck's later protests that the press was alone responsible for the disturbing fears of war might have been more convincing if the official *Norddeutsche* (April 11) had not promptly agreed with the *Post's* concern as to France's immediate intentions in an article which he instructed Hohenlohe to cite in Paris as having his approval.[112]

That Bismarck's purpose in this press campaign was not to prepare an offensive war against France is now generally admitted. The most convincing argument is still the fact that Germany had more to lose than to gain by a war when it was by no means certain that the rest of Europe would remain neutral.   In spite of the difficulty of deciphering his real aims from what he wrote and said, it is nevertheless fair to conclude that he wished to discourage France from attempting to use Germany's diplomatic difficulties for her own advantage and to frighten her as to the consequences of her rearmament.[113]   He failed to attain either purpose.   To argue as the official German press did a few days later that the unanimous affirmation of peaceful intentions in France was itself a notable achievement assumes the existence of aggressive plans for which there is no evidence.   If Bismarck had

---

[110] Ballhausen, *Bismarck-Erinnerungen,* p. 72 (April 11); Bismarck, April 10. *G. P.,* I, 234.

[111] The *Magdeburgische Zeitung* (April 9) insisted that this was the real explanation.

[112] Bismarck, April 10. *G. P.,* I, 254.

[113] Herzfeld successfully disposed of Fuller's theory that Bismarck was prepared to go to war if France did not slow up her rearmament and has shown, convincingly on the whole, that he had no intention of presenting a formal demand for a limitation of her armaments. *Cf.* Herzfeld, *Deutsch-französische Kriegsgefahr,* p. 57; J. F. Fuller, "The War Scare of 1875," *Am. Hist. Rev.,* XXIV, 226.

France alone to deal with, the result would have been different, but England and Russia had an interest in checking the use of Germany's power and in assuring France's undisturbed recovery. England was incredulous when Bismarck explained that France, not Germany, was the real danger to peace,[114] for Derby, her foreign minister, had Germany in mind when he told France that he could be certain of peace for only the current year. In St. Petersburg, Alexander and Gorchakov were more cordial and sympathetic than ever. "Our two countries," the Tsar assured the French ambassador, April 15, "have interests in common and if, as I do not believe, you are one day threatened, you will know it very quickly. You will know it from me."[115] His foreign minister went much further, even hinting, if Le Flô's report is to be trusted, that the Alsace-Lorraine question, or at least the status of Lorraine, might be reopened. It was, Gorchakov said, a matter of time and opportunity. During his visit to Berlin with the Tsar in May, they would do "everything in their power to restrain Berlin's impatience and to see that moderate and peaceful ideas prevail."[116]

In Germany Bismarck's policy had aroused a degree of hostile criticism for which there had been no precedent since the Luxemburg crisis and, what was doubtless more important from his point of view, strong opposition in the court. The Emperor and the Crown Prince assured France that she need fear no attack, and William called upon Bismarck for an explanation of the alarmist articles.[117] Partisan motives do not entirely explain the reaction of independent opinion. Commercial and industrial interests, just beginning at this time to recover from the collapse of the inflationary movement caused by the French indemnity, resented an unnecessary crisis. The supposedly docile public refused to take its opinion ready-made from the official press or to believe that France intended to attack within a calculable period. Even the nationalist *National Zeitung's* first reaction (April 10)

---

[114] Bülow to Münster, April 11.   *G. P.*, I, 249, 250.
[115] Le Flô, April 15   *D. D. F.*, (1), I, 403, 404.
[116] Le Flô, April 20.   *Ibid.*, (1), 412, 413.
[117] Bismarck's amazing reply was that the *Kölnische Zeitung* article may have been a maneuver by the Paris Rothschilds for a fall on the Bourse.   Bülow to William, April 12.   *G. P.*, I, 255–257.

was that concrete decisions could not be based upon the vague assumptions in the *Post's* article, although, as if alarmed by its own temerity but more probably under official pressure, it changed its tone to one of complete approval the next day. The Berlin correspondent of the National Liberal *Schwäbische Merkur* wrote (April 8) that it was impossible to take the *Kölnische Zeitung's* article seriously, for the usual preliminary warnings of a serious crisis had not occurred. He accepted the panic in Paris which had followed the publication of the note to Belgium as evidence of France's peaceful disposition, for otherwise she would have used it as an excuse to attack.[118] Insisting that France was wedded to the *revanche,* the *Gegenwart* (May 15, 1875) nevertheless admitted that no immediate danger existed. The *Kölnische Zeitung,* in spite of its own contribution to the war scare, was informed from Berlin that public opinion was not so nervous as the *Post* had pretended, and the *Berliner Börsen-Courier* asserted that "they will never be able to convince us that there is any justification for this frightful alarm."[119] Liberal and Progressive opinion, as expressed by such journals as the *Frankfurter Zeitung* (April 12), the *Vossische Zeitung,* and the *Volks-Zeitung* (April 11), was incredulous, since it was absurd to suspect the still insecure Republic of aggressive designs. Even those who insisted that the French were bent upon the *revanche* sometimes admitted that they would be *"arg bestürzt"* if the word were suddenly to become a reality.[120] The ultra-Conservative *Kreuz-Zeitung* (April 11) minced no words in denouncing the misuse of the official press; instead of performing its legitimate functions of correcting errors and of interpreting the government's policy, it created confusion by "expecting the public to believe the opposite of what it had been told the day before, perhaps under the threat of being charged with hostility to the Empire (*Reichsfeindlichkeit*)." Conditions in Berlin at this time disturbed men who were in a position to know what was going on behind the scenes, for General Werder, then the Emperor's personal representative at the Russian court, wrote that "not only something but much is rotten

---

[118] Cf. *Augusburger, Abendzeitung,* April 12.
[119] *Post,* April 11.
[120] *Im neuen Reich,* 1875, I, 756.

in Berlin." It was in his opinion a misfortune "that bad humor, that anger at a subordinate (*ein Ärger über einen Kanzleidiener*) should shake all Europe. . ."[121]

It was probably the unfavorable reaction abroad to his press campaign that decided Bismarck to beat a strategic retreat after the *Post's* article.[122] On April 14, France was assured that Germany desired nothing better than a century of peaceful relations; and a note smoothing over the Church question was sent to Belgium. The Emperor spoke rather vaguely of the failure of those who had tried to make trouble between the two countries, and Bismarck warned Gontaut-Biron to guard himself against the exaggerations of the press.[123] An announcement in the official *Provinzial-Correspondenz* (April 14) that nothing justified the fear of an immediate crisis marked the end of the systematic press campaign. Nevertheless, no one acknowledged that a mistake had been made; instead, those journals which had been most active in creating alarm insisted that they had performed a real service in calling the attention of their readers to the dangerous character of the *revanche* sentiment. War, said the *Magdeburgische Zeitung* (April 14), would always remain a possibility "as long as so powerful a state as France refuses to recognize the status quo as determined by the Treaty of Frankfurt. . . ." The *Post* (April 15) insisted that its much-maligned article had strengthened the forces for peace in France by putting the French on guard against the machinations of the chauvinists. "The present peaceful and friendly tone of the French press," wrote the *Norddeutsche* (April 18), "is the result of the alleged 'provocations' of the German sheets." Its attempt to prove that the French newspapers had been filled with the most violent chauvinism moved the liberal *Frankfurter Zeitung* (April 19) to a

---

[121] Nothing has been found that throws light upon this interesting but mysterious remark, which appears in a private letter to Schweinitz (Berlin, April 14). *Briefwechsel des Botschafters General v. Schweinitz* (Berlin, 1928), pp. 103, 104. Werder was then in Berlin on a special mission from St. Petersburg. Wahl, *Vom Bismarck der 70er Jahre,* pp. 89, 90.

[122] Herzfeld attributed the change to a more moderate attitude in Berlin to a more accurate understanding of the French *loi des cadres.* See his *Deutsch-französische Kriegsgefahr,* pp. 26, 27. It may have been true of the general staff, but the press had already given this interpretation.

[123] Gontaut-Biron, April 17. *D. D. F.,* (1), I, 408, 409.

vigorous protest. The power of initiative, in its opinion, could not be attributed to the French government, for everyone in Europe knew that the question of peace or war would be settled in Berlin.

France's irreconcilable hostility and her indubitable progress toward recovery had unquestionably suggested to Bismarck the advantages of a preventive war. In other countries similar conditions have also given rise to the same temptation. The sincerity of his repudiation of this expedient after the end of the crisis on the ground that "one can never be certain as to God's providence" may be granted,[124] for the danger of foreign intervention was too great to be risked. It was, however, to Germany's interests as he understood them that France should feel herself to be under the menace of an attack.[125] To this end he not only wrote approvingly more than once of a preventive war, but also, in his diplomatic correspondence with Paris, he stated the circumstances which would justify it.[126] Nor did he reserve the discussion of this dangerous subject for confidential documents, since its effectiveness in exerting pressure upon France would be augmented by publicity. The *Norddeutsche* (April 3, 1874) frankly acknowledged that Germany would consider immediate action if war with France was inevitable. "Should Germany," asked Treitschke's organ a few days after the *Post's* article (April 9, 1875), "allow the enemy to arm at his leisure until the favorable moment for an attack? . . . If France intends to attack in two years, self-defense may compel us to precipitate it earlier." [127] The subject was probably much discussed in diplomatic and military circles. At a dinner given by the British ambassador, April 22, Radowitz expounded the theory of a preventive war to Gontaut-Biron with so considerable a variety of favorable arguments as to suggest either definite instructions or long familiarity with the

---

[124] To William I, Aug. 13, 1875. Busch, *Tagebuchblätter,* II, 287. *Cf.* his speech in the Reichstag, Feb. 9, 1876. *Verhandlungen,* II Leg. Per., III Sess., II, 1328, 1329.

[125] He acknowledged this in his letter to the Emperor, Aug. 13, 1875.

[126] See his dispatches to Arnim, Feb. 2, May 12, 1872, Oct. 30, 1873. *G. P.,* I, 116, 117, 163, 221. See also his circular of January 23, 1874. *Ibid.,* I, 235 and n.

[127] *P. J.,* vol. 35, p. 452 (April 12, 1875). Cf. *Magdeburgische Zeitung,* May 5. *Das augenblickliche Verhältnis Frankreichs zu Deutschland und die Friedensaussichten,* von einem Deutschen in Paris (Duisburg, 1874), reviewed by L. Richter, in *Gegenwart,* VI, 325 (Nov. 21, 1874.)

theme.[128] Bismarck's connection with this pronouncement has never been established, but that he was not displeased is evident from the favor which Radowitz continued to enjoy. In fact, it may have been intended as a part of a new effort to suspend or to slow up France's armaments. Only two days later (April 24) the *Kölnische Zeitung* said that Germany would be forced to give "more weight to France's deeds than to her words" if she did not suspend her army law of March 13. It also repeated an earlier allegation that France's preparation would be completed in 1877. Essentially the same point of view was brought to France's attention indirectly through diplomatic channels after Bismarck and Moltke told the Belgian minister some days later that France would either soon be guilty of a *coup de tête* or would curtail her military establishment, and Moltke gave the British ambassador to understand that her military measures would end in war.[129] Bismarck, it is clear, had not yet abandoned hope of forcing France to yield on the army question. In South Germany the press continued to attribute the entire crisis to this purpose.[130]

The renewal of pressure, which could only mean that Bismarck was not yet ready to accept France's right to rearm at her own discretion, and Decazes' diplomatic maneuvers discount the sincerity not only of Decazes' suggestion of a Franco-German understanding but also of Bismarck's favorable reply, although it has recently been interpreted as the beginning of his attempt to conciliate France.[131] Decazes' offer, at any rate, was merely a smoke screen to cover the preparations for his diplomatic counter-offensive. As soon as it was fairly clear that France was not in danger of an immediate attack, he laid his plans for an interna-

---

128 Of Radowitz wrote the Berlin correspondent of the *Augsburger Abendzeitung* (March 29): "beim Reichskanzler *persona gratissima* — durfte . . . für einen hohen Post auserkoren sein." On the same day (April 22) Moltke asked Miquel, the finance minister: "Wie würde man es im Lande aufnehmen wenn wir noch in diesem Jahre einen Offensivkriege begännen?" *Cf.* Treitschke to Hirzel, April 25. W. Kloster, *Der deutsche Generalstab und der Präventivkriegs-Gedanke* (Stuttgart, 1932), p. 18.

129 Gontaut-Biron, May 7. *D. D. F.*, (1), 441, 442. The British military attaché, writing on May 1, regarded the preservation of peace as "extremely doubtful" and as dependent "on the will of one man." Taffs, "War Scare of 1875," II, *Slavonic Review*, IX, 633n.

130 This explanation appears in a Berlin dispatch to the *Nürnberger Korrespondent* (May 10). Cf. *Bayerische Kurier*, May 13.

131 Wahl, *Vom Bismarck der 70er Jahre*, p. 108; Langer, *European Alliances and Alignments*, p. 54; P. B. Boring, *The Bismarckian Policy of Conciliation with France, 1875–1885* (Philadelphia, 1935), pp. 42–49.

tional action against Germany at the time of the visit to Berlin (May 10) by the Tsar and his foreign minister. His first step was to furnish Blowitz, the Paris correspondent of the London *Times,* with the material for an alarmist article, which was to be held in reserve for publication at a favorable moment. Rado- witz' statement of the preventive war theory, supported by re- ports from St. Petersburg of similar remarks there in February, ensured Decazes' success. Gorchakov rose from his sick-bed and laid the matter before the Tsar, who at once confirmed his earlier assurances.[132] In London, where an agreement with Russia (May 8) assuring England against the occupation of Merv in Central Asia momentarily disposed of a serious obstacle to Anglo-Russian coöperation, Decazes found an equally favorable audience. Rus- sell, in Berlin, was instructed to offer England's good offices and to support such action as Russia might take. Of the powers most concerned, only Austria refused to join this concerted pressure upon Bismarck, largely because Andrássy anticipated advantages from Bismarck's probable resentment at Russia's interference.

On May 6, the London *Times* opened the final phase of the crisis with Blowitz' article "A French War Scare," attributing the alleged panic in France to the frightful terms which the war party in Germany intended to impose upon France after a new invasion. Equally significant, though less known, was the *Morn- ing Post's* (May 6) explanation of the importance of the approach- ing meeting in Berlin and its emphasis of Alexander's power to decide the question of war or peace. In Germany these articles were generally and correctly appraised as a French maneuver to arouse suspicion of Germany and sympathy for France,[133] but opposition newspapers agreed that the recent stand taken by the official press and the vogue in certain quarters of the preventive war theory justified their alarmist tone to a certain extent.[134] Far more important, however, was the successful culmination of De- cazes' diplomacy. Bismarck could only plead innocence in reply to England's and Russia's representations. Although William's

---

[132] Le Flô, May 6. *D. D. F.,* (1), I, 439.

[133] *Frankfurter Zeitung,* May 7; *Kölnische Zeitung,* May 9; *Magdeburgische Zeitung,* May 10; *Kreuz-Zeitung,* May 11.

[134] The Catholic *Germania* (May 10) said that the intentions ascribed to the German war party were the views of the *Preussische Jahrbücher.*

assurances that no cause for alarm existed apparently satisfied the Tsar,[135] Gorchakov was probably more interested in the effect upon France's rearmament. On this point, Bismarck's defeat was complete. Decazes had made up his mind that he could safely refuse to entertain any suggestions for disarmament or for the slowing up of France's preparations.[136] "We should," he wrote, "congratulate ourselves that the right to reorganize France's military forces at our own discretion has been recognized without reserve." [137] The results of the crisis were equally disappointing if Bismarck's intention had been to test European opinion. "He now has its response," was Derby's comment.[138]

The official press at this time surpassed its earlier misrepresentation. In suggesting that Alexander's visit meant the renewal of the League of the Three Emperors it was guilty of a complete distortion of the facts. This result, it was said, would show France that she could hope for nothing from Russia.[139] The official *Norddeutsche* (May 11) greeted him with fulsome compliments and asserted on his departure (May 14) that the traditional Russo-German friendship had been strengthened. His welcome in Germany, according to the *Provinzial-Correspondenz* (May 12), was the result not only of the family ties between the two reigning houses but also of "the community of their interests." To the semi-official press was left the task of denying the shrewd suspicion that the Russian guests had not been wholly sympathetic. "It is not true," wrote the Berlin correspondent of the *Kölnische Zeitung* (May 13), "that the Tsar used his visit to convert Bismarck and Moltke to peaceful views. Not for a moment has contact with Russia been broken." [140] As late as May 19 the *Post* wrote of the calming influence which the demonstration of Russo-German friendship had exerted upon France. Bis-

---

[135] Gorchakov repeated his earlier encouragements at this time. Gontaut-Biron, May 11. *D. D. F.*, (1), I, 452, 453.

[136] He affirmed this as his unshakable determination in reply to Italy's tentative offer of mediation. Decazes, May 11. *Ibid.*, I, 450.

[137] Decazes, May 18. *Ibid.*, (1), I, 459, 460.

[138] Gavard, London, May 12. *Ibid.*, (1), I, 455. Though he felt that no one could deny France the right to arm as she pleased, Russell believed that she would henceforth go slow. Berlin, June 6. Taffs, "War Scare of 1875," II, *Slavonic Review*, IX, 648.

[139] *Kölnische Zeitung*, May 9; *Magdeburgische Zeitung* (April 27) *Augsburger Post-zeitung*, April 29.

[140] The *Frankfurter Zeitung* (May 14), however, wrote that he had acted the part of a good friend of peace "in making pacifists of our official press and its patrons."

marck, of course, was under no illusions as to Gorchakov's part in his discomfiture. From this incident dated the personal animosity which envenomed Russo-German relations for years, and when he wrote his memoirs twenty years later Bismarck's resentment was still acute.[141] England's action also excited his wrath. "If she had shown in 1870," he wrote, "a tenth part of her present boundless zeal in preventing France's attack, the bloody war could have been averted." Her conduct proved that "she would arouse Europe against us and in favor of France if we ever, which will certainly never occur, took military or diplomatic steps against a renewal of France's attack." [142] The German foreign office attributed to England the chief responsibility for the current suspicions as to Germany's purposes.[143]

After the publication of Gorchakov's famous telegram, "Peace is now assured," and the London *Times'* (May 14) statement that England and Russia had restrained the German war party had made it increasingly difficult to pretend that the Berlin interviews had resulted advantageously for Germany, Bismarck tried to place the responsibility for the crisis upon the newspaper press. The official *Norddeutsche* (May 11) declared unblushingly that it alone had been responsible for the recent alarmist rumors and prognostications of war. Bismarck turned against the official press as if it had betrayed him. On May 30, the Progressive *Volks-Zeitung* reported prematurely the abolition of the press section of the foreign office, but by the end of the year the Chancellor was openly affirming his intention to break all connections between the government and the press. There would no longer be, he told the Reichstag, February 9, 1876, an official newspaper nor would any other journal receive any official information or directions.[144] It is difficult to say how seriously he was taken; his recognition of the useful services of the press to the government of any great country justified some doubt as to his intentions. "So he says," remarked a guest when he spoke of breaking

---

[141] Bismarck, *Gedanken und Erinnerungen*, II, 202.

[142] Bismarck, May 14. *G. P.*, I, 279-282.

[143] Bülow, June 3, *Ibid.*, I, 284, 287. As early as October 1874, Hohenlohe had attributed to English diplomats a systematic campaign to arouse suspicion of Bismarck's purposes. Herzfeld, *Deutsch-französische Kriegsgefahr*, p. 16, citing Hohenlohe, *Denkwürdigkeiten*, II, 140.

[144] *Verhandlungen*, II Leg. Per., III Sess., II, 1328, 1329.

with the press at a parliamentary reception, "but he will continue to use the press as much as ever." [145]   A considerable group of independent newspapers showed enough self-respect to repudiate any share of responsibility for the crisis and placed it squarely upon the official journals, where it rightly belonged. "The reptile press," said the *Breslauer Zeitung* (June 2), "has deceived our faith in the German feeling for justice . . . and right-thinking people will have nothing to do with its frivolous intrigues." Even the *Kölnische Zeitung* (June 2), conveniently forgetting its own sins, wrote that the inspired press "had really denied the blue of the heavens." Leading opposition journals directed their attack against Bismarck's conduct of Germany's foreign policy. The *Post's* article (April 9) led the Catholic *Germania* (April 10) to question the value of the League of the Three Emperors as a guarantee of peace. [146]   From the danger that Germany would face a coalition in her next war, it (June 1) drew the conclusion that Bismarck should at least assure a united nation by liquidating the *Kulturkampf*. It even predicted a possible encirclement of Germany by hostile powers, with the result that a true peace policy might one day require "that *we try to break through* it at any price . . . (*dass wir dieselbe um jeden Preis zu durchbrechen versuchen müssten* . . .)." [147]   More and more people, according to the *Historisch-Politische Blätter,* were drawing the conclusion that Bismarck had been as seriously over-rated as Louis Napoleon had been in his day. To the Progressive *Volks-Zeitung* (May 11), the crisis and its results had confirmed its opinion that the League of the Three Emperors was in reality an advantage to France in giving her time to re-arm while it restrained Germany. "We are not so confident of the future," it concluded, "as patriots are now expected to be." Of the international *Kulturkampf* the ultra-Conservative *Kreuz-Zeitung* (May 27) wrote that it "had accomplished nothing and had aroused suspicion everywhere."

Nothing had occurred, according to nationalist opinion, that required a revision of its earlier point of view. On the contrary, insisted the *Post* (May 23), Germany had not been sufficiently

---

145 Brockhaus, *Stunden mit Bismarck,* p. 151 (Dec. 18, 1875).
146 The *Frankfurter Zeitung* (April 9) had expressed the same opinion.
147 The italics are the *Germania's.*

chauvinistic. "To be sensitive in regard to the international position of one's country is an essential characteristic of a great
people." The *Magdeburgische Zeitung* (May 21) saw no reason
for renouncing the preventive war theory. Since it had been
communicated to the powers in January 1874, it should have
occasioned no more alarm than "the news that Vesuvius is a
volcano to the Neapolitans." Nor did the crisis leave the *Preussische Jahrbücher* in a chastened mood, for it insisted that nothing had been changed. Germany still desired peace and France
the *revanche*. In its opinion, Germany had been justified in informing the powers that "she would not permit France to choose
the most favorable moment if she were bent upon war."[148] The
conclusion, nevertheless, could not be escaped that the crisis had
been productive of more harm than good, but the nationalists,
refusing to accept the blame for themselves, the official press, or
for the government, vented their wrath upon the meddlesome
powers. Although Russia's part was obvious from Gorchakov's
telegram, they generally overlooked it to concentrate upon
England, for it was less dangerous and more satisfactory to their
native prejudices to twist the lion's tail than to prod the Russian
bear.[149]

The war scare of 1875, as later events were to show, closed the
period of readjustment after the Franco-Prussian War. From
the beginning, a serious conflict of interests existed between
Germany and the rest of Europe, although many Germans cherished the illusion that her satisfaction with the status quo and her
desire to prevent France from again disturbing the peace should
convince Europe that Germany's interests were its own. Germany's chief worry was France's recovery, while Europe desired
without exception a stronger France as a balance to a disturbingly
strong neighbor or rival. Until the autumn of 1873, Bismarck's
comparative moderation and reserve minimized the diplomatic
consequences of this conflict of interest and facilitated the formation of the League of the Three Emperors (Oct. 1873). That
this promising policy was not continued was largely the result of

---

[148] Vol. 76, p. 67 (1875).
[149] *Post*, May 20; *Magdeburgische Zeitung*, May 27. The *Kölnische Zeitung's* (June
19) London correspondent protested against this discrimination between England and
Russia to the former's disadvantage.

Bismarck's international *Kulturkampf*. The fear and suspicion thereby everywhere aroused rallied invaluable support to France when Bismarck made an issue of the activities of the Catholic clergy in France and of the rapid progress of French rearmaments. For Russia, however, it was not so much a question of protecting a clerical government as it was of freeing France's rearmament from the menace of Bismarck's veto. England, apparently, was seriously apprehensive of a German offensive.

The nervous tension which made Bismarck's nights sleepless, increased his irritation, and caused him to think of resigning, may be a partial explanation, but it is not a justification of the policy that precipitated the war scare and in the end assured to France the support of Russia and England and the tacit acknowledgment once and for all of her right to rearm at her own pleasure. An official of the Russian foreign office justly remarked during the crisis: "I wasn't aware that the nervousness or bilious condition of a statesman could be considered a diplomatic argument." [150] Fortunately for Germany, the union of France, England, and Russia—the members of the future Triple Entente—was only temporary, thanks to Bismarck's caution in stopping short of a specific demand to France for the limitation or the suspension of her military activities. By this wise restraint Bismarck not only kept the control over the question of peace or war in his own hands but also allowed time for the reappearance of friction between England and Russia in Central Asia. Thus he avoided the ultimate disaster which had been implicit in his policy since the autumn of 1873, but the crisis left deeply rooted suspicions and a personal quarrel with Gorchakov as new sources of difficulties.

The rôle of German opinion in this period was distinctly less important that it had been during the struggle for unification. Few references to its reactions appear in the diplomatic correspondence. The printed documents for the crisis of 1875 may be searched in vain for the criticism aroused by Bismarck's alarmist press campaign. The solution of the German question

---

[150] Le Flô, April 23, 1875. *D. D. F.*, (1), I, 421.

diminished his need of considering public opinion.   On the other hand, his tentative use in 1874 of tension with France to secure a favorable majority in the Reichstag for the army bill fore-shadowed a more expert use of public opinion upon foreign affairs for the purposes of his domestic policies.   The alarmist press campaign in April of the following year, however, was not intended so much to excite German opinion as to impress France. Bismarck so far had shown little interest in educating public opinion as to the objectives of his foreign policy or awareness of the value of its united support.   He doubtless counted upon his immense prestige to secure that support, but his failure to win the Progressives and the Centrists, his treatment of them as *Reichsfeinden,* made their hostility inevitable.

CHAPTER IV

Between Austria-Hungary and Russia, 1876-1881

> Unser gutes deutsches Reich steht ein wenig eigenthüm-
> lich in der Mitte der europäischen Mächte. In Sachen
> der hohen Diplomatie, die Krieg und Frieden macht, sind
> wir gar sehr ostmächtlich geworden; in Sachen des Volks-
> lebens, was man so "Handel und Wandel" nennt, gestattet
> man uns westmächtlich zu sein.
>
> *Volks-Zeitung*, May 16, 1876.

> Unser Reichskanzler kann versichert sein, bei seiner
> gegenwärtigen Politik das deutsche Volk hinter sich zu
> haben. Schon bei der deutschen National-Versammlumg
> in der Paulskirche verlangte man auf der einen Seite Aus-
> schliessung Oesterreichs aus dem Deutschen Reiche, zu-
> gleich aber auf der anderen ein möglichst enges Bündnis
> mit dem stammverwandten Oesterreich.
>
> *Kölnische Zeitung*, Sept. 23, 1879.

The menace of a coalition declined as England and Russia clashed in Central Asia and the Balkans. Only a few weeks after the Berlin interviews, Derby and Gorchakov were both pro- testing to Berlin that no unfriendliness had been intended by their recent advice.[1] The value of Germany's good-will rose rapidly when the revolt in Herzegovina (July 1875) threatened the integrity of the Turkish Empire in Europe and brought Russia into conflict with Austria and England. For several years, Russia displaced Germany as the chief danger to the peace of Europe, with important diplomatic advantages to the latter. Without Germany's support or friendly neutrality, Russia could

---

[1] Wahl, *Deutsche Geschichte*, I, 368. See above p. 126.

not safely advance in the Balkans or seek to realize her ambitions in the Straits.   Both England and Austria would have welcomed Germany's active coöperation in the defense of Turkey. Even France, preoccupied with an acute political crisis at home and reluctant to jeopardize her financial and other interests in the Ottoman Empire, could not safely be counted upon to side with Russia.   Germany clearly had no reason to fear isolation.

Bismarck, nevertheless, continued the reserve which had marked his relations with Russia and Austria since 1871.   Participation in an anti-Russian coalition would mean, in his opinion, Russia's enduring hostility, an eventual Franco-Russian alliance, and perhaps the chief burden of a war whose benefits, if any, would accrue to Austria and England, because he had no desire for Russian territory.   Since a moderate tension between the other powers was advantageous to Germany, he saw no reason to take the lead himself in an effort to remove the causes of friction.   Germany, he insisted, had no economic or political interests in the Balkans that required her interference.   A leading part in the search for a solution of the Balkan imbroglio, he informed England in an effort to discover a basis of coöperation with her, might tend to identify Germany with Russia or with Austria.[2]   Not for a moment admitting that Germany's predominant power in Europe implied any wider responsibility than the defense of her own interests, he refused to do more than to second the search of the more directly interested powers for a peaceful solution.   There is no reason to doubt the sincerity of his signature to the Andrássy note (Dec. 1875), of his bid for England's coöperation (Jan. 1876),[3] or of his participation in the Berlin Memorandum (May 1876), although his confidence in the success of these measures was slight.   If the Balkan insurgents could be induced to lay down their arms for a promise of reforms in the Turkish administration, the danger that a European war might compel Germany to choose between the belliger-

---

[2] Russell, Berlin, Jan. 3, 1876.   D. Harris, "Bismarck's Advance to England, January, 1876," *Journal of Modern History*, III, pp. 444, 445.

[3] The official press frankly hoped that England's appreciation of the danger of the situation would induce her to join the League. *N. A. Z.*, April 22, 1876. His advances to England doubtless were intended to safeguard Germany against the danger either of an Austro-Russian understanding or war. *Cf.* Harris, *A Diplomatic History of the Balkan Crisis of 1875–1878; The First Year* (Stanford, Calif., 1936), pp. 174, 175.

ents would be avoided. The failure of these negotiations was not Bismarck's fault. It was caused mainly by the dissatisfaction of the insurgents at the lack of adequate guarantees in the Andrássy note and by England's refusal to identify herself with the League of the Three Emperors by signing the Berlin Memorandum. Had Bismarck made full use of Germany's great influence, however, the result might have been different.

The danger which he had hoped to avoid by remaining in the background became a reality after the failure of the several efforts to impose reforms upon Turkey. With the encouragement of the Pan-Slavs, if not that of the Russian government, Serbia and Montenegro declared war upon Turkey in July 1876. The atrocities then perpetrated by the Turkish irregulars in Bulgaria inspired Gladstone's campaign in England to drive the Turk, "bag and baggage," out of Europe. London and Vienna nevertheless declared more and more firmly for the maintenance of Turkey's territorial integrity in reply to ever more strident demands of the Pan-Slavs for the satisfaction of Russia's racial and historic interests. In these circumstances, Bismarck's reserve became increasingly difficult. Since the well-being of the Balkan peoples meant nothing to him in comparison with Germany's interest in peace and friendly relations with both Russia and Austria, he suggested a radical solution of the crisis by a partition of the Balkans and the Near East between the great powers.[4] He returned to this scheme repeatedly in later years, but it is difficult to agree with those who believe that he seriously expected better Austro-Russian relations to follow the assignment to Austria of the Western and to Russia of the Eastern Balkans as spheres of influence or, for that matter, that he expected good feeling to result from the establishment of France in Syria and of England in Egypt. The multiplication of contacts between rival states in disputed areas does not usually make for peaceful relations. Because this adventurous leap in the dark appealed to no one, Bismarck was forced by events to consider the effect of the various possibilities of war upon Germany's interests. Far from alarming him, an Anglo-Russian conflict would work to Germany's

---

[4] He broached the project to Russell in January 1876. Harris, *The First Year*, p. 174.

advantage, since it would weaken each without endangering the existence of either.[5]   An Austro-Russian war, however, would not only dissolve the League of the Three Emperors but it might also eliminate one of them as a great power, with vastly greater dangers for Germany because she would then face one powerful state in Central and Eastern Europe instead of two whose antagonism helped to assure Germany's security.   Bismarck's preference therefore was for an understanding between Austria and Russia; he was willing to risk the comparatively slight danger that their association might diminish their gratitude for Germany's friendship.[6]   With his blessing but without his participation, Andrássy and Gorchakov arranged at Reichstadt, where they were accompanied by their respective sovereigns (July 1876), an agreement defining in a general way the attitude of their respective governments during and after the war.

As a support for the balance he hoped to maintain between Austria and Russia, Bismarck desired a quiet and disciplined public opinion.   Nothing but difficulties could be expected from a strong expression of opinion in favor of one of these powers. Thus the *Norddeutsche* (Jan. 1, 1876) wrote that Bismarck's achievements imposed upon the political parties the duty of "keeping their theoretical and sentimental preferences to themselves." To a greater extent than before, the purposes of Germany's policy were explained by the official press and to the Reichstag,[7] although not a word was said of his scheme to divide the Balkans or of his indifference toward an Anglo-Russian war.   German opinion generally approved neutrality as the proper policy.[8] Before the Russo-Turkish War, only the leading newspapers expressed any editorial opinion as to the daily grist of news from the Near East, and even their columns were normally filled with endless discussion of the church conflict and with the debate preceding the change from free trade to the protective tariff

---

[5] Bülow, Nov. 27, 1876.   *G. P.,* II, 108.

[6] Bismarck, Aug. 30, 1876.   *Ibid.,* II, 34, 35.

[7] For an affirmation of Germany's policy of observation and reserve as early as September 23, 1875, see the official *Reichsanzeiger.*   Wertheimer, *Andrássy,* II, 270.

[8] I know of but one specific approval of a Russo-German war at this time.   It was represented as the inevitable result of Russia's challenge to Germany's hegemony in Europe.   C. J. Cremer, *Europa, Russland und die orientalische Frage* (Berlin, 1876), pp. 33, 34.

(1878). The Bulgarian atrocities failed to arouse much interest in the fate of the Balkan peoples; one observer pointed to the anti-Turkish campaign in England as an example worthy of emulation and protested without appreciable effect that "it is high time for us to assert our Christian sentiments or, as Gladstone justly says, our common humanity." [9] That Germany might be involved in war by events in the Balkans seemed so remote a possibility that it received slight consideration. This indifference, however, did not include the problem of Germany's relations with Austria and Russia, because the same preferences for Austria which had assured the popularity of the reconciliation of 1871 were stronger than ever. To avoid the danger that the pro-Austrian tendencies of German opinion might antagonize Russia was the task of the official press. The *Norddeutsche* deprecated the persistent reports of the Tsarevich's anti-German bias, it praised Alexander II's peaceful disposition as a reliable guarantee against the hostility of the Pan-Slavs,[10] it rehearsed Russia's services to Prussia and Germany, and it accepted without question her assurances that she had no intention of annexing territory in the Balkans.

Many Conservatives and National Liberals needed no official prompting to declare for a policy of friendship with Russia. Treitschke wrote of Russia as "the best ally Germany ever had," and another observer claimed that a Russian alliance "would enable Germany to face the future with entire confidence." [11] The inspired press, like Bismarck, warned Austria more emphatically than Russia that Germany's armed support could not be counted upon in the Balkans,[12] but, of course, it did not attempt to arouse bad feeling against Austria. Even Russia's partisans occasionally betrayed uneasiness as to Austria's fate, for the National Liberal *National Zeitung* (March 28, 1876) repeated the old saying that "he deserved hanging who should even speak

[9] *Zur orientalischen Frage. Ein Mahnruf an die öffentlichen Meinung,* von einem Deutschen in Oesterreich (Berlin, Sept., 1876). Cf. *Deutschlands Umkehr und seine Stellung zur orientalischen Frage* (Berlin, 1876); Sayve, Berlin, Sept. 29, 1876. *D. D. F.,* (1), II, 94.

[10] Cf. *National Zeitung,* June 23, 1876.

[11] Treitschke, "Die Türkei und die Grossmächte," *P. J.,* vol. 37, p. 675 (June 1876). Cf. *Zur orientalischen Frage,* pp. 9, 10.

[12] *Oesterreich und die Orientfrage* (Vienna, Budapest, Leipzig, 1876); "Oesterreich und die türkische Krisis," *Grenzboten,* 1877, I.

of Austria's dissolution." The Conservative *Kreuz-Zeitung* (Nov. 15, 1876) reminded Russia that an attack upon Turkey would cause either a European intervention or a general war. No sympathy or appreciation of Germany's diplomatic interests restrained, however, the bitter denunciation of England. Her support of Turkey against the "fresh, pulsing life" of the Balkan peoples, or, as Treitschke put it, her "hateful enmity of young and struggling nations," marked her as a reactionary influence in European affairs.[13] Her refusal to sign the Berlin Memorandum meant, according to the National Liberal *Magdeburgische Zeitung* (June 14, 1876), that "she had learned nothing and had forgotten everything"; and what she had forgotten, wrote the satirical weekly, the *Kladderadatsch* (Jan. 16, 1876), was her earlier sacrifices for the cause of freedom. She now counted tons, not hearts. Admiration for England among the Progressives, henceforth a not insignificant cause of the anti-English sentiment of their Conservative opponents, evoked an indignant protest from an anonymous pamphleteer, who argued that she had never reciprocated Germany's friendship and that her influence in Germany had produced "nothing but discontent, impoverishment, demoralization and corruption, decline of patriotism, and emigration."[14] Treitschke had commenced his venomous tirades. The fall of the British Empire, he believed, was approaching, for sea power was not the determining cause of history in the age of nation states and of national armies that it had once been. "The day must and will come," he wrote, "when Gibraltar will belong to the Spanish, Malta to the Italians, and Heligoland to the Germans."[15] The satisfaction of anti-English sentiment at the prospect of an Anglo-Russian war was only restrained by the danger that Austria might become involved. Even Bismarck weighed its chances with comparative indifference,[16] and, in contrast to his attitude toward an Austro-Russian conflict, he wrote, "to prevent it is not a necessity for us."[17]

Bismarck and his followers had nothing but contempt for the

---

[13] *Deutschlands Umkehr*, p. 16.

[14] *Russland und England*, von Junius Junior (Berlin, Feb. 1877), pp. 4–6, 17.

[15] Treitschke, "Die Turkei und die Grossmächte," *P. J.*, vol. 37, (June 20, 1876). The *National Zeitung* (July 1, 1876) gave these views in its blanket endorsement.

[16] Hohenlohe, *Denkwürdigkeiten*, II, 202 (Sept. 29, 1876).

[17] Bülow, Nov. 27, 1876. *G. P.*, II, 108.

critics of his policy of friendship with Russia. It was not, however, easy to dismiss them, according to his usual practice, as unworthy of consideration, for they expressed perhaps the prepon-
derant trend of German opinion. In addition to the opposition
parties everywhere, South Germany was almost unanimously
anti-Russian and pro-Austrian. Even the National Liberals of
that section agreed with the Catholics in their hatred of Russia.[18]
That the *Kölnische Zeitung* and the *Allgemeine Zeitung* (Augsburg), two of the most influential of German newspapers, refused to support Bismarck's policy was especially significant, since
they could not be suspected of systematic opposition. They irritated Bismarck but nevertheless commanded his attention, because his frequent use of them insured Russia's sensitive reaction
to their advocacy of Germany's coöperation with her enemies.[19]
Neither gave any credence to Russia's allegedly unselfish support of the oppressed Balkan peoples and both welcomed every
hint of Turkey's increased power of resistance.[20] Catholic and
Progressive opinion expressed these views still more emphatically.
Russia's support of the reform program, according to the Progressive *Volks-Zeitung* (May 9, 1876), had never been sincere; her
agents had secretly worked against it. Few of Bismarck's critics
admitted that Russia had any real justification or excuse for her
Balkan ambitions, nor did they show much sympathy for the
Balkan peoples. The superficial observance of Christian formalities in the Balkans meant nothing, according to the *Kölnische
Zeitung* (April 20, 1876), because they had no scruples against
murder and theft. The independence of the semi-barbarous Slavs
would be no improvement over the Turkish administration; it
would result in discrimination against German commerce (Aug.
14, 1876). The Progressives saw no loftier motives for Serbia's
declaration of war than Russia's influence and her own land-
hunger. They denied that an aggressive policy was being forced
upon Russia by the Pan-Slavs, since the Russian press was notoriously under official control. More important for the develop-

---

18 See the speech by Fischer, a National Liberal member of the Bavarian Landtag, in
Augsburg (Jan. 7, 1877). *Augsburger Abendzeitung*, Jan. 8, 1877.
19 *Bayerische Kurier*, May 9, 1877; *Kölnische Zeitung*, June 10, Aug. 14, Oct. 22,
1876; *Volks-Zeitung*, May 20, July 11, 1876.
20 *Kölnische Zeitung*, April 14, 1876; *Allegemeine Zeitung*, June 10, 1876.

ment of critical opinion in Germany was the feeling that Russia's success would be an incalculable catastrophe. The *Kölnische Zeitung* (Nov. 14, 1876) insisted that the possession of Constantinople would place the domination of Europe within Russia's reach. Its inevitable result, wrote the Progressive *Volks-Zeitung* (July 8, 1876), would be the dissolution of Austria-Hungary.

During the summer and autumn of 1876 the crisis moved inexorably toward war. The Reichstadt agreement (July 1876), which the official press had applauded as a guarantee of peace between Russia and Austria, failed, as the opposition had foreseen, to remove the underlying causes of their rivalry.[21] Germany's inaction caused increasing uneasiness for the safety of her commercial interests at Constantinople and for her vital interest in Austria's security.[22] The *Allgemeine Zeitung* (Aug. 23, 1876) even spoke of Austria's interests in the Balkans as identical with those of Germany. It was, however, easier to condemn Bismarck's complaisance toward Russia than to propose a better policy. To the *Allgemeine Zeitung* (June 10, 1876), a new league including Austria, England, and Germany, which it later referred to as a coalition of the Germanic races against the Slavs (Aug. 18, 1876), seemed the only effective solution. In England this trend of opinion aroused hope of Germany's support against Russia. The London *Times* (Oct. 16, 1876) wrote that Bismarck had "never before held in his hand so much power for good or evil," and that "if any country can thus save the world from a tremendous war, it is Germany." The family ties between the Hohenzollerns and the Romanovs would make it unnecessary for Germany to adopt a dictatorial tone. "One plain word from Bismarck," it concluded, "would stop Russia even on the brink of the abyss into which a very little more pressure would make her plunge." Influenced more by its Austrian sympathies than by any partiality for England, Catholic opinion agreed that Germany's predominant power entailed the obligation to act in the interests of peace. "The world," wrote a Catholic student of the crisis, "has a moral right to expect the power that possesses

---

[21] *Volks-Zeitung,* July 11; *Germania,* July 15.

[22] The Russian press attributed the failure of the reform policy to Germany's ungrateful refusal to apply the necessary pressure at Constantinople. *Germania,* Aug. 22, 1876; *National Zeitung,* Sept. 27, 1876.

the hegemony of Europe to act vigorously against any disturbance to its peace." [23]   To a less partisan observer it seemed that Germany would serve her own as well as Europe's interests if she were to use her full influence against Russia's policy. [24]   The *Kölnische Zeitung,* however, found it difficult to define its stand. On October 21, it acknowledged its reluctance to sacrifice Russia's friendship, since she had been "Germany's best and only ally," and thereby to risk a Franco-Russian alliance for an immediate war of revenge.   But Germany could coöperate with Austria and England for the maintenance of peace without definitely breaking with Russia.   It would be "a certain, yes, an infallible means of preventing the Russo-Turkish war and the success of the Pan-Slavic plans."   A few weeks later (Nov. 18, 1876) it lamented the failure to act more energetically.   "How proud we once were of the influence that would be united Germany's."   The plea that Germany should assume the responsibility of assuring peace was of course summarily dismissed by those who approved the official policy.   Germany, according to the *National Zeitung* (Nov. 3, 1876), had enough to do in protecting her own interests without acting as the policeman of Europe.   After Disraeli's Guildhall speech (Nov. 9) and the Tsar's reply at Moscow (Nov. 10) had increased the danger of an Anglo-Russian war, the same journal asked (Nov. 12) that she be spared the task "of defending the Himalayas on the Rhine and the Vistula."   Treitschke rejected the suggested coöperation with England and Austria as a typical example of the complete ignorance of European politics among the German radicals, but he admitted that "only the government and some important liberal organs in Berlin, Suabia, and the Hanseatic towns still retained their sanity." [25]

"These demonstrations," wrote the official *Norddeutsche* (Oct. 27, 1876) of the demand for a new policy, "do not count and will not be considered even if the moment should come for a

[23] G. F. Haas, "Die orientalische Frage in ihrem gegenwärtigen Stadium," *Historisch-Politische Blätter,* vol. 79, p. 306 (Feb. 1877).

[24] J. von Hartmann, "Zur orientalischen Frage," *Deutsche Rundschau,* IX, 449, 450 (Dec. 1876).

[25] Treitschke, "Deutschland und die orientalische Frage," *P. J.,* vol. 37, pp. 672, 673 (Dec. 15, 1876).

change." In its opinion, the mistreatment of a German student at the *École des Beaux Arts* and the demonstrations in Paris against the playing of selections from Wagner's *Götterdämmerung* showed the dangers of alienating Russia. In the meantime, Bismarck, who had written sarcastically, "Who is Europe?" when Gorchakov claimed that the Balkan question was a European problem,[26] discouraged William's vague feeling that he should act in some manner either in Constantinople or at St. Petersburg for the maintenance of peace.[27] Germany, he said, could perhaps persuade Russia to keep the peace, but it would be at the cost of an anti-German coalition.[28] He preferred to encourage Russia's Balkan plans, counting upon his own skill to safeguard Germany and even Austria from the dangers of a Russo-Turkish war, and upon the losses of the war to weaken Russia. He had already sent Marshal Manteuffel to Warsaw for the Russian maneuvers with assurances of Germany's friendly sentiments whatever the Tsar's decision might be. The envoy also carried a personal letter from William in which he informed his nephew that the memories of Russia's aid would "guide my policy toward Russia no matter what happens."[29] Although Schweinitz was not then with the Tsar, he probably knew whereof he spoke when he said that Manteuffel, perhaps with Bismarck's oral approval, had exceeded his instructions by encouraging the Tsar to attack Turkey.[30] Years later Bismarck argued that the Russian army would have been turned against Austria if they had not found employment against the Turks.[31] There is convincing evidence that Russia's rulers were not only confident of Germany's moral support but that they interpreted Bismarck's attitude as a positive encouragement to declare war. According to the Russian finance minister, Bismarck made suggestive references to Russia's honor, to the decline of morale in her army, and to the harm that a weak conclusion of the crisis would do the monarchical prin-

[26] Marginal note, Gorchakov, Livadia, Oct. 21/Nov. 2, 1876. *G. P.,* II, 86, 87.

[27] Radowitz, Oct. 10, 1876. Bülow, Oct. 16. *Ibid.,* II, 63, 64, 67.

[28] Bülow, Nov. 10, 1876. *Ibid.,* II, 95, 96. German historians believe that this purpose not only explains but justifies Germany's policy. Rachfahl, *Deutschland und die Weltpolitik,* p. 104.

[29] Bismarck's memorandum, Aug. 30, 1876; William, Sept. 2; Manteuffel, Sept 6. *G. P.,* II, 37–39.

[30] Schweinitz. *Briefwechsel,* pp. 115, 116.

[31] Bismarck, May 27, 1885. *G. P.,* IV, 125.

ciple.[32]   Only a complete certainty as to Germany's attitude during a Russo-Turkish war explains Alexander's request for an assurance of her continued neutrality if it should develop into a war between Austria and Russia.[33]   To Bismarck, who had hoped to avoid this issue, the question was *"unverschämt* (shameless)," [34] yet Russia was quite justified in asking it after his encouragement to attack Turkey.   He succeeded most adroitly, however, in averting the danger of antagonizing her and at the same time in preserving his freedom of action.   If Russia wished to raise embarrassing questions, he was ready to do the same; the idea had already occurred to him that the Near Eastern crisis might be used to secure her guarantee of Germany's possession of Alsace-Lorraine and her consent "to work over the French thoroughly once more (*die Franzosen nochmals gründlich zu verarbeiten*)." [35]   Knowing Russia's desire to reserve France as a possible ally or as a balance to Germany, Bismarck almost certainly counted upon a negative reply when he instructed Schweinitz to say that his price for an alliance would be a guarantee for Alsace-Lorraine.[36]   Nor had he erred, for Gorchakov replied laconically: "Such treaties have no value these days." [37]   Schweinitz could then say with less danger of giving offense that Germany's neutrality in an Austro-Russian war would last until the existence of either of the belligerents was seriously threatened.   To make this warning more palatable he explained that Germany's sympathies would be with Russia in a war with Turkey, and, in effect, that she would do what she could to assure the neutrality of Austria and England.[38]   Gorchakov's disappointment betrayed the hopes he had built upon Bismarck's encouragement.   "We expected great things from you," was his reply, "you have brought nothing that we have not long since known." [39]   The first step in the reorientation of Germany's policy, which Bismarck's critics had demanded in vain, had been taken.

[32] Ziekursch, *Politische Geschichte,* II, 66.
[33] Werder, Livadia, Oct. 1, 1876.   *G. P.,* II, 53.
[34] Bismarck, Oct. 4.   *Ibid.,* II, 59.
[35] Ballhausen, *Bismarck-Erinnerungen,* p. 93 (Sept. 25–28).
[36] Becker, *Bismarcks Bündnispolitik* (Berlin, 1923), pp. 17, 18.
[37] Schweinitz, *Briefwechsel,* p. 141.
[38] Bülow, Oct. 23.   *G. P.,* II, 76.
[39] Schweinitz, Jalta, Nov. 1.   *Ibid.,* II, 80, 81.

Bismarck now resorted to public statements to supplement his confidential encouragement of Russia's Balkan projects, to reassure Austria, and to lecture German opinion. He chose an informal occasion, a dinner for members of the Reichstag (Dec. 1, 1876), to say that Germany would intervene to protect Austria from serious dangers if she were involved in the impending Russo-Turkish war.[40]   In the general satisfaction inspired by this support of Austria, his acceptance of a Russo-Turkish war as inevitable and an unfavorable reference to mediation attracted little notice. For the more difficult task of mollifying Russia, he preferred the weightier circumstances of a full-dress speech to the Reichstag (Dec. 5, 1876). There was little comfort in it for Austria or her German friends. He affirmed his attachment to Russia's friendship, his desire for the unimpaired survival of the League of the Three Emperors, and the absence of any friction between Russia and Austria. The first of his aims was the maintenance of Germany's friendships, and, following this, the preservation of peace, "so far as that could be done through friendly mediation with no comminatory gestures on our part." It was his intention to localize the war which might break out in the Near East. Addressing Russia's critics in Germany, he said: "The gentlemen may do as they please, but I assure them that as long as I stand here they will not succeed in disturbing our good and solid relations with Russia or in driving a wedge in our century-old friendship."[41]   For those who had been encouraged by the first and more informal statement to hope for a marked change in Bismarck's policy this speech was a disappointment. "Some fine illusions," said the *Frankfurter Zeitung* (Dec. 5) "have met a sudden end," although the same journal believed that he wished both Russia and Austria to expect Germany's support. He had, according to the *Kölnische Zeitung* (Dec. 7), donned an Austrian uniform only to change it immediately for a Russian. In general, Bismarck's intervention failed to effect any significant changes in the tendencies of public opinion. For observers like

---

[40] He approved the publication of his remarks "in order that the speech he intended shortly to deliver in the Reichstag might be better understood." Brockhaus, *Stunden mit Bismarck*, p. 161 (Dec. 3, 1876).

[41] *Verhandlungen*, II Leg. Per., IV, Sess., I, 583–585.

Treitschke [42] and for the *National Zeitung* (Dec. 7) there was nothing to add to or to subtract from his exposition, although the Conservative *Kreuz-Zeitung* (Dec. 13) accepted his support of Russia chiefly for the reason that force alone would check the ambitions of the Pan-Slavs. Bismarck's critics nevertheless continued their protest against complete neutrality, which seemed in their eyes an unworthy subservience to Russia. [43] The moderate *Vossische Zeitung* (Dec. 7) even suspected that his peaceful assurances and assertions of friendship really covered a substantial service to Russia.

Less hopeful than ever of positive results from diplomatic negotiations, Bismarck looked for nothing but recrimination from the conference which met on December 11 in Constantinople at England's invitation. He instructed Germany's representative to support anything that Austria and Russia agreed upon, but persisting in his reserve, he refrained from exerting the pressure which might have brought them together. [44] His caution was unavailing, for the Russians and the French charged him with the responsibility for the failure of the conference even before its collapse. [45] On January 8, 1877, Decazes hinted to the powers that Bismarck had blocked a promising compromise between Russia and Turkey, and the same charge appeared in the French press. [46] His patience was strained when Russia, after failing to confide her desires to him, complained of his lack of support. "They accept our services," he exclaimed, "as if they were obligations and then do not treat us as equals." [47] The *National Zeitung* (Jan. 23), forgetting its earlier blanket endorsement of Russia's policy, decided that Russia was responsible for her own failure.

The ensuing press controversy, embittered by Russia's disappointment at the meager returns from Germany's friendship, turned Russian sentiment more definitely toward France. "It is marvelous," wrote Le Flô, the French ambassador in St. Peters-

---

[42] Treitschke, "Deutschland und die orientalische Krisis," *P. J.,* vol. 37, p. 670 (Dec. 15, 1876).

[43] *Volks-Zeitung,* Dec. 5, 1876; *Germania,* Dec. 9.

[44] Bülow, Dec. 18. *G. P.,* II, 119, 120.

[45] The conference dissolved, Jan. 24, 1877, when Turkey promulgated a new constitution without regard to its recommendations.

[46] *D. D. F.,* (1), II, 134, 135; *Magdeburgische Zeitung,* Jan. 16, Paris, Jan. 13.

[47] Bismarck, Jan. 24, 1877. *G. P.,* II, 127, 128.

burg, "how everyone dwells with complaisance upon our incomparable wealth, our limitless resources, and the improvement of our military forces." [48]   Russia made no diplomatic proposals to France at this time, but Bismarck was not in the habit of waiting for the development of an unfavorable situation before acting. As one means of strengthening Germany's position, he apparently weighed the possible advantages of approaching England and Austria, but his proposals to the former met with no succeess.[49] Occasional instances of diplomatic coöperation with France, such as the negotiations following the murder of the French and German consular officials at Salonica,[50] counted for little against his suspicion of MacMahon's clerical and monarchist tendencies. The alleged presence of an abnormally large number of cavalry regiments between Paris and the Vosges frontier furnished a convenient excuse for a warning. Preliminary flourishes in other newspapers, which drew a protest from the French ambassador,[51] were followed by the *National Zeitung's* (Jan. 19, 1877) statement: "France . . . will find sympathy and good-will if she devotes herself to her domestic reorganization, but a France which pursues a policy of intrigue and trouble-making necessarily stands on the verge of a catastrophe."   For weeks, until France's actions proved that she had no intention of using the Russo-Turkish war as an occasion for the *revanche* or for an active diplomatic offensive, Franco-German relations remained under the shadow of a crisis which never quite became a reality.   Threatening gestures were soon followed by reassurances.   According to the Russian embassy in Berlin, Bismarck had scented a plan for a sudden occupation of Alsace in the concentration of the French cavalry,[52] but, in his conversations with Gontaut-Biron, he blamed the press for the tense atmosphere.[53]   On the same day that Russia declared war against Turkey (April 24, 1877) Moltke told the Reichstag that the forces on the French side of the frontier required an increase of the Alsatian garrisons;[54] resulting alarm in

[48] Le Flô, Jan. 30, 1877.   *D. D. F.*, (1), II, 134, 135.
[49] Langer, *European Alliances and Alignments*, p. 111.
[50] Mitchell, *The Bismarckian Policy of Conciliation*, pp. 55, 56.
[51] Gontaut-Biron, Jan. 15.   *D. D. F.*, (1), II, 136, 137.
[52] Gontaut-Biron, March 7.   *Ibid.*, (1), II, 145, 146.
[53] Gontaut-Biron, March 24.   *Ibid.*, (1), II, 151, 152.
[54] *Verhandlungen*, III Leg. Per., I Sess., II, 743.   Two weeks later, Lasker, a National

Paris was partially quieted when the full text of his speech reported him as saying that France's preparations were really due to her fear of an attack by Germany.[55]   Nevertheless, France asked in vain for a public statement, either by Germany alone or in conjunction with herself, to reassure a nervous public opinion;[56] for Bismarck evidently counted upon a chronic moderate tension to restrain France during the Russo-Turkish war.

In regard to Russia's aggressive intentions, Bismarck was as indulgent as ever when the spring opened the roads in the Balkans, since a war with Turkey would, in his opinion, not only serve as a safety valve for the Pan-Slavic passions but it would also divert Russia's attention from her Western frontiers, and it might make her more contented with her situation in Europe.[57] He renewed his earlier pledge of Germany's neutrality and again promised his best efforts to prevent the intervention of Austria and England.[58]   He persisted in his skeptical reserve toward measures for the maintenance of peace, for he agreed to take part in a final effort to secure Turkey's acceptance of the recommendations of the Constantinople Conference, chiefly, as he told William, to avoid offending the Tsar, from whom the suggestion had come.[59]   The Emperor, however, still felt an obligation to do something to prevent war.   When England wished to add a provision for a simultaneous Russo-Turkish disarmament to Russia's proposal, he found it "a very happy turn in the critical situation" and was ready to pass the idea on to the Tsar.   Alexander, he thought, would listen to what Germany had to say, but again Bismarck chose to let events take their course, this time to Russia's declaration of war, April 24, 1877.[60]   In May 1877, the public was informed that the Emperor, though he wished to spare his

---

Liberal leader, explained (with Moltke's approval) that this increase had been necessary as a result of technical rather than political reasons. *Ibid.*, 1877, 1st Sess., II, 787–789. Yet Moltke had expressed privately his opinion that the French perhaps intended to attack.   Ballhausen, *Bismarck-Erinnerungen*, p. 109 (April 11). In March Hohenlohe had been asked not to emphasize the peacefulness of opinion in Paris to avoid strengthening William's resistance to the garrison increases. Hohenlohe, *Denkwürdigkeiten*, II, 211.

[55] *Augsburger Abendzeitung*, May 4.
[56] d'Harcourt, London, March 17.   *D. D. F.*, (1), II, 149; Gontaut-Biron, May 9. *Ibid.*, (1), II, 165, 166.
[57] Bülow, Jan. 13, 1877; Bismarck, Jan. 24.   *G. P.*, II, 122, 123, 128, 129.
[58] Bülow, March 8.   *Ibid.*, II, 138.
[59] Bismarck, March 4.   *Ibid.*, II, 134–136.,
[60] Bismarck, March 14.   *Ibid.*, II, 139; Bismarck, March 16.   *Ibid.*, II, 139.

people and all Europe the horrors of war, could not command Russia to keep the peace—as Queen Victoria was reported to have twice asked the German Chancellor. The consequences, it was said, would injure Germany. If Russia refused, Germany would be involved in a war that did not concern her or she would incur Russia's blame for England's interests.[61]   His critics sensed Bismarck's responsibility from the logic of the situation and from his failure to coöperate effectively with Austria and England.[62] "Germany's policy is pro-Russian," wrote the *Allgemeine Zeitung* (June 5), "no one knows to what extent." It was evident, according to the Catholic *Germania* (Sept. 8), that Russia had acted with Germany's consent, since she would not otherwise have dared to attack Turkey against the wishes of the other powers. "Only one word by Berlin would have sufficed," it said, "for the Russian sword to have remained in its sheath; that word was not spoken." Support for this indictment was found in the official press. The *Norddeutsche* (April 26) continued to extol Russia as Germany's best friend and affirmed with some exaggeration that Germany's "best wishes accompanied her armies." Its obsequious deference at last aroused a storm of protest. The *Kölnische Zeitung* (Aug. 28) feared that Austria was about to be betrayed, it recalled the time when a misguided Prussian policy had seen its only salvation in the Tsar Nicholas, and it insisted, with the *Allgemeine. Zeitung's* approval (Aug. 29), that the Russophile press of Berlin could not claim to speak for Germany. "The nationally-minded press of South Germany," it affirmed, "does not believe that Germany's interests are to be found in the camp of the Russian Grand Dukes." [63]   In rebuttal the *Norddeutsche* (Sept. 4) could only cite an article from the *Schwäbische Merkur* (Stuttgart), but the official connections of this newspaper were too well-known for the reply to carry much conviction. It

---

[61] Busch, *Tagebuchblätter*, II, 437, 438 (May 14, 1877). *Cf.* "Friedensengel," *Grenzboten*, 1877, II, 316–319. According to Lothar Bucher, Bismarck regarded this article, which he had not seen before its publication, as too strong. Busch, *op. cit.*, II, 441.

[62] *Korrespondenz von und für Deutschland*, in *Allgemeine Zeitung*, Aug. 29, 1877.

[63] It had, however, declared (May 31, 1877) for neutrality and the maintenance of the League of the Three Emperors. The *National Zeitung* (Sept. 8) admitted that the memories of Russia's reactionary influence in Germany and the hatred of the Roman Catholics for the Orthodox church had turned South German opinion against Russia.

was inconceivable, according to the *Nationalliberale Correspondenz,* an organ of the National Liberal party, that a journal "whose tone is that of a Russian serf can represent the views of the German government." This opinion, it believed, not only had the support of the *Kölnische Zeitung* and the *Allgemeine Zeitung* but also that of the independent press in general.[64]

With the beginning of hostilities, the most devoted friends of Russia became less confident of her disinterested support of the Balkan peoples. "No conquests!" exclaimed the *National Zeitung* (April 29, 1877). "Good, Russia has given her word, Europe has heard it." It became increasingly difficult to identify Germany's interests with a Russian victory. Windthorst, the Centrist leader, correctly described the Reichstag's silence when Jörg, his party associate from Bavaria, denounced the official view that Germany's interests were not involved as a significant expression of public opinion.[65] The *Norddeutsche* (Aug. 17) felt that the unexpectedly effective resistance of the Turks at Plevna would benefit Germany by increasing Russia's appreciation of her friendship, while independent opinion undoubtedly hoped that the war would end in a stalemate.[66] A significant change occurred in that part of German opinion which followed Bismarck's lead when the Russian armies broke the last resistance of the Turks in the passes of the Balkan mountains and advanced toward Constantinople and the Straits. It was prepared to approve a free hand for Russia in Asia Minor and the Straits regardless of England's reactions. All Europe would protest, wrote the *National Zeitung* (May 12, 1877) in connection with the presence of the British fleet in the Aegean, against a firmer establishment of England's influence, adding (July 12, 1877) that the free passage by Russian warships through the Straits would soon be accepted as a matter of course. Treitschke looked forward with satisfaction to any weakening of Turkey as a humiliation of England.[67] "England's interests in the Straits," wrote the Conservative *Post* (Jan. 6, 1878), "are hostile to those of Europe." The

---

[64] Cf. *Allgemeine Zeitung,* Sept. 6.
[65] *Verhandlungen,* III Leg. Per., I Sess., II, 782, 783 (April 26, 1877).
[66] *Volks-Zeitung,* Sept. 12, 1877.
[67] Treitschke, "Die europäische Lage am Jahresschlusse," *P. J.,* vol. 40, p. 671 (Dec. 1877).

official *Norddeutsche* (Jan. 18) more tactfully assured England that her interests were not involved, since Egypt and the Suez Canal were her "exclusive domain." As for Asia Minor, Russia's gains there would, it was said, relieve the pressure upon Austria, and if England objected to them, that was not Germany's concern.[68] Even the *Kölnische Zeitung* (May 3, 1877), again diverging from the main trend of critical opinion, wrote of an Anglo-Russian conflict over Asia Minor: "Good—it would be a war between two Asiatic powers." In its opposition to the establishment of Russian influence in the region from which the mouth and the lower course of the Danube could be controlled, it had the increasingly explicit support of governmental as well as opposition opinion, since it was generally agreed that Germany's commercial interests would be affected. The dangers confronting Austria turned German opinion still more definitely against an exclusively Russian settlement of the Balkan question.[69] Austria was encouraged to prepare for her own defense. As early as May 12, 1877, the *National Zeitung* advised her to place one hundred thousand men on the *Siebenbürgen* frontier in a position to threaten the communications of the Russian army, and the Conservative *Post* wrote that Austria's reluctance to "play an active rôle in the Balkans" was the chief difficulty of the situation.[70]

From the beginning of hostilities, the official press rejected every suggestion that Germany should take an active part in a movement for peace. The *Norddeutsche* (April 29, 1877) stigmatized a proposal from Progressive sources that she should lead a general condemnation of Russia's declaration of war as a *"kolossal blödsinnige Lächerlichkeit."* A few weeks later, the *Provinzial-Correspondenz,* replying to a speech by Professor Virchow, a Progressive leader, in which he had appealed for action to restore peace, denied that Germany had any responsibility, wrote that the proposed course implied an exaggerated estimate of her power, and pointed out that Germany would have to be ready to support an initiative of this kind with her army.[71]

---

[68] *National Zeitung,* Sept. 12, 1877.
[69] *Germania,* May 26, 1877.
[70] *Augsburger Abendzeitung,* May 12, 1877.
[71] *Ibid.,* June 3, 1877. Cf. *N. A. Z.,* May 30.

When Liebknecht, the Social Democratic leader, called for mass demonstrations to force the government "to maintain at least an honorable neutrality," the *Norddeutsche* (Jan. 6, 1878) dismissed the incident as "ridiculous" and as significant only for the light it threw upon the "pathology of the entire Social Democratic movement." This was obviously Bismarck's point of view. In July 1877 he had declared that Germany would consider mediation only on Russia's express invitation,[72] and in the following November he had condemned all other schemes for peace as requiring the use of pressure upon Russia.[73] The course of events, however, brought further changes in Bismarck's policy for which public opinion had long since called without result. Since the League of the Three Emperors had enabled Russia to deal with Turkey as she chose, wrote the reactionary *Kreuz-Zeitung* (Dec. 18, 1877), its voice must be heard in the peace settlement;[74] and it then recommended that the entire problem, with the exception of Russia's annexation of Batum and Bessarabia, should be referred to a European conference (Dec. 20, 1877). On January 23, 1878, the *Provinzial-Correspondenz* asserted bluntly that the two belligerents must accept the collaboration of the European powers for the settlement of certain problems. Five days later Bismarck reached the parting of the ways when Andrássy informed him that war or a conference were the only alternatives, since he had rejected Russia's terms of peace as an inadmissible unilateral revision of existing treaties.[75] Without consulting Russia or waiting for an official communication of her terms, Bismarck agreed in principle to a conference, although he disliked Andrássy's protest as forecasting an unwelcome Anglo-Austrian intimacy. Even then he felt that Austria could accomplish more "by precautionary preparations and an ultimatum than by a conference."[76] The principles of Bismarck's own *Realpolitik* had brought him a step closer to the views

---

[72] Kurowski, July 31. *G. P.*, II, 160.

[73] H. v. Bismarck, Nov. 25. *Ibid.*, II, 160, 161.

[74] The *National Zeitung* had expressed this opinion after Russia's first defeats at Plevna. *Bayerische Kurier*, Aug. 24, 1877.

[75] Andrássy, Jan. 28, 1878, *G. P.*, II, 169–171. Yet the frequently inspired *Grenzboten* (1878, I, 1) insisted that the treaty of peace would not affect German interests in the slightest.

[76] H. v. Bismarck, Jan. 29; Bismarck, Jan. 30. *Ibid.*, II, 173, 175.

of his critics. "In Turkey," he wrote at this time, "we have no interests which we cannot sacrifice to Russia, but we do have such interests in Austria. Germany has a direct and a European interest in standing well with Austria, and in the maintenance of a friendly and reliable minister [Andrássy] there." Germany therefore could not support Russia at the price of Andrássy's defeat and of an unfriendly successor.[77]

During the closing phase of the war German opinion was more Austrian in its sympathies than ever. The Conservatives and a part of the National Liberals hoped that Russia would be satisfied with gains in Asia Minor and perhaps with a favorable solution of the Straits question.[78] To the *Frankfurter Zeitung* (Feb. 13, 1878), which had all along been distinguished from the rest of the liberal press by its advocacy of independence for the Balkan peoples, it was obvious that Germany could not be expected to work for the restoration of Turkish rule in Europe. Opposition opinion, from the Social Democrats to the National Liberals of the Rhineland and South Germany, insisted, however, that Germany should act in agreement with the other powers for a return to the program of the Constantinople Conference for the reform of the Turkish administration.[79] Nor should this combination, wrote the *Allgemeine Zeitung* (Feb. 15) in an article that brought a specific rejoinder from Bismarck in his speech on the nineteenth, be merely a temporary expedient, because there was no more effective security for peace than an alliance with Austria and England, which Germany's open support at this critical juncture would assure. The danger of a Franco-Russian alliance would be increased if Russia were given a free hand in the Balkans. Such was the background of Bismarck's speech of February 19, 1878. To prevent action on the part of the Social Democratic group, certain Progressive deputies persuaded Lasker, the National Liberal leader, to interpellate the

[77] *Bismarck,* Feb. 2. *Ibid.,* II, 180–182.
[78] *Kreuz-Zeitung,* Feb. 8; *Post,* Feb. 13.
[79] *Kölnische Zeitung,* Feb. 8; *Volks-Zeitung,* Feb. 7. Liebknecht, who had the greatest influence upon Social Democratic opinion in regard to the Near Eastern situation, believed that Germany should support England and Austria. Moved by a bitter hatred of Russia, he discounted reports of discontent among the Balkan peoples as 99/100 Russian lies. H. Hertneek, *Die deutsche Sozialdemokratie und die orientalische Frage im Zeitalter Bismarcks* (Berlin, 1927), pp. 10, 11, 13, 17.

government on its Near Eastern policy.[80] Bennigsen, who delivered the main speech in support of the motion, devoted his major efforts to reassuring Austria. "Above all," he said, speaking of the possibility that Russia might impose exorbitant terms on Turkey, "we in Germany have an interest . . . that events in the Near East do not seriously injure Austria or lead to an appreciable weakening of her position." [81]   Bismarck's offer of his services as an "honest broker" and the argument that the Near East was not "worth the bones of a Pomeranian grenadier" enriched the vocabulary of European politics, but his efforts to appease Russia justified some doubt as to his impartiality. The *Allgemeine Zeitung's* article of the preceding day, which he specifically repudiated, gave him a convenient occasion to deny that he had any intention of sitting in judgment upon Russia or of joining with Austria and England to force her to make concessions. At least in regard to the Straits question, he affirmed his support of Russia's interests, for it involved, he declared, nothing vital to Germany. Russia was left to conclude from his remark that this issue was not worth a European war, that she might win her point if she stood her ground. In any event, he would never ask the Emperor or the Bundesrat to approve a war, "except for the protection of our independence abroad, for our unity at home, or for those interests which are so clear that they will assure not only the unanimous vote of the Bundesrat but also the full approval and enthusiasm of the nation. . . ." A recent critic of Bismarck's Russian policy believes, without going into the question thoroughly, that nothing would have been more popular than a war with Russia,[82] but the contemporary evidence shows that few of Bismarck's opponents expected war to follow Germany's diplomatic coöperation with Austria and England. Liebknecht, on behalf of the Social Democrats, and Windthorst for the Centrists, declared their approval of neutrality after Bismarck's speech. But, according to Liebknecht,

---

[80] It was the first interpellation relating to foreign affairs presented by a member of the National Liberal or Conservative groups since 1867. Brockhaus, *Stunden mit Bismarck*, pp. 185, 186.

[81] *Verhandlungen*, III Leg. Per., II Sess., I, 93.

[82] U. Noack, *Bismarcks Friedenspolitik und das Problem des deutschen Machtverfalls* (Leipzig, 1928), p. 78.

Bismarck's neutral policy had worked to Russia's exclusive advantage by keeping Austria, England, and the Poles quiet. He thought that Bismarck's refusal to play the part of a schoolmaster or judge sounded well, but in practice this admirable moderation had not been observed in Germany's relations with France. Lacking the necessary documents, Windthorst could not be certain that the peace, which was admittedly Bismarck's objective, would be temporary or permanent, yet he did know that to permit Russia to acquire the control of the Straits would give her world power.[83] For those who had hoped for an official confirmation of a change in Germany's policy, Bismarck's speech was a disappointment. Its reticence as to Germany's connection with the Russo-Turkish war and its vague references to her future policy colored their first reactions.[84] Bismarck had been, according to the *Kölnische Zeitung* (Feb. 20), as pro-Russian as he could decently be in his discussion of the questions which were to be referred to the European powers. More comforting, however, was the attitude of the Reichstag. All parties, observed the moderate *Vossische Zeitung* (Feb. 20), agreed unanimously in the need for defending Austria's interests. "The German Reichstag," affirmed the Catholic *Germania* (Feb. 20), "had declared as one for the integrity of the Austro-Hungarian monarchy." Even the *Kölnische Zeitung* (March 8) thought, after a little reflection, that Bennigsen's reference to Austria had been intended to supplement Bismarck's speech.[85] Yet the French ambassador was informed that only concessions by Austria could avert an Austro-Russian war, since Russia knew that Bismarck would not resort to extreme measures.[86]

On March 3 Turkey signed the dictated peace of San Stefano. The establishment of a great Bulgarian state extending from the Danube to the Aegean and from a point within striking distance of Constantinople far into the Western Balkans, and the territorial gains it stipulated for Serbia and Montenegro, without any compensations for Austria, confirmed the worst fears as to Russia's intentions. Austria's friends were stunned. The *Allge-*

---

[83] *Verhandlungen*, III Leg. Per., II Sess., I, 99, 102, 103, 112, 113 (Feb. 19, 1878).

[84] *Volks-Zeitung*, Feb. 20.

[85] *Kreuz-Zeitung*, Feb. 21.

[86] Saint-Vallier, Feb. 24. *D. D. F.*, (1), II, 260, 261.

meine Zeitung (March 28) despaired of any considerable revision, and the *National Zeitung* (April 3) recommended a direct understanding between Russia and Austria as the most satisfactory solution of Austria's problems, on the condition that the latter would acquire Bosnia and Herzegovina. According to the *Frankfurter Zeitung* (March 27), opinion was generally indifferent, and this liberal journal insisted that Russia's annexation of Bessarabia alone affected German interests. Catholic opinion, however, demanded action. If Germany abandoned Austria in spite of her repeated assurances of support, if she permitted Russia to surround her and thus to prepare a future menace for herself, the German army, asserted the *Germania* (March 21), should be disbanded. The nationalist press was perturbed by the possibility that Austria might, in her desperation, act as England's tool in a war against Russia. Not a man, not a dollar, exclaimed the *National Zeitung* (April 10), should be sacrificed for England's commercial or political interests, especially since she lacked the means of doing her part (April 3). This contemptuous estimate of England's power, though characteristic of certain groups, was by no means universal, for the Conservative *Post* (March 27) warned Russia that an attack upon India would fail and that she could not compete with England's financial resources.

Encouraged by the *Norddeutsche's* declaration (April 6) that Germany would not be indifferent to the danger of a European war, the *Allgemeine Zeitung* (April 21) argued that Germany needed only to say a word to play the part of Napoleon III at the Congress of Paris. Bismarck had already accepted England's thesis that the Treaty of San Stefano must be submitted in its entirety to the proposed congress,[87] which, on Russia's suggestion, was to meet in Berlin.[88] He made certain the thorough revision of the treaty and therefore assumed a share of the responsibility for Russia's defeat when he obtained Russia's consent.[89] Circumstances had again forced him to resort to measures which he had earlier rejected. Faced by the danger of an Anglo-Russian con-

[87] Bülow, March 16. *G. P.,* II, 221, 222.
[88] Bülow, March 3. *Ibid.,* II, 207.
[89] Bismarck, May 31. *Ibid.,* II, 313.

flict from the proximity of the Russian army and the British fleet
at the gates of Constantinople, he abandoned his former reserve,
offered his mediation, and secured the withdrawal of both forces
to a safer distance.[90]   He had at last acted effectively in the interest of peace, but, at the same time, he had avoided an open
choice between Austria and Russia.

All Germans were united in the feeling of pride that the capital of the young Empire was the host to the most important
diplomatic assembly since the Congress of Paris and that its great
Chancellor presided over its sessions.   These considerations, together with the colorless communiqués as to its work, restrained
public discussion and discouraged the expression of anti-Russian
sentiment.   That Russia's gains would be seriously curtailed was
sufficiently obvious, as the *National Zeitung* (July 7) pointed out,
from her surrender on the vital question of the complete or partial review of the San Stefano settlement.   Russia had accepted the
inevitable after Bismarck's failure to support her, thus enabling
England before the meeting of the Congress to conclude with her
a preliminary agreement for a partition of Bulgaria, while leaving
the determination of the boundaries to be arranged in Berlin.
His change of front, because it greatly diminished the risks of a
stand against Russia, also facilitated England's secret arrangements with Austria and Turkey, by which she consolidated the
anti-Russian alignment and acquired Cyprus as a base from
which to resist the renewal of Russia's advance in the Balkans
and in Asia Minor.   With these preparations, Bismarck of course
had no direct connection, but his occasional support of Russia
during the Congress scarcely balanced the advantages to her opponents from his pressure upon the Congress for speedy decisions.[91]   Russia had to yield on the crucial question of the Bulgarian frontier.   Of the San Stefano settlement, the final Treaty
of Berlin left unchanged Russia's annexation of Bessarabia and
her partial control of Batum, but greater Bulgaria was reduced
to a small principality under Turkish suzerainty north of the
Balkan Mountains, while the southernmost portion was uncon-

---

90 Bismarck, April 9. *Ibid.*, II, 262, 263.
91 Ziekursch, *Politische Geschichte*, II, 87.

ditionally restored to Turkish rule and Eastern Roumelia was placed under a Christian governor.[92] Not even in the Straits question, notwithstanding Bismarck's earlier hints, did Russia gain her point, since the Congress adjourned without deciding between the Russian and the English views. Russia's protégés, Serbia and Montenegro, were deprived of some of their gains, and Austria, whose interests had been ignored in the Treaty of San Stefano in contravention of the Reichstadt agreement (July 1876), secured the right to occupy and administer Bosnia and Herzegovina, with the optional privilege of establishing garrisons at strategic points in the Sanjak of Novi-Bazar between the two small Slavic states.

"Victorious Russia," wrote the Progressive *Volks-Zeitung* (July 12), "received virtually no reward in Europe for her expensive victory." Except as a check to her ambitions, the Treaty of Berlin occasioned surprisingly little satisfaction among the critics of Bismarck's policy. They saw in it a fruitful source of future trouble. The partition of Bulgaria would not long survive the renewal of Russia's pressure, and the disintegration of Turkey would continue to disturb the peace of Europe.[93] "Only for the moment can people safely speak of peace," wrote a leading Catholic review, "in the sense that for today and probably tomorrow the great powers will not shoot at each other." [94] Austria's acquisition of Bosnia and Herzegovina was the cause of more concern than satisfaction to the opposition press because many feared that it would increase the perils that surrounded her. To secure her coöperation in the Bulgarian question, England had promised to support her claims to these provinces, but Bismarck had also encouraged them, perhaps as a step toward an eventual partition of the Balkans. He had been prepared as early as April 1878 to use his influence at Constantinople to secure Turkey's consent.[95] He had even been willing that Austria should present the Congress with a *fait accompli* by marching her troops

---

[92] On the first hint of these terms the *National Zeitung* (May 28, 1878) immediately claimed that peace would be cheap at this price.

[93] *Allgemeine Zeitung*, July 9, 1878; *Germania*, July 7; *Historisch-Politische Blätter*, vol. 82, pp. 329, 330 (Aug. 1878).

[94] *Historisch-Politische Blätter*, vol. 82, p. 875 (Nov. 1878).

[95] Bülow, April 30; Radowitz, July 26. *G. P.*, II, 342, 343, 344.

into both provinces.[96]   The risks of an aggressive policy in the
Balkans, although Bismarck was indifferent to them at this time,
impressed many of his critics.   "By adding to her Slavic subjects," wrote the Progressive *Volks-Zeitung* (April 12, 1878),
"Austria courts the danger of complete dissolution, for her only
defenses against the forces of disintegration are the predominance of her German provinces and the love of freedom of the
Hungarian nation." [97]   Austria, according to a Catholic review,
was certain to be involved by the convulsions which would inevitably result, for more Balkan territory would be required to
assure her control of Bosnia and Herzegovina.[98]   Even Treitschke noted the perils of Austria's new course.[99]

That Germany could not be indifferent to Austria's fate was
generally recognized.   In an article from Vienna (Aug. 5),
which may have derived from Austrian or even from German
official sources, the National Liberal *National Zeitung* (Aug. 8,
1878) called attention to the intimacy of Austro-German relations
as shown by the close contacts between Bismarck and Andrássy
at the Congress of Berlin, by Bismarck's friendly attitude in all
questions affecting Austria's interests, and by the gains Austria
had won with his support.   It asserted that German opinion as
well as German policy in general envisaged a definite alliance for
mutual defense against an attack from the East and West.   Because Bismarck had not yet decided in favor of an alliance, this
article, if he had any connection with it, was perhaps intended
for its effect upon Russia.   Russia, at any rate, was assured that
she had no real cause for complaint.   According to the *Post*
(July 11), it was to her own advantage that "Pan-Slavism has
breathed out its soul in Berlin"; Russia had Germany to thank
for the chance to make peace without being attacked by half of
Europe, a service which more than settled Germany's debt to her.
The *National Zeitung* (July 25) thought that Russia's increased
prestige in the Balkans, the proximity of Bulgaria and Eastern
Roumelia (where her influence would be predominant) to Con-

---

[96] Marginal note, Stolberg, Vienna, May 25. *G. P.*, II, 318, 319.
[97] Cf. *Kölnische Zeitung*, Jan. 7, 1878; *Allgemeine Zeitung*, March 31.
[98] "Die drei Stadien der orientalischen Frage," *Historisch-Politische Blätter*, vol. 82.
p. 217.
[99] *P. J.*, vol. 73, p. 709.

stantinople, and the deathblow she had dealt Turkey ("which no English bandage could cure") were sufficient gains. Bismarck privately distinguished between Gorchakov—"who is a calamity to Russia and her friends"—and the Russian state,[100] although he discoursed to Busch (Feb. 27, 1878) on the history of Russo-German relations since 1813 in a thoroughly critical spirit.[101] He did not deny having told Blowitz, as the latter reported in an interview (London *Times,* Sept. 7, 1878), that Russia's gains would have been more substantial if his relations with her foreign minister had been more cordial since the war scare of 1875.[102] The Tsar himself had taken offense; he declared that the Congress was controlled "by the European coalition under Prince Bismarck's leadership." [103]

For the moment, the Russian press nevertheless suspended its attack upon Bismarck and Germany and turned against Austria, England, and the mistakes of Russia's own diplomatic and military policy. A sustained anti-German campaign first began with the publication in Germany (Feb. 1879) of the Austro-German agreement for the abrogation of Article V of the Treaty of Prague (1866) providing for an eventual plebiscite in northern Schleswig. This elimination of an offensive obligation looked suspiciously like Austria's payment for the services Germany had rendered during the Congress, although it is now known that this agreement had been arranged before the meeting of the Congress.[104] The official *Provinzial-Correspondenz* (Feb. 5, 1789) and the *National Zeitung* (Feb. 7) assured their readers that it merely proved Austria's disinterested friendship, but the Conservative *Post,* whose opinion on such matters commanded attention, agreed with the Russians in drawing the obvious, if in this case, incorrect conclusion. "These services," it acknowledged, "were rendered during the three-year Near Eastern crisis and especially

---

100 Marginal comment, Radowitz, Aug. 8, 1878. *G. P.,* III, 3–6.

101 Busch, *Tagebuchblätter,* II, 552–554. The result of this conversation was a leading article in the *Grenzboten* (1879, I, 413–431, March 13, 1879), "Gortschakoff'sche Politik," the text of which was submitted to Bismarck in page proof. Busch carefully distinguished between Alexander and Gorchakov, charging that the latter was responsible for the attacks upon Bismarck in the *Golos.*

102 The *Volks-Zeitung* (Sept. 11) and the *Post* (Sept. 14) accepted the interview as authentic.

103 I. Grüning, *Die russische öffentliche Meinung und ihre Stellung zu den Grossmächten 1878–1914* (Berlin, 1929), pp. 53 ff.

104 Langer, *European Alliances and Alignments,* pp. 173 ff.

in its conclusion."[105]   Still more offensive to Russia was Bismarck's support of Austria during the protracted labors of the committees left over from the Berlin Congress, especially after the warning that the best way to appease Russia's resentment would be to act with her in the future.[106]   The London *Times* (Aug. 2, 1879) added to these multiplying reasons for Russo-German friction by attributing the Treaty of Berlin "in great measure to the influence exerted by Prince Bismarck.   It was in some respects, as he once said, his own treaty, and he has maintained a natural interest in insuring its full execution.   It is worth observing that, close as have been the relations between Russia and Prussia, yet whenever during these transactions a distinct difference has arisen between the claims of the Western Powers and Russia, Germany under Prince Bismarck's influence has, in the end, inclined the balance in favor of the West."[107]   Bismarck's reply, if the *Norddeutsche's* comments may be taken as reflecting his views, that the *Times'* purpose was to divide Germany and Russia, failed to satisfy the Tsar.   Alexander complained bitterly to the German ambassador that his country was supporting Austria on every occasion.   He then spoke of the anti-German agitation in the Russian press and asserted, resorting to French, which he habitually used when he was especially aroused, *"cela finira d'une manière très sérieuse."*[108]   This veiled menace was sufficiently serious from Bismarck's point of view (it would, he wrote, force him to side with Austria[109]), but the Tsar's personal letter, August 15, 1879, was still more ominous. Was it true statesmanship, Alexander asked, to permit a personal quarrel (between Bismarck and Gorchakov) to poison the relations of their countries?   He reminded William that he had promised never to forget Russia's services in 1870, and, in conclusion, he appealed to the seriousness of the situation, since "the consequences may be disastrous for our two countries."[110]   It

---

[105] *The Saburov Memoirs; or Bismarck & Russia*, J. Y. Simpson, ed. (N. Y., 1929), p. 51.

[106] Noted as a cause of Russia's irritation by the following: *Kölnische Zeitung*, Aug. 19; *N. A. Z.*, Aug. 20; *P. J.*, vol. 44, p. 317 (Sept. 6).

[107] Wertheimer, *Andrássy*, III, 13.

[108] Schweinitz, Aug. 8, 1879. *G. P.*, III, 10.

[109] Bismarck's undated note. *Ibid.*, III, 13.

[110] Alexander, Aug. 15. *Ibid.*, III, 15.

was impossible, Bismarck remarked to Saburov, the Russian special envoy, to dismiss this as a family letter from a nephew to his uncle, for the nephew had two million bayonets at his disposal.[111]

These threats—and reports of Russian approaches to France and Italy—at last convinced Bismarck that the mutual confidence and good-will between the two sovereigns were no longer adequate guarantees against the anti-German forces in Russia. He at once advised William that concessions would merely confirm the argument that Russia needed only resort to threats to attain her ends[112] and began the difficult task of winning his approval for an alliance with Austria. It was desirable, he admitted, only in default of dependable relations with Russia, yet, in his opinion it had important advantages of its own. Not only would it block a possible Franco-Austro-Russian alliance, to which England might be attracted, but it would also restore the assurance of Austria's aid against Russia which the old Confederation had offered, and, finally, in Austria Germany would have an ally whose own need of support would be a guarantee of her loyalty.[113] He talked of the ties of blood, the possession of a common language, and of historical memories—the same general considerations which had earlier been the strength of the Great German movement and which were still largely responsible for the pro-Austrian tendencies of German opinion. This alliance, he said, "would be more popular in Germany and therefore perhaps more permanent than one with Russia."[114] Nevertheless William refused to listen[115] and against Bismarck's advice he visited the Tsar at Alexandrovo, a small station across the Russian frontier, at some sacrifice of his personal comfort. This difference of opinion between the Emperor and his Chancellor, a hint of which appeared in the *Norddeutsche*,[116] left public opinion free to draw its own conclusions as to the direction of German policy;[117] but the *National Zeitung* (Sept. 6), as if unable

---

[111] Simpson, *Saburov Memoirs*, p. 73.

[112] Bismarck, Aug. 15, 24. *G. P.*, III, 13, 14, 18.

[113] Bismarck, Aug. 31, Sept. 1, Sept. 5. *Ibid.*, III, 25–36, 41, 42; Busch, *Tagebuchblätter*, III, 561, 562 (Oct. 6, 1879). *Cf.* "Neue Friktionen," *Grenzboten*, 1879, IV, 91, 92 (Oct. 16).

[114] Bismarck, Aug. 24. *G. P.*, III, 20.

[115] William I, Sept. 10. *Ibid.*, III, 63.

[116] Cf. *National Zeitung*, Sept. 4.

[117] *Frankfurter Zeitung*, Sept. 5.

to break away from old habits, again wrote of an epoch-making event in Russo-German relations. In view of recent events and of Bismarck's attitude, the visit did not alarm Austria's friends,[118] and the public discussion largely centered around the suspected differences between William and Bismarck.[119] Alexander's assurances persuaded his uncle that an alliance with Austria would mean a betrayal of Russia,[120] but Bismarck stood his ground, for, as he explained to the Emperor, the Russian army was still on the frontier,[121] the Tsar was still under the influence of the Pan-Slavs, and, what was equally ominous, he had learned from Waddington of Russia's diplomatic approaches to France.[122] He hastened to Vienna, even without a definite assurance of the Emperor's approval, in order to get something on paper while the friendly Andrássy was still in office.

Within three days, the Austro-German alliance was drawn up, which remained the foundation of German foreign policy until the collapse of the Dual Monarchy in 1918. William's scruples were partially appeased by a declaration in the preamble of friendly sentiments toward Russia and of the alliance's defensive purposes and by an engagement to communicate its essential terms to Russia in the event that her military preparations should assume dangerous proportions. Bismarck's concessions were probably greater than Andrássy's, since it was more likely that Germany would be called upon to make good her promise of support against a Russian attack than Austria, and since Austria refused to assume any obligations against an attack by France alone; this disparity was perhaps not unjust in view of Bismarck's not inconsiderable part in encouraging Austria's aggressive policy in the Balkans since the Congress of Berlin. He did not expect

[118] *Volks-Zeitung*, Sept. 9.

[119] The Conservative *Deutsche Zeitung* drew the conclusion from Bismarck's apparent decision to break Germany's traditional friendship with Russia that he might be a revolutionary if necessary. Cf. *Frankfurter Zeitung*, Sept. 5.

[120] Radowitz, Sept. 9. *G. P.*, III, 59.

[121] Only against Germany, Bismarck caused Busch to write, could its startling increase (of about 400,000 men) be directed. "Neue Friktionen," *Grenzboten*, 1879, IV, 91, 92 (Oct. 16). *Cf.* Busch, *Tagebuchblätter*, II, 564 (Oct. 6).

[122] Bismarck, Sept. 15. *G. P.*, III, 81. *Cf.* Rachfahl, *Deutschland und die Weltpolitik*, p. 260. The Paris *Soleil* printed at this time Gorchakov's statement that his support of France's rearmament in 1875 had earned Bismarck's hatred. Cf. *Kölnische Zeitung*, Sept. 14; *Kreuz-Zeitung*, Sept. 19; *Historisch-Politische Blätter*, vol. 84, p. 626. Busch revealed Russia's advances to France and her rebuff in "Zur Geschichte des deutsch-österreichischen Bündnisses," *Grenzboten*, 1880, I, 482 (March 18).

the alliance to endure forever,[123] but it was by no means intended as a temporary expedient to meet an immediate danger. Russia's military and financial weakness after the Russo-Turkish War and the failure of France to respond to her diplomatic approaches practically assured peace for the next few years. A time limit of five years, with provisions for renewal, meant in effect that Bismarck and Andrássy thought the alliance would be permanent. Although purely defensive, the alliance was the first step toward the division of Europe into two armed camps.

He was doubtless aware that the alliance might involve Germany in quarrels and wars having no direct connection with her own interests. Andrássy's assurance to Emperor Francis Joseph that Austria had received a free hand in the Balkans in fact made it evident that the alliance might not be limited in practice to its specific terms.[124] Even Bismarck acknowledged that the fear of a Russian attack might cause Austria to assume the aggressive, a remark that elicited William's far from pointless comment: *"Also doch offensiv?"* [125] When the French ambassador inquired whether Germany intended to support Austria if her advance toward Salonica should provoke a Russian attack, the Chancellor replied evasively that only Russia's seizure of Constantinople would cause Austria to depart from the terms of the Treaty of Berlin.[126] The press called attention to these dangerous possibilities. The *Frankfurter Zeitung* (Oct. 2, 1879) insisted that the supposed Pan-Slavic danger, if it existed at all, had been greatly exaggerated, and it opposed (Sept. 25, 1879) anything more than close commercial and friendly diplomatic relations with Austria on the ground that an alliance would mean "the support of the Viennese annexationists in their march to Salonica rather than the defense of Austria against a Russian menace." To the moderate *Vossische Zeitung* (Sept. 22), Germany's lack of interest in the Austro-Italian problem was a sufficient reason to oppose a formal alliance, and Treitschke admitted that Austria must control the road to Salonica to be secure in her possession of

---

[123] Hartung, *Deutsche Geschichte*, p. 30.
[124] Ziekursch, *Politische Geschichte*, II, 106; Noack, *Bismarcks Friedenspolitik*, p. 109.
[125] Bismarck, Vienna, Sept. 24. *G. P.*, III, 95.
[126] Saint-Vallier, No. 14. *D. D. F.*, (1), II, 588.

Bosnia and Herzegovina. Austria, he wrote, had revived in modern form the ambitious plans of Prince Eugene.[127]

Because of Austria's insistence upon secrecy, the official press studiously avoided for some time any mention of an alliance,[128] but its hints were sufficiently precise to convey the impression that a specific agreement had been concluded. The *Norddeutsche* (Sept. 21) preferred a general understanding based upon an identity of interests [129] and asserted that the "entente" guaranteed Austria against Pan-Slavism and gave Germany complete security against alliances which would serve France's *revanche*.[130] Written alliance or general understanding, the difference was of secondary importance to public opinion, for the fact that Germany had at last turned from Russia to Austria sufficed for almost unanimous approval.[131] Bismarck's critics could not resist the temptation to claim that he had been converted to their point of view.[132] After recalling Bismarck's warning that his opponents would never succeed in disturbing the century-old Russo-German friendship, the Catholic *Germania* (Oct. 29) maliciously remarked that "he had himself played the part of the grave-digger for that friendship." What of the earlier assertions, asked the National Liberal *Allgemeine Zeitung* (Sept. 23), that Germany must inevitably side with Russia if she had to choose between her and Austria? Satisfaction with recent developments failed to win the Progressive *Volks-Zeitung's* (Sept. 28) forgiveness for Bismarck's encouragement of Russia in the war with Turkey or for the weaknesses of the Treaty of Berlin which, in its opinion, he could have prevented. The Nationalist and Conservative press asserted that Germany's indifference to the Balkan situation would not now carry as much conviction as had formerly its approval of non-intervention.[133] While public opinion was perhaps not one of the determining causes of Bismarck's

---

[127] Treitschke, "Unsere Aussichten," *P. J.*, vol. 44, 567–569 (Nov. 15).

[128] In "Das deutsch-österreichische Präventivbündnis," (*Nord und Süd*, 1881, I, 118–135, Jan.), "Rhenanus" gave a surprisingly good account of the background of the alliance and described its purposes as purely defensive. The author, however, pretended to no knowledge of its terms. Cf. *Augsburger Abendzeitung*, Jan. 6, 1881.

[129] Cf. *Kölnische Zeitung*, Sept. 22, etc.

[130] *Provinzial-Correspondenz*, Sept. 24.

[131] *Historisch-Politische Blätter*, vol. 84, p. 786 (Nov. 12).

[132] *Kölnische Zeitung*, Sept. 29.

[133] *National Zeitung*, Oct. 5.

change of front,[134] it nevertheless helped to secure the support of the other ministers in winning William's consent.[135]   The Chancellor pointed to the popularity of the alliance with all parties "except the Nihilists and Socialists," and he argued that the sacrifice of German interests to Russia would have had a more disastrous effect upon German opinion than the humiliation of Olmütz.[136]   William seems to have been impressed, for he wrote of the alliance "as existing in German opinion" when he explained its reasons to Alexander.[137]   The popularity of the alliance influenced even Bismarck, for, without public approval, he would scarcely have urged its publication, its ratification by the two parliaments, or its insertion in the constitutions of the two countries.[138]

Unsatisfactory relations with Russia inevitably increased the value of Austria's support and of good relations with the Western powers.   For the moment it seemed possible that Bismarck might approach France and England.   France's strict neutrality during the Russo-Turkish war diminished his suspicions and accordingly the general tension during the spring of 1877.   MacMahon's *coup d'état* (May 1877)—the dismissal of the Simon ministry and the calling of new elections—did not disturb his watchful reserve,[139] and when the moderate Republicans gained control of the Chamber of Deputies in October Bismarck established indirect relations with Gambetta, their most influential leader, with a view to winning him to at least a businesslike relationship.   Nor did Gambetta's sudden cancellation of the interview, which had been arranged for April 1878, for fear of its effect on French opinion, change the general lines of Bismarck's more conciliatory pol-

---

[134] He told the French ambassador, however, that the national sentiment which he had defied in 1866 at the risk of his life and of his reputation in history ". . . imposes the alliance with Austria upon me just as it commanded me in 1866 not to mutilate her as soon as I decided not to destroy her." Saint-Vallier, Nov. 14. *D. D. F.*, (1), III, 582.

[135] *G. P.*, III, 105, 106. *Cf.* Ballhausen, *Bismarck-Erinnerungen*, pp. 173–176 (Sept. 28, 1879).

[136] Bismarck, Oct. 3. *G. P.*, III, 108, 109.

[137] William, Nov. 4. *Ibid.*, III, 126.

[138] Bismarck, Nov. 10. *Ibid.*, III, 129, 130. *Cf.* Becker, *Bismarcks Bündnispolitik*, p. 36; Ballhausen, *Bismarck-Erinnerungen*, p. 171; conversation with Dr. Edward Cohen, Jan. 14, 1884. *B. G. W.*, VIII, 499. Busch, in an inspired article, represented Bismarck as desiring the ratification of the alliance by the parliaments of the two countries. "Zur Geschichte des deutsch-österreichischen Bündnisses," *Grenzboten*, 1880, I, 482 (March 18). *Cf.* Busch, *Tagebuchblätter*, II, 570, 571 (March 9).

[139] *Cf. National Zeitung*, Aug. 3, 1877.

icy.[140]   He encouraged and supported the French delegation during the Congress of Berlin and, like Salisbury, the British foreign secretary, encouraged Waddington, the French foreign minister, to add Tunis to the French colonial empire.   If the French did not at once pluck the Tunisian pear, as Bismarck advised them to do, it was largely because of political conditions at home. Whatever changes the future might bring, the success of the Republicans in gaining control of both Chambers, MacMahon's resignation in 1879, and the election of the moderate Grévy were as reliable guarantees of a peaceful France as the uncertainties of politics, and especially those of France, could offer.

Bismarck's more conciliatory attitude toward France was not, however, the best indication of his Western orientation, since he believed that nothing more intimate than courteous relations was possible with her.   At the most, France's willingness to act as Russia's second in current diplomatic negotiations might be diminished.   England's friendship was the obvious alternative to an association with Russia and the natural supplement to the alliance with Austria.   Colonial friction and naval competition were not then the fatal obstacles to an understanding which they became in later years; the Disraeli government's hostility toward Russia and its increasing irritation at France's activities in the Mediterranean now worked in Germany's favor.   Alexander's threats not only caused Bismarck to negotiate the Austrian alliance, but they also led him, even before its conclusion, to ask for England's support.   This at least was the sense of his instructions to the German ambassador in London,[141] but Münster, who apparently thought that he understood Germany's needs better than the Chancellor, gave Disraeli the impression that Bismarck was chiefly interested in what England would do if France threatened to intervene in a Russo-German war instead of asking what action England would take during a Russo-German conflict. Disraeli's favorable, even enthusiastic, reply nevertheless opened the way for an Anglo-German agreement.   He approved the idea of an Austro-German alliance, and to strengthen it he was ready by an Anglo-German alliance to guarantee France's neu-

---

[140] Mitchell, *Bismarckian Policy of Conciliation*, pp. 69–85.
[141] Bismarck, Sept. 14.   *G. P.*, IV, 3, 4–6.

trality if Russia attacked Germany.[142] Never in the future was England to offer so much; yet Bismarck made no use of this unparalleled opportunity. Disraeli's failure to give a definite assurance of England's aid against an attack by Russia alone, although what he had offered amounted to a guarantee of Germany's possession of Alsace-Lorraine, drew his caustic comment: "Is that all?" [143]

Saburov's arrival in Berlin with new offers was undoubtedly the chief factor in Bismarck's decision to suspend these negotiations.[144] The Chancellor still believed that the best solution of Germany's problems in Central and Eastern Europe was the League of the Three Emperors. Yet Saburov's first proposals of a Russo-German alliance were unacceptable, for they would have meant the annulment of the alliance with Austria. Among five great powers, he held that Germany must have two on her side. He would, he said, never make an alliance with Russia alone.[145] A few weeks later he caused Germany's attachment to the new ties with Austria to be affirmed in an article that was accepted everywhere as officially inspired.[146] It was in the hope of persuading Russia to resume negotiations with Austria that he sacrificed the best opportunity Germany ever had for an alliance with England. For more than a year his efforts were balked by his personal quarrel with Gorchakov and by the mutual suspicion between Russia and Austria. That he succeeded at last in uniting them in the Alliance of the Three Emperors (1881) was the result in large measure of circumstances for which he had little or no responsibility. France's refusal to surrender Hartmann, the Nihilist, to the Russian police cooled Russia's French proclivities,[147] and Gladstone's victory in the parliamentary elec-

---

142 In view of Professor Geffcken's well-known connections with the Crown Prince, it is of interest that he approved a union with England for Russia's definitive defeat if she would pledge her support for the Austro-German Balkan policy and her opposition to the *revanche*. J. H. Geffcken, "Russland und England in Mittelasien," *Deutsche Rundschau*, XXII, p. 266 (Feb. 1880).
143 Langer, *European Alliances and Alignments*, pp. 186–190.
144 *Ibid.*, pp. 190 ff.
145 Waldersee, *Denkwürdigkeiten*, I, 200, 201. (Feb. 6, 1880). He was still suspicious of the troop movements on the Russian frontier. Bismarck, Feb. 3, 6, 1880. *G. P.*, III, 141, 143, 144.
146 Zur Geschichte des deutsch-österreichischen Bündnisses," *Grenzboten*, 1880, I, 481–484 (March 18). *Cf.* Busch, *op. cit.*, II, 571.
147 Saint-Vallier, Dec. 22, 1880. *D. D. F.*, (1), III, 74, 75.

tions of April 1880 increased Bismarck's own eagerness for a definite arrangement with Russia, because the Liberals in England had long since sympathized with Russia's support of the Balkan peoples.[148]   He accordingly increased his pressure upon Austria, advising her that she had nothing to lose, while something might be gained from a treaty relationship with Russia. Not until the assassination of Alexander II, however, was Russia ready to accept a compromise with Austria in order to present a common front against the danger of revolution.   The alliance of the Three Emperors was based upon Bismarck's favorite plan for the partition of the Balkans.   In return for Russia's recognition of Austria's right to the eventual annexation of Bosnia and Herzegovina and for her promise to satisfy Austria before launching another attack upon Turkey, she received an inclusive recognition of her Balkan interests by her two partners, their approval of the eventual union between Bulgaria and Eastern Roumelia, and, what was even more significant of Bismarck's disregard of England's interests, assurances of Austria's and Germany's diplomatic support in forcing Turkey to close the Straits to British warships.   Bismarck had repaired the tenuous line to St. Petersburg by consenting in principle to the scrapping of a large part of the Treaty of Berlin.

This eagerness to profit by Russia's advances was not the only reason for Bismarck's failure to complete the Western orientation of his policy by a diplomatic association with England.   Since he shared with many Germans the belief that an Anglo-Russian war was probably inevitable, the possibility that an alliance with Germany might increase England's bellicose disposition may have been a minor argument against it.[149]   He also thought that an alliance might disturb the good relations between France and England, which he valued as a check upon France's continental policy and upon British imperialism.   Moreover, recent developments in French politics and France's neutrality during the Russo-Turkish War had diminished his immediate concern as to France and therefore the need of a guarantee such as Disraeli had offered.   Like a large part of German opinion, Bismarck was not

[148] Simpson, *Saburov Memoirs*, pp. 128, 129.
[149] Bismarck, Nov. 10.   *G. P.*, III, 131.

at all confident that Germany would, in an alliance with her, succeed in thwarting England's supposedly traditional use of a continental ally for her own selfish aims. "We should not," he wrote,
"permit ourselves to be used for England's aggressive purposes." [150]   The fear that Germany would not be able to maintain
complete equality with England was almost an obsession with
certain sections of German opinion. That Germany refused to
pull England's chestnuts out of the fire was a favorite expression,
and a rumor of a possible alliance was at once followed by protests that she should not be dragged into a war with Russia for
English interests. The moderate *Vossische Zeitung* (Feb. 10,
1880) thought of treason, the bones of the famous grenadier, and
of English mercenaries.[151]   Even England's friends among the
Progressives and Social Democrats were cool to the prospect of
an Anglo-Russian war.[152]   As for the nationalist and Conservative circles, their normal anti-English sentiment was as usual
strengthened by the prestige England enjoyed among their political opponents.[153]

It was not so much Bismarck's ultimate purposes as his methods
that aroused opposition during the Near Eastern crisis, for his
critics were no less desirous of protecting Germany from its
dangers. They denied quite sincerely the insinuation in his
speech of February 16, 1876 that they favored war with Russia.
As they saw it, his reserve during the period of negotiations for
Turkish reforms, his manifest benevolence toward Russia's aggressive purposes, and his friendliness during the war would lead
to Russia's predominance in the Balkans, to Austria's destruction,
and thus, eventually, to a deadly menace to Germany's own security. Bismarck's method of guarding against these dangers
was to retain Russia's friendship by encouraging her ambitions,
especially at England's expense, while suggesting to Austria that
an advance in the Western Balkans would be her best defense,
although he saw just as clearly as his critics that he must protect
Austria's existence as a great power. Opposition opinion denied
that Germany's interests would be served best by virtually giving

---

[150] Marginal comment, Reuss, Vienna, Nov. 6, 1879. *G. P.*, III, 128, 129.
[151] Cf. *National Zeitung*, Feb. 21, 1880.
[152] *Germania*, Dec. 17, 1879.
[153] *Reichsbote*, Jan. 11, 1880.

Russia a free hand in the Balkans. Instead, it advocated energetic coöperation with Austria and England, as their leader if necessary, to satisfy the Balkan insurgents, then to prevent Russia from declaring war, and finally to restore peace. This counsel, according to Bismarck and his followers, proved only their ignorance and political ineptitude, yet events gradually forced him to similar conclusions. He could still argue, admittedly with some justification, that Russia's military weakness after the war and the rise to power in France of the moderate Republicans diminished the danger of thwarting Russia's interests, whereas earlier action would have meant a Franco-Russian alliance.

His critics had been willing to risk even a Franco-Russian alliance, provided that Russia might be checked in the Balkans and the security of Austria assured. Since their concern was with the immediate crisis, they did not usually draw the obvious conclusion as to the future direction of German foreign policy. Nevertheless, they felt, more as a result of sentiment and instinct than of a critical analysis of the situation, that Germany's fate was inseparably associated with Austria's. To this extent, they had the support of German opinion as a whole, as was unmistakably shown by the applause that followed the Austro-German understanding in September 1879. On this issue, Bismarck was at one with German national sentiment and the greater part of public opinion.[154] Generally speaking, only the Social Democrats and some Progressives were partisans of an alliance with England; the majority of Bismarck's critics had urged nothing more permanent than coöperation for the duration of the crisis. What the reaction of German opinion would have been to Disraeli's offer is a matter of speculation, but its inveterate suspicion of England's motives and purposes might well have more than balanced the favorable effect of the proposed guarantee of France's neutrality and therefore of Germany's possession of Alsace-Lorraine. Once the pressure of the immediate crisis had diminished, it seems clear that, with the exception of the Progressives and Social Democrats, German opinion had no objection to the restoration of diplomatic ties with Russia. Its reaction to the meeting between William

---

154 "Neue Friktionen," *Grenzboten*, 1879, IV, 92 (Oct. 16).

and Alexander III in Danzig (Sept. 1881), the first indication of the restored Russo-German friendship, was favorable, on the condition that Austria must always be Germany's first love.[155]   "We can conclude a friendship with all who desire and deserve it," wrote the *Germania* (Sept. 6), "but a *mariage à trois* and still less *à quatre* does not exist."

---

[155] *Kölnische Zeitung, Magdeburgische Zeitung,* Sept. 10, 1881.   Even the Progressive *Volks-Zeitung* (Sept. 7) approved the meeting as a warning to France that she could not expect an alliance with Russia.

CHAPTER V

Colonial Expansion,
Egypt, and the Western Powers, 1882-1885

... Die Frage der Zukunft lautet folgendermassen: Wird die
auf den Boden Aegyptens in Wirksamkeit gesetzte Gemein-
schaft, die man als Quadrupleallianz bezeichnen könnte, sich
durch den weiteren Verlauf der egyptische Dinge so befesti-
gen, dass alle innereuropäischen Konflikte dadurch be-
schwichtigt werden; oder werden diese Konflikte früher oder
später aktuell werden, und damit England die Gelegenheit
verschaffen, sich des aegyptischen Bodens allein zu bemäch-
tigen?

Preussische Jahrbücher, vol. 55, p. 206 (Jan. 1885).

... Trotzdem hat man sich weder hier noch dort Illusionen
hingegeben; die Wolken einer tausendjährige Geschichte
werfen ihre tiefen Schatten zu weit voraus, als dass vorüber-
gehende schwache Sonnenstrahlen zu mehr dienen könnten,
als zu einem Augenblickslichtbilde.

Berliner Tageblatt, Aug. 4, 1885.

Not until France accepted the Treaty of Frankfort without
reservations and Pan-Slavism renounced its aggressive aims
could Germany hope for complete and permanent security.
Nevertheless, her position was never stronger than at the beginning of the eighties. Bismarck was not satisfied with the diplomatic advantages that arose automatically when the other powers
shifted their attention from Germany to the Balkans and to colonial expansion. For more substantial guarantees, he relied
upon Germany's strong right arm and upon a system of alliances
that included a number of discontented countries for the defense
of the status quo. Need of Germany's aid assured the acceptance
of purely defensive terms, but all, from Austria to Roumania,

counted more or less definitely upon her support as an extra dividend from these alliances for either territorial gains in the future or for more effective diplomatic influence in the present.

Bismarck had long been indifferent to Italy's desire for an alliance; he regarded her military and political weakness and her irredentist aspirations as liabilities. He made no attempt to conceal his contempt for her past record, her untrustworthiness and boundless ambitions, and he did not hesitate to sacrifice her interests in Tunis. That the establishment of a French protectorate there (1881) with his encouragement and support not only increased Italy's hostility to France but also her desire for Germany's support were desirable results, if not primary motives, of Bismarck's policy. He continued to tell Italy that the road to Berlin passed through Vienna,[1] and he left her to find the way alone until a new outburst of Pan-Slavism reminded him of the uncertainty of Russia's friendship. In January 1882, General Skobelev, a Pan-Slav leader, speaking to Serb students in Paris, called upon the Slavs everywhere to prepare for an inevitable conflict with the Germans. Bismarck took no official notice of the speech, and the inspired press, following the example of St. Petersburg, explained that Skobelev did not express the views of the Russian government. The effect upon German opinion was nonetheless serious. The moderate *Vossische Zeitung* (Feb. 23, 1882) wrote of the much-prized Russian friendship as depending solely on Bismarck's services and even of a war on two fronts, in which Germany would remain on the defensive against France while launching an attack upon Russia for the purpose of permanent annexations.[2] The speech reminded Bismarck of the instability of the Alliance of the Three Emperors and, with the friendly attitude of the Gambetta ministry in France toward Italy,[3] it increased the value of an alliance which would release a part of the Austrian army for use against Russia and immobilize a part of France's forces. Enlarging upon his earlier approval of a simple neutrality agreement, he advised

---

[1] This advice appeared in Bismarck's own words in the *National Zeitung* (Oct. 22, 1881) on the occasion of King Humbert's visit.

[2] Saint-Vallier attributed this article to official inspiration. E. Bourgeois, G. Pagès, *Les origines et les responsabilités de la grande guerre* (Paris, 1922), pp. 373, 374.

[3] Wahl, *Deutsche Geschichte*, II, 14, 15.

Vienna to join Berlin in a pact with Italy pledging their aid if France attacked her.[4] In return for this assurance, the Triple Alliance (1882) provided for Italy's support of Germany against an attack by France alone, but Austria, unwilling to undertake extensive obligations toward Italy, asked only that the latter should remain neutral if Russia attacked her alone. Indeed, Bismarck was skeptical of anything more than Italian neutrality, confessing once that he would be satisfied if a corporal with the Italian colors and a drummer appeared on the French frontier in time of war.[5]

Central Europe, united in one alliance system from the Baltic to the Mediterranean, soon attracted lesser states. For Bismarck it was chiefly a question of perfecting a defense against Russia, whose talk of peace, he complained, was contradicted by the pistol she pointed at Germany.[6] He advised Austria to extend the "League of Peace" to Roumania, Serbia, and Turkey.[7] With his approval, Austria took advantage of Serbia's resentment at Russia's support of Bulgaria to conclude a defensive alliance (1881) which made Serbia an Austrian satellite for a generation. Fear of Russia and a desire to recover Bessarabia, the same complex of defensive and offensive aims which accounted for Italy's eagerness for an alliance, moved Roumania to approach Austria, but Bismarck's decided negative of Bratianu's aggressive hints [8] assured the defensive character of the final terms. Nor were the limits of Germany's diplomatic influence fixed by these formal alliances. Bismarck's support of Turkey's intervention in Egypt for the suppression of the native rebellion in 1882 gave her a foothold in Constantinople, but apparently nothing was done to attach Turkey to the "League of Peace." Symptomatic of Germany's prestige, but of less practical diplomatic importance, were the tendencies of the Scandinavian states to follow Germany's lead and Spain's friendliness, as manifested by King Alphonso's visit to Berlin in 1883.

---

[4] Busch, Feb. 28, 1882, *G. P.,* III, 212.
[5] A. F. Pribram, *The Secret Treaties of Austria-Hungary,* 2 vols. (Cambridge, Mass., 1921), II, 49.
[6] Hohenlohe, *Denkwürdigkeiten, II,* 340 (Sept. 6, 1883).
[7] Bismarck, Aug. 12, 1883. G. P., III, 263.
[8] Bismarck, Sept. 15, 1883. *Ibid.,* III, 268, 269.

These alliances were well enough known to assure the support of Bismarck's foreign policy by the greater part of public opinion. His own evaluation of the alliance system as a league of peace was usually accepted without question. Time had dimmed the memory of his unpopular support of Russia during the Near Eastern crisis. Only the Social Democrats unequivocally condemned his conduct of foreign affairs as guided by considerations of power (*Machtpolitik*) rather than the interests of the masses. They refused him the credit for blocking a Franco-Russian alliance, insisting that the Russian Nihilists and the French democrats were responsible. Social Democratic leaders followed Germany's foreign affairs closely, but their views on these questions were a minor factor even in the growth of their own party and their influence beyond its ranks was negligible. When they ventured to intrude upon the sacred ground of foreign affairs in the Reichstag, the government's spokesmen and others rarely replied to their questions or criticisms. The Center party had ceased its systematic opposition with the gradual termination of the *Kulturkampf,* while the Progressives, having acquired new recruits from the left wing of the National Liberal party following its split on the tariff issue, generally limited their criticism to Bismarck's domestic policy.

Confidence increased with the development of Bismarck's alliances. "Eighty millions of Central Europeans, including fifty million Germans," wrote the Catholic *Germania* (Sept. 14, 1789), "stand shoulder to shoulder against a threat from any direction." Bismarck often spoke of his "League of Peace," but it did not suit his purposes that public opinion should place too much reliance upon it. He used the official press to excite public opinion for the renewal of the Septennate early in 1880, with an increase of twenty-six thousand men and a longer period of service for the reserves, especially after the Progressives offered to trade their support in return for a reduction in the period of service in the infantry from three to two years.[9] This maneuver served merely to harden his insistence upon his own terms rather than to bring about the smallest concession to the principle of

---

[9] *Volks-Zeitung,* Jan. 24, 1880.

the parliamentary control of the army. It would be "no less amazing than disheartening," observed the London *Times* (March 1, 1880), if Bismarck should pretend that Germany was in danger of an immediate French aggression or that she was unprepared to meet it. "The power of Germany, vast as it is, cannot afford to sever itself from the moral support of European opinion." Neither the memorandum that accompanied the army bill nor Moltke's supporting speech (March 1) claimed that an immediate danger existed. Instead, Moltke reminded the Reichstag that the Swedes, the French, and even the Germans had made Germany a wasteland for centuries, and asked: "Are not the ruins on the Neckar and Rhine permanent monuments of our former weakness and of our neighbors' wantonness?"[10] A reference to the "peaceful and friendly relations with all foreign powers" in the speech from the throne at the beginning of the session was embarrassing. The arguments of the government's spokesmen were too threadbare to impress a public which hoped that increased security would mean lighter military burdens. "The German press outside of Berlin," acknowledged the *National Zeitung* (Jan. 24, 1880), "regards the bill with great reserve."[11] To the official press was assigned the task of creating the impression of an immediate peril. While Bismarck privately assured France that the bill contained nothing to alarm her (for it was Russia's armaments that required counter-measures), that he would caution the government's speakers not to use the specter of a French attack,[12] the *Norddeutsche* (Feb. 12) cited the numerical superiority of the French army, the eighty per cent increase in France's military budget since 1870, and the chauvinist sentiments of Catholic and Monarchist journals to prove that the army bill could not rightly be charged with the responsibility for an armament race. "It follows from the attitude of these parties," it concluded, "that they will plunge France into war as soon as they attain power in order to maintain themselves in control with the aid of Bonapartist methods." After an ominous reference to Russia's intrigues (Feb. 19), it

---

[10] *Verhandlungen,* IV Leg. Per., III Sess., I, 182, 183.
[11] Cf. *Post,* Jan. 25.
[12] Saint-Vallier, Feb. 10. *D. D. F.,* (1), III, 19, 22, 23.

asserted (Feb. 23): "The colossal armaments of both countries
. . . must therefore mean an aggressive policy."[13] Treitschke's organ painted an even darker picture.   France's true aims,
it wrote, were not to be found in the peaceful tone of the moderate Republican press, for that was a blind to conceal the intention of choosing a suitable moment for the *revanche.* "We
must not deceive ourselves; we are on the verge and are perhaps already in a world which will require us to stake our existence as a nation and as a world power."[14]

Bismarck explained his motives with cynical frankness.   To
Hohenlohe, then in Berlin, he said that he had written the
Norddeutsche's (Feb. 23) article merely to win votes for the army
bill.   "He laughed," wrote Hohenlohe in his diary, "when I
explained its effect."[15]   The French ambassador was told that
it had been necessary to choose between the press and the tribune
and that in any event the alarm would cease with the bill's
passage.   "Given the state of sentiment in Germany," Bismarck
added, "it was absolutely necessary to stir up opinion."   As a
demonstration of his continued good-will, he assured France that
he wished to act in complete accord with her and Austria in
Near Eastern questions,[16] and it was doubtless on his suggestion
that the Emperor and Empress dined at the French embassy for
the first time since 1870.[17]   Confident of the Reichstag's approval
of the bill, he directed the *Norddeutsche* (Feb. 24.) to reverse its
position within twenty-four hours by acknowledging that Russia's fortifications were no more valid as evidence of aggressive
purposes that Germany's forts in Königsberg or Posen.   This
was too much even for the press.   "The conduct of the official
journals," said the *National Zeitung* (Feb. 25), "becomes each
day more amazing."   The National Liberal *Magdeburgische
Zeitung* (Feb. 25) reminded the government's press bureau of
its responsibilities and condemned its latest exploit as "a base
and irresponsible deception of public opinion."   Conservatives

---

[13] Not a word did it say of the dynamiting of the Winter Palace in St. Petersburg only
a few days earlier, for it would not have fitted into the picture of a dangerous Russia.
[14] *P. J.*, vol. 45, pp. 206–223 (Feb. 11, 1880).
[15] Hohenlohe, *Denkwürdigkeiten*, II, 290 (Feb. 22, 1880).
[16] Saint-Vallier, Feb. 25.   *D. D. F.*, (1), III, 29–32.
[17] Saint-Vallier, Feb. 29.   *Ibid.*, (1), III, 41.

approved the moderate *Vossische Zeitung*'s (Feb. 26) sharp criticism. "Faced by such conduct," wrote the reactionary *Reichsbote* (Feb. 26), "one stands in amazement and asks, 'What does it mean?'" The *Kreuz-Zeitung* (Feb. 26) recalled the *Post's* scare article of 1875 and characterised the *Norddeutsche's* attitude as destructive of public confidence.

The lessening of foreign tension now permitted the full expression of partisan sentiment on domestic questions. A period of intense party strife began. As the *Kulturkampf* declined after 1878, its place was taken by Bismarck's attempt to destroy the Social Democratic party. Anti-Socialist laws became pawns in the shuffling and reshuffling of party groups in the Reichstag. The Progressives believed that the time had come to liberalize united Germany, and, after Bismarck broke with the National Liberals in 1878 on the protective tariff, the left wing of that party joined the Progressives in support of a responsible ministry. Bismarck's tax recommendations met an obstinate resistance that eventually suggested to him the limitation of the universal franchise. In this mood, the liberals were not impressed when the official *Provinzial-Correspondenz* (Sept. 21, 1881) announced that the nation's gratitude to Bismarck for his services in uniting Germany and in maintaining peace against untold dangers would decide the Reichstag elections (October 1881). A vote against the Bismarck ministry, it declared, would undermine the foundations of peace. According to the *Norddeutsche* (Oct. 9), a success for the Progressives would lead to increased instead of diminished military burdens, because their political ineptitude would soon involve the country in serious foreign complications. Although the *Volks-Zeitung* (Aug. 25), acknowledging the nation's indebtedness to Bismarck's foreign policy, concentrated its attack upon his domestic policy, and although Catholic *Germania* (Sept. 22) admitted the possibility of critical developments in foreign affairs in the event of Bismarck's fall, still the National Liberal press insisted that credit was also due to its party and to the nation in general. "The reaper was Bismarck," the *Magdeburgische Zeitung* (July 3, 1881) asserted, "but the sower was German liberalism. Without its patient work, there would have been no harvest." It protested (Sept. 22) against the introduction of foreign affairs into an election whose issues were primarily domestic; it indignantly denied that a vote for the same National Liberal principles which Bismarck had approved in the sixties would endanger peace. Bismarck's failure to establish an alliance with Austria and Turkey during the Near Eastern crisis, wrote the *Kölnische Zeitung* (Sept. 27), had surrounded Germany with enemies, for Russia's crushing defeat of Turkey had freed her hands in that direction. The moderate *Vossische Zeitung* (Sept. 25) likewise thought that too much credit had been given Bismarck; Germany's military strength, her need of peace, the Emperor's aversion to war, the incompleteness of France's military preparations, and the revolutionary movement in Russia had all helped to keep the peace. Although the results of the election were completely satisfactory neither to the government nor to the liberals, the latter's gains were sufficiently important for the official press to argue from the favorable reaction abroad, especially in France, that Germany had been weakened.[18]

In the meantime, the agitation for colonial expansion was attaining the proportions of a national movement. As late as February 15, 1879, the *National Zeitung* argued that Germany's energies could be more profitably employed in colonizing her own undeveloped territory, and the Conservative *Post* (March 15, 1879) commented unfavorably upon Dr. Friedrich Fabri's *Bedarf Deutschland der Kolonien?* (Gotha, 1879),[19] one of the most influential propagandist pamphlets of the agitation. Thenceforth progress was rapid. For the influential industrialists, who required assured sources of raw materials and larger markets, nothing could be more desirable than colonies where both might be found under the protection of the German flag, since the trend toward protective tariffs abroad threatened the free development of German trade. Colonies also offered a theoretical outlet for the surplus population which was being

---

[18] The increase of the Progressive vote since the election of 1877 was larger than that of any other party, and the total vote of that party, with that of the *Freisinnige Vereinigung*, its ally on the constitutional question, was only slightly less than that of the Center, whose popular vote was the largest. *Frankfurter Zeitung*, July 17, 1882.

[19] This pamphlet, according to a leading German authority on Bismarck's colonial policy, gave the first impulse to the movement for expansion. For an analysis of its contents, see M. von Hagen, *Bismarcks Kolonialpolitik* (Stuttgart, 1923), pp. 25, 26.

drained off chiefly to the United States. That the unclaimed areas suitable for white settlement and for agricultural purposes were limited failed to discourage the use of this favorite argument. Tropical colonies would provide careers for the young men of the middle classes who could find no attractive openings at home. These influences were at work in other countries, but Germany was alone in her total lack of colonies. Although it placed her at a tremendous disadvantage in the new period of imperialism, this handicap was an ally in the conversion of public opinion. Germany had gone through none of the disillusioning experiences of colonial administration which assured a strong, if unsuccessful, opposition to imperialism in other countries. The enthusiasm elsewhere aroused by such resounding phrases as "the white man's burden," a *"mission civilisatrice"* was created in Germany by arguments that resembled the American slogan "manifest destiny." That colonies were necessary to complete her stature as a great power, that they were the just reward for her achievements, were constantly recurring themes. After a period of satisfaction with political unity, many Germans suddenly awoke to a feeling that without colonies they were somehow inferior to Englishmen and Frenchmen. Thought in terms of overseas possessions was natural for a people whose commerce had already penetrated to the ends of the earth, whose sons and daughters had played a considerable part in the settlement of the New World, and whose press made a specialty of exhaustive reports from distant lands.

Public opinion was ready to respond to this new challenge to the nation's energies. A vague feeling of chagrin that no further obstacles remained to be conquered had followed, as a German historian has recently written, the attainment of political unity.[20] The Progressives insisted, of course, that the most important of all problems remained, that of adding *Freiheit* to *Einheit,* but this constitutional problem aroused little enthusiasm. They were encouraged by the prospect of a new régime under the Crown Prince and his English consort but they never succeeded in restoring the earlier union between middle-class liberalism and na-

---

[20] H. Oncken, *Das Deutsche Reich und die Vorgeschichte des Weltkrieges,* 2 vols. (Leipzig, 1933), I, 123.

tional sentiment with its more effective emotional appeal, while the working classes were rapidly going over to the social revolutionary philosophy of Marxian Socialism. Not many, even among the middle classes, were willing to risk the consequences of another constitutional conflict with Bismarck and the conservative forces of the nation. Colonial expansion struck a far more responsive chord, especially when Bismarck began to take an interest in it, for the idea certainly occurred to the National Liberal leaders that it might serve as a bridge for a retreat from their uncomfortable association with the opposition. The agitation was most successful at first in the industrialized districts of the Rhineland, Central and South Germany, while the free-trade sentiment of the ports and the agricultural interests of old Prussia was critical. Windthorst was one of many to note that the colonial fever varied directly with the distance from the sea.[21] The German Colonial Society (*Deutsche Kolonialverein*) was founded in Frankfort in 1882 (the same year which saw the organization of the *Ligue des Patriotes* in France) and the majority of its branches were established in Central and South Germany. In spite of the sectional origins of the movement, its speakers and weekly organ, the *Deutsche Kolonialzeitung,* addressed themselves to the nation irrespective of party or regional differences.

The prospects were not at first encouraging. The abandonment of the Great Elector's station on the West coast of Africa in the seventeenth century left Prussia with empty hands at the close of the first wave of imperialist expansion in the next century. The Portuguese, Spanish, and Dutch Empires rose and declined, the French won and lost an empire, and England had long since become the greatest of the naval and colonial powers, but the flag of the new Germany in 1871 covered not an inch of colonial territory. In Bismarck's hands lay the decision as to whether or not Germany should share in the partition of Africa foreshadowed by the French protectorate in Tunis (1881) and the British occupation of Egypt (1882), and whether or not Germany would participate in the division of the islands of the

---

[21] *Verhandlungen,* V Leg. Per., IV Sess., II, 1054, 1055 (June 26, 1884).

South Seas. Heretofore he had not regarded colonial expansion as within the range of practical politics. Germany, in his opinion, was too poor to afford colonial extravagances and her position in Europe too exposed to risk the additional animosities which might be expected from a policy of expansion. He reserved the future by giving the governments of the North German Confederation and of the Empire the power to acquire colonies in the constitutions of 1866 and 1871, but his failure to act upon the petitions for the acquisition of French colonial territory during the peace negotiations in 1871 was a more significant index to his intentions. Nevertheless, even Bismarck was not immune to the forces behind the colonial agitation. The increasing financial burdens of a military empire placed a premium upon its industrial and commercial development. His anti-Socialist laws, although intended for other purposes as well, served the interests of the employers. Still more important, for it was the first significant use of the state's power in behalf of industry, was the adoption of the protective tariff in 1878. That the industrialists as a group favored colonial expansion was therefore a fairly good assurance of his benevolent interest.[22]

From the first he had left a clear field to the colonial agitation. He privately told its leaders that nothing could be done without the clear support of public opinion,[23] but the official press gave more and more space to the reports of their speeches and meetings. Political and diplomatic circumstances, far more than the pressure of opinion, doubtless explain his partial conversion. It was hastened by the Reichstag's opposition to his domestic policies and by England's obstructive tactics against divers imperialist projects of a comparatively minor character. In April (1881) the Progressives were largely responsible for the defeat of his proposal to subsidize the *Deutsche See-Handelsgesellschaft* for the salvaging of the bankrupt Godeffroy enterprises in the

---

[22] While Hagen concludes that no final judgment as to Bismarck's early attitude toward colonial expansion is possible until all of the archival evidence is evaluated, he clearly inclines in favor of the traditional view as stated above. Professor Townsend believes, however, that he was converted at an early date and that he refrained from adopting a colonial policy for opportunist reasons. Hagen, *Bismarcks Kolonialpolitik*, p. 45; M. E. Townsend, *The Rise and Fall of Germany's Colonial Empire* (N. Y. 1930), p. 60.

[23] Townsend, *op. cit.*, p. 76.

South Seas and, in 1884, of a still more definitely imperialist bill to subsidize a steamship line to the Far East. That the Reichstag's opposition was an incident in the struggle for a constitutional ministry was not of course calculated to check his drift toward colonial expansion. The movement's increasing popularity recommended it as an ally against the Reichstag's factious opposition and as a means of conciliating the considerable part of the middle classes which the protective tariff had alienated. The opposition of the Progressives, the *Freisinnige Vereinigung,* and the National Liberals meant a dangerous cleft between the government and the middle classes. Of at least equal importance was the growing friction with England, which was intensified by Bismarck's dislike and suspicion of the Gladstone government. Her delay in settling the claims arising from the ejection of German merchants from the Fiji Islands as long ago as 1875 was a long-standing grievance. In reality England's attitude was not so much the result of systematic ill-will as of a failure to estimate correctly the importance Bismarck attached to these questions. His repeated denials of any interest in colonies helps to explain, if not to justify, Granville's failure to act promptly when Bismarck asked if England would protect Lüderitz' enterprises in Angra Pequena and then if she claimed the region beyond the bounds of Walfisch Bay. The foreign office turned the second request over to Lord Derby at the colonial office, whence it was leisurely forwarded to the Cape, where a change of governments, with other circumstances, delayed the answer month after month. Pressed for action by the energetic Bremen merchants and irritated by England's silence, he finally ordered the German consul at Cape Town to place Angra Pequena under Germany's protection (April 24, 1884).

Bismarck soon found an occasion to assure moderate opinion and the interested foreign powers that official support would be given only to enterprises initiated by private individuals or groups and that Germany's resources would not be dissipated in a reckless search for unclaimed territory. Like most Germans, he believed that the difficulties with England in Angra Pequena, the Cameroons, East Africa, and in the Pacific meant that Germany must expect her selfish and obstinate resistance everywhere. England seemed to be developing a kind of Monroe Doctrine in Africa. Her apparently systematic obstruction should have occasioned no surprise, for it was quite in character with the motives which most Germans had always attributed to her. The shock was nevertheless severe, for the colonial propaganda had usually ignored the effect of expansion upon Germany's foreign relations. In 1890—that is, after he had launched Germany as a colonial power—Bismarck is said, on his son's

Kladderadatsch, November 2, 1884.

Figure 6.—In a word:
England has grown so fat that she can't button her coat!

(Herbert's) authority, to have explained his colonial policy as a means of making the Crown Prince's English sympathies powerless for harm by the friction it would cause with England,[24] but this Machiavellian purpose was perhaps an afterthought. One of his objections to a colonial policy had always been the danger that it would antagonize England and therefore add unnecessarily to Germany's problems. In any event, once committed to the acquisition of colonies, Bismarck, like the greater part of German opinion, felt that England's irritation was not a legiti-

[24] Ziekursch, *Politische Geschichte,* II, 156–158.

mate argument against expansion and that the question should be decided on its own merits. He intended that Germany's new activities should be kept within well-defined limits, but it was by no means certain that circumstances, the mounting pressure of the colonial agitation, and his own irritation with England would permit this in the long run. Windthorst was one of the few who publicly called attention to the probably fateful consequences. "Germany," he told the Reichstag (Jan. 19, 1885), "has taken a step which will make her a sea power . . . with a fleet, in my opinion, equal to the strongest in the world." He even foresaw that events "would justify or force Germany to take up arms against England." Bismarck quite properly condemned the Centrist leader for raising the specter of war, for it was evidently not his intention to use more forceful methods than diplomatic pressure to secure respect for Germany's interests, and he assured the Reichstag that serious injury to Anglo-German relations could always be avoided by skilful diplomacy.[25] Even then (Jan. 19, 1885) he was showing how this could be done by his clever manipulation of Germany's relations with the two Western powers, but Windthorst's predictions proved to be more accurate under Bismarck's less adroit successors.

For almost a year after the Angra Pequena affair, Bismarck was strongly influenced by his difficulties with England. For this reason his attempt to conciliate France became a factor of primary importance. It is therefore useful at this point to discuss this development more carefully than was possible in the preceding chapter. Its beginnings dated only from the fairly secure establishment in power of the Republican parties. France was informed in unmistakable terms that a Republican government was an essential condition of his favor, but it is extremely doubtful that it was thereby strengthened, especially as his goodwill was consistently offered with the reservation that France must renounce Alsace-Lorraine.[26] His refusal to participate in the Paris Exposition of 1878, in spite of the favorable reaction of German opinion, was meant as a stroke against the MacMahon

[25] *Verhandlungen,* VI Leg. Per., I Sess., I, 530–539 (Jan. 10, 1885).

[26] *N. A. Z.,* Jan. 16, 1876. The French, wrote the *Volks-Zeitung* (Oct. 18, 1877), could easily see that the official press favored the Republic, because it would be a source of weakness for France.

government.[27] To impress upon the French electorate the importance of a Republican victory in the October elections of 1877, a result which Bismarck thought would be facilitated by representing the Republican parties as standing for peace,[28] the *Norddeutsche* (Sept. 2) explained that the best guarantee of an enduring peace with Germany would be France's emancipation "from the ultramontanist yoke and the establishment of that form of government which would cause the least partisan strife." The possibility of a *coup d'état* moved Bismarck to suggest that the press should discuss the calling of the Reichstag to consider the situation.[29] Fortunately MacMahon accepted the verdict of the election, with the result that Gontaut-Biron, who had always been a thorn in Bismarck's flesh, was replaced at the French embassy in Berlin by the more businesslike and therefore the more acceptable Saint-Vallier. In Paris, Decazes was followed by Waddington, whose English ancestry, American wife, German brothers-in-law, and Protestant faith offered some promise of a less nationalist point of view at the Quai d'Orsay. This change of personnel was completed in 1879 by the election of the moderate Grévy to the presidency.

Saint-Vallier's arrival in Berlin in the spring of 1878 drew from Bismarck his belated approval of a selection of paintings from the German galleries for the Paris Exposition, as a reply to France's friendly *carte de visite*. Suspicion was, however, too deeply imbedded in the minds of Germans to be entirely eradicated by the success of the Republicans, who were indeed regarded by the Catholics as the real *revanche* party.[30] Many continued to believe that all Frenchmen, regardless of party distinctions, were devotees of the *revanche*. Even the aversion of French opinion to an active participation in foreign affairs was considered an abnormal and objectionable preoccupation with

---

[27] *Kölnische Zeitung*, April 6, 1876; *National Zeitung*, March 29; *Volks-Zeitung*, Sept. 16. Achenbach, the minister of commerce, wrote in the *N. A. Z.* (Sept. 24, 1876) as if Germany's participation had been decided. Relatively insignificant incidents in Paris were used as the excuse for the Bundesrat's negative decision, December 6, 1876 (*Provinzial-Correspondenz* Dec. 13), and the formal announcement misrepresented the facts by claiming an unfavorable reaction of public opinion.

[28] Bismarck, June 29, 1877. *G. P.*, I, 324–327.

[29] Busch, *Tagebuchblätter*, II, 485 (Oct. 11, 1877).

[30] *Historisch-Politische Blätter*, vol. 81, p. 120 (1880).

the results of 1870.[31]   The unpopularity of France's participation in the Congress of Berlin irritated the *Norddeutsche* (March 8, 1878), whose correspondent wrote of the pride of the Parisians in the success of the Exposition as merely another form of the *revanche*.[32]   The popular demonstration for the army, July 14, 1880, when Grévy presented its new flags, betrayed to nationalist observers traces of "entirely different ideas" from those of the President's inoffensive speech.[33]   The revival of the organized *revanche* sentiment in the early eighties was closely watched by the German press.   Gambetta's famous appeal to an "immanent justice" in his Cherbourg speech (Aug. 9, 1881), and to the "majesty of right and justice" in his Belleville speech a few weeks later, caused his political opponents in France and many Germans to cry, *"Gambetta, c'est la guerre!"* [34]   Bismarck spoke of a Gambetta ministry as certain to have the effect upon Europe of the beating of a drum in a sick man's chamber.   Nevertheless, *la grande ministère* came and went the way of many French cabinets, bringing neither war nor an explosion of chauvinist sentiment in France or Germany, although its defeat after a few months was appreciated.[35]   Déroulède and the League of Patriots—organized in 1882 ostensibly to supplement the work of the national system of elementary schools under the Ferry laws for the development of patriotic sentiment—occasioned more astonishment than alarm.   The *National Zeitung* (Sept. 8, 1882) thought it necessary to warn its readers not to be deceived by the comic element in Déroulède's postures, since abnormal personalities always played a part in popular movements in France. That German opinion was able to view the situation with some equanimity was due not only to its confidence in Germany's military and diplomatic strength but also to its recognition that

---

[31] *Kölnische Zeitung*, Feb. 3, 1879.

[32] *N. A. Z.*, May 4, 1878.   An army officer who was soon to have the ear of Prince William, later William II, believed, after a visit to the Exposition, that the *revanche* would be attempted soon after 1880.   Waldersee, *Denkwürdigkeiten*, I, 179.

[33] *National Zeitung*, July 15.   The Progressive *Volks-Zeitung* (July 16) paid a high tribute to France's contributions to civilization and liberty.

[34] The reaction in Germany stressed Germany's will to defend herself.   *Kladderadatsch*, Sept. 4, 1881.

[35] "Gambetta und die Lage in Frankreich," *Grenzboten*, 1881, II, 261.   Grévy's peaceful disposition and the ministry's program of domestic reforms reassured Treitschke's organ.   *P. J.*, vol. 49, p. 212 (Feb. 13, 1881).

France's disappointment in Egypt, that the economic effect of Germany's industrial superiority, and that the influence of Alsatian exiles contributed to chauvinist sentiment as well as hatred of Germany.

Nevertheless, had it not been for Bismarck's policy of conciliation, which accounts for the generally reserved attitude of the official press, the reaction to these events would doubtless have been less moderate. He was lavish with assurances that Gambetta's accession to power would not affect his desire for good relations,[36] and he was as willing to meet Gambetta as he had been in 1878.[37] No complaints, he directed, should be made to the French authorities after the League's attack upon a German *Turnverein* in Paris, "for such things are better ignored," and he asked that the press should not give unusual attention to the incident.[38] His patient and accommodating attitude was not at first intended to win France's support for Germany in any diplomatic problem, but, as he explained more than once, to divert her attention from the Rhine. In an exceptionally sane discussion of Franco-German relations, the moderate *Vossische Zeitung* (June 8, 1876) predicted that the success of the Republicans would mean in the long run a cautious foreign policy, since moderation in domestic affairs would eventually discourage any desire for warlike adventures. "We neither ask nor desire anything more." Desirous of more substantial and speedier results, Bismarck extended to France, though in a different form, his policy of aiding those countries whose support was useful or whose hostility he wished to disarm. He was careful to assure her that the Austro-German alliance was not directed against France,[39] and he encouraged and supported not only her colonial but to a certain extent her diplomatic activities. France had his good-will when she departed from her diplomatic reserve in 1881, for the first time, to support the Greeks in their

---

[36] Ternaux-Compans, St. Petersburg, Sept. 16, 1881. *D. D. F.,* (1), IV, 129; Saint-Vallier, Oct. 3. *Ibid.,* (1), IV, 147–151; Hatzfeldt, Nov. 15. *G. P.,* III, 402; H. Bismarck, Nov. 16. *Ibid.,* III, 402.

[37] Lothar Bucher, one of his satellites in the foreign office, anticipated with much satisfaction the end of Gambetta's career if the interview occurred. Busch, *Tagebuchblätter,* III, 54 (Oct. 25).

[38] Busch, Sept. 16, 1882. *G. P.,* III, 404.

[39] de Bort, Vienna, Sept. 26, 1879. *D. D. F.,* (1), II, 561, 562.

efforts to secure a more favorable frontier in Thrace, according to a promise in the Treaty of Berlin. The German delegate at the Madrid Conference (1880) helped her to secure equality of commercial opportunity in Morocco with the powers there represented. From his diplomatic support of France's colonial enterprises in Tunis, Madagascar, and Tonkin, he counted upon a twofold advantage to Germany: the diversion of France's attention from the Vosges, and the friction resulting therefrom between France and the countries whose interests were adversely affected. He confessed during the Tunis affair that "it is to our interest if they [Italy and England vs. France] are at odds." [40] In Morocco he saw an invaluable source of difficulty between France and England, which should never be sacrificed. [41]

His promises to back France "from Guinea to Belgium" and to support "her legitimate policy of expansion in the Mediterranean" were usually followed by positive action. [42] It was precisely in the Egyptian question, upon which the French felt most keenly, that his support was entirely withdrawn or offered with unacceptable conditions. The development of Bismarck's policy and of German opinion in this connection deserves attention in view of the importance of Egypt in his diplomatic campaign against England after the Angra Pequena affair and its part in his policy of conciliation. His approval of the Anglo-French dual control of Egyptian finances, [43] as an occasion for that friendship between them which he valued as a check upon France's chauvinism and British imperialism, suddenly ended with Gambetta's and Granville's joint note (January 1882) to Ismail Pasha, the Khedive, encouraging his resistance to Arabi Bey, the leader of the Egyptian nationalists. [44] From the joint intervention therein foreshadowed, Bismarck expected either a dangerously intimate diplomatic association, in which French influence would predominate, or differences which might lead to war. He had, nevertheless, as little liking for separate action by either country, for that might even more seriously endanger

[40] Busch, *Tagebuchblätter*, III, 37, 38 (May 4, 1881).
[41] Bismarck, June 16, 1884. *G. P.*, III, 412.
[42] Bismarck, April 8, 1880; Busch, July 16, 1881. *Ibid.*, III, 395, 396, 401.
[43] *D. D. F.*, (1), II, 450, 451, 474, 475.
[44] Hatzfeldt, Jan. 15, 1882. *G. P.*, IV, 30, 31.

peace, besides placing Germany in an uncomfortable position between the two powers. As between their respective claims, he favored those of England, since Egypt, on account of the Suez Canal, was in his opinion a more vital interest to England than to France. "It is like the nerve," he told Busch, "that unites the spine with the brain." [45] To avoid these pitfalls and to keep Egypt as a kind of Alsace-Lorraine between the two countries, Bismarck threw his influence in favor of Turkey's intervention at the Constantinople Conference, which England and France had summoned largely because of the latter's desire for a mandate for their joint action. Dread of its disturbing effect upon her Mohammedan subjects in Algeria and Tunis made Turkey's intervention the least acceptable solution to France, but he refused to compromise Germany's recently acquired influence with the Sultan by any pressure in France's behalf. [46]

In July 1882, without waiting for the Conference to conclude its long-winded and perhaps futile discussions, England bombarded Alexandria, destroyed the forts there, and landed troops to protect the lives of Europeans, alleging the need of immediate action. German no less than French opinion rose in wrath. England had broken her word, said the *Kölnische Zeitung* (July 11), assuming the leadership of the anti-English chorus which it was to retain for years, not to act alone for the duration of the Conference. The renown of the British lion, according to the Catholic *Germania* (July 15), had been buried under the ruins of Alexandria. "It is high time," it added, "to tear away the hypocritical veil of 'humanity' and 'civilization' from British policy, and in the interest of all Europe and of the subject peoples under England's domination to reveal the naked, cold egoism of England's *Krämerpolitik*." True to its traditional friendship for England, the Progressive *Volks-Zeitung* (July 16) defended her on the ground that her strength was essential to the cause of progress and liberalism, but it admitted that the majority of the Progressive newspapers had joined her maligners. Not until ample time had elapsed for the full expression of this indignation did Bismarck intervene to prevent too

---

[45] Busch, *Tagebuchblätter*, III, 84–86 (June 9, 1882).
[46] Courcel, June 16, 1882. *D. D. F.*, (1), IV, 367.

drastic a disturbance of the balance he wished to maintain between England and France. The *Norddeutsche* (July 17) recommended reserve and good relations with all, since Germany's
interests were not involved; and it condemned the *Kölnische
Zeitung's* stand on the ground that its normal support of the government would mislead other countries as to Germany's real
policy. An obviously inspired communication in the *Kölnische
Zeitung* (July 17) likewise advised moderation, but by assuring
England that Germany would welcome any agreement satisfactory to France, it suggested an identity between French and
German interests.[47] It even hinted that, under certain circumstances, Germany might intervene. Only by an attitude of reserve, it said, "will Germany be able to say the decisive word at
a suitable moment." For once, the *Volks-Zeitung* (July 21)
was pleased by the use of official influence on the press, but
opinion gradually crystallized in support of the essential solidarity of European interests against England's. "Will Europe,"
asked the *Germania* (July 23), "permit the boundless egoism of
this people to assume the leading rôle in Egypt and, at that, in its
name?" Already, Treitschke's organ had declared for a settlement by the European powers.[48]

The prospects, in the opinion of the liberal *Frankfurter Zeitung*
(July 19), were excellent for the coöperation of the powers under
the leadership of France and Germany. Overestimating the
courage of the French Chambers, it expected them to grant Freycinet, the President of the Council and foreign minister, the necessary credits for the occupation of the Suez Canal. Freycinet,
however, turned in vain to Bismarck for his indispensable aid in
securing a European mandate from the Conference, which alone
might quiet the fears of a panicky public opinion. To his repeated
pleas, Bismarck replied that he would neither openly oppose a
mandate nor support it in public, out of consideration for Turkey.[49]
The French statesman therefore had nothing at hand before the
decisive vote, July 29, by which the Chamber rejected the credits
for active participation with England, except Bismarck's make-

---

[47] This was the *Frankfurter Zeitung's* (July 17) interpretation of the article.
[48] *P. J.*, vol. 50, p. 100 (July 13, 1882).
[49] Courcel, July 20, 1882. *D. D. F.*, (1), IV, 437.

shift proposal that each power should use its warships to protect the transit of its own ships through the canal.[50]   Whatever his motives, Bismarck's withdrawal of his support at this critical juncture left England alone in Egypt and gave Frenchmen some reason to believe that he would always retreat after maneuvering France into an advanced position.

The Egyptian question nevertheless continued to be a potential basis for Franco-German coöperation as long as France refused to recognize England's exclusive occupation.   German opinion was still favorable to action in defense of European, if not French, interests, and especially for the restraint of British imperialism, in spite of the evident disappointment that followed the negative vote of the French parliament.[51]   "Only by a European cure, not under England's yoke," declared the *National Zeitung* (Aug. 6), "can Egypt find health."   It still hoped (Aug. 17) that the powers would be clever and strong enough to curb England's unbearably pretentious spirit.   "England talks big," wrote the Catholic *Germania* (Aug. 9), "the powers are silent even when incontestable rights are sacrificed.   The proud Briton is becoming still prouder.   *Wie lange noch?*"   The *Kölnische Zeitung* (Aug. 4) regretted "that European diplomacy had accepted the shameful act (*Schandthat*)" at Alexandria without a protest; for it expected the British lion, "now that it had tasted the nourishing blood of the weak," to gorge itself until the entire Near Eastern question would be reopened.   This movement of opinion reached its logical conclusion in the *Preussische Jahrbücher's* warning that England would do well not to count too much upon Germany's reserve.   "It depends largely upon herself," it declared, "whether England repeats Russia's experiences at the Congress of Berlin." [52]

Courcel, the French ambassador, accepted this trend of opinion as a reliable index to Bismarck's policy.   "Germany," he wrote, "is preparing the stage with rare skill for the definitive settlement of the Egyptian question. . . .   His methods are those of 1876 and 1877, when Russia was quietly led from the triumph of San Stefano to the disillusionments of the Treaty of Berlin." [53]   The

[50] Freycinet, July 27; Courcel, July 28.   *D. D. F.,* (1), IV, 455, 460, 461.
[51] *Magdeburgische Zeitung,* Aug. 1; *National Zeitung,* Aug. 3.
[52] *P. J.,* vol. 50, p. 201 (Aug. 19).
[53] Courcel, Aug. 20.   *D. D. F.,* (1), IV, 487–490.

absence of documentary evidence as to Bismarck's attitude for some weeks after the vote of July 29 is itself evidence of a kind that Courcel had misinterpreted a watchful reserve for a deep-laid plan for England's undoing. In spite of his dislike of the Gladstone government, Bismarck had nothing to gain at this moment by leading or by participating in a diplomatic campaign against England. France's obvious reluctance to challenge her was itself a reason for reserve. If the press scented a disposition in Paris to arrange matters directly with England,[54] it is reasonable to assume, especially in view of the concern with which he had always regarded a too intimate Anglo-French understanding, that Bismarck was equally alert. In December 1882, explaining to Prince William the current friendliness toward England, he said that it was necessary "to prevent an alliance between France and England and to divide them if possible. That is the key to German policy."[55] England met the danger of European complications while engaged in Egypt by friendly advances to both France and Germany. The *Times* assured France of England's desire to consider her interests, since an "Anglo-French alliance" was more important than Egypt, but the Prince of Wales spoke to the Crown Prince, who at once informed Bismarck, of the growing feeling in England that a close association with Germany would be the most effective guarantee of peace.[56] This was a welcome opportunity for Bismarck to clarify his position in the Egyptian question. Dismissing the anti-English tone of the German press as a typical example of the tendency of Germans to interfere and of their penchant for homiletics, and even as being the product of "foreign money," he assured England that he had no intention of playing the game of "other powers" by quarreling with her if she exceeded the limits which, in his opinion, moderation should fix for her policy. He pledged Germany's and Austria's friendship, but he declined an alliance with thanks because there could be no guarantee of its permanence under the British parliamentary system and because it would endanger his good relations

---

[54] *P. J.*, vol. 50, 319 (Sept. 9); *Kölnische Zeitung*, Sept. 23; *Volks-Zeitung*, Nov. 19.
[55] Ballhausen, *Bismarck-Erinnerungen*, p. 243 (Dec. 16).
[56] Frederick William, Sept. 4, 1882. *G. P.*, IV, 31, 32.

with Russia and France.[57] No conceivable developments in Egypt, in his opinion, would be so disadvantageous to Germany as a permanent offense to British national sentiment.[58] Nor was he satisfied with these assurances. During his conversations in London at this time, Herbert Bismarck came close to encouraging England to annex Egypt. His father thought, he said, that England could avoid many difficulties by working through Turkey, but if she "should prefer to annex Egypt, she would not meet with opposition from Germany. The solid and lasting friendship of the British Empire is much more important to us than the fate of Egypt." [59]

Reports of England's desire for an alliance were coolly received by the German press. A frequently inspired periodical pointed to the necessary instability of an alliance with a country where a hostile government might rise to power at any time.[60] Much was made of England's supposed unreliability. Bitter experience, according to the *National Zeitung* (Oct. 1, 1882), had shown that England's military support could not be depended upon. Even Germany's friends in England would neither have the power nor probably the desire, according to the Conservative *Post* (Dec. 17, 1882), "to assure her active intervention on Germany's side." In fact, it was better, wrote the *Preussische Jahrbücher,* that Germany should not commit herself to England in any respect, because her friendship and her hostility would be equally unimportant in a war. Her financial support was no longer essential, her army was too small for operations on the continent, and even her fleet would not save Germany if the latter's own armies were defeated. England's inaccessibility to a continental enemy would enable her to withdraw at any time, whereas Germany's very existence would be at stake. "John Bull has so conducted himself toward his cousin Michel," it concluded, "that the latter has every reason to expect ingratitude for fighting in his interest." [61] It must nevertheless have been obvious to French

---

[57] Bismarck, Sept. 7. *G. P.,* IV, 32–34. *Cf.* Rothfels, *Bismarcks englische Bündnispolitik,* pp. 73, 74.

[58] Busch, Sept. 7. *G. P.,* IV, 34, 35.

[59] *Ibid.,* IV, 36, 37 (Sept.).

[60] "Aegypten und die Allianzgerüchte." *Grenzboten,* 1882, IV, 110, 111.

[61] "England und Deutschland," *P. J.,* vol. 51, pp. 1–8 (Jan., 1883).

observers that Germany's support in Egypt was not available. The official *Norddeutsche* (Oct. 27, 1882) again disavowed the *Kölnische Zeitung's* persistently anti-English tone; [62] it asserted, however, that the government had at first been England's sole friend in Germany. "Under no circumstances will the Eastern powers," said the *Grenzboten*, "help the French to recover the position they have renounced by not participating in the war." [63] Less obviously inspired publications affirmed Germany's willingness to accept any settlement satisfactory to England which would not endanger the peace of Europe or lead to the dissolution of the Turkish Empire.[64]

The crisis left relations between the three powers essentially unchanged. The trend of German opinion in favor of a union of the continental powers against England had been checked by France's failure to defend her own interests and, perhaps to a less extent, by Bismarck's reserve. Public attention was soon recalled to the more familiar Russian peril and to French chauvinism. The brief campaign against Russia in December 1882 is one of the less-known instances of Bismarck's use of the press to stir up alarm. Criticism of the Austro-German alliance among the Magyars on the ground that Hungary had no interest in a Franco-German war and among the Slavs because they preferred an Austro-Russian offensive against Turkey for the partition of the Balkans,[65] uncertainty as to the purpose of Giers' (Gorchakov's successor's) visit to Vienna (Nov. 1882), and the nervousness of the military authorities in Germany at Russia's armaments probably explain Bismarck's decision to exert pressure upon Russia.[66] At any rate, the *Kölnische Zeitung* (Dec. 13) announced that Austria and Germany were not united by a general understanding but by a formal alliance signed by the two sovereigns, that its duration was for five years, that its renewal was certain before its expiration (October 15, 1884), and that (doubtless for the benefit of the Magyars) the *casus foederis* would

---

[62] Its admonition was approved by the Progressive *Volks-Zeitung* (Oct. 31) and the Conservative *Kreuz-Zeitung* (Oct. 28).

[63] "Die Lage in Frankreich," *Grenzboten*, 1882, IV, 59.

[64] *Deutsche Rundschau*, vol. 33, p. 162 (Sept. 1882); *National Zeitung*, Oct. 1.

[65] *Kölnische Zeitung*, Nov. 21, 1882.

[66] Waldersee, *Denkwürdigkeiten*, I, 223 (Dec. 11, 1882).

arise if either member were attacked by two powers. It hastened
to add, however, that nothing prevented one member from supporting the other if only one power attacked. The same journal
(Dec. 15) then described Russia's feverish construction of railways on the Austrian and German frontiers as possibly indicative
of aggressive designs.[67] Even the *Vossische Zeitung* (Dec. 17),
which usually did not lend its services to such purposes, clipped
a St. Petersburg dispatch from the *Nova Reforma* of Cracow
asserting that Russia was on a war footing. The storm passed
over more quickly than usual. After the appearance in the
German press of Katkov's moderate editorial, the *Norddeutsche*
(Dec. 22) denied that the alarmist deductions were justified by
Russia's railway construction, affirmed Germany's complete confidence in Austro-Hungarian policy, and praised the good relations between the three Emperors. On the same day, the *Kölnische Zeitung* (Dec. 22) was informed from Berlin that its
revelations as to Russia's armaments and the Austro-German
alliance had served their purpose by clearing the air. Again the
use of official influence to stimulate alarm aroused caustic criticism, even by the moderate *Vossische Zeitung* (Dec. 23), notwithstanding its own perhaps unintentional contribution to the
brief war scare.[68]

In 1883 both Bismarck and the military authorities continued
to give their chief attention to Russia's armaments,[69] but it was
against the *revanche* movement in France, in spite of Bismarck's
earlier directions to neglect it, that they aroused public opinion.
That the French chauvinists talked far more of German provocations and of Bismarck's aggressive purposes than of a French
offensive [70] did not make the professional zeal of General Thibaudin, France's energetic minister of war, less suspicious to

[67] Cf. *Kreuz-Zeitung*, Dec. 15. Bismarck, according to Busch, attributed this article
to the military authorities, but the same witness represents him as anticipating a possible
war in 1883. Busch, *Tagebuchblätter*, III, 134 (Dec. 20, 1882).

[68] "Was uns doch nicht alles zugemuthet wird!" wrote the *Germania* (Dec. 28) of a
N. A. Z. article celebrating Bismarck's peace policy. "Erst werden durch blinden
Kriegslärm die Geschäfte lahm gelegt, die Course gedrückt und nachdem so Tausende
von Familien in tiefe Bekümmernis versetzt worden sind, wünscht man
ihnen einen fröhliches Weihnachtsfest!"

[69] Hohenlohe, *Denkwürdigkeiten*, II, 340 (Sept. 6, 1883); Waldersee, *Denkwürdigkeiten*, I, 227 (Sept. 30, 1883).

[70] The Paris correspondent of the *N. A. Z.* (Aug. 23, 1883) admitted the truth of
this interpretation of French public opinion.

German observers or the doings of Déroulède and the League of Patriots less irritating. The German press, according to the *Norddeutsche* (Aug. 22, 1883), had not given much heed to the "ceaseless war" waged by "the newspapers of all parties," but the conclusion was unescapable that the situation could not endure much longer without endangering peace.[71] "What is happening today," it concluded, "illustrates with particular force the truth of the popular saying that when the devil is conjured up too frequently, he actually appears in the end." It was doubtless not a coincidence that the *Kölnische Zeitung* (Aug. 22) decided on the same day that France's fortification of her Eastern frontier betrayed an offensive rather than a defensive psychology, since the forts there could be used as the base for an attack (*Ausfallspforte*). In view of France's greater military effectiveness, German opinion was more easily impressed by the danger of a French than of a Russian attack. Even the Catholic *Germania* (Sept. 5) approved the *Norddeutsche's* article, and the Progressives questioned only the immediacy of the peril.[72] In Paris, Ferry, then at the beginning of his long ministry, asserted that "optimism doesn't pay. *Ce plat aîgre doux donne froid dans le dos.*"[73] As Bismarck doubtless intended, the *Norddeutsche's* article was generally interpreted in France to mean that her fear of an attack might become a reality.[74] Thibaudin at once cancelled his plans for a test mobilization on the Eastern frontier and the press, with one accord, protested that no one in France had advocated an aggressive war.[75] German observers remained skeptical. For the *Magdeburgische Zeitung* (Aug. 29) protestations of innocence illustrated the Jesuitical maxim, *si fecisti, negra,* and the *Post* (Aug. 27), while conceding their sincerity, held that Frenchmen had lost "the capacity of weighing accurately the significance of their own outpourings (*Aus-*

---

[71] d'Aubigny, Berlin, Aug. 22. *D. D. F.*, (1), V, 92, 92. Hohenlohe dutifully defended this indictment of the French press (Hohenlohe, *Denkwürdigkeiten*, II, 340, Aug. 23), but the French officials continued to insist upon its essential injustice. *D. D. F.*, (1), V, 92n.

[72] *Volks-Zeitung*, Aug. 23; *Dresdener Nachrichten*, in *Volks-Zeitung*, Sept. 11.

[73] Challemel-Lacour, Aug. 28. *D. D. F.*, (1), V, 92n.

[74] The official organ in Alsace-Lorraine wrote: "France would not be permitted to select the moment for her attack." *Elsass-Lothringen Zeitung*, in *National Zeitung*, Aug. 28.

[75] *National Zeitung*, Aug. 23; *Post, Kölnische Zeitung*, Aug. 24.

lassungen).'' Nevertheless, the *Norddeutsche* (Aug. 30) was satisfied—since its article had been intended as a warning and not as a threat—that the eyes of many Frenchmen had been opened to the dangerous character of the chauvinist campaign.

Bismarck had closed the incident promptly to avoid the danger of driving France into England's arms. In reply to the complaint of a leading Paris newspaper (*Journal des Débats*) that

Kladderadatsch, September 23, 1883.

Figure 7.—The *Times* insists up and down that Bismarck is pushing France into a colonial policy to get her into trouble with England. The world journal therefore advises France urgently to concentrate upon the *revanche*.

Germany had been trying since 1871 to isolate France, the *Norddeutsche* (Sept. 4), tactfully evading the point, explained that a sincere acceptance of the status quo would assure not only the best of relations but also complete freedom of action wherever France might wish to extend her influence. If Bismarck disliked a too intimate relationship between the two Western powers, the hint of a Franco-German rapprochement, remote as it then seemed, was a far greater danger to England, for it might be the first step toward a hostile continental union. The London *Times* intervened to avert this danger. After defending the French press from the charge of chauvinism,[76] it (Sept. 4) reminded France that her vital interests were in Europe, as the attitude of the official German press had recently made clear, although it was doubtless true that Germany would create no difficulties if her Tonkin adventure led to war with China.   Nor did it agree (Sept. 6) with the *Norddeutsche's* version of Germany's attitude toward France or its own Berlin correspondent's tribute to her as "the peacemaker of Europe," for it found her method of keeping the peace "a little blustering and minatory."   Germany is not to be satisfied, it continued, even when France shows her, in contrast to "other countries," "the utmost deference" and when "she speaks . . . with bated breath," since "she probably thinks all the more, as the German semi-official organ almost pathetically complains."   Scenting a treacherous intent to stimulate bad feeling between France and Germany, the *Norddeutsche* (Sept. 15) again tempted France with the golden rewards of Germany's good-will, and warned the *Times* that "German opinion might easily acquire an interest in a friendship which perhaps would not be so difficult to obtain."   The *Times* (Sept. 17) at once changed its tone to the satisfaction of the Berlin semi-official journal by affirming "our hearty wish for the development of Germany's might and prosperity under the protection of her fine army." [77]   This triangular exchange of reproaches, insinuations, and compliments is more enlightening for the tendencies of official policy than for the attitude of public opinion in Germany. For the moment no crisis gave importance to these questions. The Conservative *Post* (Sept. 29), one of the few journals to discuss at this time a Franco-German rapprochement, regretfully concluded that two centuries of strife stood in the way of the coöperation which could be of such great service to both countries.   From the Progressive *Volks-Zeitung's* (Sept. 16) point of view, it seemed that the understanding with France, which was highly desirable for its own sake, had been suggested chiefly as a move against England.

Such was the situation when England's conduct during the

---

[76] *Kölnische Zeitung*, Sept. 1, London, Aug. 31.
[77] *N. A. Z.*, Sept. 25.

Angra Pequena affair gave Germany a concrete and important grievance for the first time since her neutrality during the Franco-Prussian War. Bismarck's hands were comparatively free, should he decide to teach her the value of a friendlier attitude. His assiduous cultivation of Russia, which in Schweinitz's opinion was scarcely consonant with Germany's dignity,[78] at least momentarily relieved the pressure from the East. In spite of his partiality for England in the Egyptian crisis of 1882, of the brief press campaign against France a year later, and of the street demonstrations in Paris against Alfonso of Spain while en route to Berlin in the fall of 1883, Bismarck had continued his policy of diverting France's attention from the Vosges by services elsewhere. Ferry's slow assimilation of Tonkin had his good-will,[79] and he coolly refused Germany's support for Italy's ambitions in Morocco, the Red Sea, Tunis, and Egypt.[80] In June 1884 he wrote that "the slightest meddling in Morocco would excite strong animosity in France." [81] With his own reasons for hostility toward England, which had been lacking in 1882, it seemed possible that he might finally support France in Egypt as a part of a general campaign against her. German opinion had once (1882) declared emphatically for action in defense of European interests against a purely British solution. Two years later, England's rebuff of his offer of Germany's diplomatic support in return for satisfactory relations in Africa and the South Seas and for the cession of Heligoland turned him more definitely against her even in Egypt.[82] Intensely irritated, he talked of publishing Münster's reports revealing her unfriendly treatment of Germany, "without consideration as to the effect upon public opinion," and he threatened, "if justice cannot be had from her

---

[78] Schweinitz, *Briefwechsel,* p. 204 (May 12, 1884). He vetoed at this time the Crown Princess' cherished plan for her daughter's marriage with Prince Alexander of Battenberg and Bulgaria whose independence had embroiled him with the Tsar. E. C. Corti, *Alexander von Battenberg* (Vienna, 1920), pp. 165 ff.

[79] Hohenlohe, *Denkwürdigkeiten,* II, 348.

[80] Bismarck, April 6, 1884. *G. P.,* III, 410, 411.

[81] Bismarck, June 16. *Ibid.,* III, 412.

[82] England naturally did not agree with Bismarck's argument that he was offering more than he asked. At any rate, Münster, who opposed colonial expansion, stressed the request for Heligoland. Münster, May 8, 1884. Bismarck, May 11. *Ibid.,* IV, 53, 55, 56, 59–62.

[England], to approach the other seafaring powers, and especially France," for "German opinion will not permanently tolerate England's monopolistic methods and pretensions." [83]

England's initiation of the London Conference between the powers represented on the Egyptian Debt Commission for the purpose of securing a reduction of the interest charges on Egyptian bonds immediately brought Ferry and Bismarck together. For the former it meant the arrival of England's *"quart d'heure de Rabelais"* because, as Ferry thought and wished, the Conference would concern itself, whether England liked it or not, with the entire Egyptian question. Bismarck agreed that England could not deny to the powers who had tolerated her action "the right to demand a complete accounting." [84] Two days later, the *Norddeutsche* (April 26) asserted that Gladstone's Egyptian policy had been a complete failure.[85] Nevertheless, France's desire that the Conference should endorse her tentative agreement with England for the evacuation of Egypt as soon as possible after January 1, 1885 did not interest Bismarck. Much as he disliked the Gladstone government, he knew that Russia's coöperation was not to be had for any scheme that might precipitate its fall and lead to a Conservative cabinet, which would oppose Russia's interests in the Near East. He therefore told Russia's delegate, her ambassador in London, that Europe would in effect approve England's present occupation even if the Conference agreed with France's desire to fix a date for its termination. Nothing more definite than an agreement to maintain a watchful reserve and to coöperate at a suitable moment was arranged between the members of the Alliance of the Three Emperors.[86] With the approach of the Conference, England tried to avoid the danger by a more accommodating attitude toward Germany's colonial interests. The protracted Fiji Islands

[83] Bismarck's marginal comment, Hatzfeldt, May 24. Bismarck, June 1. *G. P.*, IV, 57–62. *Cf.* Rothfels, *Bismarcks englische Bündnispolitik,* pp. 77 ff.

[84] Ferry, April 17. *D. D. F.*, (1), V, 257; Courcel, April 24. *Ibid.*, V, 264. The *Frankfurter Zeitung* (May 1), doubted that France had a well-thought-out plan.

[85] Even moderate observers doubted the ability of the British Empire to survive. *Deutsche Rundschau,* vol. 40, p. 148 (June 1884).

[86] Staal, 20 June/2 July 1884. A Meyendorff, *Correspondance diplomatique de M. de Staal (1884–1900)*, 2 vols. (Paris, 1929), I, 36. Staal's instructions during the conference were to exert a moderating influence. *Ibid.*, I, 29, 63–65, 67, 68, 73.

dispute was finally arranged and an objectionable Anglo-Portuguese treaty, giving Portugal the control of the mouth of the
Congo, was abandoned.   On June 16 Granville communicated
to Herbert Bismarck, the Chancellor's son, England's recognition of Germany's sovereignty in Angra Pequena.   These concessions cooled Bismarck's interest, for the time being, in common action with France.   The official press promptly moderated
its tone.[87]   Instead, therefore, of carrying out his threat to reveal
England's obstructive tactics, Bismarck stressed, during the colonial debate in the Reichstag, the moderation of his own policy.[88]
This promising beginning came to a sudden end when the Cape
government annexed territory (July 16) between the Orange
River and the Portuguese colony of Angola, which German colonial enthusiasts had reserved for the future expansion of Angra
Pequena.[89]   In reply to the first hint of England's desire for
Germany's aid during the Conference, the *Norddeutsche* (Aug.
4) wrote that England could scarcely expect Germany to pull
the English chestnuts out of the French fire, especially after the
Times' clumsy efforts to fan the antagonism between France and
Germany.   It was Germany's proposal that the Conference
should discuss the sanitary measures in Egypt against the plague,
a topic upon which agreement between the continental powers
would be easy, which decided England in favor of an indefinite
adjournment; [90] and if Münster voted against France's motion
to fix October 20 as the date for the resumption of its sessions,
Bismarck censured him a few days later.[91]

The English press was justified in celebrating the result as a
substantial victory; France had failed to unite Europe.   "On the
Right Line at last," exclaimed the *Pall Mall Gazette* (Aug. 5).
"The trap we set for ourselves has been smashed to atoms before
we had time to step into it." [92]   The danger of a continental

[87] Courcel, June 25.   *D. D. F.*, (1), V, 338.
[88] *Verhandlungen,* V Leg. Per., IV Sess., II, 1061 (June 26, 1884).
[89] An article in the *Fortnightly Review*, signed "G" and advocating an Anglo-Franco-
Russian understanding, attracted attention in Germany at this time.   *Frankfurter Zeitung,*
June 7.
[90] *Pall Mall Gazette,* Aug. 5.   A supposedly inspired communication in the *Magdeburgische Zeitung* cleared Germany of any responsibility for its failure.
[91] Bismarck, Aug. 12.   *G. P.,* III, 415n.
[92] The *Times* (Aug. 7) announced that England henceforth had no obligations to
France in Egypt.

union, however, had not been averted; indeed it soon became more threatening than ever. German opinion again declared strongly for a settlement of the Egyptian question in accord with the general interests of Europe. The National Liberal *Berliner Börsen-Zeitung* (Aug. 6) noted with pleasure, but without much justification, that "England's insolent treatment of the powers had been richly repaid." Bismarck not only talked of teaching her a lesson but he also studied the problem of doing so. On July 22, he told the ministry that he still intended to have a reckoning with England, although it was too late to do anything at the London Conference.[93] He reprimanded Münster for deserting France, warning him that too much consideration for England's interests and sensibilities would increase her presumption. Münster, he concluded, had not made sufficiently clear that, if England continued her present treatment of German interests, "she will compel us to consolidate our contacts with France," a result which might only be averted by "a decisive and, if necessary, a sharp attitude on our part." [94] As a reminder of his impatience, the *Norddeutsche* (Aug. 14) fired the opening gun of a press offensive, declaring that England's conduct, which was a poor return for Germany's "unselfish support," would end in enduring ill-will. "German policy will continue to be friendly to its friends and hostile" to those who unjustly injure German interests.[95] Nor were matters improved by the *Standard's* (Aug. 15) reply that "the substratum of all this edifice of indignation is amazingly slight," that "it is childish to make an international question of casual incidents in the conduct of a Cabinet," and that "sober Statesmanship" should take "no great account" of the foreign office's dilatory methods. The attempt to deprive Angra Pequena of the sole opportunity for its natural development, countered the *Norddeutsche* (Aug. 20), was no casual incident, and nothing in international law, it asserted, relieved England of responsibility for the actions of her colonial governments. This strong stand was approved as a clear and necessary statement of

---

[93] Ballhausen, *Bismarck-Erinnerungen*, p. 296.
[94] Bismarck, Aug. 12. *G. P.*, IV, 77, 78.
[95] This warning appears almost word for word in the report of the cabinet meeting of July 22. Ballhausen, *op. cit.*, p. 296.

Germany's position.[96]   The government, said the *National Zeitung* (Aug. 17), would have the support of all parties in throwing her influence against England in every international question. Even the Progressive *Volks-Zeitung* (Aug. 19), England's staunchest friend in the German press, could find no more effective defense than that she had been moved chiefly by self-interest. Germany, it acknowledged, should follow her example.

In the meantime, relations with France improved as those with England grew worse. Official influence was used to prevent any serious harm when a chauvinist mob in Paris hauled down a German flag (July 14) from the Hotel Continental which that fashionable hostelry had raised in honor of its Wittelsbacher guest. Neither the French government nor the French people, it was said, should be blamed for the irresponsible conduct of the rabble.[97] The prompt removal of the prefect of police was accepted, even by nationalist opinion, as a satisfactory settlement. It was the liberal *Berliner Tageblatt* (July 15) that talked of the occasional need of a *"Kaltwasserstrahl"* for the Paris hotheads and the Catholic *Germania* (July 18) which referred to a possible reversal of public opinion in France with men of Déroulède's stamp replacing moderate statesmen like Ferry and Grévy. Following the flag incident, the *Figaro's* article *"Nos amis les allemands, nos ennemis les anglais,"* advocating a Franco-German alliance, had a skeptical reception.[98] To the *Kölnische Zeitung* (July 28), whose "Anglophobist tirades" could only be paralleled, according to the Berlin correspondent of the *Times* (Aug. 19), by the most violent anti-Prussian articles in the French press after 1866, an "open, honorable and unreserved alliance with France would be the ideal which one meets ordinarily only in the most beautiful of dreams." It would mean unqualified security for both countries and—"if they wish—the mastery of the world." [99] That the *Figaro* had spoken for millions of Frenchmen was admitted by the *National Zeitung* (July 30), but, unfortunately,

---

[96] *National Zeitung*, Aug. 14; *Tägliche Rundschau, Germania*, Aug. 15.

[97] *Kölnische Zeitung, Tägliche Rundschau*, July 16; *Post*, July 17.

[98] The silence of the Paris press was noted as a significant phenomenon. *Augsburger Abendzeitung*, July 30. The *Frankfurter Zeitung* (July 29) warned its readers that the *Figaro* did not represent the dominant trend of opinion in France.

[99] See Barrère's similar remarks to Herbert Bismarck, Sept. 6. *G. P.*, III, 427.

French opinion was still dominated by the chauvinists. The failure of a single spectator to condemn the insult to the German flag was, according to the *Kreuz-Zeitung* (July 31), more significant than the *Figaro* article. If France were a true democracy, wrote the *Berliner Volksblatt* (Aug. 2), the chief organ of the rapidly increasing but still relatively weak Social Democratic party, she would welcome an alliance with Germany, but the liberal bourgeoisie were just as hypnotized as the Bonapartes and Bourbons had been by the glory of war and conquests.

Bismarck had no thought of proposing an alliance; when he directed (Aug. 7) that negotiations should be initiated in Paris, he had nothing more ambitious in mind than a limited coöperation for the establishment of free trade in the unappropriated regions of Central Africa.[100] To this was later added the question of indemnities arising from England's bombardment of Alexandria as a possible basis of an understanding. These offers, which drew from Courcel the complaint that they affected "only the distant periphery of the globe," were not calculated to arouse much enthusiasm in Paris, where the burning desire was to reopen the entire Egyptian question. If Bismarck's proposals fell far below France's hopes, his suggestion that she should call a conference of the continental naval powers to meet in Paris, or lead them against England in some other way, opened such dangerous perspectives that it apparently received no serious consideration.[101] Because of the introduction at this time of armor plate and of heavier armaments in naval construction, a coalition might have wrested the control of the seas from England,[102] but, granting the very doubtful point that France ever seriously contemplated war in support of her Egyptian interests, Ferry, his colleagues, and a large section of French opinion feared that Bismarck's real purpose was to maneuver France into an advanced position against England and then to sell her out by a separate agreement assuring Germany's own interests. "He [Bismarck] has undoubtedly suggested to England or told her," Ferry wrote some weeks later, "that Egypt would go to her. . . .

100 Bismarck, Aug. 7.   *G. P.*, III, 413, 414; Courcel, Aug. 11.   *D. D. F.*, (1), V, 365.
101 Hatzfeldt, Aug. 11; W. Bismarck, Aug. 15.   *G. P.*, III, 415–417, 418, 419.
102 Langer, *European Alliances and Alignments,* p. 302.

His tendency is manifestly to push us forward while promising to follow; our rôle is to wait and not to take one step without the certainty of Europe's support."[103] Bismarck was perhaps equally doubtful of Ferry's loyalty, although the evidence is not as clear. The French statesman had good reason for his suspi-

Kladderadatsch, October 26, 1884.

Figure 8.—A "Dutch-treat" trip to the Congo.

cions. Bismarck thought for a moment (Aug. 23) of making "difficulties for England in all diplomatic questions" when Granville refused his suggestion that England should prove her goodwill by "discountenancing the proposals of Cape Colony," but he finally decided to wait and see if she were bent upon breaking with Germany—since France might require the return of Lorraine as the price of her support.[104] Only a week later Herbert Bismarck wrote Granville that Egypt, in his opinion, had nothing to do with the prevailing irritation in Germany and "that our relations will be brought back to the former satisfactory state they were in at the moment that you treat us in the same friendly way in colonial questions as we have treated you in all

[103] Ferry's memorandum, Oct. *D. D. F.,* (1), V, 442.

[104] W. Bismarck's memorandum, Aug. 23. *G. P.,* IV, 78, 79; E. Fitzmaurice, *Life of Granville,* 2 vols. (London, 1906), II, 359, 360.

political questions until now." [105]   Still England held back, unable or unwilling to disregard the hostility of her colonies toward Germany's colonial enterprises.   Since France could not be induced to accept the leading rôle in a continental union, Bismarck continued and completed his negotiations for a limited coöperation with her for the following purposes: free trade in Central Africa, effective occupation as a test for any annexations on the west coast of Africa, and free transit on the Niger.   As a modest encouragement to France's interest in Egypt, he agreed to act with her in the question of the membership of the Debt Commission and in that of the indemnities. [106]   Early in October, Herbert Bismarck's protracted conversations in Paris finally produced a joint invitation to the interested powers to meet in Berlin for the discussion of the topics relating to Central Africa. [107] Bismarck had thus agreed in a limited sense to accept the lead for Germany, but the ever-delicate Egyptian question had again been thrust into the background.

Meanwhile, the English press became definitely conciliatory after the *Norddeutsche's* attack (Aug. 12).   Africa, wrote the *Times* (Aug. 20), was large enough for both countries.   The *Pall Mall Gazette* (Aug. 20) was still more cordial in an article that attracted much attention in Germany.   *"Sine Germania nulla salus* should be engraved," it declared, "above the doors of the Foreign Office" and no "sentimental preferences on the part of individual statesmen for other alliances will be allowed to disturb the good relations which have existed, which now exist and which always must exist between the German Empire and Great Britain."   Even the Conservative *Standard* (Aug. 30) became more accommodating as it considered the possibility of a continental union.   On September 1, Gladstone gave his blessing to Germany's colonial activities in a speech at Edinburgh: "I wish them God speed in the work as far as . . . the British nation is concerned." [108]   With the Cape Colony's action a recent memory, these friendly advances met a distinctly skeptical response.   Very

[105] H. Bismarck, Aug. 30.   *G. P.,* IV, 82.
[106] Hatzfeldt, Aug. 25.   *G. P.,* III, 421–423; Hohenlohe, *Denkwürdigkeiten,* II, 351.
[107] H. Bismarck, Oct. 6.   *Ibid.,* III, 435, 436.
[108] *Times,* Sept. 2, 1884.

good, replied the nationalist *Tägliche Rundschau* (Aug. 22), we will see if they are translated into acts. The National Liberal *Berliner Börsen-Zeitung* (Aug. 23) discounted the value of friendly gestures when they were the result of compulsion; a really friendly attitude could not be expected, in its opinion, from either the Whigs or the Tories.   Replying to the theory advanced in France that Bismarck wished to force England into an alliance, the Conservative *Post* (Aug. 21) explained that every child in Germany knew that a no more useless thing existed than an English alliance in which Germany would be left to do all of the work.[109]

German opinion continued to regard a continental union and an arrangement with France as the natural results of Anglo-German and Anglo-French friction.   Circumstances, according to the Catholic *Germania* (Aug. 27, 29), were unusually favorable, because a rapprochement would be based upon a clear perception of common interests.   As usual, however, those who were most eager were also, unfortunately for the future of Franco-German relations, the most definite in their demands for France's renunciation of the *revanche*.[110]   In return, dazzling gains were offered—at England's expense.   Treitschke's organ wrote of a "far more fruitful and magnificent objective" which would be within France's reach if she followed Austria's example in sacrificing her great German interests and Italy's in renouncing her irredentist aspirations.[111]   Germany, wrote the *Kölnische Zeitung* (Aug. 17), could do nothing to remove the spiritual causes of France's discontent, but she could remove its material sources. "Power and fame," it declared, "will again be hers when she plants her boot on the neck of her English opponent. . . ." More moderate opinion, refusing to entertain definitely hostile plans against England, hoped that developments in France might lead to a friendly coöperation.   Many, like the *Vossische Zeitung* (Aug. 16), were skeptical.   The Progressive *Volks-Zeitung* (Sept. 4), remembered *"dass eine Schwalbe noch keinen Sommer macht."*   The Social Democratic *Berliner Volksblatt*

---

109 This article was translated by the Berlin correspondent of the *Standard* (Aug. 21).
110 *Post,* Aug. 31.
111 *P. J.,* vol. 54, pp. 362, 363 (Sept. 1884).

(Sept. 3) felt that politics would prevent the realization of a "magnificent aim." The Paris correspondent of the moderate *Berliner Tageblatt* (Sept. 4) wisely deprecated the discussion of an alliance which would reopen old wounds. A definite renunciation of Alsace-Lorraine, however, was not in his opinion an essential condition for a close association based upon common interests. What he had in mind was substantially Bismarck's policy of conciliation, for he predicted that a virtual renunciation would follow the benefits of diplomatic coöperation. This more modest view probably reflected at least the greater part of liberal German opinion. Although the *Frankfurter Zeitung* was as unyielding in regard to Alsace-Lorraine as the most ardent nationalist journal, it (Sept. 13, 14), counted upon the existence of common interests to bring the two countries together. It thought of "France's association with the union of the Central European powers under Germany's leadership" (Sept. 18), not as a definitely hostile move against England,[112] but as a "new guarantee of peace and as an opportunity for France's diplomatic activity." This association, it predicted, would prevent England from solving the pending questions of world politics for her own exclusive profit, and if she forced war then the united fleets of Europe would more than equal hers. Even the nationalist *Münchener Neueste Nachrichten* (Oct. 4) was content to await the rapprochement that similar grievances would inevitably accomplish.

The continental union remained a mirage. Bismarck suggested to William that the text of the Alliance of the Three Emperors might be examined during his approaching interview with Alexander III and Francis Joseph at Skierniewici (Sept. 15–17, 1884) for an application to the "present situation,"[113] but nothing came of this proposal, in spite of Giers' forebodings, because Russia's support was, as always, unavailable for any step that might cause Gladstone's fall. After the meeting, Kálnoky,

---

[112] It discountenanced (Oct. 19) apparently inspired suggestions in France that the Berlin Conference would be directed against England, insisting that it could accomplish nothing without her approval.

[113] Bismarck, Aug. 21. *G. P.*, III, 364. He assured France that if Egypt were discussed it would be to affirm the validity of all treaty rights. Courcel, Sept. 12. *D. D. F.*, (1), V, 404.

the Austrian foreign minister, advised Bismarck to remain
strictly within the existing provisions of the alliance.[114]   Nor had
England expected a serious threat from that quarter, for she
announced, without consulting the interested powers, the suppression of the sinking fund for the Egyptian debt—a step which
might well have brought the continental powers together—the
day after the three Emperors had separated.   The German press

Kladderadatsch, December 21, 1884.

Figure 9.—If by any chance Gallia occasionally forgets about the old
flame and it almost dies out, the gentlemen of the Paris press come and
fan the flames anew.

at once predicted an effective resistance,[115] and Bismarck told
Courcel that he was urging the powers to unite.[116]   Nevertheless,
nothing more dangerous to England followed this incident than
France's declaration that she regarded it as null and void.   The
attack launched against Ferry by the Monarchists and the intransigeant Republicans as Bismarck's tool or dupe undoubtedly
favored the skeptics in Germany, although the most extreme
anti-English press discounted it as a political maneuver.[117]   Fer-

114 Reuss, Vienna, Sept. 19.   G. P., III, 369–372.
115 National Zeitung, Sept. 21; Kreuz-Zeitung, Sept. 23.
116 Ferry, Sept. 21; Courcel, Sept. 25.   D. D. F., (1), V, 417, 425.
117 Post, Oct. 11.

ry's difficulties were increased rather than diminished when the *Kölnische Zeitung* (Oct. 12) asserted that an alliance existed at least for specific purposes, when the *Post* (Dec. 24) gave some credence to a rumor that Bismarck intended to visit Paris, and when it claimed that "the French forgive Bismarck everything except that he is not a Frenchman and not their statesman." Bismarck, however, was more seriously impressed by the situation. "I can see," he told Courcel, "how little it takes to restrain you, to make you hesitate even in secondary matters. Your government is afraid of compromising itself with me; it hasn't the courage to show itself publicly in Germany's company."[118] What was happening in Paris would show, according to the moderate press, the value which France placed upon Germany's coöperation. The moderate *Vossische Zeitung* (Oct. 10) drew the conclusion that treaties or agreements meant "precious little if they are not based upon the sentiment of the peoples concerned and are not supported in a crisis by public opinion."[119]

The most serious grievances of neither France nor Germany were on the agenda of the Berlin Conference. When the nationalist *Münchener Neueste Nachrichten* (Nov. 18) affirmed England's "complete diplomatic isolation," it not only greatly exaggerated the importance of the Conference but it also gave a mistaken impression of the relations between the three powers. Public opinion in Germany soon lost interest in the protracted discussion of Central African questions. Instead of the full understanding which supposedly united France and Germany in all colonial questions, these powers were as suspicious of each other's loyalty as ever. France's negotiations with England relating to her difficulties with China over Tonkin, and especially Granville's offer of England's good offices, caused Bismarck to question the stability of the Franco-German coöperation, and Ferry, for his part, suspected that the Chancellor had already come to terms with her.[120] As to the work of the Conference, England disconcerted the proponents of a continental union by

---

[118] Courcel, Nov. 29. *D. D. F.*, (1), V, 496.

[119] It was one of the few journals to note the obviously inspired dispatch in the *Temps* declaring that the Franco-German agreement was limited to a few innocuous subjects.

[120] Courcel, Nov. 12. *D. D. F.*, (1), V, 469. Ferry, Nov. 14. *Ibid.*, (1), V, 471.

accepting principles for the protection of the natives and of the weaker colonial powers in the partition of Central Africa. In fact, the Conference had little or no influence upon the development of the diplomatic situation or on German opinion.[121]

Both the Egyptian question and Germany's quarrel with England again became acute at the beginning of 1885, while the Conference was still in session. Granville's scheme to purchase Germany's support in Egypt by the cession of Heligoland came to nothing; nor did the project of a joint demand by the European powers for the settlement of the debt question by an international conference have more positive results.[122] If Bismarck still maintained his reserve in regard to Egypt, he acted vigorously in his own feud with England. On December 9 appeared a White Book containing documents relating to the Angra Pequena affair. In it, wrote the *Berliner Tageblatt* (Jan. 12, 1885), expressing the general reaction of German opinion, Germany's English cousins could find ample justification for the increasing anti-English sentiment. It was the first of a bombardment of White and Blue Books relating to past and present colonial controversies in which each government sought to prove its own innocence and the other's iniquity.[123] That Bismarck's purpose was to drive Gladstone from office has long been suspected but never proved, but it is a fact that he expressed no objection to the scurrilous attacks upon the Prime Minister in the German press. He referred at this time (Feb. 3) to the *Kölnische Zeitung* as the "representative of educated opinion," [124] when it had only the day before savagely attacked Gladstone's policy in the Sudan for covering its obviously strategic and economic purposes by a hypocritical pretense of duty. "No word is so shamefully misused in the England of Mr. Gladstone as the word 'duty.' It is the most serious cause of the disrepute into which the Liberal statecraft of England has fallen." A premature report of his fall after Gordon's death and the massacre at Khartoum pleased it immensely. "The judgment of history," it declared, "has been

---

121 The *Frankfurter Zeitung* (Feb. 27, 1885) remarked at its close that there had been no victors and no vanquished.
122 *Kölnische Zeitung,* Jan. 21, 1885; *National Zeitung,* Jan. 23.
123 *Cf.* Sass, *Deutsche Weissbücher,* pp. 111, 112.
124 Bismarck, Feb. 3. *G. P.,* IV, 99, 100.

pronounced upon the Gladstone cabinet." Since anti-English sentiment was as strong as ever,[125] there was still much confidence in the prospect of effective coöperation with France. Ferry, wrote the *Kölnische Zeitung* (Jan. 5), represented the great majority of the French people.[126] The *Frankfurter Zeitung* (Jan. 8, 1885) accepted General Campenon's removal from the war ministry as proof that Ferry and even the army had repudiated the *revanche*. Another general, it was noted, had said that the French army should not remain hypnotized by the Vosges frontier.[127]

A vigorous diplomatic action against England, it was evident, would still have the support of German opinion. Her friends among the Progressives had been reduced to comparative silence. The only vigorous criticism of Bismarck's policy came from the Catholics. The *Germania* (Jan. 6) scouted the prospects of a new conference on the Egyptian question and discounted the new relations with France as depending upon the political fortunes of one French statesman. "With no assurance as to France, Germany has completely antagonized England." In the Reichstag, Windthorst foresaw a war as the ultimate result of colonial expansion and of the naval rivalry which, in his opinion, it would entail.[128] Bismarck's assurances to France were as generous as ever.[129] He continued his diplomatic support in the Tonkin affair and even suggested, with apparently no response, a personal interview with Ferry in Luxemburg, Belgium, or Monaco.[130] Of course, both statemen were still playing a double game. If Ferry assured Bismarck of his "determination to continue his former policy,"[131] Courcel, in Berlin, referred in his correspondence with Paris to "large concessions" in Egypt as the means by which "England could assure France's disinterestedness and dissolve perhaps forever the coalition against British policy."[132]

---

[125] Even the Social Democratic *Berliner Volksblatt* (Feb. 13) sympathized with German opinion's *Schadenfreude* at England's misfortunes.
[126] Cf. *Kreuz-Zeitung*, Jan. 15; P. J., vol. 55, pp. 98, 99 (Dec. 1884).
[127] *Berliner Tageblatt*, Jan. 20, 1885.
[128] *Verhandlungen*, VI Leg. Per., I Sess., I, 530, 531, 539 (Jan. 10, 1885).
[129] Bismarck, Jan. 24. G. P., III, 439, 440.
[130] Courcel, Jan. 30. Bourgeois, Pagès, *Origines et responsabilités*, pp. 390, 391.
[131] He said that his task would be easier if the German press did not talk of an alliance. Hohenlohe, Jan. 27. G. P., III, 441, 442.
[132] Courcel, Jan. 19. D. D. F., (1), V, 551.

The obstacles to an Anglo-French arrangement in Egypt were, however, much more serious than those in the way of an Anglo-German settlement, because English opinion had been less aroused against Germany than against France. "Germany," surmised the Russian ambassador to London, "will change her fire as soon as the Gladstone cabinet falls. . . . Today England is isolated. Tomorrow she will not be." [133] Bismarck, in fact, had decided to try again for a settlement with England. Although he assured the Reichstag (Jan. 10) that relations with France were more satisfactory than they had ever been since 1866, he left a door open to England on the condition that she would not support the anti-German attitude of her colonies. As usual he threatened to support her opponents "and to present her with a *do ut des.*" [134] On January 25, only a day after he had asked for and secured assurances from Ferry, he made a direct bid in London for an arrangement. Egypt, he wrote, had merely a secondary interest for him, while the colonial question, thanks to the popular demand for expansion, was of vital concern especially to his domestic policy. Münster was therefore to remember that Germany was "entirely indifferent" to Egypt and that for Germany Egypt "is only a means of overcoming England's resistance to our colonial enterprises. The smallest part of New Guinea or West Africa, no matter how worthless it may be, is more important for our purposes than all of Egypt and its future." [135] Nor did Granville's claim (Feb. 27) that Bismarck had offered Egypt to England change the essentials of his policy. He denied the charge in his speech of March 2, 1885, explaining that he had merely advised, after repeated requests for his opinion, an indirect control through Turkey, but he also denied the existence of serious differences between the two countries and affirmed that "England's friendship is more important to us than the fate of Egypt." [136]

Encouraged by the *Norddeutsche* (March 4), the German press represented the criticism of English policy and Bismarck's pleasant references to France as more significant than the hand

[133] Staal, 14/26 Feb. Meyendorff, *Correspondance de M. de Staal*, I, 161.
[134] *Verhandlungen*, 1885, VI Leg. Per., I Sess., I, 532, 541, 542.
[135] Bismarck, Jan. 25. *G. P.*, IV, 96, 97.
[136] *Verhandlungen*, VI Leg. Per., I Sess., vol. III, 1501–1504.

which he had obviously offered to England.[137]   The speech was
followed, however, by a comprehensive settlement of the colonial
controversies largely as a result of the warning signs of a serious
Anglo-Russian crisis caused by Russia's steady advance toward
British India.   On a special mission to London, Herbert Bismarck
found the officials there in a most accommodating mood.   Gladstone assured him of England's benevolence in all colonial questions and, on March 12, welcomed Germany in the House of
Commons as an "ally and partner"; and Granville promised to
say as much in the House of Lords.[138]   The latter's speech,
drafted in conference with Bismarck's son, was received in Germany with great satisfaction.[139]   This sudden change of front
was not merely an example of the official influence upon the
German press and public opinion; the causes were more complex.
Bismarck's prestige was undoubtedly a factor,[140] but still more
important was the feeling that France could not be depended
upon,[141] the belief that German interests were not directly involved in Egypt, the limited success of the propaganda of the
bitterly anti-English press led by the *Kölnische Zeitung*,[142] the
hope that England had at last seen the error of her ways,[143] and,
finally, the pleasing thought that she had been forced to yield.
"The Press here," reported the *Times* (March 10, Berlin correspondent), "is tolerably unanimous that Lord Granville's statement was a humble apology to Prince Bismarck."   From Bismarck's point of view, however, England's readiness to yield and
his own desire to keep out of the Anglo-Russian quarrel were
more important considerations than uncertainty as to France's
attitude; Ferry's political position in fact seemed as secure and
his loyalty to the policy of coöperation as reliable as at any time
since the preceding autumn.[144]

---

[137] *Berliner Tageblatt*, March 3; *Germania*, March 4; *P. J.*, vol. 55, p. 581 (April 1885).
[138] H. Bismarck, March 7.   *G. P.*, IV, 102–107.   *Cf.* Langer, *European Alliances and
Alignments*, p. 308.
[139] Bismarck's skill in choosing the psychological moment for a settlement was much
admired.   *Kreuz-Zeitung*, March 7; *Deutsche Rundschau*, vol. 43, p. 145 (March 1885).
[140] *Germania*, March 6.
[141] Even the *Kölnische Zeitung* (March 11) welcomed the elimination of Egypt as a
source of difficulties, but it preferred to wait for a confirmation of England's friendlier
attitude in other fields.
[142] *Berliner Börsen-Zeitung*, March 6.
[143] *Kreuz-Zeitung*, March 7.
[144] Berlin's support of Russia's claims, according to the *Frankfurter Zeitung* (March

Events were to show that Bismarck had definitely declared for England in the Egyptian question and that his decision had the support of German opinion. The Anglo-Russian crisis nevertheless promptly revealed the limits of this friendlier attitude. Not even the sympathetic Progressives favored anything more helpful than the strictest neutrality during the Penjdeh crisis when the Russians advanced toward Afghanistan beyond an agreed-upon line.[145] The Catholic *Germania* (May 3), much less militantly anti-Russian than when Austria's interests were involved, found England's desire of Germany's aid *"lächerlich."* To the Conservative *Post* (March 29) it was naïve. The danger was that Germany's attitude might again encourage Russia to aggressive action, as in 1877. The Conservative press frankly urged her to take what she wanted. Although the *Kreuz-Zeitung* was doubtless sincere in its disavowal of any desire for war, it (March 6) reminded Russia that England's relations with Germany and Austria "secured her [Russia] against Britain's lust for war," and (April 16) it assured her that there could be no question as to Germany's choice in the final analysis. The *Post* (May 21) counted upon Russia's advance to the Indian Ocean to diminish her pressure upon the German and Austrian frontiers and thus to serve Germany's interests. After its violently anti-English tirades it was logical that the *Kölnische Zeitung* should be partial to Russia, despite its exactly opposite attitude during the Near Eastern crisis. Russia's movement toward India, it asserted (March 27), was as inexorable as that of a glacier; England's preparations to resist it made her the laughing stock of the world. As for England—"the modern Carthage"—her complete isolation left her no choice, according to the *Kölnische Zeitung's* Berlin correspondent (April 13, 25), but to accept peace on Russia's terms. Bismarck, like the *Post,* confidently expected the same advantages for Germany from an Anglo-Russian conflict that had accrued to her from the Russo-Turkish War in diverting Russia's attention from Austria and in weakening her army.[146] It is true that he did not directly encourage a Russian

---

6), itself partial to England, was due to the desire to make trouble for England, and especially, for Gladstone.

[145] *Volks-Zeitung,* April 17.

[146] Hohenlohe, *Denkwürdigkeiten,* II, 358 (June 1885).

attack,[147] but the extreme partiality of the German press, including the official *Norddeutsche,*[148] and his efforts in Constantinople, Vienna, and even Paris to assure Turkey's neutrality and the closure of the Straits to the British fleet greatly reduced the risks for Russia; these circumstances would practically guarantee Germany's benevolent neutrality and the inaccessibility to England of the Crimean battlefields.[149] An inspired communication to the press announced that the Central powers stood behind the neutrality of the Straits and declared that "perhaps Germany and her friends would use more than sentimental measures" to oppose any attempt to violate it.[150] The prospect of a peaceful settlement, however, cooled even the *Kölnische Zeitung's* zeal; before the end of the crisis it was (April 30) generously recognizing England's financial power, her capacity for dogged resistance, and (May 8) voicing the hope that she had learned the need of completing her armaments and of giving Germany enduring proof of her "steadfastness, loyalty and honorableness." Its earlier Anglophobia, it explained, had been due to a legitimate concern for Germany's interests.[151] The fall of the Gladstone cabinet and the organization of the Salisbury government removed the personal factor in Anglo-German differences and improved Bismarck's temper, while German opinion foresaw—with the usual reserve that experience must be the final test—if not a permanent improvement, at least a franker and more sincere relationship.[152] The *Kreuz-Zeitung* (June 16), however, advised Salisbury to

---

147 Münster, in London, was reported as displeased at the prospect of a peaceful settlement. Staal, 23 April/5 May. Meyendorff, *Correspondance diplomatique de M. de Staal,* I, 210. Bismarck acknowledged to William the advantages of war but denied that he had done anything to further it. *G. P.,* IV, 124–126 (May 27).

148 *Frankfurter Zeitung,* March 28.

149 He had not waited for Russia's request before acting. Bismarck, April 9, *G. P.,* IV, 113, 114; Schweinitz, St. Petersburg, April 13. *Ibid.,* IV, 114; Courcel to Hatzfeldt, April 14. *Ibid.,* IV, 116. For Bismarck's advance to France and her favorable reaction, see Courcel, April 11, 12. *D. D. F.,* (1), VI, 6, 7, 10, 11; Freycinet, April 12. *Ibid.,* (1), VI, 8, 9.

150 This statement, first appearing in the *Kölnische Zeitung* (April 18) as a dispatch from Constantinople, was clipped by the *N. A. Z.* (April 24). The *Frankfurter Zeitung* (May 2) declared for neutrality even if the British fleet should force the Straits. Bismarck, according to the *Münchener Neueste Nachrichten* (May 3), had expressed the same opinion.

151 A compromise frontier was finally arranged between England and Russia by direct negotiations, without making use of an earlier arbitration agreement, September 10, 1885.

152 *Kölnische Zeitung,* June 15; *National Zeitung,* July 8; *Post,* June 11, 28; "Der Ministerwechsel in London," *Grenzboten,* 1885, III, 5.

resist the pressure of his party for a more active foreign policy, at least in regard to Germany, for the attitude of Russia and France would make it easy for Bismarck to prepare "new humiliations" for England.

There was no indication that Bismarck intended, after the settlement of the colonial controversies with England, to abandon his conciliation of France. Only in Egypt was his support definitely denied. His conversations with the Chinese envoy in Berlin aided Ferry's peace negotiations with China. Bismarck's support gave an effective weapon to the opposition parties in France, and its denial in Egypt had much the same result, because it could be said with some reason that Bismarck's real intentions were to involve France in dangerous complications and then himself to withdraw.[153] These suspicions contributed to the nervousness of French public opinion and thus to Ferry's fall (March 30, 1885) after a relatively insignificant reverse of the French troops in Tonkin. His disappearance from power later seemed a turning point in the history of Franco-German relations, as the beginning of a new period of concentration upon continental affairs and of renewed tension with Germany, but the immediate effect was not great. Almost a decade was to pass before Ferry's successors initiated new colonial enterprises, but Tonkin was not only not abandoned but its pacification, facilitated by the treaty with China which Ferry had practically completed before his defeat, was successfully terminated. In Germany few sensed the renewal of tension. Freycinet, the foreign minister in the Brisson cabinet, was regarded as a moderate in spite of his association with Gambetta in 1870–1871.[154] The same circumstances which had determined Ferry's policy would force, it was thought, his successors to follow the same course.[155] Bismarck invited and secured France's aid in maintaining the closure of the Straits to England during the Penjdeh crisis, and (April 22) avowed his interest in Freycinet's suggestion of a settlement of outstanding differences between the two countries in Western

---

[153] Courcel expounded this reasoning to Bismarck as that of a large part of the French press. Courcel, May 15. *D. D. F.*, (1), VI, 24, 33.

[154] *National Zeitung*, April 8; *Kreuz-Zeitung*, April 10.

[155] *Vossische Zeitung*, March 31; *Kölnische Zeitung*, April 1; *National Zeitung*, April 1, 3; *Germania*, April 8.

Africa and the Southern Pacific.[156]   He nevertheless tended more and more toward the conclusion that France could not be trusted to stand firmly against England and that no French government could withstand the pressure of the extremists. His advice that France should follow Ferry's example was undoubtedly sincere, but he could scarcely have expected positive results from his offer to secure the support of the Central and Eastern powers for France if she would guarantee her steadfastness in an advanced position against England in Egypt and West Africa.[157] "It is not to Germany's interest," he wrote to Hohenlohe, "to antagonize either France or England unnecessarily, to facilitate their intimacy, or to encourage war between them."[158]   He had returned to his earlier view that Germany's interests would be best served by a controllable tension between the Western powers.

Even the nationalist press saw no reason, after Ferry's fall, to fear an immediate danger from France. The parade of the schoolboy battalions and the decoration of the Strasburg statue in the *Place de la Concorde* (July 14) amused the *Tägliche Rundschau* (July 16). The campaign leading to the parliamentary elections in the autumn precluded, wrote the Paris correspondent of the *Kölnische Zeitung* (July 18), any thought of war, and he meant with England, not with Germany. Occasional chauvinist speeches by Republican politicians were explained as intended to convince a sensitive electorate as to the purity of their patriotism.[159]   Clemenceau's advocacy of "social justice" as preparing the way for a "peaceful *revanche*" was balanced against his appeal for a stronger army.[160] Talk of the need of concentrating France's strength at home occasioned a certain uneasiness, and Ferry's statement in the chamber that colonies could never take the place of Alsace-Lorraine was regarded as a surrender to chauvinism.[161] Although the activities of the League of Patriots

[156] Freycinet, April 30.   D. D. F., (1), VI, 17.

[157] Courcel, May 10. Bourgeois, Pagès, *Origines et responsabilités*, pp. 392–394;
D. D. F., (1), VI, 21–27.

[158] Bismarck, May 25, 1885. G. P., III, 445, 446.

[159] Arthur Levysohn, in *Berliner Tageblatt*, July 20.

[160] *Ibid.*, July 25.

[161] *Ibid.*, Aug. 3; *National Zeitung*, Aug. 4. The French documents show that Freycinet's chief desire was Germany's aid in getting England out of Egypt. D. D. F., (I), VI, 33 (May 24), 47–49 (May 29).

aroused comparatively little concern at this time, Bismarck nevertheless used the official press against France for the first time
since August 1883. The *Temps* (July 24) furnished the occasion
when it reprinted an excerpt from a technical military review,
without identifying its source, advocating the transfer of additional cavalry regiments to the Eastern frontier. Such independent observers as paid any attention to the article were chiefly
impressed by its technical inaccuracies in estimating the number
of troops on the two sides of the border,[162] but the *Norddeutsche*
(Aug. 3), after more than a week's reflection, came to the conclusion that it was extremely ominous. When the most influential representative of moderate bourgeois opinion in France discussed the possibility of war, it was, according to this official
journal, far more significant than the excesses of a Déroulède or
of a Cassagnac. It was forced to conclude that Germany's conciliatory policy had failed and that "France is only waiting for a
favorable opportunity to fall upon us," although "Germany has
no intention of attacking her." As usual, the *Kölnische Zeitung*
(Aug. 4) went the Berlin journal considerably more than one
better. Germany's friendliness, instead of diverting into less
dangerous channels the restless energies which had produced the
"forest of bayonets in Eastern France from the crest of the Vosges
to Paris," had, it suspected, been attributed to fear. It invited the
French to acquire a more accurate understanding of German
character. Fame and glory inspired the French soldier to his
greatest efforts, but the German soldier fought best "when his
love of peace" was threatened. To release its *furor teutonicus,*
to awaken its slumbering "berserker rage," the German people
needed only to be shown "that an enemy filled with hatred lives
on its frontier, who . . . will not be satisfied until he spreads the
flames of war through the German land. The German reservist
will then go to war with a terrible rage, not merely to defeat but
to destroy that enemy, when he is certain that security, peace, and
economic progress cannot be his until the Parisian volcano has
been extinguished."

These grandiose threats were not so serious as they seemed.

---

162 *National Zeitung,* Aug. 4: *Berliner Tageblatt,* July 29.

The *Kölnische Zeitung* let the cat out of the bag in its concluding sentence: "Germany's patience has its limits and the sovereign French people, whose overwhelming majority desire peace, will do well to keep this in mind when it selects the men to whom it trusts its fate." These articles were in fact intended for their effect upon the approaching parliamentary election in France. Unless Germany made her views clear, reasoned an official of the foreign office, the election might be dominated by chauvinist phrases, even if a real desire for war did not exist. "The *Norddeutsche Allgemeine Zeitung's* article was only a pawn moved against the exploitation of *revanche* phrases, because the Chancellor believed that the majority of the non-Parisian population desired peace. It was not directed against the French government and was intended merely as an appeal to the peace-loving majority." [163] Without echoing the talk of the *furor teutonicus* and the "berserker rage," the Conservative and National Liberal journals found nothing objectionable in these articles. Neither denials nor affirmations of peaceful purpose nor even the minister of war's repudiation of the *Temps'* article satisfied them. It was the fate of Franco-German relations that ultimate dangers could always be used to create alarm in the absence of an immediate menace. "Today no one in France seriously desires war," the *Kölnische Zeitung* (Aug. 5) was informed by its Paris correspondent, "but let a favorable opportunity appear, and they will all desire it." Few noticed that Frenchmen believed themselves under the menace of a German attack, and criticism of the official press was this time largely limited to the opposition newspapers. If speculators had been responsible for the disturbance to business caused by the alarmist articles, wrote the Progressive *Volks-Zeitung* (Aug. 5), they would be liable to prosecution. The press, it asserted (Aug. 8), was not the proper vehicle for communications intended for effect abroad. The *Vossische Zeitung* (Aug. 5) believed that there had been a backfire, for the alarm in Germany had exceeded that in France. The *Berliner Tageblatt* (Aug. 8) was amazed by the *Norddeutsche's* self-laudatory claim that it had assured peace. Bismarck's interven-

---

[163] Rantzau's memorandum, Aug. 26. *G. P.*, III, 451.

tion, it is safe to say, did more harm than good. Frenchmen were not disposed to listen to advice from Berlin, and if the moderate Republicans carried the October elections, it was in spite of rather than because of Bismarck's efforts in their behalf.[164]

German opinion was not permitted nor was it disposed to rest content with the comparative security of Bismarck's system of alliances. Instead of inculcating confidence, he systematically used the press to misrepresent ultimate dangers as immediate, either to secure the enactment of military legislation, as in February 1880, or for effect abroad, as in December 1882, August 1883, August 1885, and repeatedly during the colonial controversy with England. Increased security in Europe enabled the small minority of colonial enthusiasts to awaken a large section of the German people to the need of a colonial empire, and finally to win Bismarck for a policy of expansion. Thanks to the size, if not the real value, of the colonies acquired in 1884-1885, to the moderation of Bismarck's plans, and to the hopes still cherished by the enthusiasts, it was not yet what it later became: a source of enduring dissatisfaction with Germany's international situation; but the Anglophobe tendencies of German opinion had been greatly strengthened.

There resulted, however, no permanent changes in Germany's foreign policy in general or in her relations with England and France in particular. In spite of Bismarck's irritation with England and the temporary community of interest with France, the revolutionary project of a continental union always had an air of unreality, inasmuch as neither Germany nor France was prepared to make the requisite sacrifices. Neither had any taste, under these circumstances, for the *"le grand jeu"* of a coalition against England. Bismarck's readiness to sacrifice France at a critical moment limited even Ferry's desire to profit by Germany's aid. Bismarck was at least equally suspicious of the ability of any French government to resist the extremists and even of a possible Anglo-French arrangement at Germany's expense. After all, in spite of their professed desire for as intimate an association as France would accept, neither Bismarck nor

---

[164] The recently published French diplomatic documents contain only one reference to this incident, and that occurred in October. Freycinet, Oct. 1. *D. D. F.,* (1), VI, 96.

German opinion was willing to sacrifice important interests to secure it. Any concession as to Alsace-Lorraine was of course out of the question; but both the demands in the German press for a formal renunciation and Bismarck's own ominous warnings played into the hands of the proponents of the *revanche* in France. His support, although valuable to France where it was given, cost Germany little or nothing, and it was denied in the critical Egyptian question when it meant the sacrifice of a possible arrangement with England. In abandoning the scheme for a continental union and in using England's difficulties with Russia and France for the liquidation of the colonial quarrel, he practically assured England's exclusive control of Egypt and substantially reaffirmed the primacy of continental problems. A diplomatic association with England, as the Anglo-Russian crisis immediately made clear, was not his purpose; it would have poisoned his relations with Russia and France. Nor did he, at first, intend to scrap his conciliatory policy toward the latter. Franco-German relations nevertheless steadily reverted to their earlier condition of mutual suspicion and tension. The Catholic *Germania* was one of the few to note and to regret the passing of the opportunity for a friendly association. "Cool relations with England and good relations with France," it wrote (Aug. 6, 1885), "might have been of the greatest value to Europe. If Austro-German policy had been able to establish a relationship with France like that between Germany and Austria, it would have been the greatest triumph of diplomacy."

CHAPTER VI

Facing Russia and France, 1886-1888

... les inquiétudes propagées par la presse allemande n'auraient d'autre but que de pousser au vote du projet militaire; si elles visent plus particulièrement les rapports de l'Allemagne avec la France, ce serait par suite de l'impossibilité de mentionner le véritable objectif des measures de précaution reconnues nécessaires, c'est-a-dire la Russie.
Bleichröder to Herbette, December 24, 1886.
D. D. F., (1), VI, 397.

Bismarck's support of those countries which he desired to conciliate naturally ended where Germany's vital interests began. That point was first reached in his relations with France. Renewed tension in Franco-German relations nevertheless failed to weaken his confidence in the general value of this policy. By a judicious distribution of favors to Russia, Austria, Italy, and England, all of whom were anxious for his support in the Near East, he was able to employ intimidating tactics against France without giving rise even to a temporary coalition like that of 1875. The tenuous wire to St. Petersburg was kept open, but Russia's attempt with his encouragement to control Bulgaria threatened to precipitate an Austro-Russian conflict, because Austria feared for her position in Bosnia-Herzegovina and the Sanjak, and for her interest in the route to Salonica. To avert this clash, with its dangerous consequences for Germany, he hoped to restrain Austria and to persuade Italy and England to support her in case of need. The partition of the Balkans was still his favorite solution for the Austro-Russian problem. However illusory it may have been as a basis for a lasting peace, at least it proves—though proof is scarcely necessary—that Bismarck had no hand in Bulgaria's resistance to Russia. Russia's own army officers and civilian officials alienated Bulgarian national sentiment and made Prince Alexander of Battenberg, whose election by the Sobranje in 1879 had been approved by Alexander II, a national hero. To show his disinterestedness, Bismarck vetoed the Crown Princess's plan for her daughter's marriage with the Bulgarian prince. He minced no words in urging Alexander to make his peace with the Tsar. In Bulgaria, Bismarck was, as always, Russian.

In September 1885, the Philippoppolis Revolution, Prince Alexander's acceptance of Eastern Roumelia's union with Bulgária, and its sanction by Bulgarian national sentiment first drew the attention of German opinion to the crisis. Foreseeing incalculable dangers from the reopening of the Near Eastern question, German opinion united in a demand for a return to the status quo ante.[1] Even the liberals, under the mistaken impression that Bulgaria was still a Russian satellite, joined the chorus. Turkey, it was agreed, should be entrusted with the task of coercing Bulgaria,[2] but neither her failure to act nor the fruitless negotiations of the great powers resulted in any serious demand for active measures. Bismarck likewise was indifferent when Serbia suddenly announced her claim to territorial compensations as a balance to Bulgaria's gains. Austria's failure to prevent the Serbian declaration of war against Bulgaria drew his lively reproaches.[3] He would not permit, he told an English banker, "two millions of sheep thieves to disturb the peace of Europe." [4] Nor did Austria's intervention when her small ally was promptly and completely defeated improve his temper, since Russia would certainly resent the appearance of Austrian armies in the Balkans. He continued his admonitions during the protracted negotiation

---

[1] But public opinion, according to Bebel, soon accepted the *fait accompli* when it was seen that the union was directed against Russia and was not a Russian intrigue. A. Bebel, "Deutschland, Russland und die orientalische Frage," *Die neue Zeit; Revue des geistigen und öffentlichen Lebens,* vol. IV, 510 (1886).

[2] *National Zeitung,* Sept. 20; *Kölnische Zeitung,* Sept. 21; *Post,* Sept. 22; *Volks-Zeitung,* Sept. 22. Bismarck, however, advised Turkey against the use of force in Eastern Roumelia for fear of trouble in Macedonia. Courcel, Sept. 22, Oct. 22. *D. D. F.,* (1), VI, '89, 126.

[3] H. Bismarck, Sept. 29; Bismarck, Oct. 3. *G. P.,* V, 9–12. Austria, on the other hand, had not encouraged Serbia. J. V. Fuller, *Bismarck's Diplomacy at Its Zenith* (Cambridge, 1922), pp. 37, 38.

[4] Conversation with Hicks Gibbs, Oct. 1885. *B: G. W.,* VIII, 533. See the *National Zeitung* (Nov. 8) for a remarkably similar statement.

of the briefest treaty of peace in history, "Peace is restored." He questioned the value to Austria of a strong Serbia, discouraged her increasing hostility toward Russia, and denied the existence of any serious sympathy for Serbia among her South Slav subjects. A break with Russia without a reliable assurance of the support of the two Western powers might, he said, lead to an Anglo-Franco-Russian coalition.[5] He reminded Vienna that the Dual Alliance required Germany's armed support only if Russia attacked and that England's backing was thoroughly unreliable.[6] German opinion was equally cool to the prospect of war. The Catholic *Germania* (Nov. 17), Austria's loyal partisan, had called for neutrality, and the Social Democratic *Berliner Volksblatt* (Jan. 5, 1886), although it believed in an inevitable war between Germany and Russia, asserted that nothing would justify it at this time. The independence and national unity of the Balkan peoples were not worth the sacrifice of German blood.

Toward Russia Bismarck was tactful and accommodating. He continued to ignore the plight of the Baltic Germans, he tightened the anti-Polish legislation, and Russia had only to mention her desire for the full title to Batum to secure his approval, although he declared for the integrity of the Treaty of Berlin against Bulgaria's union with Eastern Roumelia.[7] In contrast to his restraint of Austria, nothing was said to Russia of the limits beyond which she might not safely go; indeed, Bismarck's partition plan always figured chiefly in his correspondence with Vienna. His suit for Russia's favor nevertheless failed to check the growth of anti-German sentiment in the Russian press. Occasionally, as in its reaction to Déroulède's enthusiastic if unofficial reception in Russia (July 1886), Germany's long-suffering foreign office suggested that Germany might adopt a more independent policy,[8] but her diplomats were apparently satisfied by Russia's assurances that the press attack was merely

---

[5] Bismarck, Dec. 13. *G. P.*, V, 36. Bismarck repeatedly blamed England for the crisis (Fuller, *Bismarck's Diplomacy*, p. 48), although the *Kölnische Zeitung* (Dec. 11) was unusually tactful, minimizing earlier differences as without significance.

[6] H. Bismarck, Dec. 6. *G. P.*, IV, 263, 264; Bismarck, Dec. 6. *Ibid.*, V, 27.

[7] Busch, *Tagebuchblätter*, III, 207 (Jan. 25, 1886); Berchem, June 27, 1886. *G. P.*, V, 43, 44; Courcel, Oct. 22, 1886. *D. D. F.*, (1), VI, 125. *Cf.* Fuller, *Bismarck's Diplomacy*, pp. 55, 56.

[8] Rottenburg, July 22, 1886. *G. P.*, VI, 92, 93.

a harmless safety valve for revolutionary sentiment.[9] "Only Austria is hated," said Giers, the friendly foreign minister, after Prince Alexander's forced abdication.[10] The Tsar spoke of the Germanophobe outbursts in the press as *"Dummheiten"* which would soon be forgotten, "but what they say against Austria is the truth."[11] Yet Bismarck was far from indifferent: he wrote, evidently for the benefit of his foreign office, that the press campaign might increase the difficulties of his own friendly policy.[12]

On the night of August 20–21, 1886, a group of Bulgarian army officers, presumably in Russia's pay, forced their way into the palace in Sofia, extorted Alexander's abdication, and hustled him out of the country. His return ten days later in response to a strong popular appeal was promptly followed by a second abdication, virtually at the Tsar's command.[13] The chronic tension flared at once into a serious crisis, for Russia was generally expected to occupy Bulgaria or to impose a ruler of her own selection. Probably without immediate responsibility for Russia's menacing attitude (although she would scarcely have acted had it not been for his friendly assurances), Bismarck stood between two fires. In London, Salisbury blamed him for Russia's initiative, and the Tsar, isolated at Livadia against the danger of assassination, suspected Germany of treachery.[14] The official German press at once came to Russia's defense, attributing Alexander's abdication to the ingratitude of the Bulgarian people. As late as three weeks after his second abdication, the *Norddeutsche* (Sept. 27) insisted that Russia "had not worked against the Prince in Sofia."[15] To support Alexander, it added (Sept. 30), would mean a Franco-Russian alliance, while a war with Russia

---

[9] H. Bismarck, Dec. 3, 1886. Schweinitz, *Briefwechsel*, p. 227. *Cf.* H. T. von Falkenstein, *Bismarck und die Kriegsgefahr des Jahres 1887* (Berlin, 1924), pp. 7, 8.

[10] Schweinitz, Nov. 23, 1886. *G. P.*, V, 84.

[11] Schweinitz, Dec. 8. *Ibid.*, V, 92.

[12] Bismarck's marginal comment, Berchem, Aug. 5, 1886. *Ibid.*, V, 47. Courcel believed that the meeting of the German and Austrian Emperors at Gastein with their principal ministers was intended as a warning to Russia. *D. D. F.*, (1), VI, 283 ff. (Aug. 9, 1886).

[13] Corti, *Prince Alexander von Battenberg*, pp. 272–274.

[14] Salisbury, Sept. 5. Cecil, *Salisbury*, IV, 1, 2; B. v. Bülow, Nov. 15. *G. P.*, V, 69.

[15] Bismarck dictated this article. E. Marcks, A. v. Brauer, A. K. v. Müller, *Erinnerungen an Bismarck: Aufzeichnungen von Mitarbeitern und Freunden des Fürstens*, 2nd ed. (Stuttgart, 1915), pp. 350–352.

would at once involve France. Austria, according to the *Post* (Sept. 24), was mistaken in thinking of Russia's predominance in Bulgaria as a danger. Russia's future plans, it concluded, "do not concern us."

In the meantime, Bismarck took steps against the danger that Germany might be involved in a war over Bulgaria. He invited the German consul in Sofia to pay more attention to German interests and less to the welfare of the Bulgarian people; Germany's interests, he wrote, were not involved.[16] He urged Austria again to agree to a partition and warned her that the alliance of 1879 did not require Germany's support even if Russia's occupation of Bulgaria should provoke her to an attack.[17] But Austria was not the only source of danger to his Russian policy. A group of generals, of whom Waldersee was close to Prince William, feared that Bismarck's peace policy had caused Germany to miss a favorable occasion to wage the war with Russia which would be imposed upon her when conditions were less auspicious. He was, they felt, an obstacle to the further development of Germany's greatness.[18] Not for a moment did Bismarck consider a preventive war. Territorial conquests at Russia's expense would merely increase the difficulties of the Polish question, and his good fortune during the wars of unification might not be repeated. Still firmly determined to defend Austria's existence as a great power, he rejected Russia's amazing suggestion of an alliance for her partition and warned Russia that Germany's neutrality could not be counted upon beyond the first few battles.[19] As to Russia's interests in the Balkans, his assurances were more lavish than ever. The British cabinet shrewdly suspected him of more extensive concessions than the "sacrifice of Prince Alexander."[20] In November, he pledged Germany's consent to Russia's seizure "of the bolt as well as the key to the Straits" and recorded at the same time his decision to drop the partition plan, apparently because Russia had refused to agree

---

[16] Rantzau, Oct. 6. *G. P.,* V, 137.

[17] H. Bismarck, Dec. 3. *Ibid.,* V, 146; Rantzau, Sept. 23. *Ibid.,* V, 124–126. *Cf.* Szechenyi, Jan. 14, 1887. Corti, *Alexander von Battenberg,* pp. 245, 246.

[18] Loë, Nov. 14, 1866. Waldersee, *Briefwechsel,* I, 54.

[19] H. Bismarck, Oct. 17. *G. P.,* V, 66; Bismarck, Oct. 22. *Ibid.,* V, 78n.

[20] Salisbury, Sept. 7. *Letters of Queen Victoria,* (3), I, 202.

that Serbia should be a permanent part of Austria's sphere of influence.[21]

Russia's rough treatment of Prince Alexander aroused much sympathy in Germany. The *National Zeitung* (Aug. 26), which could not be accused of an animus against Russia, noted the "unprecedented power and unanimity" of opinion in Berlin. Nothing like this popular enthusiasm had occurred in Germany since 1870. The prince's German blood and his rank as an officer in the German army were useful and effective arguments for those leaders who supported him as a bulwark against Russia's influence in the Balkans.[22] Catholic and Progressive newspapers throughout Germany, and even a part of the National Liberal press, united in a strong protest against Bismarck's support of Russia. Not a single independent journal, according to Bebel, defended him.[23] "His attitude," wrote the *Germania* (Aug. 26), "has seriously damaged the popularity of his foreign policy. . . . In the long run governments cannot act with impunity contrary to the ideas and sentiments of the people. . . . The people do not understand how Bulgaria and the entire Balkans can be turned over to the Russian despotism." A stream of denunciation poured from the Conservative and inspired press against Bismarck's critics. Windthorst and Richter, the Centrist and Progressive leaders, were held up to scorn for their temerity in discussing affairs beyond their ken. Their arguments were represented as attacks upon the Empire.[24] Their support of Prince Alexander was sufficient, it was said, to condemn his cause on the principle that a man is known by the company he keeps.[25] The explosion of popular indignation was dismissed as merely another example of the incurable sentimentalism and political incapacity of the German people. Its leaders were charged with exploiting the idealism of the masses for an attack on Bismarck.[26]

---

[21] H. Bismarck, Nov. 16. *G. P.*, VI, 102; Bismarck's marginal comment, Schweinitz, Nov. 16. *Ibid.*, V, 75. Schweinitz believed a more correct foreign policy and good relations with her neighbors should be required as conditions for Germany's support of Russia in the Straits question. *Ibid.*, VI, 101 (Nov. 9).

[22] *Germania*, Aug. 24.

[23] A. Bebel, "Deutschland, Russland und die orientalische Frage," *Neue Zeit*, vol. IV (1886), p. 511.

[24] *N. A. Z.*, Sept. 2.

[25] *Ibid.*, Aug. 29.

[26] *National Zeitung*, Aug. 30; *N. A. Z.*, Sept. 4, 20; *Post*, Sept. 26.

"They have tried," asserted a National Liberal party organ, "to use a momentary explosion of popular sentiment to destroy Bismarck's prestige." It predicted the direst consequences to Germany from their success. "That success would seriously weaken her influence and therewith the most dependable guarantee of world peace." [27]

The most serious item in the indictment was, just as ten years earlier, the opposition's alleged desire for war or its support of policies which could only result in a conflict. "The question of the day is a world war," said the *Norddeutsche* (Sept. 2), "which would be disastrous to the Empire even if it were successful." [28] According to the Conservative *Post* (Aug. 29), the opposition demanded that "Germany should fight in Bulgaria's defense and thus force a French alliance upon Russia." This charge was as ill-founded as at the time of its first appearance. The denunciation of Bismarck's supposedly peace-at-any-price policy in a communication to the *Berliner Tageblatt* (Sept. 12), whose editor disavowed it, came almost certainly from the military clique, for its reasoning was essentially that of the generals. Not a few opposition journals suggested fairly definite diplomatic combinations by which Russia might be peacefully restrained. When Emperor William was reported as working for a reconciliation between the Tsar and Prince Alexander, the *Vossische Zeitung* (Sept. 1) wrote that German opinion desired nothing better, and it denounced those who claimed that Bismarck's critics desired war. The *Germania* (Sept. 1) recommended that Germany and Austria, with the coöperation of England and Turkey, should strengthen Prince Alexander's position (he had just returned to Sofia) by a definite recognition of Eastern Roumelia's union with Bulgaria and by the organization of a Balkan league between Bulgaria, Roumania, and Serbia as a barrier to Russia's ambitions.

The *Germania's* recommendations were either scornfully rejected, ignored, or misrepresented. Germany might, according to the Conservative *Post* (Sept. 12), persuade Russia to accept

---

[27] *National-Liberale Korrespondenz*, in *Kölnische Zeitung*, Sept. 7.

[28] On September 25, it charged the opposition with the desire to use the Bulgarian question to secure his dismissal. This article was dictated by Bismarck. E. Marcks, A. v. Brauer, A. K. v. Müller, *Erinnerungen an Bismarck*, pp. 345–349.

Alexander, but it would mean a Franco-Russian alliance and a tense situation that would inevitably lead to war. Even an Austro-German victory, which it believed probable, would not be worth its terrific cost, whereas Germany could accept Russia's advance toward Constantinople with equanimity. She would be mad, it concluded, to fight Russia while the power most concerned (England) stood aside. The persistence of Austro-Russian tension again turned Russia's German friends against her, although Bismarck was then making his most extensive concessions. The ease with which Batum was acquired had convinced her, according to the *Kölnische Zeitung* (Nov. 6), that she need fear nothing. So she proceeded "by corruption, treachery, and force" on her chosen course. Nevertheless, it was England's, not Germany's, task to check her, and when Salisbury's Guildhall speech (Nov. 9) sounded a firmer note, this journal gave the credit to Germany's masterly inactivity. It threatened war, however, if Russia should reply to the Anglo-Austrian rapprochement by allying herself with France. "It is definitely known on the Neva," it asserted, "that a forest of bayonets will be instantly set in motion if Russia extends her hand to France." To Bismarck's critics this change of attitude meant their own vindication. They concluded, quite erroneously, that Bismarck had turned against Russia. The *Berliner Tageblatt* (Nov. 15) was convinced that the pressure of public opinion had forced him to warn Russia or, at least, to advise moderation. "Public opinion," wrote the Progressive *Breslauer Zeitung,* "has compelled the hesitating diplomats to follow it. The independent press has forced the inspired press to agree with its point of view. It has shown that ordinary common sense can determine the large aims and fundamentals if not the details of foreign policy." [29]

Events promptly disposed of the hope that Bismarck would restrain Russia. On November 17, the day after his most tempting offers, the withdrawal of General Kaulbars with all of the her consuls and Russia's refusal of further relations with Bulgaria greatly increased the danger of an Austro-Russian war. Bismarck doubtless agreed with those who accepted a war upon

---

[29] *Freisinnige Zeitung,* Nov. 17.

two fronts as possible, since it was generally believed that a French attack would follow the beginning of fighting on Germany's eastern frontier. Some believed that France would even attack on the beginning of hostilities between Austria and Russia, although Herbette, the new French ambassador, had done his best to allay suspicion as to France's intentions and, in fact, was still asking for Bismarck's support in Egypt.[30] Nevertheless, there was sufficient reason for uncertainty to justify Germany in looking to her defenses. Although the Septennate would not expire until April 1888, a new army bill was naturally the first step, since, as a result of the recent increases of her army, France was maintaining under arms a larger percentage of her population than Germany. According to the general staff, the minimum increase must be 41,000 men to provide a peacetime army of 468,000, the constitutional limit of one per cent of the population. From the first, Bismarck could have had no illusions as to the Reichstag's action. The election of 1884 had disappointed his hope that a policy of colonial expansion would assure a nationalist majority; the Centrist and Progressive delegations had then won gains which assured them a majority with the coöperation of the smaller dissenting groups. Had they desired war with Russia, they would have welcomed the government's proposal and, in fact, after having made so much of the danger of Russia's Balkan ambitions, they were willing in principle to approve such increases as would strengthen Germany in view of the immediate crisis. What they objected to was the use of a temporary danger to impose higher burdens upon the country for the next seven years.[31] The government's case was first presented by Bronsart von Schellendorf, the minister of war, and Moltke. Both followed the example of the speech from the throne in appealing to the general diplomatic situation, the armaments of Germany's neighbors, rather than to an imminent danger. In fact, Bronsart specifically denied that the danger was immediate and admitted that the bill would have no practical value for the immediate future, since many months must elapse

---

[30] Herbette, Oct. 31, Nov. 4, 12, 13, 24. *D. D. F.,* (1), VI, 343, 348, 349, 357–363, 373, 374.
[31] *Cf.* the speech by Hänel, a Progressive deputy, to the Liberal Club in Kiel. *Freisinnige Zeitung,* Nov. 30.

before the additional troops could be equipped and trained.[32] To the opposition, which insisted that permanent military increases would merely increase the perils of Germany's position by precipitating an armament race, this statement was far from convincing. Nevertheless, a majority was assured at any time for a bill with a time limit of three years.

To recognize the Reichstag's right to determine the duration of military legislation was far from Bismarck's intention. Moreover, the army bill might be used, with the aid of the international crisis, to create a clear-cut issue with the recalcitrant majority, to dissolve the Reichstag, and then to secure a dependable majority in a new election by creating a wave of national sentiment. In his impatience Bismarck even considered a *Staatsstreik* against the Reichstag and the universal franchise.[33] By one stroke the technical requirements of the general staff might be satisfied, the political problem solved, and a plain warning addressed to France and Russia. A more effective preparation than Bronsart's and Moltke's arguments was, however, necessary. The specter of war on two fronts would probably increase the already strong anti-Russian tendencies of German opinion, to the embarrassment of Bismarck's general policy. His critics suggested that the moment had arrived for a "dash of cold water" against Russia, but diplomatic strategy pointed to France as a more suitable recipient of a *Kaltwasserstrahl*. An alarmist campaign might reasonably be expected to divert attention from Russia and to discredit the opposition to the Septennate.

After he had abandoned his policy of conciliation, Bismarck's decisions in relation with France were more influenced by the exigencies of his policy elsewhere than by her political situation. As a matter of fact, the Boulangist agitation was more pregnant with revolutionary disturbances within France than with aggression against Germany. Many of the *brav' général's* most ardent followers hoped, like Clemenceau, who secured his appointment as minister of war early in 1886, to use his popularity to secure radical changes in the constitution. Even the official press in Germany occasionally noted this political factor as a reason for

---

[32] *Verhandlungen*, VI Leg. Per., IV Sess., I, 1, 83 (Dec. 1); pp. 94, 95 (Dec. 3); *Frankfurter Zeitung*, Jan. 1, 1887.

[33] E. Zechlin, *Staatsstreikpläne Bismarcks und Wilhelms II, 1890–1894* (Stuttgart, 1929), pp. 23, 24.

confidence. The *Norddeutsche* (July 14, 17, 1886) wrote that the unusually imposing military display on Bastille Day, which marked the beginning of the more hysterical phase of the movement, was intended to strengthen the Republic against its Monarchist enemies. That the influence of the *revanche* press had been exaggerated was the *National Zeitung's* (July 15) conclusion from the presence of a German speaker at the dedication of a monument to Diderot only a day before the national holiday. General von Loë refused to agree that Boulanger was a serious menace. "A couple of Paradise apples every night," he wrote contemptuously, "are dearer to him than all the laurels in the world. . . . We should not in any case do him the favor of playing the part of the wolf. They desire nothing more than that we should attack them." [34]   The flood of chauvinist publications which attained unprecedented heights after July 14, 1886 caused no little alarm in Germany,[35] but reasons were not infrequently found for minimizing its significance. The *National Zeitung* (April 21), of whose sensitive nationalism there could be no question, had interpreted Barthèlemy's chauvinist pamphlet, *Avant la Bataille,*[36] with Déroulède's bellicose introduction, as intended to cure public opinion of its lack of confidence and its fear of Germany's military power. While this state of mind might serve as a psychological preparation for war, it was not a definite incitement to the attack, and Villaume, the German military attaché, noted this distinction in his discussion of the *revanche.*[37]   When the possibility of a war on two fronts became the object of general concern during the Bulgarian crisis, it was rather the result of uncertainty as to France's reaction to a war in Eastern Europe than to an anticipation of an independent attack by her.[38]   Déroulède's enthusiastic reception in Russia during the summer foreshadowed the possible result if Boulanger became a dictator. Only during the sixties had there been, according to

---

[34] Loë, June 9, 1886. Waldersee, *Briefwechsel,* I, 25.

[35] It meant, according to an observer who had once been connected with the official press bureau, France's persistent refusal to accept the existence of a united Germany. C. Rössler, "Französische Masken," *P. J.,* vol. 57, p. 399 (March 1886).

[36] Münster, in Paris, told Freycinet that this pamphlet was attributed in Berlin to official influence. Freycinet, May 10. *D. D. F.,* (1), VI, 250. *Cf.* the Berlin letter in the *Politische Correspondenz* (Vienna), *N. A. Z.,* April 19; Fuller, *Bismarck's Diplomacy,* p. 61n.

[37] Villaume, April 29. *G. P.,* VI, 133.

[38] *Frankfurter Zeitung,* Dec. 15.

the *Kölnische Zeitung* (Nov. 23), as much talk of an inevitable conflict. That Bismarck's policy was one of peace was not decisive, wrote Loë, because he no longer was able to move figures at his pleasure on the European chessboard.[39] If his critics conceded the danger of a Franco-Russian rapprochement, they used it as an argument in favor of checking Russia's expansion in the Balkans.[40] To encourage this expansion, as Bismarck did, would, they said, strengthen France.

In the meantime, Bismarck had rejected Freycinet's repeated requests for his aid in forcing England to fix a date for the evacuation of Egypt, but he encouraged him to act alone and to secure Russia's coöperation for this purpose even in spite of reports that the Pan-Slavs were trying to establish contacts with France.[41] The day had passed when he considered it worth while to coöperate with the French government. When Münster, Hohenlohe's successor in Paris, emphasized the peaceful tendencies of French opinion,[42] he covered the ambassador's reports with question marks, and lectured him when he attempted to bring his moderate interpretation to the Emperor's attention. The most serious error of Münster's otherwise fair analysis was its neglect of the ever-present danger that an unpredictable frontier incident might play into the hands of the chauvinist minority. Villaume's reports, which were far more biased in their meticulous cataloging of chauvinist pamphlets and of rumors as to military preparations, won Bismarck's approval. Like the Chancellor, he was convinced that the peaceful sentiment of the great majority was less significant than the "value attributed by the government, the parties, and the army to this product of French patriotism."[43]

[39] Loë, Dec. 3. Waldersee, *Briefwechsel*, I, 56, 57.

[40] The *Frankfurter Zeitung* (Dec. 9) mentioned France, in a statement supposedly derived from official sources in St. Petersburg, as "Russia's distinguished reserve."

[41] An official of the German embassy in London had predicted a favorable response. Floriau, Sept. 24. *D. D. F.*, (1), VI, 316. *Cf.* Herbette, Oct. 26, Nov. 12, 13. *Ibid.*, (1), VI, 336; H. Bismarck, Sept. 28, Münster, Oct. 1, *G. P.*, VI, 137, 138; 151, 152; *Deutsche Rundschau*, vol. 49, p. 49 (Oct.); *P. J.*, vol. 58, pp. 515, 516 (Oct.); "Wieder die ägyptische Frage," *Grenzboten*, 1886, IV, 259.

[42] He deprecated Berlin's alarm in conversation with Freycinet. Freycinet, May 10. *D. D. F.*, (1), VI, 250.

[43] Villaume, Feb. 28, 1886. *G. P.*, VI, 127, 128. The Crown Prince asked Captain Hoiningen, Villaume's successor, to report a more moderate view of the situation. E. Bourgeois, "L'Allemagne et la France au printemps de 1887," *Revue des sciences politiques*, March 1924, p. 12. *Cf.* Carroll, *French Public Opinion*, p. 120.

To disillusion those who still hoped for the success of moderate opinion in France, Bismarck used Villaume's conclusions. On March 10, 1886, the *Kölnische Zeitung* printed verbatim the military attaché's report of February 28 as a Paris dispatch under the date of March 7, .whence it was clipped by the *Norddeutsche* (March 11) and other less official journals, with flattering comments as to the author's services. The *Post's* reaction (March 18) betrayed the purpose of this maneuver. The article, it wrote, contained nothing new, but it should convince all that no hope remained for a Franco-German reconciliation. Germany would be justified in expecting a French attack but she would not take upon herself the odium of an aggression. Although the general effect strengthened the view that chauvinism had won the upper hand in France,[44] for the Social Democratic *Berliner Volksblatt* (March 23) was one of the few to insist that the *revanche* sentiment was declining and that friendly relations were still possible, opinion remained skeptical as to the existence of an immediate danger. Waldersee thought *"dass alles Komödie ist"* and he wrote in his diary that Villaume had been astounded by the use which had been made of his report.[45] The *National Zeitung* (March 14) saw no reason for alarm. Ferry's defeat and Déroulède's candidacy for the Chamber were, in its opinion, the only definite reasons for concern, whereas those conditions which made a Franco-Russian alliance an impossibility would compel France to keep the peace.

After reading for months of the growth of chauvinism in France, the news of Freycinet's defeat (Dec. 3) and of Boulanger's retention as the war minister in the Goblet government inevitably suggested to German observers that the extremists were about to acquire control. *"C'est maintenant l'inconnu,"* was Herbert Bismarck's first comment to the French ambassador.[46] The moderate *Berliner Tageblatt* (Dec. 6) thought that the majority in the French chambers would no longer tolerate a government which did not reject every appearance of coöpera-

---

[44] The *Preussische Jahrbücher* (vol. 57, pp. 413, 414, March, 1886) had asserted this for months. Cf. *Post*, March 18.

[45] Waldersee, *Denkwürdigkeiten*, I, 281 (March 15), 284 (March 22).

[46] Herbette, Dec. 7. *D. D. F.*, (1), VI, 381.

tion with Germany and which did not openly declare for the *revanche*. To remove this impression France exerted herself to the utmost both in Berlin and in Paris through official as well as unofficial channels. Herbette affirmed the new government's intention of continuing Freycinet's foreign policy, its modest efforts for a peaceful settlement of the Bulgarian crisis, and its indifference to an alliance with Russia. He maintained that France's chief interest was the solution of the Egyptian question. His insistence upon the peaceful character of Republican opinion was not without effect, for Herbert Bismarck assured him that no greater significance should be attributed to the polemics of German newspapers than he himself attached to those of the *France*.[47] After an interview with Goblet, Münster touched upon perhaps the most serious cause of concern, at least on the part of the German government: the danger of France's intervention in a Russo-German war. "He and the existing government," wrote the ambassador, "are determined to maintain the strictest neutrality."[48] Goblet refused to defy chauvinist opinion by permitting the publication of this statement, but he publicly affirmed France's desire and need of peace a few days later to the stock exchange agents, and President Grévy voiced the same sentiments at his New Year's reception. Conservative and nationalist opinion in Germany doubted their sincerity and attributed the practically unanimous affirmation of peaceful purposes by the press and even by Boulanger to official influence. The National Liberal *Berliner Börsen-Zeitung* (Jan. 4, 1887) suspected a plot "to lull Germany's suspicions in order to prepare secretly for a surprise attack." Boulanger's moderation, in its opinion, was the result of the German army bill and was therefore the best of reasons for its passage. The *Post* (Jan. 6) likewise scented unavowed designs, and the nationalist *Tägliche Rundschau,* although it admitted Goblet's sincerity, insisted (Jan. 4) that "the logic of the international situation would be stronger than the will of individuals." In the French government's refusal to receive the Bulgarian delegation then seeking support against Russia, the *Kölnische Zeitung* (Jan. 11) saw evidence of

---

[47] Herbette, Dec. 15, 21; Flourens, Dec. 17. *D. D. F.,* (1), VI, 384, 387, 399.
[48] Münster, Dec. 26. Falkenstein, *Bismarck und die Kriegsgefahr,* p. 34.

its "lust for revenge against Germany," yet it found nothing objectionable when Bismarck made the same decision. France's peaceful assurances did not convince even the liberal *Berliner Tageblatt* (Jan. 3). It regarded Goblet's and Boulanger's recent speeches as a guarantee against an immediate offensive, but it found the key to the change in France's attitude in the recent reports of an improvement in Russo-German relations and in official influence rather than in a sincere conversion to a peaceful policy.

Herbette was confident from the first signs of a new alarmist campaign that it was intended to influence the Reichstag's vote, and was not the prelude to an attack. What seriously alarmed him, besides the increasing fear of an inevitable war, was Bismarck's belief that France would immediately join Russia at the beginning of a war in Eastern Europe.[49] He therefore urgently advised the Quai d'Orsay that the utmost caution was necessary, that no attention should be given to the Bulgarian question, and that the greatest indifference should be affected in regard to the friction between Berlin and St. Petersburg.[50] It is probably true that the exceptional moderation of the Paris press at this time followed, if it was not wholly the result of, an official appeal. Nevertheless, this restraint was important, whatever its causes. "We have had no occasion for weeks," acknowledged the National Liberal *Berliner Börsen-Zeitung* (Jan. 4), "to register one of the Germanophobe demonstrations which formerly were the best of form in France." All sections of the Paris press, according to the *National Zeitung* (Jan. 6), had suddenly filled their columns with the most conciliatory comments and with wolf-and-lamb idyls. The nationalist *Münchener Neueste Nachrichten* (Jan. 3) admitted that the future could be regarded with greater security when the entire French press overflowed with assurances of peace and neutrality in a possible Russo-German war. Europe had witnessed, said the liberal *Frankfurter Zeitung* (Jan. 4), a unanimous expression of French public opinion, although complete confidence would not be possible until it had

---

[49] The French cannons would, it was said, go off of themselves in the event of a Russo-German war. "Deutsche und englische Politik in Bulgaria," *Grenzboten*, 1886, IV, 4.

[50] Herbette, Jan. 1, 1887. *D. D. F.*, (1), VI, 401.

been translated into deeds. The Progressive *Volks-Zeitung* (Jan. 9) thought it especially significant that every candidate for an elective office in France had affirmed his support of peace, for it guaranteed the sincerity of the government's efforts to avoid foreign entanglements.

For the present and immediate future, there was less danger of war than there had been since the beginning of the crisis.[51] France had gone as far as she could in reassuring Germany without a formal renunciation of Alsace-Lorraine and without dismissing Boulanger. Bismarck knew that Russia would refuse to renew the Alliance of the Three Emperors, but on January 10 Peter Shuvalov, the Russian ambassador to England, handed to him the draft of a Russo-German agreement, which apparently proved Russia's desire to remain on friendly, even close, terms. None of the serious dangers to Germany's position had been removed, but there was little reason to fear an immediate attack from any direction. Bismarck certainly did not agree with the views of the military clique that a circle of hostile powers had closed around Germany and that it should be broken by a sudden attack on Russia in the manner of the Great Frederick. Nor was it his intention, in his speech (Jan. 12) on the army bill, to block the road that had been opened for a return to friendlier relations with Russia by exciting opinion against her. Except as a *Kaltwasserstrahl* for France, the speech was perhaps chiefly intended to enlist support for the bill and for the government parties in the election which would follow its probable defeat.

Bismarck was, according to the Berlin correspondent of the London *Daily News* (Jan. 12), "bland, conciliatory, almost deferential" in his discussion of Germany's relations with Russia. Nothing had disturbed them since the days of Alexander II, and nothing was to be gained by a quarrel over Bulgaria, since Germany's interests were not involved. He repeated the familiar charge that the *Berliner Tageblatt, Freisinnige Zeitung, Volks-Zeitung,* and the *Germania* had worked for a Russo-German war

---

[51] Professor Japikse, the Dutch historian, also discounts the danger of a French attack. Boulanger, in his opinion, did not himself know his own desires. Japikse, *Europa und Bismarcks Friedenspolitik*, pp. 174, 175.

as an excuse to reprimand the opposition press for its anti-Russian attitude and to reassure Russia. "I considered," he said, "this press agitation laughable." Not a hint did he give of his encouragement of Russia's ambitions in the Straits, and he suggested, if somewhat vaguely, that she need not be unduly alarmed by Germany's obligations to Austria in the Dual Alliance. As for the military bill, "the arguments for it drawn from our relations with Russia have, in my judgment, no foundation." [52]   Turning to France, his tone, according to the same journalist, became "stern, defiant, and almost menacing." Germany, he said, had long since forgotten France's annexation of Metz, Toul, and Verdun—which he said was the beginning of the historic antagonism between the two countries. Since then France had compelled almost every generation of Germans to draw the sword in self-defense. His support of her interests everywhere except on the Rhine had been in vain. No French ministry had ever dared publicly to renounce Alsace-Lorraine, "because public opinion in France was against it, because France is like an overcharged boiler in which a spark, a clumsy motion, may cause an explosion, in other words, a war." If he could be persuaded that France's present leaders (Boulanger's name was not mentioned) would remain in power for a reasonable period, Germany would not need to increase her army. Neither their moderation nor the desire for peace among the masses constituted, however, a reliable guarantee, for the history of France proved that energetic minorities always determined official decisions at difficult moments. Germany, he declared, would never attack, but "we must expect war by a French attack in ten days or ten years, . . . depending on the duration of the present government in France." It would come the moment she was confident of her military superiority, a state of mind which might follow the attainment of a numerical advantage, a more powerful artillery, a better rifle; or an attack might be launched as a diversion from domestic problems. In any event, the loser would be "bled white" for the next thirty years. The defeat of the army bill, he concluded, would be the

---

[52] The *Novosti* (St. Petersburg) ascribed more significance to his failure to endorse specifically Russia's claim to predominant influence in Bulgaria than to his friendliness in other respects. *D. D. F.*, (1), VI, 413 (Jan. 22, 1887).

equivalent of a voluntary surrender of Metz; each had the value of one hundred thousand men.[53]

It would be futile to criticize this speech as an impartial analysis of the international situation. Its points were carefully selected and its emphasis distributed for their effect abroad and at home. His account of the French danger and his optimistic view of Russo-German relations omitted important facts which, if they had been given their due weight, would have materially changed the tone of the speech. He ignored the Pan-Slavs and exaggerated the forces for peace in Russia, but he underestimated the resistance to the chauvinists in France and failed to mention the fear of a German attack as an important factor in the reactions of French opinion. That the speech had much practical influence upon the international situation is doubtful. In France, the chorus of peaceful assurances, whose sincerity was discounted as usual by the Conservative and nationalist press in Germany as intended to weaken the campaign for the military bill,[54] had antedated it. Only a negligible minority were frightened into advocating a formal renunciation of Alsace-Lorraine, the equivalent according to patriotic opinion of a second signing of the Treaty of Frankfort.[55] Although Bismarck's assurance that Germany would not attack, which Flourens eagerly noted as a binding guarantee,[56] undoubtedly relieved alarm for a moment, the Chancellor's scarcely veiled reference to Boulanger as the chief danger to peace and the implicit invitation to dismiss him strengthened rather than weakened the war minister's position.[57] It might be argued more legitimately that Goblet's veto of Boulanger's proposed personal letter to the Tsar [58] and Boulanger's promise not to move a single regiment toward the frontier without the consent of his colleagues [59] were services to peace which should rightly be credited to Bismarck if the crisis which he had

[53] *Verhandlungen*, VI Leg. Per., IV Sess., I, 336–339.

[54] *Kölnische Zeitung*, Jan. 15; *National Zeitung, Kreuz-Zeitung*, Jan. 18.

[55] Carroll, *French Public Opinion*, p. 124.

[56] Flourens, Jan. 14.   *D. D. F.*, (1), VI, 409.

[57] *Krieg oder Frieden? Politische Betrachtungen* . . . , gewidmet von F-y (Leipzig, Basel, 1887), p. 18.

[58] The *National Zeitung's* report of this incident occasioned comparatively little discussion, although it was specific evidence of the government's ability and willingness to restrain Boulanger. *Tägliche Rundschau*, Feb. 12.

[59] Herbette, Feb. 4.   *D. D. F.*, (1), VI, 437.

precipitated had not been the cause of these incidents. Nor did Bismarck's tactful treatment of Russia bear immediate fruit. Weeks passed without a word as to Shuvalov's project for a Russo-German agreement, for the Tsar had refused to approve a proposal which had been presented to Bismarck without his knowledge.[60] Russia's continued coolness at last moved the Chancellor to retract something of what he had told the Reichstag. When asked, Prussia's representatives in the South German courts were to explain that "I had spoken more favorably of our relations with Russia than I really thought," [61] and Busch was instructed to reveal in the press the reservations which had not appeared in Bismarck's speech.[62]

Scarcely a voice was raised in criticism. The "well-informed" press found in it (which was not surprising) a confirmation of its own views,[63] and the more independent nationalist and Conservative journals approved his emphasis of the French danger.[64] The *Tägliche Rundschau* (Jan. 14) applauded his assurance that Germany would never attack France, fear of which it had already identified (Jan. 13) as the determining factor of French opinion, because it disposed of the alleged danger which she had used to cover her own aggressive designs. From St. Petersburg, Schweinitz, the German ambassador, wrote his American wife that the Pan-Slav press had attacked Germany more bitterly than ever since Bismarck's speech,[65] but Bismarck's followers in the press discounted this campaign while the friendly Giers remained in office. The generally favorable reaction of the opposition apparently pointed to the passage of the military bill. Bismarck had expressed, wrote the Progressive *Freisinnige Zeitung* (Jan. 12), the opinion of all groups in the Reichstag. That the French

---

[60] Bismarck, Feb. 17. *G. P.*, V, 218, 219. Giers denied that Russia would support France against Germany diplomatically or otherwise. Falkenstein, *Bismarck und die Kriegsgefahr*, p. 64.

[61] Bismarck, Jan. 24. *G. P.*, V, 117.

[62] He confided to his henchman his doubts as to Pan-Slavism and as to Russia's attitude in the event of a Franco-German war. Busch, *Tagebuchblätter*, III, 211 ff. (Jan. 27). They were expressed in "Die Kriegswolke im Westen," *Grenzboten*, 1887, I, 249–258.

[63] *Kölnische Zeitung*, Jan. 12.

[64] *National Zeitung*, Jan. 12; *Kreuz-Zeitung*, Jan. 13; *Unsere Zeit*, 1887, I, 283 (Jan. 20).

[65] Schweinitz, *Briefwechsel*, p. 231 (Jan. 17).

government might be tempted to wage war as a diversion from its domestic difficulties was conceded by the Progressive *Volks-Zeitung* (Jan. 12). The *Frankfurter Zeitung* (Jan. 15) accepted the recognition in France of Bismarck's denial of aggressive intentions "as evidence that she had sincerely feared an attack," but, except for the Social Democratic *Berliner Volksblatt* (Jan. 14), few ventured to deny the validity of Bismarck's indictment. His mild interpretation of Russia's attitude and his fairly clear refusal to support Austria in a war over Bulgaria were, of course, regretted.[66] "The Reichstag," wrote the *Freisinnige Zeitung* (Jan. 12), "is perhaps less optimistic in regard to Russia." Practically the entire opposition press agreed, nevertheless, that Bismarck's own analysis of the international situation was a convincing argument for its case against the army bill, since a peaceful Russia would deprive France of a favorable opportunity for an attack and block a Franco-Russian alliance.[67] His critics could not, wrote the *Frankfurter Zeitung* (Jan. 13), have argued more effectively.

On January 14, the opposition mustered a majority for the Stauffenberg amendment granting all of the requested increases for a period of three instead of seven years. Bismarck immediately dissolved the Reichstag and ordered new elections for February 21; peace and war apparently trembled in the balance during the intervening six weeks. Even Herbette, who was, unlike Flourens in Paris, confident that Bismarck had no intention of attacking, viewed with alarm the growing feeling that war was inevitable for which the German press was chiefly responsible, the consequences to France of a war in the East, and the possible defeat of the government parties. Except for these unpredictable contingencies, he argued that Bismarck's electoral purposes not only explained his exaggeration of the crisis but also foreshadowed its peaceful settlement. He was substantially correct.[68] The political stakes in the election were great enough to explain, if not to justify, Bismarck's use of the foreign crisis for domestic purposes. It is not too much to say that the future

---

[66] *Vossische Zeitung,* Jan. 12.

[67] *Verhandlungen,* VI Sess., IV, vol. I, 341 (Windthorst, Jan. 11); *Vossische Zeitung, Berliner Tageblatt, Volks-Zeitung,* Jan. 12.

[68] Herbette, Jan. 1, 4, 14, 29, Feb. 4, 10. *D. D. F.,* (1), VI, 401, 402, 408, 409, 430, 437, 438, 450, 451.

development of parliamentary institutions, as well as the fate of the army bill, depended upon the election.

The bitterness of the campaign equalled the importance of these issues. Nothing was omitted that would discredit the opposition. Windthorst and Richter were practically charged with treason on the ground that their obstructive tactics would encourage Germany's enemies to count upon Germany's domestic dissension.[69] Moltke was the first (Jan. 11) to argue that the defeat of the army bill would mean war,[70] but thenceforth this view played a leading part in the official propaganda and undoubtedly contributed to the opposition's defeat. The joint electoral appeal of the Conservative parties stressed it: "The result of the election means war or peace." "A Windthorst majority," wrote the *Post* (Jan. 26), "would make the danger of war an immediate reality. . . . A decisive majority would mean defeat." Waldersee privately confessed his inability to see why France would be restrained from an aggression by the addition of a few thousand soldiers,[71] but the *National Zeitung* (Feb. 6) insisted that the best way to preserve peace "was to strengthen the government's hands, for upon its prestige and strength and upon them alone depends the peace of Europe!" To support these arguments, every rumor of France's military preparations was exploited to the limit. The *Kölnische Zeitung* (Jan. 21) reported the purchase of lumber in the Black Forest for the construction of barracks on the frontier, and the *National Zeitung* (Jan. 21) mentioned an impending embargo upon the export of horses in response, as in 1875, to alleged French orders. In view of the significance often attributed to France's increased purchases of picric acid, an ingredient in the manufacture of explosives, in Germany, it is not without interest that certain German chemical concerns had secured, according to the *Vossische Zeitung* (Jan. 25), the government's consent for these sales, with the advice to demand prompt payment.[72] The German embassy nevertheless was informed that representations to France in regard to these

---

[69] *Verhandlungen*, VI Leg. Per., IV Sess., vol. I, 361 (Helldorf); A. Fränkel, *Russlands Verhältnis zu Deutschland und Russlands wirthschaftliche und militärische Zustände* (Hanover, 1887), p. 26.

[70] *Verhandlungen*, VI Leg. Per., IV Sess., vol. I, 328, 329.

[71] Waldersee, *Denkwürdigkeiten*, I, 310 (Jan. 22).

[72] It is to be regretted that Flourens' telegram of January 27 containing "precise in-

and other military preparations were being considered,[73] and two days later Bismarck tried unsuccessfully to secure England's support against France.[74]   To neutralize the effect of these reports upon public opinion, the opposition press affirmed France's peaceful disposition more definitely than before.[75]   The tone of the inspired press, wrote the Progressive *Freisinnige Zeitung* (Jan. 26), would not have been different if it had been commissioned to force a war.

It seemed possible toward the end of January that Bismarck might ask for an explanation of France's military preparations. The first hint appeared in the *Politische Correspondenz* of Vienna—a journal which the great powers used occasionally for *ballons d'essai*—in a communication from Berlin on the French menace.   The peaceful tone of the press, it declared, deceived no one; a bolt of lightning would not be surprising, since Bismarck's warning of January 12 had not been taken seriously enough. What that bolt might be was foreshadowed in the last sentence: "It remains to be seen if the French government is willing or able to give a plausible explanation of these purchases." [76]   Since the *Norddeutsche* clipped this article, with the exception of the concluding statement, its purpose was doubtless to frighten France and to strengthen the government's position in the electoral campaign by the additional tension which it would cause. The London *Daily News* (Jan. 24) at once concluded, however, that Germany was about to demand an explanation of France.[77] Events were swiftly working toward a crisis in spite of the peaceful intentions of the German Emperor and the French government.   "The first movement will probably be on the part of Germany, which it is reported will on an early date ask France what is the meaning of recent military movements towards the frontier." [78]   Since the recent attitude of the German inspired

---

formation" as to these purchases was not included in the published French documents. *D. D. F.,* (1), VI, 427 n.

[73] Bismarck, Jan. 22.   *G. P.,* VI, 166, 167.

[74] Salisbury, Jan. 24.   *Letters of Queen Victoria* (3), I, 262.

[75] *Vossische Zeitung,* Jan. 21.

[76] This sentence was quoted by Herbette, Jan. 23.   *D. D. F.,* (1), VI, 415.

[77] The *Nation,* a Progressive weekly, traced the article to its source in Vienna and Berlin.   *Freisinnige Zeitung,* Feb. 2.   Cf. *Reichsbote,* Jan. 26; *Frankfurter Zeitung,* Jan. 25.

[78] Cf. *Germania,* Jan. 25.

press gave a degree of plausibility to this prophecy, it was followed by a panic which sent prices crashing on all European stock exchanges, although immediate denials appeared in London, Paris, and Berlin. In Germany, the *Norddeutsche's* denial (Jan. 25) was weakened by a report in another column that the Alsatians expected war,[79] but the London journal was roundly chastised for its irresponsible playing with fire.[80] Although the *National Zeitung* (Jan. 25) had suggested that France might be questioned, it wrote two days later that the *Daily News* must have known that France was bound to reply that she was merely keeping abreast of Germany. "That," it concluded, "would have meant war." Thanks to the skeptical reaction of the French press and to its revelation of the Havas Agency's misrepresentation of the *Daily News'* article,[81] the incident had an unexpectedly favorable effect upon German opinion. "After France's unanimously peaceful assurances, only an interested pessimism can still believe," wrote the moderate *Vossische Zeitung* (Jan. 27), "in her alleged plans for war in the immediate future." If the National Liberal *Berliner Börsen-Zeitung* (Feb. 2) credited the change to the drastic cure Bismarck had administered, it nevertheless recognized France's admirable restraint. A temporary amelioration of the Bulgarian crisis persuaded the reactionary *Reichsbote* (Jan. 26) that the prospects of peace had improved. The National Liberal *Magdeburgische Zeitung* (Feb. 2) saw no reason to believe that the causes for war were any more serious than they had long since been. If peace had been maintained to the present, the prospects, which to this nationalist journal were the results of Germany's military strength and the fear it inspired, were good for peace in the immediate future.

It was not Bismarck's interest to permit the normal development of this moderate tendency. German opinion, no less than the French, must be reminded from time to time of the inherent dangers of the Boulangist agitation. "Because of General Boulanger's increasing prominence," wrote Herbert Bismarck, "we no longer have any confidence in peace. We believe that he will

---

[79] Fuller, *Bismarck's Diplomacy*, p. 137.
[80] *Kölnische Zeitung*, Jan. 25; *Kreuz-Zeitung*, Jan. 28; *Berliner Börsen-Zeitung*, Feb. 5.
[81] Carroll, *French Public Opinion*, p. 126.

be forced into war as soon as he attains power in order to save his prestige; and that may happen more quickly than he himself desires." [82] "If General Boulanger becomes the President of France or of the Council," his father told the French ambassador, "it will mean war." [83] The Chancellor, according to the *Berliner Börsen-Zeitung* (Feb. 2), "racked France's nerves to the point of exhaustion, since she could be impressed only by threats." Public opinion was constantly reminded of the reality of the French menace. According to the opposition, which still included the Centrists in spite of the Pope's instructions,[84] the future of constitutional government was the real issue. It labored desperately to divert opinion from the foreign crisis, which it incessantly described as essentially artificial, and to minimize the necessity of the army bill. Indeed, as the nationalist *Münchener Neueste Nachrichten* (Jan. 10) admitted, the difference between seven and three years was relatively unimportant and therefore scarcely an effective electoral argument for either of the contesting groups. Defeat would mean, so the opposition argued, the Reichstag's permanent subordination to the executive, additional indirect taxes for the masses, and perhaps a limitation of the universal franchise. The prospect that a defeat for the government would be followed by a constitutional conflict was a double-edged argument, for it alienated the timid, who either shrank from its inevitable risks or who feared that such progress toward liberalism as had been attained would be lost.

A new wave of alarmist articles appeared at the end of January. On January 27, the Conservative *Post* wrote that France's failure to follow Bismarck's example in officially denying offensive purposes betrayed unavowable plans. A correspondent of the *Magdeburgische Zeitung* (Jan. 28) asserted that "one of those moments is approaching when the accumulating electricity in France threatens to discharge against her neighbor." A Boulangist cabinet was represented as an imminent prospect.[85]

---

[82] *G. P.*, VI, 168, 169 (Jan. 31).

[83] Herbette, Jan. 29. *D. D. F.*, (1), VI, 426–430.

[84] In a letter from Cardinal Jacobini to Cardinal Pietro, the Papal Nuncio in Munich, Jan. 21. For an explanation of the Pope's motives by the French ambassador to Rome, see Mouy, Feb. 9. *D. D. F.*, (1), VI, 447, 448. *Cf.* Lefebre de Béhaine, *Léon XIII et le prince de Bismarck; fragments d'histoire diplomatique* (Paris, 1898), pp. 206, 207.

[85] *National Zeitung*, Jan. 25; *Tägliche Rundschau*, Jan. 28.

The campaign culminated in three manifestly inspired articles which betrayed its double purpose of intimidating France and of frightening the German electorate. War, admitted the *Norddeutsche* (Jan. 30), probably would not come immediately, but it insisted that the peaceful assurances of neither Germany nor France could change the fundamental causes of alarm in view of the ever-increasing expectation of an inevitable conflict.[86] Since the "situation remains as serious as ever," the most reliable guarantee of peace would be to discourage an attack by making Germany overwhelmingly powerful. The *Kölnische Zeitung* (Jan. 31) referred mysteriously to facts in its possession so serious as to make their revelation inadvisable, and described France's military measures, if not as evidence of an impending attack, then "as serious and even threatening." "Those who are bent upon defeating the army bill," it said, "wish either war or the surrender of Alsace-Lorraine." Then appeared the *Post's* (Feb. 1) more famous article "On the Razor's Edge," representing Boulanger's political position in France as unassailable. Ceaseless agitation had finally excited the "peace-loving or, more accurately, the war-hating masses" to the extent that they would no longer support a peaceful statesman. The opposition's misrepresentations, it asserted, required a frank statement of the truth; Boulanger had become the master of the situation, thanks to the scope and speed of his war preparations and to the increasing confidence in his leadership. "The situation presses toward its logical conclusion." Only France herself under her best and most enlightened leaders, the *Post* concluded, could avert the danger, but it left its readers to estimate for themselves the prospects of this solution.[87] At the same time, the government ordered 71,000 reservists to Alsace, ostensibly to be trained in the use of a new rifle.[88]

The opposition press, struggling against almost hopeless odds,

---

[86] Herbette had mentionel this as perhaps the most serious aspect of the crisis. *D. D. F.,* (1), VI, 437 (Feb. 4), 451 (Feb. 10).

[87] Herbert Bismarck assured Herbette that the *Post,* whose editor had shown too much zeal, was not an inspired journal, and promised to restrain the press as much as he could. When reminded of his promise a few days later, he referred vaguely to the difficulty of changing electoral methods. Herbette, Feb. 1, 7. *D. D. F.,* (1), VI, 436 n, 437.

[88] Flourens asked for "categorical explanations." *Ibid.,* (1), VI, 441 (Feb. 8).

did what it could to restore confidence. Not a shadow of justification existed, the *Berliner Tageblatt* (Feb. 1) asserted, for the
alarmist campaign which was ruinous to many (Feb. 5).[89] The
Vossische Zeitung (Feb. 5) predicted that the *Post's* attempt to
force Boulanger's dismissal would merely strengthen his position.[90] Its Paris correspondent wrote, after reading the scare
articles in the German press: "Are we deaf? blind? . . . Neither
the press, nor the people, nor the ministry desire war. . . . Boulanger is so far from being the master of the situation that he
would not even be the war minister without the support of
Germany's hostility." To parade the danger of war at a time
when the "fear of war had completely disappeared" was, according to the Catholic *Germania* (Feb. 4), a cynical electoral
maneuver, and it identified the possibility of a Franco-Russian
alliance, which the inspired press denied, as the real danger.
Those who had been chiefly responsible for the crisis could not
deny that the reaction in France to the latest press campaign was
reassuring, but the credit, they insisted, was Bismarck's.[91] According to the *Post* (Feb. 6), "Germany's firm determination not
to be the victim of a *saigner à blanc*" had cooled France's zeal for
the *revanche*. Her reserve, said the *National Zeitung* (Feb. 9)
was the product of the "diplomatic-journalistic reconnaissance."
This implied what others stated specifically, that the improvement was only temporary. The *Tägliche Rundschau* (Feb. 15)
in fact saw in it a plan to assist the opposition in the approaching
election. That a new Masonic lodge in Paris had been named
Alsace-Lorraine was noted as symptomatic of the permanent
trend of French opinion.[92]

Although Bismarck wished to center alarm against France, her
attitude was only one and perhaps not the most ominous phase
of an unfavorable international situation. Uncertainty as to
Russia's intentions exerted at least as much influence upon his

---

[89] Cf. *Volks-Zeitung*, Feb. 3.

[90] Cf. *Frankfurter Zeitung*, Feb. 1; *Vossische Zeitung*, Feb. 3; *Volks-Zeitung*, Feb. 12.
A part of the National Liberal press agreed. See *Münchener Neueste Nachrichten*
(Feb. 4) and the *Hamburgischer Korrespondent*, in *Freisinnige Zeitung* (Feb. 5). Flourens
asked Herbette to explain that the attacks upon Boulanger would have this result.
D. D. F., (1), VI, 436 (Feb. 3).

[91] *Kölnische Zeitung*, Feb. 4.

[92] *Tägliche Rundschau*, Feb. 15; *Berliner Börsen-Zeitung*, Feb. 17.

foreign policy. Since Shuvalov's first approach (Jan. 10), nothing more had been heard of her desire for a substitute for the Alliance of the Three Emperors. Her silence was a compelling reason for the repairing of Germany's diplomatic fences. Because she desired a friend in the Mediterranean against France, England exchanged letters (Feb. 1) with Italy—with Bismarck's blessing and encouragement—in which she acknowledged a community of interests while retaining her freedom of action.[93] England at last was now associated with the Central Powers, though not by too substantial ties. Austria's exposed position toward Russia and the possibility that Germany might be forced to fight on both fronts greatly increased Italy's strategic value, since even her neutrality would simplify the military problems of Germany as well as of Austria. Bismarck's eagerness for the renewal of the Triple Alliance therefore increased Italy's bargaining power and enabled her in the agreements signed February 20, the day before the Reichstag elections, to secure not only a promise of Germany's armed support if France's action in Tripoli or Morocco should result in war but also a vague approval of Italy's territorial aspirations in North Africa.[94] That Italy expected positive advantages from these terms was demonstrated beyond question when, in the fall of 1887, she agreed to send a part of her army north of the Alps to the Rhine in the event of a Franco-German war. Bismarck may have granted these concessions, which were responsible for the single offensive feature of the Triple Alliance, in the expectation, as has been suggested,[95] of evading payment on his promises at the crucial moment. It is, however, equally probable that he would have used a Franco-Italian war as an opportunity to remove France as a serious factor and he certainly would have intervened to protect Italy from the consequences of her defeat.

In the meantime, the party lines were more clearly defined than ever as the Reichstag elections approached. The opposition continued to insist that the only cause of the crisis with

---

[93] These letters were a part of the first Mediterranean accord. Pribram, *Secret Treaties*, I, 94–97.

[94] There is evidence that Bismarck even contemplated supporting Italy's irredentist aspirations at France's expense. Fuller, *Bismarck's Diplomacy*, p. 155.

[95] Langer, *European Alliances and Alignments*, p. 395.

France, at least so far as an immediate danger was concerned, was the alarmist press campaign. A local Centrist committee offered a prize of a thousand marks for irrefutable proof of the alleged danger and invited Bronsart, the war minister, and Moltke to serve as the judges.[96] The Progressive *Freisinnige Zeitung* (Feb. 20) headed its dispatches from Paris, Budapest, and St. Petersburg on the eve of the election with the caption *"Friedensversicherungen* (Assurances of Peace)." Every effort was made to concentrate attention upon the reactionary consequences of a victory for the governmental parties. "On February 21," wrote the Social Democratic *Berliner Volksblatt* (Feb. 17) on behalf of the entire opposition, "the dice will decide whether the German parliament will be a shadow or if the German people desires that its representatives shall have a voice in the problems of state." The choice, according to the *Vossische Zeitung* (Feb. 20), was between a constitutional and a police state. If the government wins, wrote the *Berliner Tageblatt* (Feb. 20), "proposals for the abolition of the annual discussion of the budget and the annual sessions of the Reichstag, for the limitation of parliamentary immunity, and for the revision of the press and penal laws in a reactionary sense will be revived in sharper form than ever."[97] Government spokesmen assured those, especially among the National Liberals, who were impressed by these arguments that a victory for the opposition would alone precipitate a constitutional conflict. This threat had sufficed to secure the surrender of National Liberal journals, like the *Münchener Neueste Nachrichten* (Jan. 12, 13), which had acknowledged their aversion to the army bill. *"Still in the throes of development,"* it said (Jan. 18), *"the Empire can tolerate no conflict between the Reichstag and the executive."*

The absence of dramatic incidents in Russo-German relations had favored the thesis that France was the sole important source of danger. Almost at the last moment, Russia suddenly, if unofficially, intervened, declaring her intention of opposing a dis-

---

[96] The *Tägliche Rundschau* (Feb. 19) admitted the impossibility of citing chapter and verse for the aggressive intentions of Germany's enemies. They were not capable of demonstration like a mathematical proposition.

[97] See also the *Frankfurter Zeitung's* (Feb. 1) comments on the *Kölnische Zeitung's* article (Jan. 31).

turbance of the balance of power, in a communication from St. Petersburg to the *Politische Correspondenz* (Vienna, Feb. 17) and in the better-known article of the *Nord* (Brussels, Feb. 20).[98] These pronouncements were of course discounted by the government press as merely the expression of Pan-Slavic opinion,[99] but the *Kreuz-Zeitung* (Feb. 22) claimed that Boulanger now could choose the moment for the conclusion of a Franco-Russian alliance. The nationalist *Tägliche Rundschau* (Feb. 22) represented Giers, the Russian foreign minister, as at last yielding to Katkov and the Pan-Slavs. On the day of the election, the *Norddeutsche* (Feb. 21) noted an open letter to Bismarck in the *Grashdenin* warning him that France's defeat would merely transfer the danger for Germany from her western to her eastern frontier. Russia's last-minute intervention, of course, had no influence upon the outcome of the election, and its general effect, such as it was, doubtless worked against the opposition. The government parties placed the army bill at the head of their final electoral appeals.[100] It was a question, asserted the *Kölnische Zeitung* (Feb. 18), of a permanent, not a temporary, danger. Nothing had changed since Bismarck's speech. "He who votes against an avowed friend of the Septennate," it concluded, "endangers peace and increases the prospect of war." "Here Bismarck and Moltke," exclaimed the *Post* (Feb. 20), "there Windthorst, Richter, and Grellenberger! Here security abroad and peaceful, constitutional development at home, there weakness abroad and the kindling of domestic strife and the prospect of a new crisis and then war." The opposition leaders and press were denounced as the allies of Germany's enemies.[101] More definitely than before, the voters were asked to return a nationally-minded majority in the place of the motley coalition whose opposition to the government was its sole bond of union.

Except for the success of the entire list of protesting candidates

---

[98] Both articles stressed Russia's disapproval of a Franco-German war. The *Nord* was generally recognized as an organ of the Russian foreign office.

[99] *Kreuz-Zeitung*, Feb. 20.

[100] *Kölnische Zeitung*, Feb. 18; *N. A. Z., National Zeitung*, Feb. 19.

[101] *Kölnische Zeitung*, Feb. 18. The *Kreuz-Zeitung* (Feb. 19) mentioned the *Freisinnige Zeitung, Berliner Tageblatt, Vossische Zeitung, Frankfurter Zeitung,* and the *Germania*.

in Alsace-Lorraine, which the *Norddeutsche* (March 2) tried to explain away as an ingratiating gesture toward France,[102] no other imperial election was ever so satisfactory from the government's point of view. Only the Center among the opposition parties maintained its strength, while the Progressives were practically eliminated as a serious factor in the Reichstag.[103] Bismarck had attained his desire for a pliant majority, for the Conservative parties united with the National Liberals in the Cartel no longer depended as before upon the Center for a majority. On March 9, the Septennate was passed with only forty-eight negative votes. Reluctant to admit the lukewarmness of public opinion on the constitutional issue, the embittered opposition attributed the result to Bismarck's unscrupulous exaggeration of the French danger[104] and to the systematic participation of administrative officials.[105] Industrial corporations, according to the *Freisinnige Zeitung* (Feb. 23), had threatened to dismiss their employees if they voted against the government. Bismarck, it was evident, had shrewdly chosen the issue which aroused national sentiment most effectively. "He reads the German mind," acknowledged the *Berliner Tageblatt* (Feb. 23), "like an open book."

Events soon showed more clearly than ever that Bismarck had misrepresented the international situation. Although doubts were still expressed as to the sincerity of France's apparently peaceful disposition,[106] little was heard of the French danger after the election. "Public sentiment being peaceful for the moment," wrote the Conservative *Post* (April 13), "the war party cannot think of assuming the responsibility for a war." After the *Politische Correspondenz* and the *Nord* articles, Russia took France's place as the chief source of concern. Those who had

---

102 *Cf.* Herbette, March 4. *D. D. F.,* (1), VI, 470.

103 The Progressive *Freisinnige Zeitung* (April 28) found some consolation in the numerical majority of 324,711 for the opposition parties.

104 The middle classes, formerly the bulwark of liberalism, had believed the lie, according to the *Frankfurter Zeitung* (Feb. 22), that the Septennate meant peace. Cf. *Berliner Tageblatt,* Feb. 24.

105 *Berliner Volksblatt,* Feb. 25.

106 *Kreuz-Zeitung,* Feb. 27, March 2; *Reichsbote,* Feb. 27; *Unsere Zeit,* 1887, I, 431 (Feb. 26).

recently attributed the most sinister designs to France now represented Russia as having encouraged her to attack.[107] "Not from
the West but from the East comes as always the threat of war,"
wrote the National Liberal *Berliner Börsen-Zeitung* (Feb. 26),
after acknowledging the moderation of the French press. The
opposition insisted that recent events had proved that Russia was
the real source of danger, as it had always maintained.[108] To the
Norddeutsche's great indignation, the Progressive *Freisinnige
Zeitung* (Feb. 25) noted that Russia had followed Bismarck's
example with her own "dash of cold water." Even Russia's best
friends among the German press, like the *Kreuz-Zeitung* (March
1) and the *Post* (March 13), suspected that her real purpose was
to use Germany to extort concessions from Austria. They insisted that Germany could not be blackmailed; yet Bismarck
had already repeated his assurances that Bulgaria was a matter
of indifference to him and that Germany, under the Dual Alliance, had no obligations relating thereto.[109] He also told Russia
that she need not be alarmed by his intentions in regard to
France, that he had spoken of a *saigner à blanc* to restrain her,
and that he would have offered peace, at any rate, after the first
few battles.[110] There were still differences of opinion as to the
proper method of dealing with Russia. To the military clique,
war was the only satisfactory solution. Loë admitted that Russia's ambitions in Bulgaria should be encouraged, not however
to win her friendship as Bismarck desired, but to precipitate the
war which France, because Boulanger knew that her army was
not prepared and because the French feared war even more than
the German people, would not initiate.[111] Schweinitz, in St.
Petersburg, hit the nail on the head when he predicted that a
quiet France would reduce the Russo-German friction to comparative insignificance,[112] while the Social Democratic *Berliner*

---

[107] *Kölnische Zeitung,* Feb. 23; *P. J.,* vol. 59, p. 271 (Feb. 1887).
[108] *Berliner Volksblatt,* March 8.
[109] H. Bismarck, Feb. 23 Falkenstein, *Bismarck und die Kriegsgefahr,* p. 90. *Cf.* the
Norddeutsche's statement (Feb. 26): *"Das Wort vom 'bischen Herzegovina' gilt noch
heute."*
[110] Bismarck, Feb. 25. *G. P.,* VI, 177, 178. *Cf.* Schweinitz, *Briefwechsel,* p. 234.
[111] Waldersee, *Briefwechsel,* I, 77–79 (April 6).
[112] Schweinitz, *op. cit.,* p. 233 (March 2).

Volksblatt (March 8) pointed to a friendly relationship with France as an infallible solution of the Near Eastern question.

In France the chauvinist agitation declined after the German elections. Déroulède resigned (April 1887) as President of the *Ligue des Patriotes* in protest against the government's weakness in the face of Germany's provocations.[113] Twice there was a good deal of discussion of a Franco-German reconciliation or at least a *détente*. Since February the *Figaro* had discussed from time to time the possibility of Pope Leo XIII's mediation for a disarmament agreement,[114] but Germany's reaction was far from encouraging. Bismarck informed the Vatican that the territorial status quo would not interest France, especially since the rise of Boulanger, and that Germany would never purchase peace by concessions in Alsace-Lorraine.[115] The *Kölnische Zeitung* (April 9) characterized the suggestion of a neutralized Alsace-Lorraine as "more than baroque," and its Paris correspondent expressed the sentiment of most Germans when he wrote (April 12) that "it is high time for France to realize that Alsace was German, is German, and will remain German as long as the German Empire endures." Equally barren of positive results, although it occasioned a more amicable discussion, was Ferdinand de Lesseps' visit to Berlin in March 1887, ostensibly to confer upon Herbette a promotion in the Legion of Honor.[116] The creator of the Suez Canal heard nothing that had not been endlessly repeated in the press: Germany would not attack, but she had feared the possibility of a French offensive. The visit occasioned some satisfaction in the German press—and more skepticism. For the *Kölnische Zeitung* (March 14) only the fact that the visit was possible had any significance, since the clouds had already lifted. He had, according to the *Preussische Jahrbücher,* incorrectly estimated the sentiment of his own people. That no one thought of an immediate war was not, in its opinion,

---

113 Carroll, *French Public Opinion,* p. 128.

114 The idea apparently originated with certain journals which were connected with the Vatican. Béhaine, *Léon XIII et le prince de Bismarck,* p. 207. According to Béhaine, the Pope had no thought of mediation.

115 H. Bismarck, March 5. *G. P.,* VI, 178, 179.

116 The visit, it appears from the French documents, was Lesseps' own idea. *D. D. F.,* (1), VI, 484 (March 18).

a sufficient guarantee for a political friendship between the two countries.[117] Note was taken of a French army order forbidding officers to employ German maids, of the government's continued toleration of Boulanger, and of the *Ligue des Patriotes* as ample justification for "more energetic language and measures."[118] Few Germans favored a radical reorientation of German policy.

To the necessarily slow return of confidence the nationalists of both countries were insuperable obstacles. They strengthened instinctive suspicions by exaggerating relatively unimportant incidents. It was a reliable indication of latent tension when the unfortunately normal use of spies became the cause of international friction. After the nationalist press in Paris had named the German military attaché as the receiver of military secrets and had called for the dismissal of all foreign military attachés, journals of the same stripe in Germany asserted that "the withdrawal of the German ambassador should be the reply," and that France had disregarded the "gentlemen's agreement to observe a decent silence on such matters."[119] Of greater moment was the brief but intense crisis which followed the arrest of Schnaebelé (April 20), a French police commissioner of Alsatian birth, at Pagny-sur-Moselle on the Lorraine frontier, following his condemnation *in absentia* by the German Supreme Court on the charge of espionage. It was the sensation of a week. The immediate reaction in France, as the German press admitted,[120] was comparatively moderate. Probably owing to Goblet's decision that France should at last demonstrate her capacity for resistance, the semi-official Havas Agency gave the nationalists their cue by representing the affair as a deliberate provocation.[121] They succeeded in arousing French opinion.

Meanwhile the two governments busied themselves with the facts and with the fine points of international law. France's case was simple. Disregarding Schnaebelé's earlier activities in Alsace, she first demanded his release on the ground that the arrest had occurred on French soil and—when Germany pre-

---

[117] *P. J.*, vol. 59, p. 375 (March, 1887).
[118] *Kreuz-Zeitung*, March 17.
[119] *Post*, April 2; *N. A. Z.*, April 3.
[120] *Kölnische Zeitung*, April 23; *Post*, April 24.
[121] Carroll, *French Public Opinion*, p. 130.

sented evidence to the contrary—that Gautsch, the German police official, had invited him to a conference on official business. On April 25, when Herbette submitted photographic reproductions of Gautsch's letters containing this invitation, Herbert Bismarck recorded his opinion, though reluctantly, that the prisoner must be released in order to assure the transaction of routine business.[122]

German opinion had been assured that no serious trouble was to be expected. "Peace between Germany and France," wrote the *National Zeitung* (April 22), "will not be disturbed by the arrest." This incident, according to an evidently inspired statement, should not create more alarm than others of a similar nature.[123] Nevertheless, the *Norddeutsche's* announcement (April 24) that Germany's thesis as to the place of the arrest and as to Schnaebélé's activities as a spy had been proved seemed to foreshadow the refusal of his release. From its silence as to proofs, the opposition newspapers scented a weak case. The absence of a comprehensive statement of the facts, asserted the Social Democratic *Berliner Volksblatt* (April 24), would strengthen the suspicion that a provocation had been intended. When the moderate *Vossische Zeitung* (April 23) ventured to predict that Germany would yield if either of France's contentions proved correct, the *Norddeutsche* (April 26), doubtless in ignorance of the official negotiations, bitterly condemned it as an ally of France. Lack of reliable information encouraged fantastic rumors. An absurd tale that Schnaebelé had bitten Gautsch's thumb in the struggle preceding his arrest was widely circulated,[124] and a report that the arrest had been made at Novéant at some distance within the German frontier was copied by many journals.[125] Schnaebelé's release was foreseen and approved by a few good nationalists,[126] but others, like the *National Zeitung* (April 25) asserted that France must resign herself to the main-

---

122 H. Bismarck, April 25. *G. P.*, VI, 185. *Cf.* Herbette, April 25. *D. D. F.*, (1), VI, 518, 519.

123 *Berliner Politische Nachrichten*, in *Berliner Tageblatt*, April 23.

124 *Rheinisch-Westfälische Zeitung* (Essen), *Hannoversche Zeitung*, in *Freisinnige Zeitung*, April 24; *Post* April 24.

125 *National Zeitung*, April 23; *Freisinnige Zeitung*, April 24; *Strassburger Post*, in *Post*, April 26.

126 *Berliner Börsen-Zeitung*, April 24.

tenance of the arrest and to Schnaebelé's trial. The failure of
the opposition press at once and unreservedly to champion the
German thesis may explain the government's delay in taking the
public into its confidence.   After France communicated Gautsch's
letters, the *Norddeutsche* hinted at Schnaebelé's probable release,

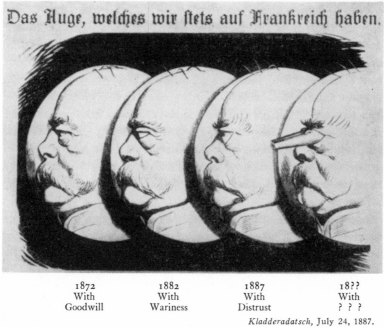

Das Auge, welches wir stets auf Frankreich haben.

1872	1882	1887	18??
With	With	With	With
Goodwill	Wariness	Distrust	? ? ?

Kladderadatsch, July 24, 1887.

Figure 10.—The eye we ever have fixed on France.

but these documents were not even mentiond in its elaborate
report (April 28) of the incident.[127]

Nevertheless, the decision to free Schnaebelé was communicated to France on April 28, with the formal reservation that
the Emperor's approval must be secured.   On April 29 the
necessary order was given, and it appeared in the press on the
30th.   As to the need of action against France's espionage in
Alsace, the government had the opposition's full support, except
in regard to the steps to be taken.   The *Vossische Zeitung* (April

---

[127] *Kölnische Zeitung*, April 29, Berlin, April 28.

28, 29, 30) had urged Schnaebelé's immediate release with an acknowledgment that a mistake had occurred, in order to strengthen Germany's case in dealing with the larger question. Instead, the inspired press continued to defend the legality of the arrest and to explain the final action "as a demonstration of good-will" as well as the result of circumstances (Gautsch's letters) of which the government had known nothing.[128]   That the case against Schnaebelé was again rehearsed in the formal memorandum which closed the incident is no proof of the French thesis that Bismarck had tried systematically to provoke France. It now seems clear that, while he had known of the Leipzig decision against Schnaebelé, the arrangements for the arrest had been made without his cognizance and still less with his sanction. The inspired press of course defended Germany's case to the end with loud denunciations of French espionage, but the absence of provocative articles such as had appeared in earlier crises is evidence of a sort that the incident had surprised Berlin as much as Paris.

In the long run, the affair, although Bismarck's fairly prompt surrender of a bad cause assured an acceptable solution, damaged Germany's position morally if not materially.   For the powerful groups that shaped French opinion it furnished additional proof of Bismarck's and Germany's brutality.   It confirmed their unshakable conviction that he was determined to provoke France, and it furnished another item in the long indictment of Germany before world opinion.   These unfavorable results developed slowly; the immediate effect in stressing the need of greater caution on France's part was perhaps a positive gain.   Three weeks later, a ministerial crisis was precipitated for the specific purpose of getting rid of Boulanger.   Rouvier's success in securing the support of both chambers for a cabinet without the popular war minister and the latter's return to his army post were the definite measures against the chauvinists for which Germans had repeatedly called.   In Germany the reaction was favorable at first, especially since the *Figaro's* publication (May 21) of Le Flô's correspondence during the war scare of 1875 apparently

---

[128] *Post,* May 1.

indicated Russia's intervention in Boulanger's behalf.[129] With Boulanger's fall, acknowledged the *Post* (May 24), disappeared the danger of a ministry under his direction. The *Kölnische Zeitung* (June 1) gave all the credit to the French people, disclaiming any responsibility for Germany. "May 30," wrote the *National Zeitung* (June 2), "has dispelled the fear of a dictatorship and of war for the immediate future and perhaps forever." This favorable impression unfortunately was soon overshadowed by the feverish development of the Boulangist agitation, although its immediate objective, after his dismissal, was the overthrow of the French government. Bismarck at first confided to France his satisfaction at Boulanger's fall as a sign of peace and his decision to delay a pending project for an anti-espionage law,[130] but he soon made it clear that nothing had changed between the two countries. "How long?" was his reply to Herbette's assurance of France's desire to coöperate with Germany. He had pursued that mirage for sixteen years. As always, France's moderation was at the mercy of agitators. Germany could never count upon sufficient good-will in France to balance the hostility which the support of her Egyptian policy would cause in England. The truth was, he concluded, that France was waiting until Germany should be defenseless or occupied elsewhere to stab her in the back.[131] There were, of course, echoes in the press. For the *Post* (June 19), just a fortnight after Boulanger's fall, wrote: "France's real desire is to reverse all that has been done in Germany since 1815, and preferably since 1808." On June 26, the *Kölnische Zeitung* devoted a long article, studded with *revanche* songs, to the Boulangist agitation, and a popular review spoke of measures that might be necessary against it.[132] Boulanger's dismissal had left Franco-German relations unchanged.

However, France had now ceased to be, except indirectly, the chief preoccupation of German diplomacy. In Russia, the contest between Giers and Katkov for the Tsar's confidence promised to exert a decisive influence upon Russo-German relations. To

[129] *Kölnische Zeitung,* May 23. Cf. *Germania,* May 24. There is nothing in the published French documents to support this rumor.
[130] H. Bismarck, June 3. *G. P.,* 192, 193. There is no trace of this reaction in Herbette's reports.
[131] H. Bismarck, July 5, and Bismarck's comments, June 8. *Ibid.,* VI, 192–196, 199.
[132] *Unsere Zeit,* 1887, II, 282.

strengthen the former, Bismarck had repeated at the end of February his assurances of support for Russia's interests in Bulgaria and the Straits. With the aid of Katkov's violent criticism of Russian foreign policy in the *Moscow Gazette* (March 7), they turned Alexander toward Germany, and, for his part, Bismarck raised no objection to the sacrifice of the Alliance of the Three Emperors.[133] Russia was advised that the possibly impending change of rulers in Berlin (a reference to the Crown Prince's English sympathies) might prevent the successful conclusion of a separate agreement.[134] The suspended negotiations were revived during the Schnaebelé affair, in spite of a lively press controversy as to Germany's attitude since the Congress of Berlin. To Pan-Slavic charges of betrayal, the *Norddeutsche* replied with an extensive historical exposition (April 20, 28, May 2, 3) of Germany's friendliness in the past, and, what was more to the point, Bismarck not only approved Russia's desire to replace the Bulgarian regent with one of her own selection[135] but also tried to secure England's acceptance in return for concessions by Russia on the Afghanistan frontier.[136] A *ukase* against the ownership or management of agricultural properties by foreigners in the western provinces, a measure primarily directed against Germans, increased his eagerness for a Russo-German understanding. He refused, nevertheless, to promise Germany's neutrality in an Austro-Russian war precipitated by a Russian aggression, although this reservation caused Russia to insist upon the same freedom of action in the event of a German attack upon France.[137]

The famous Reinsurance Treaty (June 18, 1887) was intended to prevent Russia's intervention in a war caused by a French aggression and, indirectly, to minimize the risk of a Franco-Russian alliance. For Russia's promise of a limited neutrality during a period of three years Bismarck paid a high price: an assurance of Germany's neutrality if Russia were forced to fight in defense of her interests in the Straits (for the limitation of this

---

133 Becker, *Bismarcks Bündnispolitik*, pp. 89, 90.
134 H. Bismarck, March 8; Schweinitz, *Briefwechsel*, pp. 236, 237.
135 Bismarck's marginal comment, Giers, May 28, June 9. *G. P.*, VI, 178, 179.
136 Bismarck, May 21. *Ibid.*, V, 175, 176.
137 Giers, May 25. *G. P.*, V, 239.

obligation in Article I to an attack upon Russia by a third power was virtually set aside in the protocol, at least in regard to the Straits) and a promise to support Russia's efforts to organize an acceptable (i.e., an obedient) government in Bulgaria. It is difficult to escape the conclusion that Russia fared much better. Her one obligation, whose fulfillment depended upon the Tsar's ability to resist the Pan-Slavs, was essentially passive, while the several to which Bismarck committed Germany required positive diplomatic support in questions which might cool Germany's relations with Austria and England. Whether he was justified in paying this exorbitant price for an uncertain advantage depends, in the final analysis, upon the soundness of the conclusion, which he stated at least for the Emperor's benefit, that a French attack was more probable than a war in the Near East.[138] It is, of course, impossible to prove that Bismarck was mistaken, but it is at least to be noted that the French government, less than three weeks before the conclusion of the treaty, had unmistakably repudiated Boulanger. Its ability to survive the rising tide of popular enthusiasm for the *brav général* was the chief justification of uncertainty as to France's policy. The odds were at least even.

Having read the full text of the Austro-German alliance to the Russian diplomats and specifically reserved his freedom to protect Austria from a Russian attack, Bismarck believed that the new alliance was not inconsistent with the Dual Alliance. Austria would scarcely have agreed, although he was willing to test her reaction, had Russia been agreeable, by publishing its text. Francis Joseph, he admitted, might have taken offense,[139] and Austrian opinion, as well as that of the opposition parties in Germany, would certainly have been outraged by the support he had formally pledged to Austria's enemy. Bismarck relied with much reason upon her need of Germany's support to mitigate her resentment.[140] It is still more difficult to reconcile Germany's obligations in the Reinsurance Treaty with the second Mediterranean Agreement (December 12, 1887) for the defense of the

---

[138] Bismarck, July 28. G. P., V, 268.
[139] Bismarck, July 28. *Ibid.*, V, 265, 266.
[140] Becker, *Bismarcks Bündnispolitik*, p. 103.

status quo in Bulgaria and the Straits, whose conclusion he had welcomed and encouraged. Against the same changes for which he had pledged Germany's support to Russia he had helped to organize a defense by Austria, England, and Italy, the three powers most directly concerned, in such a way as to conceal his own part. By maintaining the wire to St. Petersburg, by providing Austria with allies, he had served Germany's immediate interests, but it is more than doubtful that these complicated arrangements had a fair chance of solving any of Germany's fundamental problems. Schweinitz, in St. Petersburg, was far from confident that the Reinsurance Treaty would insure the Tsar's resistance to the Pan-Slavic agitation.[141] "I only think," wrote the Crown Princess to her mother, Queen Victoria, "that all this obliging is of no use and of no avail and that the Russians . . . will ally themselves with the French whenever they think convenient." [142]

Between the diplomatic accord, whose secrecy was well observed, and the public relations between the two countries, there was a fatal incongruity. Tension soon became more acute than ever. Instead of cooling the zeal of the Pan-Slavs for a French alliance, Katkov's death (Aug. 1) apparently removed, strange as it may seem, a moderating influence; for Katkov had not advocated an immediate alliance.[143] Déroulède again aroused much enthusiasm during his second visit for the editor's funeral.[144] Even Giers protested his inability to check the more intense Pan-Slavic agitation, which in fact had the sympathy of men as highly placed as himself. It inevitably had repercussions in the German press.[145] Russia's discriminations against Germans in her western provinces had been followed by an inspired press campaign against the investment of German capital in Russian paper, the prelude to the prohibition of its use as security for the Reichsbank's loans (Nov. 1887).[146] Foreign office officials

---

[141] Schweinitz, June 23. G. P., V, 256, 257.
[142] *Letters of the Empress Frederick*, Sir F. Ponsonby ed. (London, 1928), p. 217 (April 29, 1887).
[143] Grüning, *Die russische öffentliche Meinung*, p. 125.
[144] Russia was reminded that Germany would have deported a Polish, Hungarian, or a Bulgarian agitator. Berchem, Aug. 29. G. P., VI, 113.
[145] Fuller, *Bismarck's Diplomacy*, p. 202.
[146] H. Feis, *Europe, the World's Banker* (New Haven, 1930), pp. 212, 213.

not infrequently expressed themselves in a manner not usually regarded as good form between allies, and even Bismarck's diplomatic ingenuity failed to prevent the Bulgarian question from adding to the increasing strain. The first mention of Prince Ferdinand of Coburg as a candidate for the Bulgarian princely honors was followed by an assurance of the Chancellor's opposition and of his determination to act in accordance with St. Petersburg's wishes.[147] He promised his full support on the condition that Russia should take the initiative in replacing Ferdinand with the Russian General Enroth. After the Coburg prince's election by the Sobranje (Aug. 1) and his proclamation ending with "Long live free and independent Bulgaria!", the *Norddeutsche* (Aug. 16) presented Germany's motives in more palatable form for the benefit of German opinion. Germany could not approve the violation of the Treaty of Berlin resulting from Ferdinand's manifest disregard of Turkey's suzerain powers.

While Bismarck advised Russia to accomplish her purpose indirectly by getting Turkey to appeal to the powers for Ferdinand's removal, he was willing to accept any solution that would satisfy her. The other interested powers were less open-minded. Russia's advance into Bulgaria, Austria informed her ally, would mean war, but Bismarck's sole comment was, "not for Germany."[148] Austria, he said, should remain quiet and refrain from threats.[149] For the delays that Russia encountered, thanks to the secret combination between Austria, England, and Italy, she blamed Germany, and the famous "Bulgarian documents" placed in the Tsar's hands by the French seemed to prove Bismarck's connivance in the election of Prince Alexander of Battenberg and therefore his double-dealing.[150] In Germany, the powerful *Kölnische Zeitung* had come to the support of anti-Russian sentiment. It confessed (Sept. 2) its complete disillusionment as to the possibility of friendly relations with Russia. Bismarck, it intimated, might not succeed in restoring the former confidential association. War was possible. Katkov's death would perhaps

---

147 Rantzau, July 8. *G. P.,* V, 187.
148 Bismarck's comment, Berchem, Aug. 19. *G. P.,* V, 192, 193.
149 *Ibid.,* V, 194, 195.
150 Fuller, *Bismarck's Diplomacy,* p. 213.

not spare Germany the need of proving to Russia, sword in hand, how fatal his theories were. Germany should neither humiliate herself by unworthy competition with France for Russia's favor nor should she ever lose sight of Austria's interests. On September 18, the same journal nevertheless conceded the practical advantage of supporting Russia's incontestable rights—which it left undefined—in order to strengthen the Tsar's resistance to the Pan-Slavs.[151] Since articles of a similar character appeared in the Conservative *Post,* another frequently inspired journal, Bismarck perhaps intended to season his secret assurances with an indirect warning, a conclusion that finds support in the parallel campaign against Russian securities. A pamphleteer, who favored war with Russia and who thought that it would be popular, believed that these signs pointed to Bismarck's abandonment of his peace policy.[152] The military clique agitated for a settlement by force of arms. Waldersee disagreed with Bismarck's decision for neutrality at the beginning of an Austro-Russian conflict, arguing that Austria, if left alone, would hasten to make peace with Russia after the first few battles. Thus Germany would be isolated, and to avoid this danger, he believed that she should force the issue, since an Austro-Russian war was inevitable.[153] From Constantinople, Colonel von der Goltz, the head of the German military mission, insisted that Germany should take the initiative, for Russia regarded her as her real enemy.[154] The general staff also believed war to be inevitable, and Deines, the Germany military attaché in Vienna, urged Austria, probably on Waldersee's direction, to hasten her preparations.[155] Moltke also thought that Russia's actions meant war, although he may not have shared his subordinates' desire to precipitate it.[156]

Bismarck had no patience with these ideas. "As long as I am minister," he wrote, "I will never give my consent to a prophylactic war."[157] While the general staff's independence in urging

---

[151] Raindre, Berlin, Oct. 5. *D. D. F.,* VI, 617, 618.

[152] Fränkel, *Russlands Verhältnis zu Deutschland,* p. 50. *Cf.* W. Eisenhart, *Der nächste Krieg mit Russland und seine politische Folgen* (Halle, 1888).

[153] Waldersee, *Denkwürdigkeiten,* I, 337, 338 (Nov. 23, 26).

[154] Waldersee, *Briefwechsel,* I, 136, 137 (Dec. 12).

[155] Rantzau, Dec. 15. *G. P.,* VI, 28, 29.

[156] *Ibid.,* VI, 24, 25n.

[157] Bismarck, Dec. 15. *Ibid.,* VI, 25.

Austria to prepare incensed him as an invasion of his exclusive control of foreign policy, he could not safely ignore the possibility of war. He not only communicated Moltke's report on Russia's armaments to Austria, but he also approved direct communications between the two general staffs.[158] As to France, he considered the possibility, perhaps for the first time, that she might not attack at the beginning of a Russo-German war. He believed in that case that Germany should assume the aggressive (perhaps even in an Austro-Russian war) in order to crush France and then to turn with her full strength against Russia.[159] He of course wished to prevent the circumstances which might necessitate a recourse to these measures from arising, but account should be taken of his readiness to force a war upon France in the interest of his general policy.

His mastery of diplomatic finesse was never better illustrated than at this time. Fearful that Russia, knowing the defensive character of the Dual Alliance, wished to provoke Austria, he repeatedly advised Austria to be cautious,[160] and warned her not to expect Germany's aid if she assumed the aggressive.[161] He encouraged her at the same time to perfect her preparations,[162] and promised that Russia's mobilization on the Galician frontier would be followed by Germany's.[163] He hoped, however, to avoid the necessity for this dangerous decision by developing the first Mediterranean Accord into a more effective barrier against Russia's aggressive purposes, or, if fighting began, to provide a defense for Austria. Austria's success in October in enlisting Turkey's coöperation with the three Mediterranean powers won his approval. To persuade England to accept more binding engagements was not too difficult, for the Salisbury government felt a community of interests with Germany and the Central powers against Russia and France. Since July 1887, when these powers had blocked Turkey's ratification of the Drummond-Wolf agreement for the definitive settlement of the Egyptian

---

[158] G. P., VI, 24, 25n.
[159] Bismarck, Dec. 15, 27. Ibid., VI, 27, 68. Cf. Becker, Bismarcks Bündnispolitik, p. 131.
[160] Rantzau, Nov. 24. G. P., VI, 12.
[161] Bismarck's comment, Kálnoky, Dec. 22. Ibid., VI, 64.
[162] H. Bismarck, Nov. 30; Bismarck, Dec. 27. Ibid., VI, 12, 13, 68, 69.
[163] Bismarck's comment, Reuss, Jan. 8, 1888. Ibid., VI, 77.

question, Anglo-French relations were severely strained. There were moments when Salisbury thought of encouraging Bismarck to buy a free hand in the West by the surrender of Constantinople to Russia.[164] He had recently written that there was "a silver lining even to the great black cloud of a Franco-German war."[165] Much praise has been lavished upon Bismarck's management of England at this critical juncture, but Salisbury was under no illusions as to his motives. Bismarck, he believed, wished England, Austria, and Italy "to lift a weight which he will not touch with one of his fingers. . . ."[166] He suspected that the Chancellor would cover himself at St. Petersburg by disavowing any responsibility for the new league,[167] and that he desired nothing better than "a nice little fight between Russia and the three powers" so that he might "make France a harmless neighbour for some time to come."[168] His dislike of this "unscrupulous game" nevertheless was more than balanced by England's interest in securing support against Russia's designs upon the Straits and, to a less extent, by his desire to secure a position from which he could observe and perhaps check Bismarck's plans.[169] To reassure the suspicious Salisbury as to Prince William's pro-Russian tendencies, Bismarck expounded at great length the conservative and peaceful factors of German policy, which no sovereign or minister could change, and he communicated the text of the Dual Alliance as proof of its defensive character.[170] His efforts culminated in England's adherence, December 12, to the second Mediterranean Accord.

Bismarck also resorted to publicity to supplement his complex diplomatic arrangements. On May 11, 1887, he had secured Austria's consent to the eventual publication of the Dual Alliance, with the single exception of its time limit, and had, a few days later, read the entire text to the Russian ambassador. Its appear-

[164] Cecil, *Salisbury*, IV, 50, 51 (Aug. 10, 1887).
[165] *Ibid.*, IV, 48, 49 (July 20).
[166] *Ibid.*, IV, 69 (Oct. 29).
[167] *Ibid.*, IV, 69, 70 (Oct. 28).
[168] *Ibid.*, IV, 71 (Nov. 2).
[169] *Ibid.*, IV, 69, 70 (Oct. 28).
[170] Hatzfeldt, London, Nov. 11; Bismarck, Nov. 22. *G. P.*, VI, 367, 368, 376-380, 393n.

ance in the *Staats-Anzeiger* (Feb. 3, 1888), minus the article containing its time limit, followed a series of alarmist reports of troop movements in Russia,[171] and was explained as a move to allay doubts as to its defensive character. It was also intended to correct the exaggerated views of Germany's obligations recently expressed in the Hungarian parliament, to restrain Russia,

Jn der Galerie „Bismarck".

Kladderadatsch, February 12, 1888.

Figure 11.—"I beg Your Majesty to give your especially gracious attention to this work of art—which always gives me peace and confidence."

and, what was in Bismarck's opinion of equal importance, to assure the support of German opinion for the defensive war which might arise from it. "In my judgment," he wrote, "this is more valuable than a considerable number of army corps."[172] Knowledge of the terms of the alliance elicited the same unanimous approval which had greeted its conclusion in 1879,[173] but its publication under the circumstances was naturally regarded more

[171] *Post*, Jan. 19, 22; *National Zeitung*, Jan. 24. The *Kölnische Zeitung* (Jan. 19) traced these reports to the *Militär-Wochenblatt*, an organ of the general staff. There was more than a little talk of a Russian attack upon Germany. *P. J.*, vol. 61, p. 93 (Jan. 1888). Among the skeptics were: *Berliner Tageblatt*, Jan. 3; *Kölnische Zeitung*, Jan. 9; *National Zeitung*, Jan. 24.

[172] *G. P.*, V, 282.

[173] Rantzau, Jan. 22, 1888. *Ibid.*, V, 284, 285.

definitely as a warning to Russia than as an admonition to Austria. If the *Norddeutsche* (Feb. 4) wrote vaguely of "the needs of an abnormal situation," the *Post* (Feb. 5) compared it to the "emplacement of a large calibre cannon showing the strength of the defense to those who are thinking of war." The *Kölnische Zeitung* (Feb. 4) represented it as a reply to the concentration of Russian troops on the Austrian, German, and Roumanian frontiers and to the presence in Russia of Floquet, of *"Vive la Pologne, Monsieur!"* fame.[174] The opposition press stressed even more definitely its significance as a warning to Russia. The *Berliner Tageblatt* (Feb. 4) felt that the government had confidential information of the utmost importance as to the Russian danger.

Uncertainty was a striking characteristic of German opinion early in February. "Hope and fear, affirmation and doubt, confidence and alarm," wrote the *Vossische Zeitung* (Feb. 6), "meet and contradict each other." Germany, and all Europe, awaited Bismarck's speech (Feb. 6) in hope of reassurance and enlightenment. Occasioned by the first reading of a supplementary army bill, its essential purpose was to serve his foreign policy, since the passage of the bill was assured.[175] Spoken in a low tone audible, it was said, only to the first rows of the Reichstag, it was heard, nevertheless, by all Europe. He was confident of peace. Again, as in his speech of January 12, 1887, he declared that Germany would never attack any one: the Reichstag would quite justifiably refuse credits for an offensive war. The Alliance of 1879 was defensive and was not intended to augment Germany's prestige. Nor was its publication, he hastened to assure Russia, intended as a menace. He did not believe that Germany's neighbors planned to attack her. As to France, there had been, he acknowledged, a great improvement, for the moderate Grévy had been followed by the still more peaceful Carnot, and dangerous members of the cabinet had been dropped. He insisted, nevertheless, that France would certainly attack in the event of a Russo-German war. In regard to relations with

---

[174] It acknowledged (Feb. 6), however, that a Franco-Russian alliance was no longer "the *Sehnsucht* of French hearts" nor the bugbear of Germans.

[175] *Volks-Zeitung*, Feb. 5.

Russia, he was extremely circumspect, deprecating any need for alarm in view of the Tsar's pacific intentions. Her troop movements threatened neither Austria nor Germany, for they were intended to strengthen Russia's diplomacy. In his speech of January 12, 1887, he had studiously neglected the Pan-Slavic agitation; he now spoke of it in connection with the Russian press. Its menaces were not to be taken seriously, for the newspapers lacked the power of the French press. Compared with the Tsar's will, it lay a featherweight in the balance. Its tirades were merely "printer's ink," but a warning accompanied this contemptuous dismissal. "Every country," he said, "is responsible in the long run for the windows broken by its press; the bill will be presented sooner or later in the form of the ill-will of the other country." He repeated his assurances of Germany's support in Bulgaria on the condition that Russia would take the initiative, but he presented the *furor teutonicus* of 1813 as the alternative to Germany's friendship. "We Germans," he concluded, "fear God but nothing else in the world." [176]

His speech was sufficiently firm in its treatment of Russia to earn the enthusiastic approval of public opinion. Since their overwhelming defeat in the February elections, 1887, the opposition parties had maintained an embittered reserve, convinced that they were the victims of an unscrupulous trick. They now joined the cartel parties in a demonstration of national unity.[177] The *Berliner Tageblatt* (Feb. 7) stressed his repudiation of a preventive war as an accurate reflection of German opinion, and the opposition press generally agreed that his purpose had been to strengthen peace. Only the Social Democratic *Berliner Volksblatt* (Feb. 9, 10) refused to join the chorus of approval. Bismarck's own exposition proved the failure of his policy, the relative decline of Germany's military strength in comparison with that of her opponents, and hence the certainty of war. Its own advice was to approach the two Western powers at any price. Bismarck's following in the press was less certain of the speech's

---

176 *Verhandlungen*, VII Leg. Per., II Sess., II, 724–734.
177 *Volks-Zeitung*, Feb. 7; *Vossische Zeitung*, Feb. 7; *Germania*, Feb. 7, 8; *Weser Zeitung*, in N. A. Z., Feb. 10; *Nation*, Feb. 11. The unanimity of opinion was welcomed by the *Kölnische Zeitung* (Feb. 7) and the N. A. Z. (Feb. 7).

peaceful character than the newspapers which had often been charged with desiring war with Russia. Russia must choose, wrote the Berlin correspondent of the *Kölnische Zeitung* (Feb. 7), between peace and war for the solution of the Bulgarian question; and the *Post* (Feb. 8) refused to accept Bismarck's repudiation of a preventive war as anything more than a concession to a temporary situation.

Russia was closely watched for evidence of a change of heart. She therefore had Germany's (and France's) support when she asked Turkey to act against Ferdinand, but when she turned to the other powers she found that England, Austria, and Italy would do nothing without definite information as to her intentions after his removal. Russia thereupon retreated into an extreme reserve. The crisis had passed without war, but it was only too clear that its underlying causes remained. In Germany, the enthusiasm and confidence which had followed Bismarck's speech soon changed to discouragement and pessimism. The Progressive *Nation* (Feb. 11) doubted that the speech would improve the situation permanently, and the Conservative *Preussische Jahrbücher* feared that it would not assure peace for more than the current year.[178] "Everything remains the same," wrote the moderate *Vossische Zeitung* (Feb. 17), and four days later it referred to a Franco-Russian alliance almost as an accomplished fact. The military authorities hastened preparations for a war on two fronts, until Russia's passive acceptance of the check in Bulgaria diminished the immediate danger.[179]

The view that Bismarck's diplomacy and use of publicity had maintained peace during this disturbed period assumes a real danger of a French attack and of an Austro-Russian war arising from the Bulgarian question. If these assumptions were well-founded, Bismarck's policy was a masterpiece of intimidation, conciliation, and a nice balancing of national interests. But the maintenance of peace does not prove that it had been dangerously threatened. It seems indisputable that a good deal of the crisis was of Bismarck's own contrivance. He undoubtedly exag-

---

[178] *P. J.*, vol. 61, p. 291 (March 1888).
[179] Falkenstein, *Bismarck und die Kriegsgefahr*, p. 54; Blumenthal, Feb. 21. Waldersee, *Briefwechsel*, I, 63.

Die dreizehnte Arbeit des Herkules.

Kladderadatsch, July 8, 1888.

Figure 12.—The Chancellor's position since 1870.

gerated the menace from France to serve his domestic policy, and the threat of a Russian occupation of Bulgaria would have been less serious without his repeated assurances of support. The result was a first-rate crisis in the Near East, which his diplomatic genius, after contributing to it, kept from eventuating in war. The Reinsurance Treaty, which is often regarded as his greatest diplomatic success, probably had a smaller part in the maintenance of peace than the second Mediterranean Accord, which he helped to establish in direct contravention of its terms and spirit. Nor did the treaty materially improve the public contacts between the two contracting powers, for their relations were never so tense as during the period following its conclusion.

For the first time, Germans had faced the real or supposed danger of a war on two fronts. The opposition parties struggled in vain against the fears it aroused. With the additional dread of a constitutional conflict, those fears swept away their control of the Reichstag and satisfied Bismarck's desire for a rubber-stamp majority. On any issue concerning relations with France, the opposition had the instinctive reactions of national sentiment, excited by systematic press campaigns, against them. It was even divided against itself, for a part of its press merely questioned the imminence of the French danger. Only the Social Democrats asserted France's essentially peaceful intentions and supported an understanding with her (and England) as the only satisfactory solution for the problems of German foreign policy.[180] Bismarck's tactics had failed at first to unite German opinion, but the publication of the Dual Alliance and his speech of February 6, 1888, achieved this result, the Social Democrats alone dissenting. Never since July 1870 had there been an equal unanimity in support of Bismarck's foreign policy.

---

[180] It would, according to the *Berliner Volksblatt* (Feb. 17, 1888), eliminate the most important cause of the Russian danger.

CHAPTER VII

New Leaders and Old Policies, 1888-1895

Unseres Erachtens wäre es das Richtigste gewesen, nach
dem Abgang des Begründers des deutschen Reiches den ehrlichen Versuch zu machen, Bismarcksche Politik ohne den
Fürsten Bismarck zu machen.
Kölnische Zeitung, Feb. 12, 1891.

Unsere Politik könne aber und solle nur eine einfache sein.
Caprivi, May 30, 1890. *G. P.,* VII, 29, 30.

Das heisst doch nicht Anderes, als dass die Politik des
'neuen Kursis' ihre Aufgabe darin gesehen hat, die Dinge zu
nehmen, wie sie gekommen sind, und lediglich zu sorgen,
dass Deutschland bei diesem 'einfachen Verlaufen' desselben
nicht zu Schäden käme. Das ist die Politik des Gehens and
Gehenlassens, das Nehmens und Geschehenlassens, wie der
liebe Gott es fügt! . . .
E. Bauer, *Caveat Populus!* (Berlin, 1892), pp. 45, 46.

I

The last two years of Bismarck's career were disturbed by no
serious international crises. His system of alliances discouraged
Russia from pressing her claims in Bulgaria, and the collapse of
the Boulangist agitation reduced the danger from France. Russia's aversion to republican institutions and lack of confidence in
France's foreign policy strengthened the doubtful defense against
a Franco-Russian alliance in the Reinsurance Treaty. During
this period, the details of foreign affairs were less significant than
the protracted struggle for power within Germany. The political situation at first left little to be desired from Bismarck's point
of view. Only the Social Democrats continued openly to criticize
his foreign policy after the elections of 1887. He had nothing to
fear from the demoralized opposition, unless the accession of
Crown Prince Frederick should lead to an alliance between the
Emperor and the liberals.

During William I's long reign Bismarck's control had acquired a deceptive appearance of permanence. Nevertheless, the prospect that a change of rulers might suddenly terminate it contributed for years to his sleepless nights. He saw in Frederick's liberalism a menace to the Empire and in the English connections and sympathies of the Crown Princess a threat to his foreign policy. The thought of the venerable ruler's approaching death moved him to tears.[1] The immediate problem he solved by depriving Frederick of any real influence; with the Emperor's approval, Bismarck had rarely taken him into his confidence in regard to foreign affairs. In 1884, he sent Prince William, instead of his father, to represent Germany at Alexander III's coronation. The desire for a barrier to Frederick's liberalism was probably among the reasons why he sought a nationalist and conservative majority in the Reichstag elections of 1887.

The Crown Prince's fatal illness dealt a rude blow to the liberals. With only a few months to live after his succession to the throne (March 9, 1888), Frederick reluctantly reconciled himself to the impossibility of setting a new course for German policy. The Empress Frederick, Queen Victoria's daughter, nevertheless refused to abandon without a struggle her dream of reducing Prussia's influence in Germany and of instituting reforms upon English models.[2] She had undoubtedly planned that Bismarck's dismissal should be one of her husband's first official acts. "As you cannot gather grapes from thorns or figs from thistles," she had recently written to her mother, "so can you not expect from him that which modern Germany lacks and which it thirsts for, and that is peace among its classes, races, religions and parties, good and friendly relations with its neighbors."[3] Bismarck correctly regarded her as his most dangerous opponent. His ruthless attack is, for this study, the chief interest of Frederick III's brief and tragic reign.

The conflict seemed hopelessly unequal. Alone, Bismarck was a formidable enemy, but, on the issue of liberalism, he had the

---

[1] Courcel, May 28, 1885. *D. D. F.*, (3), VI, 45, 46.
[2] See her moving letter to Queen Victoria on the day of Frederick's funeral (June 15). C. Radziwill, *The Empress Frederick* (N. Y., 1934), p. 223.
[3] Ponsonby, *Letters of the Empress Frederick*, p. 272 (Jan. 5, 1888).

support of the powerful nationalist and Conservative groups. He could have desired no more favorable conditions for the contest. The two Bismarcks easily enlisted Prince William. His father's reign, he said in June 1887, would destroy Germany;[4] in a toast on Bismarck's birthday following his grandfather's death, he spoke of the Chancellor as the leader toward whom all eyes were turned at a time when the commander-in-chief lay dead and the chief-of-staff was mortally wounded.[5] Except for her friends among the Progressives, the Empress stood alone, since Frederick could give her little support, and Bismarck's constant surveillance made impossible any other than secret and indirect contacts with her political allies.[6] Nevertheless, Bismarck did not underestimate the danger: his pulse, he said, increased fifteen beats under the new government.[7] Although he arranged a kind of armed truce in his personal relations with the Empress, he launched a savage campaign, which did not spare even the sick ruler. No reference to Frederick's accession (on the excuse that a regency might be established[8]) appeared in Minister Puttmaker's speech at the opening session of the Prussian Abgeordnetenhaus, and the president of that assembly closed his remarks with the equivocal invocation: *"Gott schütze das Vaterland!"*[9] The *Kölnische Zeitung* (March 14) callously informed its readers that the Emperor's recovery was impossible and (March 25) that Germany's foreign policy would remain unchanged. Thus, according to the Catholic *Germania* (April 10), Frederick was denied the right to have any opinions of his own.[10]

The Empress' revival of the Battenberg marriage project against

---

[4] *Aus 50 Jahren; Erinnerungen, Tagebücher und Briefe aus dem Nachlass des Fürsten Philipp zu Eulenburg Hertefeld* (Berlin, 1925), pp. 136, 183.

[5] *Post*, in *Frankfurter Zeitung*, April 4, 1888. The *Norddeutsche* changed the text, making it appear less offensive to the mortally ill Emperor. *D. D. F.*, (1), VII, 105 (April 9).

[6] Feder, *Bismarcks grosses Spiel*, p. 341 *passim*.

[7] Busch, *Tagebuchblätter*, III, 237 (April 8, 1888). A recent writer has said of this incident that it was "the last and decisive struggle by German liberalism for the possession of political power." G. Beyerhaus, "Die Krise der Liberalismus und das Problem der 99 Tage," *P. J.*, vol. 239, p. 1.

[8] *Liberale Korrespondenz*, in *Volks-Zeitung*, March 10.

[9] *Volks-Zeitung*, March 11.

[10] The Catholic press was said to have surpassed the Progressive newspapers in its zealous defense of the Emperor. *P. J.*, vol. 61, pp. 517, 518 (April 1888).

the advice of her Progressive friends and her invitation to Prince Alexander to visit the court in Berlin challenged Bismarck on a question intimately affecting his foreign policy, thereby giving him a distinct advantage in the contest for power.[11] He at once represented the project as a gratuitous offense to Russia, which would profit England alone. England, wrote the *Kölnische Zeitung* (March 15), must pull her own chestnuts out of the Russian fire. A week later (March 23), Bismarck developed the same theme to the imperial council. When he stressed the necessity of reserve in the Bulgarian question—frequently interjecting the remark that "he could work for a German, never for an English policy"—Frederick approved, doubtless not entirely because of his physical condition, for he was still reluctant to break with the traditions of Germany's foreign policy.[12] On April 4, Bismarck's ultimate victory was assured when he obtained the cancellation of Prince Alexander's visit by threatening to resign.[13] To make his success doubly certain, he informed Frederick that Queen Victoria had been responsible for the revival of the Battenberg marriage project, and, on the same day, he asked Russia for a statement that the visit would have been offensive to her.[14] Giers, however, refused to play Bismarck's game. Although he had earlier explained Russia's objections to the marriage, he replied, to Bismarck's great annoyance, that the visit would not have weakened Russia's confidence in Germany's friendship.[15] The Chancellor was not more successful in trying to use England. Salisbury had instructed Malet, the British ambassador in Berlin, to "discourage any leaning to English notions of policy" on the part of the Empress, for her proper rôle was "to be mildly Bismarckian and intensely German," but he refused to intervene against the marriage.[16] By this time, Queen Victoria had lost

---

11 The liberal *Frankfurter Zeitung* (April 13) approved Bismarck's stand on this question.

12 Ballhausen, *Bismarck-Erinnerungen*, pp. 441, 442.

13 The *Kölnische Zeitung* announced this decision on April 7.

14 *G. P.*, VI, 287, 288 (April 4), 281, 282 (April 4).

15 Schweinitz, St. Petersburg, April 5; Bismarck, April 8. *Ibid.*, VI, 289–291; Meyendorff, *Correspondance de M. de Staal*, I, 414, 415 (Giers, April 6). *Cf.* E. Wolfe, *Kaiser Friedrich; Die Tragödie des Übergangenen* (Helleran bei Dresden, 1931), pp. 281, 272.

16 Cecil, *Salisbury*, IV, 96, 97 (March 14); Malet, April 9. Ponsonby, *Letters of the Empress Frederick*, p. 297.

her earlier enthusiasm for this family alliance; yet she refused to give up her plan of visiting Berlin at Bismarck's behest.[17] Bismarck's bark was louder than his bite. In Berlin the Queen was "agreeably surprised to find him so amiable and gentle."[18] Frederick's renewed approval of his policy (April 12) apparently satisfied him that the last had been heard of the Battenberg affair, although in reality the Empress' heart was still immovably set upon it.[19]

In the meantime, public opinion had been appealed to on Bismarck's behalf. Notwithstanding his probable success after the cancellation of Prince Alexander's visit (April 4), the *Kölnische Zeitung* announced on the next day (April 5), that Germany might lose the services of her great Chancellor.[20] On April 7, Bismarck furnished Busch with the material for a bitter attack upon the Empress and her marriage project. Busch's article represented Frederick as in agreement with Bismarck, while the Empress was depicted as acting in England's interests. She had always remained, wrote Busch, an Englishwoman at heart. It was an arguable point whether she valued the title of German Empress more highly than that of Princess Royal of England.[21] The nationalists and Conservatives at once rallied to him. The marriage, according to the National Liberal *National Zeitung* (April 10), was inconceivable. A flood of petitions protested against the possibility of Bismarck's resignation. "The thought that he may one day no longer be at the head of the German Empire," wrote the *Nation* (April 14), a Progressive weekly, "seems so dreadful to many that they turn from this prospect as from the head of a Medusa." Denying that even Bismarck was indispensable, the opposition retained its equanimity, insisting that the German people had other able leaders. The Progressive *Freisinnige Zeitung* (April 29) found nothing more

---

[17] *Letters of Queen Victoria* (3), I, 397 (April 8).
[18] *Ibid.,* (3), I, 404, 405, (April 25). On April 24, the *Frankfurter Zeitung* noted that the campaign in the inspired press against England and Queen Victoria had ceased.
[19] Ballhausen, *Bismarck-Erinnerungen,* p. 447; Feder, *Bismarcks grosses Spiel,* p. 371.
[20] Feder, *Bismarcks grosses Spiel,* pp. 342, 343 (April 21); Ballhausen, *Bismarck-Erinnerungen,* p, 446.
[21] Busch, *Tagebuchblätter,* III, 237. *Cf.* "Fremde Einflüsse," *Grenzboten,* 1888, IV, 153–167 (Nov. 17).

mysterious in the success of his foreign policy than the exploitation of differences between other countries. "Every period," said the Catholic *Germania* (April 7), "will produce its necessary leaders and others will take the rudder after Bismarck."

II

Frederick's death (June 15, 1888) removed one threat to Bismarck's control of German policy, but William II's accession raised another that was more serious. Against his parents, William had sided with the Chancellor, but, lacking his grandfather's steadfastness and his father's self-abnegation, there was little assurance that this agreement would continue. His exalted conception of the crown, his self-confidence, his youthful eagerness to try his hand at the business of government, and his mercurial temperament made a clash practically inevitable. To encourage it in order to bring about Bismarck's fall was the purpose of not a few ranking officers in the army, of highly placed officials in the foreign office, and even of reigning princes. Their intrigues were in part responsible for the recurring friction between the young Emperor and the aged Chancellor.

William's accession revived earlier fears abroad as to the future course of German policy. A Marcus Aurelius, it was said in France, where much had been expected of the Emperor Frederick, had been followed by a Commodus.[22] Salisbury spoke of the German ship of state as leaving the harbor for the open sea, which was covered with "white horses."[23] William's first public pronouncements were disquieting, although the usual assertions of peaceful purposes appeared on the appropriate occasions. A reference in his speech at the opening of the Reichstag to the strength of the Triple Alliance as a guarantee of peace and as a basis for good relations with Russia disturbed even Giers, the friendly Russian foreign minister.[24] Disregarding the precedent set by his father in addressing his first proclamation to the nation, William singled out the army for this honor and stressed his feeling of identity with it. A few weeks later, in reply to a rumor

---

[22] Carroll, *French Public Opinion*, p. 145.
[23] Cecil, *Salisbury*, IV, 96.
[24] Meyendorff, *Correspondance de M. de Staal*, I, 429 (June 15, 1888).

that his father had been willing to discuss the return of Alsace-Lorraine,[25] he publicly affirmed the willingness of the entire army to die on the battlefield rather than to yield an inch of Germany's conquests. The German people, acknowledged the *National Zeitung* (Aug. 19, 1888), needed time to adjust itself to this sort of thing, but to army officers like Waldersee, William's sabre-rattling was a healthy sign.[26] These speeches, so unlike those of William I, furnished the first public evidence that Bismarck's control had weakened and that Germany's future was henceforth to depend, as never before, upon the caprices of her sovereign.

Friction had already appeared between the Emperor and Chancellor. Intervals of satisfactory relations alternated with serious differences of opinion during the next two years. Relations with Russia had occasioned a clash even in Frederick III's brief reign. Under the influence of Waldersee and the military clique, William had turned against Bismarck's policy of conciliation.[27] He agreed with them that the Tsar had neither the desire nor the ability to resist the pressure of the Pan-Slavs, and with Kálnoky, the Austrian foreign minister, that Russia should have been destroyed in the autumn of 1887.[28] To defend his Russian policy as well as his own power, Bismarck had embittered Frederick's last days and had stopped at nothing in his persecution of the Empress Frederick, but he dared not resort to similar methods against their self-willed son. Instead of attempting to intimidate William, even when he was still the Crown Prince, Bismarck recommended a war with France. He coolly enumerated its advantages: it could be precipitated more easily and terminated more speedily than one with Russia, and it could be represented to the public as the necessary price of a permanent peace.[29] Although it is not clear that either William or Waldersee had in mind an immediate war with Russia,[30]

[25] *National Zeitung,* Aug. 19, 1888.
[26] Waldersee, *Denkwürdigkeiten,* I, 398, 399 (May 10).
[27] Oncken, *Vorgeschichte des Weltkrieges,* II, 361.
[28] William II's comments. Reuss, Vienna, April 28, 1888. *G. P.,* VI, 301, 302. See also Bismarck, May 3, with William II's and Bismarck's comments. *Ibid.,* VI, 302, 303.
[29] Bismarck, May 9. *Ibid.,* VI, 304-307.
[30] Waldersee, *Denkwürdigkeiten,* I, 398, 399 (May 10).

Bismarck's advice, which was manifestly inconsistent with his earlier policy, may perhaps best be explained as a move to attract William from Waldersee's dangerous influence, both to show the Crown Prince that the advocates of a war with Russia did not understand the correct approach even to a warlike solution of Germany's difficulties and to establish his own influence with William. Nevertheless, the Chancellor went to considerable trouble to give the impression that he was thinking of war. He told the ministry that less care would henceforth be exerted to avoid a war with France. Germany, would not provoke a conflict, but another Schnaebelé affair or the crisis which might arise in connection with the succession question in Luxemburg would result in war if it were allowed to take its natural course.[31] William, it seems, seriously expected a war with France to follow his father's death,[32] and Waldersee, who had at first discounted Bismarck's stand as a reply to William's criticism of his Russian policy, thought that the establishment of more stringent passport regulations on the Alsatian frontier was the first step in that direction.[33] No scare articles appeared, however, in the press, a fairly reliable indication that Bismarck's talk of war was intended to serve other purposes. The official *Norddeutsche* (May 29) explained the new passport regulations as a measure for the more effective assimilation of the conquered provinces. Far from desiring war, Germany had "carried respect for our neighbor's independence to the extent of tolerating the most unjust hatred of us."

By July 1888 the differences between the Emperor and Bismarck had been temporarily made up, for William informed Queen Victoria that "I am quite *d'accord* with Prince Bismarck. . . ."[34] St. Petersburg was selected for the first of his many visits to foreign capitals. His coolness toward England, which had not been entirely overshadowed by his suspicions of Russia, and his Austrian sympathies were taken into account in the *aides-mémoires,* which were to guide William and Herbert Bismarck

[31] Ballhausen, *Bismarck-Erinnerungen,* p. 452 (May 13).

[32] Waldersee, *Denkwürdigkeiten,* I, 399 (May 16).

[33] *Ibid.,* I, 398, 399 (May 16), 400 (May 17). These regulations were announced before Emperor Frederick's death. *Frankfurter Zeitung,* May 28.

[34] *Letters of Queen Victoria,* (3) I, 425 (July 6).

in their conversations. Bulgaria was excluded from Germany's approval of Russia's interests, but that approval explicitly covered her desire for the control of the Straits and Constantinople.[35] The visit, though a social success, produced no significant political results. Soon there appeared a perceptible coolness in the public discussion of Russo-German relations when the *Norddeutsche* (July 16) reported that the *Novoe Vremja* had attributed the visit to Bismarck's initiative. Even the Conservatives' Russian sympathies had decidedly cooled. Nothing remained, according to the *Preussische Jahrbücher,* of their warm attachment; only those who had investments in Russia or who feared a great war favored an understanding with her at the sacrifice of Austria's interests. So few were the newspapers which favored a Russo-German agreement at this price that they deserved a place in the museums.[36] Yet the Progressives as well as the Nationalists and Conservatives agreed that the visit was a good thing, for it at least prolonged the appearance of an understanding and demonstrated Germany's peaceful policy. "It may soon be worth while," wrote the Progressive *Nation* (July 2), "that European opinion should think of Germany as working sincerely for the maintenance of peace." Indeed, Bismarck's Russian policy was temporarily strengthened toward the end of 1888 by William's doubts as to Austria's loyalty, and in the following spring by the desire of the general staff for time in which to complete the rearmament of the infantry.[37] In June 1889 the truce was broken when Bismarck refused the Emperor's request for a press attack against Russia after her decision to transfer her loans from Berlin to Paris.[38] Herbert Bismarck prevented an open break, but, according to Waldersee, the turning point had arrived. "In his heart," wrote the general, "William has broken with the Bismarcks, father and son . . . and since then he has merely played a game." [39] The rift was widened when the *Norddeutsche* and the *Hamburger Nachrichten* were charged with advising William to make war upon Russia, because

---

[35] *G. P.,* VI, 311–314 (July 6).
[36] *P. J.,* vol. 62, p. 413 (Sept. 1888).
[37] Waldersee, *Denkwürdigkeiten,* II, 13 (Nov. 1), II, 48 (April 15).
[38] Bismarck, *Gedanken und Erinnerungen,* III, 142–144.
[39] Waldersee, *op. cit.,* II, 54, 55 (July 7, 1889).

the Emperor felt that this criticism was directed against himself.[40] Such incidents as William's visit to Constantinople in
the autumn of 1889 revealed his increasing disregard of Bismarck's advice, while his own vanity was wounded by the numerous reminders which he encountered of the Chancellor's prestige abroad.[41] Nevertheless, he could not bring himself to
break with Bismarck on the issue of Russo-German relations.[42]
In October 1889, he agreed to abandon the idea of a second visit
to Russia, doubtless unaware that Bismarck feared the results
of a prolonged intimacy between the impulsive Emperor and the
reserved and suspicious Tsar.[43]

Relations with England were even less responsible than those
with Russia for the widening breach. At first, Queen Victoria
and the Prince of Wales resented the treatment of the Empress
Frederick. The Queen hoped that "we shall be very cool,
though civil" in official relations with William and Bismarck.[44]
In the autumn of 1888, an open break between the Emperor and
Prince Edward, his uncle, was narrowly averted when William
refused to meet his uncle in Vienna because the latter had, it
was said, represented the Emperor Frederick as having been
ready to return Alsace-Lorraine to France. Edward's familiar
manners were distasteful to his nephew as lacking in respect.[45]
These family quarrels did not seriously affect the official relations between the two countries, although the incompatibility
between uncle and nephew survived to poison them in later
years. The Queen agreed with Salisbury that England's interests required good relations, and her daughter, the Empress
Frederick, wrote that "Prince Bismarck's wickedness and William's folly" should not be permitted to disturb them.[46]

As nationalist opinion lost its illusions in regard to the traditional friendship with Russia, it flirted with the idea of a close
union with England.[47] In August 1888 Bismarck brought to

40 Waldersee, Denkwürdigkeiten, II, 60–62 (July 18).
41 E. Gagliardi, Bismarcks Entlassung (Tübingen, 1927), pp. 295–297.
42 Conversation with Frau von Spitzenberg, Dec. 5, 6, 1889. B. G. W., VIII, 672.
43 Bismarck, Gedanken und Erinnerungen, III, 144, 145.
44 Letters of Queen Victoria (3), I, 429 (July 7, 1888).
45 Ibid., (3), I, 439 (Oct. 13, 1888).
46 Ponsonby, Letters of the Empress Frederick, p. 359 (Nov. 2, 1888).
47 National Zeitung, Aug. 8, 1888; Hartmann, Zwei Jahrzehnte, p. 358 (Aug. 1888).

England's attention the decisive influence that might become hers in assuring a permanent peace by joining the satisfied powers (he meant, of course, the Triple Alliance) after increasing her own military forces.[48] Nevertheless, he was strangely indifferent to English sentiment, for he continued his vendetta against the German liberals and the memory of Emperor Frederick. Sir Robert Morier, at this time the British ambassador to Russia, was charged with having abused his position as the British minister in Munich in 1870 and his close relations at that time with Frederick by furnishing the French with information as to the movements of the German armies during the Franco-Prussian War. The London *Times* immediately launched an indignant denial,[49] but the incident undoubtedly stimulated anti-English sentiment in Germany and offended English susceptibilities. "Never," affirmed the Progressive *Nation* (Jan. 12, 1889), "has so severe a blow been struck at England's sympathies." Yet Bismarck chose this moment for an offer of an alliance to England. On January 11, he asked Hatzfeld, the ambassador to England, to explain that a secret alliance would assure England's defense against France and that an open alliance, ratified by the two parliaments, would deter France from attacking her. Although Salisbury was willing to agree that England's interests were in general those of the Triple Alliance, Bismarck's offers were far from satisfactory, for the proposed alliance was to be directed solely against France; Germany, Bismarck insisted, must retain her freedom of action in an Anglo-Russian war.[50] This reservation, not to mention England's traditional isolation, was sufficient to account for Salisbury's dilatory tactics and for his failure to communicate the offer either to the foreign office or to the Queen.[51] In reply Salisbury said merely that he could only "leave it on the table, without saying yes or no." [52] He was even less favorably impressed by Chamberlain's

---

[48] Berchem, Aug. 21, 1888. *G. P.*, IV, 399, 400.
[49] *Nation*, Jan. 5, 1889.
[50] Bismarck, *G. P.*, VI, 400–403.
[51] Hatzfeldt, Jan. 16, 1889. *Cf.* Japikse, *Europa und Bismarcks Friedenspolitik*, p. 190. For the political difficulties confronting an alliance, see the Earl of Derby's explanations to the French ambassador. Waddington, Jan. 3, 1888. *D. D. F.*, (1), VII, 5–7.
[52] H. Bismarck, March 22. *G. P.*, VI, 404–406.

suggestion of an exchange of Heligoland for German Southwest Africa as the first step in a general liquidation of the colonial differences between the two countries; he could see no value for the British Empire in the latter territory and none for Germany in Heligoland.[53]

Meanwhile, William's attitude toward England improved. The English were ready to meet him halfway. Although Salisbury had refused Bismarck's offer of an alliance, he advised the Queen to respond to her grandson's advances.[54] In June 1889, William was delighted with his appointment as an admiral of the British fleet. "Fancy wearing the same uniform as St. Vincent and Nelson," he wrote to Malet, "it is enough to make one giddy." [55] A visit to England soon completed the reconciliation, but he accepted Bismarck's advice to await a later occasion when England's need for Germany's support would make her more generous before renewing the interrupted conversations for an exchange of colonial territory for Heligoland.[56] In Russia, William's visit to England was regarded as evidence of at least a rapprochement,[57] an opinion which was shared by some German observers, but in reality not much progress had been made. If Salisbury viewed askance an association with the Triple Alliance, Bismarck had no intention of permitting him to use an improvement in Anglo-German relations to disturb Germany's relations with Russia.[58] Neither Russia nor Germany wished to withdraw from the Reinsurance Treaty, although the heyday of their friendship had passed.

Even the fact that the treaty was to expire in June 1890 failed to give Germany's relations with Russia a decisive influence in the final clash resulting in Bismarck's dismissal. Those relations were used by both protagonists—by Bismarck to defend his position and by William to attack it—but the real quarrel was over the control of domestic policies. Although William's dis-

[53] H. Bismarck, March 27. *G. P.*, VI, 406–409.
[54] Salisbury, March 9. *Letters of Queen Victoria* (3), I, 477.
[55] William II, June 14. *Ibid.*, (3), I, 504.
[56] Berchem, June 21. *G. P.*, VI, 413, 414; Bismarck's comments, H. Bismarck, June 21. *Ibid.*, VI, 415–417.
[57] Giers, Aug. 9, 1889. Meyendorff, *Correspondance de M. de Staal*, II, 48; *P. J.*, vol. 64, 382–384 (Aug. 1889).
[58] Ballhausen, *Bismarck-Erinnerungen*, pp. 500, 501 (Aug. 17, 1889).

regard of the Chancellor's prerogatives under an old administrative rule (1852) that no minister should consult the Emperor except in the Chancellor's presence furnished the occasion
for Bismarck's resignation, the crisis was actually precipitated by
William's determination to abandon the use of force against
the Social Democrats. William had been won by Waldersee,
Hofprediger Stöcker, and the city mission group to the idea
that they might yield to kindness after they had refused to bow
to persecution. He dreamed of winning popularity for himself among the working classes and of reconciling them to the
Empire. As a substitute for Bismarck's anti-Socialist laws, whose
renewal the Reichstag was almost certain to refuse,[59] he proposed an international congress in Berlin on the hours of labor
in coal mines. Simulating approval, Bismarck coöperated in
drafting the invitation to the powers (Feb. 5), but at the same
time he secretly encouraged them to accept Switzerland's invitation to a similar congress in Berne. What William's reaction
would have been if he had been aware of this deception is not
difficult to imagine, but Eulenburg, the Emperor's friend, persuaded Switzerland to postpone her own congress and thus
avoid an immediate clash. Bismarck's good fortune, however,
had at last deserted him. On February 20, owing to the absence
of a stirring issue, to his own strange inactivity (he was absent
from Berlin during most of the campaign), and to popular
discontentment with high prices and taxes, the opposition won a
clear majority in the Reichstag elections, reversing the decision
of 1887. The increase of the Social Democratic group from
eleven to thirty-five and of its popular vote by 1,500,000 votes
proved the failure of Bismarck's policy of repression.[60] Even the
Progressives more than recovered the ground which they had
lost three years earlier by winning thirty-one seats, making a
total of sixty-nine.

These results were acclaimed as signifying the collapse of Bis-

---

[59] L. Bergsträsser, *Geschichte der politischen Parteien in Deutschland* (Mannheim, 1928, 5th ed.), p. 120.

[60] W. Mommsen, *Bismarcks Sturz und die Parteien* (Berlin, 1924), pp. 16, 17. Thanks to the absence of an immediate crisis, the *Norddeutsche's* (Feb. 17) plea that the need of a demonstration of national unity to moderate France was as great as in 1887 had little effect. "Heute," wrote the *Kölnische Zeitung* (Feb. 19), "muss das kühle Pflichtgefühl dem ruhigen Bürger den Weg zum Wahltisch weisen."

marck's domestic policy.[61] "February 20," wrote Friedrich Engels, Karl Marx's collaborator, "is the beginning of the end of the Bismarckian era." Among the causes were, he said, the popular discontent with the colossal armaments and the international tension which Bismarck's treatment of France had produced.[62] According to Liebknecht, the German people had passed judgment upon Bismarck.[63] Already the rancorous Holstein had foreseen that a defeat of the government would put him in such isolation as he had never been in since 1866.[64] It was clear, in any event, that a new period of parliamentary obstruction was about to begin. On February 25, Bismarck expounded a plan of action to the Emperor which he described in general terms as one of repeated dissolutions of the Reichstag. Having maneuvered William into agreeing by expressing doubt of his firmness in repressing the Social Democrats, should they cause trouble, he then soothed his misgivings by speaking of legislation in behalf of the working classes and finally clinched a temporary success by offering to introduce a bill for the increase of the peacetime army by eighty thousand men (although Bismarck doubted its need).[65] William for the moment was dazzled; he repeated Bismarck's exclamation at the close of the interview, "No surrender (*Keine Übergabe*)!" [66] During the next few days, he nevertheless listened to those who desired Bismarck's dismissal and to the Conservatives who advised him against an open conflict with the Reichstag. Waldersee saw that the reports of the consul at Kiev (which Bismarck had withheld to avoid exciting William against Russia) representing Russia as actively preparing for war were brought to William's attention. The Emperor at once concluded that he had been deceived; he was strengthened in this feeling when Bismarck consulted with Windthorst, the Centrist leader, as to a union between the Conservatives, the National Liberals, and the Centrists, without informing him.[67]

---

[61] *Germania*, Feb. 22.
[62] *Sozial-Demokrat*, March 8, in Mommsen, *Bismarcks Sturz*, p. 175.
[63] *Verhandlungen*, VIII Leg. Per., I Sess., I, 103 (May 16, 1890).
[64] W. Schüssler, *Bismarcks Sturz* (Leipzig, 1922, 3d ed.), p. 132 (Jan. 7, 1890).
[65] Bismarck, *Gedanken und Erinnerungen*, III, 74.
[66] Schüssler, *Bismarcks Sturz*, pp. 137, 138; Zechlin, *Staatsstreichpläne Bismarcks*, pp. 32, 33.
[67] Schüssler, *Bismarcks Sturz*, p. 212.

The two-year struggle for power came to an end on March 17, when William insisted on Bismarck's resignation because the Chancellor stood his ground on the administrative rule of 1852. While the decision was chiefly the result of personal differences and of domestic politics, distrust of Russia influenced Waldersee, the Grand Duke of Baden, and Holstein to encourage William in his determination to break with Bismarck. Little was said of this factor either publicly or in private, since public opinion might demand Bismarck's retention if his resignation could be represented as the result of a clash of opinion in regard to foreign affairs.[68] That his control of foreign policy was necessary to conserve Germany's prestige abroad was an argument that played a considerable part in Bismarck's tenacious defense.[69] He counted upon it, according to the Austrian ambassador, to prevent a complete break and to assure at least his control of the foreign office.[70] It was to the needs of Germany's foreign policy that he appealed when he asked the ministry (March 17) for a strong statement in his behalf.[71] As in 1888, he tried to enlist Russia's support by confiding to Shuvalov, her ambassador, that relations with her as well as domestic questions were contributing to his involuntary resignation.[72] In the hope of securing his father's recall, Herbert Bismarck a few days later in vain misrepresented the Tsar as unwilling to negotiate the renewal of the Reinsurance Treaty with anyone else. *"Warum nicht?"* was William's sole comment.[73] Herbert's own retirement soon followed.

Bismarck's own views of the German constitutional system meant that the loss of William's favor would leave him defenseless. Despite the respect he had always shown for William I, he had considered himself as the ultimate source of power, even as the embodiment of the state. He told Schweinitz in 1884, *"Moi, je suis l'état,"* in the manner of Louis XIV.[74] He had never tried, except for a moment in 1888 against the influence

68 Eulenberg, *Aus 50 Jahren*, p. 287 (Jan. 8, 1890).
69 Ballhausen. *Bismarck-Erinnerungen*, pp. 509, 510 (Jan. 24, 1890).
70 Széchényi, April 26, 1890. Schüssler, *op. cit.*, p. 291.
71 *Ibid.*, p. 212.
72 Schweinitz, St. Petersburg, April 3, reporting Giers statement. *G. P.*, VII, 14.
73 H. Bismarck to William, March 20. R. Frankenberg, *Die Nichterneuerung des deutsch-russischen Rückversicherungsvertrage im Jahre 1890* (Berlin, 1927), pp. 48, 49.
74 Zechlin, *Staatsstreichpläne Bismarcks*, pp. 66, 67.

of the Empress Frederick, to enlist public opinion against the crown. On the contrary, he had used the Reichstag as a tool, encouraging the subdivision of its parties in order the more easily to dominate it; he had never recognized public opinion as a legitimate ally but only as an instrument for the attainment of his purposes. This is merely another way of saying that the only methods he ever contemplated for retaining the sovereign's favor were those of persuasion or intrigue. Bismarck had none of the ideology of the modern dictator.

Of an appeal to public opinion in his behalf there was scarcely a trace. Only the *Hamburger Nachrichten,* whose editor, Hermann Hofmann, had been in contact with him since 1888, spoke of the support which gratitude for his services should arouse.[75] The response to this timid *ballon d'essai* was not encouraging. Only a few voices were raised to demand his retention. Széchényi, the Austrian ambassador, was amazed by the indifference of the social world in Berlin.[76] The *Konservative Korrespondenz* (March 21) was scandalized by the coolness of the "better journals," the *Deutsch-Evangelische Kirchenblatt* (March 22) merely regretted that Bismarck had not resigned immediately after the election,[77] and the Conservative *Post* soon became silent after saying (March 19) that he should be retained at least for the control of the foreign office. The absence of acute tension abroad had furnished, according to the *Preussische Jahrbücher,* a convenient occasion for a change of Chancellors.[78] The organ of the Colonial Society was more critical of than grateful for his colonial acquisitions; it obviously expected more from the new régime.[79] The *Kreuz-Zeitung* (March 19) coldly denounced any attempt to enlist public opinion for him. "If Prince Bismarck cannot persuade his sovereign as to the correctness of his views, he must retire," it wrote, "and an effort to arouse the *vox populi* against the will of the King must be forbidden as anti-monarchical." The opposition had too many grievances against Bismarck;

---

[75] *Freisinnige Zeitung,* March 18; H. Hofmann, *Fürst Bismarck 1890—1898,* 9th ed., 3 vols., (Stuttgart, 1922), I, 3.

[76] Schüssler, *op. cit.,* p. 271.

[77] Mommsen, *Bismarcks Sturz,* pp. 180, 182.

[78] *P. J.,* vol. 65, pp. 460, 461 (March 22).

[79] *Deutsche Kolonialzeitung,* April 12.

it feared and hated his political philosophy too deeply for it to protest against his dismissal. It had, however, only contempt for the Conservatives' swift desertion. "Those who slavishly burned incense to him," wrote the *Vossische Zeitung* (March 18), "are the first to turn against him." "The rats," said the *Berliner Tageblatt* (March 21), "have already abandoned the ship." Liebknecht included Bismarck's foreign policy among the reasons why his party welcomed his fall, because that policy, although admittedly designed to maintain peace, had embittered other nations by its provocative use of the inspired press.[80] He spoke, however, only for his own party. Practically the entire non-Socialist press approved the assurance in William's parting letter to Bismarck that Germany's foreign policy would remain unchanged.[81] The National Liberal *Berliner Börsen-Zeitung* (March 26) refused to admit that he and his policy were inseparable. "The German Empire was not worth establishing," it wrote, "if its existence depended upon one man (*auf zwei Augen*). Even the greatest statesman is not irreplacable." Hopeful that their political position in Germany would benefit by Bismarck's fall, the Progressives did not object to his foreign policy. That the system of alliances had survived two changes of rulers was, according to the *Vossische Zeitung* (March 19), an assurance of continuity. Public opinion undoubtedly approved the Triple Alliance and the maintenance of good relations with Russia and England, but to infer that the Reinsurance Treaty was popular is not permissible, since its existence was neither known nor generally suspected.

III

The uncertainty as to the future course of German policy, expressed in *Punch's* famous cartoon "Dropping the Pilot," was characteristic of German as well as of foreign opinion. To Bismarck and his partisans, it gave grave concern, but the majority undoubtedly regarded the future with hope. Whereas personal rancor had most influenced the leaders of the intrigue against

---

[80] *Verhandlungen,* VII Leg. Per., I Sess., I, 101, 103 (May 16, 1890).
[81] *Berliner Börsen-Zeitung,* March 21; *Tägliche Rundschau,* March 23, 27; *National Zeitung,* March 23; *Kreuz-Zeitung,* March 23; and so forth.

Bismarck, the Progressives and Centrists were hopeful that his dismissal would at last give them a real share in the government. William's attitude encouraged each group to expect a favorable consideration of its point of view. Speaking on shipboard at Bremerhaven, April 21, 1890, and referring to a maneuver which had brought together the dispersed units of a naval squadron, he coined a phrase, the "new course," and applied it to Germany's future policy, which was sufficiently elastic to appeal to all who desired innovations of one kind or another. The liberal *Berliner Tageblatt* (April 22) and the Catholic *Germania* (April 23) wrote warmly of the entire nation's enthusiastic approval. While the opposition thought that the "new course" would mean a policy which they could approve, the nationalists, the colonial enthusiasts, and most Conservatives thought that it would lead to a more aggressive attitude in European politics and to a more active policy of colonial expansion. The *Preussische Jahrbücher* protested that Germany should no longer be regarded as a saturated state. Already she was experiencing premonitory pangs of hunger; not for her was the *fin de siècle* spirit of skeptical lassitude.[82] Karl Peters, a founder of German East Africa and one of the most active leaders of the movement for colonial expansion, was irritated by the constant references to Germany as a guarantor of peace. Her first responsibility, he told an audience in Frankfort, was the defense of German interests: "Let the French, English, and Russians safeguard peace if they wish."[83]

Abroad, Bismarck's fall seemed ominous for the more or less distant future but not as an immediate danger of war. Even in France not a few forgot their grievances; they now acknowledged, in retrospect, the value of his steadiness. "It is true—most unhappily—," Salisbury had written before William's accession to the throne, "that all Prince William's impulses . . . will henceforth be political causes of enormous potency."[84] Széchényi, the Austrian ambassador, doubted his capacity for self-control in a serious crisis.[85] Bismarck's successor was ex-

---

[82] *P. J.*, vol. 66, p. 190 (July 1890).
[83] *Nation*, Sept. 20, 1890.
[84] *Letters of Queen Victoria* (3), I, 398 (April 21, 1888).
[85] Schüssler, *Bismarcks Sturz*, p. 281.

pected to be the young Emperor's pliant tool, an opinion which history has unjustly echoed. Instead of appointing Waldersee, whose hostility toward Russia made him the most dangerous of candidates, William followed Bismarck's advice in selecting General von Caprivi, a former minister of the marine. The new Chancellor's political and diplomatic inexperience—he felt in taking office that he was entering a dark room[86]—was not devoid of advantages to Germany. If it played a part in the non-renewal of the Reinsurance Treaty, it explains in part his resistance to the pressure for an aggressive European and colonial policy. He spoke in one of his earliest speeches of further colonial expansion as a valuable stimulus to national sentiment, but he promptly qualified this assertion by affirming the need of caution.[87] There would be, he said, no occasion for claiming that "Bismarck's departure endangers peace." [88] "The situation," he told the Reichstag, May 16, 1890, "requires no initiative on our part, because the facts are so simple and clear that it can be left alone (*dass sie eben weiter laufen können*)." [89] Although Marschall von Bieberstein was later to show a high degree of diplomatic skill as the ambassador to Constantinople, his experience as a public prosecutor in Baden and as that state's envoy to the *Bundesrat* scarcely prepared him for effective work as the head of the foreign office. Herbert Bismarck, his predecessor, said that he did not know "the A, B, C of foreign affairs." [90]

What the Chancellor and foreign minister lacked in professional diplomatic training was possessed in abundance by Friedrich von Holstein, from his long and intimate association with Bismarck. By the not inconsiderable part which he had played in Bismarck's dismissal,[91] Holstein had assuaged his long-concealed hatred of his benefactor and master, dating from the early seventies, when Bismarck had forced him to reveal in open court his treacherous spying upon Harry von Arnim in Paris.

---

[86] O. Hammann, *Der neue Kurs; Erinnerungen* (Berlin, 1918), p. 17.

[87] *Verhandlungen*, VIII Leg. Per., I Sess., I, 41 (May 12, 1890); Caprivi, May 23, 1890. *G. P.*, VII, 29, 30.

[88] Waldersee, *Denkwürdigkeiten*, II, 121 (March 22, 1890).

[89] *Verhandlungen*, VIII Leg. Per., I Sess., vol. I, 112.

[90] Crewe, *Rosebery*, 2 vols. (London, 1931), II, 362, 363.

[91] Eulenberg wrote that Machiavelli might have learned something from him. Eulenberg, *Aus 50 Jahren*, p. 245.

Nevertheless, his undoubted intellectual power, his capacity for work, his mastery of detail, and his reputed command of Bismarck's technique and policy gave him the commanding influence upon German's foreign policy that was to remain his until he resigned in 1906. He became at once, according to one of his colleagues, "the guiding genius of the political division . . . the *Wettermacher* of the entire [foreign] office . . . the chief representative of the great tradition." [92] Much has been made of his pathological aversion to publicity and to normal social life, which by some is attributed to the ostracism organized by Arnim's relatives and friends. More important was his refusal to accept a degree of responsibility proportionate to his actual power; as *vortragener Rat* (Councillor) he could intrigue, pull wires, and initiate policies with comparative impunity. The blame for failure as well as the credit for success went to the foreign minister, while Holstein, in the obscurity of his office, retained the substance of power. It is now impossible, after the publication of his private correspondence, to doubt his patriotic devotion to Germany's interests as he understood them.[93] He ruined his health by tireless labors, and he was capable of sacrificing his personal feelings in the service of his country. But his influence on the whole was baneful, because the direction which he gave to German foreign policy was too often determined by ideas derived from a fallacious analysis of the changing facts of European politics. In the following pages, he will frequently be seen at work.

In rejecting Russia's advances, Germany's new leaders committed a fatal blunder, even if the logic of circumstances worked against a permanent alliance with her and in favor of a Franco-Russian rapprochement. Germany's interest was manifestly to keep the Reinsurance Treaty alive as long as possible. William, at first, favored its retention, once he had freed himself of Bismarck's tutelage.[94] Caprivi might have agreed, although he shared the army's view that Germany must one day fight on two

---

[92] J. von Eckhardt, *Aus den Tagen von Bismarcks Kampf gegen Caprivi* (Leipzig, 1920), pp. 1, 2.

[93] *Friedrich von Holstein: Lebensbekenntnis in Briefen an eine Frau*, H. Rogge, ed. (Berlin, 1932).

[94] See above, p. 283.

fronts and although he doubted his ability to keep so many diplomatic balls in the air, for he had informed the foreign diplomats that ill health was the cause of Bismarck's resignation.[95] The final word was spoken by Holstein and his associates in the foreign office; it was their influence that definitely turned the Chancellor and Emperor against renewal. To maintain a formal treaty relationship with Russia was, according to Holstein, not only in conflict with Germany's obligations to Roumania and Austria but her relations with Austria and England might also be disturbed at any time by Bismarck's revelation of the treaty. The foreign office also disliked the probable protests which a revelation of an alliance with Russia would evoke from the opposition.[96] Against these arguments William was unable or unwilling to stand his ground; in May 1890, the historic wire to St. Petersburg was cut, in spite of Giers' willingness to accept something less than a formal treaty.[97]

Nevertheless, Holstein wished to maintain friendly relations with Russia. A large part of the memorandum which recorded Germany's final decision might indeed have been written by Bismarck himself, for it repeated many of his arguments and approved Germany's support of Russia in certain questions. It urged that Germany's influence in Vienna should, if necessary, be continued in favor of Russia's claim to a paramount position in Bulgaria and that Russia's attention might be diverted to the Straits, where she would come into conflict with England and France.[98] Unfortunately the public discussion of Russo-German relations gave Russia some reason to suspect Germany of hostile purposes. An anonymous pamphleteer depicted Russia as the national enemy and represented war with her as merely a question of the time required for the Pan-Slavs to establish their domination over the Tsar and his ministers.[99] Although he agreed that France's armaments proved her hostile intentions,

---

[95] W. L. Langer, *The Diplomacy of Imperialism, 1890–1902*, 2 vols. (N. Y., 1935), I, 5.

[96] Frankenberg, *Nichterneuerung des Rückversicherungsvertrage*, p. 128.

[97] Schweinitz, May 15. *G. P.*, VII, 18. Russia was willing to forego the assurance of Germany's support in Bulgaria contained in the Reinsurance Treaty.

[98] Berchem, March 25, 1890. *G. P.*, VII, 4–10.

[99] Professor Oncken identifies the author as Major, later General, von Bernhardi. Oncken, *Vorgeschichte des Weltkrieges*, II, 711. It is usually attributed to Professor

she would not, in his opinion, precipitate war without a reliable ally; Russia, accordingly, held the key to the situation. Russia's purposes were clearly shown by the anti-German campaign in the Baltic provinces and by her concentration of troops against Germany. Germany should therefore have made use of the exceptionally favorable circumstances in the autumn of 1887 for an offensive war; after crushing France, Russia should have been dealt with.[100] These views, for which he predicted a great success, won Waldersee's warm approval.[101] Kardoff, a Conservative deputy, told the Reichstag that they reflected the opinions of the court, a charge that moved Caprivi to affirm (May 16, 1890) the continuity of Bismarck's foreign policy.[102] The articulate reaction to what was essentially the program of the military party was, for the most part, unfavorable. The *Kreuz-Zeitung,* in spite of its earlier strong partiality for Russia, was one of the journals to approve,[103] but the liberal *Berliner Tageblatt* (April 23) and the Catholic *Germania* (May 20) condemned the resort to war. The discussion occasioned by this pamphlet apparently led to the beginning of Bismarck's attack in the *Hamburger Nachrichten* upon the government's support of Austria's Balkan ambitions. Austria, wrote this journal (April 26), should turn for aid to England, France, and Italy, as the more directly interested powers, rather than to Germany. "Germany's complete disinterestedness in Balkan affairs has a certain justification, even if the Russian press does hope for a free hand from her. That in fact has always been so except when Austria's existence was at stake." [104] A second anonymous pamphlet appeared in Bismarck's defense, protesting that the theory of a preventive war really meant the perpetuation of war and arguing that the restoration of Russo-German friendship was to Germany's best interests.

Theodor Schiemann of the University of Berlin. Since its publication was noted by the *Berliner Tageblatt* on April 23, 1890, the pamphlet was in press at the time of Bismarck's dismissal.

[100] *Videant consules ne quid res publica detrimenti capiat* (Kassel 1890). Cf. *Hamburger Nachrichten,* Hofmann, *Fürst Bismarck,* I, 262, 263.

[101] Waldersee, *Denkwürdigkeiten,* II 125, 126 (April 28, 1890).

[102] *Verhandlungen,* VIII Leg. Per., I Sess., I, 107 (May 16).

[103] Hofmann, *op. cit.,* I, 262.

[104] *Ibid.,* I, 256. In 1913, this passage was quoted as Bismarck's testament as to Austro-German relations. * * *, *Deutsche Weltpolitik und kein Krieg!* (Berlin, 1913), pp. 22, 23.

Nor would Russia's good-will be difficult to recover "if we only make use of the lessons and traditions of history and close our ears to misleading voices which would have us pull England's chestnuts out of the Russian fire on the hypocritical pretence of defending civilization against barbarism." [105] Friedrich Schultze was courageous enough to reject an agreement with Russia which would implicate Germany in her guilty ambitions and even to advocate the return of Alsace-Lorraine to the Alsatians and Lorrainers (though not to France) as the only adequate solution to the problems of German foreign policy.[106]

There was substance for alarm as well as for comfort for both Russia and Austria in this lively discussion. If Bismarck's stand pleased Russia, the slight chance of his return to power diminished its practical value; and Caprivi's assurance as to the continuity of German policy was not wholly reassuring after the non-renewal of the Reinsurance Treaty. Neither the Russians nor the Germans were entirely pleased with William's visit to the Russian court at Narva, August 17–22, 1890. It was preceded by a note from St. Petersburg in the *Politische Correspondenz* (Vienna) to the effect that it would not change Russia's freedom of action, and it was criticized in Germany as an unworthy suit for Russia's favor.[107] Like William's first visit, it had no political results.[108] Russo-German relations, it was said, were worse than ever.[109] A pamphleteer wrote that Russia now knew that she need pay no attention to Germany.[110] Bismarck's press campaign for a return to a friendship with Russia was doubtless more alarming to Austria than comforting to Russia.[111] To allay

---

[105] *Cedant arma togae!* Antwort auf *Videant consules* (Berlin, 1890), pp. 11, 25, 26 and *passim*.

[106] *Ne quid nimis!* (Berlin, 1890), pp. 5, 19, 21, 22.

[107] *Allgemeine Zeitung*, June 11, 1890; *Post*, June 14; (J. von Eckhardt) *Berlin-Wien-Rome; Betrachtungen über den neuen Kurs und die neue europäischen Lage* (Leipzig, 1892), pp. 85, 86; J. von Eckhardt, *Fürst Bismarck und Russlands Orientpolitik*, von einem dreibundfreundlichen Diplomaten (Berlin, 1892), pp. 14, 15.

[108] Langer, *Diplomacy of Imperialism*, I, 8.

[109] H. Robolsky, *Die mitteleuropäische Friedensliga* (Leipzig, 1891), pp. 287, 288; ****,*Wilhelm II und Alexander III* (Dresden, 1892), p. 9.

[110] E. Bauer, *Caveat Populus (Deutsches Volk, sei auf der Hut)!*, wider den *Neuen Kurs* (Leipzig, 1892), p. 61.

[111] In 1891, one of Bismarck's partisans claimed that the former Chancellor had spoken of a dissolution of the Triple Alliance and of an agreement with Russia for the partition of Austria. M. Brewer, *Der Untergang Oesterreichs* (Dresden, 1891). Cf. Eckhardt, *Fürst Bismarck*, pp. 10–12.

the former's concern, Caprivi explained to her ambassador that "we are disposed to give greater emphasis than ever to our relations with our allies." [112] German diplomacy in fact identified itself more than usual with that of the Triple Alliance by the communication of the text of the Reinsurance Treaty to Austria and by an active support of her policy in Bulgaria. The Bismarck fronde probably hastened, if it did not cause, the anti-Russian trend of German policy.

The press, as well as the diplomats, was curiously silent as to the future of Anglo-German relations. None of the above-mentioned pamphlets discussed the problem and none called for a close understanding with England. But the same logic which had turned Bismarck toward her as a substitute for Russia in Germany's diplomatic arrangements exerted even greater influence upon his successors.[113] The Heligoland-Zanzibar Treaty (July 1890) was the first occasion for the public discussion of a rapprochement with England based upon the elimination of outstanding differences between the two countries. Despite the denials of the Bismarckian press, its negotiation began under Bismarck; if the idea of a diplomatic arrangement had been dropped in the hope that England's greater need at some future time would secure more valuable concessions than Heligoland, a tentative agreement had been reached for the arbitration of colonial differences. The widening of the breach with Russia inevitably turned Germany's new leaders against those Russian interests which they had at first been inclined to support and in favor of a diplomatic understanding with England. This change was especially evident in Bulgaria and the Straits. Caprivi agreed with Salisbury that Russia's ambitions in the Straits required the military defeat of Austria and that the road to Constantinople passed through Vienna; he believed that Roumania should be encouraged to erect a barrier of fortresses as a defense against a new Russian invasion of the Balkans.[114] Holstein cited Russia's desire for German support in closing the Straits as a reason for rejecting her second attempt to revive the Reinsurance Treaty, on

---

[112] Széchényi, May 28, 1890. Schüssler, *Bismarck's Sturz*, p. 296.
[113] Frankenberg, *Nichterneuerung des Rückversicherungsvertrage*, pp. 128, 129.
[114] He was not, however, disposed to go too far without a definite assurance of England's support in a war with Russia. Caprivi, May 11, 1890. *G. P.*, IX, 28-33.

the ground that it would alienate England as well as Austria, Roumania, and Italy.[115] Coincident with this diplomatic rapprochement in the Near East, direct negotiations were substituted for arbitration in the elimination of friction in Africa and conversations were resumed in regard to Heligoland.[116] England yielded fairly promptly on the two points which the German diplomats regarded as essential: that the African hinterland should belong to the power in possession of the coast, and that there should be no corridor under British sovereignty along the eastern shore of Lake Tanganyika joining the British colonies north and south of German East Africa.[117] To assure England's offer of Heligoland, which the German diplomats valued as much for its effect in reconciling German opinion to the accompanying concessions to England as for its strategic location commanding the mouths of German rivers and the western opening of the Kiel Canal then under construction,[118] and to effect a speedy conclusion to the negotiations, Marschall offered a high price. It included the surrender of Germany's claims to Uganda Witu, Somaliland, and Zanzibar.[119] In the final treaty, Germany secured Heligoland, the title to the coast opposite Zanzibar, and the political satisfaction of a common frontier between German East Africa and the Congo Free State. But its chief value was undoubtedly as a move toward a diplomatic rapprochement.

There remained the problem of publishing the treaty in such a way as to secure a favorable reaction of public opinion in both countries, for it contained much that might offend their sensibilities. On June 12, the *St. James's Gazette* (London) revealed Germany's colonial concessions without mentioning Heligoland, obviously to reduce the shock which would certainly follow the announcement that European territory had been ceded.[120] If the Germans had agreed to this partial revelation, their consent was

[115] *G. P.,* VII, 22, 23 (May 20).
[116] *Ibid.,* VIII, 11n. (May 1890).
[117] Hatzfeldt, May 14. *Ibid.,* VIII, 11–14.
[118] Marschall, June 4. *Ibid.,* VIII, 21, 22.
[119] Hatzfeldt, May 23. *Ibid.,* VIII, 16.
[120] M. Sell, *Das deutsch-englische Abkommen von 1890 über Helgoland und die afrikanischen Kolonien im Lichte der deutschen Presse* (Berlin, 1926). Sell does not mention the *St. James Gazette's* revelation. His monograph is an excellent analysis of press comment upon each of the treaty's terms. My own material was collected before I had an opportunity to read this study.

perhaps given in the hope that the complete text would seem the more satisfying to German opinion after the first unfavorable impression. The news that far-reaching claims had been abandoned with little or no compensation was received in Germany with almost complete silence. The first to comment was the official *Norddeutsche* (June 16); it explained that the removal of differences with England—the treaty's real purpose—was worth the necessary sacrifices. So, undoubtedly, thought Caprivi and the foreign office. As a soldier, Caprivi disliked colonial expansion; he also feared that the friction it would cause with England would force her into an agreement with France and even with Russia. But the official organ's frank argument that England's friendship was worth a high price drew the fire of the anti-English press. The *Allgemeine Zeitung* (June 17), second only to the *Kölnische Zeitung* as a representative of National Liberal opinion, was amazed that England's platonic sympathies should be purchased by substantial sacrifices, *"dass man Redensarten mit Thaten bezahlen soll,"* because her friendship would never extend to military support. Germany's friendship, it argued, was in fact more necessary to England than England's was to Germany. The publication of the complete text of the treaty (*Staats-Anzeiger,* June 17), including the cession of Heligoland, by no means dispelled criticism. Even the liberal *Frankfurter Zeitung* (June 18) found that England had received the lion's share of the bargain, although it was disposed to approve Germany's sacrifices.[121] Nevertheless, public opinion was at first generally favorable.[122] That a bit of German territory and a kindred folk had been united with the fatherland contributed more to the first wave of enthusiasm than the island's strategic advantages. Yet something was made of the argument that the possession of Heligoland would strengthen Germany's defense against a possible blockade in time of war.[123] Equally gratifying was the value which England apparently placed upon Germany's friendship, for the cession of European territory otherwise seemed

---

[121] Cf. Sell, *Das deutsch-englische Abkommen,* p. 91.

[122] *Berliner Börsen-Zeitung,* in *N. A. Z.,* June 18; *National Zeitung,* June 18; *Tägliche Rundschau Germania,* June 19. Cf. Berlin despatches in the *Morning Post* and *Standard* (London), June 19.

[123] O. Hammann, *Der neue Kurs,* pp. 19, 20.

inexplicable. The English sympathies of the opposition press were aligned at once in favor of an entente, and its anti-imperialism left it indifferent to the price. It pointed to the cession of Heligoland as an irrefutable proof of England's sincerity; it explained the value to Germany and to the Triple Alliance of her diplomatic coöperation.[124] In this as in most questions, the Social Democrats were primarily concerned with their partisan interests, but they were in principle favorable to a rapprochement with England.[125] The National Liberals, as a government party, were not free to express their resentment at Germany's colonial concessions. The *Kölnische Zeitung* was filled with contradictory opinions, but a few days later it joined the outspoken critics of the African settlement.[126] The official thesis that the treaty left Germany with sufficient territory in East Africa to absorb her energies for an indeterminate period and that it assured England's friendship was echoed by the *National Zeitung* (June 18), and the National Liberal *Berliner Börsen-Zeitung* (June 18) wrote that the accord guaranteed "intimate and friendly relations with England for the calculable future." Conservative opinion stressed Heligoland's military value, but it was divided in regard to the other provisions of the treaty. The *Kreuz-Zeitung's* (June 18) immediate reaction, even to its colonial terms, was generally favorable, in spite of the conclusion, which the *Reichsbote* (June 18) shared, that England had received more than her due. The *Post* (June 19) voiced the normal coolness of the agrarian Conservatives to colonial expansion when it spoke of German East Africa as sufficient to occupy Germany for decades.

The disparity between Heligoland's slight intrinsic value and Germany's sacrifices incensed the colonial enthusiasts and the opponents of an entente. With a land surface of less than a square kilometer and with a population of less than two thousand, the possession of Heligoland could not long sustain the first wave of enthusiasm. The *Allgemeine Zeitung* (June 18) foresaw the time when the North Sea would wash it away. Too

---

[124] *Vossische Zeitung*, June 17, 19; *Germania*, June 19; *Freisinnige Zeitung*, June 19, 20.
[125] *Berliner Volksblatt*, in Sell, *op. cit.*, pp. 95–98.
[126] Sell, *op. cit.*, p. 79.

much sentiment had been aroused, however, for a frontal attack to be launched against this provision of the treaty. The colonial setdement proved more vulnerable; almost every detail gave offense to one section or another of German opinion. The establishment of clearly defined boundaries between the British and German colonies was regarded as a fatal blow to the hopes of the expansionists. Karl Peters, whose treaties with the native chieftains in Uganda were annulled almost at the moment of their conclusion, returned to Germany protesting loudly that he had been betrayed. The gains of German commerce in Zanzibar were remembered with regret. There was increasing talk that Heligoland was not an adequate proof of the friendly generosity which to many Germans seemed an essential condition of an understanding with England, for she had always exploited her friends. To the *Allgemeine Zeitung* (June 18), the cession of the island, valueless to England, meant nothing so far as her attitude was concerned.

Nor were the comments of the London press calculated to make a good impression. The reaction of the *Times* (June 18), it is true, left little to be desired. It spoke of the two countries as "natural and necessary allies," of the settlement as a "good thing," and of an alliance as "one of the main guarantees of the peace of the world." To the Conservative *Standard* (June 18), "Germany's friendship is a valuable asset," but, referring to the gains which more and more Germans were regarding as utterly inadequate, it wrote that Germany had received "more than she . . . was entitled to" with "effusive gratitude." In regard to England's own gains, even the *Times* (June 18) was only moderately appreciative; it considered them as merely "adequate" and the agreement in general "not as in itself all that could be desired." The Conservative *Morning Post* (June 18) felt that no essential interests had been surrendered, but other important journals denounced the cession of Heligoland in no uncertain terms. The *St. James's Gazette* (June 18) hoped that parliament would refuse to ratify the treaty, for (June 19) Heligoland would not prevent Germany from composing her differences with Russia, with France, or with both "by the sacrifice of British interests." Salisbury's "surrender to Germany," wrote the Conservative *Pall Mall Gazette* (June 18), is "shameful to the last degree." England's humiliation, according to the *Daily Chronicle* (June 18), a Liberal journal of imperialist inclinations, was "so abject that up to now no representative of this great country would dare to propose it." There was, in short, little trace of the sympathetic understanding of Germany's needs which might have made the treaty more palatable.

Meanwhile, the friends of the treaty outraged the colonial enthusiasts by attacking the policy of expansion. The official *Norddeutsche* (June 17) practically announced its abandonment by speaking of the exploitation of Germany's existing colonies as her main problem. Still more offensive was the Progressive *Freisinnige Zeitung's* (June 19) statement that the treaty was an acknowledgement of England's hegemony (*Vormacht*) in Africa. "The more Germany withdraws from East Africa," it wrote, after asking if England had another small island to exchange for African territory, "the better it will be for German interests." The reply was an increasingly violent campaign against the treaty.[127] The rejoicing over the acquisition of Heligoland," wrote the Berlin correspondent of the London *Standard* (June 21), "has been succeeded by an outcry in the press about Germany's losses." Heligoland had been paid for tenfold, affirmed the *Allgemeine Zeitung* (June 20); what guarantee was there, it asked, that England's friendship would continue under Salisbury's successor? The treaty should, it insisted, either be withdrawn or England should be required to hand over Walfisch Bay. Since she could never arrange her differences with Russia and France peacefully, greater concessions, according to the *National Zeitung* (June 20), could have been secured from her.[128]   In July 1890, the Colonial Society cancelled its plans for a meeting in celebration of Germany's colonial achievements. When the Conservative *Post* (June 24) denied that the colonial enthusiasts could speak for German opinion as a whole, the *Allgemeine Zeitung* (June 25) referred to the flood of communications it had received from all parts of Germany opposing the treaty,

---

[127] *Vossische Zeitung*, June 19.
[128] This long article has interesting similarities with the doctrinaire point of view which later played a disastrous part in Holstein's management of German foreign policy. The Conservative *Reichsbote* (June 24) echoed the demand for additional concessions.

and it insisted that the great majority of the middle classes and of the military circles agreed with its point of view.[129] "The prestige of the Berlin statecraft," it wrote, "has been seriously compromised, at least in South Germany." The first enthusiasm, wrote the *Preussische Jahrbücher,* "has changed completely." [130]

At this juncture the government intervened with a communication to the press to check the unfavorable development of opinion.[131] Even the *Kreuz-Zeitung* (July 30) and the *Reichsbote* (July 30), in spite of their anti-English views, agreed that the treaty would avert the bitterness which otherwise would inevitably arise and that it would consolidate the friendship of the two countries.[132] Nevertheless, the *Kreuz-Zeitung* regretted that England could now be certain that Germany would not go to war in defense of her interests in Africa; this possibility could no longer be used to exert pressure. The *Denkschrift* did not, of course, accomplish a complete reversal of public opinion. It was impossible to eradicate the impression that Germany had made a bad bargain, and a part of Conservative opinion continued to insist that England could not be counted upon to reciprocate Germany's friendly sentiments.[133] The government's intervention, however, restrained at least the leading organs of National Liberal opinion from systematic opposition. The *National Zeitung* (July 31) acknowledged that the *Denkschrift* had been well received, and the *Kölnische Zeitung* (July 31), admitting that the time for regrets had passed, welcomed the determination to make full use of Germany's remaining colonies. *"Volldampf voraus!"* should henceforth be, it exclaimed, the order of the day.

The polemic against the treaty and an entente with England continued intermittently for years, with Bismarck eventually taking a leading part. The *Hamburger Nachrichten,* his chief partisan in the press, remained neutral until Caprivi, desirous of enlisting Bismarck's prestige for the rapprochement, quoted to

---

[129] This was true, at least, of Waldersee. *Cf.* his *Denkwürdigkeiten,* II, 131, 132.
[130] *P. J.,* vol. 66, pp. 90, 91 (June, 1890).
[131] "Denkschrift über die Beweggründe zu dem deutsch-englischen Abkommen," *Staats-Anzeiger,* July 29; *N. A. Z.,* July 30.
[132] Sell, *op. cit.,* pp. 74–76.
[133] *Post,* July 31; Bauer, *Caveat Populus!* p. 69.

the Reichstag (Feb. 5, 1891) the former Chancellor's comment upon a diplomatic document that England's friendship was worth more than Zanzibar and all of East Africa. From this statement, which misrepresented the fundamental principles of his policy, dates Bismarck's open conflict with the government. He denied that he would have signed the Zanzibar treaty, arguing that the international situation had not required it while he remained in power. Because the needs of Salisbury's foreign policy assured England's friendship for Germany as long as that statesman remained in power, gifts of territory to a world empire that already had a surplus of colonies would accomplish nothing.[134]   Relations with Russia were the chief reason for his concern, but what most aroused German opinion were the sacrifices made to England in the colonial field.   It brought the most extreme of the colonial enthusiasts and the nationalists together in the *Allgemeine Deutsche Verband,* the predecessor of the Pan-German League,[135] but that is a subject which will be discussed in the following chapter.

Despite this hostile opinion, German diplomacy attempted to work with England on not a few occasions after the Zanzibar-Heligoland Treaty.   Its intentions were excellent.   Only through practical coöperation, with the exercise of patience and with the subordination of immediate to ultimate aims, might the understanding become an actuality.   While the negotiations were still in progress, Germany's agent in Cairo was instructed to work with the British consul general rather than with the Egyptians, after the latter had proposed a scheme for the conversion of the public debt.[136]   Concerted action between London and Berlin followed France's protest that Germany's surrender of her claims to Zanzibar had violated an earlier agreement by which Germany had been pledged to respect the Sultan's sovereign rights.[137] So far, however, neither power had been required to sacrifice its vital interests.   The test of Germany's determination to continue

[134] *Hamburger Nachrichten,* Feb. 8, 11, 15, 19, 1891.   Hofmann, *Fürst Bismarck,* I, 315–319, 320, 321, 323, 328; Bismarck, *Gedanken und Erinnerungen,* III, 147; Robolsky, *Die mitteleuropäische Friedensliga,* p. 300.

[135] Karl Peters, the colonial enthusiast, was its first leader.   Hammann, *Der neue Kurs,* p. 108.

[136] Marschall, June 2, 1890.   *G. P.,* VIII, 156.

[137] Hatzfeldt, July 24; Caprivi, July 25.   *Ibid.,* VIII, 34–36.

upon her new course at whatever cost came when such interests were involved. She experienced a first serious rebuff when she asked England to approve Italy's acquisition of Tripoli at some future time in order to strengthen Italy's loyalty to the Triple Alliance and to moderate her resentment at Germany's failure to support her in the latest quarrels with France over Tunis.[138] For Salisbury the maintenance of England's influence in Constantinople was more important than the satisfaction of Italy's ambitions; he feared that a guarantee such as Italy desired would convince the Sultan that Russia of all the powers would despoil him least. "I do not like," he wrote, "to disregard the plain anxiety of my German friends. But it is not wise to be guided too much by their advice now. Their Achitophel is gone. They are much pleasanter and easier to deal with; but one misses the extraordinary penetration of the man." [139] Nor was Germany more willing to risk Russia's enmity when Salisbury asked for her support in a protest against the Sultan's permission for the passage of the Straits by the Russian volunteer fleet. It would, Caprivi believed, make friendly relations with Russia impossible.[140] The prospects of an Anglo-German rapprochment were not improved when the correspondent of the *Times* in Zanzibar charged Germany (Sept. 15, 1890) with reopening the slave trade. The Germans in East Africa, according to the editorial comment of the Liberal *Daily News,* were evidently making a bid for the business after England had closed the slave markets. The Conservative *Post* (Sept. 21) promptly replied that England, dissatisfied with her enormous gains, wished to deprive Germany even of East Africa. A brief but violent outburst followed against England's assumption of moral superiority. The *Norddeutsche* (Sept. 20) warned England that friendship required mutual respect and the recognition of each other's rights (*die beiderseitige Anerkennung der Gleichberechtigung*). This con-

---

[138] Engelbrecht, Rome, June 27, 1890. Waldersee, *Briefwechsel*, I, 384, 385; Münster, Paris, July 25. *G. P.*, VIII, 259. Caprivi, like Bismarck, believed that Tunis was not a legitimate *casus foederis* for the Triple Alliance. Caprivi, July 17, 19, Aug. 5; Holstein, July 29, Aug. 13; Marschall, Aug. 10. *Ibid.*, VIII, 245–249, 255, 256, 264, 265, 266–269, 270, 271.
[139] Cecil, *Salisbury*, IV, 374, 375 (Aug. 12, 1890).
[140] Raschdau, July 18. *G. P.*, VII, 347; Caprivi, Aug. 8; Marschall, Aug. 31. *Ibid.*, IX, 46, 47, 50.

ception remained an important factor in the relations between the two peoples. None of these instances of friction were serious, but taken together they indicated the diplomatic and emotional barriers to an effective Anglo-German rapprochement. Neither country had shown, by the end of 1890, much willingness to yield when important diplomatic interests were involved. Each had its own reasons for suspicion.

IV

When Caprivi spoke of the need of sacrifices to cultivate England's friendship during the debate in the Reichstag on the Zanzibar-Heligoland Treaty (Feb. 5, 1891), he stated a salutary truth but he also strengthened the enemies of an entente.[141] The *Allgemeine Zeitung* (Feb. 8, 1891) immediately concluded that Germany had drawn away from Russia, that their relations were *"im Stadium der aufgezogenen Brücken,"* whereas Germany's true interests were in a revival of the Alliance of the Three Emperors. Bismarck, from his retirement, resisted Caprivi's attempt to foist a part of the responsibility for the Zanzibar treaty upon him and advised against the sacrifice of Russia's friendship.[142] But a return to Bismarck's policy was not the only alternative to receive public consideration. At least a part of the anti-English press regretted that Bismarck's effort to conciliate France in 1884 had failed.[143] The development of moderate opinion in France, the dissolution of the League of Patriots, and the collapse of the Boulangist agitation in 1889 had been powerless to change the traditional opinion of France's intentions. That she was bent upon war at the earliest possible moment was shown, it was said, by the increase in the term of military service from two to three years and by the benevolence of the moderate Tirard cabinet toward Antoine when this Alsatian member of the Reichstag left Germany to become a Frenchman.[144] Even those who believed in an inevitable war with Russia were not im-

---

141 *Verhandlungen*, VIII Leg. Per., I Sess., II, 1329–1335.

142 *Hamburger Nachrichten*, Feb. 11, 1891, in Hofmann, *Fürst Bismarck*, I, 322, 323. The *N. A. Z.* (Feb. 9) promptly denied that any change for the worse had occurred in Russo-German relations. The official policy was endorsed by the *National Zeitung*, (Feb. 11), the *Germania* (Feb. 11), and the *Post* (Feb. 15).

143 *Post*, Sept. 21, 1890.

144 *P. J.*, vol. 63, pp. 415, 416 (March 1889); vol. 64, p. 378 (Aug. 1889).

pressed by Colonel Stoffel's plea for a Franco-German alliance in a pamphlet that appeared on the eve of Bismarck's dismissal, because he specified the return of Alsace-Lorraine as its essential condition.[145] Wilhelm Schultze, in his contribution to the discussion of Russo-German relations, was one of the few to make some concessions, though not enough to satisfy French patriotic sentiment; his proposal was for an autonomous government under a Hohenzollern prince whose neutrality would be guaranteed by the powers.[146] In reply the *Norddeutsche* (Feb. 3, 1890) wrote of the twenty offensive wars which France had waged against Germany and of future attacks from the same source. It repeated the customary explanation that the *revanche* was the result of the military defeats which France had suffered rather than of the loss of Alsace-Lorraine. Already the nationalist *Tägliche Rundschau* (Feb. 1) had said that the Alsace-Lorraine question did not exist for Germany. Even the liberal parties deprecated the talk of an alliance with France as productive of no good or they ignored it. The Catholic *Germania* (Feb. 5) opened its columns only to the unfavorable comments in the Russian press upon Stoffel's pamphlet, and the liberal *Berliner Tageblatt* (April 28, 1891) expressed a practical interest in nothing more than *"ein leidliches Verhältnis."* According to Liebknecht, the less said of an alliance the better it would be for Franco-German relations, although he favored a plebiscite in the two provinces to determine their political allegiance once and for all.[147] Not even the return of Alsace-Lorraine to France, declared Hänel, a Progressive leader in the Reichstag, would assure a permanent peace, because men of his generation knew from their reading of Hugo, Musset, and Thiers that France's lust for the left bank of the Rhine was the real cause of her dis-

---

[145] C. Stoffel, *De la possibilité d'une future alliance franco-allemande* (Paris, 1890), pp. 30, 32, 35.

[146] "Deutschland möge auf den Besitz von Elsass-Lothringen als Reichsland verzichten und das Land den Elsass-Lothringen überlassen, die es dankbaren Herzens aus den Händen eines hochherzigen Kaisers,. . . annehmen würden. Das Land möge der Herrschaft eines deutschen Fürsten, eines Hohenzollern, und seine Neutralität der Garantie von ganz Europa anvertraut werden." W. Schultz, *Post tenebras lux!* Im Anschluss an *Videant consules* . . . (Cassel, 1890) p. 19.

[147] *Verhandlungen,* VIII Leg. Per., I Sess., I, 102 (May 16, 1890). Bebel predicted that France's victory would mean the loss of the left bank of the Rhine as well as Alsace-Lorraine. *Ibid.,* VIII Leg. Per., II Sess., I, 306 (Dec. 13, 1892).

satisfaction.[148] The increasing moderation of French opinion was regarded with reserve by the greater part of articulate German opinion. Too many agreed with General von Loë that it would be instantly discarded if war broke out between Germany and Russia.[149]

Hostility to England—and, to a certain extent, to the United States, whose McKinley tariff law was regarded as America's industrial declaration of independence—produced a friendlier attitude on the part of precisely those Conservatives who had formerly been most uncompromising. During the slave-trade controversy the Conservative *Post* (Sept. 21, 28, 1890) not only referred regretfully to the failure of conciliation in the past but it also recommended that an effort be made to induce France to join a Central European customs union. Others noted what was thought to be a lessened enthusiasm in France for an alliance with Russia and a better understanding of German policy; they even agreed at the beginning of 1891 that the increasing stability of republican institutions might have a favorable effect upon Franco-German relations.[150] A contributor to the *Preussische Jahrbücher,* who favored a definite reassurance to France, found incomprehensible the indifference with which German public opinion regarded her moderate statesmen and publicists "as if the cause for which they are fighting were not also Germany's, indeed her most important and significant." [151] Was it merely a coincidence that William decided with startling abruptness after the appearance of this article to capitalize on the development of moderate opinion in the interest of a reconciliation? The responsibility was obviously his own, for the foreign office was not likely to initiate a forlorn hope of this kind. He had, at any rate, shown great consideration for the French delegation at the Berlin labor conference in 1890. He now began an intense courtship with a personal message of condolence to the *Académie des Beaux Arts* after Meissonnier's death (Jan. 21, 1891). En-

---

[148] *Verhandlungen*, VIII Leg. Per., I Sess., I, 108. *Cf.* F. H. Geffcken, *Frankreich, Russland und der Dreibund* (Berlin, 1893), pp. 8, 9.

[149] Waldersee, *Denkwürdigkeiten*, I, 361, 362.

[150] *National Zeitung*, Jan. 1, 1891; *Kölnische Zeitung*, Jan. 3; *N. A. Z.*, Jan. 6; *Allgemeine Zeitung*, Jan. 7; *Kreuz-Zeitung*, Feb. 11.

[151] M-t-s, "Das Verhältnis Deutschlands zu Frankreich," *P. J.*, vol. 67, pp. 101, 102 (Jan. 1891).

couraged by the favorable reaction of such indubitably patriotic journals as the *Journal des Débats* and the *Figaro,* by France's award of the cross of the Legion of Honor to Helmholtz, the German scientist,[152] and alarmed by the possibility that the French sympathies of Rudini, Crispi's successor as the Italian Prime Minister, might lead to a Franco-Italian rapprochement,[153] William soon sought more positive results than the exchange of courtesies. A convenient occasion for a dramatic gesture presented itself with the consent of the Paris Society of Artists, with the government's unofficial approval, to participate in the Berlin exposition. At her son's request, the Empress Frederick spent a week in Paris under the transparent pseudonym of Countess Lindau.

No one was deceived by the pretense that her visit was merely a shopping excursion, nor was it believed that her purpose was simply to assure a large and representative showing for French art in the Berlin exposition. Events might have taken a different course if William had waited for Münster's estimate of the situation; the ambassador explained that the moderate (*anständige*) press could not be counted upon to resist the pressure of the chauvinists, owing to its fear of being charged with a lack of patriotism.[154] The chauvinists, in fact, immediately took offense at the political significance attributed to the visit by the German press; it was, by common consent, a conciliatory gesture by the Emperor himself.[155] Even the liberal journals, which prided themselves on their understanding of the imponderables of foreign affairs, quite unwittingly and with the best of intentions, offended French susceptibilities. For the first time since 1871, a member of the Hohenzollern family, they said, had entered France. The *Vossische Zeitung* (Feb. 21) even suggested the possibility of a future visit by William himself, as if his mother's had already been successful; it congratulated Germany's new leaders for their progress in solving the fundamental problems

---

152 *N. A. Z.,* Feb. 16; *National Zeitung,* Feb. 19.
153 W. L. Langer, *Franco-Russian Alliance,* (N. Y., 1929), pp. 138, 139.
154 *G. P.,* VII, 271-274 (Feb. 19).
155 *Vossische Zeitung,* Feb. 19, 21; *Berliner Tageblatt,* Feb. 19; *Rheinische Kurier,* in *Post,* Feb. 22.

of European politics. The Progressive *Freisinnige Zeitung* (Feb. 20) spoke of a test of moderate sentiment in France. According to the nationalist *Magdeburgische Zeitung,* Germany had done her part; it was now time for France to do hers.[156] The Empress contributed to the failure of her mission by tactless visits to Versailles, where the German Empire had been proclaimed, and to St. Cloud, where the château had been burned during the siege of Paris. It was easy for Déroulède and his followers, who had been in eclipse since the collapse of the Boulangist agitation, to assert themselves. On the evening of February 21, they adopted a series of violent resolutions attacking the government for its traitorous dalliance with the idea of a Franco-German entente and affirming France's friendship for Russia.[157]

Of the chauvinist excesses in Paris, German opinion was at first tolerant.[158] The nationalist *Tägliche Rundschau* (Feb. 24) wrote of the spirit of absinthe, but it also exclaimed: "How tiresome politics would be without the amusement France always provides *(wenn nicht Frankreich für allerhand Scherze sorgte)!"* That neither the government nor public opinion had the courage or the desire to defend the cause of friendlier relations with Germany was considered much more significant.[159] It was obvious, according to the Progressive *Freisinnige Zeitung* (Feb. 27), that both could still "be terrorized by an insignificant minority," and the Progressive *Nation* (Feb. 28) found therein "a danger for the French as well as for the world." France, wrote the National Liberal *Allgemeine Zeitung* (Feb. 27), had not changed since 1870, and the Conservative *Post* (March 1), forgetting its recent interest in conciliation, agreed that the chauvinists would be able to force the government into war.

The great majority, however, neither expected nor demanded any sort of punitive action against France. The liberal press

---

[156] *Post*, Feb. 22.

[157] They included a reference to a future visit by the Emperor and to a demand for disarmament. Carroll, *French Public Opinion*, p. 150.

[158] *Kölnische Zeitung,* Feb. 23; *Germania, National Zeitung,* Feb. 24; *N. A. Z.,* Feb. 25.

[159] *Allgemeine Zeitung,* Feb. 26; *N. A. Z.,* Feb. 25; *P. J.,* vol. 67, p. 390 (Feb. 1890).

redeemed itself by denying that the Paris chauvinists represented French opinion and by advising coolness.[160] The *Vorwärts* (March 1), the *Berliner Volksblatt's* successor as the leading organ of the Social Democratic party, insisted that the experiences of no individual, no matter how highly placed, should affect the relations between two nations. Of the Conservative press, the *Reichsbote* (Feb. 25, 27) was the most sensible. It spoke of "the childish impressionableness and the emotional instability" of the French temperament; the incident should not be permitted to obscure the real improvement in Franco-German relations. There was a moment of uncertainty, before the Empress Frederick left Paris, as to Germany's official attitude. An article in the *Kölnische Zeitung* (Feb. 26), promptly clipped by the Paris press, caused the French police to fear for her safety.[161] "Every German," it wrote, "who has any appreciation of the nation's dignity feels himself the victim of a deadly insult in the person of the Emperor. The German people have a right to expect the French government and people to furnish an adequate satisfaction and to erase the stain upon France's honor by the severe punishment of the wretches whom we Germans consider the dregs of human society." Although William told the Austrian ambassador a few days later that "peace had hung by a hair," there was, fortunately, little foundation for the rumor that he had taken steps to mobilize the German army.[162] The official *Norddeutsche* (Feb. 27) dispelled some of the alarm by remarking that "the character of the persons responsible for the provocation makes further excitement unnecessary." On February 28, Münster was instructed to say nothing—and later, March 4, to maintain his reserve in regard to the efforts of a few artists to revive the subject of the Berlin exposition—unless the foreign minister initiated a conversation; even then he was to refrain from any criticism and, indeed, to recognize that the attitude of the French government had been irreproachable.[163]

William, of course, abandoned his attempt to conciliate France; *"Ja,"* was his sole comment on Münster's (Feb. 27) remark

[160] *Berliner Tageblatt*, Feb. 27; *Nation*, Feb. 28.
[161] Münster, Feb. 28. *G. P.*, VII, 279–282.
[162] Langer, *Franco-Russian Alliance*, p. 143.
[163] *G. P.*, VII, 279, 286.

that coöperation in non-political questions had produced nothing of value. Nor was France to be let off without an indirect warning, for the stringent passport regulations of May 22, 1888, were revived on the Alsatian frontier.[164] This time, the official *Norddeutsche* (March 1) minced no words. "These measures," it wrote, "should convince France . . . that Alsace-Lorraine belongs to Germany for all time, that a trench separates it from France, and that this trench . . . can be made wider and deeper." This abrupt change from "excessive friendliness" to "equally disproportionate unfriendliness" perturbed the Conservative *Reichsbote* (March 1) as well as the liberal press, but even the foreign office now trained its guns upon France. She was told that her moderate opinion should heed the warning and support the government more effectively.[165] In spite of the regrets expressed by Ribot, the French foreign minister, Holstein (March 30) thought of making representations as to the maneuvers to be held that autumn on the German frontier. An evasive or negative reply, he wrote, would throw light upon France's intentions.[166] "Nonsense!! Absurd!" wrote William on Münster's reports of France's essentially moderate policy—reports which had convinced him that Münster was not the right man for the Paris embassy.[167] The possibility of war may have been considered, for an official of the foreign office went to the trouble of carefully summarizing the arguments against it: an unfavorable public opinion would alienate England, and German opinion was almost unanimously hostile to an aggression or to a provocation which would justify, from the point of view of the neutrals, a French declaration of war.[168] That the *Kölnische Zeitung* (June 26, 1891) spoke of another military defeat of France as the only permanent guarantee of Germany's possession of Alsace-Lorraine was a better index to the views of an inner circle than to the general current of public opinion.

164 *Staats-Anzeiger*, in *Post*, March 1.
165 Marschall, March 4. ·*G. P.*, VII, 286, 287.
166 *Ibid.*, VII, 290.
167 *Ibid.*, VII, 293 (April 6); William II, May 9. *Ibid.*, VII, 295, 296.
168 *Ibid.*, VII, 296–298. For a reference to the state of German public opinion as a conclusive argument against a preventive war, see E. Loewentheil, *Der Kampf um die europäischen Suprematie, oder die Konsequenzen einer französisch-russischen Allianz* (Berlin, 1890), p. 91.

By scrupulously avoiding occasions for friction, the development of moderate French opinion might have been encouraged. Nothing was to be gained by seeking speedier results. It is difficult to place William's gesture in the general scheme of German foreign policy, except perhaps as his personal contribution to Caprivi's program of conciliation. Having rejected the Reinsurance Treaty, having turned toward a rapprochement with England, there could have been no serious thought of a continental league against England. Better Franco-German relations undoubtedly would have improved Germany's bargaining power with England by reducing the advantages which the latter automatically derived from an irreconcilable Franco-German antagonism, but William was probably less influenced by this statesmanlike consideration than by a passing impulse. The failure of his gesture, at any rate, quickly changed his optimistic appraisal of Franco-German relations. In May 1890 he accepted the word of an American industrialist and of an army officer of the same nationality as sufficient evidence that France intended to precipitate war that summer.[169] The effect upon public opinion was unfortunate. Although there was no demand for war, it was generally agreed that Germany had done all she could to improve relations with France. The National Liberal *Hamburgischer Korrespondent* expressed the views of most Germans when it warned the French "that the first step in the restoration of neighborly relations will certainly not be taken by Germany." [170]

V

Meanwhile, Germany's experiments in her relations with the Western powers had alarmed Russia. In view of Germany's frank acknowledgment that she regarded the Heligoland-Zanzibar Treaty as the foundation of an entente with England, Russian diplomats, like Staal in London, not unnaturally concluded that Germany would henceforth coöperate in all international problems with Russia's most powerful enemy.[171] William's intense flirtation with France did nothing to quiet Russia's sus-

---

[169] von Hoiningen, May 15, 1891. *G. P.*, VII, 299, 300.
[170] *N. A. Z.*, March 8, 1891.
[171] Staal, 19 June/July, 1890. Meyendorff, *Correspondance de M. de Staal*, II, 88.

picions. In St. Petersburg, the agitation of the French chauvinists against an entente with Germany during the Empress
Frederick's visit was regarded with satisfaction; indeed, Münster
thought that it could be traced to a payment of Russian money
to the *Matin*.[172] "Not a single newspaper," reported the German military attaché in the Russian capital, "said a word against
the tactless chauvinist demonstrations.[173] According to Lamsdorff, a high official of the Russian foreign office, a repetition of
1870 would have been preferable to "the possibility of a gradual rapprochement, which might, little by little, smoothe out the
hostility between Paris and Berlin," because a new Franco-
German war would perhaps enable Russia to "become the arbiter
between them" and to "attain our national interests in the
East."[174] Since it was manifestly to Russia's interest to stiffen
the French against Germany's blandishments, she therefore
adopted a warmer tone in her communications with Paris, approving France's conduct during the Empress' visit, affirming her
interest in an entente as necessary for a "just balance of power
in Europe," and speaking of the accord as "solid as granite."[175]
Alexander III chose this moment to confer the Cross of St.
Andrew upon President Carnot. Although the Russians were
not prepared for an alliance which would erect a permanent
barrier between them and Germany, those Germans deceived
themselves who, like a good many Englishmen,[176] believed such
an alliance to be impossible. William quickly agreed with the
French generals who said that Russia's confidence in France's
support under any circumstances would prevent the formation of
an alliance.[177] *"Les Russes,"* said one, *"regardent la République
Française comme une cocotte que l'on peut avoir quand on la
désire, sans mariage."*[178] Some comfort was derived from a

---

[172] *G. P.*, VII, 281 (Feb. 28, 1891). Cf. *Lettres de la princesse Radziwill au
Général de Robilant*, 4 vols. (Paris, 1933), I, 69 (March 13, 14).

[173] Villaume, 21 Feb./5 March. *G. P.*, VII, 196–200.

[174] Langer, *Diplomacy of Imperialism*, I, 16, quoting Lamsdorff, *Dnievnek, 1891–
1892*.

[175] Ribot, March 9, 1891. *Livre jaune: l'alliance franco-russe* (Paris, 1918). pp.
2, 3.

[176] *Daily Telegraph*, May 23, 1890; *Standard*, June 13, 1891.

[177] Funcke, Paris, April 13, 1891, *G. P.*, VII, 201, 202. For similar opinions, see
Reichsbote (June 18, 1891) and *Post* (July 14).

[178] *"Sehr gut,"* wrote William. Münster, June 24. *G. P.*, VII, 193, 194.

report that Russia had refused to promise military support to France during the Empress' visit,[179] and the German press professed confidence, with suspicious unanimity, that differences of interest would be an insuperable obstacle. France's defeat of Germany, wrote the *Kölnische Zeitung* (June 22, 1891), would deal a deathblow to Russia's ambitions in Asia Minor and in the Straits.[180] According to the Conservative *Reichsbote* (July 1), France could not possibly desire Russia's conquest of Constantinople nor could Russia desire Germany's humiliation. Occasional expressions of doubt in the French press as to the desirability of an alliance were noted with satisfaction. It was perhaps the *Figaro's* appeal for an understanding with Germany on the basis of the return of Lorraine and of the neutralization of Alsace, and Barthélemy Sainte-Hilaire's warning (in *Gil Blas*) that France might suffer Poland's fate as a consequence of an alliance with Russia, that elicited the most far-reaching plan for the solution of the Alsace-Lorraine question to appear in the non-Social Democratic press since 1871.[181] Again, the Conservative *Post* (July 8) blamed the contemptuous intransigeance of German opinion for the weakness of moderate opinion in France. "What good does it do us," it asked, "to say every time, 'I won't give anything?' The *revanchards* naturally reply by telling their moderate compatriots: 'There is your reply, fools who dream of a reconciliation with Germany.'" Provided that Luxemburg were assured to Germany, the *Preussische Jahrbücher* was willing to discuss the surrender of Metz, if not Alsace, but it admitted that the idea had been flouted by the entire German press.[182] To these important organs of Conservative opinion, a settlement with France, even at the price of Germany's conquests, was preferable to the sacrifices required by an entente with England.

German diplomacy, of course, did not share this view any more than did the greater part of German opinion. Since it could not rely upon the supposed impossibility of a Franco-

---

[179] *G. P.*, VII, 205-207 (May, 1891). Echoes of this report appeared in *Berliner Tageblatt* (June 22), *Kölnische Zeitung* (June 22), and the *Freisinnige Zeitung* (June 24).
[180] Cf. *Freisinnige Zeitung*, June 22.
[181] Cf. *Kölnische Zeitung*, June 22, July 5; *Germania*, July 8.
[182] *P. J.*, vol. 68, p. 125 (June 1891).

Russian alliance, it turned once more to the task of attaching England to the Triple Alliance. An indirect approach was chosen. On May 6, 1891, when the Triple Alliance was renewed, a protocol was added in which England was mentioned as an associate of the allied powers (by virtue of the Mediterranean agreements of 1887) for the defense of the status quo in the Near East.[183] Thus was checkmated France's attempt to detach Italy from the Triple Alliance.[184] The three Central powers also agreed to enlist England's aid against France by persuading her to support the status quo in North Africa as well as the Near East.[185] The results of this diplomatic maneuver were disappointing; not only did England fail to respond, but the press discussion in England and Germany after the renewal of the Triple Alliance brought Russia and France more closely together than ever. Salisbury expressed his satisfaction, because he still valued the Triple Alliance as a check upon France and Russia, but, rejecting Italy's plea for a formal alliance, he promised nothing more than a reconsideration of the text of the Mediterranean accord.[186] There were indications, however, that fairly close relations had been established between England and the Triple Alliance. On June 29, 1891, Rudini spoke to the Italian senate of England's co-operation for the maintenance of peace and of the status quo in the Mediterranean. The charge that she had become the fourth member of the alliance was supported on the floor of the House of Commons by an appeal to no less an authority than King Victor Emmanuel in a statement to Prince Jerome Bonaparte.[187] Even the cabinet's explanation, denying that any formal engagements had been made and affirming England's freedom of action, left some room for speculation, because it admitted that Italy could count upon England's support for the status quo in the Mediterranean. There was much to please Germany in the London press. The Conservative *Standard* (June 4) wrote of England's "good-will and preference" as the "natural and inevitable at-

---

[183] Marschall, May 7. *G. P.*, VII, 98, 99.

[184] Langer, *Franco-Russian Alliance*, pp. 151–156; *idem, Diplomacy of Imperialism*, I, 10, 11. For Clemenceau's attempt to secure pressure from England for this purpose, see J. L. Garvin, *The Life of Joseph Chamberlain*, 3 vols. (London, 1932–1934), II, 459.

[185] *G. P.*, VII, 103.

[186] Hatzfeldt, May 23. *Ibid.*, VIII, 48.

[187] *Morning Post*, June 4.

titude of this country" in view of the defensive character of the Triple Alliance. The correspondent of the Liberal *Daily News* (June 29) attributed Italy's consent to the renewal of the alliance to England's influence, and the imperialist *Daily Telegraph* (June 30), despite its hostility to the Zanzibar-Heligoland Treaty, wrote that "England heartily agrees with the policy of Germany, Austria, and Italy, so far as it is pacific and defensive." On July 1 the *Times* wrote of the alliance as a "League of Peace" and of its hope that the "union of Germany and England in the cause of peace and civilization may be as solid and valuable as if it were embodied in a formal treaty." It even spoke of "a conjunction of the forces of the greatest naval Power with those of the greatest military Power in the world" if "the necessity [were] to arise in the future as it has arisen in the past." Thus, as Salisbury acknowledged, the impression arose that England's relations with the Triple Alliance were closer than the facts warranted;[188] in reality, Salisbury was unwilling even to strengthen the terms of the Mediterranean accord.[189]

German opinion, with the possible exception of the Social Democrats, received the renewal of the alliance with satisfaction; even the Catholic *Germania* (Aug. 15) defended it.[190] Not only was it approved as an assurance of Germany's security, but also as a warning to her neighbors, who, according to the official *Norddeutsche* (June 29), might be tempted to disturb the peace. Its effect in St. Petersburg and Paris, said the Conservative *Kreuz-Zeitung* (July 1), would be that of a peal of thunder. William's visit to England in the summer of 1891 drew Bismarck's fire as an indication that all was not well with Russo-German relations,[191] but it strengthened the impression of a practical, if not a formal, connection between England and the Triple Alliance. The warmth of the *Times'* reaction (July 4) was undeniably encouraging. "Germany," it wrote, "does not excite in any class among us the slightest feeling of distrust or antipathy." She

[188] Cecil, *Salisbury*, IV, 380, 381.

[189] *G. P.*, VIII, 72 n.

[190] *Germania*, July 1; *Reichsbote*, July 4. The *Kreuz-Zeitung* (July 6) noted the criticism of Liebknecht and Singer.

[191] *Hamburger Nachrichten*, in *Berliner Tageblatt*, June 29. This liberal journal condemned his attitude as more harmful to the state than Harry von Arnim's had ever been.

was so powerful that she needed no help, "but if her hour of trial were to come again, as it has come for nations as proud and powerful, there is no country to which she can more confidently look for sympathy and support than to our own." The liberal press in Germany naturally assumed that the rapprochement had occurred. According to the *Berliner Tageblatt* (June 30), a Quadruple Alliance virtually existed, and it wrote (July 9) of William's entrance into London as an event that would be recorded in the annals of history in golden letters. In England's Mediterranean interests and in her differences with Russia and France, the moderate *Vossische Zeitung* (July 3) discovered that community of interests which alone gave viability to alliances and treaties. The nationalist and Conservative press was less enthusiastic but it too exaggerated the extent of the Anglo-German rapprochement. The *Kreuz-Zeitung* (July 1) acknowledged its reluctant approval "in view of the critical situation," in spite of England's selfish policy and of the certainty that she would always insist upon her freedom of action. The success of the visit, which the Conservative *Reichsbote* (July 9) described as an event of world significance, was due, in the *Post's* opinion, (July 5) to Germany's strength, for England's unscrupulous exploitation of the weak was well-known, and the National Liberal *National Zeitung* (July 4) insisted that the understanding was no more necessary to Germany than to England.

But even William's brief visit was not to conclude without a discordant note. True, the Conservative *Standard* (July 6) spoke of a conversation at Windsor "which may affect the course of history"; the Conservative *Morning Post* (July 11) said that "the days of isolation . . . are, happily, dead" and "that British foreign policy will not be altered by any change in government." These journals—and the *Times* (July 13)—represented the community of interest between England and the Triple Alliance as making a treaty unnecessary, but Salisbury assured Chamberlain after William's departure that England was free "to take any action which it might think fit in the event of war." Nevertheless, he also "considered the friendship of the Central Powers . . . almost essential to us." [192] Many Germans, of course, sus-

---

[192] Garvin, *Chamberlain*, II, 461 (July 16, 1891).

pected Salisbury of these or similar reservations, but all could see from the London press that public opinion by no means unanimously favored close relations with the Triple Alliance, especially after it became clear that an Anglo-German rapprochement would bring Russia and France more closely together. The *Daily Telegraph* (July 6) hastened to assure its readers that "we are . . . no parties to any new coalition against France or Russia," although it acknowledged that England could not but approve the effort to keep "France from a dash on the Rhine and Russia from another raid across the Balkans." Much more disquieting were the views of the Liberal *Daily News,* for they were regarded in Germany as a reliable index to the policies of the next Gladstone government. The exchange of royal courtesies, it wrote (July 6), could not affect British foreign policy, nor did the cheers accorded to the Emperor mean that the British people had declared for the Triple Alliance. It (July 11) condemned any attempt "to isolate France" and to deprive her of "her legitimate influence in continental affairs" as "doomed to failure" and as a possible cause "of infinite mischief before it failed." It affirmed (July 14) England's friendship for all countries, but, as if moved by the spirit of Bastille Day, it suggested at the same time a solution of the Alsace-Lorraine question. "If the Emperor, rising above all scruples and difficulties, dared to do that supreme act of justice [that is, return Alsace-Lorraine to France] he would deserve to be remembered by the latest posterity as the noblest member of his illustrious house." In response to Clemenceau's suggestion that England should work for this solution of the problem, Chamberlain said that Germany would reply by asking England "to mind our own business." [193] This, in fact, was substantially the reaction of the German press. For the Emperor to cede any part of Alsace-Lorraine was as inconceivable as for the Queen to cede Ireland or Wales.[194] "Every German newspaper," wrote the *National Zeitung* (July 21), "must refuse to discuss the status of German territory once and for all. The argument over Metz was settled with cannons in 1870, and only cannons can reopen it."

---

[193] Garvin, *Chamberlain*, II, 458, 459.
[194] *Allgemeine Zeitung,* July 16.

The German diplomats still felt no compulsion to sacrifice vital interests in order to make the apparent rapprochement a reality. They were as confident as ever that England's own difficulties with Russia and France would eventually align her with the Triple Alliance, and that she needed Germany's friendship as much or more than Germany needed England's. The indifference, to say the least, of Liberal opinion in England was doubtless another argument in favor of reserve, in view of a possible change of government. At any rate, William's visit led to no commitments by either country.[195] If England refused to join the Triple Alliance, Germany remained silent in regard to the Straits.[196] Russia drew the obvious, if mistaken, conclusion from William's visit to England, from that of Victor Emmanuel and Francis Joseph to the British squadron at Fiume and from the renewal of the Triple Alliance.[197] Russia's response was the first step toward an alliance with France. "A closer association between Russia and France is not merely the desire of the Russian people," wrote a St. Petersburg correspondent of the *Politische Correspondenz* (Vienna), "it is also an inescapable necessity."[198] Acting upon a hint from Paris, Russia invited France to send a naval squadron to Kronstadt, although it was England more than Germany whom she wished to impress. Neither Giers nor the Tsar had any thought at this time of a formal alliance,[199] but Kronstadt (July 1891) was followed in August by Russia's consent to consult with France with a view to common action if either power should be in danger of an attack.

In Germany, the press tried without much success to cover its real concern with ironical reflections as to autocratic Russia's sudden affection for republican France. Referring to a French naval attack during the Crimean War, the *Kölnische Zeitung* (July 25) wrote that the French this time were bombarding Kronstadt with champagne corks. The *National Zeitung* (July 26) felt that the French and Russians wished to add their quota

195 *Cf.* Garvin, *Chamberlain*, II, 461 (July 16).
196 *Cf.* Hatzfeldt's opinion, July 21. *G. P.*, VII, 66–69.
197 Schweinitz, Aug. 22. *Ibid.*, VII, 217.
198 *Freisinnige Zeitung*, July 10.
199 Meyendorff, *Correspondance de M. de Staal*, II, 141, 142 (12/24 July 1891).

to the toasts of the preceding weeks "in order at least to restore a rhetorical balance of power." That the democratic Republic should throw itself info the arms of a "despotism tempered with assassination" was, according to the liberal *Berliner Tageblatt* (July 27), amusing rather than alarming. "The Russians are mistaken," observed the Conservative *Kreuz-Zeitung* (Aug. 2) of a report that a group of French naval officers had been embraced by a crowd of Russian peasants, "if they think that we are jealous." When the Tsar himself listened with bared head to the Marseillaise on the deck of the French flagship, it was not easy to ignore its political significance. France reminded Russia that her support could not be counted upon as a certainty by sending her naval squadron to Portsmouth on its return from Kronstadt, but Portsmouth was also a demonstration of England's intention to retain her freedom of action between the two groups of powers.[200] While he spoke of peace and the status quo as a bond of union between England and the Central powers in his Mansion House speech (July 29), Salisbury had already denied the existence of any commitments to the Triple Alliance. These leads were followed even by those London journals which had been most cordial to Germany during her Emperor's recent visit. They now agreed with the *Daily News* as to England's "impartiality in Continental friendships." [201] No wonder that the celebration of Sedan Day (Sept. 2) was clouded by doubts as to Germany's security. Serious dangers from abroad, wrote the Conservative *Kreuz-Zeitung* (Sept. 1), had been added to the Social Democratic menace at home. The Conservative *Post* (Sept. 2) resented the talk in France and Russia of the need to restore the balance of power "as if we had disturbed it, as if Germany's strength had not been used exclusively for the maintenance of peace in Europe." A shadow, according to the Berlin correspondent of the *Kölnische Zeitung* (Sept. 2), lay upon many a German heart. Public opinion expected Germany to look to her defenses.

---

[200] Portsmouth, according to the *Preussische Jahrbücher* (vol. 67, p. 271, July 1891), had deprived Kronstadt of all significance by showing that a little courtesy sufficed to attract France. It had apparently forgotten the Empress Frederick's visit to Paris.

[201] *Times*, July 29; *Morning Post*, Aug. 5; *Standard*, Aug. 6. The *Morning Post* (July 27) and the *Daily Telegraph* (July 25) promised a cordial welcome to a Russian squadron.

Opinion was divided, however, as to the most serious source of danger. Bebel regarded Russia as the real menace: against that country he pledged the support of the masses although his party counted upon a general war to precipitate a social revolution.[202] It was of France that William was most suspicious. He agreed with the military attaché in Paris that *"Vive la Russie!"* meant *"À bas l'Allemagne!"* Of Schoen's moderate reports, he wrote that the chargé looked at the French scene through rose-colored glasses, and he contradicted Münster's opinion that France would be content for a time with her diplomatic successes. If a Franco-Russian alliance existed, it was offensive in character.[203] The inspired press was used to convince a public opinion, which perhaps did not need its suggestion, that France was the real danger. Although the *Kölnische Zeitung* (Aug. 4) reported the presence of troop movements on the Russian frontier as an ominous development, it gave first attention to the danger that France might set the world in flames now that the chauvinists were confident that she had recovered her former commanding position.[204] The official *Norddeutsche* (Aug. 4) wrote of her increased self-confidence as a potential danger. Even the liberal *Berliner Tageblatt* (July 30) expressed the opinion that her union with Russia would cause France to seize the first opportunity to recover Alsace-Lorraine and her lost hegemony. Nevertheless, most Germans probably remained skeptical as to the prospects of a formal Franco-Russian alliance, and the government took no steps to correct this illusion. It seemed unlikely that Russia would accept its burdens since she could count upon France's aid in any event.[205] On September 27, 1891, Caprivi declared at Osnabrück that Kronstadt had not changed in essentials a permanent international situation, an opinion which had already appeared in the press.[206] Russia's obvious indifference to

202 *Vorwärts,* Oct. 5, 1891.
203 William's comments, Funcke, Aug. '30; Schoen, Aug. 20, Sept. 30; Münster, Oct. 5. *G. P.,* VII, 218–223, 224, 225, 236, 314–316.
204 The Catholic *Germania* (Aug. 5) was reminded of the *Post's* article "War in Sight" of 1875. *Cf.* Berlin letter, *Politische Correspondenz,* in *National Zeitung* (Aug. 10); *Berliner Tageblatt* (Aug. 10); *Standard* (London, Aug. 10).
205 *Freisinnige Zeitung,* July 28; *Vossische Zeitung,* July 29.
206 *Nation,* July 25; *Kreuz-Zeitung,* July 28. *Cf.* Langer, *Franco-Russian Alliance,* p. 197.

Alsace-Lorraine would, it was thought, restrain France; a possible Franco-Russian union would thereby be deprived of its dangerous character.[207] William, on the other hand, agreed with Schweinitz that France's influence might diminish the Tsar's resistance to the pressure of the Pan-Slavs.[208]

Striking similarities existed between the reactions in Germany to the Franco-Russian rapprochement and those which had preceded Bismarck's *Kaltwasserstrahlen*. There was the same sense of insecurity, the same fear of war upon two fronts, and also the same tendency to single France out as the chief danger. Perhaps events had gone too far in 1891 for the successful use of Bismarck's tactics. However that may have been, the alarmist press articles in this case were not followed by a crisis. The usual signs indicated, on the contrary, that the government had resigned itself to the new situation. An illuminating communication from Berlin appeared in the *Politische Correspondenz* (Vienna), a journal which all Europe watched for hints as to the policies of the great powers, only a few days after Kronstadt: "That the Russians intend to sacrifice themselves for France's interests may be regarded as impossible. Europe has no reason for alarm on account of an alliance between these countries for the defense of their common interests, because none of the other powers have any intention of attacking them." [209] Far from calling France to account for her supposed intentions, according to Bismarck's usual practice, Germany moderated the stringent passport regulations on the Alsatian frontier—a concession which one of Bismarck's partisans denounced as an encouragement to the French to expect other benefits from their relations with Russia.[210] Differences of opinion as to the details of the army increases—which all admitted were necessary—doubtless had more to do with the delay of more than a year in presenting a military bill to the Reichstag than concern for the reaction of France or Russia. Caprivi spoke rather definitely of Germany's need to prepare for a war on two fronts in his defense

[207] *Kreuz-Zeitung*, Aug. 2; *Kölnische Zeitung*, Aug. 4.
[208] *G. P.*, VII, 211 (Aug. 5). Cf. *Allgemeine Zeitung*, Aug. 6, 7.
[209] *Berliner Tageblatt*, Aug. 1, 3; *Kreuz-Zeitung*, Aug. 1; *Allgemeine Zeitung*, Aug. 1. See *Times* (Aug. 3) for a translation of this article.
[210] Bauer, *Caveat Populus!* p. 68.

Das ewige — *Brautpaar.*

Figure 13.—As long as he will not agree to wait on her lap dog, there is little expectation that the marriage will be solemnized in the near future.

Kladderatsch, July 24, 1892.

of the proposed increase of 83,000 men for the peacetime army, but there was less saber-rattling than in Bismarck's time.[211] An historical controversy with the former Chancellor in regard to the origins of the Ems Dispatch gave his successor an opportunity to affirm Germany's peaceful intentions. Replying to newspaper articles minimizing his part in the founding of the Empire,[212] Bismarck maintained in the *Hamburger Nachrichten* (Nov. 11, 1892) that he had "deserved well of Germany (*sich um Deutschland verdient gemacht hat*)" by the publication of the Ems Dispatch, which, he acknowledged, had provoked France's declaration of war, for that war had united Germany.[213] He may thereby have scored a point against an ungrateful sovereign, but he also did his country incalculable harm by enabling her enemies to represent the Franco-Prussian War as the result, according to his own evidence, of an unscrupulous falsification. In an effort to prove that no falsification had occurred and that the war was the result of France's refusal to accept Prince Leopold's renunciation of the Spanish crown, Caprivi revealed the text of Abeken's original telegram from Ems, July 13, 1870. Prussia, he declared, did not provoke war in 1870, nor did she intend to do this in 1892 or later.[214] He had, in fact, recently advised that colonial disputes with France should be avoided in the absence of support by Germany's allies and England. In his opinion, the colonial problem would not be settled in Africa but on the Rhine.[215]

VI

After rejecting the use of diplomatic pressure to check the Franco-Russian rapprochement, Caprivi doubtless hoped to achieve a gradual improvement in Germany's position by avoid-

---

[211] *Kölnische Zeitung, Berliner Tageblatt,* Nov. 24, 1892.

[212] *Das Ende des Fürsten Bismarck in der auswärtigen Politik* (Berlin, 1891). There is an analysis of this anonymous pamphlet in the *Freisinnige Zeitung* (Aug. 21, 1891).

[213] Hofmann, *Fürst Bismarck,* II, 167.

[214] *Verhandlungen,* VIII Leg. Per., II Sess., I, 10, 11 (Nov. 23, 1892). His position had the approval of Liberal opinion (*Volks-Zeitung, Vossische Zeitung,* Nov. 24), while Bismarck's version had been developed by H. Delbrück, "Der Ursprung des Krieges von 1870," *P. J.,* vol. 70, p. 738. Most of the German historians who henceforth gave much of their time to the origins of the War of 1870, until another and later war monopolized their attention, accepted Bismarck's account, arguing, however, that France would in any case have declared war.

[215] *G. P.,* VII, 329 (Sept. 19, 1892).

ing such friction as would hasten the union of her neighbors and alienate England. Not content with this passive policy, Caprivi negotiated commercial treaties with Austria, Italy, Switzerland, and Holland (1891) for the reduction of tariff barriers. His purpose was not only to strengthen the Triple Alliance and to open wider markets for her expanding industries, but also to improve Germany's diplomatic relations with her neighbors.[216] In 1893, he initiated negotiations for a similar agreement with Russia. This tacit confession that Germany no longer played the tune to which Europe danced was inevitably offensive to national sentiment. Nor were its modest aims likely in the long run to have William's support; its success required, in any case, a long period of patient reserve. Caprivi's aims, though admirably adapted to Germany's needs in many respects, therefore lacked the necessary support at home.

Yet the international situation was not entirely unfavorable. Neither England nor Russia, themselves at odds in Asia, contemplated a definitely hostile policy. Although an entente with England seemed as remote as ever, in part because Germany refused to identify herself with England's policy in the Straits, the latter's difficulties with France and Russia and her common interests with Italy (the Mediterranean Accord of 1887 still existed) worked in Germany's favor. Salisbury still held back, directing the British ambassador in Rome to refuse any "definite engagements" when Germany sought his aid against France's designs upon Tuat (an oasis in Morocco near the Algerian frontier) in the autumn of 1891. He suspected that Berlin wished to use England to attract Italy from France's "illegitimate embraces," and he was unwilling to do more in Rome than to stress "the note of mutual interest, esteem, and affection."[217] In August 1892, Salisbury's fall and Gladstone's return to power further diminished the prospects of an Anglo-German entente. The foreign office believed that the antipathies of the Liberal party would eventually color England's official policy, although no immediate change was expected,[218] but it also deprecated an unfriendly at-

---

216 Oncken, *Vorgeschichte des Weltkrieges,* II, 398, 399.
217 *G. P.,* VIII, 301, 304–312; Marschall, May 4, 1892. *Ibid.,* VIII, 318, 319; Cecil, *Salisbury,* IV, 383, 384.
218 Raschdau, July 20, 1892. *G. P.,* VIII, 76, 77.

titude, since it was to Germany's interest that Rosebery should continue as the new foreign secretary in view of his known approval of Salisbury's policy.[219] Rosebery soon proved a disappointment. His assurance that British opinion would probably endorse measures for the defense of Italy against a "groundless" attack seemed to German diplomats a retreat from Salisbury's position.[220] Accordingly, they began to insist more vigorously upon Germany's point of view. In reply to the "offensively hostile" attitude of the British ambassador in Constantinople to the development of Germany's railway interests in Asia Minor, they talked of opposing Egypt's desire to increase her military forces.[221] England's prompt change of front was followed by Germany's return to her normal support in Egypt; she advised the Sultan not to listen to France in regard to Egyptian affairs and to arrange, on the contrary, an understanding with England, and later, not to embarrass her by referring the Egyptian question to the European powers.[222] Hatzfeldt reported that Rosebery was "extraordinarily grateful" and that the foreign secretary sought even closer relations, but the German ambassador's counsel to maintain a cool reserve reflected his government's dislike and distrust of the Liberals.[223]

Doubts as to England's practical value as an ally or as a friend in a continental war had always been a restraining factor in Germany's efforts to approach her. They were greatly strengthened during the summer of 1893 by her attitude during the crisis in Anglo-French relations in Siam—a question that did not concern Germany at all. At first, it seemed probable that England would defend her interests to the limit when France, after sending gunboats (July 13) to blockade Bangkok, was reported (July 30) as having demanded the departure of the British warships. Rose-

---

[219] Hatzfeldt, Aug. 20, 1892. *G. P.,* VIII, 82. Salisbury had urged the incoming cabinet to maintain the contacts he had established with Italy. Cecil, *Salisbury,* IV, 404, 405 (Aug. 18, 1892).

[220] Hatzfeldt, Sept. 7, 11, 1892; Solms-Sonnenwalde, Sept. 26, 1892. *G. P.,* VIII, 84, 85, 87, 91.

[221] Marschall, Jan. 7, 1893. *Ibid.,* VIII, 185, 186.

[222] Marschall, Jan. 28, 1893; Hatzfeldt, Jan. 30, July 24, 1893. *Ibid.,* VIII, 188–191, 214.

[223] Hatzfeldt, May 27, 1893; Marschall, July 21. *Ibid.,* VIII, 100, 101, 213, 214.

bery at once approached Germany; he even hinted that the time had perhaps arrived for a quadruple alliance. At Cowes, where William was attending the races, the Emperor lost his head for a moment when Ponsonby, ashen-faced, reported that France was threatening war; he felt that Germany, in the midst of the reorganization of her army, was not prepared for a European conflict and even that the British fleet was unready.[224] In Berlin, Caprivi was not, however, averse in principle to war, provided that "an English ship, by firing the first shot," would insure England's active participation with the Triple Alliance. Not one of the allies, he said, would give even her diplomatic support without this assurance, because she might otherwise suddenly arrange her quarred with France and abandon her friends. But, if England stood her ground, Germany, he told Hatzfeldt (in reply to the latter's hypothetical qu stion as to the government's attitude toward war), had no reasc a to avoid war: "It would not be undesirable from the point of view of domestic politics, and the military factor is as favorable now it is ever will be."[225] Rosebery's advances had been dictated solely by France's alleged ultimatum; he had already decided that England had too many irons in the fire to "keep the police of the world," although France's treatment of Siam had been, in his opinion, "base, cruel, and treacherous."[226] He therefore yielded at once after learning that no ultimatum had been presented to the British naval authorities. Instead of fighting, he accepted a solution which kept France from the left bank of the Mekong River and which maintained Siam as a buffer state between Burma and French Indo-China. England's apparent surrender—for the facts as to the supposed ultimatum were not generally known—greatly diminished her prestige throughout Europe. In Germany respect for the practical value of her support sank to a new low point.[227]

---

[224] Eulenburg reported that William, watching the races the next day, acted as if "he had forgotten the political sensation of the night before as though it had never been." J. Haller, *Philip Eulenburg: the Kaiser's Friend*, 2 vols. (New York, 1930), I, 142 (July 30).

[225] Caprivi's marginal comments, Hatzfeldt, July 31. *G. P.*, VIII, 108–110.

[226] Crewe, *Rosebery*, II, 425–427 (July 26).

[227] Langer, *Franco-Russian Alliance*, pp. 325–332; idem, *Diplomacy of Imperialism*, I, 43–45. Neither of these accounts mentions Caprivi's theoretical readiness for war.

VII

The Siam crisis practically completed the disillusionment of Germany's new leaders in regard to their original plan of substituting England for Russia in their diplomatic arrangements. They promptly informed London that Germany's support could not be counted upon without a definite treaty.[228] In September 1893 they charged the British colonial officials with systematic ill-will and presented England with a long list of colonial grievances.[229] Some of these complaints were arranged without much difficulty,[230] but their general effect increased the coolness of Anglo-German relations. In the meantime, a gradual change occurred in Germany's attitude toward Russia. Among Caprivi's domestic policies, the more lenient treatment of the Poles and the army law (1893)—whose enactment had been assured by the vote of the Polish group—strengthened Russia's impression of Germany's fundamental hostility.[231] Nevertheless, Holstein wrote at the beginning of 1893: "We want a good understanding with Russia, but without committing political adultery," [232] and William assured the Tsarevich Nicholas that the Triple Alliance, instead of being directed against Russia, was essentially a union of the conservative powers against radicalism and a nucleus for commercial pressure against the United States.[233] Germany, it is evident, was reverting to Bismarck's Russian policy, although her leaders did not openly seek the restoration of the Reinsurance Treaty. A Conservative review had already described the attempt to avoid offense to Russia as repugnant to many good Germans.[234]

For almost three years Russia's refusal to enter a formal alliance with France kept the door at least partially open to an improvement in Russo-German relations. She had no liking for the simultaneous mobilization by which the French hoped to provide against the dangers to which they were exposed by their

[228] Marschall, Aug. 4, 1893. *G. P.*, VIII, 115, 116.
[229] Rotenhan, Sept. 10. *Ibid.*, VIII, 402–405.
[230] *Ibid.*, VIII, 405–413 (Sept. 16, Nov. 16, 1893).
[231] R. Geis, *Der Sturz des Reichskanzlers Caprivi* (Berlin, 1930), p. 25.
[232] Haller, *Philip Eulenburg*, I, 140, 141 (Jan. 29, 1893).
[233] Marschall, Jan. 25, 1893. *G. P.*, VII, 243, 244.
[234] H. Delbrück in *P. J.*, vol. 70, p. 122 (June 1892).

undefined relations with Russia. The Tsar's aversion to republican institutions was a plausible excuse for the persistent skepticism as to a Franco-Russian alliance; Maximilian Harden's
Zukunft wrote caustically of Alexander's insistence upon wearing gloves in dealing with the unclean Republic.[235] Nevertheless, the first announcement that a Russian naval squadron would
visit Toulon in the autumn of 1893 caused Caprivi to think for
a moment of war. "Not much would be required," he wrote,
"to produce the most serious consequences. . . . Our situation is
very different from that of Bismarck during the Schnaebelé affair; we cannot now tolerate as much as then. If a provocation
is offered the Triple Alliance in any form, I believe that the
initiative should be left to Italy in order to make sure of her
support." [236] Despite the caution of the French press in avoiding
the mention of Alsace-Lorraine, the festivities in Toulon and Paris
probably occasioned more concern in Germany than had Kronstadt. It could not be denied that Russia had taken France's
proffered hand. Although the simultaneous appearance of a
British squadron in the Italian harbor of Taranto suggested that
England was the main reason for the appearance of Russian
warships in the Mediterranean,[237] German observers rightly concluded that the Franco-Russian rapprochement would, in the
long run, be directed against Germany. Nor was the moderation
of the French press reassuring, although the *Preussische Jahrbücher* found some consolation in the hope that Russia's indifference to Alsace-Lorraine would eventually turn France toward
a reconciliation with Germany.[238] That moderation was attributed to the Quai d'Orsay or even to Russia.[239] The *Kölnische
Zeitung* (Oct. 15) reminded its readers of Gambetta's dictum
never to talk of but always to remember Alsace-Lorraine. On
October 28, 1893, the official *Norddeutsche* endorsed the opinion
of the liberal *Vossische Zeitung* that Toulon had not changed
the international situation in any essential respect, but the nationalist *Münchener Neueste Nachrichten* doubtless expressed the

235 H. Wachenhausen, "Die Russen in Paris," *Zukunft*, Oct. 21, 1893.
236 Caprivi, Sept. 24, 1893. *G. P.*, VII, 247.
237 Langer, *Franco-Russian Alliance*, pp. 347, 348.
238 *P. J.*, vol. 74, p. 396 (Oct. 21, 1893).
239 *Kölnische Zeitung*, Oct. 15; *Kreuz-Zeitung* in *Post*, Oct. 21, 1893.

views of a more numerous group when it wrote of the salvos at Toulon and Paris as a "warning of future battles more destructive than any of the past." [240]

In January 1894 Russia finally agreed to an alliance with France; in return for a promise to mobilize in reply to Germany's mobilization, she secured the same assurance by France in the event of a similar action by any member of the Triple Alliance. France had paid a high price, because the obligation to mobilize, becoming effective on Austria's action, would inevitably bring Germany in. She secured other compensations, since Germany was mentioned as the chief enemy, since Russia agreed to use a large force against her, and since the alliance was to have the same duration as the Triple Alliance. These terms remained a closely guarded secret until after the World War; even German diplomats were at first under the illusion that France and Russia had not advanced beyond the stage of a flirtation. In March 1894 Münster thought that the meeting between William and the Tsar in Copenhagen had disillusioned France as to the existence of an alliance.[241] Nevertheless, Toulon had been an unmistakable indication of at least a close rapprochement—a sufficient motive, it would seem, for the diplomats to renew their efforts for an entente with England and for them not to haggle over the price. England was evidently in a more receptive mood than at any time since the new orientation of German policy. She regarded Toulon and the subsequent talk of a permanent Russian naval squadron in the Mediterranean as a menace. To the Conservative *Daily Telegraph* the blow was more serious than any England had received since Trafalgar.[242] Work began at once upon the modernization and expansion of the British fleet, and approaches were made to Austria and Italy for their aid in assuring France's neutrality during an Anglo-Russian war.[243] Yet Germany remained essentially indifferent. Resentment at England's failure to respond to her own advances and an ineradicable confidence

---

[240] *Post*, Oct. 19, 1893.

[241] G. P., VII, 257 (March 17). Alexander was reported to have assured William that Russia would never draw the sword for Alsace-Lorraine. Geffcken, *Frankreich, Russland und der Dreibund*, p. 167.

[242] Meyendorff, *Correspondance de M. de Staal*, II, 231 (July 29, 1894).

[243] G. P., IX, 131–134.

in England's quarrels with Russia and France caused Germany to miss a good opportunity to attach England to the Triple Alliance. Austria pleaded in vain for Germany to support her own and England's interests in the Straits. The *Kölnische Zeitung* (Oct. 17, 1893) had revealed something of the official attitude toward England even at the time of the Toulon demonstration. Of course, it cheerfully envisaged England's aid for Italy in a Mediterranean war, but it discouraged in no uncertain terms such references as had appeared in the English press to the desirability of England's membership in the Triple Alliance. The Mediterranean problem—and more particularly England's interest in it—was not, in its opinion (Nov. 3, 1893), worth the bones of the famous Pomeranian grenadier. Berlin opposed England's overtures in Vienna and Rome; without a definite treaty relationship, Germany had no interest in supporting England.[244] On the contrary, her interest, according to Caprivi, was in a free hand between England and Russia.[245]

Anglo-German relations became worse rather than better during 1894. Although Caprivi reaffirmed his desire for a good understanding, and in spite of his aversion to an active colonial policy, he approved a strong stand against England in colonial questions on the erroneous theory that the friction thus engendered would not affect the general problems of European diplomacy.[246] The Franco-Russian alliance had scarcely been concluded when Germany sought concessions from England by bringing pressure to bear upon her. An accord with France (Feb. 4), defining the frontier of German Southwest Africa, was followed by a more reserved attitude on the part of Germany's agents in the Egyptian debt question.[247] At the same time, England was reminded that the satisfaction of Germany's desire for the full and exclusive possession of the Samoan Islands would cause "such a reversal of German public opinion" that Germany would be able to support England's elsewhere.[248] Nor was England considerate of

[244] Hatzfeldt, Dec. 29, 1893. *G. P.*, VIII, 127, 128.
[245] *Ibid.*, IX, 134–137 (March 8, 1894).
[246] Hatzfeldt, June 1. *Ibid.*, VIII, 436.
[247] Hatzfeldt, April 14, 17; Marschall, April 17. *Ibid.*, VIII, 413, 414, 215–217, 414, 415.
[248] Marschall, April 17; Hatzfeldt, April 23. *Ibid.*, VIII, 414, 415, 419–423. *Cf.* "Samoa," *Zukunft*, May 26, 1894. Caprivi once referred to Samoa as worthless in

Germany's sensibilities. She brusquely rejected the suggestion in regard to Samoa, referring to the probable reaction of British opinion as an excuse.[249] On May 12 was signed the Anglo-Congo agreement by which England secured a lease of the western shore of Lake Tanganyika in return for a lease of the Bahr-el-Gazel to the Congo Free State. The first provision deprived the Heligoland-Zanzibar Treaty of one of its chief advantages to Germany by giving England a corridor uniting Uganda and Rhodesia. After rejecting England's bid for her coöperation against France in West Africa,[250] Germany agreed to parallel her negotiations for the annulment of the Tanganyika corridor with those of France, who wished to defeat the proposed lease of the Bahr-el-Gazel in order to remove a barrier on her route to the Upper Nile. She even discussed France's favorite idea of a conference as a means of checking England.[251] If England yielded to Germany first, in order to remove a cause of an embarrassing Franco-German coöperation,[252] the French agreed that Germany had acted in good faith—and they, in turn, soon attained their purpose. The consequences were more serious than the public suspected. The *Times* (June 23) wrote of a misunderstanding and described the solution as "a signal proof of the firm foundations upon which their [England's and Germany's] good relations now rests." Rosebery, however, thought that the tone taken by the Germans in their official communications, "though not unusual, . . . was thoroughly insufferable"; he found their use of France equally objectionable.[253] Although the *Times* (June 23) congratulated Germany on her resistance to the pressure of extremist opinion, the German foreign office had been deeply aroused. It rejected the pleas of Austria and Italy for a more conciliatory attitude toward England,[254] and about Egypt it continued to maintain a studied reserve.[255] England, it was thought,

---

comparison with a rapprochement with England. Caprivi, May 28. *G. P.,* VIII, 430–432.

[249] Hatzfeldt, April 24. *Ibid.,* VIII, 423, 424.

[250] Marschall, May 2; Hatzfeldt, May 10. *Ibid.,* VIII, 425, 426.

[251] Marschall, June 8, 15; Hatzfeldt, June 12. *Ibid., VIII,* 442, 449, 454.

[252] Marschall, June 18. *Ibid.,* VIII, 465.

[253] Crewe, *Rosebery,* II, 448, 449 (June 14).

[254] Eulenburg, Vienna, June 15; Marschall, June 15; Bülow, Rome, June 20. *G. P.,* VIII, 130–133, 455, 456.

[255] Rotenhan, June 29. *Ibid.,* VIII, 221, 222.

would not have yielded so quickly had it not been for the possibility of a European conference for the settlement of the Egyptian question.[256] But Egypt, as in Bismarck's time, was too useful a means of keeping England and Frace at loggerheads for Germany to identify herself with France; the German agent was instructed to avoid too intimate relations with Turkish, Egyptian, and French circles.[257]

Given the prevailing temper in Berlin, only important and tangible sacrifices by England could have revived the earlier interest in anything short of a hard and fast alliance. Nor was there much eagerness for an alliance, thanks to the fear of being used for England's purposes. The hopes formerly cherished of England were transferred to Russia. The final stages of the Franco-Russian negotiations coincided with the Russo-German conversations leading to the commercial treaty of 1894. Because Russia considered the tariff war with Germany as an obstacle to improved diplomatic relations, Caprivi hoped that its termination would bring an improvement.[258] The commercial treaty, he thought, would be a step in "gradually attracting Russia from France," [259] since it granted favorable duties to her agricultural products. To Szögyény, the Austrian ambassador, he confided his expectation of significant progress within the current year in working out a compromise between Russia's interests and those of Germany's allies.[260] Caprivi had William's support in this partial return to Bismarck's policy, for the Emperor, since the autumn of 1893, had affirmed Germany's indifference to the Near Eastern problem.[261] The same means by which Caprivi hoped to induce Russia to return to Germany's orbit contributed to his own fall: the reduced tariff rates upon agricultural products turned the Conservatives against him. After the military bill of 1892–1893 had shattered their hopes of a share in the government, the Progressives had resumed their normal opposition. Caprivi's policy of kindness had encouraged the development of a moderate, evo-

---

[256] Rotenhan, July 5. *G. P.*, VIII, 222, 223.
[257] Rotenhan, July 9. *Ibid.*, VIII, 226, 227.
[258] Ibekken, *Staat und Wirtschaft*, p. 174 *passim*.
[259] Caprivi, March 8. *G. P.*, IX, 137.
[260] Caprivi, April 23. *Ibid.*, IX, 144.
[261] Langer, *Franco-Russian Alliance*, pp. 371, 372.

lutionary movement within the ranks of the Social Democrats, but their systematic opposition had not been surmounted. William's dream of winning the acclaim and affection of the working classes had not been realized; in his disappointment, he promptly concluded that their demands were insatiable.[262] No reliance, he felt, could be based upon their gratitude. In 1890, Bismarck's desire to use force against the Social Democrats contributed to his dismissal; William's support of the same policy in October 1894 played a part in Caprivi's resignation. There was, however, no immediate change in foreign policy, for Hohenlohe's long association with Bismarck, and perhaps his own large estates in Russia, assured his support in the attempt to recover Russia's friendship. Only a few days after his appointment William, with the Chancellor's approval, rejected Austria's request for aid against Russia's designs upon the Straits. "Russia," said William, "needs her house key for her fleet and this is no concern of ours." [263] In foreign affairs as well as in domestic politics, the Emperor was now prepared to reverse the results of his dismissal of Bismarck. He told Shuvalov, the Russian ambassador, that the Reinsurance Treaty might be revived and that the *Dreibund* might be made a *Vierbund* by the inclusion of Russia.[264]

VIII

As an obvious escape from the embassassing problem of choosing between Russia and Austria in the Balkans, German diplomacy had always been benevolent toward Russian imperialism in the Far East. Japan's victory in the Sino-Japanese War (1894–1895), by menacing Russia's interests in Manchuria, offered the first opportunity for a dramatic service—and for public opinion to pass judgment upon the attempt to recover her favor. Nevertheless, it was not at first clear that Germany would support Russia, for she might follow an independent course with a view to sharing in the partition of China. When China appealed to the European powers, William's first impulse was to insist that For-

---

[262] Geis, *Sturz des Reichskanzlers Caprivi*, p. 103.
[263] Fürst Chlodwig zu Hohenlohe-Schillingsfürst, *Denkwürdigkeiten aus der Reichskanzlerzeit*, K. A. von Müller, ed. (Stuttgart, 1931), p. 8 (Nov. 2, 1894).
[264] *Ibid.*, p. 29 (Jan. 14, 1894).

mosa should be Germany's part of the booty,[265] but his opinion, opposed by Hohenlohe and the foreign office,[266] had no immediate influence upon German policy. By refusing, like the United States, England's proposals of a joint intervention (from October 1894 to January 1895), Germany aided Japan by keeping the circle while she completed China's defeat, a service which might have served as the basis of a friendly relationship.

The exigencies of European politics soon required a different course of action. If Germany had oscillated between England and Russia, England's earlier partiality for the Triple Alliance was followed by a persistent effort in the nineties to reach an understanding with Russia. The Conservatives worked for an agreement that would free England's hands in the Near and Far East, and the Liberals, under Rosebery, had even less reason for uncompromising hostility in view of their traditional sympathies for Russia's patronage of the Balkan peoples. Divided as they were by imperialist rivalries in China, England and Russia were at first united by the desire to maintain the integrity of China against Japan's territorial ambitions. It was this community of interest that attracted public attention to a possible Anglo-Russian understanding in the autumn of 1894. In the Liberal *Daily News* (Nov. 7), "Diplomaticus" proposed a delimitation of spheres of interest in the Near and Far East; he even urged (Nov. 10) the inclusion of France in a triple entente. Rosebery himself spoke of England's cordial relations with Russia and of friendly relations with France in a speech, November 9, at the Lord Mayor's banquet.[267] The *Times* (Nov. 10) affirmed as a fact that "the last subject of controversy between the two powers is being removed . . . in Central Asia." Of Russia's apparent desire for closer relations, as indicated by the courtesies with which she surrounded the British official mission to the funeral of Alexander III, the Conservative *Standard* (Nov. 19) wrote: "There are no reasons, on our side at any rate, why this most desirable state of things should not be brought about." The theme was, of course, extremely disagreeable to Germans, with whom an irreconcil-

---

[265] Hohenlohe, *Denkwürdigkeiten aus der Reichskanzlerzeit*, p. 8 (Nov. 2, 1894).
[266] *Ibid.*, pp. 15, 16; Marschall, Nov. 17, 1894. *G. P.*, IX, 246, 247.
[267] See H. Preller, *Salisbury und die türkische Frage im Jahre 1895* (Stuttgart, 1930), p. 29.

able Anglo-Russian hostility was axiomatic. The Conservative *Reichsbote* (Nov. 16) drew the conclusion that "England rates her relations with Germany in the third or fourth order," and the Conservative *Kreuz-Zeitung* (Nov. 27) suspected her of planning to reduce Germany to the status of a satellite. For the most part, however, German opinion refused to take the danger of an Anglo-Russian understanding seriously. It was impossible, according to the *Kreuz-Zeitung* (Dec. 18), as long as England remained at odds with France. The National Liberal *Schlessische Zeitung* saw nothing more than an effort on England's part to secure a few crumbs from Russia's bountifully laden table, and the Hamburger *Nachrichten,* Bismarck's organ, dismissed the talk of an entente in the English press as a mere pretense whose real purpose was to attract Germany to England's side for a stronger stand against Russia.[268]

The danger was taken more seriously by the German foreign office. As Japan's victories increased the prospects of a dictated peace, it tried to moderate her demands in order to avoid an occasion for a joint intervention which might bring England and Russia together and, at the same time, to attract Russia away from England.[269] Germany maintained an experimental balance as late as March 1895. England was permitted to hope for a favorable response to her proposal of intervention, although William wrote: "We must sell our support at a high price." [270] Russia was assured a few days later that "our interests in the Far East do not clash with Russia's," and that "we are therefore ready to exchange opinions with her in view of common action." [271] Disregarding Germany's advice, Japan forced China to sign the Treaty of Shimonoseki, April 17, 1895. China agreed, among other things, to cede Port Arthur and the peninsula of Liaotung, Formosa, and the Pescadores Islands, to pay a large indemnity, to grant Japan the most-favored-nation clause in a new commercial treaty, and to open seven additional ports to the commerce of the world. England now executed a *volte face.* Accepting Japan's new status as a great power in spite of the

---

[268] *Post,* Nov. 27.
[269] Langer, *Diplomacy of Imperialism,* I, 177.
[270] Hohenlohe, March 19, and William's comment. *G. P.,* IX, 253–258.
[271] Marschall, March 23. *Ibid.,* IX, 258, 259.

danger that she would soon appear as a competitor and rival in the Yangtze valley—England's special sphere of interest—, England decided that Japan's friendship was worth more than China's, since Russia was unwilling to strike a bargain. Moreover, others might undertake the task of forcing Japan to surrender her territorial booty. Japan's peace terms therefore were received in London with reserve.

Germany now openly joined Russia—and France—in forcing a revision of the Treaty of Shimonoseki.[272] The official press soon revealed Germany's effort to secure more moderate terms and also, after its failure, her coöperation with Russia.[273] The nationalist and Conservative press had already supported intervention, but there was much more talk of defeating Japan's plans for the economic regimentation of China than of restoring the broken ties with Russia.[274] Many began to talk of a Yellow Peril.[275] Anticipating by several months William's famous sketch of himself as leading the peoples of Europe against the menace of the yellow races, the *Kölnische Zeitung* (April 22) wrote that all Europe must unite. The *Kreuz-Zeitung* (April 25) even associated the United States with the Yellow Peril as the great danger to European interests in the Far East. If this sensational version of Germany's action in the Far East was intended to make the coöperation with Russia more palatable to public opinion, the effort was largely a failure. On no occasion since 1887 had an issue in foreign affairs aroused as much opposition. Not only did Germany's part in the political and military reorganization of Japan create a strong current of sympathy for Japan, but it was feared that German policy in the Far East lacked a sense of the realities. Harden would have required a binding assurance of Formosa as a condition for Germany's coöperation with Russia and France.[276] Although the *Hamburger Nachrichten,* as was to be expected of Bismarck's organ, accepted intervention as a favor to Russia, it insisted that complete neutrality would have

---

[272] Tschirschky, March 25, Brandt, April 8, Marschall, April 17. *G. P.,* IX, 259, 265, 270.
[273] *Kölnische Zeitung,* April 20; *N. A. Z.,* April 21.
[274] *Kreuz-Zeitung,* April 1; April 11; *National Zeitung,* April 17.
[275] *Kreuz-Zeitung,* April 17; *Reichsbote,* April 23.
[276] Harden, "Das Theezeitalter," *Zukunft,* April 27, 1895.

served the same purpose without alienating Japan.[277] Opposition opinion stood strongly against intervention and in favor of neutrality.[278] The cultivation of Japan's friendship was Germany's true interest, said the Catholic *Germania* (April 24), and this journal proposed (April 26) an interpellation in the Reichstag as a check upon the official policy.[279] The liberal *Vossische Zeitung* (April 17) preferred Japan to Russia as a partner, and, like the *Frankfurter Zeitung,* it expected (April 22) nothing but ingratitude for pulling Russia's chestnuts out of the fire. The position of the liberal *Berliner Tageblatt* (April 21) was less clear: it believed that Germany should participate in the approaching partition of China, but it also spoke of Germany's coöperation with Russia and France as "rather peculiar." It condemned the government's failure to explain its motives and it regretted the loss of Japan's friendship. It feared that the foreign office did not itself see the ultimate consequences of its anti-Japanese policy. Concern for Germany's commercial and, less directly, for her imperialist interests was the chief factor in the reaction of German opinion. According to the nationalists and Conservatives, these interests required Japan's defeat. While dislike of an association with Russia doubtless contributed to the opposition's criticism, the feeling that Germany was backing the wrong horse in her support of Russia and that she had more to gain by neutrality was decisive. The greater part of German opinion had little liking for the direction taken by German policy in the Far East.

To avert the danger that Germany's temporary associates might represent her to Japan as the ringleader in the intervention, Marschall directed that her diplomatic agents should not seem more "intolerant" than those of Russia and France.[280] Nevertheless, her part in the operation, which deprived Japan of most of the fruits of her victory, produced no permanent advantage and eventually much harm by preparing the way for the later Anglo-Japanese Alliance (1902). William's desire to acquire a foothold in China remained unsatisfied, for the powers had no inten-

---

[277] Hofmann, *Fürst Bismarck,* II, 298 (May 7, 1895).
[278] *Volks-Zeitung,* in *Post,* April 23.
[279] Cf. *National Zeitung,* April 25.
[280] *G. P.,* IX, 279 (April 24).

tion of proceeding immediately with the partition of China after compelling Japan to disgorge her conquests. It seemed, at first sight, that coöperation with Russia and France had relieved, as William had hoped,[281] the pressure upon Germany's eastern frontier, but Russia might have been still more deeply involved in the Far East by leaving the Treaty of Shimonoseki intact, for the Russo-Japanese war would doubtless thereby have been advanced several years. The *Norddeutsche* (April 29) was convinced that good would accrue to Germany's peace policy by her association with Russia and France, and the National Liberal *Hannoversche Zeitung* claimed the approval of public opinion for the policy of coöperation, as an expedient which had averted a dramatic demonstration of the Franco-Russian rapprochement and which would assure commercial advantages to Germany.[282] By the middle of June, the latter journal was calling, however, for proof *"dass das Eine nicht Schein, das Andere nicht Täuschung gewesen ist."* [283]

Perhaps the one definite sign of Russia's gratitude was the pressure which she exerted upon France to secure her participation in the international naval demonstration at the opening of the Kiel Canal. The French flag at last flew in honor of a German achievement, but the results were disappointing. William's recent condolences after the assassination of President Carnot had made a good impression, but the reference to Alsace-Lorraine as not open to discussion in the speeches exchanged between the Emperor and Bismarck at Friedrichsruh needlessly increased the difficulties of moderate French opinion in defending the presence of French warships at Kiel.[284] Again, as in 1891, the German press showed too much zeal in counting the pulse of French opinion. The French authorities naturally used every opportunity to prove that Kiel had no diplomatic significance. They saw to it that the French flagship followed that of the Russian squadron into the canal,[285] and much bad feeling was caused in Germany

[281] William II's comment, Brandt, April 9. *G. P.,* IX, 268; E. Brandenburg, *From Bismarck to the World War* (London, 1927), p. 67.
[282] *Deutsche Rundschau,* vol. 83, pp. 474, 475 (June 1895). Holstein, it is said, wished to prevent a *"Bluttaufe"* for the alliance. Hammann, *Der neue Kurs,* p. 113.
[283] *Freisinnige Zeitung,* June 15.
[284] *National Zeitung,* March 29.
[285] *Kölnische Zeitung,* June 24.

by an order forbidding shore leaves to the French crews and visits by civilians to the French warships.[286] In the Chamber of Deputies, Hanotaux, the foreign minister, denied that France's freedom of action had been affected in any way. Kiel, instead of serving the cause of conciliation, emphasized once more the fallacy of expecting good results from a dramatically staged fraternization. When Pasteur refused Prussia's highest decoration, *Pour le mérite,* Harden warned his readers against the talk in France of a reconciliation. "The gentlemen," he wrote, "who wax enthusiastic for a brotherhood of Germans and Gauls are parlor Socialists, anarchistic adventurers, or, very often, young men who, desirous of literary connections in Germany, wish to get their names in the newspapers at any price." [287]

Kiel was followed by a series of incidents culminating in a public acknowledgment of the Franco-Russian Alliance. The Tsar conferred the Order of St. Andrew upon President Faure; and Ribot, a former foreign minister who had had charge of the negotiations with Russia, spoke in the Chamber of an alliance as existing between the two countries. Continuing its wilful blindness, the German press attempted to explain away the clear meaning of these events. The Russian newspapers, it said, had totally ignored Ribot's statement, and Lobanov, the Russian foreign minister, was reported as telling Montebello, the French ambassador, *"Mais il n'y a rien d'écrit."* [288] Many of the arguments which had been used to diminish the significance of Kronstadt and Toulon were repeated. The *Vossische Zeitung* (June 17, 18) once more maintained that no changes had occurred in the international situation. Ribot's statement was discounted by some as a maneuver to force Russia to show her colors or as a consolation to the chauvinists after France's participation in the Kiel festivities.[289] Russia would never draw her sword in the interest of the *revanche;* her sole aim was France's support, and that was assured to her with or without an alliance.[290] By sharing with France rather

[286] *Politische Correspondenz* (Vienna), in *Vossische Zeitung,* June 24. Cf. *Freisinnige Zeitung,* June 25.

[287] Harden, "Kiel," *Zukunft,* June, 1895.

[288] *Hamburgischer Korrespondent,* in *Post,* June 18; *Kreuz-Zeitung, Reichsbote,* June 18.

[289] *Dresdner Journal, Strassburger Post,* in *Post,* June 15.

[290] *Vossische Zeitung,* June 18.

than with Germany the loan which was to enable China to pay the indemnity to Japan, Russia nevertheless gave due warning that she had no intention of changing the direction of her foreign policy. "Experience has shown again," wrote Hatzfeldt, "as after the last Turkish war, that Russia willingly accepts and exploits our aid, but also that she acknowledges no gratitude without our complete subordination." [291] Openly to take offense would have been to risk the complete failure of the attempt to approach Russia; the foreign office therefore pretended that Germany's exclusion from the Chinese loan had no diplomatic significance.   Russia was left in no doubt as to Germany's resentment, for she was told that Germany would henceforth merely fulfil the letter of her engagements and that the unfavorable reaction of public opinion would require great caution.[292] Coöperation with Russia and France had clearly not improved her diplomatic position in Europe.   Not only had it led to a public affirmation of the Franco-Russian Alliance, but it had also suggested to British observers that Germany's ultimate aim was a continental union for the evacuation of Egypt and for the acquisition of Walfisch Bay.[293] She seemed in danger of falling between two chairs after the failure to establish a rapprochement with England and to repair the broken ties with Russia.

IX

In contrast to the praise usually lavished upon Bismarck, the conclusions presented in this study have been critical.   There is, of course, another side to the picture.   His extraordinary command of diplomatic technique cannot be denied.   No statesman of his generation, and none of his successors in Germany equaled his skill in using the interests of other countries to advance those of his own.   Since the maintenance of the status quo would assure Germany's preëminent position in Europe, there is no reason to doubt his desire for peace.   Few of his achievements were lasting (even the national unity which he hastened was more superficial than real), but their immediate value was inestimable.   He as-

---

[291] *G. P.*, IX, 353 (June 18).
[292] Rotenhan, July 6. *G. P.*, IX, 305, 306; Holstein, July 8. Hohenlohe, *Denkwürdigkeiten aus der Reichskanzlerzeit*, p. 84.
[293] *Morning Post*, May 6.

sured Germany's security and predominance in Europe for twenty years. If, for ulterior purposes, he often represented latent as immediate dangers, if he sometimes purposefully increased existing tension, he always succeeded in keeping the decision for peace or war in his own hands. He was partly responsible for Germany's reputation abroad for brutality and unscrupulousness, but his system of alliances insured her against the hardening of this unfavorable opinion into a hostile coalition. If his greatest successes were palliatives rather than permanent solutions, statesmanship perhaps may not fairly be judged by a more exacting standard. His foreign policy, nevertheless, is open to criticism from the point of view of its methods, its relation to the dominant economic and social trends in Germany, and especially its use of public opinion. He would have been remiss in his duty had he not taken advantage of international tensions, but Germany's permanent interests were not served by purposefully increasing them. He may not have been directly responsible for the Franco-Italian friction in Tunis, but Italy's membership in the Triple Alliance, which that antagonism made possible, was never more than of limited value, because the approach to England which it opened was not effectively exploited. His encouragement of the friction between England and France in Egypt was extremely skilful; but, because their statesmen saw through his game, it tended to defeat its own purposes. It added to the already abundant suspicion and dislike of Germany on the part of the Western powers. Much has been made of Germany's fear of being used as England's lightning rod or sword upon the continent; but England also suspected that Germany valued her friendship chiefly as a tool against France, and suspicion of Bismarck's intentions was likewise an important cause of the failure of Franco-German cooperation under Ferry. His manipulation of the Austro-Russian rivalry in the Balkans is often regarded as his greatest diplomatic achievement. His encouragement of Russia to attack Turkey in 1877 doubtless served Germany's immediate interests by diverting Russia's attention from Central Europe, but the powerful Pan-Slavs, and even the Russian government, never forgave Germany for Bismarck's failure to support her interests during and after the Congress of Berlin. By maneuvering Russia back into his system of alliances in 1881 and 1887, he erected a temporary defense against these dangers; but the belief that Russia's friendship was essential to Germany's security, for which he was largely responsible and which revived in many quarters after his fall, was not an unmixed blessing. It tended eventually to deprive German foreign policy of the adaptability to circumstances which her situation required.

That Germany was and should remain primarily a continental power was one of Bismarck's basic assumptions. He believed that colonial expansion should be left to the initiative of individuals rather than that of the state, although he was responsible for the acquisition of almost all of the colonies which Germany possessed before 1914. There was much to be said for this point of view. An imperialist policy was certain to increase the friction with the established world empires—England, France, and Russia—but it was toward this result that the most significant economic and social movements in Germany were working. The rapid industrialization of Germany, accelerated by Bismarck's adoption of the protective tariff system of 1878, with the attendant rapid increase of population, created a powerful demand for markets, sources of raw materials, and suitable areas for colonization. Some of this dissatisfaction might have been averted by the negotiation of commercial treaties opening new and widening old markets or by legislative support for the settlement of the surplus population upon Germany's own soil. But Bismarck showed no interest in using his incomparable diplomatic ability for the benefit of German industry, nor did he even consider the possibility of extending the social security laws to an attack upon the great landed estates. His entire career shows that, in his opinion, diplomacy, commerce, and industry were entirely different branches of statecraft. He had no adequate solution for the problems that were pointing Germany toward imperialism.

Although public opinion was certainly not among the more obvious of the determining factors of Bismarck's foreign policy after the establishment of the Empire, his attitude toward it had momentous consequences both to himself and to Germany after his fall. Not until the problem of Germany's relations with Russia and Austria became acute, when popular sentiment

threatened the nice balance which he wished to maintain between
these powers, did he show much appreciation of its importance.
Through the press bureau of the foreign office and in his speeches
to the Reichstag he gave a good deal of attention to the education of opinion in regard to the proper solution of this fundamental problem. The results, though difficult to estimate, were
doubtless considerable, but even more important was his success. The nationalist sections of the middle classes united with
the Conservatives in an unquestioning support of his foreign policy, but it was nevertheless under Bismarck that a cleft developed
between the official conduct of German policy and a section of
public opinion that neither he nor his successors ever bridged.
For the most part, neither the Progressives nor the Social Democrats—who were making good their claim of speaking in the
name of the working classes—accepted his aims and methods
as those which were required by the country's true interests.
While the former applauded his strong speech against Russia,
February 6, 1888, their reaction would have been different if
they had been aware of the Reinsurance Treaty. Neither of
these opposition parties had any sympathy for the principles of
Machtpolitik, and both saw Germany's salvation in a diplomatic
association with the Western powers. They also agreed in condemning Bismarck's use of the press. The existence of official
and semi-official newspapers was a standing grievance; but even
more offensive was the publication of alarmist communications
—the famous *Kaltwasserstrahlen*—during periods of international tension. Innumerable protests were directed against the
practice of exaggerating foreign dangers to drum up sentiment
for increases in the army and to secure pliant majorities in the
Reichstag. By his abandonment of the *Kulturkampf,* Bismarck
neutralized the Centrists' criticism to a considerable extent, but
his domestic policy, especially in its refusal of any concession to
the principle of ministerial responsibility and in its reliance
upon indirect taxes, which bore most heavily upon the working
classes, continued to alienate liberal opinion. Taxation and
military service bore most heavily upon the masses, but their
spokesmen were refused any real voice in German policy at
home or abroad. Instead, Bismarck dismissed them cavalierly

as *Reichsfeinde* or as sentimentalists who were incapable of understanding the realities of international politics. No wonder that his dismissal was accepted not only with indifference but even with the hope that it would mean a change for the better. If he was largely responsible for the divorce between German policy and the masses, his influence upon nationalist opinion had serious consequences. He knew that every country must pay for the windows broken by its press; Germany eventually paid the bill for Bismarck's use of the press for alarmist purposes in the form of a public opinion that was increasingly susceptible to panic and hysteria. He was responsible to no small degree for the conviction that the chauvinists would always dictate France's action in a crisis—an assumption which inevitably militated against a cool steadiness in relations with her —and for the ingrained suspicion that England would never be a reliable friend.

It is customary to trace the first weakening of Germany's diplomatic position to Bismarck's fall and the subsequent failure to renew the Reinsurance Treaty. While his advanced age made impossible a much longer period of power, even a few more years of contact with him might have steadied the Emperor. The circumstances of his dismissal undoubtedly weakened Germany's prestige abroad and, eventually, that of the Empire at home as an act of ingratitude. Despite the increasing alienation between German and Russian public opinion, it was of value to Germany that a diplomatic relationship should be retained as a barrier to the dangerous pressure of popular passions for as long a period as possible, especially in the absence of a clearly thought-out substitute. The failure to act on Russia's desire for the renewal of the treaty was, as events proved, an irreparable blunder never to be corrected by later efforts to repair the broken line to St. Petersburg. It did more to win Russia for an alliance with France than the latter's ardent courtship.

Yet the judgment of history has been less than fair to Caprivi, owing to the fact that the history of the German Empire has usually been written by admirers of Bismarck. It is true that Caprivi was responsible for the non-renewal of the Reinsurance Treaty and that he left Germany in a weaker position than that which had been hers. Nevertheless, his most serious mistake was not the failure to renew the treaty with Russia but rather his failure to carry through to its conclusion the rapprochement with England. The difficulties were self-evident: it takes two to make an international as well as a personal friendship. It should have been clear that England was not easily to be won for a close association with Germany and the Triple Alliance and that German opinion would react unfavorably to important concessions for this purpose. Knowing these obstacles, it was Caprivi's duty, after committing Germany to this new course, to make use of every possible approach and to develop it patiently, persistently, despite temporary disappointments, even at the price of serious sacrifices and in the face of popular opposition at home. The beginnings were auspicious. By the surrender of important interests and claims in the Heligoland-Zanzibar Treaty, many potential causes of friction in Africa were removed and a way was opened for diplomatic coöperation. Germany, in fact, continued for a brief period to work with England in Egypt and elsewhere.

Conciliation was characteristic of Caprivi's orientation of German policy in domestic as well as in foreign affairs. In approaching England, he had no intention of turning against Russia. He at least tolerated William's amateurish gesture of friendship in the Empress Frederick's visit to Paris. At home, he refused to renew Bismarck's repressive laws against the Social Democrats, thereby encouraging the development of a moderate tendency within their ranks, which was in a few years to result in Eduard Bernstein's revisionist movement. His commercial treaties with Austria, Holland, and Switzerland in 1891 and with Russia in 1894 opened new markets for German industry. Nor did he resort to his predecessor's *Kaltwasserstrahlen* when the dramatic incidents of the Franco-Russian rapprochmements revealed all too clearly the weakening of Germany's diplomatic position. In fact, less use was made, at least temporarily, of official newspapers. The carefully managed tension which had been an integral part of Bismarck's statecraft was notably absent in that of his successor.

The "new course" unfortunately soon lost its attraction for

its official sponsors. Disappointed by the skeptical reserve of the working classes toward his advances, William reverted to Bismarck's policy of force. In 1894 he supported the Conservatives when the commercial treaty with Russia made them more determined than ever to force the Chancellor out of office; lacking the Emperor's confidence, Caprivi had no other choice than to resign. That no substantial progress was accomplished in approaching the Western powers was, of course, not entirely Germany's fault. Their response was admittedly discouraging. But the Empress Frederick's visit presented to French opinion much too brusquely the choice between reconciliation with Germany and loyalty to historic grievances. It played into the hands of the extremists, because the government could not, if it would, oppose their agitation without opening itself to the charge of unpatriotic conduct and of endangering the progress already attained in winning Russia's friendship. The negotiations with England showed at first a sounder appreciation of political realities. Instead of inviting a certain rebuff by a forthright offer of an alliance, the German diplomats counted upon their colonial sacrifices in the Heligoland-Zanzibar Treaty, their support in Egypt, their willingness to coöperate elsewhere, and the interests England had in common with Italy in the Mediterranean to win England's friendship and eventually her association with the Triple Alliance. No one factor adequately explains the ultimate failure. Distrustful of the new régime in Germany, reluctant to abandon the advantages of a free hand in European politics and to identify herself with Germany and the Triple Alliance against Russia and France, England was exasperatingly slow in responding. She continued to disregard Germany's interests, notably in Asia Minor and in the Anglo-Congo Treaty (1894), in spite of the latter's colonial concessions. Nevertheless, it should have been clear that England, with her world empire, would not agree with Germany's own estimate of her sacrifices and that the business of winning her support would demand infinite patience and especially the subordination of immediate to ultimate advantages. Caprivi was undoubtedly handicapped by the opposition of nationalist opinion, but, after all, his own failure and that of his advisers to support England against Russia in the Straits question betrayed a fatal reserve. Despite their decision to seek England's friendship, they could not free themselves from the presuppositions of many Germans as to her essential unreliability, her self-centered policy, and her desire to use the German army in her quarrel with Russia. They abruptly abandoned their attempt gradually to solidify Anglo-German relations by practical coöperation when England's supposed surrender to France in the Siam crisis seemed to demonstrate her worthlessness as a friend. England's refusal of a formal alliance, which Germany now said was an essential condition for her support, was followed by a belated return to Bismarck's policy of conciliating Russia. The "new course" in foreign affairs had become an ineffective copy of the old.

Caprivi had written, July 1890: "We must give more attention to public opinion than in Bismarck's time." [294] While it would not be easy to prove that German public opinion caused the failure of his plans for an Anglo-German rapprochement, its influence must have been considerable. This appears most clearly in connection with colonial affairs. He had aroused the hopes of the expansionists by speaking of a vigorous colonial policy as a valuable stimulus to patriotic and national sentiment, only to dash them in the Heligoland-Zanzibar Treaty. Henceforth the exceedingly articulate colonial enthusiasts joined the nationalists in attacking the government's weak attitude toward England. This pressure at home helps to explain the suggestion that appeared more than once in the official correspondence: that England's aid in securing new colonies would alone satisfy Germany's doubts as to the sincerity of her good-will. The official policy eventually alienated the greater part of public opinion. Approving Caprivi's position that Germany should develop her existing colonies rather than seek new territory, endorsing his approach to England and his milder attitude in foreign affairs, the liberal parties broke with him over the military bill (1893). They disliked the renewed courtship of Russia, and they united in a protest against coöperation with her against Japan in the Far East. Caprivi's policy of inaction, according

---

[294] G. P., VII, 347 (July 18).

Kladderadatsch, April 1, 1895.

Figure 14.—His old ship.

to nationalist opinion, was unworthy of Germany's power.[295] In the absence of a great issue which might have occupied the restless energies of the nation, domestic politics had degenerated into unedifying intrigues. Bismarck and his partisans continued their campaign against the "new course" and especially against the attempt to approach England. After William's superficial reconciliation with Bismarck in 1894, the foreign office quailed under the fear of his return to power.[296] The *Kladderadatsch* revealed the ambitions of the triumvirate—Holstein, Kiderlen-Wächter, and Eulenburg—in an unpleasant light.[297] With the lapse of years, youthful zeal ceased to be a convincing excuse for the Emperor's vagaries, the cumulative effect of which seriously compromised his popularity.

Disillusionment in regard to Germany's new leaders combined with failures in foreign policy to diminish confidence in Germany's security. Even Caprivi, despite his essential moderation, thought occasionally of desperate measures. He was ready for war in 1893 if England would fire the first shot against France in the Siam crisis. Toulon moved him to dire forebodings. There was, however, surprisingly little discussion in the press of a preventive war in connection with the Franco-Russian rapprochement. Confident that the Russians would never go beyond an innocent flirtation with the French—a point of view which doubtless influenced the diplomats who allowed the Reinsurance Treaty to lapse—the press failed for the most part to enlighten the public as to the extent of the unfavorable development of the international situation since Bismarck's fall. The resulting misapprehension averted a violent explosion of nationalist opinion, but it also weakened a powerful argument in favor of a rapprochement with England.

---

[295] Bauer, *Caveat Populus!* pp. 45, 46.
[296] Haller, *Eulenburg,* I, 182–184.
[297] "Kladderadatsch," *Zukunft,* April 7, 1894.

CHAPTER VIII

Weltpolitik and European Reactions, 1895-1899

Den besten Prüfstein für die Leistungsfähigkeit unserer auswärtigen Politik bildet für uns die Art und Weise, wie sie ihre Stellung zwischen Russland und England nimmt. Geschieht dies in richtiger Weise, so wird dadurch eine Basis geschaffen, die alle Operationen Deutschlands auf dem Gebiete der überseeischen Politik ausserordentlich erleichtert; geschieht es in verkehrte Weise, so entstehen daraus so viele Nachteile für die deutschen Interessen, dass alle Aufwendungen für die Flotte und für andere zur Betreibung einer Weltpolitik nothwendige Mittel dadurch in ihre Wirkung mehr als paralysiert werden.

> *Hamburger Nachrichten*, in *Post*, Dec. 14, 1899.

Das Festhalten an einer Mittellinie zwischen der sich immer gegensätzlicher gestaltenden russischen und englischen Politik ist dadurch erleichtert, dass wir nicht darauf angewiesen sind, weder von der einen, noch von der anderen Seite Unterstützung für irgend etwas zu begehren. . . . Gott sei Dank, wir sind in der Lage, freie Hand nach beiden Seiten zu haben, und auf eigenen Füssen stehen zu können.

> *Westdeutsche Zeitung,* in *Post*, May 21, 1899.

I

Under Caprivi, dissatisfaction with the conduct of foreign policy was largely the result of his indifference to colonial expansion.[1] The Bismarck fronde lamented the breaking of the wire to St. Petersburg, but Russo-German relations excited no unusual concern. The timely appearance of serious Anglo-Russian and Anglo-French differences and the fact that the alliance between France and Russia showed no aggressive tendencies removed any

---

[1] This was the opinion of the semi-official and Conservative press: *Kölnische Zeitung*, Nov. 10, 1894; *Post*, Dec. 15, 1894; *Reichsbote*, Jan. 1, 1895.

immediate reason for fear. Caprivi, indeed, hopefully resumed the courtship of Russia during his last year of power, and Hohenlohe, his successor, aided by the accession of the youthful, easily led Nicholas II to the Russian throne (1894), continued it with even greater zeal. The change of Chancellors also meant a more forceful participation in world affairs, although the usual assurances appeared as to the continuity of German foreign policy.[2] No government, said Hohenlohe in his first speech in the Reichstag, could ignore the popular desire for expansion. "It springs from a stronger national unity."[3] The nationalists also were optimistic. To one journal, the Chancellor's sympathy with the nation's aspirations assured a more glorious period in German history.[4] Even the Pan-Germans, whose standards in this respect were high, looked forward to a stronger support of Germany's interests abroad.[5]

Imperialist sentiment was stronger than ever. Although emigration had already begun to decline, it was possible to argue that agricultural colonies could alone save for Germany her surplus population, since her industries and commerce were unable to support it at home. The cry for raw materials and markets was louder than ever. Great banks like the *Deutsche Bank,* the *Diskontogesellschaft,* and the *Darmstädter Bank* secured concessions for German industries and invested millions in Turkey, the Far East, and South America, and then looked to the government for protection. Great industrial combines depended increasingly upon foreign commerce for the profitable operation of the mass system of production. Efficient agents brought Germany's trade to the world's doorstep and paved the way for the expansion of her political influence. Except among the Socialists and the Progressives, there was little articulate opposition. The economic factor was perhaps more potent in Germany than in England, France, Russia, or the United States, for these countries already possessed an abundance of undeveloped

---

[2] Hohenlohe, *Denkwürdigkeiten aus der Reichskanzlerzeit,* p. 17 (Nov. 25, 1894); William to Victoria, Oct. 28, 1894. *Letters of Queen Victoria,* (3), II, 435.

[3] *Verhandlungen,* IX Leg. Per., III Sess., I, 22 (Dec. 11, 1894).

[4] *Leipziger Tageblatt,* in *Post,* Dec. 14, 1894.

[5] *Alldeutsche Blätter,* Jan. 6, 1895. Henceforth this weekly, the official Pan-German organ, will be cited as *A. B.*

territory,[6] but the appeal of a *Weltpolitik* to a society and a government which retained many feudal characteristics owed much to psychological and political factors. Only an acute threat to Germany's position in Europe might have made her immune to the imperialist trend of world politics. The landlord and the aristocratic diplomat who thought in terms of Germany's predominance in Europe could not easily remain indifferent while other countries, in less need of expansion, competed in Africa for the remains of a continent and prepared to share in the impending partition of China. In the progress of Germany's trade and industry, in her administrative efficiency, and in her cultural achievements, almost all Germans saw a just claim to a liberal share in the spoils. Germany's future was at stake. If there was less talk than in England of the "struggle for survival" and of the "survival of the fittest,"[7] the Darwinian view of national interests and policy had no little influence upon public opinion. Unless Germany acquired coaling stations, naval bases, spheres of influence, and colonies—unless her expansion equalled that of the other powers—she would, it was feared, sink to the level of the second- or third-rate powers. Bebel, Liebknecht, and their Social Democratic followers insisted that Germany's future depended rather upon the solution of the social problem, but the appeal to national prestige spoke the language of the upper and of a large section of the middle classes. The Pan-Germans became vociferous partisans of colonial expansion, because they felt that world dominion had become the essential test of a great power.[8] Even the agrarian Conservatives went along with the current, without much enthusiasm, however, since a good price was exacted for their votes on imperialist legislation.

More surprising than the strength of imperialist sentiment was the government's adoption of a *Weltpolitik*. Scarcely a member of the diplomatic service abroad or of the foreign office was drawn from the industrial and commercial groups. If the

---

[6] Oncken, *Vorgeschichte des Weltkrieges*, II, 421.

[7] Langer, *Diplomacy of Imperialism*, I, ch. 3.

[8] The Pan-Germans were not alone. in this point of view. *Allgemeine Zeitung*, Jan. 15, 1900. *Cf.* Lamprecht's address at the University of Leipzig in commemoration of von Treitschke. *Zukunft*, July 18, 1896.

landed aristocrats used their control of German foreign policy for imperialist purposes, it was not to enrich a small minority of contractors, speculators, and investors. Imperialism became a national interest because it was expected to strengthen the Empire against the rising tide of the Social Democracy,[9] because it would increase Germany's stature in the world, and because William II was its ardent partisan. The numerous references in the diplomatic correspondence to the popular demand for colonies is in part explained by the desire to secure concessions from other countries, especially England, but political advantages at home were also foreseen. In March 1895 William spoke of imperialism as an issue that might secure the election of a more tractable Reichstag. Although the Emperor once referred to the advantages that would accrue to the shipbuilding industry from the naval program, although it was at the launching of a passenger liner that he spoke of Germany's place upon the seas, the economic advantages of *Weltpolitik* interested him less than its contributions to German power and prestige. It was in addressing the army or navy that he waxed most eloquent in regard to Germany's place in the world.

The unprofitableness of Germany's colonies discouraged neither the official circles nor public opinion. Even poor colonies added to the territory under the German flag, and they might serve as stepping stones to something better. The fact that little territory adaptable to white settlement remained unclaimed was seen as an argument for prompt and vigorous action. Germany should ever be alert, it was said, to participate in any revision of the colonial balance of power. Ernest Hasse, the president of the Pan-German League, spoke for a wider circle than this extremist group: "One of the conventional lies of history is that the world is already divided. History, on the contrary, is merely the record of the partition and repartition of the world."[10]   A

---

[9] In neither the Reichstag nor the lower house of the Prussian parliament was there a majority for its legal suppression. There was talk again of a *Staatsstreik*. Hammann, *Der neue Kurs*, pp. 140, 141.

[10] *A. B.*, Sept. 13, 1896. ". . . es wird manche Auftheilungen vorgenommen werden, solange es überhaupt eine Welt geben wird. Staatengebilde entstehen, ändern sich oder verschwinden auch ganz. Der Mächtige nimmt an dieser Umgestaltung zu seinem Gunsten theil!" *Münchener Neueste Nachrichten*, Dec. 20, 1897. *Cf.* V. A. Schroeder, "Bedarf Deutschland einer Vergrösserung seines colonialen Besitzes," *Grenzboten*, 1899, I, 409.

good deal of Germany's offensive assertiveness and alarming nervousness derived from the feeling that these years would be decisive for her future as a world power. England and France were evidently about to complete the partition of Africa, and the choicest sections of China might soon be staked out as British, Russian, or Japanese spheres of influence. The Monroe Doctrine, which the Germans, like most Europeans, regarded as a typical example of Yankee imperialism, further narrowed the available outlets for German energies. Even the government was inevitably vague as to the specific objectives and methods of *Weltpolitik*.[11] "It is easy," wrote the Catholic *Germania* (Jan. 26, 1896), "to wax enthusiastic for a German world policy, but it is more difficult to form a clear, well-defined picture of it." Unlike those of England and France, Germany's colonies were surrounded by the territory of European powers. The dread of antagonizing Russia led her to affirm repeatedly that her interests in Turkey, including the Bagdad Railway, were exclusively economic. German imperialism was therefore necessarily opportunist in character. It developed slowly, according to no discernible plan. It was Germany's misfortune that the interests of other powers were already established, more often than not, in those regions (Samoa, South Africa, the Philippines, China) where she hoped to expand. The resulting friction inevitably had repercussions upon her position in Europe. Instead of seeking first and always a secure position in Europe, as in Bismarck's time, her foreign policy was subordinated to the advancement of her *Weltpolitik*.

This change of emphasis acquired greater significance from the fact that it occurred during a transition in European politics. Almost every great power reviewed its diplomatic commitments. Permanent alliances suffered from stresses and strains that arose chiefly from divergent imperialist interests. Russia's indifference to Alsace-Lorraine and her desire for better Franco-German relations cooled the enthusiasm of French opinion, if not the government's loyalty, for the alliance. The most ardent *revanchards* forgot their hatred of Germany when England forced France, under the threat of war during the Fashoda crisis, to

11 Brandenburg, *From Bismarck to the World War*, p. 206.

abandon her claims to the Upper Nile. The miscarriage of justice in the Dreyfus affair strengthened the pacifist and Socialist movements as well as the left-wing bourgeois parties, while the numerous polls of public opinion revealed a decline in the more extreme aspects of the *revanche* spirit.[12] If these circumstances favored Germany, others were sapping the foundations of the Triple Alliance. The nationalist aspirations of the Czechs and the South Slavs menaced the German and Magyar domination of the Dual Monarchy and weakened the military efficiency of Germany's one reliable ally. By many the aged Francis Joseph was regarded as the sole cause of Austria's continued existence. Italy's loyalty to the Triple Alliance declined still further with her repeated disappointments in the colonial field. When Germany's friendliness toward Turkey showed how little her help in securing Tripoli could be depended upon and Italy's first attempt to conquer Abyssinia ended in the catastrophe of Adowa (1896), the Italians decided to put an end to the ten-year tariff war with France and to approach her diplomatically (1900–1902). Shimonoseki was only the first example of a trend toward an "interpenetration of alliances." Members of opposing groups patched up their differences, like Austria and Russia in 1897 in regard to their Balkan interests, or reached agreements for the attainment of specific purposes, as did France and Italy in 1900 with reference to Tripoli and Morocco. Unrest in Armenia, Macedonia, and Crete threatened to reopen the Near Eastern question and to precipitate the long-expected partition of Turkey. Many Englishmen to whom their country's traditional isolation no longer seemed "splendid" seriously considered the establishment of a close friendship with a continental power as a protection against an uncertain future.

Events had again played into Germany's hands; the advantages of her situation, at least for the immediate future, were clearly greater than its dangers. Her potential enemies were farther apart than ever. Thanks to this favorable situation, her diplomats could strengthen Germany's position in Europe, advance the interests of her *Weltpolitik,* or undertake the difficult task of combining these purposes. Bismarck had little advice

---

[12] Carroll, *French Public Opinion,* ch. IX.

to give that was pertinent to these problems. Written in 1891 and published after his death in 1898, the first two volumes of his political testament, the *Reflections and Reminiscences,* assumed that she was still essentially a continental power.[13] Given the powerful economic, social, and political pressures that were working in favor of imperialism, it was doubtful if Germany could stand aside while the world was being divided. At any rate, the diplomats decided to use Germany's exceptional advantages in the interest of colonial expansion, confident that her strength and their own skill would be equal to such perils as might arise. The greatest of these dangers was the possibility that England might side with France and Russia; the balance of power in Europe would thereby be turned against Germany and her allies. A challenge to England's interests in South Africa or China, a demand for territorial concessions as the price of German neutrality or friendship, or an attempt to profit by her distress during the Boer War, might well drive her into the arms of Germany's enemies. On the other hand, a friendly arrangement would certainly imperil the success of the renewed effort to approach Russia. Germany's relations with England constituted therefore the crucial problem of German foreign policy. Again there were three possibilities: a frankly hostile attitude and a Russo-German rapprochement, an Anglo-German understanding directed more or less openly against France and Russia, and a middle course based upon a balanced position between England and Russia. It was natural, if not inevitable, that the third alternative was chosen, since the diplomats had decided to give first place to *Weltpolitik*. Nothing seemed easier for Germany than to sell her favors from time to time to the other powers, but these profits might be lost if England should decide to throw in her lot with France or Russia. To sense the moment when England would prefer this course rather than to pay Germany's price and then to come to terms with her or with Russia was the necessary condition for a successful policy of the "free hand."

Germany had embarked upon a tortuous but entirely legitimate course. Bismarck himself had not only taken advantage

---

[13] Oncken. *Vorgeschichte des Weltkrieges,* II, 469.

of differences between other countries but he had even encouraged them. That the diplomats were able more or less to ignore public opinion, as was shown during the Boer War, was a favorable augury, but, unfortunately, their freedom of action was far from complete. Because it made almost inconceivable a definitive break with Russia, Bismarck's influence was a handicap. The leaders shared with public opinion its suspicions of England's good faith, of her ability to follow a steady policy, and of her value as a friend. The fear that she wished to use the German army to fight her battles almost eliminated even the possibility of an Anglo-German rapprochement. Holstein's excessive confidence in the permanence of the antagonisms between England, France, and Russia made him blind to the moment when, the balanced position between England and Russia no longer being tenable, a choice between them should have been made. William's vagaries likewise caused serious difficulties. Hohenlohe loosened the reins which Caprivi had held more tightly, for fear that a dangerous man would be his successor. "If I had not been prepared to do this," he wrote to Holstein in March 1896, "I should not have entered this office. Having accepted it, I must take the Emperor as he is." [14] While William's occasional flashes of insight had little practical influence, his extravagant speeches and personal diplomacy had serious consequences.[15] Such statements as "Germany's place is upon the seas" and "Germany has become a world empire" captured the popular imagination,[16] but they also encouraged hopes of colonial gains beyond any reasonable prospect of achievement and thus prepared for a dangerous dissatisfaction. His oscillation between excesses of friendliness and hostility toward England, Russia, and France weakened confidence in the stability of German policy.[17] The zigzag course—in a measure the inevitable result of the "free-hand policy"—had commenced.[18] In South Germany William's changeableness was said to be com-

---

[14] Hohenlohe, Denkwürdigkeiten aus der Reichskanzlerzeit, p. 192.

[15] Brandenburg, From Bismarck to the World War, pp. 21, 22.

[16] R. Denner, Bedeutung und Ziele deutscher Weltpolitik (Minden, 1898), pp. 10, 11.

[17] Harden, "Karlsruh-Darmstadt," Zukunft, Nov. 6, 1897.

[18] O. Mittelstadt, Vor der Flute; sechs Briefe zur Politik der Gegenwart (Leipzig, 1897), pp. 135, 136.

parable to the aberrations of Ludwig II, the mad King of Ba-varia.[19]

II

Only in the sense that friction existed between England, Rus-sia, and France did Germany have anything like a "free hand." To use it effectively was, however, extremely difficult. The per-sonal factor—William's relations with Prince Edward and Salis-bury—and conflicting interests made a cool detachment in Anglo-German relations almost impossible. Compared to the causes of bad feeling with England, the differences with Russia were insignificant, at least until the Bagdad Railway question reached a more advanced stage. It was chiefly at England's expense that Germany could ever hope to attain her vague but far-reach-ing imperialist aspirations. Because the Germans had attributed a greater sympathy and capacity for *Realpolitik* to the Conserva-tive party, they believed that Salisbury's cabinet, which took office in June 1895, would be more sympathetic than Rosebery's Liberal government.[20] This hope was soon disappointed. Anglo-German relations steadily deteriorated, although no really seri-ous crisis occurred until the Jameson Raid at the end of the year.

William's visit to Cowes that summer for the regatta had unfortunate results. To Prince Edward, his officious demeanor was intolerable. William himself never forgave Salisbury for breaking an engagement when Queen Victoria suddenly sum-moned him to London. German opinion was likewise out-raged by the ironical and patronizing tone (Aug. 5) of the Conservative *Standard's* comments. After paying its respects to Germany's military power, to the abilities of her ruler, and to the value of her friendship, it spoke of the "want of courage and of self-confidence" which "would never be ascribed to the young Emperor." It recalled Goethe's saying, "No youth can be a master," and drew the conclusion that William had much to learn from his grandmother. Germany's "tendency to try diplo-

---

[19] Monts, Munich, July 8, 1897. *Erinnerungen und Gedanken des Botschafters Anton Graf Monts,* Nowack, Thimme, eds. (Berlin, 1932), p. 372.
[20] *Germania,* June 25; *Freisinnige Zeitung,* June 27.

matic experiments" in her recent coöperation with Russia and France reminded the *Standard* of the "dexterous, not to say, ambidexterous tactics of her first Chancellor." What was really an expression of irritation at Germany's recent dealings with Russia and France convinced the Germans that their estimate of England's attitude was correct. "This affair," wrote the Conservative *Post* (Aug. 10), "brings to the surface the dislike of Great Britain which many Germans have in their blood." The press rehearsed most of Germany's traditional grievances. England still refused to see that her friendship could only be had on terms of complete equality.[21] The nationalist *Leipziger Neueste Nachrichten* insisted that England should be the one to make concessions, since her present and future needs were greater than Germany's.[22] The *Standard's* use of the word "Fatherland" betrayed, said the *Hamburger Nachrichten* (Aug. 13), as much contempt as the Frenchman's *"la Prusse"* and *"prussien."* [23] Bismarck's press organ spoke for many in attributing to England the desire to use Germany against Russia.[24] Moderates joined extremists in an indignant protest. While the Progressive *Freisinnige Zeitung* (Aug. 11) admitted that harm had been done to the cause of friendly relations, the Pan-Germans insisted that William, "after this latest product of her shamelessness," should not visit England for the next ten years.[25]

The German foreign office was just as quick as public opinion to impute the worst of motives to England. Although Salisbury's proposal for an international understanding for the partition of the Turkish Empire was obviously intended as a precautionary measure,[26] it seemed to Holstein good evidence of a deep-laid plot to divide Germany and Russia, to make Albania a bone of contention between Austria and Italy, and to precipitate a continental war in order to divert France from Egypt

---

[21] *Kölnische Zeitung, Hannoversche Courier,* in *Post,* Aug. 8; *National Zeitung,* Aug. 9.

[22] *Post,* Aug. 13.

[23] Hofmann, *Fürst Bismarck,* II, 317, 318.

[24] *Post,* Aug. 9; *Dresdner Journal,* in *Post,* Aug. 10; *Hannoversche Courier,* in *Post,* Aug. 13; *Zukunft,* Aug. 17. Cf. *Times,* Aug. 8.

[25] *A. B.,* Aug. 18, 1895.

[26] F. Meinecke, *Geschichte des deutsch-englischen Bündnisproblems, 1890–1901* (Munich, 1927), pp. 55, 56; Langer, *Diplomacy of Imperialism,* I, 196; Brandenburg, *From Bismarck to the World War,* p. 73.

and Russia from the Far East.[27]   William dismissed the project as *"echt Englisch"* and agreed—on Holstein's advice—to maintain an attitude of strict reserve if Salisbury raised the question. Later Holstein saw more merit in it when he learned that Russia would receive Constantinople and that Germany would be compensated (probably in Africa), but it was then too late, for William's strained relations with the Prime Minister prevented any good results from this change of heart.[28]   While Germany's reserve may largely be explained by her suspicions of England's purposes and by concern for Russia's reaction, she was already thinking of the profits of a balanced position between these powers. "Germany," wrote William who expected to ask England for concessions in Zanzibar and elsewhere when she turned to him for aid, "is now in the fortunate position of being able to look on calmly and wait, for no one in Europe can achieve anything without us."[29]   "We wish to keep a free hand," wrote an official of the foreign office, "in order to demand something for ourselves at the psychological moment, even if not in the Mediterranean. . . ."[30]   From London, Hatzfeldt also advised against any definite commitments, although he did not share Holstein's suspicions.[31]   Salisbury's warning, scarcely a month after William's visit to Cowes, that his views might change was not calculated to disturb the equanimity of the German foreign office;[32] a return to England's normal policy of defending the integrity of Turkey would, on the contrary, serve Germany's purposes. As for Russia, the possibility that Salisbury might win her for his partition plan had moved William to suggest that the Central powers should themselves support her aims in the Straits in return for suitable concessions to Austria in the Balkans.[33]   In October 1895 Salisbury's definitive abandonment of his scheme —when a temporary improvement in the Armenian problem gave Turkey a new lease on life—apparently removed the danger

---

[27] *G. P.,* X, 19, 20.
[28] *Ibid.,* X, 23, 24.
[29] Brandenburg, *From Bismarck to the World War,* p. 72.
[30] Rotenhan, Aug. 5, 1895. *G. P.,* X, 21.
[31] *Ibid.,* X, 30-32 (Aug. 16).
[32] Hatzfeldt, Aug. 31. *Ibid.,* X, 34.
[33] William II's comments, Eulenburg, Aug. 18. *Ibid.,* X, 33.

of an Anglo-Russian rapprochement [34] and revived, as Germany believed, England's need of good relations with Austria and the Triple Alliance. It was not, however, to Germany's interest that the relations between Russia and England in the Near East should be strained to the breaking point, for trouble there might involve Austria; she therefore encouraged Russia's expansion in the Far East as an equally fruitful and less dangerous source of Anglo-Russian friction. William addressed Nicholas before going to Cowes as the representative of European civilization in the Far East,[35] but he then proceeded to spoil the effect by presenting the famous allegorical painting (it was based upon his own rough sketch) of himself as Saint George at the head of the Western nations against a distant Buddha, the symbol of the Yellow Peril. In his reply Nicholas spoke of the "charming picture that Moltke brought." [36]

Meanwhile, the Armenian crisis furnished a less dangerous opportunity for Anglo-German coöperation. Russia and France had reluctantly joined England when Salisbury, following Rosebery's example, tried to secure relief for the Armenians against their Turkish oppressors. Neither power was willing, however, to use force. To watch and to restrain England were Russia's chief purposes, and France merely wished to do her ally a favor, since she had a large financial stake in Turkey's integrity.[37] The Armenian triplice therefore did not mean that England had joined Germany's enemies; uncertainty as to the ultimate disposition of the French naval forces in fact kept Salisbury from using the British fleet to intimidate the Sultan. Even if Germany was justified in refusing to participate in a plan for the partition of Turkey, she might easily have made a good impression in London by offering her coöperation in securing reforms for Armenia. Among the liberals and religious groups the Armenians enjoyed much sympathy. Germany's allies were eager. Goluchowski, the Austrian foreign minister,

---

[34] Hatzfeldt, Oct. 24. *G. P.,* X, 81.

[35] William II, July 10. M. Semenoff, *Correspondance entre Guillaume II et Nicolas II, 1894–1914* (Paris, 1924). p. 12; Rotenhan, *G. P.,* IX, 358, 359.

[36] "He has," exclaimed the disappointed William, "not the slightest notion of what it is all about!" Eulenberg, Oct. 1. Hohenlohe, *Denkwürdigkeiten aus der Reichskanzlerzeit,* p. 111.

[37] Langer, *Diplomacy of Imperialism,* pp. 146 ff.

protested against the anti-English tone of a part of the German press; Austria, he insisted, needed her aid against Russia.[38] Fearing that Germany would eventually support Russia against England, he warned her that Austria would never agree to the Russia's establishment at Constantinople.[39] Italy also spoke strongly for a rapprochement with England. When Germany was at odds with England, she was, said her foreign minister, in the position "of a child of divorced parents." England's cooperation with the Triple Alliance was, according to Blanc, his lifework.[40]

At first Germany had worked with Salisbury to a limited extent, advising Turkey more than once to yield to his demand for the appointment of a humane governor.[41] She soon reverted, however, to the reserve which she had maintained toward the partition scheme. From his retirement, Bismarck protested against the sentimental campaign in favor of the Armenians.[42] A friendly Turkey was a necessary condition for the success of such imperialist enterprises as the Bagdad Railway. Confident that England would never consent to the concessions which alone would give permanence to the Armenian triplice, the foreign office saw no compelling need to abandon the "free hand." Holstein insisted that Germany should burn none of her bridges, especially since England wished to delay the inevitable Anglo-Russian war by pushing France and Russia into an attack upon the Central powers.[43] The pleas of Germany's allies availed nothing against the incurable suspicions of England. In Italy's offer of her fleet for a naval demonstration in the Dardanelles and in Austria's suggestion that an international fleet should be sent through the Straits, William scented an English plot to commit the Triple Alliance to an initiative against Russia.[44] With his approval, Germany had earlier refused to exert pres-

[38] Lichnowsky, Oct. 28, 1895. *G. P.,* X, 145, 146.

[39] Lichnowsky, Oct, 30; Eulenburg, Nov. 8. *Ibid.,* X, 147, 157.

[40] Bülow, Dec. 3, 7. *Ibid.,* X, 218, 219, 227.

[41] *Ibid.,* X, 42, 44, 45, 56, 57–59. *Cf.* Preller, *Salisbury und die türkische Frage,* pp. 37, 38.

[42] K. Kron, *Russland oder England? Ein Mahnruf* (Vienna, 1900), pp. 34, 35.

[43] Holstein, July 14, 1895. Monts, *Erinnerungen und Gedanken,* p. 350.

[44] William II's comments, Bülow, Rome, Nov. 9; Hohenlohe, Nov. 11; Eulenburg, Nov. 11. *G. P.,* X, 169–173.

sure upon England, France, and Russia at Turkey's request;[45] he now directed that Austria and Italy should be restrained from these dangerous enterprises. A report from Constantinople that Russia had ceased to coöperate with England confirmed Germany's aversion to active measures.[46] This inaction had disadvantages, for it diminished the value of Germany's friendship to the powers more directly concerned. Nicholas' discouraging coolness in an exchange of letters (Nov. 8, 9) was a reminder of the value of the Triple Alliance and of the need to keep a door open to London.[47] Momentarily impressed by the solidity of the Franco-Russian Alliance, even William soon agreed that Austria's English proclivities should be encouraged. The results, however, were meager. In reply to Austria's proposal for the strengthening and extension of the Mediterranean Accord of 1887, Salisbury refused to extend its original terms,[48] and Austria's proposal for an international naval demonstration was vetoed by France and Russia. The outcome merely confirmed Germany's belief that England had intended to use Austria as a tool.[49] Hohenlohe, whose responsibility for the conduct of German foreign policy was greatest, still believed that England might be attracted to the Triple Alliance, provided that dangerous crises with France and Russia were avoided.[50]

Except in regard to the Armenian problem, public opinion had no clear views as to the problems of Germany's foreign policy at this time. Salisbury's proposed understanding for the partition of the Ottoman Empire seems to have remained a secret. In January 1896, almost six months after its communication to Germany, an even more ambitious scheme appeared in

---

[45] William II's comments, Saurma, Therapia, Aug. 10, 1895. *G. P.*, X, 48, 49.
[46] Saurma, Therapia, Oct. 29. *Ibid.*, X, 91.
[47] Hohenlohe, Nov. 12. *Ibid.*, X, 99-101. No concessions, wrote Holstein, should be made to Russia at the expense of the Triple Alliance as long as the Franco-Russian Alliance endured. Hohenlohe, *Denkwürdigkeiten aus der Reichskanzlerzeit*, p. 119 (Nov. 8).
[48] Hohenlohe, Nov. 14. *G. P.*, X, 203. *Cf.* Langer, *Diplomacy of Imperialism*, I, 208.
[49] *G. P.*, X, 121, 207, 207-209; Hohenlohe, *op. cit.*, p. 122.
[50] Hohenlohe, Nov. 22, Dec. 17. *G. P.*, X, 112, 234; Marschall, Dec. 23. *Ibid.*, X, 244. Salisbury's refusal of Italy's request—which Germany seconded—for permission to use Zeila in British Somaliland for her campaign against Abyssinia was scarcely encouraging. Marschall, Dec. 13, 28. *Ibid.*, X, 214, 215, 223.

the Conservative *Preussische Jahrbücher* under the title *Politische Träumereien*. The anonymous author allotted Asia Minor, Constantinople, the Straits, the islands of Lesbos, Chios, and Rhodes to Russia, while the Balkans were to be divided between its native peoples. Austria was to be compensated by the formation of a new Poland, created from Austrian, German, and Russian territory, as a third partner in the Dual Monarchy. For her sacrifices Germany was to secure Russia's Baltic provinces— while Russia would move her capital to Moscow. The return of Metz to France and Germany's annexation of Luxemburg were proposed as a solution of the Franco-German problem. England was assigned Egypt, Italy was to receive Tripoli, and France was to be given Morocco and the Congo. In many respects a remarkable forecast of future changes in the maps of three continents, this scheme nevertheless excited little discussion. It was either entirely ignored or bitterly condemned. The official *Norddeutche* dismissed it as a dream,[51] and the Pan-Germans marvelled that a review calling itself *"preussisch"* dared to suggest the retrocession of Metz on the twenty-fifth anniversary of the proclamation of the German Empire. To them the author was *"weder preussisch noch deutsch."*[52] Yet there were significant tendencies in public opinion during the last half of 1895. The popular sympathy for the Armenians evoked many a lecture from the semi-official press and from Bismarck and his partisans as to the need of a realistic view of foreign policy. Interests, not sentiment, should be the guide; yet nothing was done to check the bad feeling toward England. It permeated even the foreign office, to the extent that one of its officials suspected her of instigating the Armenian insurrection. That England was exceedingly irritating and that some justification for suspecting her intentions doubtless existed cannot be denied, but the incitement of opinion against her was scarcely a proper preparation for the policy of a "free hand" or for her eventual association with the Triple Alliance. The popular response to the Kruger Telegram was the natural result of these tendencies.

---

[51] *P. J.*, vol. 83, pp. 2 ff.
[52] "Vir pacificus," "Politischer Ernst," *ibid.*, vol. 83, p. 412.

III

A brief but intense crisis in Anglo-German relations at the beginning of 1896 threatened to change the direction of German foreign policy. Its origins go back to Bismarck's establishment of German Southwest Africa twelve years earlier, a step which might have led at that time to a challenge of British supremacy in South Africa. The resulting suspicions in Cape Colony and, to a less extent, in England soon became permanent factors of the situation. Bismarck chose, however, to retreat at the critical moment. Faced by dangers in Europe, he finally dropped his vigorous protests and recognized (May 7, 1885) the establishment of a British protectorate over Bechuanaland and the seizure of St. Lucia Bay on the East Coast,[53] although England's manifest purpose in both instances had been to prevent a direct contact between German territory and the Transvaal. Moreover, he had implicitly accepted Article IV of the London Convention (1881) allowing the British government to veto the Transvaal's treaties and alliances, except in the case of the Orange Free State,[54] by submitting a commercial treaty with the Boers to its approval. Neither his preoccupation with European politics nor Caprivi's later coolness to imperialism was able to check the economic and political forces that gradually resulted in a relationship with the Transvaal approaching that of an unofficial protectorate.

The discovery of gold gave the little country an economic importance which it had formerly lacked. By the middle of the nineties, German capital controlled at least a fifth of the foreign investments, including a large share in the projected railway from Pretoria to the frontier of Portuguese Mozambique. Not a few German concerns had thriving branches in Pretoria and Johannesburg. A regular steamship service was established, with the aid of a governmental subsidy, between Germany and the port of Lorenzo Marques on Delagoa Bay. Enterprising Germans had acquired the profitable whiskey and dynamite monop-

---

[53] J. A. Wüd, *Die Rolle der Burenrepubliken in der auswärtigen und kolonialen Politik des Deutschen Reiches in den Jahren 1883–1900* (Nuremberg, 1927), pp. 70, 71.

[54] Hammann, *Der neue Kurs*, p. 121.

olies.[55] Still more significant were the sympathy which the Boers enjoyed in Germany, President Kruger's confidence in her support, and her unmistakable benevolence toward the Transvaal's resistance to British imperialism. If the British imperialists, with Cecil Rhodes at their head, regarded the Boers as an obstacle to progress and to the more efficient exploitation of the gold mines, the Germans, for the most part, thought of them as a small people of Germanic blood struggling to maintain their independence. The colonial enthusiasts had long since earmarked the Transvaal as a desirable possession. A more numerous group, unwilling to go this far, saw in her a barrier to British supremacy in South Africa and therefore a means of reserving the future until Germany's interests were more clearly defined. Such was doubtless the government's point of view, for there is no reason to believe that immediate annexation was contemplated. Germany, it is clear, intended to have a voice in any change of the balance of power in South Africa.

While Germany cautiously advised Pretoria against any provocations that might give England an excuse to act,[56] a number of incidents increased England's suspicions during 1895. On January 27, President Kruger, speaking to a group of Germans in Pretoria, expressed his gratitude for Germany's support in the past and his confidence in her future aid. Germany by no means improved matters by replying to England's protest that the Transvaal could conclude no treaty without her consent by declaring that her interests required an "economically independent" Transvaal and an open communication from Pretoria to Delagoa Bay.[57] William emphasized the point when he telegraphed in July his congratulations on the completion of the Pretoria-Lorenzo Marques railway. At the same time the extremists in Germany urged strong measures. The Colonial Society pledged its full support for the defense of the Transvaal's independence,

---

[55] Langer, *Diplomacy of Imperialism*, II, 218, 219.

[56] Germany nevertheless encouraged the Transvaal's efforts in 1894 to prevent England from taking Delagoa Bay from Portugal, from gaining control of the Pretoria-Lorenzo Marques railway to the Portuguese frontier, and Portugal from placing a loan in London. Marschall to Herff, Dec. 3, 1894. Hallgarten, *Vorkriegs Imperialismus*, pp. 332, 333.

[57] Marschall, Feb. 1, 1895. *G. P.*, XI, 3–5. Cf. *Deutsche Kolonialzeitung*, Feb. 2.

and the Pan-Germans called for a *"Hände weg!"* command.[58]
As to Germany's assurance that her sole desire was the maintenance of the status quo, as defined by the London Convention,
the English were naturally incredulous, since they now interpreted
Article IV as confirming their status as the suzerain power.
They suspected Germany of unavowed designs upon Mozambique as well as upon the Transvaal. Malet, the British ambassador, seasoned the amenities of his last interview with Marschall
in October with a warning that Germany's attitude might cause
serious trouble,[59] and—if William's word can be trusted—he
spoke to the Emperor of war.[60] From this vehemence the Germans drew the conclusion that their worst fears were justified,
an inference which was strengthened by the news of an impending revolt among foreigners in the Transvaal and of warlike
preparations by Cecil Rhodes' South African Company. Even
Hohenlohe agreed, in spite of his recent confidence in an
eventual rapprochement between England and the Triple Alliance, that the situation was serious.[61] William promptly declared
for the dispatch of naval reënforcements to Delagoa Bay, and
Hatzfeldt, in London, was instructed to insist that England
should respect the Transvaal's independence.[62]

On December 31 the startling news arrived in Berlin that Dr.
Jameson, the commander of the Chartered Company's private
troops, had crossed the Transvaal frontier with a force of six
hundred men. While it was clear that he intended to support
the expected insurrection among the *Uitlanders,* the fact that he
was also bent upon forcing England's hand was not known until
later. But the Germans concluded, like the greater part of the
non-British world, that the raid foreshadowed the immediate
absorption of the Transvaal by the British Empire. From London Hatzfeldt promptly reported that the government not only
was not responsible for the raid but that it was embarrassed by
Jameson's action. It was to no avail, however, for only the form

---

[58] *Deutsche Kolonialzeitung,* June 15; *A. B.,* June 16.
[59] *G. P.,* XI, 6.
[60] William to Nicholas, Oct. 25. Semenoff, *Correspondance entre Guillaume II et Nicolas II,* p. 22.
[61] Monts, Jan. 7, 1896. Monts, *Erinnerungen und Gedanken,* pp. 401, 402.
[62] A reference to the Convention of 1884 left some room for doubt as to Germany's meaning. Marschall, Dec. 28. *G. P.,* XI, 15, 16.

of Germany's action was uncertain. "Now we must act," wrote Marschall in his diary.[63] The Boers were immediately encouraged by the communication of the instructions that Haztfeldt should insist upon England's respect for their independence.[64] Next came a warning that she must not count upon the differences between the continental powers to prevent their concerted action and instructions to Hatzfeldt to demand his passports if England approved the raid.[65] Only Salisbury's weekend absence from London and Chamberlain's swift disavowal of Jameson, followed by an order for his recall, prevented the delivery of a sharp note.[66] If Jameson's defeat and capture removed the immediate reason for diplomatic pressure upon England, Germany's displeasure was made abundantly clear. She would, London was informed, never accept a treaty that diminished the Transvaal's international status,[67] and Hatzfeldt was instructed to tell Salisbury that the outcome alone had averted the need of painful measures.[68]

Chamberlain's guilt was chiefly one of omission rather than of commission, as most Germans thought then and later. While he must be acquitted on the charge of direct complicity, the documents recently published in Mr. J. L. Garvin's biography show that he was aware of Rhodes' plans and that he did not move a finger against them. However, German observers found support in the London press for their suspicions concerning the sincerity of Chamberlain's disavowal of Jameson. If the Conservative *Daily Telegraph* (Jan. 2) described the raid as a "piece of filibustering, inadmissible, impossible" and the Liberal *Daily News* (Jan. 2) as "this gross outrage upon the decencies of civilization," equally important journals tempered their disapproval with the reflection that Jameson was perhaps a better judge of conditions in Johannesburg than were officials in London.[69] That his actions were blameworthy but that his motives were sound was, according to the *Times* (Jan. 2), the judgment of

---

[63] Langer, *Diplomacy of Imperialism*, I, 233.
[64] Marschall, Dec. 30. *G. P.*, XI, 16.
[65] Marschall, Dec. 31. *Ibid.*, XI, 17–19.
[66] Marschall, Dec. 31, Jan. 2; Hatzfeldt, Jan. 1, 3. *Ibid.*, XI, 19, 24, 25, 28, 29.
[67] Marchall, Jan. 2. *Ibid.*, XI, 26, 27.
[68] Marschall, Jan. 3. *Ibid.*, XI, 30.
[69] *Pall Mall Gazette*, Jan. 1, 2; *Morning Post*, Jan. 2.

public opinion. Not an iota of England's thesis as to her relations with the Transvaal, it was said with one accord, would be
surrendered. The *Times* (Jan. 2) wrote that the "status is one of
vassal to suzerain"; the *Daily Telegram* (Jan. 2), that "this is . . .
a domestic business" and (Jan. 3) that "we will wash our own
dirty linen at home and without the help of German, French, or
other laundresses." Infuriated by the raid and certain of England's complicity,[70] German opinion ignored this warning. Although Salisbury told Hatzfeldt (Jan. 1) that anything like a
threat would make negotiations impossible,[71] the semi-official press
encouraged its readers to expect a strong stand. The *Norddeutsche*
(Jan. 3) clipped and approved an article from the *Kölnische
Zeitung* promising the defense of the Transvaal's complete independence (*volle Unabhängigkeit*) as a "pressing interest of
several European powers and especially that of Germany. Germany, at least, will strongly support her own interests . . . according to her unquestioned right, *und es wird sich dazu von
keinem Staate die Erlaubnis holen.*" Like the Pan-Germans,[72]
the *Kölnische Zeitung* (Jan. 5) advised a sharp command:
"Halt!" The National Liberal *Magdeburgische Zeitung* (Jan.
2) wisely recommended a "policy of peaceful negotiation" and
suggested that some concessions might be made to the *Uitlanders,*
but the indignation of the moderate and Social Democratic
journals is the best evidence that public opinion stood squarely
with the Transvaal and that it favored diplomatic intervention.
The moderate *Vossische Zeitung* (Jan. 2) warned England that
Germany needed "no instruction as to the extent of her interests
in South Africa and that the Transvaal had a right to turn to
Germany for support. The Republic is in no sense an English
vassal." The Progressive *Freisinnige Zeitung* (Jan. 2) approved
intervention and predicted "England's inevitable defeat." According to the Social Democratic *Vorwärts* (Jan. 3), England's
claim that the rights of other countries were not involved was
an "absurdity," since the entire civilized world was interested in
the defeat of Jameson's piratical adventure. The *Kölnische*

---

[70] *Standard,* Jan. 2, Berlin, Jan. 1; *Kreuz-Zeitung,* Jan. 3.
[71] *G. P.,* XI, 24, 25.
[72] *A. B.,* Jan. 5.

Zeitung (Jan. 3) was substantially correct in claiming that German opinion as a whole "approved the energetic intervention of the German government." The moderate *Vossische Zeitung* (Jan. 1) even spoke with favor of something more than diplomatic intervention. Like other liberal journals, its sympathies were with a people "which looks trustfully to *Mutter Germania.*" While the press as a whole did not neglect the racial relationship, it stressed the maintenance of the balance of power in South Africa as a more substantial reason for action.[73]

After Chamberlain's repudiation of Jameson, there was no immediate need of hasty action, even if the suspicions of England's ultimate aims were well-founded. Indeed, an attitude of reserve on the part of the government would have helped to moderate the anti-English tendencies of public opinion. To the immense satisfaction of an excited public opinion, German policy was in part determined by William's hysterical demand for action and by the desire of his advisers to teach England that her best interests lay in an association with the Triple Alliance. The Jameson Raid, the last of a series of irritating experiences with England, seems to have deprived the Emperor of his limited sense of proportion. On January 3, Bronsart, the war minister, described his appearance as "not entirely normal."[74] His first reaction is said to have been to draft a telegram to President Kruger containing an assurance of Germany's support and a proposal that the Transvaal should place herself under her protection.[75] Fortunately this telegram was not sent. Of the men who were most influential in shaping German foreign policy, Holstein apparently had no desire for action, but neither he nor Marschall was averse to threatening England with a continental union. Some discussion of this idea had appeared in the press even before the Jameson Raid. An Austrian publicist who supported German imperialism and admired Bismarck at the same time proposed a delimitation of Austrian and Russian interests in the Balkans and Austria's mediation between Germany and France as a basis for intervention in the Egyptian

---

[73] *National Zeitung,* Jan. 1; *Kölnische Zeitung,* Jan. 2; *Allgemeine Zeitung,* Jan. 1.
[74] Hohenlohe, *Denkwürdigkeiten aus der Reichskanzlerzeit,* p. 151.
[75] Langer, *Diplomacy of Imperialism,* I, 235, 236, citing K. Lehmann, "Die Vorgeschichte der Krügerdepesche," *Archiv für Politik und Geschichte,* V, 159–177.

question for a more equitable distribution of the undeveloped parts of the world.[76] The response in the German press seems to have been negligible; France was still the chief obstacle. She would never, wrote the Conservative *Post* (Aug. 20, 1895), accept colonial expansion as her true interest until she recognized Germany's invincibility, even against a combined Franco-Russian attack.[77] The foreign office nevertheless may have been encouraged by reports that France had declared in favor of the localization of a war in the Near East.[78] At any rate, William and Marschall both spoke of a continental union to British agents,[79] and Marschall approached France on January 1.[80] The project failed for substantially the same reasons which had caused its defeat in 1884. While France's unshakable attachment to Alsace-Lorraine was still the ultimate barrier, the same reservations in Germany's attitude inevitably aroused her suspicions. Marschall's silence in regard to Egypt was bound to cool France. In fact, Holstein's omission of India and Persia as well as Egypt from his enumeration of the areas in which a continental union might oppose England showed that she was by no means ready to identify Germany with England's enemies.[81] The French decided wisely enough that their interest was not in a maneuver which might be abandoned after Germany had secured concessions for herself.[82]

Meanwhile William contemplated such fantastic measures as the dispatch of German officers or troops to Pretoria and the support of the Transvaal in a war with Cape Colony while Germany remained at peace with England.[83] His civilian ministers had no taste for these adventures. During the famous meeting of January 3 at the Chancellor's palace between the Emperor, Hohenlohe, Marschall, and the naval officials—Holstein listened from an adjoining room with Kayser, the colonial min-

---

[76] K. Kron, *Aegypten und die aegyptische Frage* (Leipzig, 1895).
[77] A. Peez, "Zur neuesten Handelspolitik," in *Mitteleuropa und der Handelspolitik der Zukunft*.
[78] Marschall, Dec. 10; Münster, Dec. 12. *G. P.*, X, 226, 227.
[79] William II, Dec. 20, 1895. *Ibid.*, X, 254.
[80] *Ibid.*, XI, 71 n.
[81] *Ibid.*, XI, 67-69. He insisted that England's vital interests must be respected. *Ibid.*, XI, 73 (Jan. 3).
[82] Herbette, Jan. 1, 1896. Bourgeois, Pagès, *Origines et responsabilités*, p. 257.
[83] Langer, *Diplomacy of Imperialism*, I, 236.

ister—the Chancellor warned William that his proposals would mean war. The idea of a congratulatory telegram originated with Marschall (though its text was drafted by Kayser, the colonial minister), who doubtless wished to avoid something worse, but the first draft failed to satisfy William. It was, according to Marschall's account, the Emperor who determined the final text of the Kruger Telegram:

> I express to you my sincere congratulations that you and your people, without appealing to the aid of friendly powers, have

Kladderadatsch, January 12, 1896.

Figure 15.—The *Times* explains how dangerous the British lion can be when excited. But did someone laugh?

> succeeded, by your own energetic action against the armed bands which invaded your country as disturbers of the peace, in restoring peace and in maintaining the independence of the country against attacks from without.[84]

As an implicit endorsement of the Transvaal's claim to complete independence, the concluding phrase was certain to give grave offense to England, and the plain hint that Germany would have welcomed an appeal for her aid was scarcely less

---

[84] Langer, *Diplomacy of Imperialism,* I, 237.

serious. Holstein, who left before the definitive text was approved, alone had no share in the responsibility for this ill-considered action; the others were all involved to a greater or less
degree. It is not unlikely that, anxious as they were to prevent
William from carrying out his more dangerous ideas, they gave
little thought to England's probable reaction,[85] especially since
a clear reminder of Germany's displeasure was consistent with
their larger diplomatic purposes. They were by no means averse
to a crisis, provided that the Transvaal should appear as the prime
mover. Hohenlohe dissuaded the Emperor from sending his
aide-de-camp to Pretoria,[86] but Marschall, although he still advised against a direct provocation of England,[87] recommended
that the Transvaal should offer to submit her case to a European
congress.[88]

Not war with England but her ultimate association with the
Triple Alliance was Marschall's aim and, indeed, Hohenlohe's
and Holstein's. He relied chiefly upon intimidation: *"Und
bist du nicht willig, so brauch' ich Gewalt!"* He assured Chirol,
the correspondent of the London *Times,* that the Kruger Telegram was not merely an expression of the Emperor's personal
sentiments but a formal document "drawn up at a conference
of ministers" having therefore "the character of a state action." [89]
England refused to be intimidated, insisting more firmly than
ever that her relations with the Transvaal were a purely domestic problem. The alarm was sounded most dramatically by
the Liberal Imperialist *Daily Chronicle.* "There can be no
doubt," it wrote, "that at an early hour on Saturday morning
the British Empire was in a state of some peril." Both the

---

[85] Hohenlohe dismissed the momentous meeting of January 3 with one sentence:
"Marschall schlug ein Telegram an Krüger vor, das akzeptiert wurde." Hohenlohe,
Denkwürdigkeiten aus der Reichskanzlerzeit, p. 151.
[86] Hohenlohe, Jan. 4. Wüd, *Die Rolle der Burenrepubliken,* pp. 155, 156.
[87] Marschall to Herff, Jan. 5. *G. P.,* XI, 35, 36.
[88] Marschall, Jan. 3, 5. *Ibid.,* XI, 31, 35, 36. *Cf.* Hohenlohe, Jan. 7. *Ibid.,* XI,
37; *National Zeitung,* Jan. 9; *Allgemeine Zeitung,* Jan. 11; *Berliner Börsen-Zeitung,*
Jan. 12. At the same time Holstein was urging Marschall through Bülow, their mutual
friend, to do nothing against England's vital interests. *G. P.,* XI, 72, 73 (Jan. 3).
[89] *Times,* Jan. 4, Berlin, Jan. 3; *Morning Post,* Jan. 4; *Cf. Frankfurter Zeitung,*
Jan. 4; *Münchener Neueste Nachrichten,* Jan. 5; *Zukunft,* Jan. 11. According to Hammann, Marschall also asked Chirol to use his influence for a moderate reaction in the
London press. O. Hammann, *Der missverstandene Bismarck* (Berlin, 1921), pp. 48,
49. The complexities of German policy at this time make this not unreasonable.

Times (Jan. 4) and the Conservative *Standard* (Jan. 4) asserted her intention to resist the intervention of any power. Chirol's theory (*Times,* Jan. 7, Berlin, Jan. 6) that Germany's real purpose was to convince England "that she could only find salvation in closer contact with Germany and her allies" only made matters worse.[90] England, wrote the *Times* (Jan. 7), "will concede nothing to menaces and will not lie down under insult." "A kick," said the Conservative *Pall Mall Gazette* (Jan. 9) "may be intended for a veiled caress, but it should not be too roughly administered." According to the Liberal *Daily News* (Jan. 8), England "could not yield an inch to threats, or be turned from [her] straight course by unmanly impertinence. . . ." "She is determined," it added (Jan. 9) "to win our love by an ostentatious display of the possibilities of her hatred." There was much support for a reply that would be a convincing demonstration of England's ability and readiness to fight. Only thus, wrote an "occasional correspondent" of the *Times* (Jan. 7), in a review of Anglo-German relations, could Germany's friendship be secured. With this view the *Times* (Jan. 7) was in substantial accord: "The sure way for the restoration of friendly relations is to demand courteously but firmly some explanation of what was at least unfriendly conduct." It even wrote favorably "of an approach to Russia and France."[91] While the government had no intention of going too far, it was nevertheless determined to stand its ground and to prepare for all contingencies. Warships were dispatched to Delagoa Bay and a flying squadron, whose formation had been discussed during the recent tension with the United States over the Venezuela affair, was brought together in the English Channel.[92] The Queen was all for moderation. If Prince Edward spoke of the telegram as "a most gratuitous act of unfriendliness," she deprecated any retaliatory action and asked Salisbury if he could not "hint to our respectable papers not to write violent articles to excite the people. These newspaper wars often tend to provoke war, which would be too awful."[93]

---

90 Cf. *Daily News,* Jan. 6, Berlin, Jan. 5.
91 Cf. *Daily Chronicle,* Jan. 9.
92 Goschen, Jan. 10. *Letters of Queen Victoria,* (3), III, 16, 17.
93 Knollys, Jan. 4; Victoria, Jan. 8, 11. *Ibid.,* (3), III, 7, 8, 13, 19, 20.

An almost unanimous and ecstatic approval greeted the tele-gram in Germany.[94] While the Social Democratic *Vorwärts* (Jan. 5) assured the English that it expressed merely the Em-peror's personal opinion, representative journals of every other party described it as an accurate reflection of popular sentiment.[95] "Nothing that the government has done for years," wrote the National Liberal *Allgemeine Zeitung* (Jan. 5), "has given as complete satisfaction. . . . It is written from the soul of the German people." "The friends of England," affirmed the *Na-tional Zeitung* (Jan. 6), "are silent." Positive action was de-manded.[96] The *Allgemeine Zeitung* (Berlin, Jan. 5) believed that Germany's interests required a command to halt the further advance of British imperialism in South Africa.[97] For the first time since Bismarck, said the National Liberal *Schwäbische Merkur,* German opinion was confident that England's presump-tion would be resisted.[98] The entire nation, wrote the Con-servative *Kreuz-Zeitung* (Jan. 8), approved the protection of the Transvaal's rights and was prepared for the possible con-sequences. Karl Peters, the explorer, told a Berlin audience that men, arms, and money should be sent by private initiative if the government did not act.[99] Forgetting its earlier moderation, the National Liberal *Magdeburgische Zeitung* (Jan. 4) desired a close relationship with the Transvaal, which, however, it did not define. Even the moderates succumbed for the moment. On January 10, the Progressive *Volks-Zeitung* approved the fol-lowing demands, which the Transvaal, according to rumor, was about to present to England: the elimination of Article IV of the London Convention, the annulment of the South Africa Company's charter, and the surrender of England's option for the purchase of Delagoa Bay from Portugal. This journal was in strange company; the Pan-Germans had already asked the

---

[94] *Reichsbote,* Jan. 5; *Berliner Tageblatt,* Jan. 5; *Germania,* Jan. 8.
[95] "Unsere Presse ist vorzüglich," Marschall noted in his diary. "Alle Parteien einig, sogar die Tante Voss will kämpfen." F. Thimme, "Die Krüger-Depesche; Genesis und historische Bedeutung," *Europäische Gespräche,* May-June 1924, p. 213 (Jan. 3).
[96] *Kölnische Zeitung,* Jan. 4; *Allgemeine Zeitung,* Jan. 4, Berlin, Jan. 3.
[97] Cf. *Berliner Börsen-Zeitung,* Jan. 4.
[98] *Post,* Jan. 10.
[99] *Germania,* Jan. 4.

Chancellor to support these demands.[100]   The chief value of the
Telegram, said the liberal *Berliner Tageblatt* (Jan. 8), was its
"clear and firm" definition of "our relations with England."
There were differences of opinion from the first, but German
opinion was undoubtedly thoroughly hostile.   The Kruger Telegram, however, was responsible for its extreme virulence.

First in the opposition and then in the semi-official press
doubts soon appeared as to the expediency of a direct challenge
to England.   Sympathy for the Boers, wrote the Progressive
Freisinnige Zeitung (Jan. 5), "is expressed in a perhaps exaggerated form."   The *Frankfurter Zeitung* (Jan. 6) broke its
silence to agree that the Transvaal should receive satisfaction
and guarantees, but it soon maintained (Jan. 9) that the greater
part of public opinion was opposed to the armed support of the
Boers.   Bismarck's organ, the *Hamburger Nachrichten,* spoke
of domestic development, the maintenance of peace, the avoid-
ance of a "French" policy of prestige as Germany's true interests;[101] it mentioned Bismarck's speech of February 6, 1888 as
a warning against the use of pressure upon another country.[102]
The Progressive *Weser Zeitung* deprecated the prevailing hatred
of England, since it made an alliance with the greatest naval
power impossible.   "The center of international politics," it
pointed out, "is in Europe, certainly not in Africa, as the colonial enthusiasts seem to imagine." [103]   Russia, according to the
leading Catholic review in South Germany, was the most dangerous enemy.[104]   The Conservative *Post* (Jan. 5) pointed out
that England's naval supremacy fixed the limits of Germany's
freedom of action, but, like the National Liberal *Magdeburgische
Zeitung* (Jan. 5), it advocated the construction of a fleet rather
than conciliation.[105]   While Tirpitz, then an admiral and soon
to become the minister of marine, welcomed the decline of
Anglomania and the beginnings of a movement for naval ex-

---

[100] *A. B.,* Jan. 19.
[101] Defending the official policy, the *Berliner Tageblatt* (Jan. 9), pointed out that
"resistance to the disturber of peace also serves the cause of peace."
[102] *National Zeitung,* Jan. 23.
[103] *Post,* Jan. 16.
[104] *Historisch-Politische Blätter,* vol. 117 (Jan. 24).
[105] The National Liberal *Augsburger Abendzeitung* (Jan. 6) called for the construction of a fleet second only to that of England.

pansion, he condemned the official policy and the anti-English trend of public opinion as the products of an unrealistic view of Germany's strength and as directing against Germany the wrath which had first been aroused by the United States in the Venezuela question.[106] The violence of England's reaction, which was said to have surpassed that of Germany,[107] mystified the Germans. No provocation had been intended; William had merely expressed the sentiment of the entire civilized world, as the attitude of the Paris press showed.[108] The British government itself had repudiated Jameson. England's excitement and naval measures were, according to the German press, a tacit confession of her support of Jameson and of her responsibility for the raid.[109]

Since France's aversion to "unnatural alliances" made a continental union impossible, the danger that England might be driven into the arms of Germany's enemies exerted a moderating influence. If the Pan-Germans called for the completion of what had been commenced,[110] the more influential journals soon changed their attitude. Germany, they said, had never thought of establishing a protectorate in the Transvaal. Nor would she summon a European congress.[111] The *Kölnische Zeitung* reverted to the silence which the *Norddeutsche* had maintained. In spite of Hohenlohe's advice (Jan. 7) that Germany should support President Kruger if he took the initiative in calling a congress, William (Jan. 8) wrote directly to his grandmother. "Never was the telegram," he said with less than complete candor, "intended as a step against England or your government." On the contrary, his sole desire had been to insure the obedience of the "rebels" to the Queen.[112] Wishing to relieve the tension,

---

[106] A. von Tirpitz, *Erinnerungen* (Leipzig, 1920), pp. 54, 55 (Feb. 13, 1896).

[107] U. R. von Bieberstein, "Englands Wehrmacht und strategische Situation Deutschland gegenüber," *Nord und Süd*, vol. 76, pp. 350, 351; *Verhandlungen*, IX Leg. Per., IV Sess., II 934 (E. Richter, Feb. 13).

[108] *Magdeburgische Zeitung*, Jan. 7.

[109] *National Zeitung, Magdeburgische Zeitung, Vorwärts*, Jan. 5; *Vossische Zeitung*, Jan. 6; *Freisinnige Zeitung*, Jan. 7; *Konservative Korrespondenz, Hamburger Nachrichten*, in *Post*, Jan. 8; *Germania*, Jan. 8; *Deutsche Rundschau*, vol. 86, pp. 306, 307 (Feb. 1896).

[110] *A. B.*, Jan. 12.

[111] *Berliner Tageblatt*, Jan. 6; *Kölnische Zeitung, Freisinnige Zeitung*, Jan. 7.

[112] S. Lee, *King Edward VII; a Biography*, 2 vols. (London, 1927), I, 726, 727.

Salisbury now opened a way for Germany's retreat. He agreed (Jan. 7), even before the arrival of William's letter, to accept a return to the status quo in South Africa, without any reference to England's suzerain powers over the Transvaal. A few days later, he advised the Queen to accept William's explanations "without enquiring too narrowly into the truth of them. . . ." [113] Germany's concession was a warning to Dr. Leyds, the Transvaal's agent in Berlin, that the raid must not be used as an excuse to denounce the Transvaal's obligations in the Treaty of 1884. [114]

The attempt to force England into an association with the Triple Alliance had failed. Salisbury may have calmly discussed a rapprochement at the height of the crisis, [115] but his mind was set against any formal obligations, "because the English people would never consent to go to war for a cause in which England was not manifestly interested. . . ." [116] Hohenlohe drew the conclusion that "the attempt to commit England to a firm agreement for the event of war has no prospect of success." There should be, he directed, no move even for the strengthening of the Mediterranean accord of 1887. [117] To attract England within Germany's orbit had been an important, but not the only, purpose of the Kruger Telegram; this motive was, at least as far as the development of German opinion was concerned, less important than the desire to teach England a lesson. Most German historians agree that the Telegram was a tactical error, but a good many contemporary observers believed that Germany had won a substantial success. That England had accepted the status quo was, according to Holstein, "a small diplomatic success for Germany and a small political lesson for England." [118] She had been compelled, wrote the *National Zeitung* (Jan. 10, 11), to abandon her plan of absorbing the Transvaal. Just as the London press represented the return to a comparatively moderate attitude in Germany as the result of Eng-

---

[113] Hatzfeldt, Jan. 7. *G. P.*, XI, 40, 41; *Letters of Queen Victoria*, (3), III, 20, 21 (Jan. 12).

[114] Marschall, Jan. 11. *G. P.*, XI, 51.

[115] Langer, *Diplomacy of Imperialism*, I, 250.

[116] *Letters of Queen Victoria*, (3), III, 20, 21 (Jan. 12).

[117] *G. P.*, XI, 95, 96 (Jan. 23).

[118] *Ibid.*, XI, 48, 49 (Jan. 10).

land's strong defense of her rights,[119] so the German newspapers
attributed the similar change in England to their *"stramme
Haltung,"* to their *"kühle Ruhe."* [120]   Bebel, the Social Democratic leader, condemned the anti-English campaign as the "most
perverted, the most fatal imaginable," for Austria and Italy
would never be effective allies in a war; [121] his views, however,
had little influence outside his own party.

Even the prospect that England had been permanently alienated was faced without a sense of serious loss.[122] The *Hamburger Nachrichten* catalogued historical examples of her indifference or open hostility to German interests.[123] The Progressive *Volks-Zeitung* (Jan. 20) was less concerned with England's
alienation, which it acknowledged to be complete, than with
Germany's alleged dependence upon Russia. Except among the
Social Democrats, there was little fear of unfavorable repercussions upon Germany's diplomatic position, in spite of a minor
Anglo-French understanding in regard to Siam. The semi-official *Norddeutsche* (Jan. 2) dismissed an Anglo-Franco-Russian
entente as an impossibility. The Conservative *Kreuz-Zeitung*
(Jan. 14, 17) based its confidence in Germany's security on the
anti-English tone of the Russian press and on the cool response
of France and Russia to the *Times'* advances. In her distress,
England was crying, wrote the reactionary *Reichsbote* (Jan. 22):
"Ein Königreich für ein Bündnis!" "It is difficult to see," added
the *Hamburger Nachrichten,* "upon what friends she can count
in the event of war." [124] Moderate opinion also saw no reason
to fear that England would join Germany's enemies. That she
could enter no alliance without parliament's consent and that
every country had a bone to pick with her were sufficient reasons, in the *Vossische Zeitung's* opinion, (Jan. 13), for complete
skepticism. Arthur Levysohn, a contributor to the *Berliner Tageblatt* (Jan. 19), described the talk in England of a triple entente
as a bluff as long as Russia and France refused to abandon their

---

119 *Morning Post,* Jan. 9; *Times,* Jan. 10.
120 *Augsburger Abendzeitung,* Jan. 4; *Vossische Zeitung,* Jan. 10.
121 *Verhandlungen,* IX Leg. Per., IV Sess., II, 939 (Feb. 13).
122 *P. J.,* vol. 83, pp. 399–402 (Jan. 1896); *Münchener Neueste Nachrichten,* Jan.
11, 18.
123 Hofmann, *Fürst Bismarck,* II, 350–352 (Jan. 28).
124 *National Zeitung,* Jan. 24.

historic interests in the Straits and in Egypt. The violent hostility of the London press, which the correspondent of the *Berliner Tageblatt* (Jan. 31) reported as rivaling that of the most extreme chauvinists in France, was not at the time taken very seriously. It was a serious error. The *Morning Post* (Jan. 11) thought that a return to more normal relations would not change the essentials of the situation: "We must ever be prepared for wild acts inconsistent with the laws of international friendship." On February 1, the Conservative *Saturday Review* opened its virulent campaign. It insisted that the similarity between the economic interests of the two countries made a conflict not only inevitable but desirable: "Were every German to be wiped out tomorrow, there is no English trade, no English pursuit that would not immediately expand. Were every Englishman to be wiped out tomorrow, the Germans would gain in proportion. Here is the great racial struggle of the future. . . . One or the other has to go; one or the other will go." While the great majority of Englishmen doubtless regarded this tirade as arrant nonsense, the Kruger Telegram and the campaign against Germany's commercial competition—which led to the passage of the "made-in-Germany" law—left an indelible impression upon public opinion.[125] "If you want to send a telegram to Oom Kruger," shouted the London crowd to Prince Albert of Prussia during the Queen's Jubilee in June 1898, "you'll find a post office round the corner on the right." [126]

IV

If the return to the status quo ante in South Africa was a meager gain, it could be argued with some plausibility that Germany had substantiated her claim to a larger influence in world affairs and that her weakness upon the seas had alone prevented a more dramatic success. William was more than willing to give himself the benefit of the doubt as to the results of his personal intervention in high politics. It was not as one who had suffered a recent defeat that he addressed the Reichstag and the

---

125 R. J. S. Hoffman, *Great Britain and the German Trade Rivalry, 1875–1914* (Philadelphia, 1933), pp. 244 ff.
126 Langer, *Diplomacy of Imperialism*, I, 254, citing Bülow, *Memoirs*, I, 21, 476.

nation in celebrating the twenty-fifth anniversary of the German Empire (Jan. 18). He spoke first of the need to conserve the work of the fathers, but he pointed with greater zest to the tasks that remained. "The German Empire," he cried, "has become a world empire (*Aus dem deutschen Reiche ist ein Weltreich geworden*)." Germany's trade, her mercantile marine, and her sons had penetrated to the ends of the earth. "Yours is the solemn duty," he said, "to help me to attach this greater German Empire to the one at home."

This pronouncement, like Germany's imperialist aspirations, was extremely vague. The moment was inopportune for a public announcement of William's determination to build a fleet. Nevertheless, the obvious inferences were drawn, either with enthusiastic approval or with alarm. The speech, wrote the Conservative *Schlessische Zeitung* (Breslau), was an appeal for the nation's support against the dangers arising from the Anglo-German economic rivalry.[127] Its purpose, said the nationalist *Münchener Neueste Nachrichten* (Jan. 22), was to reassure public opinion that the "success" won in the recent crisis would be consolidated.[128] The Pan-Germans were elated. "It was," wrote their official organ, "a Pan-German toast; we find in it our own aims and it therefore fills us with confidence."[129] On the issue of *Weltpolitik,* the opposition parties, which had in general approved the Kruger Telegram, parted company with the Emperor. His speech, according to the moderate *Vossische Zeitung* (Jan. 24), was ominous. At first, the liberal *Frankfurter Zeitung* (Jan. 21, Berlin, Jan. 19) thought it portended merely a greater emphasis upon the cultural community of Germans everywhere and perhaps a more active support to Germans abroad, but certainly not an active *grossdeutsch* policy. It was, however, impossible to maintain this confidence in the face of the trend in the nationalist and Conservative press. On January 26, the same liberal journal protested against the talk of a great fleet on the ground that the larger part of public opinion was opposed to one, and it insisted that naval expansion would weaken Ger-

127 *Germania,* Jan. 23.
128 Clipped by the *Post,* Jan. 23.
129 *A. B.,* Jan. 26.

many's financial and military strength. "The worst that could happen to us," wrote the Catholic *Kölnische Volkszeitung,* "would be a transition to a *Weltpolitik.*" [130]

William's speech had little immediate effect upon the conduct of Germany's foreign affairs. Less confident than public opinion of England's inability to approach France and Russia, the foreign office was more concerned with her diplomatic activities in Europe than with distant adventures. Some discussion appeared in English and French newspapers of a definitive settlement of the Egyptian question. When Russia called Germany's attention to the Anglo-French negotiations, Holstein betrayed no uneasiness, arguing that England would always be among France's enemies and that her differences with Germany were relatively insignificant. [131] He spoke a different language, however, in his instructions to Hatzfeldt. If England yielded even in the smallest degree to France in Egypt, "we—and the Triple Alliance— would approach Russia," since it would then be clear that England had definitely rejected coöperation with Germany. [132] The same views were communicated to Austria, with a hint that European politics might soon take a new direction, in order doubtless to cool her interest in closer Anglo-German relations. [133] While conditions were not yet ripe for an Anglo-French rapprochement, it was Italy's Abyssinian adventure and the annihilation of her army at Adowa (March 1) that enabled German diplomats to undo what had been accomplished in that direction. William suggested (March 3) that England might send troops to Dongola in order to relieve the pressure upon the Italians and to protect the Sudan, [134] and Germany later supported her against France and Russia on the question of financing the expedition from the Egyptian treasury. "Hurrah!" wrote the Emperor on a report of France's displeasure, [135] "The end has been attained. England . . . is compromised, and the flirtation with France and Russia has been disturbed; that is all I wished to do." [136]

---

[130] *Post,* Jan. 25.
[131] *G. P.,* XI, 57 (Feb. 20, 1896).
[132] *Ibid.,* XI, 136 (Feb. 21).
[133] Marschall, Feb. 23. *Ibid.,* XI, 139.
[134] Hohenlohe, March 4. *Ibid.,* XI, 235, 236.
[135] William II's comment, Münster, March 13. *Ibid.,* XI, 151.
[136] William II's comment, Radolin, March 27. *Ibid.,* XI, 167, 168.

This turn of events caused England, despite the memories of the Kruger Telegram, to speak favorably of Germany's friendship and of coöperation with the Triple Alliance.[137]   Egypt had again served Germany well.   The indifference of her foreign office effectively discouraged Russia and Turkey from proposing a European congress, although Germany was still willing to approve Russia's seizure of the Straits and to moderate the reaction of the other powers.[138]   It was, however, no part of Germany's intentions to work for a general understanding with England. Her attitude in the Egyptian question had been intended to divide England and France, and, as Marschall said, to aid the Italians: "We had no reason for making concessions to England after recent events." [139]   Italy pleaded in vain for a renewal of the ministerial declaration of 1882 that the Triple Alliance would never be directed against England.   It was, according to the foreign office, pointless; the insuperable hostility between England, France, and Russia made England's participation in an attack upon the Triple Alliance impossible.[140]   That St. Petersburg and Paris should be sounded was William's first reaction to a report of an impending demonstration by a British naval force in the Persian Gulf; by no means had he lost interest in a continental union, for he spoke of it as a wise provision against the day when England might be tempted to seize Germany's colonies.[141]

The trend in German foreign policy was, however, definitely toward a balanced position—the "free hand"—between England and Russia.   The fears of the Progressives and Catholics that the country was reverting to its former subservience to Russia were without foundation; nothing was done to establish more than cordial relations.   When Bismarck revealed, in October 1896, the terms of the Reinsurance Treaty of 1887, as a reminder that a treaty relationship with Russia was essential to Germany's security, William, enraged, spoke of treason (*Landesverrat*), and

---

[137] Marschall, March 13.   *G. P.*, XI, 242.
[138] Holstein, Aug. 28.   Hohenlohe, *Denkwürdigkeiten aus der Reichskanzlerzeit*, pp. 258, 259; Radolin, Dec. 27.   *G. P.*, XII, 67–69.
[139] *G. P.*, XI, 155 (March 16).
[140] *Ibid.*, XI, 272 (March 30), 273–275 (March 31), 275, 276 (April 2), 279, 280 (April 28, 29), 282 (May 30).
[141] *Ibid.*, XIII, 3, 4 (Oct. 25, 1896).

the official *Staats-Anzeiger* asserted its confidence that Germany's reputation abroad for loyalty would not be shaken.[142] The result was doubtless disappointing to the former Chancellor, in spite of the favorable reaction of the Conservative press. It was with mixed feelings that Germany learned in the spring of 1897 that Austria had arranged an understanding with Russia.[143] Despairing of England's support against Russia and of Germany's for an aggressive policy in the Balkans, Goluchowski, her foreign minister, accepted an agreement for the maintenance of the status quo in the Balkans and for a common policy in the event of its being disturbed. If William approved warmly and if the *Hamburger Nachrichten* called for a continental union against England, "the common enemy," [144] the foreign office feared that the elimination of the ancient Austro-Russian feud would diminish Austria's need of Germany's aid and therefore her loyalty to the alliance. An Austrian diplomat had in fact brought these possibilities to Germany's attention months earlier.[145] Domestic conditions in the Dual Monarchy soon gave some support to these views. The understanding with Russia encouraged the nationalist agitation among the Slavs and the attack upon the predominance of the Austrian Germans. Many Catholics denounced not only the "disgraceful dependence upon Russia" but also the "hypocritical and unnecessary" alliance with Italy.[146] In Germany, the Catholics of the South regretted that an empire "calling itself German" had thrown itself into the Tsar's arms; it remained to be seen whether he would be grateful.[147] Holstein, fearful that the Dual Alliance would be weakened, could see no value in the Austro-Russian agreement, except as an assurance that Russia desired peace for at least a few years.[148] Next to neutrality,[149] good, but not too close, relations

---

142 *Hamburger Nachrichten*, Oct. 24, in Hofmann, *Fürst Bismarck*, II, 372. *Berliner Neueste Nachrichten, Berliner Börsen-Zeitung, Münchener Neueste Nachrichten*, in *Post*, Oct. 29; *Leipziger Tageblatt*, in *Post*, Oct. 29.

143 Professor Meinecke represents Germany's reaction as one of relief. Meinecke, *Geschichte des deutsch-englischen Bündnisproblems*, pp. 75, 76.

144 *Historich-Politische Blätter*, vol. 119, p. 768 (May 12, 1897).

145 Lichnowsky, Feb. 29, 1896. *G. P.*, XI, 117, 118.

146 Lichnowsky, May 5, 1897. *Ibid.*, XII, 292, 293.

147 *Historisch-Politische Blätter*, vol. 119, p. 766 (May 12, 1897).

148 *G. P.*, XII, 303.

149 *Ibid.*, XII, 169, 170, 309. Cf. *Post*, Oct. 1897.

with Russia continued to be the chief aim of German policy during the complicated negotiations during the Cretan revolt and
the Greco-Turkish War, 1896–1897.[150]   To the extent that Germany worked for a stronger Turkey, on the mistaken theory that
Russia's point of view had been changed by her ambitions in the
Far East, she laid the foundations at this time for future difficulties with her Eastern neighbor.

In the meantime, Germany's relations with England continued
to suffer from mutual suspicions, from commercial competition,
and from the development of her *Weltpolitik*. Her diplomats
still saw a plan to bring about a continental war and thereby to
acquire a free hand in South Africa in England's alleged efforts
to push Austria forward during the Near Eastern crisis. Although it is clear now that nothing would have been more
objectionable to England than Turkey's dissolution and a general
conflict,[151] these purposes were read into the reported revival of
Salisbury's earlier partition scheme.[152]   Anti-German sentiment
in England reached unparalleled heights as a result of the invasion of English markets, of allegedly unscrupulous commercial
and industrial practices, and of the feeling that Germany stood
in the way of British imperialism in South Africa. Although
the Conservative *Saturday Review* had declined in influence and
is said to have lost subscribers,[153] its pronouncement (Sept. 11,
1897), *Germaniam esse delendam,* played a part in the development of Anglo-German antagonism that was out of all proportion
to its intrinsic importance and, indeed, to its immediate effect.
"What Bismarck realized," wrote this Conservative weekly, "and
what we too may soon come to see, is that not only is there the
most real conflict of interests between England and Germany,
but that England is the only Great Power that could fight Germany without great risk and without doubt as to the issue."
Not a few German statesmen, publicists, and historians later
used this article to prove that England was determined to destroy
Germany as a economic and colonial competitor, but its imme-

---

[150] *G. P.,* XII, 199, 200, 409.
[151] Salisbury, Feb. 17, 19. *Letters of Queen Victoria,* (3), III, 133, 137.
[152] *G. P.,* XII, 195, 196, 256, 345, 346.
[153] E. L. Woodward, *Great Britain and the German Navy* (Oxford, 1935), p. 42.

diate effect in Germany was slight. There is, in fact, little evidence that it attracted general attention. The *Kölnische Zeitung* was perhaps unaware of its existence when it advocated a more moderate tone in the discussion of Anglo-German relations.[154] From a few delayed and scattered comments, it appears that the Conservative and nationalist press represented the *Saturday Review* as a reliable mirror of English public opinion.[155] The *Post* (Nov. 25, 1897) was chiefly impressed by the claim that England served the cause of civilization by working for her own selfish interests as a typical example of English hypocrisy: "Never was a purely piratical policy more shamelessly concealed behind the mantle of a divine mission." In any event, Germany had no desire at this time to close the door to improved relations. A sometimes well-informed Austrian publicist insisted two years later that Germany should have approached England after the Austro-Russian accord.[156] Neither the government nor public opinion was opposed in principle to a rapprochement then or later, always provided that England was sufficiently considerate of German sentiment and accommodating to German interests. Writing in the Conservative *Kreuz-Zeitung* (Jan. 6, 1897), Professor Schiemann, the leading political commentator for this important journal, a member of the faculty of the University of Berlin, and soon to become one of the Emperor's intimates, affirmed his confidence in the possibility of an understanding if England would finally see that she could no longer ignore Germany's interests throughout the world. His tone, however, was scarcely calculated to serve the cause of an understanding. "England," he wrote, "is still the state which has least adjusted itself to the fact that Germany is the strongest power on the continent, and that she is prepared, if necessary, to compel this recognition."[157] Marschall coupled his approval of good relations with the condition that "we must . . . proceed on the basis of

---

154 Its advice was accompanied, however, by a catalogue of Germany's grievances. The *Times* (Sept. 21, 1897) replied with a favorable discussion of an entente with France and Russia!

155 *Hamburger Nachrichten,* Dec. 25, 1897.

156 K. Kron, *Der Transvaalkrieg und die deutsche Reichspolitik* (Vienna, 1899), pp. 26–28.

157 T. Schiemann, *Deutschland und die Grosse Politik,* I, 11, 12.

complete reciprocity. . . ."[158]   The prospect that Germany's interests might be advanced with England's aid was naturally the most powerful argument in favor of coöperation. Appropriate proposals accordingly followed the annexation of the Hawaiian Islands by the United States. Hatzfeldt suggested an understanding in regard to the Samoan Islands only a few days after the appearance of the *Saturday Review* article. Despite its normal animus against England, the *Post* (Nov. 14) wrote approvingly of "a free, friendly relationship."

Germany was still extemporizing in her relationships with England and Russia; she had not yet definitely rationalized her precarious balance between them as the policy of a "free hand" when she launched her program of naval construction in the first naval law of 1898. A large fleet was a natural corollary to the *Weltpolitik,* just as a powerful army was essential to Germany's continental policy. The navy's rôle in Germany's armaments was necessarily of comparatively slight importance as long as security in Europe remained the chief aim of her foreign policy. It was significant that, under Bismarck, two generals, Stosch and Caprivi, were the ministers of the marine. Until the adoption of a *Weltpolitik,* the functions of the navy were limited to the protection of Germany's commercial interests abroad, of her coasts at home, and to raids against the enemy's mercantile marine. These purposes, requiring only a comparatively small number of cruisers and destroyers, became inadequate with the adoption of an imperialist policy. If Germany was determined henceforth to make her voice felt in world politics, she needed a large fleet. A strong case can be made against the wisdom of Germany's *Weltpolitik*—with reference to her own permanent interests—but not against the necessity of a fleet as a support for imperialism. Some of the arguments advanced by the naval enthusiasts were, however, decidedly weak. They maintained, for example, that Germany's commercial expansion had been tolerated because of her naval weakness and that a powerful fleet would alone protect her against the withdrawal of this toleration.[159] Others were franker

---

[158] *G. P.,* XIII, 15.

[159] E. von Hartmann, "Deutschland im zwanzigsten Jahrhundert," *Gegenwart,* Jan. 6, 1900.

and more realistic. They placed greater emphasis upon the strategic and diplomatic factors. Since Germany could not count upon England's support, she must be prepared to control the Baltic Sea and to meet the French and Russian fleets on even terms.[160] They pointed out the need of controlling the North Sea during a war in order to defend Germany against a blockade and to assure adequate food supplies.[161] A fleet strong enough to make its weight felt would, it was said, increase her ability to contract alliances, her *Bündnisfähigkeit*.[162] At first, France and Russia were thought of in this connection, but England eventually became the country that was thus to be attracted. The possibility that an ambitious program of naval expansion would precipitate an armaments race was usually ignored. While Bebel protested that a strong navy would be a challenge to England's control of the sea,[163] the naval propagandists insisted then as later that the problem should and would be solved, without reference to any other power, according to Germany's own needs.[164] These arguments contained many contradictions. The control of the North Sea could not be secured except at England's expense, nor could Germany use her navy for the benefit of her *Weltpolitik* without in some degree challenging the strongest naval power. "We seek no trouble with anyone on the high seas," wrote the *Kölnische Zeitung* (Dec. 6, 1897), "but we wish to be able to put a heavy hand on the scales wherever the map of the world may be revised."

The naval bill was the result neither of England's attitude nor of the pressure of public opinion. Beginning with Captain von Tirpitz's memorandum of June 1894, the ministry of the marine had declared for a fleet strong enough to attack an enemy upon the high seas. It was no longer satisfied with a force sufficient

---

160 *P. J.*, vol. 86, p. 403 (Jan. 24, 1897). In 1898, Germany had 13 battleships not older than fifteen years while Russia and France had a total of 28. The disproportion of those under construction was even larger. Woodward, *Great Britain and the German Navy*, App. I.

161 *P. J.*, vol. 90, p. 179 (Sept. 26, 1897); *Post*, Nov. 28, 1897. This, according to Tirpitz's later account, was the first aim of his policy. Tirpitz, *Erinnerungen*, p. 81.

162 *N. A. Z.*, Nov. 29, 1897. William also used this argument. Hohenlohe, *Denkwürdigkeiten aus der Reichskanzlerzeit*, p. 311 (March 7, 1897).

163 *Verhandlungen*, IX Leg. Per., V. Sess., III, 1746, 1747 (March 19, 1897).

164 *Ibid.*, IX Leg. Per., IV Sess., III, 5174 (Benningsen, March 19, 1897); Karl Peters, "Die Flottenfrage," *Zukunft*, Oct. 9, 1897.

only for commerce raiding.[165]   With William's approval, the
naval experts decided by the autumn of 1895 that the battleship
should take the cruiser's place as the basic unit.   If the recurring
friction with England since the Anglo-Congo Treaty of 1894 may
have had some indirect influence, these decisions had no connection with the Jameson Raid,[166] but William welcomed the explosion of anti-English sentiment for the support it might assure to
a naval bill.[167]   Delay enraged him,[168] but public opinion was not
yet prepared for an expensive naval program.[169]   Consultations
with party leaders convinced Hohenlohe that a bill had no prospect of passage.[170]   William might boast that he was ready to
build the fleet and then to submit the costs to the Reichstag (his
eighteen army corps, he said, would soon dispose of the democratic South),[171] but his ministers had no intention of precipitating a new constitutional conflict.   They were quite aware of the
importance of enlisting the support of public opinion for a policy
that would add to the already high taxes.   Partly to arouse public
opinion, new men were summoned to Berlin.   Count Bernhard
von Bülow was recalled from Rome to take Marschall's place as
secretary of state for foreign affairs.   His mission, according to the
Emperor, who agreed with those who feared that England would
crush Germany before she had acquired the means of defending herself, as she had crushed Denmark at Copenhagen in 1807,[172]
was to assure the security of Germany's industry and commerce
while the fleet was being constructed, and to use his powers as a
charmer of men to secure a favorable vote in the Reichstag.[173]
To Tirpitz, who succeeded Admiral Hollmann as minister of
marine, was entrusted the task of winning the support of public
opinion.

By September 1896, the Pan-Germans had already launched a

---

165 Woodward, *Great Britain and the German Navy*, p. 19.
166 E. Kehr, *Schlachtflottenbau und Parteipolitik, 1894–1900* (Berlin, 1930), p. 51.
167 See his earlier reference to anti-English sentiment, *G. P.*, XI, 12 (Oct. 25, 1895).
168 William II, Jan. 8, 1896. Kehr, *op. cit.*, p. 464; Hohenlohe, *Denkwürdigkeiten aus
der Reichskanzlerzeit*, pp. 153, 154.
169 *Vorwärts*, Jan. 21; *Reichsbote, Vossische Zeitung*, Jan. 24; *Germania*, Jan. 28.
170 Hohenlohe, Jan. 14, 1896. Hohenlohe, *op. cit.*, pp. 156, 157.
171 *Ibid.*, p. 311 (March 7, 1897).
172 Stosch, Jan. 12, 1896. Tirpitz, *Erinnerungen*, pp. 53, 54.
173 Bülow, *Denkwürdingkeiten*, I, 59 (Aug. 3, 1897).

campaign in behalf of naval increases, collecting ten thousand marks as a freewill offering and thirty thousand for propagandist purposes.[174] From the first organization of this group after the Heligoland-Zanzibar Treaty (1890), it had combined an ardent imperialism with fantastic schemes for the direct or indirect association of all Germans in a greater German Empire. Its first considerable increase in membership coincided with its propaganda in favor of naval expansion—suggesting that imperialism was more popular than racial theories.[175] Since it was recruited to a large extent from the teachers, governmental officials, businessmen, and retired army and navy officers, its influence was doubtless greater than its numerically insignificant membership suggests; Dr. Lehr, its business manager, received official encouragement before the enactment of the naval law in 1898.[176] Nevertheless, the Pan-Germans were probably a minor factor in the education of public opinion in comparison with larger propagandist groups, such as the Colonial Society. Progress was discouragingly slow. "There is," wrote Delbrück in the Conservative *Preussische Jahrbücher* (April 1897), "not the slightest prospect of a favorable solution of the naval question." [177] The opposition parties were still overwhelmingly hostile to *Weltpolitik* and all its works. While the agrarian interests resented the emphasis upon industrialism that was implicit in naval expansion, the South German particularists had no liking for the increasing predominance of Prussia.[178] Germany was embarking upon a course, wrote a critic in Munich to Hohenlohe, which would eventually ruin her. Her true policy was to economize, to concentrate upon her defenses against France and Russia, and to rely "upon her single reliable support, the rural population, since our industry is not worth much in any event." [179] "Why should we help Prussia,"

174 M. S. Wertheimer, *The Pan-German League 1890–1914* (N. Y., 1924) pp. 84, 88. Cf. *Historisch-Politische Blätter*, vol. 121, p. 217.

175 The increase was almost one hundred per cent, rising from 7,715 to 15,401. Wertheimer, *op. cit.*, p. 54.

176 H. Class, *Wider den Strom; vom Werden und Wachsen der nationalen opposition im alten Reich* (Leipzig, 1932), pp. 82, 83. Class became the president of the League in 1908, after serving for several years on its executive committee.

177 *P. J.*, vol. 88, p. 172.

178 "Vom Deutschenhass," *Grenzboten*, 1898, II, 511.

179 Volderndorff, Nov. 9, 1897. Hohenlohe, *Denkwürdigkeiten aus der Reichskanzlerzeit*, p. 401.

asked a South German newspaper, "to build a powerful fleet?"[180]
Because the navy served the interests of the wholesale trade rather
than agriculture, the *Deutsche Tageszeitung*, the chief agrarian
journal in North Germany, insisted that its claims were not so
important as those of the army.[181] From Bismarck's point of
view, the proposed change in the character of the navy was thoroughly distasteful. Battleships, he said, were *Paradeschiffe*, intended primarily to augment Germany's prestige.[182]

Under Tirpitz's direction, the ministry of marine took an active
part in the effort to enlist public opinion. Popular excursions
were organized to the naval bases; retired naval and army officers
were sent on lecture tours. Numerous professors offered their
services, and writers contributed "bundles" of pamphlets and
romances. Nor did Tirpitz neglect the press. More than a thousand newspapers received propaganda,[183] but an agent sent to
arouse the South German press had little success until he revealed
his official status; even then some newspapers refused.[184] Relations with England inevitably played a part in this campaign.
Much was said of her jealousy of Germany's commercial progress, although any thought of challenging England's control of
the seas was vigorously denied.[185]

While this publicity campaign, which continued with varying
intensity to 1914, ultimately did much to envenom Anglo-German
relations, it was perhaps less immediately effective in securing a
majority for the first naval law than the occupation of Kiaochow
(Nov. 16, 1897). Tirpitz had opposed this measure on the
ground that Germany, without a strong fleet, should not risk a
war,[186] but this first success in *Weltpolitik* did more to arouse
public opinion than his elaborate propaganda machine. Since the
naval bill was given to the press only a few days before the public
announcement of the acquisition of the Chinese port,[187] it reaped

---

[180] *Landauer Zeitung*, Dec. 22, 1897, in Kehr, *Schlachtflottenbau*, p. 132n.
[181] *Post*, Dec. 7, 1897.
[182] Harden's interview with Bismarck, in *Zukunft*, Sept. 1897. Kehr, *op. cit.*,
pp. 88, 89.
[183] Tirpitz, *Erinnerungen*, pp. 96, 97.
[184] William II, Aug. 20, 1897. Bülow, *Denkwürdigkeiten*, I, 137–139.
[185] *A. B.*, March 8, 1896.
[186] Tirpitz, Nov. 10, 1897. Hohenlohe, *Denkwürdigkeiten aus der Reichskanzlerzeit*, 412.
[187] *Staats-Anzeiger*, in *N. A. Z.*, Nov. 28, 1897.

the full profit of the subsequent enthusiasm. The opposition soon began to retreat. Except among the Social Democrats, few denied the value of a foothold from which German commerce might penetrate China more freely; it was only a short step to an acknowledgment of the need of a stronger fleet for its protection.[188] Some of the less determined opponents of naval expansion were doubtless impressed by Hohenlohe's and Tirpitz's assurances that the bill satisfied the country's maximum needs, although it might easily have been foreseen that further requests would in time be supported with the argument that new circumstances required a greater effort.[189] The debate on the Kiaochow affair became a patriotic demonstration. "The 8th of February," wrote the official organ of the Pan-Germans, "was one of the Reichstag's great days."[190] In March 1898, Lieber, the Centrist leader, made the passage of the naval bill certain by delivering sixteen votes in return for the promise that the costs of construction would not be met by indirect taxes.[191] Even the agrarian Conservatives, unwilling to defy patriotic sentiment by voting with the opposition, joined the majority. The German people were thus committed to a policy whose ultimate results no one could foresee, without much thought of its effect upon Germany's foreign relations. By the end of the fiscal year 1903–1904, the fleet was to consist of nineteen battleships, twelve large and thirty small cruisers, and eight armored coast-defense ships, a program that required the construction of seven new battleships and two large cruisers in addition to those already on the stocks.[192]

Both the occupation of Kiaochow and Germany's naval projects had immediate repercussions upon her position between England and Russia. It is a mistake to assume from the absence of diplomatic representations that England was indifferent even to the moderate naval program. It would not seriously weaken her control of the seas, but the London press, nevertheless, made no attempt to conceal its irritation. The *Times* (Dec. 1, 1897)

[188] *Historisch-Politische Blätter,* vol. 121, p. 121 (Jan. 12, 1898).

[189] The reaction of the other powers, according to the *Historisch-Politische Blätter* (vol. 121, 213, Jan. 28, 1898), would decide the question of further demands.

[190] *A. B.,* Feb. 20, 1898.

[191] Kehr, *op. cit.,* pp. 138–140, 152. The final vote was 212 to 139. "Flottengesetz und Zentrum, *Die neue Zeit,* 1897–1898, II, 33 (March 30, 1898).

[192] Woodward, *Great Britain and the German Navy,* p. 25.

felt that assurance as to the finality of its terms might serve parliamentary purposes, "but for the purposes of naval strategy, we cannot but regard it as worthless." Putting the implication of the *Times* into definite words, the Conservative *Daily Telegraph* (Dec. 1) acknowledged that no legitimate ground for objection existed without further increases. It was a fact, nevertheless, that the bill as it stood would ultimately destroy the two-power standard which had been the aim of British sea power since 1889.[193] At any rate, there was a good deal of talk about immediate increases. Germany's plans, wrote the Conservative *Standard* (Dec. 1), would probably "cause the English navy, already so strong, to be made stronger still." The Conservative *Morning Post* (Nov. 30) drew the worst conclusions. Germany's program exceeded "anything [she] can possibly require for the maintenance of her own interests. The results will constitute a direct menace to the other Naval Powers, and more especially to this country. . . . Can any one doubt that it is the British Empire which is threatened, that these battleships are intended to aid in gaining the command of the Channel and the North Sea, that these cruisers are designed to attack British commerce?" Like the Liberal press in general, the *Daily News* (Dec. 1) was more moderate, but it could not refrain from congratulating the "German Government on its denial of any intention to compete with first-rate naval powers." To commercial competition and the Kruger Telegram another cause of suspicion had been added by Germany's naval program.

Even the occupation of Kiaochow caused some resentment. "If this occupation is to be permanent," wrote the Conservative *Pall Mall Gazette* (Nov. 23, 1897), "it is regarded as a slap for us. There is too much of a slap all round in German policy these days." For the most part, neither the press nor the government showed much concern at Germany's establishment in a part of China that was so far removed from the British sphere of in-

---

[193] Even without additional construction by the other powers, a Russo-German combination after the completion of the German program would align 36 battleships against England's 29, while France and Germany would have a total of 44. Woodward, *Great Britain and the German Navy*, app. I.

fluence in the Yangtze Valley. The *Times* (Nov. 23) was moved merely to ironical amusement at Germany's disproportionate enthusiasm. While her secrecy was not to Salisbury's liking, he felt that no British interests had been injured.[194] William's famous "mailed-fist" speech at Kiel, on his brother's departure for the Far East, occasioned more amusement than foreboding. According to the *Times* (Dec. 17), it showed a notable lack of a sense of humor.[195] The real danger was Russia's reaction, for it might nullify everything that had been done to restore cordial relations with her.[196] William's advisers did not share his obstinate interest in a continental union; there was, however, no disagreement as to the desirability of conciliating Russia and of increasing the friction, if possible, between her and England. The first objective seemed to have been attained by William's successful visit to St. Petersburg in August 1897, although the pleasant reflections inspired by Muraviev's assurances that he preferred Germany to France as an ally were interrupted by the reference to *"amies et alliées"* exchanged between the Tsar and President Faure on the deck of the "Pothuau" at Kronstadt. Russia had been told repeatedly that she need not fear for the security of her Western frontier while concentrating her energies upon her plans in the Far East.

Germany, however, was just as eager to acquire a foothold in China as she was to conciliate Russia. In March 1896, an official carefully summarized the evidence of a popular demand for a port.[197] William's impatience steadily increased; it was with some difficulty that the more cautious foreign office and Chancellor finally persuaded him to abandon his idea of a *fait accompli* and to wait until China should furnish a convenient excuse for action.[198] From the German point of view, there was no neces-

---

[194] Salisbury, Jan. 12, 1898. *British Documents on the Origins of the War* (London, 1927) I, 4. This work will henceforth be cited as *B. D.*
[195] Cf. *Daily Mail, Daily Telegraph,* Dec. 17, 1897.
[196] See Langer, *Diplomacy of Imperialism,* I, 445 f., from which the following brief account is largely drawn.
[197] He mentioned nine newspapers and numerous petitions from individuals and from local branches of the Pan-German League. Klehmet, March 18, 1896. *G. P.,* XIV, 25, 26.
[198] Klehmet, Nov. 28, 1896. *Ibid.,* XIV, 45, 46.

sary conflict between her imperialist aspirations in China and her diplomatic interest in Russia's good-will, in view of her assistance in the revision of the Treaty of Shimonoseki. Having received no compensation, her claims were naturally regarded as unusually strong. Steps were taken to ascertain Russia's attitude even before the German experts had settled upon Kiaochow, while England, France, and Japan were not consulted. The results of carefully guarded inquiries seemed encouraging; [199] indeed, Russia had no objection to Germany's proposed action if it led to increased Anglo-German friction or if it further alienated Japan. The case of Kiaochow was somewhat different, since its northerly location and the right of "first anchorage" which Russia possessed created interests that Germany could not safely ignore. William mentioned the name of this port during his visit to St. Petersburg in August 1897, but, speaking merely of the impending arrival of a German naval squadron at this port, a serious misunderstanding arose. Unwilling to offend Germany, the Tsar replied rather favorably, although he carefully ignored the question of a German occupation, whereupon William drew the mistaken conclusion that Russia would not seriously object.[200]

Before final arrangements were completed,[201] the murder of two Catholic German missionaries in the province of Shantung provided the long-desired excuse for action. The editor of the nationalist *Berliner Neueste Nachrichten* had warned Hohenlohe, even before the news of the tragedy arrived in Berlin, that the government must have a success in the Far East.[202] In complete sympathy with this view, William thereupon declared for complete and immediate annexation. It was high time, he wrote, that "Germany should at last show the Chinese with great sternness and with brutal ruthlessness (*mit voller Strenge und brutalen Rücksichtlosigkeit*) that the German emperor cannot be trifled with." [203] The Tsar's cool response to William's final inquiry, refusing to approve or to disapprove Germany's proposed

199 *G. P.,* XIV, 12 n; Marschall, Jan. 31, 1896. *Ibid.,* XIII, 59; Hohenlohe, *Denkwürdigkeiten aus der Reichskanzlerzeit,* p. 296 (Feb. 3, 1897).
200 Bülow, Aug. 17, 1897. *G. P.,* XIV, 59, 60.
201 Brandenburg, *From Bismarck to the World War,* p. 99.
202 Hohenlohe, *op. cit.,* p. 398 (Nov. 1, 1897).
203 William II, Nov. 6, 1897. *G. P.,* XIV, 67.

action, had no effect.[204]   William, in fact, was encouraged by it. Russia's protest of November 9, stating her own interests, therefore burst like a bombshell upon an unprepared Berlin. Holstein, who had frowned upon the Kiaochow enterprise from the beginning, talked of war or peace as the choice.[205]   England's good-will suddenly acquired supreme importance. She was told that Germany had refused Russia's offer of a continental alliance and that she had also rejected China's advances in regard to a port near the British sphere of influence.[206]   While Berlin considered an offer of a free hand in South Africa and a threat to join Russia and France if England proved unreasonable, Hatzfeldt, in London, proposed Germany's support in a protest against the annexation of the Hawaiian Islands by the United States in exchange for concessions in Samoa as a basis for coöperation in the Far East.[207]   Salisbury, however, had no intention of questioning America's action or of yielding anything at this time in Samoa, but his indifference to Germany's establishment at Kiaochow undoubtedly contributed to her success. Confident that Russia had no intention of sacrificing the possibility of securing her support against England,[208] Germany ordered her ships to remain and, on November 12, troops were landed. These calculations were well-founded. In possession of Germany's assurance that she would not object to the occupation of Port Arthur, Russia withdrew her support of China's resistance to the German ultimatum,[209] and, on March 6, 1898, Germany secured a ninety-nine-year lease of the port and its adjacent territory, with various railway and mining concessions.

Unaware of Russia's protest, public opinion had no reason to express its opinion on the relative value of Russia's good-will and Germany's imperialist interests in China. It was even informed that Germany and Russia were in essential agreement.[210]   Rus-

---

[204] Hohenlohe, Nov. 6. *G. P.*, XIV, 68; Nicholas II, Oct. 26, Nov. 7, *Correspondance entre Guillaume II et Nicolas II*, p. 33.

[205] Hohenlohe, *Denkwürdigkeiten aus der Reichskanzlerzeit*, p. 411 (Nov. 9).

[206] Hohenlohe, Nov. 30, *G. P.*, XIV, 81–83; Bülow, Nov. 19, Dec. 19. *Ibid.*, XIII, 90, XIV, 129.

[207] Brandenburg, *From Bismarck to the World War*, 104.

[208] Rotenhan, Nov. 11; Hohenlohe, Nov. 16. *G. P.*, XIV, 77, 78, 86, 87.

[209] Radolin, Dec. 4. *Ibid.*, XIV, 107, 108.

[210] *Post*, Nov. 21, 1897; *Berliner Börsen-Zeitung*, in *Post*, Nov. 30; *Münchener Neueste Nachrichten*, Nov. 26.

sia's occupation of Port Arthur late in December, giving her the control of the Gulf of Pechili and of the most direct route to Peking, averted any permanent damage to Russo-German relations by giving her an interest in Germany's friendship as a check upon England and Japan. At first William seemed responsive. The two countries, he telegraphed the Tsar, now stood at the entrance to the Yellow Sea like "St. George and St. John shielding the Holy Cross . . . and guarding the gates to the continent of Asia."[211] Even the *Hamburger Nachrichten,* with its acute sensitiveness to any differences with Russia, accepted Germany's approval of Russia's action as a satisfactory proof of an understanding. William, however, was chiefly concerned with the future development of German interests in China. The relations with Russia should, in his opinion, be determined by circumstances: *"Das Spätere werde sich später finden."*[212] In the Far East, as in Europe, Germany now found herself between Russia and England, with Japan's attitude—who secured nothing, while England, Russia and France successfully demanded compensations—as a further argument against a too intimate association with Russia.[213] She balanced her approval of the seizure of Port Arthur with the announcement of her intention to administer Kiaochow as a free port in the hope of conciliating England.[214] Her press was instructed to avoid any jubilation at the prospect of Anglo-Russian friction when England occupied Weihaiwei,[215] and Japan was indirectly informed that Germany would welcome her establishment on the mainland opposite Formosa.[216] Germany's interest in Japan as a partner in the development of China was doubtless not as keen as her satisfaction at the thought of the friction that would inevitably have followed in Anglo-Japanese relations. The Japanese naturally had no intention of antagonizing England, in view of their new grievances against Russia and Germany.

---

[211] *G. P.,* XIV, 129, 130.

[212] *Bülow,* Jan. 2, 1898.   *Ibid.,* XIV, 135-137.

[213] *Bülow,* Jan. 8. *Ibid.,* XIV, 143, 144.

[214] Bülow, Jan. 5. *Ibid.,* XIV, 141.

[215] William II, April 6, 1898; Bülow, April 7. *G. P.,* XIV, 166; *Hamburgischer Korrespondent,* in *N. A. Z.,* April 26, 1898.

[216] Bülow, Dec. 13, 1898. *G. P.,* XIV, 120, 121.

V

Germany had emerged from the Far Eastern crisis in an apparently advantageous position between Russia and England. Her interest in an understanding with England ended swiftly with the flaring up of Anglo-Russian tension over Port Arthur. England, on the other hand, was debating the desirability of a change in the direction of her foreign policy. Since 1895, crisis had followed upon crisis; the Venezuela affair, the various complications in the Near East, the Kruger Telegram, Kiaochow, and Port Arthur had all involved British interests more or less directly. South Africa remained a chronic source of trouble, and France's challenge in the Niger Valley and in the Upper Nile was rapidly taking form. A hostile coalition could no longer be dismissed as a negligible danger after Russia and Austria had at least temporarily composed their differences in the Balkans and in view of France's adjournment of the *revanche* in favor of colonial expansion in Africa. Prudence advised an arrangement whereby England might share with others the burden of her imperialist interests or which would divide her potential enemies. In the Salisbury cabinet, the leading representative of this point of view was Joseph Chamberlain, the colonial secretary and an ardent imperialist. Convinced that the interests of the Empire should decide the direction of British foreign policy in this age of imperialism, he was prepared to abandon England's "splendid isolation" and to seek alliances. His position in the cabinet stood second only to that of Salisbury, the Prime Minister and foreign secretary. A successful industrialist without professional experience in diplomacy, he drove directly and sometimes tactlessly toward his goal. His first advances to the United States and Japan were without result. Nor was Salisbury's offer to Russia of a general delimitation of interests in the Near and Far East more successful.[217] The choice of a continental friend was therefore narrowed to Germany and France, and of these powers, the former was apparently the less dangerous in the spring of 1898. There followed Chamberlain's offer of an alli-

---

[217] *B. D.*, I, 5–18 (Jan.–March 1898).

ance, which seemed to confirm the theories of the German foreign office as to the strength of Germany's position.

Some evidence of England's desire for closer relations had already appeared. Even during Salisbury's negotiations with Russia, Queen Victoria moderated the anti-German tone of the London press.[218] The Duke of Cumberland told Münster, the German ambassador in Paris, of England's sincere wish for a rapprochement and assured him that the Prince of Wales would not be an insuperable obstacle.[219] Germany therefore was not unprepared for Chamberlain's proposal. The occasion was furnished by Eckardstein, the secretary of the German embassy, when, acting without instructions from Berlin, he brought Hatzfeldt and Chamberlain together in the interest of an understanding to which he was devoted for personal reasons. Hatzfeldt, the German ambassador, had already heard Balfour, the acting foreign secretary, affirm (March 25) his personal desire for better relations and his belief that the two countries were divided by no serious differences. The ambassador's reply, while it emphasized Germany's grievances, left the door open for further conversations.[220] They were continued with the colonial secretary on March 29 and April 1.

Much that was formerly obscure in these negotiations has been cleared up by the recent publication of Chamberlain's memoranda,[221] for the historian has heretofore been forced to rely chiefly upon German sources.[222] A brief summary here will suffice. Even the most cursory survey must note the fact that Chamberlain's offer had the cabinet's approval and that Salisbury, while more skeptical, agreed that an approach should be made, because the German documents seemed to show that Chamberlain had acted upon his own responsibility. Hatzfeldt clearly did not question Chamberlain's authority to speak in the name of his colleagues,[223] nor was the unfavorable reaction in Berlin appar-

[218] Martin, Jan. 13, 14, 16, 1898. *Letters of Queen Victoria,* (3), III, 224, 225.

[219] Hohenlohe, *Denkwürdigkeiten aus der Reichskanzlerzeit,* p. 431.

[220] Hatzfeldt, March 25, 1898. *G. P.,* XIV, 195, 196.

[221] Garvin, *Chamberlain,* III, 259, 260, 263–266, 271, 272.

[222] For a detailed account making use of the latest information, see Langer, *Diplomacy of Imperialism,* II, ch. XV. Since the negotiations were not conducted by the British foreign office, its archives contain no material bearing upon them.

[223] G. Ritter, *Die Legende von der verschmähten englischen Freundschaft* (Freiburg, 1929), p. 19.

ently determined by any uncertainty on this point. The ambassador even exaggerated Chamberlain's repudiation of the policy of "splendid isolation." Eager for an understanding, in spite of his own dislike and distrust of the colonial secretary's unconventional methods, Hatzfeldt reported his advances in the most favorable light in the hope of converting the opposition of the German foreign office. When Chamberlain spoke (March 29) of a "Treaty or Agreement . . . , for a term of years, . . . of a defensive character based upon a mutual understanding as to policy in China and elsewhere," he wrote simply of an offer to join the Triple Alliance.[224] When the secretary said (April 1) that the alliance should be used to stop Russia's advance in China and implied that Germany should act as a buffer between England and Russia in the Far East, Hatzfeldt omitted as many of these details as possible, mentioning only the minister's recognition of Russia's existing sphere of influence and his opposition to its further extension.[225] The alliance, which was obviously intended as a bait to make the Far Eastern agreement more palatable, was to be published and ratified by the British parliament. Chamberlain, in contrast to Balfour, was confident of a favorable vote.[226]

It was with good reason that Hatzfeldt edited Chamberlain's offers, for his superiors in Berlin were certain to reject an alliance directed against Russia. In spite of Germany's establishment in Kiaochow, she still had a diplomatic interest in Russia's continued activity in North China as a service to Austria, and the growth of the nationalist agitation among Austria's Slavic subjects, by weakening the Triple Alliance, increased the value of Russia's friendship. "We must," wrote William a few weeks before Chamberlain's offers, "prepare a firm bridge to Russia while there is time." [227] Still suspicious of the Austro-Russian understanding of 1897, Holstein believed that Austria should be reminded that "the road from Vienna to St. Petersburg is longer than that from Berlin to St. Petersburg." [228] Chamberlain's ad-

224 Garvin, *Chamberlain*, III, 260; Langer, *op. cit.*, II, 494, 495.
225 Langer, *op. cit.*, II, 496.
226 *Ibid.*, II, 496.
227 William II's comments, Eulenburg, March 1, 1898. *G. P.*, XIII, 113–115.
228 Hohenlohe, *Denkwürdigkeiten aus der Reichskanzlerzeit*, p. 433 (March 4, 1898).

vances, even as Hatzfeldt had reported them, therefore clashed with the official opinion in Berlin as to Germany's interests. There was, however, no need of a brusque refusal. Hatzfeldt therefore suggested (April 1) to Chamberlain that England, facing a probable war with Russia and France, should settle her differences with Russia in order to deal with France alone, since Russia would not support her ally in a conflict over West Africa. In all probability Germany neither desired nor expected England to follow this advice, since the elimination of the Anglo-Russian antagonism would destroy what was, from the German point of view, one of the most favorable features of the international situation; but nothing was less probable in view of the collapse of the earlier Anglo-Russian negotiations. Although Hatzfeldt's enquiries as to the permanence of a secret alliance under the parliamentary system and as to the ratification of a public alliance were more symptomatic of doubt than of a desire for information, his conversation with Chamberlain (April 1) concluded without a definite break in the negotiations.

While it was once believed that Holstein was responsible for the refusal of Chamberlain's offer,[229] it is now clear that Bülow and the Emperor shared the responsibility. William scented a maneuver to align Germany against Russia and to prevent the former from adopting an anti-English policy. The British navy, he wrote, could be of no assistance against Russia; the immediate hostility of Russia and France would more than balance any benefits of an alliance. Nevertheless, he was overjoyed at Chamberlain's advances as a proof of the failure of England's "splendid isolation." England, he informed the foreign office, had placed a valuable card in Germany's hand, which could be played against Russia; it would help to maintain a profitable balance between the two countries.[230] He therefore believed that England should be encouraged to hope for a favorable reaction in the future. Like his advisers, William counted upon her increasing difficulties to keep her desire for an alliance alive and even to increase her offers. Meanwhile, he was aware of the importance of keep-

---

[229] Cf. E. Fischer, Holsteins grosses Nein (Berlin, 1925).
[230] Langer, Diplomacy of Imperialism, II, 501.

ing "official sentiment in England favorable to us and hopeful." [231]

His own efforts had, on the whole, characteristically unhappy results, although his telegram of congratulations (April 9) to Queen Victoria on the victory of the British forces at Atbara against the Dervishes in the Sudan made a favorable impression.[232] "His Latest and Best," read the headlines of the Conservative *Pall Mall Gazette* (April 11). "It will go a long way to wipe out such feelings of resentment as time and incidental changes had not effaced already." After Balfour's reference in the House of Commons (April 5) to the identity of interests in China between England and Germany, the London press not unreasonably, but inaccurately, interpreted the telegram as a move in the direction of an understanding. Such was the conclusion of the Liberal *Daily News* (April 11). It was, according to the Conservative *Standard* (April 11) a plain indication not only that William's sympathies were with England in Egypt but also that he favored "a beneficial coöperation in other fields." The reaction in Germany proved that Bülow was correct (April 3) in using the anti-English trend of public opinion as an argument against an alliance.[233] On the same day, the Conservative *Post* (April 3) wrote of the "long experience which has made us skeptical of the friendliness of the English press," and it described William's telegram (April 15) as merely an act of courtesy in his capacity as a British army officer. "Material interests, not emotion or sympathy," it wrote, "are decisive for German policy." England's sudden friendliness, according to the nationalist *Münchener Neueste Nachrichten,* the nationalist *Rheinisch-Westfälische Zeitung* and the National Liberal *Hamburgischer Korrespondent,* was solely the result of her difficulties.[234] The *Hamburger Nachrichten* noted with satisfaction the denials in the Progressive press that the telegram had any significance for Germany's foreign policy or for her relations with Russia.[235] Of these views, the *Times'* Berlin correspondent observed (April

[231] *G. P.,* XIV, 217 (April 10). *Cf.* Garvin, *Chamberlain,* III, 270.
[232] *Letters of Queen Victoria,* (3), III, 242.
[233] Bülow, *G. P.,* XIV, 206.
[234] *Post,* April 13; *Times,* April 11, Berlin, April 10.
[235] *Post,* April 16; *Times,* April 14, Berlin, April 13, quoting the *Vossische Zeitung.*

14, Berlin, April 13) that they expressed the "general feeling among the Germans." Germany "could not if it would and would not if it could support the policy of the British Empire in any part of the world."

In the meantime, Eckardstein visited the Emperor at Homburg and, after his return to London, he assured Chamberlain (April 22) that William eagerly desired the successful conclusion of the negotiations.[236] Since there was no essential difference between the foreign office and the Emperor as to the undesirability of an alliance, it seems clear that Eckardstein had either been misled at Homburg or, as it has been recently maintained, that he completely misrepresented the Emperor's attitude in the hope of rushing the negotiations to a successful conclusion.[237] The notorious unreliability of his memoirs and the known inaccuracy of his diplomatic reports tend to support the view that he was responsible for Chamberlain's false hopes. There is, however, some reason to believe that the blame was not wholly Eckardstein's. Unfortunately, no record seems to have been made of the conversation at Homburg,[238] but, in view of William's remarks (April 10) at about the same time as to the need of encouraging England to hope for a favorable response in the future, it is not unreasonable to suppose that, with his usual impulsiveness, he made use of his visitor for this purpose. In reporting the Emperor as eager for the immediate conclusion of the alliance, Eckardstein was doubtless guilty of an exaggeration that was not without serious consequences, since Chamberlain drew the most unfavorable conclusions as to the reliability of German foreign policy when Hatzfeldt, shortly thereafter, definitely rejected his offer. Neither the ambassador's mention of an indirect approach to Germany through an agreement with Austria and Italy nor his vague reference to a more favorable occasion in the future was an adequate substitute. Chamberlain closed the discussion some-

---

236 Garvin, Chamberlain, III, 271, 272.

237 Langer, Diplomacy of Imperialism, II, 502.

238 Eckardstein's own account is too brief and general to be enlightening. It merely states that he left Homburg confident that the negotiations would succeed. This vagueness of course supports Professor Langer's view to a certain extent. H. von Eckardstein, Lebenserinnerungen und politische Denkwürdigkeiten, 3 vols. (Leipzig, 1929), I, 295.

what ominously with a quotation from the French: *"le bonheur qui passe."* [239]

Although the men who controlled Germany's foreign policy doubted England's ability to contract an alliance and to observe its obligations, these considerations do not explain their refusal of an offer which they then regarded in general as sincere and as practicable. They were not aware of the full significance of the facts—such as Salisbury's continued confidence in England's splendid isolation and the difficulties which an increasingly anti-German public opinion would create for an alliance—which have convinced some historians that there was no real prospect for an alliance. [240] The reasons for Germany's decision must be sought elsewhere. Her leaders did not feel that she had arrived at a diplomatic crossroad. The results of the occupation of Kiaochow seemed to show, after a moment of panic, that the differences between England and Russia were more powerful than any grievances which either power might hold against Germany. There was indeed no immediate danger of offensive action by the Franco-Russian Alliance and therefore no pressing necessity to secure England's support. [241] Nor is there any evidence that the German diplomats even suspected that an irrevocable decision had been made in repulsing Chamberlain's advances. They were confident that her difficulties with France and Russia would eventually compel England to seek Germany's friendship with worthwhile colonial concessions and without unacceptable claims upon Germany's aid against Russia. Chamberlain's warning that the refusal of his offers might be followed by other arrangements left them unmoved. For the present, the prospect that England might join the enemies of Germany was slight; in the Far East she was almost at swords' points with Russia, and a few months later the Fashoda crisis brought England and France to the verge of war. The mistake was in relying upon the permanence of these hostilities. If the English had made up their minds to

---

239 Garvin, *Chamberlain*, III, 274.

240 Langer, *Diplomacy of Imperialism*, II, 514 ff. *Cf.* Ritter, *Die Legende von der verschmähten englischen Freundschaft*, *passim*.

241 Ritter, *op. cit.*, pp. 17, 18.

abandon their isolation, as the Germans had reason to believe, they would not be likely to permit their relations with both France and Russia to remain in a state of perpetual tension to Germany's advantage. This potential danger was underestimated not only because the professional diplomats believed mistakenly that the clash between the national interests of the other powers were incapable of accommodation but also because they expected, like a large section of public opinion, to use these conflicts for the advancement of Germany's imperialist aspirations. For this purpose, the "free hand" was the natural policy. William wrote of the "prospect of winning from England colonial and commercial advantages," and Bülow, after affirming that Germany must be the "tongue of the balance between England and Russia instead of an oscillating pendulum," unsuccessfully tried to persuade Chamberlain that Germany's neutrality should be assured by colonial concessions. "The sole result of efforts to win Germany's alliance against Russia," wrote the Berlin correspondent of the *Times* (May 5, 1898), would be to place her in the "balance between England and Russia" and to give her "a handsome commission as an 'honest broker' from both sides."

There was much in England's attitude, even after the refusal of Chamberlain's advances to support the calculations of the German diplomats. No essential change had occurred in the situation which had led to the discussion of an alliance. It was not until June 1898 that an arrangement was made with France in regard to the Niger Valley, and the settlement of that problem was soon followed by the more serious contest for the possession of the Upper Nile. Salisbury, for one, resented Germany's methods. "You ask too much," he complained to Hatzfeldt, "for your friendship." The colonial secretary nevertheless still believed that England must find an ally and that it should be Germany. On May 13 he appealed for the first time to public opinion in a speech at Birmingham in behalf of Anglo-American friendship and, less explicitly, for an alliance with Germany. Of England's relations with Russia he said, "Who sups with the devil must have a very long spoon," and added that, "We must not reject the idea of an alliance with those Powers whose interests are most nearly approximate to our own." The press reaction in London was surprisingly favorable, although the Conservative *Saturday Review* (May 16) dismissed his talk of Anglo-Saxon solidarity as "claptrap." If the Liberal *Daily News* (May 18) feared that his frank acknowledgment of the perils of isolation would cause Germany to raise her price, at least it was not unfavorable to the suggested change in the direction of British foreign policy. The Liberal *Daily Chronicle* (May 16) spoke of "gathering clouds," the Conservative *Morning Post* (May 17) of the "too long silent tone of Canning and Chatham," of the "rejoicing" with which the world would greet the first act of a really national policy, and the Conservative *Standard* (May 14) of "concentrated and un-adulterated truth." An alliance for the defense of the "open door" in China won the unreserved approval of the *Pall Mall Gazette* (May 14) and the *Morning Post* (May 17). The *Times* (May 16) was prepared to accept the full consequences "to others as well as to ourselves" of the abandonment of isolation, although it saw no reason for concession on England's part. Like Chamberlain, a considerable section of opinion had at least temporarily, under the pressure of difficulties with France and Russia, accepted the idea of an alliance with Germany as a necessity, provided that the price were not too high.

The reaction of the German press to Chamberlain's speech resembled that of the official circles to his earlier advances. There was the same unyielding refusal of an association directed against Russia. According to the Conservative *Post* (May 15), the speech approximated a declaration of war; to the National Liberal *National Zeitung,* it was an open acknowledgment of the bankruptcy of England's power.[242] Where, asked the moderate *Frankfurter Zeitung* (May 14), could England find allies in the existing circumstances? "Germany has no reason to call Russia to account for her procedure in China." It was not to the interest of Germany's "free hand" that, after Chamberlain's offer had been rejected, this rather violent outburst of anti-English feeling should continue. The semi-official press therefore intervened to emphasize the more favorable aspects of England's attitude. From the *Hamburgischer Korrespondent,* the *Norddeutsche* (May 18)

---

[242] *Times,* May 16, Berlin, May 15.

clipped an article pointing out the colonial secretary's friendly attitude; from the *Berliner Börsen-Courier,* it took (May 18) another referring to the differences between England and Germany as merely economic in character and expressing astonishment that the German press should be doing the work of Russia. As to an alliance, there was but one opinion, except among the Social Democrats and a few liberals.[243] The moderate *Weser Zeitung* (Stettin) rejected it, while insisting at the same time that Germany had no reason to rejoice at England's troubles, since the commerce of the two countries would prosper or decline together.[244] The revival among the Progressives [245] of interest in a rapprochement with England was checked by the *Frankfurter Zeitung's* (May 16, 1898) approximately accurate revelation of the Austro-Russian entente (1897), because it was generally associated with the Dual Alliance of 1879 as a force for peace. Although the more influential sections of German opinion were thoroughly hostile to an alliance with England,[246] there was no strong demand for a close association with Russia, except among Bismarck's partisans. It was in favor of a balanced position between these countries that the government used its influence upon the press. "We can," wrote the *Hamburgischer Korrespondent* in an article that was clipped by the *Norddeutsche* (May 29), "comfortably play the part of a spectator with the consciousness that our policy . . . will pull no country's chestnuts out of the fire." Only the Social Democrats objected, however, to the use of Germany's "free hand" for the benefit of her *Weltpolitik.*

With the remainder of Africa about to be divided between England and France and with all the signs of an approaching partition of China, it seemed imperative to the German imperialists that every favorable opportunity should be seized to secure a share. William was the first to act. In his personal influence upon the Tsar, he saw a chance to derive a profit from Chamberlain's recent advances. On May 30 he informed his cousin

---

[243] The *Hamburger Nachrichten* continued to denounce it as a maneuver to attract Germany away from Russia. *Post,* May 28.

[244] *N. A. Z.,* May 19.

[245] *Post,* June 19.

[246] A few German historians have attempted to show that a class alignment existed on the question of an alliance with England. *Cf.* Langer, *Diplomacy of Imperialism,* II, 534, referring to Meinecke and Kehr.

Nicholas that he had twice refused England's offers and that, for the third time, there was before him "enormous offers showing a wide and great future for my country. . . ." The motive behind this astonishing prevarication was obvious. What would Nicholas pay, asked William, to insure his refusal? The reply, he wrote, must be "clear and open without any reservations." [247] William had miscalculated his ascendancy over the Tsar and the latter's independence of his official advisers. Nicholas' answer was a definite refusal. Not only did he offer nothing but he revealed the shocking information that Russia had also received "many tempting proposals" from England, which had been rejected "without thinking twice." As to William's reply, it must be decided, wrote the Tsar, by the interests of his own country.[248] The first attempt to exploit England's difficulties for Germany's imperialist interests was a signal failure. Bülow was chiefly impressed by the unreliability of her foreign policy, since Chamberlain's advances had clearly been preceded by negotiations with Russia. Henceforth it would be necessary, he informed Hatzfeldt, to observe great caution in dealing with her.[249]

This disappointment by no means diminished Germany's impatience for tangible gains. There is perhaps no better statement of her point of view and hopes than in Salisbury's speech in Albert Hall, May 4, 1898. "You may," he said, "roughly divide the nations of the world as the living and the dying . . . the weak States are becoming weaker and the strong States are becoming stronger . . . the living will gradually encroach on the territory of the dying. . . ." [250] If the extremists in Germany counted upon the eventual disintegration of the British Empire for opportunities to expand, the government hoped to share in the colonial heritage of the weaker powers. The financial difficulties of the Portuguese government in the summer of 1898 seemed to offer promising possibilities. Burdened with a national debt whose interest charges exceeded her income, Portugal had applied to England for a loan, to the great alarm of her

---

247 Semenoff, *Correspondance entre Guillaume II et Nicolas II*, p. 38.
248 Nicolas, May 22/June 3. *G. P.*, XIV, 250, 251.
249 *Ibid.*, XIV, no. 3804, 3805.
250 Garvin, *Chamberlain*, III, 281.

German and French creditors and their governments. The Germans, fearing that the power or powers with whom the loan was placed would eventually acquire the Portuguese colonies, at once decided to bid for a share. From the legal point of view, their case was weak, since Portugal, as a sovereign state, could seek a loan where it pleased and arrange such security as was satisfactory to herself and her creditor. In fact she was about to agree to give England a voice in the administration of Delagoa Bay, the use of all her ports, and the control of the railway to the Transvaal frontier in time of war, and to promise that no concessions would be granted in the vicinity of Delagoa Bay without England's consent. Moreover, England had interests arising from an ancient alliance and from a more recent agreement (1891) giving her an option upon the southern part of Mozambique, which Germany could not rival. She was therefore certain to resent Germany's intrusion, but the latter held a number of trump cards which could not safely be ignored. However indifferent she might be to Germany's need of colonies, England was keenly aware of the danger that the Germans might support the Boers in the conflict of which there were already many signs. France's attitude was another reason for not rejecting Germany's claim out of hand, since Madagascar gave her some interest in the disposal of the mainland. One of Bülow's first moves was to offer Hanotaux, the French foreign minister who had been willing more than once to coöperate with Germany in colonial affairs, a general agreement as a basis for common action against England in the question of the Portuguese colonies,[251] without result, however, for Delcassé, his successor at the Quai d'Orsay, never replied. Franco-German coöperation at Lisbon nevertheless lasted long enough to persuade Portugal to suspend the negotiations for the loan.

Germany had already informed London that her neutrality in South Africa "has its price like everything else in the world," and that price was an agreement for a joint Anglo-German loan and for the eventual partition of the Portuguese colonies.[252] Since Germany's first proposal placed Delagoa Bay in the British sphere,

---

251 Bülow, June 17. *G. P.,* XIV, 266.
252 Bülow, June 8. *Ibid.,* XIV, 251, 252.

although William had assured Dr. Leyds in January 1896 that he would never permit England to secure the possession of Lorenzo Marques, England soon gave up her original contention that the loan was a purely private affair between herself and Portugal. This concession persuaded Germany to abandon the Boers.[253] Germany asked a high price: Mozambique north of the Zambesi River and all of Angola. Only these gains would, she argued, reconcile public opinion to the sacrifice of her interests in the Transvaal. England's dogged efforts to give to Germany as little as possible and to safeguard Portugal's integrity were exasperating. The Germans threatened to come to terms with Russia or France.[254] According to Bülow, Anglo-German relations were at the crossroads: "They will either be much better or much worse."[255] Enraged at Salisbury's attitude, William persuaded his mother to write Queen Victoria attacking her Prime Minister as an obstacle to an understanding.[256] He even threatened to withdraw Hatzfeldt if the negotiations failed.[257] Eventually, England won a substantial victory in Germany's implicit abandonment of the Boers and by securing as a part of her share of Portugal's colonies the Transvaal's most convenient outlet to the sea. To Chamberlain, the cost of Germany's surrender of an untenable position seemed extortionate, even "blackmail." "Well," he concluded, "it is worth while to pay blackmail sometimes. . . ."[258] On paper, Germany's profits in the agreement of August 30, 1898 were impressive: the greater part of Mozambique north of the Zambesi River, generous slices in northern and southern Angola, and the Portuguese part of the Island of Timor.[259] She also secured England's promise not to secure any special privi-

---

[253] Bülow, June 19. *G. P.*, XIV, 269; Salisbury, June 21, *B. D.*, I, 49; Wüd, *Die Rolle der Burenrepubliken*, p. 158. However, Hallgarten attributes the decision to the pressure of such great financial institutions as the *Deutsche Bank* and the *Darmstädter Bank*, whose interests, as holders of shares in the Transvaal mines, were similar to those of Rhodes—in contrast to the industrial concerns which were seeking concessions from the Boers. Hallgarten, *Vorkriegs Imperialismus*, pp. 158, 159.

[254] Salisbury, July 20. *B. D.*, I, 59; Hatzfeldt, July 22, Richthofen, July 22. *G. P.*, XIV, 301, 302, 305.

[255] *Ibid.*, II, XIV, 323, 324 (Aug. 20).

[256] Langer, *Diplomacy of Imperialism*, II, 527.

[257] William, Aug. 22. *G. P.*, XIV, 333, 334; Lascelles, Aug. 22. *B. D.*, I, 69.

[258] Garvin, *Chamberlain*, III, 315.

[259] In addition to the southern part of Mozambique, England secured the surrender by Germany of her extraterritorial rights in Zanzibar.

leges for herself in the Portuguese colonies prior to their actual partition without similar advantages for Germany. Not an inch of Portuguese territory in fact ever passed into Germany's possession, for the English took more seriously than the Germans the endorsement of Portugal's "integrity and independence," which had been incorporated in the agreement. Germany's eagerness for the prompt arrangement of the Anglo-German loan [260] only irritated England, since she regarded the agreement as strictly conditional upon Portugal's financial collapse. The Germans, according to Salisbury, wished "to force the pace of destiny." [261] Having secured what they desired and acknowledging no obligation to hasten Portugal's bankruptcy, England apparently advised Lisbon to place the loan in Paris rather than in London and Berlin. The renewal of the Anglo-Portuguese Alliance in 1899, of which Berlin soon learned,[262] came to be regarded in Germany as a betrayal and as conclusive proof that England would never be a reliable friend. Englishmen could always argue, however, that no promise had been broken, since the agreement had provided for the maintenance of Portugal's independence and integrity. The German diplomats had been decisively out-maneuvered.

That the Portuguese agreement would have no positive results Germany perhaps could not have foreseen. There was, however, no mistaking the unfavorable reaction of German opinion to the rumors that the Boers had been abandoned. The Conservative *Post* (Sept. 7, 1898) was one of the few journals to approve a deal in South Africa, on the ground that Germany's interests, not "fruitless emotional outbursts (*unfruchtbare Herzensaufwallungen*)," must determine her policy. The same newspaper acknowledged, however, that "betrayal of the Boers" was a phrase that had frequently appeared in the press. The Pan-German *Alldeutsche Blätter* (Sept. 25) thought it "impossible to conceive of compensations sufficient to balance the sacrifice of a

---

[260] The *Darmstädter Bank* was asked to arrange the German part. A. Vagts, *Deutschland und die Vereinigten Staaten in der Weltpolitik*, 2 vols. (N. Y., 1935), II, 1528.
[261] Salisbury's minute, Balfour, Sept. 1, 1898. *B. D.*, I, 76.
[262] Bülow, *Denkwürdigkeiten*, I, 274. Bülow places the date "about the turn of the century." Meanwhile Portugal had dropped the idea of a foreign loan.

racially related people" in connection with the reported surrender of Germany's claims to Delagoa Bay. For many nationalists and Conservatives, what mattered was not so much the desertion of a related and friendly people as the loss of an opportunity to acquire an important foothold in Southeast Africa. The Nationalist *Münchener Neueste Nachrichten* (Sept. 27) feared that too much was being paid for an otherwise desirable understanding with England: the German people would not tolerate another Heligoland-Zanzibar Treaty. "Every German-feeling man," wrote the National Liberal *Berliner Börsen-Zeitung* (Sept. 15), "is asking himself: Are we again on the eve of a first-class diplomatic humiliation?" The Leipzig section of the Colonial Society protested (Oct. 7) against the abandonment of the policy of 1896 in South Africa.[263] Despite occasional and probably official reassurances,[264] the question became a permanent cause of bad feeling toward England. In time something was learned of England's obligations to defend the integrity of Portugal's colonial possessions in the alliance that was renewed in 1899. "Can Germans be blamed," asked an observer in 1903, "when they speak of a 'punic faith' or apply Faust's words, 'They speak English when they lie,' to these events? Such things are never forgotten; their influence endures for decades and centuries."[265] In the long run, however, it was more significant that the nationalists first began at this time seriously to doubt the ability of Germany's leaders to achieve worth-while results in *Weltpolitik*.

If Germany's impatient efforts to secure a share in the Portuguese colonies were an irritant in her relations with England, her desire to become one of the heirs of the Spanish colonial empire was largely responsible for the growing feeling in the United States that Germany was unfriendly. Friction between the two countries had developed before the Spanish-American War, but heretofore no serious conflict of national interests had occurred. The ruling classes in Germany, when they thought at all of the

[263] *Münchener Neueste Nachrichten*, Oct. 11.

[264] *Hamburgischer Korrespondent*, in *Post*, March 28, 1899. The *Staats-Anzeiger* (Dec. 29, 1899) denied the *Lokal-Anzeiger's* (Dec. 27) claim that the lion's share had gone to England in the South African agreement. E. Bauer, *England und das Deutsche Reich; eine Abrechnung zur Jahrhundertwende* (Leipzig, 1900), pp. 54, 55, 57.

[265] E. von Liebert, "Deutschland und England in Africa," *Deutsche Revue*, vol. 28, pp. 190, 191.

Americans, returned their dislike of German institutions with interest. In spite of the important place which the German-Americans had earned in all walks of American life, they probably had no small part in the development of this mutual aversion, since many, as fugitives from the reaction after the Revolution of 1848, had every reason to dislike the institutions of Imperial Germany. Their letters to relatives and friends—their influence is an unexplored problem—probably contributed to the growth of social discontent in Germany and therefore indirectly to the unfriendly feeling among the Conservatives toward the United States. Among Americans there was much admiration of Germany's great achievements in science, industry, and higher education. Such definite instances of friction as occurred prior to 1890 were chiefly the result of Germany's tariff policy and, indirectly, of the relatively insignificant rôle of the United States in Bismarck's diplomatic calculations. To the great Chancellor, the reaction of the United States to the irritating restrictions and prohibitions upon American agricultural products in the early eighties and to his refusal in 1884 to permit the Reichstag to receive Congress' resolution of condolence on the death in the United States of Eduard Lasker, the Progressive leader, was apparently a matter of indifference. Until 1890, the competition of American agriculture, cattle, and meat products in Germany's domestic markets had been the chief cause of resentment; the McKinley tariff of that year threatened to close the American market to the industrial products of Germany and of other European countries. The prospect that a protest would probably cause Congress to raise the tariff barrier still higher alone prevented the German and other European governments from yielding to the pressure of industrial and commercial interests for concerted action. William II continued, however, to talk of a Central European and even of a continental tariff agreement as a necessary weapon in the economic conflict with the United States.[266]

---

[266] He represented the continental union as an accomplished fact to the Tsar at Görlitz in September 1896. *G. P.*, XI, 358–360. For an exhaustive study of the more imaginary than real "American Danger," see Vagts, *Deutschland und die Vereinigten Staaten*, I, ch. V.

In Germany, as in other European countries, there was much resentment against the Monroe Doctrine, both on the part of the government and of public opinion, as a device by which Yankee imperialism reserved an entire continent for its own selfish interest. Even the Pan-American movement was distasteful, for it was feared that it would eventually weaken the loyalty of the large German settlements in Brazil and elsewhere.[267] Since the German government had no intention of challenging the most fundamental of the national interests of the United States, there was no other outlet for the popular feeling on these questions than acrimonious newspaper articles and pamphlets. The beginnings of American imperialism in the Pacific and especially the approach of the war with Spain presented apparently less dangerous opportunities for action in behalf of Germany's interests. In 1897, when the Americans were about to annex the Hawaiian Islands, Germany approached England with a proposal for coöperation in order to secure their neutralization or the exclusion of the United States from the Samoan Islands,[268] but England, having recently retreated in the Venezuela affair in preference to risking a conflict, was in no mood to engage in a new controversy with the United States. At first William II was eager to act upon Spain's request for Germany's leadership in a European mediation when her quarrel with the United States reached a crisis after the sinking of the "Maine" (Feb. 15, 1898), in the interest of the monarchical principle and as a lesson to the English as well as to the Americans. Although the foreign office persuaded the Emperor to abandon a measure that would have centered America's hostility upon Germany, it coöperated with the other powers in the collective note to Spain and the United States (April 7), encouraged Austria and the Papacy to assume the leadership which it did not itself desire, and recommended Spain to turn to France.[269] The German ambassador in Washington was instructed to act only in concert with the representatives of the other powers.[270]

William saw that nothing was to be gained by further protests

---

[267] R. Denner, *Bedeutung und Ziele deutscher Weltpolitik* (Minden, 1898), pp. 31, 32.
[268] *G. P.*, XIII, 28, 29 (July 18, 1897), 29, 30 (July 22), 42.
[270] Bülow, April 4. *Ibid.*, XV, 19, 20.
[269] Rotenhan, Sept. 29, 1897; Bülow, Sept. 30; Feb. 15, 1898. *Ibid.*, XV, 3–6, 7, 8.

after repeated efforts to organize European mediation had failed. When England proposed a second collective note representing Spain's consent to suspend hostilities in Cuba as an acceptable satisfaction,[271] he exclaimed: "I believe that it is entirely out of place (*verfehlt*), pointless, and therefore harmful!" [272] From the beginning of the war, Germany maintained a strict neutrality, without officially proclaiming it as her policy, with the approval of Spain's warmest friends and of the most zealous expansionists. The liberal *Frankfurter Zeitung* (May 19), like the greater part of the German press, condemned American imperialism, but it was moved by reports of anti-German feeling in the United States to insist that Germany's interests required a strict neutrality. As in most European countries, the sympathies of public opinion were definitely with Spain as the victim of an aggression and as the representative of the Old World and of the monarchical principle. The defeat of the United States would undoubtedly have been popular. While there were few who seriously expected this result, the predictions of a long war indicated the contemptuous estimate of America's military strength even on the part of the professional or amateur military experts.[273] The probable effect of a victory upon American policy occasioned considerable concern. The United States intended, according to the *Hamburger Nachrichten*, to expel from the Western Hemisphere those powers which already possessed colonies there and thus to extend the meaning of the Monroe Doctrine.[274] Lombroso predicted in Harden's *Zukunft* (Aug. 1898) that the United States was entering a period of militarism and colonial conquests. Professor Blumentritt of the University of Cologne foresaw that a Yankee victory would be followed by other attempts to impose America's will upon Europe.[275] Among the liberals there was no little regret that the republic was about to follow the example of the Old World powers, but the moral indignation at American imperialism on the part of the colonial enthusiasts had a false ring, for

---

[271] Germany signed it. Oncken, *Vorgeschichte des Weltkrieges,* II, 481.
[272] Vagts, *Deutschland und die Vereinigten Staaten,* II, 1315, 1316.
[273] *Ibid.,* II, 1312, 1313. Bülow and William agreed with this view.
[274] *Historisch-Politische Blätter,* vol. 121, p. 761 (May 12, 1898). White included this view as among the most important causes of anti-American sentiment. Vagts, *op. cit.,* II, 1345.
[275] *Kölnische Volkszeitung* (April 20), in *Historisch-Politische Blätter,* vol. 122, p. 297.

Kladderadatsch, August 14, 1898.

Figure 16.—The new world order: A glimpse into the future.

they frankly acknowledged their hope that Germany would share in the spoils of the war. The Pan-German *Alldeutsche Blätter* (May 8) believed that the desire of both belligerents for Germany's friendship should enable her to secure America's withdrawal from the Samoan Islands (McKinley directed Andrew D. White, the American ambassador, to refuse to discuss this point) [276] and to acquire Fernando-Po, the Caroline, and the Marianne Islands, if the United States insisted upon territorial annexations. Foreseeing the collapse of the Portuguese, Danish, and Dutch as well as the Spanish colonial empires, one of the more moderate of the Conservative journals hoped that Germany would not stand aside "when the hour strikes for the partition of these valuable properties, for Germany belongs among those nations which will become stronger." [277] According to the *Frankfurter Zeitung* (June 13), the newspapers which had condemned the United States as an *Angreifer,* a *Räuber,* and a *Rechtsbrecher* were precisely those that most eagerly desired a German occupation of the Philippines.

Provided that it could be done without making an enemy of the United States, the government would gladly have taken advantage of the war to add something to Germany's colonial possessions. In November 1897, William had spoken of the collapse of the Spanish monarchy as an opportunity for expansion.[278] Washington was informed, after the beginning of hostilities, that Germany's friendship could be had—at a price. Impressed by reports of anti-German feeling in the United States,[279] for which it blamed the English press and the Associated Press, the foreign office professed a desire for an understanding in return for concessions in the form of colonial territory.[280] Particular care, however, was taken to show no interest in the West Indies, in spite of Holleben's advice from Washington to play for time, in view of the possibility that an unfriendly policy might be desirable.[281]

[276] Vagts, *Deutschland und die Vereinigten Staaten,* II, 1349.
[277] *Schlessische Zeitung,* in *N. A. Z.,* June 5, 1898.
[278] Vagts, *op. cit.,* II, 1358, 1359.
[279] Richthofen, July 6, 1898. *G. P.,* XV, 48, 49.
[280] Holleben was asked to estimate the relative weight of opinion for an Anglo-American and a German-American understanding, the latter to provide Germany with naval bases and coaling stations. Bülow, July 1; Hatzfeldt, July 8. *Ibid.,* XV, 44, 45, 52, 53.
[281] *Ibid.,* XXV, 109, 110.

William rejected the Dominican Republic's offer of a commercial treaty and of a naval base.[282] The Philippines were a different matter, since the Monroe Doctrine did not apply to them. Moreover, the American ambassador, himself an opponent of an imperialist policy, and without definite information as to the attitude of his government, spoke encouragingly of Germany's aspirations,[283] as if it were more important that her restlessness should be satisfied and that her friendship should be sought than that his own government's freedom of action should be preserved. The islands had, in fact, already attracted Germany's attention. In 1896 Hohenlohe had thought for a moment of offering her assistance to Spain for the suppression of a native rebellion.[284] For Tirpitz, the possession of the Philippines was a national necessity; he hoped that the Spanish-American War would be delayed until the completion of Germany's naval program.[285] There was considerable discussion in Berlin after the outbreak of hostilities as to the proper form of Germany's intervention. No one seems to have been willing to risk independent action, for Bülow recommended an understanding with the United States and England or with England alone for the partition of the islands or their neutralization.[286] If William was favorably impressed by any arrangement that would delay their disposal until some future time, he discountenanced a favorable reply to the request from the rebel leaders for a German protectorate and a German prince.[287] It was unfortunate for the future of German-American relations that the Germans abandoned the normal methods of diplomacy in favor of direct action. When Admiral Diedrich anchored in Manila Bay after Dewey's easy victory with a naval squadron that was superior in fighting strength to the American forces, he created a tense situation.[288] The most damaging reports of the German admiral's threatening conduct—and of Eng-

---

[282] Bülow, Sept. 2. *G. P.*, XV, 110, 111.

[283] L. B. Shippee, "Germany and the Spanish-American War," *A. H. R.*, XXX, 770.

[284] Hohenlohe, *Denkwürdigkeiten aus der Reichskanzlerzeit*, p. 284 (Dec. 2).

[285] Vagts, *Deutschland und die Vereinigten Staaten*, II, 1325, citing Bülow, *Denkwürdigkeiten*, I, 188 (March 16, 1898).

[286] *G. P.*, XV, 33–38 (May 14).

[287] Bülow, May 18. *Ibid.*, XV, 39.

[288] For a critical comparison between the reports of the two admirals, see J. Keim, *Forty Years of German-American Political Relations* (Philadelphia, 1919), pp. 216, 217.

land's friendliness—were doubtless exaggerated, but the important thing is that they were then and later widely circulated in the United States. It was Germany's right to safeguard her interests at a time when the Americans were not yet sufficiently strong to take control of Manila and to maintain order. Her maintenance of an unusually powerful squadron there for an unnecessarily long period was a serious mistake, to which William apparently consented when Tirpitz urged that it would stimulate a demand in Germany for a stronger fleet.[289]   In any event, this incident was more effective than the efforts of Spring Rice, the British ambassador in Washington, and of the English press to arouse suspicions of Germany's intentions. She would, it was generally believed, assert her claims at a favorable moment.

That moment never came. The Treaty of Paris (Nov. 1898) gave the United States the entire archipelago in return for the payment of twenty-five million dollars. The same unwillingness to risk a definite break which had restrained Germany during the war closed her ears to Spain's plea for support during the peace negotiations. The attention of German opinion was centered at this time upon the Fashoda crisis, but its reaction to the terms of peace was clearly unfriendly. The Progressive *Volks-Zeitung* (Nov. 30) was one of the few journals to welcome America's annexation of the Philippines, on the ground that it would insure her coöperation with England in the latter's inevitable conflict with the Asiatic peoples. "Germany's future," it wrote, returning to its earlier partiality for England, "lies in an alliance with these powers; in a union against them she will dig her own grave in spite of the efforts of our Anglophobes to obscure the facts." The first indication of the peace terms had moved the National Liberal *National Zeitung* (Nov. 2) to invite the intervention of the powers which were interested in the Far East. As the leader, the Paris correspondent of the moderate *Berliner Tageblatt* (Nov. 14) recommended France, arguing that it would enable France to recover the prestige which she had recently lost in her capitulation to England. The Catholic *Germania* (Dec. 13) spoke of the "shameless exploitation of their opponents' weak-

---

ness," which the Americans would themselves one day regret. Only the mutual suspicions among the European powers had saved the United States, according to the *Kölnische Zeitung,* from an irresistible mediation.[290]   In the hope of securing something from Spain's collapse, the foreign office did not hesitate to explain to the Americans that the colonial enthusiasts would create serious difficulties for the government if it emerged with empty hands.   It was needlessly alarmed.   If the State Department did not agree with White's willingness to give Germany a naval station in the Philippines, it had no desire for the rest of Spain's island possessions in the Pacific.   Germany was therefore able (Feb. 12, 1899) to purchase from Spain the Caroline, the Pelew, and the Marianne Islands (with the exception of Guam). These gains occasioned only moderate satisfaction in Germany; their economic value was obviously slight, and the circumstances of their acquisition added nothing to Germany's prestige.

Germany's restless search for colonial possessions was accumulating difficulties that might one day react unfavorably upon her position in Europe.   England had not yet turned against her, for Chamberlain and others still hoped that an alliance might still be arranged.   It is also true that the chances were perhaps against the success of the negotiations during the spring of 1898, yet Germany's desire to profit by the friction between England and Russia was one of the causes of her failure to make the fullest possible use of England's willingness to talk.   Even Chamberlain thought of "blackmail" in connection with the price which Germany asked for her abandonment of the Boers.   The Americans reached the same conclusion from her attitude during the Spanish-American War.   "There is," wrote John Hay, the Secretary of State, "to the German mind something monstrous in the thought that a war should take place anywhere and they not profit by it." [291]   It is easy to understand and to sympathize with Germany's needs, but the resentment which her methods occasioned is also comprehensible.   However justifiable these methods may have been from her own point of view, success would ultimately be the sole justification.   A conditional understanding

---

[290] *Volks-Zeitung,* Nov. 30, 1898.
[291] Langer, *Diplomacy of Imperialism,* II, 518.

with England for a situation which might never exist and some
hundreds of tiny islands in the distant Pacific were meager advantages in comparison with the actual or potential damage done
to Germany's relations with England and the United States.

VI

France played no small part in Germany's confidence that adventures in *Weltpolitik* would not seriously endanger her security
in Europe.   No reason existed for immediate alarm either in the
Franco-Russian Alliance or in the *revanche*.   Few Germans questioned the sincerity of Russia's professed indifference to Alsace-
Lorraine; [292] since they had always assumed that she would fight
only for her own interests and never for those of her ally, her
understanding with Austria (1897) and her imperialist enterprises in the Far East furnished convincing proof of her desire
for peace in Europe.   For her part, France had no intention of
putting her army at the service of Russia's Balkan interests.   If
her government did not agree with the embittered chauvinists
that Russia's failure to support the *revanche* deprived the alliance
of its value, it expected little more from Russia's association than
a stronger voice in international affairs.   The dream of attacking Germany single-handed had largely been dispelled by the
rapid increase in Germany's population.   It seemed not impossible that important changes were about to occur in the attitude
of French opinion toward foreign affairs in general and toward
Germany in particular.   The growth of Socialism, trade union-
ism, and intellectual radicalism, and the humanitarian sympathies
aroused by Dreyfus agitation, gave a powerful impetus to pacifism
and anti-militarism.   Even the Conservatives and nationalists in
Germany finally admitted the strength of these moderate tendencies.[293]   Writing of the *Mercure de France's* (Dec. 1897) round
robin on the *revanche*,[294] the Paris correspondent of the Conservative *Post* (Dec. 7, 1897) paid a tribute to the patriotic Frenchmen
who were willing to approve the "ever stronger" peace movement

---

[292] Osten-Sacken, Berlin, 8/20 March 1896. Meyendorff, *Correspondance Diplomatique de M. de Staal, II,* 313, 314.   The *Post* (Sept. 24, 1898) spoke of Russia's attitude as having forced France to a practical renunciation of the *revanche* and as the
best of reasons for a Franco-German rapprochement.

[293] Eckardstein, *Lebenserrinerungen,* I, 237; Hohenlohe, *Denkwürdigkeiten aus der
Reichskanzlerzeit,* 237.

[294] Carroll, *French Public Opinion,* p. 186.

and to concede something to Germany's aspirations. The apostles of the *revanche*, wrote the Paris correspondent of the *Kölnische Zeitung* (Dec. 10, 1897), would have few successors "when time gathers them to their fathers." The *Münchener Neueste Nachrichten* (Dec. 17, 1897) believed that the efforts to excite nationalist sentiment would make no impression upon "the increasing skepticism" of the French people. For Münster the poll was a fair index to the views of the younger generation.[295]

Nevertheless, it occurred to few in Germany that something might be done to encourage or to hasten these changes. The government and the greater part of the press alike remained interested but indifferent spectators of the struggle for justice in the Dreyfus affair, although the German war office could have proved the innocence of the prisoner of Devil's Island. To no avail did the Paris correspondent of the Jewish-owned *Frankfurter Zeitung* (Dec. 17, 1897) call for the publication of the pertinent correspondence, for it was thought to be Germany's interest that France should be weakened by internal dissension. The discussion in the French press of a solution of the Alsace-Lorraine question as the basis of an understanding was addressed to deaf ears. Except among the Social Democrats, only an insignificant minority even admitted the existence of the question. There was a strong feeling that a compromise of any kind—the exchange of Lorraine for a French colony, the creation of a buffer or neutralized state, the establishment of an autonomous government—would cause a resurgence of *revanche* sentiment as a confession of weakness. "'Nach Berlin!' would be France's reply," wrote the National Liberal *National Zeitung*.[296] Nor were the Germans more willing now than they had been in Bismarck's time to sacrifice important diplomatic advantages for the creation of a continental union when the state of French opinion and the direction of French policy seemed favorable. An association with France and Russia against England might drive Italy into the latter's arms in consequence of her vulnerability to the power that controlled the Mediterranean.[297] Egypt was still a principal obstacle; next to France's

---

295 *G. P.*, XIII, 108, 109 (Dec. 11, 1897).
296 *Post*, July 9, 1895.
297 Rotenhan, Aug. 3, 1895. *G. P.*, X, 19.

own reluctance to burn her bridges and to her traditional attitude toward Germany, its omission from the questions in which Germany had offered her support at the time of the Jameson Raid did more than anything else to prevent a continental union. It was not strange that the *Temps* (Jan. 8, 1896) rejected it as an "unnatural alliance," or that the French ambassador in London, according to a report which had a lasting influence upon German policy, spoke of Germany as France's sole enemy.[298] With the lessening of tension shortly after the Kruger Telegram and with Germany's gradual drift into a balanced position between England and Russia, England found that she could usually depend upon Germany's support in Egypt. It was still the most effective means of dividing the two Western powers. William's continued flirtation with the idea of a continental league took no more definite form than expressions of sympathy after the disastrous Charity Bazaar fire and the attempted assassination of President Faure,[299] for he counted upon Russia, as he told the Tsar in August 1897, to decide France's action.[300] The scattered evidence at hand gives the impression that the German Conservatives and nationalists were favorable to an anti-English combination.[301] While France's unofficial advances were rejected with the warning that only formal proposals could be considered,[302] there was some appreciation in the German press of Hanotaux's business-like attitude. "To a certain point," wrote the nationalist *Münchener Neueste Nachrichten* (March 30, 1898), "the peaceful powers can depend upon him. . . . Germany values in him as good a neighbor as any Frenchman can be and wishes for him a long period of power with all the prestige compatible with peace." Delcassé, his successor, not only failed to reply to Germany's advances but he explained on the eve of the Fashoda crisis

---

[298] Hohenlohe, Dec. 8, 1896. *G. P.,* XI, 332; Bülow, Sept. 2, 1898. *Ibid.,* XIV, 361. Both Marschall and Hatzfeldt had refused to believe that Germany's reserve in Egypt accounted for France's attitude, since coöperation in South Africa would improve the latter's position in Egypt. Marschall, May 24, 1896. *Ibid.,* XI, 200, 201.

[299] *Ibid.,* XIII, 97, 98, 101 (May 7, June 13, 1897).

[300] William II, Aug. 20, 1897. Bülow, *Denkwürdigkeiten,* I, 139.

[301] *P. J.,* vol. 88, p. 370 (May 1897). This was especially true at the time of the Jameson Raid and of the Austro-Russian understanding.

[302] *G. P.,* XI, 320-323 (June 23); 324-331 (Sept. 19); Münster, Oct. 6, 1897. *Ibid.,* XI, 388; Hohenlohe, *Denkwürdigkeiten aus der Reichskanzlerzeit,* 296, 297.

·that the state of public opinion made impossible anything more than parallel action in specific cases.[303]

The theories of the German diplomats were again justified when (Sept. 1898) Captain Marchand challenged England's claims to the Sudan and threatened to precipitate the entire Egyptian question by raising the French flag at Fashoda. Germany's diplomatic position was never stronger. In the absence of important interests in the disputed territory and without any diplomatic commitments to either power, her freedom of action was apparently complete, but the situation did not permit the effective use of her advantages. The traditions of German foreign policy were all against supporting France in Egypt. Although the Pan-Germans thought that Germany should help the French to make good their claims, in order to block the all-British Cape-to-Cairo route,[304] the greater part of German opinion doubtless preferred the maintenance of the status quo and perhaps the restoration of British control in the Sudan.[305] For diplomatic reasons as well as the interests of her *Weltpolitik,* an energetic effort to profit from England's troubles seemed inadvisable. On August 21, William had read into Lascelles' remark that his government was ready to associate itself with the Triple Alliance an official offer by the British cabinet.[306] Moreover, the agreement for the future partition of the Portuguese colonies (Aug. 30) had just been concluded. The moment was therefore inopportune for opposition to her interests in a vital question. William in fact telegraphed his congratulations (Sept. 4) to Queen Victoria on the victory at Omdurman, telling her that he had announced "the joyous tidings to the regiments at the foot of the Waterloo column" in Hanover.[307] The bitterness of France's reaction to the demand for Marchand's unconditional evacuation nevertheless was a temptation which he could not resist. From Palestine, where he was courting Turkey and the Mohammendan world, William asked the Tsar, evidently with a view to a continental union, what

---

[303] Holstein was not averse to this limited coöperation, since Germany would be free to withhold her support at discretion. Monts, *Erinnerungen,* p. 355 (July 10, 1898).

[304] *A. B.,* Oct. 16, 1898.

[305] *Historisch-Politische Blätter,* vol. 122, p. 523 (Sept. 24).

[306] Ritter, *Die Legende,* p. 19 f.

[307] *Letters of Queen Victoria,* (3), III, 274.

Russia would do in the event of an Anglo-French war.[308] The
certainty of Russia's and Germany's support might well have encouraged France to stand firm, but Russia, through Muraviev, her
foreign minister, who was then in Paris, made it clear that she
would not fight in support of her ally's African interests.[309] The
Tsar's cool and evasive reply [310] and France's surrender were decisive for William, although he regretted, as he informed Nicholas,
that France had not taken advantage of her "splendid situation
to act in the interest of us all." [311] Of a report that opinion in
Paris desired an understanding he wrote, "A little late! It should
have been made three years ago during the Transvaal affair." [312]
"Too late, Sir!" was his reaction to the support of a continental
union by Count Witte, the Russian finance minister, *"Jetzt will
ich nicht."* [313]

In maintaining a neutral and passive attitude, the German foreign office probably acted in accordance with the desires of public
opinion. France's withdrawal of Marchand confirmed earlier
doubts as to her resistance,[314] and the danger of an Anglo-French
rapprochement seemed more remote than ever. Chamberlain,
Berlin was informed, had said that England would present her
"bill to France not only in Egypt, but all over the globe; and
should she refuse to pay, then war." [315] The momentary fear
that England's naval preparations were directed against Germany
as well as France soon disappeared.[316] Germany, it was felt, had
only to watch the development of a favorable situation. "The
diplomats," wrote the *Berliner Tageblatt* (Nov. 8), "may count
upon a profound hostility between France and England. . . .
Germany will watch the game with interest." The Anglo-French
tension interested the Progressives chiefly as an argument against
the need of naval and military increases.[317]

---

308 Bülow, Oct. 28. *G. P.*, 382, 383.
309 Münster, Oct. 20. *Ibid.*, XIV, 377. For a fairly accurate analysis in the press
of Russia's attitude, see *Zukunft* (Nov. 26), *Freisinnige Zeitung* (Dec. 4).
310 *G. P.*, XIV, 385, 386 (22 Oct./Nov. 3).
311 Semenoff, *Correspondance entre Guillaume II et Nicolas II*, p. 53.
312 Münster, Nov. 9. *G. P.*, XIV, 392.
313 William II's comments, Radolin, Dec. 20, 1898. *Ibid.*, XIII, 197.
314 *Historisch-Politische Blätter*, vol. 120, pp. 937, 938.
315 Metternich, Nov. 6. *G. P.*, XIV, 388.
316 *Post, Vossische Zeitung*, Nov. 3; *Germania*, Nov. 11.
317 *Volks-Zeitung*, Nov. 7.

From England's demonstration of her strength and of her capacity for action arose a more general interest in an understanding with her than at any time since 1890. Those who had regarded her friendship as without practical value in continental affairs were noticeably impressed. Fear that she would succeed in using Germany against her enemies declined with her demonstrated ability to cope with them herself. "With this England we can treat," wrote the Conservative *Kreuz-Zeitung*, ". . . an understanding is entirely in accordance with our views." [318] England's firmness was an agreeable surprise for the Conservative *Post* (Nov. 10). If it rejected a full alliance and insisted upon *"absolute Parität,"* it agreed that an understanding would be to the interest of both countries. The Progressive *Volks-Zeitung* (Nov. 10) approved the closest of alliances, but the Social Democratic *Vorwärts* (Nov. 15) came out unexpectedly for neutrality, because France's retreat had cleared the ground or a definitive settlement between England and Russia. In a speech at Manchester, November 15, Chamberlain again affirmed the community of interests with Germany and—for the first time—with Japan in China. It was his strong tone toward France that chiefly concerned the London press, but his reference to Germany did not pass unnoticed. According to the Conservative *Pall Mall Gazette* (Nov. 17), Chamberlain had "simply said what all believe," and the Liberal-Imperialist *Daily Chronicle* (Nov. 17) spoke of a promising solution of Far Eastern problems, provided that England's interests were adequately safeguarded. The mention of China was sufficient, however, to check the trend in Germany in favor of an understanding. The *Kölnische Zeitung* (Nov. 18) insisted upon complete parity for Germany and spoke of "the good and friendly relations which exist today between Germany and Russia," while the National Liberal *National Zeitung* (Nov. 19) would await events for proof that Chamberlain's assurance that Germany's commercial competition was not a legitimate grievance would be followed by an improvement in England's attitude toward her colonial interests. Time alone, wrote the Conservative *Post* (Nov. 20) and the Catholic *Germania*

---

[318] *Times,* Nov. 10, Berlin, Nov. 9.

(Nov. 18), would show whether he was right in representing the two countries as divided by no serious differences. Although the liberal *Frankfurter Zeitung* agreed with the British colonial secretary that the two countries were separated by no insuperable obstacles, it insisted that Germany had no interest in strengthening "the might of England at the expense of France or Russia." [319]

The Berlin correspondents of the London press erred for once on the side of moderation in their reports of German opinion. Of the newspapers with any claim to "serious political convictions," only the *Post,* they said, had maintained its "inimical tone towards Great Britain." The "jealous and often contemptuous ill-will which for many years past has marked the attitude of most German newspapers towards this country" had disappeared or diminished.[320]   With an eye to France, Salisbury advised the Queen to encourage this friendlier attitude by arranging William's first visit since 1895.[321]   On December 8 Chamberlain attempted to meet some of Germany's objections in his Wakefield speech. "We do not want them," he said, "to pull our chestnuts out of the fire and we are not going to pull out chestnuts for them. . . . I can assure our German friends that if our interests are not the same . . . we will not ask for and will not wish for their assistance." Applauded in England,[322] this clarification pleased the Germans. Although the Conservative *Kreuz-Zeitung* (Dec. 9) advised delay in order that Chamberlain's fair words might be checked with England's deeds, it approved coöperation wherever the interests of the two countries were identical. His moderation toward Russia removed the objection of the *National Zeitung* (Dec. 9) to a limited understanding. The moderate *Vossische Zeitung* (Dec. 9) was not only skeptical of Chamberlain's ability to put his ideas into effect, but it also insisted that England's difficulties with France and Russia made her need greater than Germany's; yet it had no objection in principle to a practical coöperation. The Conservative *Post* (Dec. 11) even used the occasion to lecture the anti-English extremists and to say that Germany

[319] *Times,* Nov. 19, Berlin, Nov. 18.
[320] *Morning Post,* Nov. 18, Berlin, Nov. 17; *Times,* Dec. 8.
[321] *Letters of Queen Victoria,* (3), III, 312 (Nov. 17).
[322] *Times, Standard,* Dec. 9.

could not afford to oppose England under all circumstances. Its position nevertheless helps to explain the failure to reach an agreement and indeed the absence of negotiations at this time. From the elimination of the sources of discord with England, the *Post* expected above all an improvement in Germany's bargaining power rather than a diplomatic association. "Only in this way can Germany maintain her neutrality between the Eastern and Western powers and thus protect her interests. . . . The more guarantees we have for our independence [the famous 'free hand'], the higher the price we can ask for our friendship—the ultimate goal of a true *Realpolitik*. . . ." Since France's retreat obviously reduced England's immediate need of German support, nothing was done to profit by the favorable diplomatic situation and the receptive attitude of public opinion in both countries.

Many of the same considerations determined Germany's reaction to the talk of a rapprochement in the French nationalist and chauvinist circles. The traditional hatred of Germany was for the moment submerged in an access of rage against England that was expressed in terms more bitter than any that had been used of Germany since 1870.[323] If the German ambassador attributed this movement of opinion to the fear of a war with England, to mistrust of Russia, and to the dread of isolation,[324] it was nevertheless no negligible factor in the general situation; yet Russia's cool response to William's advances had destroyed its value for Germany. At any rate, France made no official advances to Berlin, for Delcassé did nothing to give effect to his threat to Monson, the British ambassador, to seek Germany's aid.[325] It was not until February 14, 1899, when France had already decided to liquidate the question of the Upper Nile, that Hohenlohe heard that the French foreign minister had spoken of the transfer of Alsace-Lorraine for a French colony in a conversation with an Alsatian merchant.[326] The German foreign office was sufficiently interested, however, to send an unofficial agent to Paris, whence he reported, among other astonishing things, that

---

[323] Carroll, *French Public Opinion*, p. 176.
[324] Münster, Nov. 24, 1898. Hohenlohe, *Denkwürdigkeiten aus der Reichskanzlerzeit*, 470.
[325] *B. D.*, I, 196, 197 (Dec. 9).
[326] Hohenlohe, *op. cit.*, III, 483.

Delcassé had asserted his willingness to sponsor a Franco-German understanding in the chamber.[327] Without a solution of the Alsace-Lorraine question, a Franco-German understanding could be nothing more than an academic question.

The German press left the French in no doubt as to Germany's intransigeance on this question. No compensation, wrote the *Kölnische Zeitung* (Dec. 3), could ever pay Germany for what she had bought with her blood. No understanding was possible until "the word Alsace-Lorraine has been dropped from the vocabulary of the French statesmen and of the French press." Germany's security, wrote the National Liberal *Allgemeine Zeitung* (Dec. 4), required an uncompromising refusal; there would never be the slightest difference on this question between the most ardent patriot and the most peaceful Emperor. The National Liberal *Magdeburgische Zeitung* explained that "what the French call a question is for us a fact based upon the highest justice. . . ." Nor were the liberals more conciliatory.[328] "This idea," stated the Progressive *Volks-Zeitung* (Dec. 13), "has not the slightest prospect of success. . . ." "No one in Germany," wrote the moderate *Vossische Zeitung* (Dec. 15), "knows of an Alsace-Lorraine question. The Treaty of Frankfort solved it once and for all. . . . Germany would not exchange even Metz for the entire French colonial empire."

The English assumed correctly that Alsace-Lorraine would prevent an understanding, but the Berlin correspondent of the Liberal *Daily News* (Dec. 13) erred in reporting that France's advances had not made "any impression here." On the contrary, they were frequently regarded as evidence of a significant change in French opinion. The devotion to the lost provinces had become, it was said, little more than a formal tribute to patriotic sentiment. "Most frequently," wrote the Conservative *Post* (Dec. 13), "the wish is guardedly expressed that Germany should offer some kind of moral compensation for the sacrifice of the sentimental attachment to the *Rheinland* in order to save France's face." What intelligent Frenchmen dared not publicly acknowledge, they were, asserted the Conservative *Kreuz-Zeitung* (Dec. 21), saying

---

[327] *G. P.*, XIII, 247–254 (Dec. 5, 1898).
[328] *Post*, Jan. 21, 1899.

privately. Even Münster, the German ambassador in Paris, doubted that the French were as deeply attached to Alsace-Lorraine as they pretended.[329] The *Kölnische Zeitung* (Dec. 10) nevertheless informed France that no progress could be made toward an understanding "until she accepts the Treaty of Frankfort without reserve . . . until she recognizes once and for all that no territorial, monetary, or blood debt exists between us. . . ." Outside the ranks of the Social Democrats, there was no support for any concessions in regard to Alsace-Lorraine, but some difference of opinion existed as to requiring a formal renunciation of the *revanche*. The leading Catholic review in South Germany described it as "rather childish." France had signed away the two provinces for all time. "But a treaty has never prevented a state from undertaking a new war for the reconquest of lost territory. This silent reservation is always assumed. Nothing more can be expected of France than what she has already done. . . ."[330] No French government would ever yield, as the *Kölnische Zeitung* doubtless knew, to a demand which practically required a second signing of the Treaty of Frankfort. That the Germans had no intention of conciliating France is best shown by the attitude of their government during the Dreyfus affair. The general staff instructed Schwartzkoppen, the military attaché in Paris, to do nothing that would establish the authenticity of his note, the famous *petit bleu*, to Esterhazy, the traitor for whose crime Dreyfus was being punished.[331] Bülow had already decided that Germany's interests would be served best "if the affair continued to disrupt the army and to scandalize Europe."[332] One of the few voices raised in favor of positive measures for the encouragement of opinion in France for an understanding was that of the Pan-German *Alldeutsche Blätter* (Dec. 18, 1898). They might "one day bear splendid fruit."

There was indeed no compelling reason for Germany at the close of 1898 to throw in her lot with either England, France, or Russia. She was courted on all sides. "The Kaiser," wrote the

---

[329] *G. P.*, XIII, 254, 255 (Dec. 18, 1898).
[330] *Historisch-Politische Blätter*, vol. 123, p. 364 (Feb. 15, 1899).
[331] *Militärattaché von Schwartzkoppen: die Wahrheit über Dreyfus*, B. Schwertfeger, ed. (Berlin, 1930), pp. 140, 141.
[332] *G. P.*, XIII, 307 (Sept. 29, 1898).

Conservative *Standard* (Nov. 21, 1898), "may at least congratulate himself on the fact that he now stands almost in the position of the late Tsar. The most powerful nations are rivals for his friendship." The Germans were keenly alive to the advantages of this situation.[333] As an expression of this satisfaction, the *Kölnische Zeitung* (Dec. 10) quoted Goethe: *"Prophete rechts, Prophete links, das Weltkind in der Mitte,"* but it also warned against any illusions as to the motives of Germany's suitors. While Chamberlain's oratorical advances were undoubtedly regarded with greater favor and given more serious consideration than those of the French chauvinists, the tendency nevertheless was to insist upon a free hand. There was little difference of opinion that Germany's imperialist interests should be the guide in using this freedom of action. It was easy for the *Kölnische Zeitung* (Dec. 10) and the Pan-German *Alldeutsche Blätter* (Jan. 1, 1899) to urge a "healthy egoism"; [334] it was more difficult to define the details of a policy of enlightened self-interest. If the *Berliner Tageblatt* (Dec. 11) spoke of the Caroline Islands, if the Pan-Germans, as yet in the dark as to the abandonment of the Boers in the Anglo-German agreement of August 30, 1898, talked of preventing England's occupation of Delagoa Bay,[335] the government doubtless had its eye upon Germany's prospective share of the Portuguese colonies—and, with the strong support of public opinion, upon the undivided control of the Samoan Islands. The responsibility for the profitable use of Germany's advantageous position, said the Conservative *Post* (Jan. 22, 1899), belonged to the diplomats. Bülow and the foreign office had long since fixed the course of German policy. "Refusing to be drawn into the orbit of either England or Russia," he wrote, "it follows only German interests while maintaining good relations with both." [336]

In their tendency to confuse temporary with permanent diplomatic advantages, the Germans were themselves responsible for the most serious threat to the success of the "free-hand" policy. The antagonism between England, France, and Russia was at

[333] *Berliner Tageblatt,* Dec. 11, 25, 1898; *Kreuz-Zeitung,* Dec. 15.
[334] Cf. *Allgemeine Zeitung,* Nov. 20, 1898, Berlin, Nov. 19.
[335] *A. B.,* Jan. 1, 1899.
[336] *G. P.,* XIV, 399 (Nov. 15, 1898).

this time greater than that between any one of these powers and Germany, but its duration would depend upon the confidence of each of these powers in the strength of its position and in the absence of a greater fear of Germany. The first of these factors was illustrated by the relations between France and England in the spring of 1899. To believe that France would remain at swords' points with the latter power after Russia's refusal to support her and after Germany's attitude had confirmed her isolation was seriously to underestimate the suppleness of her diplomacy and the sense of national interests on the part of her public opinion. On January 16, 1899, Delcassé informed England that he was ready to discuss every question at issue between the two countries,[337] and he spoke confidently (Jan. 23) of an amicable arrangement during the debate on the Fashoda affair in the Chamber. This disturbing development was followed by the final press discussion of a Franco-German rapprochement. Speaking with unusual favor of an understanding, the *Kölnische Zeitung* (Jan. 28) invited the historian Valfrey, who, as "Whist," had urged a colonial accord in the *Figaro* (Jan. 14), to state his understanding of its conditions. Nothing came of this newspaper debate. Its conclusion, preceded by William's acceptance (Feb. 2) of his grandmother's invitation to visit England,[338] appeared with the *Kölnische Zeitung's* curt remark, *"Schlusse der Debatte,"* when Valfrey spoke of opening such regions as Siam to German capital in return for Germany's support in less important questions relating to Egypt.[339] In the meantime, neither the improvement of German opinion toward England nor William's sometimes embarrassing assurances [340] prevented the English from responding to France's move for a peaceful settlement of the questions arising from the Fashoda crisis. The *Post's* (Jan. 29) forecast of an improvement in Anglo-French relations became a reality in the agreement of March 21, 1899, giving France extensive, though economically worthless, lands south of

---

[337] *B. D.*, I, 199.
[338] *Letters of Queen Victoria*, (3), III, 336, 337.
[339] *Figaro*, Feb. 4. *Cf.* Carroll, *French Public Opinion*, pp. 178 ff.
[340] On December 19, 1898, he told Lascelles, referring to "the agreement he had made with me . . . in August," that Germany would come to England's aid if she were attacked by two powers, even if England were not similarly obligated to Germany. *B. D.*, I, 101–104 (Dec. 21).

Tripoli in return for the evacuation of the Bahr-el-Ghazel. Of course, the two countries were still far from the entente cordiale; the main issues in the Egyptian question, among many other problems, remained unsettled. William was confident that England's selfishness would prevent results that might be dangerous for his country; [341] to Holstein, France's alliance with Russia would prevent an understanding with England.[342] That a considerable part of moderate opinion in France had declared for a general understanding with England should have been a warning against an opinionated reliance upon the theory of a perpetual interest conflict between these powers. A few unofficial observers were less confident. The Conservative *Post* (March 26) predicted that France's increased freedom of action would have serious results. A turning point of world importance had been passed, according to a Catholic review, for the question as to the evacuation of Egypt now belonged on the scrap heap (*zum alten Eisen*).[343] An understanding with England may have been the foreign office's ultimate goal, but scarcely any consideration was given to the possibility that Germany's "free hand" might be lost in a few years. There was as yet little serious alarm as to Germany's security and still less feeling that a new orientation of her policy might be necessary. If the Social Democrats and a part of liberal opinion favored an understanding with one or both of the Western powers, they were influenced more by general considerations than by a sense of impending dangers. Among the Conservatives and nationalists, the affirmation of Germany's military power was becoming the characteristic reaction to foreign dangers, a point of view that discouraged the serious consideration of a new foreign policy. "Confident in her power and preparedness and in the support of her reliable allies," wrote the *Post* (March 26, 1899), "Germany can quietly watch the course of events."

---

[341] William II's comments, Münster, March 22, 1899. *G. P.*, XIV, 423–425. *Cf.* the impressions of the *Kölnische Zeitung's* (March 24) Paris correspondent. Bülow, less indifferent, offered Germany's support to Italy if she would attempt to block the Anglo-French agreement. *G. P.*, XIV, 436 (April 29).

[342] *G. P.*, XIV, 535, 536 (April 17, 1899).

[343] *Historisch-Politische Blätter*, vol. 123, p. 606 (April 12, 1899).

CHAPTER IX

Weltpolitik and European Reactions, 1899-1903

So günstig für Deutschland liegen die Verhältnisse nicht.
Und deshalb wird eines Tages der Entschluss, ob mit, ob
gegen England, eben gefasst werden müssen.
K. Kron, *Der Transvaalkrieg und die Reichspolitik,* Vienna, 1899, p. 20.

Das Wort von der 'Politik der verpassten Gelegenheiten,'
und von der 'Politik der Verbeugungen' macht die Runde
durch ganz Deutschland und ist bereits zu einem geflügelten
geworden.
Alldeutsche Blätter, July 11, 1903.

I

Imperialism brought important changes in Germany's outlook
in foreign affairs. Still content with her diplomatic and territorial status in Europe, with respect to her world interests she
was thoroughly dissatisfied. Her diplomatic relations with other
powers reflected this change. Generally speaking, their interests
could no longer be used as easily as in Bismarck's time to advance
those of Germany, since the aims of her *Weltpolitik* could usually
be attained only at their expense. Some friction was therefore
inevitable, but many, confident of Germany's military and diplomatic strength, were aware of no compelling need to keep this
friction at a minimum. The dislike and hostility which were
arising on all sides gave them little concern; would not the
differences between England, Russia, and France prevent a coalition?[1] No one seemed to remember that the same argument

---

[1] "Ob man hasst uns oder liebt," wrote Holstein, April 22, 1899, "darauf kommt es
nicht viel an, denn bei der heutigen komplizierten Weltpolitik möchte keine von den
beiden grossen Interessengroupen Deutschland gegen sich haben—weder die Eng-
länder noch die Russen." Holstein, *Lebensbekenntnis,* p. 193.

had been advanced in regard to France and Russia. There was no lack of irritation at the unfavorable attitude of world opinion, which by many observers was attributed to England's control of the cables, to the wide influence of her newspapers, and to the biased reports of the American Associated Press. Only the Social Democrats blamed the issues and methods of German foreign policy. Convinced of the justice of Germany's claim to a larger place in the world, most Germans felt that the world should adjust itself to the necessary changes. The circumstances could scarcely have been less favorable for the solution of the main problem of German foreign policy: the selection of the moment to abandon the "free hand" and to choose between England and Russia.

The problem was by no means pressing in 1899. Since there was no immediate danger of a hostile coalition, Germany apparently risked little in pushing her interests at the expense of England and Russia. It was against the former that she first acted after the Anglo-American bombardment of Apia in the Samoan Islands, March 15–17, 1899. To obtain the undivided control of these islands—the birthplace of German imperialism—or a high price for the surrender of her share had been a lesser aim of German policy and among the principal aspirations of German public opinion since the agreement of 1889 dividing the control between England, Germany, and the United States. England had been approached more than once without result,[2] and it was doubtless to obtain her purposes indirectly that Germany supported the claims of the pretender in a civil war against the puppet king who enjoyed the favor of England and the United States. The destruction of German property during the bombardment furnished a convenient excuse. Since the American government expressed its official regrets in the note of March 31, whereas Salisbury denied that British guns had destroyed any Germany property,[3] Germany's wrath was concentrated against England—partly because of mounting irritation at the disappointing results of the agreement for the partition of the Portuguese

---

[2] G. P., XIII, 37–39 (Aug. 21, 1897). Cf. Brandenburg, From Bismarck to the World War, p. 125.
[3] G. P., XIV, 622.

colonies and at England's indifference to her colonial aspirations elsewhere.

From London, Hatzfeldt wisely but vainly advised against unsupported threats.[4] Nor did the Anglo-French accord of March 21, arising from the Fashoda crisis, exert a restraining influence. William, so England was informed, would remain friendly only if a prompt and satisfactory solution were found,[5] and Bülow, with the Emperor's consent, even instructed Hatzfeldt to break off diplomatic relations unless England agreed to the dispatch of an arbitrator to Samoa with power to arrange the differences between the representatives of the three powers.[6] There was undoubtedly strong support in Germany for a firm stand.[7] When the Conservative *Standard* (April 5) spoke of the "taunting, threatening" attitude of the German press, the Conservative *Post* (April 9) denounced its insolence (*hochtrabener Ton*) and said that the time had long since passed when England could deal as she pleased with a weakened and divided Germany. The leaders of every party group in the Reichstag, except the Social Democrats, signed an interpellation by Lehr, the business manager of the Pan-German League. All disapproved, however, when he spoke of the League's aims as the proper objectives of German foreign policy,[8] and Bülow's statement that Germany intended to defend her treaty rights while respecting those of other powers was generally applauded.[9] Salisbury, who may have expected an ultimatum, likewise yielded something, perhaps under the pressure of Germany's opposition in the Egyptian Debt Commission: on April 15, the day after the Reichstag debate, he agreed that the Samoan commission's decisions should require a unanimous vote.[10]

Despite Cecil Rhodes' cordial reception in Berlin and William's

---

[4] *G. P.*, XIV, 594 (April 1).

[5] Bülow, April 1. *Ibid.*, XIV, 590–592.

[6] *Ibid.*, XIV, 601, 602 (April 11).

[7] The restlessness of German opinion was cited more than once as a reason for a favorable settlement. Bülow, April 1. *Ibid.*, XIV, 590–592; Lascelles, March 24. *B. D.*, I, 111.

[8] The nationalist *Münchener Neueste Nachrichten* denounced this repudiation of Lehr's chauvinism as a "shameful exhibition." *Post*, April 18.

[9] *Verhandlungen*, X Leg. Per., I Sess., II, 1754–1759 (April 14).

[10] Oncken, *Vorgeschichte des Weltkrieges*, II, 492, 493.

friendliness to the Cape-to-Cairo project,[11] the Samoan question remained for months a source of friction. Hope of England's generosity declined still further. Chamberlain, it was said, had lost interest in an Anglo-German alliance.[12] "The policy of the German Empire," he wrote to Salisbury, September 18, 1899, "has always been one of undisguised blackmail." [13]　The German foreign office was more certain than ever of Salisbury's systematic hostility. On its advice, William had omitted, during the Fashoda crisis, a mild criticism of Muraviev in a telegram to the Tsar, but Bülow did not object when the Emperor attacked the British Prime Minister in a personal letter to Queen Victoria, charging him with incivility toward Germany. Salisbury's attitude, he wrote, had the effect of "an electric shock" upon the German people; it had given the impression that he "cares for us no more than for Portugal, Chili, or the Patagonians." Germany's "national Honour" and "self-respect," said William, were involved.[14]　Nor did these indiscretions appear only in William's private correspondence, for he asked Lascelles to "tell your people to behave themselves," [15] and then cancelled his visit to Cowes.[16]　Had it not been for his grandmother's refusal to take offense, and especially for the increasing tension in South Africa, William's letter might have had more serious consequences than Victoria's mild reproof.[17]

Meanwhile, Germany's methods caused resentment elsewhere, especially in Russia. When Nicholas (Aug. 1898), hoping to avoid the sacrifices necessary if Russia were to keep pace with Germany's new artillery, astonished the world with his proposal of a conference for the limitation of armaments, German public opinion was not wholly displeased. The Social Democrats and liberals looked forward hopefully, in spite of their normal suspicion of all things Russian, to a relief from increasing military burdens, while others took pleasure in the manifest chagrin of the

---

[11] G. P. Gooch, *History of Modern Europe* (N. Y., 1923), p. 303.
[12] Hatzfeldt, April 22. *G. P.*, XIV, 612, 613.
[13] Garvin, *Chamberlain*, III, 334.
[14] *G. P.*, XIV, 615, 616. Here dated May 22, this letter is printed as of May 27 in *Letters of Queen Victoria*, (3), III, 375–379.
[15] Lascelles, May 26. *B. D.*, I, 117, 118.
[16] Oncken, *Vorgeschichte des Weltkrieges*, II, 494.
[17] Victoria, June 12. *G. P.*, XIV, 620, 621.

French nationalists.[18] If the thought of surrendering the nation's liberty of action was no more attractive to her leaders than to those of other countries, it was not certain that the conference would ever meet, and, at any rate, the diplomats understood at first the desirability of permitting some other country to assume the responsibility for its failure.[19] Germany therefore agreed to attend, although she delayed the appointment of her delegation until the last moment.[20] To William his cousin's initiative was a blow at Germany's security; if he promised to participate in the *"Conferenzkomödie,"* he would appear sword at his side. Bülow's caution unfortunately had no effect upon Germany's attitude at the Hague. While the other powers were chiefly interested in the use that could be made of the conference for their foreign policies, that was not an adequate reason why Germany should block the serious consideration of armament limitation. She emerged definitely the loser; if her part in the failure of the conference had apparently no serious effect upon her relations with Russia, it undoubtedly injured her with world opinion.

Of greater concern to the Russians were Germany's increasing influence at Constantinople, where Marschall von Bieberstein had already succeeded in weakening England's position, and the progress of the Berlin-Bagdad Railway. In view of the recent efforts to conciliate Russia, the foreign office naturally was at first reluctant to support Marchall's ambitious plans in the Near East.[21] Even after Bismarck's fall, Germany had continued to affirm her lack of interests there and her support of Russia's ambitions in the Straits and in Constantinople. By 1899 a significant change had occurred in German policy. William had advertised his warm approval of the enterprises of the *Deutsche Bank* by his visits to the Near East in 1889 and 1898. At Damascus, in November 1898, he said that the Mohammedans had no better friend than Germany. No other phase of German imperialism was more popular than economic expansion in the

[18] *Vossische Zeitung, Freisinnige Zeitung, Berliner Zeitung,* in *Post,* Aug. 31, 1898.
[19] Bülow, Aug. 26, 1898. *G. P.,* XV, 146. Cf. *Kölnische Volkszeitung,* in *Post,* Aug. 31.
[20] H. Wehberg's Memorandum, in *Die Vorgeschichte des Weltkrieges im Auftrage des Ersten Unterausschusses* (E. Fischer, et al., eds.) V, (2), (Berlin, 1929), p. 8.
[21] W. Becker, *Fürst Bülow und England, 1897–1909* (Greifswald, 1929), p. 8.

Near East. Russia's attitude made little impression upon the liberals and Catholics, who had always stood for a firm resistance to her advance in the Balkans and against a diplomatic association with her, and the Pan-Germans were frankly eager for the expansion of Germany's political influence into Asia Minor. The diplomats tried to remain on good terms with Russia and, at the same time, to advance Germany's new interests. While negotiating for the railway concession from Konia to Bagdad and beyond (Dec. 22, 1899), they assured Russia that it was a question merely of the economic penetration of Asia Minor and Mesopotamia, a non-political enterprise to which she could not legitimately object.[22] Russia, nevertheless, was justified in refusing to accept this explanation, for it was reasonable to believe that economic penetration was soon to lead to political influence. She refused to be appeased even by definite assurances as late as April 1899 of Germany's consent to her control of Constantinople and of the adjacent territory; Germany's interests were too clearly becoming identified with a strong Turkey. To test Germany's good faith, the Russians proposed a delimitation of spheres of influence and a formal assurance of Germany's support of Russia's exclusive control of the Straits. While England's certain objection was itself sufficient to insure Berlin's refusal, the foreign office could not accept without imposing undesirable limitations upon its new policy. William was highly incensed at Russia's presumption. "How very kind and generous!" was his comment. "So must Nicholas I have spoken to Frederick William IV! But not to me! Heels together and stiff as a ramrod, Herr Muraviev, when you speak to the German Emperor!" [23] The Near East had become a source of serious friction with Russia.

It was perhaps not a coincidence that Russia agreed at this time to strengthen her alliance with France and to narrow the range of her differences with England in China. At the end of April 1899, Russia promised not to seek any railway concessions in the Yangtze Valley in return for a similar promise by England in

[22] Bülow, May 14, 1899. *G. P.*, XV, 196, and William's comments.
[23] William II's comments, Radolin, June 29, 1899. *Ibid.*, XIV, 554. Holstein presented the same arguments against Russia's offers as he had against the renewal of the Reinsurance Treaty in 1890. Becker, *Bülow und England*, p. 11.

Auf der russischen Bärenjagd.

Kladderadatsch, September 16, 1900.

Figure 17.—Diplomacy in Bismarck's footsteps.

regard to the region north of the Great Wall. This arrangement apparently left Germany indifferent, since she continued unmoved her invasion of Russia's historic preserves. The Conservative *Post's* comments were enlightening. Although it had been one of the few journals to sense the possibilities of the Anglo-French agreement (March 21, 1899), it now (May 14) chided those who were alarmed by the Anglo-Russian accord, on the ground that it would be powerless to remove the fundamental antagonism between the two countries. "This," it concluded, "is intended for the pessimists who prophesy catastrophe from every political incident in Europe." Russia, nevertheless, continued to strengthen her diplomatic position in view of the change in Germany's Near-Eastern policy. Believing that the existence of Austria-Hungary was threatened by the nationalist agitation among her subject peoples and fearful that the breakup of the Dual Monarchy would be followed by Germany's absorption of Austria, Delcassé hastened to St. Petersburg (Aug. 1899), and persuaded the willing Russians to agree that the duration of the military alliance should henceforth depend upon the diplomatic understanding between the two countries rather than upon the existence of the Triple Alliance and that the maintenance of the balance of power should be one of its purposes. Not until after the World War did these significant changes become generally known, but it was reasonably obvious at the time that Germany's diplomatic situation had been weakened. Italy's unreliability, for example, was no secret. "It is scarcely worth the trouble," wrote a Catholic observer as early as 1897, "to speak of her as a member of the Triple Alliance." [24] If the commercial treaty of November 1898 bringing the Franco-Italian tariff war to an end was received with favorable comments, [25] it was doubtless the result of official influence, for the removal of one of the most solid guarantees of Italy's loyalty to the Triple Alliance would otherwise have scarcely occasioned satisfaction. More illuminating for the attitude of public opinion were the multiplying charges of inefficiency directed against the conduct of Germany's foreign policy. Maximilian Harden was especially caustic. Something was

---

[24] *Historisch-Politische Blätter,* vol. 119, pp. 114, 115.
[25] *Allgemeine Zeitung,* Nov. 29, 1898; *Post,* Dec. 2, 1898.

wrong, he said, when Bülow's witticisms were celebrated as great victories. "The people no longer have confidence in the foreign policy of their leaders; there is no clear orientation, no assurance that the helm is in firm hands." [26] Public opinion, it was said, was not adequately informed as to the government's purposes.[27] "A certain nervousness has unfortunately appeared in recent years . . . ," wrote the Conservative *Post* (Oct. 21, 1899) "instead of the quiet confidence with which the German people once watched the doings of their leaders."

II

In October 1899, the beginning of hostilities in South Africa restored to Germany the advantages which had been compromised by her recent differences with England and Russia. To a certain extent, the Boer War placed in her hands the control of England's relations with the continental powers, since Germany's attitude would determine the success or failure of any attempt to mediate or to intervene. For the moment England had taken Germany's place as the object of almost universal dislike. Events had again apparently proved the justice of her calculations. Like the Fashoda crisis, the Boer War seemed to show that England's difficulties would eventually compel her to sue for Germany's good-will and to pay a high price for it. The German diplomats, however, had no hand in the development of this extraordinarily favorable situation. They had even advised President Kruger, through the Dutch government, to make enough concessions in the *Uitlander* question so that it would be difficult for England to precipitate war.[28] Clearly Germany had no interest in making good her abandonment of the Boers until the moment for the partition of the Portuguese colonies arrived.

How to capitalize the war for Germany's profit was the fundamental question. The situation offered a variety of possibilities: the hope of sharing the booty of the Portuguese colonial empire might be sacrificed in favor of coöperation with Russia and

26 Harden, "Chromotrop," *Zunkunft*, April 15, 1899.
27 *Berliner Börsen-Courier*, in *Post*, April 16, 1899.
28 Wüd, *Rolle der Burenrepubliken*, pp. 124, 126, 129 (May 11, 12, July 4, Aug. 31, 1899).

France in striking a mortal blow at England, England's friendship might be sought by preventing a continental league, or her
difficulties might be used for the benefit of Germany's imperialist
ambitions. In any case, the government's choice was to be determined by Germany's interests. Even before the outbreak of
hostilities Bülow directed that the press should avoid the emotional sympathies for the underdog, which had embarrassed the
government during the Spanish-American War,[29] although he
later discovered that anti-English sentiment might be useful. German opinion was, however, too strongly aroused in favor of the
Boers for its reactions to be determined wholly by official influence. Nothing in the *Kladderadatsch* or the *Simplicissimus* perhaps equalled the vulgarity of the Parisian *Rire's* caricatures of
Queen Victoria and Prince Edward, but they were just as bitter.
To the denunciations of the nationalists and Conservatives was
added the possibly more disinterested disapprobation of England's friends. Even the Social Democrats desired her defeat,
unless a Liberal government with a peace program should be
organized.[30] The military operations were followed as if Germany's own armies were in the field, and the first victories of the
Boers were celebrated as if they had been won by German arms.[31]
Because England's success would prevent the expansion of Germany's colonial possessions in South Africa, the Pan-Germans asserted in an appeal for funds that the Boers were "shedding their
blood in our interest."[32] The government at once minimized
this current of opinion as a harmless expression of German sentimentality.[33] Bülow soon protested that Saunders, the Berlin
correspondent of the *Times,* was misrepresenting German opinion in his dispatches by culling extremist statements from obscure journals.[34] Saunders, however, was not withdrawn, nor
did he change the character of his reports. Not only did he

---

[29] *G. P.,* XV, 395, 396 (Sept. 20, 1899).

[30] *Vorwärts,* Dec. 16, 1899.

[31] Monts, Munich, Nov. 2, 1899. Monts, *Erinnerungen,* p. 390; *P. J.,* vol. 98, p.
586 (Dec. 1899); O. Umfried, "Intervention und Gefühlspolitik," *Gegenwart,* March
10, 1900.

[32] *A. B.,* Nov. 5, 1899.

[33] *Tägliche Rundschau,* March 9, 1900; P. Rohrbach, *Deutschland unter den Welt-
volken* (Berlin, 1903), p. 130.

[34] *G. P.,* XV, 412, 413, 415 (Nov. 15, 24, 1899); Bülow, *Denkwürdigkeiten,* I,
318, 319.

stand his ground against the *Post's* attack but he also frankly acknowledged that his purpose had been to show "that the hostility of the German press to the British Empire is not a thing of yesterday . . . but that it has been of long standing and of great persistence and rancour." [35] The press, he said, "simply expresses the feelings and aspirations not of some but of all classes of the community, except, I presume, those directly responsible for the conduct of foreign policy." [36] However biased Saunders may have been, Germany's own leaders admitted his substantial accuracy. The Emperor did not hesitate to speak to Queen Victoria of the hatred which the German people felt for England, attributing it to the " 'poison' which Bismarck poured into the ears of the people." [37] Bülow was even more forthright: "It is doubtless true that, in general, English sentiment is much less anti-German than German sentiment is anti-English. Those Englishmen are therefore the most dangerous who, like Chirol and Saunders, know from their own observation the sharpness and depth of the German antipathy to England. If the English public were fully aware of the dominant sentiment in Germany, a great change would occur in its views in regard to Anglo-German relations." [38] While nothing would have been more welcome than England's defeat, not even the most ardent partisans of the Boers expected or desired the government to contribute to it. The most hotheaded fire-eater recognized that Germany could not afford, with her small fleet, to risk a war with the dominant naval power. "Far be it from us," wrote the official organ of the Pan-German League, "to demand a policy for which we lack the necessary support. . . ." [39] Spokesmen of the Bismarckian tradition warned against the folly of completely alienating England, since the broken ties with Russia would never be completely repaired. [40] For a long time there was scarcely any

---

[35] *Times*, Oct. 17, 1899, Berlin, Oct. 16. Saunders was violently attacked by the German press in the spring of 1900. *Kölnische Zeitung, Hamburger Nachrichten, Leipziger Tageblatt,* in *Post*, April 15, 1900.

[36] *Times*, Nov. 11, Berlin, Nov. 10.

[37] Journal, Nov. 21. *Letters of Queen Victoria* (3), III, 421.

[38] *G. P.*, XV, 419 (Nov. 24, 1899).

[39] *A. B.*, Oct. 8, 1899.

[40] *Hamburger Nachrichten*, in *N. A. Z.*, Oct. 12, 1899; K. Kron, *Russland oder England? Ein Mahnruf* (Vienna, 1900), pp. 23, 24.

discussion and still less approval of common action with Russia and France. The Conservative *Post* (Sept. 14, 29, Oct. 8, Nov. 19, 1899) repeatedly cited the indifference of these powers as an unanswerable argument in favor of neutrality.[41] It was therefore with the support of public opinion that the government rejected the opportunity to deal England a fatal blow. Although the anti-English trend of opinion was used to emphasize the value of Germany's friendship and to win popular support for additional naval construction, Germany never diverged from a policy of strict neutrality. England had achieved the essential purpose for which she had concluded the agreement for the partition of the Portuguese colonial empire.

As to the reward for this valuable service, there was little difference of opinion. A diplomatic rapprochement was clearly out of the question; while the diplomats still felt that the moment for it had not yet arrived, an association with the despoiler of the Transvaal would have scandalized the most sincere of England's friends. The Germans were almost unanimous in feeling that England should at last show a generous comprehension of their colonial needs. For the officials and doubtless the imperialists, it was a question of the price that she might be forced or persuaded to pay. Bülow had strongly insisted on the eve of the war that the press should not give the impression that Germany wished "to exploit England's hour of need for her own profit," but he felt that it would be a stupid blunder not to make use of the opportunity for a favorable settlement of the Samoan problem and of other questions.[42] The *Kölnische Zeitung* indiscreetly revealed the general direction of German policy when it explained, to Saunders' great indignation, that Germany's freedom of action would be used "to serve such purposes as are proportionate to her power." If this was to be Germany's official attitude, "the British answer to such a challenge would," wrote the correspondent of the *Times*, "ring out clearly enough for the whole world to hear. . . ."[43] Bülow, who was rightfully confident that the British foreign office would take a more realistic

---

[41] Cf. *Freisinnige Zeitung*, Oct. 4, 1899; *Vorwärts*, Oct. 13.
[42] *G. P.*, XV, 396 n. (Sept. 21, 1899).
[43] *Times*, Oct. 20, 1899, Berlin, Oct. 19.

view of the situation, pressed upon Salisbury with extraordinary vehemence the German solution of the Samoan question as the only way to restore good relations and to secure Germany's friendship.[44] Even Saunders saw the point, for he reluctantly admitted "that the pacification of the German Press by an acceleration of the Samoa negotiations would be desirable." To William's intense irritation, Salisbury delayed in coming to terms, but Chamberlain finally abandoned his support of the Australians and the New Zealanders who opposed Germany's claim. After Germany's refusal of the first offer of other islands in the Pacific and of a generous slice of West Africa, the colonial minister finally approved a compromise sacrificing England's share of the Samoans in return for compensations in the Solomon and Tonga groups, the surrender of Germany's extra-territorial rights in Zanzibar, and a share of the neutral zone between Germany's Togoland and the British Gold Coast.[45]

Because the public announcement of the main terms of this agreement coincided with the Tsar's visit to Berlin, the English tried to give the impression that a diplomatic rapprochement had occurred. Salisbury affirmed publicly "that at the present moment our relations with the German people are all that could be desired."[46] The Germans at once hastened to explain that the settlement of the Samoan question in no way affected their relations with Russia. Germany's hands were still free.[47] Although the *Times* (Nov. 13) was irritated by the claim that Germany had agreed to nothing but the settlement of specific questions, the general reaction in both countries was favorable. In England those who grumbled at the price also appreciated Germany's neutrality.[48] Even the colonial office was satisfied that England had received at least as much as she had given.[49] In Germany, the long-delayed acquisition of "the firstborn of her colonial policy" aroused a degree of enthusiasm which, according to the ultra-Conservative *Reichsbote* (Nov. 10), was entirely dispropor-

---

44 Salisbury, Oct. 6; Lascelles, Oct. 10, 1899. *B. D.,* I, 125–127.
45 Garvin, *Chamberlain*, III, 324 f.
46 *Standard*, Nov. 10, 1899.
47 *Reichsbote, Berliner Tageblatt*, Nov. 9.
48 *Standard, Daily News*, Nov. 9; *Daily Chronicle*, Nov. 11.
49 Garvin, *Chamberlain*, III, 341.

tionate to its value. The Pan-Germans and others truthfully but tactlessly stressed the services of the Boers in bringing the English to reason,[50] but the view more generally held was that the elimination of friction between two countries would diminish the dangers arising from the anti-English tone of public opinion.[51]

On November 20, 1899, William, accompanied by Bülow, arrived in England, giving that visible demonstration of Germany's neutrality for which Chamberlain had yielded in the Samoan question. Although the Liberal *Daily News* (Nov. 20) acclaimed the visit as a tacit confession that Germany needed England's friendship, it was more characteristic of the prevailing opinion that the *Saturday Review* was as friendly as it had once been hostile. A better understanding of Germany's virtues would, it wrote (Nov. 25), lessen her unpopularity. "We say this in the belief that Germany is destined to play no mean part in the development of Africa and the East, and that Great Britain would do better work with her than against her." To the greater part of the German press a diplomatic association was, however, utterly unacceptable.[52] The official assurances that the visit was only a courtesy call were powerless to silence those who felt that the government had betrayed national sentiment.[53] Not a few Conservatives insisted for once that a greater consideration should be shown for public opinion,[54] while the liberals, reversing their usual point of view, applauded the decision to ignore it.[55] In London, William referred more than once to the attitude of German opinion. To Chamberlain he denied that it would be a barrier to further negotiations. "I am," he said, "the sole master of German policy and my country must follow me wherever I go." He was ready to tell all who would listen that "he was himself German public opinion and the Germans think the way he wishes them to think."[56] At the same time, he urged England in her own interest to show consideration for the "sensi-

[50] *A. B.*, Nov. 19, 1899. *Cf.* E. Bauer, *England und das Deutsche Reich; eine Abrechnung zur Jahrhundertwende* (Leipzig, 1900), pp. 33, 34.

[51] *Freisinnige Zeitung*, Nov. 9; *Berliner Neueste Nachrichten, Frankfurter Zeitung, Vossische Zeitung, Berliner Tageblatt, Hannoversche Zeitung,* in *N. A. Z.,* Nov. 10.

[52] *Vossische Zeitung,* in *Post,* Nov. 22.

[53] *Kreuz-Zeitung,* Nov. 15; *National Zeitung,* Nov. 17.

[54] *Reichsbote,* Nov. 11.

[55] *Berliner Tageblatt,* Nov. 19.

[56] Bülow, *Denkwürdigkeiten,* I, 317, 318 (Nov. 22, 1899).

tive, dogmatic and distinctly sentimental Germans. . . ." [57] William paid almost as little attention to the advice of the German foreign office as to the reactions of public opinion. While Holstein deprecated any political discussion on the ground that Salisbury could not be moved from his preconceived opinion that Germany demanded too much for her friendship and that Chamberlain was interested solely in enlisting Germany's aid against Russia, the Emperor stressed the value of Germany's neutrality and referred to the many points upon which the two countries could agree. [58]

In spite of the unfavorable verdict of public opinion, Germany had to this point played her cards to fairly good advantage. England had already yielded in one question. Unfortunately, the imperialists had far-reaching (though essentially vague) ideas as to what her contribution to Germany's greatness should be, a contribution that England, distracted as she was by her difficulties with France and Russia and by the Boer War, was still unwilling to make. The officials, however, were not unreasonable. They knew that England's conversion to the desired state of mind would take time. If much was expected from the new naval program which was taking shape during the summer of 1899, they were content for the moment with what were, in their opinion, modest requests. England was not to be driven too far, for fear that she might attack before Germany could defend herself. Tirpitz had already insisted that an anti-English policy was an impossibility until "we have a fleet equal to England's." [59] The extravagant aims of the Pan-Germans and of other extremists were not a reliable index to the official policy. Instead of yielding to the anti-English opinion, Bülow even gave the impression during the visit to England that he was interested in a diplomatic rapprochement. He was, however, extremely vague. He talked of England's need of Germany's friendship and of his own desire for Chamberlain's aid in improving German-American relations, but when the colonial minister mentioned the partition of Morocco and coöperation in the construction of the Bagdad Railway

[57] Bülow, Nov. 24. *G. P.*, XV, 413, 414.
[58] Bülow, *Denkwürdigkeiten*, I, 311, 312.
[59] Hohenlohe, *Denkwürdigkeiten aus der Reichskanzlerzeit*, 464 (Oct. 24, 1898).

as the basis of an understanding, he remained silent.[60]   Although his emphasis upon Germany's good relations with Russia was a further reason for skepticism, Chamberlain, as he always maintained thereafter, understood that Bülow would welcome a public demonstration of England's friendship.   On November 30, within twenty-four hours after the departure of her guests, the colonial minister spoke at Leicester of Germany as England's natural ally and of an understanding between England, the United States, and Germany that was "perhaps better than an alliance." [61]

The speech evoked a storm of protest in Germany.   Never, wrote the Conservative *Kreuz-Zeitung* (Dec. 1), had public sentiment been equally aroused.   "With an unscrupulous, grasping, and dishonorable policy like that of England in South Africa," affirmed the Conservative *Reichsbote* (Dec. 3), "no alliance or general understanding is possible, only definitely limited negotiations. . . ."   "The Liberal and Radical German Press," reported Saunders of the *Times* (Dec. 2), ". . . reads Mr. Chamberlain a terrible lecture." [62]   The London press hastened to say that England's interest in a formal alliance was no greater than Germany's and that what Chamberlain had spoken of was merely an understanding on specific questions.[63]   By playing up this point of view, the official newspapers succeeded in moderating the first explosion.   No one, it was said, would object to the recognition of the value of Germany's friendship or to the existence of friendly relations, in so far as they were compatible with Germany's interests. "If Herr Chamberlain," wrote the Conservative *Kreuz-Zeitung* (Dec. 6), "wishes to call the absence of differences an entente, we have no objection, but it is under no circumstances an alliance." This incident showed that it was within the government's power to restrain the more extreme expression of anti-English sentiment. It was in fact a commonplace that German policy should be determined by national interests rather than by sentiment,[64] but one

---

[60] See p. 486.

[61] Garvin, *Chamberlain*, III, 507, 508.

[62] *Cf.* Bauer, *England und das Deutsche Reich*, pp. 39, 40.

[63] This is the gist of clippings from the *Daily News, Daily Chronicle*, and *Times*, in the *N. A. Z.*, Dec. 2.

[64] M. von Brandt, "Die Transvaalfrage vom deutschen Standpunkte," *Deutsche Revue*, vol. 24, pp. 369, 370 (Dec. 1899); *National Zeitung*, Dec. 3; *Kreuz-Zeitung*, Dec. 6.

of these national interests was the enlistment of public opinion for the new naval bill, whose principal terms had already been announced. For this purpose, the maintenance of bad feeling toward England was desirable and useful. There was much truth in the Social Democratic *Vorwärts'* argument that the case for naval increases would be ridiculous if friendly relations existed. "The adventurers of *Weltpolitik*," it wrote (Dec. 4), "would convince no one by their talk of a blockade, of starvation, and of overpopulation without the assumption of an irreconcilable economic and political conflict with England. Except for this, there would be no excuse for a new naval bill." Bülow, therefore, ignored Chamberlain's Leicester speech and adopted an almost hostile attitude in his survey of foreign affairs to the Reichstag, December 11. His reference to Germany's colonial aspirations contained a warning. "In any event," he declared, "we cannot permit any foreign power, any foreign Jupiter to tell us: 'What can be done? The world is already partitioned.' We do not wish to offend any power, but we will not permit anyone to tread on our toes. . . ." He spoke then of Germany's desire to live with England in peace and friendship on terms of complete reciprocity and of the need of a fleet to resist an attack from "any power." [65] In England, Chamberlain felt himself the victim of an unscrupulous deception; he "had been made," he wrote, "to pull the chestnut out of the fire for him [Bülow]." [66] Although England's interests compelled him to accept this rebuff in silence, he decided to drop the idea of an alliance, "at least for the duration of the war." [67] Because neither country wished to drive the other too far, the official relations were not so strained as these incidents and the state of public opinion might suggest, but Bülow's speech was a reminder that Germany must be reckoned with when the famous "Black Week" brought a succession of disasters to British arms in South Africa.

Scarcely a fortnight passed before England's detention of the German postal steamers, the "Bundesrat" (Dec. 28) and the *General* (Jan. 8, 1900) raised the question of Germany's legal rights

---

[65] *Verhandlungen*, X Leg. Per., I Sess., IV, 3293.
[66] Garvin, *Chamberlain*, III, 512 (Dec. 12).
[67] *Ibid.*, III, 513 (Dec. 28).

and revealed England's lack of confidence in the loyalty of her neutrality. Anti-English sentiment mounted to new heights as the negotiations for the release of these ships dragged along, with Bülow himself noting, prophetically, that the rights of neutral commerce might become a life-and-death question for Germany in a future war. The government, nevertheless, refrained from measures that would have definitely alienated England. It agreed that the disposition of the ships should be settled by direct negotiations rather than by arbitration, as it had first proposed. What was more important for England, it rejected Russia's proposals for intervention by the continental powers, even in the face of England's coolness to the hint that the cession of Zanzibar would assure Germany's consent to the occupation of Delagoa Bay—a step that would cut the Transvaal's communication with the outside world. On January 12, 1900, while indignation against England was still at its peak, Bülow evaded Muraviev's questions as to Germany's intentions if the occupation occurred, suggesting that France was more directly concerned than Germany, in view of the proximity of Madagascar.[68] His reply foreshadowed the general direction of German policy. When Russia at last (March 3, 1900) formally proposed the joint mediation of the powers, after England's first important victory, Bülow named France's explicit acceptance of her eastern frontier for a period of years as the essential condition for Germany's coöperation.[69] Germany's reply was, as England had already been informed, "an unmistakable negative," [70] for France was certain to refuse a demand which she was bound to consider as one for a second signing of the Treaty of Frankfort. Instead of the uncertainties of a continental league, Germany preferred the diplomatic advantages and the prospective profits of neutrality. The decision was, on the whole, in accord with the views of public opinion. The lead, according to one observer, should be Russia's.[71] As to France's attitude, Paul Deschanel's address on taking his chair in the *Académie Française* had been interpreted as convincing proof of the de-

[68] *G. P.*, XV, 506–508.
[69] *Ibid.*, XV, 516.
[70] Lascelles, Berlin, Feb. 16, 1900. *B. D.*, I, 130, 131.
[71] L. Lendschau, "Die Zukunft Südafrikas," *Gegenwart*, Feb. 5, 1900.

cline of moderation and of the vitality of the *revanche*.[72] Even the Pan-Germans did not object in principle to Germany's refusal to coöperate with England's enemies but only to the publicity given this decision. "England," declared their official organ, "will now be able to do anything she pleases." [73]

The mention of Zanzibar meant that the Samoan agreement should be merely the first payment for Germany's services. While Bülow hoped that England's statesmen would gradually appreciate their value, the Emperor hastened to call their attention to what Germany had done.[74] In 1898 William had informed Russia of England's advances; he now confided to England that Russia and France had proposed intervention and that Germany had refused. First he told the Prince of Wales that "Sundry Peoples" were "preparing to take liberties and foster intrigues and surprises," and then he informed the British ambassador that "I have kept those two tigers apart." [75] Nor did William's unprecedented concern for England's welfare stop with this important diplomatic service: he so far forgot his former sympathy with the Boers as to submit a long list of aphorisms to the British officials on the proper conduct of the war.[76] Having rejected the common front with the other continental powers, it was doubtless with some sincerity that Germany more than once assured England of her desire that she should emerge from the war with her strength unimpaired, since a strong England would be useful as a balance to Russia and France. Nevertheless, the English were not so favorably impressed as Berlin desired. If Prince Edward finally acknowledged that "William . . . wishes to be our true friend" and that "he indeed deserves our thanks and confidence," [77] Salisbury was, with some justification, less confident of Germany's good-will. The naval inferiority, which was mentioned in the unfavorable reply to France's proposal for diplomatic

---

[72] *National Zeitung, Post, Kölnische Zeitung,* Feb. 2; E. Richter, "Eine Kontinentalunion," *Gegenwart,* Feb. 17, 1900.

[73] *A. B.,* Feb. 18, 1900.

[74] *G. P.,* XV, 431 (Dec. 22, 1899).

[75] Lee, *Edward VII,* I, 768 (Feb. 23, 1900); Lascelles, March 2, 1900. *B. D.,* I, 253, 254.

[76] Lascelles, Feb. 9, 1900. *B. D.,* I, 249–252.

[77] *Letters of Queen Victoria,* (3), III, 499, 500 (March 5, 1900); *ibid..* (3) III, 527 (April 10, 1900).

coöperation, October 28, 1899,[78] would probably have given the leadership of a continental league to France and Russia. It was more significant that William to a certain extent encouraged Russia to attack India. According to his own account of a conversation with Osten-Sacken, the Russian ambassador, on January 13, 1900, during the excitement over the seizure of the "Bundesrat," he refused a proposal for a continental naval league, unless England should force him into it, and then promised Germany's neutrality in an Anglo-Russian war. The Russian ambassador, however, did not mention in his report his own proposal but rather stressed William's assurance that no other power would move if Russia should attack the British in India.[79] Although Professor Meinecke accepts the Russian diplomat's version,[80] the difference between the two reports is not, for present purposes, of great importance; for the promise of Germany's neutrality, the essential consideration from Russia's point of view, appears in both. Moreover, Osten-Sacken continued to believe after the conversation that Germany might still be won for a continental league.[81]

Among the influences that shaped German foreign policy during the Boer War, none was more effective than the decision to secure the Reichstag's approval for a new program of naval construction. Its ultimate objectives, like those of the first naval law, included the strengthening of Germany's value as an ally—her *Bündnisfähigkeit*—but for the present it prevented any real improvement in Anglo-German relations. Even if England ignored Germany's ambitious naval plans in order to safeguard herself against the danger of intervention, a close friendship with England would have strengthened the opposition in the Reichstag to the new naval bill, besides arousing nationalist sentiment against the government. The naval question also worked against coöperation with Russia and France; a continental league might cause England to destroy Germany's young fleet before it became a serious menace.

The navy had in fact become one of the government's chief

---

[78] William II, Oct. 29, 1899. *G. P.,* XV, 406–408.
[79] Bülow, Jan. 13, 1900. *Ibid.,* XV 509, 510; Osten Sacken, 6/19 Jan. 1900. Meyendorff, *Correspondance de M. de Staal,* II, 448, 449.
[80] Meinecke, *Geschichte des deutsch-englischen Bündnisproblems,* p. 156.
[81] Langer, *Diplomacy of Imperialism,* II, 664.

concerns. Under Tirpitz' influence, preparations for a new bill began soon after the enactment of the law of 1898. On April 30 of that year the Navy League was organized in Berlin under official auspices. Prince Henry of Prussia, the Emperor's brother, agreed to act as its sponsor, and Prince zu Hohenlohe-München, the Chancellor's son, was elected to its executive committee. The appointment of Victor Schweinburg, the business manager of the Nationalist *Berliner Neueste Nachrichten,* was equally significant of the forces behind the naval agitation, for this journal was owned by the Krupps.[82] Members of reigning families throughout Germany permitted the league to use their names. Decorations frequently rewarded services to the cause. With a minimum fee of fifty *pfennige,*[83] its membership soon far surpassed that of the Pan-German League and of the Colonial Society. Its aims had the support of almost all nationalist groups. The *Flotte,* its official organ, rapidly attained a circulation of hundreds of thousands. The Samoan affair, it was said, proved the need of a stronger fleet.[84] The Pan-Germans had earlier professed their satisfaction with a fleet designed for defensive purposes; the bombardment of Apia was followed by a barrage of telegrams from their local branches for one that would be capable of offensive operations.[85] Spain's defeat and France's retreat from Fashoda were accepted as warnings of the fate that awaited Germany unless she was prepared to defend her interests upon the seas.[86] While William was soon to repudiate German opinion in his conversations at Windsor (Nov. 20), he agreed with Tirpitz that the wave of anti-English sentiment would sweep aside the opposition to the naval bill and urged its prompt introduction into the Reichstag. Ten days after the beginning of hostilities in South Africa and only a month before his visit to England, William spoke at Hamburg (Oct. 18) of "a strong German fleet" as a "bitter necessity." As late as October 24 the *Norddeutsche* de-

[82] Kehr, *Schlachtflottenbau,* pp. 169, 170. Writing to Tirpitz, Prince Salm-Horstmar, the president of the Navy League, urged the passage of a new navy bill as a means of raising prices on the stock market. Hallgarten, *Vorkriegs Imperialismus,* p. 164.

[83] *Post,* May 3, 1898.

[84] *Ibid.,* April 16, 1899; *Allgemeine Zeitung,* April 18.

[85] *A. B.,* April 16.

[86] *Allgemeine Zeitung,* Nov. 9, 1898; Tirpitz, *Erinnerungen,* pp. 102–104.

nied that a new bill was impending and, two days later, Hohenlohe warned the Emperor that the reaction to his Hamburg
speech was too weak to secure a majority.[87]   On October 27 the
Post called for immediate action and the *Norddeutsche,* ignoring its recent denials, announced on the following day that the
government would ask for a fleet of forty battleships by 1917.

In spite of the immense propaganda machine, of the government's influence, and of the more intangible but nevertheless
powerful force of circumstances, the prospects for a favorable vote
were unfavorable.   The Centrists and the Progressives were at
first determined to vote with the Social Democrats, and these
groups, with the agrarian Conservatives, who disliked the emphasis which the naval program would place upon industry, controlled the Reichstag.[88]   Tirpitz was therefore overjoyed by England's seizure of the "Bundesrat."   In conference with the Emperor and the Chancellor when the news arrived, he proposed that
the British commanders should be decorated.   "Now," he cried,
"we have the wind that will blow our ships into port; the naval
bill will pass." [89]   William insisted that the bill should immediately be submitted to the Reichstag.[90]   There was, however, a more
complicated story behind its enactment.   Promises of protection
for their agricultural interests and for the digging of an important
canal in North Germany secured the votes of the Conservatives.[91]
The dread of a new election, the fear of losing the chance of securing a measure of power, and a sense of the futility of opposition resulted in the desertion of a fraction of the Center party,
while a few of the Progressives finally yielded to the glamor of
imperialism.   In the final vote, June 12, 1900, the opposition
numbered only one hundred and three against two hundred and
one.   A propaganda campaign of unparalleled intensity and
scope, a war in which Germany was not involved, a political bargain, and the inseparable connection between imperialism and
navalism carried the day for a program that would give Germany

[87] Hohenlohe, *Denkwürdigkeiten aus der Reichskanzlerzeit,* 534 (Oct. 26).
[88] Kehr, *Schlachtflottenbau,* pp. 182, 183.   *Cf.* a Berlin correspondent in the *Pall
Mall Gazette,* Feb. 9, 1900.
[89] Ziekursch, *Politische Geschichte,* III, 127.
[90] William II, Jan. 10, 1900.   Hohenlohe, *op. cit.,* 555, 556.
[91] Kehr, *op. cit.,* pp. 203, 204.

a fleet of thirty-eight battleships within twenty years. This total, judging by recent experience, might be increased on the plea of changed conditions; it would, in all probability, never be reduced.

The exact fulfilment of this program henceforth had the consent, if not the enthusiastic support, of the greater part of public opinion, although the later proposals for its increase always encountered bitter opposition. To what extent the Reichstag's approval of a greatly enlarged fleet, while maintaining the most powerful army in Europe, was the result of anti-English sentiment is difficult to say. It is, however, evident that domestic considerations exerted considerable influence. A large fleet had always been an article of faith on the part of the ardent imperialists. While the Conservatives drove a hard bargain, their conversion was partly the result of their sympathy with any increase in Germany's power and prestige. The nationalist point of view was also not without weight among the liberals. The naval question was only one of the vital issues on which they were unable to maintain a united front. For the National Liberals and the *Freisinnige Vereinigung,* the group which had seceded from the Progressives on the issue of the protective tariff, it was sufficient that the fleet added to Germany's power, although they were influenced by their strong anti-English sentiment. Under Eugen Richter's leadership, the majority of the Progressives expressed their hatred of *Machtpolitik,* their defense of the Reichstag's right to control the annual budget, their opposition to "limitless naval programs" by their hostile votes, but a minority was influenced by the party's early interest in a fleet. The first steps toward the creation of a German navy had in fact been taken by the Frankfort Parliament; and in Bismarck's time the Progressives had not included the navy in their systematic opposition to armament appropriations. The naval propagandists translated these general considerations in terms that were more easily understood by the general public. Evading the charges that the law of 1900, like that of 1898, would be followed by still larger requests and that Germany's overseas interests were threatened by no serious dangers,[92] they argued that a great fleet was a necessity for the de-

---

[92] *Freisinnige Zeitung, Vossische Zeitung,* in *N. A. Z.,* Oct. 31, 1899.

fense of her rapidly expanding foreign commerce, for protection against a *Verhungerungsblockade*,[93] and to secure her rightful share in the partition of colonial territory.[94] It was Tirpitz' desire that the naval program should be supported and carried out on its own merits, in order to reduce the danger of a premature clash with England. That the fleet was to be directed against England could not, however, be entirely concealed,[95] although this aspect of the question was ignored as much as possible. The government doubtless had no intention of challenging England's control of the seas in the sense of building up to or beyond her naval strength. She would, it was evident, sooner or later seek to maintain a safe margin by increasing her own rate of construction. While the opposition made good use of this point, it was fundamentally ineffective, because the experts believed that even a second-rate fleet would serve Germany's purposes. The famous "risk theory," which appeared in the memorandum accompanying the bill of 1900 and in the press,[96] assumed the existence of a sufficiently strong fleet to inflict such serious losses upon the most powerful navy that it would be at the mercy of a third power. England's need of protecting her imperial possessions and communications, it was agreed, would prevent the concentration of her entire fleet in the North Sea, so that the margin of her superiority would be less than it seemed on paper. Tirpitz, defending the bill in the Reichstag, left no doubt as to the enemy. Germany must be prepared for the "most dangerous naval war," and, while he denied that the fleet was intended for offensive purposes,[97] he defined its function as that of keeping the North Sea open in the event of war.[98] Therein lay a challenge to England's naval supremacy in waters which were essential to her security.

---

[93] *Deutsche Zeitung*, in *N. A. Z.*, Jan. 17, 1900; Montgelas' speech in Munich, *N. A. Z.*, March 9, 1900.

[94] *Bitter Noth ist uns eine starke deutsche Flotte; Gedanken eines Vaterlandfreundes* (Berlin, 1899); *National Zeitung*, Nov. 13, 1899; *A. B.*, June 11, 1899. William also stated this point of view in his New Year's speech to the officers of the Berlin garrison. *N. A. Z.*, Jan. 2, 1900.

[95] One pamphleteer frankly acknowledged that her humiliation was the government's secret purpose. P. J. Thiel, *Rache für Transvaal! Deutschlands Wehgeschrei und Zukunftsprogramm* (Elberfeld, 1900), pp. 19, 20.

[96] Tirpitz, *Erinnerungen*, p. 105; *Kölnische Zeitung*, Jan. 26; *Allgemeine Zeitung*, Jan. 27.

[97] See for the opposite view, the *Vorwärts* (Oct. 20, 1899) and the *Freisinnige Zeitung* (Oct. 20).

[98] *Verhandlungen*, X Leg. Per., I Sess., V, 3955, 4024 (Feb. 8, 9, 1900).

In spite of half-hearted attempts to moderate the more extreme forms of anti-English sentiment during the Boer War, that feeling was encouraged in the interest of the naval bill. The Conservative *Post* (Jan. 6, 1900) predicted the destruction of Germany's mercantile marine if the Reichstag failed to grant the government's request. "We must then," it wrote, "quietly permit a larger naval power to sink our merchant ships and to bombard our ports. . . ." By implication Bülow attributed aggressive designs to England in his argument to the finance committee of the Reichstag. He could no longer say, as he had two years before, that no danger of war existed,[99] or, according to his own account, describe the "risk navy" as the only reliable assurance of peace between the two countries.[100] Her attention absorbed by the war in South Africa, England took little heed of a program whose results would not make themselves felt for years.[101] She was, however, far from indifferent to the multiplying signs of Germany's ill-will. Although the *Times* accepted Germany's naval plans without visible alarm, it contained a warning. Englishmen, it wrote (March 7, 1900), had "learnt the truth in these past few months . . . and they will not readily forget the painful lesson. They may not say much about it, but they will reflect upon it, and they will frame their future acts and policy upon it." What England would do was a matter of serious concern to not a few Germans. Bebel, describing England as Germany's natural ally, raised a warning voice in the debate on the naval bill.[102] Germany, according to Delbrück, could either develop her world policy in agreement with England or against her. "With England—peace; against England—war." [103] There was, however, as yet little serious alarm, even when an understanding with Russia or with France was mentioned in the London press. "Any one who is not a dilettante in politics," wrote the Conservative *Post* (March 17, 1900), "will merely laugh at these schemes." Germany was prepared for all contingencies. "Confident in her

[99] E. von Heyking, *Tagebücher aus vier Weltteilen* (Leipzig, 1926), pp. 315, 316 (April 1, 1900) in Kehr, *Parteipolitik und Schlachtflottenbau*, p. 201.

[100] Bülow, *Denkwürdigkeiten*, I, 414.

[101] Woodward, *Great Britain and the German Navy*, pp. 48–51.

[102] *Verhandlungen*, X Leg. Per., I Sess., V, 4012, 4013 (Feb. 10, 1900).

[103] *P. J.*, vol. 98, pp. 588, 589 (Dec. 26, 1899).

strength," it affirmed, as it had a year earlier, "she can as always ward off all missiles from abroad."

III

The three years that followed the naval law of 1900 were decisive for the future of Anglo-German relations. During this period occurred Germany's failure to choose between Russia and England and England's decision to compose her differences with France. Anglo-German relations became increasingly difficult, not because of the naval law, although the Germans were mistaken in thinking that it would make their friendship more desirable, but because of a series of incidents precipitated by divergent diplomatic and imperialist interests and by the irascibility of leaders. No small part was played by Germany's diplomatic methods. There is little doubt that she misplayed her hand at almost every turn. The Boer War, the Anglo-Russian conflict in Asia, and the differences between England and France in Africa placed Germany in an extraordinarily favorable position, but its advantages were frittered away without proportionate gains. Samoa was a small return for saving England from the menace of a continental league, and there were those in England who regarded even that comparatively small sacrifice as blackmail. Germany quite legitimately refused to align herself with England against Russia in the Far East, but her efforts to advance her imperialist interests in China at England's expense eventually limited her freedom of action. She reasoned correctly that England had no other choice but to yield, but that country would not always be embarrassed by the South African War.

At first it seemed possible that China might become the basis of an understanding. Whatever their ultimate intentions may have been, England and Germany both stood for the "open door" and against her partition at the time of the Boxer Rebellion.[104] Germany's original intention of coöperating merely as one of the many intervening powers yielded to William's emotional reaction to the murder of von Ketteler, the German minister (June 19, 1900), and his desire that Germany should play the leading

---

[104] Bülow, June 30, 1900. *G. P.*, XVI, 25, 26

part. Had not events justified his views as to the Yellow Peril?
To his country's great misfortune, he instructed the German expeditionary force to make the German soldier as feared as the
Hun had been of old (July 27). His efforts to secure the supreme
command of the international army for a German general placed
him in a somewhat ridiculous position. After England's refusal
to propose Waldersee's name, he finally persuaded the Tsar to do
him this service, but Peking was actually relieved before Waldersee had even left Germany. Moreover, it was Russia's troops, not
Germany's, that led the way into the Chinese capital. This was
a small matter; but Russia's request for the consent of the powers
to the withdrawal of her contingent to Tientsin—in the interest
of her separate negotiations with China—gave serious offense to
the Emperor as an obstacle to the drastic punishment of China.
He now turned to England, although he had earlier refused her
suggestion that Japan be given an exclusive mandate to act in
behalf of the powers,[105] for a separate understanding.[106] He was
determined, he confided to the Prince of Wales, August 22, to
block Russia's plans for a "rotten peace," but a reference to Germany's commercial interests in the Yangtze Valley as second only
to those of England threw a flood of light upon his desire for an
Anglo-German agreement for the maintenance of the "open
door."[107]

If the British foreign office agreed to negotiate in the expectation that William's irritation would assure Germany's coöperation
against Russia in Manchuria, it was grievously mistaken. Bülow,
who had just succeeded Hohenlohe as Chancellor, hoped to use
the Boxer Rebellion as an approach to St. Petersburg. "Our
proposal," he wrote, September 16, of a demand for the surrender
of the leaders of the Boxers, "can and should be the bridge between Russia and us."[108] Placed between England and Russia
in Asia as well as in Europe, Germany had no intention of identifying herself with either. Her purpose was evidently to prevent
England's permanent and exclusive establishment in the Yangtze

---

[105] Lamsdorff, 18 June/1 July, 1900. G. P., XVI, 29; Lascelles, Aug. 1, B. D., II,
5, 6.
[106] Langer, Diplomacy of Imperialism, II, 698 ff.
[107] Ibid., II, 700.
[108] G. P., XVI, 133, 134.

Valley. The future of this rich area had been discussed more than once by the German diplomats during the summer of 1900. Its neutralization and a concerted action by the interested powers under Germany's leadership against England's control were among the suggested solutions.[109]   Any thought of coöperating with Russia and France was, however, swiftly discarded after England's icy reaction to their first advances (July 26),[110] whereupon William approached England directly with the proposal for joint action in defense of the "open door." [111]   The need to keep Germany in a good humor during the Boer War seems the only satisfactory explanation for England's consent to the final text with its vague pledge "to hold the open door for all Chinese territory as far as they [England and Germany] can exercise influence."   Germany's attitude should have disposed of any hope that she would help England to prevent Russia's establishment in Manchuria.

The reaction of the German press to the publication of the full text of the Yangtze accord convinced British observers that the agreement was not intended to include Manchuria.   By the newspapers which were usually read for information as to the views of the German government, the accord was recommended as providing for the defense of Germany's commercial prospects in the Yangtze Valley, as a barrier to the partition of China, and as proof of Germany's ability to arrange friendly understandings with England as well as with Russia.[112]   Such doubts as it occasioned arose from the apprehension of the Bismarckian, agrarian, and nationalist press that Russia might take offense,[113] and were chiefly significant of the dislike which these groups felt for any agreement with England.   To allay concern for relations with Russia, considerable publicity was given Bülow's visit to the Russian embassy at the time of the accord's publication,[114] and the *Norddeutsche* (Oct. 20) explained that "Germany is under no obligation to interfere where other countries have acquired special

---

[109] Bülow, June 30. *G. P.*, XVI, 199; Derenthall, July 27. *Ibid.*, XVI, 201.

[110] Derenthall, Aug. 20. *Ibid.*, XVI, 211, 212.

[111] William II, Aug. 22. *Ibid.*, XVI, 212, 213.

[112] *Kölnische Zeitung*, Oct. 20.

[113] The Pan-German *Alldeutsche Blätter* (Nov. 4) cited the following journals as expressing this concern: *Deutsche Tageszeitung, Tägliche Rundschau, Hamburger Nachrichten, Rheinisch-Westfälische Zeitung, Leipziger Neueste Nachrichten, Augsburger Abendzeitung.* Cf. *Reichsbote*, Oct. 23; Harden, "Englisches Pflaster," *Zukunft*, Oct. 27.

[114] *Berliner Tageblatt*, Oct. 20; *Times*, Oct. 22, Berlin, Oct. 21.

rights." The Conservative *Post* (Oct. 21) and the nationalist *Berliner Neueste Nachrichten* [115] both insisted that the absence of German interests in Manchuria settled the question once and for all. The liberal *Berliner Tageblatt* (Oct. 21) was more receptive to the English interpretation, for it argued that Germany's relations with Russia would not suffer, since the agreement provided for consultation prior to any action. For the Social Democratic *Vorwärts* (Oct. 23), on the other hand, the agreement had no significance, since it was not directed against Russia's ambitions. Nor was the London press in any doubt on this score. The Conservative *Morning Post* (Oct. 22) suspected Germany at once of having made an arrangement with Russia. "It is absurd to regard the agreement," wrote the Berlin correspondent of the Liberal *Daily News* (Oct. 22), "as a move against Russia—at least as far as Germany is concerned. . . ." "The Anglo-German understanding," reported the correspondent of the Conservative *Standard* (Oct. 22), "is in no way directed against Russia. . . ." In the *Times* (Oct. 22) Saunders warned against the mistake of thinking that "the treaty is interpreted on this side of the water as an Anglo-German guarantee against Russian aggression. . . ."

Although Lansdowne, the new British foreign minister, did not pretend in his conversations with Haztfeldt that Germany had assumed any obligations in regard to Russia, the accord left a good deal of soreness in England. The impression grew that Germany had gone back upon her word, and, from the German press comments, that she had tricked England into conceding equal rights in the Yangtze Valley. If there remained any uncertainty as to the attitude of German opinion, it was removed by the reaction to William's visit in January 1901 to the deathbed of Queen Victoria. When the *Daily Mail* (Jan. 30) wrote that "we are brought nearer to Germany" by William's visit, the ultra-Conservative *Reichsbote* complained that it was thinking of an earlier German Emperor's pilgrimage to Canossa.[116] "The incident," according to the agrarian *Deutsche Tageszeitung,* "is no concern of the German people." [117] To Englishmen, William's

[115] *Times,* Oct. 23, Berlin, Oct. 22.
[116] *Germania,* Feb. 10, 1901.
[117] *Ibid.,* Feb. 23.

visit was a friendly gesture as well as a demonstration of filial piety; to many Germans, however, it meant that their ruler had violated the sentiments of his people. It would, it was said, increase the alienation between the Emperor and the nation.[118] All true monarchists, affirmed the *Staatsburger Zeitung,* would join in the cry: "Kaiser, turn back! Turn away from English flattery, from British praises, to the homely speech of your people." [119] Bülow's primary purpose in assuring the Reichstag, March 15, 1901, that the Yangtze agreement did not cover Manchuria was to avoid offending Russia, especially since her victory in the impending war with Japan was believed to be certain; but his explanation and the bitter reaction to it in England nevertheless showed plainly enough that no compromising arrangements had been made.[120]

That the moment had arrived to abandon the policy of the "free hand" and to approach England was a possibility that received some discussion in the spring of 1901. "We must keep a careful watch upon these tendencies," wrote the Conservative *Post* (March 23) of England's reaction to Bülow's speech, "to prevent an error in our calculations." At the time of his visit William feared that "he could not continue indefinitely to oscillate between the Russians and the English, for he might end by falling between two chairs." [121] Even Holstein felt that the moment for final decisions was at hand, that England, overwhelmed by difficulties in the Far East and in South Africa, was about ready to pay Germany's price for an alliance.[122] This opinion was not without some foundation, in spite of Salisbury's dislike of the Germans and of his refusal to abandon England's traditional isolation.[123] In 1900 he, like Chamberlain, had spoken of a partition of Morocco giving Germany the Atlantic coast, as a barrier

---

[118] *Kreuz-Zeitung,* in *Germania,* Feb. 10; *A. B.,* Feb. 16.

[119] *Historisch-Politische Blätter,* vol. 127, p. 441 (March 12), citing the *Leipziger Neueste Nachrichten, Tägliche Rundschau, Kreuz-Zeitung.*

[120] *Verhandlungen,* X Leg. Per., II Sess., II, 1870; *Morning Post,* March 22. *Cf.* Langer, *Diplomacy of Imperialism,* II, 722.

[121] Metternich, Feb. 4, 1901. *G. P.,* XVI, 295, 296. "Enormously" displeased at Russia, William talked of an Anglo-German union to which France's artistic and creative genius would act, when she became associated with it, "like pepper on the beefsteak." William, Jan. 29; Eckardstein, Feb. 2. *Ibid.,* XVI, 291, XVII, 24–29.

[122] Holstein, March 20. Eckardstein, *Lebenserinnerungen,* II, 281.

[123] Langer, *Diplomacy of Imperialism,* II, 281.

to French ambitions. Chamberlain grew indifferent to an arrangement with Germany because of her refusal to coöperate against Russia in the Far East; but Lansdowne was favorably disposed toward a rapprochement in some form as a substitute for an untenable isolation. Unfortunately, Eckardstein, in order to convert his doubtful superiors in Berlin and to hasten the negotiations to a successful conclusion, represented Lansdowne and the cabinet as more eager than was justified by the facts. Believing that Germany now had the whip hand, Holstein tried unsuccessfully to secure satisfaction for relatively unimportant claims arising from the Chinese indemnity and from the South African War; they were, he wrote, more important than an alliance. These demands naturally caused some irritation in England, but it was not one of the major causes of the failure of the Anglo-German negotiations from March to June, 1901. The real obstacle was England's unwillingness, in spite of the draft of an alliance which Lansdowne prepared as a basis for discussion, to assume the specific obligations that were essential to an alliance.

The responsibility for the failure to arrange a more general understanding as a basis for diplomatic coöperation was, however, Germany's. When Lansdowne proposed an accord "in reference to particular questions or in particular parts of the world," Metternich, Hatzfeldt's successor as the ambassador in London, replied "unhesitatingly" that "no such minor proposal" would interest his government, that "it was a case of 'the whole or none.' " [124] In 1898 Germany, perhaps for sufficient reasons, had rejected Chamberlain's offer of an alliance; three years later her blunt refusal of an entente ended the possibility of a diplomatic association which might have averted the worst consequences of naval, economic, and imperialist rivalry. No equally favorable opportunity was again to present itself. Nevertheless, no sudden change had occurred in the diplomatic interests of the two countries. England still regarded Russia and France as her most serious enemies; neither her government nor her public opinion had yet awakened to the menace of the German fleet. The "free hand" was, as before, the basis of German policy. Did it leave

---

[124] Landsdowne, Dec. 19, 1901. *B. D.*, II, 82.

Germany no other choice than to refuse Lansdowne's proposal? Granting that an understanding for the defense of the "open door" in Manchuria would have alienated Russia, there were other regions, such as Morocco, where Russia was manifestly indifferent, to which this objection did not apply. The Eastern Mediterranean and the Persian Gulf—which Lansdowne had in mind —were, of course, only less objectionable than Manchuria, for Russia had claims there. In any event, what Germany desired was not a general understanding, but an alliance with precisely defined obligations, as a guarantee against England's unreliability and against her practice of using her friends for selfish purposes. The value of an entente, never great in her eyes, had been further diminished by England's renewal of her alliance with Portugal in the autumn of 1899—as Germany soon learned—for it deprived the agreement for the partition of the Portuguese colonies (Aug. 1898) of its value. Even the Atlantic coast of Morocco was not sufficiently attractive to win her for anything else than a formal alliance; she counted upon securing greater concessions by enabling France, through her inaction, to proceed with the peaceful penetration of the Moroccan Empire. Germany, in short, still believed that she could afford to wait. Although Holstein expressed the opinion in March 1901 that a turning point had been reached in Anglo-German relations, in October of the same year he denied the need of hastening the natural forces which, sooner or later, would bring the two countries together.[125] Bülow felt that it would be well to encourage England to hope that an arrangement was still possible, but also advised against any appearance of "impatience or haste."[126]

Public opinion in both countries, and perhaps even more in Germany than in England, was a serious if not insuperable obstacle to the conclusion of an openly acknowledged diplomatic association and especially to its effective operation. This factor gave Salisbury an argument against an alliance.[127] William, like the German diplomats, frequently used the attitude of German opinion in his efforts to secure concessions, but he continued, neverthe-

---

[125] *G. P.*, XVII, 105 (Oct. 31, 1901).
[126] *Ibid.*, XVII, 109 (Nov. 1).
[127] *B. D.*, II, 68, 69 (May 29, 1901).

less, to assert his complete indifference to it. England, he said, had only "to keep me in good humor, the rest does not signify. . . ." [128] He acknowledged to King Edward, after Lansdowne's advances had been rejected, that the newspapers of both countries were "awful," "but here," he insisted, "it [the press] has nothing to say, for I am the sole arbiter and master [of] German foreign policy, and the Government and Country must follow me, even if I have to face the music!" [129] Notwithstanding his pronounced divergence from German national sentiment during the Boer War and his admiration for English society, his reactions to the problems of Anglo-German relations were often similar to, if they were not influenced by, those of public opinion. Even in patriarchal Germany, "the Emperor cannot," said the Duke of Connaught, in advising against William's visit to England, "carry out a correct policy without regard to popular sentiment." [130] The newspapers placed before him and the persons close to him were probably unfriendly to England. At any rate, his impulsive dispatches from London reflect the same suspicions and preconceptions, the same tendency to mistake the defense of British interests for systematic hostility, that characterized a large part of the press. [131] He contradicted Metternich when the ambassador acquitted England of the charge, on which she had long stood condemned in the eyes of the German people, of seeking to maneuver the continental powers into war. He insisted, against Metternich's opinion, that she might one day attack Germany before the completion of the fleet in order to destroy her commerce. [132] He spoke of her statesmen as "unmitigated noodles" and said that he would no longer "stick" to an England that paid no heed to his wishes. [133]

Not long before Lansdowne's rebuff, the Germans acquired a new grievance. On October 25, 1901, Chamberlain, defending

[128] Lascelles, Feb. 28, 1901. *B. D.,* I, 258, 259.
[129] William II, Dec. 30, 1901. *G. P.,* XVII, 111.
[130] Bülow, *Denkwürdigkeiten,* I, 503.
[131] To a certain extent this was also true of Holstein. He agreed (Feb. 11, 1901) with "99/100 of the German people" in believing that England would repudiate her engagements in a serious crisis after making use of an arrangement for her own profit. *G. P.,* XVII, 34.
[132] William II's comments, Metternich, June 15, 1901. *Ibid.,* XVII, 7.
[133] Eckardstein, *Lebenserinnerungen,* II, 298; Lascelles, Nov. 9, 1901. *B. D.,* I, 261.

the record of the British troops in South Africa in a speech at Edinburgh, declared that their conduct compared favorably with that of the continental armies. His reference to the conduct of the German troops in the war with France was not less offensive to German patriotic sentiment because he included the French, Austrian, and Russian armies among those that had furnished ample precedents in *Schrecklichkeit*. It "evoked," Saunders reported to the *Times* (Oct. 28), "a perfect storm of protest in the German press." [134] Resounding resolutions were drawn up at public meetings, especially by university students and veterans. Although the government waited almost three months before it replied, nothing was done to restrain this explosion of popular resentment. The *Kölnische Zeitung* (Nov. 8), on the contrary, condoned it as a natural expression of patriotism, but this incident probably had no part in Germany's reply to the British colonial secretary. If there had been more interest in a rapprochement with England and less in the price that she might be forced to pay for it, public opinion would not have been a serious obstacle. William's affirmations of indifference to popular sentiment and to the press were louder than ever after Chamberlain's speech.[135] The prestige of *Realpolitik* had sufficed to win opinion for a policy of neutrality during the war; it might well have assured the acceptance, if not enthusiastic approval, of an agreement represented as required by Germany's interests. The *Kreuz-Zeitung* (Nov. 27, 1901) told France, at any rate, that Germany's official relations with England had not been disturbed by Chamberlain's speech. The diplomats still looked forward to an eventual understanding.

Disquieting evidence of Italy's drift away from the Triple Alliance should have been a warning against further friction with England. On December 14, 1901, Prinetti, the Italian foreign minister, announced an agreement with France in regard to Morocco and Tripoli, an important step in the rapprochement which the commercial treaty of 1898 had foreshadowed. Although Italy had assured Germany of her loyalty, the obligation

---

[134] At least two violent pamphlets appeared immediately: *Der Lügner Chamberlain* (Berlin, 1901); *Protest gegen Chamberlain* (Berlin, 1901).
[135] *G. P.*, XVII, 34 (Feb. 11, 1902).

to send an army north of the Alps had already been cancelled.[136] There could be no doubt that the chief reason for Italy's original participation in the alliance no longer existed when Barrère, the French ambassador in Rome, explained that the Mediterranean question had ceased to be a source of difficulty in Franco-Italian relations.[137] Yet the German leaders did not question the essential soundness of their policy. Since England's differences with France and Russia would always be greater than those with Germany, Italy's need of good relations with England, the strongest naval power in the Mediterranean, would never, they reasoned, permit her to join the Franco-Russian Alliance.[138] The Franco-Italian rapprochement was even said to be directed against England, as a reply to her surrender of territory adjacent to Tripoli in the accord with France in 1899.[139] It seems more probable, however, that the Italians, doubtful of Anglo-German relations, wished to acquire not only a guarantee of their interests in Tripoli but also an anchor to windward, in the event that England should turn against Germany.

When Bülow spoke to the Reichstag, January 8, 1902, the international situation was clearly not so favorable to Germany as it had been. Confident nevertheless that the stars in their courses were working for Germany's interests, he believed that he could safely teach Chamberlain a lesson, reassure nationalist opinion,[140] and, at the same time, warn Italy. He approved the patriotic protest against the British minister's slur upon the army and quoted Frederick the Great: "Let the man talk . . . he is biting on granite." He spoke of Italy with studied confidence. While the Triple Alliance was an insurance society, not an association for profit, while it was no longer essential to Germany's policy of peace, it was still useful as a friendly union of countries united by common interests. Germany's good-will, he implied, had limits, although, like a good husband, she had no objection to Italy's extra dance with an old suitor. Germany, he said in conclusion,

---

[136] Richthofen, Dec. 17, 1901. *G. P.*, XVIII, 507, 508. Cf. *Ibid.*, XVIII, 702 (July 20, 1901).

[137] *Post*, Jan. 4, 1902.

[138] Bülow, Nov. 30, 1900. *G. P.*, XVIII, 503.

[139] *Grenzboten*, 1901, II, 433–436.

[140] He told the Prince of Wales that he "had to consider public opinion." Lascelles, Jan. 31, 1902. *B. D.*, I, 271, 272.

must be strong, "so that, as now, our friendship may be valuable to everyone and our hostility a matter of indifference to none." [141] Lacking the first Chancellor's understanding of the realities of the international situation and facing, in a sense, more delicate problems, Bülow failed to achieve the results that had followed Bismarck's great speeches. Relations with England, as he must have foreseen, became still more difficult. Chamberlain emphatically reaffirmed his earlier statements in a speech at Manchester, January 11,[142] and the London press concluded that the Chancellor's purpose had been to clear himself of the charge of being England's friend.[143] "He drew the cheers of his hearers," wrote the *Times* (Jan. 9), ". . . but he has done a bad day's work for the promotion of the friendly relations between the two countries. . . ." His tone, acording to the Conservative *Standard* (Jan. 9), had been "little short of offensive. . . . They [the Germans] will do well to realize that we are beginning to be seriously moved by the campaign of taunts and degrading accusations leveled against us at public meetings and in the newspapers of the Empire." For the Conservative *Morning Post* (Jan. 10, Berlin, Jan. 9), Bülow had worked for a political success at England's expense by encouraging anti-English sentiment. Although the offensive remarks of Liebermann von Sonnenberg were stricken from the official record of the Reichstag's debates, the London press was informed that the Pan-German deputy had spoken of the British army as "a pack of thieves and brigands" and of Chamberlain as "the most accursed scoundrel on God's earth." [144] "Seldom, if ever," wrote the *Times* (Jan. 11), "has a friendly nation been so grossly insulted in a foreign Parliament." [145] Because Bülow had not rebuked Liebermann with sufficient severity, the weekly *Spectator* (Jan. 18) drew the conclusion that "for the time we have no more unreasonable enemy than the German people." Nor is there any reason to believe that Italy was influenced by Bülow's warning, for she agreed later in 1902 to remain neutral, even if France attacked Germany after a

---

[141] *Verhandlungen*, X Leg. Per., II Sess., IV, 3209.
[142] *Times*, Jan. 13, 1902.
[143] *Pall Mall Gazette*, Jan. 9.
[144] Langer, *Diplomacy of Imperialism*, II, 775; *Times*, Jan. 11.
[145] The comments of the *Saturday Review* (Jan. 18) were more moderate.

provocation like the Ems Dispatch or Schnaebelé's arrest. If Holstein had known of this arrangement, it is doubtful that Italy's consent to renew the Triple Alliance (June 28, 1902) would have caused him much satisfaction.[146]

In his blunt rejoinder to Chamberlain, the Chancellor had, it was generally agreed, satisfied Germany's outraged honor. Even the extremists acknowledged that he had acted in accordance with popular sentiment. Ernest Hasse, a National Liberal deputy and the president of the Pan-German league, objected only to Bülow's slowness in replying.[147] The nationalist press was enthusiastic.[148] There was also warm approval in these quarters for the affirmation of Germany's ability to stand alone. What Bülow had said on this point was elaborated by the *Süddeutsche Reichskorrespondenz,* a news circular that was sometimes used by the government: no serious difficulties would arise even if the loss of Italy should be followed by Austria's defection, since a hostile coalition would be forced to disperse its forces to distant parts of the globe.[149] In the Reichstag, Liebermann, the Pan-German, declared: "The German Empire needs no allies. It can defend its interests, thank God, against a world of enemies."[150] This apparent indifference to the danger of isolation meant, according to the Conservative *Post* (Jan. 11), that Italy could expect no concessions, such as tariff reductions, to assure her loyalty to the Triple Alliance. The possibility of Italy's desertion nevertheless occasioned concern. It was betrayed by the explanation that the Franco-Italian rapprochement was directed against England; France would not otherwise have sacrificed her interests in Tripoli.[151] From this position to one of outright alarm was only a step, since geography and history made it difficult to believe that the Italians no longer considered England's friendship to be essential to their security. While the Social Democrats and the Progressives had joined the Centrists in applauding Bülow's de-

---

[146] Holstein, *Lebensbekenntnis,* pp. 212, 213 (Aug. 25, 1902); *G. P.,* XVIII, 609.
[147] *Verhandlungen,* X Leg. Per., II Sess., IV, 3339 (Jan. 13).
[148] *Tägliche Rundschau,* Jan. 9; *Magdeburgische Zeitung,* Jan. 9, 10; *Reichsbote,* Jan. 10.
[149] Cf. *Schlessische Zeitung,* in *Post,* Jan. 14.
[150] *Verhandlungen,* X Leg. Per., II Sess., IV, 3278 (Jan. 10).
[151] *Reichsbote,* Jan. 10; P. Asmussen, "Bündnisfragen," *Gegenwart,* Feb. 1, 1902.

fense of the army's honor,[152] they were unmistakably alarmed. The threatening crisis, wrote the *Vossische Zeitung* (Jan. 9), would test the capacity of her leaders. "It is unthinkable that the German Chancellor is reconciled to the idea of a splendid isolation. . . . The situation of our foreign policy is dark and confused as never before." The liberal *Berliner Tageblatt* (Jan. 12) thought it impossible that Bülow could have spoken of the Triple Alliance as he had without something like the Reinsurance Treaty with Russia. A week later (Jan. 19), it complained that the Chancellor had made Chamberlain the most popular man in the British Empire. The Social Democrats found no redeeming feature in the conduct of German foreign policy. Bülow, according to the *Vorwärts* (Jan. 10), was neither a statesman nor a diplomat; he had needlessly alienated England, he had dismissed the Triple Alliance with "a couple of miserable jokes." "He doesn't know what to do from one day to the next."

The possible consequences of driving England too far occasionally alarmed even the most confident. The Conservative *Post* (Jan. 19, 1926) revealed the insincerity of its professed indifference by speaking of Chamberlain as the chief cause of Germany's displeasure. Bülow's expression of a desire for good relations should, according to the *Kölnische Zeitung* (Jan. 9), close the Chamberlain incident. The nationalist *Tägliche Rundschau* (Jan. 9) affirmed its interest in an amicable relationship, provided that England would reciprocate Germany's friendliness; the moderate *Vossische Zeitung* (Jan. 14), distinctly alarmed, talked of the general forces that would eventually bring the two countries together. A different note was sounded, however, by the *Allgemeine Zeitung,* a journal which occasionally expressed official opinion. The German people, it wrote, should remember that Chamberlain's popularity and political influence had not been impaired by his support of an understanding with Russia and France.[153] There was indeed ample reason for fear. A complement to the anti-German tendencies of English opinion had peared in the agitation for a treaty of arbitration in both London and Paris. On January 30, 1902, Metternich reported that Cham-

---

[152] *Verhandlungen*, X Leg. Per., II Sess., IV, 3235. Cf. *Volks-Zeitung*, Jan. 13.
[153] *Volks-Zeitung*, Jan. 14.

berlain was negotiating with France for an understanding to be based upon a compromise in Morocco and elsewhere.[154] Somewhat perturbed, William again affirmed his repudiation of German opinion; the hostility of the German press, he told Lascelles (in an effort to persuade King Edward not to abandon his projected visit to Germany), did not count, "as he himself is the master in Germany."[155] He believed, however, that the friction between England and Russia in the Far East would improve Germany's position, a factor which he hoped to strengthen by giving his blessing to the negotiations for an Anglo-Japanese alliance.[156] His action, however, was short-sighted. If England's association with Japan might create new difficulties with Russia, it would certainly free England's hands in the Far East—unless France, by going to the aid of her ally, should necessitate her participation in a war—with the result that she would be able to concentrate the major part of her navy at home. The Germans, moreover, seemed unaware that the Anglo-Japanese Alliance (1902) might be an even more important step toward an Anglo-French entente than the rapprochement between France and Italy, although their own belief that England would always let other countries fight her battles should have warned them that she would try to prevent France's participation in a Russo-Japanese war in order to keep out of it herself. Even this ancient *idée fixe* was powerless, when it might have served Germany well, to weaken her faith in the conflict of interests between England and Russia.

The press, like the diplomats, could see nothing but advantages in the alliance. If the Conservative *Post* (Feb. 16) was careful to explain (for Russia's benefit) that Germany had had no part in its negotiation, the general reaction was most satisfactory.[157] The alliance, as the *Kölnische Zeitung* (Feb. 13) pointed out, would delay the partition of China and thus serve the "open-door" policy.[158] The nationalists were completely reassured as

---

[154] Oncken, *Vorgeschichte des Weltkrieges*, II, 530.
[155] Lascelles, Jan. 22, 1902. *B. D.*, I, 270.
[156] It was signed on January 30, 1902.
[157] Hans Delbrück, in *P. J.*, vol. 108, p. 186 (April, 1902).
[158] *Kreuz-Zeitung*, Feb. 19, 1902, Schiemann, *Deutschland und die Grosse Politik*, II, 75.

to the strength of Germany's diplomatic position. There was, according to the National Liberal *National Zeitung* (Feb. 12), no further need of concern in regard to the talk in the London press of an understanding with Russia. Opinion differed, however, as to the means by which Germany should profit from the Anglo-Russian conflict, which was regarded as more certain than ever. If the National Liberal *Magdeburgische Zeitung* (Feb. 13) discussed the prospects of a new period of coöperation with Russia and France, if the *Hamburger Nachrichten* welcomed the opportunity for a return to Bismarck's policy of a close association with Russia, the nationalist *Tägliche Rundschau* (Feb. 12) emphatically rejected both suggestions in favor of a temporary reserve. "Germany's word will then be the weightier at the decisive moment. . . . When they turn to us, we will then dictate our conditions." The ultra-Conservative *Reichsbote* (Feb. 19) spoke with satisfaction of mediating when the two countries reached the point of exhaustion. Nor were the liberals much clearer as to the probable course of events. Somewhat surprised by England's decision to enter a formal alliance and more than a little alarmed by the instability of the Triple Alliance, the moderate *Vossische Zeitung* (Feb. 12) contented itself with an expression of confidence that Germany's strength and the skill of her leaders would enable her to profit by the situation. The Progressive *Friesinnige Zeitung* (Feb. 13) saw no reason for alarm, since Germany's interests were adequately protected by the Yangtze accord. In the Progressive *Volks-Zeitung's* (Feb. 12) scandalized protest was clearly expressed the change that had occurred in the attitude of liberal opinion toward England. She was the first Western power to make an alliance with the Yellow race, "because she could find no other ally. She had even enlisted the Negroes against the whites in South Africa." The Social Democratic *Vorwärts* (Feb. 14) foresaw no worse consequences than a strengthened opposition to German expansion in China and additional requests for the army and navy.

The Franco-Russian declaration of March 19, 1902, made this satisfaction complete.[159] France's promise to consult with her

---

[159] *D. D. F.*, (2), III, 177, 178.

ally in regard to common action in the Far East pointed to her participation in a Russo-Japanese war and therefore, thanks to her alliance with Japan, to England's entrance as well. The Conservative *Post* (March 22) felt that international relations had at last become stabilized, that "the formation of diplomatic groups is terminated." England's drift away from Germany was sufficiently ominous to impress the latter's leaders. Holleben's dispatch (April 1898), reporting the British ambassador's proposal for a second joint note against America's armed intervention in the Cuban question, and William's unfavorable comment were published (Feb. 12, 1902) to counteract statements in the English press and in the House of Commons as to Germany's responsibility.[160] Metternich's warning, "I wouldn't give two-pence for Anglo-German relations," disturbed even Bülow; the English press, in his opinion, was more hateful than Germany's, chiefly because of Saunder's reports to the *Times*.[161] That there was little to choose between the extremists of both countries was shown, however, by the reaction of nationalist opinion in Germany at the close of the Boer War. The British victory was "a very serious blow," asserted the *Rheinisch-Westfälische Zeitung,* since it left Germany to face British imperialism alone in South Africa.[162] More offensive from the English point of view was the Conservative *Post*'s prophecy (June 3, 1902) that the Boers would become a second Irish problem. The Pan-Germans predicted that England's freedom of action would be limited by the need to immobilize a large part of her military strength in South Africa.[163] While Bülow hoped that the Emperor's popularity in England might be useful in improving relations, William was himself alarmed at the possibility of an English attack before Germany was prepared to defend herself. In the autumn of 1902, he therefore refused to see the Boer generals, in spite of the clamor of public opinion. "I am," he wrote on a report of anti-German sentiment in England, "the only restraint upon the English; without me they would attack immediately and my fleet is

---

[160] K. Wuppermann, *Deutsche Geschichtskalendar für 1902,* pp. 212, 213.
[161] Bülow, March 13, June 24, 1902. ·G. P., XVII, 151, 152.
[162] *Post,* June 3, 1902.
[163] *A. B.,* June 7, 1902.

not yet ready. . . ."[164] A visit to Sandringham, where he talked with Chamberlain and Salisbury, confirmed his anxieties and strengthened his belief that caution was necessary, "for they will not stand much more. Caution above all! Here they have thirty-five battleships in service and we eight!" His advice was excellent: the German press should be moderate and friction should be avoided.[165] Nevertheless he had not contributed much to the cause of appeasement, for his uncle, King Edward, said after his departure, "Thank God, he's gone!"[166] The visit, in fact, served mainly to emphasize the unfriendliness of public opinion in both countries. While the Conservative *Saturday Review* (Nov. 8) extended a cordial welcome and noted the unusual moderation of the German press at this time, the *Times* (Nov. 8) recalled the earlier "inflammatory Anglophobia" and the "campaign of scurrility." The Liberal *Daily Chronicle* (Nov. 8) reminded its readers that Germany was England's second most dangerous commercial rival and asserted that her "venomous hostility . . . cannot be obliterated by the fairest professions now." If, in Germany, there was less of the violent repudiation of William's suspected partiality for the English which had accompanied his earlier visits, this moderation was doubtless the result to a large extent of official influence. The Conservative *Post* (Nov. 8) saw no reason why the relations with England should be worse than those with Russia, but it definitely rejected the idea of an alliance.[167] *"Keine Liebe, aber auch nicht unüberlegten Zorn"* was, according to the principal Catholic review in South Germany, the proper tone for Anglo-German relations.[168] Delbrück's warning that "England must have no delusions upon the point that she is hated in Germany . . ." received more attention in England, however, than more moderate opinion. The *Daily Mail* (Nov. 7) drew from it the conclusion that the German people would reject an alliance and that, therefore, "it must be worthless."

The rapid deterioration of Anglo-German relations continued

---

[164] Eckardstein, Oct. 4, 1902. *G. P.,* XVII, 229, 230.
[165] William II, Nov. 12, 1902. *Ibid.,* XVII, 115–117.
[166] Lee, *Edward VII,* II, 153.
[167] "Zum neuen Jahr," *Grenzboten,* 1903, I, 4 (Jan. 1).
[168] "Deutsch-Englisches," *Historisch-Politische Blätter,* vol. 130, p. 859 (Dec. 1902).

unchecked. Naval rivalry was beginning to exert a serious influence upon public opinion in both countries. In England the specter of an invasion made its first appearance. England, according to J. R. Seeley, one of the major prophets of imperialism, was the one country which offered a "reasonable prospect of immediate success to the attacking side . . . ," while German publicists, doubtless taking their cue from Tirpitz or other officials, argued that England might suddenly decide to destroy the young German fleet, as she had that of Denmark in 1807.[169] The diplomats added to the increasing ill-will by their bitter wrangles over China. Seeking to defend Germany's foothold in the Yangtze Valley, her foreign office opened itself to the charge of sharp practices soon after William's visit to England and his advice against unnecessary friction. On October 7, England was informed that Germany must have guarantees from China that no special privileges would be given another country in that region before she would withdraw her troops from Shanghai, although these guarantees, as England soon discovered, had already been given (Oct. 5). Irritated by Germany's distrust of England's loyalty to the Yangtze agreement, Lansdowne refused to agree that the chronological succession of these events was a matter of no importance.[170] The incident, revealed, to Germany's displeasure, by the publication of a Blue Book, raised a storm of protest in London. "In our insular life, the man," wrote the Conservative *Morning Post* (Dec. 4, 1902), "who is considered not to 'play fair' is regarded as a person with whom it is prudent to have as few dealings as possible." "Such exhibitions of pseudo-Bismarckian diplomacy," affirmed the Conservative *Standard* (Dec. 4), "are calculated to impress the world with the inconveniences of common action with the German Government." The *Times* (Dec. 5) even spoke of a "lie," and the Liberal *Daily Chronicle* (Dec. 4) charged Germany with "a piece of sharp practice to limit British influence in Central China for her own advantage." From the German point of view, England's reaction merely meant a refusal to admit that Germany had a legitimate right to defend her interests.

---

[169] John Seeley, "The Cause of European Peace," *The National Review*, vol. 40, pp. 738–745 (Jan. 1903); H. J., "Seerüstungen," *Grenzboten*, 1903, II, 11.
[170] *B. D.*, II, 150 (Nov. 28, 1902).

It was almost impossible for the two governments to work together anywhere. While the Boer War had shown that the
German government could ignore anti-English sentiment if it
suited its purposes, the English government could not, if it so
desired, disregard the increasing aversion of public opinion against
any association with Germany, especially when it threatened to
disturb England's good relations with the United States. England first suggested, in the autumn of 1902, to a somewhat reluctant Germany, that the two countries should act together to
secure a financial settlement with Castro, the Venezuelan dictator,
but she quickly withdrew when anti-American feeling in Germany and the bombardment of a Venezuelan fort and ships by the
Germans raised the prospect of a serious crisis with the United
States. To the partisans of an entente with Russia and France,
like the *Spectator* (Dec. 13, 1902), coöperation with Germany
was at best a disagreeable necessity. Britain's straightforward
but naïve diplomats, it was feared, would be no match for the
wily Germans. The talk in Germany of using the "mailed fist,"
of setting the Monroe Doctrine aside,[171] and of ignoring the
United States entirely [172] discouraged the English—who had never
shared Germany's far-reaching expectations.[173] King Edward
declared for immediate withdrawal soon after the incident at
Fort Carlos.[174] "The English ministers," wrote Harden, "had
to invent a thousand excuses and stammer daily apologies because they had dared to agree to an alliance with Germany, although it had been limited to a single question." [175]

Still less fortunate were the results of Germany's efforts to
secure England's participation in the construction of the Bagdad
Railway, in spite of the fact that the motive was more financial
than political. Again the foreign office was forced by popular
clamor [176] to retract its consent, given at the time of its withdrawal

[171] K. von Strantz, "Deutschland und die Monroelehre," *Gegenwart,* Jan. 10, 1903.
[172] *A. B.,* Jan. 10, 1903. Otto Hoetsch advised those who were contemptuous of
the Americans to read the writings of President Roosevelt and the accounts of the
Battles of Chattanooga and Gettysburg. *Ibid.,* March 7, 1903.
[173] *Kreuz-Zeitung,* Feb. 13. Schiemann, *Deutschland und die Grosse Politik,*
III, 55. The *Post* (Jan. 24) counted upon this affair to restore the good relations
with England which Bismarck had regarded as necessary.
[174] Metternich, Jan. 29, 1903. *G. P.,* XVII, 281.
[175] Harden, "Venezuela," *Zukunft,* Feb. 27, 1903.
[176] Lansdowne, April 7. *B. D.,* II, 185.

from the Venezuelan affair.[177]   While the friends of an understanding with Russia and France were perhaps the most determined in their protest that Germany should not be aided against
Russia,[178] they had the support of a large part of the London
press.   "The nation," wrote the popular *Daily Mail* (April 4,
1903), "with the example of the Venezuela affair fresh in its
memory, is not prepared to accept another Anglo-German agreement."   It was time, said the Conservative *Morning Post* (April
4), for the nation to wake up.   "The German Government is as
pushing and as little scrupulous as ever, witness the late transaction relating to the evacuation of Shanghai."   England, according
to the *Times* (April 22), had no interest in helping Germany to
build a railway that would compete with her own Eastern communications.   When Balfour announced England's refusal in
the House of Commons, he explained it as the result of the failure
to provide adequate provisions for international control, but the
Germans, of course, were not deceived.   The reason was the
opposition of opinion in and out of parliament to any association
with Germany.

IV

Each period of German history since the beginning of Bismarck's drive for political unity influenced, in varying degrees, its
future development.   None perhaps was more significant than
the eight years from 1895 to 1903.   At home, the industrialization
of Germany continued, with consequences that affected the whole
complex of social and political problems and which changed, in
vital respects, Germany's position in foreign affairs.   Increasing
prosperity, whose benefits were chiefly shared, though unequally,
between the middle classes and the workers, gradually weakened
the hostility of some of the opposition parties to the imperial
régime.   Until his death in 1902, Eugen Richter's leadership assured the hostility of perhaps the majority of the Progressives to
Macht- and *Weltpolitik,* but the insidious influence of large profits, already manifest in the attitude of the secessionists in the
Freisinnige Vereinigung, was slowly working toward the aban-

---

[177] Lansdowne, Feb. 27. *B. D.,* II, 179.
[178] *National Review,* April 1903; *Spectator,* April 3.

donment of earlier hopes. Military, naval, and colonial appropriations were approved by members of the Reichstag who had
been irreconcilable in Bismarck's time. The Catholic Center had
no objection in principle to supporting these measures, in return
for concessions or in the hope of sharing eventually in political
power. In the long run, favorable economic conditions were to
moderate the attitude of the Social Democrats, but the immediate
effect of industrialism immensely strengthened the social revolutionary movement. Its following multiplied as emigration declined with Germany's increasing capacity, thanks to industries
and foreign commerce, to support a larger population. By the
beginning of this period, it was clear that William had failed to
win the industrial workers and that the majority were and would
remain the enemies of the existing régime. Although the party's
allegiance to revolutionary methods was perhaps even at this time
mainly theoretical, it was, however, firmly committed to the
social control of an industrial system—to whose existence and
development it had no objection—for use rather than for profit.
It was, however, one of the most interesting features of the situation that the landlords, although they had been one of the pillars
of the Empire and continued to furnish most of the army
officers, administrative officials, and diplomats, had little liking
for the government's support of industry, in the form of the protective tariff and of commercial treaties, or for ambitious naval
programs. Their opposition nevertheless was not a serious danger. Although agriculture was in a chronic state of depression
during the nineties, this group supported the government on
critical issues, such as the naval question, when it secured promises of legislative favors.

The economic changes through which Germany was passing
made little or no impression upon the Empire's constitutional system. The Emperor and the administration remained in theory
above all parties and classes. To examine the question as to
whether or not this theory was carried into practice is beyond the
province of this study. It is necessary to note that the German
system placed the decision as to the nature of national interests
more definitely in the hands of the executive—or in those of the
Emperor—than did the constitutions of the democratic powers.

Since he was supposed to be independent of party strife, his function was to guide German policy for the nation's permanent profit—subject, especially in domestic affairs, to the approval of the Reichstag. From this point of view, the fact that millions of workers differed on all issues with his conception of national interests was not important. There is, however, undoubtedly a good deal of truth in the Marxian argument that German policy was actually determined, at least in domestic affairs, by the interests of the ruling classes. The government's favor shifted between the great industrialists and the landlords, according to political expediency. It is more doubtful whether class interests exerted the same determining influence upon foreign policy. Bismarck's efforts to safeguard Germany's continental security were determined by geographical and political factors that certainly had little or no connection with class interests, although his dislike of England's parliamentary institutions may have had a part in his preference for a diplomatic association with Russia. By no means does it follow, as Socialist historians have argued, that the rivalry between the agrarians and the great industrialists for the government's favor explains the collapse of the Anglo-German negotiations in 1898 and 1901. The foreign office continued, in fact, to count upon an eventual understanding.

The launching of Germany's *Weltpolitik* in the period of industrial expansion was not a coincidence; here as elsewhere the demand for markets and raw materials was a cause of imperialism. The economic factor was, however, far from the whole story. Whatever truth there may be in the thesis that imperialism is the last phase of a declining capitalist system, it does not offer a satisfactory explanation; for the desire of the German government to enhance national prestige and to strengthen Germany in dealing with the world powers was far more important in determining the attitude of William, Tirpitz, and other officials. Moreover, a large section of the propertied classes, including the merchants of the Hanseatic cities, the Progressives, and the agrarians, were at first definitely opposed; their later conversion was in part the result of considerations that had nothing to do with economic interests. The question may, after all, be essentially academic; since a young, self-confident, and ambitious state like

Germany could not easily have limited itself to purely continental interests in this age of imperialism.

Be that as it may, Germany's decision to enter the race for a share of the still available colonial territory, for naval bases and coaling stations, for economic concessions—in short, for "a place in the sun"—was the most important event during this critical period. It changed the entire emphasis of German foreign policy. International affairs were no longer carefully weighed with primary reference to Germany's security in Europe; they were evaluated in the light of her imperialist aspirations. The attempt to conciliate Russia was abandoned in favor of a balanced position between England and Russia. Germany came to rely almost exclusively upon the interest conflicts between these and other powers to provide opportunities for her own expansion. This policy—and that of the "free hand" in general—should not be dismissed as an aberration of Holstein's possibly abnormal mind. Bismarck had followed a somewhat similar course in 1884 in establishing the colonial empire. It had the hearty support of William, Hohenlohe, Bülow, and that of a large section of public opinion. Even the Progressives endorsed it, since it seemed an assurance against Bismarck's alliance with Russia and since their sympathy for England declined with her coolness toward Germany's colonial aspirations. There was, in fact, much to be said for the analysis of the international situation upon which this policy was based. No immediate threat menaced Germany's security in Europe. It was a matter of common knowledge that Russia's indifference to the *revanche,* the Austro-Russian understanding of 1897, and Russia's preoccupation with the Far East adjourned the danger of hostile action by the Franco-Russian Alliance or by France alone. Far less tension existed in relations with Russia than in the days of the Reinsurance Treaty, and France, discouraged by Russia's attitude, weakened by the Dreyfus affair and the growth of anti-militarism, and enraged by England's treatment of her claims in the Upper Nile, showed no disposition to create serious trouble. Like Ferry, Hanotaux was willing to work with Germany for colonial purposes; even Delcassé, who succeeded him at the Quai d'Orsay in June 1898, approached Berlin more than once, though indirectly and only when he despaired of the understanding with England which he undoubtedly preferred. Events, moreover, seemed to justify Holstein's confidence that no conceivable diplomatic arrangement could change the enmity that divided England from Russia and France into a reliable friendship. The Germans learned from the Tsar himself that Russia had refused England's advances during the winter of 1897–1898. During the Fashoda crisis in the autumn of 1898, France and England were on the verge of war only a few months after the agreement of June in which their differences in West Africa were arranged. The settlement of their conflicting interests in the Upper Nile (March 1899) did not prevent France from taking a leading part in the anti-English agitation during the Boer War or from supporting Russia's move for intervention.

In the light of these circumstances, it is evident that Germany's diplomatic position was one of great strength. How to use its advantages for her interests was the task of her statesmen. The problem would have been comparatively simple if the chief aim had been to increase Germany's security in Europe, since a policy of reserve would have served that purpose; but Caprivi's experience had shown this course to be virtually impossible for a German statesman. William's imperialistic pronouncements raised the expectations of a large part of public opinion. Accordingly, the sole question was in regard to the proper time and the most effective procedure for advancing Germany's imperialist interests, while the other powers quarrelled. There were two possibilities: to go the limit in the hope of acquiring important gains immediately, for example by joining Russia and France in a continental union against England during the Boer War or by joining England against Russia in China; or to accept such minor concessions as England, in particular, was willing to grant in return for German neutrality. Since the first alternative meant the burning of Germany's bridges, a leap in the dark whose consequences were incalculable, her diplomats chose to retain their "free hand" between England and Russia and to seek as many immediate concessions as possible, in the confident expectation that they need only wait until England, in dire distress, should pay the price for Germany's friendship. The results were disappointing. The Samoan settlement, the purchase of the Caroline and Marianne Islands from Spain, the lease of Kiaochow and of Shantung, the rapidly diminishing prospects of a share of the Portuguese colonial empire—these gains were insignificant in comparison with Germany's diplomatic advantages and, especially, with her expectations. In the meantime, an essential condition of the "free hand," the possibility of coming to terms with England, had been compromised, if not entirely lost. A strong case can be made for the refusal of Chamberlain's advances, for their purpose was clearly to secure Germany's support against Russia—an arrangement which would probably have alienated Russia, although she might conceivably have been stimulated to compete with England for Germany's friendship. There were equally valid reasons, from England's point of view, against the German invitation to join the Triple Alliance; if she did, England's obligations arising from Austria's Balkan interests would have far exceeded the value of Germany's aid against an attack by two powers. Although it might have paid Germany to continue the negotiations with Lansdowne in the autumn of 1901, her greatest mistake after all was not perhaps in failing to come to terms—since any agreement had no great prospect of permanence so long as the naval program endured—but in her choice of the methods for securing her wishes. From her procedure in the affairs of the Portuguese colonies and of Samoa, even Chamberlain, the strongest partisan of an alliance in the cabinet, talked of "blackmail," and many Englishmen resented Germany's obvious intention to make what she could out of their troubles. The Yangtze accord, perhaps unjustifiably, and the controversies arising in connection with the evacuation of Shanghai, gave the impression of sharp practices. These incidents finally culminated in the repudiation of a diplomatic association with Germany in any form on the part of English public opinion in connection with the Bagdad Railway. Although the Germans continued to hope for important advantages from the Anglo-Japanese Alliance, there was less prospect than ever of a direct arrangement with England.

German opinion played a part during this period scarcely less significant than that of German diplomacy. William repeatedly discounted its influence—Germany's neutrality was often, though not entirely accurately, cited as proof—but the general hatred of England inevitably poisoned her attitude. Saunders' reports and those of other less well-known correspondents perhaps exerted as much influence upon the course of events as the dispatches from the British embassy. While the German foreign office urged Saunders' recall, on the ground that his estimate of German opinion was biased, the government did not try very hard to moderate the anti-English agitation, partly because a certain tension in Anglo-German relations was useful in converting a reluctant Reichstag to the naval program and in reconciling public opinion to its burdens. The effect of the increasing criticism of the government and of its conduct of foreign affairs was slower in making itself felt, but it eventually became a factor in Germany's increasing nervousness and excitability. It is a question that merits careful examination. There was a good deal of dissatisfaction, especially in the press, with the personal characteristics of Germany's leaders. William's flamboyance, his emotional and tactless speeches, and his choice of favorites were regarded as unworthy of a German sovereign. Much was expected of Bülow on his appointment in 1897 as minister of state for foreign affairs, but even his suavity and the literary allusions of his speeches that charmed the liberals as a welcome change from Bismarck's brutal directness turned many against him. His *"rednerischen Bonbonièren"* was a frequently used expression. Since the publication of his memoirs, with their ungenerous attempt to saddle all of Germany's mistakes upon the Emperor and upon his colleagues, Bülow's reputation has passed into an eclipse. The pendulum has perhaps swung too far, but it seems clear that he may justly be burdened with a considerable share of the responsibility for the failure to make better use of Germany's diplomatic advantages. He did nothing to correct the fixation of the foreign office upon the supposedly irreconcilable interest conflicts between Germany's actual or potential enemies. He encouraged William in his most dangerous characteristics with flattery, for, like Hohenlohe, he did not dare to oppose him openly. While his use of the press occasioned much less criticism than Bismarck's, his reply to Chamberlain was a demagogic appeal to mass psy-

chology and his pretended indifference, in the same speech, to
the fate of the Triple Alliance increased rather than allayed
alarm.

More important than the criticism of personalities was the increasing doubt of the effectiveness of German foreign policy. The
contrast between the aspirations of the imperialists and the government's accomplishments was perhaps the most potent source
of dissatisfaction. If the diplomats consoled themselves for the
disappointingly meager results of the "free hand" with the theory
that Germany had only to wait for more adequate returns, England's progress in South Africa, Russia's penetration of Manchuria, France's advance in Central Africa, and the annexation
of the Philippines and of Porto Rico by the United States caused
many Germans to think that it was a question of now or never.
It seemed that perhaps the last opportunity to become one of the
select circle of world powers was about to be lost. Reasons for
criticism were also found in the European situation. Bismarck's
admirers pursued Bülow with a continuous barrage of denunciations for his failure to restore the broken wire to St. Petersburg.[179]
The Social Democrats condemned the entire range of German
policy; the only salvation, from their point of view, was the
abandonment of the naval program, the withdrawal from the
race for colonies, and an alliance with England. The greater
part of German opinion doubtless preferred a middle course between England and Russia, yet the inevitable shifts required by
this policy were themselves productive of uneasiness. From this
came, to a considerable extent, the charge of a *zickzack Kurs*.
Irresponsible commentators were not the only persons to view
the future with some concern. Even William occasionally felt
he could not permanently remain in a condition of suspension
between them. "We are beginning," wrote Monts, soon to become the ambassador to Italy, "to harvest the fruits of our foreign policy, with its restlessness and unpredictability."[180] Signs
of weakness and dissolution in the Triple Alliance disturbed
even those who believed that Germany should preserve her free-

---

[179] Harden, "Diagnose," *Zukunft*, March 2, 1901; Harden, "An den Kanzler,"
ibid., March 16, 1901; *Hamburger Nachrichten*, in *Post*, April 25, 1902.
[180] Monts, *Erinnerungen und Gedanken*, p. 413 (Jan. 17, 1903).

dom of action. In addition to Italy's rapprochement with France and the revival of irredentism, the increasing agitation among Austria's subject nationalities threatened the stability and value of Germany's alliances. Moreover, the anti-German press in London continued to talk of an Anglo-Franco-Russian entente. In November 1901, reprints of an article on "British Foreign Policy," signed by A. B. C. and advocating a diplomatic understanding with Germany's continental enemies, were sent by the *National Review* to many German editors in order, according to the *Post* (Nov. 2), to excite them to new outbursts against England.[181] "We are faced by a concert of ill-will," the *Kölnische Zeitung* (May 8, 1901) had already written of the anti-German campaign in the foreign press, "that only awaits its director (*Kapellmeister*) to strike up the battle march." Were Germany's leaders capable of meeting these dangers? The *Dresdner Zeitung,* for one, was skeptical. *"Playing with international fireworks,"* it wrote, *"is dangerous;* children and inexperienced persons would do better not to touch them."[182] There was still much confidence in Germany's armed forces and in her diplomatic advantages. Instead of enlightening its readers as to the dangerous reality, the *Post,* desirous that the *Weltpolitik* should not be disturbed by alarm as to the European situation, encouraged the feeling of security. Of Delcassé it wrote as late as November 15, 1902: "We have no reason to doubt his love of peace and his moderate views as to France's foreign policy," and of his "loyal and truly friendly sentiment" on the occasion of Edward VII's visit to Paris in May 1903.[183]

Especially significant was the dissatisfaction among the nationalists and Conservatives, for these groups had hitherto been the main pillars of the Empire. Their attachment to the monarchy was a restraining influence, except in the case of the Pan-Germans. Admittedly a small minority, the influence of this extremist group far transcended its small membership. Many of its members occupied key positions in the business world, in the professions, and even in the administration. Alfred Hugenberg, soon to be-

---

181 Schiemann received two copies from different sources. *Kreuz-Zeitung* (Dec. 4, 1901). Schiemann, *Deutschland und die Grosse Politik,* I, 395.
182 *Kölnische Zeitung,* Nov. 24, 1901.
183 *Post,* April 11, 1903.

come a director of the Krupp corporation, was, for example, active in its affairs at an early date. Although the League had appeared under a different name, as a protest against Germany's concessions to England in the Heligoland-Zanzibar Treaty of 1890, it attracted little public attention until the agitation for the first naval law in 1898, when its services were acknowledged by the government.[184] The League owed its chief strength to its extremely nationalist point of view rather than to its rather vague program. Its anti-Semitism, its exaltation of Germanism, which were drawn, according to Heinrich Class' interesting memoirs, from the writings of Paul Lagarde, Gobineau, and Houston Stewart Chamberlain, were quite generally ignored, although Hugenberg's articles on the Polish question presented a point of view which the government later put into effect by subsidizing German settlers in the eastern provinces.[185] Nor did the League's far-reaching ideas as to Germany's expansion in Europe have much appeal. On the other hand, its blunt condemnation of the government's record in *Weltpolitik,* its insistence that the official policy must have its roots in popular sentiment,[186] and its demand for more forceful measures expressed the point of view of many who had no use for its fantastic schemes. In 1903, sixty thousand copies of Class' pamphlet, *Die Bilanz des neuen Kursis,* a violent attack upon the whole course of German policy since Bismarck's fall, were sold in a few weeks.[187] To the Pan-Germans, the same methods which were alienating foreign, especially English, opinion were woefully weak. In calling for a firmer, a more energetic, and a more sustained support of Germany's interests everywhere, based upon an unshakable confidence in her strength, they spoke for nationalist and Conservative opinion. The government was soon to act in the spirit of this advice.

---

[184] Wertheimer, *The Pan-German League,* p. 54; Class, *Wider den Strom,* pp. 82, 83.

[185] Class, *Wider den Strom,* pp. 86, 87.

[186] The Social Democratic gains in the Reichstag elections of 1903 were the result, according to its official organ, of the government's failure to identify itself with public opinion during the Boer War. *A. B.,* June 27, 1903.

[187] Class tells of an approving letter from a leader of the Free Conservative party who nevertheless continued to affirm his support of the government in public. Another prominent politician explained his refusal to support Class as a candidate for election to the Reichstag on the ground that he could not afford to endanger the career of his sons, who were in the government service. Class, *op. cit.,* pp. 94–97.

CHAPTER X

The First Offensive Against Encirclement, 1904-1907

Man male sich in Deutschland keine Schreckbilder an die Wand von Koalitionen und furchtbaren Gefahren; gegenwärtig haben wir gar nichts zu fürchten. Man ist im Auslande nicht gut auf uns zu sprechen und wünscht uns Pest und Pestilenz ins Haus; aber die Herrschaften haben alle Ursache, uns die nächste Zeit in Ruhe zu lassen.
Reichsbote, April 10, 1906.

Wenn man weiter nichts anstreben, als heute auf morgen die Beruhigung zu haben, dass niemand uns überfallen wird, dann können wir in den nächsten Jahren vielleicht ruhiger schlafen als bisher. Aber das sind die politischen Ideale eines abstirbenden Volkes und so weit sind wir hoffentlich doch noch nicht.
Alldeutsche Blätter, July 7, 1906.

Gegenüber allen vielbesprochenen Einkreisungs—und Isolierungsversuchen ist von deutsche Seite wiederholt hervorgerufen worden, dass ein Staat von der tatsächlichen Macht Deutschlands unmöglich aus dem europäischen System ausgeschaltet werder kann.
Norddeutsche Allgemeine Zeitung, August 11, 1907.

Since 1871 a hostile coalition had never entirely ceased to be a possibility. Bismarck suffered from his famous *cauchemar* in spite of his alliances. His successors nevertheless learned that the Franco-Russian Alliance was not a serious menace, nor did they fear that an Anglo-French rapprochement would threaten Germany's security in Europe. Of greater concern was its probable effect upon her imperialist interests. Other powers, as Bülow foresaw in 1900, would be attracted. "This group would control every sea, and the colonial expansion of all nations would then depend upon its good-will." [1] Holstein thought that the time had perhaps arrived to ask France to state her intentions. "I am not certain," he confessed to the Chancellor, "that we should not take preventive and serious diplomatic steps in Paris." [2] Recovering from this momentary panic, the diplomats permitted the negotiations of 1901 to founder on England's refusal to join the Triple Alliance.

Chamberlain's suggestion in January 1901 of an understanding based upon Morocco and reserving its eastern coast for Germany was not followed up. [3] In fact, only the Pan-Germans called for territorial annexations in that part of Africa. Germany's unimpressive share in Morocco's commerce meant nothing to them in comparison with her needs. [4] "Even if we had no established interests there, our desire to become a world power gives us a right to a place at the table when a cake is to be divided." [5] By 1900 the *Alldeutsche Blätter* demanded ports on the Atlantic coast with their hinterland, but German opinion either ignored the subject, opposed an active policy, or called for the maintenance of Moroccan independence. [6] Even the Pan-Germans were willing that the bill for policing Morocco should be paid by the English or the French, but they fully counted upon sharing the benefits. The liberals had already said that England should do this work, [7] but the Pan-Germans felt that more could be secured from France. [8] Only a few weeks before the publication of the Anglo-French Entente, April 9, 1904, E. Hasse, the president of the League, called for an agreement with France for the acquisition of Rabat, Casablanca, and Mogador. [9] While the government

[1] Bülow's comments, Hatzfeldt, May 21; Bülow, June 5. *G. P.*, XVII, 305, 318–321.
[2] Bülow, *Denkwürdigkeiten*, I, 435.
[3] *G. P.*, XVII, 298 n.
[4] It was only slightly more than a fourth of England's, less than a third of France's, and larger than Spain's by only a small margin. E. N. Anderson, *The First Moroccan Crisis, 1904–1906* (Chicago, 1930), p. 2. *Cf.* F. T. Williamson, *Germany and Morocco before 1905* (Baltimore, 1937).
[5] *A. B.*, June 3, 1900. *Cf.* J. Wiese, "Marokko und die europäischen Mächte," *Gegenwart*, Jan. 10, 1903; W. Hemeling, "Marokko," *Grenzboten*, 1903, I, 202–204 (Jan. 22).
[6] *Magdeburgische Zeitung*, in *Post*, June 4, 1898.
[7] *Weser Zeitung*, in *N. A. Z.*, June 7, 1898; *Vossische Zeitung*, Dec. 8, 1898.
[8] *A. B.*, July 13, 1901.
[9] *Ibid.*, March 5, 1904.

clearly did not share these territorial ambitions, there is reason to believe that it wished to keep the question open. Of England's alleged desire for the Atlantic coast Bülow wrote, "It would seriously weaken the German government at home, and abroad it would make any coöperation impossible for an indefinite period: it would compel us, almost at any price, to turn to Russia and France." [10] The hope of diplomatic advantages was more influential in the decision against a Moroccan agreement than the problematical gains of a more or less distant future. Caprivi's dictum that Morocco should be maintained as a bone of contention between England and France still reflected the foreign office's point of view. [11]

As to an arrangement with France, Holstein dismissed it as worthless without a formal renunciation of Alsace-Lorraine. [12] Repeatedly, unofficial approaches from Franco-Russian and Spanish sources for a continental league were coolly rejected. [13] A watchful reserve was the obvious alternative to active intervention in Morocco. "We must," wrote Bülow, "remain completely reserved until further notice and act the part of the sphinx." [14] A year later Holstein said that this attitude should be continued as long as the existing alignment of the European powers endured, even if "France advanced south of the Atlas Mountains as far as Cape Juby." [15] Instead of encouraging Morocco to expect Germany's aid, the Sultan was advised to come to terms with France. [16] Schiemann, the Emperor's friend, began to write at the end of 1902 of the "open door" as Germany's sole interest. [17] The foreign office perhaps was not pleased by William's assurance to the King of Spain at Vigo, March 1904, that Germany desired only the "open door," for this unnecessarily limited its freedom of action.

[10] Bülow's comment, Hatzfeldt, May 21, 1900. *G. P.*, XVII, 305.

[11] *Ibid.*, VIII, 229, 230 (July 20, 1891).

[12] *Ibid.*, XVII, 341 (Aug. 8, 1901). According to Radolin, the ambassador in Paris, Bülow did not agree that a formal renunciation should be demanded. F. Thimme, "Aus dem Nachlass des Fürsten Radolin," *Berliner Monatshefte*, Sept. 1937, p. 746.

[13] Mühlberg, July 19, 1901. *G. P.*, XVII, 336, 337.

[14] Bülow's comments, Hatzfeldt, May 21, 1900. *Ibid.*, XVII, 305.

[15] *Ibid.*, XVII, 333 (July 8, 1901).

[16] Meinzingen, July 9, 1901. *Ibid.*, XVII, 334.

[17] *Kreuz-Zeitung*, Dec. 3, 1902, Jan. 28, 1903. Schiemann, *Deutschland und die Grosse Politik*, II, 406, III, 29, 30.

Germany had extended her "free hand" to Morocco. There, as elsewhere, she intended to await developments, in the expectation that the interest conflict between France and England would keep them apart and would lead to an Anglo-German rapprochement. These calculations were mistaken. Germany's passive attitude permitted the Western powers to come to terms. Instead of allowing Morocco to remain a source of friction, England chose to sacrifice her political interests there to secure France's renunciation of her claims in Egypt and to reduce the number of her potential enemies upon the continent. With the beginning of these negotiations in 1903, an Anglo-German rapprochement probably ceased to be within the range of practical politics. Germany had missed the psychological moment. "The art of politics," wrote Delbrück after the public announcement of the entente, "consists in making sacrifices at the right moment. To persuade one's own nation to accept a retreat requires much more strength and determination than to stimulate it to aggressive action." [18] For the moment, the diplomats had no alternative policy, and none occurred to a confused public opinion. Bülow clung to his illusions, arguing that France would never risk offending Russia.[19] Eckardstein, he said, was the only diplomat who seriously believed in the possibility of a triple entente.[20] In the press, the same mistaken optimism yielded gradually to alarm. A conservative observer even argued that the increasing tension in Anglo-German relations would attract France toward Germany.[21] In spite of earlier warnings in connection with Edward VII's visit to Paris, the Conservative *Post* (April 5, 1903) said that "everything will remain as before," because England would never accept France's leadership.[22] More satisfaction was derived from Russia's probable resentment and from reports of opposition in England and France to an understanding.[23] The Tsar's visit to Wiesbaden, November 1903, was

[18] *P. J.,* vol. 116, pp. 379, 380 (April 24, 1904).
[19] *G. P.,* XVII, 348 (Feb. 20, 1903).
[20] *Ibid.,* XVII, 570 (May 13, 1903).
[21] Dr. Hecksher, "German Ambitions," *P. J.,* vol. 114, p. 148 (Oct. 1903).
[22] Cf. *Post,* Feb. 6, May 9, June 28, 29, 1903.
[23] *Kreuz-Zeitung,* Feb. 25, 1903. Schiemann, *Deutschland und die Grosse Politik,* III, 65, 66; *Times,* April 6, 1903, Berlin, April 5; K. von Strantz, "Die Vereinsamung Deutschlands oder ein Dreikaiserbündnis," *Gegenwart,* Nov. 14, 1903. Holstein shared this view. Oncken, *Vorgeschichte des Weltkrieges,* II, 543.

encouraging.[24] Meanwhile the Social Democrats charged the government with complete failure, and the liberals claimed, despite their general approval of Bülow's foreign policy, that favorable opportunities had been lost.

More significant was the nervousness of the statesmen and of nationalist opinion. War was occasionally regarded as a possibility. Schiemann wrote (*Kreuz-Zeitung,* Feb. 25, 1903) that an Anglo-French understanding giving France the exclusive control of Morocco would "make a war between the great powers of Europe highly probable. . . ." The *Post* (June 23, 1903) warned France that "the German sword, though sheathed, is still sharp." Other reasons for suspicion were discovered: France's refusal to coöperate in the financing of the Bagdad Railway and the popular furor that followed when a Socialist told the Chamber of Deputies that France had practically abandoned the *revanche.*[25] To the Pan-Germans, France's willingness to sacrifice her historic interests in Egypt meant a desire to win England's support for an attack.[26] William's attitude and that of the foreign office showed that Germany's reserve had its limits. There was no interference in the Anglo-French negotiations, but reports that these countries were about to satisfy Spain's claims were followed by an unsuccessful effort to secure territory—either a part of Morocco or Fernando Po, an island off the western coast of Central Africa. The reply, silent as to Fernando Po, made it clear that Spain desired the same part of Morocco which interested Germany.[27] While the Emperor's renunciation of territorial aspirations at Vigo blocked any further discussion of annexations in Morocco, William himself informed the Chancellor that "we must . . . acquire Fernando."[28] Indifferent to Morocco, William was seriously alarmed by the European situation; yet he increased England's irritation and confirmed the Quai d'Orsay's belief in the aggressiveness of German policy. "What a sacrilegious affront to England's sacred memories!" wrote Paul Cambon, summing up

---

[24] *Post,* Nov. 14, 1903.

[25] Rosen, Oct. 29, 1903. *G. P.,* XVII, 456; *Post,* Nov. 28, 1903.

[26] *A. B.,* Oct. 17, 1903.

[27] These aims were stated by the Conservative *Deutsche Zeitung,* in the *Post,* Sept. 30, 1903.

[28] Richthofen, Sept. 24; Radowitz, San Sebastian, Sept. 29, 1903. *G. P.,* XVII, 354–356, 359, 360.

the reaction of English opinion to William's speech in Hanover, December 19, 1903, in which he claimed that Blücher and the Hanoverian regiments had saved the day for the English at Waterloo. "Never since the celebrated Kruger Telegram has any statement by a sovereign irritated the English so much." [29]   In January 1904 William committed an amazing indiscretion during a conversation with King Leopold of Belgium. After Leopold had refused an alliance, which he attempted to make more attractive by suggesting that Belgium might recover the ancient glories of the Burgundian Kingdom at France's expense, William, according to Bülow's version, resorted to threats, which the Belgian King communicated to the French foreign office. [30] William was not in the habit of being trifled with. "In the event of a European war, he who is not for me will be against me." If Belgium was not Germany's ally in her time of need, his decisions, like those of Frederick the Great in regard to Saxony in 1756, "would be determined solely by strategical considerations." [31] Leopold and the French of course drew the conclusion that the Germans intended to attack France through Belgium.

Reasons for confidence were found in the tension between Russia and Japan. If France, to prevent the dissipation of Russia's strength, worked for a peaceful arrangement, William brought all of his influence to bear upon the impressionable Tsar, against the advice of Bülow and Holstein, for an aggressive policy. [32] The foreign office had little confidence in William's ability to organize a continental league. Even Bülow failed to dissuade William; yet the diplomats, after Japan suddenly attacked Port Arthur (Feb. 1904), were not blind to the advantages of the conflict in the Far East. If Russia won, as was generally expected, her attention would be diverted from Constantinople and the Balkans; a defeat would so diminish her strength and prestige that for years she would be a negligible factor in Europe.

---

[29] *D. D. F.*, (2), IV, 99.

[30] M. Paléologue, *Un grand tournant de la politique mondiale, 1904–1906* (Paris, 1934), pp. 17–19.

[31] Bülow, according to his later account, insisted that Belgium's neutrality must be respected, unless it was first violated by France or England. Bülow, *Denkwürdigkeiten*, II, 75.

[32] R. J. Sontag, "German Foreign Policy, 1904–1906," *Am. Hist. Rev.*, XXXIII, 281, 282.

"The danger," wrote Holstein, "that Russia and France will fall upon Germany has been averted for an indefinite period."[33] The war was expected to increase the friction between England and Russia either in China, if Russia were victorious, or in the Straits, if she were defeated. Bülow increased his efforts to restrain William, reminding the Emperor of his duty to German interests when William advised the Tsar to go to Moscow and to preach a "Holy War."[34] That popular sympathy was largely with Japan doubtless meant little to the Chancellor,[35] but the feeling abroad that Germany was encouraging Russia doubtless contributed to the proclamation of Germany's neutrality. He promptly instructed the press to explain that everything had been done to avert hostilities and to stress her comparative disinterestedness.[36] The semi-official press nevertheless exulted at Germany's improved diplomatic situation. The war, wrote the *Kölnische Zeitung,* would again make "Berlin the center of European politics," and impose a greater modesty upon France.[37] A demand arose that the situation be used to advance German imperialism.[38] The Pan-Germans rehearsed the gains acquired during the Boer War and recommended an immediate arrangement with France giving Germany either a few ports or the entire Atlantic coast of Morocco.[39] The prospects, they insisted, were more favorable than ever, "for Russia would not fight in defense of French interests and because England, having withdrawn, could be counted upon not to intervene." Quick action,

---

[33] Holstein, *Lebensbekenntnis,* p. 228 (Jan. 21, 1904). That the war with Japan forced Russia, because of her need of German loans—the French market being temporarily closed to her—to renew the commercial treaty of 1894 without any concessions to her agrarian interests does not, as Hallgarten suggests, prove that the economic factor exerted a decisive influence upon Germany's policy. Hallgarten, *Vorkriegs Imperialismus,* pp. 177, 178.

[34] *G. P.,* XIX, 62, 63 (Feb. 14, 1904).

[35] A section of the press, according to the *Post* (Jan. 11, 1904), was more Japanese than the Japs themselves. The diplomatic corps believed that sympathy for Russia was limited to official circles and to the upper classes. *D. D. F.,* (2), IV, 347, 348 (Feb. 12, 1904).

[36] Bülow, Feb. 7, 1904. *G. P.,* XIX, 165. *Cf.* O. J. Hale, *Germany and the Diplomatic Revolution* (Philadelphia, 1931), p. 37. If England became involved, wrote a nationalist, she should not be permitted to attack in the Baltic Sea. F. Eisenhart, "Deutschlands Neutralität in Astasien," *Gegenwart,* Feb. 13, 1904.

[39] *A. B.,* Feb. 13; E. Hasse, "Marokko," *ibid.,* March 5, 1904.

[38] *Rheinisch-Westfälische Zeitung,* in *N. A. Z.,* Feb. 14, and in *Tägliche Rundschau,* April 12.

[39] *A. B.,* Feb. 13; E. Hasse, "Marokko," *ibid.,* March 5, 1904.

they insisted, was the principal need.[40]   The foreign office was in no position to follow this advice.

The Anglo-French negotiations had been hastened to a conclusion to prevent the war from spreading to Europe.   The published terms of the Entente Cordiale of April 8, 1904 revealed a comprehensive settlement extending from Newfoundland to Siam.   What concerned Germany was the recognition of France's interests in Morocco, with the reservation that the "open-door" should be maintained for thirty years, and France's abandonment of her historic interests in Egypt, for these terms meant the end of some of the conditions which had favored her *Weltpolitik*. Egypt had ceased to be the Alsace-Lorraine of Anglo-French relations, and Morocco could not be counted upon to turn England toward Germany.   Few Germans were optimistic enough to believe that the entente had no positive diplomatic significance. The secret terms, which were not revealed until 1911, occasioned much speculation; in fact they provided for the partition of Morocco between France and Spain in the event that a change in the status quo should become necessary, with France receiving the lion's share, since only the Mediterranean coast opposite Gibraltar should go in perpetuity to Spain, and for corresponding changes in Egypt.   Not only was it clear that the status quo in Morocco had been destroyed, but there was also reason to fear that the colonial settlement would develop, when the occasion arose, into a general diplomatic coöperation.[41]   There is, however, no proof in the British diplomatic correspondence that England intended that the understanding should be directed against Germany, nor is the recent suggestion of a German historian convincing that compromising documents were suppressed in order that they might not be submitted to parliament.[42]   There is no satisfactory evidence that she had any long-range purpose in mind except the removal of differences with the country which then seemed to be the least dangerous to the British Empire;[43]

---

[40] E. Hasse, "Versäumte Gelegenheiten," *ibid.*, Feb. 27; P. S., "Eine Wendung in der Marokkofrage," *ibid.*, April 2, 1904. From Tangier a diplomatic agent reported that conditions were ripe for the occupation of Agadir and of the surrounding country. Meintzingen, April 5. *G. P.*, XX, 202.

[41] *Cf.* Brandenburg, *From Bismarck to the World War*, p. 203.

[42] Oncken, *Vorgeschichte des Weltkrieges*, II, 545.

[43] Brandenburg thinks that her real desire was to return to the balanced position

let the future take care of itself, since British imperial interests had profited—this seems to have been the attitude of the British diplomats. Least of all had they any intentions of siding with France in the ancient Franco-German feud. The French foreign minister naturally spoke of his desire to change the entente into an alliance only to his colleagues,[44] but he frankly told Lansdowne that he wished to exclude Germany from Morocco. That the French would try to bring Russia into the entente was clear to Lord Cromer, the British pro-consul in Egypt. "Indeed," he wrote, November 27, 1903, "I cannot help feeling that, to the French government, this is one of the main attractions of the whole scheme." Like Cromer, Lansdowne expected Germany to take offense. "I have felt from the first, and so has Cambon," he wrote, November 17, 1903, "that we shall have to reckon with Germany."[45] In the comments of the anti-German press in England, there was indeed much to justify Germany's fears. The *Times* (April 9, 1904) refused to accept a narrow interpretation of the entente. The understanding was important "as a substantial pledge of the essential unity of our interests and desires" and not merely as a settlement of colonial differences. It was France, however, that furnished the immediate grievance. In Delcassé's failure to communicate the entente with the usual formalities, Germany saw a studied slight which she intended to hold in reserve as an excuse for her own intervention.

To excite opinion did not suit the government's purposes, since no immediate action was contemplated. The semi-official press adopted an attitude of qualified approval or of resignation. Its London and Paris correspondents predicted that the understanding "would furnish no grounds for objection to other powers."[46] If the door were left open for her commerce, Germany would benefit,[47] the *Kölnische Zeitung* (March 26) acknowledged, by the restoration of order. Public opinion was therefore forewarned when Bülow told the Reichstag, April 12, that the Anglo-

---

between the two diplomatic groups and that Germany's Moroccan policy forced her to change this plan. Brandenburg, *From Bismarck to the World War*, p. 269.

[44] Paléologue, *Un grand tournant*, p. 12 (Feb. 1, 1904).

[45] Lord Newton, *Lord Lansdowne: A Biography* (London, 1929), p. 285.

[46] *Kölnische Zeitung*, March 21. Cf. *Allgemeine Zeitung*, March 22; *National Zeitung*, March 19.

[47] Bihourd, March 25. *D. D. F.*, (2), IV, 505.

French understanding was not directed against Germany. It was even an advantage, since the quarrels between England and France "might endanger the world peace which we are sincerely trying to maintain." There was no reason to fear that Germany's commercial interests would be injured.[48] The *Vossische Zeitung* (April 11, 15) agreed that the entente was a welcome defense against war, but the reasons sometimes given in favor of the government's policy were scarcely flattering. At the end of March, the *Hamburger Nachrichten* expressed, according to the French ambassador, the major reaction of German opinion when it welcomed the diversion of France's attention from her eastern frontier,[49] but after Bülow's speech it wrote that the mediocrity of Germany's leaders condemned her to a passive rôle. "Doubtless we no longer have an active policy like Bismarck's, but nothing can be done about it. In the absence of a Bismarck we must take our leaders as they are. . . ." A change of ministers would do no good in view of the Emperor's interference.[50] The approval of the Social Democrats—Bebel spoke of the entente as a model for German diplomacy [51]—was scarcely a source of satisfaction.

The speech, according to the general verdict, was not one of Bülow's best. "There was no trace of the firm, confident tone," wrote the National Liberal *Hannoversche Kurier*, "which is most effective at home and abroad. . . ." [52] The Social Democratic *Vorwärts* (April 15) described it as "feeble and colorless. . . ." The moderate *Berliner Tageblatt* (April 17) spoke of "ringing figures of speech without tangible substance." Nationalist opinion had already protested against an attitude of resignation. On April 10, the *Magdeburgische Zeitung* spoke of the entente as the first step in France's new *revanche* policy.[53] Morocco's fate would be that of Tunis, although Germany's claim to the Atlantic coast was as good as France's. *"Auf den Westen Marokkos haben wir dasselbe Anrecht wie Frankreich, und das müssen wir uns wahren."* It was not too late, it said, to defend Germany's rights.

[48] *Verhandlungen*, XI Leg. Per., I Sess., III, 2022, 2023.
[49] Bihourd, April 1. *D. D. F.*, (2), IV, 529. Cf. *Post*, March 30.
[50] *Tägliche Rundschau*, April 15.
[51] *Verhandlungen*, XI Leg. Per., I Sess., III, 2058, 2059 (April 14).
[52] *Tägliche Rundschau*, April 15.
[53] Cf. *Post*, Feb. 6, 1904.

Bülow had once spoken of Germany's place in the sun. "We must not lose the last opportunity!" [54] Loudest were the complaints of the Pan-Germans. Of the claim that the "open door" was assured and that Germany desired nothing more, their official organ wrote "a maximum of nonsense in a minimum of words." [55] It was with shame and discouragement that von Reventlow, a Pan-German and big-navy publicist, listened to Bülow's speech. Germany had missed a favorable opportunity; it was not true that she had no interest in the antagonisms between other countries. [56] When Bülow asked if war should be declared for the conquest of Morocco, Heinrich Class, later to become the president of the Pan-German League, replied with another inquiry, Did the Chancellor "prefer peace at any price? Under any circumstances it is a poor statesmanship that conceives of only two alternatives, war or surrender." [57] Hitherto, according to the League's organ, peace had been maintained because Germany's enemies believed her to be ready for war. "And now Count Bülow cries from the housetops that he will not wage war with France for the sake of Morocco." [58] That Germany had been ignored "like a second-rate power" was the result, said the nationalist *Tägliche Rundschau* (April 17), of England's knowledge that Germany would not fight.

Nevertheless there was still some confidence. Many believed an Anglo-Russian war to be inevitable and saw in the Entente Cordiale a diplomatic preparation for it. [59] Even Delbrück agreed. [60] From Paris the *Kölnische Zeitung* (April 8) was informed that England wished to involve France in Morocco to weaken her, in view of the possible extension of the Russo-Japa-

---

[54] In the same article appeared perhaps the first warning that France intended to organize a native army in Morocco. The *Hamburger Nachrichten* took issue with all of these points. If Germany had a rightful claim to Moroccan territory, she could as justly claim any part of the world. The danger of a Berber army was a phantom; that of the *revanche*, a reality. "Does any one believe the latter would be disarmed or weakened by creating serious trouble for France in Morocco?" *Tägliche Rundschau*, April 13.

[55] *A. B.*, April 9.

[56] *Verhandlungen*, XI Leg. Per., I Sess., III, 2053, 2054.

[57] H. Class, *Marokko verloren? Ein Mahnruf in letzter Stunde* (Munich, 1904), p. 12. A part of this pamphlet—one of the publications of the Pan-German League (vol. XVII)—was written before Bülow's speech.

[58] *A. B.*, April 23.

[59] *Post, Reichsbote*, April 9.

[60] *P. J.*, vol. 116, pp. 189, 190 (March 27).

nese War. "From the Entente Cordiale," wrote the *Allgemeine Zeitung's* (April 12) London correspondent, "is hoped Russia's isolation." Schiemann believed it self-evident that France had deserted her ally,[61] and the nationalist *Leipziger Zeitung* asserted that "England was systematically preparing for the great settlement of her accounts with Russia." [62] Russia's reaction was awaited with satisfaction. "The May Days of the Franco-Russian love affair," wrote the moderate *Vossische Zeitung* (April 9), "are gone forever." Little encouragement was to be found in Russia, the Conservative *Post* (March 19) had already written, for the propaganda of the press coterie in London that favored a new triple alliance. From London Dr. Hans Plehn, the journalist and historian, vigorously protested against the facile optimism which counted upon England to force a war with Russia. She was essentially peaceful: "Her foreign policy is far more passive than is commonly supposed on the continent." [63] As for Russia, a Paris correspondent of the liberal *Berliner Tageblatt* (April 13) wrote that "Delcassé has done everything with *Russia's* full approval," for she hoped through France and England to secure better terms from Japan.

For a large part of German opinion, isolation was already or would soon be a fact. Bülow's denial that the entente was directed against Germany carried little conviction.[64] Had not the Conservative *Morning Post* (April 9) written: "Never in our recollection has Great Britain given away so much for nothing"? This feeling was not, of course, new. "All of the world makes friends," a nationalist had exclaimed in the preceding autumn, "while Germany is snubbed or treated with a minimum of courtesy." [65] Never before was pessimism so general or so forcefully expressed. Harden regretted that no one had replied to Bülow: "Germany faces . . . an immediate danger of isolation." Even her allies could not be counted upon. "If we were today forced

---

[61] *Kreuz-Zeitung*, April 12. Schiemann, *Deutschland und die Grosse Politik*, IV, 120.
[62] *Tägliche Rundschau*, April 13.
[63] *Ibid.*, April 14.
[64] *Post*, March 24; *Kölnische Zeitung*, March 26; *P. J.*, vol. 116, pp. 189, 190 (March 27); *Leipziger Tageblatt*, in *Tägliche Rundschau*, April 13; *Reichsbote*, April 13; *Kreuz-Zeitung*, *Allgemeine Zeitung*, April 15; *Berliner Tageblatt*, April 17.
[65] K. von Strantz, "Die Vereinsamung Deutschlands oder das Dreikaiserbündnis," *Gegenwart*, Nov. 14, 1903.

to fight Russia and France, not a single rifle would be fired in Italy and Austria."[66] Writing from England, Karl Peters warned his countrymen that Russia probably would be unable to resist the attraction of an Anglo-French alliance.[67] To the inference in Bülow's statement, "the strong is the most alone (*Der Starke ist am mächtigsten allein*)," that isolation should have no terrors for Germany, the *Berliner Tageblatt* (April 17) opposed another proverb, "Many hounds mean the death of the hare (*Viele Hunde des Hasen Tod sind*)." All Germans, wrote Delbrück, should realize "the danger to our position in world politics and should understand its reasons." Only with "a very strong armament on land as well as on sea" could Germany keep the world open against England for the expansion of other peoples.[68] Against the inevitable war, whose horrors would transcend anything that Germany had ever experienced, there remained, according to one observer, no recourse other than Bismark's system of alliances. She was powerless to remove the reasons for the hostilities that encircled her.[69] While the Social Democrats continued to support a policy which to others seemed a betrayal of Germany's interests—the renunciation of imperialism, the abandonment of the naval program, and even the return of Alsace-Lorraine—and although the extreme nationalists favored a stronger assertion of these interests and an avowed reliance upon the country's armed strength, moderate public opinion was largely at a loss as to Germany's future policy.[70]

On April 20 Bülow lectured the press. Since Germany was judged in part by her newspapers, their duty, he informed the director of the press bureau, was to discuss foreign affairs with restraint. He offered as a model the patriotism and sense for national interests of the English and French newspapers in recent crises.[71] The resulting article, "The Press and Foreign Countries," in the *Kölnische Zeitung* (April 22), diverged, however, in important respects from his admonitions. Not only did

---

[66] Harden, "Der neue Trust," *Zukunft*, April 23, 1904.

[67] *Finanz-Chronik*, in *Post*, April 20.

[68] *Post*, April 20.

[69] *P. J.*, vol. 116, pp. 375, 376 (April 24).

[70] Fokke, "Englische Freundschaft," *Gegenwart*, June 18, 1904.

[71] O. Hammann, *Bilder aus der letzten Kaiserzeit* (Berlin, 1921), pp. 42, 43. For a translation of a part of Bülow's memorandum, see Hale, *Germany and the Diplomatic Revolution*, pp. 40, 41.

it omit the praise of English and French journalism, but it also condemned the anti-Russian caricatures of the satirical reviews (*Witzblätter*) instead of the demand for Morocco. Nothing came of this effort to restrain nationalist opinion. Despite Bülow's official optimism, the diplomats and statesmen were alarmed. What Holstein feared, although he set no great store upon imperialism himself, was the creation of an insuperable barrier to the overseas expansion, upon which public opinion had set its heart. "No colonial policy," he wrote, "is possible against the opposition of England and France." [72]   His colleagues, however, did not share his confidence as to Germany's security in Europe. From Rome came the word that Delcassé was working to bring Russia into the entente.[73]   Not until June 26 did King Edward acknowledge to Bülow his desire for an understanding with Russia,[74] but the German foreign office did not need definite information to suspect that France and England were trying to form a triple entente. Bülow showed increased concern for Germany's prestige in Europe and for the loyalty of her allies. He quickly abandoned his efforts to secure Fernando Po and tried (March, May, 1904) to induce Italy publicly to pledge her fidelity to the Triple Alliance during the visit of President Loubet. Her silence, he had said, "would mean, in my opinion, *'le glas funèbre'* of the Italo-German Alliance." [75]   The results were disappointing, for Victor Emmanuel's mention of the Triple Alliance in his toast to the Emperor during William's visit to Naples and in a speech to the Italian parliament was a poor substitute for his silence to the French President, yet Bülow chose to swallow the affront rather than to acknowledge an unsatisfactory state of Italo-German relations.[76]   Within twenty-four hours after the

---

[72] "England und Frankreich werden uns schwerlich angreifen, das ist es nicht, was ich fürchte, aber wir sind ausser Stande, irgendwelche überseeische Erwerbungen zu machen." Colonial acquisitions did not interest him, "aber eine Masse Menschen Schreien danach und wundern sich, dass nichts für Deutschland abfällt." Holstein, *Lebensbekenntnis*, p. 231 (April 10).

[73] Monts, April 26. *G. P.*, XX, 26.

[74] Bülow, June 26. *Ibid.*, XX, 187, 188. The King had already spoken to Izvolski in Copenhagen in the same sense. Lee, *Edward VII*, II, 284 (April 14).

[75] Bülow, March 6, 15, 1904. *G. P.*, XX, 40, 45.

[76] Monts, May 21. *Ibid.*, XX, 77. Monts, however, suspended his visits to the Italian foreign office until Tittoni called upon him. *Ibid.*, XX, 74, 75. By a badly timed telegram thanking Victor Emmanuel for his reception, William weakened the effect of Bülow's pressure. Anderson, *The First Moroccan Crisis*, pp. 144–146.

Chancellor's optimistic speech of April 12 an official of the foreign office advised the acquisition of Agadir, in order to rehabilitate German prestige. "We need," he wrote, "a success in foreign affairs, since the Anglo-French Entente and the Franco-Italian rapprochement will be generally regarded as a defeat." [77] There was, however, little or no thought, in official circles, of direct action. Thoroughly pessimistic, William expected England to abandon every consideration for Germany, but he vetoed a proposal for a naval demonstration in Moroccan waters and refused—on Bülow's advice that it would strengthen the opponents of further naval increases—to coöperate with England, France, and Spain. [78]

In the meantime, Germany tried to dissolve the Entente Cordiale and the Franco-Russian Alliance, and twice to create a continental union against England. Differing as to procedure, William, Bülow, and Holstein were in accord as to the ultimate objective. [79] Germany, they felt, could no longer afford to wait. Striving feverishly to recover the initiative, they turned in succession to France, to England, to Russia, back to France, and finally to Russia again.

An agreement with France was regarded with considerable favor. The Pan-Germans, expecting a part of Morocco, supported it vigorously—even if force had to be used. Monts, the ambassador to Italy, believed it to be a necessity. [80] In February 1904, Count Graeben, the councillor of the Paris embassy, resigned because his chief, Prince Radolin, was convinced that France could be detached from the Russian alliance. [81] The Emperor himself had never entirely abandoned his dream of a reconciliation. Applauding Radolin's illusions, William did his best to meet President Loubet during his visit to Italy. [82] Since France

---

[77] G. P., XX, 203 (April 13).

[78] Tschirschky, Messina, April 3; Bülow, April 6; William II, Syracuse, April 19. Ibid., XX, 22, 23, 199–201.

[79] Sontag, "German Foreign Policy, 1904–1906," Am. Hist. Rev., XXXIII, 278.

[80] Monts, Erinnerungen und Gedanken, pp. 415–417 (End of May, July 11, 1904).

[81] Paléologue, Un grand tournant, p. 16.

[82] In accordance with Bülow's directions, the German press played up every bit of evidence of Italy's loyalty, although important liberal journals, like the Vossische Zeitung and the Frankfurter Zeitung, spoke of her defection and of the consequent weakening of Germany's position. Hale, Germany and the Diplomatic Revolution, pp. 46–48.

was still attached to Alsace-Lorraine, and since Germany had no intention of yielding an inch on that question, Delcassé was probably justified in thinking that the interview would do more harm than good.[83]   In vain, William hovered about the Italian coast in the *Hohenzollern*. With characteristic abruptness, he abandoned his cruise at Venice, and, returning to Germany, served notice upon France that his brief courtship was at an end.[84] Spain was thus assured of a favorable reaction to her request for Germany's support in regard to Morocco.   With advice, Bülow was generous: Spain should delay negotiations as long as possible, since an improvement in the Far Eastern situation might lessen England's attachment to the Entente Cordiale; she should demand the utmost in economic concessions.   If the Chancellor expected to be rewarded with Fernando Po or a Moroccan port, he was mistaken, for Spain continued the negotiations resulting in the agreement with France of October 1904.   By trying to use Spain's needs for the benefit of German imperialism, he had missed an opportunity to create difficulties for France.   There was still the possibility of a direct intervention in Morocco.   Without waiting for a reply to his inquiry as to England's attitude, Bülow decided (Aug. 17) to dispatch an ultimatum demanding satisfaction for certain claims within three months and threatening to stage a naval demonstration.   Again, William prevented a measure which would have inspired doubts abroad as to the sincerity of his Vigo statement.   In Morocco, Germany had still to show her hand.[85]

While William maneuvered for a meeting with President Loubet, the foreign office attempted to arrange a general understanding with England.   Bülow agreed, April 19, that "all remaining questions, large and small," should be discussed as a condition for Germany's approval of proposed changes in the Egyptian administration.   He even included a treaty of arbitration to show that Germany's good-will equalled that of France.[86] The prospects were not encouraging.   Having just completed the

83 Paléologue, *Un grand tournant*, pp. 56, 57 (April 20).
84 For Delcassé's reaction, see *ibid.*, pp. 113, 114 (July 11, 1904).
85 Anderson, *The First Moroccan Crisis*, pp. 147-158.
86 *G. P.*, XX, 124.

entente with France, the British foreign office had no desire to diminish its value in her eyes by making a similar agreement with Germany.[87] The German navy enthusiasts did not improve matters by launching a campaign for additional construction.   On April 16, the executive committee of the Navy League, meeting at Dresden with the Crown Prince of Saxony in the chair, announced that the construction by 1912 of three double squadrons with a total of forty-eight modern battleships would be one of the League's aims and that a *"grossartige Agitation"* would at once be organized.[88]   England's reaction was not improved by the disavowal of any intention of building up to her strength [89] (the *Reichsbote,* April 21, claimed that a fleet half the size of England's would force her to show a satisfactory consideration for German interests), since the British naval authorities knew that their entire fleet would never be concentrated in or near the North Sea.   Whatever Tirpitz' own views may have been, the government contemplated no new bill at this time; but it did hope to persuade England to pay a high price for an understanding and was perhaps not entirely displeased by the League's action.   Had not England given more than she received in the Entente Cordiale and should not Germany have the same treatment as France?   Only "a large compensation," England was informed, May 4, would reconcile German opinion to the renunciation of Germany's rights in the control of the Egyptian finances.[90] But Germany's expectations far exceeded her financial interests, for her nationals owned only one quarter of one per cent of the Egyptian bonds.   Her desire to discuss the Samoan question, the indemnities arising from the South African War, and the Canadian preferential tariff in connection with a "perfectly innocuous arrangement" seemed to Lansdowne "like a great piece of effrontery," and not less so because she spoke at the same time of a possible arrangement with Russia and France.[91]   She demanded, he complained, "the advantages which France had secured with-

---

[87] Hale, *Germany and the Diplomatic Revolution,* p. 50.   Cf. *Spectator,* June 4.

[88] A report of this meeting appeared in the semi-official *Norddeutsche* (April 19). The League claimed at this time a total of 3595 local branches and a membership of about seven hundred thousand. *Die Woche,* April 30.

[89] Eissenhart, "Zur kommenden Flottenvorlage," *Gegenwart,* Aug. 20, 1904.

[90] *G. P.,* XX, 127, 128.

[91] Newton, *Lansdowne,* p. 328 (May 6).

out offering any return," whereas Russia, Italy, and Austria had accepted the Khedival Decree without further ado.[92]   Awakening at last to the folly of irritating England with so little prospect of profit, Germany finally abandoned the attempt to reach an understanding and approved (June 1904) the changes in Egypt in return for assurances in regard to German local rights and interests.[93]   The momentary tension had no immediately serious consequences; it was even followed by a perceptible improvement. At Kiel, King Edward assured William that no serious political differences existed between the two countries, and, on his suggestion, German warships visited Plymouth late in June.[94]   While the arbitration treaty of July 12 was soon forgotten, Bülow believed that he had learned something of value.   England's promise to support France in Morocco, he wrote, need not be taken too seriously; she might be even more willing to recognize the community of Anglo-German interests.   While Metternich was convinced that England would aid France in establishing herself in Morocco, he also thought that she favored a narrow interpretation of her obligations in the entente.[95]   Lansdowne had told him: "I could at any rate say that it was not at all probable that, if any third Power were to have occasion to uphold its Treaty rights, we should use our influence in derogation of them." [96] The first attack upon the entente had nevertheless clearly failed.

For a rapprochement with Russia the prospects seemed better. If the Entente Cordiale had not seriously weakened Russia's loyalty,[97] the Anglo-Japanese Alliance and the Russo-Japanese War had greatly increased her ill-will toward England.   There was, on the contrary, no question as to Germany's friendliness. Never had William's personal ascendancy over the Tsar been more marked than in their correspondence in 1904,[98] an influence which William used to urge a desperate offensive against Japan.[99]

[92] Metternich, June 2.   G. P., XX, 139.

[93] Anderson, The First Moroccan Crisis, p. 150.

[94] The newspapers of both countries regarded these incidents with suspicion.   Hale, Germany and the Diplomatic Revolution, pp. 48, 53.   Cf. G. P., XX, 211 (July 21).

[95] G. P., XX, 211, 221 (July 21, Aug. 15).

[96] Lansdowne, Aug. 14.   B. D., III, 54.

[97] Some thought that France would withdraw her financial support.   "Russlands grosse Zukunft," Historisch-Politische Blätter, vol. 134, p. 537 (Oct. 1904).

[98] Oncken, Vorgeschichte des Weltkrieges, II, 549.

[99] During the war, he advised the Russians to launch their naval forces in the Far

Even Bülow's critics rejoiced that the specter of a war on two fronts had been allayed for many years.[100]   After the withdrawal of Russian troops from the German frontier Germany made a significant change in her plan of campaign: the Schlieffen plan, adopted somewhat later, provided for a purely defensive position against Russia, a crushing attack upon France through Belgium, and a holding operation on the Alsace-Lorraine frontier.[101]   In September William wrote of the removal of five infantry divisions from the East Prussian frontier as something which Moltke and Bismarck had longed for in vain and for which he had ceased to hope.[102]   A new commercial treaty suggested the possibility of further coöperation; yet it was not easy for Germans to abandon the "free hand." "We believe," wrote an important review in June, "that it would be a mistake for Germany to depend on one country; but that will certainly happen if we break with the other. We should keep the door open in both directions." [103] The liberals were almost as opposed to an association with Russia as the Social Democrats. Any move, wrote the *Vossische Zeitung* (April 18, 1904), "to place German policy at her service against England will meet the forthright opposition of the German people." For those who believed that Bismarck had spoken the last word on foreign policy, there was, however, no question as to what should be done. One spoke of Bismarck's *Gedanken und Erinnerungen* as "a textbook of the first order for German foreign policy" [104] and Harden insisted that Germany would pay for Russia's weakness, because the stronger England became, the

East against the Japanese fleet to weaken it, in view of the coming of their main fleet under Rodjestvenski, and to send their warships in the Black Sea through the Straits without consulting the powers. Semenoff, *Correspondance entre Guillaume II et Nicolas II*, pp. 107, 109 (Sept. 1904).

[100] Monts, *Erinnerungen und Gedanken*, p. 415 (End of May, 1904).

[101] According to Paléologue, a traitor on the German general staff revealed the details of an essentially similar plan in the spring of 1904. Paléologue, *Un grand tournant*, pp. 63–65 (April 25). When this revelation first appeared in the *Revue des deux mondes* (June, 1931; Oct. 1932), German critics at once attacked its authenticity, arguing that no plan like this had yet been adopted. Paléologue nevertheless repeated the story without any modification in his book. W. Foerster, "Ist der deutsche Aufmarsch 1904 an die Franzosen verraten worden?" *Berliner Monatshefte*, X, 1053–1067; Foerster, "Zu Paléologues neue Mitteilungen zum Verrat des deutschen Aufmarsch-Planes," *ibid.*, XI, 156–160.

[102] *G. P.*, XIX, 252 (Sept. 25). *Cf.* Oncken, *Vorgeschichte des Weltkrieges*, II, 550, 551.

[103] "Deutschlands Stellung zu England und gewissen deutschfeindlichen Treibereien," *Grenzboten*, II, 666 (June 23, 1904).

[104] Dr. F. C. W., "Deutschland und Russland," *Gegenwart*, May 20, 1904.

greater would be the obstacles to her expansion.[105]   Fearing a disturbance of the good relations with the United States and the recently improved relations with England, and increased demands by Russia during the negotiation of the commercial treaty, the foreign office waited some months before it agreed to William's offer of an alliance to the Tsar.   An unfriendly press campaign in England played a part: the *Times* charged that Germany had made a separate agreement with Russia against England, that she had blocked China's ratification of an Anglo-Thibetan treaty, and, finally—in its Paris correspondence—that she had warned Russia of the presence of Japanese destroyers in the North Sea and that she was therefore responsible for the loss of lives when the Russian fleet fired upon the British fishing vessels on the Dogger Bank.[106]   This, however, was only one aspect of an unfavorable world situation.   From France's efforts to attract Russia into the Entente Cordiale, from the danger of the renewed tension between Russia and Austria in the Balkans, and from the possibility that England might decide to come to terms with Russia arose the fear that the situation might be even worse after the end of the Far Eastern war.[107]   A rapprochement with Russia would avert the greatest of these dangers.

Again Germany asked for too much.   Counting upon the Dogger Bank affair to secure Russia's acquiescence, Bülow and Holstein encouraged the willing Emperor to offer Nicholas a general defensive alliance in Europe, although they argued that Germany in fact ran the risk of a British attack from the agreement to coal the Russian fleet at Kiaochow.[108]   Nicholas, at first enthusiastic, asked for a draft of the proposed alliance.   France, he said, would be compelled "to join her ally."[109]   It is pointless to spec-

---

[105] Harden, "Der Krieg," *Zukunft,* Oct. 22, 1904.

[106] Hale, *Germany and the Diplomatic Revolution,* pp. 56–62. To each of these charges the Germans replied with a formal denial. *G. P.,* XIX, 295, 298 (Nov. 4, 7).

[107] *Cf.* Alvensleben, St. Petersburg, Aug. 25. Oncken, *Vorgeschichte des Weltkrieges,* II, 551.

[108] William II, Oct. 24, 1904. *G. P.,* XIX, 303, 304. The offer antedated the allegations in the English press of German responsibility for the Dogger Bank affair (Oct. 29). On November 2 was brought to the attention of the Quai d'Orsay Prince Radolin's statement that France would have to choose between Russia and Germany on the one hand and England on the other. Paléologue, *Un grand tournant,* pp. 157, 158.

[109] Nicholas II, Oct. 29. *G. P.,* XIX, 305. The draft was sent October 30. *Ibid.,* XIX, 307, 308.

ulate as to the result if the German foreign office had proposed merely a new Reinsurance Treaty, providing for neutrality in the event of an attack by a third power.   This offer convinced Lamsdorff, the Russian foreign minister, that Germany desired a complete reorientation of Russian policy.   With England's consent to the arbitration of the Dogger Bank affair, thanks to France's effective work in London and St. Petersburg,[110] the danger of war disappeared and with it the strongest argument in favor of William's proposal.   In Paris, Delcassé warned Russia that France would never sacrifice England's friendship or join a Russo-German alliance.[111]   Lamsdorff had already triumphed.   On November 7 Nicholas submitted a proposal differing fundamentally from William's offer: the purpose of the alliance was to be the localization of the Russo-Japanese War, its duration the period of hostilities in the Far East, and the text was to be communicated to France before its ratification.[112]   While these terms safeguarded Germany against the dangers arising from the coaling of the Russian fleet, their limited character and the provision for their communication to France were offensive.   Germany's second offer, largely based upon Holstein's ideas, defined the purpose of the alliance as the maintenance of peace, fixed the duration at one year, and specifically withdrew the provision for coöperation during the Russo-Japanese peace negotiations.[113]   In vain William warned the Tsar against England's intention of intervening in Japan's favor and of establishing her influence "once and for all" in Thibet; to no avail he spoke encouragingly of an aggressive movement toward India or Persia.[114]   Nicholas' enthusiasm had cooled.   When he insisted that the terms must first be communicated to France, William spoke of "kalte Füsse."[115]   Rather no agreement at all than to put it in Delcassé's power to inform London.[116]   Germany's hopes were again dashed.   As a substitute for a formal alliance, Russia's promise of military support if Eng-

[110] Anderson, *The First Moroccan Crisis*, p. 112.

[111] Paléologue, *Un grand tournant*, pp. 160 (Nov. 4), 171 Nov. 9).

[112] Nicholas II, Oct. 25/Nov. 7. *G. P.*, XIX, 311.

[113] William (undated). *Ibid.*, XIX, 312–315.

[114] William II, Nov. 15, 19. *Ibid.*, XIX, 390, 393, 394. *Cf.* Anderson, *First Moroccan Crisis*, p. 112.

[115] William II, Nov. 23. *G. P.*, XIX, 316. *Cf.* Oncken, *Vorgeschichte des Weltkrieges*, II, 558.

[116] *G. P.*, XIX, 318, 319 (Nov. 24).

land attacked Germany in connection with the coaling question left Holstein cold, for the English could easily find another excuse to attack.[117] The result left William in the depths of despair. To Nicholas he professed his continued friendship, but, writing to Bülow, he spoke of the outcome as "entirely negative" and as "the first defeat of my experience." [118] His subsequent marginal comments show a distinct leaning toward Japan and the United States.[119]

The failure of these negotiations had more than a negative significance. England became more unfriendly than ever, the excitement in the anti-German press increasing on reports of a Russo-German understanding.[120] On November 7, Paléologue handed to Lansdowne all of the information in France's possession relating to Germany's courtship of Russia.[121] The effect was immediate. On December 6 ships were forbidden to leave British ports with coal for the Russian fleet—an order that most affected German vessels. Four battleships were promptly detached from the Mediterranean fleet for service in the home waters.[122] Rumors of a permanent shift in British naval strength so excited William that he threatened to regard it as a *casus belli.* "It would rightly be considered," he wrote, "as a menace of war." [123] At the same time, the German naval attaché's reports arguing from a few chauvinist articles in the *Army and Navy Gazette* and *Vanity Fair* that the theory of the preventive war was gaining ground were taken seriously in Berlin.[124] Despite Bülow's moderate speech to the Reichstag (Dec. 5),[125] there developed a "private" war scare in Berlin in November and Decem-

---

[117] Holstein's comments, Alvensleben, Dec. 12. *Ibid.,* XIX, 328, 329.
[118] Semenoff, *Correspondance entre Guillaume II et Nicolas II,* p. 139. (Dec. 21); William II, Dec. 28. *G. P.,* XIX, 346, 347.
[119] Oncken, *Vorgeschichte des Weltkrieges,* II, 561, n. 3.
[120] Bülow admitted this. Lascelles, Dec. 28. *B. D.,* II, 57.
[121] Paléologue, *Un grand tournant,* pp. 169, 170.
[122] Oncken, *Vorgeschichte des Weltkrieges,* II, 560.
[123] William II, Nov. 23. *G. P.,* XIX, 316, 317.
[124] *Ibid.,* XIX, 353. These articles, according to a witness writing in the Pan-German official organ, had been ignored by almost all newspapers of any influence. H. Plehn, "Die englische Presse und Deutschland," *A. B.,* Jan. 21, 1905.
[125] *Verhandlungen,* XI Leg. Per., I Sess., V, 3374, 3375. In an interview with Bashford (Nov. 15), an English journalist, Bülow denied that the German fleet was intended to serve other than defensive purposes. The *Alldeutsche Blätter* (Dec. 10) protested that he should have asserted Germany's right to build the kind of a fleet required by her interests.

ber 1904. Naval units in the Far East were ordered home.[126] Holstein confessed, for the first time, that he feared an attack by England.[127] The full resources of the diplomatic service were enlisted in a review of Anglo-German relations. Metternich was summoned from London and his chief assistants were asked to submit memoranda. All believed that England would not attack immediately unless an unforeseen incident like the Dogger Bank affair occurred. Against the danger of a triple entente, a Russo-German alliance was generally regarded as the only effective defense, and Metternich asserted that it must be kept secret from France.[128] As the source of greatest danger, he correctly pointed to the fears current in both countries and to the inability of each to understand the reasons.[129] To the German press, only her jealousy of Germany's mercantile marine could explain England's alarm, while its own fears were justified.[130] The danger of an attack by England was indisputable. "The moment they are ready," wrote one pamphleteer, "she will fall upon us . . . in order to assure her survival." [131] Even the diplomats were not reassured by the predominantly peaceful tendencies of her public opinion,[132] for they believed that the aggressive minority would prevail in a crisis.[133] In this atmosphere of suspicion, the efforts of those who desired a better understanding had little prospect of success. In vain was Germany's point of view explained in the English press by her spokesmen and *vice versa*.[134] So long as the underlying economic and political conflicts remained, good

[126] Hale, *Germany and the Diplomatic Revolution*, p. 67.

[127] *G. P.*, XIX, 359 (Dec. 5). A fortnight later, he told Lascelles that the government's failure to check the anti-German press campaign suggested "that they do not disapprove it." *B. D.*, III, 58.

[128] Hale, *Germany and the Diplomatic Revolution*, pp. 67, 68.

[129] Metternich, Dec. 18. *G. P.*, XIX, 332. *Cf.* Newton, *Lansdowne*, p. 332.

[130] F. Eisenhart, "Die Gründe der Abneigung gegen Deutschland," *Gegenwart*, Jan. 7, 1905; E. Reventlow, *Deutschland in der Welt voran?* (Berlin, March 1, 1905), pp. 16 ff.; "Eine englisch-deutsche Verständigung," *Grenzboten*, II, 63 (April 13, 1905).

[131] A. Gildemeister, *Deutschland und England; Randbemerkungen eines Hanseaten* (Berlin, 1905), pp. 48, 49; *Reichsbote*, Feb. 11, 1905.

[132] Of the influence of public opinion in England an experienced observer wrote that it "can scarcely be exaggerated. Public opinion is almost sovereign in England." H. Plehn, *Nach dem englisch-japanischen Bündnis* (Berlin, 1907), pp. 109, 110.

[133] Schulenburg, Dec. 13; Eulenburg, Dec. 15. *G. P.*, XIX, 362, 363.

[134] Professor Paulsen denied that the admitted cooling of German opinion toward England meant a desire for war, in an article that appeared in the *Deutsche Rundschau* (Nov. 1904) and in the *Contemporary Review* (Dec. 1904). Hale, *Germany and the Diplomatic Revolution*, p. 69.

feeling was at the mercy of an incident, of a press campaign, or of an alarmist statement from official quarters. The Germans promptly feared the worst when Arthur Lee, the first civil lord of the admiralty, asserted (Feb. 2, 1905) that the North Sea would henceforth be the crucial area and that "the British Navy would get its blow in first, before the other side had time even to read in the papers that war had been declared." [135] Nothing could convince German opinion that this statement was not a threat. Only an official repudiation, William told the British ambassador, would prevent a "colossal" expansion of the naval program under the pressure of an excited public opinion.[136] The nationalists at once demanded a stronger fleet.[137] "England," wrote the *Reichsbote* (Feb. 11), ". . . will be Germany's enemy in the coming war, and she gambles everything upon a rapid offensive." Even the Social Democratic *Vorwärts* (Feb. 5) admitted that no speech had ever been pointed so directly against Germany. Anglo-German friction had become perhaps the major problem of German foreign policy. Delbrück wrote a few months later: "World politics during the next generation will center in the Anglo-German antagonism." [138]

Many Germans were at a loss to explain the increased unfriendliness of foreign opinion. The record, they believed, was clear. Other countries had compelled the German people to fight for their national unity, but "what nation would have been less intoxicated by success? Surely there is no other example of a victorious nation consecrating itself so exclusively to the solution of its domestic problems instead of embarking upon further conquests." [139] Innumerable editorials asserted that Germany's armaments on land and sea were purely defensive, that the maintenance of peace in Europe for a generation was the result of the fear inspired by her army, and that the fleet would serve the same useful purpose. Even her *Weltpolitik*, rightly regarded, should not be a cause for animosity, for it was inspired not by hostility but by necessity and the consciousness of Germany's

---

[135] *Standard*, Feb. 4.
[136] Hale, *Germany and the Diplomatic Revolution*, p. 72.
[137] *P. J.*, vol. 121, p. 370 (July 23, 1905).
[138] H. Delbrück, "Die Wahrheit über das deutsche Volk," *Deutsche Revue*, 1904, I, 97 (Jan. 1904).
[139] "Wozu der Lärm?" von einem Diplomat, *ibid.*, 1905, II, 13 (April).

merits. The unfriendliness of foreign opinion must therefore be the artificial product of the French and English control of the distribution of news, chiefly through the British-owned cables. The fact remained, however, that Germany's position in world affairs had changed for the worse and that her efforts to improve it by the normal methods of diplomacy had failed. Her security in Europe became more definitely the chief cause of uneasiness. William's reaction was symptomatic. "The situation," he wrote, "begins to resemble more than ever that which preceded the Seven Years' War." [140] Officials warned against the expectation of a weakened Franco-Russian Alliance and against France's efforts to bring England and Russia together.[141] Moved by jealousy of Germany's achievements, England had approved, said the *Reichsbote* (Jan. 1, 1905), "France's lust for revenge." Public opinion was increasingly disturbed by criticisms of German foreign policy. A Pan-German dismissed as unsound its basic assumptions: Germany never had maintained a balance between Russia and England, because any differences with one of these powers inevitably required a dependence upon the other.[142] Harden continued his caustic attacks. "Bülow," he wrote, "is a wonderful captain for quiet seas to amuse the passengers on the promenade deck; he is not to blame if the times are greater than he is." [143] "Nothing seems so desirable," wrote Monts, "as perpetual change. It is painful to see how the advantages of a situation are always missed." [144] This dissatisfaction was a constant temptation to try more forceful methods.

Moreover, Germany remained, in spite of the fact that the military law was renewed in 1904 for the first time without significant increases,[145] the strongest power in Europe. Germany, according to a widely read article, was like a fortress that must always be prepared to withstand a siege, and to remain a great power she must become a world power. Her military

---

140 *G. P.*, XIX, 316, 317 (Nov. 23, 1904).
141 A communication to this effect in the *Süddeutsche Reichskorrespondenz* was reprinted by the *Norddeutsche Allgemeine Zeitung* (Feb. 11, 1905).
142 K. Mehrmann, "Die britische Hegemonie als nächste Erscheinungsform der Weltpolitik," *A. B.*, Sept. 3, 1904.
143 Harden, "Moritz und Nina," *Zukunft*, March 18, 1905.
144 Monts, *Erinnerungen und Gedanken*, p. 418.
145 Graf Westarp, *Konservative Politik*, 2 vols. (Berlin, 1935), I, 219.

strength gave her the right to a voice in all questions and the power to enforce her claims against the strongest rivals, including the United States. Every opportunity should be used to reduce the long lead of the United States, England, and Russia.[146] These ideas, welcomed by the Pan-Germans as essentially their own,[147] were shared to some extent by official circles. Whatever might be said publicly, there was no intention of acquiescing in the unfavorable change in the balance of power or of abandoning Germany's imperialist aspirations. The Moroccan question furnished a convenient excuse for action; the timing and form of the initiative alone remained uncertain. It was evident, by the beginning of 1905, that the policy of reserve played into France's hands. She had done nothing to satisfy Germany.[148] On the contrary, she had already made an appreciable advance toward a paramount position in Morocco by refunding the debt (July 1904) and she was about to take an even longer step toward that end by sending an agent to Fez to secure administrative reforms and the organization of a military police under her own direction. Germany's aims were not entirely clear. In spite of the Emperor's Vigo statement, the Pan-Germans continued to hope for territorial acquisitions. The idea appeared more than once in the negotiations with Spain, but the foreign office had not in fact adopted it as its chief objective. As early as June 1904 a fairly accurate statement of the official view appeared in the *Grenzboten*. Chiding those who demanded territory, because the first step in that direction would give "the signal for the union of all powers against us," it declared for the maintenance of Moroccan independence and of the "open door." [149] Representing the interests of all countries and demanding no special ad-

---

[146] "Weltpolitik," *Grenzboten*, 1904, IV, 2 (October 6).

[147] "The *Grenzboten* and other periodicals," wrote the *Alldeutsche Blätter* (Oct. 29, 1904), "condemn us Pan-Germans without seeing that our ideas have unconsciously become their own."

[148] The possibility that France might eventually include Germany in her arrangements had been one of the reasons for the policy of reserve. Richthofen's comments, Bruening, April 23, 1904. *G. P.*, XX, 203-205.

[149] "Deutschlands Stellung zu England und gewisse deutschfeindlich Treibereien," *Grenzboten*, 1904, II, 667, 678 (June 23). In the competition between the Krupps and Schneider-Creusot munition companies, which reached an acute stage in Constantinople at this time, Hallgarten discovers the real cause of the Moroccan crisis. Rottenburg, the Krupp agent in Morocco, hastened back to Berlin to arouse the foreign office against France. Hallgarten, *Vorkriegs Imperialismus*, pp. 187, 188.

vantages for herself, Germany, said Bülow, had a strong position.[150]   France's "peaceful penetration" had in fact antagonized
most of the representatives of the powers in Morocco; [151] there
was even some reason for doubting England's support of France
against Germany.[152]   If the German foreign office had invited
France to discuss the situation and if other powers had been consulted, support might have been won, but this procedure was regarded as offensive to Germany's dignity and interests.   To ask
France to state her purposes would perhaps lead, it was thought,
to the recognition of conditions which would permit her steadily
to continue her peaceful penetration.[153]   Nor would a quiet discussion with France, it seemed to German diplomats, have contributed anything to the solution of the larger problems.   For
Bülow and Holstein, the Moroccan question was chiefly significant as a convenient terrain for an attack upon the Entente
Cordiale.   To compel France to change her foreign policy, to
impress upon her the consciousness of her weakness and the
folly of depending upon England's support were the objectives
which they hoped to attain by forcing her to yield in Morocco.
The first step was the inclusion of Tangier in the itinerary of the
Emperor's spring cruise.

In addition to Russia's decisive defeat at Mukden (March 1–10),
the domestic situation in France seemed encouraging.   There
was, for the moment, little evidence of a strong national sentiment.   Neglected by the anti-clerical ministries, the army and
navy were in no condition to fight.   That French public opinion
would not support an aggressive foreign policy when faced by the
danger of war was generally believed.   Officially, France might
"embrace the Japanese, the Venezuelans, and the Hottentots, if
they declare for the revision of the Treaty of Frankfort," wrote
a nationalist observer; but the people had no intention of going
to war with Germany.[154]   "In reality," wrote the ultra-Conservative *Reichsbote* (Feb. 4, 1905), "no Frenchman, not even a na-

---

[150] *G. P.,* XX, 281 (March 29).
[151] Hale, *Germany and the Diplomatic Revolution,* pp. 88–91.
[152] See p. 502.
[153] Hale, *Germany and the Diplomatic Revolution,* pp. 88–91.
[154] F. Wugk, "Deutschland und die äussere Politik Frankreichs," *Grenzboten,* 1905,
II, 18–25 (April 6).

tionalist, has any taste for measures which might force France
to draw the sword against any country. . . . And nothing but an
emotional upheaval can change this peaceful state of mind."
There was less justification for confidence that England would
not support France and for the acceptance of President Roosevelt's declaration of disinterestedness in China as a favorable
augury.[155]   The attempt to intimidate France was based upon a
fatal weakness. The foreign office counted chiefly upon her unpreparedness for war, but Germany was not herself ready to resort to extreme measures. The Emperor refused to accept Morocco as a sufficient cause for war and Bülow finally agreed with
him. The Chancellor warned the Sultan that "Germany cannot
declare war upon France for the sake of Morocco" and to quiet
William's doubts about the Tangier visit he explained that "there
is no question of Your Majesty's risking a war with France." [156]
Unreliable in many respects, Bülow's *Memoirs* reveal the motives
and aims of his Moroccan policy accurately enough. "Trusting
in my skill and strength to force Delcassé's fall without resorting
to extreme measures, I did not hesitate to confront France with
the danger of war." [157]   France's ministry, "in which even the
minister of war is a stockbroker," wrote the Chancellor, February 11, 1905, could be counted upon to yield.[158]

History, said William at Bremen just before his departure, had
taught him the folly of world domination. "The world empire
of which I have dreamed is merely the newly established Germany enjoying on all sides the absolute confidence which is the
due of a quiet, honorable, and peaceful neighbor." [159]   The nationalists were frankly disappointed,[160] but the liberals hoped
that the speech foreshadowed a reasonable settlement of the
Moroccan question.[161]   In fact, Bülow feared that William might
not land at Tangier. To prevent this, the Chancellor had the
Norddeutsche (March 21) announce that the visit to Tangier
was a certainty; he then assured his sovereign, in spite of Metter-

155 *G. P.*, XIX, 349, 350 (Feb. 5, 1905).
156 *Ibid.*, XX, 247, 275 (Jan. 30, March 26).
157 Bülow, *Denkwürdigkeiten*, II, 108.
158 *G. P.*, XX, 252.
159 *N. A. Z.*, March 24.
160 *Rheinisch-Westfälische Zeitung*, in *Tägliche Rundschau*, March 25.
161 *Berliner Tageblatt, Vossische Zeitung*, March 23. Cf. *Vorwärts*, March 24.

nich's report from London that the English press was more French than the French themselves, that the "French government . . . cannot count upon strong support from England" and that Delcassé would claim a last-minute change of plans as a diplomatic victory.[162]   Counting upon the resulting uncertainty to frighten the French, Germany let the visit speak for itself. France and England, Bülow wrote, March 24, should draw their own conclusions. Germany's representatives were to remain silent to all questions "with an impassible and serious countenance.   Our attitude in this affair is, for the time being, like that of the Sphinx, which, surrounded by curious tourists, betrays nothing."[163]   This reserve was by no means complete.   In London, Germany's dissatisfaction was attributed to France's presumption in claiming a mandate from the powers in demanding reforms.[164]   In St. Petersburg, Bülow expressed his "painful surprise" at the sympathy for France in the Russian press.[165]   A similarly indefinite attitude was reflected by the official press at home.   On March 23, the *Norddeutsche* asserted "that the attempt to represent the Emperor's journey as the point of departure for a new policy will fail."[166]   The *Kölnische Zeitung* (March 25) admitted that the visit would have "a certain political significance" and then, three days later, it said that the Emperor naturally did not wish "to miss the colorful life of the Orient at the very gates of Europe."   France's failure to communicate her agreement with England deprived her of the right, it was said, to speak in the name of Europe in dealing with Morocco.[167]   A somewhat more definite stand was taken on the very eve of the visit.   "The political significance . . . which Paris seeks to deny," asserted the *Süddeutsche Reichskorrespondenz,* "consists in the demonstration that *Germany has not withdrawn her relations with the sovereign Sultan of Morocco and will not withdraw them.*"[168]   On March 28, Bülow told the Reichstag, however,

---

[162] Bülow, March 20, 29, Metternich, March 28, *G. P.,* XX, 263, 281, 601.
[163] Bülow, March 24. *Ibid.,* XX, 274.
[164] Bülow, March 22. *Ibid.,* XX, 269.
[165] Bülow, March 27. *Ibid.,* XX, 277, 278.
[166] Cf. *Berliner Lokal-Anzeiger,* March 23.
[167] Hale, *Germany and the Diplomatic Revolution,* p. 104.
[168] *Vossische Zeitung,* March 29.

that the interests which Germany could and would protect were commercial.[169]

Meanwhile public opinion became receptive to a separate bargain with France. The nationalists welcomed Tangier as a promise of a more forceful effort to profit by the favorable international situation, but doubts of the government's ability to accomplish anything of real value cooled their enthusiasm.[170] No diplomatic action, wrote the *Rheinisch-Westfälische Zeitung,* ever had a worse preparation, since no preliminary arrangements had been made with France or Morocco: "The opportunity is favorable, but the stage setting is all wrong. We have had more than enough of melodrama and fireworks, but we are almost resigned to disappointments and missed opportunities."[171] The *Leipziger Tageblatt* predicted that "John Bull will laugh in his sleeve,"[172] while the staunch guardians of the Bismarckian tradition, the *Hamburger Nachrichten* and Harden's *Zukunft,* regarded a crisis with France as a high price to pay for a share in the thankless task of policing Morocco and the Tangier visit as in contradiction to William's Bremen speech, Theodor Wolff, the Paris correspondent of the *Berliner Tageblatt,* approved on the condition that the visit would be followed by a friendly agreement. The circumstances, he said, were favorable: Delcassé was now aware of the dangers of his foreign policy and Germany had something to trade. That moment "which always comes to those who know how to wait" was at hand. German diplomacy was in a position, "if it would only understand," to win France's friendship and gratitude by offering to support her reform program.[173] This procedure was, however, utterly distasteful to Bülow. He instructed Germany's representatives to denounce the report from Paris that an understanding had already been reached recognizing France's supremacy in Morocco as the work of "an international press intrigue."[174]

There is no need to tell again what happened at Tangier. The

---

[169] *Verhandlungen,* XI Leg. Per., I Sess., III, 5709.
[170] *Magdeburgische Zeitung,* in *Tägliche Rundschau,* March 23.
[171] *Tägliche Rundschau,* March 23.   Cf. *Berliner-Börsen Zeitung,* March 29.
[172] *Tägliche Rundschau,* March 23.
[173] *Berliner Tageblatt,* March 24, 31, Paris, March 22, 29.   The editors were in complete accord with this point of view. *Ibid.,* March 29.
[174] Bülow, March 24.   G. P., XX, 270, 271.

clearing of the weather toward noon of March 31 removed the last argument against landing. Bülow's advice was carried out, except in one particular. To the Sultan's uncle, William asserted Germany's intention of protecting her interests: for this

Simplicissimus, April 11, 1905.

Figure 18.—Tangier.

purpose he would establish direct relations with the Sultan, whom he regarded as a sovereign prince. On the reform question (which was France's chief interest) he advised prudence and consideration for the religious sentiments of the people. Speaking privately to the French *chargé d'affaires,* he involved France more directly than the Chancellor and the foreign office had intended. He counted upon her respect for the agreement which he intended to negotiate with the Sultan for the equal treatment of Germans.

That France might be forced to choose between diplomatic humiliation and war, there was at first no clear indication. The continued silence of official quarters left some room for optimism. In the face of Holstein's desire that the *Norddeutsche* should call for an international conference as the only peaceful solution, Hammann, the chief of the press bureau, persuaded Bülow that a threat was inadvisable, since public opinion was even more definitely against war than the press.[175] Indeed, it seemed not impossible that Franco-German relations might improve. In France, the fear of a serious crisis produced a distinctly conciliatory attitude.[176] Instead of charging Germany with seeking to destroy the Entente Cordiale—the immediate reaction of the English press—the press admitted that Delcassé had been at fault. The weakness of his position, resulting from the momentary uncertainty as to the extent of England's support, the doubtful adequacy of France's army and navy, and the aversion of public opinion to an adventurous policy, forced him to abandon his earlier intransigeance. While he had no intention of asking Germany to explain her intentions and even less of abandoning his Moroccan policy, he was ready, if Germany took the first step, to give additional assurance as to Morocco's independence and the "open door," and to discuss the complaint that the Entente Cordiale had not been communicated to her. That the Quai d'Orsay was anxious to talk things over was clear in André Tardieu's articles in the *Temps,* in Delcassé's speeches, and in the dispatch of unofficial agents to Berlin. Delcassé was willing, he informed the Chamber of Deputies, April 7, to dispel such misunderstanding as remained. He repeated this statement to Radolin, the German ambassador, on April 13, and to the Berlin embassy, with instructions that it should be communicated to the

---

[175] Holstein, April 3. Hammann, April 3. *G. P.,* XX, 297–299, 300, 301; O. Hammann, *Zur Vorgeschichte des Weltkrieges; Erinnerungen aus den Jahren 1897–1916* (Berlin, 1918), pp. 136, 137.

[176] Anderson, *First Moroccan Crisis,* pp. 193, 194; Hale, *Germany and the Diplomatic Revolution,* pp. 102, 103.

German foreign office.[177] If Monts' post-war (1926) statement that he offered Casablanca, a second port on the Atlantic, and France's financial assistance in the construction of the Bagdad Railway if Germany would initiate direct negotiations seems inconsistent with his policy, it is a fact that Barrère, the French ambassador in Rome, approved the private conversations which Luzzatti, a member of the Italian ministry, had initiated with Monts in the interest of Franco-German relations.[178]

To these unofficial advances, the German foreign office and the semi-official press maintained a cold reserve.[179] There was, it was said, no occasion for discussions. "Germany," a Berlin correspondent wrote in the *Allgemeine Zeitung* of Munich (April 3), *"asks and expects nothing* and therefore has no reason to negotiate. . . ." According to the *Kölnische Zeitung* (April 3), Germany should watch *"mit Gelassenheit"* the development of events. Bülow's critics spoke bitterly of disappointed hopes, but few, if any, called for direct conversations with France. The Pan-Germans applauded the Tangier visit, but they drew the worst conclusions when the *Norddeutsche* denied that Germany wished to acquire a part of Morocco. Another opportunity had been lost. "A day of hope has again faded away, like many others." [180] Harden, too, was at a loss to explain the government's purposes. If the question was one of commercial rights, the Treaty of 1890 with Morocco, giving her the benefit of the most-favored-nation clause, had never been denounced. If the purpose was to humiliate France, "no responsible politician could approve it after Germany's experiences since 1871, least of all those who had been most active in trying to bind Marianne's hands with chains of roses and to force her love." An insignificant bargain would be a blow to Germany's prestige after the

[177] Radolin, April 14. *G. P.,* XX, 329; Delcassé, April 14, Bihourd, April 18. *D. D. F.,* (2), VI, 356, 360–362, 377–379.

[178] Monts' contemporary report contains a vague reference to "a striking satisfaction." *G. P.,* XX, 362 (May 2). *Cf.* F. Rosen, *Aus einem diplomatischen Wanderleben* (Leipzig, 1931), 2 vols., I, 137, 138. Luzzatti's record of these conversations contains no definite reference to concessions by France. *D. D. F.,* (2), VI, 447–451 (May 1), 477, 478 (May 5). Theodor Wolff recently dismissed this advance by Delcassé as "a birdcatcher's trick." T. Wolff, *Through Two Decades* (London, 1936), p. 52.

[179] *G. P.,* XX, 310, 311, 329, 344, 345, 347, 361–364, 372.

[180] H. Class, "Marokko," *A. B.,* April 1; *ibid.,* April 8.

brave beginning at Tangier. There should have been no visit "if Germany was not prepared to fight." [181] Even the Social Democratic *Vorwärts* (April 5) did not think it worth while to urge the initiation of discussions. Theodor Wolff saw no point in reiterating his point of view, and Arthur Levysohn, the editor of the *Berliner Tageblatt* (April 2), was evidently torn between the hope that France might be induced to adopt a fairer attitude and the fear that Delcassé might decide, under pressure, to purchase an alliance with England at any price. The moderate *Vossische Zeitung* (April 20) affirmed Germany's desire for a really peaceful relationship with France, provided that it was based upon mutual respect, but it saw no need of seeking it immediately. "Germany," it wrote, "is fortunately able to wait."

The foreign office may at first have considered a separate treaty with Morocco, but a different course was soon charted. Bülow and Holstein agreed that a defense of the international character of the Moroccan question under the Madrid Convention of 1880 would best serve their purposes. An international conference might give Germany a double advantage, by winning the sympathy of the other countries and by forcing France to yield. Holstein had immediately taken the position that the hostility of the English press should be ignored (*totgeschwiegen*) and the foreign office gave little heed to the reports that England would support France.[182] The reaction to the first unofficial approaches on the question of the conference was, however, not encouraging. Spain and Italy intended to follow England's example.[183] Sensing Germany's purpose from the comments of her semi-official press, Delcassé promptly warned the powers that France would refuse, and he succeeded in securing the assurances of several that they would do likewise.[184] Even from the American state department he received some encouragement.[185] Nor did the Sultan immediately respond to the first suggestion that he should call a conference. Instead, he discussed the question of reforms

---

[181] Harden, "Fantasia," *Zukunft*, April 8.

[182] Metternich, April 6, Radolin, April 10, *G. P.*, XX, 593, 594, 604.

[183] Anderson, *First Moroccan Crisis*, pp. 206, 207.

[184] *D. D. F.*, (2), VI, 331, 332 (April 10), 342, 343 (April 12), 365, 366 (April 15).

[185] Germany's hope of American support was brought to the attention of the Quai d'Orsay in an article in the *Lokal-Anzeiger*, April 5. *D. D. F.*, (2), VI, 302, 303. *Ibid.*, (2), VI, 364, 365 (April 14), 374, 375 (April 17).

with Taillandier, the French agent, although he did propose that the powers should guarantee France's promise to withdraw her military instructors after their work had been completed.[186] Meanwhile, no really favorable changes had occurred in European politics. The placing of a loan with Russia, following the latter's failure to secure acceptable terms from the Paris bankers, had no immediate effect upon her diplomacy.[187] In Spain, the persistent efforts to secure support, to persuade King Alfonso to attend the German maneuvers, and thus to separate Spain from the Entente Cordiale, merely united England and France in an effort to stiffen Madrid's resistance.[188] In spite of these unfavorable developments, Germany adopted the conference as the central point of her policy. Delcassé's offer (April 13, 14) to clear up the remaining misunderstanding was promptly followed by Tattenbach's departure from Tangier for Fez, with the obvious purpose of strengthening the Sultan's resistance to Taillandier. The French even suspected that Germany desired a separate treaty. On May 28, before the arrival of Lowther, the British minister, who had been sent to support the French agent, the Sultan agreed to invite the interested powers to a conference.[189]

If Germany hoped to weaken France's resistance by prolonging the uncertainty as to her intentions, the results were not wholly satisfactory. Popular dissatisfaction with Delcassé's policy increased, and the foreign minister was sufficiently impressed to apply the brakes to the peaceful penetration of Morocco by instructing Taillandier not to seek any exclusive economic privileges. On the conference, Delcassé was, however, unyielding, because he believed that Germany was bluffing and that he could count upon England's support. England indeed favored a strong resistance. She was just as active as France in stiffening Spain. The King's sympathies were on her side. "The Tangier incident," he wrote to Lansdowne, April 15, "was the most mischievous and uncalled-for event which the German Emperor has ever engaged in since he came to the throne. . . . He is no more

---

[186] D. D. F., (2), VI, 332, 333 (Fez, April 5), 365–369 (Fez, April 11), 436 (Fez, April 29).
[187] Ibid., (2), VI, 202, 203 (March 18), 466, 467 (May 4).
[188] Ibid., (2), VI, 271, 272 (April 1) passim.
[189] Tattenbach, May 28. G. P., XX, 392.

or less than a political *'enfant terrible.'* "[190]   On April 25, the British foreign office submitted to the Quai d'Orsey an agreement condemning Germany's action, assuring Delcassé of its support, particularly against any move by Germany to acquire a port in Morocco, and urging him to give England every opportunity to arrange measures of defense.[191]   Three days later, the French minister learned that Lansdowne had spoken of his resignation as "a European calamity."   Early in May, King Edward insisted that Delcassé should be included among the guests at social affairs organized in his honor during his visit to Paris.   His confidence remained unshaken when Paléologue returned from Berlin believing that his policy, if persisted in, would mean war.[192]

Delcassé's fall seemed more clearly than ever a necessity if Germany hoped to compel France to change her foreign policy. Bülow perhaps understood the difficulties France would meet in negotiating directly with Germany after the sacrifice of her minister,[193] but it was to force his dismissal that Germany's chief energies were directed from early in May.   Unofficial and indirect attacks upon French foreign policy culminated in undisguised pressure against its author.   Delcassé's name does not appear in the record of the Luzzatti-Monts conversation in Rome, May 1, but the German ambassador spoke of war as a possibility if no change occurred in France's attitude.   The Moroccan question, said Monts, was chiefly important as a means of clarifying Franco-German relations.   If the result was unsatisfactory, "Germany will continue in that state of suspicion and hostility from which conflicts arise.   May God save us from a war!"   Of the consequences to France if Germany were defeated upon the sea, Monts said: "We would be able to secure compensations in France. . . ."[194]—a threat which had an electrifying effect in France when it appeared in the German press some six weeks later.   On May 7 and 8, Prince Henckel von Donnersmarck, a wealthy Silesian mine owner, spoke with Rouvier, the President

[190] Lee, *Edward VII*, II, 240.
[191] *D. D. F.*, (2), VI, 414, 415.
[192] Paléologue, *Un grand tournant*, pp. 307–310, 311 (April 26, 28).
[193] Luzzatti's second interview with Monts, May 5. *D. D. F.*, (2), VI, 477; Bülow, May 3. *G. P.*, XX, 363.
[194] *D. D. F.*, (2), VI, 449. Monts' full report of this conversation was omitted from the *Grosse Politik*, the editors explaining that it added nothing of importance to the ambassador's brief dispatch of May 2. *G. P.*, XX, 362.

of the Council, and with Francis Charmes, a former official of
the Quai d'Orsay, who was at this time the political editor of
the *Revue des deux Mondes,* in a similar vein. There is no
definite evidence that the Prince was officially commissioned to demand Delcassé's dismissal, but the fact that he had served as Bismarck's agent and was still an important personage was sufficient
to convince the French officials that he expressed more than his
own views.[195]   No detailed record of his remarks to the Premier
exists in print, but Charmes reported in full to the Quai d'Orsay,
with his own alarmist conclusions, what von Donnersmarck had
told him. Like Monts, he spoke of Morocco as a question of
secondary importance.   France must not only treat Germany like
the other powers but she must also agree to "intimate" relations;
otherwise France will make an alliance with England and "that
we will not tolerate at any price." "The present affair," he concluded, "will be decisive.   Our relations will either be definitely
cordial or hostile." Delcassé, according to Charmes, had become
"a national peril."[196]   Even the foreign minister was momentarily shaken. The military situation was manifestly bad: no
help from Russia, so the experts said, could be expected for a
period of not less than three years; Brugère, the chief of staff, had
resigned and his successor had not yet been appointed; two of
the five armies on the frontier were without commanders; and
Hervé, at this time a militant left-wing Socialist, had threatened
that a strike among the reservists would paralyze a mobilization.[197]   Relations with England occasioned concern.   Edward
VII endorsed Delcassé's Moroccan policy, but he also spoke favorably of a *détente* in Franco-German relations.[198]   The protracted
stay of the Russian fleet on the coast of French Indo-China irritated England.[199]   Delcassé soon recovered his confidence. From
Russia he secured an order for the departure of her fleet,[200] but

---

195 For a convincing attack upon the accuracy of the *Gaulois'* famous article of
June 17, which became the chief basis for the belief that von Donnersmarck was an
unofficial agent of the German government, see Hale, *Germany and the Diplomatic
Revolution,* Ch. VI. Only in the sense that it envenomed Franco-German relations
has this article any historical importance.
196 Paléologue. *Un grand tournant,* pp. 320–322 (May 9).
197 *Ibid.,* pp. 316–318 (May 5).
198 *Ibid.,* p. 315 (May 2), 319 (May 7).
199 *Ibid.,* p. 325 (May 12), quoting the *Times.*
200 *D. D. F.,* (2), VI, 391 (April 20), 469 (May 4).

what most strengthened his resolution, in spite of the fact that he practically stood alone, were England's strong assurances.

Rouvier, who did not share Delcassé's belief that Germany was bluffing and who had a keener appreciation of the aversion of public opinion for an adventurous policy, was more amenable. England, he believed, wished to use France as a cat's-paw against Germany. At first he defended his foreign minister because he feared the effect of a manifest surrender to Germany, but he soon let Berlin know that he intended to get rid of Delcassé in the hope that Germany would then consent to direct negotiations. In his eagerness to prove his desire for an understanding, he spoke of Delcassé to German agents—whose reports were sometimes intercepted and decoded by the Quai d'Orsay—in a manner that could only encourage Germany to continue her pressure.[201] So fearful was the Premier that he refused to act when the way seemed to open for a closer relationship with England.[202] Interpreting England's willingness to discuss ways and means for resisting Germany as amounting to a bid for an alliance, Delcassé was eager to profit by this exceptional opportunity; but Rouvier was only the more eager to dismiss his dangerous colleague.[203]

---

[201] Anderson, *First Moroccan Crisis,* pp. 212, 213, 217–219.

[202] On May 12, Delcassé agreed, on the advice of Barrère, Paul Louis, and Paléologue, to ask England if France could count upon her full support if Germany used the Moroccan question as an excuse for war. Paléologue, *Un grand tournant,* p. 325. Cambon, according to his own report of his conversation with Lansdowne, May 17, presented the question in a more general form than here indicated. Lansdowne replied with a reference to the need of "absolute confidence" between the two powers, to a full exchange of information, and to the importance of discussing in advance future contingencies, or, according to Cambon's more detailed version, with an assurance of "the British government's readiness to reach an agreement with the French government on necessary measures if the situation became alarming." Cambon secured, according to his report, Lansdowne's consent to inform Delcassé that the British government was ready to agree upon the necessary measures in the event of a serious danger of an unprovoked attack. Lansdowne, May 17. *B. D.,* III, 76; P. Cambon, May 18. *D. D. F.,* (2), VI, 523.

[203] For the text of Lansdowne's written communication to Paul Cambon of May 25, see *B. D.,* III, 77, 78; *D. D. F.,* (2), VI, 558–560. It repeated his general assurances of May 17 but it contained no reference to an unprovoked attack by Germany. Cambon noted this omission, only to represent the foreign secretary's new position as even more significant. Lansdowne, he wrote, "rectifie sur ce point, en lui donnant une portée plus large et plus prochaine, le sens de sa déclaration. Ce n'est plus à une entente en cas d'agression qu'il nous convie, c'est à une discussion immédiate et un examen de la situation générale. . . . Accepter la conversation, c'est entrer dans la voie d'une entente générale qui constituerait en réalité une alliance. . . ." P. Cambon, May 29. *D. D. F.,* (2), VI, 558; Delcassé, May 30. *Ibid.,* (2), VI, 563, 564. At a meeting with President Loubet, Delcassé, Paul Cambon, and Barrère (May 15), Rouvier had declared against a closer union with England. Paléologue, *Un grand tournant,* 346 n.

Even Paul Cambon, who shared the foreign minister's illusions as to England's intentions, privately urged him not to defy the President of the Council.[204] The stage was set for the last act. On May 27 Russia's collapse was completed by the destruction of her fleet at Tsushima. Within twenty-four hours there followed the Sultan of Morocco's invitation, backed by Germany, to a conference. Two days later (May 30), Bülow wrote to Radolin in Paris describing Delcassé as the tool of a "foreign inspiration" and instructing him to remind Rouvier again of "the serious concern for Franco-German relations which would necessarily arise if Herr Delcassé remained in office." To make his meaning still plainer, he was sending a special agent to speak in the same sense.[205] On June 4, Monts furnished the final impulse that moved Rouvier to action. Speaking to Tittoni, the Italian foreign minister, the German ambassador declared, on instructions from Berlin, that Taillandier had handed an ultimatum to the Sultan of Morocco: "If the French troops cross the Moroccan frontier . . . the German troops will invade France at the same time." [206] Delcassé promptly denied that anything like an ultimatum had been delivered and asserted that Germany, sensing the approaching collapse of her policy, was losing her head. He correctly expected this latest proof of Germany's nervousness to increase his difficulties with Rouvier. When Barrère's dispatch was handed to the Premier on the morning of June 5, Rouvier hurried to President Loubet and insisted that the ministry must choose between him and Delcassé. "M. Delcassé," he said, "is leading us into war." [207] Abandoned by his colleagues the following morning (June 6), Delcassé could no nothing but resign. The decisive argument, according to the one adequate first-hand report of the discussion, was neither the pressure of public opinion nor a desire for a direct understanding with Germany, but France's unpreparedness for war. It was generally agreed that Germany was not bluffing, that England's aid (the ministry apparently believed, like Delcassé, that her offer amounted to an

---

[204] Cambon, June 1. Paléologue, *Un grand tournant*, pp. 346, 347.
[205] *G. P.*, XX, 389.
[206] Barrère, June 4. *D. D. F.*, (2), VI, 585, 586. The *Grosse Politik* throws no light upon this incident.
[207] Paléologue, *Un grand tournant*, pp. 347, 348.

alliance) would not save France from a possibly disastrous defeat, and that Germany would regard France's signature to an agreement for common action with England as an excuse for war.[208]

For the moment, Germany glowed with satisfaction. Holstein placed the fall of Delcassé, "our cleverest and most dangerous enemy," first among the political achievements of the preceding six months.[209] The semi-official press refrained from open exultation, but the Conservative *Post* (June 7) wrote of a "manifestly great diplomatic success." When a German statesman was even the remote cause of the fall of a French minister, it was, wrote the Catholic *Historisch-Politische Blätter,* "an event of almost world significance, for French statesmen had been wont to overthrow German princes."[210] There was a ring of confidence in the diplomatic dispatches. In dismissing Delcassé, France had acknowledged her unwillingness to risk the dangers of a frankly anti-German policy and of a too close association with England. The Entente Cordiale was weakened more than Germany realized. Since France could not, as Balfour informed King Edward, "be trusted not to yield at the critical moment of a negotiation and was therefore no longer an effective force in international politics," England would have to make other arrangements to prevent Germany from acquiring a port.[211] The entente, Lansdowne informed Bertie, the British ambassador in Paris, "is quoted at a much lower price than it was a fortnight ago."[212] By encouraging President Roosevelt's mediation in the Russo-Japanese War, the German diplomats believed that they had prevented an initiative by England and France and thus had stopped a possible step toward a quadruple alliance.[213] How to use this improvement in Germany's diplomatic position to her permanent

---

[208] J. Chaumié, "Note sur le conseil des ministres où M. Delcassé a donné sa démission," *D. D. F.,* (2), VI, 601–604. The following sentences doubtless refer to Lansdowne's note of May 24 and show that Chaumié at least had no doubt as to its significance. "Il [Delcassé] lit le texte de la dernière qui, sans entré dans le détail d'exécution, dit très nettement l'offre par l'Angeterre de cette action commune. Il estime qu'il y a tout intérêt à conclure cette alliance."

[209] Holstein, *Lebensbekenntnis,* pp. 239, 240 (June 16).

[210] Vol. 136, p. 39 (July 1905). The Center party was now united with the Conservatives in the governmental "blue-black *bloc*."

[211] Lee, *Edward VII,* 344 (June 8).

[212] Newton, *Lansdowne,* p. 341 (June 12).

[213] Hale, *Germany and the Diplomatic Revolution,* pp. 153, 154; Anderson, *First Moroccan Crisis,* p. 240.

advantage was the problem. Never, in some respects, had the prospects for a rapprochement with France been so favorable. That public opinion had repudiated Delcassé's policy was freely acknowledged.[214] Rouvier's sincerity in seeking a direct understanding was above suspicion; of Germany, he immediately asked for "an explanation of her intention to adopt a friendly policy toward him."[215] Even in the press, there was, however, only weak support for the abandonment of the demand for a conference or for a direct understanding. It was chiefly among the supporters of a frankly anti-English policy that a conciliatory policy found favor. The *Hamburger Nachrichten* (June 7) continued its advocacy of an arrangement with France. "Only a Franco-German rapprochement," wrote a pamphleteer whose views were endorsed by the official organ of the Pan-Germans, "can permanently block an alliance between England and France and prevent a world war."[216] The *Alldeutsche Blätter* thought at once of a continental league.[217] While the liberal press favored a change of policy toward France, its position was developed wtih no great force. The *Frankfurter Zeitung* (June 7) deprecated talk of her defeat and asserted that Germany was more concerned with an agreement. The *Vossische Zeitung* (June 7) believed that France, in her chastened spirit, would not meet with excessive difficulties in Berlin. At first, Theodor Wolff was silent; but, on June 14, he complained in the *Berliner Tageblatt* that Germany had not taken advantage of an unusually favorable opportunity.

Germany's attitude had invited the inference that Delcassé's removal would moderate her policy; but indications had already appeared that it would not be changed. The most violent press polemics, like those of the *Allgemeine Zeitung,* sometimes paraded an ostentatious indifference.[218] Delcassé's unpopularity in France, according to the *Kreuz-Zeitung* (April 12), was the result

---

[214] *Deutsche Tageszeitung,* June 6; *Kreuz-Zeitung, Tägliche Rundschau, Vorwärts,* June 7; *National Zeitung,* June 8.

[215] Flotow, June 6. *G. P.,* XX, 404.

[216] *Krieg mit Frankreich? Wohin muss die deutsche Marokkopolitik führen?* Berlin, 1905, in *A. B.,* Nov. 9, 1906.

[217] Mehrmann, "Die Mächtegruppierung nach der Seeschlacht bei Tsuschima," *ibid.,* June 17, 1905.

[218] *D. D. F.,* (2), VI, 322, 323 (April 8), 406, 407.

of his personal characteristics and therefore had no larger significance. The liberal *Berliner Tageblatt* (April 23) spoke of an
interest conflict in Morocco as the real issue between the two
countries. There would be no justification, asserted the *Kölnische Zeitung* as early as April 25, for celebrating his fall as a
diplomatic victory. The government in fact shared this point of
view. "Our position in regard to France," wrote Bülow May 6,
"is so strong that it is a matter of indifference to us who happens
to be her foreign minister. In fact, Delcassé's mistakes make him
. . . the best man for the place." [219] The demand for a conference was continued in order to force France to abandon her machinations and to restore Germany's damaged prestige. Tattenbach's suggestion that Germany should claim a sphere of influence fell upon deaf ears.[220] "We have," wrote Holstein (June
16), "achieved much during the last six months. . . . There is
nothing that we especially desire. Our action was intended to
show that we must be consulted (*dass es ohne uns nicht geht*)
and, above all, to force Delcassé's fall." [221] As to the conference,
Theodor Wolff doubted "that the prospective gains are really
worth the risks involved," [222] and the agrarian *Deutsche Tageszeitung* (June 11) thought that "it is fairly certain that we will be
outvoted by a firm union between France, England, Spain, and
Italy," while Bülow himself foresaw that it would merely delay
for a few years France's inevitable attainment of a paramount
position in Morocco.[223] The rule of unanimity, it was thought,
would protect Germany against an unfavorable result. The foreign office's predilection for formulas may have contributed to
the decision against a direct understanding with France, but the
claim that Morocco could not be abandoned after she had issued
the invitation on Germany's advice was manifestly nonsense.
The desire to complete an unfinished lesson to France was far
more important. Rouvier must show by deeds that he intended

[219] *G. P.*, XX, 370; Bülow's comments, Radolin, May 13. *Ibid.*, XX, 378.
[220] Bülow, *Denkwürdigkeiten*, II, 125.
[221] Holstein, *Lebensbekenntnis*, p. 240.
[222] *Berliner Tageblatt*, June 16. Monts also believed that a Franco-German understanding should have followed Delcassé's fall. Monts, *Erinnerungen und Gedanken*,
p. 419 (June 22).
[223] Bülow, May 4. *G. P.*, XX, 364-367.

to pursue a different policy.[224] The French must become even more amenable; they must be brought to the realization that England could not save them, and the diplomats perhaps hoped to show England that France could not be depended upon in a crisis.[225] On June 5, Bülow accepted the Sultan's invitation and immediately informed the powers, although he knew that Delcassé's fall was probably a matter of days or of hours.[226] Two days later, the *Kölnische Zeitung* (June 7) attributed the ministerial crisis to the pressure of public opinion and announced that Germany's policy would remain unchanged, at least until Rouvier had shown that he really intended "to respect the rights of others." Delcassé's resignation, said the nationalist *Tägliche Rundschau* (June 9), had settled nothing. The future, according to the agrarian *Deutsche Tageszeitung* (June 7), depended upon Rouvier. For Schiemann, only a sympton had been eliminated; the disease itself must be cured. "It is," he said, "a question of Germany's isolation." [227]

In Paris, Rouvier took charge of the Quai d'Orsay, expecting that an arrangement with Germany would soon enable him to return to the more congenial ministry of finance.[228] His chief concern, hitherto, had been to guard against the dangerous consequences of Delcassé's policy; in his new post, he was obliged— the permanent officials of the Quai d'Orsay seem to have been largely responsible—to give greater emphasis to France's interests. Nevertheless he was willing to make concessions. He immediately instructed Taillandier to suspend his negotiations with the Sultan and indirectly offered Germany a general understanding, like the entente with England, based upon Morocco, the Bagdad Railway, and the Far East.[229] On June 10 came the great disillusionment. Radolin repeated the demand for a conference, saying that Germany would otherwise not recognize any changes in Morocco. "Germany," said the ambassador, "will support Sultan

[224] This was the sense of his private letter to Radolin, June 14, which Herr Thimme uses to show Holstein's conciliatory disposition. Thimme, "Aus dem Nachlass des Fürsten Radolin," *Berliner Monatshefte*, Oct. 1937, p. 845.
[225] Brandenburg, *From Bismarck to the World War*, p. 225; *Post*, June 9.
[226] *G. P.*, XX, 413–415.
[227] *Kreuz-Zeitung*, June 14. Schiemann, *Deutschland und die Grosse Politik*, V, 168.
[228] Paléologue, *Un grand tournant*, p. 354 (June 7).
[229] Anderson, *First Moroccan Crisis*, p. 238.

Abd-el-Aziz with all her strength." [230]   From this interview there emerged one ray of light, for Rouvier pointed to a prior under-standing in regard to reforms as a possible basis for France's acceptance. [231]   To discourage him completely was not Berlin's desire.   William, who apparently knew little or nothing of France's earlier advances, was favorably impressed: *"Ja,"* and *"Gut: alles was wir wollen,"* were his comments, which Bülow echoed, on Rouvier's plea for friendly coöperation.[232]   Meanwhile, the efforts to win support for the conference were unsuccessful. From Russia, Austria, Portugal, Denmark, and Italy came the reply that they would follow the example of England and France, and England recommended a direct understanding with France. After a first cool response, President Roosevelt, hoping to avoid complications that might endanger the success of his mediation between Russia and Japan, agreed to advise France to yield.   To the need of securing France's consent as a reason for continued pressure was added a report from the French capital (June 7) that England had offered an alliance.[233]

Some months later, Holstein blamed William's conciliatory conversations with General Lacroix, the leader of the French delegation to the Crown Prince's wedding, for France's stiffer resistance.[234]   Bülow promptly warned the French that a "serious danger of war would arise if they thought that His Majesty had changed his point of view." [235]   Such encouragement as may have been derived from Lacroix's report was a minor factor in French policy.   After Germany's failure to meet him halfway, Rouvier listened more receptively to those who, like Paul Cambon, believed that her talk of war was a bluff.   At any rate, Bülow's arguments that the conference would be a mere formality and that it would only delay the full attainment of France's aims a few years left him cold.[236]   To the suggestion that an agreement

---

230 Paléologue, *op. cit.,* p. 238. *Cf.* Radolin, June 11, *G. P.,* XX, 430; Brandenburg, *From Bismarck to the World War,* p. 226.

231 Radolin, June 6. *G. P.,* XX, 426.

232 Radolin, June 11. *Ibid.,* XX, 407–409.

233 Anderson, *op. cit.,* pp. 236, 237.

234 Bülow, *Denkwürdigkeiten,* II, 123. What chiefly impressed Lacroix, judging by his conversation with Paléologue, was William's excited remark, June 7: "Delcassé, I assure you, was leading your country into a catastrophe . . . , yes, I repeat, into a catastrophe." Paléologue, *Un grand tournant,* p. 362 (June 13).

235 Bülow, June 10. *G. P.,* XX, 429, 430.

236 Bülow, June 11, *Ibid.,* XX, 407–409.

regarding the agenda could be reached after France had accepted the conference,[237] Rouvier replied (June 21) in an open note that he would yield if Germany agreed to recognize France's interests on the Algerian-Moroccan frontier. More than ever, it was clearly a question of prestige that divided the two countries; by insisting upon a prior understanding, France hoped not only to protect her Moroccan interests but also to moderate the reaction abroad to her surrender. French public opinion responded to the challenge with an increasing acceptance of war, a reaction that was immensely strengthened when Holstein used the press to turn France against England. From the report that England had offered an alliance he had drawn the conclusion that she was seriously contemplating a war. While he did not hesitate to confront the British ambassador with these charges in the privacy of his office,[238] he used Professor Schiemann, the Emperor's intimate, to launch the famous "hostage (*Geisel*)" theory in the *Kreuz-Zeitung* (June 14).[239] Delcassé, wrote Schiemann, had made the mistake of thinking that the Anglo-German antagonism would enable France peacefully to devour the Moroccan artichoke, whereas the tension between England and Germany really contained a serious danger for France. "Germany," he concluded, "can only conduct a war with England . . . in France."[240] The Catholic *Kölnische Volkszeitung* (June 16) stated the idea even more forcefully: "France must serve us as a hostage for the good conduct of her foreign office."[241] When the Paris *Temps* Berlin correspondent asked (June 21) if France could remain neutral in an Anglo-German war, Schiemann replied that she would be compelled to choose between the combatants.[242] On June 16, the Paris correspondent of the *Kreuz-Zeitung* (June 17) reported that public opinion "remained reserved and quiet" and that its resentment was still primarily directed against Delcassé,[243] but within a week there occurred a strong resurgence of national-

[237] Bülow, June 12. *G. P.*, XX, 431.

[238] Lascelles, June 12. *B. D.*, III, 80, 81.

[239] Hammann, *Der missverstandene Bismarck*, p. 123. Later Bülow claimed that Schiemann exaggerated one of Holstein's offhand remarks. Bülow, *Denkwürdigkeiten*, II, 80.

[240] Schiemann, *Deutschland und die Grosse Politik*, V, 170, 171.

[241] Hale, *Germany and the Diplomatic Revolution*, p. 145.

[242] Carroll, *French Public Opinion*, pp. 214, 215.

[243] Cf. *Post*, June 18.

ist sentiment. The *Gaulois'* sensational story (June 17) of the Henckel von Donnersmarck mission, the *Temps'* interview with Schiemann (June 21), and, finally, Bülow's reply (June 23) that an agreement was impossible on the basis of Rouvier's note of June 21, aroused the nation.[244] June 23, according to the *Hamburger Nachrichten* (June 24), was a day of panic in Paris. The French press accepted the "hostage" theory as conclusive proof of Germany's will to dictate France's friendships.[245] "No surrender" was the advice of the German chauvinists. Speaking at Worms to the annual congress of the Pan-German League, June 15, Ernst Hasse, its president, said that Germany had learned how to "convince France that she was powerless."[246] "If Germany will only remain firm and self-confident," wrote the *Rheinisch-Westfälische Zeitung,* "success must be ours, for Paris has neither the leader nor the courage to fight us."[247] On June 27, Germany restated her position—first, acceptance of the conference and, then, negotiations in regard to France's interests.[248] For the most part, however, German opinion was not prepared for a strong stand. Not until the French had become excited did the "hostage" theory attract much attention.[249] No pressure would be required, according to the *Hamburger Nachrichten* (June 19) and to Theodor Wolff in the *Berliner Tageblatt* (June 24), to restrain France from fighting for England's interests. On June 20, the Social Democratic *Vorwärts* promised the French workers that "the working classes of Germany would resist with all their might the criminal folly of those who wish to precipitate a war. . . ." The German workers, asserted another Socialist organ, "do not ask, they demand, peace—if necessary with their fists on the table."[250] Only Bülow's intervention in Paris prevented Jaurès

---

[244] Bülow, June 23, 26. G. P., XX, 462, 463–478. Cf. *Kölnische Zeitung,* June 22: "*Die Note des Herrn Rouvier macht Delcassé-Politik ohne Delcassé.*" *Vossische Zeitung,* June 23.

[245] *Allgemeine Zeitung,* in *Tägliche Rundschau,* June 23; *Kölnische Zeitung,* June 24, quoting Jaurès in *Humanité; Vossische Zeitung,* June 26; *Kölnische Zeitung,* June 27, Paris, June 26.

[246] *A. B.,* June 24.

[247] France, it insisted, must not be given time to organize an anti-German *bloc. Tägliche Rundschau,* June 27.

[248] Hale, *Germany and the Diplomatic Revolution,* p. 162.

[249] The French, wrote Wolff, understood that "dieser Krieg sich auf ihrem Boden abspielen wurde, dass sie die zerbrückenen Töpfe bezahlen müssten." *Berliner Tageblatt,* June 24, Paris, June 21. Cf. *Vossische Zeitung,* June 26, Paris, June 24.

[250] *Neue Gesellschaft,* in *Post,* July 6, and in *Deutsche Tageszeitung,* July 7.

from going to Berlin.[251]   Berlin impressed a special correspondent of the Paris *Figaro* (June 25) as profoundly quiet and completely unaware of the war scare in Paris.[252]   "Germany," wrote the Conservative *Post* (June 23), "has not the slightest intention of going to war for the sake of Morocco, least of all to precipitate a preventive war."   The National Liberal *National Zeitung* (June 24) rejected Rouvier's note of June 21 as a basis for an understanding but it also asserted "that Morocco is not a sufficient cause for war for either country."   What was generally accepted as an official communication in the *Preussische Korrespondenz* deprecated the alarmist rumors: "Neither now nor in the predictable future can there be any question of war, since the French and German peoples have no desire for a bloody conflict over Morocco." [253] Schiemann now explained that he had launched the "hostage" theory as a rejoinder to the report of an English offer of an alliance.[254]

The weakness of the Moroccan question as occasion for an attack upon French policy had been revealed; neither the diplomats nor public opinion regarded it as a sufficient justification for war.   No diplomatic support was forthcoming from other countries.   Gratitude for Germany's support in his mediation between Russia and Japan did not, as had been hoped, cause Roosevelt to influence France as Germany desired.   Sympathetic with the French and irritated by Germany's apparently empty threats, he urged her to accept the note of June 21 and finally withdrew, after an ineffectual suggestion that both countries should enter the conference without any commitments except those which they may have contracted with third powers.[255]   On July 8, after a last week of feverish negotiations, a compromise was reached: in return for France's acceptance of the conference and for her recognition of the sovereignty, independence, and territorial integrity of Morocco, and of the principle of the "open door," Germany

---

[251] The *Vorwärts* (July 9) printed a German translation of Jaurès' undelivered speech under the title, "Die Friedensidee und die Solidarität des internationalen Proletariats."

[252] Hale, *op. cit.*, p. 159.

[253] *Deutsche Tageszeitung*, June 24.

[254] *Kreuz-Zeitung*, June 28.   Schiemann, *Deutschland und die Grosse Politik*, V, 185.

[255] Hale, *op. cit.*, 162–166.   For a higher estimate of Roosevelt's influence, see Anderson, *op. cit.*, p. 252 f.

promised not to injure France's "legitimate" interests during the deliberations and to recognize at once France's special interest in the maintenance of order on the Moroccan-Algerian frontier. France's concessions were received with some satisfaction.[256] Even the Pan-Germans were moderately pleased—they had always supported a direct understanding—but their approval was given on the condition that the conference "would mark a beginning in Morocco." If the "open-door" proved to be the limit of Germany's gains, wrote the *Alldeutsche Blätter* (July 15), "the chapter of German history which she shall then have finished should be entitled, 'Much Ado about Nothing'."

In spite of France's sacrifices, it was clear that the diplomatic situation had not improved. England's support was blamed for France's stubbornness, and there was little reason for believing that it would be withdrawn. No one knew that Rouvier had communicated the text of the July 8 agreement to London before approving it, but the English press frankly said that England would attend the conference as France's friend.[257] During the visit of the British fleet to Brest (July 12–17) and that of the French to Plymouth a month later, English newspapers outdid the French in talking of an alliance. The British fleet, the Paris *Gaulois* (July 12) reported Delcassé as saying, had alone saved France from an attack. Harden depicted the situation in somber colors. The agreement of July 8, he wrote, was a Pyhrric victory: "The *Zweibund* between the Western powers, originally loose, has been tightened by a common hatred. . . . England has again learned to think in terms of a European war, and Italy resents the prospect of being forced to choose between her old and new friends." [258] For the first time since 1900 a meeting was called of the Bundesrat's foreign affairs committee.[259] The time when a rapprochement with England might have appealed to many Germans had long since passed; the *Frankfurter Zeitung* (July 14) was practically alone in urging an effort to clear up the misunderstanding between the two countries. Differences

---

[256] According to the *Kölnische Zeitung* (July 12) and to the *Post* (July 12), the press reaction was favorable.

[257] Hale, *op. cit.*, pp. 169, 170.

[258] Harden, "Marokko," *Zukunft*, July 8.

[259] *N. A. Z., Post*, July 13.

of opinion had, however, appeared between those who still believed that the Entente Cordiale should be weakened by exerting pressure upon France. If the Conservative *Post* (July 13) revived the "hostage" theory by reminding France that "the bill would be presented in Paris if the German fleet succumbed to the British" and that "she would not get off as easily as she had at Frankfort" if Harden insisted that France be forced to show her true colors,[260] the attitude of the *Kölnische Zeitung* suggested that some official consideration was being given to a conciliatory policy. "We wish," it wrote of the conference, "to work with and not against France. . . ." [261]   Tattenbach was instructed not to seek any economic concessions in Morocco prior to the conference. No fundamental change, however, had occurred in German policy. On July 10, the foreign office informed Paris that no coöperation would be possible so long as "a notorious chauvinist" like Révoil continued to influence French policy. Holstein even urged Rouvier to resign in favor of Dupuy, the editor of the *Petit Parisien,* who had acted as the Premier's intermediary in earlier negotiations, for an understanding with him would be a simple matter.[262]   At Kiel, William worked upon the Prince of Monaco to secure "a general change of front on the part of French policy." [263]

The failure of the frontal attack upon the Entente Cordiale inevitably suggested a new approach to Russia. A convenient occasion appeared when William, cruising in the Scandinavian waters, arranged a meeting with the Tsar at Björkö. Bülow and Holstein were both agreeable, for they hoped to prevent Russia from beginning negotiations for a triple entente after the peace with Japan; [264] in reply to the Emperor's request, they sent him the text of a defensive alliance. William felt that at last he was about to win a decisive diplomatic triumph. Grateful for Germany's

---

[260] Harden, "Der Polarstern," *Zukunft,* July 29.

[261] *Deutsche Tageszeitung,* July 11. On August 4, Holstein asked Radolin in a private letter if one of France's spokesmen had suggested a partition of Morocco into zones, which might eventually become spheres of influence. The reply, August 22, was negative. Thimme, "Aus dem Nachlass Fürsten Radolin," *Berliner Monatshefte,* Oct. 1937, p. 855.

[262] Richthofen, Holstein, July 10; Radolin, July 14. *G. P.,* XX, 521, 523, 527.

[263] Tschirschky, July 13. Monts, *Erinnerungen und Gedanken,* p. 438.

[264] Bülow, July 20. *G. P.,* XIX, 436. *Cf.* Holstein, July 21, 22. *Ibid.,* XIX, 437, 438, 441, 442.

friendliness and hopeful of her support in the negotiations with Japan, Nicholas was more than half won even before the interview on the "Polar Star," July 24. It was therefore child's play to arouse his anger against France by reminding him that she had practically chased Rodjestvenski from her Far Eastern waters to his doom at Tsushima. After William explained that France's refusal to accept Germany's challenge meant the end of the Alsace-Lorraine question, Nicholas, according to the Emperor's vivid account (July 25), was ready to sign anything. The Tsar's signature to the alliance seemed to William the work of divine providence. "Thus has the morning of July 24, 1905 at Björkö become a turning point in the history of Europe. . . ." [265] "On that day," wrote William two months later, "a new page of history began." [266] It remained to be seen whether the Russian autocrat would be able to reverse his country's foreign policy. However, William was the first to experience difficulties from his advisers. So bitter was Bülow that William had agreed to limit his promise of support to Europe if Germany or Russia was attacked by a third power that he threatened to resign, because this change would discourage Russia from attacking British India,[267] but a hysterical appeal from the Emperor sufficed to change his mind.[268] The failure of the negotiations during the preceding autumn seems to have disturbed him no more than it had the Emperor himself.

The secret of Björkö was well guarded, but the meeting between the two sovereigns itself aroused speculation. In Germany, satisfaction equaled the anxiety of the English and the French. Even the liberals could not object to the friendly relations with Russia which, according to the *Norddeutsche* (July 30), had been established.[269] For the Social Democrats, however, any contact with her was intolerable. "The German people," wrote the *Vorwärts* (July 25), "hates and despises the Russian absolutism; it rejects any and every rapprochement with the barbarous and

---

[265] Tschirschky, July 24, William II, July 25. *G. P.*, XIX, 454-456, 459. *Cf.* Fay, *Origins of the World War*, I, 172-175.
[266] William II, Sept. 27. Semenoff, *Correspondance entre Guillaume II et Nicolas II*, p. 171.
[267] Bülow, Aug. 2. *G. P.*, XIX, 481.
[268] Bülow, *Denkwürdigkeiten*, I, 146.
[269] Cf. *Deutsche Tageszeitung*, July 25.

sanguinary tyranny." Conservative journals were manifestly pleased, but their desire seems to have been to assure France that no one had any intention of disrupting the Franco-Russian Alliance.[270] The announcement (July 29) that the British fleet would hold its autumn maneuvers in the Baltic had every appearance of being England's reply to Björkö. Even the Björkö alliance failed to reassure Bülow as to Germany's security. In the event of an English attack, he informed the foreign office, ultimata must immediately be presented in Brussels and in Paris demanding a declaration "for or against us within six hours," and he also spoke of the invasion of Belgium as a necessity, regardless of Belgium's reply. Russia would side with Germany, and even France might be bought off by an offer of a part of Belgium for her sacrifice of the *revanche*.[271] On the same day, the *Norddeutsche* (July 30) quoted a speech by von Wallwitz, the minister to Belgium, to the German colony in Brussels, as evidence of Germany's respect for the rights of all countries. "Germany," he said, "desires a strong Belgium, economically and politically; the maintenance of the treaty guaranteeing her independence is axiomatic for us Germans." Bülow's calculations also envisaged a peaceful arrangement with France. On July 31, he told the foreign office that it must be prepared "to give the French a free hand in Morocco as the price of her association with the Russo-German entente. For us no better use could be made of Morocco; it would be far and away the best conclusion of our Moroccan campaign."[272] Unfortunately France was beginning to see that she could use the conference for her own purposes.

As late as a month after the announcement of the British maneuvers in the Baltic, William was still bitter. He informed the Tsar, August 25, that he had ordered the fleet to shadow the British squadron, to anchor near it, to invite its officers to the best of dinners, and then to weigh anchor.[273] Neither this incident nor the renewal of the Anglo-Japanese Alliance (Aug. 12) seriously alarmed German opinion. Even a navy enthusiast agreed

[270] *Post*, July 25; *Kreuz-Zeitung*, Aug. 2. Schiemann, *Deutschland und die Grosse Politik*, V, 234.

[271] Bülow, July 30, *G. P.*, XX, 531, 532.

[272] *Ibid.*, XX, 531.

[273] Semenoff, *Correspondance entre Guillaume II et Nicolas II*, p. 186.

that a visit by the British warships to a German port would show that no offense had been intended, and a nationalist commentator deprecated further naval propaganda as unnecessary, since everyone had already been converted.[274]   England's association with Japan was still regarded as a certain cause of friction with Russia.[275]   The embassy in London was less confident, so strong was, in its opinion, the desire for understanding with Russia that an attempt would be made to secure it regardless of the results of the impending parliamentary elections.[276]   The causes of Germany's dissatisfaction indeed remained unchanged.   For the Conservative *Post* (Sept. 27), England had acquired from her new treaty with Japan a greater freedom of action in Europe.   "No Russian alliance," wrote Harden, "would enable Germany to make headway against England's reinsurance system." [277]   Bülow, however, had no desire for a new effort to intimidate France. Although Germany's agents had, in violation of her promises during the negotiation of the agreement of July 8 and contrary to the Chancellor's directions,[278] secured a contract for the construction of harbor works at Tangier and a loan to the Sultan,[279] he took advantage of Holstein's illness to send Friedrich Rosen to Paris in place of Radolin, whose firmness against the French was doubted, to negotiate an agreement upon the agenda, with permission to depart somewhat from the legalistic basis of Germany's earlier policy.[280]   Bülow now hoped for nothing better than a compromise; in his opinion there should be *"ni vainqueurs, ni vaincus,"* but he did suggest that Rouvier should be warned as to the consequences of a break.[281]   Rosen found Révoil a stubborn opponent.   The understanding of September 25 provided that the policing of the Algerian-Moroccan frontier should not be

---

[274] E. von Reventlow, "Die Kanalflotte in der Ostsee," *Zukunft,* Sept. 9; G. Hartmann, "Die deutsche Presse und die britische Frage," *Grenzboten,* 1905, III, 573 (Sept. 15).

[275] Greindle, Berlin, Sept. 23. *Belgische Dokumente,* VI, 2; *Kreuz-Zeitung,* Oct. 4. Schiemann, *Deutschland und die Grosse Politik,* V, 277, 278; *Münchener Neueste Nachrichten,* in *G. P.,* XIX, 638 (Sept. 8).

[276] *G. P.,* XIX, 636, 637 (Sept. 8).

[277] Harden, "Pax Britannica," *Zukunft,* Sept. 9.

[278] Brandenburg, *From Bismarck to the World War,* p. 227.

[279] To the French, the loan was, according to the German ambassador, *"wie ein Blitz aus heiteren Himmel. . . ."* *G. P.,* XX, 549, 550 (Aug. 29).

[280] Rosen, *Aus einem diplomatischen Wanderleben,* pp. 150-152; Bülow, Sept. 8, Richthofen, Sept. 10. *G. P.,* XX, 560, 564, 565.

[281] Bülow, Sept. 20, 26. *G. P.,* XX, 575, 586.

discussed at the conference and that the agenda would include the organization of the police in the remainder of Morocco, the establishment of a state bank, the suppression of contraband trade, and questions relating to the public finances and services. As a concession to France, Algeciras instead of Tangier was selected as the meeting place. German opinion was cool. The *Norddeutsche* (Oct. 1) commended the understanding as "a basis for further coöperation," but the partisans of an active policy in Morocco were disappointed. Nothing like this had been expected at the time of the Tangier demonstration, said the Pan-Germans, although the memory of the Kruger Telegram and the subsequent abandonment of the Boers had occasioned doubts.[282] "Germany's far-reaching concessions," wrote the nationalist *Tägliche Rundschau* (Oct. 1), "were understandable only if they were intended to serve larger purposes," such as "France's release from England's encompassments and her rapprochement with Germany." There was, said Harden, no saving feature. "France," he said, "has triumphed for the first time." There was more justification for demanding Rouvier's official head than Delcassé's, since the Premier had "led our *Excellenzen und Durchlauchtigen* around by the nose."[283]

Behind Germany's accommodating attitude was the desire to attract France into the Björkö alliance. France's attitude was not encouraging. During the recent negotiations Rouvier spoke of the Cameroon, and the Bagdad Railway as a basis for coöperation, but Révoil mentioned the Near East and the admission of the shares of the Bagdad Railway to the Paris Bourse, only to dismiss the subject on the ground that there was no country against which a Franco-German understanding could be directed![284] The German leaders, nevertheless, were eager to complete the work commenced at Björkö. Already William had appealed to the Tsar to use his influence, for only thus could England's ambitions be thwarted and France's subservience to her be broken.[285]

---

[282] P. S., "Der Rückzug aus Marokko," *A. B.*, Oct. 7.

[283] Harden, "Die Bescherung," *Zukunft*, Dec. 23.

[284] Rosen, *Aus einem diplomatischen Wanderleben*, pp. 190, 191; Radolin, Sept. 29. *G. P.*, XX, 593, 594.

[285] William II, Sept. 26. Semenoff, *Correspondance entre Guillaume II et Nicolas II*, p. 193.

"We must," wrote Bülow, September 30, "make use of every opportunity to create a community of interest with France." [286] On Rosen's advice, he granted interviews to André Tardieu of the *Temps* and to a representative of the *Petit Parisien;* to both he insisted upon the justice of Germany's grievances against Delcassé, but he also asserted his desire for and hope of good relations.[287] While a great cry went up in Paris that the Entente Cordiale was in danger, the reaction of the German press was more than favorable. The Liberal *Berliner Tageblatt* (Oct 4, 8) rejoiced that the government had at last seen the advantages of an understanding. For the improvement of relations with France, the anti-English *Reichsbote* (Oct. 6) pledged the assistance of the press. To quiet France's apprehensions, the Conservative *Post* (Oct. 7) assured her that nothing more was desired than the same unprejudiced and conciliatory treatment which she accorded to England. Germany, wrote the National Liberal *National Zeitung* (Oct. 7), had no intention of disturbing France's diplomatic arrangements or of objecting to an Anglo-Russian understanding in the Far East. When the *Norddeutsche* (Oct. 8) broke its silence, it pointed to Germany's proven love of peace as the reason for her desire for friendly relations with France. [288] "For the great majority of the German people," it concluded, "the old accounts of the Moroccan affair are closed . . . and at the head of the new stands the welcome Franco-German understanding." At the two extremes of public opinion, there were some who saw that Germany's attitude could not quickly be forgotten or easily forgiven. Bülow had given France the impression, wrote the *Vorwärts* (Oct. 4), that he wished to dictate her foreign policy. To the chauvinist *Rheinisch-Westfälische Zeitung,* it was absurd to expect France to be attracted by the diplomatic objectives which alone could justify Bülow's concessions. Of Franco-German relations, the Chancellor, according to the nationalist *Leipziger Neueste Nachrichten,* had spoken in a "rich, lyrical tone, but could an enemy be conciliated by giving him a

---

[286] *G. P.,* XX, 595.
[287] The Tardieu interview appeared in the *Temps* (Oct. 3) and the second in the *Petit Parisien* (Oct. 2). *Cf.* Carroll, *French Public Opinion,* p. 218.
[288] Cf. *Post,* Oct. 7.

black eye?" If Bülow had told the truth, Germany ought to be pleased, it supposed, "that our friend also has friends—Russia, Italy, and England—who also enjoy Japan's amity. *Gott, wie ist die Welt so schön! Beglückwünschen wir uns!*" [289]

Bülow's appeal to French public opinion was shortly followed by the revelation that England had offered France armed support. Claiming Delcassé as his authority, Stéphane Lauzanne wrote in the Paris *Matin* (Oct. 6, 7, 8) that she had proposed, before the foreign minister's fall, to land one hundred thousand men in Schleswig in case of war. Not a shred of supporting evidence is to be found in the diplomatic documents. While the diplomats and the military experts were in all probability satisfied that this fantastic offer had never been made, the possibility that so much smoke might conceal some fire and that England might have offered her military assistance was sufficiently disturbing. At any rate, the government failed to convince public opinion that it was satisfied with England's official and public denials. *"Faule Ausreden!"* was William's incredulous reaction. "The King promised it personally and directly to Delcassé." [290] Fearing an anti-English press campaign, Bülow advised against personal attacks upon King Edward and against an open discussion of a continental league; this moderate counsel was weakened, however, by the directions that the press should explain Germany's success in "destroying at a critical moment the net that was about to be thrown over her," and that it should say that her "strength on land and sea" would protect her from a possible attack.[291] On October 12—the date of Bülow's directions to the press—the *Norddeutsche* clipped a Berlin dispatch from the *Kölnische Zeitung* claiming that Lauzanne's revelations should "be taken seriously and not as comical fantasies." Delcassé's strange confidence required an explanation.[292] William believed that England should be asked for a more positive statement and that Metternich should be recalled on an indefinite leave if the reply was unsatisfactory, but Bülow, pointing to the inadvisability of in-

[289] The excerpts from these nationalist journals are taken from the *Tägliche Rundschau*, Oct. 7.
[290] William II's comments, Metternich, Oct. 9. *G. P.*, XX, 663, 664.
[291] *Ibid.*, XX, 665 (Oct. 12).
[292] *Kölnische Zeitung*, Oct. 13.

creasing anti-German feeling in England, prevented this dangerous step and succeeded in imposing a cool reserve on the foreign
office.[293]   Public opinion drew the conclusion, however, that the
government was not taken in by England's denials.   On October
15, an article appeared in the *Norddeutsche* which Lascelles, the
British ambassador, was assured in advance would show that
England's statement had been accepted.   Contrary to the ambassador's prediction, the article did not have a calming influence.   While the British embassy translated its most important
passage in terms that confirmed his impression ("this communication was accepted on the German side in the same straightforward spirit in which it was given"),[294] the German press drew an
entirely different conclusion from the original text (*"dass sie
[England's confidential communication] deutscherseits ebenso
loyal, wie sie gegeben wurde, entgegengenommen ist."*)   The
liberal *Vossische Zeitung* (Oct. 16) and the Social Democratic
Vorwärts (Oct. 17), still more bluntly, condemned this statement as an example of the diplomat's use of words for a double
purpose; according to the second journal, it was intended to
confirm the general reaction to the *Matin's* revelations.   The
Post (Oct. 17) asserted that the English and the French denials
carried no conviction.   In fact, Bülow wanted the press to give
the impression that England was egging France on.[295]

England seemed more than ever to be Germany's worst enemy.
"We must henceforth keep in mind," wrote the *Rheinisch-Westfälische Zeitung,* "that she has never been so hostile.   Wherever
she can, she will zealously and joyously create difficulties for us." [296]
The National Liberal *National Zeitung* (Oct. 13) branded her as
an *"agent provocateur,"* and the ultra Conservative *Reichsbote*
(Oct. 18) as the "greatest enemy of human progress."   Nor were
Bülow's instructions against personal attacks upon King Edward
obeyed, for the nationalist *Tägliche Rundschau* (Oct. 22) wrote
that "he is the inspiration and leader of anti-German policy."
The Conservative *Schlessische Zeitung* foresaw an inevitable war,

---

[293] *G. P.,* XX, 666–668 (Oct. 14, 15).
[294] Lascelles, Oct. 15, 16.   *B. D.,* III, 84, 85.
[295] *G. P.,* XX, 668, 669 (Oct. 15).
[296] *National Zeitung,* Oct. 13.

because England had always destroyed her rivals.[297]   Even the *Berliner Tageblatt* (Oct. 24) betrayed an unacknowledged animosity by printing an appeal for Germany's intervention in behalf of Egyptian independence from Mustapha Kemal, who, it asserted, was a true friend of Germany.   The *Matin*'s revelations revived alarm.   They had, according to Delbrück, "clearly shown the terrible seriousness of Germany's position. . . ."[298]   Torn between fear for her security and a desire for a greater place in the world, the *Reichsbote* (Oct. 11) asserted that the duty of German diplomacy was to preserve the peace for many years in the interest of German expansion, and it warned England in the same article "that Germany would rise in her entire might *'mit dem furor teutonicus'*" to free Europe from her eternal intrigues "if she succeeds in precipitating a war."[299]   William asserted Germany's armed strength in a dramatic fashion.   "The second glass to the future and to the present!" was his toast at the unveiling of a statue to Moltke.   "Gentlemen, you have seen how we stand in the world.   Therefore, keep your powder dry and swords sharp, your vision clear, your strength alert, and away with the pessimists!   I drink to our nation in arms!   The German army and its general staff.   Hurrah!   Hurrah!   Hurrah!"[300]

The bitterness of feeling toward England strengthened the conciliatory attitude toward France.   Harden explained the *Matin* revelations as a typical journalist scoop: *"Demandez le Matin!"* he wrote, "was heard for a few days in the streets of two continents."[301]   To France's credit was still placed the repudiation of Delcassé.   The *Kölnische Zeitung* (Oct. 18) was confident that her people would overthrow any Chamber or ministry which might be tempted to thrust the nation into war.   Germany, affirmed the *Post* (Oct. 9), had never intended to interfere with France's diplomatic arrangements or to violate her patriotic attachment to Alsace-Lorraine.   Germany desired, according to

---

[297] *Post.* Oct. 18.

[298] *P. J.,* vol. 122, p. 358 (Oct. 29).

[299] Many Germans, according to Greindl, the Belgian envoy, believed that England was either seeking allies for an aggression or that she was working to provoke a war, whose profits she would collect without participating herself. *Belgische Dokumente,* III, 87 (Oct. 27).

[300] *N. A. Z.,* Oct. 28.

[301] Harden, "Oktober Equus," *Zukunft,* Oct. 21.

the *Süddeutsche Reichskorrespondenz,* merely a colonial agreement.[302]   Once the French understood that she wished nothing
more than neighborly relations, Lauzanne's articles, wrote the
Berliner Tageblatt (Oct. 15), would redound to Germany's advantage.   Delbrück asserted that the Moroccan question would
never again be permitted to become a cause "of general tension
with France."[303]   These friendly gestures were occasionally accompanied, however, by an ominous reference to France's fate if
her response was unsatisfactory.   While the *Kölnische Zeitung*
(Oct. 16) scouted the idea that Germany had any intention of
forcing her hegemony upon France, it also called for military
measures, "so that the hotheads will see that a conflict with us
would mean, as Bismarck said, a *saigner à blanc.*"   In June
France might have accepted a colonial understanding, if not a
union, with Germany and Russia against England, but by October
it was too late.   Seven months of pressure and of attacks in the
press had created a strong spirit of resistance, and time had meas-
urably strengthened the impression that Germany was bluffing.
"There is not a single politician in France," wrote the Belgian
minister in Paris, October 14, "who would dare to support a rapprochement with Germany."[304]   Morocco, said Radolin to an
official of the Quai d'Orsay, was a detail which the conference
could speedily arrange, but he complained that no one would
discuss with him the "much more important questions from
which great catastrophes might arise."[305]   By this time Rouvier
had practically adopted Delcassé's policy.   "If the people in
Berlin think they can intimidate me," he told Georges Louis, a
leading official at the Quai d'Orsay, "they are mistaken.   I will
yield nothing more . . . come what may."[306]   When the Quai
d'Orsay heard that William had invited Spain to concentrate two
hundred thousand men on the French frontier in the event of
war, the report was communicated to London, and the first conversations began between the French military attaché and General
Grierson, the chief of the British general staff.[307]   Rouvier had

[302] *Vossische Zeitung,* Oct. 14.
[303] *P. J.,* vol. 122, p. 358 (Oct. 29).
[304] *Belgische Dokumente,* III, 69 (Oct. 14).
[305] Paléologue, *Un grand tournant,* p. 407 (Nov. 4).
[306] *Ibid.,* p. 410 (Nov. 9).
[307] *Ibid.,* p. 416 (Dec. 18), 419 (Dec. 22), 420 (Dec. 23), 421 (Jan. 3, 1906).

lost his earlier aversion to a closer relationship with England.

The conditions which had made Germany's diplomatic successes possible no longer existed on the eve of the Algeciras Conference. In September the Treaty of Portsmouth diminished Russia's need of her support and increased the value of the French alliance. Her defeat in the Far East was certain sooner or later to revive Russia's aspirations in the Balkans and in Constantinople and her rivalry with Austria. The Tsar's advisers were even less willing to approve the Björkö alliance than they had been to respond to Germany's advances in the autumn of 1904.[308] Lamsdorff again persuaded Nicholas to retreat. On November 23 the Tsar told William that the alliance could not apply to a Franco-German war, because the obligations incurred by his father could not be "struck off by a stroke of the pen." Nor were the Russians satisfied with this great service to France; "as a true friend," the Tsar suggested that William might "order Tattenbach to cool down."[309] Thus ended William's dream of separating Russia and France and of a continental league. Although the Björkö alliance was never formally denounced, it was consigned to the archives, never to emerge. Meanwhile, the approach of the conference brought England and France together more closely than ever; Sir Edward Grey, the secretary of state for foreign affairs in the Liberal Campbell-Bannerman ministry, believed that France's loyalty could only be assured by helping her in Morocco and against Germany. On January 10, 1906, five days before the first session of the Algeciras Conference, Paul Cambon "put the great question" when he asked if England would come to France's aid against a German attack occasioned by Morocco.[310] The reply enabled the French to enter the conference with increased confidence. A positive assurance was impossible under the English constitutional system, but Grey did say—and he was to repeat the statement more than once before 1914—that British opinion would be strongly influenced in France's favor if a German attack should arise from the Entente Cordiale. Moreover, he approved, without consulting any members of the cabinet except

---

[308] About the middle of October, France warned Russia that her association with Germany was impossible. *B. D.*, IV, 211 (Oct. 14).

[309] Nicholas II, Nov. 10/23. *G. P.*, XIX, 524.

[310] Grey, Dec. 21, 1905, Jan. 15, 1906. *B. D.*, III, 162, 177.

the Prime Minister, the conversations between the military experts relating to the dispatch of British troops to the continent,
although he stipulated that the technical arrangements should in
no sense limit the government's freedom of action.[311]   To Germany Grey explained his attitude in even more precise terms
than those he used a few days later to Cambon.[312]   For their
part, the French were doing what they could to improve Anglo-
Russian relations.   Early in October 1905, Bompard, the French
ambassador in St. Petersburg, persuaded the influential *Novoie
Vremja* to say that the renewal of the Anglo-Japanese Alliance
required no countermeasures,[313] and there is some evidence that
Paul Cambon, the French ambassador in London, promised to
inform the British foreign office when the moment was favorable
for negotiations with Russia.[314]

Germany's prospects at the beginning of the conference were
indeed gloomy.   From Rome came the warning not to count
upon Italy's support.[315]   Already William had jumped to the
premature conclusion "that the military coalition *à trois* exists." [316]
Much pessimism was abroad.   Delbrück believed as early as October 1905 that a Liberal electoral victory in England would have
no effect upon British foreign policy, since "hostility to us is no
longer a party dogma but instead a kind of popular supersti-
tion." [317]   A round robin in a French newspaper on Germany's
claims as a world power convinced him that all countries were
united "in a kind of public secret alliance against us."   Against
this overwhelming coalition the best defense, in Delbrück's opinion, would be to avoid threats and to refrain scrupulously from
every misuse of Germany's power.[318]   Bülow spoke of isolation
at the conference as something that must be avoided at all costs.[319]
An offer to recognize France's supremacy in Morocco was discussed in official circles as well as in the press.   Metternich spoke

---

[311] Grey, Jan. 11.   *B. D.*, III, 173.
[312] Metternich, Jan. 3.   *G. P.*, XXI, 46.
[313] Hardinge, St. Petersburg, Oct. 8.   *B. D.*, IV, 208, 209.
[314] Spring Rice, St. Petersburg, Jan. 26, 1906.   *Ibid.*, IV, 222.
[315] Monts, Jan. 6, 1906.   *G. P.*, XXI, 58.
[316] *Ibid.*, XIX, 523 (Nov. 26, 1905).
[317] *P. J.*, vol. 122, p. 358 (Oct. 29).
[318] *Ibid.*, vol. 122, p. 569 (Nov. 25).
[319] *G. P.*, XXI, 14, 15 (Nov. 23, 1905).

of it early in November 1905 as one of three possible policies.[320]
That it should not be lightly dismissed was the conclusion of a
conference between Bülow and the officials of the foreign office
on Christmas Day, provided that France would make substantial
concessions.[321] Harden doubted that the opportunity would ever
be repeated.[322] Against this sensible view worked the fear that
Germany would emerge with empty hands. "We would in that
case," was the decision of the conference, "prefer war. If there
is no question of trying to humiliate France, a French triumph
at our expense would be intolerable." [323] Even William, in spite
of his indifference to Morocco and despite his later complaint
that Holstein had ignored his instructions that the Algeciras Conference should "be a stepping stone to an agreement between
France and Germany," [324] would assuredly have balked at an
open acknowledgment of failure. In the end, Holstein won
Bülow's support for a last effort to defeat France. On December 29, 1905, the Chancellor instructed Radolin to convince
France that Germany was not bluffing and that she faced the
danger of a serious conflict.[325]

Germany went to Algeciras determined to hold out to the end
not only against the grant of an exclusive mandate to France for
the policing of Morocco but also against its division between
France and Spain—for Spain, she thought, would be a French
puppet—and against any special privileges for France in the state
bank. Holstein was confident of success. France, he believed,
might be willing to accept a real rapprochement when she realized that England's "platonic" support would not suffice for the
establishment of her control of Morocco.[326] More clearly than
ever, it was a question of a willingness to fight, and neither the
Emperor nor public opinion was prepared for war. William
later spoke of his astonishment when Bülow repeatedly asked

---

[320] *G. P.*, XX, 676–678 (Nov. 2).
[321] *Ibid.*, XXI, 28, 29.
[322] Harden, "Algeciras," *Zukunft*, Feb. 3, 1906.
[323] *G. P.*, XXI, 28, 29.
[324] William II's comments, Stumm, April 17, 1907. *Ibid.*, XXI, 567.
[325] *Ibid.*, XXI, 30, 31. *Cf.* Mühlberg, Dec. 25. *Ibid.*, XXI, 29. *"Aha, tant. mieux!"* was Bülow's reaction to a report that French opinion was becoming uneasy. Flotow, Dec. 20. *Ibid.*, XXI, 26.
[326] Holstein, Feb. 22. *Ibid.*, XXI, 206–208.

him whether he desired war with France.[327]   In the Chancellor's effort to persuade public opinion that it was hopeless to expect a satisfactory arrangement with France, there is some evidence of a desire to prepare it for war.   The optimistic view of French opinion, he informed the press bureau, should be corrected;[328] he also drafted an article pointing out the decline of moderate and Socialist influences and predicting that France would, with England's tacit approval, force Germany to choose between "a serious loss of prestige and an armed conflict."[329]   To a policy that would stop at nothing, William, however, was opposed, and Holstein's support of it was weakened by the resignation (Jan. 1, 1906) of von Schlieffen, the chief of the general staff, who had advised a preventive war.

During the conference, Germany relied upon the support of the other powers and upon her ability to intimidate France.   To the French proposal of a Franco-Spanish mandate for the policing of the ports under some form of international supervision, she proposed three alternatives: each of the powers at Algeciras to receive a mandate for one port; one or more of the smaller countries to be given an exclusive mandate; or, the Sultan himself to organize the police everywhere, with foreign officers in command at designated points.   In reply to the proposal for the division of the shares of the state bank between France, Spain, Great Britain, Germany, and Italy, with percentages varying in this order and a preferential interest in the Moroccan loans for France, she proposed a strictly equal allotment of the shares and no preferential rights in the placement of loans.[330]   Germany soon found herself in danger of isolation, while France was strongly supported by England, whose representative, Sir Arthur Nicolson, coldly rejected Tattenbach's approaches.   Russia's attitude was disappointing, for she explained that her financial needs made it necessary to support France.   Even Italy advised Ger-

---

[327] William II's comments, Stumm, April 17, 1907. *G. P.,* XXI, 567.

[328] The peaceful character of French public opinion was acknowledged in the German press on the eve of the conference. "Zur Lage in Frankreich," *Historisch-Politische Blätter,* vol. 137, p. 144 (Jan. 1906); "Frankreich vor den Wahlen," *Grenzboten,* 1906, I, 4; Ajax, "Ein Ueberzeugender Beweis von Friedensliebe," *Gegenwart,* Jan. 27.

[329] O. Hammann, *Bilder aus der letzten Kaiserzeit* (Berlin, 1921), pp. 43–45.

[330] Anderson, *First Moroccan Crisis,* p. 353.

many to yield on crucial questions. If Austria was more loyal, she had no desire for war. Nor were the French to be moved by direct pressure or threats. Supported by an excited public opinion, Rouvier refused outright when Germany attempted, February 13, to shift the decision of the important problems from Algeciras to Paris; Germany had insisted upon the conference, and France did not intend to question its authority.[331] Holstein's offer (Feb. 20–22) of a not unfavorable compromise providing for the eventual recognition of France's exclusive control a few years later was rejected for the same reason.[332] Germany had now reached the crossroads; she must either fight or yield. By the middle of March, she accepted the compromise sponsored by Austria. From this moment Holstein, who still believed that Germany could secure Rouvier's repudiation by a frightened French opinion or the intervention of the neutral powers by forcing the dissolution of the conference, lost his influence upon German policy, and early in April the Emperor astonished him by accepting one of his numerous offers of resignation.[333] France's obstinacy on what the other powers regarded as minor points might eventually have improved Germany's position, but England's loyalty remained the decisive factor. The preliminary agreement of March 27 was confirmed by the General Act of April 7. Serving a term of five years, the officers for the native police in four ports were to be French, in two Spanish, and in the remaining two—Casablanca and Tangier—both French and Spanish, while all.were to be inspected at least once each year by a Swiss officer stationed at Tangier. The latter, as the French had desired, was to report to the Sultan—and to send copies of his observations to the diplomatic corps in Tangier. As to the bank question, the principle of international control fared no better; the censors, appointed by the participating powers, were to supervise the operations of the bank with a view to its financial interests rather than to those of the signatory powers, while the shares were divided according to the French scale. Superficially, Germany had won her point. France had pledged her respect

---

[331] Anderson, *First Moroccan Crisis*, p. 353. *Cf.* Paléologue, *Un grand tourant*, p. 429.
[332] Anderson, *op. cit.*, p. 376.
[333] Oncken, *Vorgeschichte des Weltkrieges*, II, 595; *G. P.*, XXI, 153; Holstein, *Lebensbekenntnis*, p. 246 (April 4).

for the independence and sovereignty of Morocco and for the principle of the "open door" for an indefinite period; she had accepted a settlement by an international conference as superseding that which Delcassé had arranged with England, Spain, and Italy. Few of the delegates probably expected, however, anything more to result from the General Act than a delay in the advance of French influence. The failure to achieve the larger diplomatic purposes for which William had landed in Tangier—the weakening or dissolution of the Entente Cordiale and a lasting change in French foreign policy—was even more pronounced.

Nevertheless, the semi-official press claimed that Germany's aims had been attained. Both the *Norddeutsche* (April 3) and the *Kölnische Zeitung* (April 3) asserted that Bülow's slogan—*ni vainqueurs ni vaincus*—was an accurate description of the settlement, and the *Norddeutsche* added that the principle of international control was the real victor. This desirable result, it was said, could not have been achieved by a separate agreement with France.[334] Even the nationalist journals at first thought that the Entente Cordiale had been set aside and that Morocco had been saved from the fate of Tunis.[335] Silent in regard to the intrinsic value of the agreement, the Conservative *Post* (April 4) argued that a separate arrangement with France would have destroyed the legal basis of Germany's intervention and that it might not have accomplished better results. In a speech to the Reichstag, which was suddenly terminated by his collapse, Bülow presented a weak defense. Germany had shown, as she had intended, that she could not be treated as a *quantité négligeable*. Her interests in Morocco were not important enough to justify a war; Germany and France could both be satisfied.[336] This attempt to prevent an explosion of dissatisfaction was unsuccessful. Although the moderate *Vossische Zeitung* (April 1) welcomed the peaceful solution, although it assured the Chancellor (April 6) that his Moroccan policy had the support of the liberal parties, it soon confessed (April 12) its doubts of the loyal application of the General Act and acknowledged (April 19) that

---

[334] *Kölnische Zeitung*, April 3.
[335] *Tägliche Rundschau*, April 1; *Reichsbote*, April 3.
[336] *Verhandlungen*, XI Leg. Per., II Sess., III, 2622, 2623.

its earlier optimism had not been shared by public opinion. The official assurances that all was well were not believed. Among the nationalists, the first indication of the terms had excited a storm of protest. The *Dresdner Nachrichten* saw at once that they provided no adequate guarantees against the progress of France's peaceful penetration.[337] "A beginning with drums and trumpets, with brave words and startling stage effects," wrote the *Rheinisch-Westfälische Zeitung,* "now a quiet, self-effacing retreat. So it was in South Africa, in China, and in Venezuela."[338] "First a fanfare," said the agrarian *Deutsche Tageszeitung* (April 3), quoting Bismarck, "now a chamade. . . . Germany has emerged with a black eye." "We started out in search of a kingdom," lamented the National Liberal *Hannoversche Courier,* "and we are now bringing home a donkey."[339] To France had gone the real gains, wrote the *Hamburger Nachrichten* (April 3); from Germany had come the vital concessions. The Pan-Germans promptly concluded that France would henceforth be the effective sovereign in Morocco; they insisted that Germany was like the merchant who revealed his unsatisfactory accounts when his real purpose was to secure new credits; the world knew what to think when she rattled her sword.[340] From the beginning of the crisis, these critics asserted, the methods of German diplomacy had been badly adapted to its professed purposes.[341] If a rapprochement with France had been the aim, "our first steps," wrote the *Hamburger Nachrichten* (March 31), "were utterly wrong, showing a complete misunderstanding of French psychology." It was a mistake, asserted the *Berliner Neueste Nachrichten* (April 1), to threaten France for the sake of "the general inspector of the Moroccan police; the shares of the state bank were not worth a European war." That statesman was Bismarck's heir, wrote the *Rheinisch-Westfälische Zeitung,* who pursued the nation's larger interests with cool, iron determination, not he who was a slave to a formula.[342]

---

[337] *Tägliche Rundschau,* March 31.
[338] *Ibid.,* March 31.
[339] *Ibid.,* April 1.
[340] *A. B.,* April 7.
[341] *Deutsche Tageszeitung,* April 3.
[342] *Berliner Neueste Nachrichten,* April 3.

Kladderadatsch, April 15, 1906.

Figure 19.—After the Algeciras days.

As a cause of dissatisfaction, the Moroccan settlement was less important than the broader results of the crisis. Italy, it was evident, was unreliable. "We will do well," wrote William in March, "to . . . write off this ally as smoke." [343] He was willing, he told the Austrian ambassador, that Austria should teach the Italians a lesson,[344] and the press insisted that the Italo-German relations required reconsideration. Extraordinary guarantees "should be demanded of Rome," wrote the National Liberal *Magdeburgische Zeitung* (April 4), "as a condition for the next renewal of the Triple Alliance; an avowed enemy is preferable to a doubtful friend." The agrarian *Deutsche Tageszeitung* (April 17) was concerned less with her bad faith than with her weakness. At this juncture, the eruption of Vesuvius furnished an opportunity to show Germany's dissatisfaction.[345] Among the messages of condolence that poured into Rome, there was none from William. Many Germans were doubtless humiliated by his failure to observe the ordinary amenities,[346] but others approved.[347] "In any event," wrote the moderate *Vossische Zeitung* (April 17), "we cannot permit the tragedy to interrupt the settlement of our accounts with her." To Austria William was all smiles; he congratulated Goluchowski, her foreign minister, on his services as a "brilliant second" and promised Germany's aid "in a similar case." England's strong support of France was no less offensive because it was not entirely unexpected,[348] but Russia's attitude was a cruel disappointment. True to its Bismarckian traditions, the *Hamburger Nachrichten* (April 5) advised Berlin to open its coffers to prevent her from placing loans in London and Paris, but even the Conservatives joined the Centrist speakers in the Reichstag (April 5) in warning German capital against Russian paper, an incident that foreshadowed the closing of the Berlin

---

[343] William II's comments, Monts, March 8. *G. P.*, XXI, 353.

[344] Pribram, *Secret Treaties of Austria-Hungary*, II, 138. *Cf.* Anderson, *First Moroccan Crisis*, p. 398 n.

[345] *Berliner Neueste Nachrichten*, April 18.

[346] The *Hamburger Nachrichten* (April 18) and the Conservative *Schlessische Zeitung* (*Tägliche Rundschau*, April 18) protested against the surrender to an emotional resentment.

[347] *Reichsbote*, April 20.

[348] *Deutsche Zeitung*, in *Post*, April 15; H. Jacobi, "Die Weltlage nach dem Schluss der Algeciras-Konferenz," *Grenzboten*, 1906, II, 36, 37 (April 5).

market.[349] Isolation, according to the pessimists, was a reality. The nationalist *Berliner Neueste Nachrichten* (April 1) believed that public opinion understood at last that little aid could be expected in a war. "Germany," wrote the leading Catholic review, ". . . suffers one diplomatic humiliation after another. While we act and talk as if our situation is of the best, our world position can be described most accurately by two words: '*Endlich allein!—aber auch ganz allein.*' "[350] Many still felt that the situation was merely temporary and therefore no real reason for alarm. In Rome, Monts conceded that the circle of enemies around Germany had been closed, "but," he added, "great coalitions are seldom capable of action. . . . In the long run the English will not follow their royal *commis voyageur.*"[351] If Germany remained true to herself, wrote an unofficial observer, "even isolation, which is after all the result of passing combinations, will not be important."[352] To the nationalist *Tägliche Rundschau* (April 20), an Anglo-Russian entente still seemed improbable. "Between the possibility and the *fait accompli*," wrote the moderate *Vossische Zeitung* (April 7), "there is still a long way." What the extremist press (April 10), like the *Reichsbote,* feared most was not an immediate menace to Germany's security, but rather insupportable restrictions upon Germany's expansion.[353]

Despite the general dissatisfaction with Germany's foreign policy, there were few signs of an impending change. Nationalist opinion called for a strong and unwavering policy, based upon an ever more powerful army and navy, and it protested against further attempts to court other countries.[354] For the future, Bülow's support of a closer union with Austria "as Germany's sole dependable ally" was significant as the first step away from the leadership which Bismarck had always insisted upon.[355]

---

[349] *Tägliche Rundschau,* April 6.
[350] *Historisch-Politische Blätter,* vol. 138, pp. 234, 235 (July 1906).
[351] Monts, *Erinnerungen und Gedanken,* pp. 424, 425 (April 10).
[352] "Deutschland und die auswärtige Politik," *Deutsche Revue,* 1906, II, 375 (June).
[353] *A. B.,* July 7.
[354] *Reichsbote,* April 7; *Tägliche Rundschau,* April 17; *Deutsche Tageszeitung,* April 18; Ajax, "Vom seligen Dreibund," *Gegenwart,* May 12.
[355] Bülow, May 31, 1906. *G. P.,* XXI, 360. *Cf.* H. Delbrück in *P. J.,* vol. 124, p. 390 (April 22). Delbrück, according to Holstein, accepted his cue from Hammann of the press bureau. Monts, *Erinnerungen und Gedanken,* p. 365.

Austria's domestic troubles discouraged, however, the expression of this view in the press. Not yet was opinion prepared to admit that Germany must depend upon a country so torn by domestic dissension. As to France, judgment was suspended; Germany's attitude would depend upon the fate of the General Act. "The future of Franco-German relations," wrote the Conservative *Post* (April 6), "depends upon France." The Moroccan crisis was, according to Schiemann, "a fencing match, not a duel, and now that the rapiers have been sheathed, we see no reason for refusing to shake hands."[356] The success of the Republican parties in the parliamentary election, according to a thoughtful observer, was a promising augury.[357] Meanwhile increasing tension with England again revived the discussion of a rapprochement. The beginnings antedated the Algeciras Conference, when England made several friendly gestures. The time, wrote Metternich, December 4, 1904, was ripe.[358] In a letter to William, King Edward denied that England had any hostile intentions and he spoke of the baneful influence of the press.[359] Thomas Barclay, who had helped to prepare for the Anglo-French entente, addressed the Rhineland and Ruhr industrialists in behalf of an Anglo-German reconciliation.[360] During the conference William showed an accommodating spirit. "My policy," he replied to his uncle, "is clear as crystal. . . . It's no use to cry over spilt milk! Let bygones be bygones!"[361] Unfortunately, neither country was willing to sacrifice anything of importance. Germany's earlier demands were remembered by the British foreign office. "Past history has shown," wrote Eyre Crowe, the leading proponent of an anti-German policy, "that a friendly Germany has usually been a Germany asking for something, by way of proving our friendship."[362] Not only William, but a considerable part of

---

[356] *Kreuz-Zeitung*, April 4. Schiemann, *Deutschland und die Grosse Politik*, VI, 122.
[357] "Frankreich nach den Wahlen," *Grenzboten*, 1906, II, 453, 454.
[358] *G. P.*, XX, 681, 682.
[359] Lee, *Edward VII*, 525 (Jan. 27, 1906).
[360] The *Alldeutsche Blätter* (Feb. 3, 1906) believed, however, that he wished to thrust the responsibility for the certain failure upon Germany, since he had stipulated a Franco-German understanding as a necessary condition. Besides many intellectuals, the financiers seem to have been most active in the agitation for an understanding. Hallgarten, *Vorkriegs Imperialismus*, p. 196.
[361] Lee, *Edward VII*, II, 526 (Feb. 1).
[362] Crowe's minute, Lascelles, May 24, 1906. *B. D.*, III, 258.

public opinion undoubtedly thought that England, not Germany, should make concessions. "Why should we always take the first step?" exclaimed the Emperor when Haldane, the British minister of war, spoke of the Bagdad Railway, "The railway is already ours." [363]   Germany could expect, according to an anonymous commentator, to surrender more than she received. [364]   The English, it was noted, were careful to assure France during the summer of 1906 that the visit of the German *Bürgermeister* and journalists would have no effect upon the entente. [365]   For France's benefit, an anonymous observer, who expressed, according to the British ambassador in Paris, the views of the highest German officials, spoke of an Anglo-German friendship as the best guarantee for France's security. [366]   The Germans, it was evident, did not wish to lock the door.   In July 1906, the foreign office vetoed a plan to transfer the reserve officers who resided in the United States to German Southwest Africa on the outbreak of war. [367]   An agreement in regard to the conference that was to meet at the Hague in 1907 aroused William's interest as a means of establishing "intimate" relations.   By the autumn of 1906, he had, however, given up hope for any immediate progress toward this goal.   "England will not change," he wrote in October, "until we are strong enough on the sea to become a desirable ally." [368]

He nevertheless rebuked those who were undermining public confidence.   He could not tolerate a pessimist, he said, in a speech at Breslau, September 8: "He who will not coöperate, let him, if he wishes, seek a better country." [369]   Perhaps no pronouncement by a German sovereign ever occasioned so much indignation as this repudiation of a part of his people.   The *Schwarzseher,* asserted the National Liberal *National Zeitung,* represented the views of the majority; moreover, he performed a necessary serv-

[363] William II's comments, Stumm, May 19.   *G. P.,* XXI, 434, 435; Grey, June 15. *B. D.,* VI, 343.

[364] "Deutschland und die auswärtige Politik," *Deutsche Revue,* 1906, II, 368 (June).

[365] The visit, according to the Belgian minister, had no effect upon English opinion. *Belgische Dokumente,* II, 151 (June 23); *cf.* Crowe's minute, June 26.   *B. D.,* III, 359, 360.

[366] "Deutschland und die auswärtige Politik," *Deutsche Revue,* 1906, III, 322, 323 (Sept.); Bertie, Sept. 6.   *B. D.,* III, 385, 386.

[367] *G. P.,* XXI, 440, 441 (July 9).

[368] William II's comments, Metternich, Oct. 14.   *Ibid.,* XXI, 464.

[369] "Schwarzseher dulde ich nicht.   Und wer sich zur Arbeit nicht eignet, der scheide aus, und wenn er will, suche er sich ein besseres Land."

ice.[370] Even Delbrück admitted that many reasons for pessimism existed, yet he believed that fear rather than an aggressive purpose was bringing the other powers together. In his opinion, Germany should renounce her imperialist aspirations and should concentrate upon her industrial development.[371] The officials were less philosophical. Rumors of Anglo-Russian negotiations moved William to speak of the net being drawn around Germany. "A fine prospect!" he exclaimed. "In the future, we can reckon with the Franco-Russian Alliance, the Anglo-French Entente Cordiale, and the Anglo-Russian Entente, with Spain, Italy, and Portugal as satellites."[372] A general conflict would inevitably follow if England succeeded in detaching Italy from the Triple Alliance.[373] Metternich had already warned Grey, July 31, 1906, that Germany was too strong to permit herself to be hemmed in diplomatically and "that a situation might arise which would make it necessary for her to break through the circle."[374] The presence of General French, the chief of the British general staff, at the French maneuvers again raised the question of England's readiness to support France with her armed forces.[375] The time had come for a public statement, especially since Bülow's break with the Catholic Center and the resulting press campaign against the administration of the colonies required the formation of a new governmental majority to take the place of the "blue-black" *bloc*. For this purpose, a stronger leadership in foreign affairs was desirable. On November 14, 1906, Bassermann, the National Liberal leader, interpellated the government in the Reichstag; England, he said, was encircling Germany. Although his main purpose was, in accordance with an arrangement with the Chancellor, to provide an occasion for the speech which Bülow had carefully prepared during the summer, Bassermann did not hesitate to charge that the government's im-

---

[370] *Post,* Sept. 11. If William had his way, wrote a nationalist, he would stand alone with his advisers, his adjutants, and his lackeys. Ajax, "Die allgemeine Lage," *Gegenwart,* Nov. 24.

[371] *P. J.,* vol. 126, p. 191 (Sept. 18).

[372] William II's comments, Miquel, Sept. 19. *G. P.,* XXV, 23.

[373] William II's comments, Wedel, Nov. 2. *Ibid.,* XXI, 444, 445.

[374] *Ibid.,* XXI, 444, 445. William, Bülow wrote to the foreign office, should express the same point of view to King Edward during his visit to Homburg in August. *Ibid.,* XXI, 449 (Aug. 13).

[375] William II's comments, Radolin, Nov. 4. *Ibid.,* XXI, 530, 531.

pulsiveness had reduced Germany's prestige abroad.[376] Bülow's facile optimism had largely disappeared. If he disavowed the Pan-Germans and asserted that Germany had no intention of interfering with England's arrangements with Russia and France, he also said that the existence of exclusive friendships "without good relations . . . with Germany would endanger the peace of Europe." Encirclement would be impossible "without a certain amount of pressure. But pressure produces counterpressure, and pressure and counterpressure may eventually produce an explosion." As to what should be done, he was necessarily vague, for the government itself did not know. Nevertheless, Bülow did say that force would not win England's friendship (fruit would not ripen more quickly by placing a lamp under it) and he did assure Austria that Germany was ready to return the service which she had rendered at Algeciras. In any event, Germany need not feel like a frightened child lost in the forest. "A nation of 60 millions with an army like Germany's is never isolated so long as it does not falter." [377] The reaction in Germany disappointed Bülow. It proved, he said, the public's profound ignorance of foreign affairs and its political immaturity.[378] By a practical admission that a hostile coalition existed, the speech confirmed the reasons for alarm, and the Pan-Germans felt more aggrieved than ever. They reminded the Chancellor that "their political aims— sometimes initiated in the face of a hostile public opinion—had often been taken over by the majority of the German people." [379] Two months later, Cartwright, the British consul in Munich, noted "a feeling of despondency and uncertainty as to [the] future," although he also acknowledged that "the mass of the people ask only for peace and quiet." [380]

Hoping to recover a working majority in the Reichstag, Bülow decided early in December 1906, like Bismarck in January 1887, to dissolve the Reichstag and to appeal to the country on a popular issue. That issue was found in the colonial question. His ap-

[376] Hammann, *Bilder aus der letzten Kaiserzeit*, pp. 45, 46; *Verhandlungen*, XI Leg. Per., II Sess., V, 3621.

[377] *Verhandlungen*, XI, Leg. Per., II Sess., V, 3623–3631.

[378] Hammann, *Bilder aus der letzten Kaiserzeit*, pp. 45, 46.

[379] *A. B.*, Nov. 24, 1906.

[380] *B. D.*, VI, 4 (Jan. 12, 1907).

pointment as colonial minister of Bernhard Dernburg, the director of the *Darmstädter Bank,* whose political sympathies were with the Progressives, was a clever move.   Not only did the liberal middle classes see in it a friendly gesture, but Dernburg's strong defense of the colonial administration against the attacks of the Centrists and the Social Democrats won much acclaim. Having secured the Emperor's consent and that of the Bundesrat, Bülow dissolved the Reichstag on December 13 and set the election for January 25, 1907.   His aim was a new combination between the Conservatives and the three middle-class liberal parties —an unnatural alliance which the imperialist trend of liberal opinion alone made possible—but a timely insurrection among the Herreros in Southwest Africa was followed by an appeal for national unity and for the defense of national honor.   Although the Centrists had played the more important part in the parliamentary crisis, the attack was concentrated against the Social Democrats.   Abroad, and especially in England and France, Germany's enemies had made no secret of their desire for the eventual triumph of the Social Democrats, as an assurance against the misuse of Germany's power or, as most Germans believed, as a weakening influence.[381]   At home, it was good politics to attack the Socialists.   "For the national honor," would be, according to the Conservative *Post* (Dec. 14), the slogan.   The election would show, wrote the *Norddeutsche,* "whether Germany is capable of becoming a world power."[382]   On Bülow's suggestion, a society was formed to combat the Social Democrats, and all of the numerous nationalist propaganda groups aided the cause.[383] These tactics won a notable success.   Although the Social Democratic vote increased by eight per cent, the party lost almost half of its seats, its representation falling from eighty-one to forty-three.   The Center increased its total of one hundred and four seats by one.   The chief gains went to the parties upon which the government was to rely for its majority: the Conservatives

---

[381] Lalaing, London, Feb. 8, 1907.   *Belgische Dokumente,* VI, 59.   Cartwright, in Munich, advised his government to cultivate the dissatisfied elements in South Germany.   *B. D.,* VI, 9 (Jan. 12, 1907).   Cf. *Kreuz-Zeitung,* Jan. 30.   Schiemann, *Deutschland und die Grosse Politik,* VII, 39; *A. B.,* Feb. 2, 1907.

[382] *Post,* Dec. 19, 1906.

[383] *Ibid.,* March 8, 1907.

won eight to make a total of sixty and the liberal parties thirteen.[384] The celebration of the demise of the Social Democratic
party was premature; for the moment, however, it seemed a great
victory. "The national idea," proclaimed the Pan-Germans, "has
won a victory for which even the most optimistic scarcely dared
to hope." [385] "The Emperor and Chancellor now know," wrote
the Conservative *Post* (Feb. 9, 1907), "that the nation is with
them despite the Socialists' anti-patriotic campaign." To the
British ambassador William voiced the hope that the world "will
eventually grasp the meaning of the recent elections, which, by
diminishing the power of the Social Democrats, will increase that
of the German Empire and thus furnish an extra guarantee for
the maintenance of peace, as any Power who wishes to attack
Germany will now hesitate." [386]

The day had long since passed when a German election could
change the diplomatic situation. A new reason for uneasiness
had already appeared. In October 1906, Clemenceau's rise to
power in France banished the hope for the loyal application of
the General Act of Algeciras. In the face of his record, his peaceful assurances carried no conviction; [387] German opinion believed
that he intended, with England's aid, to seduce Austria and solve
his difficulties at home by a foreign diversion.[388] William spoke
of Jules Cambon, the new French ambassador, as one of Germany's most dangerous enemies.[389] But Germany had no desire
for another crisis. Hers was the passive rôle, wrote the Conservative *Post* (April 14, 1907); France must henceforth take the
initiative in any effort to improve relations. The Germans made
no attempt to conceal their alarm when Edward VII visited the
Kings of Spain and Italy during the spring of 1907. William
assumed at first an air of disdainful indifference. *"Ich bleibe
ruhig!"* he wrote, *"und seh' ich herab von meinem Thier auf das*

---

[384] I. Eschenburg, *Das Kaiserreich am Scheideweg* (Berlin, 1929), p. 57.
[385] *A. B.,* Feb. 2, 1907.
[386] Lascelles, Jan. 21, 1907. *B. D.,* VI, 12.
[387] "Clemenceau," the *Hamburger Nachrichten* stated, "hates Germany." *Cf.* Vi-
deus, "Frankreich und das Ministerium Clemenceaus," *Historisch-Politische Blätter,*
vol. 138, p. 929 (Dec. 5, 1906).
[388] The British government, according to the Belgian minister, shared this opinion
of Clemenceau's policy. *Belgische Dokumente,* III, 175 (Feb. 4, 1907).
[389] Carroll, *French Public Opinion,* p. 225.

Gesindel unter mir." [390]   He was, however, alone in this Olympian calm. "The day before yesterday," wrote Lascelles, the British ambassador, "Berlin went stark raving mad. There was a fall of six points in German securities on the Bourse and a general impression that war was to break out between England and Germany. . . ." To isolate Germany, wrote the *Kölnische Zeitung,* was Edward's manifest purpose.[391]   Ten days passed before the government, in an unofficial statement to the correspondent of the London *Daily Mail* (April 30), repudiated this "nervous unrest." "The diplomatic position, as viewed from Berlin," wrote the correspondent, "has undergone no changes requiring the outburst of the *furor teutonicus* from the Reichstag and the forum as had been urged in various quarters." The foreign office was manifestly uneasy. The Anglo-Spanish and the Franco-Spanish exchange of notes, May 15, 1907, pledging the three powers to the maintenance of the status quo in the western Mediterranean, on the coast of Morocco, and in the adjacent waters of the Atlantic, was followed by feverish efforts to learn from Madrid whether England or France had taken the initiative. While the Franco-Japanese accord of June 9, 1907 was another reminder that the interest conflicts which had played so large a part in her calculations were fast being arranged, Germany could not object, since her interests were not directly involved, but St. Petersburg was asked to explain its intentions in the understanding with Japan (July 1907) for the maintenance of the status quo in the Far East. Izvolski was gratifyingly unwilling openly to offend Germany; Russia, he said, was not a party to any negotiations for an anti-German coalition, and she would inform Berlin if German interests were affected by any of her arrangements.[392] The fact remained that the network of alliances and understandings was almost complete by the summer of 1907. "These agreements," wrote the Belgian minister in Berlin, "are all being concluded . . . between powers who are, for one reason or another, hostile to Germany." [393]

---

[390] William II's comments, Monts, April 18, 1907. *G. P.,* XXI, 496, 497.
[391] Lascelles, April 19, Cartwright, April 23. *B. D.,* VI, 28, 29.
[392] Schoen, June 19, 1907. *G. P.,* XXV, 59.
[393] Greindl, May 13. *Belgische Dokumente,* III, 205.

By 1907 Germany was probably powerless to prevent the completion of the Anglo-French diplomatic system, but it was still within her power to effect a gradual improvement of foreign opinion. A favorable opportunity was missed in connection with the Second Hague Conference. There was sufficient opposition to the American and English proposal for the inclusion of the limitation of naval armaments in the agenda to assure its defeat, and Bülow agreed at first that it would be a mistake to flout the world-wide peace sentiment.[394] Besides William's refusal to endanger Germany's naval program, the possibility that England might announce her willingness to drop one of the three dreadnoughts from her naval budget, in return for suitable concessions, and the desire to take advantage of Russia's sympathy diverted Germany from a policy of reserve. Bülow, in fact, led the opposition to a discussion of naval armaments. First he rejected Grey's advances.[395] When Aehrenthal, Austria's new foreign minister, suggested a new *Dreikaiserbund,* he urged Russia to join Germany and Austria in asking that the English proposal be dropped as a condition for attending the conference.[396] Izvolski, then in charge of the Russian foreign office, had no desire, however, to offend England at a time when Russia was seeking an understanding with her and with her Japanese ally.[397] On April 30, 1907, the Chancellor openly stated his position to the Reichstag and thereby probably assured England's consent to the Havas Agency's revelation of the Anglo-Spanish and Franco-Spanish notes (May 15).[398] Another step, according to German opinion, had been taken toward isolation.[399] England was promptly outvoted when she moved that the limitation of armaments should be brought before the conference, and Germany then led the

---

[394] Oncken, *Vorgeschichte des Weltkrieges,* II, 606. Cf. *P. J.,* vol. 128, pp. 369, 370 (April 27).

[395] Brandenburg, *From Bismarck to the World War,* p. 275.

[396] *G. P.,* XXIII, 116, 117 (Feb. 10); 120 (Feb. 12); 123 (Feb. 15); 127, 128 (Feb. 18).

[397] Schoen, April 3. *Ibid.,* XXIII, 197.

[398] For the contents of these notes, see above, p. 559. Grey acknowledged his satisfaction with Bülow's statement. Stumm, May 3. *G. P.,* XXIII, 221, 222. *Cf.* Hardinge, March 25, 1907. *B. D.,* VII, 17.

[399] *Kreuz-Zeitung,* June 19, 1907. Schiemann, *Deutschland und die Grosse Politik,* VII, 233; *Belgische Dokumente,* VII, 233 (June 22). K. Mehrmann, "Spanien unter englisch-französischer Kontrolle," *A. B.,* July 6; R. von Bieberstein, "Der Zusammenschluss der Westmächte," *Historisch-Politische Blätter,* vol. 140, p. 269 (Aug.).

movement to exclude questions relating to national interests and honor from the International Court of Arbitration.   In comparison with the blame which Germany everywhere incurred, the united front which Marschall, the leader of the German delegation, later claimed had been maintained by the Triple Alliance,[400] was a mediocre advantage.   Even Marschall conceded that the conference had increased England's prestige.   The world, he said, was taken in by her claim to represent the interests of humanity.[401]

The complexity of international politics nevertheless enabled the Germans to discover reasons for optimism, even on the eve of the Anglo-Russian entente.   Forgetting its recent doubts of Italy's loyalty, the Conservative *Post* (July 15, 1907) spoke of the renewal of the Triple Alliance as a more significant service to peace than the Hague Conference.   Italy might not fulfil her obligations in wartime, but she would at least remain neutral.   The Anglo-Japanese Alliance was still expected to turn the United States toward Germany.[402]   Relations with England were momentarily better; during Edward VII's visit to Wilhelmshöhe in August, a return visit to England was arranged for the autumn. Mindful of Delcassé's failure to consult Germany during the negotiation of the Entente Cordiale, Russia took particular pains to inform her as to the progress of the negotiations with England.[403] Assurances were given as early as May 1906 of Russia's full recognition of Germany's interests in the Bagdad Railway.[404]   Not until Izvolski had ascertained that Berlin would not object did he venture to begin negotiations for an understanding.[405]   In St. Petersburg, German diplomacy adopted, according to a British diplomat, "a suave and conciliatory attitude"; in London, on the other hand, Metternich told Haldane that he "would have to abandon his belief in England's friendly aims" if England should arrange an entente with Russia without "first making the same

[400] *G. P.*, XXIII, 289, 290 (Nov. 30, 1907).
[401] *Ibid.*, XXIII, 282 (Oct. 28).
[402] "Die Beziehungen des Deutschen Reiches in den Vereinigten Staaten von Amerika," *Grenzboten*, 1907, II, 538, 539 (June 13).
[403] Bertie, Oct. 22; Nicolson, Nov. 7. *B. D.*, IV, 243, 412, 413.
[404] Schoen, May 24. *G. P.*, XXV, 14.
[405] Nicolson, Nov. 7, 1906. *B. D.*, IV, 412, 413.

proposals to Germany."[406]   Nevertheless, public opinion was assured that an Anglo-Russian understanding in Asia would be unobjectionable, since Germany's interests in Persia were exclusively commercial.[407]   The visits of Nicholas II and Edward VII in August caused some satisfaction.   The meeting of the Russian and German sovereigns at Swinemunde, according to the semi-official press, resulted in a substantial agreement.   The *Norddeutsche* (Aug. 3) wrote of "a welcome similarity of views . . . on all current questions," asserting at the same time that nothing had been done to disturb the alliances of either country.   The *Kölnische Zeitung* hinted that Nicholas' visit was more than a mere courtesy call,[408] and the Conservative *Post* (Aug. 1) suggested a parallel between Russia's position and that of Italy.   For the nationalist *Berliner Neueste Nachrichten* (Aug. 2), the presence of Bülow and Stolypin, the two Chancellors, meant that the Anglo-Russian understanding would not be directed against Germany.   William, in fact, had offered to support Russia and Austria if they were able to agree upon a common policy in the Balkans.[409]   At Wilhelmshöhe, according to Hardinge, the representative of the British foreign office, there was "no real intimacy" and no political discussion between Edward and William.[410]   While Bülow was silent on the naval question and the Bagdad Railway, he did say that "he could warmly welcome the conclusion of an Agreement between Great Britain and Russia," since the latter had also assured him that Germany's interests were not involved.   As to Morocco, he affirmed the intention of defending German rights under the General Act, but he took particular pains to express a conciliatory attitude as to Germany's relations with France.[411]   While the semi-official press in general warned opinion not to expect too much, the *Norddeutsche* (Aug. 18) asserted "that Anglo-German relations are not at present shadowed by any clouds. . . ."   Before Edward's arrival, the Con-

---

[406] Nicolson's report for 1906, Jan. 2, 1907. *B. D.*, IV, 257; *G. P.*, XXV, 12n (May 7, 1907).

[407] "Deutschland, Russland und England," *Deutsche Revue*, 1907, I, 131 (Feb.); *Verhandlungen*, XII Leg. Per., I Sess., II, 1253 (Bülow, April 30, 1907); Tschirschky, Sept. 11, 1906. *G. P.*, XXV, 118.

[408] *Reichsbote*, Aug. 2.

[409] Brandenburg, *From Bismarck to the World War*, p. 306.

[410] Hardinge, Aug. 21. *B. D.*, VI, 46.

[411] Hardinge, Aug. 19. *Ibid.*, VI, 43-46.

servative *Post* (Aug. 9) spoke of England's recognition of the part played by "an unscrupulous press" in the recent tension as "an opening for friendly relations" and of the successes of German diplomacy in restoring the balance of power. "The significance," it wrote, "of the strengthening of the Triple Alliance, of the rapprochement with Russia, of the beginning of a *détente* with France, of America's friendship; and of many other achievements of German statesmanship should not be underestimated."

Scarcely a week elapsed after Edward's departure when a confidential exchange of views between Bülow, William, and Tirpitz showed that the naval question was still a fundamental cause of friction. If William agreed with the Chancellor's protest against boundless naval programs, he also insisted upon the exact fulfilment of the law of 1900, and Tirpitz believed that a threat of an increase in the annual construction of dreadnoughts to three after 1911 would be useful in negotiating with England.[412] The Anglo-Russian Entente (Aug. 31, 1907), based upon a series of compromises in Afghanistan, Thibet, and Persia, was nevertheless accepted by the government as satisfactory. Bülow, ignoring his alarmist speech of November 1906, directed the press not to write of an alliance or "unnecessarily to speak of a violation of German interests. . . ."[413] These moderate counsels were reflected in the semi-official press.[414] Both parties to the new understanding, the *Norddeutsche* (Sept. 29) acknowledged, had kept Germany informed. Even the government's great influence could not silence those who felt that England's "great sacrifices" meant unavowable purposes. The agrarian *Deutsche Tageszeitung* (Sept. 26) refused to believe in the sincerity of the official optimism. "Of what value to us," it asked, "is the so-called 'guarantee of world peace,' when it diminishes the assurances of our own peace? . . . We have no reason . . . to welcome the settlement of differences between other countries, the existence of which was sometimes extremely useful to us." The liberal *Berliner Tageblatt* (Sept. 29), now definitely critical of Bülow's foreign and domestic policy, also felt that Germany had suffered a defeat.

---

[412] Hammann, *Bilder aus der letzten Kaiserzeit*, pp. 57, 58.
[413] Bülow's comments, Miquel, Aug. 31. *G. P.*, XXV, 40.
[414] *Kölnische Zeitung*, Sept. 27; *N. A. Z.*, Sept. 29. Cf. *Post*, Sept. 3, 26; *Berliner Neueste Nachrichten*, Sept. 28.

The extent of Russia's gains might be questioned, but it certainly was "bad business for the German Empire. Again we are pretending a satisfaction which we do not feel. We are everything to all peoples." For a different reason, the Social Democrats were also disappointed; in England's abandonment of her traditional opposition to Russia, they saw the strengthening of the Russian autocracy and therefore a danger for the revolutionary movement.[415] Even the Conservative *Post* (Oct. 5) finally acknowledged that England's position in world affairs was greater than ever.[416] Not indifference but a sense of the folly of irritating England by "useless recriminations" was, according to the Belgian minister, the reason for the moderation of the greater part of the press. William was soon to visit England. The officials had no illusions as to the situation. William understood that the new entente would make itself felt in Europe even more than in Asia.[417] While Bülow became more cautious on the naval question, the Emperor reverted to an attitude of defiance, writing, "Let it come on, it will be surprised at its warm reception!" when it was suggested that Germany must henceforth reckon with a *"Syndikat"* of the other powers.[418]

In these circumstances, William's visit to England had a more than ordinary significance. If the original invitation had been intended to moderate Germany's reaction to the Anglo-Russian Entente, it also opened the door for an improvement in Anglo-German relations, provided, as Grey pointed out, that it was not achieved "at the expense of our friendship with France."[419] It was precisely this reservation that caused the British government to object to Bülow's presence. To Grey's intense displeasure, because he was forced to make something like an apology, the *Times* (Oct. 10) frankly expressed the hope that the Chancellor had at last seen that his attitude during the Boer War had not been "very worthy of himself or of his position."[420] Yielding gracefully, Bülow remained in Germany. "We should not," he

415 M. Beer, "Der britisch-russische Ausgleich in Mittelasien," *Neue Zeit*, Oct. 12, 1907.
416 *Cf.* L. Martin, "Das anglo-russische Abkommen," *Gegenwart*, Oct. 19, 1907.
417 William II's comments, Miquel, Sept. 25. *G. P.*, XXV, 44, 45.
418 William II's comments, Miquel, Sept. 27. *Ibid.*, XXV, 46, 47.
419 Hardinge, Oct. 2. *B. D.*, VI, 84.
420 Grey, Oct. 10. *Ibid.*, VI, 86.

wrote, "try to force anything upon England or to rush her." [421] William, convinced that the encirclement of Germany was still England's aim, regarded the invitation as a mere maneuver "for the purpose of throwing sand in the eyes of the stupid." The sending of General French to Russia only three weeks before seemed unprecedented.[422] Alleging a passing indisposition as an excuse, he tried to send the Crown Prince in his place, but he changed his mind when Edward reminded him of the probable effect upon public opinion.[423] The Emperor's reception was most cordial, especially since the French press had made no secret of France's desire for better Anglo-German relations to lessen the danger of a war that would not concern her own interests.[424] The London press took the position that England's diplomatic arrangements must not be disturbed, but it was also prepared to welcome better relations with Germany.[425] "On this occasion," wrote the Conservative *Pall Mall Gazette* (Nov. 9), "England holds out to Germany the hand of friendship." "The feeling of distrust," averred the liberal *Daily Chronicle* (Nov. 12), "has faded away like mist before the rising sun." "We believe," said the sensational *Daily Mail* (Nov. 11), "that relations frank, courteous, and businesslike between Germany on the one side and England and France on the other are compatible with the closest intimacy between both the Western Powers." William's speeches contributed to the general good-will. In Germany, moderate opinion welcomed the opportunity, after a coolness of many years, again to affirm its traditional sympathy for England. Who, asked the *Vossische Zeitung* (Nov. 9), could object to her present policy? "The island empire can make as many agreements as it desires; no one believes any more that it is organizing an aggressive coalition against us." Theodor Wolff, now the editor of the *Berliner Tageblatt,* assured the English (Nov. 9) of the German people's good-will. Even the *Kölnische Zeitung*

---

[421] Bülow, Oct. 21. Hammann, *Bilder aus der letzten Kaiserzeit,* p. 49.
[422] William II's comments, Miquel, Oct. 9. *G. P.,* XXV, 47, 48.
[423] William II, Oct. 31. Lee, *Edward VII,* II, 554.
[424] *Spectator* (London), Nov. 9.
[425] The Conservative *Standard* (Nov. 11) spoke favorably of coöperation in matters of common interest like the Macedonian question and the Bagdad Railway, but it insisted that no basis existed for an arrangement like England's understandings with France and Russia.

(Nov. 14) spoke of the elimination of suspicion between the two countries. The Conservative *Post* (Nov. 15) echoed this opinion and recommended "an Anglo-German entente" to be built upon the improvement of public opinion. There were, inevitably, discordant voices. The Conservative *Zeitfragen* reminded its readers that imperial visits to England had never benefited Germany.[426] It was nonsense, wrote the nationalist *Berliner Neueste Nachrichten* (Nov. 10), to think that a couple of after-dinner speeches meant a diplomatic rapprochement. For the agrarian *Deutsche Tageszeitung* (Nov. 13), "a mutual recognition of equality, the absence of which was the principal cause of earlier differences," was the essential condition for an understanding, although it professed to accept England's friendliness at its face value.[427] The *Berliner Tageblatt's* enthusiasm soon cooled. It would (Nov. 14) wait to see if England's world policy would reflect the friendly sentiment of her people. In any event, Grey believed that the visit had improved Anglo-German relations "without in the least weakening our relations with France."[428]

England had succeeded in moderating Germany's reaction to the Anglo-Russian Entente. The nationalist *Tägliche Rundschau* (Nov. 17) believed that England would henceforth find it necessary to give more heed to German interests. Actually the inveterate suspicions of her intentions and the naval question made it impossible to secure any permanent advantages. On Bülow's advice and under the mellowing influence of English hospitality, William offered his hosts a share in the construction and the control of the terminal section of the Bagdad Railway, but nothing came of this, because Bülow, fearing that Germany would be outvoted, refused Grey's suggestion that Russia and France should be included in the conversations.[429] What the Chancellor desired was an agreement that would weaken the Triple Entente, but,

---

[426] *Deutsche Tageszeitung,* Nov. 10.

[427] One observer insisted upon the inclusion of the United States as the condition for an understanding. A. von Flöckher, "Grossbritannien und Deutschland," *Grenzboten,* 1907, IV, 329 (Nov. 14).

[428] *B. D.,* VI, 102.

[429] Haldane, Nov. 15. *B. D.,* VI, 96, 97. Bülow, however, did agree with Schoen's suggestions from St. Petersburg that the question should be discussed separately with each of the three powers and that all four should sign the final agreement. *G. P.,* XXIV, 19 (Nov. 20).

unwilling to trust all of Germany's eggs in England's uncertain basket, he was also seeking to associate the United States with Germany and China against British imperialist interests in the Far East. The initiative was possibly China's, but Bülow welcomed the idea and passed it on to Washington as an effective means of defending the integrity of China and of assuring the maintenance of the "open door" against Japan.[430] In vain Sternburg held out to President Roosevelt the prospect of Germany's military support in a war with Japan; the President's interest did not extend beyond a limited diplomatic coöperation in specific questions.[431] Nevertheless, William continued to hope for American aid against England's efforts to cripple Germany in Europe and to seize the Yangtze Valley. The American fleet, then on its world cruise, should, he thought, be stationed near the Philippines until Germany was prepared to relieve it.[432]

Meanwhile, Germany served notice that she would not sacrifice any part of her naval plans. On November 19, the *Norddeutsche* printed the text of a new bill reducing the service of capital from twenty-five to twenty years. While such nationalist journals as the *Deutsche Zeitung,* the *Rheinisch-Westfälische Zeitung,* the *Berliner Neueste Nachrichten,* and the *Tägliche Rundschau* criticized the modesty of the government's proposals,[433] even the moderate press said little about England's probable reaction.[434] The question, insisted the *Kölnische Zeitung* (Nov. 19), was purely technical. Bebel was the only member of the Reichstag frankly to point out that England was bound to regard the increase of the German fleet as a challenge. The sole practical result would be, he said, the danger of a surprise attack like Japan's upon Russia, for Germany certainly could not hope to build up to England's strength.[435] This indictment could not be ignored, because the English might seize upon it for their own purposes. Tirpitz therefore hastened to assure the Reichstag and the British

---

[430] Bülow, Oct. 17, 1907. *G. P.,* XXV, 74, 75.

[431] Sternburg, Nov. 8. *G. P.,* XXV, 78, 79.

[432] William, Dec. 30, 1907. *Ibid.,* XV, 88, 89. The Japanese-American Declaration of December 1, 1908 affirming the principle of the "open door," disposed of these schemes once and for all. Bernstorff, Jan. 2, 1909. *Ibid.,* XXV, 97.

[433] *Post,* Nov. 19.

[434] *Berliner Tageblatt, Vossische Zeitung,* Nov. 19.

[435] *Verhandlungen,* XII Leg. Per., I Sess., IV, 2729 (Jan. 29, 1908).

naval attaché that it was fantastic to suppose that Germany would dream of building up to England's strength and that the real difficulty was the commercial competition between the two countries.[436] The English were naturally incredulous. Having counted upon the first dreadnought (1906) to establish their naval supremacy once and for all, the fact that Germany was also building dreadnoughts, despite the need of widening the Kiel Canal, and that she now planned to speed up the replacement of her older ships was more enlightening than anything Tirpitz could say.[437] Even after he explained the technical reasons for its impossibility,[438] the British foreign office continued to believe that she had seriously considered the invasion of England. Replying to William's famous letter to Lord Tweedmouth on the foolishness of the fear of the "German danger," since the British fleet was five times as strong as Germany's, King Edward wrote that "the great increase in the building of the German ships of war . . . necessitates our increasing our navy as well." [439] The issue was now joined. On February 28, 1908, Germany was duly warned that "the security of the British Empire requires that the standard and proportion of the British navy to those of the European countries which has been upheld by successive British governments must be maintained." [440] The point of view of the German government, though never as clearly defined, had also taken form. The naval program must be carried through, regardless of the size of the British budget.[441] The English, wrote William, "must reconcile themselves to our fleet and we must tell them from time to time that it is not directed against them." [442] Probably the Social Democrats alone disagreed with the official view that no power could be permitted to dictate the size of Germany's fleet and that it was intended for the defense of her economic and political interests.

"Either England's 'encirclement policy' has never existed,"

---

436 *Verhandlungen*, XII Leg. Per., I Sess., IV, 2730, 2731; Dumas, Feb. 3, 1908. *B. D.*, VI, 115, 116.

437 This, according to William, was the real reason for England's nervousness. William II's comments, Metternich, March 7. *G. P.*, XXIV, 46.

438 Minutes by Crowe and Hardinge, Feb. 3. *B. D.*, VI, 115, 116.

439 Lee, *Edward VII*, II, 606 (Feb. 14).

440 *G. P.*, XXIV, 37.

441 Cf. *Post*, Feb. 25.

442 William II's comment, Metternich, March 7, 1908. *G. P.*, XXIV, 46.

wrote an unofficial observer at the beginning of 1908, "or it has been suspended."[443] Not many Germans thought of the Triple Entente as an immediate menace, no matter how objectionable an obstacle it might be to their imperialist interests. While Grey foresaw that the Triple Entente would be powerful enough "ten years hence . . . to dominate Near Eastern policy," he had few illusions as to its present strength.[444] The memories of recent diplomatic defeats and the fear of others had become a permanent cause of uneasiness. As to the best defense against an uncertain future, the leaders of public opinion were roughly divided between those who advised caution and those who supported an adventurous course. Hertling, a Centrist leader, belonged to the first group. He advised Bülow against any enterprise that would strengthen foreign suspicion.[445] Bassermann, the National Liberal leader, whose sympathies were Pan-German, expressed the views of a more vociferous group in criticizing Germany's policy as lacking in force, as giving "too much emphasis to Germany's love of peace," for other countries were thereby encouraged to take advantage of her.[446] A correspondent of the *Kölnische Zeitung* who resided abroad expressed (May 14, 1908) essentially the same point of view: "Authorized and unauthorized persons alike preach continuously, 'Peace, peace, and always peace,' with the result that it is more and more generally believed abroad that it is safe to take any liberty with Germany, since she will resent nothing." This false interpretation, according to the editors, was most dangerous, for it might expose "Germany's love of peace" to impossible tests. There was some irresponsible talk of an invasion and of other ways of making England feel the weight of Germany's power.[447] From these sources Crowe and other British diplomats, as well as a countless public throughout the world, drew material for the denunciation of Germany's aggressive purposes.

---

[443] "Neujahrsgedanken, erbauliche und unerbauliche," *Grenzboten*, 1908, I, 3, 4.

[444] Grey, Feb. 24, 1908. *B. D.*, IV, 616, 617.

[445] *Verhandlungen*, XII Leg. Per., I Sess., V, 4222 (March 23, 1908); *Germania*, May 28, 1908.

[446] *Verhandlungen*, XII Leg. Per., I Sess., V, 4223 (March 23, 1908).

[447] On April 27, 1908, the British military attaché in Berlin noted the publication of a pamphlet, *Die Offensiv-Invasion gegen England*, as a significant sign of the times. *B. D.*, VI, 147.

Germany's resentment against the Entente Cordiale was the key to German foreign policy during these four years. The Wilhelmstrasse's first concern was its *Weltpolitik;* the new situation, it was evident, meant the beginning of the end of the interest conflicts, which had been the most promising assurances of success. Bülow and Holstein both foresaw a perhaps insuperable opposition to German expansion. Like William, the nationalists soon spoke of Germany's isolation, but even they understood that the Russo-Japanese War would prevent an attack by France and Russia for many years. As to Germany's reply, public opinion varied all the way from the anti-imperialism of Social Democrats to the nationalists' stand for a strong assertion of German interests. Between these extremes, the moderates accepted Bülow's leadership, confident that he would secure Germany's due without serious trouble. The Pan-Germans were practically alone in demanding a part of Morocco. At first Germany's counter-offensive was caused less by the fear of an immediate menace in Europe than by the desire for that freedom of action which seemed essential to the *Weltpolitik*.

Two procedures were employed. In attempting to approach England and to secure a defensive alliance with Russia, Germany relied upon the interests of these countries. Exaggerated territorial or political expectations contributed to her failure, but in neither instance were the results seriously damaging. Against France, Germany resorted to direct pressure, counting upon her own military superiority, Russia's preoccupation with the Japanese war, the limitations of England's loyalty to the Entente Cordiale, and the aversion of French public opinion for an adventurous policy to secure the repudiation of Delcassé. The advance of French influence toward a paramount position in Morocco furnished the occasion. Those who desired territorial acquisitions and those who preferred a direct understanding with France were far less numerous than those whose prime concern was the defense of Germany's treaty rights. The foreign office showed an interest at various times in all of these views; but, foreseeing the ultimate establishment of French control, its chief aim was the improvement of Germany's diplomatic position. An international conference seemed to be the most effective way to force France to change her foreign policy and her foreign minister, destroy the Entente Cordiale, and defend Germany's economic interests. At first, this campaign was strikingly successful. Delcassé fell when his colleagues, believing that Germany meant business, turned against him, and was succeeded by the conciliatory Rouvier. It was a critical moment; circumstances had never been more favorable for an understanding. Delcassé was thoroughly discredited. Not for Morocco's sake were Frenchmen prepared to fight. If public opinion had been confronted with a demand to drop the entente with England, it would doubtless have refused, but it was sufficiently suspicious of England's intentions and apprehensive of Germany's to be receptive to a direct settlement of the Moroccan question. Germany rejected Rouvier's advances. Although a few publicists supported an understanding, the government, with the approval of the greater part of the press, continued to insist upon a conference, yet Rouvier's reluctant acceptance failed to produce the hoped-for diplomatic gains. Germany's surrender of a good part of her original aims in the preliminary agreements of July 8 and September 25 made little impression upon France. Rouvier stiffened under continued pressure, and a large section of French opinion, drawing the worst conclusions from the hostage theory, gradually steeled itself to the idea of war. With France's increased firmness, England's support was renewed. Too late, the German government and press sought a direct and friendly settlement. Threatened with isolation at the Conference of Algeciras, Germany finally had to choose between a diplomatic defeat and a war. Holstein may have been prepared for the latter, but the issue was decided when Bülow sided with William in favor of peace. Among the causes of this decision, the feeling that public opinion did not regard Morocco as a sufficient cause for war was not the least important. If less dramatic than Delcassé's fall, Holstein's resignation had more important consequences. Germany, it was clear, would not fight to prevent an unsatisfactory outcome of the conference or the completion of the Triple Entente. To the intense displeasure of public opinion, she accepted the General Act of Algeciras and professed her satisfaction with the Anglo-Russian Entente.

The first campaign against encirclement had failed. The Entente Cordiale emerged stronger than ever. Under Germany's fire, England had not only supported France at Algeciras but also had given her reason to count upon England's aid against a German attack. Contrary to Germany's expectations, it was the Liberal government that assumed the responsibility for this development of the entente toward complete diplomatic coöperation. By 1907 the British foreign office was unwilling, even in the expansive atmosphere of William's visit, to discuss important problems without consulting France and Russia.

These developments produced a chronic uneasiness. Even the unshaken confidence in the army was powerless to check the alarm. Isolation and encirclement were becoming household words. Germany was no longer satisfied with her position, either in world politics or in Europe. The press had little constructive advice to offer. From the Center leftward, the moderates and liberals either accepted Bülow's leadership unquestioningly or recommended a cautious attitude. Except for the Social Democratic press, only a few journals like the *Berliner Tageblatt* ventured occasionally to take a stand for a new orientation. Even the nationalists, who talked much of a more vigorous attitude based upon the country's military supremacy, had few ideas as to what should be done in a specific crisis. Their point of view was, however, the most dangerous feature of public opinion. They counted upon fear to attain Germany's aim peacefully, for the few who frankly advocated war and who discussed an invasion of England did not represent even the Pan-Germans; they were, however, prepared to fight if intimidation failed. These views were limited to no one group. Under the pressure of circumstances, even moderate opinion might be influenced by them. In spite of the nationalists' running fire of criticism, the government's ultimate decisions reflected the moderate rather than the extremist position. If Bülow's Moroccan policy failed in its diplomatic objectives, the chief responsibility was his and William's, for they were not prepared, in the final analysis, to fight rather than to yield.

CHAPTER XI

The Weakening of the Triple Entente: The Bosnian Crisis, 1908-1910

> Der deutsche Standpunkt ist von Anfang an gewesen, dass
> wir die Wahrung der Grossmachtstellung Oesterreich-Un-
> garns auch als ein eminentes Interesse der deutschen Politik
> betrachten; dass wir deswegen ohne Zögern an die Seite
> unseres Bundesgenossen getreten sind; dass wir nach allen
> Seiten über unsere feste Entschlossenheit, uns nicht von Oester-
> reich-Ungarn abdrängen zu lassen, Klarheit gegeben haben.
> . . . Zu der Leitung der verbündeten Monarchie aber haben
> wir das Zutrauen, dass sie am besten beurteilen kann, welches
> die unentbehrlichen Voraussetzungen ihrer Grossmachtstel-
> lung sind. Ihr steht es auch allein zu, in den Einzelheiten
> die entscheidenden Entschlüsse zu fassen; und von Deutsch-
> land kann sie mit Recht erwarten, dass es keinen Schritt
> tun werde, der als unerbetene Einmischung oder als Bevor-
> mundung ausgelegt werden könnte.
> *Norddeutsche Allgemeine Zeitung,* January 3, 1909.

> Durch die Nation geht es wie Aufatmen nach schwerem
> Druck, und frische Winde kunden der Morgen.
> "Die politische Lage," *Grenzboten,* July 1, 1909.

The "encirclement" scare was never more intense than in the early summer of 1908. For a moment, it seemed as if the Triple Entente might become a triple alliance.[1] President Fallières' visit to London, May 25, had disquieting implications. When André Tardieu stipulated (*Temps,* May 27) England's adoption of universal military service as the essential condition for an alliance,[2] many newspapers drew the conclusion that France was

---

[1] *Kölnische Volkszeitung,* May 27, Berlin, May 26.
[2] During the summer of 1907, Clemenceau spoke in this sense to J. A. Spender, the editor of the *Westminister Gazette,* and to King Edward at Marienbad. Spender, *Fifty Years of Europe* (London, 1933), pp. 290, 306; Lee, *Edward VII,* II, 628, 629.

preparing to attack.[3]   The foreign office soon received reassuring reports.   Radolin wrote that French public opinion disagreed with Tardieu, "the *enfant terrible* of the pen," in his "current delusion of grandeur," and Metternich was told that "there was no question of an alliance."[4]   Although the King and the President exchanged toasts to the *entente resserrée* and to the *entente permanente,* the London press made it clear that England was not interested in too close a relationship.[5]   Even the entente, some German newspapers informed the French, was acceptable to England only because it served her own interests.[6]   France's cool reaction to Tardieu's proposal was reassuring, but a part of the nationalist press still remained nervous.[7]   The *Berliner Neueste Nachrichten* (June 3) advised the foreign office against a mistaken confidence.   "To French public opinion should be brought" Germany's awareness that it was no longer a question of playing with fire but of downright arson.   "The sound of festivities on the Thames," reported the British consul in Munich, "has considerably ruffled the equanimity of the German press. . . . Everywhere I notice a sullen discontent. . . ."[8]   No one was more aroused than the Emperor; his defiant remarks to the army officers at Döberitz (May 29) followed Fallières' visit by only a few days.   For the means to quiet William's alarm, Bülow turned to Metternich.   The visit, said the ambassador, had changed nothing.   "The English momentarily desire neither alliances nor war."[9]

Close on the heels of the French President's cordial reception came King Edward's visit to Reval, June 9, 10, the first ever paid by a British sovereign to Russia.   Nothing would be done, Germany was told, to which she could object.   In the House of Commons, Grey said that no new engagements would be con-

[3] *Deutsche Tageszeitung, Berliner Neueste Nachrichten,* May 27; *Reichsbote, Germania,* May 28.

[4] Radolin, May 27; Metternich, May 29.   *G. P.,* XXIV, 60–62.

[5] *Pall Mall Gazette, Daily News, Standard,* May 28; *Saturday Review,* May 30.   Cf. *Augsburger Abendzeitung,* May 29.

[6] *Kölnische Zeitung,* May 29; *Reichsbote,* May 30.   By permitting herself to be used as England's tool, France, wrote the *Münchener Neueste Nachrichten* (May 27), had become responsible for the most serious danger to peace.

[7] *N. A. Z.,* May 31; *A. B.,* June 5.

[8] Cartwright, June 1.   *B. D.,* VI, 150–152.

[9] Bülow, June 1; Metternich, June 5.   *G. P.,* XXIV, 64, 68.

tracted; to the German ambassador, he explained that the King had not seen the Tsar for seven years and that the visit had long been under discussion.[10] Protesting his desire for "the most cordial relations," Izvolski denied any intention of tightening the entente and spoke of an understanding on the question of reforms in Macedonia as the possible result of the meeting.[11] He instructed the *Rossija* to condemn the agitation in the Russian press for a strong anti-German coalition;[12] and the Tsar hastened to assure William that "political questions were hardly touched upon" at Reval.[13] The conversations, in fact, dealt with matters of interest to Germany. While Izvolski argued that Russia could not afford to incur the hostility of the Central powers over the Macedonian question, his interest was aroused by the suggestion that Russia might build a railway through Persia to the Persian Gulf, and he eagerly pressed for England's support against Austria's railway projects in the Sanjak of Novibazar. He would not "hesitate to take strong measures" to prevent a violation of the Treaty of Berlin. In effect, Hardinge encouraged Russia to take a firmer stand. England had no desire to "irritate or exasperate" Germany, but she did not intend to sacrifice her own "legitimate interests or those of humanity at large." From the distrust of Germany's "unnecessarily" large naval increases, from England's countermeasures and the mounting tax burden, "a critical situation might arise" in seven or eight years and then Russia might become, if she were strong enough in Europe, "the arbiter of peace."[14]

Reval almost caused a panic in Germany.[15] Although the lib-

---

[10] Of Grey's speech the *Times* (June 10) wrote that it should convince Berlin that there was no question of an alliance.

[11] Pourtalès, May 26. *G. P.*, XXV, 441.

[12] William II's comments, Pourtalès, June 5. *Ibid.*, XXV. Cf. *Post*, June 10. Berlin was informed a few days later that the Russian press still represented the Triple Entente as a means of restraining Germany. Pourtalès, June 9. *Ibid.*, XXV, 448-450.

[13] William II, June 11. *Ibid.*, XXV, 450. In reply, William congratulated his cousin on his appointment as a British admiral and expressed the hope that, as Nicholas had said, "nothing has changed." William II, June 12. *Ibid.*, XXV, 451.

[14] Hardinge, June 12. *B. D.*, V, 237-245. Writing after the World War, Hardinge said that the widening of the Kiel Canal, which he saw on his way to Reval, had given him the impression that Germany was preparing for war. *Times*, March 13, 1922. *B. D.*, VI, 200.

[15] P. Rohrbach, *Das politische Krisengebiet Europas, 1908-1909* (Berlin, 1909), p. 1.

eral *Frankfurter Zeitung* (June 16) spoke of "baseless fears," the confidence of the semi-official press was unconvincing.[16] The announcement of an agreement upon Macedonian reforms convinced German opinion that the Anglo-Russian entente had been

Die eingetreifte Germania

Simplicissimus, July 6, 1908.

Figure 20.—We'd better let her alone—she' got her sword along.

[16] *Allgemeine Zeitung* (Munich), June 13; *Süddeutsche Reichskorrespondenz,* in *Germania,* June 16. Cf. *Times,* June 15, Berlin, June 14.

extended to Europe [17] and that the Austro-Russian understanding of 1897 had collapsed.[18] The *Preussische Jahrbücher* saw a threat to German imperialism in England's alleged plan to connect Egypt with India by a chain of protectorates.[19] Indeed, the fear of increased obstacles to Germany's expansion was fully as important as concern for her security in Europe in causing the climax of the "encirclement" scare.[20] The nationalist *Münchener Neueste Nachrichten* (May 31) exclaimed, *"König Eduard in Russland!"* The new *Dreibund,* wrote the Catholic *Germania* (June 11), had been completed, even if it had not been officially announced. "Encirclement," said Harden, "is a fact." [21] "Never," writes Professor Hoetzsch, who was then lecturing at the University of Edinburgh, "will I forget the clear-cut impression . . . of the immense danger which confronted my country and her foreign policy." [22] Even those who believed that the Liberal government in England would exert a restraining influence upon the Triple Entente resented the attacks in the English and Russian newspapers.[23]

For years, the nationalists had complained that the lack of firmness encouraged the belief that Germany would never fight. The time had come for a change. Anglo-Russian coöperation in the Balkans would threaten Austria's interests and therefore Germany's. Calling for a defense of Austria even where Germany had no immediate interests, the *Kölnische Zeitung* (June 12) foreshadowed the abandonment of Bismarck's interpretation of the Dual Alliance. *"Treue um Treue!"* should be the watchword, according to a leading nationalist journal in South Germany.[24] The best defense would be an assertion of Germany's strength and of her willingness, if necessary, to use it. The agra-

---

[17] *Augsburger Abendzeitung,* May 25; *Deutsche Tageszeitung,* June 11; *N. A. Z.,* in *Kölnische Zeitung,* June 12; *Süddeutsche Reichskorrespondenz,* in *Germania,* June 16; *Münchener Neueste Nachrichten,* June 17.
[18] *Reichsbote,* June 7; *Vossische Zeitung,* June 11.
[19] *P. J.,* vol. 133, p. 182 (June 1908).
[20] *Augsburger Abendzeitung,* May 25, June 9; *Deutsche Tageszeitung,* June 11. That King Edward had been accompanied by General French and Admiral Fisher was regarded as particularly significant. *Kölnische Volkszeitung,* June 17.
[21] *Zukunft,* June 13.
[22] O. Hoetzsch, *La politique extérieure de l'Allemagne de 1871 à 1914* (Geneva, 1933), p. 60.
[23] *Frankfurter Zeitung,* June 14, London, June 9.
[24] *Münchener Neueste Nachrichten,* June 17.

rian *Deutsche Tageszeitung* (June 3) advised that "a jet of cold water" should be directed against France. The *Münchener Neueste Nachrichten* (June 3) feared that Germany, tired of provocations, would be forced to "remember how Frederick II had suddenly foiled the plans of a circle of enemies. . . . The French are mistaken if they think that Germany is afraid of a war upon two fronts; therein lies a grave danger to peace." While Harden did not specifically advise drastic measures, he nevertheless believed that a change of policy was imperative.[25] The official Pan-German organ called for a vigorous defense of German interests in the Near East. "To retreat again," it wrote, "will destroy respect for us abroad. . . . Our love of peace notwithstanding, we should not abandon our position even at the cost of war."[26] There was, however, little or no desire that Germany should precipitate a conflict. Even the *Kladderadatsch's* (June, 1908) significant cartoon, picturing the black clouds as rolling up from England, France, and Russia, represented Michael as undecided whether he should fire the rain-making mortar at his side.

The officials were no less disturbed than public opinion. One warlike rumor, wrote the Catholic *Kölnische Volkszeitung* (June 17), followed another in military and political circles. On a report that a hostile diplomatic campaign was in preparation, William wrote: "Therefore a reform of the imperial finances! Many indirect taxes! A strong fleet and a powerful army! Dry powder!"[27] William's gesture of defiance at Döberitz on May 29 was not objectionable to his advisers. "Now," the Emperor was reported to have said, "it seems that they wish to encircle us. We will know what to do. The German has never fought better than when he has had to defend himself on all sides. Just let them attack (*Sie sollen uns nur kommen*). We are ready."[28] An official denial would be, said Bülow, contrary to

---

[25] *Zukunft,* June 13.
[26] *A. B.,* June 19.
[27] William II's comments, Pourtalès, June 12. *G. P.,* XXV, 454.
[28] First circulated in St. Petersburg by a Russian army officer, the world read the text in the *Dortmunder Zeitung.* Pourtalès, June 12. *G. P.,* XXV, 456; *Kölnische Zeitung,* June 16. Brandenburg's version is more moderate than the text which appeared, without an official correction, in the contemporary press. Brandenburg, *From Bismarck to the World War,* p. 312.

Kladderadatsch, June 14, 1908.

Figure 21.—Michel: "Humph! The clouds are moving dangerously close together! I wonder if it's time to begin firing the weather cannon?"

precedent; "a true word at the right moment," was his reaction.[29] The liberals and Social Democrats promptly condemned the speech as a personal interference in foreign affairs.[30]   According to the *Berliner Tageblatt* (June 18), the Bundesrat's committee on foreign affairs should meet.   Social Democratic mass meetings in Berlin during the next few weeks affirmed the people's will for peace.[31]   The semi-official press evidently wished to reassure opinion at home and abroad and, at the same time, to show that the government was alive to every possible danger. William had expressed, wrote the *Kölnische Zeitung* (June 16) and the nationalist press,[32] what the great majority were thinking.   In a leading article, "On the Situation," the *Norddeutsche* (June 19) asserted that the Emperor had only praised the army's efficiency and affirmed its readiness for any emergency, that Germany's purposes were not aggressive, and it insisted that the general feeling of insecurity proved the existence of a hostile coalition.   It concluded, however, on a more disturbing note: "It would, however, be a mistake to deny that difficult diplomatic conflicts may occur."

The effect was scarcely quieting.   The article meant, by general consent, that the government recognized the seriousness of the situation and that it was prepared to face it squarely.   The public's response, wrote the nationalist *Berliner Neueste Nachrichten* (June 21), was far more unanimous than was usually the case after a similar pronouncement.   To the ultra-Conservative *Reichsbote* (June 21), the article was a *kalter Wasserstrahl* like Bismarck's.   Its purpose was "to show the foreign powers that Germany is on guard, that she . . . sees through everything. . . . It means . . . 'do not misunderstand us, we know what is in progress and are ready to protect our interests and our honor.'" "Its language is timely," wrote the moderate *Vossische Zeitung* (June 20), because it felt that a belief in Germany's weakness would be the most serious threat to peace.   In the reference to the army's *Schlagfertigkeit,* the Conservative *Post* (June 20) found the article's chief significance.   It was "a serious admoni-

29 Bülow, *Denkwürdigkeiten,* II, 317, 318.
30 *Vorwärts,* June 16.
31 *A. B.,* July 24, 1908.
32 *Berliner Neueste Nachrichten, Deutsche Tageszeitung,* June 16.

tion to the other powers." "Certainly we desire peace," it continued, "but it must be peace with honor. If our national honor is attacked, if we are so hemmed in that the most vital of our interests are imperilled, then we will draw the sword without a moment's hesitation." The press and the government were agreed, according to the Belgian minister, in warning the outside world that Germany's love of peace was not unconditional.[33] "The greater part of public opinion," wrote an observer, "has approved the government's attitude and is determined to prosecute to the limit a war imposed by Russia and England. The nation understands that Germany's honor and interests are at stake."[34] The National Liberal *Augsburger Abendzeitung* (June 25) definitely rejected the idea of a preventive war, but it wrote that any attempt "to deprive the nation of air and light, to restrict or hinder its natural development," would find it united and determined. More than one journal dwelt with emphasis upon the military virtues of the German people. The French were correct, said the National Liberal *Allgemeine Zeitung* (June 27), in describing the spirit of the German army as that of the "brutal offensive." A somewhat different conclusion was drawn, however, by the Berlin correspondent of the London *Morning Post* (June 22), for he reported that the *Norddeutsche's* article had spread "nervousness and uneasiness among wider circles." The Catholic *Germania* (June 20) was almost alone in openly doubting the government's ability to cope successfully with an admittedly dangerous situation.

In view of the widespread criticism of Bülow's foreign policy, the talk of *Einkreisung* was naturally distasteful to him. "We have always been encircled," he told William, "we live in the center of Europe."[35] The Chancellor believed that the Triple Entente was still essentially defensive. That it might become an alliance was the danger which Germany must guard against; this consideration guided his reconsideration of German foreign policy late in June. Nothing could be done to remove the funda-

[33] *Belgische Dokumente*, IV, 89, 90 (June 22).
[34] G. Roloff, "Deutschland zwischen England und Russland," *P. J.*, vol. 133, p. 185 (June, 1908).
[35] Bülow, *Denkwürdigkeiten*, II, 319.

mental causes of the Triple Entente "without voluntarily sacrificing" Germany's economic progress and the increased political influence for which it was responsible. There were, however, reasons for confidence. Russia was weak; her understanding with England was restricted to Asia. Time was on Germany's side, because France was declining in population and in military strength. For the future, "loyal coöperation with Austria-Hungary should remain the highest principle of German foreign policy." Like a large part of public opinion, Bülow believed that England held the key to the situation, since neither Russia nor France would risk an open break. Germany, he believed, should conciliate Russia, avoid a conflict with France, and refrain from measures irritating to England. With the support of a moderate press and public opinion, this policy would enable Germany to face the future with confidence.[36]

There was much to be said for these views. Their failure was largely the result of their inconsistencies and their inadequate provision for Germany's interests. A close coöperation with Austria made the success of the proposed conciliation of Russia improbable. Without a solution of the naval question, differences with England were bound to arise. Never had the Chancellor been more favorably disposed toward an understanding. To reject all negotiations, he wrote late in August, would cause "a fundamental and permanent change" in English sentiment and an increased naval construction at a time when Germany needed peace for several years.[37] Unfortunately, the Chancellor made no headway against the opposition to any important concessions of his sovereign, his colleagues, and public opinion. The attitude of Bethmann-Hollweg, then the Prussian minister of the interior and within a year to become Bülow's successor, illustrates the prevailing state of mind. Favorable in principle to a rapprochement, he shared the widespread anger at England's supposed leadership in the conspiracy against Germany. In August 1908, he let himself go to Lloyd George, the British chancellor of the exchequer, who was then in Berlin seeking information in regard

[36] Bülow, June 25. *G. P.*, XXV, 474–481. This dispatch to the principal German courts is mistakenly dated July 25 in the Chancellor's memoirs. Bülow, *Denkwürdigkeiten*, II, 326.

[37] Bülow, Aug. 26. *G. P.*, XXIV, 151.

to the social-insurance legislation. While he made it clear that he did not fully approve the naval program, he gave his guest to understand that King Edward was regarded in official circles as working for "a Confederacy with a hostile purport against Germany." There is no reason to doubt the essential accuracy of Lloyd George's account of his "extraordinary outburst." "'An iron ring!' he repeated violently, shouting out the statement, and waiving his arm to the whole assembled company. 'England is embracing France. She is making friends with Russia. But it is not that you love each other; it is that you hate Germany!' And he repeated and literally shouted the word 'hate' thrice."[38]

In the meantime, the naval question increased the friction between the two countries. Against William's and Tirpitz' refusal to consider the reduction or slowing up of naval construction, Bülow could only try to dispel England's fears of a German attack; but Grey and other British ministers replied by insisting upon the necessity of maintaining Britain's supremacy. For the first time, it was suggested that a naval understanding would be impossible without a political rapprochement as an assurance that England's diplomatic arrangements would not be "misused against us." Even this idea did not interest William. "We shall never be dictated to," he exclaimed, "on the constitution of our armaments." To every suggestion of change in the official program, he returned an emphatic negative. Lloyd George's mention of a three-to-two ratio moved him to speechless indignation. A proposal for a naval conference at the Hague would, he wrote, "be regarded as a declaration of war." When Metternich suggested that the question might be considered after a period of quieter relations, he replied, "No, we will never discuss it. I have no desire for good relations with England at the cost of the expansion of Germany's fleet."[39] Alive as Bülow was to the dangers of complete intransigeance, he nevertheless had recently told Vienna as well as Munich, Stuttgart, and Dresden that Germany "would take up arms" against a concrete

---

[38] *War Memoirs of David Lloyd George*, 5 vols. (London, 1933–1936), I, 30, 31.
[39] Metternich, July 16 and William II's comments. *G. P.*, XXIV, 103 ff.

proposal for a reduction of her existing program.[40]   Sir Charles
Hardinge's tactless remark during King Edward's visit to Cronberg in August, "You must stop or build ,slower," excited the
Emperor to the point that he spoke of war.[41]   At bottom William
desired an improvement in Anglo-German relations; like Bülow,
he tried in vain to convince the British diplomats that the German fleet was not a menace.   To Hardinge, he spoke of his
services during the Boer War.   Nothing, however, was to be
gained, in his opinion, by a tactful attitude.   With Englishmen,
brutal frankness, he told Bülow, was the proper procedure.   He
was himself half an Englishman.[42]   "They are," he told Lascelles,
"stark, raving mad." [43]   To William Bayard Hale, an American
publicist, he spoke of England, knowing that the interview would
be published, as a traitor to the white race and of her ministers
as "ninnies" for having made an alliance with Japan.[44]   On the
naval issue, William was scarcely more rational than the Pan-
Germans, whose official organ claimed that an agreement for the
limitation of naval armaments, of which the *Vossische Zeitung*
spoke with favor as the result of the Cronberg meeting, would
mean "the end of Germany's political influence." [45]

Nor did Bülow succeed in avoiding friction with France.
Even the hostage theory was occasionally revived, because it was
feared that England might use the French army against Germany.[46]   A German diplomat told Tardieu that France could not
possibly remain neutral in the inevitable Anglo-German war.[47]

[40] Conrad von Hötzendorf, *Aus meiner Dienstzeit*, 5 vols. (Vienna, 1921–1925),
I, 95.

[41] Hammann, *Bilder aus der letzten Kaiserzeit*, p. 144. *Cf.* Hardinge, Aug. 16.
B. D., VI, 185, 186. From the refusal of the Germans to consider any modification
of their naval program, Hardinge concluded that "they realize the chauvinistic spirit
of the German public, and that they know that they must take it into account." *B. D.,*
VI 188 (Aug. 16).

[42] Bülow, *Denkwürdigkeiten*, II, 323.

[43] *G. P.,* XXIV, 123 (Aug. 11).

[44] After strenuous efforts, the foreign office succeeded in suppressing the edition of the
American *Century Magazine* containing Hale's article. W. H. Hale, "Thus Spoke the
Kaiser," *Atlantic Monthly,* May 1934, pp. 517–523. Enough got into the press, how-
ever, to irritate the English. Lee, *Edward VII,* II, 622.

[45] *Cf.* de Salis, Aug. 17. *B. D.,* VI, 198; *A. B.,* Aug. 28.

[46] "Therein," wrote Schiemann, "lies the real danger of the world situation."
Kreuz-Zeitung, Dec. 7, 1908. Schiemann, *Deutschland und die Grosse Politik,* VIII, 377.

[47] Wangenheim, July 14, 1908. *G. P.,* XXIV, 308, 309. William agreed with
Clemenceau's statement to Izvolski that Germany would attack France in certain circumstances. William II's comments, Aehrenthal, Sept. 26, 1908. *Ibid.,* XXVI, 38.

Morocco remained a source of difficulty, for Germany was determined to maintain the General Act of Algeciras. William averted a serious crisis in December 1906 when his advisers thought of sending warships, as did France and Spain, to Tangier. But he demanded an impossible price—a formal alliance —for the surrender of Germany's claims.[48] When France bombarded and occupied Casablanca,. August 1907, she was nevertheless assured of Germany's good-will,[49] and William advised the strictest reserve. "There is," he said, "no reason to provoke the French or to frighten them."[50] At first, nothing was done to support Mulai Hafid against his brother Abdul Aziz, the Sultan, even after the pretender controlled the greater part of the country and when France's inactivity gave some color to the suspicion that she wished to prolong the state of anarchy. Occasional references to the General Act reminded Paris that Germany was not asleep.[51] Both Mulai and France were told that Germany desired the former's recognition, but the foreign office maintained, in general, a tactful reserve.[52] Finally, after England had been informed (July 31, 1908) that no complications were expected and that the most cordial relations existed with Jules Cambon,[53] France was informed that "our unconditional promise to wait for her approval before recognizing Mulai Hafid could no longer be considered binding, in view of the changed circumstances."[54] Further delay would enable her to secure from Mulai such concessions as would be fatal to the General Act and to Germany's interests. From his summer retreat at Nordeney, Bülow advised against independent action, but the foreign office nevertheless notified Paris that Germany intended to remind the powers of the need to hasten Mulai's recognition and to send an agent, Dr. Vassel, to Fez.[55] The Chancellor's forebodings were soon justified. In Paris, Pichon, the foreign minister, was

[48] Brandenburg, *From Bismarck to the World War*, pp. 336–339.
[49] Tschirschky's comments, Jules Cambon's *Note verbale*, Aug. 7, 1907. *G. P.*, XXIV, 217, 218.
[50] *G. P.*, XXIV, 221 (Aug. 16).
[51] Bülow, April 24, May 6, 1908. *Ibid.*, XXIV, 251, 280.
[52] Schoen, May 28, June 15, 1908. *Ibid.*, XXIV, 291, 299.
[53] *B. D.*, VI, 157.
[54] Stemrich, Aug. 27. *G. P.*, XXIV, 384.
[55] Bülow, Aug. 29, Stemrich, Aug. 31. *Ibid.*, XXIV, 388, 392.

"extremely intransigeant," protesting that the prospects for improved relations would be spoiled. The effect in England was even more unfavorable. The London press, according to Stumm, the German *chargé d'affaires,* was again more French than the French themselves: "There can be no question but that the recent incident has appreciably increased the mistrust and suspicion of the aims and methods of German policy." [56] France's delay in recognizing Mulai was, according to the British diplomats, regrettable, but Crowe believed that Germany was about to "resort to another bullying campaign intended to frighten and cow France into a yielding mood." [57] England, Germany was informed, would support France's desire for definite guarantees of Mulai's acceptance of the General Act before his recognition. Whatever the original intentions of the German foreign office may have been, it beat a prompt retreat. In Tangier, Wangenheim described the Franco-Spanish note of September 14, incorporating the French point of view, as dangerous to German interests, but Schoen told Cambon in Berlin that "a kind of a Truce of God" in Morocco would be highly desirable. A few days later, he accepted the French conditions in principle,[58] in large part doubtless because of England's attitude.

The great need in Morocco, Metternich explained to Bülow, was an immediate arrangement *à trois* with England and France. Nothing, however, came of the Chancellor's conference with the foreign office.[59] On September 25, the arrest of three German deserters from the Foreign Legion by the French military police at Casablanca threatened to precipitate a new and more serious crisis, for the dragoman of the German consulate, who was escorting them to a ship, was struck during the melée. The first reaction in both countries was moderate. "This disagreeable affair," wrote Bülow, who wished to avoid open friction with France, "should be quickly and cordially arranged without any legal quibbling on either side." It would be desirable if the newspapers of both countries would refrain from exaggerating

[56] Hammann, *Bilder aus der letzten Kaiserzeit,* p. 145.
[57] Lascelles, Sept. 11, and minutes. *B. D.* VII, 91, 92; Crowe's minute, Bunsen, Sept. 7. *Ibid.,* VII, 90.
[58] Wangenheim, Sept. 15; Schoen, Sept. 18, 22. *G. P.,* XXIV, 418, 426–428.
[59] Bülow, Sept. 12. Hammann, *Bilder aus der letzten Kaiserzeit,* p. 50.

the incident.[60]   Although his reference to the nation's honor
boded no good, William also desired a prompt arrangement.
Three deserters who had fled from their military service in Germany were not worth the damage to the improved relations with
France.[61]   The semi-official press nevertheless insisted that the
French police had acted illegally, that the government would
defend Germany's interests with the requisite firmness, that
France might be expected to repudiate her erring agents; there
was, however, little trace of a desire to excite opinion.   On September 28, the *Kölnische Zeitung's* Berlin correspondent acknowledged that differences existed between the French and German versions and that France desired a peaceful settlement.[62]
The semi-official *Norddeutsche* (Oct. 4) finally broke its silence
to explain that no official statement could be expected from
either government until the arrival of exhaustive reports from
Casablanca.   The liberal press had little to say, but the moderate
Vossische Zeitung (Oct. 1) surveyed the larger problem of
Franco-German relations in a conciliatory spirit.   "If the French
are ready," it wrote, "to offer their hand, we will certainly accept it."

The nationalist newspapers differed, however, only in the
degree of their violence.   To the Conservative *Post* (Sept. 28),
the incident furnished France with a good opportunity to show
that she did not regard Casablanca as French territory.   The
Berliner Neueste Nachrichten (Sept. 28, 29) saw no inconsistency
between its opinion that no crisis existed and the three demands
which it urged (Sept. 30) the government to address to France:
satisfaction for the mistreatment of the consular official, the surrender of the German deserters, and the clarification of the status
of the Foreign Legion in international law.[63]   The release of
the deserters, wrote the agrarian *Deutsche Tageszeitung* (Sept.
28), was a matter of national honor: "If they are not freed
soon, *the prestige of our name and flag in Morocco will suffer*

---

[60] Carroll, *French Public Opinion*, p. 226.   Three other deserters, an Austrian, a
Russian, and a Swiss, were also arrested.
[61] Jenisch, Oct. 4.   *G. P.*, XXIV, 441.
[62] This article was clipped by the *National Zeitung*, the *Post*, and the *Berliner
Neueste Nachrichten*, Sept. 28.
[63] On October 1, this journal practically withdrew the third point.

a serious blow. . . ." The moderation of the semi-official and the indifference of the liberal press incensed the Pan-Germans. Pichon, according to the *Rheinisch-Westfälische Zeitung* (Oct. 1), should be satisfied. "Why isn't a *warship* sent to Casablanca?" it asked after demanding apologies from France. "Does anyone really believe," asked the *Alldeutsche Blätter* (Oct. 9), "that our prestige is so great that we can tolerate such treatment?" Writing to Bülow, the Crown Prince endorsed the *Rheinisch-Westfälische Zeitung's* demand for the dispatch of a warship and its denunciation of the semi-official press. He believed, like the Pan-Germans, that the French wished to test "our love of peace." "Our honor is at stake; it is high time that the insolent fellows in Paris should again be shown what our Pomeranian grenadiers can do." The Chancellor discouraged, however, a resort to strong measures. By no means was it certain, he replied, October 11, that the consul had a right to protect the deserters; in any event, no war could be undertaken without serious risks for the dynasty unless its popularity was assured.[64] The official policy nevertheless agreed in certain respects with the nationalists' point of view. After the withdrawal of Schoen's original suggestion of a limited arbitration, France was asked, October 15, before she had time to present her own version of the affair, to discipline her police officials, to apologize to the German consul, and to release the German deserters. On the other hand, there was no thought of sending a warship to Casablanca, and the offer to reprimand Lüderitz, the consul, and to refrain from encouraging desertion from the Foreign Legion would probably have enraged the extremists.[65] Arguing that the police had acted within their rights, the French refused to yield and proposed that the entire question, the legal issues as well as the facts, should be referred to the Hague Court for arbitration. The same reply was given when Bülow and Schoen proposed, October 19, an exchange of regrets and the arbitration of the legal questions.[66] Here the affair rested until the end of the month.

[64] Bülow, *Denkwürdigkeiten*, II, 410, 411.
[65] Schoen, Oct. 15. *G. P.,* XXIV, 346, 347.
[66] Schoen, Oct. 19; Radolin, Oct. 21. *Ibid.,* XXIV, 351–353.

Bülow's personal responsibility was perhaps greater for the failure to conciliate Russia than for the continued friction with the Western powers. While he was beginning to see the need of relieving England's anxieties, he supported Austria at a time when her attitude threatened to make Russia a bitter enemy of the Central powers. Aehrenthal, who succeeded the more cautious Goluchowski as the foreign minister in October 1906, had already launched a diplomatic offensive in the Balkans. He told the Delegations, late in January 1908, that Austria intended to construct a railway through the Sanjak of Novibazar to Mitrovitsa. In this forward movement toward Salonica was everywhere seen an unwelcome disturbance of the status quo in the Balkans. To Russia it meant the end of the truce maintained since 1897, but Izvolski, lacking an assurance of England's support, dared not object. There was, however, every reason to believe that Russia would not abandon the Serbs, who, since the palace revolution of 1903 and the accession of the Karageorgevich dynasty, looked to her for protection. The test came when the Young Turks, after seizing power in July, attempted to strengthen the Empire's hold upon its outlying provinces. The danger that the presence of deputies from Bosnia-Herzegovina in the new Turkish parliament would imperil Austria's rights and that the Serbs would profit by the resulting uncertainty moved Aehrenthal to action. In return for Russia's consent to the formal annexation of Bosnia-Herzegovina he offered to approve the opening of the Straits to her warships. With one of Russia's historic aspirations apparently within his grasp, Izvolski promptly abandoned the Serbs during his conversation with Aehrenthal at Buchlau, September 16. He had failed, however, to reckon with the Pan-Slavs and with England. Believing that his part of the bargain was assured, Izvolski was not seriously perturbed when he heard, October 4, just before his arrival in Paris, that the annexation was an accomplished fact. A warning from his own government that the Serbs must not be sacrificed and England's refusal to agree to the opening of the Straits, although Grey spoke vaguely of a future arrangement, finally awakened him to the fact that he had been outwitted. Henceforth he was an ardent champion of the Serbs and Aehrenthal's bitter personal enemy.

By his annexation of the two provinces and by his approval of Prince Ferdinand's assumption of the title of Tsar, Aehrenthal had torn up an important part of the Treaty of Berlin without the consent of the signatory powers, thereby dangerously disturbing the status quo in the turbulent Balkans. Germany's diplomatic interests were directly involved.[67] Serbia's national aspirations left her cold, but she was concerned by Austria's failure to secure Italy's consent to the annexation and, even more, by Turkey's probable reaction. Germany, nevertheless, had done nothing to restrain the adventurous Austrian minister. From the beginning of his aggressive foreign Balkan policy, her attitude had been encouraging.[68] Even a moderate diplomat like Metternich had said that the strengthening of Vienna's influence in the Balkans would be "entirely desirable from our point of view."[69] No discouraging word came from Berlin, although it was known that Aehrenthal was considering the annexation of the two provinces. On September 1, he explained that a final decision had not yet been reached and asked that the subject should not be discussed in the press.[70] After his conversation with Schoen at Berchtesgaden, September 4, there remained little uncertainty except as to the date, for Aehrenthal then said that it was only a question of time. According to his memoirs, Schoen protested when the Austrian minister said that he intended "to suppress the Serbian revolutionary nest once and for all," warning him that the annexation would cause international complications and that the use of force against Serbia "seemed to me very extravagant."[71] His contemporary report tells a somewhat different story. Favorably impressed by Aehrenthal's assurances that an advance toward Salonika had been abandoned, that the Sanjak of Novibazar would be evacuated at the time of the annexation, and that the prospects for an understanding

[67] The case against Aehrenthal was stated by no one more strongly than by Marschall, the German ambassador in Constantinople, who foresaw the loss of Germany's influence in Turkey. *G. P.,* XXIV, 99.

[68] Bülow later assured Hardinge that "they had, when the opportunity presented itself, given moderating advice." Hardinge, Feb. 10, 1909. *B. D.,* V, 668.

[69] *G. P.,* XXIV, 306 (Feb. 7, 1908).

[70] B. E. Schmitt, "The Bosnia Annexation Crisis," *Slavonic Review,* IX, 321. *Cf.* Brockdorff-Rantzau, Sept. 1. *G. P.,* XXVI, 21.

[71] W. von Schoen, *The Memoirs of an Ambassador* (N. Y., 1923), p. 78.

with Russia were good, he maintained an attitude of reserve, except in speaking of an enlarged Bulgaria as a possible danger.[72] There is still another version of Schoen's attitude. Speaking to the imperial council, Aehrenthal (Sept. 10) represented Schoen as expressing "merely a certain degree of astonishment that Austria-Hungary's aspirations in regard to Turkish territory were so moderate and modest," [73] but the need of winning the Hungarians for the annexation doubtless caused him to misrepresent what Schoen had said. To do Austria a service without giving Russia the impression that Germany was urging her on was Bülow's chief aim.[74] He accordingly remained silent, September 26, when Aehrenthal wrote that he had decided to proceed with the annexation while withdrawing from the Sanjak, "in the confident expectation of Germany's support . . . in a critical hour," but the minister's request that the Emperor should receive Szögyény, the Austrian ambassador, on October 5 or 6 was a pretty clear indication of the date.[75] Foreseeing that William would object, he directed the foreign office not to forward these documents to William without an explanation of the need to prove "our unconditional reliability." [76]

William therefore did not learn until the evening of October 5 what the Chancellor had known for more than a week. To Szögyény's announcement of the annexation (Oct. 6), the Emperor made no serious objection, accepting without demur the explanation that the decision had been communicated to Schoen on September 4 and to Bülow on September 26.[77] In reality, he

[72] Except for a rectification of the frontier, Austria, according to Aehrenthal, would annex no Serbian territory. Most of it would go to Bulgaria. *G. P.,* XXVI, 27–29 (Sept. 5).

[73] *Oesterreich-Ungarns Aussenpolitik von der bosnischen Krise 1908 bis zum Kriegsausbruch 1914,* 8 vols. (Vienna, 1930), I, 79. This work will henceforth be cited as *Ö.-U. A.*

[74] See Bülow's comments relating to Bulgaria's confiscation of her section of the Orient Railway. *G. P.,* XXVI, 72 (Sept. 23).

[75] It seems to the present writer that too much has been made of the fact that Aehrenthal did not confide the exact date of the annexation to Germany. Surely, there were definite indications that it would occur very soon; yet Bülow wrote, September 30, as if there would be time for William to advise Francis Joseph to treat Turkey tactfully. *Ibid.,* XXVI, 46. On the other hand, an official of the foreign office informed Marschall on October 3 that information at hand pointed to the publication of the proclamation on October 7. *Ibid.,* XXVI, 98.

[76] Bülow's comments, Tschirschky, Sept. 28; Bülow to Foreign Office, Sept. 30. *Ibid.,* XXVI, 43–46.

[77] William II's comments, Bülow, Oct. 5. *Ibid.,* XXVI, 53; *Ö.-U. A.,* I, 156.

was enraged at Bülow's silence. He was, he complained, "the last man in Europe to hear anything."[78]   The work of twenty years in seeking Turkey's friendship would be lost and Edward VII would take his place at Constantinople.   Back in Berlin, he greeted Bülow with the excited proposal of "a complete change of direction" in Germany's foreign policy.[79]   Never, never would he approve Prince Ferdinand's action, and he would force Austria to withdraw her annexation decree and to dismiss Aehrenthal. Again William's impulsive reaction might have served his country better than the reasoned policy of his ministers, but, as usual, he quickly permitted himself to be won over by the argument of a diplomatic necessity.   When Russia, with the support of the Western powers, demanded that the question be referred to an international conference, no one was more zealous than he in supporting Austria.

Germany's problem was to aid her ally and, at the same time, to remain on as good terms as possible with Russia and with the Western powers.   To keep Turkey from going over to the Triple Entente was another reason why the press and the diplomats unanimously protested that Germany had not been consulted. The circumstances, it was said, left Germany no choice, for the Dual Alliance was the best guarantee of peace, as the experience of thirty years had shown.   The *Berliner Lokal-Anzeiger* (Oct. 7) was at once corrected when it reported that the Archduke Francis Ferdinand had confided Austria's plans to William and Bülow during the recent army maneuvers.[80]   If the foreign office soon admitted that Aehrenthal had "mentioned" the annexation of Bosnia-Herzegovina and Prince Ferdinand's action as "remote contingencies,"[81] the *Kölnische Zeitung* (Oct. 7) insisted that Germany would have advised less dangerous methods if an opportunity had presented itself.   After all, it was argued by Austria's sympathizers, the annexation was merely a formal recognition of a condition which had existed for thirty years.[82]   No one

---

[78] William II's comments, Bülow, Oct. 5. *G. P.*, XXVI, 53.
[79] Bülow, *Denkwürdigkeiten*, II, 341.
[80] *N. A. Z.*, in *Frankfurter Zeitung*, Oct. 11; *Berliner Neueste Nachrichten*, Oct. 11.
[81] Lascelles, Oct. 6, 7. *B. D.*, V, 397, 402.
[82] *Kölnische Zeitung*, Oct. 5; *Kölnische Volkszeitung*, Oct. 6; *Vossische Zeitung*, Oct. 6, 7; *Germania*, Oct. 7.

had ever supposed that the provinces would be returned to Turkey, and Austria's claims had been strengthened by the beneficial results of her occupation and by her evacuation of the San-jak.[83] With these views even the *Hamburger Nachrichten* (Oct. 7) agreed. Resentment was directed, for the most part, against Bulgaria, while excuses were found for Austria. Bülow, how-ever, was moved to write that the press should avoid unnecessary offense to "the coming nations." In regard to German policy in general, he thought it should explain "that we have no interest in taking a leading position in the crisis," and that Germany should localize the conflict if war broke out in the Balkans.[84] Such in fact had already been the predominant reaction of the press.[85] Even the government's influence and the sympathy which the Catholics and the liberals normally felt for Austria did not prevent a good deal of criticism. Like Grey, the liberal *Frankfurter Zeitung* (Oct. 9) condemned Austria. According to the *Berliner Tageblatt* (Oct. 8), Germany's obligations as an ally should not blind her to the violation of a treaty. "We can-not understand," it wrote, "why the German foreign office did not give our ally better advice." What an important section of the nationalist press resented especially was not so much Austria's offense against international law as the danger that Germany might have to fight without any prospect of gaining something for herself. As early as October 8 the *Hamburger Nachrichten* insisted that Austria's Balkan policy had only disadvantages for Germany and that the text of the Dual Alliance and Bis-marck's counsel proved conclusively "that Germany is under no obligation to support it." The moderate *Vossische Zeitung* (Oct. 9) regarded Austria's aggressive action as a welcome refuta-tion of those who predicted her approaching demise, but the chauvinist *Rheinisch-Westfälische Zeitung* (Oct. 7) viewed her revival with mixed feelings, fearing that the leadership might pass from Berlin to Vienna. Germany, it wrote (Oct. 9) had incurred universal "disfavor and suspicion" without any hope of securing the slightest advantage. Like the *Hamburger Nach-*

---

[83] *Vossische Zeitung*, Oct. 6; *Germania*, Oct. 7.
[84] *G. P.*, XXVI, 137 (Oct. 7).
[85] Cf. *Freisinnige Zeitung*, Oct. 7.

richten, this journal, the organ of the heavy industrialists of Essen, denied that Germany had any obligation to pull Austria's chestnuts out of the Balkan fire. Austria, in its opinion (Oct. 11), was no longer a German state. "For a *Slavic Danubian monarchy* we have *not a single pfennig and not a drop of blood* —except as expressly stipulated in the alliance." The official organ of the Pan-Germans was willing that Austria should enjoy Germany's sympathy, but not her active support.[86]

There was a note of regret in the most cordial approval of Austria's action. "The best proof that she counts upon Germany's loyalty," wrote the *Kölnische Zeitung* (Oct. 10), "is her courage in exposing it to the present test." Although the foreign office promised, after a protest from Vienna,[87] that the Cologne journal would not again offend, the feeling that German interests were not directly involved and the unfavorable comparison between the weakness of Germany's recent foreign policy and Austria's aggressiveness combined with the encirclement scare to produce a strong undercurrent of dissatisfaction.[88] It reached the flood tide with the *Daily Telegraph* (Oct. 28) interview containing the Emperor's remarks to Colonel Whortley during his visit to England in the autumn of 1907. Like William, more than a few newspapers thought that his services therein related would impress England favorably.[89] That the Emperor had foiled the plans of Russia and France to intervene during the Boer War should, according to the National Liberal *Magdeburgische Zeitung* (Oct. 29) and the *Hamburger Nachrichten* (Oct. 29), open England's eyes to the purposes of her associates. Edward VII, wrote the chauvinist *Rheinisch-Westfälische Zeitung* (Oct. 29), would probably lose no time in seizing the proffered hand—in the hope of winning William's support for England's Balkan interests. The National Liberal *National Zeitung* (Oct. 29) promptly identified William's policy with that of the German nation. This favorable reaction, however, was

---

[86] *A. B.,* Oct. 9.

[87] Szögyény, Oct. 11. *Ö.-U. A.,* I, 189.

[88] The government's chief fault, according to the Catholic *Kölnische Volkszeitung* (Oct. 18), had been its failure to proclaim its unreserved support of Austria.

[89] Nothing but a reduction in the naval program, wrote the Social Democratic *Vorwärts* (Oct. 30), could win England for an understanding. Cf. *Vossische Zeitung,* Oct. 29.

immediately submerged by a storm of protest. "The cannon," wrote one observer, "has, in a sense, discharged backward, wreaking havoc in our own ranks." [90] William's efforts to conciliate England were offensive to nationalist opinion.[91] Not only was the contrast which he had drawn between his own friendship and the hatefulness of German opinion during the Boer War regarded as an unpatriotic disavowal of his own people,[92] but it was also clear that the desired effect in England had not been obtained.[93] Never had there been so unanimous a demonstration against William's personal interference in foreign affairs. "Our diplomats," wrote the nationalist *Berliner Neueste Nachrichten* (Oct. 29), "will have to work for a long time to correct the results of this blow." The uproar increased when the *Norddeutsche* (Oct. 31) argued that William had merely intended to correct England's mistaken impressions as to his aims, and especially when it asserted that he had consulted the Chancellor prior to the publication of the interview. Indeed, Bülow's responsibility was almost as great; instead of reading the manuscript which the Emperor had sent to him, he returned it to the foreign office, where a subordinate official merely corrected a few factual errors, and then, apparently, he approved its publication. In any event, the *Norddeutsche's* article sufficed to direct a part of the popular indignation against the Chancellor. Even the Conservative *Post* (Nov. 1) was dissatisfied when William refused to accept Bülow's resignation. The liberal *Berliner Morgenpost* advised the Reichstag to make no provision for his salary.[94] Although the liberals as a group wished to use the incident for the establishment of ministerial responsibility and some of them even planned to secure for the Reichstag the right to approve a declaration of war,[95] the view gradually prevailed that nothing was to be gained by a change of Chancellors. The *Kölnische Zeitung*

---

[90] Von Leyden, "Pro Imperator," *Deutsche Rundschau*, 1909, I, 184 (Feb.).

[91] *Deutsche Tageszeitung*, Oct. 29; *Leipziger Neueste Nachrichten*, in *Tägliche Rundschau*, Oct. 30; *Reichsbote*, Oct. 30.

[92] *Frankfurter Zeitung*, Oct. 29; *Reichsbote*, Nov. 4; *Deutsche Tageszeitung*, Nov. 5. The Catholic *Kölnische Volkszeitung* (Oct. 29) suspected that he read nothing but the Pan-German newspapers.

[93] *Daily News, Morning Post, Pall Mall Gazette, Standard*, Oct. 29.

[94] *National Zeitung*, Nov. 2.

[95] Ziekursch, *Politische Geschichte*, III, 195.

(Nov. 2) emphasized the difficulties of the international situation. It was useless, according to the National Liberal *National Zeitung* (Nov. 2), to talk of a return to Bismarck's methods and policies in view of the changed circumstances. It was the foreign situation that persuaded the *Post* (Nov. 4) to reverse its original position in favor of Bülow's resignation.

To bring the entire incident before the Reichstag was the purpose of the interpellations asking Bülow if he would assume the responsibility for the interview which almost all groups presented at the first session, November 4. The Conservatives had characteristically omitted the Emperor's name in their interpellation, but, on the following day, their executive committee showed an unprecedented independence in declaring that his remarks had often created difficulties and in expressing the hope that he would be more reserved in the future.[96] What every section of public opinion desired was an assurance that William's meddling in the affairs of state would stop. Never were the circumstances so favorable for the establishment of effective restraints, but neither the Reichstag nor the Chancellor proved equal to the opportunity. Concerned primarily with their own partisan interests, the parliamentary groups failed to reach an agreement in regard to procedure before the crucial debates of November 10, 11. Scarcely a deputy spoke in William's defense, but the refusal of the Conservatives to participate in any direct pressure prevented the formulation of the joint address for which the spokesmen for almost every other party declared.[97] To avert a serious constitutional crisis was Bülow's chief aim. Not a word did he say in his speech of November 10 of his own negligence; he permitted the Reichstag to exhaust itself in oratory without speaking in the Emperor's defense. The semi-official and inspired press at once rose in protest. The like of this debate, wrote the *Kölnische Zeitung* (Nov. 12), should never be repeated, and the *Norddeutsche* (Nov. 15) agreed that no monarchist could ever desire its renewal. In spite of the position taken by the Bundesrat's committee on foreign affairs, November 15, that the Chancellor should use his full authority to restrain the Emperor, and

---

[96] Eschenburg, *Kaiserreich am Scheideweg*, p. 136.
[97] Westarp, *Konservative Politik*, I, 47.

in spite of Bethmann-Hollweg's statement to the Prussian ministry that Bülow should say to the Emperor, *"Bis hierher und nicht
weiter,"* the Chancellor accepted William's moderately apologetic
statement (Nov. 16) as satisfactory.[98] No real guarantees were
secured. In the absence of determined leadership, public opinion
rapidly accepted this disappointing result, which the *Rheinisch-
Westfälische Zeitung* (Nov. 18) denounced as "a *brutal denial*
of the people's will as well as that of the Reichstag and the Bundesrat." The liberal *Berliner Tageblatt* (Nov. 18) continued for
a few days to insist that the situation was ripe for the establishment of parliamentary government, but the Conservatives and
many nationalists would certainly have balked at a serious revision of the constitution. The executive committee of the Pan-
German League called for Bülow's dismissal, on the ground that
men, not measures, were the issue, and the *Alldeutsche Blätter*
(Nov. 7) declared against any limitation of the Emperor's powers.

The Catholic *Kölnische Volkszeitung* (Nov. 10) indicated accurately the trend of opinion. Since no trace of a considered
system could be found in Bülow's foreign policy, there was nothing to be gained by giving him the full control. "Diplomatically,
Prince Bülow," it concluded, "has always lived from hand to
mouth." Two of the most important of the liberal journals, the
Frankfurter Zeitung (Nov. 18) and the *Vossische Zeitung* (Nov.
18), thought that the Emperor had conceded about as much as
could be expected, while the nationalist *Tägliche Rundschau*
(Nov. 18) was willing to give the government an opportunity to
remedy its errors and to pursue "the quiet, courageous, and
purposeful policy which we desire so much." Bassermann, the
National Liberal leader, approved the solution in the *Roter Tag,*
and the *National Zeitung* (Nov. 18) spoke of it as "temporarily
satisfactory." What decided the outcome perhaps more than
anything else was the aversion of the Conservatives to any change
in the political and social balance of power. Having argued
(Nov. 17) that a "limitation of the rights of the Crown would be

---

[98] The editors of the *Deutsche Zeitung,* the *Leipziger Neueste Nachrichten,* and the
Tägliche Rundschau, all nationalist journals, were present. Class, *Wider den Strom,*
p. 139.

a serious blow to Prussia's presidial power," it was natural that the *Post* (Nov. 18) should describe the settlement as "admirable in every respect." The chief danger had been, according to Heinrich Class, Hasse's successor as president of the Pan-German League, that the federated states might be strengthened at the expense of the Empire.[99]   Opposition to constitutional changes did not imply an approval of the *Daily Telegraph* interview,[100] nor did the tame conclusion mean that the crisis had no important results for German foreign policy.   Far from being grateful to Bülow, the Emperor never forgave his failure to defend him more effectively.   Henceforth the Chancellor could not count upon his confidence, especially when it was most necessary, during the approaching contest with Tirpitz.   This rift may have encouraged Bülow to seek a dramatic success in the Bosnian crisis in the hope of recovering William's favor.

Among the harmful results of the domestic crisis, not the least significant was the reaction abroad to the *Daily Telegraph* interview.   Incensed by the revelation of Russia's proposed mediation during the Boer War at a time when England's support was needed most, the Tsar showed Nicolson, the British ambassador, while concealing its date (Nov. 17, 1904), William's letter recommending a military demonstration on the Indian frontier.   "From this moment," writes Nicolson's son and biographer, "his [Sir Arthur Nicolson's] judgment was coloured by the conviction that Germany cherished tortuous and malignant designs against the British Empire."[101]   In France, the interview was regarded as another attempt to weaken the Entente Cordiale, with the result that there was less inclination than ever to yield in the Casablanca affair.   That question had remained dormant since the rejection of Bülow's proposals of October 19.   Schoen spoke to Jules Cambon as late as October 28 of the Emperor's and his own desire for a general understanding that would include more than Morocco.[102]   The next day, October 29, he asked for a speedy ar-

---

[99] *A. B.*, Nov. 27.

[100] Delbrück spoke of the interview as responsible for Prussia's most serious diplomatic defeat since Olmütz.   *P. J.*, vol. 134, p. 575 (Nov. 28).

[101] Nicolson, *Lord Carnock*, p. 289. Pourtalès, the German ambassador, regarded Nicolson as responsible for Izvolski's stiff attitude during the Bosnian crisis. *G. P.*, XXVI, 309 (Dec. 4, 1908).

[102] Schoen, Oct. 28. *G. P.*, XXIV, 223, 224.

rangement, adding that public opinion would insist upon an explanation when the Reichstag met on November 4. Although the government's real difficulties would certainly arise from the domestic crisis, Bülow suddenly demanded, October 30, the immediate release of the three German deserters and a suitable satisfaction for the mistreatment of the consular official. Upon France's answer, said Bülow, would depend not only the further development of the entire Moroccan question but also that of "the diplomatic relations between us and France."[103] Not to force a war but to create a diversion from the serious domestic crisis or perhaps to secure an easy diplomatic success was evidently the Chancellor's purpose, for France was informed, on the same day, that Germany would accept her conditions for Mulai Hafid's recognition.[104] The French still insisted upon the arbitration of the facts as well as of the legal issues. To the demand for satisfaction, they replied with a firm negative.[105] Schoen, for a moment, thought of action. Writing from his sickbed, he said that the heavy artillery must be brought up and that a warship might even be sent to Casablanca.[106] However, a retreat began almost immediately.[107] The demand for the release of the deserters, wrote Schoen, should be abandoned.[108] The insistence upon a direct apology was soon dropped. On November 2, Jules Cambon's proposal for an exchange of regrets and for the arbitration of the entire question was accepted in principle. Only the wording of the joint expression of regret remained in dispute, but it involved the prestige of both countries, since Germany tried to secure and France to prevent the adoption of a formula that would place the blame upon the latter or her agents.

While the question was being threshed out in the chancelleries, the revelation of Germany's demands in the French press aroused a defiant spirit,[109] and, in Germany, the nationalists replied in

---

[103] Bülow, Oct. 30. *G. P.,* XXIV, 355. On the same day, the *Alldeutsche Blätter* printed the same demands, with the warning that the government's success in securing satisfaction would be the test of its "ability to protect Germany's prestige and honor."

[104] Schoen, Oct. 30. *G. P.,* XXIV, 455.

[105] Radolin, Oct. 31. *Ibid.,* XXIV, 357, 358.

[106] Schoen's comments, Flotow, Nov. 1. *Ibid.,* XXIV, 357, 358.

[107] Austria's withdrawal of her demand for the release of her own national may have influenced this decision.

[108] Schoen's comments, Radolin, Nov. 1. *G. P.,* XXIV, 357.

[109] Carroll, *French Public Opinion,* p. 228.

kind. The chauvinist *Rheinisch-Westfälische Zeitung* (Nov. 5) described an exchange of regrets as "the middle road of indecision and weakness." The French should see that "they are facing the most serious decision since 1870"; a refusal would be conclusive proof "that they are bent upon a *war with Germany*." To count upon the domestic crisis to save them would be folly, wrote the *Hannoversche Courier;* all patriots would unite in defense of the national honor.[110] There could be no discussion: "A definite and unconditional apology is indispensable." The nationalist *Tägliche Rundschau* (Nov. 5) claimed "good authority" for the announcement that *"Germany will stand firmly behind the demand for an apology,"* because France's efforts to test her "already seriously compromised leadership" made it a question of national honor. "French Insolence (*Frankreich wird frech*)!" screamed the headlines of the *Post* (Nov. 4). A refusal, according to the *Berliner Neueste Nachrichten* (Nov. 5), could not be tolerated; France wished to use Germany's domestic crisis "to humiliate her." The East Prussian *Königsberger Allgemeine Zeitung* spoke of war.[111] To the *Münchener Neueste Nachrichten* (Nov. 6) one thing was clear: "Germany will accept the consequences rather than yield on the question of honor." Justice was so clearly on her side, wrote the agrarian *Deutsche Tageszeitung* (Nov. 6), that a retreat "would cost us every bit of our prestige in world affairs." Only France, insisted the *Allgemeine Zeitung* (Munich, Nov. 7), could find anything objectionable in Germany's moderate demands. "Dissatisfied with the usual tolerance of France's susceptibilities," the nation approved, wrote the ultra-Conservative *Reichsbote* (Nov. 6), the government's vigor; but the violence of the nationalist press was doubtless partly a reaction against the feeling of frustration arising out of the domestic crisis. Austria's friends had no desire to see Germany's attention diverted by a serious clash with France. Public opinion, wrote the Catholic *Kölnische Volkszeitung* (Nov. 6), was by no means excited. "Much ado about nothing," was the moderate *Vossische Zeitung's* (Nov. 6) view. The Conservative *Post* con-

---

[110] *Kölnische Zeitung*, Nov. 6; *Tägliche Rundschau*, Nov. 8.
[111] *Berliner Tageblatt*, Nov. 5.

tinued to insist that Germany's honor must be safeguarded, but it admitted (Nov. 6) that both governments probably desired a peaceful settlement. As early as November 5, the National Liberal *National Zeitung* took the position that the right to satisfaction did not mean "that the question must result in war." The talk of war over the fate of a couple of deserters was, according to the Catholic *Kölnische Volkszeitung* (Nov. 9), a scandal. Many felt that the demand for an apology was intended as a diversion from the constitutional problem. "After our recent experiences," wrote the *Frankfurter Zeitung* (Nov. 5), "anything can happen." Even the *Rheinisch-Westfälische Zeitung* (Nov. 5) found in Bülow's desire for a diplomatic success the reason for the adjournment of the debate on the *Daily Telegraph* interview to November 10. While the liberal *Berliner Tageblatt* (Nov. 5) agreed that satisfaction must be secured for the violence done to the German consular agent, it charged the government, nevertheless, with yielding to the Pan-Germans.[112] The plan, according to the Social Democratic *Vorwärts* (Nov. 6), was to intimidate the Reichstag with a wave of national sentiment. To this charge, the semi-official press replied that the demands had been presented to France on October 18, ten days before the publication of the *Daily Telegraph* interview, and that no change had occurred since then.[113] One nationalist observer even blamed France for the crisis. "It was," he wrote, "not a little surprising when France, the day after the appearance of the interview, suddenly rejected the German proposal."[114]

Instead of giving the Chancellor a timely diplomatic success, the incident emphasized the weakness of Germany's position. England, and probably Russia, supported France loyally. Khevenhüller, the Austrian ambassador in Paris, suspected that England was encouraging the aggressiveness of the French, a charge

---

[112] It was during the Casablanca affair that Schoen assured Reventlow, the editor of the *Alldeutsche Blätter*, that the government welcomed a strong nationalist opposition. Class, *Wider den Strom*, pp. 145, 146.

[113] At first, the *Berliner Lokal-Anzeiger* (Nov. 4) and the *Kölnische Zeitung* (Nov. 4) merely said that the demands had been made earlier than October 28, but the semi-official *Norddeutsche Allgemeine Zeitung* (Nov. 7) referred specifically to the demands of October 18 as Germany's last word. Cf. *National Zeitung, Münchener Neueste Nachrichten*, Nov. 6; *N. A. Z.*, Nov. 8.

[114] *Grenzboten*, 1908, IV, 355.

later repeated by Schoen,[115] but there is no supporting evidence in the British diplomatic correspondence. Grey and the British foreign office were convinced of France's moderation by her willingness to arbitrate the entire question. Only the fear of doing more harm than good prevented Grey from speaking in Berlin on her behalf.[116] Although England was apparently not asked as to what she would do in the event of war,[117] Grey nevertheless examined the question and decided, as usual, that the final decision would depend upon the reaction of public opinion. Overt preparations, he wrote November 5, might precipitate a Franco-German war. "But I think," he added, "the Admiralty should keep in readiness to make preparations in case Germany sent an ultimatum and the Cabinet decided that we must assist France."[118] In questions that concerned Anglo-German relations, Grey was, however, distinctly considerate. He urged the need of a tactful attitude in regard to the *Daily Telegraph* affair,[119] and, on November 7, he assured Metternich that cooperation in such questions as the Turkish finances would be welcome.[120]

The long-delayed Dordé report, containing the evidence collected by the French agents at Casablanca, presented a strong case for the argument that the consular agent had not made known his identity until after he was struck by the French military police.[121] Kiderlen-Wächter, recalled from Bucharest to take Schoen's place at the foreign office, saw at once, November 10, that only an immediate settlement could save. something for Germany.[122] Fearful that a serious crisis would weaken Germany's support and that it would insure France's ardent cham-

[115] *Ö.-U. A.,* I, 419 (Nov. 11); Schoen, *Memoirs,* pp. 90, 91. King Edward, according to Tardieu, promised that "five divisions of infantry and one division of cavalry" would be placed at France's disposal. G. P. Gooch, *History of Modern Europe* (New York, 1923), p. 460.

[116] Grey's minute, Nov. 5. *B. D.,* VII, 118.

[117] Grey, Nov. 10. Nicolson, *Lord Carnock,* p. 285.

[118] *B. D.,* VII, 119.

[119] *Ibid.,* VI, 206, 207, (Nov. 7).

[120] Metternich, Nov. 9. *G. P.,* XXIV, 368, 369.

[121] Later, Schoen explained that the report reached his hands on the evening of November 7. *Verhandlungen,* XII Leg. Per., I Sess., p. 6107 (Dec. 10, 1908).

[122] E. Jäckh, *Kiderlen-Wächter, der Staatsmann und Mensch,* 2 vols. (Berlin, 1925), II, 12, 13.

pionship of Russia, Austria had meanwhile exerted her influence in favor of a solution. The withdrawal of her own demand for the release of the Austrian deserter was followed by Francis Joseph's plea, itself suggested by Paris, for an arrangement during his conversation with William at Schönbrunn, November 6.[123] The Dordé report moved the Emperor to declare for a prompt settlement, for fear that Germany might end by making apologies herself.[124] On November 9, the *Kölnische Zeitung* announced that the new light upon the incident made it impossible for Germany to insist upon her demands, and, the next day, it added that the phraseology of mutual regrets was relatively unimportant.[125] The nationalists, of course, were bitterly disappointed. "A new defeat," announced the *Tägliche Rundschau* (Nov. 10). The *Deutsche Tageszeitung* (Nov. 10) reminded its readers of the boasts that the government would never yield, and it pointed out that Germany now enjoyed "peace and the Hague tribunal" instead of France's apologies. *"Rückwärts, rückwärts, stolzes Deutschland,"* was, said the chauvinist *Rheinisch-Westfälische Zeitung* (Nov. 10), the order of the day. "Germany barks but doesn't bite. What was said after Olmütz, '*Avilir la Prusse et puis démolir,*' we hear again." While the *Reichsbote* (Nov. 11) admitted that the outcome, given the facts, was inevitable, it insisted that a better-informed diplomatic service could have avoided a humiliating defeat. To the *Alldeutsche Blätter* (Nov. 14), the government's timidity explained everything. The *Norddeutsche* (Nov. 15), announcing the text of the joint expression of regrets, sought to correct the impression of a diplomatic defeat by denying that Germany had ever insisted upon an apology and by representing public opinion in the two countries as satisfied. At least of moderate opinion this was true.[126] What irritated even Schiemann most was not so much the outcome of the affair as the support which France had received from England and Russia. He could not refrain from a warning. "Not even the

---

[123] Khevenhüller, Nov. 4; Aehrenthal, Nov. 7. *Ö.-U. A.,* I, 382, 407; Jenisch, Tschirschky, Nov. 7. *G. P.,* XXIV, 242, 366, 367.
[124] William II's comments, Bülow, Nov. 7. *G. P.,* XXIV, 367.
[125] Cf. *N. A. Z.,* Nov. 10.
[126] *Berliner Tageblatt, Vorwärts,* Nov. 10. Cf. *Hamburger Nachrichten,* Nov. 11.

most sincere assistance," he wrote, "always gives effective protection." [127]

In a crisis concerning her own interests, Germany had yielded, but she continued unfalteringly to support her ally in the more dangerous Bosnian question. Bismarck's warnings were ignored or regarded as inapplicable to the existing circumstances. "No longer is Germany the director of the European concert," wrote the National Liberal *National Zeitung* (Nov. 2), "A 'Remember Bismarck!' (*Ein 'Denke an Bismarck!'*) . . . is either useless or dangerous to any occupant of the Wilhelmstrasse." Opinion continued to be sharply divided as to the proper interpretation of Germany's treaty obligations. In favor of Austria worked the hatred of autocratic Russia, the belief that Germany's fate was inseparably associated with that of her ally, and the interests of the Roman Catholic Church. It was a curious paradox that Austria had many ardent champions among the moderates, who condemned an adventurous policy in support of Germany's own interests. On October 28, the *Vossische Zeitung* insisted that the alliance had always been interpreted as providing for the defense of each other's position as great powers. With Austria's unexpected energy, the nationalists were in general pleased; their sympathies were clearly with her in the quarrel with Serbia. Many frowned, however, upon the use of military force and they resented especially the injury done to Turkey.[128] Far more important, from their point of view, was the danger that the leadership in the alliance might pass to Vienna and that Germany might be involved in a war for other interests than her own. The appeal to Germany's gratitude for services rendered during the Algeciras Conference made little impression upon them; the circumstances, they said, were essentially dissimilar, since there had been no real danger of war in 1906. Austria's attitude toward the Casablanca incident released Germany, according to the argrarian *Deutsche Tageszeitung* (Oct. 16), from any obligation, and the Pan-Germans mentioned Aehrenthal's earlier announcement that the Dual Alliance did not extend to

---

[127] *Kreuz-Zeitung*, Nov. 11. Schiemann, *Deutschland und die Grosse Politik*, VIII, 343.

[128] *Deutsche Tageszeitung*, *Reichsbote*, Oct. 14; *Leipziger Neueste Nachrichten*, in *Tägliche Rundschau*, Oct. 15.

the North and Baltic Seas as justifying a refusal to support "every conceivable aim and activity of his policy. . . ." [129] The situation, wrote the *Hamburger Nachrichten,* required a revision of the alliance to secure a more exact definition of Germany's obligations.[130] In the opinion of the *Deutsche Tageszeitung* (Oct. 18), no change in the text was necessary, for the alliance merely required Germany's armed support against an attack by Russia: "Not a word is said in it of diplomatic support." Bülow himself tried to restrain this movement of opinion. Addressing the press bureau, he wrote, October 28: *"Under no circumstances must we become involved in a press war with Vienna! . . .* It will merely discourage and perhaps alienate Austria, while cementing the entente of the Western powers with Russia." All newspapers that were receptive to official influence—he mentioned the *Deutsche Tageszeitung* and the *Tägliche Rundschau*—should be requested "to stop their academic discussion of the value and scope of the alliance." [131] Two days later, the *Alldeutsche Blätter* (Oct. 30) nevertheless noticed an increasing appreciation in the press of the "danger of identifying Germany with Austria's foreign policy."

Aehrenthal had abundant reason to believe that he could count upon Germany's unconditional support. In regard to the demand for an international conference, William had taken the position, October 7, even before he knew what Austria's intentions were, that the recognition of the *fait accompli* should be required as the essential condition for its acceptance.[132] Scarcely a fortnight passed before he gave the Austrians even more positive encouragement. On October 21, on the eve of Izvolski's arrival (Oct. 24) in Berlin, he told the Austrian ambassador: "The Emperor Francis Joseph is a Prussian field marshal; he has therefore only to command and the entire Prussian army will obey." Should war come, which he did not believe, he intended to fulfil his obligations with "real passion." [133] Nor were these indiscretions the limit of Germany's encouragement. To all sugges-

---

[129] *A. B.,* Oct. 16.
[130] *Deutsche Tageszeitung,* Oct. 18.
[131] *G. P.,* XXVI, 222.
[132] William II's remarks, Jenisch, Oct. 7; Metternich, Oct. 15; Bülow, Oct. 30. *Ibid.,* XXVI, 113, 175, 176, 224.
[133] Szögyény, Oct. 22. *Ö.-U. A.,* I, 278.

tions that she should use her influence in Vienna to secure such concessions for Russia and her Serbian and Montenegrin protégés as would enable them to accept the annexation peacefully, she turned a cold shoulder. Instead, Germany performed positive services for her ally. Serbia was told that she should disarm and suppress her war party.[134] The importance of Bulgaria's friendship was called to Austria's attention.[135] Austro-Turkish relations were an object of particular concern. To Turkey, Berlin suggested the abandonment of her boycott of Austrian goods, and, December 6, Austria was advised, as the press had repeatedly suggested, to weaken the legal position of the entente powers by securing Turkey's recognition of the *fait accompli* in return for a money payment.[136] To a certain extent the responsibility for Aehrenthal's intransigeance was therefore Germany's; she had, at least, indentified herself with a policy that would, as Metternich pointed out,[137] add the Balkans to Morocco as a source of friction.

On December 8 Austria refused the Russian agenda for the proposed conference without consulting Berlin. Germany's loyalty to the alliance and her stake in the crisis gave her the right, wrote Kiderlen, to be informed as to her views;[138] yet Germany's attitude remained essentially unchanged. On December 7, Bülow told the Reichstag that Germany undoubtedly had "the right and duty" of deciding the degree to which she should support Austria's special interests; but even this vague reservation did not appear in his speech of December 10.[139] He wished, according to the Belgian envoy, to show the Triple Entente that it "should not count upon the dissatisfaction aroused by Baron Aehrenthal's adventurous policy."[140] By the end of 1908 his real aims had become distinctly more ambitious. Whatever his objections to the annexation may have been, he came to see in the crisis an opportunity to improve Germany's diplomatic position. Turning to Russia, he offered to support her

---

[134] Schoen, Dec. 2. *G. P.*, XXVI, 281.

[135] Szögyény, Nov. 30. *Ö.-U. A.*, I, 530.

[136] O. H. Wedel, *Austro-German Diplomatic Relations, 1908–1914* (Stanford, 1932), p. 75.

[137] *G. P.*, XXVI, 167 (Oct. 14).

[138] *Ibid.*, XXVI, 459.

[139] *Verhandlungen*, XII Leg. Per., I Sess., VII, 6047, 6106.

[140] *Belgische Dokumente*, IV, 115, 116 (Dec. 11).

ambitions in the Straits, a move which William thought might lead to the revival of the Three Emperors' League;[141] but, after the Tsar's cool response,[142] Bülow was even more definitely in favor of an aggressive policy. When Izvolski rejected a direct agreement with Aehrenthal, he withheld this information from the Austrian minister for fear "that he might weaken," and directed that Russia's purpose should be represented "as the encirclement of Austria in the Balkans."[143] Scarcely a week after Kiderlen's criticism of Austria, the Chancellor spurred Vienna on against the Serbs and Montenegrins. The moment, he told Szögyény, would never be more favorable. He confessed, as a sincere friend and ally, that "it would be highly desirable if a sign of life should be manifested again in international politics."[144] A similar point of view appeared in the semi-official press. In reply to the criticism in the Austrian press of Bülow's alleged lukewarmness,[145] the Norddeutsche's (Jan. 3) assurances were so comprehensive as to constitute almost a carte blanche. There had never been, it insisted, any doubt of Germany's support: "We are confident that the leaders of the allied monarchy know best what is essential to its existence as a great power. It alone can decide what is to be done in specific questions (Einzelfragen); and they have the right to expect that Germany will do nothing susceptible of being construed as uninvited meddling or dictation."[146] This significant article was preceded by the first letters of an important correspondence between Hötzendorf and Moltke, the chiefs of the Austrian and German general staffs. In reply to the former's inquiry, January 1, Moltke wrote, January 21, "with the knowledge" and therefore with the approval of the Emperor and Chancellor, that a Russian mobilization during an Austro-Serbian war would be followed by similar action on the part of Germany. Since both governments apparently regarded

---

[141] G. P., XXVI, 371–381 (Dec. 13, 19).

[142] "We have got difficulties enough," replied Nicholas, "if I may say so, plenty of diplomatic food to digest for many months to come." Ibid., XXVI, 387, 388 (Dec. 15/28).

[143] Bülow's comment, Pourtalès, Dec. 11. Ibid., XXVI, 320.

[144] Szögyény, Dec. 16. Ö.-U. A., I, 607.

[145] Reichspost (Vienna) in Germania; Dec. 29.

[146] Cf. Deutsche Tageszeitung, Jan. 4, 1909; Kölnische Zeitung, Jan. 5; Berliner Neueste Nachrichten, Jan. 6.

this understanding as a binding agreement, the change in the character of the Dual Alliance which was causing so much criticism had occurred without a revision of its text.[147]

Two of Germany's ablest ambassadors feared the consequences of this policy. From London, Metternich stressed the danger of being involved in a war which not only did not concern her directly but which, if successful, might make of Austria a South Slavic empire.[148] Of a general war Monts wrote from Rome: "We can win nothing and we may lose everything, . . ." including the Austrian alliance.[149] Bülow's policy, in which Aehrenthal's intransigeance had become a useful factor, was based, however, upon the confidence that Russia was too weak to fight, and, especially that neither England nor France would support her in a war.[150] Russia, he felt certain, would restrain the Serbs and the Montenegrins rather than risk an armed conflict herself or a defeat for her Balkan protégés.[151] He dismissed as a bluff the talk in the English and Russian newspapers of war in the spring. A stiff attitude, he advised Austria, would convince Izvolski more effectively than any concessions that England's support could not be depended upon.[152] There was much truth in this analysis of the situation. Despite Grey's leadership in the demand for a conference, France held the key to the situation. Without the certainty of her military support, Russia could not think of war, and France desired above all a peaceful solution, and without France England would not move. France's emphasis upon the similarity between her interests and those of Germany in the Near East may perhaps be explained on tactical grounds,[153] just as her sympathetic attitude toward Austria was influenced by the desire to secure her assistance during the Casablanca affair.

---

[147] B. E. Schmitt, *The Coming of the War 1914,* 2 vols. (N. Y., 1930), I, 13–18. While Professor Fay holds that the agreement was essentially technical in character, he admits that "it did tend to give the alliance a potentially offensive . . . character." Fay, *Origins of the World War,* I, 343, 344.

[148] *G. P.,* XXVI, 392 (Jan. 5, 1909).

[149] Jäckh, *Kiderlen-Wächter,* II, 20 (Jan. 6).

[150] Bülow, Oct. 13. *G. P.,* XXVI, 155, 156, 161; Szögyény, Nov. 30. *Ö.-U. A.,* I, 530. Cf. *Kreuz-Zeitung,* Nov. 4. Schiemann, *Deutschland und die Grosse Politik,* VIII, 341.

[151] Bülow, Nov. 30, 1908. *G. P.,* XXVI, 513.

[152] Bülow, Dec. 12, 1908. *Ibid.,* XXVI, 516.

[153] Schoen, von der Lancken, Oct. 10, 14, 1908. *Ibid.,* XXVI, 145, 448, 449. Cf. *Post,* Oct. 13.

She was, moreover, strongly averse at this time to a war over Russia's Balkan ambitions.[154] The *Kölnische Zeitung* (Jan. 3, 1909) noted with satisfaction the strength of the peace sentiment in France and the fact "that her diplomacy had done nothing to sharpen the tension during the Bosnian crisis."[155] She was, according to the Catholic *Kölnische Volkszeitung* (Jan. 19), the "honest broker." "France," wrote Schiemann, "desires war no more than Germany."[156] The *revanche,* it was said, was little more than a sentiment.[157] To encourage this useful attitude, Bülow caused to be distributed, according to his memoirs, one hundred thousand marks to the Paris press for the expression of the opinion that France should not help Russia and England to pull their chestnuts out of the fire.[158] For those who, like Bülow, desired a successful and also a peaceful solution of the crisis, the weakness of the Triple Entente was a heartening sign. Delbrück, for example, was confident that it would "never hang together to the point of war."[159] Nevertheless, William was fearful. On New Year's Day 1909, he read to a group of generals the conclusion of General Schlieffen's unsigned article in the *Deutsche Revue,* painting a vivid picture of a concentric attack by the armed millions that surrounded Germany.[160] Public opinion, according to Harden, was not unusually nervous, but the Emperor's pessimism was undoubtedly regarded as a reason for concern.[161]

Since Germany's aims included the weakening of Russia's attachment to the Triple Entente, the relations with France and England should have played a vital part in her general policy. A rapprochement with either of the Western powers was manifestly

---

[154] Carroll, *French Public Opinion,* p. 262.

[155] *Cf.* Rohrbach, *Das politische Krisengebiet Europas,* p. 11.

[156] *Kreuz-Zeitung,* Jan. 6, 1909. Schiemann, *Deutschland und die Grosse Politik,* IX, 1, 2.

[157] Lichnowsky, "Die Friedensfrage in militärischer und politischer Betrachtung," *Deutsche Revue,* 1909, I, 166, 167.

[158] Bülow, *Denkwürdigkeiten,* II, 240, 241.

[159] *P. J.,* vol. 134, p. 181 (Dec. 28, 1908).

[160] "Der Krieg in der Gegenwart," *Deutsche Revue,* 1909, I, 22, 23. The incident, according to the *Kölnische Volkszeitung* (Jan. 8), had been brought to public attention by the *Tägliche Rundschau.* Cf. B. D., VI, 228 (Jan. 8). In the *Kölnische Volkszeitung's* (Jan. 9) opinion, the article showed that the army condemned Germany's official foreign policy.

[161] *Kölnische Volkszeitung,* Jan. 6, 1909; Harden, "Der Kriegsartikel," *Zukunft,* Jan. 16.

desirable, but, unfortunately, neither the foreign office nor public opinion was prepared for the necessary sacrifices. In regard to Morocco, Germany was ready for a new arrangement that might lessen the risk of complications. That France's neutrality in a war between Russia and the Central powers could be assured Bülow did not believe, but he conceded the possibility of eliminating Morocco as a cause of friction after a period of quiet relations.[162] The foreign office saw no reason for delay. When Jules Cambon made it clear, January 9, 1909, that France would welcome an understanding, since a general war might arise "from matters being of little concern to either country," Schoen coolly replied that the gravest questions were involved, but his advisers held that such terms should be arranged, in view of the indifference of public opinion to Morocco, as would save something from Germany's continual retreat.[163] Only the lateness of the train bringing Cambon with his government's consent prevented the signing of the accord, as the Germans desired, before the arrival of Edward VII in Berlin. The published terms included a renewal of France's pledge to respect the independence and the territorial integrity of Morocco, and an agreement to encourage the economic coöperation of the two countries in return for Germany's recognition of the preponderance of French political influence. In a secret exchange of letters, Germany also promised that France's greater interests would be recognized in any coöperation and that, from the date of the accord, her nationals would not accept employment under the Sultan.

In more than one respect, the reaction abroad to the agreement of February 9 showed the value it might have had for Germany. Aehrenthal thought that it would attract France from England's *Vormundschaft*—a result, in his opinion, as desirable as the weakening of the Anglo-Russian Entente.[164] The British diplomats who accompanied King Edward to Berlin assured their hosts, and the London press echoed this opinion, that the effect

162 *G. P.*, XXIV, 464, 465. The foreign office was perhaps influenced by its irritation at the loud claims of the Mannesmann brothers based upon a concession which, according to Hallgarten, one of them secured from Mulai Hafid by a gift of 20,000 francs. Hallgarten, *Vorkriegs Imperialismus*, pp. 232, 233.
163 Erckert, Jan. 8; Schoen, Jan. 9. *G. P.*, XXIV, 476.
164 Tschirschky, Feb. 9. *Ibid.*, XXIV, 493.

upon Anglo-German relations would be favorable,[165] and Grey himself was not entirely easy about the future of the Entente Cordiale. He wrote to Bertie, the ambassador in Paris, of the need "to keep the *Entente* . . . as fresh and vigorous in the sunshine as it had been during the storms of the Algeciras Conference. . . ."[166] Only the extreme chauvinists in France were openly critical, for the greater part of public opinion thought that a new period in Franco-German relations was perhaps beginning.[167] That the accord might serve Germany's general policy scarcely occurred to her press. The *Berliner Tageblatt* (Feb. 10) spoke of it and of Edward's VII's visit as evidence of better relations with the Western powers, and the *Frankfurter Zeitung* (Feb. 10) placed some value upon England's apparent approval, but neither of these liberal journals drew any conclusion as to its effect upon the Bosnian crisis. In what were, for the most part, colorless comments, the governmental press stressed the limited scope of the agreement and minimized its diplomatic significance. Assuming that both countries were sincere, the *Kölnische Zeitung* (Feb. 9) thought that the provision for economic coöperation might have useful results and that the general effect upon Franco-German relations would be good. The *Norddeutsche* (Feb. 14) saw in the elimination of Morocco as a source of friction a negative, and in the agreement upon specific questions a positive, advantage. The first point was repeated in a cautious statement in the *Süddeutsche Reichskorrespondenz,* in which the accord was described as restricted "to a definitely defined group of African interests. . . ."[168] Nor did the independent press see in it much more than a welcome improvement in the relations with France or, at the most, a vague service to peace. Although the *Berliner Tageblatt* (Feb. 10) spoke of the accord as the arrangement which it had recommended in 1905, it apparently expected nothing more than a

---

165 Hardinge Feb. 11. *B. D.,* VI, 230; Bülow, Feb. 13. *G. P.,* XXVIII, 90; *Daily News, Daily Chronicle, Morning Post,* Feb. 10; *Times,* Feb. 10, 13; *Standard,* Feb. 11.

166 *B. D.,* VII, 142 (Feb. 16).

167 Carroll, *French Public Opinion,* pp. 233, 234. For a recognition by a German journalist of the relief expressed by French public opinion, see *Berliner Neueste Nachrichten,* Feb. 11, Paris, Feb. 10. *Cf.* Khevenhüller, Feb. 20. *Ö.-U. A.,* I, 858.

168 *Vossische Zeitung, Freisinnige Zeitung, Germania,* Feb. 10; *N. A. Z.,* Feb. 11.

relief from incidents like the Casablanca affair.   To the *Vossische Zeitung* (Feb. 10), it was chiefly significant as a proof that the two powers could negotiate "without grasping their revolvers." Like this moderate journal and also the Progressive *Freisinnige Zeitung* (Feb. 10), the Catholic *Germania* (Feb. 10) saw nothing that was not already in the General Act of Algeciras.   In its opinion, the last obstacle to France's peaceful penetration of Morocco had been surmounted, but it also conceded the possibility that a beginning had been made toward a real rapprochement. The *Frankfurter Zeitung* (Feb. 10) spoke of economic coöperation as the only practical advantage, but said that only the future could determine its value.   True to its Bismarckian traditions, the *Hamburger Nachrichten* (Feb. 10) regarded the encouragement of France's Moroccan ambitions as a step in the right direction. The attitude of the nationalist press was one of bitter resignation.   The plea that a service had been rendered to peace did not impress the *Tägliche Rundschau* (Feb. 10): "We would gladly see our diplomats win other laurels than the palm for international unselfishness."   From the certain establishment of a French protectorate, the ultra-Conservative *Reichsbote* (Feb. 10) hoped at least for an improvement in Franco-German relations, but the agrarian *Deutsche Tageszeitung* (Feb. 9) expected that nothing would come of the proposed economic coöperation and it lamented the sacrifice of the last shreds of Germany's prestige in Morocco.   The accord, wrote the chauvinist *Rheinisch-Westfälische Zeitung* (Feb. 10), meant a full retreat and the complete sacrifice of German interests.   "Morocco is lost!" wailed the Pan-Germans.[169]   That the Moroccan policy was bankrupt was the *Münchener Neueste Nachrichten's* (Feb. 11) conclusion; Paris had finally understood that, "after so many proud retreats," Germany's warnings need not be taken seriously.   The *National Zeitung* (Feb. 10) sought, however, to give the impression that all was not lost: "The first and second matches for Morocco ended in a draw, the third is now beginning."

In a rapprochement with England Bülow apparently saw better prospects, for he made a brief, although unsuccessful, effort

---

[169] *A. B.*, Feb. 19.

in December 1908 to settle the crucial naval question. On his suggestion (Dec. 11), Metternich brought to the attention of the British foreign office the possibility that Germany might reduce her annual construction of battleships from three to two during the next few years.[170]   Grey was favorably impressed. He had every reason to welcome an arrangement that would reduce the financial burden of a naval race and even an improvement in Anglo-German relations in general, if it could be accomplished without the sacrifice of his diplomatic arrangements with France and Russia.   The friendly remarks of almost every speaker during the debates of November 10, 11 in the Reichstag had been noted with satisfaction,[171] and Grey had offered to coöperate in such questions as the Turkish finances.   He therefore replied that England would follow Germany's example if she reduced her naval program.[172]   Bülow seems to have been ready for an agreement; in a letter to Tirpitz, December 25, he practically endorsed Admiral Galster's proposal that the battleship should be subordinated to coastal defenses, small cruisers, and submarines. The chief aim, he argued, must be to avoid a war with England during the next few years.[173]   Against Tirpitz' opposition he could, however, make no headway.   The battleship was, the minister of marine argued, indispensable even to a strictly defensive policy, and as to the danger of an immediate war, it did not exist.   A reduction in the tempo of construction would be followed by his own resignation.[174]   In this clash between Germany's diplomatic and naval interests the latter won because Bülow, doubtful of his own standing with the Reichstag, knew that Tirpitz had the Emperor's favor.[175]   In the first flush of his anger at Austria's action in the Bosnian question, William had spoken favorably of a rapprochement with England,[176] but he doubtless never intended that it should be arranged at the cost of

---

[170] Bülow, Dec. 11; Metternich, Dec. 20.   G. P., XXVIII, 24, 34.

[171] Metternich, Nov. 27.   Ibid., XXVIII, 20.

[172] Metternich, Dec. 20.   Ibid., XXVIII, 35.

[173] Ibid., XXVIII, 38, 39. Theodor Wolff later acknowledged Galster's "secret advice and assistance" in the Berliner Tageblatt's campaign for a reduction of the naval program as a basis for an understanding with England.   Wolff, Through Two Decades, p. 60.

[174] Tirpitz, Jan. 4, 1909.   G. P., XXVIII, 51.

[175] Hammann, Bilder aus der letzten Kaiserzeit, p. 64.

[176] William II's comments, Marschall, Oct. 11.   G. P., XXVI, 154.

the fleet. Bülow, accordingly, bowed to the navy, covering his retreat with a reference to Tirpitz' superior competence in technical questions,[177] but he did not completely abandon hope that his opposition might still be overcome. While he instructed Metternich to drop the subject, he also asked the ambassador to

Simplicissimus, 1909.

Figure 22.—"How can we shake hands?"

explain to the British foreign office that England's naval construction was, after all, a matter of indifference to Germany.[178] What he had in mind was, he informed Metternich, "a political

177 Bülow, Jan. 5, 1909. *G. P.,* XXVIII, 5, 6.
178 Bülow, Jan.. 11. *Ibid.,* XXVIII, 59.

equivalent," [179] by which he meant an assurance of England's neutrality during a continental war; with this diplomatic triumph he could almost certainly win the Emperor for a modification of the naval laws. The psychological moment for a proposal of this kind, replied the ambassador, had occurred during the summer of 1908.[180] Blind as the Chancellor was to the difficulties of his own project, he saw at once the impractical character of Tirpitz' idea of a naval ratio of three to four during the next ten years. He would, he wrote, have the minister of marine try his hand at negotiating an agreement of this kind.[181]

Bülow's defeat was complete. In disgust, he suggested to Tirpitz that he should himself formulate a reply if the question of a naval understanding were raised.[182] Metternich agreed with the Chancellor. Standing between the two ministers on the platform awaiting Edward's train, the ambassador warned Tirpitz that the visit would be the last a British sovereign would ever pay to Berlin, unless he agreed that Bülow should settle the naval question.[183] The subject, however, was not discussed. From the point of view of the British foreign office, the visit was merely a courtesy call or, at the most, a means of improving the atmosphere between the two countries.[184] The circumstances were not encouraging for an initiative on Germany's part, even if Tirpitz had been agreeable. In the Catholic press, whose chief concern was the Bosnian crisis, there was some support for a naval understanding,[185] but recent incidents had given rise to new grievances. Much feeling had been aroused at the end of January by a report that the British fleet would be concentrated in the North Sea.[186] In England, the fear of an invasion became almost hysterical; Gerald du Maurier's play, "An Englishman's Home," had just commenced its sensational run to packed houses.[187] "King Edward brings with him," wrote the *National*

[179] Bülow, Jan. 17. *G. P.*, XXVIII, 66.
[180] Metternich, Jan. 20. *Ibid.*, XXVIII, 73.
[181] Tirpitz, Jan. 20. *Ibid.*, XXVIII, 69.
[182] Bülow, Jan. 11. *Ibid.*, XXVIII, 64.
[183] Bülow, *Denkwürdigkeiten*, II, 419.
[184] Grey, Jan. 7; Hardinge, Feb. 11. *B. D.*, VI, 227, 230–232.
[185] *Kölnische Volkszeitung*, Oct. 26, 1908.
[186] *Germania, Berliner Neueste Nachrichten*, Jan. 30.
[187] *Neue Freie Presse* (Vienna), in *Kölnische Volkszeitung*, Feb. 4; *Daily News*, Feb. 6; *Frankfurter Zeitung*, Feb. 7, London, Feb. 5.

Zeitung (Feb. 7), "the *'Invasions-Spektakelstück,'* *an increase in the naval budget of about 60 million marks,* and the establishment of the so-called home fleet as England's principal naval force." If the moderate *Vossische Zeitung* (Feb. 9) said that Germany

Kommt Eduard?

Kladderadatsch, January 16, 1909.

Figure 23.—A stove, stoked with pro-English papers, has been set up at Brandenburg Gate to provide all the heat that will be necessary for Edward's reception, even if he comes in the coldest weather.

would be responsive if Edward "was cordial as well as polite," the greater part of the press was cool. Even the liberal *Berliner Tageblatt* (Feb. 8) spoke of encirclement. England's jealousy of her prosperity and fear of her commercial competition were, according to the Progressive *Freisinnige Zeitung* (Feb. 9), undeniable facts, toasts and the like to the contrary notwithstanding. The visit, wrote the agrarian *Deutsche Tageszeitung* (Feb. 7), could have no other advantage for Germany than perhaps to strengthen the opposition in England to an immediate attack. While the ultra-Conservative *Reichsbote* (Feb. 7) dismissed even the possibility of a general improvement, the Social Democratic *Vorwärts* (Feb. 7) spoke of the naval question as certain to prevent a rapprochement during the next few years. The nationalist press united in calling upon the government to reject any proposal for naval limitation.[188]

The naval problem became more acute as the Bosnian crisis approached its climax. Scarcely a month elapsed after Edward left Berlin before his government asked parliament for funds to build eight instead of six dreadnoughts during the next fiscal year. No official spokesman ever painted so dark a picture of Germany's naval program as did McKenna, the first civil lord of the admiralty; the accumulation of materials long in advance of their need and the unexpected speed of construction showed, he said, the completion of thirteen capital ships instead of nine, as announced earlier, by 1911.[189] This forecast was doubtless exaggerated, but it convinced parliament and increased the fear for England's control of the sea. "Our sea supremacy is in peril," affirmed the *Daily Mail* (March 17). Germany, wrote the liberal imperialist *Daily Chronicle* (March 17), had both the means and the determination to challenge the British control of the seas. The Conservative *Pall Mall Gazette* (March 17) agreed that the "German naval tortoise" might overtake the "British hare." England, according to the Conservative *Standard* (March

[188] *National Zeitung*, Feb. 8; *Berliner Neueste Nachrichten*, Feb. 9; *Münchener Neueste Nachrichten*, in *Tägliche Rundschau*, Feb. 9; *Hamburger Nachrichten*, Feb. 9.

[189] Before McKenna's speech, Metternich had assured Grey that the thirteen warships would not be completed earlier than the close of 1912. Grey, however, claimed that the admiralty had included large cruisers as well as dreadnoughts in its estimate. Grey, March 10, 17. *B. D.*, VI, 241–243. Metternich's statements were repeated by Tirpitz to the budget committee of the Reichstag, March 17. *Ibid.*, VI, 250.

17), no longer possessed even a parity with Germany in fighting effectiveness.   By the spring of 1909, Germany had finally awakened, as the authors of the naval policy intended, the English to the dangers of her hostility.   "The English people," wrote

Simplicissimus, April 26, 1909.

Figure 24.—The psychiatrists have a new kind of delirium to study in England.

the *Berliner Tageblatt* (March 19), "realize fully perhaps for the first time, that we may become a dangerous enemy." Among the Social Democrats, Centrists, and liberals, there was considerable support for an understanding, but Crowe, the leader of the anti-German group in the British foreign office, doubted their practical influence.[190] Nor were the English in a mood to sue for Germany's friendship, as Tirpitz had calculated. Confident that their financial superiority would be the decisive factor, they accepted the challenge, built more warships, and conserved their continental friendships. Tirpitz' defeat of Bülow meant that the completion of the naval program had, at least for the next few years, become an end in itself.

The Franco-German accord and King Edward's visit had caused, in the meantime, a temporary confusion in the international alignment. Izvolski complained, à propos of a communiqué to the German press after Edward's departure, that England had joined Germany and that France had established "better relations" with Berlin. In London, there was no thought of abandoning Russia, but Hardinge believed that Bülow "would, under certain circumstances, act with France and ourselves in the Near East. . . ."[191] Russia's fear of isolation and England's illusions were soon moderated or dispelled. Germany still stood squarely behind Aehrenthal as Serbia's excitement brought the Bosnian crisis to a head. In contrast to her earlier reticence, Austria now confided her intentions to Germany with complete frankness. On February 20, Aehrenthal informed Bülow that he intended shortly to require of Serbia a definite renunciation of aggressive purposes and the cessation of her military preparations. There could be, he said, no question of territorial concessions, but the existing commercial treaty might be extended and Serbia might be permitted the use of a railway through Bosnia to the Adriatic coast. Should the powers fail to secure her consent to these terms, the moment would then arrive for an ultimatum.[192] It was therefore with full knowledge of Austria's purposes that the German Emperor and Chancellor rejected the

190 Crowe's minute, Goschen, March 23. *B. D.*, VI, 248.
191 Nicolson, Feb. 13; Hardinge, Feb. 16. *Ibid.*, VI, 596, 597.
192 *G. P.*, XXVI, 613.

Anglo-French request, which the British foreign office regarded as the ultimate test of Germany's attitude,[193] for their coöperation in making representations in Vienna as well as in Belgrade. Like Austria, Germany would agree to nothing more than a concerted action in the Serbian capital.[194]   Not only was this decision promptly communicated to the press,[195] but the *Norddeutsche* (Feb. 28) calmly announced that the Bosnian question had ceased to exist after Turkey recognized (Feb. 24) the annexation in return for a money payment. The Austro-Serbian question, Bülow insisted, should be settled by direct negotiations without outside interference.[196] Upon Russia's support of Serbia depended the question of peace or war.

While the Austrians and the Germans continued to blame England for their difficulties, the German press praised France's moderation. Her attitude, wrote the agrarian *Deutsche Tageszeitung* (Feb. 24), would assure the localization of an Austro-Serbian war, "for Russia will not intervene against France's advice." She was, according to the Conservative *Post* (Feb. 26), sincerely working for peace. The moderate *Vossische Zeitung* (March 3) regarded her armed support of Russia as highly problematical. "The French people have no intention," wrote the *Kölnische Zeitung* (March 9), "to fight for the establishment of a new Balkan Piedmont. . . ." Since France had not gone to war over Alsace-Lorraine, she could scarcely help Russia, in the opinion of the Catholic *Germania* (March 10), to avenge Buchlau. To the ultra-Conservative *Reichsbote* (March 6), it seemed possible that French money would be used to finance a new revolution if Russia precipitated war, while the *Hamburger Nachrichten* believed that France would prevent a Russian agression.[197] With this confidence in France's reserve, William and, according to his own account, the foreign office were in agreement. "That is the basis of our policy," he said of a French diplomat's opinion that Russia could not be sure of French support in a war for Serbian interests.[198] Nevertheless, he believed that no chances

[193] Hardinge, Feb. 16. *B. D.*, V, 597.
[194] Goschen, Feb. 23. *Ibid.*, V, 617.
[195] *Kölnische Zeitung*, Feb. 23; *N. A. Z.*, Feb. 25.
[196] *G. P.*, XXVI, 640, 642 (March 2).
[197] *Tägliche Rundschau*, March 13.
[198] William II's comments, Marschall, Feb. 24. *G. P.*, XXVI, 620.

should be taken and promptly recommended practically the same procedure that was to be followed in 1914: France should be required to act with Germany in exerting pressure upon Russia and should be warned that Russia's intervention would be followed inexorably by Germany's mobilization. "France," he continued, "must be made to give a clear and binding explanation that she would not make war upon us in this eventuality. Neither immediately nor later. A neutrality declaration will not suffice. If France refuses, we must regard it as a *casus belli;* the Reichstag and the world at large must then be told that she has willed the war by refusing to coöperate with us in the only possible way of maintaining peace." [199]   The foreign office, according to the editors of the *Grosse Politik,* paid no attention to these views; but, after all, they were predicated upon an event—the outbreak of an Austro-Russian war—that did not occur.

At any rate, France was reminded of the consequences if, as a result of the failure of the intercession of the entente powers, Russia failed to restrain the Serbs.[200] Desirous, if possible, of avoiding war, Bülow asked that the German and Austrian newspapers should be reserved toward Russia while the English and the French exerted pressure upon her.[201] The maneuver failed, for Russia, without waiting for the advice of her associates, secured from Serbia a statement (March 10) promising to stop her military preparations and submitting her case to Europe. The Central powers naturally had no intention of yielding to little Serbia. Bülow promptly announced Germany's position through the semi-official press.[202] Under the somewhat deceptive title of *"Kaltes Blut!"* the *Kölnische Zeitung* (March 5) pointed out that Serbia's move had made matters worse, since Russia was obviously behind it. Austria could honorably remain at peace only if Serbia's provocations were not inspired by a great power. Without a prior recognition of the annexation, she could not agree to a conference, but fortunately Russia's weakness and isolation assured a peaceful solution.[203] To the *Norddeutsche* (March

[199] William II's comments, Tschirschky, Feb. 24. *G. P.,* XXVI, 623, 624.
[200] Schoen's memorandum, Feb. 28. *Ibid.,* XXVI, 639.
[201] Bülow, Feb. 25. *Ibid.,* XXVI, 624, 625.
[202] Szögyény, March 6. *Ö.-U. A.,* II, 39, 40.
[203] Clipped by *Berliner Tageblatt, Deutsche Tageszeitung,* March 6.

6), Austria's refusal to consider anything less than direct negotiations with Serbia was "self-evident." "There can be no question of an attempt to intimidate and to humiliate her, for it is certain to be rejected by the Dual Monarchy supported by Germany."[204] Kiderlen had written this article, he told Cambon, "in order to stiffen the people; there has been far too much criticism in the press and elsewhere of Aehrenthal and his policy." Nothing was permitted to disturb Germany's support, neither Cambon's warning that the *Norddeutsche's* statement would be interpreted abroad as meaning a desire for war, nor Austria's dispatch of fifteen more battalions to the Serbian frontier, nor the information that Russia had asked and received assurances of France's support.[205] "What the consequences of our unshakable attachment to Austria may be," wrote Bülow (March 17), "is for us to determine." Germany, William assured Szögyény in Bülow's presence, would support Austria in the event of war.[206]

It was Germany who forced a solution at the price of Russia's humiliation. On March 14, Bülow suggested that Russia should first agree to the annexation which would then, with Austria's consent, be referred to the powers for their approval in a simple exchange of notes.[207] Three days later, William exclaimed, "There! Something definite at last! Now we can go ahead," on a report that the Russian Imperial Council had decided that the country's unpreparedness might make a retreat necessary.[208] Izvolski, however, was not yet ready for a complete surrender. Accepting the German proposal in principle, he also suggested, March 20, that a conference might still meet,[209] an evasive reply which the Germans refused to consider. "So he refuses! An insolent reply," wrote William.[210] The *Norddeutsche* (March 20)

[204] Clipped by *Berliner Neueste Nachrichten, Berliner Tageblatt, Deutsche Tageszeitung*, March 6; *Freisinnige Zeitung, Hamburger Nachrichten, Rheinisch-Westfälische Zeitung*, March 7.
[205] Szögyény, March 6. *Ö.-U. A.*, II, 39, 40; Goschen, March 13. *B. D.*, VI, 678; *G. P.*, XXVI, 657, 658 (March 13); Radolin, March 17. *Ibid.*, XXVI, 574, 575. *Cf.* Fay, *Origins of the World War*, I, 390.
[206] Szögyény, March 16. *Ö.-U. A.*, II, 113, 114.
[207] *G. P.*, XXVI, 669, 670.
[208] William II's comments, Pourtalès. *Ibid.*, XXVI, no. 9451.
[209] Pourtalès, March 20. *Ibid.*, XXVI, 691, 692.
[210] William II's comment. *Ibid.*, XXVI, 692 (March 20).

doubted that the outbreak of an Austro-Serbian war could be averted, but the prospects for its localization were not unfavorable.[211] Within twenty-four hours Russia was told—the note was Kiderlen's work—that she must answer *"ja oder nein"*; a conditional reply would be regarded as a refusal. "We would then permit the affair to take its course." [212] Yet a refusal might not have precipitated war, for Germany was even then weighing an Italian suggestion that a confidential agreement to recognize the annexation might be ratified by a conference,[213] but Izvolski dared not continue his part in this game of bluff. He described the demand as "a peremptory summons" and as a "diplomatic ultimatum of the worst sort," predicting that a refusal would be followed by an Austrian invasion of Serbia. He told Nicolson, the British ambassador, who still favored a strong stand, that this danger could not be faced in view of France's attitude, although he secretly encouraged Serbia to prepare for a future accounting with Austria. A sad ending, wrote Nicolson, when Izvolski surrendered unconditionally.[214] On the issues involved in the Bosnian crisis, the Triple Entente, as Bülow had foreseen, had not maintained a united front. When France quickly accepted Germany's terms, England had no other choice but to abandon her efforts to secure a suitable satisfaction for Serbia. She could do nothing for countries that would not or could not defend themselves.[215] For the first time since the formation of the Entente Cordiale, the Central powers had won an important diplomatic victory.

To a certain extent Bülow's support of Austria had become a cover for a diplomatic offensive against the *Einkreisung*. Bismarck's literal interpretation of the Dual Alliance had been temporarily disregarded. "Here the letter kills," declared the Chancellor in his speech to the Reichstag, March 29. Of course

---

[211] This article, according to the Social Democratic *Vorwärts* (March 20), was exceedingly stupid, since Russia was obviously preparing to retreat.

[212] Bülow, March 21. *G. P.*, XXVI, 694.

[213] That it would help to reconcile Italy to Austria's increased influence in the Balkans was its chief merit from the German point of view. Szögyény, March 22; Aehrenthal, March 23. *Ö.-U. A.*, II, 160, 166, 167.

[214] Nicolson, *Lord Carnock*, p. 301 (March 23).

[215] Metternich, March 25. *G. P.*, XXVI, 709, 710. England, however, helped Serbia to draft the statement in which she agreed to accept the status quo and promised not to encourage an anti-Austrian agitation in Bosnia-Herzegovina.

he stressed the defensive aspect of his policy: the unfavorable consequence to Germany's diplomatic position from an Austrian defeat. There had been, he insisted, nothing like a contest "like that between the two Queens in the *Nibelungenliede*." Both countries had shown the same loyalty, and both should continue to cherish the *Nibelungentreue*.[216] From the crisis, however, Austria was able to derive much comfort. Whatever Germany's initial objections might be, it was fairly certain that her own interests would enable Austria to proceed without effective restraint. Too much had been made of the need to conserve the loyalty of Germany's one dependable ally not to suggest to the Austrian leaders that her aid could be counted upon under all circumstances. To the end of the crisis, the semi-official press continued to encourage these views. "Without attempting in the slightest degree to influence Austria's independent decisions, the Berlin cabinet," wrote the *Politische Korrespondenz,* "has exerted itself in every possible way to fulfil the obligations of a long and close relationship with the Dual Monarchy and to defend the position of the allied powers in the general field of European politics." [217]

If the issue had been clearly presented as one between Germany's and Austria's leadership in the alliance, public opinion would doubtless have declared itself for the former. It was, however, for the great majority of Germans a question of defending the ally to whose fate they were inseparably bound. Where Germany's interests clashed with those of Austria, as in Turkey, the loyalty of the Catholics alone remained unshaken, but this reason for criticism disappeared with the Austro-Turkish agreement of February 24. There would doubtless have been little difference of opinion if the crisis had been restricted to Austria and Serbia, for the latter's nationalist aspirations awakened little sympathy among Germans. Even the Social Democrats, who believed that Serbia's grievances were essentially economic, were cool. Working against the Serbs was the fear shared by a large part of German opinion that the mounting Slavic tide in Austria would, with Russia's aid, overwhelm the German Austrians.

---

[216] *Verhandlungen*, XII Leg. Per., I Sess., p. 7802. The critics of Germany's official foreign policy used this speech later to attack its slavish support of Austria.
[217] *Hamburger Nachrichten*, March 24.

On the main question of supporting Austria at the risk of a general war, only the Catholic press was of one opinion. "We cannot but be ashamed," wrote the *Kölnische Volkszeitung* (March 21) of those newspapers which stood for a narrow interpretation of the alliance, "that there are such faithless fellows in Germany." [218] The liberals were influenced by their traditional sympathy for Austria, their hatred of Russia, and their aversion to war. If the moderate *Vossische Zeitung* (March 6) continued its support of Bülow's policy, if the Progressive *Freisinnige Zeitung* refrained from taking a definite stand, the *Frankfurter Zeitung* (March 4) insisted that Serbia had a right to appeal to the powers and it rejected (March 27) the claim that Austria would be justified in destroying her merely because the circumstances were favorable. The *Berliner Tageblatt* (Feb. 16) was not unsympathetic toward Austria, but it still believed that Aehrenthal's excessive zeal should be restrained. "Is it one of Germany's obligations," it asked, "to agree cheerfully every time Herr von Aehrenthal wishes to hitch the German Empire to Austria's wagon?" The same difference of opinion appeared among the nationalists. To avert the danger of complete isolation, the *Tägliche Rundschau* (March 12) believed that Bismarck would have supported Austria, and the *Deutsche Tageszeitung* (March 21) asserted that only the *Hamburger Nachrichten* and the *Rheinisch-Westfälische Zeitung* among the critics of the official policy needed to be taken seriously and that a strong support of Austria furnished the only hope of maintaining peace. The principal issue, according to the *Berliner Neueste Nachrichten* (March 4), was the survival of the Central powers. In Harden's opinion, the chief reason for supporting Austria was the effort of the Triple Entente to repeat the success won at Algeciras. "That must not be." [219] Few nationalists objected in principle even to the use of force in the settlement of Austria's account with Serbia, but many continued to attack a policy that would involve Germany in her quarrel with Russia. To the end, the *Hamburger Nachrichten* was the leading exponent of this point of view. It agreed (Feb. 24) with Russia that the viola-

---

218 Cf. *Germania*, Feb. 26.
219 Harden, "Für Oesterreich," *Zukunft*, March 13.

tion of the Treaty of Berlin required more than an economic satisfaction for Serbia and it insisted that Germany should mediate between the two great powers. For Germany to fight in behalf of Austria's grievances would be, in its opinion, absurd. "We would like to see the Reichstag," it wrote, "vote credits for such a campaign." *"Los von Österreich!"* would be the cry of all Germany. When the semi-official press pledged Germany's loyalty, the same journal called upon the government (March 7) to explain its attitude to the Reichstag. Would the "blood and property of Germans be risked in a European war of incalculable consequences for Austria's Balkan interests?" *"Nein!"* was its own answer (March 19). The Pan-German press was equally hostile to an unqualified support of Austria and more definitely in favor of a rapprochement with Russia. The chauvinist *Rheinisch-Westfälische Zeitung* (March 4) could see no reason for pulling Austria's chestnuts out of the Balkan fire, which England had kindled. In its opinion, Germany should remain strictly within the letter of the alliance, and, in return for her diplomatic support, she should secure guaranties for the supremacy of the Germans in Austria. Compared to Germany's vassal-like services, France, according to the *Alldeutsche Blätter* (March 12), had maintained an independent attitude toward England and Russia. Against the argument that Austria must be supported to avoid isolation, it quoted Bülow's claim that Germany could stand alone. War might be avoided for the present, "but a precedent has been established which will seriously limit our freedom of action toward Austria-Hungary in the future." By far the worst result of Germany's policy, according to the *Deutsche Zeitung,* was the fact that it stamped her as a deadly enemy of Slavdom in Russia's eyes.[220] Her geographical situation was responsible, in the opinion of L. Raschdau, a retired diplomat, for enough difficulties, without needlessly increasing them by supporting every change in the Ballplatz' foreign policy.[221] Among the army officers there was, wrote the Belgian envoy, little eagerness for a war resulting from Aehrenthal's adventurous disposition.[222] The *Leipziger Neueste Nachrichten* would have

[220] *Hamburger Nachrichten,* March 10.
[221] *Deutsches Volk,* in *Tägliche Rundschau,* March 13.
[222] *Belgische Dokumente,* IV, 161 (March 19).

Germany follow Austria's example at Algeciras,[223] and the *Ost-deutsche Rundschau* wrote that nothing could be more contrary to German interests than Austria's transformation into a great Slavic power—the inevitable result of her victory.[224]

On March 18, three days before Bülow addressed the final demand to Russia, the chauvinist *Rheinisch-Westfälische Zeitung* confessed that its final judgment would depend upon the results: "Success will be decisive." For obvious reasons, the government advised against the celebration of Russia's surrender as a diplomatic triumph. "There should be," wrote the Berlin correspondent of the *Kölnische Zeitung* (March 29), "no distinction between the victors and the vanquished. All Europe has contributed to the victory of peace and common sense; even Russia has subordinated her Pan-Slavic aspirations to the general interest." For the most part, however, public opinion reacted in accordance with the tendencies developed during the protracted crisis. Supporters of the official policy exulted over the defeat administered to the powers which had attempted to encircle Germany. "The campaign ends," wrote Schiemann, "with a victory along the entire line." [225] The moderate *Vossische Zeitung* (March 29) joined in the chorus. "The Central European *bloc* has so clearly demonstrated its superior power that they will certainly hesitate a long time before challenging it again. . . . Only the frank and loyal coöperation of Germany and Austria-Hungary averted a catastrophe. Whether Germany was obligated by the alliance to support the latter is of no importance." According to the Catholic *Kölnische Volkszeitung* (March 30), the alliance had again shown that it was the most effective guarantee of peace: "After many years of weakness, Germany has again become the decisive factor in the council of nations, and, at the same time, she has not only served Austria but also her own interests."

Among the nationalists there was, of course, much rejoicing. The *Berliner Neueste Nachrichten* (March 29) agreed enthusiastically that the crisis had been a test of strength between the

---

[223] *Hamburger Nachrichten*, March 19.

[224] *Tägliche Rundschau*, March 9. Dissatisfaction with their allies was, according to this provincial journal, bringing France and Germany together.

[225] *Kreuz-Zeitung*, March 31. Schiemann, *Deutschland und die Grosse Politik*, IX, 122.

two diplomatic groups. "Germany," wrote one observer, "has won a war without firing a shot. . . ." The death of Francis Joseph, he was confident, would not now mean the dissolution of the Dual Monarchy.[226] "The imposing structure of the entente has shown itself to be nothing more than a house of cards," observed an important nationalist review. "One word from the German Chancellor, 'Germany stands behind her ally,' has caused its collapse."[227] "Germany, the giant," boasted another commentator, "grasped her sword and there was peace on earth."[228] The *Rheinisch-Westfälische Zeitung* changed its tone. While it foresaw a vigorous counterattack by the Triple Entente, it welcomed (March 30) "the proof, after a long time, of Germany's still unbroken power. . . ." But to most of those who had questioned the wisdom of an unconditional support of Austria, the future still seemed dark. The liberal *Frankfurter Zeitung* (March 29) saw no reason to congratulate Aehrenthal: "Such a success may be highly prized in professional diplomatic circles, but politics is not a game; when it is a question not only of the driver but also of the fate of the carriage and that of millions, it is permissible to ask for greater caution and conscientiousness. Whether the victor will enjoy his success is altogether doubtful." That Austria would ever reciprocate Germany's gratuitous services seemed unlikely to the *Hamburger Nachrichten* (March 30), but this journal foresaw "the sharpened hostility of the other great powers." Expecting the Near Eastern crisis to continue, Raschdau believed that "the sooner we recover our freedom of action, the better it will be."[229] Ernst Reventlow, now the editor of the *Alldeutsche Blätter,* condemned Bülow for appealing to the *Nibelungentreue:* "Germany has no reason for enthusiasm, since the Triple Entente will soon correct the sources of its weakness."[230] The credit for Bülow's success, according to the liberal *Berliner Tageblatt* (March 30), belonged to the army, not to his management of foreign affairs.

[226] Arendt, "Die auswärtige Politik Deutschlands," *Gegenwart,* April 17.
[227] "Zu Bülows Rücktritt," *Grenzboten,* July 8.
[228] Walburg, "Fürst Bülows Rücktritt und dessen Einwirkung auf die internationale Lage," *Deutsche Revue,* III, 138, 139 (Aug. 1, 1909).
[229] *Deutsches Volk,* in *Tägliche Rundschau,* March 30.
[230] Reventlow, "Nach dem Fest," *Gegenwart,* May 29.

The victory seemed complete. With Germany's powerful aid and encouragement, Aehrenthal had forced Europe to accept his violation of the Treaty of Berlin and to recognize Austria's title to Bosnia-Herzegovina. The Central powers had imposed their will upon the Triple Entente largely because Germany had been prepared to fight, as she had not been in 1906. The weakness of the Triple Entente had been revealed by the unwillingness of the Western powers to fight for Russia's interests; [231] there would be, for a time, little talk of "encirclement" in the German press. Historians now agree that the victory was more brilliant than real. Even Bülow's hope that it would restore him to the Emperor's good graces was disappointed. On the contrary, it convinced William that Bülow was not indispensable; when the Conservatives refused to approve the inheritance tax—the essential feature of the Chancellor's program of financial reforms—and thus dissolved the government's majority in the Reichstag, his resignation was accepted. [232] The diplomatic victory created, in fact, more problems than it solved. In Austria, the South Slavs became more troublesome than ever. Serbia, despite her promise to the contrary, soon began through secret societies to undermine Austria's authority in Bosnia-Herzegovina. Aehrenthal and the army leaders were dissatisfied, for they knew that the Serbs would not abandon their dreams of an outlet to the Adriatic and of national unity. [233] Mobilization had, in fact, been decided (March 29) when the news arrived of Russia's and Serbia's surrender. [234] Although Aehrenthal withdrew the order, his belief that Serbia must eventually be crushed remained a permanent danger to peace. In spite of these ultimately unfavorable results, Bülow deserves the credit for maintaining peace, if it is true that Russia's surrender alone could keep Austria from attacking Serbia. [235] This, however, was not the whole truth; without Bülow's support and encouragement, the danger that the Austrian armies would march surely would not have been great, and the attitude

---

[231] *Belgische Dokumente*, IV, 203 (May 16, 1909).
[232] Oncken, *Vorgeschichte des Weltkrieges*, II, 647, 651.
[233] Brandenburg, *From Bismarck to the World War*, p. 335.
[234] Fay, *Origins of the World War*, I, 392.
[235] *Ibid.*, I, 390.

of the German Chancellor was largely the result of his confidence that the Triple Entente would not accept his challenge.[236]   For the moment, England and France did not believe that their vital interests were involved, but Russia's defeat was itself a powerful reason for strengthening their ties with her.   Nicolson began to urge the need of a stronger union and Crowe believed that Germany intended to establish her hegemony in Europe as a prelude to a war with England.[237]   Izvolski awaited an opportunity to avenge what he regarded as Aehrenthal's duplicity.   The imponderables were more than ever weighted against the Central powers.   The idea of an inevitable conflict between the Teuton and Slav became a serious obstacle to a significant improvement in Russo-German relations.   In Western Europe, public opinion accepted Germany's support of her ally's treaty violations and treatment of Serbia as proof of aggressive purposes.   At home, the confidence in the strength of the Dual Alliance and in the weakness of the Triple Entente constituted, for the nationalists at least, a standing temptation to new adventures.

After a steady deterioration of Germany's diplomatic position, Bülow at last had restored Germany's prestige to a peak which it had not attained since Bismarck.   Public opinion, for the moment, forgot its doubts of the government's capacity.   To William the future seemed assured.   He may not have told Bülow that he intended to be his own foreign minister, but it is evident that he did not regard Bethmann-Hollweg's lack of experience in international affairs as a barrier to his appointment.   As long as positive proof was lacking that the circle of hostile powers had been broken through and until Germany secured some of her imperialist interests, there remained the possibility of a revival of serious dissatisfaction.   To Bülow and, still more, to Bethmann-Hollweg, it was clear that her enhanced prestige would mean comparatively little without a definite improvement in the relations with one or more members of the Triple Entente.   France received comparatively little consideration, although nothing like the accord of February 9, 1909 existed with England or Russia.

---

[236] In support of his assurance to Jules Cambon that Germany did not desire war, Kiderlen-Wächter argued that Russia's defeat would probably mean a new revolution and the establishment of a republic.   Goschen, March 13.   B. D., V, 678.

[237] Oncken, *Vorgeschichte des Weltkrieges*, II, 646, 647.

That her moderate attitude had been an important factor in the successful conclusion of the crisis, that the *revanche* sentiment was admittedly at a low ebb,[238] and that many Frenchmen were sincerely afraid of being involved in a war with Germany for English or Russian interests failed to shake the conviction that nothing could be done with her. The exchange of compliments between Pichon and William in speeches to their respective parliaments in the autumn of 1909 had no significant results.[239] The provision for economic coöperation in Morocco was productive of little more than friction.[240] In return for a loan, the Mannesmann brothers secured from Mulai Hafid extensive mining concessions, which conflicted with the interests of the French *Union des Mines;* with the aid of a vociferous nationalist and conservative press, they persuaded the government that its duty was to support their claims.[241] The obstacles to a real Franco-German rapprochement were doubtless insurmountable. Tardieu stated them without any circumlocution in the *Deutsche Revue:* France's loyalty to the past and Germany's inability to forget that Europe had once been at her feet.[242] The satisfaction of French public opinion at the unfavorable reaction in Alsace to the law of 1910— its failure to grant complete autonomy was the principal grievance—seemed to mean that the French were unwilling to accept a peaceful settlement of the problem.[243] The agreement of February 9 had marked, it was evident, the high tide of the Franco-German reconciliation.

In spite of Germany's large responsibility for her humiliation, Russia was regarded as a better prospect. Bülow discountenanced Austria's idea of a revived Alliance of the Three Emperors, but

---

[238] "Russland, Frankreich und Deutschland," *Historisch-Politische Blätter,* vol. 144, p. 325 (Aug. 1909); Heyek, "Mehr Achtung vor Frankreich," *Grenzboten,* 1910, I, 386, 387.

[239] Oncken, *Vorgeschichte des Weltkrieges,* II, 683.

[240] England, fearing its consequences to her own interests, did nothing to assure its success. *Ibid.,* II, 685.

[241] Twenty per cent of the *Union's* shares were held by Krupp, Gelsenkirchen, and Thyssen, the German steel magnates. T. Wolff, *The Eve of 1914* (N. Y., 1936), pp. 33–35.

[242] Tardieu, "Vergangenheit und Zukunft," *Deutsche Revue,* 1910, I, 153, 154. Tardieu, nevertheless, had not hesitated to exploit the idea of a Franco-German coöperation, in the hope of securing compensation from his own government in the notorious Ngoko-Sangha affair. Hallgarten, *Vorkriegs Imperialismus,* pp. 234–237.

[243] *Kreuz-Zeitung,* June 22, 1910. Schiemann, *Deutschland und die Grosse Politik,* X, 243.

his directions that the press should not talk too much of a victory at Russia's expense showed the trend of his thought.[244]   By placing the responsibility for a refusal of his final demand upon Izvolski, the Chancellor had attempted to distinguish between the Russian state and its chief minister. The *Norddeutsche* (April 2) even represented Russia as having worked with Germany in the interest of peace.[245]   However, the Russian press was more hostile than ever, and William was moved to lecture the Tsar upon the duty of monarchs to disregard the excesses of a venal public opinion.[246]   An improvement in Russo-German relations was nevertheless not impossible. Nicholas, it is true, told Nicolson, the British ambassador: "We must keep closer and closer together," [247] but his government could not easily forget that England and France had failed Russia at a critical moment. Until the Triple Entente was strengthened, it was manifestly Russia's interest to avoid serious difficulties with Germany and even to entertain the idea of a rapprochement. A skillful diplomacy might have used the situation to Germany's profit, especially after Izvolski had been replaced by Tcharykov and Sazonov (September 1909), neither of whom had his personal grievances. An opening occurred during the summer of 1909, when the Tsar assured William that he would agree to no arrangements against Germany during his visit to London.[248] "The time is clearly past," wrote one observer, "when Germany had reason to fear 'encirclement,' for all of the powers are again competing for our friendship." [249]

Under Bethmann-Hollweg, Germany at first assumed a waiting attitude. What moved her to action were Russia's intrigues in the Balkans, Italy, and Austria. She was hard at work for a Serbo-Bulgarian rapprochement as a barrier to Austria's expansion, and with Bulgaria she concluded an alliance (Dec. 1909). At Racconigi, Nicholas reached an agreement with Victor Em-

244 Bülow, March 29, 1909. *G. P.*, XXVI, 722; Szögyény, April 3. *Ö.-U. A.*, II, 240.
245 *Post, National Zeitung, Germania,* April 2.
246 William II, June 8, 1909. Semenoff, *Correspondance entre Guillaume II et Nicolas II,* pp. 253, 254.
247 Nicolson, *Lord Carnock,* p. 313 (April 14, 1909).
248 Schoen, June 18, 1909. *G. P.*, XXVI, 823.
249 *P. J.,* vol. 137, p. 169 (July 1909).

manuel providing for the defense of the status quo in the Balkans and for the division of the profits from any change among the Balkan states themselves.[250] William was sufficiently aroused to urge a firm union with Roumania and Turkey,[251] but the foreign office, where a check upon Austria's aggressive tendencies was perhaps not unwelcome, did nothing until Russia adopted a conciliatory attitude toward Austria. The fear of an Austro-Russian rapprochement was not a new experience for German diplomats.[252] From such incidents as the mention of Germany as the enemy during the maneuvers of the Russian Imperial Guard, the immediate patching up of the differences between London and St. Petersburg when Germany attempted to arrange a direct understanding with the Shah, and Russia's high price for her consent to the completion of the Bagdad Railway, the Germans felt that the Russian and Austrian ministers might conclude that the distance between St. Petersburg and Vienna was less than between St. Petersburg and Berlin.[253]

By the autumn of 1910 both Russia and Germany were ready to resume conversations; arrangements were accordingly made for a visit by the Tsar and Sazonov to Potsdam for November 4, 5. The conversations, from the German point of view, should cover the most important questions. Progress in fact was made toward an understanding. It was agreed that both countries had a common interest in the maintenance of Turkey's integrity and of the status quo in the Balkans, although Sazonov acknowledged Russia's desire for the "freedom" of the Balkan peoples. The Russian minister was even receptive to a compromise relating to Persia and the Bagdad Railway. To secure Russia's disinterestedness in the construction of the section from Bagdad to the Persian Gulf—the question that most interested the German diplomats—Sazonov was assured that Germany would seek no railway or telegraph concessions in Persia, that Russia might

---

[250] Italy, at the same time, was about to conclude an understanding with Austria which envisaged a disturbance of the status quo in the Balkans, on the condition that she should be consulted and compensated for an advance of Austria's influence. Brandenburg, *From Bismarck to the World War,* p. 355.

[251] *Ibid.,* p. 354.

[252] Tschirschky, Jan. 1909. *G. P.,* XXVII, 453.

[253] Posadowsky, Aug. 12, 1910; Bethmann-Hollweg, Sept. 15, 1910. *Ibid.,* XXVII, 511, 541.

construct a connecting line with Teheran, and that her interests would be safeguarded in any change in the control of the terminal section of the Bagdad Railway. Of greater importance for Russia's diplomatic interests was Germany's attitude toward Austria. "We can assure Sazonov," wrote Kiderlen, "that we are neither obligated nor willing to speak for Austria's ambitious plans in the Near East." Bethmann repeated substantially the same assurance to the Russian minister, although he doubted that Austria really harbored aggressive purposes.[254] The meeting ended without anything having been put in writing, but Germany had conceded so much and asked for so little that it should not have been difficult to complete a definite, though limited, agreement. But she had withheld her most significant condition until the last: in return for a written assurance that "we are neither obligated nor willing to enter the lists" for Austria's ambitions, Germany asked Russia to pledge herself in writing not to favor "England's anti-German policy."[255] This, however, Sazonov refused to do, for fear that it would destroy the Anglo-Russian Entente; nor did his offer of an oral statement satisfy Kiderlen. It would not, said the German minister, be an equivalent to the definite assurance that Germany "would not only refuse to support an Austrian attack upon Russia but also a policy even indirectly hostile to Russia in the Balkans."[256] Nevertheless, Bethmann assured the Reichstag, December 10, 1910, that the Potsdam conversations had resulted in a definite agreement that neither power would enter a hostile combination against the other,[257] but scarcely a week had elapsed before he instructed Pourtalès, the German ambassador in St. Petersburg, to abandon the effort to secure a written assurance.[258] In Kiderlen's opinion, Sazonov's attitude revealed England's purposes, for they must be known to him; it could best be described by the familiar saying, *Nur grüss mich nicht unter den Linden*.[259] Not only had Germany failed to weaken the Anglo-Russian Entente and to secure a written

---

[254] Kiderlen-Wächter, Oct. 30; Bethmann-Hollweg, Nov. 8. *G. P.*, XXVII, 832, 841
[255] Pourtalès, Dec. 2. *Ibid.*, XXVII, 859.
[256] Kiderlen-Wächter, Dec. 4. *Ibid.*, XXVII, 861.
[257] *Verhandlungen*, XII Leg. Per., II Sess., V, 3561.
[258] Bethmann-Hollweg, Dec. 19. *G. P.*, XXVII, 880.
[259] Kiderlen-Wächter, Dec. 12 (?), 20. *Ibid.*, XXVII, 878, 882.

"The flying Dutchman"

Kladderadatsch, June 20, 1909.

Figure 25.—Mother Britannica continues to tell her "little ones" the most hair-raising ghost stories.

agreement even upon specific questions, but the Potsdam visit, Bethmann's speech, and the publication by the London *Evening Times* (Jan. 6, 1911) [260] of the alleged terms of a Russo-German agreement burdened her with the odium of another attack upon the Triple Entente.

England played an even more important part than Russia in the effort to translate Germany's diplomatic victory into solid diplomatic advantages.   While a waiting attitude had been maintained toward Russia, negotiations were immediately initiated with London as soon as the tension in the Balkans declined. Again, the circumstances seemed favorable.   For the first time in many years, it was felt that Germany could approach England on equal terms and that the interests of both countries would be served by a rapprochement.   There were friends of an understanding among the higher nobility, the middle-class liberals, the Centrists, and the Social Democrats. [261]   Even the naval scare in England was not regarded as a serious obstacle.   Thanks to the use of official influence, the press remained comparatively quiet, and the invasion scare in England must have suggested to many Germans that England was or soon would be ready for a satisfactory arrangement. [262]   Bülow had done what he could, in spite of Tirpitz' obstruction, to keep the door open for a resumption of negotiations by stressing, in his speeches to the Reichstag, the community of interests between the two countries in many parts of the world.   To British diplomats he had waxed indignant at Aehrenthal's irresponsible conduct.   Even William, momentarily impressed by the danger of driving England too far, agreed that an attempt to reach an understanding should be made, and Moltke, who felt that the Bosnian crisis had shown the need of a greater emphasis upon the army, sided with Bülow against Tirpitz during the conference of June 3, 1909. [263]   With Bethmann-Hollweg also in favor of a naval agreement, the min-

[260] *G. P.*, XXVII, 890n.

[261] Rosendahl, "Deutschland und England im Ausbau ihrer Flotten," *Deutsche Revue*, II, 279 (June 1).

[262] Reventlow, *Was würde Bismarck sagen: zur deutschen Flotte, zu England-Deutschland* (Berlin, 1909); *Germania*, April 8, 1909; Goschen, April 16, 1909, July 29, 1910. *B. D.*, VI, 265, 266, 499, 500.

[263] Brandenburg, *From Bismarck to the World War*, pp. 344, 346.

ister of the marine became somewhat less intransigeant. For the next few years, Tirpitz spoke not infrequently of a ratio between the two fleets and of other projects that would have reduced the speed of the hitherto sacred building program.[264] The important thing was the diplomatic price which England could be persuaded to pay. Only in return for an assurance of her neutrality or for a weakening of her ties with France and Russia were the diplomats and statesmen willing to concede anything of importance in the naval question. Bülow had sketched the maximum and minimum terms during his last approach to London, although the British foreign office's coolness discouraged their presentation.[265] The terms of a naval agreement, said Tirpitz during the conference of June 3, must depend upon the political accord.[266] From Bucharest, Kiderlen-Wächter, who was soon to be placed in charge of the foreign office, wrote that the question was essentially political and advised that a rapprochement of some kind should be arranged before the naval experts were drawn into the discussion.[267] Although Bethmann did say that Germany's proposals should not be manifestly impossible,[268] there is no reason to believe that he objected to the use of the naval question for the weakening of the Triple Entente. Like his advisers, he insisted upon a definite agreement, rejecting not only Grey's suggestion that a repudiation of aggressive purposes by each of the great powers would lessen the tension between the two diplomatic groups but the offer of a written assurance that England harbored no hostile designs against Germany as well.[269]

Again Germany had overestimated her own bargaining power and underestimated the vitality of the Triple Entente. The British remained cold to the argument that only a political accord could persuade the German people to accept a naval agreement. It was addressed to men who usually professed a low opinion of

[264] Brandenburg, *From Bismarck to the World War*, p. 350.

[265] *Ibid.*, p. 344.

[266] *G. P.*, XXVIII, 177.

[267] Jäckh, *Kiderlen-Wächter*, II, 48–59 (Sept. 1909). *Cf.* Bethmann-Hollweg, Aug. 13, 1909; Schoen, Nov. 1, 1909. *G. P.*, XXVIII, 214, 253; Goschen, Aug. 21, 1909. *B. D.*, VI 283.

[268] *G. P.*, XXVIII, 231 (Sept. 16, 1909).

[269] Grey's minutes, Aug. 21, 31, 1909; Goschen, Oct. 28, 1910. *B. D.*, VI, 284, 288, 539, 540. Metternich, Oct. 26; Bethmann-Hollweg, Oct. 27, 1909. *G. P.*, XXVIII, 539, 540.

the political importance of German public opinion.[270]   Few Englishmen were willing to agree that the recognition of British naval supremacy was a great concession, for they regarded it as axiomatic.[271]   It was, from their point of view, no concession at all.   Even Kiderlen, who was regarded as a *Realpolitiker* of Bismarck's school, miscalculated the strength of Germany's cards; the problems of imperial defense made, he thought, Germany's benevolent neutrality just as valuable to England as England's was to Germany.   Until the English awoke to this fact, Germany could afford to wait.[272]   At one time, William suggested that England should guarantee the possession of Alsace-Lorraine in return for underwriting her control of India.[273]   Given the feeling in London that Germany's ultimate purpose was to create a situation in which she could "deal with third powers without the possibility of England's intervening" and to reëstablish her hegemony in Europe,[274] the prospects for a successful conclusion were slight.   The German position on the naval question itself was sufficient to prevent an understanding: never was there any thought of reducing the total number of warships.   "A reduction by an agreement with England," Metternich was instructed to inform Grey, "is quite impossible, in view of the state of public opinion in the press and in the Reichstag."[275]   This "communication," wrote Crowe, "amounts to the funeral ceremony of the whole negotiation."[276]   The results were indeed meager. Grey might have given a written assurance that England had no aggressive purposes, but he was unalterably opposed to a promise of neutrality or to a general agreement which would impair England's relations with France and Russia.   Nevertheless, he offered an undefined political accord, in the hope of reducing the tension between the two diplomatic groups when Germany re-

270 Goschen, Sept. 3, Oct. 15, 1909. *B. D.,* VI, 290, 293; Bethmann-Hollweg's comments, Oct. 15. *G. P.,* XXVIII, 242. *Cf.* Kiderlen-Wächter, Sept. 1909. Jäckh, *Kiderlen-Wächter,* II, 48–59.

271 Hardinge's minute, Oct. 24, 1909; Goschen, Oct. 15, Nov. 4, 1909. *B. D.,* VI, 293, 299, 304–307; *G. P.,* XXVIII, 240, 241.

272 Jäckh, *Kiderlen-Wächter,* II, 77 (Nov. 23, 1909).

273 *G. P.,* XXVIII, 353, 354 (July 26, 1910).

274 Hardinge, April 1909; Goschen, April 16, 22; Crowe's minute, Goschen, Nov. 25, 1909. *B. D.,* VI, 265, 266, 315, 450, 536, 537, 823–826.

275 Bethmann-Hollweg, Nov. 10, 1909. *G. P.,* XXVIII, 268.

276 Crowe's minute (Jan. 3, 1910); Goschen, Dec. 29, 1909. *B. D.,* VI, 315, 316.

Kladderadatsch, January 2, 1910.

Figure 26.—Panicky Englishmen see in Halley's Comet an evil omen for the new year—for it appeared in 1066, when William the Conqueror landed on the English coast.

plied not unfavorably to his proposal for the exchange of information between the two admiralties relating to the laying down of keels, to the rate of construction, and to the weight of armaments.[277] Bethmann was still uninterested, since it contained no assurance against England's support of France and Russia. Tension, in his opinion, would not diminish "unless France knows that she cannot count upon England's support for a restless policy."[278] Germany's suggestions varied between a neutrality agreement and a looser arrangement for consultation in regard to questions of mutual concern,[279] but, as it became clear that a political accord was impossible, she lost all interest in a naval understanding.[280] Only the desultory negotiations for the exchange of technical information were continued. In June 1911 an agreement in principle was reached on this lesser question.[281]

More harm than good had resulted from the effort to translate the diplomatic victory into tangible advantages. It had strengthened suspicion and had helped to tighten the Triple Entente. The diplomats were by no means indifferent to the growth of anti-German feeling; they tried as never before to convince foreign opinion that German policy was essentially moderate.[282] Bernstorff, the ambassador to the United States, publicly denied that the Pan-Germans exerted any influence upon the government and asserted that they did not even represent German opinion.[283] In London, Metternich was quoted as saying that his country was seeking not new territorial possessions but only new

277 Kühlmann, March 31, 1910. *G. P.*, XXVIII, 313; Grey, July 29, 1910. *B. D.*, VI, 501, 502: "They are none of them to be believed on their word," was Crowe's eloquent comment. Crowe's minute, Goschen, Oct. 16, 1910. *Ibid.*, VI, 531.
278 Bethmann-Hollweg's comments, Metternich, Dec. 17, 1910. *G. P.*, XXVIII, 387.
279 Bethmann-Hollweg, Aug. 13, Oct. 27, 28, 1909, May 9, 1911. *Ibid.*, XXVIII, 214, 245, 248, 414.
280 Her offer to refrain from increasing her existing program was scarcely an acceptable substitute. *Ibid.*, XXVIII, 372, 373 (Oct. 1910). *Cf.* Goschen, Oct. 16, 1910. *B. D.*, VI, 531.
281 Kiderlen-Wächter, June 27, 1911. *G. P.*, XXVIII, 423.
282 It was to be hoped, wrote one observer, that the diplomats would succeed in convincing Europe that the German armaments existed for the maintenance of peace. O. Corbach, "Europäische Politik," *Gegenwart*, Feb. 5, 1910.
283 Bethmann-Hollweg acknowledged later that the Pan-Germans had acquired a strong following among the Conservatives and the National Liberals. Bethmann-Hollweg, *Reflections on the World War* (London, 1920), p. 28. Their protest caused Schoen to circularize Germany's representatives abroad and, in a speech to the Reichstag, to exclude the *Alldeutsche Blätter* from his repudiation of irresponsible publicists. Class, *Wider den Strom*, pp. 146-148; *Verhandlungen*, XII Leg. Per., II Sess., p. 209 (Dec. 10, 1910).

markets, "with the weapons of the intellect, of industry, and of skill. . . ." [284] Pourtalès, the ambassador to Russia, spoke in a toast on William's birthday of Germany's policy during the recent crisis as a service to peace. [285] Bethmann was not entirely confident even of Austria's loyalty. The possibility of an Austro-Russian rapprochement had been one of the reasons for the negotiations with Russia. "Germany," William reminded his ally, September 21, 1910, during a visit to Vienna, "stood by her in shining armor." In the Cretan question, Aehrenthal again showed a disturbing tendency to assume the lead in the alliance. [286] So alarmed was Bethmann at the danger of isolation that he wished to keep from Austria the full extent of the friction between Germany and Russia. If a general war had to come, it was, in his opinion, in Germany's interest that it should begin with a Russian attack upon Austria, in order to assure the latter's participation. [287]

These doubts and fears were not generally shared by public opinion; Germany's diplomatic position seemed immensely improved since the summer of 1908. The Triple Entente, though still intact, was regarded as too weak to justify serious alarm, and the "encirclement" scare had been followed by a new feeling of confidence. There was reason for satisfaction in France's lukewarm support of Russia's Balkan ambitions. England's influence upon the continent occasioned some concern, and the formation of the Union of South Africa with General Botha, recently Britain's enemy, as its Prime Minister disappointed the hope that the British Empire would have its own Alsace-Lorraine problem. [288] For the moment, however, England's purposes were not regarded as aggressive. Even her naval scare, which Bethmann attributed to the Conservative politicians and press or to official influence—a view that drew a strong protest from Grey [289] —indicated a defensive psychology. A rumor that the Triple

[284] *Kreuz-Zeitung,* Feb. 2, 1910. Schiemann, *Deutschland und die Grosse Politik,* X, 42.

[285] Germany, wrote the *Alldeutsche Blätter* (Feb. 5, 1910), should not thus be exposed to "the hilarity of nations."

[286] Wedel, *Austro-German Diplomatic Relations,* p. 120.

[287] *G. P.,* XXVIII, 511 (Sept. 15, 1910).

[288] H. Delbrück, "Weshalb baut Deutschland Kriegschiffe," *P. J.,* vol. 138, p. 155 (Oct. 1909); "König Eduard VII," *Historisch-Politische Blätter,* vol. 145, p. 860 (June 1910).

[289] Goschen, Oct. 12, Dec. 2, 1910. *B. D.,* VI, 523, 524, 558.

Entente was about to be transformed into a quadruple alliance by the inclusion of Japan was noted simply as a news item.[290] Edward VII's death, it was generally agreed, meant the passing of the leader of the "encirclement" conspiracy.[291] Most comforting, however, was the successful conclusion of the Bosnian crisis, Austria's revival as a great power,[292] and, to no small extent, the implications of the Tsar's visit to Potsdam.[293] The year 1910, according to the official organ of the Pan-Germans, would mean for Germany the beginning of a new epoch, just as 1904 had for France and England. "For the first time in many years," it concluded, "we Pan-Germans can regard the present and the future with a certain satisfaction." [294]

---

[290] *Grenzboten,* 1910, III, 148 (July 18).

[291] "König Eduard," *Ibid.,* 1910, II, 280 (May 8); "König Eduard VII," *Historisch-Politische Blätter,* vol. 145, pp. 862, 863 (June 1910).

[292] Grabowsky, "Das neue Europa," *Grenzboten,* 1910, I, 380 (Feb. 19).

[293] *Kreuz-Zeitung,* Dec. 28, 1910. Schiemann, *Deutschland und die Grosse Politik,* X, 414; "Annus Domini 1910," *Gegenwart,* Jan. 1, 1911.

[294] *A. B.,* Dec. 17, 1910.

CHAPTER XII

Agadir, 1911: a Challenge and a Retreat

Sobald es der Welt klar werden wurde, dass es Frankreich geglückt, geradezu im Schutz der Algecirasakte seine alte Pläne verwirklichen, würde es offenkundig werden, dass wir eine diplomatischen Niederlage erlitten haben, deren moralische Wirkung nicht gering anzuschlagen sein durfte, ganz abgesehen von dem Entrüstungssturm, der Deutschland durchbrausen wurde.

Zimmermann, June 12, 1911. *G. P.,* XXIX, 145.

Es war ein alter Grundsatz Bismarcks, das diplomatische *Mittel* müsse dem Wert des *verfolgten Zieles* angepasst sein, und hier haben wir einigen Kongosümpfe wegen beinahe einen Weltkrieg riskiert.

Theodor Wolff in *Berliner Tageblatt,* Nov. 3, 1911.

The situation at the beginning of 1911 was by no means unfavorable. To safeguard her interests in Persia and to secure time to rearm, Russia was still receptive to a limited understanding. Little of course was to be expected of France. Delcassé's appointment as minister of the marine in the Monis cabinet seemed ominous;[1] a German historian believes that it meant a decline of the "salutary fear" of Germany.[2] Moreover, trouble was brewing again in Morocco; while France was steadily advancing toward the complete establishment of her political influence, Germany secured little or nothing from the economic coöperation promised in the accord of 1909. In England, the "Grey-must-go" faction of the Liberal party protested against the danger of being drawn into a continental war and against the government's

---

[1] The government, according to the Belgian minister, shared this opinion. Greindl, March 3. *Belgische Dokumente,* VI, 175. Cf. *Post,* March 1.
[2] Wahl, *Deutsche Geschichte,* IV, 489.

indifference to Russia's brutal treatment of Persia. Less significant perhaps was the movement for a rapprochement with Germany; the cabinet nevertheless appointed a committee to study
the political and naval aspects of the question.[3] Believing that
the British admiralty was ready to abandon the two-power standard, Tirpitz thought that the moment had never been so favorable for an understanding.[4]

Fear was the common denominator of most of these favorable
tendencies. A new war scare, however, would probably arouse a
spirit of patriotic resistance and strengthen the Triple Entente.
A policy of reserve, which had already contributed to an appreciable détente, was perhaps the best defense, and the attitude of
Germany's allies argued in its favor. Austria had no desire to
become involved in a Franco-German quarrel, and Italy's eagerness for Tripoli threatened either to weaken the Alliance or to
alienate Turkey. It seemed possible that these considerations
might decide Germany's policy. Rarely had her leaders been so
lavish with peaceful assurances; never had they come so close
to a formal engagement to restrain Austria as in the negotiations
with Russia.[5] Against these moderate influences worked the
widespread dissatisfaction at home as well as France's activities
in Morocco. The need of colonies had not been forgotten. "We
are not satisfied," wrote the Conservative *Post* (Oct. 2, 1908) on
the eve of the Bosnian crisis, "with the existing situation; . . .
our skin is becoming too tight, we demand more elbowroom as
a nation."[6] Most vociferous, of course, were the Pan-Germans,
but many others shared this point of view in its more general
aspects. The numerous nationalist societies celebrated the successful conclusion of the Bosnian crisis and the negotiations with
Russia as the beginning of an era of great achievements.[7] They

---

[3] Nicolson, March 2, 1911. *B. D.,* VI, 590, 591.
[4] Tirpitz' comments, Widenmann, March 14, 1911. Tirpitz, *Der Aufbau der
deutschen Weltmacht,* p. 188. The Belgian minister agreed with this opinion. Greindl,
March 20. *Belgische Dokumente,* VI, 183.
[5] See above, p. 634.
[6] The *Alldeutsche Blätter* (July 24, 1908) had recently referred to the *Post* as an
opponent of the Pan-Germans.
[7] *Post,* Oct. 6, 1908. According to this journal, the membership of the League of
Veterans (*Deutsche Reichskriegerverband*) numbered 500,000, the Navy League (*Flot-
tenverein*), 900,000; the Union of Landlords (*Bund der Landwirte*), 200,000; the Anti-
Social-Democratic League (*Reichsverband gegen die Sozialdemokratie*), 150,000.

valued the improvement of the diplomatic situation as a desirable end in itself and even more as a means for the attainment of Germany's interests. The Pan-Germans were especially hopeful,[8] because they felt that their views were shared by the foreign office.[9] While they had no great faith in Bethmann, his sharp refusal (March 30, 1911) to initiate negotiations for the limitation of armaments won their applause.[10] "Anyone," he said, "who studies the problem of disarmament must come to the conclusion that it is insoluble as long as men are men and states are states."[11] Kiderlen-Wächter, who had been the foreign minister since the summer of 1910, was the chief hope of the nationalists. In his policy during the Bosnian crisis, they recognized something of Bismarck's genius. Here, they said, was a man of deeds, of strong nerves; a man who would not be afraid to adopt a firm tone toward other countries; a leader who would secure for Germany a place in the world commensurate with her greatness and with her services to humanity.[12]

Kiderlen was thinking of new diplomatic triumphs. The agreement with Turkey at the end of March assuring the construction of the final section of the Berlin-Bagdad Railway meant, he informed Bethmann, the disappointment of "England's hope of bringing Mesopotamia under her exclusive influence and a defeat for France."[13] Morocco was a different story. There, as he later said, French influence, spreading like a drop of oil, had given no convenient occasion for intervention.[14] In February, the German envoy reported that "in Casablanca one can no longer escape the feeling of living in a purely French colony. . . ."[15]

---

[8] See p. 642. Cf. *Rheinisch-Westfälische Zeitung*, March 1, 1911.

[9] *Post*, March 21.

[10] Scheidemann, the Social Democratic leader, offered a resolution calling upon the government to take the lead, arguing that the favorable action of the British House of Commons and the strength of the minority in the French Chamber of Deputies imposed a duty upon Germany to respond. *Verhandlungen*, XII Leg. Per., II Sess., IX, 5982.

[11] *Ibid.*, XII Leg. Per., II Sess., IX, 6002. The moderate and liberal press regarded the Chancellor's brusqueness as a mistake. "One should never say 'never,'" wrote the *Berliner Tageblatt*, and the *Vossische Zeitung* added, "It was not a red-letter day, it was not a great speech." *Tägliche Rundschau*, April 1, 1911.

[12] *A. B.*, Jan. 7, 1911; G. Irmer, "Deutschland und Marokko," *Deutsche Revue*, 1911, III, 145 (Aug. 1).

[13] *G. P.*, XXVII, 686, 687 (*circa* March 24, 1911).

[14] Kiderlen-Wächter, July 19. Jäckh, *Kiderlen-Wächter*, II, 132.

[15] Seckendorff, Feb. 17. *G. P.*, XXIX, 73, 74.

On March 21, the *Post* printed a map showing the regions which
France and Spain had occupied since 1904 and predicted, in an
article covering almost the entire front page, that the summer
would see Morocco's complete partition.   The French, it was immediately assumed, would use the native insurrection near Fez
as an excuse for a new advance.   While the French press prepared public opinion for the dispatch of troops to the aid of the
foreigners, Cambon informed Kiderlen, April 4, that something
would probably have to be done if the situation did not soon
improve.   Thus, for the first time in years, an opportunity was
offered to halt the train of events which threatened to make of
Morocco another Tunis.   The German foreign office regarded
the situation with some satisfaction.[16]   Kiderlen's unofficial reply
when Cambon asked for Germany's views as to the occupation
of Rabat was, as the latter informed his British colleague, "a
very stiff and categorical refusal," [17] but the German minister
soon became more reserved.   While Kiderlen's views are not
entirely clear for the period before May 1911, he probably regarded the Algeciras Act and the accord of 1909 as unworkable.
The nationalists felt that the Algeciras Act had become an obstacle "to a strong and purposeful policy." [18]   Germany's prestige,
according to the *Post* (March 21), required a new settlement.
There was even some recognition of France's difficulties.   The
Sultan, a Conservative deputy told the Reichstag, March 30, was
powerless to maintain order with the country overrun by bandits
and disturbed by tribal insurrections.   No one could blame
France for seeking satisfaction for the killing of her soldiers.[19]
In any event, Kiderlen decided to permit the situation to develop
further.   Although he warned Cambon that public opinion would
react unfavorably to an expedition to Fez and although Bethmann
expressed the hope more than once that no need for action would
arise, Kiderlen said that France must decide what should be

---

[16] Kiderlen-Wächter, July 19. Jäckh, *Kiderlen-Wächter*, II, 132. *Cf.* Bethmann's
later statement to Jules Cambon. J. Cambon, Nov. 5, 1911. *D. D. F.*, (3), I, 31, 32.
[17] Goschen, April 7. *B. D.*, VII, 187. According to Cambon, Kiderlen hinted
(April 6) that Mogador, a port on the Atlantic coast, would be an acceptable price
for the recognition of a French protectorate. F. Hartung, *Die Marokkokrise des Jahres
1911* (Berlin, 1927), p. 15.
[18] *A. B.*, March 18.
[19] *Verhandlungen*, XII, Leg. Per., II Sess., IX, 5976 (Kanitz).

done, and the Chancellor did not say *"Nein."* [20]   Neither these disquieting reservations nor the warning of the British foreign office that military action might, by causing a general insurrection, lead to a permanent occupation and therefore to Germany's intervention restrained the party of action in France.[21]   The die was cast when (April 23) the ministry approved the expedition. According to the French press and diplomats, the letter and spirit of the Algeciras Act would be religiously respected: after assuring the safety of the foreigners and strengthening the Sultan's authority, the troops would be withdrawn without even entering Fez. Germany, it was said, did not and could not object.[22]

These assurances carried little conviction.   Even in the French press there were those who doubted that the foreign colony in Fez was in real danger, and skepticism was naturally more general across the Vosges.[23]   Events, said the most charitable, would probably be too strong for France. While the liberals were chiefly concerned for Germany's economic interests, the nationalists were fearful for the damage that would be done to her prestige and security if the French established themselves permanently in Fez. The *Hamburgische Korrespondent* foresaw an important increase in their military power.[24]   That the natives were to fill the gaps in France's army caused by a declining birth rate was a favorite theme among the Pan-Germans,[25] but they feared most of all the loss of the last opportunity to acquire a part of Morocco. William, however, was even less eager for action than the liberals. In his opinion, Germany should not

---

[20] Kiderlen-Wächter, April 7; Bethmann-Hollweg, April 19. *G. P.,* XXIX, 79, 80, 85, 86.

[21] Nicolson, April 6; Bertie, April 8. *B. D.,* VII, 186, 188.

[22] Carroll, *French Public Opinion,* pp. 238, 239.

[23] The worst reports, according to the *Norddeutsche* (April 24), had not been confirmed. Lister, the British minister to Morocco, later assured the French foreign minister that "the situation was one which could not possibly be allowed to continue: the capital was practically blockaded . . . and the lives of Europeans were in danger. . . . People who said the contrary were merely misinformed or wilfully blind." *B. D.,* VII, 535 (Sept. 19, 1911).

[24] *Tägliche Rundschau,* April 25.

[25] Moltke's attention had already been directed to the subject by Colonel Mangin's writings. Friedrich Rosen, at Tangier, did not agree with the chief of the general staff that the danger would become serious only when France should acquire complete control. *G. P.,* XXIX, 52–55 (March 1).

object if France wasted her wealth and soldiers upon a difficult conquest; to others should be left the task of defending the rights of the powers.[26]   In public opinion and at the foreign office there was little support for an unconditional withdrawal.   If the

Ein Zukunftsbild

Kladderadatsch, April 24, 1911.

Figure 27.—The last class of reserves.

---

[26] William II, April 22; Jenisch, April 26, 30.   *G. P.,* XXIX, 89, 93, 94, 101.

French troops remained at Fez, Kiderlen informed Cambon, April 28, Germany would regard the Algeciras Act as no longer existing and her hands as completely free.[27]   The same warning appeared in the semi-official press.   Germany, wrote the *Kölnische Zeitung* (April 29), would not object if the expedition were withdrawn within a reasonable period; if not, she would "have to consider the new situation."   The *Norddeutsche* (April 30) was more definite.   The violation of important provisions of the Algeciras Act, even if unintentional, "will restore their freedom of action to the other powers, with consequences that cannot, at present, be predicted."[28]   This statement was, according to the chauvinist *Rheinisch-Westfälische Zeitung* (May 1), "Germany's warning."   The foreign office was about to formulate a definite policy.   Thanks to France's cautious attitude, there was, according to the *Norddeutsche,* no reason to expect trouble, but Kiderlen was preparing a line of action on the assumption that France could not, if she would, keep within the terms of the Algeciras Act and that Morocco could no longer be maintained as a sovereign state.   Germany, he decided, should not attempt to maintain the international character of the question.   Nothing should be done or said until the French began to settle down in Fez; they should then be asked how long they expected to remain.   When the withdrawal did not occur by the given date, Germany might inform the world that the powers had recovered their freedom of action.   Kiderlen opposed a simple diplomatic protest, fearing that negotiations would result in another defeat, and decided to send warships to Mogador and Agadir ostensibly for the protection of German interests.   What he intended to demand in return for the final liquidation of the problem was not stated, but the mention of mineral deposits in the hinterland of the two ports suggested that he might insist upon a part of Morocco.   This policy, he pointed out, had political advantages: by securing "tangible gains," nationalist opinion could be won for the government in the next Reichstag elections.[29]   For the moment,

---

[27] Kiderlen-Wächter, April 28.   *G. P.,* XXIX, 97.

[28] Clipped by *Tägliche Rundschau, Rheinisch-Westfälische Zeitung,* May 1; *Berliner Neueste Nachrichten, Kölnische Zeitung,* May 2.

[29] *G. P.,* XXIX, 104–108 (May 3).

however, Germany should resume the sphinxlike reserve from which Holstein and Bülow had expected so much in 1905. "The more silent we are," wrote Kiderlen, May 8, "the more uncomfortable the French will become. It would be foolish to say now that we will not fight for Morocco or, as hitherto, to resort to threats which are not carried out later!! They will soon find a hair in the Moroccan soup without our help!"[30] It was generally understood that Germany would act in some way or other. Kiderlen, the Spanish ambassador informed the British foreign office, expected to find France thoroughly involved on his return fom his vacation. That would be the moment "for Germany to step in and demand her price."[31] In Vienna, Tschirschky, the German ambassador, was reported as saying that the entrance of the French troops into Fez would be followed by a peremptory demand for their withdrawal[32]—a rumor which Crowe found entirely credible, since Germany usually insisted upon "material concessions for remaining silent."[33] There was reason to believe that France, as in 1905, would yield: Caillaux, the minister of finances in the Cruppi cabinet, had already made known to unofficial German agents his willingness to grant colonial concessions in return for "the unqualified recognition of France's vital interests."[34] On May 14, the Paris *Matin* mentioned a part of the Congo.[35]

"Herr von Kiderlen," wrote a nationalist observer, "cannot check France's questionable and dangerously irregular game until he knows with certainty that all of the other playmates of Algeciras are on his side. . . ."[36] The minister, however, regarded this as an excess of caution. The use of normal diplomatic methods would be disastrous; England and Russia would rally to the support of France, while Germany could not be certain of her allies. Austria's attitude was especially disappointing. "Our rôle," the French ambassador in Vienna was told, ". . . can only

---

[30] *Grenzboten*, May 28, 1913 (G. Clenow).
[31] Nicolson, May 11. *B. D.*, VII, 236.
[32] A report was circulated in the press that three warships were about to be sent to Moroccan waters. It was denied by the *Kölnische Zeitung* (May 8) and by the *Norddeutsche* (May 9).
[33] Crowe's minute, Cartwright, May 13. *B. D.*, VII, 437.
[34] Oncken, *Vorgeschichte des Weltkrieges*, II, 690.
[35] Carroll, *French Public Opinion*, p. 239.
[36] "Herr v. Kiderlen am Scheidewege," *Gegenwart*, June 17.

be that of a mediator." [37] About the middle of May, there was a good deal of plain speaking in Vienna's semi-official press. The *Wiener Allgemeine Zeitung* was comparatively moderate; Russia's intervention in favor of a détente indicated her loyalty to the alliance with France.[38] This article was soon followed by the *Neue Wiener Journal's* declaration in favor of a free hand for the French.[39] More significant and objectionable was the stand taken by the *Sonn- und Montagszeitung* (May 15), a journal which the *Kölnische Zeitung* (May 15) asserted was inspired by the Ballplatz. German statesmen, it wrote, had learned nothing from the Algeciras crisis; they had exaggerated the improvement in Germany's relations with England and Russia. "A fair examination of the situation shows clearly that a serious conflict with France will restore the Dual Alliance and the Entente Cordiale to their full strength and thrust Germany back into the isolation from which she had, with Austria-Hungary's not inconsiderable support, emerged. These circumstances make it necessary for our statesmen to consider to what extent our destiny may be affected by Germany's policy and how these dangers may be averted." While the writer asserted that Austria had no intention of negotiating behind her ally's back, the mention of Bismarck's Reinsurance Treaty with Russia as an appropriate precedent and the claim that Germany's services during the Bosnian crisis were simply a payment for Austria's support at Algeciras were disturbing. "It is therefore desirable," it concluded, "in our own interest and, still more, in that of our alliance with Germany and Italy, that Germany . . . should guard herself against a renewed isolation." [40] The reaction in the German press was violent. The nationalist journals cried that Austria's attitude proved the truth of all they had said about her ingratitude.[41] The *Kölnische Zeitung* (May 16) protested that

[37] Pallavicini, April 25. *Ö.-U. A.*, III, 236.
[38] *N. A. Z.*, May 13.
[39] *Rheinisch-Westfälische Zeitung*, May 15. "Austria-Hungary," the editor of the *Fremdenblatt* was reported as saying, "accepts [France's assurances] in a benevolent spirit, Germany accepts them in a malevolent spirit." Cartwright, May 13. *B. D.*, VII, 237. The *Popolo Romano's* (Rome) sole objection was France's slowness. *Berliner Neueste Nachrichten*, May 18.
[40] *Kölnische Zeitung*, May 15.
[41] "Dank vom Hause Oesterreich," *Rheinisch-Westfälische Zeitung*, May 16; *Tägliche Rundschau*, *Berliner Neueste Nachrichten*, May 18; *Hamburger Nachrichten*, *Königsberger Hartungsche Zeitung*, *Hannoversche Courier*, in *Tägliche Rundschau*, May 19.

the Viennese article might more properly have appeared in an English, French, or Russian newspaper. Nor did its denial that Germany intended to provoke France entirely allay Austria's misgivings, for the *Fremdenblatt* promptly endorsed the Algeciras Act.[42]

Bent upon a direct settlement with France, Kiderlen regarded the attitude of the other powers as comparatively unimportant. The interest conflicts within the Triple Entente would, he believed, prevent a clash between the two diplomatic groups. At any rate, the decision to surprise France by the dispatch of warships to Morocco precluded any serious diplomatic preparation. His best card was undoubtedly Russia's indifference. If she told the German foreign office, as London was informed, that there could be no objection to the French expedition, she also assured the German ambassador that Germany's point of view was correct.[43] England's probable reaction was given astonishingly little consideration. In fact, Kiderlen had predicted in his memorandum of May 3 that she would not object, because Agadir was too distant from Gibraltar and the Mediterranean coast to affect her interests. Thenceforth the German minister proceeded as if she could safely be ignored. Late in June, a foreign office official spoke of a prompt agreement for the exchange of naval information as a matter of paramount importance,[44] but silence was maintained in regard to Germany's intentions in Morocco. Metternich merely paraphrased the *Norddeutsche's* article of April 30 in reply to Grey's inquiries: if France kept her troops in Fez beyond a reasonable period, the Algeciras Act would be abrogated and the other powers, including Germany, would recover their freedom of action.[45] Grey's analysis of the situation nevertheless agreed with Kiderlen's in some respects. "We are skating on thin ice," he wrote to Bertie in Paris, "in maintaining that the Act of Algeciras is not affected by all that has happened, and every week that the French remain at Fez the ice will get thinner. If the Act of Algeciras does go by the board, the partition of Morocco

[42] *Berliner Neueste Nachrichten*, May 18; *N. A. Z.*, May 19. The *Norddeutsche* was, however, satisfied by the *Fremdenblatt's* explanation.

[43] Goschen, May 4. *B. D.*, VII, 464; Pourtalès, May 9. *G. P.*, XXIX, 117.

[44] Zimmermann, June 23. *G. P.*, XXVIII, 423.

[45] Metternich, May 22. *Ibid.*, XXIX, 119.

between France and Spain will ensue. I do not suppose that it
would be impossible to get Germany's consent to this, but it
would be necessary to pay a price for the consent, though that
price need not necessarily be anything in Morocco." [46] Grey
made it quite plain, however, on which side England would be
in a crisis. To Metternich he said that her hands were free except in Morocco, but "there she is bound by the agreement with
France to support her." [47] A few days later, the British ambassador explained in Berlin that Grey had approved the expedition
to Fez and that "no pressure of any kind should be brought to
bear upon them [the French] from any quarter which might
result in their leaving their difficult task unfinished." [48]

In spite of the practical certainty of England's support of
France, of Austria's coolness, and of Italy's unreliability, Kiderlen
carried through his plan substantially without change. Spain's
occupation of Larache, June 8, indicating an approaching partition,[49] hastened the final decision. Four days later, the foreign
office again reviewed the arguments for the sending of warships;
undue delay would enable France to attain her ambitions under
the cloak of the Algeciras Act, give time to mobilize world opinion, lead to another diplomatic defeat, and leave Germany with
empty hands. Only under pressure would France offer adequate
compensations.[50] On June 20, 21, Kiderlen told Cambon at
Kissengen to bring something back from Paris; only in return
for a worth-while equivalent would Germany consent to a final
liquidation.[51] When, after his return, the French ambassador
made no advances, Kiderlen decided to act, although he might
have made allowances for the confusion in Paris following the
accidental death of the war minister, the fall of the Monis cabinet,
the organization of the Caillaux ministry, and the appointment
of the inexperienced de Selves as the minister of foreign affairs.[52] At Kiel, William yielded to the arguments of Bethmann

[46] B. D., VII, 277, 278 (June 1). Cf. Oncken, Vorgeschichte des Weltkrieges, II, 694.
[47] Metternich, May 22. G. P., XXIX, 119.
[48] Goschen, June 1. B. D., VII, 276.
[49] A. B., June 17. Princess Radziwill assumed as a matter of course that Germany
was behind Spain's action. Lettres . . . au général du Robilant, IV, 147 (June 14).
[50] Zimmermann, June 12. G. P., XXIX, 143–149.
[51] Oncken, op. cit., II, 695.
[52] Carroll, French Public Opinion, p. 240.

and Kiderlen. "Ships approved," was the latter's laconic message of June 25 to the foreign office.[53]   Schoen informed the Quai d'Orsay at noon on July 1 that the "Panther" had been sent to Agadir to protect the interests of German citizens.[54]   Its withdrawal after the restoration of order was promised, but Germany's real purpose was revealed by Schoen's oral explanation that his government was ready for a final settlement of the problem.   An appropriate suggestion would receive benevolent consideration.[55] The Norddeutsche (July 2) merely gave the official reason, adding that the local chieftains had been told that "the Panther's presence has no unfriendly implications for Morocco or the Moroccans."

While the French government exaggerated the conciliatory sense of Schoen's explanations in its communications to the press, the shock was nevertheless severe to a public opinion that had been assured there would be no important international complications.   The effect, wrote the Social Democratic Vorwärts (July 4), was like that of a fanfare.   Soon there was talk of the coup d'Agadir and of a blow upon the tapis vert of the diplomatic table.   Germany's action, said the London Times (July 3), was another example of her fondness for dramatic methods.   The Kladderadatsch (July 16) of Berlin, a satirical weekly, encouraged this interpretation.   In a malicious cartoon, it represented the smiling Kiderlen as placing a young panther on the back of President Fallières, seated with the other heads of state.   To Kiderlen's policy, this impression was essential in order to convince the French that Germany meant business.   The disadvantages of a more normal procedure had been carefully analyzed, but little or no consideration had been given to the dangers of the "Panther's" spring.   Except in Russia, the international repercussions were definitely unfavorable.   England indicated where she stood by immediately suspending the naval negotiations.   Hitherto critical in no small degree of France's Moroccan policy, her public opinion now turned against Germany, charg-

---

[53] G. P., XXIX, 152.

[54] The property of one house, according to a Berlin correspondent of the Kölnische Zeitung (July 2), had the dimensions of a principality. Cf. Post, Deutsche Tageszeitung, July 2; Freisinnige Zeitung, July 4.

[55] Kiderlen, June 30. G. P., XXIX, 153–155.

Kladderadatsch, July 16, 1911.

Figure 28.—Kiderlen-Wächter has given an innocent old gentleman a nasty fright with a harmless little panther.

ing her with the chief responsibility for the collapse of the Algeciras Act. For months, the German ambassador in Rome and the foreign office in Berlin had been afraid that Italy would suddenly descend upon Tripoli, but the possibility that Agadir might encourage her to act had apparently not occurred to Kiderlen. The larger interests of German foreign policy had again been subordinated to imperialist ambitions.

In Germany as elsewhere, people asked themselves whether the government's objective was a Moroccan port, the Atlantic coast, or colonial compensations elsewhere; and whether it was ready to fight. These questions remained unanswered for more than three months. At first, the nationalists expected a share of the Atlantic coast, and Kiderlen encouraged the Pan-Germans to believe that he would demand Southwest Morocco. The navy's objection to a base which could easily be captured in a war did not apply, he told Class, their president, in April, to a purely colonial establishment. "Demands of this kind in the press and by societies would serve," he said, "a useful purpose. Such a division of labor is desirable. I can then say, 'Yes, I am conciliatory, but public opinion must be considered. . . .' We certainly will stand our ground in Morocco (*Ganz bestimmt in Marokko werden wir durchhalten*)." [56] Nor was this his only encouragement to the extremists. On July 1, Zimmermann assured Class' representative that "we are seizing this region [Agadir] once and for all: an outlet for our population is a necessity." [57] That these promises were the ineluctable price of the nationalists' support is doubtful, for the "Panther's" spring represented the kind of diplomacy which they had always desired. They were deliriously enthusiastic. "Hurrah! A deed!" screamed the headlines of the *Rheinisch-Westfälische Zeitung* (July 2). "Action at last, a liberating deed which must dissolve the cloud of pessimism everywhere. . . ." "Care and mistrust," wrote the *Post* (July 2), "will fall from every German heart. . . ." "The word *endlich*," according to the *Tägliche Rundschau* (July 2), "will be the uni-

---

[56] Class, *Wider den Strom*, pp. 202, 203. Speaking to the Reichstag February 27, 1912, Kiderlen tried unsuccessfully to clear himself of this charge, which Class had made under oath. Hartung, *Marokkokrise des Jahres 1911*, pp. 17, 18.
[57] Class, *op. cit.*, p. 206.

versal reaction." For the *Magdeburgische Zeitung* (July 2), "the government's emergence from its reserve must have the effect of a deliverance (*Erlösung*)." "The entire nation," affirmed the Conservative *Kreuz-Zeitung,* "breathes a sigh of relief." [58] "Again it is seen," wrote the organ of the Pan-Germans, "that the foreign policy of a great nation, of a powerful state, cannot exhaust itself in patient inaction, it must will and act." [59] Confident that its own views as to Germany's purpose were also the government's, the nationalist press tacitly conceded the latter a free hand by remaining comparatively silent in regard to Morocco. In its opinion, Agadir was clearly the prelude to a partition which would assure to Germany important mineral resources, new markets, fertile land for her surplus population, and the means of immobilizing the native troops which France intended to use in Europe. Another conference, they said, would be fatal.[60] The government's insistence upon separate negotiations with France and Spain had the almost unanimous support of public opinion. Threats of war were not lacking. If France did not yield, "then may the Panther have the effect of the Ems Dispatch," wrote the chauvinist *Rheinisch-Westfälische Zeitung* (July 2). In 1909 Germany had shown her "mailed fist," it replied when the Paris press talked of securing the aid of England and Russia; they had refused the challenge at that time, "and now our sword is sharper, . . . for it is a question of fighting for German interests." Because the chauvinism of this journal was well-known, the views of the *Konservative Korrespondenz,* an organ of the Conservative party, were more significant. Agadir, it said, might have one of three results: war, the withdrawal of all French and Spanish troops from Morocco, or the full recognition of Germany's equality. "There should not be a particle of doubt that we are ready for any of these contingencies." [61]

Only the Social Democratic press, which condemned Agadir as the work of speculators, denied the validity of the government's case, and, pointing to the ample reserves of iron ore in

---

[58] *Vorwärts,* July 14.
[59] *A. B.,* July 8.
[60] *Post,* July 6.
[61] *Rheinisch-Westfälische Zeitung,* July 8.

Germany, ventured openly to criticize the official policy.[62]   The
liberal *Berliner Tageblatt* guarded its silence for more than a
week, but, on July 9, Paul Michaelis practically approved Agadir,
and Theodor Wolff expressed the opinion that it might lead to
the permanent settlement he had always supported.   For both,
the Algeciras Act had become nothing more than a scrap of
paper.   Few saw anything to object to in Germany's action from
the point of view of diplomatic procedure.   To the moderate
Vossische Zeitung (July 2), the "Panther's" spring was merely
an invitation to a parley.   "After a long period of silence," it
said, "Germany has spoken; France now has the floor."   For
Michaelis, of the *Berliner Tageblatt* (July 9), Germany had simply given forceful notice that something must be done.   If France
was justified in going to Fez, said the most important journals,
so was also Germany in going to Agadir.[63]   For the excesses of
nationalist opinion, these newspapers, however, had only condemnation; they approved the sending of the "Panther," not as a
prelude to a war or as the signal for a serious crisis, but as a step
toward an amicable settlement.   "We demand," wrote the Catholic *Germania* (July 4), "that the government do everything in
its power to prevent a serious international conflict from arising
on account of Morocco. . . ."   It was the duty of the German
people and government, according to the *Berliner Tageblatt* (July
9), "to repudiate" the irresponsible mouthings of the nationalist
press.   To the *Frankfurter Zeitung* (July 4) only chauvinists
could think that the government intended to precipitate a serious
crisis.   "No sensible person in Germany," wrote the *Hamburger
Nachrichten* (July 19), condemning the "Morocco" press in the
name of the German people, "dreams of permitting a war on
Morocco's account."   The *Vossische Zeitung* (July 10) called
upon the Conservative leaders to repudiate the *Konservative Korrespondenz'* bellicose pronouncement, but without success.   In
some respects, the nationalists showed that they understood the
realities of the situation better than the more moderate groups.
Agadir meant a test of strength, which might be transferred from

---

[62] *Vorwärts*, July 2. *Cf.* O. Hue, "Marokko und der deutsche Bedarf," *Neue Zeit,*
[63] *Hamburger Nachrichten*, July 2; *Germania*, July 4; *National Zeitung*, July 6;
Berliner Tageblatt, July 9, 10.

the chancelleries to the battlefield. When the *Vossische Zeitung* insisted that war was impossible, the *Berliner Neueste Nachrichten* (July 17) pointed out that a little research would show that this same journal had said the same thing a week before France's declaration of war in 1870. It would be better to fight than to suffer another Olmütz.

Until Germany spoke officially, no one could be certain what her purposes were. England had not been reassured by William's statement that "we will never make war over Morocco," during his visit to London (May 16–20).[64] That of Kühlmann, the German *chargé d'affaires,* to the Russian ambassador, July 1, to the effect that Germany would be satisfied with compensations outside Morocco must be discounted as a maneuver to turn Russia against an appeal from France for her support.[65] After Agadir, those newspapers which were anxiously examined for a sign of the government's intentions remained non-committal. The *Norddeutsche* was silent. For the friends of peace, the comments of the *Kölnische Zeitung* (July 4) contained, however, some encouragement; the press, it said, could contribute to a peaceful settlement by remaining quiet. The announcement that negotiations had begun with France was reassuring. Since both countries "wished sincerely to reach an understanding," there was, wrote the *Vossische Zeitung* (July 10), no reason for alarm, but they were still poles apart at the close of the first conversations on July 9. On that date, Cambon, bitter and silent, called upon Kiderlen. Who would be the first to speak? The French ambassador's, *"Eh bien?"*—a tacit invitation to state Germany's position—was countered by the minister's, *"Vous avez du neuf?"* When Kiderlen indicated his lack of interest in the Turkish public debt, the Moroccan railways, and other subsidiary matters as the possible basis of an understanding, Cambon stated definitely his country's opposition to Germany's permanent establishment in Morocco. French public opinion, he said, would never tolerate it. However, Kiderlen brightened when his visitor mentioned the Congo, but he hastened to explain that the lion's

---

[64] Bethmann-Hollweg, May 23. G. P., XXIX, 120.
[65] Benckendorff, 16/19 Aug. B. von Siebert, *Diplomatische Aktenstücke* . . . (Berlin, 1921), p. 437.

share of a bargain must go to Germany, in order to reconcile her public opinion to the sacrifice of its hopes for a part of Morocco. In conclusion, the minister warned Cambon that a press campaign for a united front on the part of the Triple Entente might have "unpleasant results." [66] An understanding seems to have been reached that there should be no communication to the press as to the progress of the negotiations.

The international repercussions of Agadir made it more desirable than ever, from Germany's point of view, to prevent a clash between the two diplomatic groups. From her allies, she had to reckon with open or concealed opposition. The Italians said at once that they could do nothing against France in Morocco and that their attitude in a serious crisis would depend upon circumstances.[67] While Aehrenthal at first spoke favorably of Agadir and of the closest coöperation, the disagreeable memories of Potsdam were still too fresh and Austria's interests too slight for the latter to show much zeal.[68] That the Triple Entente would present a stronger front than it had during the Bosnian crisis was almost certain, since Germany's action was directed against a basic tie between England and France. Nor was Russia's neutrality certain in the event of war. By asking for her approval of the elimination of Morocco as a source of international friction, Kiderlen secured a friendly reply,[69] but she would not be likely to permit France's elimination as a great power. Indeed, her first action was to approach London for the formulation of a common point of view,[70] and England used her influence to weaken Russia's rather favorable impression of Germany's policy.[71] In view of England's loyalty to the Entente Cordiale,

---

[66] Kiderlen, July 9. *G. P.*, XXIX, 173–176; Cambon, July 10. *Livre jaune: affaires du Maroc*, VI (1910–1912), pp. 403, 404.

[67] Jagow, July 1. *G. P.*, XXIX, 157.

[68] Tschirschky, July 1. *Ibid.*, XXIX, 158; Aehrenthal, July 4. *Ö.-U. A.*, III, 267, 268. To Kiderlen's irritation, the Hungarian Minister-President spoke of Morocco as beyond the scope of the Dual Alliance. Szögyény, July 11. *Ibid.*, III, 274. On July 11, the *Post* noticed Austria's coolness. *Cf.* Wedel, *Austro-German Relations*, pp. 130–133.

[69] Pourtalès, July 1; Kiderlen, July 5. *G. P.*, XXIX, 158, 159, 168.

[70] The Russian foreign minister favored a conference. Neratov, July 2. *B. D.*, VII, 330, 331.

[71] Buchanan, July 12. *Ibid.*, VII, 357, 358.

France's initiation of direct negotiations must be regarded as a success for Kiderlen's policy. The first phase of the crisis had developed as he had foreseen. Fear of war on the part of Caillaux, of French public opinion, and of the British cabinet had prevented de Selves, the French foreign minister, from sending a warship to Agadir, although Grey had thought at first of joining France in this action.[72] The idea of an international conference had also been abandoned, chiefly because of Caillaux's unwillingness to risk the loss of what France had already gained in Morocco.[73]

It was, from Kiderlen's point of view, a not inauspicious beginning. Although he knew that France would not peacefully yield a part of Morocco, Cambon had himself mentioned the Congo and had, by his silence, tacitly agreed that Germany's compensation there should be substantial. Kiderlen now turned definitely toward compensation outside Morocco. He had the Emperor's support in this decision, for William, desirous of a direct understanding with France in order to prevent the intervention of other countries, immediately consented to an exchange of territory involving Togoland and French Equatorial Africa.[74] Unfortunately, Kiderlen was determined that France should yield enough so that Germany could claim a diplomatic victory and satisfy her own nationalists. His demand for practically the entire French Congo in return for the renunciation of territorial claims in Morocco, for the recognition of a virtual protectorate, and for a part of Togoland, threatened to cause the complete collapse of the negotiations. Personally, Cambon may have regarded Morocco as worth Kiderlen's price, but he too had to consider the imponderables and, especially, the uproar which the sacrifice of an entire colony would cause in France. He professed, at any rate, intense consternation, exclaiming that it would be sufficiently difficult to win the approval of a French parliament for the sur-

---

[72] J. Caillaux, *Mes prisons* (Paris, 1921), p. 183; Grey, July 4. *B. D.*, VII, 333. *Cf.* Wolff, *Eve of 1914*, pp. 45, 46.

[73] Caillaux, *Agadir: ma politique extérieure* (Paris, 1919), pp. 114, 115. *Cf.* Carroll, *French Public Opinion*, p. 242.

[74] Treutler, July 11. *G. P.*, XXIX, 178.

render of even a part of a colony paid for by lives and money.[75] Heretofore, Kiderlen had enjoyed almost a free hand, since William was on his travels and Bethmann was satisfied with occasional reports,[76] but it now seemed possible that he might be forced to resign. Alarmed by Kiderlen's remark that strong measures would be required to secure France's acceptance and by what he thought was the united front on the part of the Triple Entente, William at once concluded that his foreign minister was bent upon war and that he must return to Berlin. The seriousness of the situation should be brought to the attention of Germany's allies; there should be no mobilization without his consent.[77] Kiderlen's intentions at this juncture were undoubtedly dangerous. While he did not desire war, he nevertheless believed that Germany must be willing to wage it in order to persuade the French government, whose parliament and public opinion were being excited by the colonial party, to make an acceptable offer. The refusal of his demand of July 15, he believed, should be followed by a proposal for the complete evacuation of Morocco and for a rigid adherence to the Algeciras Act. As in 1909, when he gambled upon Russia's unwillingness to fight, he felt certain that the French would not accept the challenge. Unless the Chancellor approved this policy, he, Kiderlen, must resign, for the failure to secure the entire Congo would so greatly increase the power of Germany's enemies that she would have to settle accounts with them sooner or later.[78] By toning down Kiderlen's memorandum and by representing Germany's prestige as at stake, Bethmann saved his colleague, but whether William approved Kiderlen's program or the Chancellor's version of it is uncertain.[79] William, at any rate, did not return to Berlin and Kiderlen retained control.

---

[75] Bethmann-Hollweg, July 15. *G. P.,* XXIX, 185. Of Cambon's indignation, William wrote: *"Er spielt gut Komödie."* For de Selves' refusal of Kiderlen's demand, see Schoen, July 19. *Ibid.,* XXIX, 190.

[76] Hammann, *Bilder aus der letzten Kaiserzeit,* pp. 86, 87.

[77] William II's comments, Bethmann-Hollweg, July 15; Treutler, July 17. *G. P.,* XXIX, 185, 187.

[78] Kiderlen-Wächter, July 17. Jäckh, *Kiderlen-Wächter,* II, 128, 129.

[79] Bethmann-Hollweg, July 18, 20. *G. P.,* XXIX, 189, 190, 192; Jäckh, *Kiderlen-Wächter,* II, 131 (July 18); William II, July 21. *Ibid.,* II, 134. William's direction "to continue the negotiations on the lines hitherto ordered" was sufficiently vague. Wolff, *Eve of 1914,* p. 51.

Meanwhile, the diplomats had found it desirable to take public opinion into their confidence. Believing that Germany's prospects would be brighter if passions were not aroused, Kiderlen had persuaded the French to agree to complete secrecy. Nevertheless he seems to have been guilty of the first indiscretion, not, however, to excite public opinion against France but to save his face with the German nationalists. On July 14, Class sent an associate to the foreign office with the proof sheets of his pamphlet *West-Marokko deutsch*,[80] in which the territorial aspirations of the Pan-Germans were set forth. The minister advised against its publication, warning that he would otherwise repudiate it, in view of the violent reaction in France.[81] On the same day, there appeared in the *Kölnische Zeitung* a partial explanation of the official attitude toward compensation. Secrecy had been arranged with France, but it was permissible to explain that Germany did not need to insist upon a part of Morocco "as certain newspapers seem to think." On the contrary, the prospects for a satisfactory settlement would be brighter if compensations were discovered elsewhere. "The chief thing is to be sure that parity exists between what the two parties secure; not the location of the lands exchanged." Earlier suggestions of this kind had been discounted as intended to mystify the French and English, but this pronouncement, whose circumlocutions sounded like a diplomatic document, had an authentic ring. It was a bitter disappointment for those who had set their hearts upon Morocco. "Is this the vaunted masterpiece?" asked the *Alldeutsche Blätter* (July 22). No one would believe that the "Panther" had gone to Agadir for this purpose. "It will be supposed that the original and much more ambitious aim has been abandoned because the government lacks the necessary firmness." That "we are again about to abandon a valuable pledge for compensations that are not compensations at all" was the opinion of an official organ of the National Liberal Party.[82] The indignation of the German press, according to the agrarian *Deutsche Tageszeitung* (July 19),

---

[80] The manuscript contained a demand for the Rhone district, so that Germany might become a Mediterranean power. Hammann, *Bilder aus der letzten Kaiserzeit*, pp. 85, 86.

[81] Class, *Wider den Strom*, pp. 208, 209.

[82] *Nationalliberale Korrespondenz*, in *Rheinisch-Westfälische Zeitung*, July 18.

"is almost universal." Even the moderates were not entirely satisfied. The Catholic *Kölnische Volkszeitung* was surprised.[83] The most valuable of colonial compensations had little appeal for the *Frankfurter Zeitung* (July 18) if they meant the abandonment of the Algeciras Act without whose protection Germany's economic interests in Morocco would be valueless. On the condition that France would abandon "her secret hostility" and that she would "accept the friendly hand which had at last been offered her and coöperate sincerely with Germany," it would cheerfully agree to Germany's withdrawal without compensations.[84] Harden even mentioned an alliance as a suitable price for Germany's recognition of a French protectorate in Morocco.[85] Hailed as a statesman *"ohne Nerven,"* Kiderlen's stock rapidly sank. He might soon expect, according to the *Vossische Zeitung* (July 20), "to be bombarded with rotten eggs." Each mail, he told the British ambassador, brought him "a pile of anonymous letters" from the Pan-Germans charging him with the surrender of the nation's vital interests.[86]

Criticism at home was less dangerous than the reaction abroad to the demand for the entire Congo. The resistance of the French government stiffened, and, after the sensational articles of the Paris *Matin* (July 19) and of the London *Times* (July 20) in which Germany's offer of the entire Togoland or of a part of the Cameroons was suppressed, public opinion in England and in France became more hostile than ever.[87] Events now showed how short-sighted Kiderlen's treatment of England had been. With all Tirpitz' baneful influence, to him belongs at least the credit for having foreseen her opposition,[88] while the foreign office had assured Austria that everything indicated "England's acceptance of the *fait accompli.*" [89] So obvious was the importance of her attitude that more than one nationalist newspaper assumed that she had given satisfactory assurances.[90] "It cannot be denied,"

[83] *Tägliche Rundschau,* July 18.
[84] This suggestion, wrote the *Temps,* was "lyricism." *Frankfurter Zeitung,* July 21.
[85] Wolff exposed the naïve assumptions of this idea. *Berliner Tageblatt,* July 21.
[86] Goschen, July 21. *B. D.,* VII, 387.
[87] Hartung, *Marokkokrise des Jahres 1911,* p. 33.
[88] He had not been consulted. Tirpitz, *Erinnerungen,* p. 181.
[89] Szögyény, July 1. *Ö.-U. A.,* III, 265.
[90] *Deutsche Tageszeitung,* July 3; *Leipziger Neueste Nachrichten,* in *Tägliche Rundschau,* July 7.

Simplicissimus, August 7, 1911.

Figure 29.—"Hell's fire! Aren't the damned toads ever going to shut their traps?!"

wrote the Catholic *Germania* (July 5), "that London, in a certain sense, possesses the key to the situation." Since the "Panther's" spring, Kiderlen had done nothing to allay England's apprehensions, even when the British foreign office suspended the negotiations for the exchange of naval information.[91] Asked if troops would be landed, Metternich could only plead ignorance.[92] Her loyalty to France was clearly indicated by her press and by official statements, although the French policy in Morocco still occasioned no little criticism.[93] Liberal and Conservative journals vied in pledging England's loyalty.[94] In Germany's professed reliance upon the recent improvement in Anglo-German relations was seen a desire to divide the Entente Cordiale; a German port on the Moroccan coast would, it was said, imperil the communications with South Africa and require further increases in the naval budget.[95] Few thought that war was imminent or that a reply in kind should be made to the "Panther's" spring, but one and all agreed that Germany must not be permitted to ignore England in questions directly affecting her interests. "No 'claims' can be admitted and no 'compensations' allowed," wrote the *Times* (July 6), "in an international matter that concerns us nearly and deeply without our participation and assent." To support France and to defend England's interests, Asquith told the House of Commons, July 6, would be England's policy.

In Germany the press nearly unanimously relegated Asquith's statement to obscure corners and paid little attention to the trend of English opinion.[96] There was at first little to fear. If Grey promptly took the position that "we must have our say," that "we cannot . . . recognize any new arrangement which comes off without us," and if he was at first in favor, like de Selves, of sending "a warship to Agadir," the cabinet decided (July 4) against this dangerous measure, and no attempt was made to dissuade France from initiating (July 9) direct negotiations with

[91] Nicolson's minute, de Salis, July 1. *B. D.*, VI, 640.

[92] Metternich, July 1. *G. P.*, XXIX, 157.

[93] *Westminster Gazette, Daily News*, July 3; *Saturday Review*, July 8.

[94] *Times, Morning Post*, July 3; *Daily Chronicle, Standard*, July 4. Cf. *Spectator*, July 8.

[95] *Times*, July 4; *Standard*, July 5.

[96] The *Post* (July 7), one of the exceptions, warned its readers that Germany would have to contend with England's opposition.

Germany.[97]   For the time being, the cabinet's chief aim was to avoid serious trouble.   While Grey regarded a solution that would keep Germany out of Morocco as "infinitely preferable," he told the French more than once, evidently with the admiralty's consent, that England would not object to her acquisition of a port if adequate guarantees were secured that it would not be fortified.[98]   England could not agree unconditionally to fight to keep Germany out of Morocco: "Her government does not consider it vital to her interests to exclude Germany from getting a foothold, . . . provided satisfactory conditions are secured from her.   They cannot make any admission of Germany into Morocco a *casus belli* unconditionally, though they could not suggest it or deal with it except in concert with France and on terms satisfactory to France." [99]   Grey may have spoken primarily for the record and to satisfy the moderate section of the cabinet, for it was evident that France, to the great satisfaction of the permanent officials of the British foreign office, would fight rather than permit a German establishment on the Moroccan coast that would immobilize a large body of metropolitan and native troops.[100]   Moreover, the crisis involved graver issues than the Moroccan question.   What moved Grey to action more than anything else and enabled him to carry the government with him was almost certainly the fear that France's prestige would be seriously damaged and that the solidity of the Entente Cordiale would be impaired.   He feared the worst from Germany's silence and especially from Metternich's angry insistence (July 14) that Germany's power entitled her to important compensations.[101]   Instead of relieving his anxieties, Kiderlen's demand for the entire French Congo (July 15) led directly to his intervention. The foreign office officials drew the worst conclusions.   "This," wrote Crowe, "is a test of strength, if anything.   Concession means not loss of interests or loss of prestige.   It means defeat. . . .   The defeat of France is a matter vital to this country."

---

[97] Grey's minute, de Salis, July 2; Grey, July 3, 4. *B. D.*, VII, 325, 326, 328, 333, 334; Metternich, July 3, 4. *G. P.*, XXIX, 164, 167.

[98] Grey, July 6, 10, 12, 18. *B. D.*, VII, 341, 346, 358, 373.

[99] Grey, July 19. *Ibid.*, VII, 376.

[100] Bertie, July 9, 12. *Ibid.*, VII, 344, 345, 352. For Nicolson's favorable reaction, see his minute, Bertie, July 12. *Ibid.*, VII, 353.

[101] Nicolson, July 18. *Ibid.*, VII, 374, 375.

Without England's support, Germany's increasing pressure would compel France, according to Nicolson, to fight or to yield. "In the latter case German hegemony would be solidly established. . . ." [102] Arguing that England's reserve might encourage Germany to increase her demands, Grey now secured Asquith's approval for a warning (July 21) that she would insist upon a voice if the Franco-German negotiations failed and that continued uncertainty would compel her to send a warship to Agadir. [103]

Announced through the usual diplomatic channels, the shock of England's intervention would have been severe in Berlin, but it need not have affected public opinion. A different method was chosen. On July 21, just before Metternich arrived at the foreign office, Grey agreed—with Asquith's approval—that Lloyd George, the chancellor of the exchequer, should read that evening a statement of his own during a speech at the Mansion House. [104] The purpose was apparently to arouse public opinion at home, to encourage the French, and to warn Germany. From this point of view, the speech was a great success. Less definite than Grey's explanation to Metternich, it spoke of the need to defend the important place and prestige that was England's and asserted that the sacrifice of her influence was a price which the speaker would not pay for the maintenance of peace. Lloyd George's well-known pacifism greatly increased the significance of this warning; nevertheless, the German press dismissed it at first as a matter of no importance. Since it contained no specific reference to Germany, there was no reason why she should take offense, for her own statesmen might have made the same speech. [105] Meanwhile, the London newspapers had crossed the *i*'s and dotted the *t*'s. If the Liberal *Westminster Gazette* (July 21) described it as "studiously conciliatory" and as a "polite reply," it was for the great majority an official announcement of the government's support of France. [106] This reaction was, from

---

[102] *B. D.*, VII, 371, 372 (July 18).
[103] Grey, July 19. *Ibid.*, VII, 377, 378.
[104] Lloyd George, *War Memoirs*, I, 43, 44.
[105] *Lokal-Anzeiger*, July 22; *Kölnische Zeitung*, July 23, Berlin, July 22; *Frankfurter Zeitung*, July 23; *Kreuz-Zeitung*, July 26. Schiemann, *Deutschland und die Grosse Politik*, XI, 241.
[106] *Morning Post*, July 22; *Times*, *Daily News*, July 24.

the German point of view, at least as important as the speech itself.[107]   The last illusions disappeared when the *Daily Chronicle* (July 22), credited in Germany with official connections, wrote that the minister had expressed "the considered judgment of the Cabinet" and that his statement was "meant as a word in season. . . ." [108]   Feeling turned against England even more violently than against France.   Practically all sections of the press joined in a bitter protest against her meddling in a question that did not concern her.[109]   It gave some support, wrote the liberal *Frankfurter Zeitung* (July 24), to the old charges of systematic obstruction to Germany's expansion.   For the *Berliner Tageblatt* (July 26), England's intervention was symptomatic of her ill-will and could not be excused as a legitimate act of self-defense. Her real aim, according to the Catholic *Germania* (July 26), was to make sure that she got something for herself.   "Whenever a country occupies one village, England immediately demands three and preferably four."   "What a pity!" it exclaimed, referring to the failure of earlier efforts to bring France and Germany together.   The extremists spoke of war.   Compensations, said the National Liberal *Börsen-Courier,* would not avert the inevitable conflict.[110]   One journal predicted the collapse of the British Empire.   *"There is not the shadow of a doubt,"* wrote the agrarian *Deutsche Tageszeitung* (July 30), *"that a war would endanger Great Britain's existence as a world and commercial power. . . ."*   The Conservative *Post* (July 29) foresaw that the British Empire would become the prey of its enemies and that Canada and the West Indies would be taken by the United States.   Although it was more circumspect, the semi-official press left no doubt that Germany would not be intimidated.   Reminding the Western powers that a practically unanimous public opinion had approved Agadir, the *Kölnische Zeitung* (July 27) spoke of the danger that the effort to hale Germany before the bar of world opinion might bring into play the imponderables which

---

[107] *Deutsche Tageszeitung, Post,* July 24; *Berliner Tageblatt, Freisinnige Zeitung,* April 25; *Berliner Börsen-Zeitung, Reichsbote,* July 26.

[108] *Freisinnige Zeitung,* July 25; *National Zeitung,* July 26.   Cf. Hartung, *Marokkokrise des Jahres 1911,* p. 38.

[109] Bebel, the Social Democratic leader, expressed his regrets some months later. *Verhandlungen,* XiI Leg. Per., II Sess., XI, 7729 (Nov. 9).

[110] *Rheinisch-Westfälische Zeitung,* July 27.

Bismarck had said were so important in politics. "The German people," it wrote, "refuse to be dictated to by foreign powers. . . ." [111] "Strong in the justice of her cause," said the *Lokal-Anzeiger* (July 26), "Germany admonishes the stupid disturbers of the peace, 'Hands off!' "

The Mansion House speech placed Kiderlen in a difficult position. While it was obviously necessary to satisfy England to some extent if he wished to continue his separate negotiations with France, to do this under pressure would weaken Germany's prestige abroad and enrage nationalist opinion at home. Nor could he safely ignore the speech, since France might be encouraged by it to break off the negotiations. In this dilemma, Kiderlen decided, instead of replying with a defiant speech, to explain confidentially Germany's attitude toward Morocco, and to ask for an explanation. On July 24, Metternich assured Grey that no troops would be landed at Agadir and that no one had ever thought of establishing a naval base on the Atlantic coast.[112] The good impression was spoiled, however, when he refused to approve a statement to this effect in the House of Commons, to entertain the idea of an international conference, and when he complained that Lloyd George's action justified suspicion as to England's intentions. After his warning that France's provocations would compel Germany to use every means to secure respect for her treaty rights, Grey replied that "the tone of their communications made it inconsistent with our dignity to give explanation as to the speech of the Chancellor of the Exchequer." [113]

The atmosphere, for a moment, was extremely tense. If Kiderlen thought that England was bluffing, he was mistaken.[114] Steps were taken to put the British fleet upon a war footing. Grey told Lloyd George and Churchill, the colonial minister: "I have just received a communication from the German ambassador so stiff that the Fleet may be attacked at any moment. I have sent for McKenna [the first civil lord of the

---

[111] This article was quoted by the British ambassador. Goschen, July 27. *B. D.*, VII, 407, 408.

[112] Kiderlen-Wächter, July 23. *G. P.*, XXIX, 204; Grey, July 24. *B. D.*, VII, 395.

[113] Grey, July 25. *B. D.*, VII, 397; Kiderlen-Wächter, July 25. *G. P.*, XXIX, 212.

[114] Szögyény, July 27. *Ö.-U. A.*, III, 285.

admiralty] to warn him!"[115] The recent military arrangements with France were even more ominous than the recall of the Atlantic fleet to its bases and the other naval measures of a precautionary character. On July 20, the conversations between Sir Henry Wilson, the chief of staff, and the army commanders in Paris ended in an agreement, which Grey still insisted did not commit his government, providing for the dispatch of an expeditionary force of 171,900 in the event of a German invasion of France.[116] Whether Kiderlen heard immediately of these precautionary measures is relatively unimportant, for Grey's reaction convinced him that something must be done to allay England's anxiety. He insisted that the demand for the entire French Congo must be maintained,[117] but, in London, he caused a more conciliatory attitude to be adopted. Nothing, according to Asquith's remarks to the Russian ambassador a few days later, "was more astonishing" than the change in Germany's tone as reflected in Grey's conversation with Kühlmann, her *chargé d'affaires*. While it is unlikely that he said anything about reducing Germany's demands, Kühlmann apparently gave the foreign secretary to understand that she had no intention of humiliating France. Her aims were "peaceful and conciliatory," and she hoped to have England's good-will in carrying them out.[118]

Less alarmed as to Germany's intentions than at any time since the beginning of the crisis, England was ready to do something to lessen the dangerous tension. Reuter's news agency at once

---

[115] Churchill, *The World Crisis*, p. 44. He had already called McKenna's attention (July 24) to the German menace: "We are dealing with a people who recognize no law except that of force between nations, and whose fleet is mobilized at the present moment. . . ." *B. D.*, VII, 625.

[116] *D. D. F.*, (3), II, 267–271. *Cf.* Oncken, *Vorgeschichte des Weltkrieges*, II, 701. This understanding, expressly conditional upon the action of parliament, was one stage of the negotiations, which had begun as early as January 1906. *Cf.* Brigadier-General Sir G. N. Nicolson, Nov. 6, 1911, *B. D.*, VII, 628. It corresponded in many respects with the views which General Foch had expressed to the British military attaché in April and whose substance Cruppi had recently repeated to Bertie. Fairholme, April 8, Bertie, April 13. *Ibid.*, VI, 619, 620; VII, 190.

[117] Goschen, July 26. *B. D.*, VII, 402–404.

[118] Benckendorff, 19/1 Aug. Siebert, *Diplomatische Aktenstücke*, p. 429. The German and the British documents are both silent in regard to this conversation, but the latter contain a report of Metternich's interview of the morning of July 27 with Grey. The ambassador urged that British interests were not involved in the Congo. In reply, Grey expressed the hope "that we might take this last German communication as a new point of departure and not go back to things which must lead to mutual recrimination." Grey, July 27. *B. D.*, VII, 411, 412.

announced that the government would not take "a direct or active part in the present negotiations. . . . No doubt is felt that if any solution is found outside Morocco which is satisfactory to France it will prove not to be prejudicial to British interests."[119] On the same day, July 27, Asquith repeated these views to the House of Commons with the cabinet's approval. To the Franco-German negotiations, he said, "We are not a party. . . , although the final decision as to British interests must be withheld until a settlement has been arranged." "The question of Morocco," he continued, "bristles with difficulties, but outside Morocco, in other parts of West Africa, we should not think of attempting to interfere with territorial arrangements considered reasonable by those who are more directly interested." There was, from the German point of view, nothing objectionable in the reaction of most of the London press, for the Conservative *Pall Mall Gazette* (July 28) was perhaps alone in the opinion that only "a moderate rectification of Franco-German frontiers in Africa" would be acceptable to France and England.[120] Asquith's reservation in regard to the final settlement was more offensive to William than Lloyd George's speech,[121] but the change in England's attitude was received by public opinion with satisfaction. Reuter's announcement had prepared the way.[122] The Prime Minister, according to the semi-official press, had served the cause of peace. To the *Kölnische Zeitung* (July 28), his views were "serious and fair"; moreover, they confirmed its own support of compensations outside of Morocco. While the *Norddeutsche* had completely ignored Lloyd George's statement, it featured (July 29) Asquith's, printing the pertinent passage in heavy type, and it explained (July 30) that the Prime Minister's purpose had been to quiet the alarm for which the London press had been chiefly responsible. The moderate press breathed a sigh of relief. "Peace or war," wrote the *Vossische Zeitung* (July 28), "hung upon Herr Asquith's words. His was perhaps

---

[119] *Daily Chronicle*, July 27. Metternich at once reported that this communiqué had been officially inspired. *G. P.*, XXIX, 221 (July 27).

[120] *Morning Post, Daily News*, July 28.

[121] Szögyény, Aug. 21. *Ö.-U. A.*, III, 311, 312.

[122] *Lokal-Anzeiger, Berliner Neueste Nachrichten, Berliner Tageblatt, Vossische Zeitung, Frankfurter Zeitung*, July 27.

the gravest responsibility of any statesman in recent years. It was a peaceful speech." "Germany," said the Catholic *Germania* (July 29), "can be content." Writing much later, Theodor Wolff placed the chief blame for England's policy during the crisis upon Kiderlen, but his own contemporary comments, even upon the Prime Minister's speech, were bitter. Friendly relations, he insisted, were impossible as long as she tried "to impose her will in every nook and corner of the globe"; there must be complete equality. The excesses of the chauvinists, were, he thought, objectionable, but they were also natural, for England had changed what was "a mere matter of business" into a question of prestige.[123] Since the factor of prestige had played a part in Kiderlen's policy from the beginning, Wolff's indictment will not hold water; it was, in any case, a prominent feature of the nationalists' reaction to Asquith's conciliatory attitude. As the Berlin correspondent of the *Times* (July 28) had predicted, they talked much of England's retreat. It could rightly be considered "a great victory," according to the *Hamburger Nachrichten* (July 28), if Germany's point of view had been squarely presented to London. The *Post* (July 28) drew the conclusion that Lloyd George's speech had been a bluff. Asquith, the ultra-Conservative *Reichsbote* (July 29) was confident, would yield even on the question of compensations in Morocco "if England's intrigues were seriously challenged." The *Rheinisch-Westfälische Zeitung* (July 28) believed that she would accept any terms if she were given a part of Morocco. On this point, the chauvinist *Tägliche Rundschau* (July 28) was less certain: "Hands off in Morocco!" was still her watchword.[124]

So far as France was concerned, there was little reason for rejoicing. Her press ignored Asquith's speech as much as possible. Not a few concluded from Germany's failure to reply to Lloyd George's challenge that she would back down if faced by a strong resistance.[125] From her silence dated, according to Bülow's post-

---

[123] *Berliner Tageblatt*, July 28. *Cf.* Wolff, *Eve of 1914*, pp. 37ff., 41ff., 50ff.

[124] Asquith, in fact, assured the Russian ambassador that no change had occurred in the English point of view. Benckendorff, 19 July/1 Aug. Siebert, *Diplomatische Aktenstücke*, p. 429.

[125] Oncken, *Vorgeschichte des Weltkrieges*, II, 703. *Cf.* Hartung, *Marokkokrise des Jahres 1911*, p. 40.

war memoirs, the revival of France's self-confidence, the *esprit nouveau*. Certain it is that de Selves and the Quai d'Orsay were determined to yield nothing more than a rectification of frontiers in the Congo, an offer which Kiderlen rejected (July 28) out of hand. Nor was the German minister more conciliatory, since the change in England's attitude probably meant that she would not seriously object if France were forced to yield the entire Congo. Soon after Lloyd George's speech, he authorized von der Lancken (July 23) to approach Caillaux through Fondère, the unofficial go-between of the earlier conversations.[126] The President of the Council, fearing that the chauvinists and the Quai d'Orsay would be encouraged by Lloyd George's intervention, was receptive. With little confidence in England's support in a war and, for the moment, still less in that of Russia, he offered to cede a considerable part of the Congo, including a generous outlet to the coast, even to transfer France's preferential right to the purchase of the Belgian Congo, provided that these concessions, as well as certain financial arrangements, should be incorporated in a general settlement providing for the recognition of a French protectorate in Morocco. To these proposals, Kiderlen turned a cold shoulder. *"Frankreich,"* he said, *"müsse ganz anders bluten."*[127] However, William still had his doubts as to an intransigeant attitude. During an interview (July 29) at Swinemunde, Bethmann and Kiderlen persuaded him that a satisfactory settlement must be secured from France, but the foreign minister seems to have concluded that the Emperor would not support him if he went too far. "There was," wrote the British ambassador, August 4, "a marked change in Herr von Kiderlen's manner and tone . . . after his return."[128] Since a similar change occurred in de Selves' attitude when he heard of Caillaux's offers to Germany from the Quai d'Orsay's secret

---

[126] Lancken's account shows that he and Kiderlen, contrary to Hartung's opinion, took the initiative. Oncken, though he used Lancken's book, evades the question. Hartung, *Marokkokrise des Jahres 1911*, p. 43; Lancken-Wakenitz, *Meine dreissig Dienstjahre, 1888–1918* (Berlin, 1931), pp. 101ff; Oncken, *Vorgeschichte des Weltkrieges*, II, 704; Caillaux, *Agadir*, p. 161.

[127] Lancken-Wakenitz, *op. cit.*, pp. 103, 104. A conversation with Kiderlen so disturbed Bethmann at this time that he spent a sleepless night. Hammann, *Bilder aus der letzten Kaiserzeit*, pp. 87, 88.

[128] *B. D.*, VII, 432.

service, the circumstances were unusually favorable for an agreement. On August 4, the Wolff agency in fact announced that the details of a settlement alone remained to be worked out; Kiderlen had decided to accept something less than the entire French Congo, and de Selves was now willing to cede a part of the coast.

The communiqué no longer corresponded with the facts when it appeared in the press. From the change in Kiderlen's attitude, de Selves apparently concluded that the seriousness of the situation had been exaggerated. He therefore announced, on August 4, that the surrender of any part of the Congo coast would be impossible. Rather than to flout nationalist opinion at home, Kiderlen also decided to try again for his maximum program. The agitation for a share of Morocco had become more intense. Forty thousand copies of Class' pamphlet *Westmarokko deutsch!* had been sold, it was said, since its publication a few days earlier.[129] What Germany needed, it claimed, was not a naval station or the swamps of Central Africa but a full share of Morocco, as an outlet for her surplus population and as a check upon France's use of the natives for military purposes.[130] The feeling that her prestige was at stake was doubtless an even more important factor in the growing tension. Even Aehrenthal now advised "a firm stand" in the interest of the alliance.[131] To yield after England's meddling, said the nationalist *Berliner Neueste Nachrichten* (July 31), would amount to another Olmütz and would encourage new encroachments upon the nation's rights. The Colonial Society resolved that the national honor was involved.[132] Harden foresaw that the Entente Cordiale would last for a generation and that the Anglo-Saxons would continue to dominate the world for a century if Germany contented herself with gestures: "With her five millions of soldiers, Germany can prescribe the conditions for the establishment of *Nouvelle France* and her brown divisions. One more humiliation, another

---

[129] *A. B.,* July 29. Advertisements of this pamphlet appeared even in the Social Democratic *Vorwärts!*

[130] The Pan-Germans frequently cited the views of a geologist-explorer, T. Fischer, "Die Seehafen von Marokko," *Meereskunde,* II, 5 (1908).

[131] Szögyény, Aug. 1, *Ö.-U. A.,* III, 290, 291.

[132] *National Zeitung,* Aug. 2.

panicky retreat, and only the sword will be able to save what the tongue and the pen have endangered. . . ." [133]   The *Freisinnige Zeitung* (Aug. 4), exasperated by what seemed to be the systematic malignment of Germany's methods and intentions in the English and French presses,[134] protested bitterly against the cession of any part of her meager colonial possessions.[135]   Except in regard to Morocco, Kiderlen was in substantial accord with the nationalist point of view.   Only recently—probably before his interview with the Emperor at Swinemunde—he had said that Lloyd George's speech and the attitude of the French press had made the demand for the entire French Congo a matter of prestige: "We must fight if necessary. . . ." [136]   It was, however, the arguments of Lindequist, the colonial minister, who protested against the surrender of the one colony that was paying for itself, that caused the withdrawal of the offer of Togoland on August 4.

To the nationalists, the Wolff Agency's communiqué seemed the last straw.   The French, they feared, had rightly counted upon the Emperor's moderation.   On August 5, Count von Preysing wrote in Harden's *Zukunft:* "Here fell a king, but not fighting." [137]   The *National Zeitung* (Aug. 4) spoke of Kiderlen as enjoying Bethmann's confidence, of the minister's determination to resign rather than to sacrifice Germany's interests, and hoped that no differences would arise between the leaders of German policy.   Although this journal dismissed ostentatiously the rumor that William had given assurances to Cambon behind Kiderlen's back, the *Post* (Aug. 4) immediately launched perhaps the most savage attack which a German newspaper had ever directed against a German Emperor.   The *National Zeitung's* article was "a bolt of lightning in a stormy night."   Kiderlen would certainly resign; no honorable statesman could assume the responsibility for the impending retreat.   "Oh! would that

---

[133] Harden, "Marokko," *Zukunft*, July 29.

[134] William shared this resentment.   To General French he said in a jocular tone, August 3, in presenting his photograph: "Here is your Arch Enemy! here is the disturber of the peace of Europe!!" *B. D.*, VII, 463 (undated note by French).

[135] Cf. *Post*, July 30; *Madgeburgische Zeitung*, in *Berliner Neueste Nachrichten*, Aug. 3.

[136] Hammann, *Bilder aus der letzten Kaiserzeit*, pp. 87, 88.

[137] *G. P.*, XXIX, 319n.   *Cf.* Wolff, *Eve of 1914*, p. 60.

we had been spared this moment of unspeakable shame, of deep ignominy, far deeper than that of Olmütz! . . . What has happened to the Hohenzollerns, who count among their ancestors a Great Elector, a Frederick the Great, an Emperor William I? Is our Emperor to be regarded as the strongest support of the English and French policy, a support worth more than fifty French divisions? We neither can nor will believe this to be true. . . ." But the English and the French newspapers were saying that his return to Berlin would assure Gemany's retreat. *"Guillaume le timide, le valeureux poltron!* Count Brandenburg died of a broken heart [after Olmütz]. We console ourselves for the Fatherland's humiliation with aesthetic tea parties, dinners, suppers, tours, inspections, and celebrations of all kinds, thereby earning the cheap applause—and the secret contempt—of the foreigners." [138] Nearly the entire German press, according to the British ambassador, condemned the *Post,* and that journal explained a week later (Aug. 11) that the article did not represent the views of the Free Conservative Party, that in fact it had been written by an underling during the editor's absence.[139] The *Norddeutsche's* remark (Aug. 6) that the *Post* deserved the *"schärfste Zurückweisung"* apparently was the only expression of official displeasure, although the author, had he been a Social Democrat, would have risked imprisonment for a year. Other nationalist journals were just as bitter, although they treated the Emperor more tactfully. The nation, wrote the *Rheinisch-Westfälische Zeitung* (Aug. 5), expected William to take a firm stand: "Let there be no mistake. Its disillusionment might throw us back, not twenty or thirty, but eighty years, and create a rift between the people and the prince, forcing the conclusion that greatness can only be attained through conflict with the sovereign. . . ." Never, cried other journals, had there been an equally unanimous demand for a strong policy.[140] War was preferable to surrender. One weekly called for an ultimatum.[141]

---

138 The British ambassador forwarded the greater part of this article, in translation, to his government. Goschen, Aug. 6. *B. D.,* VII, 439, 440.

139 Goschen, Aug. 8. *Ibid.,* VII, 443; *Deutsche Tageszeitung,* Aug. 5. The chairman of the Free Conservative Party announced that his party had broken with the *Post. Kölnische Zeitung,* Aug. 10.

140 *Berliner Neueste Nachrichten,* Aug. 7; *Deutsche Zeitung,* in *Post,* Aug. 7.

141 "Deutschland, Deutschland über Alles," *Gegenwart,* Aug. 19.

A National Liberal news circular thought that the Reichstag should be summoned and that it should demand an accounting of the government's conduct during the crisis.[142]

Since the clippings that were regularly placed before him were largely from the Conservative press, William undoubtedly felt the impact of this strong current of emotion. He immediately seized an opportunity to show his determination to defend Germany's prestige and honor. Discouraged by the refusal of his offer of a general understanding, Caillaux ceased for a moment to be a moderating influence in Paris. On August 3, after acknowledging that Kiderlen's new attitude (in the conversations with Cambon) had improved the prospects for an agreement, he told Bertie, the British ambassador, that Germany was certain to raise "other questions disturbing to peace," that he foresaw "in the not distant future a conflict in which France and England and Russia would be fighting Germany," and that he was anxious to remove every source of friction within the Entente Cordiale.[143] The exact sense of what he said to Fondère may be a matter of dispute, but it is clear that he wished to urge upon Berlin the need of a prompt settlement and that Schoen reported him as threatening to send a warship to Agadir if a solution were not found by the end of the following week.[144] William reacted even more violently than Kiderlen, who thought that the unofficial negotiations with Caillaux should be suspended until the threat had been retracted, for he at once directed that the conversations with Cambon should be broken off.[145] "I am not going to dance attendance on the French any longer," he wrote after another attack in the Catholic *Kölnische Volkszeitung* (Aug. 7). "They must at once make an acceptable offer, or we will take more, and that immediately."[146] Caillaux should be given twenty-four hours in which to apologize, and, in the meantime, arrangements should be made for a speedier mobilization of the fleet.[147] Even after the French President of the Council explained

[142] *Nationalliberale Korrespondenz,* in *Deutsche Tageszeitung,* Aug. 8.
[143] Bertie, Aug. 3.   *B. D.,* VII, 431, 432.
[144] *G. P.,* XXIX, 310 (Aug. 4).
[145] Kiderlen, Aug. 5; Jenisch, Aug. 6.   *Ibid.,* XXIX, 311, 312.
[146] *Ibid.,* XXIX, 319n.
[147] William II's comments, Jenisch, Kiderlen, Aug. 8.   *Ibid.,* XXIX, 312, 315.

that he had been misunderstood, that he had merely said that the hotheads would soon demand the dispatch of a warship, William continued his firm stand. "We will," he wrote (Aug. 13), "insist upon our demands, for it is an affair of honor for Germany." If the French refused, he would "not be satisfied until the last Frenchman was driven out of Morocco—by the sword if necessary." [148]

The negotiations had reached an impasse. What Kiderlen regarded as the minimum which Germany would accept, France was unwilling to give; what France offered for a protectorate in Morocco was inadmissible to the German minister. The temper of public opinion became dangerously tense in both countries. There was a rebirth of confidence in France. Behind Germany's refusal of her offers was seen a desire for war, and in the fate of the accord of 1909 a warning against any agreement whatever. In return for the surrender of territory, France would secure paper promises of questionable value. Germany, it was felt, demanded compensations for abandoning rights and claims which had no basis other than France's weakness. That the government might itself lose patience and by some hasty decision precipitate war was by no means impossible. "We are not," said Messimy, the war minister, "going to stand any more nonsense from Germany, no '*manque de politesse*' and . . . we have the nation back of us." [149] To what extent military preparations were undertaken is uncertain, but the German military attaché, reporting every scrap of evidence as to unusual activity, interpreted the cancellation of the fall maneuvers as a step toward a general mobilization. [150] On September 4, one day before William reviewed the German fleet, Delcassé, minister of the marine, staged a naval demonstration at Toulon, showing the improvements accomplished since he had taken office and the government's confidence that England would protect the northern coast. [151] According to de Selves, the proposals of August 4 should be

---

[148] Jenisch, Aug. 13. *G. P.*, XXIX, 229, 230. *Cf.* Goschen, Aug. 16. *B. D.*, VII, 451.

[149] Fairholme, Sept. 1. *B. D.*, VII, 635.

[150] Winterfeldt, Aug. 24. *G. P.*, XXIX, 344. The British military attaché did not question the official explanation that the prevalence of the hoof and mouth disease in Northern France was the cause. *B. D.*, VII, 634.

[151] Hartung, *Marokkokrise des Jahres 1911*, p. 55.

France's last word. Despite Russia's coolness and England's decision to call a conference in the event of the failure of the Franco-German negotiations, he favored the occupation of certain ports on the Atlantic coast of Morocco if Germany landed troops or increased her naval forces at Agadir. Caillaux, however, had taken steps to restrain his impetuous foreign minister by transferring the control of foreign policy to the cabinet. What enabled him to resist the pressure of the extremists was doubtless, in the final analysis, Germany's failure to take further action at Agadir. No troops were landed and there was no concentration of warships.[152] The President of the Council was thus able to suggest early in September that the question of compensations could be settled more easily after France had secured what she wanted in Morocco.

Meanwhile, Germany was marking time, in the hope that the tension would cause France to make an acceptable offer. Neither William nor Kiderlen wished to force the issue. The Emperor's wounded pride had apparently been satisfied by his explosive comments upon the diplomatic dispatches. If Kiderlen, under the influence of Lloyd George's ·speech, had earlier spoken of fighting, he soon decided that Morocco was not worth a war. A foothold on or near the Mediterranean would increase Germany's vulnerability; nothing was to be gained by insisting upon a return to the Algeciras Act, since France's promises would soon be broken. "Any other settlement, provided that we can honestly accept it, is therefore preferable."[153] He did not aspire to the easy popularity of a war policy.[154] So confident was he that no vital decisions were impending that he went, with his mistress, to Chamonix (of all places), August 17, where Caillaux had the local prefect extend the government's formal greetings. He perhaps counted—and not without reason—upon the Russo-German agreement of August 19 to convince France of the wisdom of satisfying Germany. By dropping the demand for a specific recognition of Persia's independence and integrity, by promising

---

[152] For the movement of the German warships at Agadir, see *B. D.*, VII, 846, 847 (App. VI).
[153] Tirpitz, *Aufbau der deutschen Weltmacht*, p. 202 (Aug. 8).
[154] Jäckh, *Kiderlen-Wächter*, II, 138 (Aug. 12).

that no concessions for the construction of telegraphs, roads, and railways would be sought in Persia, Russia abandoned her opposition to the Berlin-Bagdad Railway and agreed to build a connecting line with her own system. However, the agreement contained no assurance that the diplomatic combination to which Russia belonged was not directed against Germany; in this respect, the results of the protracted negotiations since the Potsdam conversations were disappointing.

To exaggerate their significance, at the risk of a later disappointment, was clearly not the government's intention. The point of greatest interest, according to the semi-official press, was the fact that an agreement was possible in spite of the numerous obstacles.[155] Under no obligation to be discreet, other journals, eager for encouraging signs, extracted the last shred of comfort: the irritation manifested by French opinion, the prospect of increased friction between England and Russia, and the possible existence of secret political terms.[156] It was, in any event, a welcome demonstration of Russia's freedom of action.[157] The attitude of the Progressive *Freisinnige Zeitung* (Aug. 22) best illustrates perhaps the far-reaching effect of the international situation upon public opinion. Instead of deprecating any association with Russia as had once been its wont, it was delighted with the new arrangement, whose political significance, in its opinion, far transcended its economic provisions. True, the Franco-Russian Alliance still existed, but it had been deprived of "its aggressive tendencies"; and the Chancellor's explanation after Potsdam that Russia would participate in no hostile action was still valid. "Therewith the hopes which the *revanche* politicians in Paris and the anti-German agitators in London had placed in Russia were practically buried." To a Conservative review, the accord was "the work of a real world policy and in many respects more important than the Moroccan negotiations."[158] A nationalist observer described it as "a support for Germany in the ultimate

---

[155] *N. A. Z.*, Aug. 20; *Kölnische Zeitung*, Aug. 21. Cf. *Deutsche Tageszeitung, Post*, Aug. 21.

[156] *Frankfurter Zeitung*, in *Germania*, Aug. 22; *Rheinisch-Westfälische Zeitung*, Aug. 22; *Grenzboten*, 1911, III, 277 (Aug. 23).

[157] *Germania*, Aug. 22.

[158] *P. J.*, vol. 145, p. 582 (Sept.).

decision between peace and war." [159] Although Kiderlen had hinted shortly before the conclusion of the understanding that Russia might advise her French friends not to threaten Germany with the Triple Entente, [160] there is little evidence that either the diplomats or the press expected any immediately beneficial results so far as the Franco-German negotiations were concerned. On the contrary, the German ambassador in St. Petersburg warned his government against exaggerated hopes, because Russia's most important reason for making the agreement was her need of peace and quiet. [161] "From it," wrote the nationalist *Tägliche Rundschau* (Aug. 21), "a new era of Russo-German friendship will scarcely arise." To the *Alldeutsche Blätter* (Sept. 2), it was nothing more than "a lucky move of a pawn in a game of chess." Nor did Russia exert a determining influence upon French policy. In Paris, Izvolski began to talk of the horrors of war, of arbitration by Austria, and even of the harmlessness of a German establishment at Agadir. [162] On September 1, he lectured the French foreign minister on the need of peace, for Russia's armaments were not yet *à point*. The question of compensations, he said, was unimportant in comparison with the risks of war, but de Selves reminded the ambassador of Russia's obligations as an ally. Considering France's generous offers, arbitration was impossible. Russia was not prepared to break with her ally; the Tsar reaffirmed her diplomatic and military support, should occasion require it. [163] Germany's hope of Russia's aid thus came to nothing. Izvolski's strictures, which the French suspected had German origins, were more than counterbalanced by the fair certainty of England's support. Her warning that France must shun even the appearance of responsibility for war probably exerted a greater moderating influence than anything which the Russian ambassador said. [164]

On his return to Berlin at the end of August, Kiderlen had lost much of his former confidence that Germany could afford to

---

[159] "Ernste Lage," *Gegenwart*, Sept. 2.
[160] Siebert, *Diplomatische Aktenstücke*, p. 433 (3/16 Aug.). Cf. *B. D.*, VII, 467n.
[161] Pourtalès, Sept. 1. *G. P.*, XXIX, 354, 355.
[162] Bertie, Aug. 23. *B. D.*, VII, 467, 468.
[163] Bertie, Sept. 1. *Ibid.*, VII, 471.
[164] Grey, Aug. 23, Sept. 5, 8. *Ibid.*, VII, 483, 505, 521.

wait. The financial condition of the country was disquieting. Starting with considerable losses in the American market, the always slender capital reserves were being drained by something like a run on the banks and by France's withdrawal of her large short-term loans.[165] The situation, according to the financiers, required a lessening of the tension.[166] On the other hand, Kiderlen's freedom of action was limited by the clamor of the nationalists. No longer were they welcome allies, for their demands could only be satisfied by a successful war. For that war more than a few were prepared, although the British ambassador rightly believed that the majority had no taste for a desperate gamble.[167] Not for nothing had the extremists been saying for weeks that Germany's future was at stake. "Everything—future, power, honor, and influence—depends upon the settlement." [168] In all sections of the press, wrote the British consul general in Munich, there was "a feeling of profound disappointment at [the] course of negotiations. . . ." [169] No amount of Congo territory could reconcile the nationalists to the sacrifice of Morocco. "There are," wrote one, "only three reactions anywhere in Germany: shame, anger, [and] contempt." As for the Congo, it was the place "where the fever bacillus and the sand flea say good night to each other. Ah! it is beautiful beyond description. And how many square miles! Its value is to be measured, not merely by square miles, but by standards of real worth—such as the export of bacilli or the prospect of a profitable traffic in sand for our breeders of canaries. Oh, there is far more in the affair than meets the eye! Especially sand." [170] The chief fault was the government's weakness. "What provocations have they offered these last months," exclaimed the *Berliner Neueste Nachrichten* (Sept. 2), "and what have we *quietly accepted!*" The nation had been deceived. "People should not be permitted to talk more

---

[165] Oppenheimer, Oct. 21. *B. D.*, VII, 796–805. The *Times* (Sept. 25) estimated the French withdrawals at £10,000,000. They "began long before the fateful days early in September. . ."

[166] Hartung, *Marokkokrise des Jahres 1911*, pp. 55, 56.

[167] Goschen, Aug. 26. Nicolson, *Carnock*, p. 344.

[168] "Ernste Lage," *Gegenwart*, Sept. 2.

[169] Unless opportunities were provided for Germany's expansion, "internal interests" would eventually compel, in his opinion, "a recourse to arms—to make a final bid for the hegemony of the world." Corbett, Aug. 20. *B. D.*, VII, 459.

[170] "Abstieg," *Gegenwart*, Aug. 26.

and more loudly of war if there is no intention of waging it. . . ."[171] Moltke, the chief of staff, believed that war must be envisaged if the situation was still to be saved. "If we slink out of this affair with tails between our legs, and if we do not make a demand which we are prepared to enforce with the sword, I despair of the Empire's future."[172] Even the *Kölnische Zeitung* (Sept. 5), while it frowned upon the extreme measures which the *Post* (Aug. 26) recommended, admitted that public opinion was gravely alarmed. In 1870 war had come when the Spanish throne was far less important to Germany. "And he whose function it is to feel the public's pulse is a poor diagnostician if he does not see that all classes are ready to follow the government to the bitter end, whatever the Social Democrats may say."

The concession of an unconditional protectorate in Morocco would certainly infuriate the nationalists. This, Kiderlen wished, if possible, to avoid, especially in view of the approaching Reichstag elections. Nor could he afford to give the impression to the more moderate groups that he was unable to protect Germany's interests. A review that sometimes spoke for the foreign minister pointed out that Morocco would be a source of weakness to France, since she would have to withdraw white troops from the Vosges frontier, whose value would be greater than any colored units.[173] However persuaded Kiderlen might be as to the uselessness of paper guarantees, he was nevertheless bound to save what he could of Germany's position. He was ready to recognize a practical protectorate, provided that the word did not itself appear in the agreement and that France would meet his terms in regard to Germany's economic interests. His demands (Sept. 8) were so far-reaching that the negotiations again threatened to break down. Among other matters, they included provisions for the "open door," without any time limit, and German participation in the construction and administration of all railways (except two) to the extent of seventy per cent in the Southwest and thirty per cent in the rest of Morocco. Agreement on

---

[171] "Krieg und Kriegsgeschrei," *Gegenwart*, Aug. 26.

[172] H. von Moltke, *Erinnerungen, Briefe, Dokumente, 1877–1916* (Stuttgart, 1922), p. 362 (Aug. 19).

[173] *Grenzboten*, 1911, III, 430, 431 (Aug. 30).

this basis was impossible. Not only did the French question Kiderlen's desire for a definitive settlement, but the British foreign office was aroused by the possibility of a Franco-German monopoly of railway construction.[174] The German minister, however, had asked for much in order to be sure of securing something. More than once public opinion was told that the negotiations were proceeding satisfactorily;[175] that, from the beginning, they had envisaged political freedom for France, economic guarantees in Morocco, and colonial compensations for Germany; and that, with mutual good-will, a prompt solution could be expected.[176] A press campaign against those who demanded war was launched.[177] To the *Kölnische Zeitung* (Sept. 9), an obsolete treaty which had been abandoned by all of the other powers was not worth fighting for. The *Grenzboten* charged that the Pan-German leaders were tools of the industrial interests and that the *Rheinisch-Westfälische Zeitung,* the *Tägliche Rundschau,* and the *Post,* described as the Mannesmann press, had misled public opinion in regard to the government's aims.[178] Assumptions fundamental to the nationalist point of view were questioned. That Germany's imperialist aspirations involved her honor was denied. Against the argument that Morocco was a necessary outlet for her surplus population, it was pointed out that her man power was needed at home for military purposes. Indeed, the annual influx of agricultural laborers showed that there was no surplus.[179]

The diplomatic situation made an early settlement desirable. While England advised caution in Paris, there were limits beyond which Grey was not prepared to go. She might be blamed, so Grey informed Goschen in Berlin, for unpopular concessions, with

[174] Minutes by various officials, Goschen, Sept. 8. *B. D.,* VII, 510.

[175] *N. A. Z.,* Sept. 4; *Kölnische Zeitung,* Sept. 12, Wolff Bureau, Sept. 20. *Cf.* Hartung, *Marokkokrise des Jahres 1911,* pp. 55, 56.

[176] *Kölnische Zeitung,* Sept. 7, Berlin, Sept. 6; *N. A. Z.,* Sept. 8.

[177] At Düsseldorf, September 10, the Pan-Germans adopted a resolution calling for the breaking off of the negotiations. *A. B.,* Sept. 16; *Rheinisch-Westfälische Zeitung,* Sept. 24.

[178] 1911, III (Sept. 6). The *Tägliche Rundschau* and the *Post* (Sept. 14) immediately announced that the review would have to substantiate its charge in court. During the resulting law suit, the public heard of Kiderlen's dealings with Class for the first time.

[179] "England und Deutschland," *Deutsche Revue,* 1911, IV, 16 (Oct. 1); B. Harms, "Morokko," *ibid.,* 1911, IV, 3, 4; *P. J.,* vol. 145, pp. 582, 583 (Sept.).

the result that the entent would suffer.[180]   He still feared a sudden offensive against the British fleet. "Our fleets," he told Nicolson, September 17, "should therefore always be in such a condition and position that they would welcome a German attack. . . ."[181]   The army was also alert. With the aid "of a pointer and a big map," Sir Henry Wilson explained to the committee on imperial defense the movements of the proposed expeditionary force.[182]   At the end of August—after attending the German maneuvers—he inspected the French frontier fortresses.[183] To the German diplomats it seemed significant that the English government had intervened to avert a threatened railway strike and had used the gravity of the international situation to secure concessions from the companies for the workers.[184]   While these developments were mostly unknown to the general public, there was no mystery about England's support of France. The hopes aroused by Asquith's speech of July 27 had not been fulfilled. England was blamed for France's unreasonableness. Had it not been for her meddling, wrote the nationalist *Berliner Neueste Nachrichten* (Aug. 8), "France would certainly have reached an understanding with us over Morocco." "England," said the Catholic *Germania* (Aug. 20), "rules in Paris." "Everyone knows," wrote the *Post* (Aug. 28) under the caption "England the Enemy," "that 'England, perfidious England' is the principal force behind the Republic's hostility toward us." Seeking, as usual, to profit by the quarrels of others, she was, insisted the National Liberal *National Zeitung* (Aug. 23), purposefully obstructing a Franco-German settlement.[185]   Popular feeling, according to an observer who favored an Anglo-German rapprochement, was directed against England more than against France.[186]   Another commentator regretted that France and Germany had not reached an understanding during the Fashoda crisis.[187]

Instead of discouraging this movement of opinion, the gov-

---

[180] *B. D.,* VII, 545 (Sept. 17).
[181] *Ibid.,* VII, 638.
[182] Lloyd George, *War Memoirs,* I, 51.
[183] Hartung, *Marokkokrise des Jahres 1911,* p. 55.
[184] Metternich, Aug. 22. *G. P.,* XXIX, 233–237.
[185] Cf. *P. J.,* vol. 145, p. 585 (Sept.).
[186] "England und Deutschland," *Deutsche Revue,* 1911, IV, 16 (Oct. 1).
[187] *Grenzboten,* 1911, III, 427 (Aug. 30).

ernment exaggerated the significance of Dr. Münz's alleged interview with an anonymous British diplomat in the *Neue Freie Presse* (Aug. 25) of Vienna. The views expressed therein were extremely offensive to Germany. The diplomat, who was immediately identified as Sir Francis Cartwright, the ambassador to Austria, was represented as confident that Germany, faced by the choice of war or a settlement disappointing to the Pan-Germans, would prefer the latter. What followed was still worse. "These eternal provocations are becoming serious. Behind Germany's foreign policy stands a limited group that is just as reckless as France was in 1870, not the German people. The German government does not represent public opinion." From the speed with which the German press began to attack him, Cartwright concluded that the campaign had been engineered by the German embassy in Vienna—in retaliation for his supposed part in Austria's independent attitude in foreign affairs—but it is at least true, as he pointed out, that the German government permitted the agitation to take its course without even calling attention to the need of verifying the interview's authenticity.[188] Indeed, the *Kölnische Zeitung* (Aug. 26) spoke of "a systematic effort on the part of all hostile elements to force Germany to her knees." Even the foreign office was dissatisfied with Cartwright's and Grey's denials. "Kiderlen," wrote Goschen, "only grinned, and said that the words may have been those of Dr. Münz but the sentiments were those of Cartwright." [189] For days, the diplomats debated the text of a communiqué to the press, the Germans insisting at first upon the simple statement that England had made official explanations. On September 15, three weeks after the appearance of the interview, the *Norddeutsche* announced that England's explanations had satisfied the government. However, the press remained thoroughly skeptical. The official statement, according to the *Times'* (Sept. 16) correspondent, was "greeted with a chorus of contemptuous and highly offensive comment." Lacking a definite and official repudiation of the contents of the

---

[188] Cartwright, Aug. 26, 31, Sept. 1, 14. *B. D.,* VII, 837–840, 843, 844. Aehrenthal soon began to hint in London that Cartwright should be recalled. Mensdorff, Oct. 5. *Ö.-U. A.,* III, 398, 399.

[189] *B. D.,* VII, 499 (Sept. 1).

interview—and nothing like it appeared even in Cartwright's confidential letters—the incident, though officially closed, remained a source of bitterness and was thereafter frequently cited as an example of England's ill-will.

Italy's declaration of war against Turkey, September 29, diverted public opinion from Morocco and, at least from the government's point of view, increased the desirability of a prompt settlement with France.[190]   As Italy's ally and as Turkey's friend, Germany could expect nothing but disadvantages, since Italy's defeat would probably diminish her already doubtful loyalty, and her victory might cool Turkey's friendliness toward the *Drang nach Osten*.   Either result, it was feared, would increase Italy's dependence upon England.[191]   Germany had moderately exerted herself to maintain peace on the basis of economic concessions in Tripoli, but to no avail.[192]   In fact, the fear of German infiltration into Tripoli had been one of the reasons why Italian public opinion demanded immediate action.[193]   Reticent toward Germany and Austria in regard to her plans, Italy was more communicative in her negotiations with the Triple Entente, receiving in return assurances that no objections would be raised.   England was even ready to advise Turkey to seek the assistance of the Central powers.[194]   In Germany, public opinion generally condemned Italy's *"Raubzug,"* although her superiority to Turkey as an ally assured a measure of complaisance, but it was even more definitely in favor of neutrality.[195]   Instead of urging a prompt liquidation of the Agadir crisis in order to free Germany's hands, the press charged England and France with a large measure of the responsibility for the war.[196]   "Why," asked one journal, "was the French press silent in regard to Italy's aggression, since it had condemned Agadir as an immoral use of force?"[197]   The expedition to Fez, not the "Panther's" spring, had given the signal for

---

[190] Hartung, *Marokkokrise des Jahres 1911*, p. 58.
[191] *Post*, Sept. 26.
[192] Marschall, Sept. 25; Kiderlen, Sept. 26. *G. P.*, XXX, 52, 56.
[193] *Cf.* C. W. Askew's unpublished dissertation, Duke University, "Europe and Italy's Acquisition of Libya."
[194] Grey, Sept. 19. *B. D.*, 274.
[195] The *Reichsbote* (Oct. 1) protested even when Germany took over the protection of Italian interests in Turkey during the war.
[196] England alone, wrote the *National Zeitung* (Sept. 26), would profit.
[197] *National Zeitung*, Sept. 28.

Italy's action, although one review admitted that Austria's annexation of Bosnia-Herzegovina began the series of violations of the status quo.[198] William, however, was chiefly concerned for the future. Like the *Kölnische Zeitung* (Sept. 26), he feared that the war would reopen the entire Near Eastern question. With a flash of the insight that was one of his better characteristics, he predicted that a more intense national agitation in the Balkans, together with English and Russian imperialist interests, would precipitate a European conflict. To avert it, he proposed, without any result, an understanding with France (England was not to be included) for the maintenance of the status quo in the Balkans.[199] In fact, Kiderlen had already invited France to join him in advising caution in Rome, but Cambon successfully evaded the question by making her consent depend upon the coöperation of the other powers and upon France's engagements with Italy.[200]

Thanks to William's intervention and to France's aversion to a serious clash, the raising of the German flag at Agadir, September 27, was promptly arranged without seriously interrupting the negotiations.[201] On October 11 an agreement was finally reached on the Moroccan question. Germany secured many guarantees for her economic interests—the recognition of the open door for thirty years, the perpetuation of the state bank as organized in 1906, measures against any special consideration for French interests in the construction of all forms of communication or in the customs administration, provision for branch lines between all mines and the railways, and special courts for the trial of cases between German nationals and natives until the reorganization of the judicial system. On the other hand, she had failed to secure a fixed percentage in the construction and administration of railways and other public works, a privileged position in Southwest Morocco, or the establishment of mixed courts like those of Egypt. Whether this settlement would remove Morocco as a source of friction only time would tell. There was pes-

[198] *Grenzboten,* 1911, IV, 41 (Oct. 4).
[199] Jenisch, Sept. 26, 28. *G. P.,* XXX, 65, 66.
[200] Goschen, Sept. 27. *B. D.,* IX, 279.
[201] Hartung, *Marokkokrise des Jahres 1911,* pp. 58, 59.

simism in both countries. Some of those who were best acquainted with the situation in Morocco had little confidence in
the efficacy of paper promises for the protection of Germany's
economic interests,[202] and many Frenchmen feared that the Germans would use these guarantees for political purposes, in spite
of the recognition of a French protectorate. The agreement
nevertheless enabled the diplomats to attack the problem of compensations with better prospects of success. The German newspapers withheld their verdict until the extent of France's
concessions were known, while Paul Cambon enlisted the aid of
England and Russia in keeping his government from yielding to
the last press campaign against the surrender of any part of the
national heritage. So obstinate, however, was France's insistence
that her public opinion must be reckoned with that Kiderlen,
who was anxious to bring the negotiations to a conclusion, again
yielded a considerable part of his demands of September 8. Except for a minor frontier rectification favorable to the French colony of Dahomey, no part of Togoland was surrendered and
France received only a part of the Duck's Bill in the Cameroons,
but the final accord of November 4 awarded Germany scarcely
half of what Kiderlen had earlier fixed as the irreducible minimum in the Congo, and that half included only a small part of
the coast. Nevertheless, it laid a foundation for later advances
toward a great Central African Empire. French Equatorial
Africa was trisected by two tongues of German territory extending from the Cameroons southward to the Congo and eastward
to the Ubangi River. If France refused to yield her preferential
right in the purchase of the Belgian Congo, Germany secured
from her a similar concession relating to the tiny Spanish colony of
Rio-Muni, which was now entirely surrounded by German territory.

Four months of tension had left its mark upon public opinion.
The more moderate groups had applauded Agadir, not as a threat
to the peace of Europe, but as a necessary step toward a final settlement of the Moroccan question. They were undoubtedly disappointed, but they did not believe that any of the issues of the crisis

---

[202] *Deutsche Marokko-Zeitung,* Sept. 19, Oct. 23, in Hartung, *Marokkokrise des
Jahres 1911,* p. 59.

justified a resort to force.   Doubt had been expressed, even when the tension was most acute, that public opinion would accept Morocco as an adequate reason for war.[203]   An audible sigh of relief followed the agreement of November 4. Whatever its short-comings, it was at least a peaceful solution.   This fact, according to the Catholic press, would decide the reaction of public opinion. The extremists, wrote the *Kölnische Volkszeitung* (Nov. 6), did not represent the German people: "Their press does not reflect the real public opinion any more than Berlin is Germany.   It is well that this is so, for otherwise we would have to conclude that we have become a nation of neurasthenics!"[204]   "All in all," said the *Germania* (Nov. 5), "the Morocco accord is a peaceful docu-ment and as such it should be warmly welcomed."   Even the agrarian *Deutsche Tageszeitung* (Nov. 5), which described the characteristic mood of public opinion as one of depressed resigna-tion, wrote that there would be a "general sigh of relief."   Some even spoke well of the terms.   Schiemann privately congratulated Kiderlen and publicly described the Moroccan settlement as "a masterly assurance of our real interests."[205]   Another observer, who may likewise have reflected official opinion, thought that the international organization of the state bank could be made an effective defense against France's political control,[206] and the So-cial Democratic *Vorwärts* (Nov. 5) was pleased by the mainte-nance of the "open-door."   According to the *National Zeitung* (Nov. 4), the honor of neither country had been injured.   To the disparity between the gains of the two countries, between Germany's original aims and the result, the general reaction was, however, extremely unfavorable.   The resignation of Lindequist (Nov. 3), the colonial minister, was an eloquent commentary on the value of the new possessions in the Congo.[207]   No one could say, wrote the liberal *Berliner Tageblatt* (Nov. 2), whose chief criticism of the government's policy during the crisis was directed (Nov. 5) against its methods, that they were comparable to Ger-

---

[203] *Deutsche Tageszeitung,* Nov. 1.
[204] Cf. *Vorwärts,* Nov. 10.
[205] Schiemann, Nov. 23. Jäckh, *Kiderlen-Wächter,* II, 144, 145; *Kreuz-Zeitung,* Nov. 8.   Schiemann, *Deutschland und die Grosse Politik,* XI, 321.
[206] *Grenzboten,* 1911, IV, 294 (Nov. 8).
[207] *Magdeburgische Zeitung, Leipziger Neueste Nachrichten,* in *Post,* Nov. 4. *Cf.* Lindequist, Oct. 31. *G. P.,* XXIX, 412.

many's sacrifices. In comparison with the pressure which Germany had brought to bear upon France, the results, according to the Catholic *Kölnische Volkszeitung,* were insignificant. "People are beginning to ask, *why are we sacrificing billions for naval and military armaments?*" [208] The extremists could scarcely find words to express their indignation and disillusionment. To them, the agreement was "a national shame and the last nail in the coffin of German prestige." [209] "The mountain of the 'New Course' has again labored," said the *Rheinisch-Westfälische Zeitung* (Nov. 4), "and has brought forth a mouse. . . . *'Eine Tat,'* we wrote with a joyful heart. Now it is a joke." The *Post* (Nov. 4) lamented the collapse of Germany's last hope of acquiring an outlet for her teeming millions: "Unless relief is somehow found, the result will be a succession of serious crises, until the entire nation draws the conclusion, 'Better to fight than to starve.' . . ." The *Leipziger Neueste Nachrichten* regretted that force had not been used: "We are clad in armor, millions of soldiers are ready, our sacrifices amount to billions. But we do not fight. We send a ship, excite the world, and then go to sleep. Life is a burden." [210] Once a hero, Kiderlen now was an object of abuse. Of all the statesmen involved in the crisis, he was, in the *Berliner Neueste Nachrichten's* (Nov. 5) opinion, the least able, with the possible exception of de Selves. He had presumed to speak of a German Central African Empire!

From the National Liberals and the Conservatives came a strong demand that the Reichstag should be permitted to pass judgment upon the agreement of November 4, although the ratification of treaties was not one of its constitutional powers.[211] Only the extremists could desire, given the state of feeling, a public debate. What they wanted was stated by the *Berliner Neueste Nachrichten* (Nov. 8) in no uncertain terms. The Reichstag "should declare with the greatest emphasis that it *disapproves* the present *policy of peace at any price,* that it will no longer tolerate

---

[208] *National Zeitung,* Nov. 5.
[209] This bitterness was partly explained, according to the British ambassador, by the approaching election. Goschen, Nov. 9, *B. D.,* VII, 658.
[210] *Tägliche Rundschau,* Nov. 7. It was cowardly, wrote the *Rheinisch-Westfälische Zeitung* (Nov. 4), to say that Morocco was not worth a war.
[211] *Post,* Oct. 29; *Kölnische Zeitung,* Oct. 30; *National Zeitung,* Nov. 8; *Gegenwart,* Nov. 4.

a policy of concessions and of retreat, and that it is *ready to undertake every sacrifice necessary for a strong, manly, and honest policy.*" Even the *Post* hesitated (Oct. 29), alarmed by the bitterness of nationalist feeling to which it had itself contributed, for it feared that an attempt might be made to reduce the powers of the executive. The government, nevertheless, agreed, hoping perhaps to conciliate the nationalists, in view of the approaching election. There was also the danger that silence might be interpreted abroad as sympathy for their point of view or as a confession that the government feared to oppose them openly. In his speech of November 9, Bethmann again asserted that the "Panther's" mission had been the defense of German interests, not the conquest of a part of Morocco. He wrung from the events after July 1 every possible satisfaction for German pride. The main objective had been a definite settlement of the Moroccan question by separate and direct negotiations with France. "This program," he declared, "has been accomplished. No influence, foreign or domestic, was strong enough to force us to depart from it by a single step." England had retreated, not Germany. As to Lloyd George's speech, he advanced again the specious argument that any German statesman could have delivered it and that the comments of the English and the French newspapers had alone given it importance. England, he said, had taken heed of his statement that her complaints should be made through diplomatic channels. "Thereafter the English government expressed no desire to participate in our negotiations with France." To Bismarck's great authority he appealed against the theory of a preventive war, and then he referred, like the *Norddeutsche* (Nov. 5) a few days earlier, to the brighter future which the peaceful solution of a burning issue had opened for Franco-German relations. Here, too, he hinted that a diplomatic victory had been won. Since the Moroccan question had poisoned Germany's relations with England as well as with France, its settlement "clears the table in our relations with her."[212] The Reichstag, however, took a gloomier view of the situation. "The silence was like

---

[212] *Verhandlungen,* XII Leg. Per., II Sess., XI, 7709–7713. A Social Democratic writer on international politics agreed that the chief bond between England and France had been removed. Paul Radek, "Die Liquidation der Marokkofrage," *Neue Zeit,* 1911, 1912, p. 262 (Nov. 24).

that of the grave," the *Berliner Tageblatt* (Nov. 9) reported. "Not a hand moved, no applause rang out." To the *Kölnische Zeitung* (Nov. 10) the cause of this icy reception was to be found in the government's encouragement, during the crisis, of exaggerated expectations.

Chauvinism was the prevailing tone of the debate. In varying degrees, it was expressed by the spokesmen of almost all groups, except those of the Social Democrats. Some of them singled out France as the chief enemy, in spite of the Chancellor's optimistic prophecy of better relations. Hertling, the Centrist leader, warned France not to count upon Germany's weakness; it was a mistake, in his opinion, to lay so much stress upon the latter's love of peace. That a military demonstration had not been staged on the Vosges frontier instead of sending a warship to Agadir was a matter of regret to Bassermann, the National Liberal leader. Dr. Ricklin, an Alsatian deputy, was alone in pleading for a Franco-German reconciliation, for Bebel was more concerned with the danger of an intensified armament race. In Germany and abroad, Heydebrand's attack upon England attracted by all odds the most attention. The German people, he said, were perfectly aware whence came the pretentious claim to grant or to refuse the expansion which was its due. "Gentlemen, we Germans are not in the habit of permitting this sort of thing, and the German people will know how to reply." The government's job was to decide the proper moment. "But we Germans will be ready . . . for the necessary sacrifices."[213] This intemperate speech acquired unusual significanace from the speaker's position as the leader of the Conservative Party, from the close relations between that group and the government, and as a result of the Crown Prince's hearty applause from the gallery, where he was seated with a younger brother. The Chancellor was forced to intervene. He secured a reprimand of the princes from the Emperor, and in reply to Heydebrand, he spoke far more forcefully than was his custom. "Party interests," he said, "may be served by such ill-tempered and exaggerated remarks, . . . but they injure the German Empire. . . . The strong man does not

---

[213] *Verhandlungen,* XII Leg. Per., II Sess., XI, 7718, 7722, 7730, 7737 (Nov. 9); 7764, 7765 (Nov. 10).

need to talk about his sword."[214] Never, wrote the Catholic *Germania* (Nov. 11), had a Chancellor dealt so roughly with a Conservative leader.

Nevertheless, feeling against England remained as strong as ever. Heydebrand, according to the nationalist press, had merely voiced the sentiments of every patriot.[215] While the more moderate journals deprecated his blunt language and condemned the conduct of the princes, some were quick to see a political advantage in the differences between the government and the Conservative Party and most of them felt that England had acted the part of an enemy.[216] Even the Progressives had long since ceased to urge a rapprochement with her.[217] Definite proof of England's hostility was seen in the revelations of Captain Faber, a Conservative member of her parliament, relating to the precautionary measures taken by the British admiralty.[218] Within twenty-four hours of Behmann's reply to Heydebrand, Erzberger, a Centrist deputy, spoke of England as a more determined opponent of German expansion than France. The Reichstag, according to Raschdau, a retired diplomat, agreed to a man with his opinion that this was "the greatest political lesson of the crisis."[219] Nor did the Chancellor help the cause of appeasement by the exchange of speeches with Grey. Replying to Bethmann's speech of November 9, the British foreign secretary revealed Germany's persistent silence as to the purpose of Agadir. The Chan-

---

[214] *Verhandlungen*, XII Leg. Per., II Sess., XI, 7756 (Nov. 10). The real quarrel, according to a Social Democratic deputy, was between the bureaucrats and the Junkers for power. G. Ledebour "Das Duell Bethmann-Hollweg-Heydebrand," *Neue Zeit*, 1911, 1912, p. 311 (Dec. 1).

[215] *Deutsche Tageszeitung*, Nov. 11; *Reichsbote*, Nov. 12; *Leipziger Neueste Nachrichten*, in *Tägliche Rundschau*, Nov. 12.

[216] The Social Democrats planned to use the Crown Prince's interference in the Reichstag debates during the election. F. Mehring, "Kronprinzliche Fronde," *Neue Zeit*, 1911, 1912, p. 212 (Nov. 11).

[217] *Neue Freie Presse*, Sept. 17 (Müller-Meinengen), in H. Hochwart, *Die andern und wir* (Leipzig, 1912).

[218] *Daily Telegraph*, Nov. 9. Some weeks later, the *Illustrierte Zeitung* of Leipzig (Dec. 21) argued that Faber's account of the concentration of a part of the British fleet in the English Channel indicated the intention of transporting 150,000 men to the continent. A pamphleteer, referring to the *Pall Mall Gazette's* report that a squadron of British destroyers had shadowed the German fleet on its Norwegian cruise in July, spoke of Germany's fate upon the seas as having been at the mercy of a command by wireless from London. A. von Gerschoff, *Die Kriegsbereitschaft der englischen Flotte im Jahre 1911* (Berlin, 1911), p. 15.

[219] *Verhandlungen*, XII Leg. Per., II Sess., XI, 7797 (Nov. 11); *Berliner Neueste Nachrichten*, Nov. 14.

cellor refused to let this pass. On December 5, he told the Reichstag that her intentions had been fully explained on July 1 and that a question from England would have cleared up any remaining misunderstanding. Every German, he said, agreed with England's desire for peaceful and friendly relations, but what they expected was some evidence of her good-will in her official policy.[220] That the Chancellor had atoned for the past was the verdict, according to the British ambassador, of the entire press, excepting only the Social Democratic journals; in the Reichstag Bebel alone said a good word for England.[221] To the Emperor, Bethmann confided his hope that the bitterness of German opinion would strengthen the "Grey-must-go" faction of the Liberal Party.[222] Grey, by refraining from a reply, brought the debate to a close. In view of the approaching election and of the state of German opinion, "the Chancellor," he thought, "was bound, whatever I said, to make finally the sort of speech that he did make." [223]

For most Germans, it was a cheerless task to survey the events of 1911. Bethmann's optimism deceived no one. It was true, as the *Grenzboten* pointed out, that the "Anglo-French coalition" had preferred, notwithstanding its threefold naval superiority, to negotiate rather than to fight after the "Panther's" spring and that this decision was a kind of a compliment to Germany's military strength.[224] It could not be denied that France's cession of some 170,000 square miles of her own territory in return for about 7,500 from Germany was an achievement, especially after she had pesuaded England and Italy to recognize her claims to Morocco by yielding what had not belonged to her.[225] It was also true that the danger of war had strengthened the friends of a conciliatory policy in England. Nevertheless, Kiderlen's defeat left no room for doubt. Germany's diplomatic position was weaker than it had been in the spring. The increased prestige,

---

[220] *Verhandlungen*, XII Leg. Per., II Sess., XI, 8347.
[221] Goschen, Dec. 6. *B. D.*, VII, 762.
[222] Bethmann-Hollweg, Dec. 6. *G. P.*, XXIX, 282.
[223] Grey, Dec. 29. *B. D.*, VII, 795. "The question," wrote the Belgian minister to Berlin, "has reached the point where people understand each other less the more they explain themselves." Greindl, Dec. 9. *Belgische Dokumente*, VI, 243.
[224] 1911, IV, 515 (Dec. 6).
[225] Hartung, *Marokkokrise des Jahres 1911*, p. 68.

which had been one of Kiderlen's original aims, had not been won. Like her opponents, Germany also had preferred concessions to war,[226] a choice that contributed something to the resurgence of French nationalist sentiment. From the crisis, which was essentially a test of strength, the Entente Cordiale had emerged with flying colors, for, in contrast to the Bosnian crisis, its own interests were threatened. France could count upon England's full diplomatic support more firmly than ever, while another step had been taken toward something like a military alliance. Nor had the Russo-German accord of August 19 seriously impaired Russia's relations with the Western powers.

Germany, on the other hand, had found herself in a position somewhat similar to that of Russia two years earlier; her allies more or less definitely drew back from a quarrel in which their interests were not involved, as in the case of Austria, or because they were akin to those of France, as in that of Italy. A possibly serious rift in the Triple Alliance, however, had been avoided by restricting the negotiations to France. It was even doubtful that the agreement would eliminate Morocco as a source of friction as long as Germans insisted upon a share in its economic development. Already suggestions were appearing in the press that its economic provisions could be used to save something from the wreck of German policy. A pamphlet, which was later translated into French, predicted that Morocco would yet cause a war, resulting in the partition of France and of her colonial empire between Italy, England, and Germany.[227] Most disturbing to German public opinion was England's hostility, the intensity of French nationalism, and the meagerness of Germany's gains. Lloyd George's speech, Cartwright's interview, and the revelations of the naval preparations left an indelible impression. In an affair that did not concern her vital interests, England had kept Germany from securing what was her due. As for France, Bethmann's forecast of improved relations found little credence; defiance mingled with regret that more forceful measures had not

---

226 This decision, according to a Social Democratic student of international politics, made an eventual diplomatic defeat certain. Paul Radek, "Die Liquidation der Marokkofrage," *Neue Zeit,* 1911, 1912, p. 265 (Nov. 24).

227 *Frankreichs Ende im Jahre* 19?? (Berlin, 1911); A. Sommerfeld, *Le partage de la France en l'an* 19?? (Paris, 1913).

been used characterized the debate following his speech of November 9. To her nationalists and colonial enthusiasts, the agreement was just as distasteful as it was to the corresponding groups in Germany. From her presses, according to Harden, books appeared almost every day that breathed hatred and an aggressive spirit.[228] The reluctance of the Chambers to approve the settlement,[229] the icy response to Jaurès' speech in favor of a Franco-German reconciliation, and the part played by Caillaux's unofficial negotiations with Germany in his defeat and in the formation of the Poincaré ministry left little room for hope of improved relations.[230] Dislike and suspicion of Germany had increased throughout the world;[231] little remained of the favorable impression created by her reserve after the Bosnian crisis. For public opinion, the terms of the agreement were the greatest source of dissatisfaction. "Without acquiring anything of moment," wrote Harden, "we are more unpopular than ever."[232] The claim that the government had never desired anything more than compensations in the Congo carried little conviction. That Kiderlen had promised to insist upon a part of Morocco was the firm belief of the Pan-Germans, while the more moderate opinion assumed as a matter of course that a large part of the original program had been abandoned. "If they had desired nothing more," wrote a leading Catholic review, "one is justified in saying that they shot at sparrows with cannons."[233] The government was roundly condemned for its encouragement of the nationalists.[234] Public opinion was thoroughly dissatisfied and dangerously uneasy. "Whoever," wrote one observer who condemned the nationalist

---

[228] *Zukunft*, Dec. 2.

[229] Only the absence of a practical alternative, according to the *Norddeutsche* (Dec. 24), explained the favorable vote.

[230] *Rheinisch-Westfälische Zeitung*, Dec. 21; *Deutsche Tageszeitung*, Dec. 24.

[231] To place upon Germany the exclusive responsibility for the danger of war was, according to a Social Democratic observer, contrary to the interests of the world proletariat. The only difference between Germany and the other countries was the ineptitude of her diplomacy. F. Mehring, "Freie Hand," *Neue Zeit*, 1911, 1912, p. 305 (Dec. 1).

[232] *Zukunft*, Dec. 2.

[233] "Die Auswärtige Politik am Jahreschluss," *Historisch-Politische Blätter*, vol. 149, p. 137 (Jan. 1912).

[234] The head of the press bureau later agreed that this charge was partly true. Hammann, *Bilder aus der letzten Kaiserzeit*, pp. 89, 90. One writer referred to the "frothy sentimentality" of the masses. M. von Brandt, "Die Undankbarkeit gegen die Friedenspolitik des deutschen Kaisers," *Deutsche Revue*, 1911, IV, 257 (Dec. 1).

agitation, "wished to be heard by the people (*zum Volke reden wollte*) and to avoid the suspicion of being a servile mouthpiece of the government must rant and rave (*der musste die Ader des Zorns an seiner Stirn und das Herz mit patriotischen Entrüstung schwellen lassen*)." [235] With complete sincerity and substantial truth it was often said that the German people desired peace. An increasing number, however, felt that Germany would be forced to take up arms, not in defense of her frontiers in Europe or of her colonies, but by the international conspiracy against her legitimate expansion and against her rightful influence in world affairs.

---

[235] *P. J.*, vol. 146, p. 552 (Delbrück, Dec. 1911).

CHAPTER XIII

England, the Balkans, and a New Policy, 1912-1914

Wir sind auch nicht verpflichtet, unbesehen jeden Schritt, den Oesterrich tut, im voraus gutzuheissen. Haben wir diesmal nicht die Führing im Dreibunde, so haben wir um so mehr die Pflicht, darauf zu sehen, dass im Namen des Dreibundes nur Bundespolitik und nicht Politik eines Einzelstaats getrieben werde.

Berliner Tageblatt, Dec. 11, 1912.

The vicissitudes of foreign politics had little or no immediate effect upon Germany's economic development and therefore upon the real sources of her strength. Since 1905, Germany was no longer as dangerous a competitor for England, but everywhere her foreign trade maintained its relative position and even increased its advantage in the Low Countries, Italy, Russia, the West Indies, and Latin America.[1] "There is," wrote Felix Rachfahl, the historian, in a volume commemorating the twenty-fifth anniversary of William II's reign, "no reason for discouragement or for fault-finding pessimism; we should be proud of being Germans. . . ."[2] "Give us three or four more years of peace," Hugo Stinnes, the industrial magnate, told the president of the Pan-German league, "and Germany will be the unchallenged economic master of Europe."[3] Even the pessimists were more concerned with future than with present dangers. To the mili-

---

[1] See the charts in Hoffman, *Great Britain and the German Trade Rivalry.* For a brief account of the German penetration of the French iron and steel industry, see Hallgarten *Vorkriegs Imperialismus,* pp. 250, 251.

[2] Rachfahl, *Kaiser und Reich, 1888–1913* (Berlin, 1913), p. 349.

[3] Class, *Wider den Strom,* p. 217.

tary mind, the increasing taste for luxuries seemed a serious threat to the nation's warlike virtues.[4] The rapid increase in population was generally regarded as a proof of superiority over "old" or "tired" peoples, like the French, as an assurance of adequate reserves for the army and as an unanswerable argument for a larger place in the world. Indeed, the problem of over-population was not yet acute. Industry was making a place for every worker; emigration had declined to the insignificant an-nual total of twenty thousand. In spite of the two million and more members of the trade unions and of the impressive gains of the Social Democratic Party, there was less danger than ever of a social revolution;[5] good times, among other influences, were converting the Socialists into democratic progressives. A more immediate occasion for alarm was the dependence upon food imports, for they required an increasingly favorable balance of trade. So imperative was the need of expanding markets thought to be that the agitation in England for imperial preference caused some industrialists to talk of war.[6] That England would im-mediately blockade Germany in a war was a certainty. To avert this danger was one of the most important tasks of German foreign policy.

In England, a strong movement for better relations had arisen during the Agadir crisis. A strong group in the cabinet felt that something should be done about it.[7] After the revelation of Caillaux's secret negotiations with Germany, British foreign policy was condemned as *plus royaliste que le roi*.[8] The Entente Cordiale, said the Liberal *Daily News* (Feb. 5, 1912), was dan-gerously like a military alliance. For the "Grey-must-go" radi-cals, Russia's conduct in Persia was the best of reasons for

---

[4] F. von Bernhardi, *Germany and the Next War* (N. Y., 1914), p. 14.

[5] Talking to the Bavarian envoy, Bethmann admitted that some extremists favored war as a means of checking the growth of Social Democracy. Lerchenfeld, June 4, 1914. P. Dirr, *Bayerische Dokumente zum Kriegsausbruch und zum Versailler Schulds-spruch* (Munich, 1925), p. 113. This volume will henceforth be cited as *B. D. K.*

[6] *Morning Post*, Jan. 5, 1910; *Daily Mail*, Jan. 7, 1910, in Hoffman, *Great Britain and the German Trade Rivalry*, p. 291.

[7] The Russian ambassador expected this point of view to influence British foreign policy. Benckendorff, Nov. 9/22. Siebert, *Diplomatische Aktenstücke*, pp. 737, 738 Cf. Wolff, *Eve of 1914*, p. 93.

[8] Lalaing, Jan. 15, 1912. *Belgische Dokumente*, VI, 87, 88. Cf. *Zukunft*, March 9, 1912.

approaching Germany.[9] Lloyd George told the City Liberal Club, February 3, 1912, that the world would be richer and that taxes would be lower if jealousy and fear were eliminated from Anglo-German relations.[10] The *Saturday Review* (Sept. 9, 1911) spoke in favor of "a square deal, face to face, when the present crisis has ended peaceably . . . ," and Grey told the House of Commons, November 27, that England had no desire to obstruct Germany's colonial expansion. With due allowance for the widespread suspicions of Germany's intentions, for the diplomatic interests arising from the understandings with France and Russia, and for a fundamentally unyielding attitude on the naval question, the fact remains that Grey, although skeptical, was willing to review the entire problem of Anglo-German relations. In Germany, the situation was regarded as critical. "It cannot," wrote Professor Zorn of the University of Bonn, "remain as it is today; it must become either better or worse." [11] "For the future of the entire world, nothing is more important," wrote a conservative observer, "than the relations between Germany and Great Britain." [12] Little good had resulted, it was evident, from good-will speeches or from the visits of ecclesiastics, journalists, and mayors. "We are tired," said the moderate *Vossische Zeitung* (Feb. 4, 1912), "of listening to fine words when they are all too frequently contradicted by ugly deeds." The liberal *Berliner Tageblatt's* (Feb. 2, 1912) opinion was that Germany should not needlessly increase her naval program, since her fleet was strong enough to defeat Russia and France and since England would certainly maintain her margin of superiority. Hermann Oncken preferred military to naval increases because England might fight if she were driven too far. France, in his opinion, was the more dangerous enemy.[13] With these views Bethmann was in substantial accord. He was willing to accept a limited colonial agreement, on the ground that any kind of an understanding was better than nothing and that it might lead to something better.

[9] Cambon, Feb. 3, 1912. *D. D. F.*, (3), II, 4; *Kölnische Zeitung*, Feb. 7, London, Feb. 6.
[10] *Standard*, Feb. 5.
[11] *Kölnische Zeitung*, Dec. 30, 1911.
[12] *P. J.*, vol. 147, p. 356 (Feb. 1912).
[13] H. Oncken, *Deutschland und England; Heeres-oder Flottenverstärkung* (Heidelberg, 1912), pp. 18, 19.

Unfortunately, Bethmann's point of view did not represent public opinion as a whole, nor was he able to impose it upon German policy. Believing that England was responsible for the worst of Germany's difficulties since 1904, most Germans distrusted anything less than a definite proof of England's good-will, in the form of tangible concessions and, above all, in the treatment of Germany as an equal (*Gleichberechtigung*).[14] According to Harnack, the eminent church historian, England was just as hostile to her imperialist interests as France had been after 1866 toward German unity. "It rests with her to convince us by deeds that our experience during the past year was an incident . . . and not a symptom. . . ."[15] Some envisaged war. In view of her peaceful record and of her exclusive concern "for the defense and for the development of the necessary conditions of her national existence," Germany was ready, according to Professor Zorn, to fight the entire world and to face the alternatives—*"Sieg oder Untergang"*—rather than to tolerate England's interference.[16] It was high time, wrote the nationalist *Münchener Neueste Nachrichten,* to show that Germany's was not a peace-at-any-price policy.[17] "Despite the frightful seriousness of a war, it might be," according to a pamphlet that went through six editions in 1912, "a welcome means of breaking the chains of a people growing at the rate of 850,000 every year."[18] There is no satisfactory evidence that the government encouraged these extremist views; on the contrary, the *Grenzboten,* then regarded as a semi-official organ, dismissed some of them as laughable. "What in the world do they mean," it asked of the demand for *Gleichberechtigung.* "Should the first article of an Anglo-German agreement read,

---

[14] "Die deutsch-englische Verständigung," *Deutsche Revue,* 1912, I, 135 (Feb. 1). "But between two equals," replied the Conservative *Morning Post* (London, Jan. 26, 1912), "the notion that one must buy the good-will of the other by 'concessions' is unintelligible."

[15] *Daily News, Westminster Gazette,* Feb. 17, 1912. For the German text, see *Tägliche Rundschau,* Feb. 27.

[16] "Friede auf Erden," *Kölnische Zeitung,* Dec. 30, 1911. When the *Morning Post* (London, Jan. 5, 1912) inquired if Zorn's article had been officially inspired like the Pan-German press during the recent crisis, he replied ("England und Deutschland," *Kölnische Zeitung,* Jan. 25) that his statement had expressed the predominant sentiment of the German people, as he could prove by abundant evidence.

[17] *Tägliche Rundschau,* Jan. 10, 1912.

[18] G. Hartmann, *Krieg oder Frieden mit England? Eine Studie über unsere auswärtige Politik* (Berlin, 1912), p. 13.

'The Royal Government of Great Britain recognizes the *Gleich-berechtigung* of the Imperial German government'. . . ? This is a policy of sentiment of the purest water—and we Germans pride ourselves on being *Realpolitiker!*" [19]

German foreign policy nevertheless corresponded more nearly to the extremist than to the moderate point of view. Tirpitz and William usually determined its direction, although there was much working at cross-purposes. On August 30, 1911, Tirpitz took advantage of the Agadir crisis to propose a new naval bill for the construction during each of the next six years of three instead of two battleships, for a third squadron, in order that two would always be in commission, for the more rapid replacement of obsolete cruisers, for more submarines, and for a substantial increase in the personnel of the fleet. An understanding with England was, in Tirpitz' opinion, of secondary importance. As usual, William's attitude was a compound of enthusiasm for the navy for its own sake and of confidence that it would assure to Germany her proper place in the sun and that it alone would persuade England to offer satisfactory terms.[20] Of Metternich's warning that a new navy bill would make any negotiations with England impossible, he wrote, "Bosh!" "Rot!" and "Idiocy!" [21] Tirpitz easily secured his consent, September 26, 1911, but the Chancellor was more difficult. Bethmann finally persuaded the Emperor to reduce the number of additional battleships from six to three, but he agreed, November 16, 1911, that the budget for 1912 should include an appropriation for the first of the new dreadnoughts. Nevertheless, he refused to abandon all hope of an understanding; quickly withdrawing his first instructions to Metternich to sound Grey in regard to a political understanding, the Chancellor asked the ambassador to ascertain Grey's reaction to a colonial agreement. The result merely increased his difficulties at home, for the Emperor was more impressed by Grey's excuses for delaying the discussion (the state of public opinion in Germany, the approaching Reichstag elections, and the need of consulting his colleagues) than by his friendliness toward

---

[19] *Grenzboten,* 1912, I, 356 (Feb. 21).
[20] William II's comments on the *Times,* Aug. 18, 1911. *G. P.,* XXXI, 3, 4.
[21] Wolff, *Eve of 1914,* p. 75.

Germany's eventual acquisition of a part of the Belgian Congo and of Angola.[22] Astonishingly indifferent at this time to colonies, William became more attached to the *Novelle* than ever. "So long," he wrote, "as the British government does not feel a moral *compulsion* to come to an understanding with us, just so long is there nothing to do—but to arm." [23]

The discussion of the fundamental differences between the two countries, which the statesmen failed to bring about, was accomplished by one of the few men most responsible for Germany's great economic development. Albert Ballin, the general director of the Hamburg-America Steamship Line and the Emperor's personal friend, arranged, with the coöperation of Sir Ernest Cassel, the Anglo-German banker, a visit to Berlin for this purpose by Haldane, the war minister.[24] The questions discussed included the most serious of the underlying causes of Anglo-German friction: the German navy, and the directing lines of British foreign policy. Germany's spokesmen insisted upon a formal pledge of England's neutrality in a war which she had not provoked. However, no German official would agree to, nor would public opinion have approved, the reduction of the original naval program as fixed by the law of 1900, which probably alone might have secured England's consent. Haldane's suggestion to this effect was immediately rejected.[25] Of Bethmann, Haldane had the highest regard. He was impressed "by his evident desire to meet us wherever he could" by "his absolute sincerity and good-will." The Chancellor impressed him as "an honest man struggling somewhat with adversity." [26] Bethmann's good intentions availed little, for he

---

[22] Grey, Dec. 20. *B. D.,* VI, 650, 651.

[23] For the diplomacy of the Haldane mission I am indebted to Bernadotte E. Schmitt, "Lord Haldane's Mission to Berlin in 1912," *The Crusades and Other Historical Essays; presented to Dana C. Munro by his Former Students,* Louis J. Paetow, ed. (N. Y., 1928). The recently published British documents do not materially change the main lines of the story. *B. D.,* VI, 666–762.

[24] Grey refused to go himself, afraid to offend France and of the results of a failure. Grey, *Twenty-Five Years,* I, 241. Ballin had been in touch with Cassel since 1908. B. Huldermann, *Albert Ballin* (London, 1922), p. 134. Like other German businessmen, he believed that the naval problem could be readily solved by the customary methods of business negotiations.

[25] *G. P.,* XXXI, 159, 160; Haldane, March 12. *B. D.,* VI, 710, 711.

[26] Haldane, Feb. 10. *B. D.,* VI, 678, 679, 682; R. Haldane, *Before the War* (London, 1920), p. 59. Tirpitz had a lower opinion of Bethmann's honesty, for he suspected that the Chancellor intended to secure a political agreement by promising to

secured from Tirpitz and William nothing more substantial than a delay of one year in the construction of each of the three extra dreadnoughts. Nevertheless, his hints (March 8, 12) that something less than an assurance of neutrality would be satisfactory—and Grey's own wish to satisfy his critics at home—resulted in the offer of a political formula (March 17) for a drastic reduction of the *Novelle:*

> The two powers being mutually desirous of securing peace and friendship between them, England declares that she will neither make nor join in any unprovoked attack upon Germany and pursue no aggressive policy towards her. Aggression upon Germany is not the subject and forms no part of any treaty, understanding or combination to which England is now a party, nor will she become a party to anything that has such an object.[27]

In return for a similar statement, Germany had been willing to promise Russia her disinterestedness in the Balkans, but she rejected Grey's offer because it fell short of absolute neutrality.[28] Tirpitz had triumphed. From the beginning he had probably regarded the negotiations as useless, since he confidently expected England to refuse Germany's terms.[29] The last hope of a compromise disappeared when he secured the publication of the *Novelle.*[30] Grey's offer need not be exaggerated to conclude that its refusal was a mistake, as Bethmann doubtless felt.[31] France's anxiety was a good gauge of its value; Paul Cambon predicted that Germany would claim a victory.[32] However, some British diplomats viewed any kind of a formula with almost as much disfavor as the French. In Paris, Bertie asked Poincaré to speak "with some firmness" when the British cabinet was about to make its final decision against neutrality.[33] It was felt that a grave

---

withdraw the *Novelle* and then *"die Schiffe trotzdem zu fordern . . ."* Tirpitz, March 10. Tirpitz, *Aufbau der deutschen Weltmacht,* I, 323.
[27] Metternich, March 17. *G. P.,* XXXI, 181.
[28] *Ibid.,* XXXI, 191, 192; *B. D.,* VI, 719–721 (March 19), 724 (March 22), 728 (March 26), 732 (March 29).
[29] Tirpitz, *Erinnerungen,* p. 191; idem, *Aufbau der deutschen Weltmacht,* I, 286 (Feb. 7).
[30] *N. A. Z.,* March 22. Its main provisions had already appeared in the *Kölnische Volkszeitung,* March 8. Hammann, *Bilder aus der letzten Kaiserzeit,* pp. 106, 107.
[31] Tirpitz, March 18. Tirpitz, *Aufbau der deutschen Weltmacht,* I, 329, 330.
[32] *D. D. F.,* (3), II, 144 (March 4).
[33] Poincaré, March 27. *Ibid.,* (3), II, 262, 263.

danger had been averted. "Let us," wrote Nicolson, "definitely abandon formulas, which are dangerous and embarrassing documents, and the signature of which would apparently . . . affect our relations with France." [34] "I confess," remarked Asquith, April 10, "I am becoming more and more doubtful as to the wisdom of prolonging these discussions with Germany for a formula. Nothing, I believe, will. meet her purpose which falls short of a promise on our part of neutrality: a promise we cannot give." [35] Grey, who regarded his own formula with some misgiving, was content.

While Grey hoped that the relations between the two countries would at least continue to be cordial,[36] the prospects were scarcely bright. William was in a particularly bad temper, for he had drawn the erroneous conclusion that England was ready to pledge her neutrality.[37] There was indeed some reason for believing that the main lines of an agreement, which would require only the approval of the British cabinet, had practically been agreed upon during the conversations with Haldane.[38] For this misunderstanding Haldane's sympathy for things German and his inexperience in diplomacy and naval affairs were partly responsible. While he explained that he was powerless to commit his government,[39] he gave the impression that the *Novelle,* which he had not even read, would not be an insuperable obstacle to a political agreement and that England would meet Germany's wishes in the colonial field. Kiderlen knew better; on his return to Berlin, he argued that an understanding would be impossible without the sacrifice of the three additional battleships, but the foreign minister was not consulted during the Berlin conversations.[40] William therefore felt that England was guilty of bad faith when she objected to the provisions for the third squadron,

---

[34] *B. D.,* VI, 741 (April 4).

[35] *Ibid.,* VI, 745.

[36] *Ibid.,* VI, 721 (March 19).

[37] Schmitt, "Haldane's Mission," *The Crusades and Other Historical Essays,* p. 251.

[38] So complete was the Emperor's self-deception that he described the agreement as "purely political." He expected the *Novelle* to be laid before the Reichstag, with the delay of one year, immediately after its publication. Huldermann, *Ballin,* p. 175 (Feb. 9).

[39] Haldane, Feb. 10. *B. D.,* VI, 676.

[40] Kiderlen, Feb. 22. Tirpitz, *Aufbau der deutschen Weltmacht,* I, 290, 291. For William's reprimand, see *ibid.,* I, 292 (Feb. 24). *Cf.* Jäckh, *Kiderlen-Wächter,* II, 155 (Feb. 1912).

for more submarines, for a larger personnel, and when she began to back water in regard to the colonies.[41] To a report that England was about to concentrate her fleet in the English Channel and the North Sea, he reacted violently, again threatening to treat this action as a *casus belli*,[42] and Grey's remark (March 17) that Bethmann's successor might change the direction of German policy seemed to him an impertinent interference in German affairs.[43]

Meanwhile, public opinion awaited the results of the negotiations with some hope but with more uneasiness. The Chancellor's colorless announcement (Feb. 15) that negotiations were in progress was warmly applauded by the Reichstag.[44] "This brief statement," wrote the London *Daily Chronicle* (Feb. 16) correspondent, "was received by the members with a loud roar of 'Bravo!' that seemed to come from all parties." [45] The protests of the Liberal press in London when Churchill spoke, February 9, of Germany's "luxury" fleet moderated somewhat the indignation of German opinion,[46] although the chauvinist *Rheinisch-Westfälische Zeitung* thought that any concessions would now seem like a surrender to a threat.[47] But the rumors of "all sorts of reservations" cooled even the friends of a rapprochement,[48] and the nationalists feared that Germany's freedom of action in naval matters might be compromised. The nationalist *Tägliche Rundschau* (Feb. 20) culled numerous items from the English press relating to England's naval preparations during the Agadir crisis and represented them as evidence of an aggressive purpose. There should be, it insisted (Feb. 15), no compromise "out of consideration for the tender bud of an Anglo-German understanding." By minor concessions Germany might be led, the National Liberal *Hamburger Nachrichten* feared, "to a renunciation of the absolutely necessary strengthening of her fleet. . . ." [49]

[41] *G. P.*, XXXI, 150–153; *B. D.*, VI, 704–706.
[42] Metternich, March 1; William II, March 5. *Ibid*, XXXI, 147, 155, 157.
[43] Schmitt, "Haldane's Mission," *The Crusades and Other Historical Essays*, pp. 274, 276.
[44] *Verhandlungen*, XIII Leg. Per., I Sess., I, 47.
[45] Cf. *Vossische Zeitung*, Feb. 16.
[46] *Westminster Gazette, Daily Chronicle, Daily News*, Feb. 10. Cf. *N. A. Z.*, Feb. 11; *Vossische Zeitung*, Feb. 12, 15; *Kölnische Zeitung*, Feb. 13.
[47] *Tägliche Rundschau*, Feb. 15.
[48] L. Raschdau, "Die deutsch-englische Annäherung," *Echo*, Feb. 29.
[49] *Tägliche Rundschau*, Feb. 17.

The government's attitude, finally revealed by the publication of the *Novelle,* March 22, was indicated even earlier by the inspired press. Haldane had not left Berlin when the *Norddeutsche* (Feb. 10) printed in a conspicuous place Admiral von Koester's speech calling for increased naval construction as a defense against a blockade. The *Berliner Lokal-Anzeiger* warned England that there could be no question of the reduction of existing, or of a limitation of future, armaments, while the Conservative *Deutsche Zeitung* insisted that the time was not ripe for a naval understanding of any kind.[50] The author of a widely noticed pamphlet, described by the *Tägliche Rundschau* (Feb. 27) as "a flaming admonition to the German nation" and by the British *chargé d'affaires* as officially inspired, discovered in England's advances a conclusive argument that Germany should not cease her efforts at the last moment: "Shall we put ourselves at the mercy of the dominant power, shall we perpetuate the existing situation just as we are about to attain the goal—equality of treatment (*Gleichberechtigung*)? The gods must laugh at the spectacle. . . . If we stand firm, we shall win; England and Germany can then shake hands, convinced of each other's strength and worth." [51]

When Germans talked of equality of treatment, they usually meant that England should concede something or at least cease to obstruct Germany's expansion. Never had imperialist sentiment been stronger. The pressure of population, wrote Oncken, made colonial expansion an absolute necessity.[52] Beginning in 1911, a stream of imperialist pamphlets poured from the press.[53] Expansion was a law of nature, for nations, like individuals, decay when they stop growing. A preventive war, according to Bernhardi, would alone provide the security in Europe that was essential for a world policy, Bismarck's views to the contrary

[50] *Echo,* Feb. 15. The London press greeted Haldane on his return with the argument that England could accept no agreement that did not recognize her naval supremacy. *Standard,* Feb. 10; *Westminster Gazette, Daily Telegraph,* Feb. 12; *Morning Post, Daily News,* Feb. 16.

[51] Lookout, *England's Weltherrschaft und die deutsche Luxusflotte* (Berlin, 1912), pp. 38, 40, 41. *Cf.* Granville, Feb. 29. *B. D.,* VI, 700-702.

[52] Oncken, *Deutschland und England,* p. 21. *Cf.* P. Rohrbach, *Der deutsche Gedanke in der Welt* (Dusseldorf, 1912), p. 198.

[53] O. Nippold, *Die auswärtige Politik und die öffentliche Meinung* (Stuttgart, 1912), pp. 8, 9.

notwithstanding.[54] Writing in the *Post* (Jan. 28, 1912), Dr. Fuchs offered Frederick the Great's practice of attacking first and explaining afterward as an example worthy of emulation. "We all know that blood will flow the more, the longer we wait." [55] The chauvinists were doubtless more vociferous than numerous, but public opinion in general also desired greater opportunities for expansion. Even the Social Democrats were affected by the passion for imperialism. Since it was regarded by Socialist theorists as the last phase of the capitalist system, the social revolutionary cause might be served by hastening it. Officially the party condemned imperialism,[56] but some of its writers acknowledged that the workers themselves would benefit from larger markets.[57] As to the direction in which Germany should expand, there was the greatest diversity of opinion. To one observer, the question would be answered by the disintegration of the "tired nations (*müde gewordene Nationen*)." [58] "For us," wrote Edmund Weber, "the sole aim is Germany's world rule." [59] A. Dix urged an economic union extending from the Baltic Sea through Constantinople into Asia Minor.[60] This, in general, was the program of the Pan-Germans, although they approved the direct annexation of a part of Asia Minor and all of Mesopotamia if the integrity of the Turkish Empire could not be maintained. They favored a customs union with the German peoples living

---

[54] Bernhardi, *Germany and the Next War*, pp. 39, 40. The substance of this book was presented in a cheap publication. Bernhardi, *Unsere Zukunft; ein Mahnruf an das deutsche Volk* (Stuttgart, 1912).

[55] O. Nippold, a Swiss pacifist, collected a large number of excerpts from the German press illustrating this chauvinist agitation in his *Der deutsche Chauvinismus* (Stuttgart, 1913).

[56] See Singer's resolution adopted at the Party congress in Mainz, 1900. *Protokoll über die Verhandlungen des Parteitages (Mainz, Sept. 17–21)* (Berlin, 1900), p. 154. The official weekly continued to oppose imperialism, because it might lead to war. K. Emil, "Der deutsche Imperialismus," *Neue Zeit*, 1907, 1908, pp. 148–163 (Nov. 2, 1907); K. Kautsky, "Sozialistische Kolonialpolitik," *ibid.*, 1909, pp. 33–43.

[57] K. Radek, "Zu unserem Kampf gegen den Imperialismus," *ibid.*, 1912, (1), pp. 194–199 (May 10, 1912); L. Quessel, "Auf den Weg zum Weltreich," *Sozialdemokratische Monatshefte*, 1913, I, 656, 657 (June 12, 1913).

[58] He thought that an Anglo-German war was too remote a possibility to be worthy of consideration. "Deutscher Imperialismus," *Grenzboten*, 1913, II, 346, 348 (May 21). Cleinow, the *Grenzboten's* editor, explained that he did not share all of the views of this writer. *Cf.* W. Eisenhart, *Deutsche Politik; patriotische Sorgen und Hoffnungen* (Dresden, 1912), p. 10.

[59] Weber, *Krieg oder Frieden mit England?* (*Monographien zur Zeitgeschichte*, no. 10) (Stuttgart, 1913).

[60] Dix, *Deutscher Imperialismus* (Leipzig, 1912), p. 21.

beyond the boundaries of the Empire, but the authoritative *All-deutsche Blätter* frowned upon territorial conquests at Russia's expense as impracticable. From their point of view, the abdication in Morocco eliminated Africa as a desirable sphere of expansion.[61] According to Bernhardi, England should pay for an understanding by renouncing her pretensions as a world power, by agreeing to a free hand for Germany in Central Europe and against France, and by accepting a redivision of Northern Africa.[62] Of course, the government's views were more moderate; Kiderlen even reprimanded the chauvinists. With his approval, a retired diplomat characterized the Navy League, the Defense League (*Wehrverein*), and the Pan-German League as the greatest obstacles to an effective foreign policy. A second Bismarck could have performed no more valuable service than to restrain them.[63] In so far as the leaders had definite aims, they were probably bent upon the completion of the Berlin-Bagdad Railway and upon the development of the Central African Empire, which Kiderlen had envisaged during the Agadir crisis. Article 16 of the November 4, 1911 agreement, providing that France and Germany should consult each other and the other signatory powers to the Berlin Treaty of 1885 if any proposal should arise for the modification of the territorial status quo in the Congo basin, offered a possible opening,[64] but the moment was inopportune for annexations. The official point of view seems to have been revealed by two pamphlets. In the first, published anonymously in 1913, an optimistic view was taken of the European situation. Relations with Russia were about as good as they had been under the Reinsurance Treaty. The Anglo-French understanding would survive, but, since the settlement of the Moroccan question had removed the chief reason for England's support of France, it was no longer so exclusive as

[61] L. Werner, *Der alldeutsche Verband 1890–1918* (Berlin, 1935), pp. 134, 135.

[62] Bernhardi, *Unsere Zukunft*, p. 95.

[63] "Hindernisse auf dem Wege der deutschen auswärtigen Politik," *Deutsche Revue,* 1912, III, 61 (Sept. 1). *Cf.* Jäckh, *Kiderlen-Wächter*, II, 162 (Dec. 1912).

[64] C. Bloch, "Les visées allemandes sur le Congo-Belge à la veille de la grande guerre," *Bulletin de la societé d'histoire moderne*, 12th Series, No. 12, pp. 171–177 (Oct. 1936).

formerly. Germany could therefore safely turn her energies to expansion and especially to Central Africa; an ambitious policy in Asia Minor, however, would arouse the hostility of Russia and England. Even in Central Africa, this writer favored "a commercial policy in the grand manner" rather than territorial annexations.[65] By 1914, the situation had changed for the worse, for the author of the second pamphlet, a relative of Hammann, the chief of the press bureau, believed that Germany should arm so heavily that no other power would dare to disturb the peace while she pursued her imperialist aims. Convinced that "the decision as to her world policy will be made on the continent," he professed satisfaction for the time being with a free access to world markets.[66]

Another rebuff was experienced at England's hands before the diplomats saw that her interests must be given greater consideration. In June 1912, Metternich resigned and was succeeded by Marschall who, it was hoped, would repeat his Constantinople successes. From the beginning, the German press increased his difficulties by predicting the separation of England and France. Already the Conservative *Morning Post* (May 25) had expressed the opinion that the Entente Cordiale should be changed into an alliance. Grey had no intention of going this far, but he turned a cold shoulder to Marschall's suggestion that negotiations for a political accord should be resumed. Because the *Novelle* had forced England to increase her own naval appropriations, there was, according to Grey, nothing to be gained even by "a simple monologue that we [England] had no aggressive designs and desired to be friendly," which the new German ambassador seemed ready to accept in lieu of a neutrality agreement.[67] In fact, Grey was no longer willing to limit England's freedom of action in the slightest degree: "So I hope that we shall go on with the Portuguese colonial business rather than with the possibility of a formula." Friendly discussion of current business, he assured

---

[65] *✳*✳*, *Deutsche Weltpolitik und kein Krieg* (Berlin, 1913), pp. 29, 30, 37, 38, 79. In Huldermann's *Ballin* (p. 189), the author is identified as Dr. Hans Plehn, the London correspondent of the *Kölnische Zeitung*.

[66] J. J. Ruedorffer, *Grundzüge der Weltpolitik in der Gegenwart* (Stuttgart, 1914), pp. 103–107, 198, 199. The author was Konstantin Riesler. Westarp, *Konservative Politik*, I, 234, 235.

[67] Grey, June 27. *B. D.*, VI, 558, 579.

Marschall, would be much more useful.[68] To this point of view,
the Germans gradually adapted themselves without ever abandoning the hope of securing England's neutrality. With Lichnowsky's appointment to the London embassy after Marschall's death
(Oct. 1912), Germany embarked upon a more modest policy of
diplomatic coöperation in specific questions.

The decision owed not a little to the continental situation.
France occasioned more real concern than during the Agadir
crisis. While Schoen acknowledged that the masses feared war,
he called attention to the government's encouragement of the
nationalist spirit.[69] Poincaré, the new President of the Council,
clearly would not be the restraining influence that Caillaux had
been. The military attaché was especially impressed by the declining fear of the German army.[70] Press dispatches from Paris
emphasized the revival of self-confidence. In response to a request for a statement of France's views, Tardieu, writing in the
Deutsche Revue, explained that the Moroccan agreement had
settled none of the fundamental issues between the two countries.
Because Alsace-Lorraine and Germany's lost hegemony in Europe
could not be discussed, nothing remained but questions of secondary importance. Prince Lichnowsky, soon to become the ambassador to England, agreed with these views and insisted that
Germany's great advantage in population would prevent France
from attacking without the aid of another power.[71]

To check France and to weaken the Anglo-Russian Entente,
the cultivation of Russia was, of course, elementary strategy.
The prospects seemed encouraging; the agreement of August 19,
1911 had disposed of the Bagdad Railway as a cause of serious
friction, and Russia had been cool toward France's interests during the Agadir crisis. "A principal factor in Russia's foreign
policy," wrote Pourtalès, "is her desire to maintain friendly relations with Germany." [72] Hostility to England, the *Berliner
Lokal-Anzeiger* (Jan. 2, 1912) had already written, was a common

[68] *B. D.,* VI, 760 (July 4).
[69] *G. P.,* XXXI, 396, 397 (March 12, 1912).
[70] Winterfeldt, Feb. 19. *Ibid.,* XXXI, 389.
[71] A. Tardieu, "Frankreich und Deutschland"; Lichnowsky, "Deutschland und
Frankreich," *Deutsche Revue,* 1912, III, 11, 13, 17, 19 (July 1).
[72] *G. P.,* XXXI, 427, 428.

interest, which might lead to the restoration of the Alliance of the Three Emperors.[73] At any rate, Russia invited William to visit the Tsar at Baltic Port July 4, 1912.[74] The meeting was at first regarded with great satisfaction. Bethmann and Sazonov, the Russian foreign minister, in fact exchanged the friendliest views in regard to the Balkans. He "could confirm the assurances" which he had given at Potsdam, replied the Chancellor, when Sazonov asked if Germany would restrain Austria.[75] Russia, too, was satisfied with the status quo, and so pleased was her foreign minister that he approved the idea of similar meetings in the future.[76] A rebuff, according to the German press, had been administered to England and France.[77] Schiemann was confident that Russia would not work with them against Germany.[78] These agreeable reflections were soon forgotten when it became clear that no change had occurred in the European alignment. While the concluding statement in the press communiqué recognizing the service to peace "of the present division of powers" and declaring against any need for its revision was dismissed as diplomatic verbiage and as less significant than the mention of future meetings,[79] the reaction in France and England was disturbing. Schiemann spoke of an unblushing claim that Germany had "bowed before the powers of the Triple Entente." Potsdam, he lamented, had lost its meaning.[80] Other reasons for dissatisfaction soon appeared. Poincaré's visit to St. Petersburg was promptly followed by the announcement of a Franco-Russian naval accord, of which not a word had been said at Port Baltic.[81]

---

[73] Goschen selected this article as the most significant of the many attacks upon England in the German press. *B. D.*, VI, 653 (Jan. 3).

[74] Pourtalès, Jan. 30, 1912. *G. P.*, XXXI, 427, 428. For France's efforts to prevent the meeting, see Poincaré, June 5. *D. D. F.*, (3), III, 91.

[75] *Un livre noir; diplomatie d'avant-guerre d'après les documents des archives russes, novembre 1910–juillet 1914*, R. Marchand, ed. 2 vols. (Paris, 1921), II, 336. This work will henceforth be cited as *L. N.*

[76] Bethmann-Hollweg, July 6. *G. P.*, XXXI, 440–442.

[77] Granville, July 11. *B. D.*, IX, 585.

[78] *Kreuz-Zeitung*, July 10. Schiemann, *Deutschland und die Grosse Politik*, XII, 224. Cf. *Freisinnige Zeitung* in *Echo*, July 25.

[79] *Berliner Neueste Nachrichten*, July 7. Cf. Bethmann-Hollweg, July 6. *G. P.*, XXXI, 438. Kiderlen wrote, a few weeks later, that Germany had been persuaded to recognize "the peaceful tendency of the Triple Entente." Kiderlen-Wächter's comments, Pourtalès, Aug. 11. *Ibid.*, XXXI 531.

[80] *Kreuz-Zeitung*, July 17. Schiemann, *op. cit.*, XII, 233.

[81] This silence, according to an official of the foreign office, seriously diminished the value of William's conversations with the Tsar. Zimmermann, Aug. 6. *G. P.*, XXXI, 522.

To Schiemann, this agreement, together with Russia's efforts to turn Sweden against Germany and to bring about a Serbo-Bulgarian alliance, was a strange way to maintain the balance of power: "The purpose is rather to destroy completely that balance in so far as it exists at all and, in fact, it may lead to a war such as the world has never seen." [82]   A cry went up that France wished to isolate Germany at the *Temps'* first reference to the possible withdrawal of the French fleet from the English Channel and its concentration in the Mediterranean.[83]   Italy, replied the Conservative *Post* (Sept. 17), should increase her navy, and even the Liberal *Frankfurter Zeitung* hinted that Germany might find it necessary to take defensive measures.[84]

Meanwhile, the Balkan states were preparing for the liberation of their brothers under Turkish rule. With Russia's assistance, Serbia and Bulgaria contracted an alliance in March 1912, to which Greece acceded in May and Montenegro in July, providing for the coöperation of their armies against any attempt by a great power to acquire territory in the Balkans or if disturbances in Turkey should threaten the status quo. Any differences in regard to the division of the spoils were to be referred to Russia for arbitration. What her diplomats doubtless intended should be used as a defense against Austria's ambitions was regarded by the Balkan states themselves as an offensive weapon against Turkey. Only in a limited sense was Germany to blame for this dangerous situation; by her support of Austria she had contributed to Serbia's dissatisfaction and by her failure to prevent Italy from attacking Turkey she helped to provide the occasion for the formation of the Balkan League. Like the Triple Entente, she knew of its existence,[85] but her inaction was doubtless more excusable. Even less than France and England could Germany afford to warn Russia as to the consequences of a Balkan war. Her desire for peace in the Balkans was beyond suspicion; even the French *chargé d'affaires* saw that she

---

[82] *Kreuz-Zeitung*, Aug. 7. Schiemann, *op. cit.*, XII, 260. That no hope remained of winning Russia's friendship, the *Hamburger Nachrichten* and the *Leipziger Neueste Nachrichten* refused to believe. *Echo*, Aug. 8.
[83] *Kölnische Zeitung*, Sept. 17; *Germania*, Oct, 6.
[84] *Post*, Sept. 17.
[85] Wolff, *Eve of 1914*, pp. 140, 141. *Cf.* J. C. Adams's unprinted doctoral dissertation, "European Diplomacy and the First Balkan War," Duke University.

had everything to lose and nothing to gain.[86] Turkey's victory would be only less embarrassing than her defeat, since Russia might come to the aid of her protégés. Moreover, a war might well interfere with the new colonial policy. "Can anyone imagine," wrote Jules Cambon during the crisis, "a falser position than Germany's between Italy and Turkey, between Italy and Austria, and even between Austria and Russia."[87] In spite of her friendship with Turkey, she would doubtless have preferred to remain completely indifferent. Bülow, said the National Liberal *Madgeburgische Zeitung,* had done well to lay down his flute when the European concert concerned itself with Balkan affairs rather than to play the tune called by others. The chief task was to guard Germany's roof from the flying sparks.[88]

Like England, who feared the effect upon her Mohammedan subjects, Germany was cool to the idea of exerting pressure upon Turkey to secure the reforms which would deprive the Balkan states of their excuse for action. Indeed, Austria was promptly called to order when she acted alone for this purpose.[89] Kiderlen advised the Chancellor to warn Berchtold, the Austrian foreign minister, during their meeting at Buchlau, September 7, 8, 1912. Austria had already presented her ally with too many *faits accomplis.* Since there was nothing in the Dual Alliance that required Germany's unconditional support, it should be granted according to circumstances (*"von Fall zu Fall"*). Germany had no desire to be committed without warning to a Balkan adventure.[90] Unfortunately, Bethmann did not speak with the same firmness; Berchtold, who had a low opinion of the Chancellor's diplomatic ability, concluded that he could safely act with Russia at Constantinople without consulting Berlin.[91] Kiderlen at once instructed the German ambassador to ignore the Austro-Russian action.[92] As to the desirability of maintaining peace on the basis of the status quo, all of the great powers, Germany as

[86] Manneville, Aug. 3, 1912. *D. D. F.,* (3), III, 315, 316.
[87] *Ibid.,* (3) III, 572 (Sept. 29).
[88] *Tägliche Rundschau,* Oct. 2.
[89] Kiderlen-Wächter, Aug. 15, Aug. 30. *G. P.,* XXXIII, 49, 50, 83.
[90] Kiderlen-Wächter, Sept. 2. Jäckh, *Kiderlen-Wächter,* II, 187.
[91] Berchtold, Sept. 7, 8, 20, 24. *Ö.-U. A.,* IV, 415–418, 448, 453, 465, 466; Kiderlen-Wächter's comments, Sept. 19; Kiderlen-Wächter, Sept. 21. *G. P.,* XXXIII, 108, 112.
[92] *Ibid.,* XXXIII, 116 (Sept. 25).

well as Russia and Austria, were agreed, but their feverish efforts to reach an understanding were defeated until the last moment by differences of opinion as to the nature of the reforms and as to the proper mode of action and by the feeling that a Balkan war was inevitable. Soon the powers were working, not to extinguish the flames, but to keep them from spreading. In this effort, Germany was just as active as any other power. "It is the task and aim of both countries [Germany and France]," wrote the agrarian *Deutsche Tageszeitung* (Oct. 15) after the beginning of hostilities, "to restrain Russia and Austria from measures that might lead them into conflict." There were no delays or equivocations. If Poincaré and Sazanov were the first to propose an agreement to localize a Balkan war,[93] Kiderlen suggested that Russia, supported by Austria, should warn the Balkan states that no changes in the status quo would be permitted, and he readily agreed to Poincaré's amendment giving Russia and Austria a mandate to act in the name of the other powers.[94] Moreover, he accepted Russia's suggestion that the Balkan states be assured that something would be done about the reform question.[95] By September it may have been too late to prevent the outbreak of hostilities; in any case, England was chiefly responsible for the delay in drafting the statement to be made in Constantinople and in the other Balkan capitals until October 7, when the drift toward war could no longer be checked. From the labor of the chancellories came at least a general agreement that the conflict should be localized.[96] On October 8, anticipating the Austro-Russian *démarche* by a few hours, Nicholas of Montenegro gave the Turkish envoy his passports and, the next day, fired the first shell across the frontier into a Turkish camp.

In its efforts to preserve peace and, especially, to avert a general war, the German government was supported by public opinion.

---

[93] Granville, Sept. 17. *B. D.*, IX (1), 690; Poincaré, Sept. 22. *D. D. F.*, (3), III, 549, 550.
[94] J. Cambon, Sept. 28, 29, Oct. 2; Poincaré, Oct. 1. *D. D. F.*, (3), III, 566, 567, 571; IV, 4, 5, 14, 15.
[95] Kiderlen-Wächter, Oct. 3. *G. P.*, XXXIII, 155, 156; Poincaré, Oct. 3; J. Cambon, Oct. 4. *D. D. F.*, (3), IV, 20, 40, 41.
[96] *Ibid.*, (3), III, 549, 550; IV, 20, 21, 48, 49, 55, 60, 61, 72, 74, 75; *B. D.*, IX (1), 760. *Cf.* Nicolson, *Lord Carnock*, pp. 378, 380.

The press had been less fatalistic than the diplomats, for it argued toward the end of September that mobilization in the Balkans did not necessarily mean war.[97] The foreign office, wrote the Progressive *Freisinnige Zeitung* (Oct. 13) after the beginning of the war, had adopted a reserved attitude, "in agreement with entire nation, from the extreme Right to the Social Democrats. . . ." The chauvinist *Post's* (Sept. 30, Oct. 1, 3) support of an Austrian offensive against Serbia and of an alliance with Turkey did not represent even nationalist opinion as a whole. The agrarian *Deutsche Tageszeitung* (Oct. 3) could conceive of no surer way to precipitate a general war; moreover, it was confident that Russia's trial mobilization—the reason which the *Post* had given for its stand—had no connection with the Balkans. When the inspired press spoke of a probable international agreement to localize the war and to maintain the status quo,[98] the general reaction was one of relief. "So far as we are concerned," wrote the nationalist *Berliner Neueste Nachrichten* (Oct. 3), "we cannot possibly desire a European war for the sake of the Balkans." Should a general conflict become inevitable, it was the government's duty to see that it was waged for "an understandable and popular purpose." The chauvinist *Rheinisch-Westfälische Zeitung* (Oct. 3) noted with satisfaction Berlin's apparent reluctance to don its "shining armor." The *Hamburger Nachrichten* would have Germany remain aloof; she should "do everything in her power to prevent the *casus foederis* from arising" if other powers became involved [99]—a view with which the Social Democrats were in complete accord.[100]

France's attitude earned generous applause, especially among the liberals. Of Poincaré's sincerity in trying to bring the Triple Entente and the Triple Alliance together, the *Berliner Tageblatt* (Oct. 6) had no doubt, while the *Frankfurter Zeitung* (Oct. 9) believed more firmly than ever that France and Germany had

---

[97] *Frankfurter Zeitung, Deutsche Tageszeitung, Berliner Tageblatt,* Oct. 1; *N. A. Z.,* in *Germania,* Oct. 8.

[98] *N. A. Z., Kölnische Zeitung,* Oct. 3.

[99] *Berliner Neueste Nachrichten,* Oct. 2. On October 16, this journal wrote that a war would be "unnatural," since Germany had refused to fight during the Agadir crisis when her own interests were involved. Austria should and could be restrained.

[100] Their executive committee called for peace demonstrations throughout Prussia on October 20. *Vorwärts,* Oct. 15.

much in common.   Their economic interests in Turkey, wrote
the Social Democratic *Vorwärts* (Oct. 2), guaranteed their desire
of peace; these interests should, in the *Grenzboten's* opinion, provide an effective basis for coöperation.[101]   The National Liberal
National Zeitung (Oct. 13), as well as the moderate *Vossische
Zeitung* (Oct. 19), felt that Germany and France, acting together, could localize the war.   .Neither country, according to the
agrarian *Deutsche Tageszeitung* (Oct. 15), wished to fight for
the ambitions of its ally.   Even the chauvinist *Post* (Oct. 16)
acknowledged France's efforts in the cause of peace.   As for
England, her delay in joining the other powers and Sazonov's
visit to Balmoral just before the war were regarded with suspicion.
The Catholic press was particularly skeptical;[102] the *Germania*
(Oct. 12) hoped that Germany's diplomats would see through
her game.   What she wanted most of all, according to the nationalist *Münchener Neueste Nachrichten,* was a weak and amenable Turkey.[103]   Unwelcome as the Balkan War was to German
public opinion, certain advantages were sometimes noticed.
Anglo-German relations, it was thought, might be improved by
shifting attention from the North Sea to the Balkans.   Stresses
and strains appeared in the Triple Entente.   France evidently did
not relish the thought of fighting for Russia's interests, and Russia was supposed to be resentful at England's cool reception of
Sazonov.[104]   Nor were the German journalists alone in this analysis.   In London, Paul Cambon and Nicolson expected Germany
to exploit Sazonov's disappointment by approaching St. Petersburg
and, in Berlin, Jules Cambon thought that Germany would act
either in the Russian capital or in London.[105]
    One nationalist observer was confident that Germany had
nothing to fear, whatever the results of the war might be.[106]   With

---

[101] G. Cleinow, "Deutschland und die Balkankrise," *Grenzboten*, III, 50, 51 (Oct. 9).
[102] *Germania,* Oct. 11.   Edward VII's death had not meant the end of the policy
of encirclement.   "Zur Balkanfrage," *Historisch-Politische Blätter,* vol. 150, p. 629
(Oct. 14, 1912).
[103] *Tägliche Rundschau,* Oct. 13.
[104] L. Raschdau on an article in the *Temps, Berliner Neueste Nachrichten,* Oct. 27;
Germania, Oct. 27; "Gährungen in Frankreich." *Historisch-Politische Blätter,* vol. 150,
p. 931 (Dec. 1912); *Kreuz-Zeitung,* Oct. 23.   Schiemann, *Deutschland und die Grosse
Politik,* XII, 288, 289.
[105] P. Cambon, Oct. 16; J. Cambon, Oct. 18.   *D. D. F.,* (3), IV, 188, 206, 207.
[106] *Grenzboten,* 1912, IV, 188 (G. Cleinow, Oct. 23).

this view William was in complete accord: "May the better man win!" was his reaction to the first victories of the Balkan states.[107] His advisers did not, however, share his partiality for the Balkan League. Like the greater part of public opinion and of most military experts, they were confident—as were most observers everywhere—that Turkey would win.[108] They were soon disillusioned. The Turks were decisively beaten by the Bulgarians at Kirk Kilisse on October 22 and by the Serbs at Koumanova on October 26, and a few days later the Greeks occupied Salonica. Soon the Turks were reduced to the desperate defense of Constantinople on the Tchatalja lines and of a few strongholds in the West. To William these events meant the end of Turkey's rule in Europe,[109] but Kiderlen thought at first that it might still be saved. He proposed to England and France that they should use their influence in the Balkan capitals in favor of the status quo while he acted at Vienna for the same purpose, and that Russia should merely be notified that these measures were being taken.[110] To prevent Austria from acting precipitously, Kiderlen urged her to discuss with him the terms of an acceptable Balkan settlement,[111] but Poincaré, who suspected him of trying to divide the Triple Entente by isolating Russia, hastened to affirm its unity and France's loyalty to her engagements. The moment was propitious for a strong statement, for a large part of the press was claiming that the victories of the Balkan states proved the superiority of their French armaments and training over Turkey's German equipment and strategy. Not for years had a French statesman spoken so confidently and firmly as Poincaré did at Nantes, October 27, in pledging France's loyalty to the Triple Entente. France, he said, desired peace but she was not afraid of war.[112] So little was the speech understood in

---

107 G. P., XXXIII, 120, 142, 148, 164, 165.

108 *Rheinisch-Westfälische Zeitung*, Oct. 2; *Schlessische Zeitung*, in *Tägliche Rundschau*, Oct. 8; *Deutsche Tageszeitung*, Oct. 16. *Cf.* Granville, Oct. 14. B. D., (2), pp. 21, 22.

109 He opposed any move to deprive Bulgaria of a single village. G. P., XXXIII, 253 (Oct. 25). The chauvinist *Post* (Oct. 28) also believed that the status quo had been irretrievably destroyed.

110 J. Cambon, Oct. 25. D. D. F., (3), IV, 248, 249; Kiderlen-Wächter, Oct. 26. G. P., XXXIII, 256.

111 Szögyény, Oct. 26. Ö.-U. A., IV, 707, 708.

112 Carroll, *French Public Opinion*, pp. 269, 270.

Germany that it was generally discounted as intended exclusively for its effect upon French public opinion.[113] To the *Vossische Zeitung* (Oct. 28), Poincaré was even a "good European." Meanwhile, he was busy closing the ranks of the Triple Entente, calling upon London to join with him in a statement to Berlin that Russia must be consulted and insisting that Paris should direct the conversation with London.[114] More significant was Poincaré's proposal that the powers should offer their mediation "in a spirit of absolute disinterestedness,"[115] for mediation thus conceived could only result in Turkey's partition, the strengthening of the Balkan states, and the augmentation of Russia's and therefore of the Triple Entente's influence. Berchtold refused—protesting that the lowliest Austrian citizen would charge him with treason—and with his approval, Kiderlen suggested mediation without any reference to disinterestedness.[116] The good temper of the German press was rudely disturbed by the announcement of Poincaré's proposal of disinterestedness. The liberal *Frankfurter Zeitung* (Nov. 5) found it difficult to reconcile his professed desire for European solidarity with his claim to speak in the name of the Triple Entente. How could the *Temps* pretend that the Triple Entente was "disinterested" when it spoke of that group as the Balkan League's best friend? France, said the Catholic *Germania* (Nov. 5), was ready "to place herself at the service of a Pan-Slavic policy and to pull Russia's chestnuts out of the fire." She must understand that Austria was determined to defend her interests. To the chauvinist *Post* (Nov. 5), France wished to foment disorder, and the Pan-German *Rheinisch-Westfälische Zeitung* (Nov. 5) condemned the French Premier's proposal as "an offensive presumption, even a provocation."[117] "Germany is ready," wrote the Paris correspondent of the *Vossische Zeitung* (Nov. 4), "to stand by her ally if she defends her interests with all her might." The situation was dangerously critical. Watching the march of the Serbian army toward the

[113] *Frankfurter Zeitung, Kölnische Zeitung, Deutsche Tageszeitung,* Oct. 28.
[114] Poincaré, Oct. 28. *D. D. F.,* (3), IV, 269, 270, 281.
[115] Poincaré, Oct. 30. *Ibid.,* (3), IV, 291, 292.
[116] Kiderlen-Wächter, Oct. 30; Tschirschky, Oct. 30, Nov. 1. *G. P.,* XXXIII, 261, 262, 264–266.
[117] Cf. *Hamburger Nachrichten,* Nov. 5.

Adriatic, Austria made it clear that she would never tolerate Serbia's acquisition of a port that might weaken her control of that sea and of Serbia's economic life.[118] Again William's first reactions were more statesmanlike than those of his ministers. Believing that Germany's obligations were limited to the defense of Austria's own territory, that her own vital interests were not endangered by Serbia's aspirations, and that she should make friends with the victorious Balkan League, he directed the foreign office not to support her.[119] He would never "march against Paris and Moscow on account of Albania and Durazzo . . . "; a war for such a reason would never be popular.[120] While Kiderlen was willing that Bulgaria should even take Adrianople, he approved Austria's stand for an independent Albania with boundaries that would bar Serbia from the Adriatic coast, notwithstanding Russia's sympathy for the latter's claims.[121] To the indiscreet inquiry of the Serbian envoy, November 7, as to Germany's action in an Austro-Russian war, he replied that she would recognize the *casus foederis* regardless of the manner of its beginning; and the French ambassador reported that she would support her ally even if Russia did not appeal to France.[122] The Quai d'Orsay immediately took up the challenge. "Yes," said the director of its political section to the German ambassador, "alliances sometimes produce terrible necessities," and Poincaré himself asserted that "France will have to stand by Russia just as certainly as Germany will support Austria-Hungary."[123]

The gravity of the situation worked everywhere against precipitous action. In London Asquith spoke at the Guildhall of

---

[118] Austria was willing to concede a railway communication across Bosnia to the Adriatic coast, the annexation of the Sanjak of Novibazar, or the annexation of Salonica or of any other Aegean port.

[119] William II's comments, Kiderlen-Wächter, Nov. 3; William II, Nov. 7. *G. P.,* XXXIII, 276, 295. The Austrian ambassador's impression of his attitude at this time was completely different. Szögyény, Nov. 5. *Ö.-U. A.,* IV, 773.

[120] William II, Nov. 9, *circa* Nov. 11. *G. P.,* XXXIII, 302, 303.

[121] Kiderlen-Wächter, Nov. 5. *Ibid.,* XXXIII, 280; J. Cambon, Nov. 5. *D. D. F.,* (3), IV, 365.

[122] *G. P.,* XXXIII, 293n; J. Cambon, Nov. 7. *D. D. F.,* (3), IV, 391, 392. *Cf.* Szögyény, Nov. 7. *Ö.-U. A.,* IV, 792; Goschen, Nov. 7, 10. *B. D.,* IX (2), 113, 114, 131, 132. In an article which may have influenced the Serbian diplomat, the *Post* (Nov. 6) said that Berlin knew Austria's point of view: "It is no mistake to assume that the Berlin government will not stop with *the diplomatic support* of the ally."

[123] *D. D. F.,* (3), IV, 409 (Nov. 8); Schoen, Nov. 10. *G. P.,* XXXIII, 310, 311.

England's friendly relations with all countries, and Nicolson, talking with the German ambassador, praised Austria's moderation in the face of Serbia's delusions of grandeur.[124] Poincaré's assurances of loyalty undoubtedly encouraged Russia to count upon the support of France even in an aggressive policy, yet he always insisted that France must be consulted before a forward movement in the Balkans was decided upon. So cool was French public opinion to a war for Russia's interests, that Izvolski, the Russian ambassador, soon began to bombard his government with pleas for money with which to influence the press. That Russia's sympathy for Serbian aspirations would extend to the point of war was by no means certain; Berchtold believed that she would excite the Serbs, as in 1909, only to abandon them at a critical moment, and Kiderlen believed that Russia would only do enough to maintain her reputation as their protector.[125]

In general, German public opinion remained moderate. The Pan-German agitation for annexations in Asia Minor, according to the liberal *Frankfurter Zeitung* (Nov. 11) and to the moderate *Vossische Zeitung* (Nov. 20), made little headway. The two extremes, the Social Democrats and the nationalists, were outspoken in their criticism of Austria and of the assumption that Germany was obliged to support her under all circumstances. If the Balkan victories threatened Austria's security, the blame, wrote the *Vorwärts* (Nov. 7), lay with her own harsh treatment of her South Slavic subjects. Her real purpose, it insisted (Nov. 9), was to restore her tarnished prestige; Germany should restrain her, since it was unthinkable that German blood and treasure should be placed at Austria's disposal.[126] Nor would Austria turn against the alliance, for less than ever could she afford to alienate Germany.[127] "After freeing itself from the Hofburg's clutches, should the German people consent to act as its hired soldier (*Landsknecht*)?"[128] With this aversion to an

---

[124] *Vossische Zeitung*, Nov. 11; Lichnowsky, Nov. 15. *G. P.*, XXXIII, 310, 311.
[125] Tschirschky, Nov. 13; Kiderlen-Wächter, Nov. 20. *Ibid.*, XXXIII, 338, 362. Serbia, according to the *Vossische Zeitung* (Nov. 11), would count for little in Russia's choice between war and peace.
[126] *Cf.* K. Leuthner, "Das Balkanproblem und Österreich-Ungarn," *Sozialdemokratische Monatshefte*, 1912, pp. 1417–1419 (Nov. 14).
[127] *Vorwärts*, Nov. 12.
[128] *Sozialdemokratische Monatshefte*, 1912, p. 1425 (Nov. 14).

unconditional support of Austria, a large section of nationalist opinion agreed. The *Berliner Neueste Nachrichten* (Oct. 29) spoke of her reserve during the Agadir crisis as a precedent worthy of emulation. While the National Liberal *Hamburger Nachrichten* (Nov. 1) was by no means easy about the diplomatic and military significance of the Balkan League, it asserted (Nov. 6) that the *casus foederis* should be limited to the literal text of the alliance. That any obligation existed to aid Austria if her intervention in the Balkan War resulted in an attack by Russia was, in its opinion, doubtful. The *Rheinisch-Westfälische Zeitung* (Nov. 27) was as convinced as ever that Germany's interests were not involved. From a war at this juncture, she could hope for no other advantage, according to one observer, than a closer union with Austria, and the latter's saber-rattling would be largely responsible.[129] The liberal *Berliner Tageblatt's* (Nov. 22) attitude was even more significant: if the Triple Entente backed Serbia's demand for an Adriatic port, it was ready to support Austria, but, for the present, it believed that moderating advice in Vienna was in order.

To Kiderlen, the situation seemed far more dangerous than it did to Austria's critics. The gravest issues might be precipitated if Poincaré succeeded in aligning England with France and Russia in support of Serbia's ambitions. While the German minister wished to avoid a war for Austria's Balkan interests, he felt that her diplomatic defeat would seriously damage Germany's own position. Kiderlen therefore tried to weaken the Triple Entente and to maintain the Triple Alliance. When Grey suggested that Germany might coöperate with England in seeking a solution of the crisis, he agreed, on the condition that France and Russia should not be informed.[130] He ignored Russia as much as possible, advising Archduke Francis Ferdinand against going to St. Petersburg, on the ground that more harm than good would result, while he, Kiderlen, turned to the Western powers for an understanding in regard to the terms of peace. Upon Vienna he urged the importance of securing Italy's co-

---

[129] *Grenzboten*, 1912, IV, 437, 438 (G. Cleinow, Nov. 27); H. Ilgenstein, "Das Spiel mit dem Feuer," *Gegenwart*, Nov. 30.
[130] Kühlmann, Oct. 15, 25; Kiderlen-Wächter, Oct. 20. *G. P.*, XXXIII, 228, 237, 247.

operation in warning Serbia that the Albanian question must be reserved for the general negotiations at the close of the war.[131] For a moment during the third week in November, Austria's military measures threatened these negotiations with failure. Auffenberg, the war minister, was reported as saying that Russia's inaction would mean "a free hand toward Serbia."[132] By this time, William's attitude had undergone a complete change. Forgetting his earlier caution, he wrote that he was ready for war if Russia resorted to countermeasures or if she made representations in Vienna. He was prepared, he told Francis Ferdinand, who was in Germany for the autumn maneuvers, "to fight all three of the Entente powers" if Austria's prestige required it.[133] Kiderlen, however, was not so bellicose.[134] While he rejected Poincaré's suggestion that the port of San Giovanni di Medua with a connecting corridor should be allotted to Serbia,[135] steps were taken to quiet the alarm caused by the growing tension between Austria and Russia. More than one war, wrote the *Kölnische Zeitung* (Nov. 24), would have been fought since 1871 if precautionary measures like those of Austria and Russia meant that hostilities were inevitable. To Grey's proposal (Nov. 29) that the questions which had arisen during the Balkan War should be submitted to a conference between the representatives of the great powers in London, Kiderlen replied favorably, reserving only the right of Germany and Austria to negotiate separately with Serbia.[136] Public opinion, having little taste for a war for Austria's interests, was favorable, although some newspapers felt that the most important questions should be reserved and that little would be accomplished.[137]

In Vienna, even the officials resented the critical attitude of

131 Kiderlen-Wächter, Nov. 8, 18; Tschirschky, Nov. 8. *G. P.*, XXXIII, 354, 355; XXXIV, 3; Szögyény, Nov. 18. *Ö.-U. A.*, IV, 915, 916.

132 Tschirschky, Nov. 21. *G. P.*, XXXIII, 372, 373.

133 William II, *circa* Nov. 21. *Ibid.*, XXXIII, 373, 374; Szögyény, Nov. 22. *Ö.-U. A.*, IV, 971.

134 Like William and Bethmann, Kiderlen, according to the Belgian envoy, was sincerely trying to avert a European conflagration. Beyens, *Belgische Dokumente*, VI, 263, 264.

135 Kiderlen-Wächter, Nov. 23. *G. P.*, XXXIII, 389.

136 Kiderlen-Wächter, Dec. 1. *Ibid.*, XXXIV, 11.

137 *Kölnische Zeitung, Post*, Nov. 29; *Vossische Zeitung*, Nov. 30. The *Frankfurter Zeitung* (Nov. 29) and the *Berliner Tageblatt* (Nov. 29) were willing, however, that the question of a Serbian port should be referred to it.

the German press. At last Berchtold protested when the *Norddeutsche* (Nov. 26) wrote that the powers were agreed that the terms of peace should be arranged between themselves. The article, he said, was regarded in parliamentary circles as an insult and as a reprisal for Austria's coolness during the Agadir crisis. An official correction was in order, since Serbia might be encouraged to advance still greater pretensions.[138] Nor was Berchtold satisfied with Kiderlen's lame excuse that the purpose of the *Norddeutsche's* article had been to restore confidence to the stock market.[139] To satisfy him and, at the same time, to strengthen the position of the Central powers at the London Conference, Bethmann gave formal and precise assurances of Germany's support in a speech, December 2, to the Reichstag. "Only imagine," the agrarian *Deutsche Tageszeitung* (Oct. 28) had written of Poincaré's speech at Nantes, "a statement by the German Chancellor: 'Germany is incapable of disloyalty, she cherishes her friendships and remains closely united with Austria-Hungary and Italy!' Such a statement would not be understood in Germany; it would rightly be regarded as entirely superfluous and therefore as useless." Yet all this—and more—Bethmann read with appropriate solemnity from a carefully prepared manuscript.[140] After explaining that Germany's interests in the Balkans were chiefly economic, that the powers were arranging a common point of view, which would be presented when the combatants agreed upon terms of peace, and that any power might then make known its objections, he defined Germany's understanding of the *casus foederis:* "If they [Austria-Hungary and Italy] should be attacked, contrary to all expectation, by a third power while protecting their interests and if their existence should thereby be threatened, then we, true to our obligations, will stand by their side, then we will fight (*fechten*) with our allies in the defense of our position in Europe and of our own country." [141]

---

[138] The official news agencies having suppressed the article, only those journals with independent services reproduced it. Tschirschky, Nov. 27, 28. *G. P.*, XXXIII, 424-426, 429.

[139] Szögyény, Nov. 27. *Ö.-U. A.*, IV, 1035.

[140] *Kölnische Zeitung, Berliner Tageblatt, Frankfurter Zeitung, Leipziger Neueste Nachrichten*, in *Hamburger Nachrichten*, Dec. 3.

[141] *Verhandlungen*, XIII Leg. Per., I Sess., IV, 2472.

While this statement aroused little enthusiasm,[142] it rallied the greater part of public opinion to the Chancellor's view of Germany's obligations. The Social Democrats alone objected during the debate. "Therewith," declared Ledebour, "Germany's allies, Austria first of all, receive a blank check to pursue that policy which they consider necessary for their interests." David rejected Bethmann's interpretation of the *casus foederis*. "If Austria attacks Serbia and Russia comes to the latter's assistance, we are not obligated by the alliance," he insisted, "to take up arms. This is exceedingly important, for it is our sole guarantee of peace against the military party in Vienna."[143] The *Vorwärts* (Dec. 3) was equally unwilling that Germany should "risk her blood and property (*Gut und Blut*)" for Austria. A few discordant voices were heard above the general chorus of approval. Why, asked the liberal *Berliner Tageblatt* (Dec. 3), had the Chancellor so definitely pointed his statement against Russia after the government's earlier expressions of satisfaction with the general situation? Was the moment opportune for a rattling of the sword? Must it not be concluded "that the *future* and the security of the great German Empire depends upon that of Austria-Hungary?" The German people, "blind and dumb," wrote the chauvinist *Rheinisch-Westfälische Zeitung* (Dec. 3), would accept the war "with clenched teeth," but the same journal promptly denounced (Dec. 4) Bethmann's version of the *casus foederis* as "completely false." According to the *Hamburger Nachrichten* (Dec. 3), the Chancellor had intended to say that Germany would aid Austria against Russia's "unprovoked attack" and with this position the nation would agree. Going a little further, the National Liberal *National Zeitung* (Dec. 3) drew a distinction between Austria's vital interests, which Germany must support, and her ill-founded claims,[144] but this caution was not characteristic of the general reaction of the press. For the greater

---

142 *Berliner Tageblatt, Post,* Dec. 3.

143 *Verhandlungen,* XIII Leg. Per., I Sess., IV, 2472, 2473 (Dec. 2).

144 *Magdeburgische Zeitung,* in *Post,* Dec. 3. Bethmann, in fact, did not distinguish between Austria's interests. The text, as it appeared in the *Norddeutsche* (Dec. 3), confirms that of the parliamentary report. Beyens, the Belgian envoy, wrote later that the Chancellor had intended to fix the limits beyond which Germany's support would not go. Beyens, *Deux années à Berlin* (2 vols., Paris, 1931), I, 112. The contemporary press comments do not support this view. *Cf.,* however, the *Hamburger Nachrichten,* Dec. 3.

part of nationalist opinion, the international situation and especially Russia's attitude were the decisive factors, although a Conservative spokesman in the Reichstag said that Germany would not act as Austria's vassal.[145] It was these considerations which Class expounded to the executive committee of the Pan-German League.[146] Bethmann's speech was a warning to Russia.[147] "Not until Russia speaks," wrote the *Kölnische Zeitung* (Dec. 3) under the caption "War and Peace," "will the specter of war disappear."[148] No section of public opinion was better pleased than the Catholics. The speech, wrote the *Germania* (Dec. 4), was an important "political event." In the liberal press, there was, however, a difference of opinion, for the *Berliner Tageblatt* did not agree with the *Frankfurter Zeitung's* and *Vossische Zeitung's* position that the question of Serbia's access to the Adriatic Sea constituted a serious threat to Austria and Germany.

While Russia had already decided (Nov. 10) not to go to war in support of Serbia's ambitions, Bethmann's assurances to Austria —and the renewal of the Triple Alliance (Dec. 5)—doubtless influenced his proposal at the first session of the London Conference that the northern boundary of Albania should coincide with the southern boundary of Montenegro. Austria had won her main point, but there were other and less desirable developments. On November 22 occurred Grey's exchange of letters with Paul Cambon providing for a discussion of measures to be taken in common if either France or England were in danger of attack by a third power or if the peace of Europe were threatened. Bethmann's blunt use of the verb *"fechten"* (to fight) gave unusual significance to his speech of December 2 in the opinion of the British foreign office. It was, the Austrian ambassador was told, "another example of the tactlessness of which Berlin is so

---

[145] *Verhandlungen*, XIII Leg. Per., I Sess., p. 2487 (Kanitz, Dec. 2). This speech was Kanitz's reply to the Chancellor's earlier confidential question as to whether the German people would support a war over the possession of Durazzo. Westarp, *Konservative Politik*, I, 166. Cf. *Kölnische Zeitung*, Dec. 3; *Kreuz-Zeitung*, Dec. 11, Schiemann, *Deutschland und die Grosse Politik*, XII, 344.

[146] *A. B.*, Dec. 7.

[147] *Magdeburgische Zeitung*, *National Zeitung*, Dec. 3; *Kreuz-Zeitung*, Dec. 4. Schiemann, *op. cit.*, XII, 337, 338.

[148] The agrarian *Deutsche Tageszeitung* (Dec. 3) called for an official repudiation of this article and insisted that Germany had no intention of exerting pressure upon other countries. The *Norddeutsche* soon printed a *démenti. Kölnische Zeitung*, Dec. 7.

frequently guilty."[149] More significant was Haldane's warning, within twenty-four hours of the Chancellor's speech, that Great Britain would probably be unable to remain neutral if an Austrian aggression against Serbia should precipitate a European war. She would never tolerate France's destruction as a great power and the consequent establishment of Germany's hegemony.[150] By the end of the month, Italy withdrew her promise to send five army corps over the Alps.[151] These unfavorable developments, together with the differences between Austria and Italy over Albania and the revival of the irredentist movement, argued strongly for caution. Once Serbia's claim to an Adriatic port had been defeated, Germany's influence during the protracted and often critical negotiations leading to the Treaty of London (May 30, 1913) was directed against any dangerous decisions. Jagow, who became the minister of foreign affairs after Kiderlen's sudden death (Dec. 30, 1912), continued, in the main, his predecessor's policies, although he lacked his forcefulness and color. To Germany belongs much of the credit if the fiery Conrad von Hötzendorf, who had recently been reappointed chief of the Austrian staff, was restrained from attacking Serbia. She worked fairly consistently with England to prevent a general war. Bethmann, like the Pan-Germans, was determined to secure a share of the spoils if Turkey's Asiatic possessions were partitioned, but he preferred that this question and that of the Straits should be indefinitely postponed.[152]

The friends and critics of an unconditional support of Austria were agreed that the First Balkan War had changed the balance of power in Europe against the Central powers. The French press was boasting of the five hundred thousand bayonets which the Balkan League would place at the service of the Triple Entente.[153] The Pan-Germans had initiated a campaign for a great increase in the army as early as the autumn of 1911. In September of that year, Class helped to organize the Defense League (*Wehrverein*) and, on his suggestion, August Keim, a

149 Mensdorff, Dec. 3. *O.-U. A.,* V, 22.
150 Lichnowsky, Dec. 3. *G. P.,* XXXIV, 119–122.
151 Tschirschky, Dec. 29. *Ibid.,* XXXIV, 104.
152 Brandenburg, *From Bismarck to the World War,* pp. 444 ff. (Jan. 16, 27, 1913).
153 Carroll, *French Public Opinion,* p. 274.

retired general, was made its leader.[154]   The need of training the
thousands of young men who still escaped military service—no
important additions had been made to the army since 1904—was
preached in innumerable speeches, in the *Wehr* (the weekly
organ of the Defense League), and in the chauvinist press.   At
first, the reaction of the government and public opinion was disappointing.   Von Heeringen, the minister of war, assured Keim
in December 1911 that, while he agreed in principle, there was
no hurry, for Germany had ten years in which to prepare.[155]
The Social Democrats polled more than four and one half million votes and elected the largest single group of deputies in the
Reichstag elections, January 1912.[156]   Thanks to the unwillingness of the National Liberals to coöperate with the Social Democrats, the government was able to organize a working majority
of Conservatives, National Liberals, and Centrists, and thus to
avoid a new election.   To the *Wehrverein,* the results, so far as
military legislation was concerned, were disappointing; the law
of June 14, 1912 seemed utterly inadequate, since the government,
having just secured the enactment of the *Novelle,* approved only
moderate increases for the army.   The situation was different by
the end of the year.   Turkey's defeat and the prospect of a
permanent Balkan League under Russia's influence changed public opinion and the government's attitude.   The shift of Austrian
troops from the Russian to the Serbian frontiers would manifestly
reduce the aid which Germany formerly had counted upon.   The
reaction in France to the Balkan victories was also disturbing.
Not only were they regarded there as a demonstration of the
superiority of French arms but also as assuring an important
addition to the military strength of the Triple Entente.   To German observers, France was becoming more dangerous as her
self-confidence increased.   "The disappearance or serious decline
of the fear of the German army and of its absolute superiority

---

[154] Class, *Wider den Strom,* pp. 220, 221.

[155] *"Da sehen Sie,"* Keim exclaimed to Class, *"in welchen Händen das deutsche
Heer ist!"* Class, *op. cit.,* pp. 220, 221.   Bethmann, according to Hallgarten, told the
war minister in October that he wished to anticipate and thus to prevent Tirpitz' plans
for a new navy bill by a large increase in the army.   Hallgarten, *Vorkriegs Imperialismus,*
p. 242.

[156] For the first time, a member of this party (Scheidemann) was elected as one of
the two vice-presidents of the Reichstag.

over the French army," wrote the *Schlessiche Zeitung,* "means the end of her peacefulness."[157] Paris, according to the *Rheinisch-Westfälische Zeitung* (Nov. 1), had lost its wholesome dread of a second Sedan.[158] Those who regarded England as the "real enemy" sometimes argued, in the spirit of the hostage theory, that she could only be defeated in France. "There will be," wrote a pamphleteer, "no real prospect for success upon the sea against England unless we can count upon dictating peace in Paris."[159] Even the *Kölnische Zeitung* (Nov. 23) was troubled by efforts abroad "to shatter respect for Germany's military strength and to encourage the belief that she is a colossus with feet of clay. . . ."

A demonstration of national unity in support of a new army law, said the *Kölnische Zeitung* (Nov. 23), would discourage any country from "daring to awaken the *furor teutonicus* from Memel to Lake Constance." Differences of opinion delayed the final action. For weeks, the general staff, seeking for the first time to dictate the terms of an important army bill, fought for an increase of three hundred thousand men against the more moderate views of the Chancellor and of the war minister. Even the military experts were forced to admit that a sufficient number of commissioned and non-commissioned officers could not be found, and some viewed with alarm the increasing preponderance of the industrial proletariat in the rank and file. By December 1912, an agreement in principle was reached, but Bethmann insisted that the deliberations of the London Conference should not be disturbed by a public announcement at this time.[160] The final bill, approved by Moltke and Heeringen on January 23, 1913, provided for a larger increase than any law since the establishment of the Empire; the four thousand additional commissioned and fifteen thousand non-commissioned officers with the

---

[157] *Tägliche Rundschau,* Nov. 3.

[158] On October 14, this journal devoted its entire first page to an appeal by the *Wehrverein* in behalf of an increase in the army. It claimed forty thousand members for the Defense League.

[159] H. Hochwart, *Die andern und wir* (Leipzig, 1912), pp. 59–61.

[160] G. P., XXXIX, 145, 146, 177, 178. On December 17, 1912, the *Norddeutsche* wrote that increases were envisaged only for the aviation. Hallgarten also notes the opposition to the arming of the masses which the plans of the general staff would entail. Hallgarten, *Vorkriegs Imperialismus,* p. 243.

one hundred and seventeen thousand men meant a peacetime army of more than eight hundred thousand.[161] Soon it was known that an extraordinary effort was about to be made. The *Post* (Jan. 8) referred to the forthcoming bill as the best guarantee of peace, and its main provisions were revealed by the *Berliner Lokal-Anzeiger* (Jan. 22). On January 25, the *Norddeutsche* announced that it would be introduced during the current session of the Reichstag. Speaking to a group of agricultural experts, the Chancellor himself said, February 13, that the nation desired "everyone capable of bearing arms to be a soldier *(dass der, wer wehrfähig ist, auch Soldat wird)*."[162] The enactment of the bill seemed unlikely at first, for the Centrists and the Progressives as well as the Social Democrats announced their intention of voting against it.[163] The government appealed over their heads to public opinion. In the spring of 1913, it was easy to represent the international situation as dangerous to Germany's security, but the question whether Russia or France should be emphasized was more delicate. To direct a press campaign against the former was inadvisable, in view of the improvement in Russo-German relations and because tension between Austria and Russia had lessened after the agreement to reduce their troops on the Galician frontier. To stress the French danger, as Bismarck had usually done, might react unfavorably upon Anglo-German relations; nevertheless, this course was followed.[164] Poincaré's election to the presidency was regarded by many as ominous. He had acknowledged, it was said, personal reasons, as a native Lorrainer, for hating Germany.[165] Searching his career for light upon his probable attitude, the *Kölnische Zeitung*

---

[161] The difference between the German (819,000) and the French estimates (860,-000–870,000) is probably explained by a difference of opinion as to the classification of such auxillary troops as the military police. The increase became effective on October 1, 1913. Oncken, *Vorgeschichte des Weltkrieges*, II, 766.

[162] *Freisinnige Zeitung*, Feb. 14, 1913. In view of these circumstances, the fact that the French were the first to go to parliament with a bill increasing the term of service from two to three years (March 6) does not necessarily mean that they were responsible for initiating the new armament race. Wahl, for example, argues merely that France made her decision before she knew the exact provisions of the German bill. Wahl, *Deutsche Geschichte*, IV, 596.

[163] *Kölnische Volkszeitung*, in *Freisinnige Zeitung*, Jan. 26; *Freisinnige Zeitung*, Feb. 14.

[164] From the first, Keim, the president of the *Wehrverein*, had insisted that France's attitude was the real reason for the bill. *Tägliche Rundschau*, Jan. 11.

[165] *Rheinisch-Westfälische Zeitung*, in *ibid.*, Jan. 19.

(Jan. 18) discovered in his change of colors during the Dreyfus Affair a susceptibility to the pressure of mass opinion. In his attempt to play the first violin in the European concert during the Balkan crisis was seen a predilection for a policy of prestige.[166] He was given the credit for much of France's new self-confidence and, with Millerand, the war minister, for the considerable improvement in her army.[167] That he would doubtless favor the maintenance of "correct" relations with Germany was generally admitted, while at least one nationalist observer felt that all French statesmen were alike from Germany's point of view.[168] Delcassé's appointment as the ambassador to Russia was followed by a fall of prices on the stock exchange.[169] Since his mission was to tighten the Franco-Russian Alliance and to urge the construction of strategic railways,[170] the Conservative *Post* (Feb. 21) was justified in concluding that his presence in St. Petersburg would have significant results.

Quickly abandoning its first position (March 4, 1913) that it was the Balkan War and its results which required an immediate increase of the army, the *Kölnische Zeitung* unmasked its batteries against France on March 10:

> The government will not find it difficult to show the necessity of the new bill if it frankly and clearly indicates France as the direction from which danger threatens. Never have relations with our Western neighbor been so tense, never has the *revanche* been so bluntly avowed. Never have the French so openly confessed their desire to use the alliance with Russia and the friendship with England for the reconquest of Alsace-Lorraine. . . . No matter in which corner of the world war may begin, it is certain that we will cross swords with them. When that will happen, no one knows, but France will surely march against Germany at the first opportunity. . . .[171]

---

[166] *Deutsche Tageszeitung,* in *Kölnische Zeitung,* Jan. 18; *Kreuz-Zeitung,* Jan. 18; *Leipziger Neueste Nachrichten,* Jan. 19.
[167] *Germania,* Jan. 18; *Leipziger Neueste Nachrichten,* in *Tägliche Rundschau,* Jan. 19.
[168] *Berliner Tageblatt, Tägliche Rundschau,* Jan. 18; *Berliner Börsen-Courier,* in *Tägliche Rundschau,* Jan. 19. W. von Massow, "Der Präsident der französischen Republik," *Grenzboten,* 1913, I, 299 (Feb. 12).
[169] *Belgische Dokumente,* VI, 271 (Feb. 21); *National Zeitung,* Feb. 21.
[170] Poincaré, March 3. *D. D. F.,* (3), VI, 62, 63.
[171] Schiemann pointed more definitely to France's supposed obligation to aid Russia under all circumstances as the chief danger. *Kreuz-Zeitung,* March 12, 26, May 14. Schiemann, *Deutschland und die Grosse Politik,* XIII, 75, 97, 134.

The *Kölnische Zeitung* was confident that the Balkan League would not endure and that its members would be too weak to count for much in the immediate future.[172] Events had not prepared public opinion for these views; only the nationalists, some of whom still hoped that Russia's friendship might be regained, approved the attack upon France. The *Rheinisch-West-fälische Zeitung* (March 12) welcomed it as a confirmation of its own and the *Wehrverein's* stand: "There is rejoicing at this penitent sinner." According to the *Leipziger Neueste Nachrichten,* the danger from France had not been revealed by any one incident: "Symptom added to symptom has given rise to the impression which may be moderately described by the word 'mischief-maker.'" Germany's patience, wrote the *Braunschweiger Landeszeitung,* was exhausted. It was high time that Bismarck's warning to Russia should be directed against France.[173] On the other hand, the agrarian *Deutsche Tageszeitung* condemned the alarmist article as "factually inaccurate" and as a tactical error.[174] Against the effort to divert attention from Russia, the source of the real danger, the Catholic *Germania* (March 12) protested that the *Kölnische Zeitung* was guilty of the same mistake of confusing an extremist minority with an entire nation which French observers were making in regard to Germany. The incident, it believed (March 14), illustrated the vices of an official press. The liberal *Berliner Tageblatt* opened its columns to a warning from a French journalist that the German public was being systematically misinformed as to the real character of French public opinion. To the Social Democratic *Vorwärts,* the capitalist press of both countries was playing the game of the munition patriots by their "despicable and lying provocations."[175] The attack upon France had unfortunate results for Germany's foreign affairs. Grey was unmistakably cool.[176] Mensdorff, the Austrian ambassador in London, expected Anglo-German relations to suffer. Nothing, in his opinion, had contributed more

---

[172] The article was telegraphed at once to newspapers throughout Germany. *Freisinnige Zeitung,* March 12.
[173] *Tägliche Rundschau,* March 14.
[174] *Ibid.,* March 14.
[175] *Ibid.,* March 12.
[176] Lichnowsky, March 13. *G. P.,* XXXIV, 488.

to the cementing of the Anglo-French Entente "than the stupid
and clumsy tactics of the German press," or than its "never-fail-
ing tactlessness and deficient instinct for what is timely. . . ." [177]
Steps were at once taken to correct the effect of the *Kölnische
Zeitung's* article. On March 12, Germany's representatives
abroad were informed that it was "entirely unofficial," [178] and
the *Norddeutsche* (March 13) repeated this denial and affirmed
its faith in the maintenance of peace. The army bill, it wrote,
did not need the support of a war scare, nor was there any reason
why the French press should talk of a menace.

The government nevertheless continued to use France's hostility. From the confidence that her army was as strong as Germany's, argued a memorandum prepared for the Reichstag's
finance committee three days after the *Kölnische Zeitung's* article,
"to the thought that the day of revenge . . . is at hand" was not
very far. The three-year service law would be followed by an
explosion of chauvinism, for its burdens were too heavy to be
long endured. [179] In defending the bill, Bethmann repeated
(April 7, 1913) Bismarck's analysis of the French danger (Jan.
11, 1887), but he also frankly acknowledged that a conflict between the Germans and Slavs was possible. He spoke of Russia's "astonishing economic development" and of her army as
"unparalleled in numbers, in the effectiveness of its equipment,
in its organization, and in the rapidity of its mobilization." [180]
According to the opposition, the Chancellor's statement that relations with other countries were good destroyed the force of his
own case. The proposed increases, said the liberal *Frankfurter
Zeitung,* were nothing more than concessions to the *Wehrverein*
and to the military experts. [181] The Social Democrats had an answer for each argument: France's three-year service bill was the

[177] *Ö.-U. A.,* V, 957, 958.
[178] *G. P.,* XXXIV, 488n.
[179] *Ibid.,* XXXIX, 180.
[180] *Verhandlungen,* XIII Leg. Per., I Sess., VII, 4512–4514. The Chancellor's tone
of voice and gestures, according to Jules Cambon, moderated the effect of the speech.
D. D. F., (3), VI, 345 (April 13). A few days later, the rough handling of a few
Germans at Nancy furnished another argument against France. *National Zeitung,
Kölnische Zeitung, Post,* April 15. For more moderate views, see *Germania* (April
15), *Berliner Tageblatt* (April 16), *Vorwärts* (April 18).
[181] *Kölnische Zeitung,* April 8. General Keim, wrote the *Alldeutsche Blätter* (July
5, 1913), was the bill's spiritual father.

effect, not the cause, of Germany's action; the solidarity of the Russian and the Balkan Slavs was far from certain; fairer treatment by Austria of her South Slav subjects would deprive the Balkan League of its dangerous character.[182] No group painted the perils surrounding Germany more somberly than the Catholics. Spahn, their parliamentary leader, claimed that the Franco-Russian Alliance stipulated mutual armed assistance under all circumstances, even if Russia attacked Austria or if France attacked Germany. Defeat, according to Erzberger, would mean the dissolution of the Empire as well as the loss of Alsace-Lorraine.[183] Even the Social Democrats were somewhat reconciled to the inevitable by the provision that the money would be raised by a tax upon capital.[184] The revisionists were willing to agree to complete universal service if a militia system were introduced,[185] but in the final vote, resulting in the bill's passage by a decisive majority, June 30, 1913, they joined their orthodox brethren in the minority. On June 28, the *Kölnische Zeitung* predicted that the law would have a pacific influence, just as the "risk navy" had improved Anglo-German relations. The results were quite different. To France and Russia, the increase of the German army was regarded as an imperative reason for similar measures. Against the appeal to the German menace, the opponents in France to the three-year service bill could make no headway, and she was soon urging Russia to hasten and to increase her own preparations.[186] Suspicion, instead of confidence, increased.

The government and public opinion continued to frown upon Austria's aggressive tendencies. A new situation arose when

---

[182] *Verhandlungen*, XIII Leg Per., I Sess., VII, 4518, 4519 (Hasse, April 7); *Vorwärts*, April 8. According to an article in the official Social Democratic weekly, the prospect that England would land troops in Belgium was the one plausible argument in the bill's favor. P. Lensch, "Die neuen Wehrvorlagen," *Neue Zeit*, 1913, II, 70 (April 19).

[183] *Verhandlungen*, XIII, Leg. Per., I Sess., VII, 4528, 4571 (April 7, 8). Cf. *Kölnische Volkszeitung*, July 1.

[184] L. Quessel, "Die Stellung der sozialdemokratischen Fraktion zu den Wehr- und Deckungsvorlagen," *Sozialdemokratische Monatshefte*, 1913, pp. 494, 495. The party made no great effort to defeat the bill. E. Heilmann, "Unsere Taktik im Kampf gegen die Rüstungsvorlage," *Neue Zeit*, 1913, I, 393 (June 20). Cf. Allizé, Munich, March 20, 1913. *D. D. F.*, (3), VI, 63, 64: *Kölnische Volkszeitung*, July 1.

[185] *Sozialdemokratische Monatshefte*, 1913, I, 397 (April 10).

[186] This result was foreseen by the *Frankfurter Zeitung, Tägliche Rundschau*, April 1, 1913.

Bulgaria, enraged by the compensations which Serbia had received in Macedonia for the sacrifice of her Adriatic aspirations, attacked Serbia and was then in turn forced to contend with Greece, Roumania, and Turkey. Between the Central powers arose a serious difference of opinion. Contrary to Austria's desire to maintain a strong Bulgaria, Germany felt that the war should be permitted to take its course, since it would divide the Balkan League, weaken its members, and, at the same time, diminish Russia's influence.[187] "The best course," wrote Moltke, "would be to fence the Balkans in until they exterminate each other."[188] William and the foreign office felt that the Triple Alliance should seek the friendship of Roumania and Greece rather than that of Bulgaria. Austria therefore was left to shift for herself during the negotiation of the Treaty of Bucharest (Aug. 10). On the question of Khavalla, the Aegean port whose disposition was the chief issue between Bulgaria and Greece, Germany sided with France in supporting the latter's claims, while Austria, with Russia, backed Bulgaria.[189] William's aid went to his relatives, Carol of Roumania and Constantine of Greece. While the foreign office explained to Vienna that the Emperor had acted upon his own initiative, it nevertheless approved the publication of the telegrams in which Carol had expressed his gratitude for William's assistance in making a "permanent peace."[190] William thus announced his stand against Austria's desire for the revision of the Treaty of Bucharest, and, at the same time, he appointed Constantine a field marshal in the German army.[191] Deprived of Germany's support, Berchtold, who at first bravely protested that he could not simply say *"ja und Amen"* to the decisions of the Balkan states, yielded by the end of August 1913.[192]

In the meantime, the German press was engaged in a lively

[187] Tschirschky, July 1; William II's comments, Zimmermann, July 6; Jagow, July 7. *G. P.*, XXXV, 115, 116, 129, 134; Moltke, *Erinnerungen, Briefe, Dokumente, 1877–1916* (Stuttgart, 1922), pp. 373, 374.

[188] Moltke, *op. cit.*, p. 373 (July 19).

[189] Szögyény, Aug. 3. *Ö.-U. A.*, VII, 34.

[190] Szögyény, Aug. 11, 12. *Ibid.*, VII, 102, 116; *Kölnische Volkszeitung*, Aug. 11.

[191] *Kölnische Zeitung*, Aug. 13.

[192] Tschirschky, Aug. 12. *G. P.*, XXXV, 375; Berchtold, Aug. 28. *Ö.-U. A.*, VII, 219.

discussion of German foreign policy in connection with the Treaty
of Bucharest. With few exceptions, the entire press declared
itself for or against Austria's desire for its revision. The Catholic
press came out firmly for her point of view. The *Germania*
(July 31) called for action if Russia intervened to secure Adrianople for Bulgaria, and the Straits for herself. Germany's reserve during the Balkan Wars had already damaged her own
interests.[193] The alliance, said the *Germania* (Aug. 29), had been
a handicap to Austria since Algeciras; without it, the annexation
of Bosnia-Herzegovina would not have caused serious difficulty.
To suppose that Austria could accept the Treaty of Bucharest,
wrote the *Kölnische Volkszeitung* (Aug. 14), was to expect her
to abdicate her position as a great power. In the Reichstag,
Spahn deprecated the discussion of differences within the alliance.[194] Austria alone could assure peace and Christian civilization in the Balkans.[195] While the government was doubtless
influenced by Ferdinand of Bulgaria's unreliability and by the
dynastic ties between the German, Roumanian, and Greek royal
families, the explanation for the overwhelmingly anti-revisionist
tendencies of public opinion must be sought elsewhere. There
was, it was generally felt, little choice between Roumania and
Bulgaria. More significant was the feeling that the treaty would
assure peace for the next few years. For the Social Democrats,
this end was itself sufficient, while the colonial enthusiasts desired peace in the Balkans so that Germany's expansion might
not be disturbed.[196] "To Germany, as the first industrial and
financial power of the continent," wrote a nationalist observer,
"world politics are more important than Near Eastern problems."[197] There was much criticism of Austria's Balkan policy
in general and of her interpretation of Germany's obligations in
particular. She had pursued mistaken aims since the beginning
of the first Balkan War. "Austria," wrote the chauvinist *Post*
(Aug. 11), "has followed a false route throughout the winter."

[193] *Germania*, Aug. 13.
[194] *Verhandlungen*, XIII Leg. Per., I Sess., IX, 6286, 6287 (Dec. 9, 1913).
[195] "Der Friede von Bukarest," *Historische-Politische Blätter*, vol. 152, p. 397 (Sept. 1913).
[196] ***, *Deutsche Weltpolitik und kein Krieg*, p. 62; *Vorwärts*, Aug. 11, 12; *A. B.*, Aug. 23.
[197] *P. J.*, vol. 153, p. 547 (Sept. 1913).

"It is impossible," asserted the *Rheinisch-Westfälische Zeitung* (Aug. 18), "to see in the exact delimitation of the Serbo-Bulgarian boundary a vital interest for Austria." That Germany should support a mistaken policy "no power in the world" could expect, insisted the *Vossische Zeitung* (Aug. 11). Reason, not the sentimental talk of the *Nibelungentreue,* wrote the agrarian *Deutsche Tageszeitung* (Aug. 15), should guide Germany's foreign policy, and the *Hamburger Nachrichten* (Aug. 12) described the service which her army rendered to the Triple Alliance as the best of reasons for an independent attitude. According to the *Post* (Aug. 13), there was nothing in the Dual Alliance that required Germany to support Austria's Balkan policy "even in general." The *Leipziger Neueste Nachrichten* believed that no unconditional promises had been or should be given.[198] To some of those for whom Germany's overseas interests were paramount, the Triple Alliance seemed of secondary importance, if not a handicap. "It is," wrote one observer, "only a support for us in Europe, not an instrument for the attainment of positive purposes, and we reserve, as always, the determination of our world interests for ourselves."[199] For an active policy, the Triple Alliance was, wrote the *Deutsche Revue,* "a negative factor. . . . Germany can follow an active policy only outside it. . . . Far from being useful for this purpose, the alliance with Austria is, in a certain sense, an obstacle."[200]

That Germany's own security required Austria's survival as a great power nevertheless remained the most important assumption of German foreign policy. Nor was there, on this point, any serious difference of opinion in the press. No doubt there were many who felt that Austria's failure to solve the problem of her subject peoples weighed upon Germany like a millstone, but no one dreamed of abandoning the alliance. Harden reprinted his warning, written during the Bosnian crisis (March 13, 1909), that the failure to support Austria would result in Germany's complete isolation.[201] While Wilhelm Schüssler, the

198 *Deutsche Tageszeitung,* Aug. 15.
199 "Der Inhalt des Dreibundes," *Grenzboten,* 1913, IV, 296 (Nov. 12).
200 *Kölnische Volkszeitung,* Aug. 14.
201 *Zukunft,* Aug. 16.

historian, advised her to become a military and a unitary state, with a measure of local autonomy for her subject nationalities, he believed that Russia's attitude made the alliance a necessity for Germany as well as for Austria. When all was said and done, the fact remained "that everything which concerns Austria in the present situation, and probably in the future, also concerns us, that her gain is ours, that her loss is our loss, and that we must stand or fall together." [202] Vienna soon recovered its confidence in Germany's loyalty. By October 1913, Berchtold assured his colleagues that Germany's independence had no "serious or permanent significance." [203] In fact, William was eager for active measures against the Serbs. Although he spoke to Conrad during the German maneuvers in favor of conciliation, September 7, [204] he encouraged the general a few weeks later during the celebration of the Battle of the Nations, October 16–19, at Leipzig, to settle the question by force. "I will go along," he said, "The other powers are not ready, they will not act. You will be in Belgrade in forty-eight hours. There are limits to my desire for peace. I have read a great deal about war and I know what it means, but a day finally comes when a great power can no longer remain indifferent but must take up the sword." [205] He told Berchtold in Vienna, October 26, that Serbia must be reduced to the position of a satellite in financial, commercial, and military matters, in view of the conflict between the Slavs and the Germans, which was as inevitable as the early German migrations. "The Slavs," he added, "are born to serve, not to rule; they must be taught that this is so." [206] More moderate than his advisers at the beginning of the Balkan Wars, he had characteristically gone to the opposite extreme, while Bethmann, according to Berchtold, was opposed to the use of force. [207]

If stresses and strains had arisen in the Dual Alliance during the Balkan Wars, some progress was made in approaching Eng-

[202] W. Schüssler, "Neudeutschland und Oesterreich," *P. J.*, vol. 153, pp. 400–412 Sept. (1913).
[203] *Ö.-U. A.*, VII, 399 (Oct. 3).
[204] Conrad, *Aus meiner Dienstzeit*, III, 431.
[205] *Ibid.*, III, 469.
[206] *Ö.-U. A.*, VII, 512, 513 (Berchtold).
[207] Conrad, *op. cit.*, 469.

land. The appointment of Prince Lichnowsky as Marschall's successor in the London embassy (Oct. 13, 1912) seemed an assurance that a realistic view would henceforth be adopted in regard to Anglo-German relations. Writing in the *Nord und Sud*, a review that made a specialty of the Anglo-German rapprochement, Lichnowsky had recently said that it was useless to pretend that the two countries were divided by an artificial misunderstanding. Their differences could not be completely surmounted, but there was still room for a limited coöperation.[208] The naval question, he thought, should be avoided, but the Balkan crisis,[209] the Bagdad Railway, and the colonial problems were practicable bases for common action and, perhaps, for an understanding. So much progress was made in this direction that Kiderlen, shortly before his death, paid a public tribute (Dec. 2, 1912) to the "welcome and friendly intimacy" between London and Berlin in the Balkans.[210] To this development of Anglo-German relations, the press was moderately favorable,[211] although there were not a few skeptics. The chauvinist *Post* (Dec. 4) had no objection in principle, but it spoke, as usual, of "practical results" as the indispensable test. The "Grey-must-go" agitation was regarded as hopeful. To Schiemann, it was a sign of a possible change in England's diplomatic alignment, perhaps of her withdrawal from continental affairs or even of an Anglo-German arrangement similar to the Entente Cordiale.[212] Even Kiderlen exaggerated her change of attitude. "The English," he said, "are so tame that they eat out of my hand."[213] While Bethmann had his doubts, for he felt that Grey's pro-entente policy might cause Germany to fall between two chairs (England and Austria),[214] the Chancellor nevertheless approved the new policy.

[208] *Echo*, Oct. 24, 1912.
[209] Lichnowsky, "My Mission to London," in *Heading for the Abyss* (N. Y., 1928), pp. 64, 65. *Cf.* Lichnowsky, April 13, June 23, 1913. *G. P.*, XXXIX, 38, 46, 47.
[210] *Verhandlungen*, XIII Leg. Per., I Sess., IV, 2483.
[211] *Berliner Tageblatt, Berliner Neueste Nachrichten*, Dec. 3; *Kölnische Zeitung*, Dec. 4.
[212] *Kreuz-Zeitung*, Oct. 9, 20, 27, 1912. Schiemann, *Deutschland und die Grosse Politik*, XII, 271-273, 321, 322, 331, 332.
[213] Jäckh, *Kiderlen-Wächter*, II, 162 (Dec. 1912).
[214] Bethmann-Hollweg, Jan. 30, 1913. *G. P.*, XXIV, no. 12, 763. Wedel's conclusion that Kiderlen's death changed Germany's policy in regard to England seems unfounded. Wedel, *Austro-German Relations*, p. 180.

The naval question continued to be a source of friction. Tirpitz' favorable reference in the Budget Commission to the 16-to-10 ratio, which Churchill had suggested in 1912, offended the nationalist press. Desirable as a "real" Anglo-German friendship might be, it must be preceded by "deeds" proving England's sincerity. The *Berliner Neueste Nachrichten* (Feb. 9, 1913) hoped that no agreement had been made. To the *Rheinisch-Westfälische Zeitung* (Feb. 11), the proposed ratio would only be acceptable if it were applied to the two diplomatic groups. The Pan-Germans talked of the abdication, humiliation, and vassalage that would be Germany's if England's naval supremacy were officially recognized.[215] The *Kölnische Zeitung* (Feb. 10) doubted that a satisfactory arrangement could be reached without a "good, confidential, political-diplomatic relationship." Because the subject was soon dropped, the extremists had no reason to organize a systematic propaganda campaign, and, indeed, there is evidence that the greater part of public opinion did not agree with them. The agitators in both countries, wrote one observer, the "cannon kings" and the armor-plate manufacturers, might be excited, but "except for them the entire German people supports the government on this question."[216] Some satisfaction arose from the feeling in England that Germany's new army law would mean less emphasis upon the navy, from England's dislike of French chauvinism and of Pan-Slavism, from the tactful silence of her naval budget in regard to the German fleet, from the coolness of her public opinion to the agitation for universal military service, and from Asquith's statements in the House of Commons (March 10, 24) that her hands were free. Churchill's speech, March 26, 1913, proposing a one-year holiday in the construction of dreadnoughts, was welcomed for its friendly tone and for its flattering reference to Germany's naval progress, but the suggestion itself was condemned, on the ground that the British colonies might continue to build ships and that the German shipyards would suffer. In any event, Lichnowsky dissuaded Grey from making an official proposal, and Churchill

---

215 *A. B.*, Feb. 15.
216 H. Ilgenstein, "Ein Sieg der Vernunft," *Gegenwart*, Feb. 15, 1913. Cf. *Berliner Tageblatt*, Feb. 8; *Freisinnige Zeitung*, Feb. 8, 15.

was not more successful when he revived the subject in October 1913. The nationalists, of course, viewed the whole subject of a rapprochement with skepticism. "Are they correct," asked the *Berliner Neueste Nachrichten* (March 15, 1913), "who maintain that the great historic antagonisms between nations are nothing more than noxious inventions of hotheaded chauvinists and worshippers of the past? Is it really true that a 'golden age' is dawning in which international relations will be measured according to marks and shillings. . . ?" Too much depended upon the success of the new policy for these doubts to be, at least openly, acknowledged. When King George V and Queen Mary visited Berlin, May 1913, for the marriage of the Emperor's daughter and the Duke of Brunswick, the Belgian envoy concluded that a rapprochement had been accomplished: "France will do well to give heed to this warning." [217] That Poincaré went to London only a few weeks later did not disturb the Catholic *Germania* (July 1, 1913). "We Germans," it wrote, "can be *thoroughly satisfied* with the situation. England has clearly shown that she *will have no war* with us." No issue arose during the second Balkan War to weaken this confidence. Grey welcomed the coöperation between France and Germany and between Russia and Austria as tending to lessen the tension between the two diplomatic groups, and lauded Germany's aid in preventing the war from spreading. [218]

The success of Germany's new approach to England largely depended upon its purpose. Although Haldane's warning (Dec. 3, 1912) should have discouraged excessive optimism, [219] the hope of assuring England's neutrality was never abandoned. Some observers believed that she was turning in that direction of her own accord. To the *Hamburger Nachrichten,* her friendlier attitude meant that she was preparing to stand aside in order to profit by a continental war, and the *Fremdenblatt* (Hamburg) suspected that the "honeymoon (*Flitterwochen*)" of the Triple Entente had come to an end. [220] The foreign office had learned by experience, however, that nothing was to be gained by a forth-

[217] Beyens, May 26, 1913. *Belgische Dokumente*, VI, 289.
[218] Grey, June 27, 1913. *B. D.*, X (1), p. 465.
[219] See above p. 729.
[220] *Tägliche Rundschau*, March 13, 1913.

right proposal for England's neutrality. Whatever the ultimate diplomatic goal may have been, the immediate aim was colonial expansion. On this point there was a striking similarity between Jagow's views and those of the Pan-Germans. On November 22, 1913, the *Alldeutsche Blätter* wrote that diplomatic understandings were valuable only when they produced a profit; the foreign minister instructed Lichnowsky, February 26, 1914, that "Good relations [with England] are not an end in themselves, for they are valuable only if they produce something tangible." [221] With this point of view, the greater part of public opinion was in accord; few outside the ranks of the Social Democrats favored an understanding for its own sake. Jagow had little interest in a friendly arrangement relating to the Bagdad Railway, except as a means of securing concessions elsewhere, since Germany would have to be the giver.[222] By July 1914, an agreement was nevertheless reached which yielded to England the right to construct and to control the terminal section from Basra to Koweit on the Persian Gulf and a voice in the management of the entire line.

Germany expected to be repaid elsewhere, perhaps in the negotiations for another agreement for the partition of the Portuguese colonies. Because Grey wished to show that he was not in principle opposed to her expansion, Germany's share—chiefly, Angola and the northern part of Mozambique—was more generous than that of the agreement of 1898, despite Nicolson's indignation at "the cynical business" of parceling out the property of others.[223] The agreement was never ratified, however, because Germany feared the effect it would have upon the economic interests of her nationals in the Portuguese colonies and because she was uncertain how German opinion would react to the publication of the Anglo-Portuguese Alliance, which Grey insisted upon.[224] This timidity was not unreasonable—especially since the alliance contained England's promise to defend Portugal's ter-

---

[221] *G. P.*, XXXVII, 103.
[222] *Ibid.*, XXXVII, 33 (March 14, 1913).
[223] Lichnowsky, July 7, 1913; April 1, 1914; Zimmermann, Aug. 4, 1913. *Ibid.*, XXXVII, 59, 70, 71, 116; Nicolson, *Lord Carnock*, p. 393.
[224] Lichnowsky, Feb. 8, 1914. *G. P.*, XXXVII, 101, 102. *Cf.* Oncken, *Vorgeschichte des Weltkrieges*, II, 781.

ritorial integrity. Although interest in Africa as a sphere of expansion had undoubtedly risen from its low ebb after Agadir, still there was no great enthusiasm. On March 23, 1912, William had asked Berchtold at Schoenbrunn: "Of what value to us are East and West Africa with a Negro population devoid of cultural needs, without claims upon our modern technics, and without the means of buying our products?" [225] and there is nothing to show that he had ceased to regard the Far East with greater interest. At about the same time, Delbrück could find no better arguments in favor of Central Africa than as a basis for an understanding with England, as a means of adding to Germany's prestige, and as an outlet for the graduates of German universities who were unable to make a career for themselves at home.[226] Evidence of a change in public opinion began to appear at the beginning of the following year. On January 4, 1913, the *Post* noted with gratification a favorable response to its support of a "German Central Africa." Even the *Alldeutsche Blätter,* after denouncing a bargain giving to Germany a share of the Portuguese colonies and concessions in the Belgian Congo as "a definitive surrender of the essence of world policy—increased power, and political influence paralleling the expansion of Germany's economic interests"—wrote that the Pan-Germans would not object to such an agreement if England would furnish solid guarantees that she would exert pressure upon Portugal, Belgium, and France to secure its fulfillment.[227] Bethmann's cautious references in the Reichstag to possible gains in Africa and, in connection therewith, to improved relations with England were well received.[228] Too many Germans had insisted for too many years that England's friendship was not to be depended on, without definite sacrifices on her part, for the Bagdad Railway and colonial agreements to be certain of an enthusiastic reception. One observer expressed this point of view with brutal frankness: "Great Britain . . . must reconcile herself to the thought that it is

---

[225] *Ö.-U. A.,* IV, 61.

[226] Delbrück, "Ueber die Ziele unserer Kolonialpolitik," *P. J.,* vol. 147, pp. 503–513 (March, 1912).

[227] *A. B.,* June 7, June 21. The second editorial was in part a discussion of ***, *Deutsche Weltpolitik und kein Krieg.*

[228] *Verhandlungen,* XIII Leg. Per., I Sess., IX, 6274, XIV, 8873 (Dec. 9, 1913, May 14, 1914).

not merely a question of concluding treaties for the division of spheres of interests concerning the property of other powers; she must eventually reconcile herself to the necessity of giving to her German neighbor those of her own possessions which Germany needs for the development of her colonies." [229]   The immediate cession of Walfisch Bay probably would have meant more to German public opinion, and perhaps to the government, than the more or less distant prospect of much larger gains from Portugal.

By avoiding those questions upon which agreement was obviously impossible, a limited but real improvement had been attained in Anglo-German relations.   The same caution was not observed toward Russia when Germany's own interests in the Near East were involved.   Even as late as the spring of 1914 William thought that a conflict with the Slavs arising from Austria's opposition to the union between Serbia and Montenegro would be "idiotic" and "incredible"; [230] nevertheless he approved a policy in regard to Turkey which brought Germany and Russia almost to the verge of war.   A clash over the partition of Asiatic Turkey was averted when France and England joined Germany in defeating Russia's proposal for the formation of a single autonomous province from the Armenian vilayets.   The question was arranged by direct negotiations between Berlin and St. Petersburg; the provision for two provinces, each with a separate administration, relieved Germany's fear of an impending partition. [231] In this question, she had refused to act as Turkey's adviser, [232] but in agreeing to send General Liman von Sanders with some forty other officers to Constantinople on a mission of extraordinary powers, Germany embarked upon an enterprise which Russia was bound to regard not only as an obstacle to her ambitions but also as a menace to her prestige throughout the Near East and even to her security in the Black Sea. [233]   The first suggestion

---

[229] K. Dove, "Deutsch-englische Interessengemeinschaft in Afrika," *Deutsche Revue*, 1914, I, 280 (March 1).   Cf. *Hamburger Nachrichten*, in *Echo*, March 12, 1914.
[230] Wolff, *Eve of 1914*, pp. 376–378.
[231] *B. D.*, X (1), pp. 424, 425, 463, 466, 470, 472, 517; *D. D. F.*, (3), VIII, 36. *Cf.* R. Kerner, "The Mission of Liman von Sanders," I, *Slavonic Review*, vol. VI, 26.
[232] Jagow, April 22, Sept. 20, 1913; Wangenheim, Sept. 22, 1913. *G. P.*, XXXVIII, 30, 144, 145.
[233] Kerner, *op. cit.*, *Slavonic Review*, vol. VII, 111.

was apparently made by Turkey, but it seems almost impossible that Turkey would have asked Germany (April 1913) for the services of an officer in the fortification of Constantinople without an indication of a favorable response. At any rate, the foreign office gave its consent—on William's request for its advice— without stipulating as to the officer's functions and powers.[234] To the soldiers was left the task of arranging the terms.[235] Although Germany intended to treat this affair as one that concerned Turkey alone, William spoke of the invitation to Nicholas II and George V, May 24, 1913, while they were in Berlin for the marriage of his daughter. What he told the Tsar is, however, by no means clear. If his later explanation to Berchtold can be trusted, he included the fortification of the Tchatalja lines with that of Constantinople as the purpose of the mission, counting upon Russia's desire to prevent the Bulgarians from occupying the Turkish capital to forestall her objections. It was, he felt, a masterpiece of diplomacy.[236] Unfortunately Nicholas merely told Sazonov, his foreign minister, that William had spoken of a military mission like that of von der Goltz.[237] Russia's silence during the summer of 1913 makes it reasonable to conclude that she would not have made an issue of Germany's recovery of her former influence in the training of the Turkish army. As a member of the war council in charge of training the Turkish army, and as the commander of the first army corps, with his headquarters in Constantinople, Sanders' powers far exceeded those of the earlier German missions, although the troops under his direct command were to be used for instructional purposes. These terms were approved by the foreign office,[238] but Bethmann—if he had been consulted—did not mention the sub-

---

[234] Treutler, April 2, 4, 1913; Jagow, April 5. *G. P.*, XXXVIII, 195, 196. C. Mühlmann, *Deutschland und die Türkei 1913-1914* (Berlin, 1929), pp. 8 ff. Hallgarten attributes the initiative to Major von Stempel, the military attaché in Constantinople, whose brother was a member of the Emperor's civil cabinet. Hallgarten, *Vorkriegs Imperialismus*, pp. 279, 280.
[235] G. von Jagow, *Ursachen und Ausbruch des Weltkrieges* (Berlin, 1919), p. 72.
[236] Berchtold, Oct. 26, 1913. *Ö.-U. A.*, VII, 514.
[237] S. Sazonov, *Les années fatales* (Paris, 1927), p. 125.
[238] Mühlmann, *op. cit.*, p. 9, n. 5. For text of the contract, see *ibid.*, pp. 88-92.

ject to Sazonov when the Russian foreign minister stopped in Berlin, October 22, 1913, on his way home from Paris.[239]

When Russia learned the extent of Liman's powers, she immediately warned Germany that "everything that happens in Constantinople and on the Straits is of the greatest significance for us."[240] Sazonov could not accept a situation which placed Russia's ambassador under the protection of a "German army corps,"[241] and Kokovtsov, the President of the Imperial Council, told Bethmann that Russia's objections might be satisfied either by leaving Liman in Constantinople with reduced powers or, better still, by transferring his headquarters to a provincial city such as Adrianople.[242] At first, Germany stood her ground; Szögyény, the Austrian ambassador, was told that Kokovtsov had not even mentioned the Liman mission.[243] Any concession, according to Bethmann, was impossible, because the French press would claim that Germany had retreated in the face of "Russian and French threats."[244] The foreign office seems to have been more conciliatory; even William agreed with Jagow's suggestion, December 5, that Germany should not object if Russia succeeded in persuading Turkey to transfer Liman's headquarters to Adrianople. Yet Turkey's publication on the same date (Dec. 5) of Liman's contract suggests some doubt as to the sincerity of this gesture or, at least, that the soldiers and the civilians were working at cross-purposes.[245] Thereupon Sazonov increased his efforts to secure the support of the Western powers in bringing pressure to bear upon Constantinople. Successful in Paris,[246] he

[239] Cleinow, 26 March/8 April, 1914. *G. P.*, XXXVIII, 314, 315. The Chancellor, according to Kokovtsov, pleaded ignorance of anything more than an appeal for German instructors, and Sazonov told the British *chargé d'affaires* that Bethmann had said that the affair "seemed so much in the ordinary course of things that he had not thought it worth mentioning." *L. N.*, II, 412 (Nov. 19, 1913); O'Beirne, Nov. 26. *B. D.*, X (1), p. 341.
[240] Lucius, Nov. 7, 1913. *G. P.*, XXXVIII, 206.
[241] Lucius, Nov. 17. *Ibid.*, XXXVIII, 208, 209.
[242] Bethmann-Hollweg, Nov. 19. *Ibid.*, XXXVIII, 216, 217.
[243] *Ö.-U. A.*, VII, 578 (Nov. 20).
[244] The *Temps* had revealed Kokovtsov's protest. Bethmann-Hollweg, Nov. 29. *G. P.*, XXXVIII, 227. France had in fact warned Turkey that Liman's functions were inacceptable to the Triple Entente and that France would have to ask for "moral and political compensation" if the character of the German military mission were changed to Germany's advantage. Pichon, Nov. 22. *D. D. F.*, (3), VIII, 652, 653.
[245] Jagow, Dec. 5; Treutler, Dec. 6. *G. P.*, XXXVIII, 236, 237; Szögyény, Dec. 5. *Ö.-U. A.*, VII, 609. The contract had been signed on November 27.
[246] Ministerial note, Dec. 9. *D. D. F.*, (3), VII, 752, 753.

met with a cool reception in London. Grey was willing to agree to nothing more than a question by each of the three powers as to the terms and to a statement calling attention to the danger that they might impinge upon Turkey's independence. When these rather innocuous observations (Dec. 13) accomplished nothing, Sazonov became more eager than ever for effective action by the Triple Entente. Germany, he thought, was playing with him; on her suggestion he had sent the Russian military attaché in Constantinople to see his German colleague, only to be repulsed. Believing that she would yield nothing, he insisted that the Triple Entente should ask Berlin directly what she intended to do.[247] Germany, he was confident, would yield rather than fight, but the result would clearly have been a crisis of the first magnitude. "A stiff back and hand on the sword!" wrote William on a report of the anti-German attitude of the British and French embassies in St. Petersburg.[248] Earlier, Bethmann had assured Russia that Liman was free to decide the location of his headquarters, but the Emperor himself approved (Dec. 18) Turkey's refusal to change the terms of the contract.[249] The foreign office was less intransigent, for it repeatedly explained that an agreement was possible if Germany's prestige were not directly involved and if the Triple Entente did not make "everything impossible."[250] There is no evidence of an official effort to arouse public opinion.[251] Indeed, Dr. Ullrich, the St. Petersburg correspondent of the *Kölnische Zeitung*, whose reports at this time were influenced by the German embassy, represented the Russian press and foreign policy as more moderate

---

[247] Crowe's minute, Dec. 29. *B. D.*, X (1), pp. 400–402. *Cf.* Russian embassy's note, Dec. 29. *D. D. F.*, (3), VIII, 862

[248] Pourtalès, Dec. 13. *G. P.*, XXXVIII, 256.

[249] Jagow, Nov. 23; Bethmann-Hollweg, Nov. 26, 27; Wangenheim, Dec. 16; William II, Dec. 18. *Ibid.*, XXXVIII, 217–219, 220, 221–224, 259, 262.

[250] Goschen, Dec. 31, 1913, Jan. 2, 1914; Grey, Jan. 7. *B. D.*, X, (1), pp. 405, 406, 411; J. Cambon, Jan. 2. *D. D. F.*, (3), IX, 3. Germany, according to the Russian ambassador, was doing her best to meet Russia's just claims. Sverbeiev, 3 Jan./16 Jan. 1914. *Die Internationalen Beziehungen im Zeitalter des Imperialismus; Dokumente aus den Archiven der zaristischen und der provisorischen Regierung*, (1), I, 23. This work will henceforth be cited as *Z. I.*

[251] When Grey suggested, on a hint from St. Petersburg, that the press should be restrained, Jagow replied that he had already done all he could and that the Chancellor had persuaded the party leaders not to interpellate the government on the Liman affair. Grey, Dec. 24; Goschen, Dec. 27. *B. D.*, X, (1), pp. 396, 398.

than they actually were.[252]   Only the *Kreuz-Zeitung,* according to the British ambassador, was excited by the impending action of the Triple Entente,[253] but the German foreign office undoubtedly expected the nationalists to set up a cry of "No surrender!"

That moderation finally prevailed in Berlin was in no small degree the result of England's, and even of France's, refusal to join Russia in exerting pressure upon Germany. Recognizing from the first that the command of the Turkish fleet by a retired British naval officer, Admiral Limpus, and of the police by a Frenchman, and that the contract by which the Armstrong-Vickers firm had charge of the dockyards and arsenals in Constantinople weakened England's right to protest, Grey was also restrained by doubts as to Sazonov's purposes and by his desire to maintain the recent improvement in Anglo-German relations. "I shall be very sorry," Goschen had written (Dec. 12) from Berlin, "if we have to make a big fuss . . . and thereby run the risk of reducing the biggest advantages we *have got,* besides undoing all that has been done to improve Anglo-German relations." [254]   So pleased were the Germans by England's attitude that they hoped she would moderate Russia's demands and consult with Germany before acting,[255] and Grey, while explaining that England could not help any country to attain a strong position at Constantinople because "we should find ourselves back again in our bad relations with Russia," assured her that she would be informed as to any steps which he might decide upon.[256] By suggesting direct Russo-German negotiations, England doubtless contributed to a peaceful solution.[257]   Despite her great financial stake in Turkey, France had been prepared to support Russia in such measures in Constantinople as she deemed necessary,[258] but a concerted action in Berlin was a different matter. Jules Cambon minced no words in advising against it. Germany, he

[252] A. Jux, *Der Kriegsschrecken des Frühjahrs 1914 in der europäischen Presse* (Berlin, 1929), pp. 18–20 (Dec. 5, 9, 11, 12, 1913).
[253] Goschen, Dec. 12. *B. D.,* X, (1), p. 374.
[254] *Ibid.,* X, (1), p. 377.
[255] Zimmermann, Dec. 16. *G. P.,* XXXVIII, 259.
[256] Grey, Dec. 15. *B. D.,* X, (1), 383.
[257] Minute, O'Beirne, Dec. 13. *Ibid.,* X, (1), 378.
[258] Note for the Russian embassy, Dec. 30. *D. D. F.,* (3), VIII, 869. Yet Izvolski could not guarantee France's unconditional support even in this limited respect. *Z. I.,* (1), I, 13 (2 Jan./15 Jan., 1914).

said, would immediately direct her wrath against France; the most delicate questions would be raised at once.[259] Like England, France therefore advised Russia to await the results of the discussions between Wangenheim, the German ambassador in Constantinople, who was then in Berlin, and the German foreign office.[260] Sazonov had no choice but to agree.[261] By the middle of January 1914, a satisfactory compromise was arranged; Liman's promotion to the rank of a general of cavalry, followed by his advancement in the Turkish army to that of a field marshal and his appointment as inspector general, saved everyone's face. He remained in the Turkish capital but was deprived of a direct command of Turkish troops.

The peaceful settlement brought no real improvement in Russo-German relations. There was no denying the existence of a serious interest conflict. While the press resented Germany's retreat, the government was probably not seriously dissatisfied, since Liman's influence would still be considerable. But Russia's attitude was alarming. In spite of her diplomatic success, she evidently believed that Germany would henceforth oppose the attainment of her ambitions in the Straits. Such is the inescapable inference from the consensus of opinion at the meeting of the Russian Imperial Council (Feb. 21, 1914) that the Straits question could not be solved without a European war and that the decision would be fought out on the western frontier.[262] With Kokovtsov's forced resignation disappeared a moderating influence. Meanwhile, the Russian press launched an attack that was more violent, according to Pourtalès, the German ambassador, than it had been before Germany's concessions.[263] "The beautiful days of Potsdam," wrote Szápáry, the Austrian ambassador to St. Petersburg, after listening to the pessimistic comments of his German colleague, "are past—until further notice."[264] The gloomy outlook of these diplomats was shared

259 J. Cambon, Nov. 30. *D. D. F.*, (3), VIII, 699, 701.
260 *Ibid.*, (3), VIII, 869 (Dec. 30).
261 Russian embassy's note, Dec. 31. *Ibid.*, (3), VIII, 874.
262 Fay, *Origins of the World War*, I, 538–541.
263 *G. P.*, XXXIX, 540–544 (Feb. 25, 1914).
264 The Russo-German tension, he thought, would have a good effect upon Austro-Russian relations. *Ö.-U. A.*, VII, 915 (Feb. 23, 1914). Cf. *Münchener Neueste Nachrichten*, Feb. 11, in Jux, *Der Kriegsschrecken des Frühjahrs 1914 in der europäischen Presse*, p. 26.

by the German press correspondents in the Russian capital, most of whom represented nationalist journals.[265] From the first days of February, their reports supplied the material for editorials on alleged troop concentrations on the Russian frontier.[266] The representative of the *Tägliche Rundschau* sold his house and resigned his post to escape internment in the inevitable war.[267] Russia, wrote the nationalist *Leipziger Neueste Nachrichten* (Feb. 13), wished to provoke a war before Germany had time to complete the fortification of her eastern frontier.[268] In Russia's attitude the *Post* (Feb. 24) saw ample justification for a preventive war. Events had shown that the dissolution of the Triple Entente could not be accomplished by diplomacy. Should Germany wait until the undermining of Austria's strength deprived her of all value? Should Germany voluntarily abdicate her leadership in Europe and her place in world affairs? "There are international complications and antagonisms which the sword alone can settle." Bismarck solved the German question with blood and iron. "Our present situation," it concluded, "belongs in the same category. An honorable diplomatic solution does not exist." According to the French diplomats in Berlin, many Conservatives believed war to be the only way out of Germany's difficulties,[269] but the press, generally speaking, ignored the *Post's* counsel of desperation. An equally provocative article, wrote the Catholic *Kölnische Volkszeitung* (Feb. 26), had appeared in neither the Russian nor the French press.

Far more disturbing, though less extreme, was Ullrich's dispatch from St. Petersburg in the *Kölnische Zeitung* (March 2). There was, he wrote, no reason to fear war in the immediate future, but Russia's military and naval armaments would be complete by the autumn of 1917. That they were intended for use against Germany was generally admitted. Most Russians, in Ullrich's opinion, expected war to come from the clash between

---

[265] Jux, *Der Kriegsschrecken des Frühjahrs 1914 in der europäischen Presse*, p. 2. The *Berliner Tageblatt* and the *Vossische Zeitung* were apparently represented by Russians.
[266] *Germania*, Feb. 3, in Jux, *op. cit.*, pp. 46, 47.
[267] *Ibid.*, p. 25.
[268] For various reasons all groups, including the liberals and the Social Democrats, regarded Russia's action in raising her tariff rates as unfriendly. Sverbeiev, 13/26 April 1914. *Z. I.*, (1), II, 295.
[269] Cambon, Nov. 30, 1913; Feb. 16, 1914; Serret, Feb. 15, 1914. *D. D. F.*, (3), VIII, 699, IX, 388, 395.

Russian and German interests at Constantinople. The situation was not hopeless; while Russia's alliance with France was the chief obstacle to good Russo-German relations, Russia could be made to see reason if Germany took a strong stand, for there was a good deal of bluff in her attitude. Ullrich drew the conclusion that "we know where we stand. . . . Russia's official policy should destroy the *legend* of the historical Russo-German friendship. . . ." When the Russian ambassador protested, Jagow truthfully replied that the article had not been inspired either by the embassy in St. Petersburg or by the foreign office.[270] He did not, however, disavow its contents.[271] As to his restraining the press, Jagow equivocated in saying that his efforts had been unavailing, for some of the *démentis* were so phrased as to give the impression that the article contained much truth.[272] The *Münchener Neueste Nachrichten* (March 8) was convinced, for example, that preparations must be made for a life-and-death struggle, although it spoke of the Armenian reforms as a possible basis for coöperation with Russia.[273] Even the *Kölnische Zeitung* (March 17) described its own alarmist article as "an admonition and a warning, . . . not an alarm shot." If the Austrian ambassador remained incredulous in the face of the official denials, [274] Sazonov could scarcely be blamed for doubting their sincerity. On March 12, the *Birsheviia Vjedomosti,* a St. Petersburg journal, remarked that aggressive purposes were betrayed by the criticism of that country which had summoned the Hague Peace Conference. "Russia," read the headline, "desires peace but is prepared for war." [275]

Moderate observers were, as usual, skeptical of Russia's strength. The *Vossische Zeitung* reminded its readers that no war had occurred even in Bismarck's time, when her attitude had seemed still

[270] Sverbeiev, 20 Feb./5 March, 26 Feb./11 March. Z. I., I, 384, 428. D. D. F., (3), IX, 516, 517. Cf. Pourtalès, March 6; Hammann, March 12. G. P., XXXIX, 547, 548, 549 n.
[271] Jagow claimed in his post-war memoirs that Ullrich's military information was partially correct. Jagow, Ursachen, p. 81.
[272] Berliner Lokal-Anzeiger, March 3, in Jux, Der Kriegsschrecken des Frühjahrs 1914 in der europäischen Presse, p. 64. Politische Korrespondenz, March 4. G. P., XXXIX, 549. N. A. Z., in Tägliche Rundschau, March 8.
[273] Jux, op. cit., pp. 110, 111.
[274] Szögyény, March 6. Ö.-U. A., VII, 941.
[275] Tägliche Rundschau, March 4.

more menacing.   A part of the nationalist press refused to become
excited.   Russia, wrote the *Hamburger Nachrichten,* was no better prepared than she had been for many years and she knew the
risks too well to disturb the peace; according to the *Hamburgischer
Korrespondent,* "absolutely no reason exists for a war scare." [276]
In Russia's ambitions, Dr. Reismann-Grone, the editor of the
Rheinisch-Westfälische Zeitung, saw no menace, unlike his associates in the Pan-German League.   There would be, he insisted,
no Russo-German war unless Germany supported Austria's
Balkan policy.[277]   Others argued that Russia's admittedly dangerous attitude might change for the better.   To its own article
supporting a preventive war, the *Post* (Feb. 24, 1914) printed an
anonymous reply pointing out the possibility of Russian revolution, the unpopularity of the three-year service law in France,
and the diversion of her resources to Morocco.   Another optimist
spoke in the *Berliner Tageblatt* (March 9) of the constant changes
in the diplomatic constellations: "No one can look into the future
and say that an improvement in Germany's position will not be
brought about by peaceful means."

For that improvement all too much hope was placed in the
better relations with England.   Doubtless many continued to
think that she was the "real enemy," but, for the most part, they
kept their own counsel in the spring of 1914.   By indirect means
England, it was thought, might be brought into a relationship
which would weaken her ties with the Triple Entente.   On
September 25, 1913, Jagow had told an Austrian diplomat that he
"hoped to remove an English expedition to Belgium . . . even
from the realm of hypothesis." [278]   Characteristically, William
oscillated between optimism and despair.   When Churchill said
publicly in October 1913 that the naval weakness of either power
worked against good relations, he concluded that England was
about ready to offer acceptable terms.   "A grandiose victory
for Admiral Tirpitz!" he exclaimed.   "Another proof of the
theory I have expounded time and again that the only way to

---

[276] Russia, added the second journal, could expect nothing more than "cool correctness and mistrustful attention" from German public opinion.   *Ibid.,* March 5, 8.
[277] Jux, *Der Kriegsschrecken des Frühjahrs 1914 in der europäischen Presse,* pp. 88,
89 (March 7).
[278] *Ö.-U. A.,* VII, 357.

impress the English and to compel them at last to come to an understanding is by an unreserved, manly, courageous stand for our own interests. . . . England approaches us, not in spite of, but because of the Imperial Marine! *Avis au lecteur!"* [279] William was intensely irritated that England had not sided with Germany completely. He described Grey's attitude as *"louche"* and asked, "How long will he lean toward both sides?" [280] The great difficulty was not so much Germany's assertion of her interests in Constantinople, for London was not unwilling to see Turkey strengthened against Russia, as it was the repercussions of the Liman affair on the Triple Entente. Lichnowsky feared the attitude of such journals as the *Post* and the *Kölnische Zeitung* would soon destroy "what has already been accomplished toward an improvement in Anglo-German relations." [281] More important than the press campaign was Russia's reaction to Grey's coolness. Sazonov spoke of the Triple Entente as having no more substance "than the sea serpent"; peace, he said, would not be assured until the entente had become a defensive alliance and until it was published. The danger of a new German hegemony would then disappear "and we could quietly concentrate upon our own affairs." [282] In Berlin, his purposes were no secret; Siebert, a Baltic German in the Russian embassy in London, supplied the German foreign office with copies of his chief's correspondence with St. Petersburg and with other documents sent from the Russian capital, for Benckendorff's information in regard to his government's general policy. [283] It was therefore known that Russia was behind France's interest in a formal alliance with England. The cool response of the English press was reassuring. [284] A German observer, wrote the Belgian minister in Berlin, must conclude "that the ties of the Triple Entente have loosened somewhat, . . . that it has become more of a concert than a union of powers, acting together in certain specific questions in pursuit

---

[279] William II's comment, Oct. 10, 1913. *G. P.*, XXXIX, 51.
[280] William II's comments, Wangenheim, Dec. 13, 1913. *Ibid.*, XXXVII, 265.
[281] *Ibid.*, XXXIX, 556, 557 (March 10, 1914).
[282] *L. N.*, II, 307 (6/19 Feb. 1914).
[283] Wolff, *Eve of 1914*, pp. 357-360.
[284] *Kreuz-Zeitung*, April 19, 1914. Schiemann, *Deutschland und die Grosse Politik*, XIV, 112. *Cf.* Lichnowsky, April 22. *G. P.*, XXXIX, 601.

of common interests."[285]   The general staff's calculations assumed England's participation in a war against Germany, but
Jagow apparently believed that her neutrality was practically assured, for Lichnowsky's casual remark that England would
certainly support France if she were attacked surprised him.[286]
To Stumm, the director of the political section of the foreign
office, it seemed more probable that she would act according to
circumstances and as her interests dictated.[287]   Grey, of course,
had no intention of changing the direction of British foreign
policy. He did not share Nicolson's belief that the transformation of the Triple Entente into another Triple Alliance would be
an infallible guarantee of peace "for a generation or two," but
he was willing to appease Russia by beginning negotiations for
the Anglo-Russian naval agreement, which France had persuaded
Russia to accept as a substitute for a formal alliance.[288]   In Berlin, the knowledge that England and Russia were about to be
united by a new bond, revealed by Siebert's treachery, was concealed from William, but it diminished the foreign office's confidence in the successful outcome of the courtship of England.
Writing in the *Berliner Tageblatt* (May 29, 1914), at the government's request, Theodor Wolff pointed to the obvious connection between the proposed agreement and an eventual Anglo-
Russian alliance, and, a few days later (June 2), he called the
attention of the British Liberals to the danger to the recent improvement in Anglo-German relations from a more intense naval
agitation in Germany.[289]   Whereas Wolff, doubtless in accord
with his instructions, had dealt tactfully with Grey, the nationalist
Tag (May 29) spoke definitely of a turning point in the relations
between the two countries and of the possible need of defensive
measures.[290]   Grey's evasive assurances in the House of Commons
that no agreement limiting England's freedom of action had

[285] Beyens, April 24. *Belgische Dokumente*, VI, 309. *Cf.* "Entente und Bündnis," *Grenzboten*, 1913, IV, 389.
[286] Lichnowsky, May 1; Jagow, May 13. *G. P.*, XXXIX, 611, 614. Lichnowsky
replied that England would not permit the balance of power to be disturbed by the
defeat of France. *Ibid.*, XXXIX, 616 (May 16).
[287] Stumm's comments, Lichnowsky, March 7. *Ibid.*, XXXIX, 110, 111.
[288] Nicolson, *Lord Carnock*, pp. 402, 403, 406 (Oct. 29, 1913, April 21, 1914);
Izvolski, March 27, 1914. *Diplomatische Schriftwechsel Iswolkis*, IV, 87.
[289] Wolff, *Eve of 1914*, pp. 379–386.
[290] Jagow, May 25, 1914. *G. P.*, XXXIX, 617, 618.

been made and that no negotiations were in progress for this purpose were thoroughly unsatisfactory. Officially Germany could only profess her satisfaction, but Bethmann did explain the harmful effect of an Anglo-Russian naval accord.[291] The up-shot was a more pointed warning from Grey. When the Chancellor spoke of further complications in the Balkans as a basis for common action that would leave intact the diplomatic commitments of both countries, the British foreign secretary replied that he had entered no alliances and was committed to no action, but also that he did not wish to mislead Germany into thinking "that the relations that we had with France and Russia were less cordial and intimate than they really were. Though we were not bound by engagement as allies, we did from time to time talk as intimately as allies."[292] That the relations between the two countries were, in general, better than they had been for years could not, however, be denied. Public opinion in England was inclined to take a more sympathetic attitude toward Germany's problems and aspirations. What the result of a long period of normal relations would have been is impossible to say, but it seems probable that the improvement would have continued. Even in the absence of a serious European crisis, in which it was almost certain that England would side with France and Russia, Germany's primary concern for her imperialist interests nevertheless constituted a permanent threat to this period of better feeling, for England's desire to lessen the danger of war did not mean that she was ready to satisfy those interests.

In at least one respect, the decline of tension with England diminished anxiety in regard to France. England would never consent, it was believed, to play the rôle in the reconquest of Alsace-Lorraine which Russia had obviously refused, and she might even be expected to moderate France. Not many believed that France would attack alone. The reaction to the *Kölnische Zeitung's* (March 10, 1913) alarmist article had been definitely skeptical. Winterfeldt, the military attaché, ascribed peaceful

[291] Bethmann-Hollweg, June 16. *Die deutschen Dokumente zum Kriegsausbruch* (K. Kautsky, M. Montgelas, W. Schücking, eds.), 4 vols. (Berlin, 1927), I, 4. This work will henceforth be cited as *K. D.*

[292] Grey, *Twenty-Five Years,* I, 294. *Cf.* Grey, June 24; Lichnowsky, June 24. *K. D.,* I, 7.

sentiments not only to the majority of the French people but also to the government.[293] The ambassador saw an assurance of a cautious policy for some time to come in the agitation during the parliamentary elections for a return to the two-year service law of 1905.[294] The *revanche,* as interpreted by Boulanger and Déroulède, was, according to the ambassador, out of date. No Frenchman was willing to sacrifice his sons even for Alsace-Lorraine.[295] The chauvinists impressed a leading Catholic review only moderately: "Much is said now of the possibility of war, but the great majority have no intention of fighting except in self-defense. Of those who are the most bellicose, more than three quarters would draw back at the prospect of immediate hostilities." [296] Writing at a time when the two countries were in agreement as to some of the Balkan questions, the *Kölnische Zeitung* (July 30, 1913) at least pretended a confidence that the French people would not fight for Russia's interests: "The government of a democratic country like France cannot respect a *casus foederis* which the people refuse to recognize." Not for many years had the possibility of a rapprochement attracted so much interest. In October 1913, Germany was represented at an unofficial conference in Ghent on the Franco-German problem.[297] The recently published French diplomatic correspondence reveals an astonishingly indiscreet gesture by Tirpitz in favor of an understanding. Speaking to the American-born wife of the French naval attaché at a dinner about the middle of January 1914, he developed the possibilities open to France in North Africa and dwelt upon the insincerity of England's friendship as reasons why France should abandon her sentimental attitude toward Alsace-Lorraine. On this condition, an understanding would be easy.[298] While the small German delegation to the Inter-Parliamentary Conference in Berne (May 1913) had been largely composed of Social Democrats, more than two hundred members of the Reichstag, including forty Centrists and a delegation of National Lib-

[293] *G. P.,* XXXIX, 208 (Aug. 20, 1913).
[294] *Ibid.,* XXXIX, 227 (Nov. 15, 1913).
[295] Schoen, Feb. 5, 1914. *Ibid.,* XXXIX, 250.
[296] *Historisch-Politische Blätter,* vol. 152, p. 235 (Aug. 1913).
[297] *D. D. F.,* (3), VIII, 317, 318.
[298] J. Cambon, Jan. 19, 1914, enclosing a note by the Commandant de Faramond, Jan. 17. *D. D. F.,* (3), IX, 128–131.

erals, attended the meeting at Basle (May 1914), where resolutions were adopted endorsing a continued effort to improve Franco-German relations and an independent news service to combat the influence of the French and German chauvinist newspapers.[299] France nevertheless remained for most Germans what she had always been—the irreconcilable enemy. The studied moderation of her press during the Zabern incident could not conceal the fact that her feelings in regard to Alsace-Lorraine had not changed.[300] What impressed William most in Schoen's moderate reports was his mention of Paul de Cassagnac's challenge of Lieutenant Förstner, the central figure of this example of military brutality. "Let them come on!" he exclaimed. "Then with God's help we will settle with them once and for all! . . . Otherwise we may lose our patience!"[301] In France's policy of a mathematical balance of power was seen a determination to recover the hegemony of Europe or, according to Schiemann, to reconquer the "lost provinces."[302] Harden blamed Germany's tactlessness for the failure of her radicals to resist the pressure of the militarists,[303] but most observers feared that the extraordinary burdens of the three-year service law meant a war in the near future. As usual, it was pointed out that the chauvinist minority would decide the government's action in a crisis.[304] On official suggestion, the press spoke of Colonel Civreux's pamphlet, *Le Germanisme encirclé*, as worse than anything that had appeared in Germany.[305] "We are acquainted with Germans," wrote the Paris correspondent of the nationalist *Tägliche Rundschau* (June 7, 1914), "who feel more uncomfortable in hospitable France than they did in the time of Boulanger or during the Dreyfus affair." It was noted that the directors of an art exhibition excluded a portrait of William II, while a number of

299 *Vossische Zeitung*, June 2; *Berliner Tageblatt*, June 3.

300 In part to prevent the German government from using the attitude of the French press in an appeal for unity, French diplomats advised moderation. J. Cambon, Nov. 29, Dec. 7, 1913. Allizé, Munich, Dec. 6. *D. D. F.*, (3), VIII, 687, 716, 750.

301 William II's comments, Schoen, Nov. 26, 1913. *G. P.*, XXXIX, 229, 230.

302 *Kreuz-Zeitung*, Jan. 7, 1914. Schiemann, *Deutschland und die Grosse Politik*, XIV, 6.

303 Harden, "Frankreich und Deutschland," *Zukunft*, May 16, 1914.

304 "Zur auswärtige Politik," *Historisch-Politische Blätter*, vol. 151, pp. 234, 235 (Aug. 1913).

305 *G. P.*, XXXIX, 202n. Cf. *Kölnische Zeitung, Hamburger Nachrichten*, Aug. 4, 1913.

caricatures of him were exhibited. More significant than the general but vague aversion to war seemed the enthusiastic response of a large part of the French press to the victories of the Balkan states, with their supposed demonstration of the superiority of French arms, and to the prospect of a permanent Balkan League under the influence of the Triple Entente.[306] The fear of the "German menace" and of a new attempt to humiliate France was dismissed as insincere by those who believed in their country's peacefulness and in the justice of its claims.[307] What the better-informed observers feared was not a direct attack from France but her supposed readiness to fall upon Germany the moment that Russia began hostilities, even against Austria. This view, of course, had some foundation. While it is not entirely true that Poincaré gave Russia a "blank check" during the Balkan Wars, she believed, as a result of his encouragement, that France could be depended upon to support even an offensive policy, and an important section of the French press, whether in return for Russian subsidies or because of a sense of national interests, had tried to persuade Frenchmen that their own interests would be served by fighting for Russia. In spite of these considerations and of the tension in Franco-German relations that threatened repeatedly to make serious crises of comparatively unimportant frontier incidents, France's final decision was not entirely a foregone conclusion, for the memories of the defeat of 1871 were still alive, and, what was more important, it was generally understood that England's support and the sympathy of neutral opinion in general could not be had for an offensive policy.[308] From the diplomatic if not from the military point of view, Germany had much to gain if she could force France to assume the responsibility for the declaration of war.

By all odds, the most significant changes in Germany's international position had occurred in her relations with Russia. The

---

[306] *Historisch-Politische Blätter*, vol. 152, pp. 230, 231 (Aug. 1913).

[307] *Kölnische Zeitung*, March 10, 1914; *A. B.*, April 11, 1914.

[308] "Frankreich will den Frieden nicht brechen; aber wenn er wie von selbst zusammenbrechen soll? 'Si la fatalité le voulait . . . quand l'heure de la résurrection aurait sonné . . . au moment suprême, ou l'honneur et le sang de notre race . . . l'exigeront. . . .' " L. Littmann, *Das europäische Friedenspolitik und der Balkan* (Munich, 1913), pp. 2, 3.

hope that Potsdam and Baltic Port would eventually restore the historic friendship survived the Balkan Wars only to collapse with the Sanders mission. A St. Petersburg journal, which was said to reflect Count Witte's views, declared for an understanding in the spring of 1914, without any other result than to make the French uneasy.[309] A vital interest conflict existed in Turkey. Even William was thoroughly disillusioned, although he believed that Russia's armaments would not be complete for six years.[310] "The *turmhohe* friendship between Germany and Russia," he told the Austrian ambassador, "was already a lie in Bismarck's time . . . and for twenty-five years [my] chief concern has been to maintain [merely] the appearance of friendly relations."[311] For him Russia's unconcealed interest in France's preparations raised the specter of a war on two fronts. Those who refused to see this—and the need of countermeasures—"deserve to be sent to the asylum at Dolldorf!"[312] The revelation of Russia's hostility shocked a public opinion which had been taught to believe that the personal friendship between the two sovereigns was all that mattered. Delbrück's experience was perhaps typical. Until March 1914, he continued to believe that no occasion for war would arise from Russo-German relations. Astonished at the effect of the *Kölnische Zeitung's* alarmist article (March 2), he asked Professor Paul Mitravanov, formerly his student, for an explanation. The reply convinced him that the situation was desperate. After a tedious survey of Russia's grievances since Peter the Great, his correspondent finally got to the heart of the problem: "Russia has met and meets everywhere Germany's open or indirect opposition as the ally of Austria in the solution of her most vital problem—the Near-Eastern question. The Russians at last see that . . . the road to Constantinople lies through Berlin. Vienna is really only a secondary question." Thanks to her military and economic progress, Russia was too powerful to be treated longer as Germany's satellite. Upon Germany's policy in Turkey, Sweden, and Austria, peace would henceforth depend.

[309] *D. D. F.* (3), X, 20 (March 21), 30 (March 24), 33, 34 (March 25), 66 (March 30), 100-102 (April 1).
[310] Berchtold, Oct. 26, 1913. *Ö.-U. A.,* VII, 514.
[311] Szögyény, March 12, 1914. *Ibid.,* VII, 966.
[312] William II's comments, *Lokal-Anzeiger,* June 14, 1914. *K. D.,* I, 5.

"Well, well! If it isn't Herr Michel! He's so funny! Why you can do anything to him; he's so harmless that. . . ."

Kladderadatsch, February 18, 1912.

Figure 30.—"Damnation!!"

From this letter, which he regarded as an authentic expression of Russian public opinion, Delbrück concluded that Russia would declare war if the Straits were not opened to her warships or if the South Slavs were not torn from Austria and handed over to Serbia. Even pacifists could not be indifferent if the recognition of British naval supremacy were to be followed by a surrender to Russia and by the abandonment of the two Americas to Yankee imperialism under the Monroe Doctrine. Germany's mission, according to Delbrück, was to defend Europe against Russia's lust for domination.[313]

While anxiety pervaded all groups in Germany as elsewhere to a greater or less extent, it was the Conservatives and the nationalists who were most responsible for the growing belief that war was inevitable. "Rarely," wrote Schiemann, "has there been a time during the last century when the clouds extended so far over the entire horizon."[314] During the excitement caused by the *Kölnische Zeitung's* scare article (March 2), the *Post* (March 11, 1914) predicted a European conflict within four years. "Everything we have accomplished during the last decades is at stake. A war, the like of which history has never seen, is impending."[315] Even the extremists rarely went so far as to depict Germany in the rôle of the aggressor. Whereas the alarmists in France, Russia, and England regarded her dissatisfaction as the real danger to peace, the Germans of like mind blamed the hostile plans of the first two of these powers, although the talk of "encirclement" had passed out of favor with the new courtship of England. Russia and France, it was said, would force Germany to take arms. The sole purpose of her military increases, according to Schiemann, was "to thrust back and to punish the increasingly probable attack by our Eastern and Western neighbors. . . ."[316] On April 19, 1914, the executive committee of the Pan-German League announced "that France and Russia are preparing for the decisive struggle with Germany and Austria-Hungary and that they intend to strike at the first favor-

---

[313] *P. J.*, vol. 157, 385–397 (June, 1914).
[314] *Kreuz-Zeitung*, Dec. 31, 1913. Schiemann, *Deutschland und die Grosse Politik*, XIII, 379.
[315] Jux, *Der Kriegsschrecken des Frühjahrs 1914 in der europäischen Presse*, p. 143.
[316] *Kreuz-Zeitung*, March 11, 1914, Schiemann, *op. cit.*, XIV, 87.

able opportunity."[317]   To destroy Germany, wrote a pamphleteer whose views on other matters show a good deal of insight, was the fixed purpose "of all enemies of the existing balance of power in Europe. . . ."[318]   As in other countries, the great majority probably feared war and hoped that it might be avoided. The sad truth, asserted a nationalist pamphleteer, was that "most Germans have no other desire than to give no offense to other powers."[319]   Ottfried Nippold, the Swiss pacifist, assembled an imposing collection of chauvinist utterances to prove the existence of a systematic campaign to indoctrinate the German people with aggressive nationalism, but he came to the conclusion that the claims of the nationalist press and of the *Wehrverein* generals that they spoke for the nation were ill-founded.[320]

Even less than in the Western countries was the majority in a position to determine the government's decisions. The vote of no confidence, December 3, 1913, had no material effect upon the outcome of the Zabern affair. Notwithstanding the outrageous disregard of civil rights by the army, the military court imposed an absurdly inadequate sentence upon Lieutenant Förstner,[321] and his colonel was even decorated—showing beyond question that the army was, to a large extent, a law to itself. Contributing to the passive acquiescence in this situation was the active glorification of war and an aggressive nationalism. Two examples will suffice. Pacifism, wrote the *Post* (Dec. 25, 1912), was the work of those who wished to "dull Michael's suspicions and to rob him of his strength. . . ." "War," asserted a review that addressed itself to the youth, "is the highest and holiest phase of human activity."[322]   Bethmann's weakness in supporting German interests, it was said, made it especially necessary to prepare public opinion for the war which his attitude helped to make inevitable.[323]   To measure the exact effect of this campaign is impos-

[317] *A. B.*, April 25.
[318] Littmann, *Das europäische Friedensproblem*, p. 64.
[319] W. Eisenhart, *Deutschland erwache! Ein Mahnwort zur Hebung des National-gefühls* (Leipzig, 1913).
[320] O. Nippold, *Der deutsche Chauvinismus* (Stuttgart, 1913), p. 115.
[321] On appeal, the sentence of forty-three days of detention was reduced to six.
[322] *Wochenschrift für Deutschlands Jugend*, herausgegeben vom Bunde Jungdeutschlands und der deutscher Turnerschaft, Jan. 25, 1913.
[323] *Post*, Jan. 5, 1913.

sible, but its importance was considerable. Many Germans clearly had no doubt as to the influence of aggressive minorities in France. Alarmed by the increase of Gallophobia, by the belief in the army and, among the Conservatives, in the desirability and necessity of war, Jules Cambon and Lieutenant Colonel Serret, the French ambassador and military attaché, believed that the nation could easily be aroused to support a war against France.[324] Delbrück, the editor of the influential *Preussische Jahrbücher,* was alarmed by the influence of the extremists. The Pan-Germans, in his opinion, constituted Germany's greatest danger, for they might involve her in war when the circumstances were unfavorable: "It used to be possible to console oneself with the thought that they were a small, semi-comic sect without influence. That is no longer true. The Pan-German press is widely circulated and has a very zealous following. . . . No wonder that wide circles are alarmed by its success. . . . The French learned in 1871 the consequences of the failure of the moderates to check the chauvinists." [325] According to Nippold—and the evidence tends to support his conclusion—the latter permeated the university circles and, generally speaking, the educated classes, the Conservatives, and the army. Many shared their point of view without being really aware of the fact.[326]

In Germany as elsewhere, the psychological defenses against war were weakened by the feeling that her decision would be forced by the other powers. Nor was it merely a question of resisting a direct attack upon her own frontiers, for, under the strictest interpretation, the Dual Alliance required Germany to declare war upon Russia if she attacked Austria. Moltke believed, however, that Germany could not afford to wait for Russia to declare war if she ordered general mobilization and that she must herself mobilize. According to Cambon, the chief of staff did not "desire" war, but he believed that in the above circumstances immediate action would be necessary in order properly

---

[324] *D. D. F.,* (3), IX, 388, 394, 395 (Feb. 15, 16, 1914).
[325] *P. J.,* vol. 154, pp. 574–577 (Dec. 1913).
[326] Nippold, *Der deutsche Chauvinismus,* pp. 123, 124. The Russian ambassador feared that the government might yield to the chauvinists if they were not curbed in time. Sverbeiev, 27 March/9 April 1914. *Z. I.,* (1), II, 203.

to deal with France.[327] It was theoretically possible that Bethmann and the foreign office might decide otherwise, but there
was reason to believe that their views, if they differed with those
of the army chieftains, would not prevail in a crisis. The military, not the civil, authorities decided the details of the Sanders
mission, although it is true that the latter were strong enough
to make a compromise possible. That the notoriously mercurial
Emperor would support the civilians was highly doubtful. Cambon credited him with peaceful intentions,[328] but William occasionally expressed opinions that were similar to those of the
extremists. There may have been some truth in the report that
circulated through the diplomatic corps in Berlin in November
1913 that he spoke to King Albert of Belgium during his visit
of an inevitable war with France.[329] To Davydov, the director
of the Russian special credit bureau, William was even more
brutally frank. "I fear," he said, "there will be a clash between
the Slav and the German, and I feel it my duty to apprise you
of this fact," adding in conclusion that if war should be inevitable he considered it a matter of secondary importance who would
be the first to attack.[330] Against these rash statements should
be balanced his more moderate tone in talking with the French
minister in Munich and with the Austrians in the following
spring, but, at best, he was an uncertain factor.

Less than ever was public opinion prepared to resist a decision
for war if it could be made to appear a defensive measure. Important changes had occurred in the character of the opposition
parties. According to Delbrück, the Progressives had become "a
party of a sensible *Realpolitik,*" and the Centrists, "a party of com-
placency (*Regierungsfreundlichkeit*)." Revisionism had triumphed among the Social Democrats.[331] General von Einem,
the war minister, who refused even to shake hands with Bebel,
counted upon the eventual secession of the skilled workers to the

---

[327] *D. D. F.,* (3), VI, 572 (May 6, 1913).
[328] *Ibid.,* (3), IX, 395 (Feb. 16, 1914).
[329] J. Cambon, Nov. 22. *Ibid.,* (3), VIII, 653.
[330] Kokovtsov, *Out of My Past,* p. 392.
[331] *P. J.,* vol. 154, p. 361 (Nov. 1913). In reply to a bitter attack by the Pan-
Germans, Delbrück wrote that the Social Democrats "are no longer revolutionaries."
Ibid., vol. 154, p. 574 (Dec. 1913).

middle-class parties.[332] "Indeed," wrote a spokesman of the revisionist group at the beginning of 1914, "everything points to the fact that our Party will be compelled to participate more and more actively in political and parliamentary affairs the larger it becomes."[333] These changes were reflected in the Party's attitude toward foreign affairs.[334] Few nationalists painted a darker picture of Germany's position than Leuthner, a prolific writer on international questions. The Triple Entente, he wrote, "is the most powerful and the most fearful combination of states known to history. . . . It presents a variety of dangers, which must weigh like an Alp upon the statesmen of Vienna and Berlin. Foreigners must find it difficult to understand how they are able to retain their peace of soul in the face of these perils."[335] With its increasing appreciation of the dangers surrounding Germany, the Party's determination to resist a war at all costs inevitably weakened. In view of the refusal of the Party congress (Sept. 1913), by a vote of more than two to one, to approve Rosa Luxemburg's resolution in favor of the general strike as a weapon in the class warfare,[336] there was little prospect that this drastic measure would be resorted to during the tense atmosphere of an international crisis, although the *Vorwärts* (Oct. 9, 1912) long continued to talk of the proletariat as the saviors of peace. Kautsky believed that no government would dare to go to war unless it had succeeded in arousing a war spirit, but, once in progress, "it would be useless, even fatal," to call a general strike.[337] In the Reichstag, Haase explained that the German Social Democrats had refused to agree at the congresses of the Second International to lay down their tools with the workers of other countries for fear of adding to the inevitable distress of the masses.[338] Bebel once said that he would shoulder his musket against Russia, the oppressor of the

---

[332] K. von Einem, *Erinnerungen eines Soldaten, 1853–1933* (Leipzig, 1933), p. 157.

[333] W. Kolb, "Die Militärfrage und die Sozialdemokratie," *Sozialdemokratische Monatshefte*, 1914, p. 83 (Jan. 29).

[334] See above, p. 710.

[335] K. Leuthner, "Die Entente und das Ende der deutschen Orientpolitik," *Sozialdemokratische Monatshefte*, 1912, p. 1035 (Aug. 15).

[336] *Protokol* (Berlin, 1913), pp. 337, 338.

[337] K. Kautsky, "Der Krieg und die Internationale," *Neue Zeit*, 1912–1913, p. 191 (Nov. 8, 1912).

[338] *Verhandlungen*, XIII Leg. Per., I Sess., IV, 2535 (Dec. 3, 1912).

proletariat.[339]   The French diplomats were under no illusions as to the probable attitude of the Social Democrats.   No one, according to the minister in Munich, "should count upon any obstruction to war from them." [340]   Material prosperity, the cult of success, and an endemic nervousness were bringing parties together in a kind of truce, so far as domestic politics were concerned, and in a common front against foreign dangers.[341]   No strong stand against war could be expected from the masses.   A united nation would be assured if it were shown that German security was threatened and that Russia was the source of the danger.

---

[339] *Vossische Zeitung,* Dec. 6, 1912.
[340] Allizé, Aug. 12, 1912.   *D. D. F.,* (3), III, 393, 394.
[341] Cf. *P. J.,* vol. 154, p. 361 (Delbrück, Nov. 1913).

CHAPTER XIV

July 1914: A Gamble and Its Failure

... es wurde uns vorgeführt man müsse das Gleichge-
wicht zwischen den Macht- und Mächtegruppen in Europa
herstellen, was dann in den Hintergedanken dieser Leute so
viel bedeutete, als, man müsse darauf aus sein, ein diploma-
tisches Übergewicht über die Gegengruppe zu gewinnen und
die andern, wenn auch nur auf dem Papier, demütigen zu
können.

Kölnische Zeitung, July 26, 1914.

Seit mehr als vier Jahrzehnten hat das Deutsche Reich
den Frieden bewahrt und sorglich behütet; überall ist es im
Interesse der Erhaltung des Friedens tätig gewesen.

Kölnische Volkszeitung, August 2, 1914.

Of Germany's dissatisfaction and restlessness in the spring of
1914 there can be no question. Her desire for more and better
colonies was unappeased. With France and Russia arming to
the teeth,[1] with the balance of power in the Balkans favorable
to the Triple Entente,[2] with Austria's future as a great power
uncertain, and with England and Russia negotiating for a naval
agreement, Germany's influence and prestige, if not her security,
were endangered. If the extremists felt that war was inevitable
and even desirable, a generation of researchers has failed to unearth
satisfactory proof that the German government deliberately de-

---

[1] Germany, according to a retired army officer, could expect an attack at any time
after the completion of the Russian and French armaments in 1915. The Crown Prince
congratulated the author and expressed his best wishes for the wide circulation of the
pamphlet. H. Frobenius, *Des Deutschen Reiches Schicksalstunde* (Berlin, 1914), in
Münchener Neueste Nachrichten, July 16, 1914.

[2] France used her financial power in the form of loans to supplement Russia's efforts
to consolidate the gains of the Balkan Wars. *Cf.* Hallgarten, *Vorkriegs Imperialismus,*
p. 288.

Der Mann am Steuer

Kladderadatsch, July 12, 1914.

Figure 31.—Bethmann-Hollweg: "So at last the course will be Bismarck's! Well, we'll see what will come of it!"

cided to precipitate it. Hope for improvement by diplomatic methods had by no means been abandoned. There was every indication that the latest courtship of England, although no colonies had been secured and the Triple Entente had not been dissolved, would continue. Peaceful means were sought that would improve Austria's position and strengthen the Central powers in the Balkans. William encouraged (in the rose gardens of Konopsicht, June 12–13, 1914) Francis Ferdinand's desire for a more conciliatory treatment of Austria's Roumanian subjects, as a friendly gesture to Roumania, whose loyalty to the Alliance of 1883 was far from certain.[3] Against Austria's opposition to the movement for a Serbo-Montenegrin union Germany protested— perhaps in part because of her own increasing economic interests in Serbia[4]—for William was convinced that Austria might still win Serbia's friendship. A war between the Germans and the Slavs, precipitated by Austria, "would leave us entirely cold."[5] When Austria talked of extending her frontier southward along the Dalmatian coast at Montenegro's expense—a move which Italy was bound to resent—Bethmann thought that Vienna "must . . . be firmly bridled."[6] Voices were still raised in the Reichstag against a slavish support of Germany's ally.[7] Moreover, Germany's remarkable economic progress was undoubtedly an argument in favor of peace.[8] What the entente statesmen and diplomats feared was probably not so much a direct attack as the success of Germany's diplomatic campaign or her reaction to its failure. Even the French military attaché in Berlin believed that the purpose of her armament program was not to precipitate a "definite conflict" but to obtain her aims without fighting.[9]

---

[3] Fay, *Origins of the World War, II*, 38–40. Schmitt believes that William, disappointed by Austria's failure to act upon his advice to win Serbia's friendship, dallied with the idea of a forceful settlement of the Austro-Serbian problem. Schmitt, *Coming of the War*, I, 168–170.

[4] Clement-Simon, Dec. 28, 1913; Descos, March 12, 1914. *D. D. F.*, (3), VIII, 859, 860, IX, 574, 575. *Cf.* Wirth, "Deutschland und der Balkan," *A. B.*, March 7, 1914. The *Rheinisch Metallwarenfabrik*, a German munitions company, filled a Serbian order as late as July 18, 1914. Hallgarten, *Vorkriegs Imperialismus*, p. 267.

[5] William II's comments, Griesinger, March 11, 1914; Bethmann-Hollweg, April 6, 1914. *G. P.*, XXVIII, 335, 337, 338.

[6] Flotow, May 4; Bethmann-Hollweg, May 8. *Ibid.*, XXXVIII, 348–351.

[7] *Verhandlungen*, XIII Leg. Per., I Sess., XIV, 8839, 8862 (May 14, 1914).

[8] Oncken, *Vorgeschichte des Weltkrieges*, II, 658 ff.

[9] Serret, April 20, 1914. *D. D. F.*, (3), X, 212–218.

Among these aims none was more important than Austria's maintenance as a great power—a purpose with which public opinion was agreed. "Do not say that I am supporting a sentimental policy!" exclaimed a Centrist deputy in speaking of the alliance as a "necessity." "It is a question here of imponderables of the greatest moment."[10] The *Vossische Zeitung* (June 3, 1914) warned Russia that neither threats nor trial mobilizations would deter Germany from defending her ally. The Austrian diplomats asked in vain for a firm understanding on their own terms, but there was no lack of assurances as to Germany's support.[11] William never explicitly withdrew his amazing promise of October 26, 1913 to regard as commands anything that came from the Austrian foreign office; in fact he warned Vienna that it could not afford to retreat again.[12] To Tschirschky, the German ambassador in Vienna, it seemed that Austria was "cracking in all her parts" and that the day might come when her partition would be a part of Germany's foreign policy, but, for the present, he saw "no other political constellation capable of giving us the advantages of this alliance. . . ."[13] A strong Austria was essential to Germany's security in Europe, and that security was indispensable to her world policy.

These problems became acute with the assassination of the Archduke Francis Ferdinand at Sarajevo, June 28. "The political consequences of this decree of fate," Bethmann told the Emperor, "will be of the greatest significance."[14] The responsibility of the Pan-Serbian agitation—for whose aims there was little sympathy[15]—was clearly beyond question,[16] but the same agreement did not exist in regard to the guilt of the Serbian government or to the measures which Austria might legitimately take.

---

[10] *Verhandlungen*, XIII Leg. Per., I Sess., pp. 8893, 8894 (May 15).

[11] Tisza, March 15; Berchtold, May 16. *Ö.-U. A.*, VII, 974–979, VIII, 43.

[12] *Ibid.*, VII, 514 (Berchtold); William II's comments, Griesinger, March 11, 1914. *G. P.*, XXXVIII, 335.

[13] *G. P.*, XXXIX, 364 (May 22).

[14] Bethmann-Hollweg, June 28. K. Jagow, *Deutschland freigesprochen!* (Leipzig, 1933), p. 25. To the Saxon envoy, the foreign office nevertheless spoke reassuringly. *Deutsche Gesandtschaftsberichte* (A. Bach, ed., Berlin, 1937), p. 61. This volume will henceforth be referred to as *D. G.*

[15] The Conservative *Reichsbote* (July 28) thought that Europe would return to the chaos of the Middle Ages if the claims of every small nation were satisfied.

[16] To the Russian ambassador, it seemed that the entire press placed the guilt upon the Serbian nation as a whole. Sverbeiev, 19 June/2 July. *Z. I.*, (1), V, 67, 68.

The liberal press was moderate. Serbia, wrote the *Vossische Zeitung* (June 29), should be called to account before the "civilized world" for her failure to prevent the crime, but not for an active share in its perpetration. The *Frankfurter Zeitung* went even further. On July 1, it insisted that "the Serbian government had no part in the crime" and that Austria would be "very stupid" if she resorted to forceful measures of a punitive character, because they would drive her South Slavic subjects into the Pan-Serbian movement. So forceful was its disapproval of the failure to restrain the mobs in Bosnia and its advice in favor of economic concessions to Serbia (July 3) that Vienna protested: these views would weaken the confidence of public opinion in Germany's loyalty.[17] For the Social Democratic *Vorwärts* (July 4), the assassination removed the last hope of Austria's survival as a great power and proved that Germany must arrange an understanding with England and France, cost what it might. Only as a union of autonomous and democratic peoples, according to the official Social Democratic weekly, could Austria survive.[18] Even a part of the nationalist press deprecated hasty action. The *Tägliche Rundschau* (June 30) summarized the reasons for thinking that the crime might be traced to the Serbian government or even to a member of the royal family, but until this connection was proved, "one's judgment should be reserved." The free rein given to the mobs in Bosnia justified, in its opinion, "serious fears." [19] Alarmed by the increasing violence of the press agitation in Austria, Serbia, and Russia, the National Liberal *National Zeitung* (July 7) called for self-restraint in Vienna. Surely the Austrian foreign office had sufficient common sense to see that the sincerity of Serbia's denials of responsibility could not be questioned, that the fate of any individual, no matter how highly placed, should not affect a nation's policy, and that Serbia would certainly yield to "complaints and charges" based upon

---

17 Tschirschky, July 4. *K. D.*, I, 31.

18 "Tu felix Austria!" *Neue Zeit*, 1914, p. 652 (July 10). The revisionist organ recommended the admission of the South Slavs to an equal partnership with the Germans and Magyars. L. Quessel, "Serbia Irredenta," *Sozialdemokratische Monatshefte*, 1914, p. 903 (July 16).

19 For a detailed analysis of this article, see J. F. Scott, *Five Weeks: The Surge of Public Opinion on the Eve of the Great War* (N. Y., 1927), pp. 101, 102. Scott failed to note its reservations as to Serbia's guilt.

proof. The unquestioned responsibility of the Pan-Serbian agitation, wrote the National Liberal *Magdeburgische Zeitung* (July 2), "does not justify the stamping of Serbian officials as murderers." In support of the view that Austria was herself partly at fault, this nationalist journal spoke of the carelessness and inefficiency of her police arrangements at Sarajevo and of the fact that she had been warned by the Serbian *chargé d'affaires:* "Because we are always willing and determined to support our ally when her vital interests are involved, we believe it is our right and duty to advise moderation (*an rechter Stelle auch einmal zur nüchternden Besonnenheit zu raten.*)" This article, however, was not widely clipped or much discussed.

Austria's loss, many said, was also Germany's. The friendship between William and Francis Ferdinand had been a solid assurance of her loyalty. With the latter's death disappeared the last hope that Austria would resist the centrifugal forces that threatened her destruction, for the Archduke Karl was young and untried.[20] Could she, asked the nationalist *Leipziger Neueste Nachrichten,* continue to fulfil her function as the bulwark of Germanism against the Slavic flood? "A bullet has struck down the captain of the dikes (*Den Deichhauptmann hat eine Kugel darniedergestreckt*)."[21] That Austria would take firm measures was regarded as a matter of course. A report that Serbia would be required to agree to the participation of Austrian police officials in the investigation of the origins of the crime occasioned little or no protest.[22] The liberal *Berliner Tageblatt* (July 1) spoke of it as harsh but just.[23] To the chauvinist *Post* (July 1), the Paris *Figaro's* revelation of the negotiations for a Serbo-Montenegrin union was another reason for drastic action.[24] The Catholic press pledged Germany's unconditional support. The

---

[20] *Kölnische Volkszeitung,* June 29, July 1; *Leipziger Neueste Nachrichten,* in *Tägliche Rundschau, June* 30; *Kölnische Zeitung,* July 1; *Berliner Lokal-Anzeiger,* in *Deutsche Tageszeitung,* July 5. *Cf.* Werner, *Alldeutscher Verband,* p. 197. The press apparently had nothing to say of the Archduke's unpopularity at the Austrian court.

[21] *Tägliche Rundschau,* June 30. The Catholic *Kölnische Volkszeitung* (July 4) used exactly the same sentence. *Cf.* Scott, *The Surge of Public Opinion on the Eve of the Great War,* pp. 105, 106.

[22] This rumor, which foreshadowed the most important demand in Austria's ultimatum, was promptly denied. Lerchenfeld, July 2. *B. D. K.,* p. 118.

[23] Cf. *Berliner Neueste Nachrichten,* July 1.

[24] On July 17, Sazonov advised Serbia to postpone these negotiations. Siebert-Schreiner, *Entente Diplomacy and the World,* p. 450.

Kölnische Volkszeitung (June 29) said immediately that Serbia's guilt was self-evident and that Germany's backing was assured. "Because of our own interests as well as our obligations," wrote this journal (July 1), "we will loyally stand by our ally, come what may." Writing under the headline "Serbia's Guilt in the Sarajevo Crime," the *Germania* (July 1) approved the reported demand for Austria's participation in the police investigation on Serbian soil. Few observers ventured at this stage of the crisis to discuss the effect of the crime upon international politics. The National Liberal *Hamburger Nachrichten* was one of the exceptions. Hitherto opposed to the unconditional support of Austria and favorable to an understanding with Russia, it now (July 1) insisted that Austria's security and prestige required Serbia's punishment: "The results will show whether a European power or a group of powers will intervene, whether the Serbian instigators to murder have sympathizers and protectors in Europe." [25] What many must have privately thought a few frankly acknowledged. "It means war," was a former war minister's immediate reaction.[26] "June 28, 1914," wrote the National Liberal *National Zeitung* (June 30), "will be long remembered. A black day, and perhaps not for the Dual Monarchy alone. It is impossible at this time even approximately to measure the effect of this shocking and abominable crime."

For the Triple Entente, Sarajevo and its results did not become a major problem until the Austrian ultimatum was presented to Serbia (July 23),[27] but Germany was immediately required to make decisions of the greatest importance. Should Austria be given moderating advice or a free hand? These were the alternatives, since Germany evidently could not afford to dictate what she should do. The government's choice was in no sense hampered by public opinion. There is no reason to believe that the use of Germany's influence against dangerous measures would have caused a strong protest, except among some of the extremists and

[25] According to the *Tag*, Russia's support of the Pan-Slavic agitation was indirectly responsible for the crime, and the *Vossische Zeitung* stressed her encouragement of the Serbians in the idea that Austria was on the verge of a collapse. Scott, *The Surge of Public Opinion on the Eve of the Great War*, p. 104.

[26] Einem, *Erinnerungen eines Soldaten*, p. 169.

[27] The editors of the French diplomatic documents chose this date as the beginning of the crisis. B. E. Schmitt, "France and the Outbreak of the World War," *Foreign Affairs*, XV, 518.

the Catholics. In fact, the ambassador in Vienna promptly advised caution, but William, who had hastily returned from Kiel, called him to order.[28] It was not, he wrote (June 30), for Germany to say what Austria should do, for she would be blamed if anything went wrong. In his opinion, Austria should act promptly: "Now or never. The Serbs must be settled with, and that right soon."[29] William's assurance (July 2) of support nevertheless did not satisfy Berchtold, who, like Conrad, favored an immediate war with Serbia,[30] for he remembered that Germany had opposed the revision of the Treaty of Bucharest (1913) after a similar promise.[31] To convey William's views to the Austrian foreign office, the German embassy called upon the services of the *Frankfurter Zeitung's* correspondent. "Germany," said this unofficial agent (July 4), "will support Austria through thick and thin, whatever she may decide to do against Serbia." Haste was necessary: "The sooner Austria-Hungary acts, the better it will be. Better yesterday than today, better today than tomorrow. Even if the German press, which is entirely anti-Serb now, cries again for peace, Vienna should not be led astray; the Empire and the Emperor will stand by Austria-Hungary unconditionally. A great power cannot speak more frankly to another." Berchtold wrote in the margin of this document, "Very interesting," and he directed that it should be submitted to the Emperor Francis Joseph.[32] What the foreign minister required in order to win Tisza, the Hungarian Minister-President, and Francis Joseph for an ultimatum which Serbia could not possibly accept was, however, a binding promise. For this purpose he sent Count Hoyos (July 4) to Berlin with a long memorandum from the foreign office and an autographed letter from Francis Joseph to William.[33] In the former was a carefully worked-out scheme, written before the assassination, for a new

---

[28] Zimmermann, the undersecretary in charge of the foreign office during the absence of Bethmann-Hollweg and Jagow, advised Serbia to yield and Austria (July 4) to exercise "great discretion." Schmitt, *Coming of the War*, I, 286.

[29] William II's comments, Tschirschky, June 30. *K. D.*, I, 11.

[30] Fay, *Origins of the World War*, II, 186.

[31] Berchtold, July 3. *Ö.-U. A.*, VIII, 277.

[32] *Ö.-U. A.*, VIII, 294. *Cf.* Schmitt, *op. cit.*, I, 269n.

[33] Zimmermann's advice did not arrive in Vienna until the morning of July 5—that is, after Hoyos' departure. Szögyény, July 4. *Ö.-U. A.*, VIII, 295.

Balkan alliance, including Bulgaria and Roumania, to check Russia's influence;[34] its significance was overshadowed by the concluding statement that Berchtold planned "to destroy with a determined hand the threads in which its enemies are trying to enmesh the Monarchy."[35] Germany's response to this appeal (July 5, 6) was perhaps the most important single event of the entire crisis. To the plan for a surprise attack upon Serbia and for her destruction, hinted at in the documents presented by Hoyos and stated more frankly orally, William, Bethmann, and Zimmermann offered no objections; they practically encouraged it. William told Szögyény at Potsdam, July 5, that "this action must not be delayed"; that Germany would support her ally "with her accustomed loyalty" even in the war with Russia, which he had expected for years; and that the ambassador should communicate these views to his government, although it would be necessary to secure the Chancellor's consent.[36] The Emperor's confidence that Bethmann would agree was justified. To Szögyény and Hoyos the Chancellor said (July 6) that "an immediate intervention against Serbia" would be "the most effective (*radikalste*) and best solution of our [Austria's] difficulties in the Balkans."[37] The highest officials therefore approved and in effect encouraged Austria's plans, knowing their aggressive character. Such differences of opinion as have arisen from the microscopic examination of every shred of evidence pertaining to these momentous conversations chiefly concerns the awareness of these men that Austria's action would probably result in Russia's intervention and in a general war. Because he seems to have believed that there would be ample time to experiment with Berchtold's plan for a new Balkan alliance, and because he expressed the opinion that the international situation was more favorable for Austria's purposes than it would be later, Bethmann may not have been seriously impressed;[38] but William had fewer illusions, for

[34] Schmitt, *Coming of the War*, I, 163.
[35] *Ö.-U. A.*, VIII, 250–261. *K. D.*, I, 21–30.
[36] Szögyény, July 5. *Ö.-U. A.*, VIII, 306.
[37] Szögyény, July 6, *Ibid.*, VIII, 320.
[38] The fact that Szögyény's report contained no reference to the need of informing Italy, which Jagow later stressed (*K. D.*, I, 71, 72, July 15), has caused some historians to question the Austrian ambassador's accuracy. Bethmann, however, may simply have blundered.

he said, immediately after reading Hoyos' documents, that "a serious European complication" must be expected. He told Szögyény, July 5, that Russia would think twice before going to war in the present incomplete state of her preparations, but he also said that her hostility would have to be counted upon and he pledged Germany's support even in an Austro-Russian war.[39] Of William more justly than of Bethmann it can be said that he gave Germany's blank check with full consciousness of the dangers involved in Austria's plans. The risk, he felt, was necessary in order to preserve Austria as a great power and to protect Germany from the incalculable perils which would arise from her partition. Seeking perhaps an explanation that would diminish Austria's obligation to her ally, Szögyény found it in the feeling that, since war was inevitable because of Russia's attitude, it had better be fought before she was ready and in the confidence that England would remain neutral, even if Russia and France were involved.[40]

Berchtold was satisfied. Without a careful analysis of the international situation or even of the probable effect of the annexation of a part of Serbia upon Austria's domestic problems,[41] Germany had made it possible for him to secure Tisza's and Francis Joseph's approval of his war policy. By July 14, they agreed on an ultimatum so drastic that Serbia would refuse, although Tisza carried his point that there should be no sudden attack without the usual diplomatic formalities. Berchtold rightly concluded that Germany would not insist upon a voice in the drafting of the ultimatum. She had occasionally restrained him during the Balkan Wars because his intentions then seemed incompatible with her own interests, but a different point of view prevailed in July 1914. The famous "blank check" had been given without much consideration of its effect upon Germany's aims, but her statesmen evidently concluded during the next few days that an Austro-Serbian war might be useful. This consideration was probably one of the reasons why they wished to

---

[39] Szögyény, July 5. *Ö.-U. A.*, VIII, 306.

[40] Szögyény, July 12. *Ibid.*, VIII, 407, 408. The Saxon envoy reported that these were the army's views but that the Emperor would not approve them. Lichtenau, July 2. *D. G.*, p. 62.

[41] Oncken, *Vorgeschichte des Weltkrieges*, II, 791.

localize the crisis. If they succeeded, the better relations with England might not be disturbed, Russia would lose prestige and influence in the Balkans, and Austria's value as an ally would presumably be greatly increased. To every inquiry by the entente diplomats as to the nature of Austria's demands, Germany replied that she had no information and that the matter concerned Austria alone. This was a serious blunder; no one believed her, and Austria's demands might be so extreme as to turn public opinion everywhere against the Central powers. Nevertheless, nothing was done after hearing that the terms and the date of the delivery of the ultimatum had been agreed upon except to ask politely for information so that Germany might support Austria in the European capitals.[42] Not until the afternoon of July 22, scarcely twenty-four hours before the ultimatum was handed to the Serbian government, did the full text reach the German foreign office. There was still time for a warning, if not for protracted negotiations; if Germany remained silent, it meant her approval of Austria's purposes and procedure. Since July 5 and 6, everyone in authority in Berlin knew that Berchtold intended to force a war with Serbia. They knew that he had recommended demands of such severity during the meeting of the Austrian ministry on July 7 "that their acceptance seems out of the question."[43] On July 10, the German ambassador was asked how his government would react to an ultimatum with a time limit of forty-eight hours requiring Serbia to admit an Austrian official to watch the Pan-Serbian agitation, to dissolve the nationalist societies, and to dismiss certain army officers.[44] Three days later (July 13), Jagow informed Tschirschky that he had heard, via Bucharest, of a possible demand for the participation of Austrian officials in the investigation of the crime on Serbian soil.[45] From Vienna he learned that Austria would be satisfied only with the integral acceptance of her demands, and that

---

[42] Tschirschky, July 17; Jagow, July 19. *K. D.*, I, 93, 104. Szögyény strongly advised its immediate communication to avoid irritation in Berlin. *Ö.-U. A.*, VIII, 555.

[43] Tschirschky, July 8. *K. D.*, I, 36. Nevertheless, the Bavarian envoy was merely told that the Austrian ministry had considered domestic questions, such as the conditions in Bosnia, at this meeting. *B. D. K.*, pp. 123, 124.

[44] Tschirschky, July 10. *K. D.*, I, 50.

[45] *Ibid.*, I, 59 (July 13).

the "note" would be so phrased as to be practically unacceptable.[46] While the full text remained unknown to the Germans, they knew what the general character of the demands would be and the most important in greater detail. The pretense that the question concerned Austria alone was nonetheless maintained to the last, even in response to questions from Vienna.[47] To disprove the "legend" that Germany had given her ally a free hand, Bethmann let the cat out of the bag in his post-war memoirs: "We learned through Herr von Tschirschky the broad outlines of the demands which Austria intended to present to Serbia. We believed that we could not in principle disapprove them."[48]

The official press helped Austria to keep Europe quiet until the moment arrived for the delivery of the ultimatum, which she had intentionally delayed until Poincaré should have left St. Petersburg. On July 9, a Vienna dispatch in the *Norddeutsche* announced that no diplomatic action had been agreed upon at the meeting of the Austrian ministry on July 7.[49] From the *Neues Wiener Tagblatt* was clipped (July 11) a statement that the *démarche* at Belgrade would contain nothing "that could be construed as an affront or a humiliation," although Serbia could be expected to punish the guilty individuals, to correct conditions that constituted a threat to Austria's security, and, especially, to take steps against the Pan-Serbian agitation.[50] Only if the official investigation revealed a connection between the crime and a political conspiracy in Serbia, the *Kölnische Zeitung* (July 14) was informed from Vienna, would the situation become serious. A Budapest dispatch in the *Berliner Lokal-Anzeiger* (July 14) claimed that Austria's action "would take the politest form, according to the usual practice between states." It would leave nothing to be desired in definiteness, and a particularly clear and precise answer would be required. On July 16, the *Norddeutsche*

---

[46] Tschirschky, July 14. *Ibid.,* I, 74–76.
[47] Jagow, July 11. *K. D.,* I, 52, 53. On July 14, Zimmermann expressed some confidence to the Bavarian envoy that the affair could be localized, although he said that the Austrian "note" would insist upon a direct participation in Serbia's investigation. *B. D. K.,* p. 5.
[48] Bethmann-Hollweg, *Betrachtungen zum Weltkriege,* I, 137, 138.
[49] See above, p. 779.
[50] Clipped by *National Zeitung, Vossische Zeitung, Berliner Neueste Nachrichten, Kreuz-Zeitung, Lokal-Anzeiger,* July 10. *Cf.* Biedermann, July 17, *D. G.,* p. 64.

again clipped an article from the *Neues Wiener Tagblatt* affirming Austria's desire for a peaceful settlement. While these quieting assurances disappointed the extremists, who had applauded Austria's sudden display of energy,[51] moderate opinion was doubtless relieved.[52] As to Austria's right to satisfaction, there was little difference of opinion, and her delay was generally regarded as a sign that her action would be based upon the results of the investigation that was in progress at Sarajevo.[53]

To some observers, the international situation seemed to promise a peaceful solution. According to the nationalist *Berliner Neueste Nachrichten* (July 10), Austria had displayed much diplomatic skill in winning the support of the Triple Alliance (doubtless a reference to Italy), and the same journal was confident that England would share her point of view. France and Russia were uncertain factors, but the Tsar, living as he did in a glass house, could not afford to throw stones. Both the *Hamburger Nachrichten* (July 11) and the *Vossische Zeitung* (July 12) placed some credence in the report from Vienna that the Triple Entente was using its influence in Belgrade in the interest of peace, although the latter journal was not certain that it would advise Serbia to accept Austria's "wise and moderate demands" unconditionally. The press gradually allotted more of its first-page space to other topics, such as the trial of Mme. Caillaux in Paris for the murder of Gaston Calmette, the trial before the high court at Leipzig for treason of the Alsatian satirist Johann Jakob Waltz, better known as Hansi, and the attempt upon Rasputin's life in Russia. Poincaré's visit to St. Petersburg was followed with great attention, at first, largely because of its bearing upon the general international situation. That it had been arranged before the Sarajevo tragedy, like William's cruise in Scandinavian waters, was well-known. For most German observers, the visit was chiefly significant as another step in France's subordination to Russia, which had commenced when Poincaré first went to

---

[51] *Leipziger Neueste Nachrichten*, in *Tägliche Rundschau*, July 9; *Deutsche Tageszeitung*, July 15.
[52] Rumbold, July 11. *B. D.*, XI, 36.
[53] *Frankfurter Zeitung, Vossische Zeitung*, July 10; *Berliner Börsen-Zeitung*, July 12; *National Zeitung*, July 14; *Vorwärts*, July 16, Vienna, July 14.

St. Petersburg in 1912.[54] The *Hamburger-Nachrichten* (July 21), influenced perhaps by Jules Hedemann's ecstatic reports in the Paris *Matin* of Russia's inexhaustible resources and great military power, thought that France might be trying to enlist her in the cause of the *revanche*.[55] In its opinion, the good sense of the Russian statesmen would defeat this intrigue, but it was convinced that France would attack the moment "Russia shows any intention of breaking with Germany." Other observers discussed the possibility of a connection between the visit and the Austro-Serbian crisis. The Catholic *Kölnische Volkszeitung* (July 16) thought that the visit was "the most significant political event of 1914," and the National Liberal *Magdeburgische Zeitung* (July 20) was impressed by the dangerous development of Russia's self-confidence. Would the two powers agree, asked the *Tägliche Rundschau* (July 20), to intervene "in the domestic difference between Vienna and Belgrade. . . ? Let there be no mistake: the 'France' which arrived today at Kronstadt brings no peace to poor Europe." Every word in the toasts exchanged between the French President and the Tsar was scanned for its diplomatic significance. If the reference to the maintenance of the balance of power reminded an occasional journal of the "encirclement," it was generally acknowledged that nothing had been said to which objection could be taken.[56]

After Tisza told the Hungarian Diet, July 15, that the relations with Serbia must be clarified and that war might be necessary,[57] there could be little doubt that Austria intended to show her hand in a few days. The nationalist *Münchener Neueste Nachrichten* (July 18) still insisted that Serbia would be "approached in a peaceful spirit and in a calm, friendly manner," but other journals were less confident of Austria's moderation. Even the nationalist *Berliner Neueste Nachrichten* (July 17), which had earlier approved vigorous action, now feared that Russia's enmity would be turned against Germany. In view of Germany's services, she could not be expected to pull Austria's chestnuts out of

---

[54] *Kreuz-Zeitung*, July 8; *Hamburger Nachrichten*, July 9; *Reichsbote*, July 10; *Vossische Zeitung*, July 16.
[55] Cf. *Leipziger Neueste Nachrichten*, in *Berliner Neueste Nachricten*, July 23.
[56] *Post, Germania*, July 21.
[57] *N. A. Z.*, July 17.

the fire: "We can rightly claim a position in the background. Some evidence *from the Danube* of the *Nibelungentreue* is our due." Harden was definitely critical. Proof of Serbia's guilt, he wrote, had been promised but never furnished: "And if it could be proved that a couple of fools, tramps, or criminals from Belgrade were involved in the conspiracy, would even that certainty justify the indictment of an entire nation? Serbia needs and desires peace."[58] Tisza, wrote the *Frankfurter Zeitung* (July 17), had opened the eyes of those who believed that Austria had abandoned her original intention of forcing a settlement with Serbia. The Conservative *Kreuz-Zeitung* (July 17) was delighted: "Vienna has too long evaded the problem of the future of Austro-Serbian relations and has not seen clearly enough that Austria's most vital interests are involved." Germany had long since made up her mind that a thorough clarification was needed. On July 19, the official *Norddeutsche* made a momentous announcement: a serious crisis would be avoided if Serbia gave Austria the satisfaction which all Europe recognized as her right. It was "desirable and fitting," in the interest of European solidarity, that the reckoning (*"Auseinandersetzung"*) should be localized.[59] As the first clear indication of the government's stand, the article created a sensation. It persuaded the important *Magdeburgische Zeitung* to abandon its earlier criticism of drastic measures by Austria, approving (July 20) what it believed was Austria's determination to compel Serbia to accept her demands. The press, for the most part, placed greater emphasis upon the *Norddeutsche's* declaration in favor of the localization of the Austro-Serbian conflict. Austria, wrote the *Hamburger Nachrichten* (July 20), should not be influenced by the "diplomatic bluff" of Serbia's friends. The agrarian *Deutsche Tageszeitung* (July 20) thought that neither Russia nor any other country had a right to intervene: "A clear pronouncement in St. Petersburg to this

---

[58] Harden, "Falsche Mäuler," *Zukunft*, July 18.
[59] *Berliner Neueste Nachrichten, Deutsche Tageszeitung, Hamburger Nachrichten, Frankfurter Zeitung, Magdeburgische Zeitung,* July 20; *Kölnische Volkszeitung,* July 21. Cf. *B. D.,* XI, 60; *Z. I.,* (1) IV, 266 (7/20 July). On July 21, Jagow rebuffed Ronevski, the Russian *chargé d'affaires,* when he suggested that the *Norddeutsche* article guaranteed that Austria's terms would be such as Serbia could accept. *Z. I.,* (1), V, 340.

effect would contribute to the prompt disposition of this affair."
Two days later (July 22), it assured Austria that she could
proceed with the defense of her legitimate interests in full confidence of Germany's support.

By giving Austria a free hand, Germany had largely tied her
own hands. Little or nothing was accomplished toward assuring
the indifference of the Triple Entente prior to the delivery of the
ultimatum. The minister for Alsace-Lorraine was instructed to
avoid such measures in the *Reichsland* as would excite the French
and to discourage any press polemics that might keep France
from advising moderation to Russia,[60] but the Germans relied
chiefly upon England. Her response was cool. On July 14,
Lichnowsky warned his government that Francis Ferdinand's
clericalism and the sympathies of public opinion for the principle
of nationality would operate in Serbia's favor.[61] Only if "Austrian action . . . kept within certain bounds" could he act, was
Grey's reply to a plea for his aid in keeping Russia neutral,[62] but his
hatred "of the idea of war between any of the Great Powers"
and his remark "that [if] any of them should be dragged into a war
by Servia [it] would be detestable" were encouraging.[63] The German foreign office was not discouraged. Even if England refused to restrain Russia and France by direct action, her own
neutrality would either have the same effect or it would go far
to assure a victory for the Central powers. Jagow confidently
informed the Austrian ambassador, July 21, "that England will
try to keep out of the war even if the worst comes to the worst." [64]
Germany thus departed from her policy of timely concessions by
which she hoped to approach England and, instead, hoped to
use her to strengthen her own position. But that step—moderating advice in Vienna—which would have done more than anything else for the success of this policy, Germany would not take.

---

[60] Bethmann-Hollweg, July 16. *K. D.*, I, 85.

[61] *Ibid.*, I, 64. Jagow had instructed him and Germany's representatives in Rome
and Bucharest to prepare public opinion for possible complications between Austria and
Serbia. *Ibid.*, I, 85 (July 12).

[62] Grey, July 9. *B. D.*, XI, 33, 34. *Cf.* Lichnowsky, July 15. *K. D.*, I, 77, 78.

[63] Grey, July 20. *B. D.*, XI, 54.

[64] Szögyény, July 21. *Ö.-U. A.*, VIII, 553. Such, in general, was the impression of
the representatives in Berlin of the federated states. *D. G.*, pp. 65 (July 17), 68 (July
20).

What she counted upon most was the incomplete state of Russia's preparations. With Germany standing firmly by Austria's side, Russia, it was believed, would abandon the Serbs, either voluntarily or under pressure from London and Paris, as she had in 1909. Such, in brief, was the point of view which Jagow wished the press to develop. There should be, he wrote, no unnecessary hostility toward Russia or France, in order to avoid the impression that Germany desired a general war: "There is no better means of avoiding war than to take our stand at once firmly and quietly with Austria." [65]

Almost to the last moment it was still possible for German public opinion to hope that Austria's demands would not be so extreme as to be utterly unacceptable. The *Berliner Lokal-Anzeiger* (July 23) believed that the Austrian "note" would combine courtesy with firmness: *"Fortiter in re, suaviter in modo,* would be good diplomatic practice." In fact, the "note" was at once recognized as an ultimatum of the strongest kind, but there were few who did not believe that its demands were justified. "Sharp but just," wrote the *Berliner Lokal-Anzeiger* (July 24), and it denounced Russia's increasing armaments as a betrayal of aggressive purposes.[66] Austria's manifest determination to destroy the Pan-Serbian menace was applauded as a welcome change from her usual weakness. "The Hapsburg," wrote the nationalist *Berliner Neueste Nachrichten* (July 24), "has this time worked quietly and systematically, without timid oscillations and without empty threats, toward his goal. He evidently knows what he wants and is prepared for anything. Rather an end to fright than fright without end—such is plainly the *Leitmotiv* of our ally's present action. . . ."[67] "Not for a long time have we heard," said the National Liberal *Magdeburgische Zeitung* (July 24), "such tones from the house in the Ballplatz." According to the agrarian *Deutsche Tageszeitung* (July 24), Austria's firm attitude rightly occasioned some surprise, but, in its

---

[65] *K. D.,* I, 129 (July 22).

[66] Clipped by the *Berliner Tageblatt, Vossische Zeitung, Magdeburgische Zeitung, Kreuz-Zeitung,* July 24; *Freisinnige Zeitung,* July 25; *N. A. Z.,* July 26. Jagow expressed his regrets but asserted that he could do nothing about it when the Russian *chargé d'affaires* protested. *Z. I.,* (1), V, 339.

[67] Cf. *Reichsbote,* July 25.

opinion, the change was highly commendable and should be lasting. "At last!" exclaimed the liberal *Berliner Tageblatt* (July 24) in an article which Theodor Wolff, the editor, privately disavowed on his return (July 25) from Scheveningen, the Dutch resort.[68] However, this was one of the few journals even to pretend a confidence that Serbia might yield without reservations. It wrote (July 24) of the "note's quiet and serious tone" and it insisted that there was no reason why Serbia should take offense. The foreign office may have tried for a moment to moderate the reaction of public opinion, because the *Kölnische Zeitung* (July 24) maintained that Austria's purpose was "to establish a basis for further negotiations" and because it denied that her note could be described as a formal ultimatum. In any event, the attempt failed. The liberal *Frankfurter Zeitung* (July 25) expected Serbia to refuse and Austria to declare war. To most observers, Serbia had only two alternatives: complete acceptance and peace, or rejection and war. It was a question of *"entweder-oder."*[69] Under the caption "Bend or Break,"[70] the National Liberal *National Zeitung* (July 25) insisted that Austria could not accept a conditional surrender to her demands, except at the price of "a humiliating *subjection to the will of the powers.* . . ." It was the general impression that Serbia could not possibly yield and that Austria knew it. The ultimatum, wrote the Progressive *Freisinnige Zeitung* (July 25), "left not a loophole through which the Serbs could escape. . . ." That an Austro-Serbian war might be localized seemed possible, if not certain, to many observers because Russia's preparations were incomplete, because France lacked an adequate heavy artillery, according to Senator Humbert's recent revelations, and because England was peaceful.[71] Yet there were those who recognized that a general war was probably inevitable and who felt that it might be desirable. With the exception of the Social Democratic journals, the press, according to Beyens, the Belgian minister, envisaged "the eventuality of

---

[68] Wolff, *Eve of 1914*, p. 448.

[69] *Germania*, July 24.

[70] The *Hamburger Nachrichten* (July 24) and the *Vossische Zeitung* (July 24) both used this phrase.

[71] *Kölnische Zeitung, Kreuz-Zeitung, Schlessische Zeitung, Berliner Volks-Zeitung,* July 24; *Freisinnige Zeitung,* July 26.

war, while expressing the hope that it would be localized." [72] "It [the ultimatum] means war!" was, wrote the nationalist *Berliner Neueste Nachrichten* (July 24), the natural conclusion. Russia probably would not permit Serbia to be crushed. To the agrarian *Deutsche Tageszeitung* (July 24), Europe faced momentous decisions. "The world," asserted the National Liberal *National Zeitung* (July 25), "will know within twenty-four hours whether war is inevitable or if the danger will be averted at the last moment." The *Berliner Neueste Nachrichten* (July 25) discovered reasons why the war should be fought at this time rather than later, provided that Italy's loyalty could be counted upon: "Under this condition, it would be better from every point of view to fight the great European war now rather than in 1917, for example, and, if possible, before the harvest."

The ultimatum occasioned no real protest in official circles. "Completely superfluous," wrote William when he learned that Berchtold was thinking of giving assurances to Russia that Serbia's territorial integrity would be respected, "Ass! She [Austria] must take the Sanjak again or the Serbs will reach the Adriatic." [73] Privately Jagow may have regarded Austria's demands as too steep, but he told Szögyény that his government supported them. [74] In any case, the Austrian ambassador reported that Berlin expected Serbia's refusal to be followed "immediately by our declaration of war and by military operations. . . ." [75] The *Berliner Lokal-Anzeiger's* (July 24) attitude left no doubt as to the government's satisfaction: "The German people is relieved that the Balkan situation is at last to be clarified. It congratulates its ally on the Danube for this virile decision and will prove its loyalty and readiness to help in the dark days that perhaps face Austria." [76] By far the greater part of public opinion, convinced that Austria's existence as a useful ally was at stake and, perhaps to a lesser extent, that Aus-

---

[72] *Belgische Dokumente,* 2d supplement, p. 113.
[73] William II's comments, Tschirschky, July 24. *K. D.,* I, 167, 168.
[74] *Ö.-U. A.,* VIII, 625 (July 24).
[75] *Ibid.,* VIII, 704 (July 25).
[76] Szögyény summarized this article for the Austrian foreign office. *Ö.-U. A.,* VIII, 625 (July 24). An eloquent "So!" appears in the margin of this document opposite the reference to the dark days facing Austria.

tria's display of energy should not be discouraged, approved the
ultimatum, accepted an Austro-Serbian war as probably inevitable,
and regarded a general war as a possibility. Public opinion,
reported the French minister in Munich, would approve unanimously "every decision by the Imperial Chancellor—even the most
extreme." [77] Russia's request for an extension of the time limit
in the ultimatum was generally dismissed as an unwarranted
interference.[78] Rarely had a comparable unanimity of public
opinion occurred in Germany on an important question in foreign affairs. Only the Social Democratic press and a few Pan-
German newspapers still refused to follow the government's lead.
In Wolff's absence and, according to his post-war memoirs,
against his instructions, the *Berliner Tageblatt* (July 24) asserted
that the ultimatum deserved "unconditional support." Austria,
in its opinion, had spoken her last word.[79] Because the foreign
office persuaded him that a firm support of Austria was the best
way to prevent a general war,[80] Wolff did not reverse his newspaper's stand, and the same consideration doubtless influenced
the attitude of other moderate journals. After admitting (July
24) that no state could yield to demands such as Austria's and
retain its independence, and that Russia would probably intervene,[81] the *Frankfurter Zeitung* (July 25) promptly accepted the
fait accompli: "Given the facts, there is nothing that can be done
except to limit the scope of the catastrophe as much as possible."
The *Vossische Zeitung* (July 24) at first regretted that Serbia
had no choice other than to refuse, but, in a later edition of the
same date, it denied any intention of criticizing Austria: "What
is happening at this moment is a test of the Hapsburg monarchy's
ability to survive." At this critical moment the liberal press
failed most signally to fulfil its mission of criticizing the official
policy and of revealing its dangers to public opinion. For the
small group of newspapers that continued to oppose the blind
support of Austria, its attitude was an object of contempt.

---

[77] Allizé, July 25. *D. D. F.*, (3), XI, 65.
[78] *Berliner Neueste Nachrichten, Magdeburgische Zeitung, Vossische Zeitung,* July 25.
[79] Moltke noted this article as evidence of the satisfactory state of public opinion. Moltke, *Erinnerungen,* p. 381 (July 26).
[80] Wolff, *Eve of 1914,* pp. 450, 451.
[81] Three times the Russian *chargé d'affaires* mentioned this article as an exception to the general reaction of the press. *Z. I.*, (1), V, 56, 339.

"Never," wrote the Social Democratic *Vorwärts* (July 26), "have the Progressives sinned so miserably through the most frivolous chauvinism as during these dangerous days. Instead of greeting the ultimatum of unparalleled brutality with earnest warnings and acid criticism, they have howled with triumph." To the Conservative *Post* (July 24), the *Berliner Tageblatt's* (July 24) remark that the ultimatum contained "nothing offensive" was a good illustration of that journal's naïveté: "Every sentence is a blow in the face of the Serbian government." Whereas the Progressive press had always stood for peace, the *Post* (July 25) noticed its readiness, in this instance, "to draw the sword."

How extensive the inarticulate criticism of the ultimatum and of Germany's policy may have been will doubtless never be known, but Delbrück's remark that milder terms would have increased the danger of war, as long as they included a demand for the suppression of the Pan-Serbian agitation, suggests that there were many who kept their thoughts to themselves.[82] Only two Pan-German newspapers besides the Social Democratic press refused to join the chorus of approval. The *Post* (July 24) and the *Rheinisch-Westfälische Zeitung* (July 24) stressed Austria's failure to reveal the proof of Serbia's guilt, and the latter mentioned the damaging revelations as to Austria's methods during the Friedjung trial in 1909 as another reason for skepticism.[83] To her claim that an atonement must be secured, the *Rheinisch-Westfälische Zeitung* discovered an eloquent commentary in the notorious relief betrayed by the Austrian court at Francis Ferdinand's death. In its opinion, the Pan-Serbian agitation in Bosnia had been inspired by Catholic and Slavic circles in Austria as well as by the Serbian nationalist societies. If it were true, as alleged, that Germany had not been consulted in the drafting of the ultimatum, the exclusive responsibility, according to the *Post* (July 24), belonged to Austria, although the same journal conceded the necessity of defending her against a Russian attack. For the *Rheinisch-Westfälische Zeitung* (July 24), Germany could gain nothing from the impending general war, and an in-

---

[82] *P. J.*, vol. 158, 376, 377 (July 26).
[83] The *Weser-Zeitung* also cited this case as a reason for reserve. *Rheinisch-Westfälische Zeitung*, July 25.

crease of Austria's Slavic territory at Serbia's expense would injure Germany's interests by weakening still further the predominance of the Germans in the Dual Monarchy. While the Social Democratic *Vorwärts* (July 25) took no pleasure in the company of these journals, for it attributed their views to capitalistic influences, it also denied the justice of Austria's case, adding that Germany, whether she had been consulted by her ally or not, must share the responsibility for the grave threat to the peace of Europe.[84] The greater part of the press ignored these uncomfortable questions, and even those which attempted to reply fell back upon the argument that the unconditional support of Austria was the best way to preserve the peace. Criticism of the official policy, wrote the Catholic *Kölnische Volkszeitung* (July 26), was generally regarded as a dangerous encouragement to the warlike tendencies of the Triple Entente: "Weakness, disloyalty, and selfishness will not keep the peace. . . . Even if a disloyal policy . . . proved momentarily successful, the ultimate consequences would be the more catastrophic and frightful. . . ." Credit for the temporary improvement in the situation just prior to the Austrian declaration of war against Serbia (July 28) was given to Germany's unreserved support of her ally.[85] It should therefore, wrote the *Hamburger Nachrichten* (July 27), be continued. "The world war," according to the *Königsberger Allgemeine Zeitung,* "would already be in progress" if the *Post's* and the *Rheinisch-Westfälische Zeitung's* advice had been followed.[86]

To all but one of Austria's demands, Serbia agreed, with reservations whose significance has been variously estimated, just before the expiration of the time limit at 5 p.m., July 25; moreover, she proposed that the demand for the participation of Austrian officials in the judicial investigation on Serbian soil should be submitted along with all other points to the Hague Tribunal or to the powers for arbitration. Giesl, the Austrian minister, acting upon instructions to accept nothing but an unqualified surrender,

---

[84] *Cf.* the *Volksstimmung* (Frankfort), the Social Democratic organ for Southwestern Germany. *D. D. F.,* (3), XI, 63, 64.

[85] *Deutsche Tageszeitung,* July 27.

[86] *Tägliche Rundschau,* July 30.

refused this reply and, with his staff, immediately left Belgrade. What the effect of the prompt publication of Serbia's reply upon German public opinion would have been is hard to say, for even the foreign office, in spite of repeated appeals to Vienna, did not receive a copy until almost midnight July 27, and William did not read it until the next morning. The Emperor's reaction suggests that a considerable section of the press would have been favorable. Considering the time at Serbia's disposal, it was, in his opinion, "a brilliant piece of work" and more than could reasonably have been expected. He believed that it removed every cause for war; he suggested, in a letter to Jagow (July 28), that only a *"douce violence"* should be exerted upon Serbia, that a guarantee of her good faith and a satisfaction for the Austrian army should be secured by the occupation of Belgrade.[87] However, the German people were merely informed that Serbia had rejected Austria's terms and that the latter had broken off diplomatic relations. That night (July 25) crowds filled the streets of the larger cities. Theodor Wolff recalls his definite impression that anxiety was the characteristic emotion in Berlin. To the Bavarian *chargé d'affaires,* the prominence of the "educated" classes in the demonstrations before the royal palace, the Bismarck monument, and the Austrian and Italian embassies indicated a "popular" understanding of the issues at stake, but in Wolff's opinion the lead taken by the students of the higher schools, the parading of student *Korps* in full regalia and with drawn foils meant something quite different—the presence of directing minds in the background. That the crowd finally decided in the late hours of the night, after surging up and down Unter den Linden for hours, to stage a hostile demonstration before the Russian embassy seems something more than the natural expression of mob psychology. The police were mysteriously inactive. After the war, Traugott von Jagow, the president of the police of Berlin and the foreign minister's cousin, pleaded a complete lapse of memory in regard to these events, although he recalled without difficulty that he had not interfered with a peace demonstration by the trade unions a few days later. Some violence

---

[87] *K. D.,* I, 264, II, 18.

was almost inevitable, given the growing tension. In Munich, an army band played the "Radetzky March," "I had a Comrade," and "Prince Eugene" in Austria's honor, in place of its regular program, and a mob wrecked one of the largest cafés because Serbian students whistled during the playing of patriotic airs.[88] On July 27, the Russian *chargé d'affaires* offered a copy of Serbia's reply to leading newspapers and news agencies; in their refusal to publish it he saw convincing proof of an official preparation of public opinion for an Austrian attack upon Serbia.[89] The Wolff Agency finally released the document for publication on July 28, but it was then too late for a free expression of opinion on its merits, for Austria declared war on that day and because Austria's explanations, without an acknowledgment of their authorship, were joined with it.

Meanwhile, the press had immediately represented Austria's severance of diplomatic relations as practically a declaration of war. "War!" was the caption of the Nationalist *Berliner Neueste Nachrichten's* (July 26) leading article. The National Liberal *Magdeburgische Zeitung* (July 26) announced "War between Austria-Hungary and Serbia." "Hands off!" cried the *Kölnische Zeitung* (July 26), after explaining that "the die is cast." Nor was the liberal press less precipitate, for the Progressive *Freisinnige Zeitung* (July 26) wrote that "war has been declared." While Theodor Wolff hinted his doubts as to the Austrian ultimatum, his article in the *Berliner Tageblatt* (July 26) had as its headline "The Austro-Serbian War." He had accepted the thesis of the foreign office as to the efficacy of an unreserved support of Austria. "Faced by an accomplished fact, we must draw the necessary conclusions, whether for good or evil." Weakness would only increase the danger of Russia's intervention. In Russia's hands, it was generally agreed, lay the power to decide between peace and a general war.[90] The *Kölnische Zeitung* (July 26) led in the expression of this point of view: "Everything

---

[88] Schoen, July 26. *B. D. K.*, p. 141; Allizé, *D. D. F.*, (3), XI, 95, 96; Wolff, *Eve of 1914*, pp. 456–460. On July 27, the Prussian envoy asked the Saxon minister of foreign affairs that measures be taken against demonstrations of a provocative character to avoid the impression abroad that war was desired. *D. G.*, p. 81 (July 27).
[89] *Z. I.*, (1), V, 353.
[90] *Berliner Volks-Zeitung*, July 26; *Hamburger Nachrichten*, July 28.

depends upon Russia: our decision, France's decision, and certainly England's as well." Unswerving support of Austria was the only hope. "There is," wrote the National Liberal *Magdeburgische Zeitung* (July 27), "no better way to localize the war and to preserve the peace of Europe than to show beyond the shadow of a doubt that the German army will mobilize at Russia's first move against Austria." "Only by proving that Germany is prepared for anything will an improvement in the situation be possible," wrote the *Vossische Zeitung* (July 27), "no matter how much she tries to localize the conflict." To the Progressive *Freisinnige Zeitung* (July 28), "the fear of Germany in arms is not the least of the reasons for hoping that war will be avoided." What these journals implied, the National Liberal *Hamburger Nachrichten* (July 28) frankly stated, in saying that Russia's menacing attitude was a bluff. The liberal *Frankfurter Zeitung* (July 27) was, however, sufficiently impressed to appeal to her associates in the Triple Entente: "Only if they persuade her to renounce her ambitions for increased prestige and power will there be a satisfactory and permanent solution of the crisis." While the *Kölnische Zeitung* asserted that Germany would restrain Austria just as effectively as she was supporting her if she tried to do anything more than to impose a merited punishment on Serbia,[91] it apparently occurred to few that Germany could herself contribute to a peaceful settlement. Delbrück's suggestions certainly would not have been given a moment's consideration in St. Petersburg: the dissolution of the Serbian army, the cession of a part of her territory to Bulgaria, and the establishment of an administration for the rest of her territory that could be trusted to suppress the Pan-Serbian agitation.[92] Even those who had been most critical of Austria's policy were gradually becoming reconciled to a war if Russia intervened. The Pan-German *Post* (July 27) acknowledged that its objections would be "silenced . . . the moment Austria calls for aid against a third power." A few observers argued that the European war might better be fought immediately. Memories of old "humiliations and injuries" suggested to the *Rheinisch-Westfälische Zeitung* (July 27) the ad-

---

[91] *Berliner Tageblatt*, July 28.
[92] *P. J.*, vol. 158, p. 379 (July 26).

visability of abandoning its criticism. To the National Liberal *Hamburgischer Korrespondent,* the economic losses of a prolonged crisis argued in favor of fighting without loss of time,[93] and Delbrück, confident of Italy's support, thought that conditions were as auspicious as they ever would be.[94]

There was, at least, not the shadow of a doubt as to Germany's solidarity with Austria. On July 28, Bethmann explained the government's views in a communication to the federated states: Serbia's reply contained no guarantee that the Serbian agitation would be suppressed, the peace of Europe could be preserved only by localizing the Austro-Serbian war, and Germany would support Austria if Russia intervened.[95] Nevertheless, he maintained the fiction in negotiating with the Triple Entente that the crisis was essentially a domestic problem for Austria. There should be no "test of strength between the two diplomatic groups"; indeed, the balance of power would be destroyed if Austria now backed down, for, with her surrender, she would no longer count as a great power.[96] Germany's decision "to hold the ring" while Austria settled her accounts with Serbia cost her an exceptional opportunity to develop friendly relations with England. The British foreign office, it is true, had little sympathy for Germany's purposes. In Crowe's opinion, it "would be impolitic, not to say dangerous, . . . to attempt to controvert" the view that the two groups of powers were aligned against each other; he was unconditionally against any attempt to persuade France to exert pressure upon Russia.[97] Suspicious of Germany's attitude and unwilling to run the risk of disrupting the Triple Entente, Grey refused to restrain Russia. "We can do nothing for moderation," he wrote on a report from Berlin, "unless Germany is prepared *pari passu* to do the same."[98] Yet, clinging to the hope that a London Conference like that which had helped to keep the Balkan Wars from spreading might again serve the cause of peace, Grey urged that England, France, Germany, and

---

[93] *Tägliche Rundschau,* July 26.
[94] *P. J.,* vol. 158, p. 380 (July 26).
[95] Bethmann-Hollweg, July 28. *K. D.,* II, 27–29.
[96] Bethmann-Hollweg, July 28. *Ibid.,* II, 33.
[97] Crowe's minute, Buchanan, July 24. *B. D.,* XI, 81, 82.
[98] Grey's minute, Rumbold, July 24. *Ibid.,* XI, 83.

Italy should work together through their representatives in London. To his first suggestion (July 20, 22) in favor of direct Austro-Russian conversations, Poincaré had sharply objected during his visit to St. Petersburg,[99] but it is difficult to see how it could have helped, in view of Austria's determination to force a war with Serbia. Is it not probable that she would have refused, at least until she had secured a striking satisfaction? In any event, Germany's attitude did not become of paramount importance to Grey's search for a peaceful solution until he proposed the suspension of all military operations while the representatives of the comparatively disinterested powers considered the Austro-Serbian problem.[100] Through Tyrrell, his private secretary, he had already made an interesting offer for Germany's coöperation. The localization of an Austro-Serbian war should be dropped as impracticable, but if England and Germany, working together, succeeded in preserving peace, "Anglo-German relations will be placed upon a sure foundation for all time. Otherwise everything will be uncertain."[101] When she rejected this advance on the ground that the proposed conference "would practically amount to a court of arbitration," which only Austria and Russia, as the parties directly concerned, could call,[102] Germany doubtless did not foresee that her decision would make it impossible to use the crisis in the interest of her courtship of England. On the same day (July 27), her confidence in England's eventual neutrality suffered a first and serious blow with the news that the British fleet had been kept intact after the grand review—a step comparable in some respects to the mobilization of one of the continental armies.[103] Because Lichnowsky's opinion that England would side with France and Russia could not be completely ignored, the German foreign office tried, from the evening of July 27, to convince England that sincere efforts were being made to secure Austria's acceptance of the proposed mediation between Austria and Serbia, but, at the same time, it maintained its earlier support and encouragement of her plans

99 Fay, *Origins of the World War*, II, 362–368; Schmitt, *Coming of the War*, I, 451.
100 Goschen, July 27. *K. D.*, II, 25, 26.
101 Lichnowsky, July 26. *Ibid.*, I, 232.
102 Goschen, July 27. *B. D.*, XI, 128.
103 Schmitt, *op. cit.*, II, 68.

against Serbia. Grey's suggestion was handed to Vienna, but Bethmann's primary concern, as his instructions to Tschirschky show, was not to restrain the Austrians but to make sure that the responsibility for a general war should fall upon Russia and not upon the Central powers.[104] Even more conclusive as to Germany's policy at this juncture was Jagow's assurance, according to the Austrian ambassador's report, whose authenticity has been challenged but never disproved, that she not only did not endorse Grey's proposal but that she in fact opposed it.[105]

By July 27, a part of the German press had taken cognizance of the Triple Entente's appeal to Germany to save the peace of Europe by preventing Austria from attacking Serbia.[106] Apart from the Social Democratic journals, the liberal *Frankfurter Zeitung* (July 27), continuing its oscillations between approval and criticism of the official policy, was one of the few papers whose attitude was even partly favorable. That "an ally should give its partner a free hand for a course of action which might involve all Europe in a catastrophe" was, it admitted, doubtful, but only Germans had the right to call upon their government to restrain Austria. For the most part, the press insisted that Germany's rôle was neither to encourage Austria nor to advise moderation.[107] To ask Germany to intervene was, according to the Catholic *Kölnische Volkszeitung* (July 28), in reality an attempt to relieve Russia of the responsibility for the crisis, and the *Kölnische Zeitung* (July 28), while it affirmed Germany's readiness to coöperate in any move capable of preserving peace, insisted that interference with Austria's efforts to secure a just satisfaction would do more harm than good. In its judgment, Grey's proposal was bound to be regarded as unsatisfactory. The liberal *Frankfurter Zeitung* (July 28), irritated by the failure to publish Serbia's reply to the ultimatum, denied that Grey's suggestion was worthless and warned against the frightful consequences if its refusal should lead to war. Not a few observers acknowledged his good inten-

[104] Bethmann-Hollweg, July 27. *K. D.*, I, 267, 268.
[105] Szögyény, July 27. *O.-U. A.*, VIII, 778. *Cf.* Schmitt, *Coming of the War*, II, 72–75.
[106] *Cf.* Bienvenu-Martin, July 27. *D. D. F.*, (3), XI, 106.
[107] *Kreuz-Zeitung*, July 27.

tions,[108] but the Social Democratic *Vorwärts* (July 28), speaking for its party, was doubtless alone in supporting an unconditional acceptance. Grey's move, according to the *Hamburger Nachrichten* (July 28), was a "disguised unfriendliness," and the agrarian *Deutsche Tageszeitung* (July 28) dismissed it as a maneuver to divert British public opinion from the Ulster question: "Many have said during the last few days, 'Better a frightful end than fright without end,' and Grey's conference of ambassadors would be a fright without end."

Confident of Germany's support and desirous of raising a barrier to mediation, Berchtold precipitated events on the morning of July 28 by declaring war upon Serbia before Tschirschky presented Grey's proposal.[109] In the declaration of war, the nationalist press in Germany saw Austria's reply to the British foreign minister.[110] It was, according to the *Kreuz-Zeitung* (July 29), "the only conceivable and only worthy answer. . . ." "England's questionable attempt to intervene," said the National Liberal *Hamburger Nachrichten* (July 29), "has apparently hastened Vienna's decisions." Expected by all and doubtless desired by many, Austria's action occasioned little or no criticism. The *Vorwärts* (July 29) called it "a blow to all political reason, a new offense to the peaceful majority of nations." To avert the danger of Russia's intervention, the *Hamburger Nachrichten* (July 29) counted upon the continued close coöperation between Germany and Austria. She was bluffing: *"If we remain firm and pursue our chosen course to its logical conclusion, there is still hope that we will emerge from this crisis without a European war. Only no weakness!"* Although the government shared this hope, it tried to weaken the Triple Entente, while working for the localization of the war. With the beginning of the Austro-Serbian War, the studied reserve which Germany had maintained no longer served her purposes. On July 24, the powers were told that intervention by an outsider "must lead, by the play of the alliances, to incalculable consequences." [111] In Paris, this announcement had

---

108 They insisted, however, that mediation would be impossible unless Serbia accepted the ultimatum without any reservations.

109 Schmitt, *Coming of the War*, II, 82.

110 *Deutsche Tageszeitung*, July 29.

111 *B. D.*, XI, 79; *D. D. F.*, (3), XI, 19.

unexpected results. Bienvenu-Martin, the foreign minister *ad interim,* replied, according to his own account, that Germany and Austria should not make it "too difficult" for the other powers to localize the source of the trouble, or, according to Schoen, the German ambassador, that France agreed with Germany's desire to limit the conflict to Austria and Serbia and that she would work to that end.[112] "Germany's move," wrote the Catholic and nationalist *Echo de Paris* (July 25), "amounts to this: 'Let Austria crush Serbia, otherwise you must deal with Germany.' Under the paradoxical pretext of localizing the conflict, there is threat of a collective humiliation of the Triple Entente or the prospect of a general war."[113] Pleading the need of allaying the alarm caused by this statement, but also seeking to drive a wedge between France and Russia, Schoen asked (July 26) the Quai d'Orsay to inform the press that France and Germany were "examining in a most friendly spirit and in a sentiment of peaceful solidarity the means which may be used for the maintenance of peace."[114] While this communiqué would probably have made little or no impression upon the crisis, it was rejected, probably because Russia might question France's loyalty. Only if Germany would agree to use her influence to restrain Austria was the Quai d'Orsay willing to acknowledge the existence of intimate contacts with Germany. The press was merely informed that Schoen and Bienvenu-Martin had "considered the means of action by the powers for the maintenance of peace."[115]

While Germany, assuming the certainty of France's support of Russia, gave little heed to her reactions, England's attitude was vitally important, not only for the results of the immediate crisis but also for the success of Germany's ultimate aims. A considerable part of the press apparently believed that nothing need be done to assure England's neutrality. Churchill's order holding the fleet together was not reported by the German press until July 29, a day after it was known in France,[116] and the *Post*

---

[112] *D. D. F.,* (3), XI, 19, 20; *K. D.,* I, 166, 167.
[113] Carroll, *French Public Opinion,* p. 294.
[114] *D. D. F.,* (3), XI, 93.
[115] *Ibid.,* (3), XI, 95. *Cf.* Carroll, *op. cit.,* p. 296.
[116] *Vossische Zeitung,* July 29, London, July 28; *Frankfurter Zeitung,* July 29, London, July 29; *Kölnische Volkszeitung,* July 30. *Cf.* Carroll, *op. cit.,* pp. 303, 304.

did not explain its full significance until the next evening (July 30). Russia and France, wrote the Conservative *Schlessische Zeitung* (July 30), were mistaken in thinking that they could count upon England, even if Germany had rejected Grey's mediation proposal. The ultra-Conservative *Reichsbote* (July 30) was confident she would, as usual, take good care to profit by a continental war: "She will reap nothing but advantages from it. She will wait and fall upon the victor, whoever it may be, to maintain the balance of power." Writing in the *Hamburgischer Korrespondent,* Albert Ballin, minimized the significance of Churchill's order, explaining it as required by the annual review, and drew the conclusion that "England may be ignored so far as war is concerned." [117] While Bethmann and the foreign office probably did not fully believe Lichnowsky's warnings, nevertheless they did not share the illusions of the press, for each hour made it clearer that Grey must be convinced that Germany was sincerely exerting herself in the interest of peace to gain any assurance that England would remain neutral. This was probably the most important reason why Bethmann, from the evening of July 27, began to "press the button" at Vienna with increasing emphasis, calling upon Austria to consider Grey's proposal of mediation, to agree to stop her military operations with the occupation of Belgrade, and to promise Russia to respect Serbia's territorial integrity at the close of the war.[118] To the proposal for Austro-Russian conversations, the German press was not unsympathetic, since Russia's intervention might thereby at least be delayed. "If the mediation of the other powers succeed in starting conversations between St. Petersburg and Vienna at the last moment," wrote the *Hamburger Nachrichten* (July 29), "the European crisis may be regarded as solved—at least temporarily." The liberal *Berliner Tageblatt* (July 29) agreed that Germany must continue her firm support of Austria, but it also insisted that the people expected the government to try every means to avert war. That Grey's proposal had been rejected because Germany had decided to let events take their course,

---

[117] *Kölnische Zeitung,* July 30.
[118] William suggested the third point after reading Serbia's reply to the Austrian ultimatum. Schmitt, *Coming of the War,* II, 123.

as the *Hirsche Telegraphenbureau* asserted, was promptly denied, and the National Liberal *National Zeitung* (July 29) claimed official authority in announcing that the powers were successfully mediating between Russia and Austria. No one should dismiss this move as a "farce." "In so serious a crisis, anything which improves the situation or which delays final decisions is worth while." On the evening of July 29, the *Norddeutsche* clipped, and therefore in a sense approved, an article from a Viennese journal expressing satisfaction with Grey's speech in the House of Commons in which he had endorsed direct conversations between Austria and Russia, and speaking of Germany's favorable attitude.[119] The *Berliner Lokal-Anzeiger's* (July 29) official connections lent significance to its report that Russia had suggested the "halt-in-Belgrade" plan as a basis for negotiations. On this question, there was, however, a sharp difference of opinion. The Social Democratic *Vorwärts* (July 30) argued convincingly that a promise to respect Serbia's territorial integrity would not survive the uncontrollable passions excited by the war. To the nationalist *Berliner Neueste Nachrichten* (July 29), Austria must retain a free hand "to destroy Serbia's arrogance and offensive power. She must first be eliminated as a military factor and she must also be kept in financial subjection from five to ten years. We will then talk again with Paris and St. Petersburg in the spring of 1917."

Bethmann insisted that his efforts in Vienna proved his service to peace. There was, however, at least one other aim of German policy: the diplomatic preparation for a general war, if it could not be averted without the sacrifice of German and Austrian interests. In forwarding Grey's proposal of mediation *à quatre* on the evening of July 27, Bethmann pointed out that "we must appear as being forced into war," and to the Austrian ambassador he gave the most explicit assurances that Germany was opposed to Austria's acceptance, explaining at the same time the importance of creating the impression in England and among the German people that the policy of the Central powers was de-

---

[119] The same article was reprinted by the *Berliner Neueste Nachrichten, Volks-Zeitung, Kölnische Zeitung* and the *National Zeitung,* July 29.

fensive.[120]   From this position Bethmann and the foreign office
never really withdrew, despite the increasing sharpness of their
admonitions to Vienna.   "You will very carefully have to avoid
giving the impression," read the Chancellor's instructions to
Tschirschky of July 28, "that we wish to hold Austria back.   It
is simply the question of finding a way to realize Austria's aim
of cutting the vital cord of the Pan-Serbian propaganda without at the same time bringing on a world war; and if this
cannot in the end be avoided, of improving as far as possible
the conditions under which it will have to be conducted." [121]
After the first reports of Russia's intention to order a partial
mobilization (July 29), Bethmann began "urgently and emphatically" to recommend in the early hours of July 30 his earlier
proposals as a basis of mediation, and, finally, he warned Vienna
that we "must refuse to be drawn into a world conflagration
by Austria lightheartedly and in disregard of our advice."   This
warning seemed a threat to denounce the Dual Alliance, but its
effect was weakened by its silence in regard to the invasion of
Serbia and by Bethmann's earlier references to diplomatic strategy.
In any event, the Austrian government correctly assumed that
Germany's objections could be satisfied by a promise to Russia,
the sincerity of which was not beyond question, to respect Serbia's
territorial integrity.   A variety of excuses was found for delaying the reply to the "halt-in-Belgrade" proposal.   On the morning of July 31, the Austrian Imperial Council decided to insist
that the military operations against Serbia must continue, to
demand the suspension of Russia's mobilization, and the complete
acceptance of the ultimatum as the conditions for mediation.[122]
Germany had failed to secure a change in Austria's attitude which
Russia, in view of her determination to protect Serbia, could
regard as a satisfactory basis for negotiations or which would
persuade Grey that Germany was sincerely working for peace.
If Austria had agreed to the "halt-in-Belgrade" proposal, the
objection of the British minister to a form of mediation requiring
"Russia to stand aside while Austria had a free hand to go to any

[120] See above, pp. 796, 799.   Cf. Schmitt, Coming of the War, II, 70-72.
[121] Ibid., II, 128.
[122] Ibid., II, 218.

length she pleased" might have been surmounted, but Austria refused, and Grey placed little confidence, as he informed the German ambassador, in her promise to respect Serbia's territorial integrity, since she might "turn Serbia practically into a vassal state, and this would affect the whole position of Russia in the Balkans." [123]

As suggestion after suggestion failed, public opinion and the government gradually accepted the prospect of a general war.[124] Memories of past humiliations and the feeling that the world was hostile to Germany's just interests counted for more than any immediate issue in the conversion of the Pan-German *Rheinisch-Westfälische Zeitung* (July 29), but most Germans were convinced by Russia's attitude that war might momentarily be expected. Austria's intransigeance was largely ignored; whatever her faults might be, few doubted that Russia's were incomparably greater. To demand a change of policy as late as July 29, when Russia's general mobilization seemed only a matter of hours, required a courage or an independence of judgment possessed by few. The Social Democrats remained true to their traditional pacifism, demonstrating in numerous public meetings against Austria's aggressive policy and Germany's support of it, but the danger that the Cossacks might soon be ravaging German farms and homes meant more to them than the international solidarity of the proletariat. The *Kölnische Zeitung* (July 26) predicted that the workers would march "when they see that we are forced to fight," even if their leaders speak "with the tongues of angels." There were many indications that no serious attempt would be made to prevent war by mass action. "The Social Democratic workers," wrote the *Rheinische Zeitung,* an important party journal, "will not tolerate an attack by the Tsar's Cossacks." [125] Nor was this journal, as the *Kreuz-Zeitung* (July 29) claimed, "a white raven (*ein weisser Rabe*)." The majority of the German people, wrote Friedrich Stampfer, the editor of a Social Democratic news agency, in an article which the leaders tried too late

---

[123] *B. D.,* XI, 181 (July 29).
[124] "Man verlangt nicht den Krieg," wrote the Bavarian envoy, "aber man hat sich mit dem Gedanken abgefunden." Lerchenfeld, July 29. *B. D. K.,* p. 159.
[125] *Kölnische Zeitung,* July 28.

to suppress, did not desire war, "but no one will wish Germany's defeat or will not defend our wives and children against the Cossacks." [126] In Munich, Kurt Eisner condemned war in principle but called at the same time for a union of Western and Central Europe against the Russian menace. "We are ready," he said, "to resist an attack upon the Fatherland. Bebel once said that against Russia he would shoulder a musket." [127] Bethmann himself asked Sudekum, a Social Democratic member of the Reichstag, to explain his party's intentions. After consulting some of his colleagues on the party's executive committee, Sudekum replied in writing that there would be no strikes and that the Social Democratic press would put no weapons into the hands of the warmongers of other countries. On July 30, Bethmann explained to the council of ministers that there would be no question of strikes or of sabotage.[128]

What Russia would do in reply to Austria's declaration of war against Serbia was supremely important for the government as well as for the development of public opinion. The foreign office had already explained to Russia and France that Germany would be compelled to mobilize if Russia attacked Austria or if—and this warning was more significant—she ordered a general mobilization. Henceforth Russia's military preparations were watched with the closest attention. Disturbing reports of abnormal activity on the German and Austrian frontiers soon arrived in Berlin, although it was not of course known that the Russian Imperial Council had ordered preliminary measures of a limited character as early as July 25. This situation, together with his desire to impress upon England his services to peace and to place the responsibility for a general war upon Russia, caused Bethmann to increase the pressure he was exerting in Vienna in favor of moderation. At the same time, he tried to restrain Russia by warning her of the consequences if she mobilized, and by calling her attention to his negotiations with Austria.

---

126 C. Bloch, *Les socialistes allemands pendant la crise de juillet 1914* (Paris, 1933), p. 22. This brochure is a reprint from the *Revue d'histoire de la guerre mondiale,* October, 1933.

127 Velics, July 29. *Ö.-U. A.,* VIII, 881, 882.

128 Bloch, *op. cit.,* pp. 19–21. The same statement was made to the envoys of the federated states. *D. G.,* p. 107 (July 30).

His efforts were partially successful. William's personal appeal influenced the Tsar, July 29, to withdraw his consent to a general mobilization and, to the despair of his advisers, to approve the order only for the provinces on the Austrian frontier. The effect in Germany was momentous, although it brought into existence neither of the conditions which had been defined as requiring Germany's mobilization. During the evening of July 29—that is, before the news of Russia's action had arrived—the *Norddeutsche* (July 30) asked public opinion to remain calm.[129] Some observers refused to despair of peace, even when Russia's partial mobilization was confirmed (July 30). Yet Theodor Wolff confessed to a feeling of impotence as far as public opinion was concerned. "Faced by accomplished facts (*vor fertigen Tatsachen gestellt*), public opinion can do nothing more than support the efforts to maintain peace, while remaining calm itself. . . . There should be no such thing as 'too late,' and there is no 'too late' until the last moment."[130] Other moderate observers felt, however, that Russia's action constituted a threat to Germany as well as to Austria, and that it therefore required countermeasures. To the *Vossische Zeitung* (July 30, morn. ed.), the inadequacy of Russia's railway system made it impossible to put the country upon a war footing, except by degrees; what was happening in Russia therefore amounted to a general mobilization. Germany, according to the *Frankfurter Zeitung* (July 30, eve. ed.), would have no other recourse but to act. The tone of the official press had changed overnight. If the other powers respected Germany's vital interests, honor, and obligations to her ally, Germany's policy, wrote the *Kölnische Zeitung* (July 30, eve. ed.), would remain peaceful. Otherwise the Emperor's appeal would be answered by an explosion of the *furor teutonicus* of old: *"May the thunder roll over the Rhine!"* The Conservative *Kreuz-Zeitung* (July 30) still clung in its morning edition to the belief that Russia was bluffing, but it suggested that evening that valuable time was being wasted. There was an increasing expectation and perhaps even a desire for action, and until a

---

[129] Clipped by *Vossische Zeitung, Deutsche Tageszeitung, Berliner Börsen-Zeitung,* July 29 eve. ed.; *Berliner Neueste Nachrichten, Frankfurter Zeitung,* July 30, morn. ed.
[130] *Berliner Tageblatt,* July 30, morn. ed.

denial appeared, there was nothing inherently improbable in the report that the Imperial Council at Potsdam had decided during the late hours of July 29 to address a sharp inquiry to Russia and France as to the meaning of their military measures.[131] The agrarian *Deutsche Tageszeitung* (July 30, eve. ed.) hoped that an ultimatum had been sent to Russia, for Germany's security and economic interests required a clarification of her purposes. Assuming that Russia had been asked for an explanation, the Pan-German *Post* (July 30, eve. ed.) felt that it might be impossible to wait for a reply. That afternoon (July 30), a few hundred copies of the *Berliner Lokal-Anzeiger's* special edition announcing Germany's general mobilization were sold in the streets before the police confiscated the remainder, and the editions of four other journals published by the same house, the *Berliner Neueste Nachrichten,* the *Deutsche Zeitung,* and the *Deutsche Warte,* containing the statement that the Ist, Vth, and XVIIth army corps had been mobilized were also suppressed.[132] While these false revelations may have been inspired by chauvinists or army officers, who counted upon their effect in France to force the Chancellor's hand—the *Kölnische Volkszeitung* was informed by an anonymous official that the general mobilization had been ordered—it has been clearly established that the *Lokal-Anzeiger's* special edition had no influence upon Russia's decision during the same afternoon to mobilize her entire army.[133] Like the *Paris-Midi's* somewhat similar sensational report of the same date, it was chiefly significant of popular tension.

Whether the first unconfirmed reports of Russia's partial mobilization enabled Moltke and the general staff to exert a decisive influence upon German policy is a question that need not be discussed here, for it concerns the highly technical problem of the responsibilities for the war. Important changes were undoubtedly occurring in the official point of view. Bethmann's

---

[131] *Post, Deutsche Tageszeitung,* July 30, eve. ed. Cf. *Berliner Tageblatt,* July 30, morn. ed. The Berlin correspondent of the *Frankfurter Zeitung* (July 31) thought that the council had debated a last attempt to mediate between Vienna and St. Petersburg.

[132] *Volks-Zeitung,* July 31, morn. ed.

[133] The documents of the political section of the Berlin police, most of which were burned in October 1918, contain no information relating to this affair. Wolff, *Eve of 1914,* pp. 482–487. Cf. A. von Wergerer, "Das Extrablatt des 'Lokal-Anzeigers,'" *Berliner Monatshefte,* VII, 1035–1076.

personal appeal to the Social Democrats on July 29 meant that he had about abandoned hope for a peaceful solution. While it is true that his pressure upon Austria became more severe during that night and the early hours of July 30, steps had been taken to prepare for the carrying out of the Schlieffen plan. Already (July 26) Moltke had drafted an ultimatum to Belgium demanding the free passage of the German army, in return for a promise to respect her independence and integrity at the close of the war and for territorial compensations at France's expense. A refusal would compel Germany to treat her as an enemy. On July 29, influenced perhaps by a report of preparations which might delay the capture of the Liège forts commanding the route of the German army's right wing, Moltke sent a sealed copy of the ultimatum to Brussels, with orders to deliver it upon telegraphic instructions from Berlin. Nor was it the army alone which believed that military expediency should take precedence over diplomacy, for Bethmann took steps on July 29 to ascertain what England's attitude would be in the event of war. As long as only Austria, Serbia, and Russia were involved, England's neutrality was not impossible, for Grey was still resisting the impassioned pleas of Russia and France for support and because a considerable part of the cabinet was definitely against England's participation in a European war. To a large extent it was Bethmann himself who, on July 29, weakened the position of these moderates. Hoping to detach England and France, he promised to respect the latter's territorial integrity if she remained neutral, but he made the mistake of omitting France's colonies from this promise, and he even mentioned the possibility that the German army might be compelled to violate Belgium's neutrality.[134]

The drift toward war became still more pronounced with the confirmation (July 30) of Russia's partial mobilization. Although the Imperial Council did not approve a proclamation of a state "of threatening war" as the army desired, Moltke took it

---

[134] *K. D.*, III, 95, 96; Goschen, July 29. *B. D.*, XI, 185. Jagow, who had spoken "very pessimistically" of England's neutrality a few hours earlier (Szögyény, July 29. *Ö.-U. A.*, VIII, 864), told the British ambassador the next day (July 30) that Bethmann would not have made this proposal if Grey's warning had reached him in time. Goschen, July 30. *B. D.*, XI, 195.

upon himself to urge Conrad, the chief of the Austrian staff, to mobilize immediately against Russia and to promise that Germany would do the same, in accord with the correspondence of 1909. For his part, Bethmann moderated somewhat his pressure upon Berchtold, for he no longer threatened to repudiate the alliance, and rejected Sazonov's proposal that Austria should eliminate from her ultimatum those demands which attacked Serbia's sovereignty. Since a surrender on this point would amount to the sacrifice of all he had hoped to accomplish, Bethmann took his stand upon the advice he was giving to Vienna as the maximum of Germany's service to peace. To no avail Grey invited him to propose an acceptable basis for mediation by the four less immediately interested powers, although he held out the most attractive prospects for the future of Anglo-German relations. He was thinking of "some arrangement to which Germany could be a party, by which she could be assured that no hostile or aggressive policy would be pursued against her or her allies by France, Russia, and ourselves jointly or separately." [135] He went even further during a conversation with Lichnowsky on the morning of July 31 and in a dispatch to Goschen that afternoon; if Germany "could get any reasonable proposal put forward which would make it clear that Germany and Austria were striving to preserve European peace," he would support it and "would go the length of saying that if Russia and France would not accept it His Majesty's Government would have nothing more to do with the consequences. . . ." [136] Lichnowsky's report of the above conversation reached the German foreign office only five minutes before the dispatch of the ultimata to Russia and France; although there was still time to prevent their delivery, apparently this possibility received no consideration. Late that night (July 31), Jagow told Goschen that Germany must wait for the replies of the two powers. Equally evasive was the reply to Grey's request for Germany's attitude toward the neutrality of Belgium; Germany could not commit herself without betraying her military plans. Berlin's last hesitation disappeared with the arrival of the news of Russia's general mobilization on the morning of

[135] *B. D.,* XI, 194.
[136] *Ibid.,* XI, 216.

July 31. To the Tsar, William addressed a final appeal to halt his mobilization as the only way to maintain peace, but Bethmann had already informed Austria, only two hours after hearing of Russia's action, that Germany could be expected to follow her example within forty-eight hours and that this step would mean war. Scarcely half an hour after the arrival of Nicholas' reply explaining that the mobilization could not be stopped for technical reasons but also promising that his troops would not take "any provocative action" while the negotiations with Austria continued, Bethmann instructed Pourtalès to present the ultimatum at 6 p.m. (July 31). Russia must say within twelve hours whether she intended to halt her mobilization.[137] In the absence of a reply, Germany sent her declaration of war at about 1 p.m., August 1, and, at 5 p.m., ordered her own mobilization.

While one challenge was being delivered to Russia, another was sent to France.[138] Within eighteen hours she must state her intentions in regard to a Russo-German war; for the improbable case of a promise to remain neutral, Schoen was to insist upon the occupation of the fortresses of Toul and Verdun as guarantees of good faith.[139] Too long had it been assumed that she would attack as soon as Germany was at war with another power for there to be any illusions as to her decision. In fact, the press had paid little attention to her during the crisis. France was not even mentioned in the *Norddeutsche's* (Aug. 1) elaborate defense of German policy. However, not a few observers had been impressed by her moderation and reserve. *"The French press,"* wrote the chauvinist *Rheinisch-Westfälische Zeitung* (July 27), *"is peaceful, almost anxious."* The nationalist *Berliner Neueste Nachrichten* (July 27) spoke of *"das friedliche Paris,"* and the *Kölnische Zeitung* (July 30) was informed by its Paris correspondent as late as July 30 that "there is not a trace" of a desire for war. "France," according to the Catholic *Germania* (July

---

[137] The ultimatum to Russia was published by the *Norddeutsche* on the evening of July 31.

[138] As if by official direction, a large section of the press represented the ultimata as services to peace and not as necessarily meaning war. *Kölnische Zeitung,* July 31, noon ed.; *Volks-Zeitung,* Aug. 1, morn. ed.; *Vossische Zeitung,* Aug. 2, morn. ed.; *Deutsche Tageszeitung,* Aug. 2, morn. ed.; *Germania,* Aug. 3, eve. ed. These articles had obviously been written before Germany's declaration of war upon Russia.

[139] Bethmann-Hollweg, July 31, 3:30 p.m. *K. D.,* III, 10

30), "has' no zest for war, yes, it is feared; the overwhelming majority are peaceful. . . ." France's reply to the ultimatum, that she would consult her own interests in deciding what course to follow, was no surprise, but in view of the smashing offensive through Belgium against France with which the campaign was to begin, it was obviously desirable to shift the attention to a certain extent from the eastern to the western frontier, to represent France as the first to resort to hostilities, in view of the moral effect in England. Although France ordered her general mobilization a few minutes before the Germans acted, she also held back, taking care that her troops remained ten kilometers from the frontier and that London was informed as to this order. It therefore became an important part of Germany's strategy to create the impression at home as well as abroad that France was guilty of an aggression before Germany declared war. The press lent its services to the general staff for this purpose. Frontier incidents were the inevitable result when millions of soldiers were called to the colors, but the most unauthenticated rumors received official approval in order to prepare public opinion—and England— for the declaration of war, August 3, and for the offensive through Belgium. From the general in command of the VIIIth army corps at Coblenz, a report arrived at the foreign office on the afternoon of August 2 that eighty French army officers dressed in Prussian uniforms had tried to enter Germany. Two hours later Jagow sent it to the Hague, Brussels, and London as evidence that France had violated her neutrality, and, a little later (6:15 p.m.) the general staff communicated the same report to the Wolff Agency. Jagow resorted to means which even the general staff refused to countenance, for it denied the tale which he sent to Rome (11:15 p.m.) that a French doctor had tried to infect wells near Metz with cholera germs. Bethmann forwarded to London a long list of France's alleged violations of the frontier.[140] On August 3, the press flamed with headlines charging her with acts of aggression. "French Patrols Cross the Frontier," "French Officers in Prussian Uniforms," appeared in the *Vossische Zeitung*. Under the caption "France Violates the Frontier," the liberal *Frankfurter*

---

[140] *K. D.*, III, 81, 141, 154, 155, 157, 158.

Zeitung announced that France, like Russia, had attacked without a declaration of war. The Progressive *Volks-Zeitung* cried, "The French are Attacking!" "While Germany Acts with Complete Correctness, French Airships and Flying Machines Cruise over German Territory," "French Fliers Bomb Germany," "Still More French Fliers," "Frontier Violations by the French," and "French Officers as Spies," all appeared in one edition of the Progressive *Freisinnige Zeitung,* while the headlines of the Catholic *Kölnische Volkszeitung* included the following: "France Violates the Neutrality of Switzerland," "French Invasion of Alsace Without a Declaration of War!" and "The French Begin War!" The *Magdeburgische Zeitung,* the *Deutsche Tageszeitung,* and the *Tagliche Rundschau,* all nationalist journals, not only carried equally provocative headlines but agreed in charging France with a "Violation of International Law." In this way, public opinion was prepared for the declaration of war against France and persuaded that Germany was the victim of an unprovoked attack.

Until almost the last moment, Belgium was scarcely mentioned in the press, so obvious was the need to conceal the intentions of the general staff. On July 31, the moderate *Vossische Zeitung* noticed that London newspapers were speaking of a violation of her neutrality as a reason why England might be forced into the war. Its comment was enlightening: "There is no need to discuss this wholly hypothetical and improbable contingency seriously." Writing after the violation of Luxemburg's neutrality, the *Hamburger Fremdenblatt* (Aug. 4) hastened to assure England that Germany would not violate that of Belgium or of Holland "if they show themselves to be capable of defending it." Three days after the comments of the *Vossische Zeitung,* this "hypothetical" action became a reality when the German ultimatum, omitting the promise of compensations at France's expense, was handed to the Belgian government during the evening of August 2. Refusing to sacrifice the nation's honor and to "betray" its duty to Europe, the government replied that it would resist "every attack upon its rights." Despite the resolve to pass through Belgium—the actual violation of her neutrality occurred early in the morning of August 3—Germany tried desperately to the very end to keep England out of the war. As late as the night of August 2, the ultra-Conservative *Reichsbote* (Aug. 3) still counted upon her neutrality: "As always, she will wait to see which way the cat jumps; she will remain cool whether she joins France and Russia or stands aside. If they are defeated, she will not depart from her splendid isolation. England has never identified herself with the losing side." On August 1, Albert Ballin, acting on the request of the foreign office, tried unsuccessfully to have the London *Times* print an article recognizing Germany's "tireless" efforts for peace and blaming Russia for the war which no one desired.[141] Assurances were conveyed in vain to the British foreign office and to the press that Germany would not attack the northern coast of France or use the coasts of Belgium and Holland against her and that, in view of the insignificant size of the British army, England could help France as much by remaining neutral as by entering the war. Against the emotions aroused by the violation of Belgian neutrality and against the feeling that England's own security was threatened, the Liberal press and the City, still predominantly against participation, could not stand; the Belgian question enabled Grey in his speech on the morning of August 3 to win the support of a wavering House of Commons and to carry the cabinet with him against the supporters of peace, two of whom, Lord Morley and John Burns, persisted in their determination to resign. Grey and the foreign office may have been chiefly concerned with the fate of the Triple Entente and with the possible establishment of Germany's hegemony in Europe, but it was Germany herself who put in their hands the means of uniting the great majority of the nation in favor of war. At noon on August 4, an ultimatum, requiring a pledge by midnight to respect the neutrality of Belgium, was handed to the German foreign office. The answer, a refusal, was immediately followed by England's declaration of war. Despite the many warning signs beginning with the order holding the Grand Fleet together, this decision was a shock to German opinion, which had never quite revised its contemptuous estimate of the motives behind British foreign policy and which had exag-

---

141 Schmitt, *Coming of the War*, II, 394, 395.

gerated the improvement in Anglo-German relations. Even
Bethmann, although he had probably foreseen England's intervention for days,[142] harangued Goschen, the British ambassador,
for twenty minutes, reproaching England for going to war "just
for a word, neutrality . . . just for a scrap of paper. . . . "[143]
That a kindred people with whom Germany had tried to make
friends should fall upon her back when she was faced with a life-
and-death struggle enraged the press. The liberal *Frankfurter
Zeitung* (Aug. 5) was astounded that England, "the guardian of
international morality," had placed herself on the side of Russia,
the protector of assassins. The Progressives were surpassed by
none in the bitterness of their denunciations. In England's action, the *Volks-Zeitung* (Aug. 5) and the *Freisinnige Zeitung*
(Aug. 6) saw the proof of a long-cherished plan to destroy
Germany's naval and commercial power. Not a few observers
insisted that England's decision was no surprise and that
the government had known perfectly well that the invasion of
Belgium would bring her into the war.[144] There was nothing
but praise for Bethmann's frankness in acknowledging that military necessity alone had compelled the violation of Belgium's
neutrality. "His words," wrote the Conservative *Schlesische Zeitung* (Aug. 5), "were frank and honest, manly and firm. They
were truly German." The National Liberal *National Zeitung*
(Aug. 5) thought that Bismarck would have taken the same stand.
The Chancellor, said the ultra-Conservative *Reichsbote* (Aug. 6),
had spoken "with impressive and virile frankness." The National Liberal *Magdeburgische Zeitung* (Aug. 5) was satisfied:
"In truth a policy of courageous action that is born of necessity, a
policy that alone contains hope of protection against a serious
danger, a policy worthy of a people that is so great, so brave as
the Germans." To Theodor Wolff, the occasion was not one that
warranted self-congratulations, but he was able to console himself with the reflection that Belgium was not the decisive cause of
England's action.[145] England, according to the *Hamburger*

---

[142] Hammann, *Bilder aus der letzten Kaiserzeit*, p. 75. *Cf.* Leuckart, July 30.
D. G., p. 98.
[143] *B. D.*, XI, 351 (Aug. 6).
[144] *Kölnische Zeitung, Kreuz-Zeitung, Tägliche Rundschau, Vossische Zeitung*, Aug. 5.
[145] *Berliner Tageblatt*, Aug. 5.

Fremdenblatt (Aug. 6), was following her traditional policy of attacking the strongest continental power; the neutrality of Belgium was only a pretext, because Grey knew that France would have violated it if Germany had not. Brussels, wrote the Catholic *Kölnische Volkszeitung* (Aug. 5), had not denied the report that France and England had made arrangements for a British expeditionary force to Belgium.

An unforeseen incident had changed the direction of Germany's foreign policy. Since 1904, she had attempted many times to divide the Triple Entente, but she had always stopped short of war. In spite of her unappeased imperialist appetite and of the unsatisfactory situation in Europe, her government and the greater part of public opinion still believed that her aims could be attained by peaceful methods, supported by diplomatic pressure and by powerful armaments. The Agadir crisis and the resurgence of French nationalism which followed, the unfavorable shift in the balance of diplomatic and military power as a result of the Balkan Wars, and the armaments of France and Russia undoubtedly diminished that confidence; but the cautious courtship of England had accomplished results in diplomatic coöperation and in the agreements relating to the Berlin-Bagdad Railway and the Portuguese colonies which might in the long run have weakened England's associations with France and Russia. Exaggerating the gains already achieved, the government quickly reached the conclusion that the situation after Sarajevo was favorable for a stroke that would strengthen Austria's position as a great power and, indirectly, Germany's. Perhaps the best measure of the change in public opinion since 1909 was the decline in the hitherto strong opposition to an unconditional support of Austria's Balkan policy. That the risk must be accepted was taken as a matter of course by newspapers which, five years earlier, had denounced this point of view as a betrayal of Germany's interests. No matter what the cost might be, Austria must be permitted to destroy the Pan-Serbian menace: such was the government's view, despite its belated and conditional advice of moderation in Vienna, and such was also the attitude of the greater part of articulate public opinion. For this reason, Germany practically rejected Grey's offer of mediation between Austria and Serbia by the four disinterested powers and thereby forced a trial of strength, either by diplomacy or by force of arms, between the two diplomatic groups. In the firmest of Bethmann's dispatches to Vienna there is no evidence of yielding on this point, for the "halt-in-Belgrade" and similar proposals meant an invasion, no matter how limited. Germany would doubtless have been content if Austria had been permitted to cripple Serbia in one way or another, because a general war meant the collapse of her entire foreign policy, but her insistence upon "holding the ring" for Austria forced the members of the Triple Entente, one after the other, to choose between the sacrifice of essential interests and war. For Russia, the humiliation of Serbia meant the loss of her influence in the Balkans; for France, Russia's survival as a great power with unimpaired influence in the Balkans and as a loyal ally involved her own security, prestige, and aspirations for the recovery of Alsace-Lorraine; for England, the fate of Belgium and of France raised not only the question of her sworn promises but also of her own safety. If the German government did not set out intentionally to precipitate a European war, the conflict became practically inevitable when the Triple Entente was forced to choose between these alternatives, because Russia was too confident of the strength of her rearmament and of France's loyalty to yield, as she had in 1909. The microscopic investigation of the immediate origins of the war has proved that none of the great powers was wholly innocent. From Russia came aid and comfort for the Pan-Serbian agitation, and, if it has not been proved that she was back of the Sarajevo crime, it is possible that the Serbian government would have prevented it if her support had not been counted upon. France's support of Russia was comparable to Germany's support of Austria, and England's attitude permitted France in particular to hope for and even to count upon her aid, no matter how often Grey warned her that England's hands were free. Nevertheless, the fact remains that Austria would probably never have presented her ultimatum to Serbia without the knowledge that Germany would protect her against Russia and that, without the same confidence, she would not have declared war. These were the decisive events of the crisis, for without them there would have been no reason for Russia's mobilization.

Bethmann had repeatedly insisted that his government could not be sure of the support of publc opinion in Germany unless Austria made it possible to represent Russia as the aggressor. His fears were largely groundless, for the approach of war overshadowed all differences of opinion. Indeed, the war was even popular among many nationalists and Conservatives, for it seemed to them better that it should be fought in the summer of 1914 than later, when Russia's armaments would be complete.[146] "Our enemies," wrote the *Vossische Zeitung* (Aug. 6), "intended to delay a couple of years until they were fully armed before strangling the hated Germany." By his death Francis Ferdinand had performed his last and greatest service to his own country and to Germany in precipitating war before Russia was ready. The organ of the Pan-Germans was lyrical in its enthusiasm. "The firmness of the Viennese policy has had a cleansing effect upon the unbearable European situation; a fresh wind, yes, a storm is blowing through the country, purifying and clarifying the air. We hear the tread of world events. It is a joy to live." [147] Harden condemned the attempt to localize the Austro-Serbian war as a mistake, because a victory would only increase Serbia's hatred and because her defeat would be a poor satisfaction for Austria's spirit of determination and self-sacrifice.[148] Others yielded to the counsels of desperation. People were saying, wrote the National Liberal *National Zeitung* (July 31), "Better an end to the unheard-of tension which has weighed for years upon the world. . . ." This point of view, according to the Social Democratic *Vorwärts* (July 30), explained the conversion of the capitalists and the industrialists to the idea of a general war, and, in particular, the change in the attitude of the *Post* and of the *Rheinisch-Westfälische Zeitung*. Fatalism was the order of the day: *"Better a frightful end than fright without end.* That is a policy of desperation, of madness. That is a suicidal spirit. . . . They wring their hands and permit events to take their course." As the time for final decisions approached, the frightful consequences of war weighed more heavily upon public opinion. Even the

---

[146] *Kreuz-Zeitung,* July 31.
[147] *A. B.,* Aug. 1.
[148] Harden, "Der Krieg," *Zukunft,* Aug. 1.

chauvinistic *Post* (July 31) admitted that a growing anxiety damp-
ened the boisterous enthusiasm of the Berlin crowds. Himself
shortly to die upon the battlefield, Jules Hedemann, the French
journalist and correspondent of the Paris *Matin,* partly atoned for
his recent glorification of Russia's military power by his moderate
reports from Berlin during the last days of the crisis.[149] Few
ventured to look into the future. Confident of Germany's
mighty army, the great majority doubtless counted upon victory,
but at least one warning voice was raised. The liberal *Morgenpost* predicted (July 30) that Italy would and that England would
not remain neutral, and that the latter's participation would ultimately bring Japan and the United States in on the side of the
Triple Entente. The war, in its opinion, would last from three
to five years; it would so exhaust the world that Germany could
gain nothing. Defeated or victorious, England alone would
profit, while Germany would emerge with a million dead, two
million crippled, and a gigantic debt. The Conservative
Kreuz-Zeitung (Aug. 1), doubtless wishing to steel public opinion
for a desperate struggle, painted an even darker picture, insisting
that defeat would mean the loss of Alsace-Lorraine and of the
colonies, crushing financial burdens, and even Germany's disintegration. Doubt was occasionally expressed as to the management of Germany's foreign policy. Although the *Hamburger
Nachrichten* had fully approved its most dangerous decisions, it
(Aug. 5) was moved by England's declaration of war to ask if
the "ring around us" could not have been broken through. The
Bavarian envoy in Berlin felt that the diplomatic preparation of
the war had been inadequate, even if the worst mistake, the building of a fleet, had been made years earlier.[150] These considerations made little impression upon a public opinion which believed
almost unanimously that the war was not of Germany's choosing.

With one accord, except perhaps the Social Democrats, the entire press appealed to history to prove Germany's peacefulness, as
did William himself in his speech at the opening of the Reichstag,
August 4.[151] No country of equal strength had ever used its

---

149 Wolff, *Eve of 1914,* p. 487.
150 Lerchenfeld, Aug. 3. *B. D. K.,* p. 215.
151 *Kölnische Volkszeitung,* Aug. 2; *Berliner Tageblatt,* Aug. 4.

power so moderately. By refraining from immediate action after Russia's partial mobilization, she had shown her desire for peace.[152] This impression was strengthened by the German White Book, a selection of diplomatic documents.[153] *"No nation,"* wrote the *Münchener Neueste Nachrichten* (July 31), *"ever went to war with a clearer conscience."* With Russia's general mobilization vanished the last doubts as to the attitude of the Social Democrats. "Are we determined to win?" asked the *Volksstimme* of Chemnitz. "Our answer is, Yes! . . . Germany's women and children will not be the victims of Russian bestiality, Germany will not be the booty of the Cossacks."[154] The situation, according to a revisionist, had changed completely with Russia's intervention, for the German Socialists could only serve humanity if "their own nation has ample opportunity for making its contribution. . . ."[155] The chief hope of Socialism everywhere lay in the survival and strength of the German people.[156] Even before Hermann Müller's return (Aug. 3) from his fruitless mission to Paris, where he had tried to come to an agreement with the French Socialists as to a basis for common action, the executive committee decided (Aug. 2), against the opposition of two members (Haase and Ledebour), to vote for the war credits; in fact, only one member left the Reichstag rather than vote.[157] After England's declaration of war, indignation was largely concentrated against her. William had spoken (July 30) of the crisis as the last step in her plan to crush Germany: "Edward VII dead is stronger than I am though living!"[158] England's moderation, it was said, had concealed deadly designs. "She is putting into effect," wrote the Progressive *Volks-Zeitung* (Aug. 5), "her long-cherished plan of halting Germany's economic development and her growing sea power."[159] "It is," asserted the National Liberal *Berliner Börsen-Zeitung* (Aug. 5),

---

[152] *Kölnische Zeitung, Frankfurter Zeitung, Freisinnige Zeitung,* Aug. 1.
[153] *Post,* Aug. 4.
[154] *Vossische Zeitung,* Aug. 2.
[155] J. Bloch, "Der Krieg und die Sozialdemokratie," *Sozialdemokratische Monatshefte,* 1914, pp. 1023, 1024 (Aug. 13).
[156] L. Quessel, "Das Schicksal unseres Volkes," *Ibid.* 1914, p. 1014 (Aug. 13).
[157] C. Bloch, *Les socialistes allemands pendant la crise de juillet 1914,* pp. 24–28.
[158] William II's comments, Pourtalés, July 10. *K. D.,* II, 132.
[159] Cf. *National Zeitung,* Aug. 5.

"the culmination of Edward VII's policy. . . ." Germany was surrounded by enemies, who had coolly planned her destruction.[160] Her jealous rivals, said the *Vossische Zeitung* (Aug. 1), were determined "by force to pull us down, to cripple us, to rob us of the freedom which has taken centuries to win." On August 5, its leading editorial appeared under the headline "From Encirclement to War." "Never," wrote the Liberal *Frankfurter Zeitung* (Aug. 1), "has there been a more dishonorable and immoral coalition than this, whose sole bond of union is hostility to Germany." Unlike France, where the war was accepted as an opportunity to reconquer Alsace-Lorraine, there was, at least at first, no one objective to which public opinion rallied. Speaking to the Reichstag, August 4, William disavowed any desire for conquests, but the *Berliner Tageblatt* (Aug. 4) was one of the few journals to single this statement out for approval or, indeed, to give it any emphasis. Many others besides the members of the Pan-German League hoped that the war would destroy the Triple Entente and open the way for German expansion, but public opinion was better expressed by the *Kölnische Zeitung* (Aug. 1): "We have not willed this war, but if we must fight it . . . then we will wage it with God, for Emperor and Fatherland, in such a way that the fruits of victory will be worth the sacrifice; our warriors, we hope, will secure by force that quiet (*Ruhe*) for ourselves and our children which our enemies are now disturbing."

---

[160] *Hamburger Nachrichten,* Aug. 2; *Magdeburgische Zeitung, Germania,* Aug. 5.

Index

Index

A

Abd-el-Aziz, Sultan of Morocco, 527, 585

Abeken, H., official in Prussian foreign office, 60

Aegidi, L., official in German press bureau, and the *Kölnische Zeitung* article (April 5, 1875), 114

Aehrenthal, Count, Austro-Hungarian foreign minister, 560; Balkan policy of, 589, 619; Germany's support of (1908–1909), 605; Germany and the intransigeance of, 606; and a Franco-German accord (Feb. 9, 1909), 610; diplomatic victory of (1909), 628, 629; and mobilization against Serbia (1909), 629; and the Agadir crisis (1911), 675

Agadir, 690; Kiderlen's plans (May 1911), 649; England and its distance from the Mediterranean, 652; the "Panther's" leap (July 1, 1911), 654, 655; raising of the German flag (Sept. 27, 1911), 689

Agence Havas, 53; and news for the New World, 14; revelation of Western Mediterranean agreements by (1907), 560

Albania, and the question of frontiers, 724, 725, 728, 729

Albert, King of the Belgians, 766

Albrecht, Archduke of Austria, visit of to Paris, 1870, 50

Alexander of Battenberg, Prince of Bulgaria, 220, 272; Bismarck's marriage project for, 3, 220; Alexander II and Bismarck's advice concerning, 220; abdications of (1886), 222; popularity of in Germany, 224

Alexander II, Tsar of Russia, 136; and France's right to rearm (1872), 101; and Bismarck's attitude toward France (1874), 107, (1875), 116; and Bismarck and the Congress of Berlin (1878), 154; effect of Germany's support of Austria on (1879), 155; assassination of, 163

Alexander III, Tsar of Russia, 161, 309, 331

Algeciras Conference (1906), 543–548

Alliance of the Three Emperors (1881), 162, 163, 168, 234, 245, 301, 631, 714; action of in the Egyptian question (1884), 204, 205; abandonment of by Bismarck (1887), 256

Alsace-Lorraine, 275, 278, 317, 351, 638, 713, 816, 817; France's acquisition of, 21; demands for annexation of in the German press (1866), 31, (1867) 37, (1870) 75; demand for as strategic frontier, 75, 76; and annexationist sentiment during the Franco-Prussian War, 75, 76; proposals for neutrality of (1870–1871), 77; and the question of Metz (1870–1871), 79; and the League of the Three Emperors (1873), 101; and Gorchakov (1875), 116; and Bismarck's proposal to Alexander II (1876), 138; Disraeli and Bismarck's offer of an alliance (1879), 161, 162, 165; and Germany's good-will, 234; passport regulations in (1887), 247, 248, (1888). 276, (1891) 307, 318; F. Schultze's solution of the problem (1890), 291, 302; Colonel Stoffel and a Franco-German alliance (1890), 302; and the *Daily News'* appeal to William II (July 14, 1891), 314; discussion of in the French press, 419; and Delcassé's proposal (1899), 425; French reaction to the law of 1910, 631

Andrássy, Count J., Minister-President of Austria-Hungary, 129; offers Bismarck war or a conference (Jan. 1878), 146; Bismarck and the Dual Alliance (1879), 157; the Dual Alliance and a free hand in the Balkans, 158

Anglo-French relations, Napoleon III's ambitions in Belgium, 31, 51; neutrality in the Franco-Prussian War, 71, 79, 80; England's mediation offer (1871), 79; and Bismarck, 163; the French naval

ward war, 787, 793, 794, 815; and the liberal press after the Austrian ultimatum, 788, 789; on the support of Austria and peace, 788, 790, 792, 793, 797; and mass demonstrations (July 1914), 791, 792, 802, 816; and Serbia's reply to Austria, 792; and Germany's contribution to peace, 793, 816, 817; and Grey's mediation proposal, 796, 797; adopts attitude of "better a frightful end than fright without end," 797, 815; and Austria's declaration of war on Serbia (July 28, 1914), 797; confidence of in England's neutrality, 798, 799, 811; and Austro-Russian conversations, 799, 800; and the acceptance of war, 802, 815; and Russia's partial mobilization (July 29, 1914), 804, 805; and the *Berliner Lokal-Anzeiger's* announcement of mobilization, 805; and French public opinion during the crisis of 1914, 808, 809; preparation of for attack on France, 809, 810; and Belgian neutrality, 810, 813; and England's entrance into the war, 811, 812, 817, 818; on Bethmann-Hollweg and "military necessity," 812; prophetic forebodings of, 816; and the *Kölnische Zeitung* (Aug. 1, 1914), 818

R

Racconigi, agreement between Nicholas II and Victor Emmanuel at (1909), 632, 633

Rachfahl, F., German historian, and reasons for German optimism in 1913, 700

Radolin, Prince, German ambassador to France, 574; on France and the Russian alliance, 499; on Morocco and Franco-German relations, 542

Radowitz, J. von, mission of to St. Petersburg (1875), 109; and the preventive war theory (April 22, 1875), 119, 120

Radziwill, Prince A. von, aide-de-camp of King William, report of Ems interview by (1870), 67

Raschdau, L., retired German diplomat and publicist, supports Austria, 626; on Germany and the Dual Alliance, 628; and England as Germany's worst enemy (1911), 695

Rasputin, attempted assassination of (July 1914), 781

Reform-Verein, progress of after 1861, 24

Reichstag, interpellations of on foreign affairs, 16; and Bülow's Chinese expedition (1900), 16; and the committee on foreign affairs, 16, 17; and the agreement of Nov. 4, 1911, 693–695; elections to, *see* Elections

Reinsurance Treaty (1887), 256–258, 269, 280, 287, 308, 330, 346; comparison of with the Dual Alliance (1879), 257, 258; renewal of (1890), 283, 288, 289; and public opinion, 285

Reismann-Grone, Dr., editor of the *Rheinisch-Westfälische Zeitung*, and Russia's ambitions, 754

Reptile fund, 12

Reuter Agency, 671; news service of to the New World, 14

Reval, Edward VII's visit to Nicholas II at (1908), 574 ff.

Revanche, 181; Münster's estimate of (1886), 3; and German reaction to Déroulède and the *Ligue des Patriotes*, 182, 183

Reventlow, E., editor of the *Alldeutsche Blätter*, on Bülow and the *Nibelungentreue*, 628

Rhodes, C., 364, 365; visit of to Berlin (1899), 433

Richter, E., Progressive leader, editor of the *Freisinnige Zeitung*, 7, 239; supports Prince Alexander of Battenberg (1886), 224; attitude of toward *Weltpolitik*, 475

Ricklin, Dr., Alsatian deputy, and a Franco-German reconciliation (1911), 694

Ridder, Hermann, editor of the *New Yorker Staats-Zeitung*, and Prince Henry's American visit, 7

Rio-Muni, and the agreement of Nov. 4, 1911, 690

Rome, French garrison in and Franco-Italian relations, 50

Roon, A., Count von, Prussian war minister, 63

Roosevelt, T., President of the United States, and the Moroccan crisis, 512, 524, 528, 531; and Germany's support against Japan, 567

Rosebery, Lord, British foreign secretary and Prime Minister, 331, 355, 358; Germany and (1892), 322

Rosen, F., German diplomat, 536

Rössler, C., official in the German press bureau, and the *Berliner Post's* war scare article of April 9, 1875, 114, 115;